HARMSWORTH
HISTORY
OF THE WORLD

KING EDWARD VII.

From the statue by George Wade erected at Reading

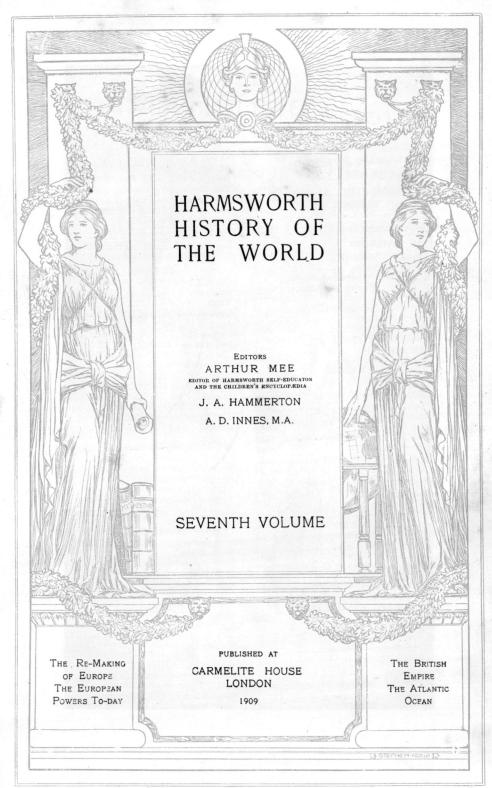

HARMSWORTH HISTORY OF THE WORLD

EDITORS

ARTHUR MEE
EDITOR OF HARMSWORTH SELF-EDUCATOR
AND THE CHILDREN'S ÆNCYCLOPÆDIA

J. A. HAMMERTON

A. D. INNES, M.A.

SEVENTH VOLUME

THE RE-MAKING
OF EUROPE
THE EUROPEAN
POWERS TO-DAY

PUBLISHED AT
CARMELITE HOUSE
LONDON
1909

THE BRITISH
EMPIRE
THE ATLANTIC
OCEAN

STEPHEN·REID

CONTENTS
OF THIS VOLUME

EUROPE
SIXTH DIVISION
THE RE-MAKING OF EUROPE

We enter now upon the last phase of completed European history—the century which has all but run its course since the decisive overthrow of Napoleon's ambitions at Waterloo. Although during this period the United Kingdom and the Eastern Powers, Russia and the whole Eastern peninsula, pursue their course in comparative independence of the complications which involve the rest of Europe, the latter being no longer in isolation sufficient to warrant us in maintaining the earlier complete separation of East and West.

Following immediately after Waterloo, we have a period of strong reaction against the political ideas of the French Revolution, a period in which the claims to power and to territory of "legitimate" dynasties are looked upon as paramount, while the control of the Sovereign People and demands for the recognition of nationalities are held in check, though Greece attains her liberation from Turkey. The second period opens and closes with two revolutions in France—the expulsion of the Bourbons and the coup d'état of Napoleon III.

During this period the demands of Constitutionalism and of Nationalism are fermenting, Germany in particular making futile efforts in the latter direction. The third period coincides with that of the Second Empire in France, and is marked by the unification of Italy and the triumph of German nationalism in the new German Empire, consummated by the Franco-German war, and attended by the establishment of the Third French Republic.

Finally we follow the fortunes of the now reconstructed Europe—the whole narrative having interludes associated with the modern Eastern Question—until we reach our own day.

GENERAL SURVEY OF THE PERIOD
By Oscar Browning, M.A.

THE CONTINENT
By Dr. H. Zimmerer, Dr. Heinrich Schurtz, Dr. Georg Adler, Dr. G. Egelhaaf, Dr. H. Friedjung, and other writers

THE BRITISH ISLES
By A. D. Innes, M.A., and H. W. C. Davis, M.A.

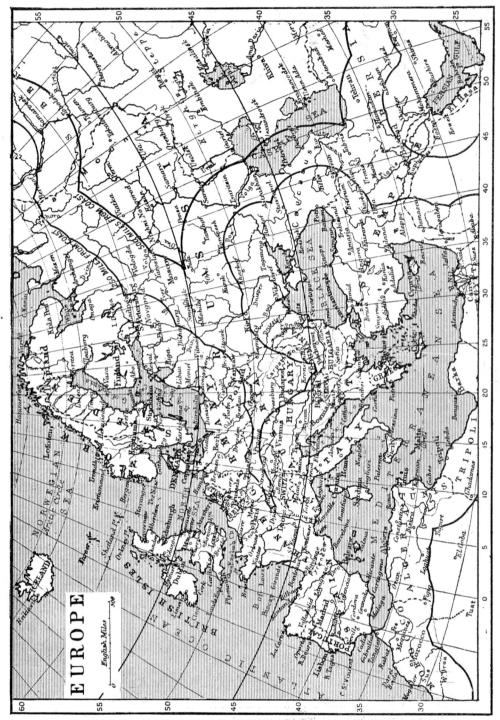

MAP TO ILLUSTRATE THE SIXTH DIVISION OF EUROPE

The above map shows the Europe of our own time, with the boundaries of the various states as we know them to-day. The period thus illustrated is not the whole of the time covered by "The Re-making of Europe," but rather the eventual settlement of the Continent, as a result of the movements which were initiated on the downfall of Napoleon, and involved such international conflicts as the Crimean War, the Italian revolt against Austria, the Franco-Prussian, the Russo-Turkish, and the Greco-Turkish wars. The changes in the map of Europe since the close of the Franco-Prussian War have been insignificant. The areas within 250 and 500 miles of the coast are also indicated.

THE RE-MAKING

OF EUROPE

GENERAL SURVEY OF THE PERIOD
By Oscar Browning, M.A.

EUROPE SINCE THE YEAR 1815

BEFORE the French Revolution Europe was in a condition of unstable equilibrium. Anyone who studies the condition of the map of Europe in the last years of the eighteenth century will perceive this to be the case. France, Spain, and Great Britain were in a fairly homogeneous situation, but the position of the rest of Europe was intolerable. The German Empire, the mere phantom of its glorious past, was honeycombed by the territories of ecclesiastical princes, while its neighbours, Hungary and Poland, better consolidated than itself, were a menace to its permanence. Russia was in the throes of expansion to the east, west, and south.

The Turkish Empire, when it crossed the Bosphorus, found itself ruling dominions which it could not hope to maintain, and which were now slipping from its grasp. Greece and Bosnia, Moldavia and Wallachia, Servia and Bulgaria were moving from a position of subjection to vassalage, from vassalage to independence. Berlin was divided from Königsberg by a long stretch of territory which could not in any sense be called Prussian. **Barriers to European Solidarity** Italy was cut up into a number of impotent and warring states, which denied it a voice in European affairs. Naples and Sicily were parts of Spain. Norway was a part of Denmark. There was no solidarity, no unity in the component parts; railways, had they existed, would have been impossible, commerce was impeded by every kind of artificial barrier. A traveller who changed a sovereign when

he crossed the Channel found it reduced to nothing before his return by the charges of perpetual discount. The awakening was rude. Sluggish Europe shook herself to resist the dangers of the Revolution. She threatened to march to Paris to punish the regicide miscreants who bore **The Rude Awakening of Europe** sway in the capital, and to restore the Bourbon to his throne. But regenerated France laughed gaily at this unwieldy Titan. She threw off with ease the attacks directed against the missionaries of a new political gospel, and carried war into the territories of those who had assailed her. Her generals were everywhere victorious; but from among them arose Napoleon, the greatest of all generals of modern times.

It is too common to represent this commanding genius as a man of blood—insatiable with slaughter, uncontrolled in ambition, and regardless of the sacrifices with which it might be gratified. The empire of Napoleon was, at least in part, a carrying out of the programme of the Directory, and the consummation of the efforts which France had originally begun to resist intrusion. When that empire had reached its height, it was either in direct government or in powerful influence, nearly coterminous with civilised Europe, with the exception of Russia and England, who remained unsubdued. Spain and Portugal were under France, Belgium and Holland were a part of her dominions, the kingdom of Italy reached to the frontier of Naples, and Naples was French.

Switzerland was devoted to the man who had given her a good government, the Confederation of the Rhine included the kingdom of Westphalia as well as the tributary states of Saxony, Bavaria, Wurtemberg, and Baden ; Scandinavia listened to the advice of the Tuileries ; Prussia was reduced to insignificance.

The Unstable Empire of Napoleon
The Grand Duchy of Warsaw, a French creation, lay as a buffer state between Prussia and Austria ; and Austria, having given an empress to the French throne, was in a position in which her best hope of influence and power lay in her alliance with Napoleon, a position which she had not the wisdom to realise.

But Napoleon's empire was itself in a condition of instability. What form it would have taken if he had continued to reign, we do not know. The claims of nationality had begun to assert themselves before his fall—indeed, they had been to a large extent the cause of his ruin ; and if he desired to rear a lasting edifice he must have found a way of reconciling them with his scheme of a European Empire. He wished for a second son, and if such a one had been born and grown to manhood, or at least to adolescence, the formation of a united Italy might have been anticipated by many years. But his empire, constituted as it was, was certain to perish at his fall, and his fall came sooner than was expected.

We do not yet completely know the causes of the great Russian war, and we cannot properly apportion the blame of it between the emperor and the tsar. He believed that this would have been his last enterprise, his last war. Russia once brought to his feet, Europe would be at peace. But he miscalculated the difficulty of the task, and the stolid stubbornness of Russian resistance. Fortune turned against him, his star paled, and his empire was no more. It is a mistake to suppose that he could have made peace at Frankfort or at Châtillon ; the terms offered him were delusive, and were intended to be so by Metternich. Had Austria obeyed the voice of honour and of interest the empire might have been preserved, but by deserting these fundamental principles, the empire of the Hapsburgs, which has made so many mistakes, committed a last fatal error, which it has since most bitterly expiated.

The Fatal Error of the Hapsburgs

The Congress of Vienna endeavoured to repair the shattered fabric, but the unprejudiced observer will not credit the diplomatists of that assembly with much wisdom or with much prescience.

Ignorant of, or ignoring, the principle of nationality, which has since governed the world with a dominating force, they were led by Talleyrand to adopt the principle of legitimacy, which they had not the courage to follow out when it became a question of punishing Napoleon's friends or rewarding his enemies. Consequently, many arrangements of Vienna have been upset. Belgium has been divorced from Holland, Norway from Sweden, Prussia has united its severed territories and secured the headship of Germany. Italy has consolidated herself at the expense of the provinces and the prestige of Austria ; and Turkey has lost, one after another, the dominions which it was a disgrace to civilisation that she should have held at all.

The change from the Restoration which succeeded the fall of Napoleon to the conditions of the present day is divided into certain well-defined epochs marked by periods of disturbance, wars, or revolutions. The period between 1820 and 1830 is one of disheartening reaction, controlled by a desire to suppress everything which could remind the world of the principles of 1789, and to undo everything which the administrative ability of the great emperor had accomplished. This led to the Revolution of July, accompanied by other disturbances in Europe, and indirectly to the emancipation of the Catholics in England and the Reform Bill of 1832. It is characteristic of our country that the only revolution which we have experienced since the close of the seventeenth century has been an alteration in our electoral system, a change quite as important as, and more permanent than, any which has taken place in any other country.

Britain's Electoral Revolution

After 1830 the democratic strivings of the nations of the Continent were either suppressed or appeased, but the fire broke out with greater intensity in 1848, when a series of revolutions either shook or shattered every throne in Europe but our own. Then followed a series of wars—the Crimean war of 1854, the Italian war of 1859, the Danish war of 1863, the Austrian war of 1866, and the Franco-Prussian war of 1870. Since

1870 Europe has been at peace, and the severance of Norway from Sweden and the final consolidation of Italy have been brought about without an actual conflict. Belgium is no longer the cockpit of Europe—that has to be sought further afield. Rivalries which have a European side to them are fought out in Asia and in Africa, and we dread the time when the horrors of war may possibly be brought within our own experience.

Yet progress, in which international jealousies must have a part, still goes on, and war, if averted, is often threatened. The world knows of many mortal struggles which have never taken place, but which have been regarded as inevitable by well-informed and responsible statesmen. At one time we were certain to have a war with Russia, at another time with France, at another time with America, and a final war with Germany is looked upon by so many as the doom of fate that they think it useless to discuss its probability or even to take means to avert it. If the possibility of these catastrophes is known to the public at large, how many are in **French Revolution of 1830** the cognisance of Ministers who are acquainted with the secrets of foreign affairs ? Happily, the past is quite sufficient to occupy the historian, without troubling too much about the future.

Let us consider separately the effect of each of these crises on the course of European politics. The Revolution of July in Paris had broken out as a quarrel between the people and the king ; it ended by establishing the authority of the people. The royal title was changed from King of France to King of the French. The Charter was a Bill of Rights on the English model, dear to the heart of Guizot. It fixed the limits within which the people were willing to accept the government of a king. It was a decided advance towards democracy. The new constitution which followed the Revolution in Belgium was framed on similar lines, and in the spirit of the English Revolution of 1688.

It laid down the principle that all power emanated from the people, and that the king possessed no authority beyond that given him by the constitution. He could do no executive act except through the Ministers, and they were responsible to the Chambers. If the Ministers failed to command a majority in Parliament, it was their duty to retire. The English

colour of these arrangements seems to have suited the character of the Belgian people and the temper of the king.

The Revolution of July produced a powerful effect upon Switzerland, and inaugurated what is called the Period of Regeneration. It began with a movement to reform the constitutions of some **Switzerland's Period of Regeneration** of the cantons, in order to give a share in the government to classes who did not possess it. The Forest Cantons, the ancient heart of Switzerland, remained passive, but the population of the others bombarded their Governments with petitions for reform, and reform was speedily accorded. Zürich was the leader of the movement. The programme of the radical party was sovereignty of the people, universal suffrage, direct election, freedom of the Press, of petition, of religious belief, and of industry.

The movement was essentially democratic, and the struggle became so severe that the Federal Government had to intervene. The Canton of Basle was separated into two half cantons, Basle Town and Basle Country. Seven cantons formed a separate confederation, and a counter league was organised to oppose it. The conflict, embittered by the presence of refugees from other disturbed countries, lasted till the convulsions of 1848.

In Spain and Portugal the struggle between the Constitutionals and the Absolutists was complicated by a disputed succession. In the first country, Isabella was the watchword of the Liberals, Don Carlos of the reactionaries, their place being taken in Portugal by Maria da Gloria and Don Miguel. In Italy the agitation was more serious. It seized upon the states which had not been affected by the previous movements of 1820. At Rome the death of Pius VIII. gave the signal. Louis Napoleon took part in the plot to make his uncle, Jerome, King **Italy in a State of Unrest** of Italy. In the Romagna and the Marches provisional governments and national guards were the order of the day. Governments of this kind, with a dictator at their head, were formed in Parma and in Modena. But the movement came to nothing. Louis Philippe would not help, and Metternich was at hand with his Austrian army. With their assistance he brought back the Duke of Modena, and pacified the States of the Church. But the " Young Italy " of Mazzini was born in the conflict, a secret society devoted to the realisation of the unity of Italy under the form of a republic. Eventually the first object was attained, but the second was not.

A similar impulse animated the Liberals of Germany, who had long been discontented with the policy of the Holy Alliance.

Poland's bold Stand for Independence The War of Liberation had only subjected them to a worse despotism than that of Napoleon. Brunswick, Hesse-Cassel, Saxony, and Hanover obtained constitutions ; in Bavaria and Baden men of enlightened minds were allowed to express themselves more freely. A stronger movement took place in Poland, then divided between two parties, the Whites and the Reds. The Whites were composed of the large proprietors, the higher officials, and the clergy. Provided that Poland was suffered to retain a nominal independence, they were content to wait for constitutional reforms. The Reds were patriots and democrats, but they were violent and impatient.

In the last month of 1830, when the emperor had mobilised the Polish army in order to suppress the revolution in France and Belgium, the national troops turned against their oppressors. The students of the Military College seized the palace at Warsaw, and the Grand Duke Constantine fled for his life. The Romanoff dynasty was deposed, and the union of Poland with Lithuania was proclaimed. Britain and France were sympathetic, but refused to give active assistance ; the Polish army was crushed by superior numbers, and a military dictator was set up. The end of Poland had arrived. In 1835 the Emperor Nicholas told the Poles plainly that unless they gave up the dream of a separate independent nationality the guns of the newly built citadel should lay Warsaw in ruins. We see, therefore, that the Revolution of July had made a great breach in the system established by the Congress of Vienna.

Political Changes in Britain The Bourbons, who based their title on the principles of legitimacy, were succeeded by a king of the barricades, professing the doctrines of 1789, and waving its flag. The British Constitution remained unshaken, but the Reform Bill of 1832 brought about a revolution in the balance of political power not less momentous than the others, because it was pacific, and destined to produce results not less important although slow in coming.

Eighteen years later the Revolution broke out with greater violence, and spread with the rapidity of a plague. It began in Switzerland in 1847, showed itself in Sicily in January, 1848, and overthrew the throne of Louis Philippe in France in February of the same year. The fall of monarchy in France gave the signal for disturbances throughout Europe. England, the Iberian Peninsula, Sweden, Norway and Russia alone escaped. In Holland, Belgium and Denmark it ran a comparatively mild course. The symptoms were more severe in Austria, Prussia, Germany, and Central Italy ; it led to bloodshed in Northern Italy, Schleswig-Holstein, and Hungary.

The outbreak in Switzerland was the result of a conflict which had been smouldering for many years. It was caused by two movements, one civil, the other religious ; one an effort to democratise the constitution, the other a desire to restrain the influence of the Roman Catholic Church. The Liberal party was divided into Moderates and Radicals, but the Moderates gradually lost their influence. The Radicals were strengthened

Revolution in Switzerland and stimulated by the refugees of other nationalities, who had found an asylum in Switzerland when driven out of their own countries. The Poles organised raids against Neuchatel and Savoy ; Mazzini used Switzerland as a place of arms. Austria and Bavaria demanded the extradition of German " patriots," and when this was refused, broke off diplomatic relations. France insisted upon the expulsion of the supposed authors of the conspiracy of Fieschi, and sealed their frontiers against the passage of the stubborn Switzers.

A few years later they asked for the surrender of Louis Napoleon, who had his home at Arenenberg. The Catholics based their hopes on the peasants, and posed as the supporters of democracy. In Schytz the two parties of " Horns " and " Hoofs " came to blows over the use of the public pastures ; in Canton Ticino, the Radicals won by force of arms ; in the Valley of the Rhone the Upper and Lower districts were in hopeless disorder. The Puritans of Zürich drove Strauss, the author of the " Life of Jesus," from his professorial chair. The Jesuits succeeded in founding Catholic Colleges at Schytz, Freiburg, and Lucerne. Argau answered this challenge by suppressing eight convents, and demanding the expulsion of the Order. The result of this prolonged tension was a civil war. In 1845 the seven Catholic cantons formed a "sonderbund," a separate league, which the government determined to suppress by force, and in three weeks General Dufour effected this object. The Radicals were victorious, the Jesuits were expelled, and civil war was averted. The result of this struggle was the formation of a new constitution, by which Switzerland, from being a statenbund—a confederation of states—became a federal state—a bundesstat. A new nation came to life in Europe.

The French Revolution of 1848 was equally a surprise for the victors and the vanquished. It raged for two days, the first of which witnessed a revolt of the reformers against Guizot, the second a revolution of the Republicans against the monarchy. At 10 a.m. on February 24th, the Palais Royal was captured; at 4.30 p.m. the throne was destroyed in the Tuileries, and shortly afterwards the Republic was proclaimed at the Hotel de Ville. The result of this was a democratic movement throughout Europe. In Holland the personal government of the king was changed into a constitutional monarchy; in Belgium the Liberals were confirmed in power; in Denmark the accession of a new king presented an opportunity for substituting a constitution for absolutism and for setting the Press free.

Italy in Revolt against Austria

Italy was shaken from Monte Rosa to Cape Passaro. The movement began in Sicily, where for a fortnight in January the insurgents fought against the Royal troops, demanding the constitution of 1812. At Naples, Ferdinand accorded a constitution based upon the French Charte, and appointed a Carbonaro as Prime Minister. At Turin, Charles Albert promulgated a constitution, which, in all the storm of conflict, has never been abrogated, and the Grand Duke of Tuscany did the same.

At Rome, Pio Nono nominated three lay Ministers, but the supreme power remained with the College of Cardinals. The passionate desire of the Italians was to shake off the hated domination of Austria. They shouted, in the words of the "Garibaldi hymn": "Va fuori d'Italia, va fuori o Stranier!" [From Italy from sea to snow, let the hated stranger go!] For this the revolution in Vienna gave an opportunity. Here the storm broke in

March, the direct consequence of the French Revolution of February. The desires of the people were voiced by booksellers, students, and Liberal clubs; they demanded liberty of religion, of teaching, of speech, and of writing, and a budget controlled by a representative government. Their cry was: "Down with Metternich! Down with the soldiery!" and Metternich was dismissed. The emperor fled to the Tyrol, and the Archduke John, the darling of the people, took his place. A Constituent Assembly met at Vienna in July. In Hungary, a country better suited for self-government, the change took a more solid shape. The seat of Parliament was transferred from Pressburg to Budapest. It issued a coinage, and formed an army under the Hungarian tricolour. Austria was compelled to weaken her garrisons in Italy in order to subdue her revolted provinces north of the Alps.

Republic of St. Mark in Venice

In March, Milan rose, and Radetsky retired within the Quadrilateral. Modena and Parma were left to themselves, and obtained constitutions. Cavour called the Piedmontese to arms; Tuscany, Rome and Naples sent their troops to join their brethren of the North. In Venice, Daniele Manin, like-named but not like-minded with the last Doge, awakened to life a Republic of St. Mark. A revolution was organised, at once Liberal, monarchical, and national, under the three colours of the Italian flag, the emblems of passion, purity, and hope.

The dream of liberty was short lived. It vanished before the approach of foreign armies. The Austrians defeated the Sardinians at Custozza, and reconquered the whole of Lombardy. A still more fatal blow fell at Novara, where Charles Albert was routed in March, 1849, and abdicated in consequence. The crown came to his son, Victor Emmanuel, who afterwards became the first monarch of a united Italy. Venice fell, after a long siege, in August of the same year. Modena and Parma, who had joined themselves to Piedmont, were occupied by Austria, and their ducal governments were restored. Tuscany suffered the same fate, and the Grand Duke was compelled by the Austrian army of occupation to abrogate the constitution of 1848, so that his country became less free than it was before the revolution. Four Catholic Powers—

The Siege and Fall of Venice

France, Spain, Austria, and Naples—offered their assistance to the Pope, but the main burden of recovering the Holy City fell upon France. Rome, defended by Mazzini and Garibaldi, was captured in June, 1849; the Cardinals came into power with Antonelli at their head. The tricolour was surrendered. Italy was again split into fragments, **Italy Split into Fragments** dependent upon foreign force. Sardinia alone remained a germ of liberty and hope. In Austria, the champion of reaction, the war of nationalities, which has always been to her a danger, now proved her salvation.

A Panslavic Congress had been summoned at Prague, which was attended not only by Bohemians, Moravians, and Silesians, but by Russians, Poles, and Servians. But the Croatians turned against the Magyars, and the South Slavs against their brethren of the North. Prague was bombarded and Bohemia conquered; the Croats marched upon Budapest. The emperor, who had fled from his capital and sought refuge in Moravia, made a common war against the German democrats and the Hungarian rebels, who had chosen Kossuth as their leader. Croats attacked Vienna from the east, Bohemians from the north. After a short struggle they were victorious; the Hungarians, who had come to the assistance of the friends of liberty, were repulsed and an absolute government was restored. Hungary held out a little longer.

A Hungarian Republic was established, with Kossuth as President. But the Russians declared themselves the enemies of revolution, and Nicholas came to the aid of his brother emperor. An army 80,000 strong entered the country from the Carpathians. The Magyars capitulated at Vilagos, preferring to fall into the hands of the Russians rather than into those of their ancient tyrants. Kossuth, after burying the Hungarian crown, sought refuge in Turkey. **The Brief Republic of Hungary** Metternich was again master, and the last state of the rebellious provinces was worse than the first. Prussia also had her " days of March," but here the middle-classes stood aloof, and the Liberals were left to fight out their battle against the army.

The chief object of their attack was the Prince of Prussia, brother of the king, who was destined at a later period to be the first Emperor of Germany. The king at first tried to temporise. He promised a constitution, withdrew his troops, and sent the Prince of Prussia to England. He adopted the German tricolour, threw himself upon the affection of his Prussians, and invoked the confidence of Germany. He granted a written constitution and a National Assembly elected by universal suffrage. But he soon discovered his mistake, and was obliged to follow the example of Austria. The army re-entered the capital, took possession of the Parliament buildings, dissolved the National Guard, and soon afterwards dispersed the Assembly. Absolute government was restored, veiled under the forms of a constitution.

The Provisional Government in France, which succeeded the Orleans monarchy, was formed by a coalition, and therefore contained within itself the seeds of dissolution. One party aimed at the establishment of a democratic republic based on universal suffrage, the other desired a democratic and social republic, the chief object of which should be the elevation of the working classes. The tricolour of 1789 was opposed by the red flag of Louis Blanc. The battle **Civil War in the Streets of Paris** raged round the organisation of labour and the establishment of national workshops. However, the Socialists had opposed to them the whole of France and half the capital, and they were unable to hold their own. A civil war broke out in the streets of Paris, and three days' fighting was required for the capture of the suburb of St. Antoine by General Cavaignac. The Socialist prisoners were shot or transported and their newspapers were suppressed. Eventually a constitution was agreed upon, which established a single chamber, a president holding office for four years, and a Council of State.

The president was to be chosen by universal suffrage, and the election took place on December 10th, 1848. Ledru Rollin was the candidate of the Socialists, Cavaignac of the Democrats, but both had to give way to Louis Napoleon, the inheritor of a mighty name, who was chosen by an overwhelming majority. This election could have no other result than the establishment of a monarchy. The coup d'état of December 2nd, 1851, dissolved the Assembly, and arrested the leaders of the Republican party. Following the example of his uncle, Louis Napoleon was first made president for ten years, and shortly afterwards Emperor. The plebiscite accepting him as Emperor of the French was taken four years, to a day, after he had been elected president.

By the events we have described absolute government was established over the whole of Europe, excepting Switzerland and the countries which had not been affected by the revolutions of 1848. However, France preserved her principle of universal suffrage, Prussia and Sardinia their constitutions, with the fixed resolve of achieving the unity of Germany and of Italy, founded on the principle of nationality, which had been ignored by the Congress of Vienna. We now pass from the epoch of revolutions to the epoch of war.

The Crimean War of 1854 belongs to those events of history of which we do not precisely know the cause. There are probably few Englishmen who feel satisfied with their country's share in it, or who support it as an act of political wisdom. There are few, also, who would deny that we were led into it by the Emperor of the French. Louis Napoleon came to the throne of France pledged by conviction **The Crimean War** and by honour to effect the liberation of Italy from the Austrian yoke. This could not be done without war, and although France was strong enough to meet Austria in the field, she could not contend against Austria and Russia united. It therefore became necessary to weaken Russia before such a war could be undertaken, and the question of the Holy Places was seized upon with great adroitness as a colourable pretext for a war with Russia.

Britain was easily, too easily, stirred to defend Turkey against aggression and dismemberment, and thus a conflict was begun of which we have little reason to be proud. Russia was prepared to meet an attack in the Baltic, in Poland, or on the Danube, but the Crimea was only feebly garrisoned. Still, Sebastopol held out, and the resources of the allies were strained to the utmost. A winter campaign became necessary in a desert country, subject to intense cold. The British lost half their troops, and no assistance came from Austria or Prussia.

In the spring of 1855 the Emperor Nicholas died, and the war no longer had a motive. However, it continued under his successor, and Sebastopol did not fall until six months afterwards. Napoleon was ready to make peace, although Palmerston wished to go on fighting, and a treaty was eventually concluded at the Congress of Paris. Turkey lost the Danubian provinces, but the integrity of her empire was guaranteed, while she promised reforms of administration which were never carried into effect. The navigation of the Danube was declared free, and the Black Sea neutral. Cavour had been **Consequences of the Crimean War** clever enough to join the alliance, although Sardinia had no interest, direct or indirect, in the questions in dispute. This gave him a right to take part in the congress, and the liberation of Italy entered for the first time into the domain of practical politics. The war undoubtedly raised the prestige of the French Emperor, and gave him a commanding position in European affairs. It called Roumania into existence, and it recognised the claims of nationality in Italy. It was another blow to the principles of the Congress of Vienna, and it weakened the influence of Austria.

It will be seen from this narrative that the Crimean War led directly to the Italian War of 1859. By adroit diplomacy Austria was induced to invade Sardinian territory, and the armies of France crossed the Alps to defend her. The two allied armies were able to concentrate at Alessandria before they could be attacked in detail. The Battle of Magenta, having been lost in the morning, was won in the afternoon, MacMahon playing the part of Desaix at Marengo.

The Austrians evacuated Lombardy and retired into the Quadrilateral to defend Venetia. After a hard struggle the Austrians were again defeated at Solferino, but the bloodshed had so unnerved the emperor, and the quarrels between his marshals had so disgusted him, that he broke his promise of setting Italy free to the Adriatic, and made a peace which secured only Lombardy to Sardinia. He received in exchange Savoy **The Damaged Prestige of Louis Napoleon** and Nice, but this second war was as fatal to his prestige as the first had been favourable. Italy alone profited by the result. Parma, Modena, and Tuscany drove out their dukes; Romagna set herself free from the Pope; provisional governments were established in these provinces, ready for incorporation with the kingdom of the House of Savoy. Cavour, who had resigned after the Peace of Villafranca, again became Prime Minister. The spell of Austrian domination was broken, and the establishment of an Italian kingdom, so long the dream of poets and patriots, became only a question of time.

The scene of our drama shifts to another quarter. What Cavour had done for Italy Bismarck was to do for Germany. The rivalry between Austria and Prussia for the leading position in Germany, and for the inheritance of the Holy Roman Empire had been active ever since the Congress of Vienna. The policy of Napoleon would have annihilated Prussia and strengthened Austria, but Metternich committed the fatal blunder of joining the coalition of which the profits were to come to his rival instead of himself.

Metternich's Fatal Blunder

There was a time when Hanover might have disputed with Prussia the first place in a Teutonic Empire, but it was impossible that such a position could be held by a King of England, and the sovereignty of the British Isles was regarded as more valuable than the chances of a Continental crown. The share which Prussia had taken in the Waterloo campaign rendered her reward certain, and the world was disposed to favour Protestant progress rather than Catholic stagnation.

Still, it is doubtful if Prussia would have gained the position which was the object of her desires unless Bismarck had been in her service, who, with a mixture of statesmanship and craft, of courage and audacity, half untied and half cut the Gordian knot of the situation. The Danish War of 1864 would probably never have taken place unless Bismarck had conveyed to the Danes the false assurance, based probably upon an intercepted dispatch, that she was certain to receive the support of Britain. The defeat of Denmark was speedy and inevitable, and the arrangements made by the Peace of Vienna ceded the duchies of Schleswig and Holstein to Austria and Prussia under conditions which made a future quarrel inevitable.

Cessions of the Peace of Vienna

The Schleswig-Holstein difficulty rose in great measure from the fact that whereas Holstein was almost entirely German—and, indeed, claimed to be a part of the old German Empire—Schleswig was more than half Danish, and yet the two duchies were united by a permanent bond which national feeling declared was never to be broken. "Schleswig-Holstein sea surrounded" was the text of their patriotic hymn. The arrangements for the joint occupation of the provinces by the two conflicting rivals provided that the German province should be occupied by Austria ; the semi-Danish by Prussia. This made a quarrel certain. The Prussian governor of Schleswig persecuted the partisans of independence ; the Austrian governor of Holstein encouraged them. The rupture was delayed for a time by the Convention of Gastein, but it came at last.

In order to attack Austria with success it was necessary that Prussia should have Italy on her side. But Italy could not act without the consent of France, and this implied the approval of the Emperor Napoleon. At the interview of Biarritz, in October, 1865, Napoleon agreed to support Prussia against Austria, and declared himself in favour of the unity of Italy, if some compensation were given to his own country by an increase of territory. He desired to tear up the settlement of Vienna, so hostile to Napoleonic ideals. Bismarck adroitly encouraged these aspirations, but took care not to commit himself. It was found difficult to overcome the distrust which the Italians felt for Bismarck. They hoped to obtain Venetia without a war, possibly by ceding the newly-created Roumania to Austria. Even King William was averse from force, and Bismarck stood alone, supported by his clear insight and his iron will. At last, in April, 1866, an offensive alliance with Italy was concluded for three months. Italy was to support Prussia in obtaining the hegemony of Germany, and was to receive Venetia in return. She asked for Trieste, but it was refused to her. Napoleon promised to remain neutral.

Italian Distrust of Bismarck

In June, Prussia declared the federative tie which bound her to Austria dissolved. But she found herself alone. Bavaria, Wurtemberg, Saxony, and Hanover, together with Hesse-Nassau, and Baden, supported Austria. Prussia had to rely upon her well-drilled army and her admirable arrangements for mobilisation. Napoleon hoped that between combatants so equally matched the war would be of some duration, and that, when both were exhausted, he could come forward as a mediator, and make his own terms. But these hopes were shattered by the rapidity of the Prussian movements. Before the end of June the army of Hanover had capitulated, Saxony was occupied, Bohemia invaded, and on July 3rd the Battle of Königgrätz, won largely by the genius of the Crown Prince Frederic, ended the struggle, and the way lay open to Vienna.

At the same time the Italians were defeated at Custozza by a force inferior in numbers, but this did not prevent the Austrians having to surrender Venetia to Napoleon, who gave it to the Italians. The southern states of Germany were incapable of effective action. They were beaten in detail; Frankfort was occupied, Austria was compelled to abandon her allies, who had no alternative but to make peace; Prussia became the undisputed head of the German confederation. Europe was dazed and bewildered by the rapidity and completeness of her success.

Napoleon found himself deceived, and every step which he took to recover his position led to new disasters. His attempt to gain possession of the Grand Duchy of Luxemburg proved a failure. He looked about in vain for allies. A triple alliance was proposed with Austria and Italy, but Austria was exhausted and dreaded another war, while Italy demanded **The Greatest War of Modern Times** the withdrawal of the French from Rome. Nothing could be obtained beyond general declarations of sympathy and friendship. A proposition made in the beginning of 1870 for a mutual disarmament came to nothing. At last, at a moment when peace seemed to be assured, war broke out with the suddenness of an earthquake. The clumsiness of a French Minister who, not satisfied with a material victory, demanded a humiliating declaration from the Prussian king, the genius of Bismarck, who seized an unequalled opportunity for precipitating a conflict which he regarded as inevitable, so as to have the nation and the sovereign on his side, caused the greatest war of modern times, by the results of which Europe is still dominated.

War was declared on July 19th, and the emperor left for the front. But he had no illusion as to the result. The empress who, stung to the heart by the taunts of Germany, had stimulated the conflict, was unable to inspire him with hope. He left St. Cloud, accompanied by his son, as a victim led to the slaughter, and the final catastrophe was not long delayed. The war of 1870 was more than a local conflict. It must be reckoned among the vital struggles which have convulsed Europe

since the fall of the Roman Empire; a scene, but probably not a closing scene, in the secular rivalry between the Roman and the Teuton.

It was said at the time that Sedan avenged Tagliacozzo, that the French emperor expiated on that field the murder of the Hohenstauffen Conradin by the **Creation of the German Empire** brother of St. Louis. Regarded from a more prosaic point of view, it upset the politics of Europe. It created a German Empire, with Prussia at its head, and gave that country a preponderance in Europe. It achieved the unity of Italy, and destroyed the temporal power of the Pope. It opened the question of the East by putting an end to the neutrality of the Black Sea. It established in France a republican government which seems to be durable, and it transferred that neutral territory between Neustria and Austrasia—which appears to have come into existence from the accident of Lewis the Pious having three sons instead of two—from the French to the German side of his dominions. Whether this arrangement will be permanent or not, none can say. It produced by force a settlement of Europe very different to those which were established at Münster, at Utrecht, or at Vienna, and we still lie under the conditions which it created.

Nearly forty years have elapsed since the war of 1870, almost as long a period as intervened between the Battle of Waterloo and the Crimean war. Can Europe be now declared to be in a state of equilibrium, or is she menaced by convulsions similar to those which we have sketched?

Political prophecy is always dangerous; rarely can the most far-sighted statesman foresee what is going to happen. The danger long dreaded frequently never comes, and the catastrophe arises in a season of complete security. Still, if we pass the map of Europe in review, we shall **The Relations of France and Britain** find a great improvement since the Congress of Vienna, and we may believe that our hopes of peaceful development for European nations rests upon a firmer basis. France appears to be firmly established in the form of a republic, and is supported by the friendship of the British Empire. Even if she were to change her government, it would not necessarily produce a European war. Spain is recovering from her disasters and entering upon a new career of prosperity, while Portugal will probably follow her example. Both monarchies are, however, menaced by the presence of a strong republican party, which is encouraged by the presence of a republic in France. The two most momentous events in the period under discussion have been the creation of a united Germany and a united Italy. Both of **Changes in Germany and Italy** these seem likely to be permanent. The divergence between the feelings and interests of Northern and Southern Germany has, to a large extent, disappeared, and the friendship which animates them has become stronger in the course of years. It was the King of Bavaria who proposed, in the great gallery of Versailles, that the King of Prussia should be Emperor of Germany, and in doing so he expressed the sentiments not only of the present, but of the future.

No one who was acquainted with Italy in the days before Magenta and Solferino can fail to recognise the change which has come over that country. The debt incurred in extending the Italian railways, in piercing the Alps and the Apennines, has been completely justified, and the prescience of those who brought it about has been proved by its success. There is a constant movement of the population between south and north, and the National Army of Italy has proved not only a potent instrument of education, but a means of creating a feeling of nationality for which the provincialism of earlier days left no scope. It has even had an effect upon the language and literature of the country. Italian has now supplanted French as the language of the higher classes, and books are now written in Italian which in old days would have been written in dialect.

The position of the Pope at Rome is still a cause of discord, but there is hope that by concessions on each side these differences may disappear. As we move **What is the Future of Austria?** further east, the outlook becomes less favourable. Who can foretell the future of Austria or of Russia? Austria, an ill-assorted congeries of discordant nationalities—Magyar and Czech, Italian and Slavonic—is held under a German head by the force of old traditions and the fear of a civil war, which might be caused by a disruption. But it is probable that even here the danger may be averted, and at the death of the present emperor means may be

found of reconciling differences, which appear irreconcilable, by the exercise of political common sense, and of a patriotism which, if not based on sentiment and affection, may at least be founded upon interest.

Russia, the unwieldy giant, a huge territory sparsely peopled by discordant elements, governed from an artificially created capital, which is removed every day further away from the centre of gravity of affairs, as the frontiers of the empire spread further to the east, may, perhaps, split up into its component elements, Asiatic and European, or, by a wise extension of constitutional government, may continue to exist for a considerable time. Many prophecies of its fall have been shown to be false, and those who know it best have the surest confidence in its stability. Turkey must always remain an apple of discord. The forces which have, during a long course of years, dismembered its territory and gradually liberated suffering provinces from its yoke will continue to be active, and, when the intelligence of Europe has leisure to attend to it, will free Constantinople from **The Startling Revolution of the Year 1908** her servitude, and drive the Ottoman Turk into Asia; unless, indeed, the startling revolution of 1908 proves the true precursor of a transformation in his character and methods without historical parallel. Portions of the world to which culture owes so much, which have had so glorious a past, which gave the world so much of Greek literature, philosophy and eloquence, which were the first to feel the awakening influence of Christianity, cannot remain for ever in a condition of inglorious slumber.

Greece, which has completely justified the enthusiasm for liberty which called her into existence, will receive not only Crete, but other provinces which once belonged to her, and the Bulgarians will enjoy the reward of their patient industry and their solid capacity for practical affairs. The world has seen the principles of territorial sovereignty, of the balance of power, of so-called legitimacy, which so long dominated the politics of Europe, receive their consecration in the Congress of Vienna. It has seen the principle of nationality, unfortunately ignored in the arrangements of that congress, create a new Germany and a new Italy, and work powerfully among the Slavs, still subject to the domination of alien masters.

It is probable that the principle which is destined to conciliate divergent interests, to reconcile rivalries, and to establish the government of Europe upon a firm basis of stable equilibrium, is the principle of federation, a mode of government which is possible only in an advanced state of civilisation, and is certain to be accepted in proportion as civilisation advances. Much of the unrest which now renders government difficult is due to the fact that legislation which benefits one part of a country is harmful to another part.

Ireland cannot be governed satisfactorily on English methods, and measures which are beneficial to Lombardy are inapplicable to Sicily. The particularism of Spain, which makes Catalonia a centre of disorder, can be remedied only by a policy which allows the provinces of that country to a large extent to govern themselves. The world is shrinking. The trend of affairs in the world of our time is towards the creation of vast empires, the formation of large political units.

But this spirit of what is sometimes called imperialism can be safely carried out only by strengthening the smaller political units of which the larger units are composed. Extensive outlooks, the management of affairs on a vast scale, cannot be indulged in unless care is taken not to weaken the intensive feelings which are equally essential to political well-being. A statesman must rely not only on the wider patriotism, which carries with it untold benefits wherever it is found, but on the domestic virtues of local and municipal patriotism, the love of our country, our province, and our town.

The tendency to foster local languages and local ties, which is sometimes regarded as injurious to the higher interests of humanity, is in reality the outcome of a natural instinct of self-preservation. Long ago the Romans taught us that the two essential bases of all government are Imperium and Libertas—ill-translated Empire and Liberty—one the exercise of firm rule, the other the concession to the freedom of individual action. The reconciliation of these two forces is to be found in federation, a form of government which is constantly making progress among us. By this every citizen owes a double allegiance, one to his municipal surroundings, which appeals to sentiments which belong to his birth, his education and his race; and the other to his imperial position, which enables him to enjoy a larger life and to take his proper share in the administration of the world. The Roman Empire, the Holy Roman Empire, have passed away; a British Empire and other similar combinations are coming into being. The scientific pursuit of this ideal, guided by the best political thought, and carried into execution by the highest political wisdom, is the only means by which we may hope to realise the theme of poets, the dream of statesmen, a goal which is yet far distant, but which is not impossible, the Federation of the World. OSCAR BROWNING

QUEEN VICTORIA AND THE PRINCE CONSORT AT THE GREAT EXHIBITION. IN 1851
From the painting by S. N. Reynolds

REORGANISING THE POLITICAL SYSTEM OF EUROPE: THE EPOCH-MAKING CONGRESS OF VIENNA

After the first fall of Napoleon, a congress of the European Powers assembled at Vienna, on November 1st, 1814, with the view of repairing the shattered fabric and reorganising the political system of Europe, which had been disturbed by the conquests of the French. The restoration of Napoleon put a sudden end to the deliberations of the congress, but its agreements were signed by the eight Powers interested on June 9th, 1815. The Powers represented were Austria, Prussia, Russia, Britain, France, Sweden, Spain, and Portugal.

EUROPE AFTER WATERLOO
THE GREAT POWERS IN CONCORD
AND THE FAILURE OF THE HOLY ALLIANCE

AT the Congress of Vienna nations were but rarely, and national rights and desires never, a subject of discussion. The Cabinets—that is to say, the princes of Europe, their officials, and in particular the diplomatists—arranged the mutual relations of states almost exclusively with reference to dynastic interests and differences in national power ; though in the case of France it was necessary to consult national susceptibilities, and in England the economic demands of the upper classes of society came into question. The term " state " implied a ruling court, a government, and nothing beyond, not only to Prince Metternich, but also to the majority of his coadjutors. These institutions were the sole surviving representatives of that feudal organism which for more than a thousand years had undertaken the larger proportion of the task of the state.

Principalities of this kind were not founded upon the institutions of civic life, which had developed under feudal society ; the rule of the aristocracy had fallen into decay, had grown antiquated or had been abolished, and as the monarchy increased in power at the expense of the classes, it had invariably employed instruments of government more scientifically constructed in **European Governments in Evolution** detail. Bureaucracies had arisen. Governments had intervened between princes and peoples and had become ends in themselves. The theory of "subordination," which in feudal society had denoted an economic relation, now assumed a political character ; it was regarded as a necessary extension of the idea of sovereignty, which had become the sole and ultimate basis of public authority in the course of the seventeenth century. The impulse of the sovereigns to extend the range of their authority, and a conception more or less definite of the connection between this authority and certain ideal objects, resulted in the theory that the guidance of **The French Idea of " The Rights of Man "** society was a governmental task, and consequently laid an ever-increasing number of claims and demands upon the government for the time being. To this conception of the rights of princes and their delegates, as a result of historic growth, the French Revolution had opposed the idea of " the rights of man." To the National Assembly no task seemed more necessary or more imperative than the extirpation of erroneous theories from the general thought of the time ; such theories had arisen from the exaggerated importance attached to monarchical power, had secured recognition, and had come into operation, simply because they had never been confuted.

Henceforward sovereignty was to be based upon the consent of the community as a whole. Thus supported by the sovereign will of the people, France had entered upon war with the monarchical states of Europe where the exercise of supreme power had been the ruler's exclusive right. It was as an exponent of the sovereign rights of the people that the empire of Napoleon Bonaparte had attempted to make France the paramount Power in Europe ; it was in virtue of the power entrusted to him by six millions of Frenchmen that the Emperor had led his armies far beyond the limits of French domination and had imposed his personal

479[1]

will upon the princes of Europe by means of a magnificent series of battles. Within a period of scarce two decades the balance of power had swung to the opposite extreme, and had passed back from the sovereign people to the absolute despot. Monarchs and nations shared alike in the task of overpowering this tyranny which

The Growing Power of the People had aimed at abolishing entirely the rights of nations as such; but from victory the princes alone derived advantage. With brazen effrontery literary timeservers scribbled their histories to prove that only the sovereigns and their armies deserved the credit of the overthrow of Napoleon, and that the private citizen had done no more service than does the ordinary fireman at a conflagration.

However, their view of the situation was generally discredited. It could by no means be forgotten that the Prussians had forced their king to undertake a war of liberation, and the services rendered by Spain and the Tyrol could not be wholly explained by reference to the commands of legally constituted authorities; in either case it was the people who by force of arms had cast off the yoke imposed upon them. The will of the people had made itself plainly understood; it had declined the alien rule even though that rule had appeared under the names of freedom, reform, and prosperity.

Once again the princely families recovered their power and position; they had not entertained the least idea of dividing among themselves the spoils accumulated by the Revolution which had been taken from their kin, their relations, and their allies; at the same time they were by no means inclined to divide the task of administering the newly created states with the peoples inhabiting them. They tacitly united in support of the conviction, which became an article of faith with all legitimists, that their position

The Subject's Duty to the State and prosperity were no less important than the maintenance of social order and morality. It was explained as the duty of the subject to recognise both the former and the latter; and by increasing his personal prosperity, the subject was to provide a sure basis on which to increase the powers of the government. However, "the limited intelligence of the subjects" strove against this interpretation of the facts; they could not forget the enormous

sacrifices which had been made to help those states threatened by the continuance of the Napoleonic supremacy, and in many cases already doomed to destruction. The value of their services aroused them to question also the value of what they had attained, and by this process of thought they arrived at critical theories and practical demands which "legitimist" teaching was unable to confute.

The supreme right of princes to wage war and conclude peace-rested upon satisfactory historic foundation, and was therefore indisputable. In the age of feudal society it was the lords, the free landowners, who had waged war, and not the governments; and their authority had been limited only by their means. Neither the lives nor the property of the commonalty had ever come in question except in cases where their sympathies had been enlisted by devastation, fire, and slaughter; to actual co-operation in the undertakings of the overlord the man of the people had never been bound, and such help had been voluntarily given. After the conception of sovereignty had been modified by the

Evil Results of the Revolution idea of "government" the situation had been changed. Military powers and duties were now dissociated from the feudal classes; the sinews of war were no longer demanded from the warriors themselves, and the provision of means became a government duty. However, no new rights had arisen to correspond with these numerous additional duties. The vassal, now far more heavily burdened, demanded his rights; the people followed his example. That which was to be supported by the general efforts of the whole of the members of any body politic must surely be a matter of general concern. The state also has duties incumbent upon it, the definition of which is the task of those who support the state. Such demands were fully and absolutely justified; a certain transformation of the state and of society was necessary and inevitable.

Few princes, and still fewer officials, recognised the overwhelming force of these considerations; in the majority of cases expression of the popular will was another name for revolution. The Revolution had caused the overthrow of social order. It had engendered the very worst of human passions, destroyed professions and property, sacrificed a countless number of human lives, and disseminated infidelity and immorality; revolution therefore must be checked, must be nipped in the bud in the name of God, of civilisation and social order. This opinion was founded upon the fundamental mistake of refusing to recognise the fact that all rights implied corresponding duties; while disregarding every historical tradition and assenting to the dissolution of every feudal idea, it did nothing to introduce new relations or to secure a compromise between the prince and his subjects.

This point of view was known as Conservatism; its supporters availed themselves of the unnatural limitations laid upon the subject unduly to aggrandise and systematically to increase the privileges of the ruling class; and this process received the name of statecraft. This conservative statecraft, of which Prince Metternich was proud to call himself a master, proceeded from a dull and spiritless conception of the progress of the world; founded upon a complete lack of historical knowledge, it equally failed to recognise any distinct purpose as obligatory on the state. Of political science Metternich had none; he made good the deficiency by the general admiration which his intellect and character inspired. His diaries and many of his letters are devoted to the glorification of these merits. A knowledge of his intellectual position and of that of the majority of his diplomatic colleagues is an indispensable preliminary to the understanding of the aberrations into which the statesmen of the so-called Restoration period fell. The restored Government of the Bourbons in France was indeed provided with a constitution. It was thus that Tsar Alexander I. had attempted to display his liberal tendencies and his good-will to the French nation; but he

The Restored Government of the Bourbons

PRINCE METTERNICH

After the fall of Napoleon, in 1815, Metternich stepped into the place vacated by the emperor as the first personality in Europe, and, as the avowed champion of Conservatism, opposed forces that were destined to ultimate triumph. He was overthrown in 1848, and died in 1859.

had been forced to leave the Germans and Italians to their fate, and had satisfied his conscience by the insertion of a few expressions in the final protocol of the Vienna Congress. Subsequently he suffered a cruel disappointment in the case of Poland, which proceeded to misuse the freedom that had been granted to it by the concoction of conspiracies and by continual manifestations of dissatisfaction. He began to lose faith in Liberalism as such, and became a convert to Metternich's policy of forcibly suppressing every popular movement for freedom. Untouched by the enthusiasm of the German youth, which for the most part had displayed after the war of liberation the noblest sense of patriotism, and could provide for the work of restoration and reorganisation coadjutors highly desirable to a far-seeing administration; incapable of understanding the Italian yearnings for union and activity, and for the foundation of a federal state free from foreign influences, the great Powers of Austria, Russia, and Prussia employed threats and force in every form, with the object of imposing constitutions of their own choice upon the people, whose desires for reform they wholly disregarded. Austria had for the moment obtained a magnificent position in the German Confederacy. This, however, the so-called statecraft of Conservatism declined to use for the consolidation of the federation, which Austria at the same time desired to exploit for her own advantage. Conservatism never, indeed, gave the smallest attention to the task of uniting the interests of the allied states by institutions making for prosperity, or by the union of their several artistic and scientific powers; it seemed more necessary and more salutary to limit as far as possible the influence of the

The Tsar's Lost Faith in Liberalism

popular representatives in the administration of the allied states, and to prevent the introduction of constitutions which gave the people rights of real and tangible value. The conservative statesmen did not observe that even governments could derive but very scanty advantage by ensuring the persistence of conditions

Austria's Surrender to Russia

which were the product of no national or economic course of development ; they did not see that the power of the governments was decreasing, and that they possessed neither the money nor the troops upon which such a system must ultimately depend. In the East, under the unfortunate guidance of Metternich, Austria adopted a position in no way corresponding to her past or to her religious aspirations ; in order not to alienate the help of Russia, which might be useful in the suppression of revolutions, Austria surrendered that right, which she had acquired by the military sacrifices of the seventeenth and eighteenth centuries, of appearing as the liberator of the Balkan Christians from Turkish oppression.

Political history provides many examples of constitutions purely despotic, of the entirely selfish aspirations of persons, families, or parties, of the exploitation of majorities by minorities, of constitutions which profess to give freedom to all, while securing the dominance of individuals ; but illusions of this kind are invariably connected with some definite object, and in every case we can observe aspirations for tangible progress or increase of power.

But the Conservatism of the Restoration period rests upon a false conception of the working of political forces, and is therefore from its very outset a policy of mere bungling, as little able to create as to maintain. Of construction, or of purification, or of improvement, it was utterly incapable ; for in fact the object of the

Defects of Restoration Period

conservative statesmen and their highest ambition were nothing more than to capture the admiration of that court society in which they figured in their uniforms and decorations. For many princely families it was a grave misfortune that they failed to recognise the untenable character of those "principles" by which their Ministers, their masters of ceremonies, and their officers professed themselves able to uphold their rights and their possessions ; many, indeed, have disappeared for ever

from the scene of history, while others have passed through times of bitter trial and deadly struggle.

From their armed alliance against Napoleon a certain feeling of federative union seized the European Cabinets. The astounding events, the fall of the Cæsar from his dizzy height, had, after all the free thinking of the Revolutionary period and the superficial enlightenment, once more strengthened the belief in the dispositions of a Higher Power. The effect on the tsar, Alexander I., was the most peculiar.

His temperament, naturally idealistic, moved him to an extreme religiosity, intensified and marked by strong mystical leanings, to many minds suggestive of the presence of something like mania. He was not without friends who encouraged him to regard himself as a special "instrument" with a religious mission, who was to raise Europe to a new level of Christianity through his power as a ruler ; in contradistinction to Napoleon, whom he probably, in common with a good many other mystics, had come to regard as Antichrist. Alexander did not pose

The Tsar Inaugurates the Holy Alliance

as the champion of a Church, but he wanted to assume the rôle of the ideal Christian monarch, and to lead his brother monarchs along the same path. Unfortunately, the conception of the divine mission developed the idea of divine monarchical authority ; so that from his early notions of Liberty he passed to the stage of identifying the cause of Absolutism and of Legitimism with the cause of Christianity. Thus, he was moved to materialise his ideals in the form of a Christian union of nations, a Holy Alliance. This scheme he laid before his brother rulers.

Frederic William III., also a pietist in his way, immediately agreed ; so did Francis I., after some deliberation. On September 26th the three monarchs concluded this alliance in Paris. They wished to take as the standard of their conduct, both in the internal affairs of their countries and in external matters, merely the precepts of Christianity, justice, love, and peaceableness ; regarding each other as brothers, they wished to help each other on every occasion. As plenipotentiaries of Divine Providence they promised to be the fathers of their subjects and to lead them in the spirit of brotherhood, in order to protect religion, peace, and justice ; and they recommended their own peoples to exercise themselves daily in Christian principles and the fulfilment of Christian duties. Every Power which would acknowledge such principles might join the alliance. Almost all the states of Europe gradually joined the Holy Alliance. The sultan was obviously excluded, while the Pope declared that he had always possessed the Christian verity and required no new exposition of it. Great Britain refused, from regard to her constitution and to parliament; Europe was spared the presentation of the Prince Regent as a devotee of the higher morality.

There was no international basis to the Holy Alliance, which only had the value of a personal declaration, with merely a moral obligation for the monarchs connected with it. In its beginnings the Alliance aimed at an ideal; and its founders were sincere in their purpose. But it soon became, and rightly, the object of universal detestation; for Metternich was master of Alexander, and from the promise of the potentates to help each other on every opportunity he deduced the right to interfere in the internal affairs of foreign states. The Congresses of **League of European Powers** Carlsbad, Troppau, Laibach and Verona were the offshoots of this unholy conception. In addition to the Holy Alliance, the Treaty of Chaumont was renewed. On November 20th, 1815, at Paris, Russia, Great Britain, Austria, and Prussia pledged themselves that their sovereigns would meet periodically to deliberate on the peace, security, and welfare of Europe, or would send their responsible Ministers for the purpose. France, which had so long disturbed the peace of Europe, was to be placed under international police supervision, even after the army of occupation had left its soil.

The first of these congresses met at Aix-la-Chapelle, and showed Europe that an aristocratic league of Powers stood at its head. Alexander, Francis, and Frederic William appeared in person, accompanied by numerous diplomatists, among them Metternich, Gentz, Hardenberg, Humboldt, Nesselrode, Pozzo di Borgo, and Capodistrias; France was represented by Richelieu; Great Britain by Wellington, Castlereagh, and Canning. The chief question to be decided by the conferences, which began on September 30th, 1818, was the evacuation of France. The Duke of Richelieu obtained on October 9th an agreement according to which France should be evacuated by the allied troops before November 30th, 1818, instead of the year 1820, and the costs of the war and the indemnities still to be paid were considerably lowered. On the other hand, he did not succeed in forming a quintuple alliance by securing the admission of France as a member **France in the Holy Alliance** into the quadruple alliance. It is true that France was received on November 15th into the federation of the Great Powers, and that it joined the Holy Alliance; but the reciprocal guarantee of the five Great Powers, advocated by Alexander and Ancillon, did not come to pass; the four Powers renewed in secret on November 15th the Alliance of Chaumont, and agreed upon military measures to be adopted in the event of a war with France. We have already spoken of the settlement of the dispute between Bavaria and Baden; the congress occupied itself also with other European questions without achieving any successes, and increased the severity of the treatment of the exile on St. Helena.

Alexander I. of Russia, who was now making overtures to Liberalism throughout Europe and supported the constitutional principle in Poland, soon returned from that path; he grew colder in his friendship for the unsatisfied Poles, and became a loyal pupil of Metternich, led by the rough "sergeant of Gatshina," Count Araktcheieff. Although art, literature, and science flourished in his reign, although the fame of Alexander Pushkin was at its zenith, the fear of revolution, assassination, and disbelief cast a lengthening shadow over the policy of Alexander, and he governed in a mystic reactionary spirit.

When it became apparent that Alexander had broken with the Liberal party, Metternich and Castlereagh rubbed their hands in joy at his conversion, and the pamphlet of the prophet of disaster, **The Tsar's Break with the Liberals** Alexander Stourdza, "On the Present Condition of Germany," which was directed against the freedom of study in the universities and the freedom of the Press, when put before the tsar at Aix-la-Chapelle, intensified his suspicious aversion to all that savoured of liberty. The conference of ambassadors at Paris was declared closed. The greatest concord seemed to reign between the five Great Powers when the congress ended on November 21st.

4795

PORTRAITS OF QUEEN VICTORIA IN THE EARLIER YEARS OF HER LIFE AND REIGN

THE BRITISH ERA OF REFORM
THE LAST OF THE GEORGES, WILLIAM IV., AND BEGINNING OF THE VICTORIAN AGE

IN the nature of things, the British nation at all times stands to a certain extent outside the general course of Continental politics. The political organism developed far in advance of other nations ; the English polity, assimilating Scotland and Ireland, had achieved long before the French Revolution a liberty elsewhere unknown. Political power had become the property not indeed of people at large, but, in effect, of the whole landowning class, a body altogether different from the rigid aristocratic castes of Europe ; and absolutism or the prospect of absolutism had long vanished. In the latter half of the eighteenth century there had been indications of a democratic movement, to which the beginnings of the French Revolution gave a considerable impulse. But its later excesses gave a violent check to that impulse throughout the classes which held political power, causing a strong anti-democratic reaction ; although a precisely contrary effect was produced in the classes from whom political power was withheld.

That is to say. Europe in general and the United Kingdom, like Europe, showed the common phenomenon of a proletariat roused by the French Revolution to a desire for political power, and rulers who were convinced that the granting of such power would entail anarchy and ruin ; while material force was on the side of the rulers. But the distinction between the composition of the ruling class in the United Kingdom and in the Continental states remained as it was before **Britain's Reactionary Ministry** the Revolution; though the existing Ministry in Great Britain was reactionary to an exceptional degree, the sympathies of the ruling class were with constitutionalism, not with absolutism. Moreover, Great Britain was free from any idea that she had a divine mission to impose her own political theories on her neighbours, and had a conviction, on the whole wholesome,

that her intervention in foreign affairs should be restricted as far as possible to the exercise of a restraining influence in the interests of peace.

Thus we find Great Britain in the nineteenth century for the most part pursuing her own way ; taking her own course of **Great Britain a Pattern to Other Lands** political development, influenced only in a very secondary degree by affairs on the Continent, on which she in turn exercises usually only a very minor influence, save as providing a pattern for reformers in other lands. Her part in world-history, as distinct from domestic history, is played outside of Europe altogether, in the development of the extra-European Empire, as already related in the histories of India, Africa, and Australasia, and to be related in the American volume. In European history, interest centres not in these islands, but in the readjustments which have issued in the reorganisation of Germany as a great and homogeneous Central European power, in the German Empire which we know to-day ; in the reorganisation of France as the Republic which we know to-day ; and in the liberation and unification of Italy, and of minor nationalities.

Great Britain had played her full part—a conspicuously unselfish one—in the Congress of Vienna and the settlements of Europe after the final overthrow of Napoleon. In the period immediately ensuing she made her influence felt, not by her intervention, but by her refusal of pressing invitations to intervene, and presently by her refusals to countenance the unwarranted intervention of other Powers. Thus the British representatives declined to join the Holy Alliance of the great Powers which was formed at Vienna in 1815 for the repression of liberal principles, and the foreign policy of the Tories was marked by a strong sympathy for the

DISTINGUISHED STATESMEN OF THE EARLY NINETEENTH CENTURY

The four statesmen whose portraits are given above—Peel, Canning, Huskisson and Palmerston—exercised a powerful influence upon the Cabinet which they joined in 1822, moderating the foreign policy of the Tories and informing it with a strong sympathy for the principles of liberty. Three of them—Peel, Palmerston, and Canning—became Prime Ministers.

principles of liberty and nationality. But this was due to the influence of the Moderates—Peel, Canning, Huskisson, and Palmerston—who joined the Cabinet in 1822. The extreme Tories sympathised with the aims of the Holy Alliance, and had resolved under no circumstances to impede its efforts. The refusal of Great Britain to assist in bolstering up the Spanish dynasty; her consent to recognise the independence of the Spanish colonies and Brazil; her defence of Portugal against the forces of Dom Miguel, the absolutist pretender, and Ferdinand VII. of Spain; her intervention to save Greece from the Sultan and Mehemet Ali—all these generous actions were the work of Canning, and would never have been sanctioned by Castlereagh, his predecessor at the Foreign Office. In domestic policy the spirit of reaction reigned supreme. During the years 1815 to 1822 class interests and the morbid fear of revolution were responsible for a series of repressive enactments which were so unreasonably severe that they increased the popular sympathy for the principles against which they were directed. After 1822 came the period in which the extreme Tories gave way tardily and with the worst of graces.

The peace was inaugurated with a new corn law, framed in the interests of the landowning classes, from which both Houses of Parliament were **Bread Riots at Manchester** chiefly recruited. This prohibited the importation of foreign corn until the price of 80s. a quarter should be reached; that is, until the poorer classes should be reduced to a state of famine. The statutory price before this date had been merely 48s. The change was naturally followed in many places by bread riots and incendiarism. The Government replied by calling out the soldiery and framing coercive measures. In 1819 a mass meeting which had assembled in St. Peter's Field, at Manchester, was broken up with considerable bloodshed; Parliament, which had already

suspended the Habeas Corpus, proceeded to pass the Six Acts giving the executive exceptional powers to break up seditious meetings and to punish the authors of seditious libels. The powers thus obtained were stretched to their utmost limits, on the pretext that such hare-brained schemes as the Cato Street Conspiracy, 1820, constituted a serious menace to public order.

It was not until 1823 that the Cabinet consented to attack the root of social disorders by making some reductions in the tariff. It began by concessions to the mercantile classes, whose prospects were seriously affected by the heavy duties upon raw materials, and to the consumers of various manufactured commodities, such as linen, silk, and cotton stuffs, upon which prohibitive duties had been imposed in the interests of British industry. But in the all-important question of the corn laws, affecting the poor rather than the middle classes, the Tories would only concede a compromise, the sliding-scale duty of 1829. The demand of the chief commercial centres for the repeal of the Navigation Laws was met by an Act

BREAD RIOTS AT MANCHESTER: THE YEOMANRY CHARGING THE MOB IN 1819
Suffering hardship in consequence of the high price of bread, the people in many places resorted to violence. The Government's reply was to call out the soldiery and frame coercive measures. A mass meeting which had assembled in St. Peter's Field, at Manchester, in 1819, was broken up, as shown in the above picture, with considerable bloodshed.

providing that the ships of any foreign Power should be allowed free access to British ports if that Power would grant a reciprocity; the Combination Acts, framed to make trades unions illegal, were repealed; considerable amendments were introduced into the criminal law. But to several reforms of paramount necessity the Ministers showed themselves obstinately averse. They would not repeal the disabling laws which still remained in force against the Catholics, although three-fourths of the Irish nation were calling for this act of justice. They would do nothing to reform the House of Commons. They would not deprive the landowning classes of the profits which the corn duties afforded.

THE SCENE OF THE CATO STREET CONSPIRACY
In Cato Street, London, shown in this picture, was conceived a plot to assassinate Castlereagh and other Ministers at a Cabinet dinner in 1820. The plot being discovered, the revolutionaries were captured, five of them being hanged and five transported for life.

It was now that the nation discovered the use which could be made of two rights which it had long possessed. Freedom of speech on political matters was guaranteed by Fox's Libel Act of 1792, which left to the jury the full power of deciding what constituted legitimate criticism of the administration. Freedom of association and public meeting existed, independently of special enactments, under the protection of the common law. These weapons were used with extraordinary skill by O'Connell, the leader of the Irish Catholics. The Catholic Association, formed in 1823, learned from him the art of intimidating without illegality by means of monster meetings. Proclaimed as an illegal body in 1825, the association contrived to continue its existence in the

DANIEL O'CONNELL
The leader of the Irish Catholics, O'Connell was foremost in the agitation for the rights of his countrymen, and patriotically surrendered personal interests for the advancement of the national cause. He died in 1847.

guise of a philanthropic society. At the Clare election in 1828 O'Connell, although a Catholic, and therefore disqualified, was returned by an overwhelming majority. Peel persuaded his colleagues that the time had come when emancipation must be granted. Bills for that purpose were accordingly passed and submitted for the royal assent. This afforded George IV., who had succeeded his father in 1820, an opportunity of asserting himself for once in a matter of national concern. A prodigal and a voluptuary, who had systematically sacrificed honour and decency to his pleasures and had broken his father's heart by his want of shame and filial piety, he now declared that nothing could induce him to accept a measure which that father had rejected. After long expostulations he broke this vow, as he had broken every other, and Catholic emancipation was finally recorded on the Statute Book.

George IV. died in 1830. He was succeeded by his brother, the Duke of Clarence, under the title of William IV., a more respectable character than "the first gentleman in Europe," but a politician of poor abilities, great tactlessness and greater obstinacy. In their resistance to the next popular agitation the Tories found him a valuable ally. The triumph of the Irish Catholics was followed by a revival, in England, of the cry for parliamentary reform, and to this purpose the tactics of O'Connell were steadily applied by the Liberals of the great manufacturing centres. The energy with which the Whigs pushed their attack is explained by their conviction that the defects of the representative system constituted the main obstacles to social, political, and fiscal reforms of the utmost weight and urgency. The House of Commons no longer expressed the opinions of the country. The most enlightened, industrious, and prosperous portion of the community were either unrepresented or ludicrously underrepresented. Since the time of Charles II. no new constituencies had been created, and of the boroughs which

KING GEORGE IV.

He became Prince Regent in 1810 owing to the mental derangement of his father, George III., and succeeded to the throne ten years later. Without any qualities that endeared him to his people, he possessed failings and vices that were conspicuously displayed, and there were few to regret his death, which occurred in 1830.

had received representation under the Tudors and the Stuarts, the greater part owed their privilege to the Crown's expectation that their elections could always be controlled. Many boroughs which formerly deserved to be represented had fallen, through the decay of their fortunes or through an excessive limitation of the franchise, under the control of the great territorial families. Close boroughs were so completely an article of commerce that the younger Pitt, when he proposed a measure of parliamentary reform, felt himself bound to offer the patrons a pecuniary

A SITTING OF THE BRITISH HOUSE OF COMMONS IN THE YEARS 1821-23

From the engraving by J. Scott.   Photo by Walker

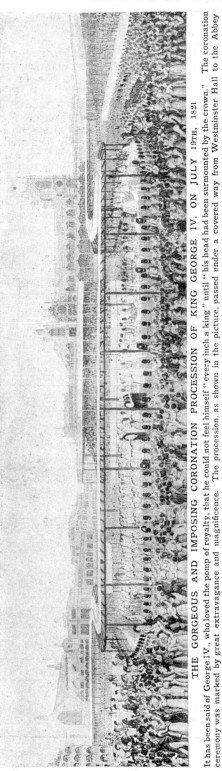

THE GORGEOUS AND IMPOSING CORONATION PROCESSION OF KING GEORGE IV. ON JULY 19TH, 1821

It has been said of George IV., who loved the pomp of royalty, that he could not feel himself "every inch a king" until "his head had been surmounted by the crown." The coronation ceremony was marked by great extravagance and magnificence. The procession, as shown in the picture, passed under a covered way from Westminster Hall to the Abbey

compensation. It was by means of "pocket" boroughs that the Whigs had held the first two Hanoverians in bondage, and that George III. had maintained his personal ascendancy for twenty years. In 1793 it was computed that 307 members of Parliament were returned by private patrons. Matters had improved in the last forty years; but still on the eve of the reform legislation 276 seats were private property. Three-fourths of these belonged to members of the Tory aristocracy. The state of the county representation was somewhat better. But the smallest shires returned as many members as the largest, with the solitary exception that Yorkshire, since 1821, returned four members in place of the usual two. The county franchise was limited, by a law of 1430, to freeholders, and the owners of large estates had established their right to plural or "faggot" votes.

The faults of this system, its logical absurdities, are glaringly manifest. With the votes of about half the House of Commons controlled by a few families, with great cities unrepresented, with small and large counties treated as of equal weight, with franchises varying in different localities, it might rather be said that there was no system at all. But it is a peculiarly British characteristic to regard anomalies as desirable in themselves, as it was characteristic of the theorists of the Revolution to discover the universal panacea in symmetrical uniformity.

Entirely apart from personal interests, the large proportion of the ruling class had a firm conviction that the constitution was incapable of improvement, that it provided the best possible type of legislator and administrator. The unenfranchised masses saw in these Olympians a group who neither understood nor cared for anything but the interests of their own class; they acquired a rooted conviction that, when they themselves obtained political power, the millennium would arrive. But among the enfranchised, the minority, who had always refused to be terrified by the Reign of Terror, now grew into a majority who believed that political intelligence existed in other sections of the community, who might be enfranchised without danger, and that flagrant anomalies might be removed without undermining the constitution. When France once more overturned the Bourbon monarchy and established the citizen-king,

GEORGE IV., KING OF GREAT BRITAIN AND IRELAND, IN HIS ROYAL ROBES
From the painting by Sir Thomas Lawrence, P.R.A.

THE CORONATION OF GEORGE IV.: THE SCENE IN WESTMINSTER ABBEY DURING THE CEREMONY

THE UNFORTUNATE QUEEN CAROLINE: HER TRIAL IN THE HOUSE OF LORDS

When George IV. ascended the throne in 1820, an annuity of £50,000 was offered to Caroline, whom he had married in 1795, if she would renounce the title of queen and live abroad, allegations having been made against her character. She refused to accept this offer, and the Government instituted proceedings against her for divorce. Public feeling was largely on the side of the queen, and after the Divorce Bill had passed the House of Lords it was abandoned by the Ministry. Desiring to be crowned along with the king, Caroline presented herself at the entrance to Westminster Abbey on the day of her husband's coronation, but was refused admittance and cruelly turned away from the door.

From the painting by Sir George Hayter

Louis Philippe, on the throne with a constitution in which the political power of the bourgeoisie was the prominent feature, effecting the change without any excesses, the phantom of the ancient Reign of Terror dwindled, and the Reform party was materially strengthened.

The king and the Duke of Wellington refused at first to believe that any change was either desirable or necessary. But they were compelled in 1830 to admit that it was necessary ; and Lord Grey was permitted to construct a reform Cabinet of Whigs and moderate Tories. Their Bills passed the House of Commons without difficulty, receiving the votes of many members whose seats were known to be doomed by its provisions. The House of Lords, encouraged by the king, endeavoured to obstruct the measure which they dared not openly oppose. But a new agitation, threatening the very existence of the Upper House, at once arose. The duke, with greater wisdom than his royal master, realised that further resistance was out of the question, and induced the Lords to give way in June, 1832.

The Reform Bill of 1832 fell far short of the democratic ideal which the English admirers of the French Revolution had kept in view. Jeremy Bentham, 1748–1832, the greatest of those writers and thinkers who prepared the minds of men for practical reform, was of opinion that the doctrine of natural equality ought to be the first principle of every constitution; but the followers of Lord Grey contented themselves with giving political power to the middle classes. This work has since been supplemented by the legislation of 1867, 1884, and 1885 ; yet even at the present day the doctrine of manhood suffrage is unknown in English law. Still less were the first reformers inclined to map out the country in new electoral districts of equal size. They enlarged the representation of some counties. They suppressed or partially disfranchised eighty-six decayed boroughs. They gave representatives to forty-two of the new boroughs. But they kept intact the old distinction between county and borough, and sedulously avoided the subdivision or amalgamation of constituencies which possessed organic unity and historical traditions. In this and other respects the later Reform Bills have been more drastic.

Changes in the Constitution of Parliament
That of 1867 abandoned the principle, which had been steadily maintained in 1832, that the franchise should be limited to those who paid direct taxes in one form or another. That of 1885 endeavoured to equalise constituencies in respect of population ; in order to attain this end, counties and boroughs were broken up into divisions, without respect for past traditions. Such legislation is necessarily of a temporary character, since no measure of redistribution can be expected to satisfy the principle of equality for more than a few years. And this is not the least important consequence of the legislative change which the nineteenth century effected in the constitution of Parliament. The Lower House in becoming democratic has ceased to represent a fixed number of communities with fixed interests and characteristics.

The reformed Parliament was not long in justifying the hopes which had been formed of it. Those, indeed, who had expected that the members returned under the new system would all be Whigs or democrats soon found reason to revise their judgment. This is not the only occasion in English history on which it has been proved that aversion to ill-considered change is a fundamental trait in the national

THE FIRST STEAMBOAT ON THE CLYDE

The early part of the nineteenth century witnessed progress along many lines, the introduction of steamboats being a noteworthy advance. The Comet, shown in the above illustration, was built by Henry Bell, and began sailing on the Clyde in the year 1812.

THE CORONATION PROCESSION OF WILLIAM IV. AND QUEEN ADELAIDE AT THE ABBEY
The third son of George III., William IV., the "Sailor King," succeeded to the throne of Great Britain and
Ireland on the death of his eldest brother, George IV., in 1830, and along with his consort, Adelaide, the eldest
daughter of the Duke of Saxe-Meiningen, whom he married in 1818, he was crowned on September 8th, 1831.
From the drawing by George Cattermole

character. The Tories, although for a
moment under a cloud, soon recovered
their spirits and a certain measure of influence in the country. Under the leadership
of Peel, they adopted the new name of Conservatives, and shook off the instinct of
dogged and unreasoning obstruction. Peel
was unable to procure a majority in the
House of Commons when first invited by the
king to form a Ministry, and accordingly left
Melbourne and the Whigs in 1835 to carry
on the government. But political opinion
was swinging round to his side;
he obtained a majority in 1841.
So far the unforeseen had
happened. On the other hand,
the work of remedial legislation proceeded
with vigour whether the Whigs were in
or out of office. In fact both parties had
become possessed by the idea that their
main business was to devise and carry
sweeping measures. Legislation was regarded as the worthiest function of a
sovereign assembly; it seemed as though
there could never be too much of legislation. Experience has brought a decline
of faith in the panacea. But it must be
admitted that for twenty years the new

**The Busy
Days of
Legislation**

Parliament had necessary work to perform
in the way of legislation, and performed it
with admirable skill. A few of the more
important measures may be mentioned.

The Emancipation Act of 1833 completed a work of philanthropy which had
been commenced in 1807. The Ministry of
All the Talents had abolished the slave
trade. The new Act emancipated all the
slaves who were still to be found in British
colonies, and awarded the owners the sum
of twenty millions as a compensation.
Costly as the measure was for the mother
country, it was still more costly for the
colonies. The sugar industry of the West
Indies had been built up with the help of
slave labour. The planters lost heavily
through being compelled to emancipate
the slave for a sum which was much less
than his market value, and the black
population showed a strong disinclination
to become labourers for hire. This was
particularly the case in the larger islands,
where land was abundant and a squatter
could obtain a sustenance with little or no
labour. The prosperity of Jamaica was
destroyed, and the West Indies as a whole
have never been prosperous since 1834.

4807

THE CORONATION OF WILLIAM IV. AND QUEEN ADELAIDE AT WESTMINSTER ABBEY ON SEPTEMBER 8TH, 1831

Free trade completed their ruin, since they had only maintained the sugar trade with the help of the preferential treatment which they received from England. The basis of their former wealth was wholly artificial, and it is unlikely that slavery and protection will ever be restored for their benefit; but it may be regretted that the necessary and salutary reforms of which they have been the victims could not have been more gradually applied in their case.

For the new Poor Law of 1834 there can be nothing but praise. It ended a system which for more than a generation had been a national curse, demoralising the labourer, encouraging improvidence and immorality, taxing all classes for the benefit of the small farmer and employer whom the misplaced philanthropy of the legislature had enabled to cut down wages below the margin of subsistence. Up to the year 1795 the English Poor Law had been, save for one serious defect, sound in principle. The defect was the Law of Settlement, first laid down by an Act of 1662, which enabled the local authorities to prevent the migration of labour from one parish to another, unless security could be given that the immigrant would not become a charge upon the poor rate.

The result of this law had been to stereotype local inequalities in the rate of wages and to take from the labourer the chief means of bettering his position. It was mitigated in 1795 to the extent that the labourer could be no longer sent back until he actually became a charge upon the rates. But about the same time the justices of the peace began the practice of giving

LORD GREY

A distinguished statesman, he succeeded his father in 1807 as the second Earl Grey; in the first reformed Parliament he was at the head of a powerful party, and passed the Act abolishing slavery in the colonies. He died in 1845.

LORD MELBOURNE

Twice Premier, he was in office at the accession of Queen Victoria in 1837. He was an "indolent opportunist," and "kept his place in the early years of Queen Victoria chiefly through the favour of the young queen." He died in 1848.

poor-relief in aid of wages, and of making relief proportionate to the size of the applicant's family. This practice was confirmed by the Speenham-land Act of 1796. The legislature acted thus in part from motives of philanthropy, in part under the belief that the increase of population was in every way to be encouraged. The Act was at once followed by a drop in the rate of agricultural wages and a portentous increase of poor-rates. In 1783 poor-relief cost the country about £2,000,000; by 1817 this sum had been quadrupled. The evils of the new system were augmented by the absence of any central authority possessing power to enforce uniform principles and methods of relief. The proposal to introduce such an authority, and in other respects to revive the leading ideas of the Elizabethan Poor Law, was made by a Royal Commission after the most careful investigations. The new Poor Law, 1834, embodied the principal suggestions of the commissioners. It provided that the workhouse test should be once more rigidly applied to all able-bodied paupers; that parishes should be grouped in poor-law unions; that each parish should contribute to the expenditure of the union in proportion to the numbers of its paupers; and that a central board should be appointed to control the system. The new Poor Law is still in force, so far as its main principles of administration are concerned. But there have been changes in the constitution of the central authority, by Acts of 1847, 1871, and 1894. The Poor-law Board has been merged in the Local Government Board; and the

Boards of Guardians, which control the local distribution of relief, are now democratic bodies, whereas, under the original Act the justices of the peace held office as ex-officio members.

The Poor Law Act was followed by others for the reform of municipal government in 1835, of the Irish tithe system in 1838, and for the introduction of the penny post in 1839. The new Poor Law and the new municipal system were also applied to Ireland by special legislation. But larger questions slumbered until the formation of great political societies forced them upon the unwilling attention of Ministers and both Houses of Parliament.

The period of 1840-1850 was peculiarly favourable to the democratic agitator. The Reform Whigs had maintained themselves in power till the death of William IV. But their majority was small, and their chief leader, Melbourne, an indolent opportunist. He kept his place in the early years of Queen Victoria chiefly through the favour

JEREMY BENTHAM
A great writer and thinker, many social and political reforms which characterised the early Victorian era were suggested by him.

of the young queen. The Conservatives, impatient for a return to power, were disposed to bid against the Whigs for popular favour. Neither party desired extreme reform. Lord John Russell expressed the general sentiment when he stated his conviction that the Reform Bill had been the final step in the direction of democracy. But neither party was strong enough to resist external pressure. The rise of the Chartist organisation in 1838 seemed likely, therefore, to produce sweeping changes. It was recruited from the labouring classes and animated by hostility to capital. It proposed the establishment of radical democracy as a panacea for the wrongs of workmen. The five points of the people's charter were manhood suffrage, voting by ballot, annual parliaments, payment of members, and the abolition of the property qualification for membership. These demands were supported in the House of Commons by the philosophic Radicals, among whom Grote, the historian, was

THE REFORM RIOTS AT BRISTOL IN OCTOBER, 1831
From the drawing by L. Haghe

DESTRUCTION OF THE HOUSES OF PARLIAMENT ON OCTOBER 16TH, 1834

This graphic scene depicts the destruction by fire, on October 16th, 1834, of the Houses of Parliament, the picture being made by the artist from a sketch taken by him by the light of the flames at the end of Abingdon Street.

From the drawing by William Heath

the most conspicuous, while in Feargus O'Connor the Chartists possessed a popular orator of no mean order. The House of Commons refused to consider the first petition of the Chartists in 1839. The refusal was, however, followed by riots in various localities; and a second attempt was made to move Parliament in 1842, when the Conservatives, under Peel, had wrested power from the Whigs. But the new Ministers were no more pliable than the old; and a series of prosecutions against prominent Chartists forced the movement to assume a subterranean character. Its

KING WILLIAM IV.

Though a Whig before his accession to the throne of Great Britain and Ireland in 1830, he became a Tory after his coronation, and used his influence to obstruct the passing of the first Reform Act in 1832. He died in 1837.

influence was felt not only in England but in Wales, where it contributed to produce the Rebecca Riots, 1843. But the next occasion on which Chartism invaded the capital was in 1848, the year of revolutions. It was announced that half a million of Chartists would assemble at a given place on April 10th, and march in procession to lay their demands before the House of Commons. The danger seemed great; extensive military preparations were made under the old Duke of Wellington, and the authorities announced on the appointed day that they would use force,

"YOUR MAJESTY!": ANNOUNCING TO PRINCESS VICTORIA THE FACT OF HER ACCESSION

On the death of King William IV. at Windsor Castle in 1837, his niece, Princess Victoria, succeeded to the throne. Riding through the night from Windsor to Kensington Palace, Dr. Howley, Archbishop of Canterbury, and the Marquess of Conyngham, Lord Chamberlain, awakened the young girl about five o'clock in the morning to tell her that she was Queen of Great Britain and Ireland. This dramatic incident is admirably represented in the above picture.

From the painting by Mary L. Gow, by permission of the Berlin Photographic Co.

QUEEN VICTORIA IN HER CORONATION ROBES

Succeeding to the throne in 1837, at the early age of eighteen years, Queen Victoria was crowned at Westminster Abbey on June 28th, 1838. The youthful queen of Great Britain and Ireland is in this picture represented in her coronation robes, standing in the dawn of the longest and most glorious reign in the nation's history.

From the painting by Sir George Hayter

THE FIRST COUNCIL OF QUEEN VICTORIA, AT KENSINGTON PALACE ON JUNE 21st, 1837

The first act of the young queen after her accession was to summon a council of her Ministers and chiefs "to receive their homage and to give her Royal assurance of maintaining the constitutions of her kingdoms." Among the illustrious personages included in the above famous picture are the Duke of Wellington, Lord John Russell, and Lord Palmerston.

From the painting by Sir David Wilkie, R.A.

THE CORONATION OF QUEEN VICTORIA: THE HISTORIC SCENE IN WESTMINSTER ABBEY ON JUNE 28TH, 1838

From the painting by Sir George Hayter

if necessary, to check the march of the procession. The Chartist leaders were cowed, and contented themselves with submitting their petition for the third time. A large number of the signatures, which had been estimated at 5,000,000, turned out to be fictitious ; and amidst the ridicule excited by this discovery the Charter and Chartists slipped into oblivion.

The collapse of Chartism was significant, for the great Chartist demonstration was contemporaneous with a series of revolutionary movements on the Continent. It meant that in England the people at

were the product of the great war. They had been established for the protection of the agricultural interest, and had altogether excluded foreign corn from the English market except while the price of English corn stood above eighty shillings, so that the price of bread was maintained at a very high figure. A modification had been introduced, by which duties were imposed on foreign corn, in place of the import being prohibited, while home-grown corn stood below eighty shillings, the amount of the duty falling as the price of English corn rose, and vice versa.

THE CORONATION PROCESSION OF QUEEN VICTORIA
From the drawing by Champion

large declined to believe in physical force as the necessary means to attaining political reforms, preferring the methods of constitutional agitation. Chartism dissolved itself in the fiasco of 1848. But the political demands of the Chartists were adopted by constitutional reformers, and were in great part conceded during the following half century—though they have not brought the millennium. The episode emphasised the sobriety of the masses ; and the result was probably in measure due to the improvement in the conditions of the industrial population owing to the repeal of the Corn Laws in 1846. We have remarked that the Corn Laws

But this did not remove the obvious fact that the cost of the staple food of the working classes was kept high artificially, in order to benefit or preserve the agricultural interest. Apart from philanthropic considerations — though these carried their due weight in many quarters— the capitalist manufacturers, now the dominant power in the House of Commons, began to perceive that if the price of bread fell the operatives could live on a lower money wage, that the wages bill would be lowered, and with it the cost of production ; that is to say, the middle classes saw that their own interests would be served by the abolition of the Corn Laws.

QUEEN VICTORIA IN HER CORONATION ROBES, 1838

From the painting by C. R. Leslie, R.A.

TO FACE PAGE 46

The Anti-Corn Law League, first formed in 1838, owed its existence to a serious depression of the manufacturing industries. Cobden, Bright, and others of the leading organisers were philanthropists who saw the iniquity of artificially maintaining the price of food when wages were low and employment uncertain. They recruited their supporters to a great extent among the starving operatives of the North and Midlands. But the funds for the Free Trade campaign were largely supplied by manufacturers. There was no thought of giving to the masses the franchise as a means of self-protection. Accordingly, the extreme Chartists hated the Free Traders, and openly opposed their propaganda, on the ground that the charter would secure to the people all, and more than all, that was hoped from the repeal of the Corn Laws. The class character of the Free Trade agitation was a source of weakness, because the working-class agitators did not believe that the labouring class would benefit by it; while the landed interest saw in it

their own prospective ruin. The working classes, however, were not convinced by the Chartist doctrine, and felt that if bread were cheaper life would be easier. An Irish famine completed the conversion of the Conservative leader, Sir Robert Peel, who had already been agitating his party for Free Trade measures and the removal or reduction of duties protecting British industries. He took a number of his colleagues with him, but not the party as a whole. Peelites and Whigs together

QUEEN VICTORIA'S FIRST OFFICIAL VISIT TO THE CITY OF LONDON
The first official visit of Queen Victoria to the City of London was on Lord Mayor's Day, November 9th, 1837, and in this picture her carriage is seen passing Temple Bar on the way to the Guildhall. The picture is interesting not only on account of its historic value, but also by reason of the glimpse which it gives of a part of London now entirely altered.

carried the repeal of the Corn Laws, but had hardly done so when the Protectionists and extreme Radicals combined to defeat the Ministry, and Peel's career as Prime Minister was closed. The Whigs, supported by Peelites, assumed the government, and were presently combined in the Liberal party.

Colonial development has been dealt with in detail elsewhere; but certain points must here be noticed. During the period under consideration nearly the whole of the Indian peninsula passed under the British dominion as a result of the great Mahratta

4817

war ; while the first Burmese war added territories beyond the Bay of Bengal. Under Bentinck's rule, progress was made in the organisation of administration and the development of education. On the north-west, however, the aggression of Persia, more or less under the ægis of Russia, produced British intervention in the affairs of Afghanistan, with disastrous consequences, of which the evil effects were at any rate diminished by the skilful operations of Pollock and Knott. In the same decade, however, the British supremacy was challenged by the Sikh army of the Punjab. Beaten in the first struggle, the Sikhs were renewing their challenge in 1848, when Lord Dalhousie arrived in India to take up the gage of battle and extend the British dominion, in 1849, over the Land of the Five Rivers up to the mountain passes, thus completing the ring-fence of mountain and ocean girdling the British Empire in India.

PRINCE ALBERT

The younger son of the Duke of Saxe-Coburg-Gotha, Prince Albert first met Queen Victoria in 1836. They fell in love, and were married in 1840, the Prince then receiving the title of Royal Highness.

In Australia the settlements, which at first had been penal in character, were assuming the form of true colonies, but were not yet emancipated. In South **The Union of British Colonies** Africa, transferred to Great Britain as a result of the Napoleonic war, a part of the Dutch population — partly in consequence of the abolition of slavery — began during the fourth decade of the century to remove itself beyond the sphere of British interference, and to found the communities which developed into the Orange Free State and the Transvaal Republic.

It was, however, almost at the moment of Queen Victoria's accession that dissatisfaction with the existing system in the colonies of Upper and Lower Canada, which had been established in the time of the younger Pitt, reached an acute stage, issuing in insurrection and in the dispatch of the epoch-making commission of Lord Durham. The report of the commissioner was the starting-point virtually of a new theory of colonial relations. It led directly to the Act of Reunion of 1842, which was gradually followed by the federal union of all the British colonies

in North America, with the exception of Newfoundland, as states of the Canadian Dominion. The foundation was laid for that system under which the colony was no longer to be treated as a subordinate section of the empire, but was to receive full responsible government—a government, that is, in which the Ministers are responsible to the representative assemblies as Ministers in England are responsible to Parliament ; to become, in fact, *mutatis mutandis*, a counterpart of the United Kingdom, practically independent except in matters affecting war and peace. Canada, indeed, did not immediately achieve this status even after the Act of Reunion ; but that Act may be regarded as initiating the change which has since been carried out in nearly all the British colonies where the white population has ceased to bear the character of a garrison. Of the religious movements in this period some account will be found in a later chapter of this section. But we have still to review here a development of English literature which has no parallel except in the Shakespearean era, for the beginnings of which we must go back to the Revolution epoch.

During three-fourths of the eighteenth century, classicalism had dominated prose and poetry alike. In place of poems, satires, epigrams, admirable essays and dissertations in verse had been produced in abundance in strict accord with rigid conventions ; no scope had been granted to the lyrical utterance of passion, and spontaneity had been repressed as barbaric or at least impolite. But the spirit which was rousing itself to a stormy attack on social and political conventions was not to spare the conventions of literature. **The Genius of Robert Burns** These were, indeed, set at naught by the lyrical genius of Robert Burns, whose first volume of poems appeared in 1786. Burns, however, was not a pioneer in the true sense—consciously promulgating a new theory. Essentially his work was the most splendid expression of a poetical type which had always flourished in Scotland outside the realms of polite literature. But its power and fascination arrested attention, and carried the conviction that subjects forbidden by the critics as vulgar were capable of treatment which was undeniably poetical. He demonstrated anew that the poet's true function is to appeal to the emotions of men, and that this may be done through the medium of language which is not at all cultured. Unlike Burns, however, the so-called " Lake School " of Wordsworth and Coleridge were conscious exponents of a theory which defied the critical dogmas of the day. But Coleridge's practice contradicted a part of his own theory, and when Wordsworth acted upon it in its entirety, he did not write poetry. Their revolt against artificial language and artificial restrictions of subject led them virtually to affirm that the best poetry may treat of commonplace matters in commonplace language.

A Group of Great Poets

The paradox becomes obvious when we perceive that Coleridge is never commonplace, and that it is precisely when he is not commonplace that Wordsworth is great, though unfortunately he never recognised that truth himself. The familiar fact must yield the unfamiliar thought ; the familiar terms must combine in the unfamiliar phrases which stamp themselves upon the mind. The current criticism erred, not in condemning the commonplace, but in identifying the commonplace with the superficially familiar, and treating conventions as fundamental laws of art. That these were errors was conclusively proved by the practice rather than by the critical expositions of the Lake school. The volume of " Lyrical Ballads," which contained " Tintern Abbey " and the " Ancient Mariner," was a sufficient refutation of the orthodox doctrines.

The poetical work which was produced in the twenty-six years which passed between the publication of the " Lyrical Ballads," 1798, and the death of Byron, 1824, travelled far enough from the standards of the eighteenth century. Within that period Sir Walter Scott adapted the old ballad form to metrical narrative, and turned men's minds back to revel in the gorgeous aspect of the Middle Ages, somewhat forgetful of their ugly side. Byron burst upon the public, an avowed rebel, whose tragic poses were unfortunately only too easy of imitation

A ROYAL ROMANCE : THE MARRIAGE OF QUEEN VICTORIA IN 1840

The interesting ceremony represented in the above picture took place at the Chapel Royal, St. James's, on February 10th, 1840. Queen Victoria was then in her twenty-first year, while Prince Albert was three months her junior.

From the painting by Sir George Hayter

by a host of self-conscious rhymesters, and gave vice a morbid picturesqueness ; but redeemed himself by the genuineness of his passion for liberty, and died at Missolonghi fighting for the liberation of Greece. Shelley, a rebel of another kind, shocked the world by his Promethean defiance of an unjust God, of tyranny in every form, but was, in fact, the prophet not of atheism and materialism, but of an intensely spiritual pantheism ; the most ethereal, most intangible, most exquisite among the masters of song. John Keats died when he was only five-and-twenty, but he had already lived long enough to win for himself a secure place in the elysium of "poets dead and gone." His poetry is the practical expression of his own dictum :

RICHARD COBDEN

"The Apostle of Free Trade," he denounced as iniquitous artificially to maintain the price of food when wages were low and employment uncertain, and to his labours was largely due the abolition of the Corn Laws in 1846.

"Beauty in truth, truth beauty ; that is all ye know on earth, and all ye need to know." Among great English poets there is no other whose work is so devoid of all ethical element, none in whom the sense of pure beauty is so overmastering or its rendering more perfect.

Among the poets whom we have named, Byron's influence alone was European; but that influence pales by the side of Walter Scott's in the realm of prose romance. There were novelists before Scott, but it was he who gave to the novel that literary predominance which at one time characterised the drama. Practically it was he who revealed the capacities of prose romance for the portrayal of character and of picturesque incident,

JOHN BRIGHT

Along with Cobden and others in the agitation against the Corn Laws, John Bright used his great eloquence both in Parliament and on the public platform to further the cause of Free Trade. He held office in later Ministries.

through the amazing achievement of the series of "Waverley Novels," whereof the first appeared in 1814. Before the close of our period, the genius of Charles Dickens

had already developed a new type of the novelist's art, in the "Pickwick Papers" ; but his great contemporary and rival, William Makepeace Thackeray, had not yet achieved fame in this field. The Bronte sisters, however, with "Wuthering Heights" and "Jane Eyre," 1847, had just given convincing proof, if any were needed after Jane Austen, Scott's contemporary, that the novel is a literary instrument which woman can handle as successfully as man. By that time all the great poets of the Revolution era had passed away, save Wordsworth, who was all but an octogenarian ; but the stars of Tennyson and Browning had already appeared above the horizon.

The time of ferment which produced this outburst of literary activity was also responsible for two new movements of English thought, the utilitarian and the idealist. Utilitarianism is the sceptical and inductive spirit of such eighteenth - century thinkers as David Hume, applied to the study of morals and social institutions. The movement began with the French Encyclopædists ; it came to England through Jeremy Bentham, 1748–1832, than whom no man has exercised a more far-reaching influence on the thought or government of modern England. Most of the social and political reforms which characterise the early Victorian era were suggested by Bentham. His two great works, the "Fragment on Government," 1776, and the "Principles of Morals and Legislation," 1789, belong chronologically to the age of the Revolution ; but it was only in later life that Bentham became a prophet among his own people. His greatest disciple was

THE CHRISTENING OF THE PRINCESS ROYAL AT BUCKINGHAM PALACE IN 1840
From the painting by C. R. Leslie

CHRISTENING THE PRINCE OF WALES, THE PRESENT KING EDWARD, IN 1841
From the painting by Sir George Hayter

DOMESTIC EVENTS IN THE LIFE OF QUEEN VICTORIA

Robert Burns, 1759–96   William Wordsworth, 1770–1850   S. T. Coleridge, 1772–1834

Jane Austen, 1775–1817   Lord Byron, 1788–1824   P. B. Shelley, 1792–1822

John Keats, 1795–1821   Thomas Carlyle, 1795–1881   Lord Macaulay, 1800–59

W. M. Thackeray, 1811–63   Charles Dickens, 1812–70   Charlotte Bronte, 1816–55

GREAT MEN AND WOMEN OF LETTERS FROM BURNS TO CHARLOTTE BRONTE

John Stuart Mill, 1806–1873, whose versatile genius never showed to more advantage than when he was handling social questions in Bentham's spirit. Mill was not so rigorous a thinker as Bentham ; but the moral enthusiasm of the younger man, his power of exposition, and his susceptibility to the best ideas of his time, gave him the respectful attention of all thoughtful minds. What Bentham did for the theory of legislation, Mill did for the theory of wealth. Mill's "Political Economy," 1848, although largely based upon the investigations of Adam Smith, Ricardo, and Malthus, marks an era in the history of that science. Mill was the first to define with accuracy the proper limits of economic study. He originated a number of new theories. He diagnosed the economic evils of his time and suggested practical remedies. Above all, however, he was the first to see the parts of economic science in their true proportions and to connect them as an ordered whole. The tendency of modern thought is to belittle the deductive school of economists which Mill represents ; but his claim to be regarded as the classic of that school has never been disputed. Similarly, by his later writings on "Liberty," 1859, and "Representative Government," 1860, he became the accredited exponent of English Liberalism ; while his essay on "Utilitarianism," 1861, by giving a larger and less material interpretation to Bentham's formula, "the greatest happiness of the greatest number," did much to bring out the common basis of belief on which Liberals and idealists have conducted their long controversy.

The idealist movement begins with Coleridge, whose philosophic writings, notably the "Aids to Reflection," published in 1825, although fragmentary and unsystematic, are the first sign of a reaction among English metaphysicians against Hume's disintegrating criticism. In a diluted and theological form the new tenets formed the intellectual stock in

SIR WALTER SCOTT
As poet and novelist Scott occupies a unique place among the world's writers. From his fertile pen came a rich library of stirring tales all aglow with the magic of romance and revealing a creative genius unmatched since Shakespeare. Born in 1771, he died in 1832.

trade of the Tractarians, whose attempt to imbue Anglican dogmas with a new significance and to destroy the insularity of the Established Church is the most remarkable phenomenon in the religious history of modern England. The idealists found a powerful though erratic ally in Thomas Carlyle, 1795–1881. In literature a romantic of the most lawless sort, unequalled in power of phrase, in pictorial imagination, and in dramatic humour, but totally deficient in architectonic skill, Carlyle wrote one history, "The French Revolution," 1837, and two biographies, "Cromwell," 1845, "Frederick the Great," 1858–1865, of surpassing interest. But his most characteristic utterances are to be found in "Sartor Resartus," 1833, and "Heroes and Hero-Worship," 1841, the first a biting attack upon formalism and dogma, the second a vindication of the importance of individual genius in maintaining and in reforming the social fabric. Carlyle's gospel of labour and silence, and his preference for the guidance of instinct as opposed to that of conscious reflection, have exercised a great, though indeterminate, influence upon many thinkers who are unconscious of their debt to him.

Carlyle's characteristics can hardly be brought out more vividly than by placing his work beside that of Thomas Babington Macaulay, no idealist, but a typical Whig, whose clear-cut antithetical style made him the past-master of popular exposition, and the still prevalent model for the essayist and the historian.

Finally, we note the appearance of John Ruskin, whose "Modern Painters" began to appear in 1842. Entering the literary field primarily as a critic of the arts of painting and architecture, Ruskin extended his criticism, constructive and destructive, to literature and economics, the essential characteristic of his teaching being insistence on the ethical basis of all human energies : teaching expressed with unsurpassed eloquence.

H. W. C. DAVIS ; A. D. INNES

AS SEEN FROM THE FANALE MARITTIMO LIGHTHOUSE

THE TOWN AND HARBOUR VIEWED FROM THE NORTH-EAST

THE FINE ANCHORAGE, WITH THE TOWN IN THE BACKGROUND

Photochrome

TRIESTE, THE CHIEF SEAPORT OF AUSTRIA-HUNGARY

THE REACTION IN CENTRAL EUROPE
AND THE ASCENDANCY OF METTERNICH

THE Austrian state, totally disorganised by the period of the French Revolution and Napoleonic wars, had nevertheless succeeded in rounding off its territories at the Congress of Vienna. In internal affairs Francis I. and Metternich tried as far as possible to preserve the old order of things ; they wished for an absolute monarchy, and favoured the privileged classes. There was no more tenacious supporter of what was old, no more persistent observer of routine than the good Emperor Francis. He was an absolute ruler in the spirit of conservatism.

He saw a national danger in any movement of men's minds which deviated from the letter of his commands, hated from the first all innovations, and ruled his people from the Cabinet. He delighted to travel through his dominions, and receive the joyful greetings of his loyal subjects, since he laid the highest value on popularity ; notwithstanding all his keenness of observation and his industry, he possessed no ideas of his own. Even Metternich was none too highly gifted in this respect. Francis made, at the most, only negative use of the abundance of his supreme power. Those who served him were bound to obey him blindly ; but he lacked the vigour and strength of character for great and masterful actions ; his thoughts and wishes were those of a permanent official. Like Frederic William III., he loathed independent characters, men of personal views, and he therefore treated his brothers Charles and John with unjustified distrust.

The Vain Emperor Francis

The only member of his family really acceptable to him was his youngest brother, the narrow-minded and characterless Lewis. On the other hand, Francis was solicitous for the spread of beneficial institutions, and for the regulation of the legal system ; in 1811 he introduced the "Universal Civil Code," and in so doing completed the task begun by Maria Theresa and Joseph II. His chief defect was his love of trifling details, which deprived him of any comprehensive view of a subject ; and his constant interference with the business of the Council of State prevented any systematic conduct of affairs.

Austria's High Position in Europe

Francis owed it to Metternich that Austria once more held the highest position in Europe ; he was therefore glad to entrust him with the management of foreign policy while he contented himself with internal affairs. Metternich was the centre of European diplomacy ; but he was only a diplomatist, no statesman like Kaunitz and Felix Schwarzenberg. He did not consolidate the new Austria for the future, but only tried to check the wheel of progress and to hold the reins with the assistance of his henchman Gentz ; everything was to remain stationary.

Reign of Suspicion and Espionage

The police zealously helped to maintain this principle of government, and prosecuted every free-thinker as suspected of democracy. Austria was in the fullest sense a country of police ; it supported an army of "mouchards" and informers. The post-office officials disregarded the privacy of letters, spies watched teachers and students in the academies ; even such loyal Austrians as Grillparzer and Zedlitz came into collision with the detectives. The censorship was blindly intolerant and pushed its interference to extremes. Public education, from the university down to the village school, suffered under the suspicious tutelage of the authorities ; school and Church alike were unprogressive. The provincial estates, both in the newly-acquired and in the recovered Crown lands, were insignificant, leading, as a matter of fact, a shadowy existence, which reflected the depressed condition of the population. But Hungary, which, since the time when Maria Theresa was hard pressed, had insisted on its national independence, was not disposed to descend from its height to the general insignificance of the other Crown lands, and the Archduke Palatine, Joseph, thoroughly shared this idea. It was therefore certain that soon there would be an embittered struggle with the government at Vienna,

Széchényi "the Greatest of the Hungarians" which wished to render the constitution of Hungary as unreal as that of Carniola and Tyrol. The indignation found its expression chiefly in the assemblies of the counties, which boldly contradicted the arbitrary and stereotyped commands from Vienna, while a group of the nobility itself supported the view that the people, hitherto excluded from political life, should share in the movement. In the Reichstag of 1825 this group spoke very distinctly against the exclusive rule of the nobility. The violent onslaught of the Reichstag against the Government led, it is true, to no result; the standard-bearer of that group was Count Stephen Széchényi, whom his antagonist, Kossuth, called "the greatest of the Hungarians."

The Archduke Rainer, to whom the viceroyalty of the Italian possessions had been entrusted, was animated by the best intention of promoting the happiness of the Lombard-Venetian kingdom, and of familiarising the Italians with the Austrian rule ; but he was so hampered by instructions from Vienna that he could not exercise any marked influence on the Government. The Italians would hear nothing of the advantages of the Austrian rule, opposed all "Germanisation," and prided themselves on their old nationality. Literature, the Press, and secret societies aimed at national objects and encouraged independence, while Metternich thought of an Italian confederation on the German model, and under the headship of Austria.

It was also very disastrous that the leading circles at Vienna regarded Italy as the chief support of the whole policy of the empire, and yet failed to understand the great diversity of social and political conditions in the individual states of the peninsula. Metternich, on the other hand, employed every forcible means to oppose the national wishes, which he regarded,

FRANCIS I. OF AUSTRIA
He succeeded his father, Leopold II., as Emperor of Germany, but in 1804 he renounced the title of German-Roman Emperor, retaining that of Emperor of Austria.

both there and in Germany, as outcomes of the revolutionary spirit. Yet the hopes of the nations on both sides of the Alps were not being realised ; the "Golden Age" had still to come.

The condition of the Austrian finances was deplorable. Since the year 1811, when Count Joseph Wallis, the Finance Minister, had devised a system which reduced by one-fifth the nominal value of the paper money—which had risen to the amount of 1,060,000,000 gulden—permanent bankruptcy had prevailed. Silver disappeared from circulation, the national credit fell very low, and the revenue was considerably less than the expenditure, which was enormously increased by the long war. In the year 1814 Count Stadion, the former Minister of the Interior, undertook the thankless duties of Minister of Finance. He honestly exerted himself to improve credit, introduce a fixed monetary standard, create order on a consistent plan, and with competent colleagues to develop the economic resources of the nation. But various financial measures were necessary before the old paper money could be withdrawn en bloc, and silver once more put into circulation. New loans had to be raised, which increased the burden of interest, in the years 1816 to 1823, from 9,000,000 gulden to 24,000,000, and the annual expenditure for the national debt from 12,000,000 to 50,000,000. The National Bank, opened in 1817, afforded efficient help. If Stadion did not succeed in remodelling the system of indirect taxes, and if the reorganisation of the land-tax proceeded slowly, the attitude of Hungary greatly added to the difficulties of the position of the great Minister of reform, who died in May, 1824. The state

The Promised Land of Restrictions of the Emperor Francis was naturally the Promised Land of custom-house restrictions and special tariffs ; industry and trade were closely barred in. In vain did clear-headed politicians advise that all the hereditary dominions, excepting Hungary, should make one customs district ; although the Government built commercial roads and canals, still the trade of the empire with foreign countries was stagnant. Trieste never became for Austria that which it might have been; it was left for Karl Ludwig von Bruck of Elberfeld to make it, in 1833, a focus of the trade of the world by founding the Austrian-Lloyd Shipping Company. Red tape prevailed in the army, innovations were shunned, and the reforms of the Archduke Charles were interrupted. This was the outlook in Austria, the "Faubourg St. Germain of Europe."

Were things better in the rival state of Prussia? Frederic William III. was the type of a homely bourgeois, a man of sluggish intellect and of a cold scepticism, which contrasted sharply with the patriotic fire and self-devotion of his people. His main object was to secure tranquillity; the

METTERNICH IN LATER LIFE
Metternich's domination of European politics after the fall of Napoleon in 1815 stands out prominently in the history of the period. He was the centre of European diplomacy, but he was only a diplomatist and not a statesman.

storm of the war of liberation, so foreign to his sympathies, had blown over, and he now wished to govern his kingdom in peace. Religious questions interested him more than those of politics; he was a positive Christian, and it was the wish of his heart to amalgamate the Lutheran and the Reformed Churches, an attempt to which the spirit of the age seemed very favourable. When the tercentenary of the Reformation was commemorated in the year 1817, he appealed for the union of the two confessions, and found much response. The new Liturgy of 1821, issued with his own concurrence, found great opposition, especially among the Old Lutherans; its second form, in 1829, somewhat conciliated

its opponents, although the old tutelage of the Church under the supreme bishop of the country still continued to be felt, and Frederic William, both in the secular and spiritual domain, professed an absolutism which did not care to see district and provincial synods established by its side. The union, indeed, produced no peace in the Church, but became the pretext for renewed quarrels; nevertheless it was introduced into Nassau, Baden, the Bavarian Palatinate, Anhalt, and a part of Hesse in the same way as into Prussia. The king wished to give to the Catholic Church also a systematised and profitable development, and therefore entered into negotiations with the Curia, which were conducted by the ambassador Barthold G. Niebuhr, a great historian but weak diplomatist. Niebuhr and Altenstein, the Minister of Public Worship, made too many concessions to the Curia, and were not a match for Consalvi, the Cardinal Secretary of State. On July 16th, 1821, Pope Pius VII. issued the Bull, "De salute animarum," which was followed by an explanatory brief, "Quod de fidelium." The king confirmed the agreement by an order of the Cabinet; Cologne and Posen became archbishoprics, Trèves, Münster, Paderborn, Breslau, Kulm, and Ermeland bishoprics, each with a clerical seminary. The cathedral chapters were conceded the right of electing the bishop, who, however, had necessarily to be a persona grata to the king.

Joseph   Széchényi
LEADERS OF HUNGARIAN INDEPENDENCE
Insisting on its national independence, Hungary was unwilling to descend to the insignificance of the other Crown lands under Austria, and both the Archduke Palatine, Joseph, and Count Stephen Széchényi assisted the movement in assemblies and elsewhere. Széchényi was described by his antagonist Kossuth as "the greatest of the Hungarians."

The truce did not, indeed, last long; the question of mixed marriages led to renewed controversy. Subsequently to 1803, the principle held good in the eastern provinces of Prussia that the children in disputed cases should follow the religion of the father, a view that conflicted with a Bull of 1741; now, after 1825, the order of 1803 was to **The Problem of Mixed Marriages** be valid for the Rhine province, which was for the most part Catholic. But the bishops of the districts appealed in 1828 to Pope Leo XII. He and his successor, Pius VIII., conducted long negotiations with the Prussian ambassador, Bunsen, who, steeped in the spirit of romanticism, saw the surest protection against the revolution in a close adherence between national governments and the Curia.

Pius VIII., an enemy of all enlightenment, finally, by a brief of 1830, permitted the consecration of mixed marriages only when a promise was given that the children born from the union would be brought up in the Catholic faith; but the Prussian Government did not accept the brief, and matters soon came to a dispute between the Curia and the Archbishop of Cologne.

It was excessively difficult to form the new Prussian state into a compact unity of a firm and flexible type. Not merely its elongated shape, its geographical incoherency, and the position of Hanover as an excrescence on its body, but above everything its composition out of a hundred territorial fragments with the most diversified legislatures and the most rooted dislike to centralisation, the aversion of the Rhenish Catholics to be included in the state which was Protestant by history and character, and the stubbornness of the Poles in the countries on the Vistula, quite counterbalanced a growth in population, now more than doubled, which was welcome in itself. By unobtrusive and successful labour the greatest efforts were made towards establishing some degree **The New Prussian State** of unity. The ideal of unity could not be universally realised in the legal system and the administration of justice. The inhabitants, therefore, of the Rhenish districts were conceded the Code Napoleon, with juries and oral procedure, but the larger part of the monarchy was given the universal common law. The narrow-minded and meddlesome system of the excise and the local variations of the land-tax system were intolerable.

The root idea of the universal duty of bearing arms, that pillar of the monarchy, was opposed on many sides. This institution, which struck deeply into family life, met with especial opposition and discontent in the newly acquired provinces. In large circles there prevailed the wish that there should no longer be a standing army.

But finally the constitution of the army was adhered to; it cemented together the different elements of the country. The ultimate form was that of three years' active service, two years' service in the reserve, and two periods of service in the militia, each of seven years. The fact that the universal duties of bearing arms and defending the country were to be permanent institutions made Frederic William suspicious. His narrow-minded but influential brother-in-law, Duke Charles of Mecklenburg-Strelitz, the sworn opponent of the reform legislation of Stein, Hardenberg, and Scharnhorst, induced him to believe that a revolutionary party, whose movements were obscure, wanted to employ the militia against the throne, and advised, as a counter precaution, that **Prussia Divided into Provinces** the militia and troops of the line should be amalgamated. But the originator of the law of defence, the Minister of War, Hermann von Boyen, resolutely opposed this blissful necessity. An ordinance of April 30th, 1815, divided Prussia into ten provinces; but since East and West Prussia, Lower Rhine and Cleves-Berg were soon united, the number was ultimately fixed at eight, which were subdivided into administrative districts.

Lords-lieutenant were placed at the head of the provinces instead of the former provincial Ministries. Their administrative sphere was accurately defined by a Cabinet order of November 3rd, 1817; they represented the entire Government, and fortunately these responsible posts were held by competent and occasionally prominent men. The amalgamation of the new territories with Old Prussia was complete, both externally and internally, however difficult the task may have been at first in the province of Saxony and many other parts, and however much consistency and resolution may have been wanting at headquarters, in the immediate vicinity of Frederic William. But the struggle with the forces of local particularism was long and obstinate. The great period of Prince Hardenberg,

Chancellor of State, was over. He could no longer master the infinity of work which rested upon him, got entangled in intrigues and escapades, associated with despicable companions, and immediately lost influence with the king, himself the soul of honour; his share in the reorganisation of Prussia after the wars of liberation was too small. On the other hand, he guarded against Roman encroachment, and assiduously worked at the question of the constitution. His zeal to realise his intentions there too frequently left the field open to the reactionaries in another sphere. Most of the higher civil servants admired the official liberalism of the chancellor, and therefore, like Hardenberg and Stein, appeared to the reactionaries as patrons of the extravagant enthusiasm and "Teutonising" agitation of the youth—

FREDERIC WILLIAM III.

He ascended the throne of Prussia in 1797, and being deeply interested in religious questions, he did much to further the union of the Lutheran and Reformed Churches.

as secret democrats, in short. Boyen was the closest supporter of Hardenberg; the Finance Minister, Count Bülow, formerly the distinguished Finance Minister of the kingdom of Westphalia, usually supported him, while the chief of the War Office, Witzleben, the inseparable counsellor of the king, who even ventured to work counter to the Duke of Mecklenburg, was one of the warmest advocates of the reform of Stein and Hardenberg. The reactionaries, under Marwitz and other opponents of the great age of progress relied on the Ministers of the Interior and of the Police, the over-cautious Schuckmann and Prince William of Wittgenstein. The latter was a bitter enemy of German patriotism and the constitution, and the best of the tools of Metternich at the court of Berlin.

The reaction which naturally followed the exuberant love of freedom shown in the wars of liberation was peculiarly felt in Prussia. Janke, Schmalz, the brother-in-law of Scharnhorst, and other place-hunters clumsily attacked in pamphlets the "seducers of the people" and the "demagogues," in

NIEBUHR THE HISTORIAN

Distinguished as a historian, Barthold Niebuhr in 1823 took up his residence at Bonn, and gave a great impetus to historical learning by his lectures in that city.

order to recommend themselves to the Governments as saviours of the threatened society. The indignation at their falsehoods was general; there appeared numerous refutations, the most striking of which proceeded from the pen of Schleiermacher and Niebuhr. The Prussian and Würtemberg Governments, however, stood on the side of Schmalz and his companions, and rewarded his falsehood with a decoration and acknowledgment. Frederic William III., indeed, strictly forbade, in January, 1816, any further literary controversy about secret combinations, but at the same time renewed the prohibition on such societies, at which great rejoicings broke out in Vienna. He also forbade the further appearance of the "Rhenish Mercury," which demanded a constitution and liberty of the Press. Gneisenau was removed from the general command in Coblenz. Wittgenstein's spies were continually active. The emancipation of the Jews, in contradiction to the royal edict of 1812, lost ground. The Act for the regulation of landed property proclaimed in September, 1811, was "explained" in 1816, in a fashion which favoured so greatly the property of the nobles at the cost of the property of the peasants that it virtually repealed the Regulation Act.

In the course of the last decade there had been frequent talk of a General Council. Stein's programme of 1808 proposed that the Council of State should be the highest ratifying authority for acts of legislation. Hardenberg, on the other hand, fearing for his own supremacy, had contemplated in 1810 giving the council a far more modest rôle. But neither scheme received a trial; and in many quarters a Council of State was only thought of with apprehension. When, then, finally the ordinance of March 20th, 1817, established the Council of State, it was merely the highest advisory authority, the foremost counsellor of the Crown, and Stein's name was missing from the list of those summoned by the king.

The first labours of the Council of State were directed to the reform of the taxation, which Count Bülow, the Finance Minister, wished to carry out in the spirit of modified Free Trade. His schemes were very aggressive, and aimed at **The Aggressive Schemes of Count Bülow** freedom of inland commerce, but showed that, considering the financial distress of the moment, the state of the national debt, which in 1818 amounted to 217,000,000 thalers, £33,000,000, the want of credit, and the deficit, no idea of any remission of taxation could be entertained. In fact, Bülow demanded an increase of the indirect taxes, a proposal which naturally hit the lower classes very hard. Humboldt headed the opponents of Bülow, and a bitter struggle broke out. The notables convened in the provinces to express their views rejected Bülow's taxes on meal and meat, but pronounced in favour of the direct personal taxation, graduated according to classes.

Bülow was replaced as Finance Minister at the end of 1817 by Klewitz—the extent of whose office was, however, much diminished by all sorts of limitations—and received the newly created post of Minister of Trade and Commerce. In Altenstein, who between 1808 and 1810 had failed to distinguish himself as Finance Minister, Prussia found a born Minister of Public Worship and Education.

In spite of many unfavourable conditions he put the educational system on a sound footing; he introduced in 1817 the provincial bodies of teachers, advocated universal compulsory attendance at school, encouraged the national schools, and was instrumental in uniting the University of Wittenberg with that of Halle, and in founding the University of Bonn in 1818. Bülow, a pioneer in his own domain, not inferior to Altenstein in the field of Church and school, adminis- **Bülow's Hand on the Customs** tered the customs department, supported by the shrewd Maassen. The first preparatory steps were taken in 1816, especially in June, by the abolition of the waterway tolls and the inland and provincial duties. A Cabinet Order of August 1st, 1817, sanctioned for all time the principle of free importation, and Maassen drew up the Customs Act, which became law on May 26th, 1818, and came into force

at the beginning of 1819, according to Treitschke " the most liberal and matured politico-economic law of those days "; it was simplified in 1821 to suit the spirit of Free Trade, and the tolls were still more lowered. An order of February 8th, 1819, exempted from taxation out of the list of inland products only wine, beer, brandy, and leaf tobacco; on May 30th, 1820, a graduated personal tax and corn duties were introduced.

Thus a well-organised system of taxation was founded, which satisfied the national economy for some time. All social forces were left with free power of movement and scope for expansion. It mattered little if manufacturers complained, so long as the national prosperity, which was quite shattered, revived. Prussia gradually found the way to the German Customs Union. No one, it is true, could yet predict that change; but, as if with a presentiment, complaints of the selfishness and obstinacy of the tariff loan were heard beyond the Prussian frontiers. What progress had been made with the constitution granting provincial estates and popular representation, **Retrogression of Frederic William** promised by the king by the edict of May 22nd, 1815? The commission promised for this purpose was not summoned until March 30th, 1817. Hardenberg directed the proceedings since it had assembled on July 7th in Berlin, sent Altenstein, Beyme, and Klewitz to visit the provinces in order to collect thorough evidence of the existing conditions, and received reports, which essentially contradicted each other.

It appeared most advisable that the Ministers should content themselves with establishing provincial estates, and should leave a constitution out of the question. Hardenberg honestly tried to make progress in the question of the constitution and to release the royal word which had been pledged; Frederic William, on the contrary, regretted having given it, and gladly complied with the retrogressive tendencies of the courtiers and supporters of the old regime. He saw with concern the contests in the South German chambers and the excitement among the youth of Germany; he pictured to himself the horrors of a revolution, and Hardenberg could not carry his point.

The Federal Diet, the union of the princes of Germany, owed its existence to the Act of Federation of June 8th, 1815, which could not possibly satisfy the hopes of a nation which had conquered a Napoleon. Where did the heroes of the wars of liberation find any guarantee for their claims ? Of what did the national rights consist, and what protection did the whole Federation offer against foreign countries ?

Even the deposed and mediatised princes of the old empire were deceived in their last hopes ; they had once more dreamed of a revival of their independence. But they were answered with cold contempt that the new political organisation of Germany demanded that the princes and counts, who had been found already mediatised, should remain incorporated into other political bodies or be incorporated afresh ; that the Act of Federation involved the implicit recognition of this necessity. The Act of Federation pleased hardly anyone, not even its own designers.

The opening of the Federal Diet, convened for September 1st, 1815, was again postponed, since negotiations were taking place in Paris, and there were various territorial disputes between the several federal states to be decided.

Disputes of Federal States Austria was scheming for Salzburg and the Breisgau, Bavaria for the Baden Palatinate ; the two had come to a mutual agreement at the cost of the House of Baden, whose elder line was dying out, and Baden was confronted with the danger of dismemberment. The two chief powers disputed about Mainz until the town fell to Hesse-Darmstadt, but the right of garrisoning the important federal fortress fell to them both. Baden only joined the Federation on July 26th, 1815, Würtemberg on September 1st. Notwithstanding the opposition of Austria and Prussia permission was given to Russia, Great Britain, and France to have ambassadors at Frankfort, while the Federation had no permanent representatives at the foreign capitals. Many of the South German courts regarded the foreign ambassadors as a support against the leading German powers ; the secondary and petty states were most afraid of Prussia.

Finally, on November 5th, 1816, the Austrian ambassador opened the meeting of the Federation in Frankfort with a speech transmitted by Metternich. On all sides members were eager to move resolutions, and Metternich warned them against precipitation, the very last fault, as it turned out, of which the Federal Diet

was likely to be guilty. On the question of the domains of Electoral Hesse, with regard to which many private persons took the part of the elector, the Federation sustained a complete defeat at his hands. The question of the military organisation of the Federation was very inadequately solved. When the Barbary States in 1817 **The Idea of a German Fleet Abandoned** extended their raids in search of slaves and booty as far as the North Sea, and attacked merchantmen, the Hanseatic towns lodged complaints before the Federal Diet, but the matter ended in words. The ambassador of Baden, recalling the glorious past history of the Hansa, in vain counselled the federal states to build their own ships. The Federation remained dependent on the favour of foreign maritime Powers ; the question of a German fleet was dropped. Nor was more done for trade and commerce ; the mutual exchange of food-stuffs was still fettered by a hundred restrictions.

How did the matter stand with the performance of the article of the Act of Federation, which promised diets to all the federal states ?

Charles Augustus of Saxe-Weimar had granted a constitution on May 5th, 1816, and placed it under the guarantee of the Federation, which also guaranteed the Mecklenburg constitution of 1817. The Federation generally refrained from independent action, and omitted to put into practice the inconvenient article empowering them to sit in judgment on "the wisdom of each federal government." Austria and Prussia, like most of the federal governments, rejoiced at this evasion ; it mattered nothing to them that the peoples were deceived and discontented.

The same evasion was adopted in the case of Article XVIII., on the liberty of the Press. The north of Germany, which had hitherto lived apparently undisturbed, and the south, which was **The Feudal System in Hanover** seething with the new constitutional ideas, were somewhat abruptly divided on this point. In Hanover the feudal system, which had been very roughly handled by Westphalian and French rulers, returned cautiously and without undue haste out of its lurking-place after the restoration of the House of Guelph. In the General Landtag the landed interest was enormously in the preponderance. Count Münster-Ledenburg, who governed the new kingdom from London, sided with the nobility ; the constitution imposed in 1814 rested on the old feudal principles. The estates solemnly announced on January 17th, 1815, the union of the old and new territories into one whole, and on December 7th, 1819, Hanover received a new constitution on the dual-chamber system, and with complete equality of rights for the two chambers. The nobility and the official class were predominant. There was no trace of an organic development of the commonwealth ; the nobility conceded no reforms, and the people took little interest in the proceedings of the chambers.

Charles insulted King George IV., and challenged Münster to a duel. Finally, the Federal Diet intervened to end the mismanagement, and everything grew ripe for the revolution of 1830.

In the kingdom of Saxony, so reduced in territory and population, matters returned to the old footing. Frederic Augustus I. the Just maintained order in the peculiar sense in which he understood the word. Only quite untenable conditions were reformed, otherwise the king and the Minister, Count Einsiedel, considered that the highest political wisdom was to persevere in the old order of things.

GENERAL VIEW OF THE TOWN OF BREMERHAVEN, FOUNDED IN 1827   Photochrome

The preponderance of the nobility was less oppressive in Brunswick. George IV. acted as guardian of the young duke, Charles II., and Count Münster in London conducted the affairs of state, with the assistance of the Privy Council of Brunswick, and promoted the material interests of the state, and the country received on April 25th in the " renewed system of states " a suitable constitution. Everything went on as was wished until Charles, in October, 1823, himself assumed the government and declared war on the constitution. A regime of the most despicable caprice and licence now began ;

Industries and trade were fettered, and there was a total absence of activity. The officials were as narrow as the statesmen. In the Federation Saxony always sided with Austria, being full of hatred of Prussia ; Saxony was only important in the development of art. Even under King Anthony, after May, 1827, everything remained in the old position. Einsiedel's statesmanship was as powerful as before, and the discontent among the people grew.

The two Mecklenburgs remained feudal states, in which the middle class and the peasants were of no account. Even the organic constitution of 1817 for Schwerin

Charles II.	Frederic Augustus	William I.

REACTIONARY RULERS OF EUROPEAN STATES

Assuming the government of Brunswick in 1823, Charles II. declared war on the constitution, and a regime of the most despicable caprice and licence went on until the Federal Diet intervened to end the mismanagement. Known as the Just, Frederic Augustus I. of Saxony followed in the old order of things, and thus the country was stunted in its industries. King of Würtemberg, William I. promised a liberal representative constitution, but did not fulfil his pledges; he died in 1821.

made no alteration in the feudal power prevailing since 1755; the knights were still, as ever, supreme in the country. The Sternberg Diet of 1819 led certainly to the abolition of serfdom, but the position of the peasants was not improved by this measure. Emigration became more common; trades and industries were stagnant. Even Oldenburg was content with " political hibernation." Frankfort-on-Main received a constitution on October 18th, 1816, and many obsolete customs were abolished. In the Hansa towns, on the contrary, the old patriarchal conditions were again in full force; the council ruled absolutely. Trade and commerce made great advances, especially in Hamburg and Bremen. The founding of Bremerhaven by the burgomaster Johann Smidt, a clever politician, opened fresh paths of world commerce to Bremen.

The Elector William I., who had returned to Hesse-Cassel, wished to bring everything back to the footing of 1806, when he left his country; he declared the ordinances of " his administrator Jérôme " not to be binding on him, recognised the sale of domains as little as the advancement of Hessian officers, but wished to make the fullest use of that part of the Westphalian ordinances which brought him personal advantage. He promised, indeed, a liberal

THE FAMOUS UNIVERSITY OF BONN, FOUNDED IN THE YEAR 1818   Photochrome

representative constitution, but trifled with the Landtag, and contented himself with the promulgation of the unmeaning family and national law of March 4th, 1817. When he died, unlamented, in 1821, the still more capricious and worthless regime of William II. began, which was marked by debauchery, family quarrels, and public discontent.

Reforms of the Grand Duke Lewis Far more edifying was the state of things in Hesse-Darmstadt, where the Grand Duke, Lewis I., although by inclination attached to the old regime, worked his best for reform, and did not allow himself to be driven to reaction after the conference at Carlsbad. He gave Hesse on December 17th (March 18th), 1820, a representative constitution, and was an enlightened ruler, as is shown, among other instances, by his acquiescence in the efforts of Prussia toward a customs union.

The most unscrupulous among the princes of the Rhenish Confederation, Frederic of Würtemberg, readily noticed the increasing discontent of his subjects, and wished to meet it by the proclamation of January 11th, 1815, that ever since 1806 he had wished to give his country a constitution and representation by estates ; but when he read out his constitution to the estates on May 15th, these promptly rejected it. The excitement in the country increased amid constant appeals to the " old and just right." Frederic died in the middle of a dispute on October 30th, 1816. Under his son, William I., who was both chivalrous and ambitious, a better time dawned for Würtemberg. But the estates offered such opposition to him that the constitution was not formed until September 25th, 1819 ; but the first diet of 1820–1821 was extremely amenable to the government. William was very popular, although his rule showed little liberalism.

Bavaria, after the dethronement of its second creator, Napoleon, had recovered the territory on the left bank of the Rhine, and formed out of it the Rhenish Palatinate, whose **Bavaria's Recovered Territory** population remained for a long time as friendly to France as Bavaria itself was hostile. " Father Max " certainly did his best to amalgamate the inhabitants of the Palatinate and Bavaria, and his premier, Count Montgelas, effected so many profitable and wise changes for this kingdom, which had increased to more than thirteen hundred square German miles, with four million souls, that much

of the blame attached to this policy might seem to be unjustified. His most dangerous opponents were the Crown Prince Lewis, with his leaning towards romanticism and his " Teutonic " sympathies and hatred of France, and Field-Marshal Count Wrede. While Montgelas wished not to hear a syllable about a new constitution, the crown prince deliberately adopted a constitutional policy, in order to prepare the downfall of the hated Frenchman.

Montgelas' constitution of May 1st, 1808, had never properly seen the light. He intended national representation to be nothing but a sham. The crown prince wished, in opposition to the Minister, that Bavaria should be a constitutional state, a model to the whole of Germany. Montgelas was able to put a stop to the intended creation of a constitution in 1814–1815, while his scheme of an agreement with the Curia was hindered by an increase in the claims of the latter. He fell on February 2nd, 1817, a result to which the court at Vienna contributed, and Bavaria spoke only of his defects, without being in a position to replace Montgelas' system by **The New Constitution of Bavaria** another. The Concordat of June 5th, 1817, signified a complete victory of the Curia, and was intolerable in the new state of Bavarian public opinion ; the " kingdom of darkness " stood beside the door. The Crown met the general discontent by admitting into the constitution some provisions guaranteeing the rights of Protestants, and thus naturally furnished materials for further negotiations with the Curia. On May 26th, 1818, Bavaria finally received its constitution ; in spite of deficiencies and gaps it was full of vitality, and is still in force, although in the interval it has required to be altered in many points.

Bavaria thus by the award of a liberal constitution had anticipated Baden, which was forced to grant a similar one in order to influence public opinion in its favour. Prospects of the Baden Rhenish-Palatinate were opened up to Bavaria by arrangements with Austria. The ruling House of Zähringen, except for an illegitimate line, was on the verge of extinction, and the Grand Duke Charles could never make up his mind to declare the counts of Hochberg legitimate. At the urgent request of Stein and the Tsar Alexander, his brother-in-law, Charles, had already announced to Metternich and

Hardenberg in Vienna on December 1st, 1814, that he wished to introduce a representative constitution in his dominions, and so anticipated the Act of Federation. Stein once more implored the distrustful man, "whose indolence was boundless," to carry out his intention ; but every appeal rebounded from him, and he once again postponed the constitutional question.

The Bavarian craving for Baden territory became more and more threatening. A more vigorous spirit was felt in the Baden Ministry after its reorganisation. At last, on October 4th, Charles, by a family law, proclaimed the indivisibility of the whole state and the rights of the Hochberg line to the succession. It was foreseen that Bavaria would not submit tamely to this. German public opinion, and even Russian influence were brought to bear in favour of a constitution. Baden was forced to try to anticipate Bavaria in making this concession. Even the Emperor Alexander opened the first diet of his kingdom of Poland on the basis of the constitution of 1815, and took the occasion to praise the blessing of liberal institutions. Then Bavaria got the start of Baden. Tettenborn and Reitzenstein represented to Charles that Baden must make haste and create a still more liberal constitution, which was finally signed by Charles on August 22nd, 1818.

Rejoicings in Liberal Germany

It was, according to Barnhagen, "the most liberal of all German constitutions, the richest in germs of life, the strongest in energy." It entirely corresponded to the charter of Louis XVIII. The ordinances of October 4th, 1817, were also contained in it and ratified afresh. The rejoicings in Baden and liberal Germany at large were unanimous. In Munich there was intense bitterness. The Crown Prince Lewis in particular did not desist from trying to win the Baden Palatinate, and we know now that even Lewis II. in the year 1870 urged Bismarck to obtain it for Bavaria. Baden ceded to Bavaria in 1819 a portion of the district of Wertheim, and received from Austria Hohengerold-seck. The congress at Aix-la-Chapelle had also pronounced in favour of Baden in 1818.

Nassau, before the rest of Germany, had received, on September 2nd, 1814, a constitution, for which Stein was partly responsible. But the estates were not summoned until the work of reorganising the duchy was completed. Duke William opened the assembly at last on March 3rd, 1818, and a tedious dispute soon broke out about the Crown lands and state property. The Minister of State, Bieberstein, a particularist and reactionary of the purest water, adopted Metternich's views. In popular opinion the credit of the first step was not given to Nassau, because it delayed so long to take the second. If Metternich looked towards Prussia, he saw the king in his element, and Hardenberg in continual strife with Humboldt ; if he turned his eyes to South Germany, he beheld a motley scene, which also gave him a hard problem to solve. In Bavaria the first diet led to such unpleasant scenes that the king contemplated the repeal of the constitution. In Baden, where Rotteck and Baron Liebenstein were the leaders, a flood of proposals was poured out against the rule of the new Grand Duke, Lewis I. ; the dispute became so bitter that Lewis, on July 28th, 1819, prorogued the chambers. In Nassau and in Hesse-Darmstadt there was also much disorder in the diets.

Unruly Scenes in the Diets

The reaction saw all this with great pleasure. It experienced a regular triumph on March 23rd, 1819, through the bloody deed of a student, Karl Ludwig Sand. It had become a rooted idea in the limited brain of this fanatic that the dramatist and Russian privy councillor, August von Kotzebue, was a Russian spy, the most dangerous enemy of German freedom and German academic life ; he therefore stabbed him in Mannheim. While great and general sympathy was extended to Sand, the governments feared a conspiracy of the student associations where Sand had studied.

Charles Augustus saw that men looked askance at him, and his steps for the preservation of academic liberty were unavailing. Metternich possessed the power, and made full use of it, being sure of the assent of the majority of German governments, of Russia, and of Great Britain ; even from France approval was showered upon him. Frederic William III., being completely ruled by Prince Wittgenstein and Kaunitz, was more and more overwhelmed with fear of revolution, and wished to abolish everything which seemed open to suspicion.

Universities the Hotbeds of Intrigues

The universities, the fairest ornaments of Germany, were regarded by the rulers as hotbeds of revolutionary intrigues ;

they required to be freed from the danger. The authorities of Austria and Prussia thought this to be imperatively necessary, and during the season for the waters at Carlsbad they wished to agree upon the measures. Haste was urgent, as it seemed, for on July 1st, 1819, Sand had already found an imitator. Karl Löning, an apothe-

The Iron Hand in Prussia cary's apprentice, attempted to assassinate at Schwalbach Karl von Ibell, the president of the Nassau Government, whom, in spite of his liberal and excellent administration, the crackbrained Radicals loudly proclaimed to be a reactionary. The would-be assassin committed suicide after his attempt had failed. In Prussia steps were now taken to pay domiciliary visits, confiscate papers, and make arrests. Jahn was sent to a fortress, the papers of the bookseller Reimer were put under seal, Schleiermacher's sermons were subject to police surveillance, the houses of Welcker and Arndt in Bonn were carefully searched and all writings carried off which the bailiffs chose to take. Protests were futile. Personal freedom had no longer any protection against the tyranny of the police. The privacy of letters was constantly infringed, and the Government issued falsified accounts of an intended revolution.

On July 29th Frederic William and Metternich met at Töplitz. Metternich strengthened the king's aversion to grant a general constitution, and agitated against Hardenberg's projected constitution. On August 1st the Contract of Töplitz was agreed upon, which, though intended to be kept secret, was to form the basis of the Carlsbad conferences; a censorship was to be exercised over the Press and the universities, and Article 13 of the Act of Federation was to be explained in a corresponding sense. Metternich triumphed, for even Hardenberg seemed to submit to him. Metternich returned with justifiable self-complacency to Carlsbad, where he found

Metternich's Reactionary Measures his selected body of diplomatists, and over the heads of the Federal Diet he discussed with the representatives of a quarter of the governments, from August 6th to 31st, reactionary measures of the most sweeping character. Gentz, the secretary of the congress, drew up the minutes on which the resolutions of Carlsbad were mainly based. Metternich wished to grant to the Federal Diet a stronger influence on the legislation of the several states, and

through it indirectly to guide the governments, unnoticed by the public. The interpretation of Article 13 of the Act of Federation was deferred to ensuing conferences at Vienna, and an agreement was made first of all on four main points. A very stringent press law for five years was to be enforced in the case of all papers appearing daily or in numbers, and of pamphlets containing less than twenty pages of printed matter; and every federal state should be allowed to increase the stringency of the law at its own discretion.

The universities were placed under the strict supervision of commissioners appointed by the sovereigns; dangerous professors were to be deprived of their office, all secret societies and the universal student associations were to be prohibited, and no member of them should hold a public post. It was enacted that a central commission, to which members were sent by Austria, Prussia, Bavaria, Hanover, Baden, Hesse-Darmstadt, and Nassau, should assemble at Mainz to investigate the treasonable revolutionary societies which had been discovered; but, by the distinct

The Te Deum of the Reactionaries declaration of Austria, such commission should have no judicial power. A preliminary executive order, to terminate after August, 1820, was intended to secure the carrying out of the resolutions of the Federation for the maintenance of internal tranquillity, and in given cases military force might be employed to effect it.

On September 1st the Carlsbad conferences ended, and the party of reaction sang their Te Deum. Austria appeared to be the all-powerful ruler of Germany. " A new era is dawning," Metternich wrote to London. The Federal Diet accepted the Carlsbad resolutions with unusual haste on September 20th, and they were proclaimed in all the federal states. Austria had stolen a march over the others, and the Federal Council expressed its most humble thanks to Francis therefor. All free-thinkers saw in the Carlsbad resolutions not merely a check on all freedom and independence, but also a disgrace; nevertheless, the governments, in spite of the indignation of men like Stein, Rotteck, Niebuhr, Dahlmann, Ludwig Börne, and others, carried them out in all their harshness. The central commission of inquiry hunted through the Federation in search of conspiracies, and, as its own reports acknowledge, found nothing of importance, but unscrupulously interfered with the life of the nation and the individual. Foreign countries did not check this policy, although many statesmen, Capodistrias at their head, disapproved of the reaction. The Students' Association was officially dissolved on November 26th, 1819, but was immediately reconstituted in secret.

There was no demagogism in Austria; Prussia was satisfied to comply with the wishes of the court of Vienna, and even Hardenberg was prepared for any step which Metternich prescribed. Every suspected person was regarded in Berlin as an imported conspirator. The edict of censorship of 1819, dating from the day of liberation, October 18th, breathed the unholy spirit of Wöllner; foreign journals were strictly supervised. The reaction was nowhere more irreconcilable than in Prussia, where nothing recalled the saying of Frederic the Great, that every man might be happy after his own fashion. The gymnasia were as relentlessly persecuted as the intellectual exercises of university training; nothing could be more detestable than the way in which men like Arndt, Gneisenau, and Jahn were made to run the gauntlet, or a patriot like Justus Gruner was ill-treated on his very deathbed, or the residence of Görres in Germany rendered intolerable. This tendency obviously crippled the fulfilment of the royal promise of a constitution—a promise in which

Frederic William had never been serious. Hardenberg and Humboldt were perpetually quarrelling; Humboldt attacked the exaggerated power of the chancellor, who was not competent for his post; Hardenberg laid a new plan of a constitution before the king on August 11th, 1819. The king, in this dispute, took the side of Hardenberg, and the dismissal of Boyen and Grolman was followed, on December 31st, 1819, by that of Humboldt and Count Beyme. Metternich rejoiced; Humboldt, the "thoroughly bad man," was put on one side and thenceforth lived for science.

Hardenberg's position was once more strengthened; his chief object was to carry the revenue and finance laws. On January 17th, 1820, the ordinance as to the condition of the national debt was issued, from which the Liberals received the comforting assurance that the Crown would not be able to raise new loans except under the joint guarantee of the proposed assembly of the estates, and that the trustees of the debt would furnish the assembly with an annual statement of accounts. Shipping companies and banks were remodelled; the capital account was to be published every three years. Hardenberg then brought his revenue laws to the front, and in spite of many difficulties these laws, which, though admittedly imperfect, still demanded attention, were passed on May 20th, 1820.

Stein Rotteck

Humboldt Eichhorn

A GROUP OF DISTINGUISHED GERMANS

Entering the service of Prussia in 1780, Baron von Stein worked for progress and laid the foundations of Prussia's subsequent greatness. Rotteck, a professor at Freiburg, was eminent as a historian and publicist; famous as a naturalist and traveller, Humboldt explored unknown lands, while Eichhorn was a prominent Prussian statesman and jurist.

In accordance with the agreement made in Carlsbad, the representatives of the inner federal assembly met in Vienna, and deliberated from November 25th, 1819, to May 24th, 1820, over the head of the Federal Diet ; the result, the final act of Vienna of May 15th, 1820, obtained the same validity as the Federal Act of 1815.

Eichhorn's Ideal of Union In the plenary assembly of June 8th, 1820, the Federal Diet pro- moted it to be a fundamental law of the Federation. Particu- larism and reaction had scored a success, and the efficiency of the Federal Diet was once more crippled. The nation was universally disappointed by the new fundamental law, which realised not one of its expectations ; but Metternich basked in the rays of success.

The question of free intercourse between the federal states had also been discussed in Vienna, and turned men's looks to Prussia's efforts towards a customs union. The Customs Act of May 26th, 1818, was unmercifully attacked ; it was threatened with repeal at the Congress of Aix-la-Chapelle, but weathered the storm, and found protection from Johann Friedrich Eichhorn. In the field of material interests Eichhorn had a free hand ; he was a hero of unobtrusive work, who with inde- fatigable patience went towards his goal— the union of the German states to Prussia by the bond of their own interests. In 1819 he invited the Thuringian states, which formed enclaves in Prussia, to a tariff union, and on October 25th in that year the first treaty for accession to the tariff union was signed with Schwarzburg-Sondershausen ; since this was extremely advantageous to the petty state, it served as a model to all further treaties with Prussian enclaves.

The German Commercial and Industrial Association of the traders of Central and Southern Germany was founded in Frank-fort during the April Fair of 1819, under **The General Commercial Association** the presidency of Professor Friedrich List of Tübingen. The memorial of the associa- tion, drawn up by List and presented to the diet, pictured as its ultimate aim the universal freedom of commercial intercourse between every nation ; it called for the abolition of the inland tolls and existing federal tolls on foreign trade, but was rejected. List now attacked the several governments, scourged in his journal the faults of German

commercial policy, was an opponent of the Prussian Customs Act, and always recurred to federal tolls. Far clearer were the economic views of the Baden statesman Karl Friedrich Nebenius, whose pamphlet was laid before the Vienna conferences. He too attacked the Prussian Customs Act ; but his pamphlet, in spite of all its merits, had no influence on the development of the tariff union. Johann Friedrich Benzenberg alone of the well-known journalists of the day spoke for Prussia. Indeed, the hos- tility to Prussia gave rise to the abortive separate federation of Southern and Central Germany, formed at Darmstadt in 1820. Such plans were foredoomed to failure. All rival tariff unions failed in the same way.

Hardenberg's influence over Frederic William III. had been extinguished by Metternich, and the Chancellor of State was politically dead, even before he closed his eyes, on November 26th, 1822. A new constitution commission under the presidency of the Crown Prince Frederic William (IV.), who was steeped in roman- ticism, consisted entirely of Hardenberg's **Reaction Again Triumphant** opponents, and would only be content with charters for the several provinces. The king consented to them. After Hardenberg's death the king could not consent to summon Wilhelm von Hum- boldt, but abolished the presidency in the Cabinet. The king contented himself with the law of June 5th, 1823, as to the regulation of provincial estates.

Bureaucracy and feudalism celebrated a joint victory in this respect. Austria could be contented with Prussia's aversion to constitutional forms, and, supported by it, guided the Federal Diet, in which Würtemberg, owing to the frankness and independence of its representative, Wangenheim, now and again broke from the trodden path. Wangenheim suggested the plan of confronting the great German powers with a league " of pure and constitutional Germany," under the leadership of Bavaria and Würtemberg, proposing to create a triple alliance. But the Vienna conferences of January, 1823, arranged by Metternich, soon led to Würtemberg's compliance. Wangenheim fell in July. The Carlsbad resolutions were renewed in August, 1824, and the Federal Diet did not agitate again, after it had quietly divided the unhappy Central Enquiry Commission at Mainz in 1828.

THE RESTORED FRENCH MONARCHY
REACTION TRIUMPHANT IN THE LATIN STATES

THE restored Bourbon monarch of France found himself in an exceedingly difficult position. At his first restoration in 1814, he had been disposed to maintain the attitude of absolutism, and had consented to grant a constitution in the form of a concession bestowed by the benevolence of the Crown. This "Charta" had established two Chambers—one of peers, nominated by the Crown, the other of representatives elected under a high franchise. But the Royalists even then had shown a zeal which Louis had not restrained for the recovery of old rights and of the old supremacy. The masses of the people had thereby been alienated.

Louis recognised his error, and was now determined to abide by his constitution; but the Royalists saw only that their side was uppermost. Like the English Cavaliers when Charles II. came back to "enjoy his own again," they hoped to get back all that they had lost with interest. **Aims of the French Royalists** But the English Cavaliers had learnt very promptly to recognise that the old order had gone never to return; the French Royalists were not equally capable of reconciling themselves to that doctrine. More royalist than the king, they made haste to seek to impose their views upon him. Socially, the democratising of France had not been swept away under the Empire, though it had been so politically. The political centralisation of the Empire was only modified by the Charta; but the Royalists aimed at reversing the social democratisation as well. Their headquarters were naturally established in the entourage of Artois, the king's brother, and the circle became known from his residence as the Pavillon Marsan.

Louis, both from calculation and from grasp of the situation, held fast to his constitution, and was involved in continued conflict with his brother and the Royalists "quand même," the party of no compromise. He had promised an amnesty, but he did not succeed in checking the "White Terror," the outbreak of royalist violence in Southern France. In Marseilles, Avignon, Nismes, Toulouse, and other places disorders broke out, in which religious fanaticism also played its part. **The "White Terror" in France** Bonapartists and Protestants were murdered wholesale, among them Marshal Brune, Generals Lagarde and Ramel; courts and local authorities were powerless to check the outrages. Fouché drew up the proscription-lists against those who were privy, or suspected of being privy, to the Hundred Days, but prudently forgot to put himself at the head of the list; and while the executions of General La Bédoyère and Marshal Ney, accompanied by the horrors in Lyons and Grenoble, were bound to make the position of the king impossible, and while the foremost men of France were driven out of the country, he was conspiring with the Duke of Orleans, being also anxious to overthrow Talleyrand.

Fouché was attacked, nevertheless, on all sides, was compelled to resign the Ministry of Police in September, 1815, and was expelled, in 1816, as a relapsed regicide. His dismissal was followed closely by that of his rival, Talleyrand, who was appointed High Chamberlain, and replaced, to the satisfaction, and indeed at the wish, of Russia, by the former governor-general in Odessa, the Duke of Richelieu, an emigré quite unacquainted with French affairs. Louis, **Favourites of the French King** who could not exist without favourites, had given his heart to the former secretary of Madame Mère, Décazes. As Fouché's successor, he sided with the Pavillon Marsan, passed sundry capricious and arbitrary measures to maintain order, but was still far too mild for the ultra-Royalists, who exercised a sort of secondary government, and procured Talleyrand's help against him.

The violence of this extreme section had found its warrant in the first election to the Chamber of Deputies in which it had effected an electioneering victory. But when the Pavillon Marsan and the deputies wished to cap the repressive measures of Décazes by making a farce of the very necessary amnesty for their political opponents,

The King Dissolves the Chambers Louis found it necessary to dissolve the Chambers, and the Royalist successes were not repeated at the new election. The majority were supporters of the moderate Richelieu, while Décazes was, comparatively speaking, a progressive.

The new Chambers passed the Electoral Law of 1817, which secured power to the middle-class, in whom the ultra-Royalists saw their strongest opponents, and the principle adopted, that one-fifth of the deputies should retire annually, in fact assured an annual increase in what may be called the existing Liberal majority. The Royalists then turned their efforts to procuring a very much lower franchise, in the belief that the peasantry would be much more amenable to the influence of clericals and landowners than the now dominant classes.

Richelieu soon found himself alarmed by what appeared to be the revival of the revolutionary spirit, emphasised at the elections of 1818 by the appearance among the new deputies of Lafayette and Benjamin Constant. His position seemed strengthened by the success of France at the Conference of Aix-la-Chapelle, where he represented her in person and procured the immediate withdrawal of the allied garrisons. Nevertheless, his representations that the electoral law must be modified to check the democratic movement failed to convince the king, and Richelieu retired in December, 1818.

The Ministry of Dessoles, which now took the lead, was dominated by Richelieu's rival, Décazes, who became Minister of the Interior. An arrangement was

Extended Liberties in France effected with the Curia on August 23rd, 1819. Freedom of the Press was encouraged, and the extraordinary laws against the liberty of the subject were repealed. The Ministry, however, at one time inclined to the Constitutionalists, at another to the ultra-Royalists, and thus forfeited the confidence of all, and depended on the personal and vacillating policy of the king, while the intensity of party feeling was increased. Even a great

batch of new peers in March, 1819, did not give the Crown the hoped-for parliamentary support. An alteration of the electoral law seemed imperative; it was essential to show fight against the Left.

On November 20th, 1819, the country learnt that Dessoles was dismissed and Décazes had become first Minister. The vacillating policy of Décazes quickly estranged all parties, and they only waited for an opportunity to get rid of him. On February 13th, 1820, the king's nephew, Charles Ferdinand, Duke of Berry, the only direct descendant of Louis XV. from whom children could be expected, was stabbed at the opera, and the ultras dared to utter the lie that Décazes was the accomplice of Louvel the murderer. The royal family implored the king to dismiss his favourite, and Louis dismissed Décazes on February 21st, 1820.

Richelieu became first Minister once more. Décazes went to London as ambassador, and received the title of duke. This compulsory change of ministers seemed to the king like his own abdication. Exceptional legislation against personal freedom was indeed

Renewed Bloodshed in Paris necessary, but it increased the bitterness of the Radicals, who were already furious at the menace of the Electoral Law of 1817. Matters came to bloodshed in Paris in June, 1820; the Right, however, carried the introduction of a new electoral law. The abandonment of France to the noisy emancipationists standing on the extreme Left was happily diverted. Richelieu administered the country in a strictly monarchical spirit, but never became the man of the ultra-Royalists of the Pavillon Marsan.

The disturbed condition of the Iberian Peninsula gave the leaders of the reaction a new justification for their policy and a new opportunity of applying it. Ferdinand VII., the king so intensely desired by the Spaniards, had soon shown himself a mean despot, whose whole government was marked by depravity and faithlessness, by falsehood and distrust. He abolished in May, 1814, the constitution of 1812, which was steeped in the spirit of the French Constituent Assembly, dismissed the Cortes, and with a despicable party or camarilla of favourites and courtiers persecuted all liberals and all adherents of Joseph Bonaparte. He restored all the monasteries, brought back the Inquisition and the Jesuits, and scared Spain once more into the deep darkness of the Middle Ages; he destroyed all benefits of government and the administration of justice, filled the prisons with innocent men, and revelled with guilty associates. Trade and commerce were at a standstill, and in spite of all the pressure of taxation the treasury remained empty. The Ministries and high officials continually changed according to the caprice of the sovereign, and there was no pretence at pursuing a

the influence of the Powers, particularly of Russia, Ferdinand was rudely awakened from the indolence into which he had fallen. Better days seemed to be dawning for Spain; but the reforming mood soon passed away.

Regiments intended to be employed against the rising in South America had been assembled at Cadiz, but at this centre a conspiracy against the Government in Madrid broke out. On New Year's Day, 1820, the colonel of the regi-

LOUIS XVIII. OF FRANCE DRAWING UP THE "CHARTA" AT ST. OUEN IN 1814

systematic policy. Such evils led to the rebellions of discontented and ambitious generals, such as Xavério Mina, who paid the penalty of failure on the scaffold or at the gallows. Even the loyalty of the South American colonies wavered; they were evidently contemplating defection from the mother country, in spite of all counter measures; and the rising world power of the United States of North America was greatly strengthened. By

ment of Asturia, Riego, proclaimed in Las Cabezas de San Juan on the Isla de Leon the constitution of 1812, arrested at Arcos the commander-in-chief of the expeditionary force together with his staff, drove out the magistrates, and joined Colonel Antonio Quiroga, who now was at the head of the undertaking. The attempt to capture Cadiz failed; Riego's march through Andalusia turned out disastrously, and he was forced on March

11th to disband his followers at Bienvenida. Quiroga also achieved nothing. But the cry for the constitution of 1812 found a responsive echo in Madrid. Galicia, Asturia, Cantabria, and Aragon revolted. The royal government completely lost heart, since it had too evil a conscience. The king, always a coward,

Reaction Triumphant in Spain capitulated with undignified alacrity, declared himself ready to gratify "the universal wish of the people," and on March 9th took a provisional oath of adherence to the constitution of 1812.

The whole kingdom was at the mercy of the unruly and triumphant Left. It was headed by Quiroga and Riego, and the Government was obliged to confer upon both these mutineers the rank of field-marshal. Quiroga was the more moderate of the two, and as Vice-president of the Cortes, which met on July 9th, endeavoured to organise a middle party. Riego preferred the favour of the mob ; at Madrid he received a wild ovation, August 30th to September 6th, and a hymn composed in his honour and called by his name was in everybody's mouth. Although his arrogance produced a temporary reaction, the party which he led was in the end triumphant. As captain-general of Galicia and Aragon, Riego became master of the situation, and the Court was exposed to fresh humiliations.

The spirit of discontent had also seized Portugal, where the reorganiser of the army, Field-Marshal Lord Beresford, conducted the government for King John VI., who was absent in Brazil. A national conspiracy against the British was quickly suppressed in 1817 ; but the feeling of indignation smouldered, and when Beresford himself went to Rio Janeiro for commands, secret societies employed his absence to stir up fresh sedition. The rebellion broke out on August 24th, 1820, under Colonel Sepulveda and Count

Portugal's Spirit of Discontent Silveira in Oporto, and Lisbon followed suit on September 15th. The juntas instituted in both places amalgamated into one provisional government on October 1st, and when Beresford returned on October 10th, he was not allowed to land. The Cortes of 1821 drew up, on March 9th, the preliminary sketch of a constitution which limited the power of the Crown, as it had already been limited in Spain. All the authorities swore to it ; Count Pedro

Palmella, the foremost statesman of the kingdom, advised John VI. to do the same. John appeared in Lisbon, left his eldest son Dom Pedro behind as regent in Brazil, and swore to the principles of the constitution on July 3rd, 1821.

In Italy, meanwhile, there was a strong movement on foot in favour of republicanism and union. But few placed their hopes on Piedmont itself, for King Victor Emmanuel I. was a bigoted, narrow-minded ruler, who sanctioned the most foolish retrogressive policy, and, like William I. at Cassel, declared everything that had occurred since 1789 to be simply null and void. There was no prospect of freedom and a constitution while he continued to reign. His prospective successor, Charles Felix, was as little of a Liberal as himself. The nobility and the clergy alone felt themselves happy. The hopes of better days could only be associated with the head of the indirect line of Carignan, Charles Albert, who in Piedmont and Sardinia played the rôle of the Duke of Orleans in France, and represented the future of Italy for many patriots even beyond the frontiers of Piedmont. In

Peaceful Rule of Duke Ferdinand Modena, Duke Francis IV. of the Austrian house did away with the institutions of the revolutionary period and brought back the old regime. The Society of Jesus stood at the helm. Modena, on account of the universal discontent, became a hotbed of secret societies.

In the papal states the position was the same as in Modena ; it was hardly better in Lucca, or in Parma, where Napoleon's wife, the Empress Marie Louise, held sway. In Tuscany, the Grand Duke Ferdinand III. reigned without any spirit of revenge ; he was an enemy of the reaction, although often disadvantageously influenced from Vienna. The peace and security which his rule assured to Tuscany promoted the growth of intellectual and material culture. His was the best administered state in the whole of Italy ; and when he died, in 1824, his place was taken by his son Leopold II., who continued to govern on the same lines and with the same happy results.

Pius VII. and his great Secretary of State, Cardinal Consalvi, had indeed the best intentions when the States of the Church were revived ; but the upas-tree of the hierarchy blighted all prosperity. Not a vestige remained of the modern civilised lay state, especially after Consalvi was removed and Leo XII., 1823–1829, assumed the reins of government. Secret societies and conspiracies budded, and brigandage took a fresh lease of life. The secret society of the Carbonari, having become too large for Neapolitan soil—1808 —maintained relations with the Freemasons, who had influence in the Italian disputes, and with Queen Mary Caroline of Naples. Later, the Government vainly tried to suppress the Carbonari, who, though degraded by the admission of the most notorious criminals had gained a hold on every stratum of society.

THE DUKE OF RICHELIEU AND DÉCAZES

The Duke of Richelieu, an emigré and formerly governor-general at Odessa, was appointed to succeed Talleyrand as High Chamberlain though he was quite unacquainted with French affairs, while Décazes, who supported the Bourbon restoration, became a great favourite of the king. He was dismissed in 1820, and went to London as ambassador.

The misgovernment of Naples and Sicily gave a plausible excuse for revolutionary agitation. King Ferdinand IV., a phlegmatic old man, full of cunning and treachery, licentiousness and cruelty, had not fulfilled one of the promises which he had given on his return to the throne, but had, on the contrary, secretly promised the Court of Vienna that he would not grant his country a constitution until Austria set him the example. On December 11th, 1816, he united his states into the "Kingdom of the Two Sicilies," and assumed the title of Ferdinand I.; and, although he left in existence many useful reforms which had been introduced during the French period, he bitterly disappointed his Sicilian subjects by abolishing the constitution which Lord Bentinck had given them in 1812. The police and the judicial system were deplorably bad; the Minister of Police was the worst robber of all, and the head of the Calderari, a rival reactionary society. The army was neglected. Secret societies and bands of robbers vied with each other in harassing the country, and the Government

A LEADER OF REVOLT

Riego was at the head of the Madrid rising of 1820; his march through Andalusia turned out disastrously, and he disbanded his followers. He was hanged at Madrid in 1823.

was powerless against them. The newly revived citizen militia was immediately infected by the Carbonari, which tempted it with the charm of a "constitution."

Guglielmo Pepe, an ambitious general, but fickle character, became the soul of the Carbonari in the Sicilian army, and gave them a considerable degree of military efficiency. He contemplated in 1819 the arrest of the king, the Emperor and Empress of Austria, and Metternich, at a review. The plan was not executed, but the spell of the Spanish insurrection and the new constitution ensnared him and his partisans. On July 2nd, 1820, two sub-lieutenants raised the standard of revolt at Nola, and talked foolishly about the Spanish constitution, which was totally unknown to them. On the 3rd this was proclaimed in Avellino. Pepe assumed the lead of the movement, which spread far and wide, and marched upon Naples. The Ministry changed. Ferdinand placed the government temporarily in the hands of his son Francis, who was detested as the head of the Calderari, and the latter accepted the Spanish constitution on July 7th, a policy which Ferdinand confirmed. On the 9th, Pepe entered Naples in triumph, with soldiers and militia; and Ferdinand, with tears in his eyes, took the oath to the constitution on the 13th, in the palace chapel. The Bourbons began to wear the colours of the Carbonari. Pepe, as commander-in-chief and captain-general of the kingdom, was now supreme; but Ferdinand hastened to assure the indignant Metternich that all his oaths and promises had been taken under compulsion and were not seriously meant.

Sicily no longer wished to be treated as a dependency of Naples, and claimed to receive back the constitution of 1812. Messina revolted, and Palermo followed the example on July 14th ; on the 18th there was fighting in the streets of Palermo. The governor, Naselli, fled, and the mob ruled; immediately afterwards a provisional government was installed. The

Flight of the Governor Naselli independent action of Sicily aroused great discontent in Naples. General Florestan Pepe was despatched to Sicily with an army, and he soon made himself master of the island. But the Crown repudiated the treaty concluded by him with the rebels on October 5th, and sacrificed Pepe to the clamour of the Neapolitan Parliament ; the gulf between the two parts of the kingdom became wider. Met-ternich had been unmoved by the tidings of the Spanish agitation, but he was only the more enraged when he heard what had occurred in the Two Sicilies. He put all blame on the secret societies, and praised the good in-tentions of Ferdinand's " paternal " government.

The insurrection in Spain had made such an impression on Alexander that in a cir-cular of May 2nd, 1820, he invoked the spirit of the Holy Alliance, and emphasised the danger of illegal constitu-tions. Metternich strength-ened the Austrian forces in Upper Italy, and stated, in a circular to the Italian courts, that Austria, by the treaties of 1815, was the appointed guar-dian of the peace of Italy, and wished for an immediate armed interference in the affairs of Naples ; but he encountered strong opposition in Paris and in St. Petersburg. Alexander, whom Metternich actually suspected of Carbonarism, advised a conference of sovereigns and Ministers ; the conference met on October 20th, 1820, at Troppau. Alexander brought with him Capodistrias, an enemy of Metternich ; Francis I. brought Metternich and Gentz ; Frederic William III. was accompanied by Hardenberg and Count Günther von Bern-storff ; the Count de la Ferronays appeared on behalf of Louis XVIII. ; and Lord Stewart represented the faint-hearted policy of his brother Castlereagh, which

JOHN VI. OF PORTUGAL
After acting as regent for his mother, he succeeded to the throne; a rebellion broke out in 1820, and the king agreed to a constitution limiting the power of the Crown.

was condemned by the British nation. It was Metternich's primary object that the congress should approve the march of an Austrian army into Naples, and he induced the congress to invite Ferdinand to Troppau. Alexander always clung closer to the wisdom of Metternich, and the latter skilfully used the report of a mutiny among the Semenoff guards as an argument to overcome the Liberalism of the tsar. Alexander saw before his own eyes how the Spanish and Italian military revolts excited imitation in the Russian army. Frederic William was equally conciliatory to Metternich, and was more averse than ever to granting a constitution on the model of Hardenberg's schemes. In the protocol of November 19th, Austria, Prussia, and Russia came to an agreement, behind the back of the two Western Powers, as to the position which they would adopt towards revolutions, and as to the maintenance of social order ; but France and Great Britain rejected the idea of changing the principles of international law. Fer-dinand took fresh oaths to his people and set out for Troppau. After Christmas the con-gress closed at Troppau, but was continued in January, 1821, at Laibach. Most of the Italian governments were represented. Metternich again took over the presidency. Ferdinand was at once ready to break his word, and declared that his concessions were extorted from him. The King of France at first hesitated. A miracle seemed to have been performed on behalf of the French Bour-bons : the widow of Berry gave birth, on September 29th, 1820, to a son, the Duke Henry of Bordeaux, who usually appeared later under the name of Count of Cham-

The "Miracle" of the French Bourbons bord. The legitimists shouted for joy, talked of the miracu-lous child who would console his mother for the death of Hector, " the stem of Jesse when nearly withered had put forth a fresh branch." The child was baptised with water which Chat-eaubriand had drawn from the Jordan. The Spanish Bourbons looked askance at the birth ; they were already speculating on the future succession to the throne, and the Duke of Orleans secretly suggested in the English

Press suspicions of the legitimacy of the child. Louis successively repressed several military revolts, but had constantly to struggle with the claims of the ultras, who embittered his reign. Although in his heart opposed to it, he nevertheless assented at Laibach to the programme of the Eastern Powers.

Austria sent an army under Frimont over the Po, and upheld the fundamental idea of a constitution for the Two Sicilies. Ferdinand agreed to everything which Metternich arranged. France did not, indeed, at first consent to that armed interference with Spain which Alexander and Metternich required. On February 26th, 1821, the deliberations of the congress terminated. The Neapolitan Parliament, it is true, defied the threats of the Eastern Powers, and declared that Ferdinand was their prisoner, and that therefore his resolutions were not voluntary. But their preparations for resistance were so defective that the Austrians had an easy task. The Neapolitan army broke up after the defeat of Guglielmo Pepe at Rieti on March 7th, 1821, and on March 24th Frimont's army marched into Naples with sprigs of olive in their helmets. Pepe fled to Spain. In Naples the reaction perpetrated such excesses that the Powers intervened ; the victims were countless, while the Austrians maintained order.

In Piedmont the revolution broke out on March 10th, 1821 ; Charles Albert of Carignan did not keep aloof from it. The tricolour flag, red, white, and green, of the Kingdom of Italy was hoisted in Alessandria, and a provisional junta on the Spanish model was assembled. Turin proclaimed the parliamentary constitution on March 11th, and the Carbonari seized the power. Victor Emmanuel I. abdicated on March 13th in favour of his brother Charles Felix. Charles Albert, a vacillating and untrustworthy ruler, who was regent until the latter's

VICTOR EMMANUEL I
King of Sardinia from 1814, he was a bigoted, narrow-minded ruler. His retrogressive policy led to a rising in 1821, and he abdicated in favour of his brother Charles Felix.

GUGLIELMO PEPE
An ambitious general, but fickle character, he became the soul of the Carbonari in the Sicilian army, and in 1820 he assumed supreme power as commander-in-chief.

arrival, accepted, contrary to his inward conviction, the new constitution, and swore to it on March 15th. Charles Felix, however, considered every administrative measure null and void which had not emanated from himself. Charles Albert was panic-stricken, resigned the regency, and left the country. Alexander and Metternich agreed that there was need of armed intervention in Piedmont. Austria feared also the corruption of her Italian provinces, and kept a careful watch upon those friends of freedom who had not yet been arrested.

At Novara, on April 8th, the Imperialists under Marshal Bubna, won a victory over the Piedmontese insurgents, which was no less decisive than that of Rieti had been in Naples. Piedmont was occupied by the imperial army ; the junta resigned, and Victor Emmanuel renewed his abdication on April 19th, at Nice. Charles Felix then first assumed the royal title and decreed a criminal inquiry. On October 18th he made his entry into Turin amid the mad rejoicings of the infatuated mob, suppressed every sort of political party, and ruled in death-like quiet, being supported by the bayonets of Austria and by the dominion of the Jesuits in Church, school, and State. The Austrians did not leave his country until 1823. On May 12th, 1821, a proclamation issued from Laibach by the Eastern Powers announced to the world that they had rescued Europe from the intended general revolution, and that their weapons alone served to uphold the cause of right and justice.

Metternich, promoted by the emperor to the office of Chancellor of State, stood at the zenith of his success when, on May 5th, 1821, Napoleon I., the man who had contested his importance and had ruled the world far more than Metternich, died at St. Helena. The black and yellow flag waved from Milan to Palermo ; princes and peoples bowed before it. Legitimacy had curbed the revolutionary craving, and Italy was further from unification than ever. The apostles of freedom and unity, men like Silvio Pellico, disappeared in the dungeons of the Spielberg and other fortresses in Austria. Russia was now on the most friendly terms with Austria. The result was soon seen when the monarchs and Ministers, still

An Era of Conspiracy and Anarchy at Laibach, received tidings of disorders in the Danubian principalities and in Greece, and the tsar, under Metternich's influence, repudiated the Greek leader, Ypsilanti, who had built on the theory that he could reckon on the warm support of Russia.

In Spain the Liberals made shameless misuse of their victory, and limited the power of the king to such a degree that he naturally tried to effect a change. His past was a guarantee that Ferdinand VII. would not be at a loss for the means to his end. He courted the intervention of the Continent; but Louis XVIII. and Richelieu preferred neutrality. The ultra-Royalists, however, became more and more arrogant in France. The Pavillon Marsan expelled Richelieu in December, 1821, and brought in the Ministry of Villèle; the reaction felt itself fully victorious, and the clergy raised their demands. The Carbonari was introduced from Italy, and secret societies were formed. New conspiracies of republican or Napoleonic tendency followed, and led to executions.

The power of the ultras became gradually stronger in the struggle; party feeling increased, and even Count Villèle was not royalist enough for the ultras. Ferdinand VII., on the contrary, favoured the Radicals, in order to employ them against the Liberals. Riego became President of the Cortes of 1822. A coup de main of the Guards to recover for Ferdinand the absolute power failed in July, 1822, and Ferdinand surrendered those who had sacrificed themselves for him. In the north guerrilla bands spread in every direction

The Tragic End of Castlereagh on his behalf; in Seo de Urgel a regency for him was established on August 15th, and an alliance entered into with France. At the preliminary deliberations for the congress intended to be held at Verona, Metternich reckoned upon his "second self," Castlereagh, now the Marquess of Londonderry; but the latter died by his own hand on August 12th, 1822. His successor in the Foreign Office, George Canning, a "Tory from inward conviction,

a modern statesman from national necessity," broke with the absolutist-reactionary principles of the Holy Alliance, and entered the path of a national independent policy, thus dealing a heavy blow at Metternich and Austria. Metternich and Alexander stood the more closely side by side.

The congress of sovereigns and Ministers at Verona was certainly the most brilliant since that of Vienna. In October, 1822, came Alexander, Francis, and Frederic William; most of the Italian rulers, Metternich, Nesselrode, Pozzo di Borgo, Bernstorff, and Hardenberg; France was represented by Chateaubriand, the Duke of Laval-Montmorency, Count La Ferronays, and the Marquis of Caraman; Great Britain by Wellington and Viscount Strangford. Entertainments were on as magnificent a scale as at Vienna. Metternich wished to annul the Spanish and Portuguese revolution, and with it the extorted constitution; the Eastern Powers and France united for the eventuality of further hostile or revolutionary steps being taken by Spain; Great Britain excluded itself from their agreements, while Chateaubriand's romanticism in-

Congress of the Powers at Verona toxicated the tsar. When the Greeks at the congress sought help against the Turks, they were coldly refused. On the other hand, an understanding was arrived at about the gradual evacuation of Piedmont by the Austrians; the army of occupation in the Two Sicilies was reduced; and good advice of every sort was given to the Italian princes. The Eastern Powers and France saw with indignation that Great Britain intended to recognise the separation of the South American colonies from Spain, and their independence, according to the example given by the United States of North America, in March, 1822. The Congress of Verona ended toward the middle of December.

Chateaubriand, now French Minister of Foreign Affairs, urged a rupture with Spain, at which Louis and Villèle still hesitated. The threatening notes of the Powers at the Verona congress roused a storm of passion in Madrid, while the diplomatists in Verona had set themselves the question whether nations might put kings on their trial, as Dante does in his Divine Comedy, and whether the tragedy of Louis XVI. should be repeated with another background in the case of Ferdinand VII. The Spanish nation revolted against the arrogance of foreign interference. The rupture was made ; the ambassadors of Russia, Austria, Prussia, and France left Spain in January, 1823. The adventurous George Bessières ventured on an expedition to Madrid ; but the Spanish hope of British help against France, which was intended to carry out the armed interference, was not fulfilled.

Louis XVIII. placed his nephew, Duke Louis of Angoulême, at the head of an army of 100,000 men, which was to free Ferdinand from the power of the Liberals and put him once again in possession of despotic power.. In the Chamber at Paris the Liberals, indeed, loudly decried the war, and trembled at the suppression of the Spanish revolution, although Canning openly desired the victory of the Spanish people. Ferdinand and the Cortes went to Seville. Angoulême crossed the frontier stream, the Bidassoa, on April 7th, and found no traces of a popular rising ; nevertheless, he advanced, without any opposition, was hailed as a saviour, and entered Madrid on May 24th. He appointed a temporary regency, and in order not to hurt the national pride, avoided any interference in internal affairs, although the reactionary zeal of the regency caused him much uneasiness, and only retained the supreme military command. But the Cortes in Seville relieved the king of the conduct of affairs and carried him off to Cadiz. Victory followed the French flag. The Spaniards lost heart, and were defeated or capitulated. Angoulême made forced marches to Cadiz, and on the night of August 31st stormed Fort Trocadero, which was considered impregnable. An expedition of Riego to the Isla de Leon ended in his arrest, and on September 28th the Cortes, in consequence of the bombardment of Cadiz, abandoned their resistance. Ferdinand VII. voluntarily promised a complete amnesty and made extensive

CHATEAUBRIAND

This eminent French writer and politician supported the Restoration monarchy from 1814 till 1824. He was created a vicomte, and for two years represented France at the British Court.

DONA MARIA II. DA GLORIA

The crown of Portugal was renounced by Pedro IV., of Brazil, in favour of his daughter, but when Dom Miguel proclaimed himself king in 1828 she returned to her father, and was restored in 1834,

professions. He was accorded a state reception by Angoulême on October 1st, and was proclaimed as absolute monarch by a large party among the Spaniards. But hardly was he free before the perjurer began the wildest reaction. Many members of the Cortes and the regency fled to England to escape the gallows, and Ferdinand exclaimed : "The wretches do well to fly from their fate !" The Powers of Europe viewed his action with horror. Angoulême, whose warnings had been scattered to the winds, left Madrid in disgust on November 4th. Riego was hanged at Madrid on November 7th, 1823 ; on the 13th Ferdinand returned triumphant, only to reign as detestably as before. Talleyrand called the war of intervention the beginning of the end ; the result of it was that Spain floundered further into the mire. The ultras tormented the country and Ferdinand himself to such a degree that he began to weary of them. The colonies in South America were irretrievably lost ; all the subtleties of the congress at Verona and of Chateaubriand could not change that fact. At Canning's proposal the British Government, on January 1st, 1825, recognised the independence of the new republics of Buenos Ayres, Colombia, and Mexico. This was a fresh victory over the principle of legitimacy, which had been always emphasised by Austria, Spain, and France, as well as by Russia and Prussia. The Spanish insurrection naturally affected the neighbouring country of Portugal. The September Constitution of 1820, far from improving matters there, had actually introduced new difficulties. Constitutionalists and absolutists were quarrelling violently with each other. Dom Pedro, son of John VI., who had been appointed regent in Brazil, saw himself compelled by a national party, which wished to make Brazil an independent empire, to send away the Portuguese troops. He assumed in May, 1822, the title of permanent protector of Brazil, and convened a national assembly at Rio de Janeiro, which on August 1st and on September 7th announced the independence of Brazil, and proclaimed him, on October 12th, 1822, Emperor of Brazil, under the title of Dom Pedro I. The Portuguese were furious, but were never able to reconquer Brazil.

Queen Charlotte, wife of John and sister of Ferdinand VII., a proud and artful woman, refused to take the oath to the Portuguese constitution, to which John swore, and, being banished, conspired with her younger son, Dom Miguel, the clergy, and many nobles, to restore the absolute monarchy. A counter revolution in February, 1823, failed, it is true, but Dom Miguel put himself at its head, and Lisbon joined his cause. The weak John sanctioned this, and cursed the constitution ; the Cortes were dissolved. John promised a new constitution, and triumphantly entered Lisbon with his son on June 5th. Portugal was brought back to absolutism. John was a mere cipher ; but Miguel and Charlotte ruled, and did not shrink even from the murder of opponents. Miguel headed a new revolt against his father on April 30th, 1824, in order to depose him. But John made his escape on May 9th to a British man-of-war. The diplomatic body took his side, and at the same time the pressure brought to bear by the British Government compelled Miguel to throw himself at his father's feet and to leave Portugal on May 13th. An amnesty was proclaimed. The return of the old Cortes which had sat before 1822 was promised, and by British mediation the Treaty of Rio was signed on August 29th, 1825, in which the independence and self-government of Brazil were recognised. On April 26th, 1826, Portugal received a Liberal Constitution by the instrumentality of Dom Pedro I. of Brazil, who after his father's death,

DOM MIGUEL

He became regent of Portugal on behalf of his niece Maria, and being ambitious, proclaimed himself king. When Maria recovered the crown, Miguel withdrew to Italy.

on March 10th, 1826, reigned for a short period over his native country as Pedro IV. Then, on May 2nd, Pedro renounced the crown of Portugal in favour of his daughter, Dona Maria II. da Gloria. On June 25th, 1828, Dom Miguel proclaimed himself king, favoured by the British Tory Cabinet of Wellington. His niece, Maria da Gloria, was forced to return to her father in Brazil.

The victory of Trocadero, which was audaciously compared by the French ultras to Marengo and Austerlitz, was of extraordinary advantage to the Government of Louis XVIII. " It was not merely under Napoleon that victories were won ; the restored Bourbons knew this secret " ; and the "hero of Trocadero" was hailed as their "champion" by the king on December 2nd, 1823. The elections to the Chambers of 1824 were favourable to them ; and a law in June of the same year prolonged the existence of the Second Chamber to seven years, which might seem some check on change and innovation. Villèle stood firm at the helm, overthrew Chateaubriand, and guided Baron Damas, his successor at the Foreign Office. But Chateaubriand revenged himself by the most bitter attacks in the Press. Louis thereupon, at the advice of Villèle, revived the censorship on political journals and newspapers, August 16th, 1824. The much-tried man was nearing his end. He warned his brother to uphold the Charta loyally, the best inheritance which he bequeathed ; if he did so, he too would die in the palace of his ancestors.

Louis XVIII. died on September 16th, 1824. France hailed Monsieur as Charles X., with the old cry, " Le roi est mort, vive le roi." But Talleyrand had forebodings that the kingdom of Charles would soon decay ; and, with his usual coarseness of sentiment, he said over the corpse of Louis: "I smell corruption here ! "

ARTHUR KLEINSCHMIDT

THE CROSS AND THE CRESCENT
REVOLT AND OPPRESSION IN RUSSIA AND THE LIBERATION OF GREECE

WE have seen that the Tsar Alexander I., when he ascended the throne of Russia, was full of liberal ideas. If he wavered between antagonism to Napoleon and alliance with him, it was, in part at least, because Napoleon's own career bore a double aspect ; if he was an aggressive conqueror who sought to impose his own will on Europe regardless of international law, he was also the incarnation of anti-feudalism. It was not until after the Congress of Vienna and the Peace of Paris that the change came over the tsar which made him a force in Europe hardly less reactionary than Metternich himself.

But it is with his domestic policy, his policy within the borders of his own empire, that we are here concerned ; his foreign policy has already appropriated a conspicuous share of earlier chapters.

The Tsar's Desire for Reforms On his accession, then, he reigned in a liberal spirit, and surrounded himself with men of the same views ; among them his Secretary of State, Michael Speranskij, was conspicuous. Magnanimous plans were proposed, and the emperor himself spoke of the burden of an absolute monarchy. There was a wish to introduce reforms on the English model, or, as Speranskij suggested, an imitation of the French Constitution. People talked, as Catharine had once done, of "the rights of the subjects, and the duty of the Government," and of the abolition of serfdom ; and a sum of a million roubles yearly was laid aside in order to buy estates with serfs for the Crown.

The German nobility of Esthonia, Courland, and Livonia took the first step by the emancipation of the Lettic and Esthonian serfs. The coercive measures were repealed, the frontier opened, the "Secret Chancery" as well as corporal punishment for nobles, citizens, priests, and church officials abolished. Schools and universities were founded, and the empire was divided into six educational districts. In place of the old boards dating from the days of Peter, real Ministries and a Council of State were created for the first time. Alexander thus reigned "according to the principles and after the heart of Catharine"

Attempt to Restore the Old Order until 1812, when he suddenly changed his views. The enemies of freedom, the Church once more at their head, strained every nerve to overthrow Speranskij, and restore the old order of things. Even the great historian, Nikolaj Karamsin, recommended serfdom and autocracy in his memoir on "Ancient and Modern Russia." Others also recommended the same policy. Speranskij was overthrown from a "wounded feeling of disappointed inclination " ; Count Alexej Araktshejev, an apostle of slavery, as an all-powerful favourite, guided the affairs of government.

Alexander did, indeed, make the attempt, to which he had always been attracted, of giving his reconstructed Poland a constitution ; but Poland was incapable of working a constitution. Another of his experiments was that of establishing military colonies all over the empire. The theory was that the soldiery, planted on the soil, would maintain themselves by agriculture, and would at the same time provide centres **New Form Of Russian Oppression** for recruiting and for military training. The practical effect, however, was merely the application of a new form of oppression to the already sufficiently oppressed peasantry. The latter years of Alexander's life were embittered by a sense of the ingratitude of mankind. Conscious of his own high purposes, he found his own people, instead of recognising their nobility, still murmuring and discontented, infected even by the mutinous spirit of the Latin peoples. He expressed repeatedly a desire to abdicate, and when he died at Taganrog in December, 1825, it was with no reluctance that he escaped from the cares of sovereignty.

He left no children. Constantine, as the elder of his brothers, would have had the next claim to the throne had he not formally renounced it in 1820 and 1822, in order to be able to marry a Polish countess, Johanna Grudzinska. The idea that his brother Nicholas had learnt nothing of this before the memorable December days of the year 1825 is no longer tenable. The homage paid by the younger brother to Constantine, who was staying in Warsaw, was a rash act chiefly due to Count Milorado-vitch, the military Governor-General of St. Petersburg at that time, and it cost trouble enough to cancel it in the days between December 9th and 24th, 1825. There is accordingly no need to suppose a noble contest of magnanimity between the two brothers. But the idea of freedom had already struck root so deeply under Alexander I. that the supporters of a constitution, who had been secretly organised since 1816, especially in the corps of officers, wished to use the opportunity of placing the liberal-minded Constantine on the **Rebellion Crushed by Nicholas I.** throne. The rumour was spread that Constantine's renunciation was only fictitious; that he was being kept a prisoner at Warsaw. The troops shouted: "Long live Constantine!" and when the cry "Long live the Constitution!" mingled with it, the troops thought that it was the name of the wife of Constantine.

Nicholas I. crushed the rebellion on December 26th, 1825, with great firmness. Several "Decabrists" were executed and many exiled. Possibly that was one of the reasons why Nicholas was throughout his whole reign a sworn enemy of popular liberty. A man of iron strength of character and energy, he was, with his immense stature and commanding presence, the personification of absolutism. But he was fully alive to the duties and responsibilities which his great position threw upon him, and he devoted all his powers to the affairs of the country. His first

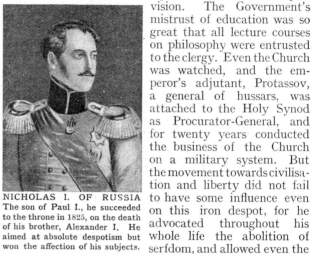

NICHOLAS I. OF RUSSIA
The son of Paul I., he succeeded to the throne in 1825, on the death of his brother, Alexander I. He aimed at absolute despotism but won the affection of his subjects.

attention was given to the publication of the legal code. His government aimed at "stopping the rotation of the earth," as Lamartine aptly puts it. He recognised no peoples or nations, only cabinets and states. The Press was therefore once more gagged, printing-offices were watched and schools were placed under strict supervision. The Government's mistrust of education was so great that all lecture courses on philosophy were entrusted to the clergy. Even the Church was watched, and the emperor's adjutant, Protassov, a general of hussars, was attached to the Holy Synod as Procurator-General, and for twenty years conducted the business of the Church on a military system. But the movement towards civilisation and liberty did not fail to have some influence even on this iron despot, for he advocated throughout his whole life the abolition of serfdom, and allowed even the peasants to acquire property. Such was the autocrat whose iron hand was to rule Russia for thirty years after his accession.

In taking up the thread of the history of the Ottoman Empire, we must note certain events in the Napoleonic period which have hitherto passed unrecorded, as standing outside the general course of our account of Europe. The movement, which has by degrees turned one after another of the provinces into practically if not completely independent states, was initiated in 1804 by a Servian revolt, caused by the violent methods of the Turkish Janissaries, and headed by George Petrovitch, otherwise known as Czerney, or Karageorge. The insurrection broke out locally at Sibnitza, Deligrad, Stalatz, and Nish. Before long, Russian influence **The Turks Defeated by the Serbs** brought to its support the Greek Hospodars, or provincial administrators of Moldavia and Wallachia, Constantine Murusiv and Constantine Ypsilanti. The flame spread, and in 1806 and 1807 the Serbs inflicted defeats on the Turks at Shabatz and Ushitze, under the command of Milos Obrenovitch, captured Belgrade, and established the popular assembly, or Skuptskina. Shortly before this, however, the Sultan Selim had set himself to overthrow the dangerous power of the Janissaries by means of a reorganisation of the army, "Nisan Jedid." A further movement in the same direction in 1807 brought disaster. The Janissaries rose; Selim was deposed and murdered. The outcome of a brief and bloody period of struggle was that the one surviving prince of the royal family, Mahmud, found himself placed on the throne, and, to all intents and purposes, in the hands of the Janissaries, who had proved themselves to be the masters of the situation. Hence the first act of Mahmud was to recognise these prætorians in a solemn Hatti-sherif, issued on November 18th, as the firmest support of the throne. The army and the population greeted the one surviving descendant of the Ottoman house with enthusiasm, and the "Chok yasha Sultan Mahmud!" resounded from thousands of throats in the mosques and on the public squares. The Ottoman dynasty had been saved as by a miracle. The sultan, who was then twenty-three years of age, was confronted by two dangerous opponents, the Serbs and Russians. The latter were supporting the Serbs and also the Montenegrins against the Turks and the French in Dalmatia. However, the war upon the Danube was continued with no great vigour. It was not until the Peace of Frederikshamn, of September 17th, 1809, when Russia acquired Finland from Sweden and secured a guarantee from Napoleon that the Polish kingdom should not be restored, that the Turkish War again took a prominent place in Russian policy. In 1810 Prince Bagration was replaced by Count Kamenskii as supreme commander over 80,000 men. He immediately crossed the Danube, and on June 3rd captured Bazarjik, which was followed by the conquest of Silistria, Sistova, Rustchuk, Giurgevo, and Nicopolis. The fear of Napoleon and of a

Opponents of the New Sultan

THE SULTANS SELIM III. AND MAHMUD II.
Sultan of Turkey, Selim III. made an effort to overthrow the dangerous power of the Janissaries, but the attempt ended in disaster, Selim being deposed and assassinated in 1808. He was succeeded on the throne by Mahmud II., during whose reign Greece established its independence. Mahmud suppressed the Janissary troops.

Polish rising prevented further enterprise. After the death of Kamenskii, Kutusoff, who was sixty-five years of age, utterly defeated the Turks on October 12th, 1811, at Slobodse and Rustchuk. This victory decided the war. The British fleet made a demonstration before the Dardanelles to prevent the sultan agreeing to the Continental embargo of Napoleon.

The Peace of Bucharest, May 12th, 1812, reconfirmed the conventions of Kütchuk-Kainarje and Jassy, ceded Bessarabia to Russia, and gave the Serbs an amnesty, greater independence, and an extension of territory. The brothers Murusi, the sultan's Phanariot negotiators, were executed upon their return home on account of the extravagance of the concessions made by them to the tsar.

The Russians had secured an influence in Servia, which Austria had obstinately disdained. When, however, in May, 1813, the Russians appeared on the Oder and Elbe the Turkish army again advanced into Servia; George Petrovitch fled to Russia by way of Austria. The Ottomans exacted a bitter vengeance upon the country, but on Palm Sunday, April 11th, 1815, Milos Obrenovitch appeared with the ancient banner of the voivodes. The people as a whole flocked to the standard, and the Turks were left in possession only of their fortresses. On November 6th, 1817, Milos was recognised by the bishop, the Kneses and people as voivode; while Karageorge, who had returned to the country to ally himself with the Greek Hetæria, was murdered. Almost contemporary with the Society of the Philomusoi, which was founded in Athens in 1812, arose in Greece the secret confraternity of the "philiki," whose energies after some years brought about the open struggle for freedom. Three young Greeks—Skuphas of Arta, Tzakaloph of Janina, and Anagnostopulos of Andritzena—founded the new Hetæria at

Odessa in 1814, and swore " to arrive at a decision between themselves and the enemies of their country only by means of fire and sword." Oaths of appalling solemnity united this growing band of comrades. It aimed at complete separation from Turkey, and the revival of the old Byzantine Empire. This yearning for liberation proceeded from and was sustained by an intellectual renascence of the nation. From the time of the conquest of Byzantium by the Turks the Greeks had been deprived of all political freedom. But under the ecclesiastical protection of their patriarch in Phanar and in monasteries, at Athos and Janina in Epirus, and in the theological school of the Peloponnese at Dimitzana, the spark of culture and freedom had glowed amongst the ashes, and was kept alive in the language of the Church and the Gospel.

The Lost Freedom of The Greeks

As was the case with the Armenians and the Jews, superior intelligence and dexterity secured the highest positions for the Greeks in the immediate proximity of the Padishah. After the position of first interpreter of the Porte had fallen into their hands, at the end of the seventeenth century, all negotiations concerning foreign policy were carried on through them; they were preferred for ambassadorial posts in foreign courts, and from the eighteenth century the Porte made a practice of choosing from their numbers the hospodars of Moldavia and Wallachia.

The opinion of an English diplomatist upon these " Phanariots," shortly before the outbreak of the Greek Revolution, is well known : " Under the oppression exercised by Turkish despotism with a daily increasing force, the Greek character acquired a readiness for subterfuge and a perversity of judgment on questions of morality, which a continuance of servitude gradually developed to an habitual double dealing and treachery, which strikes the foreigner from the first moment." However, the Greeks looked anxiously to Russian champions and liberators, notwithstanding all the apparent privileges received from the Porte, from the time of the Peace of Posharevatz, when the whole of Morea fell into the possession of the Turks. In the devastation which Russia's attempt to liberate the Morea had brought down upon Greece in 1770, when Hellas and Peloponnese suffered inhuman devas-

Greece Devastated By Enemies

tation from the Albanians whom the Turks called in, Athens and the islands had been spared ; in 1779 the Turks found themselves obliged to send Hasan Pasha to destroy the unbridled Albanians at Tripolitsa. In the Peace of Kütchuk-Kainarje in 1774, Russia had again been obliged to abandon the Greeks to the Ottomans, though the Turkish yoke became lighter as the power of the Porte grew feebler.

The Hellenes enriched themselves by means of commerce ; the sails of the merchantmen sent out by the islands covered the Mediterranean. During the French Revolution almost the entire Levant trade of the Venetians and the French fell into their hands. The number of Greek sailors was estimated at ten thousand. In their struggles with the pirates their ships had always sailed prepared for war, and they had produced a race of warriors stout-hearted and capable, like the Armatoles, who served in the armies of Europe. In the mountain ranges of Mania, of Albania, and Thessaly still survived the independent spirit of the wandering shepherds, or " klephts," who had never bowed to the Ottoman sword. The children of the rich merchants who traded with the coasts of Europe studied in Western schools, and readily absorbed the free ideals of the American Union and the French Revolution. In the year 1796, Constantine Rhigas of Pheræ sketched in Vienna a plan for the rising of his nation, and secured an enthusiastic support for his aims, which he sang in fiery ballads.

The Fate Of a Greek Patriot

When he was planning to enter into relations with Bonaparte, whom he regarded as the hero of freedom, he was arrested in Trieste in 1798, and handed over by the Austrian police, with five of his companions, to the Pasha of Belgrade, who executed him. He died the death of a hero, with the words: " I have sown the seed, and my nation will reap the sweet fruit." Adamantios Koraïs, 1748–1833, of Smyrna was working in Paris, together with his associates, before the fall of Napoleon, to bring about the intellectual renascence of the Greeks, the " Palingenesia." The only thing wanting to these associations was a leader, as was also the case with the Serbs.

This leader was eventually provided by Russia. Alexander Ypsilanti, born of a noble Phanariot family, was a grandson of the hospodar of Wallachia of the same name who had been murdered by the Turks in 1805 at the age of eighty; he was a son of that Constantine Ypsilanti who, having supported the Servian insurrection, had been deposed from the post of hospodar of Wallachia, and had fled into exile. As the tsar's adjutant during the Vienna Congress, he had inspired that monarch with enthusiasm for the Hetæria.

Relying upon the silent consent of his master, he went to Kishineff, in Bessarabia, in September, 1820, with the object of communicating with the leaders of the federation in the Danubian principalities, in Constantinople, and upon the mainland. Availing himself of the difficulties caused to the Porte by the revolt of Ali Pasha of Janina, Alexander Ypsilanti, accompanied by his brother Constantine and Prince Cantakuzenos, crossed the Pruth on March 6th, 1821, entered Jassy, sent a report on the same night to the tsar, who was awaiting the result of the congress at Laibach, and forthwith issued an appeal to the Greek nation. On March 12th he started for Wallachia; not until April 9th did he reach Bucharest with 5,000 men. But from that moment the movement **How the Tsar Regarded The Greeks** proved unfortunate. The tsar, whose hands were tied by the Holy Alliance and the influence of legitimist theories, declared the Greeks to be rebels, and the Russian consul in Jassy openly disapproved of the Phanariot enterprise. It now became manifest how feeble was the popularity of these leaders on the Danube. They were opposed by the Boyars, the peasants fell away from them, the Serbs held back, and treachery reigned in their own camp. To no purpose did the "Sacred Band" display its heroism at Dragashani, in Little Wallachia, on June 19th, 1821, against the superior forces of the Pasha of Silistria and Braila.

On June 26th, Ypsilanti escaped to Austrian territory, where he spent the best years of his life at Munkács and Theresienstadt in sorrowful imprisonment; his health broke down, and he died shortly after his liberation on January 31st, 1828. The last of the ill-fated band of heroes, Georgakis, the son of Nikolaos, blew himself up on September 20th, in the monastery of Sekko, Moldavia. The fantastic ideal of a greater Greece, embracing not only the classic Hellas, but also the Danube states of Byzantine Greece, thus disappeared for ever. The

Morea was already in full revolt against the Turks. On April 4th, 1821, the insurgents took Kalamate, the capital of Messenia, and Patras raised the flag of the Cross. The fire of revolt spread on every side, and destruction raged among the Moslems. The insurrection was led by the national hero, Theodore Kolokotroni, **Islam's Fury Against the Christians** a bold adventurer and able general, though his followers often did not obey their head; and the fleet of the islands did excellent service. The successes of the Greeks aroused boundless fury in Constantinople. Intense religious hatred was kindled in the Divan, and at the feast of Easter, April 22nd, the Patriarch Gregory of Constantinople and three metropolitans were hanged to the doors of their churches. In Constantinople and Asia Minor, in the Morea, and on the islands, Islam wreaked its fury on the Christians.

Enthusiasm for the Greek cause spread throughout the whole of Europe. The noblest minds championed the cause of the warriors, who were inspired by their noble past with the pride of an indestructible nationality, and were defending the Cross against the Crescent. Since the occupation of Athens by the Venetians in 1688, the eyes of educated Europe had turned to the city of Athene. The Venetian engineers, Vermada and Felice, had then drawn up an accurate plan of the Acropolis and of the town, which was published by Francesco Fanelli in his "Atene Attica," 1707.

Du Cange wrote his "History of the Empire of Constantinople under the Frankish Emperors" in 1657, and in 1680 his "Historia Byzantina." Since the days of George, Duke of Buckingham, 1592–1628, and Thomas, Earl of Arundel, 1586–1646, a taste for the collection of examples of Greek art had been increasing in England. Wealthy peers sent their agents to Greece and the East, or journeyed thither themselves, as did **Greek Art In Fashion** Lord Claremont, who commissioned Richard Dalton to make sketches of the Greek monuments and works of art in 1749. James Stewart and Nicholas Revett published sketches of "The Antiquities of Athens" in 1751. In 1776 appeared Richard Chandler's "Travels in Greece." In 1734 the Society of Dilettanti had been founded in London with avowedly Phil-hellenic objects. In 1764 appeared Winckelmann's "History of Ancient Art," and in 1787 Edward Gibbon completed his "Decline and Fall of the Roman Empire." From 1812 onwards Beethoven's opera, "The Ruins of Athens," had aroused tears and sympathy in every feeling heart. Numberless memories and recollections now carried away the sympathies of Europe, which had only just shaken off the yoke of the Corsican con-

Europe Inspired by Greek Songs queror. In 1821 Philhellenic unions were formed upon all sides to support the "heroes of Marathon and Salamis" with money and arms. The banker, Eynard of Geneva, the Würtemberg General Norman, the Frenchman Comte Harcourt, the United States, England, King Lewis I. of Bavaria, an artistic enthusiast, and the painter Heidegger sent money, arms, and ships, or volunteer bands. The populations of Europe were inspired by the Greek songs of Wilhelm Müller and the verses of Lord Byron "The mountains look on Marathon, and Marathon looks on the sea," and later by his heroic death, April 19th, 1824, at Missolonghi. Even Goethe, the prince of poets, with all his indifference to politics, was fascinated by the fervour of the Greek and Servian popular songs, and cast his mighty word into the scale of humanity.

The Russian people had felt ever since the beginning of the Hellenic war of independence the warmest sympathy for their oppressed brethren, and after the horrors of April 22nd the Government could no longer resist the exasperation felt against the Turks ; a storm of indignation swept through the civilised world.

The Russian ambassador, Baron Stroganoff, a Philhellene, spoke vigorously for the Christians, and suspended relations with the Porte in June ; and Capodistrias announced to the world, in his Note of June 28th, an ultimatum to Turkey that the Turks were no longer entitled to remain in Europe. A mood very unpleasing to Metternich had come over the fickle

Metternich And the Fickle Tsar tsar ; the Cabinets of Vienna and St. James saw with astonishment that Stroganoff left Constantinople in August. Metternich once more laid stress on the fact that the triumph of the Greek revolution was a defeat of the Crown, while Capodistrias was for the support of the Greeks and for war against Turkey. The Porte, well aware of the discord of the European Cabinets, showed little willingness to give way and agree to their demands.

Kolokotroni had invested the Arcadian fortress of Tripolitza since the end of April, 1821. All Turkish attempts to relieve the garrison proved futile, while the militia had been drilled into efficient soldiers, and on October 5th, 1821, Tripolitza fell. The Greeks perpetrated gross barbarities. Demetrius Ypsilanti, Alexander's brother, who also had hitherto served in Russia, had been "Archistrategos" since June of that year ; but he possessed little reputation and could not prevent outrages. The continued quarrels and jealousy between the leaders of the soldiers and of the civilians crippled the power of the insurgents. Alexander Mavrogordato, a man of far-reaching imagination, undertook, together with Theodore Negri, the task of giving Hellas a fixed political system. In November, 1821, Western and Eastern Hellas, and in December the Morea, received constitutions.

The National Assembly summoned by Demetrius Ypsilanti to Argos was transferred to Piadha, near the old Epidauros, and proclaimed on January 13th, 1822, the independence of the Hellenic

Corinth the Seat of Government nation and a provisional constitution, which prepared the ground for a monarchy. While it broke with the Hetæria, it appointed Mavrogordato as Proedros (president) of the executive council to be at the head of affairs, and in an edict of January 27th it justified the Greek insurrection in the eyes of Europe. Corinth became the seat of government. But the old discord, selfishness, and pride of the several leaders precluded any prospect of a favourable issue to the insurrection. Kurshid Pasha, after the fall of Ali Pasha of Janina, which freed the Turkish army of occupation in Albania, subjugated the Suliotes.

As a result of the objectless instigation of Chios to revolt, a fleet landed in April under Kara Ali, and the island was barbarously chastised. Indignation at the Turkish misrule once more filled the European nations, and they hailed with joy the annihilation of Kara Ali's fleet by Andreas Miaouli and Constantine Kanari on June 19th. In July a large Turkish army under Mahmud Dramali overran Greece from Phocis to Attica and Argos. The Greek Government fled from Corinth. In spite of all the courage of Mavrogordato and General Count Normann-Ehrenfels, famous for the attack on Kitzen, Suli was lost, owing to the defeat at Peta on July 16–17, and Western Hellas was again threatened. The bold Markos Botzaris fell on August 21st, 1823, with his Suliotes, in the course of a sortie against the besiegers of Missolonghi.

In his necessity the sultan now summoned to his aid his most formidable vassal, Mehemet Ali of Egypt. He first sent his son Ibrahim to Candia for the suppression of the revolt, in command of his troops, who had been trained by French officers. This leader then appeared in the Morea, February 22nd, 1825, where the bayonet and his cavalry gave him a great superiority over the Greeks, who, though brave, were badly disciplined and armed. None the less the Greeks vigorously protested against the protocol of peace, which was issued by the Powers, of August 24th, 1824, recommending them to submit to the Porte and promising the sultan's pardon, after almost the whole population of the Island of Psara had been slaughtered on July 4th. Three parties were formed amongst the Greeks themselves, one under Mavrogordato leaning upon England, that of Capodistrias leaning upon Russia, and that of Kolettis leaning upon France. British influence prevailed. On December 21st, 1825, the Tsar Alexander died at Taganrog, and the youthful Nicholas I. ascended the throne. He quickly suppressed a military revolution in St. Petersburg, and showed his determination to break down the influence of Metternich. Canning, whose whole sympathies were with the Greeks, now sent the Duke of Wellington to St. Petersburg, and on April 4th, 1826, Great Britain and Russia **The Heroic Death of Lord Byron** signed a protocol, constituting Greece, like Servia, a tributary vassal state of the Porte, with a certain measure of independence. Charles X. of France agreed to these proposals, as his admiration had been aroused by the heroic defence of Missolonghi, where Byron had fallen. Austria alone secretly instigated the sultan to suppress the Greek revolt. Even the

BYRON AS A GREEK SOLDIER
The brave fight for independence made by Greece against the Turks stirred the enthusiasm of Europe. That he might assist the Greeks, the poet Byron arrived at Missolonghi on January 4th, 1824, and died on April 19th.

help given to the Greeks at that time by Lord Cochrane and General Church, by Colonels Fabvier, Vautier, and Heydeck, did not stop the Turkish advance. On June 5th, 1827, the Acropolis again capitulated, and with it the whole of Greece was once again lost to the Hellenes. **The Sultan in a New Guise** However, a bold attack delivered at a most unexpected point shook the throne of the sultan. On May 28th, 1826, Mahmud II. issued a Hatti-sherif concerning the reform of the Janissaries. Upon the resistance of these latter they were met on the Etmeidan by the well-equipped imperial army, supported on this occasion by the Ulemas and the people, and were mown down with grapeshot. The sultan forthwith began the formation of a new corps upon European models. It was an event of the most far-reaching importance for the empire when Mahmud first appeared at the head of the faithful in an overcoat, European trousers, boots, and a red fez instead of a turban. His triumph, however, was premature, his army was momentarily weakened, and the reforms were not carried out. The invader was already knocking once again at the door of the empire. On October 6th, 1826, his plenipotentiaries signed an agreement at Akkerman, agreeing on all points to the Russian demands for Servia and the Danubian principalities, but refusing that for Greek freedom. In vain did the sultan send an ultimatum to the Powers on June 10th, 1827, representing that the right of settling the Greek problem was his alone. On April 11th, 1827, Capodistrias became President of the free state of Corfu, under Russian influence, and Russia, Britain, and France determined to concentrate their fleets in Greek waters on July 6th, a month before the death of Canning, which filled Greece with lamentation. The result of the movements was the battle of Navarino, October 20th, one of the most murderous naval actions in the whole of history; in

THE BAY OF NAVARINO AT THE TIME OF THE GREEK FIGHT FOR FREEDOM

four hours nearly 120 Turkish warships and transports were destroyed. This "untoward event," as Wellington called it—to the wrath of all Canningites—implied a further triumph for Russian policy, which had already acquired Grusia, Imeretia—Colchis, 1811, and Gulistan, 1813, in Asia, and had secured its rear in Upper Armenia by the acquisition of Etchmiadzin, the centre of the Armenian Church, in the Peace of Turkmanchai, 1828. Capodistrias, elected to the presidency of Greece, entered on that office in January. However, the sultan proved more obstinate than ever. In a solemn Hatti-sherif he proclaimed in all the mosques his firm intention to secure his independence by war with Russia, "which for the last fifty or sixty years had been the chief enemy of the Porte." He was without competent officers, and his chief need was an army, which he had intended to create had he been granted time. Thus the main power of the Porte, as at the present day, consisted in the unruly hordes of Asia, whose natural impetuosity could not replace the lack of European discipline and tactical skill. "Pluck up all your courage," Mahmud then wrote to his Grand Vizir at the

THE "MURDEROUS" NAVAL BATTLE OF NAVARINO ON OCTOBER 20TH, 1827

THE CAPITULATION OF THE TURKISH STRONGHOLD VARNA ON OCTOBER 10TH, 1828
From the drawing by Zweigle

military headquarters, " for the danger is great." On May 7th the Russians crossed the Pruth in Europe, and on June 4th, the Arpatchai in Asia. Ivan Paskevitch conquered the district of Kars and Achalzich, between the Upper Kur and Araxes, and secured a firm base of operations against Erzeroum. The Russians on the

The Grand Vizir's Army in Flight Danube advanced more slowly. It was not until the fall of Braila, on June 17th, and of Varna, on October 11th, 1828, that they ventured to attack the natural fortress of the Balkans. But the approach of winter suspended the indecisive struggle.

A second campaign was therefore necessary to secure a decision. In Eastern Roumelia the Russians seized the harbour of Sizebolu, February 15th, 1829, in order to provision their army. On February 24th, Diebich took over the supreme command, crossed the Danube in May, and on June 11th defeated and put to flight, by means of his superior artillery, the army of the Grand Vizir Reshid Mehemed, at Kulevcha. Silistria then surrendered, June 26th, and in thirteen days, July 14th–26th, Diebich crossed the Balkans with two army corps; while on July 7th Paskevitch had occupied Erzeroum in Asia. The passage of this mountain barrier, which was regarded as impregnable, produced an overwhelming impression upon the Turks, many of whom regarded the Russian success as a deserved punishment for the sultan's reforms. Diebich "Sabalkanski" advanced to Adrianople. However, Mustafa, Pasha of Bosnia, was already advancing. Fearful diseases devastated the Russian army, which was reduced to 20,000 men. None the less Diebich joined hands with Sizebolu on the Black Sea, and with Enos on the Ægean Sea, although the British fleet appeared in the Dardanelles to protect the capital, from which the Russians were scarce thirty miles distant.

Both sides were sincerely anxious for peace. However, the sultan's courage was naturally shaken by the discovery of an extensive conspiracy among the old orthodox party. The Peace of Adrianople, secured by the mediation of the Prussian

GENERAL DIEBICH

A Russian field-marshal, he fought in many campaigns, and in the Turkish war of 1829 was given the surname of "Sabalkanski," which signifies "Crosser of the Balkans."

general, on September 14th, offered conditions sufficiently severe. Before the war the tsar had issued a manifesto promising to make no conquests. Now, in August, 1828, he demanded possession of the Danube islands, of the Asiatic coast from Kuban to Nikolaja, the fortresses and districts of Atzshur, Achalzich, and Achalkalaki, with new privileges and frontiers for Moldavia, Wallachia, and Servia. The sultan, under pressure of necessity, confirmed the London Convention of July 6th, 1821, in the tenth article of the peace. The president, Capodistrias, received new subsidies, and loans from the Powers; moreover, on July 19th, 1828, the Powers in London determined upon an expedition to the Morea, the conduct of which was entrusted to France. Ibrahim retired, while General Maison occupied the Peninsula, September 7th. The Greek army, composed of Palikars, troops of the line, and Philhellenes, was now armed with European weapons; it won a series of victories at the close of 1828 at Steveniko, Martini, Salona, Lutraki, and Vonizza, and by May, 1829, captured Lepanto, Missolonghi, and Anatoliko. In 1828 the Cretan revolt again broke out, with successful results. On July 23rd, 1829, the National Assembly, tired of internal dissensions, which had repeatedly resulted in civil war, conferred dictatorial powers upon the president. The Peace of Adrianople was concluded on September 14th, 1829; this extended Russia's territory in Asia, opened the Black Sea to Russian trade, and obtained for Greece a recognition of its independence from the Porte.

Independence of Greece Established The Western Powers did not at all wish it to become a sovereign Power under Russian influence, and it was finally agreed, on February 3rd, 1830, that the independent state should be confined to as narrow limits as possible, from the mouth of the Aspropotamos to the mouth of the Spercheias, the Porte assenting on April 24th.

VLADIMIR MILKOWICZ
HEINRICH ZIMMERER

THE
RE-MAKING
OF
EUROPE

EUROPE
AFTER
WATERLOO
VI

FALL OF THE BOURBON MONARCHY
LOUIS PHILIPPE "KING OF THE FRENCH"

THE French were the first nation to put an end to the weak policy of the Restorations. Their privileged position as the "pioneers of civilisation" they used with that light-hearted energy and vigour by which their national character is peculiarly distinguished, while maintaining the dexterity and the distinction which has invariably marked their public action. The cup of the Bourbons was full to overflowing. It was not that their powers of administration were in any material degree inferior to those of other contemporary royal houses ; such a view of the situation would be entirely mistaken.

They were, however, in no direct connection with their people, and were unable to enter into relations with the ruling society of Paris. The restored emigrés, the descendants of the noble families of the period of Louis XV. and XVI., whose members had lost their lives **The Legacy** under the knife of the guillo- **Of the** tine, were unable to appreciate **Revolution** the spirit which animated the France of Napoleon Bonaparte. This spirit, however, had availed itself of the interim which had been granted definitely to establish its position, and had become a social power which could no longer be set aside. Family connections in a large number of cases, and the ties of social intercourse, ever influential in France, had brought the Bonapartists into direct relations with the army, and with the generals and officers of the emperor who had been retired on scanty pensions.

The floating capital, which had grown to an enormous extent, was in its hands, and was indispensable to the Government if it was to free itself from the burden of a foreign occupation. By the decree of April 27th, 1825, the reduced noble families whose goods had been confiscated by the nation were relieved by the grant of £40,000,000. The decree, however, did not imply their restoration to the social position they had formerly occupied ; the emigrant families might be the pensioners of the nation, but could no longer be the leading figures of a society which thought them tiresome and somewhat out of date. Louis XVIII., a well-disposed monarch, and not without ability, died on September **Charles X.** 16th, 1824, and was succeeded **King** by his brother Charles X., who **Of France** had, as Count of Artois, incurred the odium of every European court for his obtrusiveness, his avowed contempt for the people, and for his crotchety and inconsistent character ; he now addressed himself with entire success to the task of destroying what remnants of popularity the Bourbon family had retained. He was, however, tolerably well received upon his accession. The abolition of the censorship of the Press had gained him the enthusiastic praise of Victor Hugo, but his liberal tendencies disappeared after a short period. Jesuitical priests played upon his weak and conceited mind with the object of securing a paramount position in France under his protection.

The French, however, nicknamed him, from the words of Béranger, the bold song writer, "Charles le Simple" when he had himself crowned in Rheims after the old Carolingian custom. His persecution of the liberal Press increased the influence of the journalists. The Chambers showed no hesitation in rejecting the law of censorship introduced by his Minister, Villèle. When he dissolved them, barricades were again raised in Paris and volleys fired upon citizens. Villèle could no longer remain at the helm. Martignac, the soul of the new **A New** Ministry which entered on office **Ministry in** January 5th, 1828, was a **Power** man of honour, and especially adapted to act as mediator. His clear intellect raised him a head and shoulders above the mass of the Royalists. He wished for moderation and progress, but he never possessed Charles's affection, and was no statesman. Charles opposed Martignac's diplomacy with the help of his

4859

confidants, Polignac and others; and while Martignac seemed to the king to be "too little of a Villèle," public opinion accused him of being "too much of a Villèle." His laws as to elections and the Press seemed too liberal to Charles; his interference in the Church and the schools roused the fury of the Jesuits; and the Abbé Lamennais, who had been won back by them, compared the king with Nero and Diocletian. Lamennais attacked the Gallican Church of "atheistic" France, called the constitutional monarchy of Charles the most abominable despotism which had ever burdened humanity, and scathingly assailed the ordinances which

Charles had issued in June, 1828, relating to religious brotherhoods and clerical education. Martignac's government, he said, demoralised society, and the moment was near in which the oppressed people must have recourse to force, in order to rise up in the name of the infallible Pope against the atheistic king. Martignac's Cabinet could claim an important foreign success when the Marquis de Maison, who led an expeditionary corps to the Morea, compelled the Egyptians, under Ibrahim Pasha, to retreat in August, 1828, and thwarted Metternich's plan of a quadruple alliance for the forcible pacification of Russia and Turkey. But when Martignac

CHARLES X., KING OF FRANCE

On the death of Louis XVIII. in 1824, his brother, Charles X., succeeded to the throne. Prior to that, the direction of affairs had been largely in his hands owing to the weakness of the king, and by his obtrusiveness and his avowed contempt for the people he had incurred the odium of every European court. Though he was fairly well received upon his accession, he quickly alienated the sympathies of his people, and he was compelled to abdicate in 1830.

THREE NOTABLE MINISTERS OF FRANCE UNDER CHARLES X.
The rapidly-growing unpopularity of the French king, Charles X., was shared by the Ministry of Villèle, which was defeated at the polls. Martignac, the soul of the new Ministry, which entered office on January 5th, 1828, aimed at moderation and progress and met with opposition from Charles. When Martignac withdrew, in 1829, his place was taken by Polignac, but his position as head of the Bourbon Ministry did not commend itself to the people of France, and the revolt against the rule of Charles soon drove that monarch from the throne, thus ending the Bourbon regime.

wished to decentralise the French administration, and brought in Bills for this purpose in February, 1829, he was deserted by everyone. The extreme Right allied itself with the Left ; Martignac withdrew the proposals in April, and on August 8th, 1829, Polignac took his place.

The name of Jules Polignac seemed to the country a presage of coups d'état and anti-constitutional reaction. The new Ministry included not a single popular representative amongst its members. A cry of indignation was heard, and the Press made the most violent attacks on the new Minister. The Duke of Broglie placed himself at the head of the society formed to defend the charter, called " Aide-toi, le ciel t'aidera"; republicans, eager for the fray, grouped themselves round Louis Blanqui, Etienne Arago, and Armand Barbès.

The newspaper, "National," began its work on behalf of the Orleans family, for whom Talleyrand, Thiers, Jacques Laffite the banker, and Adelaide, the sister of Duke Louis Philippe, cleared the road. Even Metternich, Wellington, and the Emperor Nicholas advised that no coup d'état should be made against the Charta. Charles, however, remained the untaught emigrant of Coblenz, and did not

The Dreamer Of the Restoration understand the new era; he saw in every constitutionalist a supporter of the revolutionary party and a Jacobin. Polignac was the dreamer of the restoration, a fanatic without any worldly wisdom, whom delusions almost removed from the world of reality, who considered himself, with his limited capacity, to be infallible. The Virgin had appeared to him and

commanded him to cut off the head of the hydra of democracy and infidelity.

Polignac, originally only Minister of Foreign Affairs, became on November 17th, 1829, President of the Cabinet Council. In order to gain over the nation, **Algiers in the Hands of the French** which was hostile to him, he tried to achieve foreign successes for it. He laid stress on the principle of the freedom of the ocean as opposed to Great Britain's claims to maritime supremacy, and sketched a fantastic map of the Europe of the future ; if he could not transform this into reality, at all events military laurels should be won at the first opportunity which presented itself.

The Dey of Algiers had been offended by the French, and had aimed a blow at their consul, Deval, during an audience. Since he would not listen to any remonstrances, France made preparations by land and sea. In June, 1830, the Minister of War, Count Bourmont, landed with 37,000 men near Sidi-Ferruch, defeated the Algerians, sacked their camp, and entered the capital on July 6th, where he captured much treasure. He banished the Dey, and was promoted to be marshal of France. Algiers became French, but Charles and Polignac were not destined to enjoy the victory.

The new elections, for which writs were issued after the Chamber of Deputies had demanded the dismissal of Polignac, proved unfavourable to the Ministry and forced the king either to change the Ministry or make some change in the constitution. The Jesuits at that time had not yet adequately organised their political system,

4861

ALGIERS AS IT WAS IN THE YEAR 1830 WHEN TAKEN BY THE FRENCH
From an engraving of the period

and were in France more obscure than in Belgium and Germany. However, they thought themselves sure of their ground, and advised the king to adopt the latter alternative, notwithstanding the objections of certain members of his house, including the dauphine Marie Thérèse.

Meanwhile, the Press and the parties in opposition became more confident; Royer-Collard candidly assured Charles that the Chamber would oppose every one of his Ministries. Charles, however, only listened to Polignac's boastful confidence, and at the opening of the Chambers on March 2nd, 1830, in his speech from the throne he threatened the opposition in such unmistakable terms that doctrinaires as well as ultra-Liberals detected the unsheathing of the royal sword. Pierre Antoine Berryer, the most brilliant orator of legitimacy, and perhaps the greatest French orator of the century, had a lively passage of arms in the debate on the address with François Guizot, the clever leader of the doctrinaires, and was defeated; the Chamber, by 221 votes against 181, accepted on March 16th a peremptory answer to the address, which informed the monarch that his Ministers did not possess the confidence of the nation and that no harmony existed between the Government and the Chamber. Charles, however, saw that the monarchy itself was at stake, declared his resolutions unalterable, and insisted that he would never allow his Crown to be humiliated. He prorogued the Chambers on March 19th until September 1st, and dismissed prefects and officials; whereupon the 221 were fêted throughout France. Charles in some perturbation then demanded from his Ministers a statement of the situation. But Polignac's secret memorandum of April 14th lulled his suspicions again.

It said that only a small fraction of the nation was revolutionary and could not be dangerous; the charter was the gospel, and a peaceful arrangement was easy. Charles dissolved the Chambers on May 16th, and summoned a new one for August 3rd. Instead of recalling Villèle, he strengthened the Ministry by followers of Polignac. On May 19th De Chantelauze and Count Peyronnet came in as Minister of Justice and Minister of the Interior.

The King's Defiance of the People

The appointment of Peyronnet was, in Charles' own words, a slap in the face for public opinion, for there was hardly an individual more hated in France; he now continually advised exceptional measures and urged a coup d'état against the provisions of the Charta. In order to facilitate the victory of the Government at the new elections, he explained in his proclamation to the people on June 13th that he would not give in. But the society " Aide-toi, le ciel t'aidera " secured the re-election of the 221 ; the opposition reached the number of 272 ; the Ministry, on the other hand, had only 145 votes.

Disorders were visible in the whole of France. Troops were sent to quiet them, but the Press of every shade of opinion fanned the flame. Charles saw rising before him the shadow of his brother, whom weak concessions had brought to the guillotine ; spoke of a dictatorship ; and, being entirely under Polignac's influence, inclined towards the plan of adopting exceptional measures and re-asserting his position as king. On July 26th five royal ordinances were published. In these the freedom of the Press as established by law was greatly limited ; the Chambers of Deputies, though only just elected, were again dissolved ; a new law for reorganising the elections was proclaimed, and a chamber to be chosen in accordance with this method was summoned for September 28th. In other words, war was declared

THE CAPTURE OF THE HOTEL DE VILLE BY THE CITIZENS OF PARIS
The Paris Revolution of 1830 was brief but decisive, ending in the dethronement of Charles X. For three days—from July 26th till the 29th—Paris was in a state of revolution. The populace attacked the Hôtel de Ville and the Tuileries, the capture of the former, after a spirited defence by the National Guard, being shown in the above picture.

Thiers   Laffitte   Périer

LEADERS IN THE FRENCH REVOLUTION OF 1830

The best known political writer in France at the time, Adolphe Thiers, wrote the "Histoire de la Révolution Française," which obtained a rapid popularity. An opponent of the Polignac administration, he declared for a change of dynasty, and in his liberal policy was supported by the financiers Jacques Laffitte, and Casimir Périer, who had a large following, enjoying unlimited influence among the property-owning citizens, who were joined by some of the nobility.

upon the constitution. According to paragraph 14 of the charter, the king " is chief head of the state. He has command of the military and naval forces ; can declare war, conclude peace, alliances, and commercial treaties ; has the right of making appointments to every office in the public service, and of issuing the necessary regulations and decrees for the execution of the laws and the security of the state." Had the king, as indeed was maintained by the journals supporting the Ministry, ventured to claim the power of ruling through his own decrees, for which he alone was responsible, then all regulations as to the state of the legislature and the subordination of the executive would have been entirely meaningless. Paris, desiring freedom, was clear upon this point, and immediately set itself with determination to the task of resistance. The first day began with the demonstrations of the printers, who found their occupation considerably reduced by the Press censorship. This movement was accompanied by tumultuous demonstrations of dissatisfaction on the part of the general public in the Palais Royal, and the windows of the unpopular Minister's house were broken. On the morning of the second day the liberal newspapers appeared without even an attempt to gain the necessary authorisation from the authorities. They contained a manifesto couched in identical language and including the

LAFAYETTE

Author of the "Rights of Man" theory, and the patriarch of the Revolution, he commanded the National Guard in the rising of 1830.

following sentence : " In the present state of affairs obedience ceases to be a duty." The author of this composition was Adolphe Thiers, at that time the best known political writer in France, born in Marseilles, April 15th, 1797, and practising as advocate in Aix in 1820. In 1821 he came to Paris and entered the office of the " Constitutionnel," and co-operated in the foundation of several periodicals, writing at the same time his " Histoire de la Révolution Française," in ten volumes, 1823–1827. This work was rather a piece of journalism than a scientific history. It attained rapid popularity among the liberal bourgeois as it emphasised the great successes and the valuable achievements of the Revolution, while discountenancing the aberrations of the lamentable excesses of an anarchical society ; constitutionalism and its preservation were shown to be the results of all the struggles and sacrifices which France had undergone to secure freedom and power of self-determination to nations at large. Thiers also supported the view of the members that the charter of 1814 provided sufficient guarantees for the preservation and exercise of the rights of the people. These, however, must be retained in their entirety and protected from the destructive influences of malicious misinterpretation. Such protection he considered impossible under the government of Charles X. He was equally distrustful of that monarch's son, the Duke of Angoulême, and had already pretty plainly declared for a change of dynasty and the deposition of the royal line of the House of Bourbon in favour of the Orleans branch. Thiers and his journalistic friends were supported by a number of the advocates present in Paris, including the financiers Jacques Laffitte and Casimir Périer. They also possessed a considerable following and enjoyed unlimited influence among the property-owning citizens, who were again joined by the independent nobility excluded from court. They gave advice upon the issue of manifestoes, while Marmont, the Duke of Ragusa and military commander in Paris, strove, with the few troops at his disposal, to suppress the noisy gatherings of the dissatisfied element, which had considerably increased by July 27th. Paris began to take up arms on the following night. On the 28th, thousands of workmen, students from the polytechnic schools, doctors, and citizens of every profession, were fighting behind numerous barricades, which resisted all the efforts of the troops. Marmont recognised his inability to deal with the revolt, and advised the king, who was staying with his family and Ministers in Saint Cloud, to withdraw the ordinances. Even then a rapid decision might have caused a change of feeling in Paris, and have saved the Bourbons, at any rate for the moment; but neither the king nor Polignac suspected the serious danger confronting them, and never supposed that the Parisians would be able to stand against 12,000 troops of the line. This, indeed, was the number that Marmont may have concentrated from the garrisons in the immediate neighbourhood. In view of the well-known capacity of the Parisians for street fighting, their bravery and determination, this force would scarce have been sufficient, even granting their discipline to have been unexceptionable, and assuming their readiness to

Paris in Arms against the King

LOUIS PHILIPPE, KING OF FRANCE
After the Revolution of 1830, which drove Charles X. from the throne, Louis Philippe, the eldest son of Philip "Egalité," received the crown, and under her "citizen king" France regained some of her old prosperity.

support the king's cause to the last. The troops, however, were by no means in love with the Bourbon hierarchy, and no one felt any inclination to risk his life on behalf of such a ridiculous coxcomb as Polignac, against whom the revolt appeared chiefly directed. The regiments advancing upon Paris from the neighbouring provinces halted in the suburbs. Within Paris itself two regiments of the line were won over by the brother of Laffitte, the financier, and deserted to the revolters. During the forenoon of July 29th, Marmont continued to hold the Louvre and the Tuileries with a few thousand men. In the afternoon, however, a number of armed detachments made their way into the Louvre through a gap caused by the retreat of a Swiss battalion, and Marmont was forced to retire into the Champs Elysées. In the evening the marshal rode off to Saint Cloud with the news that the movement in Paris could no longer be suppressed by force, and that the king's only course of action was to open negotiations with the leaders of the revolt. Marmont had done all he could for the Bourbon monarchy with the very inadequate force at his disposal, and was now forced to endure the aspersions of treachery uttered by the Duke of Angoulême before the guard. This member of the Bourbon family, who had been none too brilliantly gifted by Providence, was entirely spoiled by the ultra legitimist rulers and priests, who praised his Spanish campaign as a brilliant military achievement, and compared the attack on the Trocadero to Marengo and Austerlitz. A prey to the many illusions emanating from the brain of the "sons of Saint Louis," it was left to his somewhat nobler and larger-minded father to inform him that even kings might condescend to return thanks, at any rate to men who had risked their lives in their defence.

The Soldiery Desert to the Revolters

Marmont was, moreover, mistaken in his idea that Charles could retain his throne for his family by negotiations, by

4865

the dismissal of Polignac, by the recognition of recent elections, or even by abdication in favour of his grandson Henry, afterwards Count of Chambord. The fate of the Bourbons was decided on July 30th, and the only question for solution was whether their place should be taken by a republic or by a liberal constitutional monarchy under the princes of Orleans.

Louis Philippe, son of the Duke of Orleans and of the Princess Louise Marie Adelaide of Penthièvre, had been given on his birth, October 6th, 1773, the title of the Duke of Valois, and afterwards of Duke of Chartres. During the Revolution

visited almost every country in Europe, and in North America had enjoyed the opportunity of becoming acquainted with the democratic state and its powers of solving the greatest tasks without the support of princes or standing armies.

Consequently upon his return to France he was considered a Liberal, was both hated and feared by the royal family, and became highly popular with the people, the more so as he lived a very simple life notwithstanding his regained wealth ; he associated with the citizens, invited their children to play with his sons and daughters, and in wet weather

THE DEPUTIES OFFERING THE LIEUTENANCY OF FRANCE TO THE DUKE OF ORLEANS
Meeting at the Bourbon Palace on July 30th, 1830, the deputies offered the "lieutenancy of the kingdom" to the Duke of Orleans, who had become popular with the people. He at first hesitated, but on the following day, acting, it is said, on the advice of Talleyrand, accepted the office. Reading from left to right, the figures in the above picture are : Aug. Périer, Aug. Hilarion de Kératry, Bérard, Baron B. Delessert, Duke of Orleans, General Sebastiani, A. de St. Aignan, Charles Dupin, André Gallot, Dugas-Montbel, Duchaffaud, General Count Mathieu Dumas, Bernard de Rennes.

he had called himself General Egalité, and Duke of Orleans after the death of his father, the miserable libertine who had voted for the death of Louis XVI. As he had been supported by Dumouriez in his candidature for the throne, he was obliged to leave France after the flight of that leader. He had then been forced to lead a very wandering life, and even to earn his bread in Switzerland as a schoolmaster. Forgiveness for his father's sins and for his own secession to the revolters had long been withheld by the royal house, until he was at length recognised as the head of the House of Orleans. He had

would put up his umbrella and go to the market and talk with the saleswomen. He had become a very capable man of business, and was highly esteemed in the financial world. Complicity on his part in the overthrow of his relatives cannot be proved—such action was indeed unnecessary ; but there can be no doubt that he desired their fall, and turned it to his own advantage. In his retreat at Raincy at Neuilly he received the message of Laffitte and the information from Thiers in person that the Chamber would appoint him lieutenant-general to the king and invest him with full power.

LOUIS PHILIPPE LEAVING THE PALAIS ROYAL FOR THE HÔTEL DE VILLE AFTER HIS ELECTION

Following upon his election as Lieutenant-General of France, Louis Philippe had his doubts as to how the acceptance of this office would be received by the people of France, in spite of the popularity which he had earned for himself with the people, and he decided boldly to face the situation by going through Paris from the Palais Royal to the Hôtel de Ville. The public seemed on the verge of rising against the new ruler, but no adverse movement took place, and at the Hôtel de Ville Louis Philippe was received with applause.

From the painting by Horace Vernet

4867

He then returned to Paris, and was there entrusted by Charles X. with that office in his own name and as representative of Henry V., who was still a minor. He conformed his further procedure to

The Doom of the Bourbon Monarchy the spirit of these commands as long as he deemed this course of action favourable to his own interests. As soon as he became convinced that the king's word was powerless, he announced the monarch's abdication, but kept silence upon the fact that he had abdicated in favour of his grandson. No doubt the representations of his adherents that he alone could save France from a republic largely contributed to the determination of his decision.

On July 31st it was definitely decided that France should be permanently relieved of the Bourbons who had been imposed upon her ; however, concerning the future constitution widely divergent opinions prevailed. The decision lay with the Marquess of Lafayette, the author of the " Rights of Man " theory, the patriarch of the Revolution, who had already taken over the command of the National Guard on the 29th, at the request of the Chamber of Deputies. The Republicans, who had been responsible for all the work of slaughter, and had inspired the people to take up arms, reposed full confidence in him as a man after their own heart, and entrusted him with the office of dictator. The rich bourgeoisie, and the journalists in connection with them, were, however, afraid of a Republican victory and of the political ideals and social questions which this party might advance for solution.

France's " Citizen King " That liberalism which first became a political force in France is distinguished by a tendency to regulate freedom in proportion to social rank, and to make the exercise of political rights conditional upon education and income. The financial magnates of Paris expected to enter unhindered into the inheritance of the

THE MARCH OF THE NATIONAL GUARD TO RAMBOUILLET

Realising that the nation was at last tired of the Bourbon dynasty, Charles X. abdicated in favour of his young grandson Henry V. ; but France preferred Louis Philippe, and he was called to the throne. He naturally wished to have his inconvenient cousin out of the country, and to hasten his departure a march of the National Guard to Rambouillet, where Charles was at that time residing, was organised. The march was more like a holiday procession than an intimidating movement, being joined by crowds of people, some on vehicles and others on foot, singing the Marseillaise and shouting " Vive la liberté ! " The movement, however, had the desired result, Charles leaving France for England.

LOUIS PHILIPPE TAKING THE OATH OF THE CONSTITUTION ON AUGUST 9TH, 1830

Before a brilliant assembly of the Chambers, as shown in the above picture, Louis Philippe took the oath of the Constitution on August 9th, 1830, and from that time entitled himself "The King of the French."

Legitimists, and permanently to secure the powers of government so soon as peace had been restored. For this purpose they required a constitutional king of their own opinions, and Louis Philippe was their only choice. He probably had no difficulty in fathoming their designs, but he hoped when once established on the throne to be able to dictate his own terms and address himself forthwith to the task of reducing the Republican party to impotence. He proceeded in a solemn procession to the town hall, with the object of winning over Lafayette by receiving the supreme power from his hands. The old leader considered this procedure entirely natural, constituted himself plenipotentiary of the French nation, and concluded an alliance with the "citizen-king," whom he introduced, tricolour in hand, to the people as his own candidate.

In less than a week the new constitution had been drawn out in detail. It was to be "the direct expression of the rights of the French nation"; the **France's New Constitution** king became head of the state by the national will, and was to swear to observe the constitution upon his accession. The two Chambers were retained; an elected deputy was to sit for five years, and the limits of age for the passive and the active franchise were fixed respectively at thirty and twenty-five years. The right of giving effect to the different tendencies which were indispensable to the existence of a constitutional monarchy as conceived by liberalism was reserved for the legislature. Such were the provisions for trial by jury of offences against the Press laws, for the responsibility of Ministers, **The Ex-king Charles at Rambouillet** for full liberty to teachers, for compulsory education in the elementary schools, for the yearly vote of the conscription, and so forth. The deputies chosen at the last election passed the proposals by a large majority, 219 against 38. Of the peers, eighty-nine were won over to their side; eighteen alone, including Chateaubriand, the novelist of the romantic school, supported the rights of Henry V.

In the meantime, Charles had retired from Saint Cloud to Rambouillet, retaining the Guards and certain regiments which had remained faithful; he once again announced his abdication, and that of Angoulême, to the Duke of Orleans, and ordered him to take up the government in the name of Henry V. To this demand Louis Philippe sent no answer; he confined his efforts to getting his inconvenient cousin out of the country, which he already saw at his own feet. When his representations produced no effect in this direction, his adherents organised a march of the National Guard to Rambouillet, a movement which, though more like a holiday procession than an intimidating movement, brought about the desired result. The Bourbons and their parasites showed not a spark of knightly spirit ; not the smallest attempt was made to teach the insolent Parisians a lesson, or to let them feel the weight of the "Legitimist" sword. With ostentatious delibera-

The Death of Charles X. tion a move was made from Rambouillet to Cherbourg without awakening the smallest sign of sympathy. Charles X. betook himself for the moment to England.

On November 6th, 1836, he died in Görz, where the Duke of Angoulême also passed away on June 3rd, 1844. To the Duchess Marie Caroline of Berry, the daughter of Francis I. of Naples, remained the task of stirring up the loyalists of La Vendée against the government of the treacherous Duke of Orleans, and of weaving, at the risk of her life, intrigues for civil war in France. In spite of her capture, November 7th, 1832, at Nantes, she might have been a source of serious embarrassment to Louis Philippe, and perhaps have turned his later difficulties to the advantage of her son, if she had not fallen into disfavour with her own family, and with the arrogant legitimists, on account of her secret marriage with a son of the Sicilian prince of Campofranco, the Conte Ettore Carlo Lucchesi Palli, to whom she bore a son, the later Duca della Grazia, while in captivity at Blaye, near Bordeaux. Her last son by her first marriage, the Count of Chambord, contented himself throughout his life with the proud consciousness of being the legal King of France ; however, the resources of the good Henry were too limited for him to become dangerous to any government.

France had thus relieved herself of the Bourbons at little or no cost ; she was now to try the experiment of living under the House of Orleans, and under a constitutional monarchy. The Republicans

France and its New Dynasty were surprised at their desertion by Lafayette ; they could not but observe that the mass of people who were insensible to political conviction, and accustomed to follow the influences of the moment, hailed with acclamation the new constitution adjusted by the prosperous Liberals. For the moment they retired into private life with ill-concealed expressions of dissatisfaction, and became the nucleus for a party of malcontents which was speedily reinforced by recruits from every direction. "The King of the French," as the Duke of Orleans entitled himself from August 9th, 1830, at the very outset of his government stirred up a dangerous strife, and by doing so undermined his own position, which at first had seemed to be founded upon the national will. He ought to have honourably and openly enforced the "Republican institutions" which, upon Lafayette's theory, were meant to be the environment of his royal power ; he ought to have appeared as representing the will of the nation, and should in any case have left his fate exclusively in the hands of the people. He attempted, however, to secure his recognition from the great Powers, to assert his claims to consideration among the other dynasties of Europe, and to gain their confidence for himself and France. Prince Metternich supported him in these attempts as soon as he observed that the influences of the Left had been nullified, and that the new king was making a serious effort to suppress that party. The Austrian chancellor fully recognised that Louis Philippe, in preventing

Successors of the Bourbons the formation of a Republic by his intervention, had done good service to the cause of reaction ; he readily thanked him for his erection of a constitutional throne, whereby the monarchies had been spared the necessity of again taking the field against a Republican France. The Bonapartists had proposed to bring forward an opposition candidate to Louis Philippe in the person of the highly gifted and ambitious son of Napoleon I., "le fils de l'homme," and the Archduchess Marie Louise, who had been brought up under the care of his grandfather in Vienna.

The untimely death of the excellent Duke of Reichstadt, who succumbed to a galloping consumption on July 22nd, 1832, which was not, as often stated, the result of excessive self-indulgence, freed "the citizen-king" from a danger which had threatened to increase with every year. At the end of August England recognised unconditionally and without reserve the new government in France ; her example was followed by Austria and Prussia, to the extreme vexation of the Tsar Nicholas I. The House of Orleans might thus far consider itself at least tolerated as the successor of the French Bourbons.

HANS VON ZWIEDINECK-SÜDENHORST
ARTHUR KLEINSCHMIDT

THE NEW REVOLUTIONARY PERIOD
NATIONALIST AND CONSTITUTIONAL MOVEMENTS IN THE 'THIRTIES

THE events of 1830 in Paris introduced a new revolutionary period in Europe which was to produce far more comprehensive and permanent transformations than the Revolution of 1789. From that date was broken the spell of the reactionary theory which forbade all efforts for the identification of monarchical and popular rights, and demanded blind submission to the decrees of the government.

This tyranny had been abolished by the will of a people which, notwithstanding internal dissensions, was united in its opposition to the Bourbons. Thirty or forty thousand men, with no military organisation and without preparation of any kind, had defeated in street fighting twelve thousand troops of the line, under the command of an experienced general, a marshal of the Grand Army of Napoleon I. Though gained by bloodshed, the victory was not misused or stained by atrocities of any kind; at no time was any **France Under a New Dynasty** attempt made to introduce a condition of anarchy. Upon the capture of the Louvre by bands of armed citizens, little damage had been done, and the artistic treasures of the palace had been safely removed from the advance of the attacking party. In the course of a fortnight a new constitution had been organised by the joint action of the leading citizens, a new regime had been established in every branch of the administration, and a new dynasty had been entrusted with supreme power. It had been shown that revolutions did not of necessity imply the destruction of social order, but might also become a means to the attainment of political rights.

Proof had thus been given that it was possible for a people to impose its will upon selfish and misguided governments, even when protected by armed force. The so-called conservative Great Powers were not united among themselves, and were therefore too weak to exclude a nation from the exercise of its natural right of self-government when that nation was ready to stake its blood and treasure on the issue. Other peoples living under conditions apparently or actually intolerable might be tempted to follow **Causes of National Friction** this example and to revolt. The weight of a foreign yoke, a term implying not only the rule of a conqueror king, but also that of a foreigner legally in possession of the throne, is more than ever galling if not supported upon a community of interests.

The strong aversion which springs from the contact of characters fundamentally discordant can never be overcome even by consideration of the mutual advantages to be gained from the union, however great these advantages may be. Repugnance and animosity, purely sentimental in their origin, and impossible of suppression by any process of intellectual exercise, are influences as important in national as in individual life. Irritated ambition, exaggerated pride, the under and over estimation of defects and advantages, are so many causes of national friction, with tremendous struggles and political convulsions as their consequence.

To prefer national sentiment to political necessity is naturally an erroneous doctrine, because contrary to the fundamental laws of civilisation, which define man's task as the conquest of natural forces by his intellectual power for his own good. Yet **Development of Political Vitality** such a doctrine is based at least upon the ascertained fact that, notwithstanding ages of intellectual progress, instinct is more powerful than reason, and that the influences of instinct must be remembered both by nations and individuals in the pursuit of their several needs. In nineteenth-century Europe the development of inherent national powers was entirely justified, if only because for centuries it had been neglected and thwarted, or had advanced, if at all, by a process highly irregular. Many European countries had developed a political vitality under, and as a consequence of, monarchical government; and if this vitality was to become the realisation of the popular will

The Nations In Process of Organisation it must first gain assurance of its own value and importance, and acquire the right of self-government. It was to be tested in a series of trials which would prove its vital power and capacity, or would at least determine the degree of dependency which should govern its relations to other forces.

Hence it is that national revolutions are the substratum of European political history after the Vienna Congress. Hence it is that cabinet governments were gradually forced to undertake tasks of national importance which had never before even attracted their notice. Hence, too, such nations as were vigorous and capable of development must be organised and tested before entering upon the struggle for the transformation of society—a struggle which ultimately overshadowed national aspirations and became itself the chief aim and object of civilised endeavour.

The oppression of an alien rule to which Europe had been forced to submit was, if not entirely overthrown, at any rate shaken to its foundations. The tyranny under which the Christian inhabitants of the Balkan countries had groaned since the middle of the fifteenth century, and which had entirely checked every tendency to progress, was now in process of dissolution. Among the Slav races of the Balkans the Servians had freed themselves by their own power, and had founded the beginnings of a national community. With unexampled heroism, which had risen almost to the point of self-immolation, the Greeks had saved their nationality, and had united a considerable portion of their

Greek Nationality Saved numbers into a self-contained state. In Germany and Italy the national movement, together with the political, had been crushed in the name of the conservative Great Powers and their "sacred" alliances; in this case it was only to be expected that the influence of the French Revolution would produce some tangible effect. It was, however, in two countries, where systems unusually artificial had been created by the arbitrary action of dynasties

and diplomatists, that these influences became earliest and most permanently operative : in the new kingdom of the United Netherlands, and in Poland under the Russian protectorate.

In 1813 and 1815, the Dutch had taken an honourable share in the general struggle for liberation from the French yoke; they had formed a constitution which, while providing a sufficient measure of self-government to the nine provinces of their kingdom, united those nine into a uniform body politic. They had abolished their aristocratic republic, which had been replaced by a limited monarchy; the son of their last hereditary stadtholder, Prince William Frederic of Orange, had been made king, with the title of William I., and so far everything had been done that conservative diplomacy could possibly desire. Conservatism, however, declined to allow the Dutch constitution to continue its course of historical development, and proceeded to ruin it by the artificial addition of Belgium—a proceeding which may well serve as an example of the incompetent bureaucratic policy of Prince

Belgian Union with Holland Metternich. The Orange king naturally regarded this unexpected accession of territory as a recognition of his own high capacity, and considered that he could best serve the interests of the Great Powers by treating the Belgians, whom he considered as Frenchmen, as subjects of inferior rank.

Many disabilities were laid upon them by the administration, which was chiefly in the hands of Dutchmen. Dutch trade had begun to revive, and Belgian industries found no support in Holland. Day by day it became clearer to the Belgians that union with Holland was for them a disastrous mistake, and they proceeded to demand separation. Not only by the Catholic Conservative party, but also by the Liberals, the difference of religious belief was thought to accentuate the opposition of interests. The attitude of hostility to their Protestant neighbours which the Catholic provinces of the Netherlands had adopted during 150 years of Spanish government had never been entirely given up, and was now resumed, after a short armistice, with much secret satisfaction.

Without any special preparation, the ferment became visible on the occasion of a performance of the " Revolution Opera " completed in 1828, " The Dumb Girl of Portici," by D. F. E. Auber, on August 25th,

1830. Personal intervention might even then perhaps have saved the political union of the Netherland countries. The king, however, made no honourable attempt to secure the confidence of the Belgians, and any possibility of agreement was removed by the attempt to seize Brussels, which he was persuaded to make through Prince Frederic, who had 10,000 men at his command. On November 10th, 1830, the National Congress decided in favour of the introduction of a constitutional monarchy, and for the exclusion of the House of Orange in favour of a new dynasty. Here, also, the expression of popular will failed to coincide with the hopes of the Revolution leaders, who were inclined to republicanism.

The Liberal coteries, who were forced in Belgium to act in concert with the Church, preferred government under a constitutional monarchy; if a republic were formed, an ultramontane majority would inevitably secure tyrannical supremacy, and all freedom of thought would be impossible. A royal family, if not so intellectually incapable as the Bourbons, would never consent to bind itself hand and foot to please any party, but, while respecting the rights of the minority, would unite with them in opposition to any attempted perversion of power.

The ready proposal of the Belgians to accept a monarchical government was received with satisfaction by the Great Powers, who were reluctantly considering the necessity of opposing the Revolution by force. The Tsar Nicholas had already made up his mind to raise his arm against the West; his attention, however, was soon occupied by far more pressing questions within his own dominions. Metternich and Frederic William III. were disinclined, for financial reasons, to raise contingents of troops; the **Adjusting the Dutch-Belgian Difficulty** scanty forces at the command of Austria were required in Italy, where the Carbonari were known to be in a state of ferment. Louis Philippe decided the general direction of his policy by declining to listen to the Radical proposals for a union of Belgium with France, and thereby strengthened that confidence which he had already won among the Conservative cabinets.

WILLIAM I. OF HOLLAND
On the readjustment of European affairs that followed the fall of Napoleon, Belgium and Holland were united under one sovereign, William I., who abdicated in 1840.

The British proposal to call a conference at London for the adjustment of the Dutch-Belgian difficulty was received with general approbation. On December 20th the independence of Belgium was recognised by this assembly, and the temporary government in Brussels was invited through ambassadors **Declaration of Belgian Independence** to negotiate with the conference. The choice of the new king caused no great difficulty; the claims of Orange, Orleans, and Bavarian candidates were considered and rejected, and the general approval fell upon Prince Leopold George of Coburg, a widower, who had been previously married to Charlotte of England. On June 4th, 1831, the National Congress appointed him King of the Belgians, and he entered upon his dignity in July.

It proved a more difficult task to induce the King of Holland to agree to an acceptable compromise with Belgium and to renounce his claims to Luxemburg. In the session of October 15th, 1831, the conference passed twenty-four articles, proposing a partition of Luxemburg, and fixing Belgium's yearly contribution to the Netherland national debt at 8,400,000 gulden. On two occasions it became necessary to send French troops as far as Antwerp to protect Belgium, a weak military power, from reconquest by Holland; and on each occasion diplomatic negotiation induced the Dutch to retire from the land which they had occupied.

It was not until 1838 that peace between Belgium and Holland was definitely concluded; King William had fruitlessly strained the resources of his state to the utmost, and for the increased severity of the conditions imposed upon him he had merely his own obstinacy to thank. Belgium's share of the payment towards the interest due upon the common national debt was ultimately fixed at 5,000,000 gulden. On August 9th, 1832, King Leopold married Louise of Orleans, the eldest daughter of Louis Philippe; though not himself a Catholic, he had his sons baptised into that faith, and thus became the founder of a new Catholic dynasty in Europe, which rapidly acquired importance

G   26   G

through the politic and dignified conduct of Leopold I. What the Belgians had gained without any unusual effort Poland was unable to attain in spite of the streams of blood which she poured forth in her struggle with Russia. She had been a nation on an equality with Russia, with a constitution of her own; her resistance now reduced her to the position of a province of the empire, deprived of all political rights, and subjected to a government alike despotic and arbitrary. The popular will was unable to find expression, for the nation which it inspired had been warped and repressed by a wholly unnatural course of development; there was no unity, no social organism, to support the expansion of classes and professions.

Poland under Russian Oppression

There were only two classes struggling for definite aims—the great territorial nobility, who were attracted by the possibility of restoring their exaggerated powers, which had depended on the exclusion of their inferiors from legal rights; and the small party of intelligent men among the Schlactha, the petty nobility, civil officials, military officers, teachers, etc., who had identified themselves with the principles of democracy, and were attempting to secure their realisation. Though its purity of blood was almost indisputable, the Polish race had sunk so low that the manufacturing and productive element of the population, the craftsmen and agricultural workers, had lost all feeling of national union and had nothing to hope from a national state.

Averse from exertion, incapable of achievement, and eaten up by preposterous self-conceit, Polish society, for centuries the sole exponent of national culture, was inaccessible to the effect of any deep moral awakening; hence national movement in the true sense of the term was impossible. At the outset the Polish Revolution was marked by some display of resolution and enthusiasm. It was, however, a movement animated rather by ill-feeling and injured pride than originating in the irritation caused by intolerable oppression. It is true that the government was for the most part in the hands of the Russians, but there is no reason to suppose that it was in any way more unjust or more corrupt than the monarchical republic that had passed away. It cannot be said that

The Poles Strike for Freedom

the Russian administration prevented the Poles from recognising the defective results of their social development, from working to remove those defects, to relieve the burdens of the labouring classes, and to found a community endowed with some measure of vitality, the advantages of which were plainly to be seen in the neighbouring Prussian districts. The moderate independence which Alexander I. had left to the Polish National Assembly was greater than that possessed by the Prussian provincial assemblies. The Poles possessed the means for relieving the legislature of the arrogance of the nobles, whom no monarchy, however powerful, had been able to check, and thus freeing the people from the weight of an oppression far more intolerable than the arbitrary rule of individuals, officials, and commanders.

Yet, was there ever a time when the much-lauded patriotism of the Poles attempted to deal with questions of this nature? So long as they failed to recognise their duty in this respect, their patriotism, founded upon a vanity which had risen to the point of monomania, was valueless to the nation at large. Events proved that the struggle between Poland and Russia cannot be described as purposeless. The revolutionary party had long been quietly working, and when the progress of events in France became known, was immediately inflamed to action. Its first practical steps were generally attended with a high measure of success.

Wars of the Polish Revolution

After the storming of the Belvedere, November 29th, 1830, occupied by the governor, the Grand Duke Constantine, that personage was so far intimidated as to evacuate Warsaw with his troops. On December 5th, 1830, a provisional government was already in existence. On January 25th, 1831, the Assembly declared the deposition of the House of Romanoff, and in February a Polish army of 78,000 men was confronting 100,000 Russians, who had been concentrated on the frontiers of Old Poland under Diebitsch-Sabalkanski, and his general staff officer, Karl Friedrich, Count of Toll. These achievements were the unaided work of the nobility; their military organisation had been quickly and admirably successful.

Their commander-in-chief, Prince Michael Radziwill, who had served under Thaddeus Kosciuszko and Napoleon, had several bold and capable leaders at his disposal.

If at the same time a popular rising had taken place throughout the country, and a people's war in the true sense of the word had been begun, it is impossible to estimate the extent of the difficulties with which the Russian Government would have had to deal. Notwithstanding the victories of Bialolenka and Grochow, February 24th and 25th, 1831, Diebitsch did not dare to advance upon Warsaw, fearing to be blockaded in that town ; he waited for reinforcements, and even began negotiations, considering his position extremely unfavourable. However, Volhynia and Podolia took no serious part in the revolt. The deputies of the Warsaw government found scattered adherents in every place they visited ; but the spirit of enterprise and the capacity for struggle disappeared upon their departure. It was only in Lithuania that any public rising on an extensive scale took place.

On May 26th, Diebitsch, in spite of a heroic defence, inflicted a severe defeat at Ostrolenka upon the main Polish army under Jan Boncza Skrzynecki. Henceforward the military advantage was decidedly on the side of the Russians. The outbreak of cholera, to which Diebitsch succumbed on June 10th, might perhaps have produced a turn of fortune favourable to the Poles. Count Ivan Feodvitch Paskevitch-Erivanski, who now assumed the chief command, had but 50,000

KING OF THE BELGIANS
When the independence of Belgium was recognised, the choice of a new king fell upon Prince Leopold George of Coburg, and on July 4th, 1831, the National Congress appointed him King of the Belgians.

men at his disposal, and would hardly have dared to advance from Pultusk if the numerous guerrilla bands of the Poles had done their duty and had been properly supported by the population. Never, however, was there any general rising ; terrified by the ravages of the cholera, the mob declined to obey the authorities, and their patriotism was not proof against their panic. Skrzynecki and his successor, Henry Dembinski, had 50,000 men under their colours when they attempted to resist the advance of Paskevitch upon Warsaw ; but within the capital itself a feud had broken out between the aristocrats and the democrats, who were represented

Poland Ravaged by Cholera

among the five members of the civil government by the historian Joachim Lelevel, after the dictatorship of Joseph Chlopicki had not only abolished but utterly shattered the supremacy of the nobles. The government, at the head of which was the senatorial president, Prince Adam George Czartoryiski, was forced to resign, and the purely democratic administration which succeeded fell into general disrepute. Military operations suffered from lack of concerted leadership. The storming of Warsaw on September 6th and 7th, carried out by Paskevitch and Toll, with 70,000 Russians against 40,000 Poles, decided the struggle. The smaller divisions still on foot, under the Genoese Girolamo Ramorino, Mathias Rybinski, Rozycki, and others, met with no support from the population, and were speedily forced to retreat beyond the frontier.

End of the Polish Dream of Freedom

The Polish dream of freedom was at an end. The Kingdom of Poland, to which Alexander I. had granted nominal independence, became a Russian province in 1832 by a constitutional edict of February 26th ; henceforward its history was a history of oppression and stern and cruel tyranny. However, the consequent suffering failed to produce any purifying effect upon the nation, though European liberalism, with extraordinary unanimity, manifested a sympathy which, in Germany, rose to the point of ridiculous and hysterical sentimentalism.

It was by conspiracies, secret unions, and political intrigues of every kind, by degrading mendicancy and sponging, that these " patriots " thought to recover freedom and independence for their native land. Careless of the consequences and untaught by suffering, in 1846 they instigated revolts in Posen and in the little free state of Cracow, which was occupied by Austria at the request of Russia, and eventually incorporated with the province of Galicia. The peasant revolt, which was characterised by unexampled ferocity and cruelty, made it plain to the world at large that it was not the Russian, the

| Skrzynecki | Paskevitch | Constantine |

LEADERS IN THE POLISH - RUSSIAN WARS

General Jan Boncza Skrzynecki was in command of the main Polish army at Ostrolenka, where it suffered defeat ; Count Ivan Feodvitch Paskevitch-Erivanski commanded the Russian troops opposed to Skrzynecki and Dembinski, crushing the Poles and taking Warsaw ; while the Grand Duke Constantine, brother of the Tsar of Russia and governor of Warsaw, after the storming of the Belvedere on November 29th, 1830, was so far intimidated as to evacuate Warsaw.

Austrian, or the Prussian whom the Polish peasant considered his deadly enemy and oppressor, but the Polish noble.

The revolutionary party in connection with the Revolution of July brought little to pass in Italy except abortive conspiracies and a general state of disturbance. The nation as a whole was inspired by no feeling of nationalism ; the moderate party kept aloof from the intrigues of the Carbonari, who continued their activities in secret after the subjugation of Piedmont and Naples by the Austrians in 1821. The chief Austrian adherents were to be found in the Church states ; there, however, an opposition union, that of the "Sanfedists," had been formed, with the countenance of the papacy. While striving for the maintenance of the papal power and the strengthening of religious feeling, the party occupied itself with the persecution of all Liberals, and rivalled the Carbonari in the use of poison and dagger for the attainment of its ends. Cardinal Consalvi had availed himself of the help of the Sanfedists ; but he allowed their power to extend

DUKE OF BRUNSWICK

When Charles, Duke of Brunswick, proved his incompetence, his brother William, at the request of Prussia, offered himself for the high office and was received with acclamation. King of Hanover, Ernest Augustus exhibited a weak narrow-mindedness by refusing the constitution between the nobility and the representatives of the peasants.

KING OF HANOVER

only so far as it might be useful for the furtherance of his political objects. However, under the government of Pope Leo XII., 1823-1829, the influence of the party increased considerably, and led the Cardinal Rivarola, the legate of Ravenna, to perpetrate cruelties upon the Carbonari in Faenza, a policy which contributed to increase the general ill-feeling with which Italy regarded the futile administration of the papacy. Pius VIII., 1829-1830, and Cardinal Albani supported the union of the Sanfedists ; their continued attempts at aggrandisement resulted in the temporary success of the revolution in Bologna. This movement had been long prepared, and broke out on February 4th, 1831, when Menotti in Parma gave the signal for action. The Duke of Modena, Francis IV., imprisoned Menotti in his own house ; feeling himself, however, too weak to deal with the movement, he fled into Austrian territory with his battalion of soldiers, and hastened to Vienna to appeal to Metternich for help. His example was followed by Pope Gregory XVI., elected on February 2nd, 1831, formerly

Bartolommeo Cappelleri, general of the Camaldulensian Order, whose supremacy was no longer recognised by the Umbrian towns which had broken into revolt, by the legation, or by the Marks.

The Austrian chancellor thought it advisable to maintain at any cost the protectorate exercised by the emperor in Italy; notwithstanding the threats of France, who declared that she would regard the advance of Austrian troops into the Church states as a casus belli, he occupied Bologna, March 21st, after seizing Ferrara and Parma in the first days of March. Ancona was also forced to surrender; in this town the provisional government of the Romagna had taken refuge, together with Louis Napoleon Bonaparte, son of the King of Holland and of Hortense Beauharnais, who first came into connection with the revolutionary party at this date. The task of the Austrians was then brought to completion.

On July 15th they retired from the papal states, but were obliged to return on January 24th, 1832, in consequence of the new revolt which had been brought about by the cruelties of the papalini, or papal soldiers. Louis Philippe attempted to lend some show of support to the Italian Liberal party by occupying Ancona at the same time, February 22nd. Neither France nor Austria could oblige the Pope to introduce the reforms which he had promised into his administration. The ruling powers of the Curia were apprehensive of the reduction of their revenues,

and steadily thwarted all measures of reorganisation. When Gregory XVI. enlisted two Swiss regiments for the maintenance of peace and order, the foreign troops evacuated his district in 1838.

In Germany the effects of the July Revolution varied according to differences of political condition, and fully represented the divergences of feeling and opinion prevailing in the separate provinces. There was no uniformity of thought, nor had any tendency to nationalist movement become apparent. Liberal and Radical groups were to be found side by side, divided by no strict frontier line; moreover, operations in common were inconceivable, for no common object of endeavour had yet been found. In particular federal provinces special circumstances gave rise to revolts intended to produce a change in the relations subsisting between the rulers and the ruled.

Brunswick was a scene of events as fortunate for that state as they were rapid in development. Charles, Duke of Brunswick, who had begun his rule in 1823 as a youth of nineteen years of age, showed himself totally incompetent to fulfil the duties of his high position. He conducted himself towards his relations of England and Hanover with an utter want of tact; and towards his subjects, whose constitutional rights he declined to recognise, he was equally haughty and dictatorial. After the events of July he had returned home from Paris, where he had spent his time in the grossest pleasures,

A GROUP OF NINETEENTH CENTURY POPES

Pius VII.

Leo XII.

Pius VIII.

Gregory XVI.

During the restless period in the first half of last century, St. Peter's Chair was occupied in turn by the Popes whose portraits are given above. Pius VII. died in 1823, and was succeeded by Leo XII. At his death, Pius VIII. became Pope, ruling only from March, 1829, till November, 1830. He was followed by the reactionary Gregory XVI.

4877

and immediately opposed the nobles and the citizens as ruthlessly as ever. Disturbances broke out in consequence on September 7th, 1830, and so frightened the cowardly libertine that he evacuated his capital with the utmost possible speed and deserted his province. At the request of Prussia, his brother William, who had

William Duke of Brunswick taken over the principality of Öls, offered himself to the people of Brunswick, who received him with acclamation. Notwithstanding the opposition of Metternich in the diet, the joint action of Prussia and England secured William's recognition as duke on December 2nd, after Charles had made himself the laughing-stock of Europe by a desperate attempt to cross the frontier of Brunswick with a small body of armed ruffians.

The people of Hesse forced their elector, William II., to summon the representatives of the Orders in September, 1830, and to assent to the constitution which they speedily drew up. On January 8th, 1831, the elector, in the presence of the Crown Prince Frederic William, signed the documents and handed them to the Orders; however, the people of Hesse were unable to secure constitutional government. They declined to allow the elector to reside among them in Cassel, with his mistress, Emilie Ortlöpp, whom he made Countess of Reichenbach in 1821, and afterwards Countess of Lessonitz; they forced him to withdraw to Hanover and to appoint the Crown Prince as co-regent, September 30th, 1831, but found they had merely fallen out of the frying-pan into the fire.

In August, 1831, Frederic William I. married Gertrude Lehmann, née Falkenstein, the wife of a lieutenant, who had been divorced by her husband in Bonn, made Countess of Schaumburg in 1831, and Princess of Hanau in 1853; as a result he quarrelled with his mother, the Princess Augusta of Prussia, and with

The Tyrant Frederic William the estates, who espoused the cause of the injured electress. He was a malicious and stubborn tyrant, who broke his plighted word, deliberately introduced changes into the constitution through his Minister, Hans Daniel von Hassenpflug, whom he supported in his struggle with the estates until the Minister also insulted him and opposed his efforts at unlimited despotism. Hassenpflug left the service of Hesse in July, 1837, first entering the

civil service in Sigmaringen, November, 1838, then that of Luxemburg, June, 1839, ultimately taking a high place in the public administration of Prussia, 1841.

The people of Hesse then became convinced that their position had rather deteriorated than otherwise; the Landtag was continually at war with the government, and was repeatedly dissolved. The Liberals went to great trouble to claim their rights in endless appeals and proclamations to the Federal Council, but were naturally and invariably the losers in the struggle with the unscrupulous regent, who became elector and gained the enjoyment of the revenues from the demesnes and the trust property by the death of his father on November 20th, 1847. The Liberals were not anxious to resort to any violent steps which might have provoked the Federal Council to interference of an unpleasant kind; they were also unwilling to act in concert with the Radicals.

Even more helpless and timorous was the behaviour of the Hanoverians when their king, Ernest Augustus, who had contracted debts amounting to

The brave Professors of Göttingen several million thalers as Duke of Cumberland, was so narrow-minded as to reject the constitution which had been arranged after long and difficult negotiations between the nobility and the representatives of the peasants. Seven professors of Göttingen, Jakob and Wilhelm Grimm, Dahlmann, Weber and Gervinus, Ewald and Albrecht, protested against the patent of November 1st, 1837, which absolved the state officials from their oaths of fidelity to the constitution.

The state prosecution and merciless dismissal of these professors aroused a general outcry throughout Germany against the effrontery and obstinacy of the Guelphs; none the less, the estates, who had been deprived of their rights, were too timid to make a bold and honourable stand against the powers oppressing them. A number of the electors consented, in accordance with the decrees of 1819, which were revived by the king, to carry through the elections for the General Assembly of the estates, thereby enabling the king to maintain that in form at least his state was constitutionally governed in the spirit of the Act of Federation. In vain did that indomitable champion of the popular rights, Johann Karl Tertern Stüve, burgomaster of Osnabrück, protest before the

Federal Council against the illegal imposition of taxes by the Hanoverian government. The prevailing disunion enabled the faithless ruler to secure his victory ; the compliance of his subjects gave a fairly plausible colouring to his arbitrary explanation of these unconstitutional acts ; his policy was interpreted as a return to the old legal constitution, a return adopted, and therefore ratified, by the estates themselves.

The Saxons had displayed far greater inclination to riot and conspiracy; however, in that kingdom the transition from class privilege to constitutional government was completed without any serious rupture of the good relations between the people and the government ; both King Anthony and his nephew Frederic Augustus II., whom he had appointed co-regent, possessed sufficient insight to recognise the advantages of a constitution ; the co-operation of large sections of the community would define the distribution of those burdens

THE BROTHERS GRIMM
Jakob and Wilhelm Grimm, two prominent educationists of Göttingen, were among the professors dismissed in 1837 for protesting against the absolution of state officials from their oaths of fidelity to the constitution.

which state necessities inevitably laid upon the shoulders of individuals. They supported the Minister Bernhard August of Lindenau, one of the wisest statesmen in Germany under the old reactionary regime, when he introduced the constitution of September 4th, 1831, which provided a sufficient measure of representation for the citizen classes, and protected the peasants from defraudation ; they continued their support as long as he possessed the confidence of the Second Chamber. When his progressive

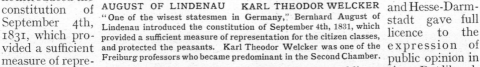

AUGUST OF LINDENAU   KARL THEODOR WELCKER
"One of the wisest statesmen in Germany," Bernhard August of Lindenau introduced the constitution of September 4th, 1831, which provided a sufficient measure of representation for the citizen classes, and protected the peasants. Karl Theodor Welcker was one of the Freiburg professors who became predominant in the Second Chamber.

tendencies proved incompatible with the favour which the Saxon Court attempted to show the Catholic Church, the two princes considered in 1843 that they were able to dispense with his services. The great rise in prosperity manifested in every department of public life under his government was invariably ascribed to his wise statesmanship and his great capacity.

Not entirely disconnected are those political phenomena which occurred in Baden, Hesse-Darmstadt, and the Bavarian Palatinate, as results of the changes which had been brought to pass in France. In these provinces it became plain that liberalism, and the legislation it promoted, were incapable of satisfying the people as a whole, or of creating a body politic sufficiently strong to secure the progress of sound economic development. Nowhere throughout Germany was the parliamentary spirit so native to the soil as in Baden, where the democrats, under the leadership of the Freiburg professors Karl von Rotteck and Karl Theodor Welcker, the Heidelberg jurist Karl Joseph Mittermayer, and the Mannheim high justice Johann Adam von Itzstein, had become predominant in the Second Chamber. The constitutions of Bavaria and Hesse-Darmstadt gave full licence to the expression of public opinion in the Press and at public meetings. But liberalism was impressed with the insufficiency of the means provided for the expression and execution of the popular will ; it did not attempt to create an administrative policy which might have brought it into line with the practical needs of the poorer classes. It hoped to attain its political ends by unceasing efforts to limit the power of the Crown and by extending the possibilities of popular representation. The result was distrust on the part of the

Discontent Encouraged by the Press dynasties, the government officials, and the classes in immediate connection with them, while the discontented classes, who were invariably too numerous even in districts so blessed by Nature as these, were driven into the arms of the Radical agitators, who had immigrated from France, and in particular from Strassburg.

The very considerable freedom allowed to the Press had fostered the growth of a large number of obscure publications, which existed only to preach the rejection of all governmental measures, to discredit the monarchical party, and to exasperate the working classes against their more prosperous superiors. The numerous Polish refugees who were looking for some convenient and exciting form of occupation requiring no great expenditure of labour were exactly the tools and emissaries required by the leaders of the revolutionary movement, and to them the general sympathy with the fate of Poland had opened every door. The first disturbances broke out in Hesse-Darmstadt at the end of September, 1830, as the result of incorporation in the Prussian Customs Union, and were rapidly suppressed by force of arms ; the animosity of the mob was, however, purposely fostered and exploited by the chiefs of a democratic conspiracy who

The Germans Preparing for Revolution were preparing for a general rising. In May, 1832, the Radicals prepared a popular meeting at the castle of Hambach near Neustadt on the Hardt. No disguise was made of their intention to unite the people for the overthrow of the throne and the erection of a democratic republic. The unusual occurrence of a popular manifestation proved a great attraction. The turgid outpourings, seasoned with violent

invectives against every form of moderation, emanating from those crapulous scribblers who were transported with delight at finding in the works of Heinrich Heine and Lewis Baruch Börnes inducements to high treason and anti-monarchical feeling, inflamed minds only too accessible to passion and excitement. As vintage advanced feeling grew higher, and attracted the students, including the various student corps which had regained large numbers of adherents, the remembrance of the persecutions of the 'twenties having been gradually obliterated.

At Christmas-time, 1832, an assembly of the accredited representatives of these corps in Stuttgart was induced to accede to the proposal to share in the forthcoming popular rising. The result was that after the émeute set on foot by the democrats in Frankfort-on-Main on April 3rd, 1833, when an attempt was made to seize the federal palace and the bullion there stored,

The Terrible Fate of the Students it was the students who chiefly had to pay for their irresponsibility and lack of common sense ; the measures of intimidation and revenge undertaken by the German Government at the demand of Metternich fell chiefly and terribly on the heads of the German students. No distinction was made between the youthful aberrations of these corps, which were inspired merely by an overpowering sense of national feeling, and the bloodthirsty designs of malevolent intriguers—for example, of the priest Friedrich Ludwig Weidig in Butzbach—or the unscrupulous folly of revolutionary monomaniacs, such as the Göttingen privat-dozent Von Rauschenplat.

Hundreds of young men were consigned for years to the tortures of horrible and pestilential dungeons by the cold-blooded cruelty of red-tape indifferentism. The punitive measures of justice then enforced, far from creating a salutary feeling of fear, increased the existing animosity, as is proved by the horrors of the Revolution of 1848.

THE
RE-MAKING
OF
EUROPE

EUROPE
AFTER
WATERLOO
VIII

THE WELDING OF THE STATES

THE GERMAN FEDERATION AND
THE GERMAN CUSTOMS UNION

DURING the period subsequent to the Congress of Vienna a highly important modification in the progress of German history took place, in spite of the fact that such expressions of popular feeling as had been manifested through the existing constitutional outlets had effected but little alteration in social and political life. This modification was not due to the diet, which, properly speaking, existed to protect the common interests of the German states collectively. It was the work of the Prussian Government, in which was concentrated the keenest insight into the various details of the public administration, and which had therefore become a centre of attraction for minds inclined to political thought and for statesmen of large ideals. In Germany the political movement had been preceded by a period of economic **Economic Progress in Germany** progress; the necessary preliminary to such a movement, a certain level of prosperity and financial power, had thus already been attained. This achievement was due to the excellent qualities of most of the German races, to their industry, their thrift, and their godliness. The capital necessary to the economic development of a people could only be gradually recovered and amassed after the enormous losses of the French war, by petty landowners and the small handicraftsmen.

However, this unconscious national co-operation would not have availed to break the fetters in which the economic life of the nation had been chained for 300 years by provincial separatism. Of this oppression the disunited races were themselves largely unconscious; what one considered a burden, his neighbour regarded as an advantage. Of constitutional forms, of the process of economic development, the nation severally and collectively had long since lost all understanding, and it was reserved for those to spread such knowledge who had acquired it by experience and intellectual toil. These two qualifications were wanting to the Austrian Government, which had formed the German **The Ignorance of Prince Metternich** Federation according to its own ideas. Even those who admire the diplomatic skill of Prince Metternich must admit that the Austrian chancellor displayed surprising ignorance and ineptitude in dealing with questions of internal administration.

His interest was entirely concentrated upon matters of immediate importance to the success of his foreign policy, upon the provision of money and recruits; of the necessities, the merits, and the defects of the inhabitants of that empire to which he is thought to have rendered such signal service, of the forces dormant in the state over which he ruled, he had not the remotest idea.

The members of the bureaucracy whom he had collected and employed were, with few exceptions, men of limited intelligence and poor education; cowardly and subservient to authority, they were so incompetent to initiate any improvement of existing circumstances that the first preliminary to any work of a generally beneficial nature was the task of breaking down their opposition. The Archduke John, the brother of the Emperor Francis, **Archduke John as Reformer** a man fully conscious of the forces at work beneath the surface, a man of steady and persistent energy, suffered many a bitter experience in his constant attempts to improve technical and scientific training, to benefit agriculture and the iron trades, co-operative enterprises, and savings banks. The Emperor Francis and his powerful Minister had one aversion in common, which implied unconditional opposition to every form of human endeavour—an aversion to pronounced ability. Metternich's long employment of Gentz is to be explained by the imperative need for an intellect so pliable and so reliable in its operations, and also by the fact that Gentz would do anything for money; for a position of independent activity, for a chance of realising his own views or aims, he never had any desire. Men of independent thought, such as Johann Philipp of Wessenberg, were never permanently retained, even for foreign service. This statesman belonged to the little band of Austrian officials who entertained theories and proffered suggestions upon the future and the tasks before the Hapsburg monarchy, its position within the Federation, and upon further federal developments. His opinion upon questions of federal reform was disregarded, and he fell into bad odour at the London conference, when his convictions led him to take an independent position with reference to the quarrel between Belgium and Holland.

FREDERIC WILLIAM IV. Crowned King of Prussia at Königsberg in 1840, he promised the introduction of reforms, which were not carried out. Becoming insane in 1857, he died in 1861.

The fate of the German Federation lay entirely in the hands of Austria, and Austria is exclusively responsible for the **Metternich's Conception of the State** ultimate fiasco of the Federation, which she eventually deserted. The form and character of this alliance, as also its after development, were the work of Metternich. People and Government asked for bread, and he gave them a stone. He conceived the state to be merely an institution officered and governed by police. When more than twenty millions of Germans declared themselves a commercial corporation with reference to the world at large, with the object of equalising the conditions of commercial competition, of preventing an overwhelming influx of foreign goods, and of opening the markets of the world to their own producers—in that memorable year of 1834 the Austrian Government, after inviting the federal representatives to months of conferences in Vienna, could find nothing of more pressing importance to bring forward than proposals for limiting the effectiveness of the provincial constitutions as

compared with the state governments, for increased severity in the censorship of the Press, and the surveillance of university students and their political activity.

Student interference in political life is utterly unnecessary, and can only be a source of mischief; but Metternich and his school were unable to grasp the fact that such interference ceases so soon as political action takes a practical turn. If Austria were disappointed in her expectations of the German federal states, her feelings originated only in the fact that Prussia, together with Bavaria, Würtemberg, Saxony, and Baden, entertained loftier views than she herself upon the nature of State existence and the duties attaching thereto.

The kingdom of Prussia had by no means developed in accordance with the expectations entertained by Metternich in 1813 and 1815; it was a military state, strong enough to repel any possible Russian onslaught, but badly " rounded off," and composed of such heterogeneous fragments of territory that it could not in its existing form aspire to predominance in Germany. Prussia was as yet unconscious of her high calling; she was wholly spellbound by Austrian federal policy, but none the less she had completed a task incomparably the most important national achievement since the attainment of religious freedom—the foundation of the pan-Germanic Customs Union.

Cotta, the greatest German book and newspaper publisher, and an able and important business man, had been able to shield the loyal and thoroughly patriotic views of Lewis I. of Bavaria from the inroads of his occasionally violent paroxysms of personal vanity, and had **Inauguration of a Federal Customs Union** secured the execution of the Act of May 27th, 1829, providing for a commercial treaty between Bavaria-Würtemberg and Prussia with Hesse-Darmstadt, the first two states to join a federal customs union. The community of interests between North and South Germany, in which only farseeing men, such as Friedrich List, the national economist, had believed, then became so incontestable a fact that the commercial treaty took the form of a customs union, implying an area of uniform economic interests.

The "Central German Union," which was intended to dissolve the connection between Prussia and South Germany, and to neutralise the advantages thence derived, rapidly collapsed. It became clear that economic interests are stronger than political, and the dislike amounting to aversion of Prussia entertained by the Central German governments became friendliness as soon as anything was to be gained by a change of attitude—in other words, when it seemed possible to fill the state exchequers. The electorate of Hesse had taken the lead in opposing the Hohenzollern policy of customs federation; as early as 1831 she recognised that her policy of commercial isolation spelt ruin.

A similar process led to the dissolution of the so-called "Einbeck Convention," of March 27th, 1830, which had included Hanover, Brunswick, Oldenburg, and the electorate of Hesse. Saxony joined Prussia on March 30th, as did Thüringen on May 11th, 1833; on May 22nd, 1833, the Bavarian-Würtemberg and the Prussian groups were definitely united. On January 1st, 1834, the union included eighteen German states, with 23,000,000 inhabitants; in 1840 these numbers had risen to twenty-three states with 27,000,000 inhabitants. In 1841 the union was joined by Brunswick, and by Luxemburg in 1842; Hanover did not come in until September 7th, 1851, when she ceased to be an open market for British goods. The expenses of administration and of guarding the frontiers were met from a common fund. The profits were divided among the states within the union in proportion to their population. In 1834 the profits amounted to fifteen silver groschen, one shilling and sixpence per head; in 1840, to more than twenty silver groschen, two shillings.

In the secondary and petty states public opinion had been almost entirely opposed to such unions. Prussia was afraid of the Saxon manufacturing industries, and Leipzig foresaw the decay of her great markets. The credit of completing this great national achievement belongs almost exclusively to the governments

Collapse of the Central German Union

THE STATELY COLOGNE CATHEDRAL   Photochrome

The foundations of this magnificent structure, regarded as one of the finest examples of Gothic architecture extant, were laid in 1248; the work was renewed in 1842, and in 1880 the building was completed according to the original plan.

and to the expert advisers whom they called in. Austria now stood without the boundary of German economic unity. Metternich recognised too late that he had mistaken the power of this union. Proposals were mooted for the junction of Austria with the allied German states, but met with no response from the industrial and manufacturing interests. The people imagined that a process of division was even then beginning which was bound to end in political separation ; but the importance of Prussia, which naturally took the lead in conducting the business of the union, notwithstanding the efforts of other members to preserve their own predominance and independence, became obvious even to those who had originally opposed the conclusion of the convention. The Würtemberg deputy and author, Paul Pfizer, recognised the necessity of a political union of the German states under Prussian hegemony, and saw that the separation of Austria was inevitable.

The Shadow of Political Separation

In 1845, in his " Thoughts upon Rights, State and Church," he expounded the programme which was eventually adopted by the whole nation, though only after long struggles and severe trials. " The conditions," he there said, " of German policy as a whole seem to point to a national alliance with Prussia and to an international alliance with the neighbouring Germanic states and with Austria, which is a first-class Power even apart from Germany. There can be no question of abolishing all political connection between Germany and Austria. In view of the danger threatening Germany on the east and west, nothing would be more foolish ; no enemy or rival of Germany can be allowed to become paramount in Bohemia and Central Germany. But the complete incorporation of Bohemia, Moravia, and Austria, together with that of the Tyrol, Carinthia, and Styria, would be less advantageous to Germany than the retention of these countries by a power connected with her by blood relationship and an offensive and defensive alliance, a power whose arm can reach beyond the Alps on the one hand, and to the Black Sea on the other."

Prussia's Relations with Germany

It was now necessary for Prussia to come to some agreement with the German people and the State of the Hapsburgs.

For more than three centuries the latter had, in virtue of their dynastic power, become the representatives of the Romano-German Empire. Their historical position enabled them to lay claim to the leadership of the federation, though their power in this respect was purely external. Certain obstacles, however, lay in the way of any settlement. It was difficult to secure any feeling of personal friendship between the South Germans and the Prussians of the old province. Some measure of political reform was needed, as well for the consolidation of existing powers of defence as for the provision of security to the individual states which might then form some check upon the severity of Prussian administration.

Finally, there was the peculiar temperament of Frederic William IV., who had succeeded to the government of Prussia upon the death of his father, Frederic William III., on June 7th, 1840. In respect of creative power, artistic sense, and warm, deep feeling, his character can only be described as brilliant. He was of the ripe age of forty-five, and his first measures evoked general astonishment and enthusiasm. But he did not possess the strong grasp of his great ancestors and their power of guiding the ship through critical dangers unaided. He had not that inward consciousness of strength and that decisiveness which shrink from no responsibility ; least of all had he a true appreciation of the time and the forces at work.

The Brilliant Frederic William IV.

Prussia's great need was a constitution which would enable her to send up to the central government a representative assembly from all the provinces, such assembly to have the power of voting taxes and conscriptions, of supervising the finances, and of legislating in conjunction with the Crown. On May 22nd, 1815, Frederic William III. had made some promises in this direction ; but these remained unfulfilled, as the government could not agree upon the amount of power which might be delegated to an imperial parliament without endangering the position of the executive. Such danger undoubtedly existed.

The organisation of the newly-formed provincial federation was a process which necessarily affected private interests and customs peculiar to the individual areas which had formerly been independent sections of the empire, and were now forced into alliance with other districts with which little or no connection had previously existed. The conflicting views and the partisanship inseparable from parliamentary institutions would have checked the quiet, steady work of the Prussian bureaucracy, and would in any case have produced a continual and unnecessary agitation. The improvements in the financial condition created by the better regulation of the national debt, by the limitation of military expenditure, and the introduction of a graduated system of taxation, could not have been more successfully or expeditiously carried out than they were by such Ministers as Bülow and Klewitz.

So soon as the main part of this transformation of the Prussian state had been accomplished, prosperity began to return to the peasant and citizen classes, and the result of the customs regulations and the consequent extension of the market began to be felt. The citizens then began to feel their power and joined the inheritors of the rights formerly possessed by the numerous imperial and provincial orders in a demand for some share in **Coronation** the administration. It was **Pledges of** found possible to emphasise **Prussian King** these demands by reference to the example of the constitutional governments existing in neighbouring territories. The speeches delivered by Frederic William IV. at his coronation in Königsberg on September 10th, 1840, and at his reception of homage in Berlin on October 15th, 1840, in which he displayed oratorical powers unequalled by any previous prince, appeared to point to an immediate fulfilment of these desires.

The king was deeply moved by the outburst of national enthusiasm in Germany which was evoked by the unjustifiable menaces directed against Germany by France in the autumn of 1840 during the Eastern complications. The Minister, Thiers, who had been in office since March 1st, suddenly broke away from the Great Powers during the Turco-Egyptian war, and initiated a policy of his own in favour of Egypt—a short-sighted departure which obliged Great Britain, Russia, Austria, and Prussia to conclude the quadruple alliance of July 15th, 1840, with the object of compelling Mehemet Ali to accept the conditions of peace which they had arranged. With a logic peculiarly their own, the

French considered themselves justified in securing their immunity on the Continent, as they were powerless against England by sea. The old nonsensical argument of their right to the Rhine frontier was revived and they proceeded to mobilise their forces. The German nation made no attempt to disguise their anger at **The Relations** so insolent an act of aggres- **of Germany** sion, and showed all readiness **and France** to support the proposals for armed resistance. Nikolaus Becker composed a song against the French which became extremely popular :

For free and German is the Rhine,
And German shall remain,
Until its waters overwhelm
The last of German name.

The nation were united in support of their princes, most of whom adopted a dignified and determined attitude towards France. Then was the time for Frederic William IV. to step forward. Supported by the warlike temper of every German race, with the exception of the Austrians, who were in financial difficulties, and by the popularity which his speeches had gained for him, he might have intimidated France both at the moment and for the future. However, he confined himself to the introduction of reforms in the federal military constitution at Vienna, and thus spared Austria the humiliation of openly confessing her weakness. The result of his efforts was the introduction of a regular inspection of the federal contingents and the occupation of Ulm and Rastatt as bases for the concentration and movements of future federal armies.

Thus was lost a most favourable opportunity for securing the federal predominance of Prussia by means of her military power, for she could have concentrated a respectable force upon the German frontier more quickly than any other member of the Federation. Moreover, the attitude of Prussia at the London conference was distinctly modest and in no **Frederic** way such as a Great Power **William a** should have adopted. The king's **Failure** lofty words at the laying of the foundation stone of Cologne Cathedral on September 4th, 1842, produced no deception as to his lack of political decision. Whenever a special effort was expected or demanded in an hour of crisis, Frederic William's powers proved unequal to the occasion, and the confidence which the nation reposed in him was deceived.

HANS VON ZWIEDINECK-SÜDENHORST

THE MASSACRE OF THE MAMELUKES BY MEHEMET ALI IN 1811
From the painting by Bida in the Metropolitan Museum of Art, New York

THE NEW KINGDOM OF GREECE
RUSSIA AND THE SUBLIME PORTE

AFTER the Porte had given its consent to the protocol of February 3rd, 1830, the Great Powers of Europe addressed themselves to the task of reorganising the Greek kingdom. Thessaly, Epirus, Macedonia, even Acarnania, remained under Turkish supremacy ; but a considerable portion of the Greek people, forming a national entity, though limited in extent, was now able to begin a new and free existence as a completely independent state.

This success had been attained by the remarkable tenacity of the Greek nation, by the continued support of Great Britain, and, above all, by the pressure which the Russian co-religionists of the Greeks had brought to bear upon the Turkish military power. The work of liberation was greatly hindered by the diplomacy of the other Great Powers, and particularly by the support given to the **Austria's Support of the Turks** Turks, the old arch enemies of Christendom, by Catholic Austria. To Austria it is due that the Greek question has remained unsolved to the present day ; that instead of developing its inherent strength the Greek nation is still occupied with the unification of its different tribes, and that the Turkish state, which was hostile to civilisation, and has justified its existence only by means of the bayonets of Anatolian regiments, still exists on sufferance as a foreign body within the political system of Europe. Once again the obstacle to a thorough and comprehensive reform of the political conditions within the Balkan Peninsula was the puerile fear of the power inherent in a self-determining nation, and, in a secondary degree, a desire for the maintenance or extension of influence which might be useful in the peninsula.

The true basis of such influence was not as yet understood. It is not the statesmanship of ambassadors and attachés which gives a nation influence abroad, but its power to assert its will when its interest so demands. National influence rests upon the forces which the state can command, upon the industry of its traders, the value and utility of its products, the creative power of its labour and capital. The Greeks were now confronted with **Greece After its Wars** the difficult task of concentrating their forces, accommodating themselves to a new political system, and making their independence a practical reality ; for this purpose it was necessary to create new administrative machinery, and for this there was an entire dearth of the necessary material. The problem was further complicated by the fact that a desperately contested war had not only unsettled the country, but reduced it almost to desolation. The noblest and the bravest of the nation had fallen upon the battlefields or under the attacks of the Janissaries and Albanians, or had been slaughtered and hurled into the flames of burning towns and villages, after the extortion of their money, the destruction of their property, and the ruin of their prosperity.

The contribution of the European Powers to facilitate the work of reconstruction consisted of a king under age and 2,400,000 pounds at a high rate of interest. Prince Leopold of Coburg, the first candidate for the Greek throne, had unfortunately renounced his project ; he would have proved a capable and benevolent ruler, and would perhaps have adapted himself to the peculiar characteristics of Greek life and thought, with the **Problem of the Greek Throne** eventual result of providing a starting-point for the introduction of more civilised and more modern methods. In consequence of his retirement, the presidency of Capodistrias continued for some time, until the murder of this statesman, who had deserved well of his people, on October 9th, 1831 ; then followed the short reign of his brother Augustine, who did not enjoy the recognition of the constitutional party, the Syntagmatikoi. Ultimately, by working on the vanity of King Lewis of Bavaria, European diplomacy persuaded this monarch to authorise his son Otto, born on June 1st, 1815, to accept the Greek throne. The government was to be carried on by three Bavarian officials until the youth attained his majority. This settlement was brought about by the London "Quadruple Convention" on May 7th, 1832, and is one of the most ill-considered pieces of work ever performed by the statesmen of the old school.

Otto King of Greece

Of the young prince's capacity as a ruler not even his father can have had the smallest idea; yet he was handed over to fate, to sacrifice the best years of his life in a hopeless struggle for power and recognition. The Greeks were fooled with promises impossible of fulfilment, and inspired with mistrust and hatred for their "benefactors." King Otto and his councillors had not the patience to secure through the National Assembly a gradual development of such conditions as would have made constitutional government possible; they would not devote themselves to the task of superintendence, of pacification, of disentangling the various complications, and restraining party action within the bounds of legality.

The Bavarian officials, who might perhaps have done good service in Würzburg or Amberg, were unable to accommodate themselves to their Greek environment; their mistakes aroused a passionate animosity against the Germans, resulting in their complete expulsion from Hellas in 1843. On March 16th, 1844, King Otto was obliged to agree to the introduction of a new constitutional scheme, the advantages of which were hidden to him by the fact that it merely aroused new party struggles and parliamentary discord. Consequently he did not observe this constitution with sufficient conscientiousness to regain the national respect. Disturbances in the East and the Crimean War proved so many additional obstacles to his efforts, which were ended by a revolt in October, 1862, when the Greeks declined to admit their king within the Piræus as he was returning from the Morea, and thus unceremoniously dismissed him from their service. In 1830, Greece was definitively separated from

The Greeks Dismiss Their King

Turkey; and at the same time the insolence of the Dey of Algiers, hitherto under the Ottoman suzerainty, gave the Bourbon monarchy the chance of trying to recover its prestige with the nation by the seizure of Algeria. The piratical activity of the Barbary States was brought to an end. In Turkey also that movement was now beginning, which will be considered later, the literary and political revolution of the Young Turkish party.

The indefatigable Mahmud, however, again resumed his efforts to secure the unity of the empire. But he was forced to give way to his Pasha of Egypt, Mehemet Ali, one of the most important rulers whom the East had produced for a long time. He was born in 1769 at Kavala, in Roumelia, opposite the island of Thasos. He had gone to Egypt in 1800 with some Albanian mercenaries; in the struggle with the French, English, and Mamelukes he had raised himself to supremacy, had conquered the Wahabites, subjugated Arabia and Nubia, and created a highly competent army by means of military reform upon a large scale. When Mahmud II. declined to meet his extensive demands in return for the help he had rendered against the Greeks, Ibrahim, an adopted son of Mehemet, a general of the highest class, invaded Syria in 1831, defeated the Turks on three occasions, conquered Akka, 1832, and advanced to Kiutahia, in Asia Minor, in 1833. Mahmud appealed to Russia for help. Russia forthwith sent 15,000 men to the Bosphorus, whilst the fleets of France and England jealously watched the Dardanelles. Mehemet Ali was obliged to make peace on May 4th, 1833, and was driven back behind the Taurus.

Russian Help for the Turks

The most important result of these events, however, was the recompense which the Sultan was induced to give to the Russians for their help. He had been shown the letters of the French Ambassador, which revealed the intention of the Cabinet of the Tuileries to replace the Ottoman dynasty by that of Mehemet. The result was the convention of Hunkyar-Skalessi, the imperial stairs on the Bosphorus, July 8th, or May 26th, 1833. In this agreement the terrified Sultan made a supplementary promise to close the Dardanelles in future against every Power that was hostile to Russia. When this one-sided convention, concluded in defiance of all international rights, became

THE BOY KING OF GREECE: OTTO I. ENTERING NAUPLIA ON JANUARY 25TH, 1833

Defeating the Turks and regaining their liberty in 1828, the Greeks accepted Otto, the youthful son of King Lewis of Bavaria, as their king in 1832. Only seventeen years of age when he came to the throne, Otto displayed but little capacity for government, and his reign was far from being a success. In 1862 he was compelled to leave Greece.

known, the Western Powers were naturally irritated, and Prince Metternich wittily designated the sultan as " le sublime portier des Dardenelles au service du tsar." The naval Powers withdrew their fleets from the Dardanelles, after entering a protest against this embargo. Meanwhile, the will of the tsar was supreme both in Athens and Stamboul.

Where the Tsar was Supreme Obeying his instructions, Mahmud refused to allow the Austrians to blast the rocks on the Danube at Orsova, or to permit his subjects to make use of the ships of the Austria-Hungarian Lloyd Company, founded in Trieste in 1836 ; notwithstanding this prohibition the company was able to resume with success the old commercial relations of the Venetians with the Levant. The Russian ambassador discountenanced the wishes of the grand vizir and of the seraskier, who applied to the Prussian ambassador, Count Königsmark, with a request for Prussian officers to be sent out, in view of a reorganisation of the army, which was in fact carried out under the advice of Moltke.

In 1837 the first bridge over the Golden Horn was built, between Unkapau and Asabkapusi ; not until 1845 and 1877 was the new bridge constructed which is known as the Valide, after the mother of Abd ul-Mejid. On August 16th, 1838, the British ambassador Ponsonby secured the completion, in the house of Reshid Pasha at Balta-Nin on the Bosphorus, of that treaty respecting trade and customs duties, which has remained the model of all succeeding agreements. By way of recompense the British fleet accompanied the Turkish fleet during all its manœuvres in the Mediterranean, until its secession to Mehemet Ali. War was declared upon him by Sultan Mahmud in May, 1839, when the Druses had revolted against the Syrian authorities in the Hauran. However, the sultan died on July 1st,

Death of Sultan Mahmud before he could receive the news of the total defeat of his army at Nisib on June 24th, and the desertion of his fleet in Alexandria on July 14th. At a later period, after his return to the Sublime Porte, Moltke vindicated the capacity which Hafiz Pasha had shown in face of the lack of discipline prevailing in his army, although the seraskier had treated the suggestions of the Prussian officers with contempt. Ibrahim did not pursue his master's troops,

as his own soldiers were too exhausted to undertake any further movements. Mahmud II. died a martyr to his own ideas and plans ; even his greatest reforms remained in embryo. However, his work lives after him ; he was the founder of a new period for Turkey, as Peter the Great, with whom he liked to be compared, had been for Russia. The difficulty of the political situation, the incapacity of his predecessors, the slavery imposed by the domestic government and court etiquette, were the real source of those obstacles which often caused him such despondency that he sought consolation in drunkenness, to the utter destruction of his powers.

Abd ul-Mejid, 1839–1861, the son of Mahmud, undertook at the age of sixteen the government of a state which would irrevocably have fallen into the power of the Pasha of Egypt had not the ambitious plans of France been thwarted by the conclusion of the Quadruple Alliance on July 15th, 1840, between England, Russia, Austria, and Prussia. The interference of the alliance forced the victorious Pasha Mehemet Ali to evacuate Syria ; after the conclusion of peace he obtained the Island of Thasos,

The Sultan's Gift to the Pasha the cradle of his race, from the sultan, as an appanage of the viceroys of Egypt, in whose possession it still remains. An important advance is denoted by the Hatti-sherif of Gülhane on November 3rd, 1839, which laid down certain principles, on which were to be based further special decrees. The reformation proclaimed as law what had in fact long been customary, the theoretical equality of the subjects of every nation, race, and religion before the law. It must be said that in the execution of this praiseworthy decree certain practical difficulties came to light. Reshid Pasha, the creator of the " hat," was not inspired by any real zeal for reform, but was anxious simply to use it as a means for gaining the favour of the Christian Powers.

As early as 1830, for example, a census had been undertaken, the first throughout the whole Turkish Empire, the results of which were valueless. No official would venture to search the interior of a Moslem house inhabited by women and children. It was, moreover, to the profit of the revenue officials to represent the number of houses and families in their district as lower than it really was, with the object of filling their pockets with the excess. The Porte, unable to secure the obedience of the Syrians by a strong government like the military despotism of Ibrahim, was equally unable to win over the country by justice and good administration, for lack of one necessary condition, an honest official service. It was not to the "hat" of Gülhane of 1856, nor yet to the later Hatti-humayun, that reform was due, but to the European Powers associated to save the crescent. These Powers suggested the only permanent solution by supplying the watchword "A la franca"; and urged the Turks to acquire a completer knowledge of the West, to learn European languages and sciences, to introduce the institutions of the West.

Literature also had to follow this intellectual change. Towards the end of the eighteenth century, a poet endowed with the powers of the ancient East had appeared in Ghalib, and a court poet in the unfortunate Selim III. Heibet ullah Sultana, a sister of the Sultan Mahmud II., and aunt of the reforming Minister Fuad, also secured a measure of popularity. These writers were, however, unable to hinder the decay of old forms, or rather the dawn of a new period, the Turkish "modern age." The study of the languages of Eastern civilisation became neglected in view of the need of the study of the West. The new generation knew more of La Fontaine, Montesquieu, and Victor Hugo than of the Moslem classics. The political need of reform made men ambitious to secure recognition for the drafting of a diplomatic note rather than for the composition of a Kassited, or of a poem with a purpose. In the East as well as in the West mediæval poetry became a lost art. By the Dardanelles Convention, which **Russia's Plans in the Black Sea** was concluded with the Great Powers in London on July 13th, 1841, the Porte consented to keep the Dardanelles and the Bosphorus closed to foreign ships of war in the time of peace. By this act the Turkish Government gave a much desired support to Russian aims at predominance in the Black Sea. In the same year it was necessary to suppress revolts which had broken out in Crete and Bulgaria. In consequence of the incursions of Mehmet

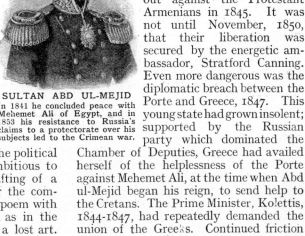

SULTAN ABD UL-MEJID
In 1841 he concluded peace with Mehemet Ali of Egypt, and in 1853 his resistance to Russia's claims to a protectorate over his subjects led to the Crimean war.

Shah into the Arabian Irak, Suleimanieh, Bagdad, Kerbela, and Armenia, a war with Persia was threatened, and the dispute was only composed with difficulty by a peace commission summoned to meet at Erzeroum. Within the Danubian principalities the sovereign rights of the Porte were often in conflict with **Persecution of Protestant Armenians** the protectorate powers of Russia. In Servia, Alexander Karageorgevitch was solemnly appointed bashbeg, or high prince of Servia, by the Porte on November 14th, 1842; Russia, however, succeeded in persuading Alexander voluntarily to abdicate his position, which was not confirmed until 1843 by Russia, after his re-election at Topchider, near Belgrade. The Roman Catholic—uniate—Armenians, who had already endured a cruel persecution in 1828, secured toleration for their independent Church in 1835 and a representative of their own. A similar persecution, supported by Russia from Etshmiadsin, also broke out against the Protestant Armenians in 1845. It was not until November, 1850, that their liberation was secured by the energetic ambassador, Stratford Canning. Even more dangerous was the diplomatic breach between the Porte and Greece, 1847. This young state had grown insolent; supported by the Russian party which dominated the Chamber of Deputies, Greece had availed herself of the helplessness of the Porte against Mehemet Ali, at the time when Abd ul-Mejid began his reign, to send help to the Cretans. The Prime Minister, Kolettis, 1844-1847, had repeatedly demanded the union of the Greeks. Continued friction ended in 1846 with a collision between the Turkish ambassador and the Greek king, with the breaking off of diplomatic relations, and with a revenge taken by the sultan upon his Greek subjects, which might almost have ended in war between Greece and Turkey, England and France. Not until September, 1847, was an understanding between the two neighbours secured, by the intervention of the tsar on the personal appeal of King Otto.

HANS VON ZWIEDINECK-SÜDENHORST
HEINRICH ZIMMERER

THE STATE OF RELIGION IN EUROPE
AND THE PROGRESS OF SOCIAL MOVEMENTS

THE great revolutions which had taken place in the political world since 1789 were not calculated to produce satisfaction either among contemporaries or posterity. Disillusionment and fear of the degeneration of human nature, distrust of the capacity and the value of civic and political institutions, were the legacy from these movements. As men lost faith in political movement as a means of ameliorating the conditions of life or improving morality, so did they yearn for the contentments and the consolations of religion. "Many believe; all would like to believe," said Alexis de Tocqueville of France after the July Revolution. However, the germs of piety, "which, though uncertain in its objects, is powerful enough in its effects," had already sprung to life during the Napoleonic period. Throughout the nineteenth century there is a general yearning for the restoration of true Christian feeling. It was a desire that

Restored Power of the Catholic Church evoked attempts at the formation of religious societies, often of a very extraordinary nature, without attaining any definite object; on the other hand, it opened the possibility of a magnificent development of the power of Catholicism.

The progress of the movement had made it plain that only a Church of this nature can be of vital importance to the history of the world, and that the revival of Christianity can be brought about upon no smaller basis than that which is held by this Church. The force of the movement which resulted in the intensification of papal supremacy enables us to estimate the power of reaction which was bound to occur, though the oppression of this supremacy will in turn become intolerable and the foundations of ultramontanism and of its successes be shattered.

The restoration of power to the Catholic Church was due to the Jesuit Order, which had gradually acquired complete and unlimited influence over the papacy; for this reason the success attained was purely artificial. Jesuitism has no ideals; for it, religion is merely a department of politics. By the creation of a hierarchy within a temporal state it hopes to secure full scope for the beneficent activity of Christian doctrine confined within the trammels of dogma. For this purpose Jesuitism can employ any and every form

The Scheming Policy of the Jesuits of political government. It has no special preference for monarchy, though it simulates such a preference for dynasties which it can use for its own purposes; it is equally ready to accommodate itself to the conditions of republican and parliamentary government. Materialism is no hindrance to the fulfilment of its task, the steady increase of the priestly power; for the grossest materialism is accompanied by the grossest superstition, and this latter is one of its most valuable weapons. While fostering imbecility and insanity, it shares in the hobbies of science, criticism and research. One maiden marked with the stigmata can repair any damage done to society by the well-meaning efforts of a hundred learned fathers.

On August 7th, 1814, Pope Pius VII. issued the encyclical *Sollicitudo omnium*, reconstituting the Society of Jesus, which retained its original constitution and those privileges which it had acquired since its foundation. At the Congress of Vienna Cardinal Consalvi had succeeded in convincing the Catholic and Protestant princes that the Jesuit Order would prove a means of support to the Legitimists, and

Jesuit Order Supported by the Papacy would, in close connection with the papacy, undertake the interests of the royal houses—a device successfully employed even at the present day. This action of the papacy, a step as portentous for the destinies of Europe as any of those taken during the unhappy years of the first Peace of Paris, appeared at first comparatively unimportant. The new world power escaped notice until the highly gifted Dutchman, Johann Philip of Roothaan, took over the direction on July 9th, 1829, and won the Germans over to the Order. The complaisance with which the French and the Italians lent their services for the attainment of specific objects deserves acknowledgment. But even more valuable than their diplomatic astuteness in the struggle against intellectual freedom were the blind unreasoning obedience and the strong arms of Flanders, Westphalia, the Rhine districts and Bavaria. At the outset of the thirties the society possessed, in the persons of numerous young priests, the implements requisite for destroying that harmony of the Churches which was founded upon religious toleration and mutual forbearance. By the same means the struggle against secular governments could be begun, where such powers had not already submitted by concordat to the Curia, as Bavaria had done in 1817.

The struggle raged with special fury in Prussia, though this state, considering its very modest pecuniary resources, had endowed the new-created Catholic bishoprics very handsomely. The Jesuits declined to tolerate a friendly agreement in things spiritual between the Catholics and Protestants in the Rhine territories, to allow the celebration of mixed marriages with the "passive assistance" of the Catholic pastor; they objected to the teaching of George Hermes, professor in the Catholic faculty at the new-created university of Bonn, who propounded to his numerous pupils the doctrine that belief in revelation necessarily implied the exercise of reason, and that the dictates of reason must not therefore be contradicted by dogma.

After the death of the excellent Archbishop Ferdinand of Cologne on August 2nd, 1835, the blind confidence of the government elevated the prebendary Klemens August Freiherr von Droste-Vischering to the Rhenish archbishopric. He had been removed from the general vicariate at Münster as a punishment for his obstinacy. In defiance of his previous promises, the ambiguity of which had passed unnoticed by the Minister Altenstein, the archbishop arbitrarily broke off the agreement concerning mixed marriages

The Defiant Archbishop of Cologne

ARCHBISHOP OF COLOGNE
Archbishop Ferdinand worthily fulfilled the duties of his high office and died on August 2nd, 1835.

arranged by his predecessor. His repeated transgression of his powers and his treatment of the Bonn professors obliged the Prussian Government to pronounce his deposition on November 14th, 1837, and forcibly to remove him from Cologne.

The Curia now protested in no measured terms against Prussia, and displayed a galling contempt for the Prussian ambassador, Bunsen, who had exchanged the profession of archæology for that of diplomacy. Prince Metternich had formerly been ready enough to claim the good services of the Berlin Cabinet whenever he required their support; his instructive diplomatic communications were now withheld, and with some secret satisfaction he observed the humiliation of his ally by Roman statecraft. The embarrassment of the Prussian administration was increased both by the attitude of the Liberals, who, with doctrinaire shortsightedness, disputed the right of the government to arrest the bishop, and by the extension of the Catholic opposition to the ecclesiastical province of Posen-Gnesen, where the insubordination and disloyalty of the archbishop, Martin von Dunin, necessitated the imprisonment of that prelate also. Those ecclesiastical dignitaries who were under Jesuit influence proceeded to persecute such supporters of peace as the prince-bishop of Breslau, Count Leopold of Sedlnitzky, in 1840, employing every form of intercollegiate pressure which the labours of centuries had been able to excogitate. In many cases congregations were ordered to submit to tests of faith, with which they eventually declined compliance.

Disloyal Prelate Punished

A more vigorous, and in its early stages a more promising, resistance arose within the bosom of the Church itself. This movement was aroused by the exhibition in October, 1844, of the "holy coat" in Trèves, a relic supposed to be one of Christ's garments, an imposture which had long before been demonstrated; an additional cause was the disorderly pilgrimage thereto promoted by Bishop Arnoldi. The chaplain, Ronge, characterised the exhibition as a scandal, and denounced

4893

the " idolatrous worship of relics " as one of the causes of the spiritual and political humiliation of Germany. He thereby became the founder of a reform movement, which at once assumed a character serious enough to arouse hopes that the Catholic Church would now undergo the necessary process of purification and

The Ruinous Influence of Jesuitism separation, and would break away from the ruinous influence of Jesuitism. About two hundred " German Catholic " congregations were formed in the year 1845, and a Church council was held at Leipzig from March 23rd to 26th, with the object of finding a common basis for the constitution of the new Church.

However, it proved impossible to arrange a compromise between the insistence upon free thought of the one party and the desire for dogma and ritual manifested by the other. What was wanted was the uniting power of a new idea, brilliant enough to attract the universal gaze and to distract attention from established custom and its separatist consequences. Great and strong characters were wanting, though these were indispensable for the direction and organisation of the different bodies who were attempting to secure their liberation from one of the most powerful tyrants that has ever imposed the scourge of slavery upon an intellectually dormant humanity. As long as each party went its own way, proclaimed its own war-cry to be the only talisman of victory, and adopted new idols as its ensign, so long were they overpowered by the determined persistency of the Society of Jesus.

Within the Protestant Churches also a movement for intellectual independence arose, directed against the suppression of independent judgment, and the subjugation of thought to the decrees of the " Superiors." The movement was based upon the conviction that belief should be

Revelations of Scientific Criticism controlled by the dictates of reason and not by ecclesiastical councils. The Prussian Government limited the new movement to the utmost of its power ; at the same time it was so far successful that the authorities avoided the promulgation of decrees likely to excite disturbance and practised a certain measure of toleration. The revelations made by the scientific criticism of the evangelical school gave a further impulse in this direction, as these

results were utilised by Strauss in his " Life of Jesus," 1835, and his "Christian Dogma, explained in its Historical Development and in Conflict with Modern Science," 1840-1841, works which made an epoch in the literary world, and the importance of which remained undiminished by any measures of ecclesiastical repression.

Among the Romance peoples religious questions were of less importance than among the Germans. In Spain, such questions were treated purely as political matters ; the foundation of a few Protestant congregations by Manuel Matamoros exercised no appreciable influence upon the intellectual development of the Spaniards. The apostacy of the Roman prelate Luigi Desancti to the Waldenses and the appearance of scattered evangelical societies produced no effect upon the position of the Catholic Church in Italy. In France, the liberal tendencies introduced by Lamartine and Victor Hugo remained a literary fashion ; the efforts of Lacordaire and Montalembert to found national freedom upon papal absolutism were nullified by the general direction of Roman policy. There was, however, one phenomenon

Lamennais the Fiery Champion of the Papacy deserving a closer attention —a phenomenon of higher importance than any displayed by the various attempts at religious reform during the nineteenth century, for the reason that its evolution displays the stages which mark the process of liberation from Jesuitism.

Lamennais began his priestly career as the fiery champion of the papacy, to which he ascribed infallibility. He hoped to secure the recognition of its practical supremacy over all Christian governments. Claimed by Leo X. as the " last father of the Church," he furiously opposed the separatism of the French clergy, which was based on the " Gallican articles " ; he attacked the government of Charles X. as being " a horrible despotism," and founded after the July Revolution a Christian-revolutionary periodical, " L'Avenir," with the motto, " Dieu et Liberté—le Pape et le Peuple." By his theory, not only was the Church to be independent of the State ; it was also to be independent of State support, and the clergy were to be maintained by the voluntary offerings of the faithful.

This demand for the separation of Church and State necessarily brought Lamennais into connection with political democracy ;

hence it was but a step to the position that the Church should be reconstructed upon a democratic basis. This fact was patent not only to the French episcopate, but also to Pope Gregory XVI., who condemned the doctrines of the "father of the Church," and, upon his formal submission, interdicted him from issuing any further publications. Lamen-

Religion in England and Scotland nais, like Arnold of Brescia or Girolamo Savonarola in earlier times, now recognised that this papacy was incompetent to fulfil the lofty aims with which he had credited it; he rejected it in his famous "Paroles d'un Croyant" in 1834, and found his way to that form of Christianity which is based upon brotherly love and philanthropy and aims at procuring an equal share for

greatly prized possession was, however, threatened by the system of the Established Church, which forced upon the congregations ministers who were not to their liking; but this was in itself merely incidental to the more important and comprehensive fact that the "establishment" was subject to civil control, and that questions affecting it might be carried for decision to a court which was Scottish only in the sense that it contained a Scottish element—the House of Peers.

The view rapidly gained ground that in matters regarded as spiritual the Church ought to be subject to no authority save its own; in other words, that it ought to be free from state control. But that view was not general, nor was the state prepared to recognise it. It only remained,

| Newman | Keble | Pusey |

LEADERS OF THE TRACTARIAN MOVEMENT

Inspired by the desire to "awaken into new life a Church which was becoming torpid by a revival of mediæval ideals and mediæval devotion," and with the aim of counteracting the "danger to religion arising from a sceptical criticism," the Tractarian movement in England had as its most notable champions Newman, Keble, and Pusey. Their teachings were in many quarters regarded as nothing but barely veiled "Popery," a view that was strengthened when Cardinal Newman went over to the Church of Rome, whither he was followed by many of his disciples.

men in the enjoyment of this world's goods. But in England and in Scotland there was considerable ferment on religious questions during the 'thirties and 'forties. German rationalism indeed would hardly have been permitted to obtain a foothold in either country; when respectability was at its zenith, German rationalism was not regarded as respectable. In Scotland the crucial question was not one of theology, but of Church government; in that country the national system of education combined with the national combativeness of character to make every cottar prepared to support his own religious tenets with a surprising wealth of scriptural erudition; and "spiritual independence" was fervently cherished. That

therefore, for the protesting portion of the community to sever itself from the state by departing from the Establishment and sacrificing its share in the endowments and privileges thereto pertaining. In the great Disruption of 1843 hundreds of ministers resigned their manses and churches rather than their principles; and the Free Church took its place side by side with the Established Church as a self-supporting religious body, although in point of doctrine there was no distinction between the two communities, which were both alike Calvinist in theology and Presbyterian in system.

The Tractarian movement in England was of a different type. On the one side, it was inspired by the desire to awaken into new life a Church which was becoming torpid, by a revival of mediæval ideals and mediæval devotion, to be attained through insistence on mystical doctrines, on the apostolic character of the priesthood, on the authority of the fathers of the Church as against the miscellaneous unauthorised and ignorant interpretations of the Scriptures, and on the historic and aesthetic attractions of elaborate ceremonial. On another side it sought especially to counteract the danger to religion arising from a sceptical criticism, and from the attacks of the scientific spirit which declined to regard convictions adopted on authority as being knowledge.

THE SOCIAL REFORMERS OWEN AND FOURIER

In the large spinning-works at New Lanark in Scotland, of which he was manager, Robert Owen put into practice his socialistic theories, but his experiment was not permanently successful. Equally futile and unsatisfactory was Charles Fourier's project of the "Phalanstère," a new social community having all things in common.

The "Tracts for the Times," from which the movement took its name, the teaching of John Henry Newman, of Keble, and of Pusey, who were its most notable champions, alarmed the popular Protestantism —the more when Newman himself went over to the Church of Rome, whither he was followed by many of his disciples ; and "Puseyism" was commonly regarded as nothing but barely veiled "Popery." Newman would have had many more imitators if the greatest of his colleagues had not maintained their view that the doctrines of "The Church" are those of the Anglican Church, and refused to sever themselves from her. They remained, and it will probably be admitted that while their movement inspired the clerical body --not only their adherents, but their opponents also—to a renewed activity at the time, it had the further effect ultimately, though not till after a considerable lapse of time, of attaching to itself a majority of the most energetic and the most intellectual of the clergy.

That Christian socialism to which Lamennais had been led by reason and experience was a by-product of the numerous attempts to settle the pressing question of social reform, attempts begun simultaneously in France and England,

and resulting in a movement which soon affected every nation. The great revolution had accomplished nothing in this direction. The sum total of achievement hitherto was represented by certain dismal experiences of "State help" in the distribution of bread and the subsidising of bakers. The phrase inscribed in the "Cahiers" of the deputies of the Third Estate in 1789 had now been realised in fact : "The voice of freedom has no message for the heart of the poor who die of hunger." Babeuf, the only French democrat who professed communistic views, was not understood by the masses, and his martyrdom, one of the most unnecessary political murders of the Directory, had aroused no movement among those for whom it was undergone.

The general introduction of machinery in many manufactures, together with the more distant relations subsisting between employer and workman, had resulted in an astounding increase of misery among the journeymen labourers. The working classes, condemned to hopeless poverty and want, and threatened with the deprivation of the very necessaries of existence, broke into riot and insurrection ; factories were repeatedly destroyed in **Factory Riots in England** England at the beginning of the century ; the silk weavers of Lyons in 1831 and the weavers of Silesia in 1844 rose against their masters. These facts aroused the consideration of the means by which the appalling miseries of a fate wholly undeserved could be obviated.

Among the wild theories and fantastic aberrations of Saint-Simon were to be found many ideas well worth consideration which could not fail to act as a stimulus to further thought. The pamphlet of 1814, "Réorganisation de la Société Européenne," had received no consideration from the Congress of Vienna, for it maintained that congresses were not the proper instrument for the permanent restoration of social peace and order. It was, however, plainly obvious that even after the much-vaunted "Restoration" the lines of social cleavage had rapidly widened and that the majority were oppressed with crying injustice.

Not wholly in vain did Saint-Simon repeatedly appeal to manufacturers, industrial potentates, business men, and financiers, with warnings against the prevailing sweating system; not in vain did he assert in his "Nouveau Christianisme," 1825, that every Church in existence had stultified its Christianity by suppressing the loftiest teaching of Christ, the doctrine of brotherly love. No immediate influence was exerted upon the social development of Europe by Barthélemy Prosper Constantin's proposals for the emancipation of the flesh, and for the foundation of a new "theocratic-industrial state," or by Charles Fourier's project of the "Phalanstère," a new social community having all things in common, or by the Utopian dreams of communism expounded by Etienne Cabet in his "Voyage en Icarie." Such theorising merely cleared the way for more far-seeing thinkers, who, from their knowledge of existing institutions, could demonstrate their capacity of transformation.

In Britain, Robert Owen, the manager of the great spinning-works at New Lanark, in Scotland, was the first to attempt the practical realisation of a philosophical social system. Owen's theories may be pronounced a definite advance, as demonstrating that capitalism as a basis of economics was not founded upon any law of Nature, but must be considered as the result of an historical development, and that competition is not an indispensable stimulus to production, but is an obstacle to the true utilisation of labour. The facts thus ascertained were worked into a socialist system by the efforts of a German Jew, Karl Marx, born in 1818 at Trèves, a man fully equipped with Hegelian criticism, and possessed by an extraordinary yearning to discover the causes which had brought existing conditions of life to pass, a characteristic due, according to Werner Sombart, to "hypertrophy of intellectual energy."

He freed the social movement from the revolutionary spirit which had been its leading characteristic hitherto. He placed one definite object before the movement, the "nationalisation of means of production," the method of attaining this end being a vigorous class struggle. Expelled from German soil by the Prussian police, he was forced to take up residence in Paris, and afterwards in London. There he gained an accurate knowledge of the social conditions of Western Europe, devoting special attention to the important developments of the English trades-union struggles, and thus became specially qualified as the founder and guide of an international organisation of the proletariat, an indispensable condition of victory in the class struggle he had proclaimed. In collaboration with Friedrich Engel of Elberfeld he created the doctrine of socialism, which remained the basis of the socialist movement to the end of the nineteenth century. That movement chiefly centred in Germany, after Ferdinand Lassalle had assured its triumph in the sixties. The social movement exerted but little political influence upon the events arising out of the July Revolution; its influence, again, upon the revolutions of the year 1848 was almost inappreciable. It became, however, a modifying factor among the democratic parties, who were looking to political revolution for some transformation of existing public rights, and for some alteration of the proprietary system in their favour.

Marx   **Lassalle**
PIONEERS OF SOCIAL DEMOCRACY
The founder and guide of an international organisation of the proletariat, Karl Marx, a German Jew, freed the social movement from its revolutionary spirit and placed before it the definite object of nationalisation of means of production. Ferdinand Lassalle was also a prominent worker in the cause of social democracy in Germany.

THE SPREAD OF LIBERALISM
AND THE COLLAPSE OF METTERNICH'S SYSTEM

THE lack of initiative displayed by the King of Prussia was a valuable help to Metternich in carrying out his independent policy. The old chancellor in Vienna had become ever more profoundly impressed with the insane idea that Providence had specially deputed him to crush revolutions,

The Zenith of Metternich's Influence to support the sacred thrones of Europe, Turkey included, and that he was the discoverer of a political system by which alone civilisation, morality, and religion could be secured. The great achievement of his better years was one never to be forgotten by Germany—the conversion of Austria to the alliance formed against the great Napoleon, and the alienation of the Emperor Francis from the son-in-law whose power was almost invincible when united with that of the Hapsburg emperor. At that time, however, Metternich was not the slave of a system; his action was the expression of his will, and he relied upon an accurate judgment of the personalities he employed, and an accurate estimation of the forces at his disposal.

As he grew old his self-conceit and an exaggerated estimate of his own powers led him blindly to follow those principles which had apparently determined his earlier policy in every political question which arose during the European supremacy which he was able to claim for a full decade after the Vienna Congress. His belief in the system—a belief of deep import to the destinies

The Tsar a Convert of Metternich of Austria — was materially strengthened by the fact that Alexander I., who had long been an opponent of the system, came over to its support before his death and recognised it as the principle of the Holy Alliance. The consequence was a degeneration of the qualities which Metternich had formerly developed in himself. His clear appreciation of the situation and of the main interests of Europe in the summer of 1813 had raised Austria to the most favourable position which she had occupied for centuries. Her decision determined the fate of Europe, and so she acquired power as great as it was unexpected.

This predominance was the work of Metternich, and so long as it endured the prince was able to maintain his influence. He, however, ascribed that influence to the superiority of his own intellect and to his incomparable system, neglecting the task of consolidating and securing the power already gained. Those acquisitions of territory which Metternich had obliged Austria to make were a source of mischief and weakness from the very outset. The Lombard-Venetian kingdom implied no increase of power, and its administration involved a constant drain of money and troops. The troops, again, which were drawn from an unwarlike

Death of the Emperor Francis I. population, proved unreliable. The possession itself necessitated interference in Italian affairs, and became a constant source of embarrassment and of useless expense. Valuable possessions, moreover, in South Germany already in the hands of the nation were abandoned out of consideration for this kingdom, and acquisitions likely to become highly profitable were declined. Within the kingdom a state of utter supineness prevailed in spite of the supervision bestowed upon it, and the incompetence of the administration condemned the state and its great natural advantages to impotence.

Far from producing any improvement, the death of the Emperor Francis I., on March 1st, 1835, caused a marked deterioration in the condition of the country. The Archdukes Charles and John were unable to override the supremacy of Metternich. As hitherto, they were unable to exercise any influence upon the government, which the ill-health and vacillation of Ferdinand I., the successor, had practically reduced to a regency. Franz Anton, Count of Kolowrat-Liebsteinsky, attempted to breathe some life into the Council of State, but his efforts were thwarted by Metternich, who feared the forfeiture of his own power.

The Tsar Nicholas upon his visit to Töplitz and Vienna, in 1835, had remarked that Austria was no longer capable of guaranteeing a successful policy, and that her "system" could not be maintained in practice, remarks which had done no good. It was impossible to convince Metternich that the source of this weakness lay in himself and his determination to repress the very forces which should have been developed. The Archduke Lewis, the emperor's youngest uncle and a member of the State Conference, was averse to any innovation, and therefore inclined to uphold that convenient system which laid down the maintenance of existing institutions as the first principle of statesmanship.

Within Austria herself, however, the state of affairs had become intolerable. The government had so far decayed as to be incapable of putting forth that energy, the absence of which the Tsar had observed. The exchequer accounts betrayed an annual deficit of thirty million gulden, and the government was forced to claim the good offices of the class representatives, and, what was of capital importance, to summon the Hungarian Reichstag on different occasions. In that assembly the slumbering national life had been aroused to consciousness, and proceeded to supply the deficiencies of the government by acting in its own behalf. Count Széchényi gave an impetus to science and art and to other movements generally beneficial. Louis Kossuth, Franz Pulszky, and Franz Deák espoused the cause of constitutional reform.

Austria Roused to Action

A flood of political pamphlets published abroad, chiefly in Germany, exposed in full detail the misgovernment prevailing in Austria and the Crown territories. European attention was attracted to the instability of the conditions obtaining there, which seemed to betoken either the downfall of the state or a great popular rising. Austria's prestige among the other Great Powers had suffered a heavy blow by the Peace of Adrianople, and now sank yet lower. Metternich was forced to behold the growth of events, and the accomplishment of deeds utterly incompatible with the fundamental principles of conservative statesmanship as laid down by the Congresses of Vienna, Carlsbad, Troppau, Laibach, and Verona.

The July Revolution and the triumph of liberalism in England under William IV. caused the downfall of Dom Miguel, "king" of Portugal, who had been induced by conservative diplomacy to abolish the constitutional measures introduced by his brother, Dom Pedro of Brazil. To this policy he devoted himself, to his own complete satisfaction. The revolts which broke out against him were ruthlessly suppressed, and thousands of Liberals were imprisoned, banished, or brought to the scaffold. Presuming upon his success and relying upon the favour of the Austrian court, he carried his aggrandisements so far as to oblige Britain and France to use force and to support the cause of Pedro, who had abdicated the throne of Brazil in favour of his son, Dom Pedro II., then six years of age, and was now asserting his claims to Portugal.

Stirring Times in Portugal

Pedro I. adhered to the constitutionalism which he had recognised over-seas as well as in Portugal, thus securing the support not only of all Portuguese Liberals, but also of European opinion, which had been aroused by the bloodthirsty tyranny of Miguel. The help of the British admiral, Charles Napier, who annihilated the Portuguese fleet at Cape San Vincent on July 5th, 1833, enabled Pedro to gain a decisive victory over Miguel, which the latter's allies among the French legitimists were unable to avert, though they hurried to his aid. His military and political confederate, Don Carlos of Spain, was equally powerless to help him.

In Spain, also, the struggle broke out between liberalism and the despotism which was supported by an uneducated and degenerate priesthood, and enjoyed the favour of the Great Powers of Eastern Europe. The conflagration began upon the death of King Ferdinand VII., on September 29th, 1833, the material cause being a dispute about the hereditary right to the throne resulting from the introduction of a new order of succession. The decree of 1713 had limited the succession to heirs in the male line ; but the Pragmatic Sanction of March 29th, 1830, transferred the right to the king's daughters,

Spain's Degenerate Priesthood

Isabella and Louise, by his marriage with Maria Christina of Naples. Don Carlos declined to recognise this arrangement, and on his brother's death attempted to secure his own recognition as king.

After the overthrow of Dom Miguel and his consequent retirement from Portugal, Don Carlos entered Spain in **Rebel Movement in Spain** person with his adherents, who were chiefly composed of the Basques fighting for their special rights, " fueros," and the populations of Catalonia and Old Castile, who were under clerical influence. The Liberals gathered round the queen regent, Maria Christina, whose cause was adroitly and successfully upheld by the Minister, Martinez de la Rosa. The forces at the disposal of the government were utterly inadequate, and their fleet and army were in so impoverished a condition that they could make no head against the rebel movement. Under the leadership of Thomas Zumala-Carregui the Carlists won victory after victory, and would probably have secured possession of the capital had not the Basque general received a mortal wound before Bilbao.

Even then the victory of the "Cristinos" was by no means secure. The Radicals had seceded from the Liberals upon the question of the reintroduction of the constitution of 1812. The revolution of La Granja gave the Radicals complete influence over the queen regent ; they obliged her to accept their own nominees, the Ministry of Calatrava, and to recognise the democratic constitution of June 8th, 1837. Their power was overthrown by Don Baldomero Espartero, who commanded the queen's troops in the Basque provinces. After a series of successful movements he forced the Basque general, Maroto, to conclude the capitulation of Vergara on August 29th, 1839. The party of Don Carlos had lost greatly both in numbers and strength, owing to the care- **Queen Regent Forced to Abdicate** lessness and pettifogging spirit of the pretender and the dissensions and domineering spirit of his immediate adherents, who seemed the very incarnation of all the legitimist foolishness in Europe. When Carlos abandoned the country on September 15th, 1839, General Cabrera continued fighting in his behalf; however, he also retired to French territory in July, 1840. The queen regent had lost all claims to respect by her intrigues with one of

her body-guard, and was forced to abdicate on October 12th. Espartero, who had been made Duke of Vittoria, was then entrusted by the Cortes with the regency.

The extreme progressive party, the Exaltados, failed to support him, although he had attempted to fall in with their views. They joined the Moderados, or moderate party, with the object of bringing about his fall. Queen Isabella was then declared of age, and ascended the throne. Under the Ministry of Don Ramon Maria Narvaez, Duke of Valencia, the constitution was changed in 1837 to meet the wishes of the Moderados, and constitutional government in Spain was thus abolished. Though his tenure of office was repeatedly interrupted, Narvaez succeeded in maintaining peace and order in Spain, even during the years of revolution, 1848–1849.

The moral support of the Great Powers and the invasion of the French army under the Duke of Angoulême had been powerless to check the arbitrary action of the Bourbons and clergy in Spain. No less transitory was the effect of the Austrian victories in Italy ; the Italian **Italy's National Disgrace** people had now risen to full consciousness of the disgrace implied in the burden of a foreign yoke. The burden, indeed, had been lighter under Napoleon and his representatives than under the Austrians. The governments of Murat and Eugène had been careful to preserve at least a show of national feeling ; their military power was drawn from the country itself, and consisted of Italian regiments officered with French, or with Italians who had served in French regiments. The French had been highly successful in their efforts to accommodate themselves to Italian manners and customs, and were largely helped by their common origin as Romance peoples. The Germans, on the other hand, with the Czechs, Magyars, and Croatians, who formed the sole support of the Austrian supremacy in the Lombard-Venetian kingdom, knew but one mode of intercourse with the Italians—that of master and servant ; any feeling of mutual respect or attempt at mutual accommodation was impossible.

A small number of better-educated Austrian officers and of better-class individuals in the rank and file, who were preferably composed of Slav regiments, found it to their advantage to maintain good relations with the native population ;

but the domineering and occasionally brutal behaviour of the troops as a whole was not calculated to conciliate the Italians. The very difference of their uniforms from all styles previously known served to emphasise the foreign origin of these armed strangers. Ineradicable was the impression made by their language, which incessantly outraged the delicate Italian ear and its love of harmony.

Of any exchange of commodities, of any trade worth mentioning between the Italian provinces and the Austrian Crown lands, there was not a trace. The newly acquired land received nothing from its masters but their money. Italian consumption was confined to the limits of the national area of production; day by day it became clearer that Italy had nothing whatever in common with Austria, and was without inclination to enter into economic or intellectual relations with her. The sense of nationalism was strengthened by a growing irritation against the foreign rule; this feeling penetrated every class, and inspired the intellectual life and the national literature.

Vittorio Alfieri, the contemporary of Napoleon, was roused against the French yoke by the movement for liberation. His successors, Ugo Foscolo, Silvio Pellico, Giacomo Leopardi, created a purely nationalist enthusiasm. Their works gave passionate expression to the deep-rooted force of the desire for independence and for equality with other free peoples, to the shame felt by an oppressed nation, which was groaning under a yoke unworthy of so brilliantly gifted a people, and could not tear itself free. Every educated man felt and wept with them, and was touched with the purest sympathy for the unfortunate **Priests' Good Work for Italy** victims of policy, for the conspirators who were languishing in the Austrian fortresses. Highly valuable to the importance of the movement was the share taken by the priests, who zealously devoted themselves to the work of rousing the national spirit, and promised the support and practical help of the Catholic Church for the realisation of these ideals. It was Vincenzo Gioberti who first demonstrated

CHARLES ALBERT
Succeeding his father as King of Sardinia, he pursued a policy of moderation; but declaring war against Austria in 1848, in the following year he abdicated the throne.

to the papacy its duty of founding the unity of the Italian nation. Mastai Ferretti, Bishop of Imola, now Pope Pius IX., the successor of Gregory XVI., who died June 1st, 1846, was in full sympathy with these views. To the Italians he was already known as a zealous **Austria Disappointed in the Papacy** patriot, and his intentions were yet more definitely announced by the decree of amnesty issued July 17th, 1846, recalling 4,000 political exiles to the Church states. Conservative statesmen in general, and the Austrian Government in particular, had granted the Catholic Church high privileges within the state, and had looked to her for vigorous support in their suppression of all movement towards freedom. What more mortifying situation for them than the state of war now subsisting between Austria and papal Italy! The Cabinet of Vienna was compelled to despatch reinforcements for service against the citizen guards which Pius IX. had called into existence in his towns, and therefore in Ferrara, which was in the occupation of Austrian troops.

When Christ's vicegerent upon earth took part in the revolt against the "legitimist" power, no surprise need be felt at the action of that repentant sinner, Charles Albert of Sardinia. Formerly involved with the Carbonari, he had grown sceptical upon the advantages of liberalism after the sad experiences of 1821. He now renounced that goodwill for Austria which he had hypocritically simulated since the beginning of his reign in 1831.

Turin had also become a centre of revolutionary intrigue. Opinion in that town pointed to Sardinia and its military strength as a better nucleus than the incapable papal government for a nation resolved to enter upon a war of liberation. Count Camillo Benso di Cavour, born August 10th, 1810, the editor of the journal "Il Risorgimento," strongly recommended the investment of Charles Albert and his army with the military guidance of the revolt. The Milan nobility were influenced by the court of Turin, as were the more youthful nationalists and the numerous secret societies which the July Revolution had brought into existence throughout Italy, by Giuseppe Mazzini, one of the most highly gifted and most dangerous leaders of the democratic party in Europe.

Austria was therefore obliged to make preparations for defending her Italian possessions by force of arms. The administration as conducted by

Austria Preparing for War

the amiable Archduke Rainer was without power or influence. On the other hand, Count Radetzky had been at the head of the Austrian forces in the Lombard-Venetian kingdom since 1831. He was one of the first strategists of Europe, and no less distinguished for his powers of organisation ; in short, he fully deserved the high confidence which the court and the whole army reposed in him. He was more than eighty years of age, for he had been born on November 4th, 1766, and had been present at the deliberations of the allies upon their movements in 1813 ; yet the time was drawing near when this aged general was to be the mainstay of the Austrian body politic, and the immutable corner-stone of that tottering structure.

A very appreciable danger menacing the progress of nations toward self-government had arisen within the Swiss Confederation, where the Jesuit Order had obtained much influence upon the government in several cantons. By the constitution of 1815 the federal members had acquired a considerable measure of independence, sufficient to permit the adoption of wholly discordant policies by the different governments. The Jesuits aimed at the revival of denominational institutions to be employed for far-reaching political objects, a movement which increased the difficulty of maintaining peace between the Catholic and the reformed congregations. Toleration in this matter was provided by the constitution, but its continuance

The Jesuits in the Swiss Confederation

naturally depended upon the abstention of either party from attempts at encroachment upon the territory of the other. In 1833 an unsuccessful attempt had been made to reform the principles of the federation and to introduce a uniform legal code and system of elementary education. The political movement then spread throughout the cantons, where the most manifold party subdivisions, ranging from conservative ultramontanists to

radical revolutionaries, were struggling for majorities and predominance. In Aargau a peasant revolt led by the monks against the liberal government was defeated, and the Church property was sold in 1841, while in Zürich the Conservatives were uppermost, and prevented the appointment of David Frederic Strauss to a professorship at the university.

In Lucerne the ultramontanists stretched their power to most inconsiderate extremes, calling in the Jesuits, who had established themselves in Freiburg, Schwyz, and Wallis, and placing the educational system in their care, October 24th, 1844. Two democratic assaults upon the government were unsuccessful, December 8th, 1844, and March 30th, 1845, but served to increase the excitement in the neighbouring cantons, where thousands of fugitives were nursing their hatred against the ultramontanes, who were led by the energetic peasant Peter Leu. The murder of Leu intensified the existing ill-feeling and ultimately led to the formation of a separate confederacy, composed of the cantons of Lucerne, Schwyz, Uri, Unterwalden, Zug, Freiburg,

Switzerland's Cantons of Refuge

and Wallis, the policy being under Jesuit control. This Catholic federation raised great hopes among conservative diplomatists. Could it be strengthened, it would probably become a permanent counterpoise to the liberal cantons, which had hitherto been a highly objectionable place of refuge to those peace-breakers who were hunted by the police of the Great Powers. At the Federal Assembly the liberal cantons were in the majority, and voted on July 20th, 1847, for the dissolution of the separate federation, and on September 3rd for the expulsion of the Jesuits from the area of the new federation.

At Metternich's proposal, the Great Powers demanded the appointment of a congress to deal with the situation. However, the diet, distrusting foreign interference, and with good reason, declined to accede to these demands, and proceeded to put the federal decision into execution against the disobedient cantons. Thanks to the careful forethought of the commander-in-chief, William Henry Dufour, the famous cartographer, who raised the federal military school at Thun to high distinction, and also to the rapidity with which the overwhelming numbers of the federal troops, 30,000 men, were mobilised, the " Sonderbund war" was speedily brought to a close without bloodshed. Austrian help proved unavailing, and the cantons were eventually reduced to a state of impotence.

The new federal constitution of September 12th, 1848, then met with unanimous acceptance. The central power, which was considerably strengthened, now decided the foreign policy of the country, peace and war, and the conclusion of treaties, controlling also the coinage, and the postal and customs organisation, and maintaining the cantonal constitutions. The theories upon the nature of the Federal State propounded by the jurist professor, Dr. Johann Kaspar Bluntschli, were examined and adopted with advantageous results by the radical-liberal party, which possessed a majority in the constitutional diet.

Bluntschli had himself espoused the conservative-liberal cause after the war of the separate federation, which he had vainly tried to prevent. Forced to retire from the public life of his native town, he transferred his professional activities to Munich and Heidelberg. The developments of his political philosophy were not **Metternich's** without their influence upon **Lack** those fundamental principles **of Courage** which have given its special political character to the constitution of the North German Federation and of the modern German Empire. The Swiss Confederation provided a working example of the unification of special administrative forms, of special governmental rights, and of a legislature limited in respect of its sphere of action, in conjunction with a uniform system of conducting foreign policy. Only such a government can prefer an unchallenged claim to represent the state as a whole and to comprehend its different forces.

Metternich and the King of Prussia were neither of them courageous enough to support the exponents of their own principles in Switzerland. Prussia had a special inducement to such action in the fact of her sovereignty over the principality of Neuenburg, which had been occupied by the Liberals in connection with the movement against the separate federation, and had been received into the confederation as an independent canton. In the aristocracy and upper classes of the population Frederic William IV. had many faithful and devoted adherents, but he failed to seize so favourable an opportunity of defending his indisputable rights by occu-

pying his principality with a sufficient force of Prussian troops. His vacillation in the Neuenburg question was of a piece with the general uneasiness of his temper, which had begun with the rejection of his draft of a constitution for Prussia and the demands of the representatives of the estates for the institution of some form of **Vacillating** constitution more honourable **King** and in consonance with the **of Prussia** rights of the people. But rarely have the preparations for imperial constitution been so thoroughly made or so protracted as they were in Prussia.

From the date of his accession the king had been occupied without cessation upon this question. The expert opinion of every adviser worth trusting was called in, and from 1844 commission meetings and negotiations continued uninterruptedly. The proposals submitted to the king emanated, in full accordance with conservative spirit, from the estates as constituted; they provided for the retention of such estates as were competent, and for the extension of their representation and sphere of action in conjunction with the citizen class; but this would not satisfy Frederic William.

The constitution drafted in 1842 by the Minister of the Interior, Count Arnim, was rejected by the king in consequence of the clauses providing for the legal and regular convocation of the constitutional estates. The king absolutely declined to recognise any rights appertaining to the subject as against the majesty of the ruler; he was therefore by no means inclined to make such rights a leading principle of the constitution. By the favour of the ruler, exerted by him in virtue of his divine right, the representatives of the original constitutional estates might from time to time receive a summons to tender their advice upon questions of public interest. As the people had every confidence in the wisdom and con- **Frederic** scientiousness of their ruler, **William &** agreements providing for their **His People** co-operation were wholly superfluous. "No power on earth," he announced in his speech from the throne on April 11th, 1847, " would ever induce him to substitute a contractual form of constitution for those natural relations between king and people, which were strong, above all in Prussia, by reason of their inherent reality. Never under any circumstances would he allow a written paper, a kind of second providence, governing by paragraphs and ousting the old sacred faith, to intervene between God and his country."

Such was the residuum of all the discussion upon the Christian state and the " hierarchical feudal monarchy of the Middle Ages," which had been the work of

The Prussian King a Victim of Delusion the Swiss Lewis von Haller and his successors, the Berlin author Adam Müller, the Halle professor Hienrich Leo, and Frederic Julius Stahl, a Jew converted to Protestantism, whom Frederic William IV. had summoned from Erlangen to Berlin in 1840. By a wilful abuse of history the wild conceptions of these theorists were explained to be the proven facts of the feudal period and of feudal society. Constitutional systems were propounded as actual historical precedents which had never existed anywhere at any time.

The object of these efforts as declared by Stahl was the subjection of reason to revelation, the reintroduction of the Jewish theocracy into modern political life. Frederic William had allowed himself to be convinced that such was the Germanic theory of existence, and that he was forwarding the national movement by making his object the application of this theory to the government and administration of his state. He was a victim of the delusion that the source of national strength is to be found in the admiration of the intangible precedents of past ages, whereas the truth is that national strength must at every moment be employed to cope with fresh tasks, unknown to tradition and unprecedented. Notwithstanding the emphatic protest of the heir presumptive to the throne, Prince William of Prussia, to the Ministry, at the head of which was Ernest von Bodelschwingh, and though no single Minister gave an unqualified assent to the project, the king summoned the eight provincial Landtags to meet at Berlin

Meeting of the United Landtag as a united Landtag for April 11th, 1847. Even before the opening of the assembly it became manifest that this constitutional concession, which the king considered a brilliant discovery, pleased nobody. The old Orders, which retained their previous rights, were as dissatisfied as the citizens outside the Orders, who wanted a share in the legislature and administration. The speech from the throne, a long-winded piece of conventional oratory, was marked

in part by a distinctly uncompromising tone. Instead of returning thanks for the concessions which had been made, the Landtag proceeded to draw up an address demanding the recognition of their rights.

The wording of the address was extremely moderate in tone, and so far mollified the king as to induce him to promise the convocation of another Landtag within the next four years ; but further negotiations made it plain that both the representatives of the nobility and the city deputies, especially those from the industrial Rhine towns, were entirely convinced that the Landtag must persevere in demanding further constitutional concessions.

The value to the state of the citizen class was emphasised by Vincke of Westphalia, Beckerath of Krefeld, Camphausen of Cologne, and Hansemann of Aix-la-Chapelle. These were capitalists and employers of labour, and had therefore every right to speak. They were at the head of a majority which declined to assent to the formation of an annuity bank for relieving the peasants of forced labour, and to the proposal for a railway from Berlin to

Dissension in the Landtag Königsberg, the ground of refusal being that their assent was not recognised by the Crown Ministers as necessary for the ratification of the royal proposals, but was regarded merely as advice requested by the government on its own initiative.

The Landtag was then requested to proceed with the election of a committee to deal with the national debt. Such a committee would have been superfluous if financial authority had been vested in a Landtag meeting at regular intervals, and on this question the liberal majority split asunder. The party of Vincke-Hansemann declined to vote, the party of Camphausen-Beckerath voted under protest against this encroachment upon the rights of the Landtag, while the remainder, 284 timorous Liberals and Conservatives, voted unconditionally.

The conviction was thus forced upon Liberal Germany that the King of Prussia would not voluntarily concede any measure of constitutional reform, for the reason that he was resolved not to recognise the rights of the people. Prussia was not as yet capable of mastering that popular upheaval, the beginnings of which could be felt, and using its strength for the creation of a German Constitution to take the place of the incompetent and discredited Federation.

HANS VON ZWIEDINECK-SÜDENHORST

EUROPE in REVOLUTION

THE FALL OF LOUIS PHILIPPE
AND ITS EFFECTS THROUGHOUT EUROPE

THE monarchy of Louis Philippe of Orleans had become intolerable by reason of its dishonesty. The French cannot be blamed for considering the Orleans rulers as Bourbons in disguise. This scion of the old royal family was not a flourishing offshoot ; rather was it an excrescence, with all the family failings and with none of its nobler qualities. Enthusiasm for such prudential, calculating, and unimpassioned rulers was impossible, whatever their education or their claims. Their bad taste and parsimony destroyed their credit as princes in France, and elsewhere their position was acknowledged rather out of politeness than from any sense of respect.

The "citizen-king" certainly made every effort to make his government popular and national. He showed both jealousy for French interests and gratitude to the Liberals who had placed him on the throne ; he sent troops unsparingly to save the honour of France in Algiers. After seven years' warfare a completion was made of the conquest, which the French regarded as an extension of their power. The bold Bedouin sheikh, Abd el Kader, whose career has been described elsewhere, was forced to surrender to La-moricière on December 22nd, 1847. Louis

The Bedouin Prisoner of Louis Philippe Philippe imprisoned this noble son of the desert in France, although his son Henry, Duke of Aumâle, had promised, as Governor-general of Algiers, that he should have his choice of residence on Mohammedan territory. The king also despatched his son, the Duc de Joinville, to take part in the war against Morocco, and gave him a naval position of equal

importance to that which Aumâle held in the army. He swallowed the insults of Lord Palmerston in order to maintain the " entente cordiale " among the Western Powers. He calmly accepted the defeat of his diplomacy in the Turco-Egyptian

Honour to the dead Napoleon quarrel, and surrendered such influence as he had acquired with Mehemet Ali in return for paramountcy in the Marquesas Islands and Tahiti. He married his son Anton, Duke of Montpensier, to the Infanta Louise of Spain, with some idea of reviving the dynastic connection between France and Spain.

While thus resuming the policy of Louis XIV., he was also at some pains to conciliate the Bonapartists, and by careful respect to the memory of Napoleon to give his government a national character. The remains of the great emperor were removed from St. Helena by permission of Britain and interred with great solemnity in the Church of the Invalides on December 15th, 1840. Louis Bonaparte, the nephew, had contrived to avoid capture by the Austrians at Ancona, and had proposed to seize his inheritance ; twice he appeared within the French frontiers, at Strassburg on October 30th, 1836, and at Boulogne on August 6th, 1840, in readiness to ascend the throne of France.

He only succeeded in making himself ridiculous, and eventually paid for his temerity by imprisonment in the fortress of Ham. There he remained, condemned to occupy himself with writing articles upon the solution of the social question, the proposed Nicaraguan canal, etc., until his faithful follower, Dr. Conneau, smuggled him into England under the name of Maurer Badinguet. Thus far the reign of Louis Philippe had been fairly successful; but the French were growing weary of it. They were not entirely without sympathy for the family to which they had given the throne, and showed some interest in the princes, who were usually to be found wherever any small success might be achieved. The public sorrow was unfeigned at the death of the eldest prince, Louis, Duke of Orleans, who was killed by a fall from a carriage on July

QUEEN OF THE FRENCH
The daughter of Ferdinand I., King of Naples and later of the Two Sicilies, Marie Amelie was married to Louis Philippe in the year 1809.

13th, 1842. These facts, however, did not produce any closer ties between the dynasty and the nation. Parliamentary life was restless and Ministries were constantly changing. Majorities in the Chambers were secured by artificial means, and by bribery in its most reprehensible forms. Conspiracies were discovered and suppressed, and plots for murder were made the occasion of the harshest measures against the Radicals; but no one of the great social groups could be induced to link its fortunes permanently with those of the House

THE ROYAL HOUSE OF ORLEANS: LOUIS PHILIPPE AND HIS FIVE SONS
In this picture, from the painting by Horace Vernet, Louis Philippe is shown with his sons, the Duke of Orleans, the Duke of Nemours, the Duke of Joinville, the Duke of Aumâle, and the Duke of Montpensier, leaving the Palace of Versailles.

of Orleans. Unfortunately for himself, the king had reposed special confidence in the historian Guizot, the author of histories of the English revolution and of the French civilisation, who had occupied high offices in the state since the Restoration. He had belonged to the first Ministry of Louis Philippe, together with the Duc de Broglie; afterwards, he had several times held the post of Minister of Education, and had been in London during the quarrel with the British ambassador. After this affair, which brought him no credit, he returned to France, and on the fall of Thiers in October, 1840, became Minister of Foreign Affairs, with practical control of the foreign and domestic policy of France, subject to the king's personal intervention. His doctrinaire tendencies had gradually brought him over from the liberal to the conservative side and thrown him into violent opposition to his former colleagues, Thiers in particular. The acerbity of his character was not redeemed by his learning and his personal uprightness; his intellectual arrogance alienated the literary and political leaders of Parisian society. The Republican party had undergone many changes since the establishment of the July monarchy; it now exercised a greater power of attraction upon youthful talent, a quality which made it an even more dangerous force than did the revolts and conspiracies which it fostered from 1831 to 1838. These latter severely tested the capacity of the army for street warfare on several occasions. It was twice necessary to subdue Lyons, in November,

LOUIS PHILIPPE, KING OF THE FRENCH

1831, and July, 1834, and the barricades erected in Paris in 1834 repelled the National Guards, and only fell before the regiments of the line under General Bugeaud. The Communist revolts in Paris under Armand Barbés and Louis Auguste Blanqui, in May, 1839, were more easily suppressed, though the Hôtel de Ville and the Palais de Justice had already fallen into the hands of the rebels.

These events confirmed Louis Philippe in his intention to erect a circle of fortifications round Paris, for protection against enemies from within rather than from without. Homicidal attempts were no longer perpetrated by individual desperadoes or bloodthirsty monomaniacs, such as the Corsican Joseph Fieschi, on July 28th, 1835, whose infernal machine killed eighteen people, including Marshal Mortier. They were undertaken in the service of republican propagandism, and were repeated with the object of terrorising the ruling classes, and so providing an occasion for the abolition of the monarchy. The doctrines of communism were then being disseminated throughout France and attracted the more interest as stock-exchange speculation increased; fortunes were made with incredible rapidity, and expenditure rose to the point of prodigality. Louis Blanc, nephew of the Corsican statesman Pozzo di Borgo, went a step further towards the transformation of social and economic life in his treatise " L'Organisation du Travail," which urged that collectivist manufactures in national factories should be substituted for the efforts of the individual employer. The rise of communistic societies among the Republicans obliged the old-fashioned Democrats to organise in their turn; they attempted and easily secured an understanding with the advanced Liberals.

The "dynastic opposition," led by Odilon Barrot, to which Thiers occasionally gave a helping hand when he was out of office, strained every nerve to shake the public faith in the permanence of the July dynasty. The republican party in the Second Chamber was led by Alexandre Rollin after the death of Etienne Garnier-Pagès and of Armand Carrel, the leaders during the first decade of the Orleans monarchy. A distinguished lawyer and brilliant orator, Rollin soon overshadowed all other politicians who had aroused any enthusiasm in the Parisians. His comparative wealth enabled him to embark in journalistic ventures; his paper "La Réforme" pointed consistently and unhesitatingly to republicanism as the only possible form of government after the now imminent downfall of the July monarchy. The action of the majority now destroyed such credit as the Chamber had possessed; they rejected proposals from the opposition forbidding deputies to accept posts or preferment from the Government, or to have an interest in manufacturing or commercial companies, the object being to put a stop to the undisguised corruption then rife. Constitutional members united with Republicans in demanding a fundamental reform of the

electoral system. Louis Blanc and Rollin raised the cry for universal suffrage. Banquets, where vigorous speeches were made in favour of electoral reform, were arranged in the autumn of 1847, and continued until the Government prohibited the banquet organised for February 22nd, 1848, in the Champs Elysées. However, Ch. M. Tannegui, Count Duchâtel, was induced to refrain from ordering the forcible dispersion of the meeting, the liberal opposition on their side giving up the projected banquet. A great crowd collected on the appointed day in the Place Madeleine, whence • it had been arranged that a procession should march to the Champs Elysées. The republican leaders invited the crowd to march to the Houses of Parliament, and it became necessary to call out a regiment of cavalry for the dispersion of the rioters. This task was successfully accomplished, but on the 23rd the disturbances were renewed. Students and workmen paraded the streets arm in arm, shouting not only "Reform!" but also "Down with Guizot!" These

THE DUKES OF ORLEANS AND AUMÂLE

The sons of Louis Philippe, they held commands in the army, and, like their brothers, "were usually to be found wherever any small success might be achieved." There was much public sorrow when the Duke of Orleans was killed by a fall from a carriage in 1842.

cries were taken up by the National Guard, and the king, who had hitherto disregarded the movement, began to consider the outlook as serious; he dismissed Guizot and began to confer with Count Louis Matthieu Molé, a leader of the moderate Liberals, on the formation of a new Ministry. Thus far the anti-dynastic party had been successful, and now began to hope for an upright government on a purely constitutional basis. In this they would

FRANCE HONOURING THE DEAD EMPEROR. NAPOLEON'S REMAINS BEING BROUGHT BACK TO PARIS FOR BURIAL

Nineteen years after the death of Napoleon on the lonely isle of St. Helena, his remains, on December 15th, 1840, were brought back to Paris that they might finally repose "on the banks of the Seine, amidst the people whom he had loved so well." Reaching Courbevoie by way of the Seine, the coffin was placed on a gigantic funeral car, and, attended by an imposing military escort, passed by way of the Place de la Concorde and the bridge of that name to the Church of the Invalides amidst a crowd of six hundred thousand spectators,

4909

have been entirely deceived, for uprightness was not one of the king's attributes. But on this point he was not to be tested.

On the evening of February 23rd the crowds which thronged the boulevards gave loud expression to their delight at the dismissal of Guizot. Meanwhile, the republican agents were busily collecting the inhabitants of the suburbs, who had been long prepared for a rising, and sending them forward to the more excited quarters of the city. They would not, in

of those incidents which are always possible when troops are subjected to the threats and taunts of the people, and in such a case attempts to apportion the blame are futile. The thing was done, and Paris rang with cries of " Murder ! To arms ! " About midnight the alarm bells of Nôtre Dame began to ring, and thousands flocked to raise the barricades. The morning of February 24th found Paris in revolution, ready to begin the struggle against the people's king. " Louis Philippe orders his

THE RECEPTION OF NAPOLEON'S BODY AT THE CHURCH OF THE INVALIDES

At the Church of the Invalides the body of Napoleon was received by Louis Philippe, the royal family, the archbishop and all the clergy of Paris. The sword and the hat of the emperor were laid on the coffin, which was then placed on a magnificent altar in the centre of the church, and after an impressive funeral service was lowered into the tomb.

all probability, have been able to transform the good-tempered and characteristic cheerfulness which now filled the streets of Paris to a more serious temper had not an unexpected occurrence filled the mob with horror and rage. A crowd of people had come in contact with the soldiers stationed before Guizot's house. Certain insolent youths proceeded to taunt the officer in command ; a shot rang out, a volley followed, and numbers of the mockers lay weltering in their blood. It was but one

troops to fire on the people, like Charles X. Send him after his predecessor ! " This proposal of the " Réforme " became the republican solution of the question.

The monarchy was now irrevocably lost ; the man who should have saved it was asking help from the Liberals, who were as powerless as himself. A would-be ruler must know how to use his power, and must believe that his will is force in itself. When, at his wife's desire, the king appeared on horseback before his

THE TOMB OF NAPOLEON AT THE HÔTEL DES INVALIDES IN PARIS

The magnificent tomb erected to Napoleon at the Hôtel des Invalides is a fitting memorial of the man who made Europe tremble and whose genius raised him to the pinnacle of power. A circular crypt, surrounded by twelve colossal figures symbolising his victories, contains the sarcophagus, which was hewn out of a single block of Siberian porphyry.

THE FLIGHT OF LOUIS PHILIPPE FROM PARIS IN 1848

Events in Paris had again been leading up to a revolution, and on February 24th, 1848, the capital of France was once more the scene of a people's rising against the monarchy. Alarmed at the course of affairs, the king abdicated in favour of his grandson, the Count of Paris, and went off to St. Cloud with the queen, afterwards escaping to England.

regiments and the National Guard, he knew within himself that he was not capable of rousing the enthusiasm of his troops. Civilian clothes and an umbrella would have suited him better than sword and epaulettes. Louis Philippe thus abdicated in favour of his grandson, the Count of Paris, whom he left to the care of Charles, Duke of Nemours, took a portfolio of such papers as were valuable, and went away to St. Cloud with his wife. The bold daughter of Mecklenburg, Henriette of Orleans, brought her son, Louis Philippe, who was now the rightful king, into the Chamber of Deputies, where Odilon Barrot, in true knightly fashion, broke a lance on behalf of the king's rights and of constitutional-ism. But the victors in the street fighting had made their way into the hall, their com-rades were at that moment invading the Tuileries, and Legitimists and Democrats joined in deposing the House of Orleans and demanding the appoint-ment of a provisional government. The question was dealt with by the "Chris-tian moralist," poet, and diplomatist,

GUIZOT THE HISTORIAN
Eminent as an historian, Guizot became chief adviser to Louis Phi-lippe on the dismissal of Thiers, and his reactionary policy did much to bring about the revolution of 1848.

Alphonse de Lamartine, whose " His-tory of the Girondists " in eight volumes with its glorification of political murder had largely contributed to advance the revolutionary spirit in France. Though the electoral tickets had fallen into the greatest confusion, he contrived to produce a list of names which were backed by a strong body of supporters ; these included Louis Garnier-Pagès, half-brother of the deceased Etienne, Ledru-Rollin, the astronomer Dominique Fran-çois Arago, the Jewish lawyer Isak Crémieux, who was largely responsible for the abdication of Louis Philippe, and Lamartine himself. The list was approved. The body thus elected effected a timely junction with the party of Louis Blanc, who was given a place in the government with four republican consulta-tive members. They then took possession of the Hôtel de Ville, filled up the official posts, and with the concurrence of the people declared France a republic on February 25th. The dethroned king and the members of his house were able, if not unmenaced, at any rate without danger,

THE PARIS REVOLUTION OF 1848: THE MOB IN THE THRONE ROOM OF THE TUILERIES

The above picture represents the scene of disorder and brutality which ensued in the Throne Room of the Tuileries after the flight of the king during the Revolution of 1848.

to reach the coasts of England and safety, or to cross the German frontier. The new government failed to satisfy the Socialists, who were determined, after definitely establishing the "right of labour," to insist upon the right of the wage they desired. The installation of state factories and navvy labour at two francs

Demands of the Socialists a day was not enough for them; they formed hundreds of clubs under the direction of a central bureau, with the object of replacing the government for the time being by a committee of public safety, which should proceed to a general redistribution of property. Ledru-Rollin was not inclined to accept the offer of the presidency of such an extraordinary body; he and Lamartine, with the help of General Changarnier and the National Guards, entirely outmanœuvred the hordes which had made a premature attempt to storm the town hall, and forced them to surrender.

Peace was thus assured to Paris for the moment. The emissaries of the revolutionaries could not gain a hearing, and it was possible to go on with the elections, which were conducted on the principle of universal suffrage. Every 40,000 inhabitants elected a deputy; every department formed a uniform electorate. Lamartine, one of the 900 chosen, obtained 2,300,000 votes in ten departments. The Assembly was opened on May 4th.

To the organised enemies of monarchy the February Revolution was a call to undisguised activity; to the world at large it was a token that the times of peace were over, and that the long-expected movement would now inevitably break out. It is not always an easy matter to decide whether these several events originated in the inflammatory labours of revolutionaries designedly working in secret, or in some sudden outburst of feeling, some stimulus to action hitherto unknown. No less difficult is the task of deciding how far the conspira-

Active Enemies of Monarchy tors were able personally to influence others of radical tendencies but outside their own organisations. These organisations were most important to France, Italy, Germany, and Poland. The central bureaus were in Paris and Switzerland, and the noble Giuseppe Mazzini, indisputably one of the purest and most devoted of Italian patriots, held most of the strings of this somewhat clumsy network. His journals "La

Giovine Europa" and "La Jeune Suisse" were as short-lived as the "Giovine Italia," published at Marseilles in 1831; but they incessantly urged the duty of union upon all those friends of humanity who were willing to share in the task of liberating peoples from the tyranny of monarchs.

From 1834 a special "union of exiles" had existed at Paris, which declared "the deposition and expulsion of monarchs an inevitable necessity," and looked for a revolution to break out in France or Germany, or a war between France and Germany or Russia, in the hope of assisting France in the attack upon the German rulers. Its organisation was as extraordinary as it was secret; there were "mountains," "national huts," "focal points," "circles," wherein preparation was to be made for the transformation of Germany in the interests of humanity.

The "righteous" had diverged from the "outlaws," and from 1840 were reunited with the "German union," which aimed at "the formation of a free state embracing the whole of Germany." The persecutions and continual "investigations" which the German Federation had carried on

Persecutions of the German Federation since the riots at Frankfort had impeded, though not entirely broken off, communications between the central officials in Paris and their associates residing in Germany. From Switzerland came a continual stream of craftsmen, teachers, and authors, who were sworn in by the united Republicans. Karl Mathy, afterwards Minister of State for Baden, who had been Mazzini's colleague in Solothurn, was one of their members in 1840, when he was called to Carlsruhe to take up the post of editor of the "Landtagszeitung."

The deliberations of the united Landtag at Berlin had attracted the attention of the South German Liberals to the highly talented politicians in Prussia, on whose help they could rely in the event of a rearrangement of the relative positions of the German states. The idea of some common movement towards this end was mooted at a gathering of politicians at Heppenheim on October 16th, 1847, and it was determined to lay proposals for some change in the federal constitution before the assemblies of the individual states.

In the grand duchy of Baden the Democrats went even further at a meeting held at Offenburg on September 12th. Proceedings were conducted by a certain lawyer of Mannheim, one Gustav von Struve, an overbearing individual of a Livonian family, and by Friedrich Hecker, an empty-headed prater, also an attorney, who had already displayed his incapacity for political action in the Baden Landtag.

To justifiable demands for the repeal of the decrees of Carlsbad, for national representation within the German Federation, for freedom of the Press, religious toleration, and full liberty to teachers, they added immature proposals, as to the practicable working of which no one had the smallest conception. They looked not only for a national system of defence and

members of the state. The king and poet, Lewis I., had conceived a blind infatuation for the dancer Lola Montez, an Irish adventuress—Rosanna Gilbert—who masqueraded under a Spanish name. This fact led to the downfall of the Ministry, which was clerical without exception; further consequences were street riots, unjustifiable measures against the students who declined to show respect to the dancing-woman, and finally bloody conflicts. It was not until the troops displayed entire indifference to the tyrannical orders which had been issued that the king yielded to the entreaties of the

EPISODE IN THE PARIS REVOLUTION: BURNING THE THRONE AT THE JULY COLUMN

fair taxation, but also for "the removal of the inequalities existing between capital and labour and the abolition of all privileges." Radicalism thus plumed itself upon its own veracity, and pointed out the path which the masses who listened to its allurements would take—a result of radical incapacity to distinguish between the practicable and the unattainable.

Immediately before the events of February in Paris were made known, the kingdom of Bavaria, and its capital in particular, were in a state of revolt and open war between the authorities and the

citizens, on February 11th, 1848, and removed from Munich this impossible beauty, who had been made a countess.

The first of those surprising phenomena in Germany which sprang from the impression created by the February Revolution was the session of the Federal Assembly on March 1st, 1848. Earlier occurrences in the immediate neighbourhood of Frankfort no doubt materially influenced the course of events. In Baden, before his fate had fallen upon the July king, Karl Mathy had addressed the nation from the Chamber on February 23rd: "For thirty years the Germans have tried moderation and in vain ; they must now see whether violence will enable them to advance, and such violence is not to be limited to the states meeting-hall ! " At a meeting of citizens at Mannheim on the 27th, an address was carried by Struve which thus formulated the most pressing questions : Universal military service with power to elect the officers, unrestrained freedom of the Press, trial by jury after the English model, and the immediate constitution of a German Parliament.

A Call to German Unity

In Hesse-Darmstadt, a popular deputy in the Landtag, one Gagern, the second son of the former statesman of Nassau and the Netherlands, demanded that the Government should not only call a Parliament, but also create a central governing power for Germany. The request was inspired by the fear of an approaching war with France, which was then considered inevitable. It was fear of this war which suddenly convinced the high Federal Council at Frankfort-on-Main that the people were indispensable to their existence. On March 1st they issued " a federal decree to the German people," whose existence they had disregarded for three centuries, emphasising the need for unity between all the German races, and asserting their conviction that Germany must be raised to her due position among the nations of Europe.

On March 1st Herr von Struve led a gang of low-class followers in the pay of the Republicans, together with the deputies of the Baden towns, into the federal Chamber. Ejected thence, he turned upon the castle in Carlsruhe, his aim being to foment disturbances and bloody conflict, and so to intimidate the moderately minded majority. His plan was foiled by the firm attitude of the troops. But the abandonment of the project was not to be expected, and it was clear that the nationalist movement in Germany would meet with its most dangerous check in Radicalism. Telegrams from Paris and West Germany reached Munich, when the newly restored peace was again broken. The new Minister, State Councillor von Berks, was denounced as a tool of Lola Montez, and his dismissal was enforced. On March 6th, King Lewis, in his usual poetical style, declared his readiness to satisfy the popular demands. However,

Radicalism the Check to Nationalism

fresh disturbance was excited by the rumour that Lola Montez was anxious to return. Lewis, who declined to be forced into the concession of any constitution upon liberal principles, lost heart and abdicated in favour of his son Maximilian II. He saw clearly that he could no longer resist the strength of the movement for the recognition of the people's rights. The political storm would unchain the potent forces of stupidity and folly which the interference of short-sighted majorities had created. When Lewis retired into private life, Metternich had already fallen.

The first act of the Viennese, horrified at the victory of the Republicans in Paris, was to provide for the safety of their money-bags. The general mistrust of the Government was shown in the haste with which accounts were withdrawn from the public savings banks. It was not, however, the Austrians who pointed the moral to the authorities. On March 3rd, in the Hungarian Reichstag, Kossuth proposed that the emperor should be requested to introduce constitutional government into his provinces, and to grant Hungary the national self-government which was hers by right. In Vienna similar demands were advanced by the industrial unions, the legal and political reading clubs, and the students. It was hoped that a bold attitude would be taken by the provincial Landtag, which met on March 13th. When the anxious crowds promenading the streets learned that the representatives proposed to confine themselves to a demand for the formation of a committee of deputies from all the Crown provinces, they invaded the council chamber and forced the meeting to consent to the despatch of a deputation to lay the national desire for a free constitution before the emperor.

Riots in the Streets of Vienna

While the deputation was proceeding to the Hofburg the soldiers posted before the council chamber, including the Archduke Albert, eldest son of the Archduke Charles, who died in 1847, were insulted and pelted with stones. They replied with a volley. It was the loss of life thereby caused which made the movement a serious reality. The citizens of Vienna, startled out of their complacency, vied with the mob in the loudness of their cries against this " firing on defenceless men." Their behaviour was explained to Count Metternich in the Hofburg, not as an

FIGHTING IN THE STREETS OF PARIS DURING THE REVOLUTION OF FEBRUARY, 1848
From the drawing by Wegner

ordinary riot capable of suppression by a handful of police, but as a revolution with which he had now to deal. Nowhere would such a task have been easier than in Vienna had there been any corporation or individual capable of immediate action, and able to make some short and definite promise of change in the government system. There was, however, no nucleus round which a new government could be formed, Prince Metternich being wholly impracticable for such a purpose.

All the state councillors, the court dignitaries, and generally those whom chance or curiosity rather than definite purpose had gathered in the corridors and antechambers of the imperial castle, were unanimous in the opinion that the Chancellor of State must be sacrificed. This empty figure-head stood isolated amid the surrounding turmoil, unable to help himself or his perplexed advisers; he emitted a few sentences upon the last sacrifice that he could make for the monarchy and disappeared. He left no one to take up his power; no one able to represent him, able calmly and confidently to examine and decide upon the demands transmitted from the street to the council chamber. The Emperor Ferdinand was himself wholly incapable of grasping the real meaning of the events which had taken place in his immediate neighbourhood. The Archduke Lewis, one of Metternich's now useless tools, was utterly perplexed by the conflict of voices and opinions.

In his fear of the excesses that the " Reds " might be expected to perpetrate, he lost sight of the means which might have been used to pacify the moderate party and induce them to maintain law and order. The authorisation for the arming of the students and citizens was extorted from him perforce, and he would hear nothing of concessions to be made by the dynasty to the people. Neither he nor Count Kolowrat Liebsteinsky ventured

LEWIS I. OF BAVARIA
Ascending the throne in 1825, he pursued a policy of reaction, which led to public discontent, and in the year 1848 abdicated in favour of his son, Maximilian II.

THE KING'S FAVOURITE
With this Irish adventuress, who masqueraded under the name of Lola Montez, Lewis I. became infatuated, but was compelled to remove her from Munich.

to draw up any programme for the introduction of constitutional principles. Even on March 14th they demurred to the word " constitution," and thought it possible to effect some compromise with the provincial deputations. Finally, on March 15th, the news of fresh scenes induced the privy councillor of the royal family to issue the following declaration : " Provision has been made for summoning the deputies of all provincial estates in the shortest possible period, for the purpose of considering the constitution of the country, with increased representation of the citizen class and with due regard to the existing constitutions of the several estates." The responsible Ministry of Kolowrat-Ficquelmont, formed on March 18th, included among Metternich's worn-out tools one man only possessed of the knowledge requisite for the drafting of a constitution in detail ; this was the Minister of the Interior, Pillersdorf, who was as weak and feeble in character as in bodily health.

In Hungary the destructive process was far more comprehensive and imposing. On March 14th Louis Kossuth in the Reichstag at Pressburg secured the announcement of the freedom of the Press, and called for a system of national defence for Hungary, to be based upon the general duty of military service. Meanwhile, his adherents, consisting of students, authors, and "jurats"—idle lawyers—seized the reins of government in Ofenpest, and replaced the town council by a committee of public safety, composed of radical members by preference. On the 15th the State Assembly of the Reichstag was transformed into a National Assembly. Henceforward its conclusions were to be communicated to the magnates, whose consent was to be unnecessary.

On the same day a deputation of the Hungarian Reichstag, accompanied by jurats, arrived at Vienna, where Magyars and Germans swore to the fellowship with all pomp and enthusiasm. The deputation secured the concession of an independent and responsible Ministry for Hungary.

This was installed on March 23rd by the Archduke Palatine Stephen, and united the popular representatives among Hungarian politicians, such as Batthyány and Széchényi, with Prince Paul Eszterházy, Josef von Eötvös, Franz von Deák, and Louis Kossuth. After a few days' deliberation the Reichstag practically abolished the old constitution. The rights of the lords were abrogated, and equality of political rights given to citizens of towns ; the right of electing to the Reichstag was conceded to "the adherents of legally recognised religions"; laws were passed regulating the Press and the National Guards. The country was almost in a state of anarchy, as the old provincial administrations and local authorities had been abolished and replaced by committees of public safety, according to the precedent set at Pest. The example of Austria influenced the course of events throughout Germany; there the desire for a free constitution grew hotter, and especially so in Berlin.

The taxation committees were assembled in that town when the results of the February Revolution became known. The king dismissed them on March 7th, declaring himself inclined to summon the united Landtag at regular intervals. The declaration failed to give satisfaction. On the same day a popular meeting had resolved to request the king forthwith to convoke the Assembly. In the quiet town public life became more than usually lively. The working classes were excited by the agitators sent down to them ; in inns and cafés newspapers were read aloud and speeches made. The king was expecting an outbreak of war with France.

Germany Preparing for War

He sent his confidential military adviser, Radowitz, at full speed to Vienna to arrange measures of defence with Metternich. He proposed temporarily to entrust the command of the Prussian troops upon the Rhine to the somewhat unpopular Prince William of Prussia. However, he was warned that

MAXIMILIAN II.—BAVARIA
He ascended the throne on his father's abdication in 1848. A noble-minded man; he made an excellent king, ruling his people on the ideal grounds of "Christian philosophy."

the excitement prevailing among the population of the Rhine province would only be increased by the appearance of the prince. Despatches from Vienna further announced the fall of Metternich. The king now resolved to summon the united Landtag to Berlin on April 17th ;

Mobs at the Royal Palace in Berlin

he considered, no doubt, that Prussia could very well exercise her patience for a month. On March 15th the first of many riotous crowds assembled before the royal castle, much excited by the news from Vienna. Deputations constantly arrived from the provinces to give expression to the desire of the population for some constitutional definition of their rights. The king went a step further and altered the date of the meeting of the Landtag to April 2nd ; but in the patent of March 18th he explained his action by reference only to his duties as federal ruler, and to his intention of proposing a federal reform, to include "temporary federal representation of all German countries." He even recognised that "such federal representation implies a form of constitution applicable to all German countries," but made no definite promise as to any form of constitution for Prussia. Nevertheless, in the afternoon he was cheered by the crowd before the castle. But the leaders of the mob, who desired a rising to secure their own criminal objects, turned gratitude into uproar and bloodshed. The troops concentrated in the castle under General von Prittwitz were busy until midnight clearing the streets.

The authorities had 12,000 men at their disposal, and could easily have stormed the barricades next morning; but the king's military advisers were unable to agree upon their action, and his anxiety and nervousness were increased by the invited and uninvited citizens who made their way into the castle. He therefore ordered the troops to cease firing, and the next day, after receiving a deputation of citizens, commanded the troops to concentrate upon the castle, and finally to retire to barracks. The arguments of such Liberals as Vincke, and of the Berlin town councillors, induced the king to this ill-advised step, the full importance of which he failed to recognise. It implied the retreat of the monarchical power before a riotous mob inspired only by blind antipathy to law and order, who, far from thanking the king for sparing their guilt, proclaimed the **The German** retreat of the troops as a **States' Distrust** victory for themselves, and **of the King** continued to heap scorn and insult upon king and troops alike. A new Ministry was formed on March 19th, the leadership being taken by Arnim. On the 29th his place was taken by Ludolf Camphausen, president of the Cologne Chamber of Commerce, who was joined by Hanseman and the leaders of the liberal nobility, Alfred von Auerswald, Count Maximilian of Schwerin, and Heinrich Alexander of Arnim.

The Ministry would have had no difficulty in forming a constitution for the state had not the king reduced the monarchy to helplessness by his display of ineptitude. That honest enthusiasm for the national cause which had led him on March 21st to escort the banner of black, red, and gold on horseback through the streets of Berlin, far from winning the popular favour for him, was scorned and flouted by the Republicans. The energy displayed in summoning the Parliament was too rapid a change, made the German states distrustful, and exposed him to degrading refusals, which embittered his mind and lowered his dignity in the eyes of his own people.

FRIEDRICH DAHLMANN
This distinguished German historian was appointed Professor of History at Bonn in 1842, and was at the head of the constitutional Liberals in the movement of 1848.

The united Landtag met on April 2nd, 1848, and determined upon the convocation of a National Assembly, for the purpose of forming a constitution upon the basis of universal suffrage. To this the Government agreed, at the same time insisting that the Prussian constitution was a matter for arrangement between themselves and the Assembly. During the elections, which took place simultaneously with those to the German Parliament, the democrats uttered their war-cry, to the effect that the resolutions of the Prussian National Assembly required no ratification. Thus the popular claim to a share in the administration disappeared, and was overshadowed by the struggle for supremacy waged by the masses under the guidance of ambitious agitators.

On March 5th, 1848, fifty-one of the better known German politicians met at Heidelberg upon their own initiative by invitation ; their object was to discuss what common action they should take to guide a general national movement in Germany. Most of them belonged to the Rhine states ; but Prussia, Würtemberg, and Bavaria were represented, and an Austrian writer who happened to be on the spot joined the meeting in order to place it in relation with Austria. The twenty representatives from Baden included the radical democrat Hecker, who even then spoke of the introduction of a republican constitution as a wish of the German people. He, however, was obliged to support the resolution of the majority, to the effect that the German nation must first have the opportunity of making its voice heard, for which purpose preparation must be made for the convocation of a German National Assembly. All were agreed upon the futility of waiting for the Federal Council to take action ; they must bring their influence to bear upon the council and the German government by their own energy, by the use of accomplished facts, and by specific demands. A committee of seven members was appointed to invite a conference on March 30th, at Frankfort-on-Main, " of all past or present members of provincial councils and members of legislative assemblies in all German countries," together with other public men of special influence. This "preliminary conference " was then to arrive at some resolutions for the election of the German National Assembly. Both the Federal **The Saving** Assembly and the majority **Force** of the German governments **of Politics** viewed these proceedings with favourable eyes ; they saw that the nation was at the highest pitch of excitement, and would be prevented from rushing into violence by occupation in political matters. The results of the Parisian revolution led them to think the overthrow of every existing form of government perfectly possible.

FIGHTING AT THE BARRICADES IN BERLIN ON MARCH 18TH, 1848

From the drawing by C. Becker

The only remaining course was to treat with the Liberals and enlist their support for the existing states and dynasties by the concession of constitutional rights. Only in Hanover and in the electorate of Hesse were there difficulties at the outset. However, the fall of Metternich shattered even the pride of Ernest Augustus and of the Elector Frederic William.

Liberal Movements in Saxony Baden sent the Freiburg professor Karl Welcker to Frankfort. On March 7th he proposed on behalf of his Government the convocation of a German Parliament to discuss and carry out the reform of the federal constitution in conjunction with the representatives of the Government. In Hesse-Darmstadt, Gagern made a similar proposal in the Chamber. The King of Würtemberg called one of the members of the Heidelberg conference, Friedrich Romer, to the head of a new Ministry, to which Paul Pfizer also belonged.

In Saxony, Frederic Augustus, after unnecessarily alarming the inhabitants of Leipzig by the concentration of troops, was obliged to give way, to dissolve the Ministry of Könneritz, and to entrust the conduct of government business to the leader of the Progressive Party in the Second Chamber, Alexander Braun. Of the Liberals in Saxony, the largest following was that of Robert Blum, formerly theatre secretary, bookseller, and town councillor of Leipzig. He was one of those trusted public characters who were summoned to the preliminary conference, and directed the attention of his associates to the national tasks immediately confronting the German people. In the patent convoking the united Landtag for March 18th, even the King of Prussia had declared the formation of a "temporary federal representation of the states of all German countries" to be a pressing necessity; hence from that quarter no opposition to the national undertaking of the Heidelberg meeting was to be ex-

Conference of the German States pected. Five hundred representatives from all parts of Germany met at Frankfort-on-Main for the conference in the last days of March; they were received with every manifestation of delight and respect. The first general session was held in the Church of St. Paul, under the presidency of the Heidelberg jurist, Anton Mittermayer, a Bavarian by birth; the conference was then invited to come to a decision upon one of the most important questions of German politics. The committee of seven had drawn up a programme dealing with the mode of election to the German National Assembly, and formulating a number of fundamental principles for adoption in the forthcoming federal constitution. These demanded a federal chief with responsible Ministers, a senate of the individual states, a popular representative house with one deputy to every 70,000 inhabitants of a German federal state, a united army, and representation abroad; a uniformity in the customs systems, in the means of communication, in civil and criminal legislation.

This premature haste is to be ascribed to the scanty political experience of the German and his love for the cut and dried; it gave the Radicals, who had assembled in force from Baden, Darmstadt, Frankfort, and Nassau, under Struve and Hecker, an opportunity for demanding similar resolutions upon the future constitution of Germany. Hecker gave an explanation of the so-called "principles" propounded by Struve, demanding the disbanding of the standing army, the abolition of officials, taxation, and the here-

Deliberations of the Frankfort Conference ditary monarchy, and the institution of a Parliament elected without restriction under a president similarly elected, all to be united by a federal constitution on the model of the Free States of North America. Until the German democracy had secured legislation upon these and many other points, the Frankfort conference should be kept on foot, and the government of Germany continued by an executive committee elected by universal suffrage.

Instead of receiving these delectable puerilities with the proper amount of amusement, or satirising them as they deserved, the moderate Democrats and Liberals were inveigled into serious discussion with the Radicals. Reports of an insignificant street fight aroused their fears and forebodings, and both sides condescended to abuse and personal violence. Finally, the clearer-sighted members of the conference succeeded in confining the debate to the subjects preliminary to the convocation of the parliament. The programme of the committee of seven and the "principles" of the Radicals were alike excluded from discussion. Hecker's proposition for the permanent constitution of the conference was rejected by 368 votes to 143, and it was decided to elect a committee of fifty members to continue the business of the preliminary parliament.

On the question of this business great divergence of opinion prevailed. The majority of the members were convinced that the people should now be left to decide its own fate, and to determine the legislature which was to secure the recognition of its rights. A small minority were agreed with Gagern upon the necessity of keeping in touch with the Government and the Federal Council, and constructing the new constitution by some form of union between the national representatives and the existing executive officials. This was the first serious misconception of the Liberal party upon the sphere of action within which the Parliament would operate. They discussed the " purification " of the Federal Council and its " aversion to special resolutions of an unconstitutional nature ; " they should have united themselves firmly to the federal authorities, and carried them to the necessary resolutions.

The mistrust of the liberals for the government was greater than their disgust at radical imbecility, a fact as obvious in the preliminary conference as in the National Assembly which it called into being. This is the first and probably the sole cause of the futility of the efforts made by upright and disinterested representative men to guide the national movement in Germany. Franz von Soiron of Mannheim proposed that the decision upon the future German constitution should be left entirely in the hands of the National Assembly, to be elected by the people ; with this exception, the constitutional ideal was abandoned and a utopia set up in its place not utterly dissimilar to the dream of " the republic with a doge at its head." Soiron, who propounded this absurdity, became president of the committee of fifty.

The National Movement in Germany

The mode of election to the National Constituent Assembly realised the most extreme demands of the Democrats. Every 50,000 inhabitants in a German federal province, East and West Prussia included, had to send up a deputy " directly "—that is to say, appointment was not made by any existing constitutional corporation. The Czechs of Bohemia were included without cavil among the electors of the German Parliament, no regard being given to the scornful refusal which they would probably return. The question of including the Poles of the Prussian Baltic provinces was left to the decision of the parliament itself. The Federal Council, in which Karl Welcker had already become influential, prudently accepted the resolutions of the preliminary conference and communicated them to the individual states, whose business it was to carry them out. Feeling in the different governments had undergone a rapid transformation, and in Prussia even more than elsewhere. On March 21st, after parading Berlin with the German colours, Frederic William IV. had made a public declaration, expressing his readiness to undertake the direction of German affairs. His exuberance led him to the following pronouncement : " I have to-day asumed the ancient German colours and placed myself and my people under the honourable banner of the German Empire. Prussia is henceforward merged in Germany."

Prussia Merged in Germany

These words would have created a great effect had the king been possessed of the power which was his by right, or had he given any proof of capacity to rule his own people or to defend his capital from the outrages of a misled and passionately excited mob. But the occurrences at Berlin during March had impaired his prestige with every class ; he was despised by the Radicals, and the patriotic party mistrusted his energy and his capacity for maintaining his dignity in a difficult situation.

Moreover, the German governments had lost confidence in the power of the Prussian state. Hesse-Darmstadt, Baden, Nassau, and Würtemberg had shown themselves ready to confer full powers upon the King of Prussia for the formation, in their name, of a new federal constitution with provision for the popular rights. They were also willing to accept him as head of the federation, a position which he desired, while declining the imperial title with which the cheers of the Berlin population had greeted him. When, however, Max von Gagern arrived in Berlin at the head of an embassy from the above-mentioned states, the time for the enterprise had gone by ; a king who gave way to rebels and did obeisance to the corpses of mob leaders was not the man for the dictatorship of Germany at so troublous a time.

Frederic William not a Favourite

Notwithstanding their own difficulties, the Vienna government had derived some advantage from the events at Berlin ; there was no reason for them to resign their position in Germany. The Emperor

Ferdinand need never yield to Frederic William IV. The Austrian statesmen were sure of the approval of the German people, even of the national and progressive parties, if they straightway opposed Prussian interference in German politics. Relying upon nationalist sentiment and appealing to national sovereignty, they might play off the German parliament against the King of Prussia. Austria was, upon the showing of the government and the popular leaders, the real Germany. Austria claimed the precedence of all German races, and therefore the black, red, and gold banner flew on the Tower of Stephan, and the kindly emperor waved it before the students, who cheered him in the castle. The offer of Prussian leadership was declined; the German constitution was to be arranged by the federal council and the parliament, and Austria would there be able to retain the leading position which was her right.

The Proud Claims of Austria

The case of the King of Prussia was sufficiently disheartening; but no less serious for the development of the German movement was the attitude of the Liberals towards the Republicans. The professions and avowals of the latter had not been declined with the decisiveness that belong to honest monarchical conviction. Even before the meeting of Parliament disturbances had been set on foot by the Baden Radicals, and it became obvious that Radicalism could result only in civil war and would imperil the national welfare.

The Struve-Hecker party was deeply disappointed with the results of the preliminary conference. It had not taken over the government of Germany; no princes had been deposed, and even the federal council had been left untouched. The leaders, impelled thereto by their French associates, accordingly resolved to initiate an armed revolt in favour of the republic. The "moderate" party had cleared the way by assenting to the proposal of "national armament." Under the pretext of initiating a scheme of public defence, arms for the destruction of constitutional order were placed in the hands of the ruffians who had been wandering about the Rhineland for weeks in the hope of robbery and plunder, posing as the retinue of the great "friends of the people." Acuter politicians, like Karl Mathy, discovered too late that it was now necessary

The Mad Schemes of Agitators

to stake their whole personal influence in the struggle against radical insanity and the madness of popular agitators. In person he arrested the agitator Joseph Fickler, when starting from Karlsruhe to Constance to stir up insurrection; but his bold example found few imitators. The evil was not thoroughly extirpated, as the "people's men" could not refrain from repeating meaningless promises of popular supremacy and the downfall of tyrants at every public-house and platform where they thought they could secure the applause for which they thirsted like actors.

Hecker had maintained communications with other countries from Karlsruhe, and had been negotiating for the advance of contingents from Paris, to be paid from the resources of Ledru-Rollin. After Fickler's imprisonment on April 8th he became alarmed for his own safety, and fled to Constance. There, in conjunction with Struve and his subordinates, Doll, Willich, formerly a Prussian lieutenant, Mögling of Würtemberg, and Bruhe of Holstein, he issued an appeal to all who were capable of bearing arms to concentrate at Donaueschingen on April 12th, for the purpose of founding the German republic. With a republican army of fifty men he marched on the 13th from Constance, where the republic had maintained its existence for a whole day. In the plains of the Rhine a junction was to be effected with the "legion of the noble Franks," led by the poet George Herwegh and his Jewish wife. In vain did two deputies from the committee of fifty in Frankfort advise the Republicans to lay down their arms. Their overtures were rejected with contumely. The eighth federal army corps had been rapidly mobilised, and the troops of Hesse and Würtemberg brought this insane enterprise to an end in the almost bloodless conflicts of Kandern on April 20th, and Güntersthal at Freiburg on April 23rd.

Defeat of the Republicans

The Republicans were given neither time nor opportunity for any display of their Teutonic heroism. Their sole exploit was the shooting of the general Friedrich von Gagern from an ambush as he was returning to his troops from an unsuccessful conference with Hecker. Herwegh's French legion was dispersed at Dossenbach on April 26th by a company of Würtemberg troops. These warriors took refuge for the time being in Switzerland with the "generals" Hecker, Struve, and Franz Siegl.

ITALY'S FRUITLESS REVOLT
AND AUSTRIA'S SUCCESS UNDER RADETZKY

AS early as January, 1848, the population of the Lombard States had begun openly to display their animosity to the Austrians. The secret revolutionary committees, who took their instructions from Rome and Turin, organised demonstrations, and forbade the purchase of Austrian cigars and lottery tickets, the profits of which went to the Austrian exchequer. Threats and calls for blood and vengeance upon the troops were placarded upon the walls, and cases of assassination occurred. Field-Marshal Count Radetzky had felt certain that the national movement, begun in the Church States, would extend throughout Italy, and oblige Austria to defend her territory by force of arms.

He was also informed of the warlike feeling in Piedmont and of the secret preparations which were in progress there. This view was well founded. Any dispassionate judgment of the political situation in the peninsula showed that the governments of the individual states were in a dilemma; either they must join the national yearning for liberation from the foreign rule and help their subjects in the struggle, or they would be forced to yield to the victorious advance of republicanism. The Savoy family of Carignan, the only ruling house of national origin, found no difficulty in deciding the question. As leaders of the patriotic party they might attain a highly important position, and at least become the leaders of a Federal Italy; while they were forced to endanger their kingdom, whatever side they took.

A Nation's Yearning for Liberation

Radetzky was indefatigable in his efforts to keep the Vienna government informed of the approaching danger, but his demands for reinforcements to the troops serving in the Lombard-Venetian provinces were disregarded. The old War Minister, Count H. Hardegg, who supported Radetzky, was harshly dismissed from his position in the exchequer, and died of vexation at the affront. Not all the obtuseness and vacillation of the Vienna bureaucracy could shake the old field-marshal—on August 1st, 1847, he began his sixty-fourth year of service in the imperial army—from his conviction that the Austrian house meant to defend its Italian possessions. He was well aware that the very existence of the monarchy was involved in this question of predominance in Italy. A moment when every nationality united under the Hapsburg rule was making the most extravagant demands upon the state was not the moment voluntarily to abandon a position of the greatest moral value.

Austria's Complicated Politics

After the outbreak of the revolt many voices recommended an Austrian retreat from Lombardy to Venice. It was thought impossible that these two countries, with independent governments of their own, could be incorporated in so loosely articulated a federation as the Austrian Empire seemed likely to become. Such counsels were not inconceivable in view of the zeal with which kings and ministers, professors, lawyers, and authors plunged into the elaboration of political blunders and misleading theories; but to follow them would have been to increase rather than to diminish the difficulties of Austrian politics, which grew daily more complicated.

In the turmoil of national and democratic aspirations and programmes the idea of the Austrian state was forgotten; its strength and dignity depended upon the inflexibility and upon the ultimate victory of Radetzky and his army. The war in Italy was a national war, more especially for the Austro-Germans; for passion, even for an ideal, cannot impress the German and arouse his admiration to the same extent as the heroic fulfilment of duty. Additional influences upon the Austrians were the military assessment, their delight in proved military superiority, and their military traditions.

National War in Italy

4925

Nationalism was indisputably an animating force among the Germans of the Alpine districts. Never did Franz Grillparzer so faithfully represent the Austrian spirit as in the oft-repeated words which he ascribed to the old field-marshal, upholding the ancient imperial banner upon Guelf soil : " In thy camp is Austria ; we are but single fragments."

The Vanished Power of the Hapsburgs It is not difficult to imagine that a statesman of unusual penetration and insight might even then have recognised that Austria was no longer a force in Germany, that the claim of the Hapsburgs to lead the German nation had disappeared with the Holy Roman Empire. We may conceive that, granted such recognition of the facts, a just division of influence and power in Central Europe might have been brought about by the peaceful compromise with Prussia ; but it was foolishness to expect the House of Hapsburg voluntarily to begin a partition of the countries which had fallen to be hers.

The acquisition of Italy had been a mistake on the part of Metternich; but the mistake could not be mended by a surrender of rights at the moment when hundreds of claims would be pressed. To maintain the integrity of the empire was to preserve its internal solidarity and to uphold the monarchical power. The monarchy could produce no more convincing evidence than the victories of the army. An army which had retreated before the Piedmontese and the Guelf guerrilla troops would never have gained another victory, even in Hungary.

In an army order of January 15th, 1848, Radetzky announced in plain and unambiguous terms that the Emperor of Austria was resolved to defend the Lombard-Venetian kingdom against internal and external enemies, and that he himself proposed to act in accordance with the imperial will. He was, however, unable **Outbreak of the Revolution** to make any strategical preparations for the approaching struggle ; he had barely troops enough to occupy the most important towns, and in every case the garrisons were entirely outnumbered by the population. Hence it has been asserted that the revolution took him by surprise. The fact was that he had no means of forestalling a surprise, and was obliged to modify his measures in proportion to the forces at his disposal. The crowds began

to gather on March 17th, when the news of the Vienna revolution reached Milan ; street fighting began on the 18th and 19th, and the marshal was forced to concentrate his scattered troops upon the gates and walls of the great city, lest he should find himself shut in by an advancing Piedmontese army.

On March 21st it became certain that Charles Albert of Sardinia would cross the Ticino with his army. Radetzky left Milan and retreated beyond the Mincio to the strong fortress of Verona, which, with Mantua, Peschiera, and Legnago, formed the "Quadrilateral" which became famous in the following campaign. Most of the garrisons in the Lombard towns were able to cut their way through, comparatively few surrendering. However, the 61,000 infantry of the imperial army were diminished by the desertion of the twenty Italian battalions which belonged to it, amounting to 10,000 men. It was necessary to abandon most of the state chests ; the field-marshal could only convey from Milan to Verona half a million florins in coined money, which was **The New Republic of Venice** saved by the division stationed in Padua, which made a rapid advance before the outbreak of the revolt. Venice had thrown off the yoke. The lawyer Daniel Manin, of Jewish family, and therefore not a descendant of Lodovico Manin, the last doge, had gained over the arsenal workers.

With their help he had occupied the arsenal and overawed the field-marshal, Count Ferdinand Zichy, a brother-in-law of Metternich, who was military commander in conjunction with the civil governor, Count Pálffy of Erdöd. Zichy surrendered on March 22nd, on condition that the non-Italian garrison should be allowed to depart unmolested. Manin became president of the new democratic Republic of Venice, which was joined by most of the towns of the former Venetian terra firma ; Great Britain and France, however, declined to recognise the republic, which was soon forced to make common cause with Sardinia. Mantua was preserved to the Austrians by the bold and imperturbable behaviour of the commandant-general, Von Gorczkowski.

The Italian nationalist movement had also spread to the South Tyrol. On March 19th the inhabitants of Trent demanded the incorporation into Lombardy of the Trentino—that is, the district of the former prince-bishopric of Trent. The appearance of an Austrian brigade under General von Zobel to relieve the hard-pressed garrison of the citadel secured the Austrian possession of this important town, and also strengthened the only line of communication now open between Radetzky's headquarters and the Austrian government, the line through the Tyrol.

The defence of their country was now undertaken by the German Tyrolese themselves; they called out the defensive forces which their legislature had provided for centuries past, and occupied the frontiers. They were not opposed by the Italian population on the south, who in many cases volunteered to serve in the defence of their territory; hence the revolutionary towns were unable to make head against these opponents, or to maintain regular communication with the revolutionists advancing against the frontier. Wherever the latter attempted to break through they were decisively defeated by the admirable Tyrolese guards, who took up arms against the " Guelfs " with readiness and enthusiasm.

On March 29th, 1848, the King of Sardinia crossed the Ticino, without any formal declaration of war, ostensibly to protect his own territories.

DANIEL MANIN

He became President of the Venetian republic in 1848, and after the capitulation of Venice in the following year escaped to Paris, where he died in 1857.

He had at his disposal three divisions, amounting to about 45,000 men, and after gaining several successes in small conflicts at Goito, Valeggio, and elsewhere, against weak Austrian divisions, he advanced to the Mincio on April 10th. Mazzini had appeared in Milan after the retreat of the Austrians; but the advance of the Piedmontese prevented the installation of a republican administration. For a moment the national movement was concentrated solely upon the

The Forces Opposed to Austria struggle against the Austrian supremacy. Tumultuous public demonstrations forced the petty and central states of Italy to send their troops to the support of the Piedmontese. In this way nearly 40,000 men from Naples, Catholic Switzerland, Tuscany, Modena, and elsewhere were concentrated on the Po under the orders of General Giacomo Durando, to begin the attack on the Austrian position in conjunction with Charles Albert.

After the despatch of the troops required to cover the Etsch valley and to garrison the fortresses, Radetzky was left with only 35,000 men; he was able, however, with nineteen Austrian battalions, sixteen squadrons, and eighty-one guns, to attack and decisively defeat the king at Santa Lucia on May 6th, as he was

Deciding Point in the Revolution advancing with 41,000 men and eighty guns. The Zehner light infantry under Colonel Karl von Kopal behaved admirably; the Archduke Francis Joseph, heir presumptive, also took part in the battle. The conspicuous services of these bold warriors to the fortunes of Austria have made this obstinate struggle especially famous in the eyes of their compatriots. Radetzky's victory at Santa Lucia is the turning-point in the history of the Italian revolution.

The Austrian troops definitely established the fact of their superiority to the Piedmontese, by far the best of the Italian contingents. Conscious of this, the little army was inspired with confidence in its own powers and in the generalship of the aged marshal, whose heroic spirit was irresistible. Many young men from the best families of Vienna and the Alpine districts took service against the Italians. The healthy-minded students were glad to escape from the aula of the University of Vienna, with its turgid orations and sham patriotism, and to shed their blood for the honour of their nation side by side with the brave " volunteers," who went into action with jest and laugh. Such events considerably abated the enthusiasm of the Italians, who began to learn that wars cannot be waged by zeal alone, and that their fiery national spirit gave them no superiority in the use of the rifle.

Radetzky was not to be tempted into a reckless advance by the brilliant success he had attained; after thus vigorously repulsing Charles Albert's main force, he remained within his quadrilateral of fortresses, awaiting the arrival of the reserves which were being concentrated in Austria; 16,000 infantry, eight squadrons of cavalry, and fifty-four guns marched from Isonzo under Laval, Count Nugent, master of the ordnance, an old comrade of Radetzky. He was an Irishman by birth, and had entered the Austrian army in 1793; in 1812 he had seen service in Spain during the War of Liberation, and in 1813 had led the revolt on the coast districts. On April 22nd Nugent captured Udine, and advanced by way of Pordenone and Conegliano to Belluno, Feltre, and Bassano, covering his flank by the mountains, as Durando's corps had gone northward from the Po to prevent his junction with Radetzky. Nugent fell sick, and after continual fighting, Count Thurn led the reserves to San Boniface at Verona, where he came into touch with the main army on May 22nd.

Meanwhile, the monarchical government in Naples had succeeded in defeating the Republicans, and the king accordingly

LEOPOLD II.
Grand Duke of Tuscany, Leopold II. granted a liberal constitution to his people, and thought he had satisfied all their demands, but a revolt broke out, and he fled to Gaeta.

recalled the Neapolitan army, which had already advanced to the Po. The summons was obeyed except by 2,000 men, with whom General Pepe reinforced the Venetian contingent. This change materially diminished the danger which had threatened Radetzky's left flank; he was now able to take the offensive against the Sardinian army, and advanced against Curtatone and Goito from Mantua, whither he had arrived on May 28th with two corps and part of the reserves. He proposed to relieve Peschiera, which was invested by the Duke of Genoa; but the garrison had received no news of the advance of the main army, and were forced from lack of provisions to surrender on May 30th. However, after a fierce struggle at Monte Berico on June 10th, in

THE BOMBARDMENT OF MESSINA IN SEPTEMBER, 1848
The town of Messina, which lately was the scene of a destructive earthquake, suffered severely in September, 1848, during the rising of Italy against Austria. Under the bombardment of General Filangieri, the town was exposed to a heavy fire; many houses were destroyed and burned and thousands of dead bodies lay in the streets.

ARRANGING TERMS OF PEACE: THE MEETING OF VICTOR EMMANUEL AND RADETZKY

In this picture there is represented the meeting of the two principals in the war between Sardinia and Austria, Victor Emmanuel II. and Count Radetzky, which took place on March 24th, 1849, at the farmstead of Vignale. An armistice was agreed to on conditions which were to serve as the basis of a peace, finally concluded in the following August.

From the painting by Aldi, in the Palace of the Signory, Siena

which Colonel von Kopal, the Roland of the Austrian army, was killed, Radetzky captured Vicenza, General Durando being allowed to retreat with the Roman and Tuscan troops. They were joined by the "crociati," crusaders, who had occupied Treviso. Padua was also evacuated by the revolutionaries, and almost the whole of the Venetian province was thus recovered by the Austrians. Fresh reinforcements from Austria were employed in the formation of a second reserve corps under General von Welden on the Piave; this force was to guard Venetia on the land side.

At this period the provisional government in Milan offered the Lombard-Venetian crown to the King of Sardinia.

Charles Albert might reasonably hope to wear it, as the Austrian Government, which had retired to Innsbruck on the renewal of disturbances in Vienna, showed some inclination to conclude an armistice in Italy. Britain and France, however, had declared the surrender by Austria of the Italian provinces to be an indispensable preliminary to peace negotiations.

Radetzky hesitated to begin negotiations for this purpose, and remained firm in his resolve to continue the war, for which he made extensive preparations in the course of June and July, 1848. He formed a third army corps in South Tyrol, under Count Thurn, a fourth in Legnago, under General von Culoz, and was then able with the two corps already on foot to

In the hope of re-establishing her ancient form of government under the presidency of Manin, Venice rose in revolt against Austria in 1848, but after a fifteen months' siege of the city the Austrians compelled it to capitulate.
From the drawing by W. Giacomelli

The enthusiasm of the citizens of Venice in their revolt against Austria was shared by all classes, even the women and children desiring to have some part in the struggle for liberty, and bringing their jewels, as shown in the above picture, to raise money for the defence of the city against the attack of their hated enemy.

SCENES IN THE SIEGE OF VENICE BY THE AUSTRIANS IN 1848-49

attack the king in his entrenchments at Sona and Sommacampagna. Operations began here on July 23rd, and ended on the 25th with the Battle of Custozza. The king was defeated, and Radetzky secured command of the whole line of the Mincio.

Charles Albert now made proposals for an armistice. Radetzky's demands, however, were such as the king found impossible to entertain. He was forced to give up the line of the Adda, which the field-marshal crossed with three army corps on August 1st without a struggle. The Battle of Milan on the 4th so clearly demonstrated the incapacity of the Piedmontese troops that the king must have welcomed the rapidity of the Austrian advance as facilitating his escape from the raging mob with its cries of treason. Radetzky entered Milan on August 6th and was well received by some part of the population. Peschiera was evacuated on the 10th. With the exception of Venice, the kingdom of the double crown had now been restored to the emperor. An armistice was concluded between Austria and Sardinia on August 9th for six weeks; it was prolonged by both sides, though without formal stipulation, through the autumn of 1848 and the winter of 1848–1849.

In Tuscany the Grand Duke Leopold II. thought he had completely satisfied the national and political desires of his people by the grant of a liberal constitution and by the junction of his troops with the Piedmont army. Since the time of the great Medici, this fair province had never been so prosperous as under the mild rule of the Hapsburg grand duke; but the Republicans gave it no rest. They seized the harbour of Livorno and also **Flight of the Grand Duke Leopold II.** the government of Florence in February, 1849, under the leadership of Mazzini's follower, Francesco Domenico Guerrazzi, whom Leopold was forced to appoint Minister. The grand duke fled to Gaeta, where Pope Pius IX. had sought refuge at the end of November, 1848, from the Republicans, who were besieging him in the Quirinal. Mazzini and his friend Giuseppe Garibaldi, who had led a life of adventure in South America after the

MARSHAL RADETZKY
Rightly called "the saviour of the Monarchy," this great marshal led the forces of Austria to one success after another during the Italian rising and quelled the Revolution.

persecutions of the 'thirties, harassed the Austrians with the adherents who had gathered round them. They operated in the neighbourhood of Lago Maggiore, where they could easily withdraw into Swiss territory, and also stirred their associates in Piedmont to fresh activity. King Charles Albert saw that a renewal **Radetzky Ready for Emergencies** of the campaign against the Austrians was the only means of avoiding the revolution with which he also was threatened. He had, therefore, by dint of energetic preparation, succeeded in raising his army to 100,000 men. He rightly saw that a victory would bring all the patriots over to his side; but he had no faith in this possibility, and announced the termination of the armistice on March 12th, 1849, in a tone of despair. Radetzky had long expected this move, and, far from being taken unawares, had made preparations to surprise his adversary. Instead of retiring to the Adda, as the Sardinian had expected, he started from Lodi with 58,000 men and 186 guns, and made a turn to the right upon Pavia. On March 20th he crossed the Ticino and moved upon Mortara, while Charles Albert made a corresponding manœuvre at Buffalora and entered Lombard territory at Magenta. He had entrusted the command of his army to the Polish revolutionary general, Adalbert Chrzanowski, whose comrade, Ramorino, led a division formed of Lombard fugitives. Radetzky's bold flank movement had broken the connection of the Sardinian forces; Chrzanowski was forced hastily to despatch two divisions to Vigevano and Mortara to check the Austrian advance, which was directed against the Sardinian line of retreat.

The stronghold of Mortara was captured on March 21st by the corps d'Aspre, the first division of which was led by the Archduke Albert. The Sardinian leaders were then forced to occupy Novara with 54,000 men and 122 guns, their troops available at the moment. Tactically the position was admirable, and here they awaited the decisive battle. Retreat to Vercelli was impossible, in view of the advancing Austrian columns.

On March 23rd Radetzky despatched his four corps to converge upon Novara. About 11 a.m. the Archduke Albert began the attack upon the heights of Bicocca, which formed the key to the Italian position. For four hours 15,000 men held out against 50,000, until the corps advancing on the road from Vercelli were **King and General in Conference** able to come into action at 3 p.m. This movement decided the struggle. In the evening the Sardinians were ejected from the heights of Novara and retired within the town, which was at once bombarded. The tactical arrangement of the Italians was ruined by the disorder of their converging columns, and many soldiers were able to take to flight. Further resistance was impossible, and the king demanded an armistice of Radetzky, which was refused. Charles Albert now abdicated, resigning his crown to Victor Emmanuel, Duke of Savoy, his heir, who happened to be present. During the night he was allowed to pass through the Austrian lines and to make his way to Tuscany.

On the morning of March 24th, King Victor Emmanuel had a conversation with Radetzky in the farmstead of Vignale, and arranged an armistice on conditions which were to serve as the basis of a future peace. The status quo ante in respect of territorial possession was to be restored ; the field-marshal waived the right of marching into Turin, which lay open to him, but retained the Lomellina, the country between the Ticino and the Sesia, which he occupied with 21,000 men until the conclusion of the peace. It was stipulated that Sardinia should withdraw her ships from the Adriatic and her troops from Tuscany, Parma, and Modena, and should forthwith disband the Hungarian, Polish, and Lombard volunteer corps serving with the army. Brescia, which the Republicans had occupied after the retreat of the **Garibaldi Withdraws from Rome** Austrians from Milan, was stormed on April 1st by General von Haynau, who brought up his reserve corps from Padua. In the preceding battles the Italians had committed many cruelties upon Austrian prisoners and wounded soldiers. For this reason the conquerors gave no quarter to the defenders of the town ; all who were caught in arms were cut down, and the houses burned from which firing had proceeded. With the defeat of Sardinia the Italian nationalist movement became purposeless. The restoration of constitutional government in the Church States, Tuscany, and the duchies was opposed only by the democrats. Their resistance was, however, speedily broken by the Austrian troops, Bologna and Ancona alone necessitating special efforts ; the former was occupied on May 15th, the latter on the 19th. Under Garibaldi's leadership Rome offered a vigorous resistance to the French and Neapolitans, who were attempting to secure the restoration of the Pope at his own desire.

The French general Victor Oudinot, a son of the marshal of that name under Napoleon I., was obliged to invest the Eternal City in form from June 1st to July 3rd with 20,000 men, until the population perceived the hopelessness of defence and forced Garibaldi to withdraw with 3,000 Republicans. From the date of her entry into Rome until the year 1866, and again from 1867 to 1870, France maintained a garrison in the town for the protection of the Pope. Venice continued to struggle longest for her independence. Manin rejected the summons to surrender **Italy's Power Crushed** even after he had received information of the overthrow and abdication of Charles Albert. The Austrians were compelled to drive parallels against the fortifications in the lagoons, of which Fort Malghera was the most important, and to bombard them continuously. It was not until communication between the town and the neighbouring coast line was entirely cut off by a flotilla of rowing boats that the failure of provisions and supplies forced the town council to surrender.

Italy was thus unable to free herself by her own efforts. Since the summer of 1848 the Austrian Government had been forced to find troops for service against the rebels in Hungary. It was not until the autumn that the capital of Vienna had been cleared of rioters ; yet Austria had been able to provide the forces necessary to crush the Italian power. Her success was due to the generalship and capacity of the great marshal, who is rightly called the saviour of the monarchy, and in no less degree to the admirable spirit, fidelity, and devotion of the officers, and to the superior bravery and endurance of the German and Slav troops. High as the national enthusiasm of the Italians rose, it could never compensate for their lack of discipline and military capacity.

THE
RE-MAKING
OF
EUROPE

EUROPE
IN
REVOLUTION
III

THE HUNGARIAN REBELLION
DEFEAT AND FLIGHT OF LOUIS KOSSUTH

THE struggle between Italy and Austria may be considered as inevitable ; each side staked its resources upon a justifiable venture. The same cannot be said of the Hungarian campaign. Under no urgent necessity, without the proposition of any object of real national value, blood was uselessly and wantonly shed, and the most lamentable aberrations and political blunders were committed. The result was more than a decade of bitter suffering, both for the Magyars and for the other peoples of the Hapsburg monarchy.

Such evils are due to the fact that revolutions never succeed in establishing a situation in any way tolerable; they burst the bonds of oppression and avenge injustice, but interrupt the normal course of development and of constitutional progress, thereby postponing improvements perfectly attainable in themselves. Both in Vienna and in Hungary the month of March had been a time of great con-

Confusion in Vienna and Hungary fusion. In the sudden excitement of the population and the vacillation of the Government, rights had been extorted and were recognised ;· but their exercise was impeded, if not absolutely prevented, by the continued existence of the state. In Vienna the most pressing questions were the right of the students to carry arms and to enter public life ; in Hungary, the creation of a special war office and an exchequer board of unlimited power.

The students were the leading spirits of political life in Vienna. There was no constitutional matter, no question of national or administrative policy, in which they had not interfered and advanced their demands in the name of the people. Movements in the capital, the seat of government, were therefore characterised by a spirit of immaturity, or, rather, of childishness. Quiet and deliberate discussion on business methods was unknown, every conclusion was rejected as soon as made, and far-sighted men of experience and knowledge of admini-

strative work were refused a hearing. Fluent and empty-headed demagogues, acquainted with the art of theatrical rant, enjoyed the favour of the excitable middle and working classes, and unfortunately were too often allowed a determining voice

Student Politicians in Vienna and influence in government circles. Any systematic and purposeful exercise of the rights that had been gained was, under these circumstances, impossible, for no one could appreciate the value of these concessions. Like children crying for the moon, they steadily undermined constituted authority and could put nothing in its place.

The students were seduced and exploited by ignorant journalists, aggressive hot-headed Jews, inspired with all Börne's hatred of monarchical institutions ; any sensible proposal was obscured by a veil of Heine-like cynicism. To the journalists must be added the grumblers and the base-born, who hoped to secure lucrative posts by overthrowing the influence of the more respectable and conscientious men. These so-called "Democrats" gained the consideration even of the prosperous classes by reason of their association with the students, who represented popular feeling.

They controlled the countless clubs and unions of the National Guard in the suburbs, and stirred up the working classes, which in Vienna were in the depths of political ignorance ; they had been, moreover, already inflamed by the emissaries which the revolutionary societies sent out into France, Switzerland, and West Germany, and were inspired with the

Democrats Dream of a New Era wildest dreams of the approach of a new era, bringing freedom, licence, and material enjoyment in boundless measure. Together with the Jews, the Poles also attained to great importance, especially after the disturbances in the Polish districts of Austria had been crushed by the energies of Count Franz Stadion, governor of Galicia, and of the town commandant of Cracow. The agitators who were there thrown out of employment received a most brilliant reception at Vienna, and their organisation of "lightning petitions" and street parades soon made them indispensable. On April 25th, 1848, was published the Constitution of Pillersdorf, a hastily constructed scheme, but not without merit; on May 9th, the election arrangements followed. Both alike were revolutionary; they disregarded the rights of the Landtag, and far from attempting to remodel existing material, created entirely new institutions in accordance with the political taste prevailing at the moment. Centralisation was a fundamental principle of these schemes; they presupposed the existence of a united territorial empire under uniform administration, from which only Hungary and the Lombard-Venetian kingdom were tacitly excluded. The Reichstag was to consist of a Senate and a Chamber of Deputies. The Senate was to include male members of the imperial house over twenty-four years of age, an undetermined number of life-members nominated by the emperor, and 150 representatives from among the great landowners; in the Chamber thirty-one towns and electoral districts of 50,000 inhabitants each were to appoint 383 deputies through their delegates.

LOUIS KOSSUTH

Leader of the Hungarian Revolution, Louis Kossuth was gifted with wonderful eloquence, and was able to impart his own enthusiasm to the people whom he led. He was appointed provisional Governor of Hungary after the National Assembly had declared the throne vacant.

From the outset the Radicals were opposed to a senate and the system of indirect election; the true spirit of freedom demanded one Chamber and direct election without reference to property or taxation burdens. Such a system was the expression of the people's rights, for the "people" consisted, naturally, of Democrats. All the moderate men, all who wished to fit the people for their responsibilities by some political education, were aristocrats, and aristocrats were

enemies of the people, to be crushed, muzzled, and stripped of their rights.

Popular dissatisfaction at the constitution was increased by the dismissal of the Minister of War, Lieutenant Field-Marshal Peter Zanini, and the appointment of Count Theodor Baillet de Latour on April 28th. The former was a narrow-minded scion of the middle class, and incapable of performing his duties, for which reason he enjoyed the confidence of the Democrats. The latter was a general of distinguished theoretical and practical attainments, and popular with the army; these facts and his title made him an object of suspicion to the "people." At the beginning of May the people proceeded to display their dissatisfaction with the ministerial president, Count Karl Ficquelmont, by the howls and whistling of the students. On May 14th the students fortified themselves with inflammatory speeches in the aula and allied themselves with the working classes; on the 15th they burst into the imperial castle and surprised Pillersdorf, who gave way without a show of resistance, acting on the false theory that the chief task of the Government was to avoid any immediate conflict. Concessions were granted providing for the formation of a central committee of the democratic unions, the occupation of half the outposts by National Guards, and the convocation of a "Constituent Reichstag" with one Chamber.

The imperial family, which could no longer expect protection in its own house from the Ministry, left Vienna on May 17th and went to Innsbruck, where it was out of reach of the Democrats and their outbursts of temper, and could more easily join hands with the Italian army. It was supported, from June 3rd, by Johann von Wessenberg, Minister of

Foreign Affairs, a diplomatist of the old federal period, but of wide education and clever enough to see that in critical times success is only to be attained by boldness of decision and a certain spirit of daring. After Radetzky's victory on the Mincio he speedily convinced himself that compliance with the desires of France and Britain for the cession of the Lombard-Venetian kingdom would be an absolute error—one, too, which would arouse discontent and irritation in the army, and so affect the conclusion of the domestic difficulty ; he therefore decisively rejected the interposition of the Western Powers in the Italian question.

Wessenberg accepted as seriously meant the emperor's repeated declarations of his desire to rule his kingdom constitutionally. As long as he possessed the confidence of the court he affirmed that this resolve must be carried out at all costs, even though it should be necessary to use force against the risings and revolts of the Radical Party. He was unable to secure as early a return to Vienna as he had hoped ; hence he was obliged to make what use **Archduke** he could of the means at his **Johann** disposal by entrusting the Arch- **as Regent** duke Johann with the regency during the emperor's absence. The regent's influence was of no value ; at that time he was summoned to conduct the business of Germany at Frankfort-on-Main, and his action in Vienna was in consequence irregular and undertaken without full knowledge of the circumstances.

On July 18th the Archduke Johann, as representing the emperor, formed a Ministry, the president being the progressive landowner Anton von Doblhoff. The advocate Dr. Alexander Bach, who had previously belonged to the popular party, was one of the members. The elections to the Reichstag were begun after Prince Alfred of Windisch-Graetz, the commander of the imperial troops in Bohemia, had successfully and rapidly suppressed a revolt at Prague which was inspired by the first Slav Congress. This achievement pacified Bohemia. On July 10th the deputies of the Austrian provinces met for preliminary discussion.

The claims of the different nationalities to full equality caused a difficulty with respect to the language in which business should be discussed ; objections were advanced against any show of preference for German, the only language suitable to the purpose. However, the necessity of a rapid interchange of ideas, and dislike of the wearisome process of translation through an interpreter, soon made German the sole medium of communication, in spite of the protests raised by the numerous Polish peasants, who had been elected in Galicia against the desires of the nobility.

A New State in Hungary The most pressing task, of drafting the Austrian Constitution, was entrusted to a committee on July 31st; the yet more urgent necessity of furthering and immediately strengthening the executive power was deferred till the committee should have concluded its deliberations. The Ministry was reduced to impotence in consequence, and even after the emperor's return to Schönbrunn, on August 12th, its position was as unstable as it was unimportant.

While these events were taking place in Vienna a new state had been created in Hungary, which was not only independent of Austria, but soon showed itself openly hostile to her. For this, two reasons may be adduced : in the first place, misconceptions as to the value and reliability of the demands advanced by the national spokesmen ; and, secondly, the precipitate action of the Government, which had made concessions without properly estimating their results. The Magyars were themselves unequal to the task of transforming their feudal state into a constitutional body politic of the modern type as rapidly as they desired.

They had failed to observe that the application of the principle of personal freedom to their existing political institutions would necessarily bring to light national claims of a nature to imperil their paramountcy in their own land, or that, in the inevitable struggle for this paramount position, the support of Austria and of the reigning house would be of great value. With their characteristic tendency to overestimate their powers, they deemed them-**The Magyars** selves capable of founding a **Demand** European power at one stroke. **Independence** Their impetuosity further increased the difficulties of their position. They were concerned only with the remodelling of domestic organisation, but they strove to loose, or rather to burst asunder, the political and economic ties which for centuries had united them to the German hereditary possessions of their ruling house. They demanded an independence which they had lost on the day of the Battle of Mohacs. They deprived their king of rights which had been the indisputable possession of every one of his crowned ancestors. Such were, the supreme command of his army, to which Hungary contributed a number of men, though sending no individual contingents; the supreme right over the coinage and currency, which was a part of the royal prerogative, and had been personally and therefore uniformly employed by the representatives of the different sovereignties composing the Hapsburg power.

The legal code confirmed by the emperor and King Ferdinand at the dissolution of the old Reichstag, on April 10th, 1848, not only recognised the existing rights of the Kingdom of Hungary, but contained concessions from the emperor which endangered and indeed destroyed the old personal union with Austria. Of these the chief was the grant of an independent Ministry, and the union of Hungary and Transylvania without any obligation of service to the Crown, without the recognition of any community of interests, without any stipulation for such co-operation as might be needed to secure the existence of the joint monarchy.

In Croatia, Slavonia, in the Banat, and in the district of Bacska inhabited by the Servians, the Slavonic nationalist movement broke into open revolt against Magyar self-aggrandisement; the Hungarian Ministry then demanded the recall of all Hungarian troops from the Italian army, from Moravia and Galicia, in order to quell the "anarchy" prevailing at home. The Imperial Government now discovered that in conceding an "independent" war ministry to Hungary they had surrendered the unity of the army, and so lost the main prop of the monarchical power. The difficulty was incapable of solution by peaceful methods; a struggle could only be avoided by the voluntary renunciation on the part of Hungary of a right she had extorted but a moment before. No less intolerable was the independent

attitude of Hungary on the financial question, wherein she showed no inclination to consider the needs of the whole community. She owed her political existence to German victories over the Turks, but in her selfishness would not save

Hungary's Debt to German Victories

Austria from bankruptcy by accepting a quarter of the national debt and making a yearly payment of one million pounds to meet the interest. The majority of the Ministry of Batthyány, to which the loyalist Franz von Deák belonged, were by no means anxious to bring about a final separation between Hungary and Austria; they were even ready to grant troops to the court for service in the Italian war, if the Imperial Government would support Hungarian action against the malcontent Croatians.

In May, Count Batthyány hastened to the Imperial Court at Innsbruck and succeeded in allaying the prevailing apprehensions. The court was inclined to purchase Hungarian adherence to the dynasty and the empire by compliance in all questions affecting the domestic affairs of Hungary. But it soon became clear that Batthyány and his associates did not represent public feeling, which was entirely led by the fanatical agitator Kossuth, who was not to be appeased by the offer of the portfolio of finance in Batthyány's Ministry.

Louis Kossuth was a man of extravagant enthusiasm, endowed with great histrionic powers, a rhetorician who was apt to be carried away by the torrent of his own eloquence, a type of the revolutionary apostle and martyr. He was undoubtedly lacking in sobriety of political judgment, and his powers were never exerted with full effect except under the stress of high excitement; he seems, indeed, to have been one of those who realise themselves only at the moment when they feel that the will of great masses of men has fallen completely under the sway of their own passion of eloquence. The ambitions of such men can never be satisfied in any

FRANCIS JOSEPH I.
Born in 1830, he became Emperor of Austria in 1848, succeeding his uncle Ferdinand I., who had been compelled to abdicate. The above portrait was taken about the year 1830.

arena less than that in which national destinies are staked. Kossuth did not enter on his political career from motives of personal aggrandisement, with a deliberate intention of overthrowing the Hapsburg rule in order that he might become the presiding genius and authoritative chief of a Hungarian Republic; but it can hardly be questioned that this would have been the outcome of the movement which he originated, had it been carried to a successful issue with Kossuth at its head.

For such national rights as the Magyars could claim for themselves full provision was made by the Constitution, which they had devised on liberal principles, abolishing the existing privileges of the nobility and corporations; every freedom was thus provided for the development of their strength and individuality. On July 2nd, 1848, the Reichstag elected under the new Constitution met together. The great task before it was the satisfaction of the other nationalities, the Slavs, Roumanians, and Saxons, living on Hungarian soil; their acquiescence in the Magyar predominance was to be secured without endangering the unity of the kingdom, by means of laws for national defence, and of other innovations making for prosperity.

Some clear definition of the connection between Hungary and Austria was also necessary if their common sovereign was to retain his prestige in Europe; and it was of the first importance to allay the apprehensions of the court with regard to the fidelity, the subordination, and devotion of the Magyars. Kossuth, however, brought before the Reichstag a series of proposals calculated to shatter the confidence which Batthyány had exerted himself to restore during his repeated visits to Innsbruck. The Austrian national bank had offered to advance one and a quarter million pounds in notes for the purposes of the Hungarian Government. This proposal Kossuth declined, and issued Hungarian

Kossuth's Demands at the Reichstag

KOSSUTH IN LATER LIFE

For some years Kossuth resided in England, the above portrait showing him during his stay in this country. He died in the year 1894.

paper for the same amount; he then demanded further credit to the extent of 4,200,000 pounds, to equip a national army of 200,000 men. He even attempted to determine the foreign policy of the emperor-king. Austria was to cede all Italian territory as far as the Etsch, and, as regarded her German provinces, to bow to the decisions of the central power in Frankfort. In case of dispute with this power she was not to look to Hungary for support. Such a point of view was wholly incompatible with the traditions and the European prestige of the House of Hapsburg; to yield would have been to resign the position of permanency and to begin the disruption of the monarchy.

It was to be feared that Hungarian aggression could be met only by force. The federal allies, who had already prepared for what they saw would be a hard struggle, were now appreciated at their true value. They included the Servians and Croatians, who were already in open revolt against the Magyars, and had been organised into a military force by Georg Stratimirovt. The Banace of Croatia was a dignity in the gift of the king, though his nominee was responsible to Hungary. Since the outbreak of the revolution the position had been held by an Austrian general upon the military frontier—Jellacic.

Though no professional diplomatist, he performed a master-stroke of policy in securing to the support of the dynasty the southern Slav movement fostered by the "Great Illyrian" party. He supported the majority of the Agram Landtag in their efforts to secure a separation from Hungary, thereby exposing himself to the violent denunciations of Batthyány's Ministry, which demanded his deposition. These outcries he disregarded, and pacified the court by exhorting the frontier regiments serving under Radetzky to remain true to their colours and to give their lives for the glory of Austria. The approbation of his comrades in the imperial army strengthened him in the conviction that it was his destiny to save the army and the Imperial house. He formed a Croatian army of 40,000 men, which was of no great military value, though its numbers, its impetuosity, and its extraordinary armament made it formidable. The victories of the Italian

The Emperor's Answer to Kossuth army and the reconquest of Milan raised the spirit of the Imperial Court. On August 12th the emperor returned to the summer palace of Schönbrunn, near Vienna, and proceeded to direct his policy in the conviction that he had an armed force on which he could rely, as it was now possible to reconcentrate troops by degrees in different parts of the empire. On August 31st, 1848, an Imperial decree was issued to the palatine Archduke Stephen, who had hitherto enjoyed full powers as the royal representative in Hungary and Transylvania ; the contents of the decree referred to the necessity of enforcing the Pragmatic Sanction. Such was the answer to the preparations begun by Kossuth.

This decree, together with a note from the Austrian Ministry upon the constitutional relations between Austria and Hungary, was at once accepted by Kossuth as a declaration of war, and was made the occasion of measures equivalent to open revolt. On September 11th the Minister of Finance in a fiery speech, which roused his auditors to a frenzied excitement, declared himself ready to assume the dictatorship on the retirement of Batthyány's Ministry. On the same day the Croatian army crossed the Drave and advanced upon Lake Platten.

The Vienna Democrats, who might consider themselves masters of the capital, had been won over to federal alliance with Hungary. The most pressing necessity was the restoration of a strong government which would secure respect for established authority, freedom of deliberation

Illiterate Deputies in the Reichstag to the Reichstag, and power to carry out its conclusions. The Reichstag, however, preferred to discuss a superficial and ill-conceived motion brought forward by Hans Kudlich, the youthful deputy from Silesia, for releasing peasant holdings from the burdens imposed on them by the overlords. The work of this Reichstag, which contained a large number of illiterate deputies from Galicia, may be estimated from the fact that it showed a strong in-

clination to put the question of compensation on one side. Dr. Alexander Bach was obliged to exert all his influence and that of the Ministry to secure a recognition of the fundamental principle, that the relief of peasant holdings should be carried out in legal form. The " people " of Vienna took little part in these negotiations ; their attention was concentrated upon the noisy outcries of the Democrats, who were in connection not only with the radical element of the Frankfort Parliament, but also with Hecker and his associates.

As early as the middle of September a beginning was made with the task of fomenting disturbances among the working classes, and the retirement of the Ministry was demanded. Great excitement was created by the arrival of a large deputation from the Hungarian Reichstag, with which the riotous Viennese formed the tie of brotherhood in a festive celebration on September 16th. The Hungarians were able to count upon the friendship of the Austrian revolutionaries after their manifestations of open hostility to the court. The Hungarian difficulty weakened the

Radical Hopes of a Republic impression made by Radetzky's victories, and radical minds again conceived hopes of overthrowing the Imperial house and forming a Federal Danube Republic. At the request of the archduke palatine, Count Louis Batthyány made another attempt to form a constitutional Ministry on September 17th, with the object of abolishing Kossuth's dictatorship ; however, no practical result was achieved.

The die had been already cast, and the military party had established the necessity of restoring the imperial authority in Hungary by force of arms. The Archduke Stephen attempted to bring about a meeting with Jellacic, to induce him to evacuate Hungarian territory, but the banus excused himself ; at the same time the palatine was informed that Field-Marshal Lamberg had been appointed commander-in-chief of the imperial troops in Hungary, and that the banus was under his orders. This was a measure entirely incompatible with the then existing Constitution. The archduke recognised that he would be forced to violate his constitutional obligations as a member of the Imperial house ; he therefore secretly abandoned the country and betook himself to his possessions in Schaumberg without making any stay in Vienna.

When Count Lamberg attempted to take up his post in the Hungarian capital he fell into the hands of Kossuth's most desperate adherents, and was cruelly murdered on September 28th, 1848, at the new suspension bridge which unites Pesth and Ofen. An irreparable breach with the dynasty was thus made, and the civil war began. At the end of September the Hungarian national troops under General Moga, a force chiefly composed of battalions of the line, defeated Jellacic and advanced into Lower Austria. They were speedily followed by a Hungarian army which proposed to co-operate with the revolted Viennese, who were also fighting against the public authorities.

It was on October 6th, 1848, that the Viennese mob burst into open revolt, the occasion being the march of a grenadier battalion of the northern railway station for service against the Hungarians. The democratic conspirators had been stirred up in behalf of republicanism by Johannes Ronge, Julius Fröbel, and Karl Tausenau ; they had done their best to inflame the masses, had unhinged the minds of the populace to the point of rebellion, and **The Minister of War Assassinated** made the maintenance of public order impossible. The uproar spread throughout the city, and the Minister of War, Count Latour, was murdered. The Radical deputies, Löhner, Borrosch, Fischhof, Schuselka, and others now perceived that they had been playing with fire and had burnt their fingers. They were responsible for the murder, in so far as they were unable to check the atrocities of the mob, which they had armed.

Once again the Imperial family abandoned the faithless capital and took refuge in the archbishop's castle at Olmütz. The immediate task before the Government was to overpower the republican and anarchist movement in Vienna. In Olmütz the Government was represented by Wessenberg, and was also vigorously supported by Prince Felix Schwarzenberg, who had hastened to the court from Radetzky's camp. He had been employed not only on military service, but also in diplomatic duties in Turin and Naples.

He declared for the maintenance of the constitutional monarchy, and supported the decree drafted by Wessenberg, to the effect that full support and unlimited power of action should be accorded to the Reichstag summoned to Kremsier for discussion with the Imperial advisers upon some mutually acceptable form of constitution for the empire. There was strong feeling in favour of placing all power in the hands of Prince Alfred Windisch-Graetz, and establishing a military dictatorship in his person, with the abolition of all representative bodies ; but for the moment this idea was not realised. Windisch-Graetz was **Crushing the Revolt in Vienna** appointed field-marshal and commander-in-chief of all the imperial forces outside Italy, and undertook the task of crushing the revolt in Vienna and Hungary. The subjugation of Vienna was an easy task.

The garrison, consisting of troops of the line under Auersperg, had withdrawn into a secure position outside the city on October 7th, where they joined hands with the troops of the banus Jellacic on the Leitha. These forces gradually penetrated the suburbs of Vienna. On October 21st the army of Prince Windisch-Graetz, marching from Moravia, arrived at the Danube, crossed the river at Nussdorf, and advanced with Auersperg and Jellacic upon the walls which enclosed Vienna.

The Democrats in power at Vienna, who had secured the subservience of the members of the Reichstag remaining in the city, showed the courage of bigotry. They rejected the demands of Windisch-Graetz, who required their submission, the surrender of the War Minister's murderers, and the dissolution of the students' committees and of the democratic unions ; they determined to defend Vienna until Hungary came to their help. Robert Blum, who, with Julius Fröbel, had brought an address from the Frankfort Democrats to Vienna, was a leading figure in the movement for resistance. Wenzel Messenhauser, the commander of the National Guard, undertook the conduct of the defence, and headed a division of combatants in person. The general assault was delivered on October 28th.

Only in the Praterstern and in **Vienna on the Point of Surrender** the Jägerzeile was any serious resistance encountered. By evening almost all the barricades in the suburbs had been carried, and the troops were in possession of the streets leading over the glacis to the bastions of the inner city.

On the next day there was a general feeling in favour of surrender. Messenhauser himself declared the hopelessness of continuing the struggle, and advised a general surrender. However, on the morning of October 30th he was on the Tower of Stephan watching the struggle of Jellacic against the Hungarians at Schwechat, and was unfortunately induced to proclaim the news of the Hungarian advance with an army of relief, thereby reviving the martial ardour of the desperadoes, who had already begun a reign of terror in

Vienna's Reign of Terror

Vienna. He certainly opposed the fanatics who clamoured for a resumption of the conflict; but he quailed before the intimidation of the democratic ruffians, and resigned his command without any attempt to secure the due observance of the armistice which had been already concluded with Windisch-Graetz. On the 31st the field-marshal threw a few shells into the town to intimidate the furious proletariat; but it was not until the afternoon that the imperial troops were able to make their way into the town. They arrived just in time to save the Imperial library and the museum of natural history from destruction by fire.

Vienna was conquered on November 1st, 1848; those honourable and distinguished patriots who had spent the month of October in oppression and constant fear of death were liberated. The revolution in Austria could now be considered at an end. The capture of Vienna cost the army sixty officers and 1,000 men killed and wounded. The number of the inhabitants, combatants and non-combatants, who were killed in the last days of October can only be stated approximately. Dr. Anton Schütte, an eye-witness, estimated the number at 5,000.

The next problem was the conduct of the war with Hungary, which had already raised an army of 100,000 men, and was in possession of every fortress of importance in the country, with the exception of Arad and Temesvar. The Battle of Schwechat, on October 30th, 1848, had ended with the retreat of the 30,000 men brought up by General Moga. The energy of the Hungarians had not been equal to the importance of the occasion. A Hungarian victory at that time would have implied the relief of Vienna, and the question of the separation of the Crown of Stephen from the House of Hapsburg would certainly have become of European importance.

Abdication of the Emperor Ferdinand

Upon the abdication of the Emperor Ferdinand and the renunciation of his brother, the Archduke Francis Charles, the Archduke Francis Joseph ascended the throne on December 2nd, 1848. On the same day Prince Windisch-Graetz advanced upon the Danube with 43,000 men and 216 guns, while General Count Franz Schlick started from Galicia with 8,000 men, and General Balthasar von Simunich moved upon Neutra from the Waag with 4,000 men. After a series of conflicts—at Pressburg on the 17th, at Raab on the 27th, at Moor on the 30th December, 1848, and after the victory of Schlick at Kaschau on December 11th, the provisional Government under Kossuth was forced to abandon Pesth and to retire to Debreczin; the banate was speedily evacuated by the national troops, as soon as Jellacic, who now commanded an army corps under Windisch-Graetz, was able to act with the armed Servians.

However, the field-marshal under-estimated the resisting power of the nation, which, as Kossuth represented, was threatened with the loss of its political existence, and displayed extraordinary capacities of self-sacrifice and devotion in those dangerous days. He was induced to advance into

The Tide Turns for Hungary

the district of the Upper Theiss with too weak a force, and divided his troops, instead of halting in strong positions at Ofen and Waitzen on the Danube and waiting for the necessary reinforcements. The Battle of Kapolna, on February 26th and 27th, 1849, enabled Schlick to effect the desired junction, and could be regarded as a tactical victory. Strategically, however, it implied a turn of the scale in favour of the Hungarians; they gradually concentrated under the Polish general Henryk Dembinski and the Hungarian Arthur Görgey, and were able to take the offensive at the end of March, 1849, under the general command of Görgey, who won a victory at Isaszégh, Gödöllö, on April 6th.

Ludwig von Melden, the representative of Windisch-Graetz, who had been recalled to Olmütz, was forced to retire to the Raab on April 27th to avoid being surrounded. The town of Komorn had offered a bold resistance to the Austrian besiegers, who had hitherto failed to secure this base, which was of importance for the further operations of the imperial army. General Moritz Perezel made a victorious advance into the banate. General Joseph Bem fought with varying success against the weak Austrian divisions in Transylvania under Puchner.

The remnants of these were driven into Wallachia on February 20th. By April, 1849, the fortresses of Ofen, Arad, and Temesvar alone remained in the occupation of the Austrians.

The promulgation of a new constitution for the whole of Austria, dated March 4th, 1849, was answered by Kossuth in a proclamation from Debreczin on April 14th, dethroning the House of Hapsburg. In spite of the armistice with Victor Emmanuel, Italy was as yet too disturbed to permit the transference of Radetzky's army to Hungary. Accordingly, on May 1st the Emperor Francis Joseph concluded a convention with Russia, who placed her forces at his disposal for the subjugation of Hungary, as the existence of a Hungarian

with three corps to Arad without coming into collision with the Russian contingents.

On August 5th Dembinski was driven back from Szoray to the neighbourhood of Szegedin, and the Hungarian leaders could no longer avoid the conviction that their cause was lost. On August 11th, Kossuth **Kossuth's** fled from Arad to Turkey. On **Flight** the 13th, Görgey, who had been **to Turkey** appointed dictator two days previously, surrendered with 31,000 men, 18,000 horse, 144 guns, and sixty standards, at Vilagos, to the Russian general Count Rüdiger. Further surrenders were made at Lugos, Boros-Jenö, Mehadia, and elsewhere. On October 5th, Klapka marched out of Komorn under the honourable capitulation of September 27th.

THE HISTORIC ARCHBISHOP'S CASTLE, NEAR OLMUTZ, IN MORAVIA

Republic threatened a rebellion in Poland. It was now possible to raise an overwhelming force for the subjection of the brave Hungarian army. General Haynau was recalled from the Italian campaign to lead the Imperial army in Hungary. He advanced from Pressburg with 60,000 Austrians, 12,000 Russians, and 250 guns. **The Imperial** Jellacic led 44,000 men and **Army** 168 guns into South Hungary, **in Hungary** while the Russian field-marshal Prince Paskevitch marched on North Hungary by the Dukla Pass with 130,000 men and 460 guns. Görgey repulsed an attack delivered by Haynau at Komorn on July 2nd; on the 11th he was removed from the command in favour of Dembinski, and defeated on the same battlefield, then making a masterly retreat through Upper Hungary

Hungary was thus conquered by Austria with Russian help. For an exaggeration of her national claims, which was both historically and politically unjustifiable, she paid with the loss of all her constitutional rights, and brought down grievous misfortune upon herself. The Magyar nationalists had expected the Western Powers to approve their struggles for independence and to support the new Magyar state against Austria and Russia ; they calculated particularly upon help from England. They were now to learn that the Hungarian question is not one of European importance, and that no one saw the necessity of an independent Hungarian army and Ministry of Foreign Affairs except those Hungarian politicians whose motive was not patriotism but self-seeking in its worst form.

AN EPISODE IN THE CAMPAIGN OF 1848: THE TROOPS RESTING BEFORE THE BATTLE OF SCHLESWIG

From the painting by I. Senne

STRUGGLES OF GERMAN DUCHIES
AND THE RISINGS OF THE SLAVS AND POLES

AN entirely strong and healthy national feeling came to expression in those " sea-girt " duchies, the masters of which had also been kings of Denmark since the fifteenth century. During the bitter period of the struggle for the supremacy of the Baltic they had but rarely been able to assert their vested right to separate administration. They, however, had remained German, whereas the royal branch of the House of Holstein-Oldenburg, one of the oldest ruling families in Germany, had preferred to become Danish. The members of the ducal House of Holstein, which had undergone repeated bifurcations, largely contributed to maintain German feeling in Schleswig and Holstein, and asserted their independence with reference to their Danish cousins by preserving their relations with the empire and with their German neighbours. In the eighteenth century the consciousness of their inde-

Results of the Vienna Congress pendence was so strong among the estates of the two duchies that the " royal law " of 1660, abolishing the assembly of the estates and establishing the paramountcy of the Danish branch of the House of Oldenburg, could not be executed in Schleswig and Holstein.

The result of the Vienna Congress had been to secure the rights of the German districts and to separate them definitely from Napoleon's adherent. Metternich's policy had bungled this question, like so many other national problems, by handing over Schleswig to the Danes, while including Holstein in the German Federation. Unity was, however, the thought that inspired the population of either country. This feeling increased in strength and became immediately operative when Denmark was so impolitic as to defraud the Germans by regulations which bore unjustly upon the imperial bank, founded in 1813. The disadvantages of Danish supremacy then became manifest to the lowest peasant. Danish paper and copper were forced upon the duchies, while their good silver streamed away to Copenhagen. The struggle against this injustice was taken up by the German patriot leaders, who were able to make the dissension turn on a constitutional point after the publication of the " open letter " of King Christian

Disadvantages of Danish Supremacy VIII. On July 8th, 1848, he announced the intention of the Danish Government, in the event of a failure of male heirs, to secure the succession to the undivided " general monarchy " to the female line, in accordance with the Danish royal law. Christian's only son, Frederic, was an invalid and childless, and the duchies had begun to speculate upon the demise of the Crown and the consequent liberation from a foreign rule.

Their constitution recognised only succession in the male line, a principle which would place the power in the hands of the ducal House of Holstein-Sonderburg-Augustenburg, while in Denmark the successor would be Prince Christian of Holstein-Sonderburg-Glücksburg, who had married Louise of Hesse-Cassel, a niece of Christian VIII. Schleswig had the prospect of complete separation from Denmark, and this object was approved in numerous public meetings and adopted as a guiding principle by the Assembly of these estates. Schleswig objected to separation from Holstein, and to any successor other than one in the male line of descent.

Christian VIII. died on January 20th, 1848, and was succeeded by his son, Fred-

The Duchies Demand Independence eric VII. This change and the impression created by the revolutions in Paris, Vienna, and Berlin confirmed the duchies in their resolve to grasp their rights and assert their national independence. Had the king met these desires with a full recognition of the provincial constitutions and the grant of a separate national position and administration, he would probably have been able to retain

4943

possession of the two countries under some form of personal federation without appealing to force of arms, and perhaps to secure their adherence for the future. He yielded, however, to the arguments of the " Eider Danes," who demanded the abandonment of Holstein and the incorporation of Schleswig with Denmark, regarding the Eider as the historical frontier of the Danish power. This party required a joint constitutional form of government, and induced the king to elect a Ministry from their number and to announce the incorporation of Schleswig in the Danish monarchy to the deputation from the Schleswig-Holstein provinces in Copenhagen, on March 22nd, 1848.

A New Government at Kiel

Meanwhile, the Assembly of the estates at Rendsburg had determined to declare war upon the Eider Danes. On March 24th a provisional government for the two duchies was formed at Kiel, which was to be carried on in the name of Duke Christian of Augustenburg, at that time apparently a prisoner in the hands of the Danes, until he secured liberty to govern his German territories in person.

The new Government was recognised both by the population at large and by the garrisons of the most important centres. It was unable, however, immediately to mobilise a force equivalent to the Danish army, and accordingly turned to Prussia for help. This step, which appeared highly politic at the moment, proved unfortunate in the result. The fate of the duchies was henceforward bound up with the indecisive and vacillating policy of Frederic William IV., whose weakness became daily more obvious ; he was incapable of fulfilling any single one of the many national duties of which he talked so glibly.

His first steps in the Schleswig-Holstein complication displayed extraordinary vigour. On April 3rd, 1848, two Prussian regiments of the Guard marched into Rendsburg, and their commander, General Eduard von Bonin, sent an ultimatum on the 16th to the Danish troops, ordering them to evacuate the duchy and the town of Schleswig, which they had seized after a victory at Bau on April 9th over the untrained Schleswig-Holstein troops. On April 12th the Federal Council at Frankfort recognised the provisional government at Kiel, and mobilised the tenth federal army corps, Hanover, Meck-

Prussian Regiments in Rendsburg

lenburg, and Brunswick, for the protection of the federal frontier. The Prussian general Von Wrangel united this corps with his own troops, and fought the Battle of Schleswig on the 23rd, obliging the Danes to retreat to Alsen and Jütland.

Throughout Germany the struggle of the duchies for liberation met with enthusiastic support, and was regarded as a matter which affected the whole German race. There and in the duchies themselves Prussia's prompt action might well be considered as a token that Frederic William was ready to accomplish the national will as regarded the north frontier. Soon, however, it became plain that British and Russian influence was able to check the energy of Prussia, and to confine her action to the conclusion of a peace providing protection for the interests of the German duchies.

The king was tormented with fears that he might be supporting some revolutionary movement. He doubted the morality of his action, and was induced by the threats of Nicholas I., his Russian brother-in-law, to begin negotiations with Denmark. These ended in the conclusion of a seven months' armistice at Malmö on August 26th, 1848, Prussia agreeing to evacuate the duchy of Schleswig. The government of the duchies was to be undertaken by a commission of five members, nominated jointly by Denmark and Prussia. The Frankfort Parliament attempted to secure the rejection of the conditions, to which Prussia had assented without consulting the imperial commissioner, Max von Gagern, who had been despatched to the seat of war, these conditions being entirely opposed to German feeling. But the resolutions on the question were carried only by small majorities ; the Parliament was unable to ensure their realisation, and was eventually forced to acquiesce in the armistice.

Prussia's Evacuation of Schleswig

Meanwhile the Assembly of the estates of Schleswig-Holstein hastily passed a law declaring the universal liability of the population to military service, and retired in favour of a " Constituent Provincial Assembly," which passed a new constitutional law on September 15th. The connection of the duchies with the Danish Crown was thereby affirmed to depend exclusively upon the person of the common ruler. The Danish members of the government commission declined to recognise the new constitution, and also demurred to the election of deputies from Schleswig to the Frankfort Parliament. Shortly afterwards Denmark further withdrew her recognition of the government commission. The armistice expired without any success resulting from the attempts of Prussia to secure unanimity on the Schleswig-Holstein question among the Great Powers. War consequently broke out again in February, 1849. Victories were gained by Prussian and federal troops and by a Schleswig-Holstein corps, in which were many Prussian officers on furlough from the king at Eckernförde on April 5th, and Kolding on April 23rd, 1849. On the other hand, the Schleswig-Holstein corps was defeated while besieging the Danish fortress of Fridericia, and forced to retreat beyond the Eider. On July 10th, 1849, Prussia concluded a further armistice with Denmark. The administration of the duchies was entrusted to a commission composed of a Dane, a Prussian, and an Englishman.

At the same time the government of Schleswig-Holstein was continued in Kiel in the name of the Provincial Assembly by Count Friedrich Reventlow and Wilhelm Hartwig Beseler, a solicitor. They tried to conclude some arrangement with the king-duke on the one hand, and on the other to stir up a fresh rising of the people against Danish oppression, which was continually increasing in severity in Schleswig. The devotion of the German population and the enthusiastic support of numerous volunteers from every part of Germany raised the available forces to 30,000 men and even made it possible to equip a Schleswig-Holstein fleet. In the summer of 1850, Prussia gave way to the representations of the Powers, and concluded the "Simple Peace" with Denmark on July 2nd. Schleswig-Holstein then began the struggle for independence on their own resources.

Discontent Under Danish Oppression

They would have had some hope of success with a better general than Wilhelm von Willisen, and if Prussia had not recalled her officers on furlough. Willisen retired from the battle of Idstedt, July 24th, before the issue had been decided, and began a premature retreat. He failed to prosecute the advantage gained at Missunde on September 12th, and retired from Friedrichstadt without making any impression, after sacrificing 400 men in a useless attempt to storm the place. The German Federation, which had been again convoked at Frankfort, revoked its previous decisions, in which it had recognised the rights of the duchies to determine their own existence, and assented to the peace concluded by Prussia. An Austrian army corps set out for the disarmament of the duchies. Though the Provincial Assembly still possessed an unbeaten army of 38,000 men fully equipped, it was forced on January 11th, 1851, to submit to the demands of Austria and Prussia to disband the army, and acknowledge the Danish occupation of the two duchies. From 1852 Denmark did her utmost to undermine the prosperity of her German subjects and to crush their national aspirations.

The Ignoble Methods of Denmark

Such ignoble methods failed to produce the desired result. Neither the faithlessness of the Prussian Government nor the arbitrary oppression of the Danes could break the national spirit of the North German marches. On the death of Frederic VII., on November 15th, 1863, they again asserted their national rights. Prussia had become convinced of their power and of the strength of their national feeling, and took the opportunity of atoning for her previous injustice.

Of the many quixotic enterprises called into life by the "nation's spring" of 1848, one of the wildest was certainly the Slav Congress opened in Prague on June 2nd. Here the catchword of Slav solidarity was proclaimed and the idea of "Panslavism" discovered, which even now can raise forebodings in anxious hearts, although half a century has in no way contributed to the realisation of the idea. At a time when the nations of Europe were called upon to determine their different destinies, it was only natural that the Slavs should be anxious to assert their demands. There were Slav peoples which had long been deprived of their national rights, and others, such as the Slovaks and part of the southern Slavs, who had never enjoyed the exercise of their rights. For these a period of severe trial had begun; it was for them to show whether they were capable of any internal development and able to rise to the level of national independence, or whether not even the gift of political freedom would help them to carry out that measure of social subordination which is indispensable to the uniform development of culture. The first attempts in this direction were

Rising of the Slavs

somewhat of a failure; they proved to contemporaries and to posterity that the Slavs were still in the primary stages of political training, that the attainment of practical result was hindered by the extravagance of their demands, their overweening and almost comical self-conceit, and that for the creation of states they possessed little or no capacity. The differences existing in their relations with other peoples, the lack of uniformity in the economic conditions under which they lived, the want of political training and experience—these were facts which they overlooked. They forgot the need of prestige and importance acquired by and within their own body, and considered of chief importance preparations on a large scale, which could never lead to any lasting political success.

THE HISTORIAN PALACKY
The Czech historian and politician, Franz Palacky, became influential at the imperial court in Olmütz. He was born in 1798 and died in 1876.

Had their action been limited to forwarding the common interests of the Austrian Slavs it might have been possible to produce a political programme dealing with this question, to demand a central Parliament, and, through opposition to the Hungarian supremacy, to assert the rights of the Slav majority as against the Germans, Magyars, and Italians. But the participation of the Poles in the movement, the appearance of the Russian radical democrat Michael Bakunin, and of Turkish subjects, infinitely extended the range of the questions in dispute, and led to propositions of the most arbitrary nature, the accomplishment of which was entirely beyond the sphere of practical politics. Panslavism, as a movement, was from the outset deprived of all importance by the inveterate failing of the Slav politicians, which was to set no limit to the measure of their claims, and to represent themselves as stronger than they were.

LOUIS MIEROSLAWSKI
A learned visionary who believed in the triumph of Democracy, he began his revolutionary work in Posen in 1848, and fought at the head of the rebels at Xions.

Greatly to the disgust of its organisers, among whom were several Austrian conservative nobles, the Slav Congress became an arena for the promulgation of democratic theories, while it waited for a congress of European nations to found Pan-Slavonic states. These states were to include Czechia—Bohemia and Moravia—a Galician-Silesian state, Posen under Prussian supremacy, until the fragments of Poland could be united into an independent Polish kingdom, and a kingdom of Slovenia which was to unite the Slav population of Styria, Carinthia, Carniola, and the seaboard. The Slav states hitherto under Hapsburg supremacy were to form a federal state; the German hereditary domains were to be graciously accorded the option of entering the federation, or of joining the state which the Frankfort Parliament was to create. The attitude of the Slovaks, Croatians, and Servians would be determined by the readiness of the Magyars to grant them full independence. Should the grant be refused, it would be necessary to form a Slovak and a Croatian state. All these achievements the members of the congress considered practicable, though they were forced to admit that the Slavs, whom they assumed to be inspired by the strongest aspirations for freedom and justice, were continually attempting to aggrandise themselves at one another's expense; the Poles, the Ruthenians, and the Croatians respectively, considered their most dangerous enemies to be the Russians, the Poles, and the Servians.

The Czech students in Prague had armed and organised a guard of honour for the congress. They made not the smallest attempt to conceal their hatred of the Germans; Germanism to them was anathema, and they yearned for the chance of displaying their heroism in an anti-German struggle, as the Poles had done against Russia. They were supported by the middle-class citizens, and the working classes were easily induced to join in a noisy demonstration on June 12th, 1848, against Prince Alfred Windisch-Graetz, the general commanding in Prague, as he had refused the students a grant of sixty thousand cartridges and a battery of horse artillery. The demonstration developed into a revolt, which the Czech leaders used as evidence for their cause, though it was to be referred rather to the disorderly character of the Czech mob than to any degree of national enthusiasm. The members of the congress were very disagreeably surprised, and decamped with the utmost rapidity when they found themselves reputed to favour the scheme for advancing Slav solidarity by street fights.

The Vienna government, then thoroughly cowed and trembling before the mob, made a wholly unnecessary attempt at intervention. Prince Windisch-Graetz, however, remained master of the situation, overpowered the rebels by force of arms, and secured the unconditional submission of Prague. He was speedily master of all Bohemia. The party of Franz Palacky, the Czech historian and politician, at once dropped the programme of the congress in its entirety, abandoned the ideal of Panslavism, and placed themselves at the disposal of the Austrian Government. Czech democratism was an exploded idea ; the conservative Czechs who survived its downfall readily co-operated in the campaign against the German democrats, and attempted to bring their national ideas into harmony with the continuance of Austria as dominant power. Palacky became influential at the imperial court in Olmütz and proposed the transference of the Reichstag to Kremsier, where his subordinate, Ladislaus Rieger, took an important share in the disruption of popular representation by the derision which he cast upon the German Democrats.

The Exploded Idea of Czech Democratism

The Austrian Slavs had acquired a highly favourable position by their victory over the revolutionary Magyars, an achievement in which the Croatians had a very considerable share. They might the more easily have become paramount, as the Germans had injured their cause by their senseless radicalism. Their fruitless attempt to secure a paramount position in Bohemia gave them a share in the conduct of the state ; this they could claim by reason of the strength and productive force of their race and of their undeniable capacity for administrative detail, had they conceded to the Germans the position to which these latter were entitled by the development of the Hapsburg monarchy and its destiny in the system of European states. The year 1848 might perhaps have afforded an opportunity for the restoration of Polish independence had the leaders of the national policy been able to find the only path which could guide them to success. Any attempt in this direction ought to have been confined to the territory occupied by Russia ; any force that might have been raised for the cause of patriotism could have been best employed upon Russian soil. Russia was entirely isolated ; it was inconceivable that any European Power could have come to her help, as Prussia had come in 1831, if she had been at war with the Polish nation.

Revolt of the Poles

Austria was unable to prevent Galicia from participation in a Polish revolt. Prussia had been won over as far as possible to the Polish side, for her possessions in Posen had been secured from any amalgamation with an independent Polish state. The approval of the German Parliament was as firmly guaranteed to the Polish nationalists as was the support of the French Republic, provided that German interests were not endangered.

Exactly the opposite course was pursued : the movement began with a rising in Posen, with threats against Prussia, with fire and slaughter in German communities, with the rejection of German culture, which could not have been more disastrous to Polish civilisation than the arbitrary and cruel domination of Russian officials and police. Louis of Mieroslawski, a learned visionary but no politician, calculated upon a victory of European democracy, and thought it advisable to forward the movement in Prussia, where the conservative power seemed most strongly rooted. He therefore began his revolutionary work in Posen, after the movement of March had set him free to act. On April 29th, 1848, he fought an unsuccessful battle at the head of 16,000 rebels against Colonel Heinrich von Brandt at Xions ; on the 30th he drove back a Prussian corps at Miloslaw. However, he gained no support from the Russian Poles, and democratic intrigue was unable to destroy the discipline of the Prussian army, so that the campaign in Posen was hopeless ; by the close of May it had come to an end, the armed bands were dispersed, and Mieroslawski driven into exile.

Failure of Polish Rising

4948

BARRICADE FIGHTING IN THE PARIS REVOLUTION: THE ARCHBISHOP OF PARIS MORTALLY WOUNDED ON SUNDAY, JUNE 25TH, 1848

THE SECOND REPUBLIC IN FRANCE
LOUIS NAPOLEON, PRESIDENT AND DICTATOR

THE European spirit of democracy which was desirous of overthrowing existing states, planting its banner upon the ruins, and founding in its shadow new bodies politic of the nature of which no Democrat had the remotest idea, had been utterly defeated in France at a time when Italy, Germany, and Austria were the scene of wild enthusiasm and bloody self-sacrifice. Democratic hopes ran the course of all political ideals. The process of realisation suddenly discloses the fact that every mind has its own conception of any ideal, which may assume the most varied forms when translated into practice.

A nation desirous of asserting its supremacy may appear a unity while struggling against an incompetent government ; but as soon as the question of establishing the national supremacy arises, numbers of different interests become prominent, which cannot be adequately satisfied by **France Declared a Republic** any one constitutional form. The simultaneous fulfilment of the hopes which are common to all is rendered impossible, not only by inequality of material wealth, but also by the contest for power, the exercise of which necessarily implies the accumulation of privileges on one side with a corresponding limitation on the other.

When the 900 representatives of the French nation declared France a republic on May 4th, 1848, the majority of the electors considered the revolution concluded, and demanded a public administration capable of maintaining peace and order and removing the burdens which oppressed the taxpayer. The executive committee chosen on May 10th, the president's chair being occupied by the great physicist Dominique François Arago, fully recognised the importance of the duty with which the country had entrusted it, and was resolved honourably to carry out the task. But in the first days of its existence the committee found itself confronted by an organised opposition, which, though excluded from the Government, claimed the right of performing its functions. Each party was composed of Democrats, government and opposition alike ; each entered the lists in the name of the sovereign people, those elected by the moneyed classes as well as **Leaders of the Radicals** the leaders of the idle or unemployed, who for two months had been in receipt of pay for worthless labour in the " national factories " of France.

On May 15th the attack on the dominant party was begun by the Radicals, who were pursuing ideals of communism or political socialism, or were anxious merely for the possession of power which they might use to their own advantage. They found their excuse in the general sympathy for Poland. The leaders were Louis Blanc, L. A. Blanqui, P. J. Proudhon, Etienne Cabet, and François Vincent Raspail. Ledru-Rollin declined to join the party. They had no sooner gained possession of the Hôtel de Ville than a few battalions of the National Guard arrived opportunely and dispersed the masses.

The leaders of the conspiracy were arraigned before the court of Bourges, which proceeded against them with great severity, while the national factories were closed. They had cost France £10,000 daily, and were nothing more than a meeting-ground for malcontents and sedition. This measure, coupled with an order to the workmen to report themselves for service in the provinces, produced the June revolt, a period of street fighting, in **The Struggle Round the Red Flag** which the radical Democrats, who gathered round the red flag, carried on a life and death struggle with the republican Democrats, whose watchword was the " République sans phrase." The monarchists naturally sided with the republican Government, to which the line troops and the National Guard were also faithful. The Minister of War, General Louis Eugène

Cavaignac, who had won distinction in Algiers, supported by the generals Lamoricière and Damesne, on June 23rd successfully conducted the resistance to the bands advancing from the suburbs to the centre of Paris. The "Reds," however, declined to yield, and on June 24th the National Assembly gave Cavaignac the dictatorship. He declared Paris in a state of siege, and pursued the rebels to the suburb of Sainte-Antoine, where a fearful massacre on June 27th made an end of the revolt. The victory had been gained at heavy cost; thousands of wounded lay in the hospitals of Paris and its environs. The number of lives lost has never been determined, but it equalled the carnage of many a great battle, and included nine generals and several deputies. An important reaction in public feeling had set in; the people's favour was now given to the conservative parties, and any compromise with the Radicals was opposed. The democratic republic was based on the co-operation of the former "constitutionalists." Thiers, Montalembert, and Odilon Barrot again became prominent figures. Cavaignac was certainly installed at the head of the executive committee; his popularity paled apace, however, as he did not possess the art of conciliating the bourgeois by brilliant speeches or promises of relief from taxation. The constitution, which was ratified after two months' discussion by the National Assembly, preserved the fundamental principle of the people's sovereignty. The choice of a president of the republic was not left to the deputies, but was to be decided by a plebiscite. This provision opened the way to agitators capable of

DOMINIQUE FRANÇOIS ARAGO
After France had been declared a republic, on May 4th, 1848, a capable public administration was demanded, and an executive committee was formed with Arago, the great astronomer and physicist, who had taken part in the Revolution of 1830, as a member.

LOUIS BLANC
Socialist and historian, he was appointed a member of the Provisional Government in 1848; escaping to London on being unjustly accused of complicity in the disturbances of that year, he there completed his "Histoire de la Révolution," returning later to France.

influencing the masses and prepared the path to supremacy for an ambitious member of the Bonaparte family, who had been repeatedly elected as a popular representative, and had held a seat in the National Assembly since September 26th, 1848. From the date of his flight from Ham Louis Napoleon had lived in England in close retirement. The outbreak of the February revolution inspired him with great hopes for his future; he had, however, learned too much from Strassburg and Boulogne to act as precipitately as his supporters in France desired. He remained strong in the conviction that his time would come, a thought which relieved the tedium of waiting for the moment when he might venture to act. He tendered his thanks to the republic for permission to return to his native land after so many years of proscription and banishment; he assured the deputies who were his colleagues of the zeal and devotion which he would bring to their labours, which had hitherto been known to him only "by reading and meditation." His candidature for the president's chair was then accepted not only by his personal friends and by the adherents of the Bonapartist empire, but also by numerous members of conservative tendencies, who saw in uncompromising Republicans like Cavaignac no hope of salvation from the terrors of anarchy. They were followed by ultramontanes, Orleanists, legitimists, and socialists, who objected to the republican doctrinaires, and used their influence in the election which took place on December 10th, 1848. Against the one and a half millions who supported

Cavaignac, an unexpectedly large majority of five and a half millions voted for the son of Louis Bonaparte and Hortense Beauharnais. As a politician no one considered him of any account, but every party hoped to be able to use him for their own purposes or for the special objects of their ambitious or office-seeking leaders. The behaviour of the National Assembly was not very flattering when the result of the voting was announced on December 20th. "Some, who were near Louis Bonaparte's seat," says Victor Hugo, "expressed approval; the rest of the Assembly preserved a cold silence. Marrast, the president, invited the chosen candidate to take the oath. Louis Bonaparte, buttoned up in a black coat, the cross of the Legion of Honour on his breast, passed through the door on the right, ascended the tribune, and calmly repeated the words after Marrast; he then read a speech, with the unpleasant accent peculiar to him, interrupted by a few cries of assent. He pleased his hearers by his unstinted praise of Cavaignac. In a few moments he had finished, and left the tribune amid a general shout of 'Long live the republic!' but with none of the cheers which had accompanied Cavaignac." Thus "the new man" was received with much discontent and indifference, with scanty respect, and with no single spark of enthusiasm. He was, indeed, without genius or fire and of very moderate capacity; but he understood the effect of commonplaces and the baser motives of his political instruments, and was therefore able to attract both the interest of France and the general attention of the whole

PIERRE JOSEPH PROUDHON
An advanced Socialist, Proudhon published works asserting that "Property is theft." In 1849 he was sentenced to three years' imprisonment for the violence of his utterances, and in 1858 received a similar sentence.

LOUIS EUGENE CAVAIGNAC
In 1848 this distinguished general became Minister of War, and carried his success on the field into his office of military dictator, promptly quelling the June insurrection. He was a candidate for the presidency of the republic when Louis Napoleon was elected.

of Europe. The president of the citizen republic was thus a member of the family of that great conqueror and subduer of the world whose remembrance aroused feelings of pride in every Frenchman, if his patriotism were not choked by legitimism; it was a problem difficult of explanation. No one knew whether the president was to be addressed as Prince, Highness, Sir, Monseigneur, or Citizen. To something greater he was bound to grow, or a revolution would forthwith hurl him back into the obscurity whence he had so suddenly emerged. But of revolution France had had more than enough. "Gain and the enjoyment of it" was the watchword, and Louis Napoleon accepted it. Victor Hugo claims to have shown him the fundamental principles of the art of government at the first dinner in the Elysée. Ignorance of the people's desires, disregard of the national pride, had led to the downfall of Louis Philippe; the most important thing was to raise the standard of peace. "And how?" asked the prince. "By the triumphs of industry and progress, by great artistic, literary, and scientific efforts. The labour of the nation can create marvels. France is a nation of conquerors; if she does not conquer with the sword, she will conquer by her genius and talent. Keep that fact in view and you will advance; forget it, and you are lost." Louis did not possess this power of expression, but with the idea he had long been familiar. He now increased his grasp of it. He knew that men get tired of great movements, political convulsion, hypocritical posing. Most people are out of breath after they have puffed themselves like the frog in the fable, and need a rest to recover their wind. As long as this desire for quietude prevailed, Napoleon the citoyen was secure of the favour of France. The moment he appealed to "great feelings" his art had reached its limits and he became childish and insignificant. His political leanings favoured the Liberalism for which the society of Paris had created the July kingdom. This tendency was shown in his appointment of Odilon Barrot as head of his Ministry, and of Edouard Drouyn de l'Huys, one of his personal adherents, as First Minister of Foreign Affairs. Desire to secure the

VICTOR HUGO
Greatest among the poets of France, Victor Hugo claimed to have shown Louis Napoleon the fundamental principles of the art of government, advising him at the first dinner in the Elysée to raise the standard of peace.

constituted authority against further attacks of the "Reds" was the dominant feeling which influenced the elections to the National Assembly. By the election law, which formed part of the constitution, these were held in May, 1849. The majority were former Royalists and Constitutionalists, who began of express purpose a reactionary policy after the revolt of the Communists in June, 1848. Fearful of the Italian democracy, into the arms of which Piedmont had rushed, France let slip the favourable opportunity of fostering the Italian movement for unity and of taking Austria's place

OVERTHROWING THE CONSTITUTION : THE COUP D'ETAT OF LOUIS NAPOLEON
Returning to France in 1848, after a few years of quiet seclusion in England, Louis Napoleon was elected deputy for Paris in the Constituent Assembly of June, and in December was elected president. But it was not long before he quarrelled with the Chambers, carrying out a coup d'état on December 1st, 1851, by overthrowing the constitution.

in the peninsula. Had she listened to Charles Albert's appeal for help, the defeat of Novara could have been avoided, and the Austrian Government would not have gained strength enough to become the centre of a reactionary movement which speedily interfered both with the revolutionary desires of the Radicals and the more modest demands of the moderate-minded friends of freedom.

Louis Bonaparte fully appreciated the fact that the sentiments of the population at large were favourable to a revival of **The Pope's** governmental energy through-**Supremacy** out almost the whole of Europe. **Restored** He saw that the excesses of the mob, which were as passionately excited as they were morally degraded, had restored confidence, among the moneyed classes and those who desired peace, in the power of religious guidance and education. For these reasons he acquiesced in the restoration of the temporal supremacy of the Pope, which the democracy had abolished, thereby rendering the greatest of all possible services to the ultramontanes.

In March, 1848, Pius IX., the "National Pope," had assented to the introduction within the states of the Church of a constitutional form of government. At the same time he had publicly condemned the war of Piedmont and the share taken in it by the Roman troops, which he had been unable to prevent. This step had considerably damped public enthusiasm in his behalf. Roman feeling also declared against him when he refused his assent to the liberal legislation of the Chambers and transferred the government to the hands of Count Pellegrino de Rossi. The count's murder, on November 15th, 1848, marked the beginning of a revolution in Rome which ended with the imprisonment of the Pope in the Quirinal, his flight to the Neapolitan fortress of Gaeta on November 27th, and the establishment of a provisional government.

The Pope was now inclined to avail himself of the services offered by Piedmont for the recovery of his power. However, the constituent National Assembly at Rome, which was opened on February 5th, 1849, voted for the restoration of the Roman republic by 120 votes against 23, and challenged the Pope to request the armed interference of the Catholic Powers in his favour. The Roman republic became the central point of the movement for Italian unity, and was joined by Venice, Tuscany, and Sicily. Mazzini was the head of the triumvirate which held the executive power ; Giuseppe Garibaldi directed the forces for national defence, of which Rome was now made the head-quarters. The "democratic republic" which was being organised in France would have no dealings with the descendants of the Carbonari, or with the chiefs of the revolutionary party in Europe. It considered alliance with the clericals absolutely indispensable to its own preservation. Hence came the agreement to co-operate with Austria, Spain, and Naples for the purpose of restoring the Pope to his temporal power. Twenty thousand men were at once despatched under Marshal Oudinot, and occupied the harbour town of Civita Vecchia on April 25th, 1849.

The president, however, had no intention of reimposing upon the Romans papal absolutism, with all the scandals of such a government. He sent out his trusty agent, Ferdinand de Lesseps, to effect some compromise between the Pope and the Romans which should result in the establishment of a moderate Liberal government. Oudinot, however, made a premature appeal to force of arms. He suffered a reverse before the walls of Rome on April 30th, and the military honour of France, which a descendant of Napoleon could not afford to disregard, demanded the conquest of the Eternal City. Republican soldiers thus found themselves co-operating with the reactionary Austrians, who entered Boulogne on May 19th, and reduced half of Ancona to ashes. On June 20th, the bombardment of Rome began, in the course of which many of the most splendid

THE POPE PIUS IX.

Succeeding Gregory XVI. in 1846, Pope Pius IX. introduced a series of reforms and won the affections of the populace. During the revolutionary fever of 1848, however, he opposed the public desire for a war with Austria, and the mob became so menacing that he found it expedient to make his escape from the Quirinal in disguise.

monuments of artistic skill were destroyed. The city was forced to surrender on July 3rd, 1849, after Garibaldi had marched away with 3,000 volunteers. By its attitude upon the Roman question, and by its refusal of support to the German Democrats, who were making their last efforts in the autumn of 1849 for the establishment of Republicanism in Germany, the French Republic gradually lost touch with the democratic principles on which it was based. Its internal disruption was expedited by the clumsiness of its constitution. A Chamber provided with full legislative power and indissoluble for three years confronted a president elected by the votes of a nation to an office tenable for only four years, on the expiration of which he was at once eligible for re-election.

Honest Republicans had foreseen that election by the nation would give the president a superfluous prestige and a dangerous amount of power ; but the majority of the Constituent Assembly had been "inspired with hatred of the republic."

Napoleon's Message to the Nation — They were anxious to have an independent power side by side with the Assembly, perhaps with the object of afterwards restoring the monarchy." This object Louis Bonaparte was busily prosecuting. On October 31st, 1849, he issued a message to the country, in which he gave himself out to be the representative of the Napoleonic system, and explained the maintenance of peace and social order to be dependent upon his own position. Under pressure from public opinion, the Chamber passed a new electoral law on May 31st, 1850, which abolished about three millions out of ten million votes, chiefly those of town electors, and required the presence of a quarter of the electorate to form a quorum. The Radicals were deeply incensed at this measure, and the Conservatives by no means satisfied. The president attempted to impress his personality on the people by making numerous tours through the country, and to conciliate the original electorate, to whose decision alone he was ready to bow.

A whole year passed before he ventured upon any definite steps; at one time the Chamber showed its power, at another it would display compliance. However, he could not secure the three-quarters majority necessary for determining a revision of the constitution, although seventy-nine out of eighty-five general councillors supported the proposal. There could be no doubt that the presidential election of May, 1852, would have forced on the revision, for the reason that Louis Napoleon would have been elected by an enormous majority, though the constitution did not permit immediate re-election. A revolt of this nature on the part of the

The Waiting Policy of Napoleon

whole population against the law would hardly have contributed to strengthen the social order which rests upon constitutionally established rights; the excitement of the elections might have produced a fresh outbreak of radicalism, which was especially strong in the south of France, at Marseilles and Bordeaux. The fear of some such movement was felt in cottage and palace alike, and was only to be obviated by a monarchical government.

No hope of material improvement in the conditions of life could be drawn from the speeches delivered in the Chamber, with their vain acrimony, their bombastic self-laudation, and their desire for immediate advantage. The childlike belief in the capacity and zeal of a national representative assembly was destroyed for ever by the experience of twenty years. The Parliament was utterly incompetent to avert a coup d'état, a danger which had been forced upon its notice in the autumn of 1851. It had declined a proposal to secure its command of the army by legislation, although the growing popularity of the new Cæsar with the

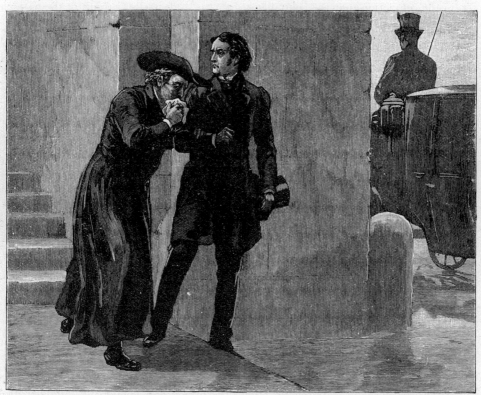

THE FLIGHT OF A POPE: PIUS IX. LEAVING THE QUIRINAL IN DISGUISE

army was perfectly obvious, and though General Saint-Arnaud had engaged to leave North Africa, and conduct the armed interference which was the first step to a revision of the constitution without consulting the views of the Parliament. After long and serious deliberation the president had determined upon the coup d'état ; the preparations were

Preparing for the Coup d'état made by Napoleon's half-brother, his mother's son, Count de Morny, and by Count Flahault. He was supported by the faithful Persigny, while the management of the army was in the hands of Saint-Arnaud. On December 2nd, 1851, the day of Austerlitz and of the coronation of his great uncle, it was determined to make the nephew supreme over France. General Bernard Pierre Magnan, commander of the garrison at Paris, won over twenty generals to the cause of Bonaparte in the event of conflict. Louis himself, when his resolve had been taken, watched the course of events with great coolness. Morny, a prominent stock-exchange speculator, bought up as much state paper as he could get, in the conviction that the coup d'état would cause a general rise of stock.

The movement was begun by the Director of Police, Charlemagne Emile de Maupas, who surprised in their beds and took prisoner every member of importance in the Chamber, about sixty captures being thus made, including the generals Cavaignac, Changarnier, and Lamoricière ; at the same time the points of strategic importance round the meeting hall of the National Assembly were occupied by the troops, which had been reinforced from the environs of Paris. The city awoke to find placards posted at the street corners containing three short appeals to the nation, the population of the capital, and the army, and a decree dissolving the National Assembly, restoring the right of universal suffrage, and declaring Paris

Paris in a State of Siege and the eleven adjacent departments in a state of siege. In the week, December 14th to 21st, 10,000,000 Frenchmen were summoned to the ballot-box to vote for or against the constitution proposed by the president. This constitution provided a responsible head of the state, elected for ten years, and threefold representation of the people through a state council, a legislative body, and a senate, the executive power being placed under the control of the sovereign people. On his appearance the president was warmly greeted by both people and troops, and no opposition was offered to the expulsion of the deputies who attempted to protest against the breach of the constitution.

It was not until December 3rd that the revolt of the Radicals and Socialists broke out ; numerous barricades were erected in the heart of Paris, and were furiously contested. But the movement was not generally supported, and the majority of the citizens remained in their houses. The troops won a complete victory, which was stated to have secured the establishment of the " democratic republic," though unnecessary acts of cruelty made it appear an occasion of revenge upon the Democrats. The exponents of barricade warfare were destroyed as a class for a long time to come, not only in Paris, but in the other great towns of France, where the last struggles of the Revolution were fought out. The impression caused by this success, by the great promises which Louis Napoleon made to his adherents, and by the rewards which he had begun to pay them,

Napoleon Becomes Dictator decided the result of the national vote upon the change in the constitution, or, more correctly, upon the elevation of Louis Napoleon to the dictatorship. By December 20th, 1851, 7,439,246 votes were given in his favour, against 640,737. Bonapartism in its new form became the governmental system of France.

" The severest absolutism that the nineteenth century has seen was founded by the general demonstrations of a democracy. The new ruler, in the early years of his government, was opposed by all the best intellects in the nation ; the most brilliant names in art and science, in politics and war, were united against him, and united with a unanimity almost unparalleled in the course of history. A time began in which wearied brains could find rest in the nirvana of mental vacuity, and in which nobler natures lost nearly all of the best that life could give. For a few years, however, the masses were undeniably prosperous and contented ; so small is the significance of mental power in an age of democracy and popular administration." It is the popular will which must bear the responsibility for the fate of France during the next two decades ; the nation had voluntarily humbled itself and bowed its neck to an adroit adventurer.

THE PROBLEM OF THE GERMAN STATES
AND THE VAIN SEARCH AFTER FEDERATION

ON May 18th, 1848, 586 representatives of every German race met in the Church of St. Paul at Frankfort-on-Main to create a constitution corresponding to the national needs and desires. The great majority of the deputies belonging to the National Assembly, in whose number were included many distinguished men, scholars, manufacturers, officials, lawyers, property owners of education and experience, were firmly convinced that the problem was capable of solution, and were honourably and openly determined to devote their best energies to the task. In the days of " the dawn of the new freedom," which illumined the countenances of politicians in the childhood of their experience, flushed with yearning and expectation, the power of conviction, the blessing that would be produced by immovable principles were believed as gospel. It was thought that the power of the Government was broken,

In "the Dawn of the New Freedom" that the Government, willing or unwilling, was in the people's hands, and could accommodate itself to the conclusions of the German constituents. Only a few were found to doubt the reliability of parliamentary institutions, and the possibility of discovering what the people wanted and of carrying out their wishes.

No one suspected that the experience of half a century would show the futility of seeking for popular unanimity, the division of the nation into classes at variance with one another, the disregard of right and reason by parliamentary, political, social, religious, and national parties as well as by princes, and the inevitability of solving every question which man is called upon to decide by the victory of the strong will over the weak.

A characteristic feature of all theoretical political systems is very prominent in Liberalism, which was evolved from theory and not developed in practice. This feature is the tendency to stigmatise all institutions which cannot find a place within the theoretical system as untenable, useless, and to be abolished in consequence ; hence the first demand of the Liberal politician is the destruction of all existing organisation, in order that no obstacle may impede the erection of the theoretical structure.

The Ideals of the Radicals Liberals, like socialists and anarchists, argue that states are formed by establishing a ready-made system, for which the ground must be cleared as it is required. They are invariably the pioneers to open the way for the Radicals, those impatient levellers who are ready to taste the sweets of destruction even before they have formed any plans for reconstruction, who are carried away by the glamour of idealism, though utterly incapable of realising any ideal, who at best are impelled only by a strong desire of " change," when they are not inspired by the greed which most usually appears as the leading motive of human action.

Thus it was that the calculations of the German Liberals neglected the existence of the Federal Assembly, of the federation of the states, and of their respective governments. They took no account of those forms in which German political life had found expression for centuries, and their speeches harked back by preference to a tribal organisation which the nation had long ago outgrown, and which even the educated had never correctly appreciated.

They fixed their choice upon a constitutional committee, which was to discover the form on which the future German state would be modelled ; they created

Obstacles to the Formation of a Constitution a central power for a state as yet non-existent, without clearly and intelligibly defining its relations to the ruling governments who were in actual possession of every road to power. Discussion upon the " central power " speedily brought to light the insurmountable obstacles to the formation of a constitution acceptable to every party, and this

4957

without any interference on the part of the governments. The Democrats declined to recognise anything but an executive committee of the sovereign National Assembly; the Liberals made various proposals for a triple committee in connection with the governments. The bold mind of the president, Heinrich von Gagern, eventually soothed the uproar. He invited the Parliament to appoint, in virtue of its plenary powers, an Imperial Administrator who should undertake the business of the Federal Council, then on the point of dissolution, and act in concert with an imperial Ministry.

The Popular Archduke John of Austria

The Archduke John of Austria was elected on June 24th, 1848, by 436 out of 548 votes, and the law regarding the central power was passed on the 28th. Had the office of Imperial Administrator been regarded merely as a temporary expedient until the permanent forms were settled, the choice of the archduke would have been entirely happy; he was popular, entirely the man for the post, and ready to further progress in every department of intellectual and material life. But it was a grievous mistake to expect him to create substance out of shadow, to direct the development of the German state by a further use of the "bold grasp," and to contribute materially to the realisation of its being.

The Archduke John was a good-hearted man and a fine speaker, full of confidence in the "excellent fellows," and ever inclined to hold up the "bluff" inhabitants of the Alpine districts as examples to the other Germans; intellectually stimulating within his limits, and with a keen eye to economic advantage; but Nature had not intended him for a politician. His political ideas were too intangible; he used words with no ideas behind them, and though his own experience had not always been of the pleasantest, it had not taught him the feeling then prevalent in Austrian court circles. For the moment his election promised an escape from all manner of embarrassments. The governments could recognise his position without committing themselves to the approval of any revolutionary measure; they might even allow that his election was the beginning of an understanding with the reigning German houses. This, however, was not the opinion of the leading party in

Germany's Imperial Administrator

the National Assembly. The Conservatives, the Right, or the Right Centre, as they preferred to be called, were alone in their adherence to the sound principle that only by way of mutual agreement between the Parliament and the governments could a constitutional German body politic be established. Every other party was agreed that the people must itself formulate its own constitution, as only so would it obtain complete recognition of its rights.

This fact alone excluded the possibility of success. The decision of the question was indefinitely deferred, the favourable period in which the governments were inclined to consider the necessity of making concessions to the popular desires was wasted in discussion, and opportunity was given to particularism to recover its strength. There was no desire for a federal union endowed with vital force and offering a strong front to other nations. Patriots were anxious only to invest doctrinaire Liberalism and its extravagant claims with legal form, and to make the governments feel the weight of a vigorous national sentiment. The lessons of the French Revolution and its sad history were lost upon the Germans. Those who held the fate of Germany in their hands, many of them professional politicians, were unable to conceive that their constituents were justified in expecting avoidance on their part of the worst of all political errors.

Hereditary Curse of the German

The great majority by which the central power had been constituted soon broke up into groups, too insignificant to be called political parties and divided upon wholly immaterial points. The hereditary curse of the German, dogmatism and personal vanity, with a consequent distaste for voluntary subordination, positively devastated Monarchists and Republicans alike. The inns were scarcely adequate in number to provide headquarters for a score of societies which considered the promulgation of political programmes as their bounden duty.

On July 14th, 1848, the Archduke John made his entry into Frankfort, and the Federal Council was dissolved the same day. The Imperial Administrator established a provisional Ministry to conduct the business of the central power till he had completed the work at Vienna which his imperial nephew had entrusted to his care. At the beginning of August, 1848, he established himself in Frankfort, and appointed Prince Friedrich Karl von Leiningen as the head of the Ministry, which also included the Austrian, Anton von Schmerling; the Hamburg lawyer, Moritz Heckscher; the Prussians, Hermann von Beckerath and General Eduard von Peucker; the Bremen senator, Arnold Duckwitz; and the Würtemberger, Robert von Mohl, professor of political science at Heidelberg.

To ensure the prestige of the central power, the Minister of War, Von Peucker, had given orders on August 6th for a general review of contingents furnished by the German states, who were to give three cheers to the Archduke John as imperial administrator. The mode in which this order was carried out plainly showed that the governments did not regard it as obligatory, and respected it only so far as they thought good. It was obeyed only in Saxony, Würtemberg, and the smaller states. Prussia allowed only her garrisons in the federal fortresses to participate in the parade; Bavaria ordered her troops to cheer the king before the imperial administrator. In Austria no notice was taken of the order, except in Vienna, as it affected the archduke; the Italian army did not trouble itself about the imperial Minister of War in the least.

At the same time, the relations of the governments and the central power were by no means unfriendly. The King of Prussia did not hide his high personal esteem of the Imperial Administrator, and showed him special tokens of regard at the festivities held at Cologne on August 14th, 1848, in celebration of the six hundredth anniversary of the foundation of the cathedral. Most of the federal princes honoured him as a member of the

HEINRICH VON GAGERN
This German statesman was president of the Frankfort Parliament in the year 1849, and it was mainly on his suggestion that an Imperial Administrator was appointed.

ARCHDUKE JOHN OF AUSTRIA
A " good-hearted man and a fine speaker," he was elected Imperial Administrator; he entered Frankfort on July 14th, 1848, and on the same day the Federal Council was dissolved, whereupon he established a provisional Ministry.

Austrian House, and continued confidential relations with him for a considerable time. The German governments further appointed plenipotentiaries to represent their interests with the central power; these would have been ready to form a kind of Monarchical Council side by side with the National Assembly, and would thus have been highly serviceable to the imperial administrator as a channel of communication with the governments. But the democratic pride of the body which met in the Church of St. Paul had risen too high to tolerate so opportune a step towards a "system of mutual accommodation." On August 30th the central power was obliged to declare that the plenipotentiaries of the individual states possessed no competence to influence the decisions of the central power, or to conduct any systematic business. The new European power had notified its existence by special embassies to various foreign states, and received recognition in full from the Netherlands, Belgium, Sweden, Switzerland, and the United States of North America; Russia ignored it, while the attitude of France and Britain was marked by distrust and doubt. Austria was in the throes of internal convulsion during the summer of 1848 and unable seriously to consider the German question; possessing a confidential agent of preeminent position in the person of the Archduke John, she was able to reserve her decision. With Prussia, however, serious complications speedily arose from the war in Schleswig - Holstein. Parliament was aroused to great excitement by the armistice of Malmö, which Prussia concluded on August 26th, without consulting Max von Gagern, the imperial state secretary commissioned to the duchies by the central power. The central power had declared the Schleswig-Holstein question a matter of national importance, and in virtue of the right which had formerly belonged to the Federal Council demanded a share in the settlement. On September 5th, Dahlmann proposed to set on foot the necessary measures for carrying out the armistice ; the proposal, when sent up by the Ministry for confirmation, was rejected by 244 to 230 votes. Dahlmann, who was now entrusted by the Imperial Administrator with the formation of a new Ministry, was obliged to abandon the proposal after many days of fruitless effort. Ignoring the imperial Ministry, the Assembly proceeded to discuss the steps to be taken with reference to the armistice which was already in process of fulfilment. Meanwhile the democratic Left lost their majority in the Assembly, and the proposal of the committee to refuse acceptance of the armistice and to declare war on Denmark through the provisional central power was lost by 258 votes to 237.

Revolution in Frankfort

This result led to a revolt in Frankfort, begun by the members of the Extreme Left under the leadership of Zitz of Mainz and their adherents in the town and in the neighbouring states of Hesse and Baden. The town senate was forced to apply to the garrison of Mainz for military protection and to guard the meeting of the National Assembly on September 18th, 1848, with an Austrian and a Prussian battalion of the line. The revolutionaries, here as in Paris, terrified the Parliament by the invasion of an armed mob, and sought to intimidate the members to the passing of resolutions which would have brought on a civil war.

Barricades were erected, and two deputies of the Right, Prince Felix Lichnowsky and Erdmann of Auerswald, were cruelly murdered. Even the long-suffering archducal administrator of the empire was forced to renounce the hope of a pacific termination of the quarrel. The troops were ordered to attack the barricades, and the disturbance was put down in a few hours with no great loss of life. The citizens of Frankfort had not fallen into the trap of the " Reds," or given any support to the desperadoes with whose help the German republic was to be founded. A few days later the professional revolutionary, Gustav Struve, met

Frankfort's Revolt Suppressed

the fate he deserved ; after invading Baden with an armed force from France, "to help the great cause of freedom to victory," he was captured at Lörrach on September 25th, 1848, and thrown into prison.

The German National Assembly was now able to resume its meetings, but the public confidence in its lofty position and powers had been greatly shaken. Had the radical attempt at intimidation proved successful, the Assembly would speedily have ceased to exist. It was now able to turn its attention to the question of " fundamental rights," while the governments in Vienna and Berlin were fighting for the right of the executive power. The suppression of the Vienna revolt by Windisch-Graetz had produced a marked impression in Prussia. The conviction was expressed that the claims of the democracy to a share in the executive power by the subjects of the state, and their interference in government affairs, were to be unconditionally rejected. Any attempt to coerce the executive authorities was to be crushed by the sternest measures, by force of arms, if need be ; otherwise the maintenance of order was impossible, and without this there could be no peaceful enjoyment of constitutional rights. It was clear that compliance on the part of the government with the demands of the revolutionary leaders would endanger the freedom of the vast majority of the population ; the latter were ready to secure peace and the stability of the existing order of things by renouncing in favour of a strong government some part of those rights which Liberal theorists had assigned to them. In view of the abnormal excitement then prevailing, such a programme necessitated severity and self-assertion on the part of the government. This would be obvious in time of peace, but at the moment the fact was not likely to be appreciated.

The Severe Measures of the Government

The refusal to fire a salute upon the occasion of a popular demonstration in Schweidnitz on July 31st, 1848, induced the Prussian National Assembly to take steps which were calculated to diminish the consideration and the respect of armed force, which was a highly beneficial influence in those troublous times. The result was the retirement on September 7th of the Auerswald-Hansemann Ministry, which had been in office since June 25th ; it was followed on September 21st by a bureaucratic Ministry under the presidency of General Pfuel, which was without influence either with the king or the National Assembly. The Left now obtained the upper hand. As president they chose a moderate, the railway engineer, Hans Victor von Unruh, and as vice-president the leader of the Extreme Left, the doctrinaire lawyer, Leo Waldeck. During the deliberations on the constitution they erased the phrase " By the grace of God " from the king's titles, and resolved on October 31st, 1848, to request the Imperial Government in Frankfort to send help to the revolted Viennese. This step led to long continued communications between the Assembly and the unemployed classes, who were collected by the democratic agitators, and surrounded the royal theatre where the deputies held their sessions.

On November 1st, 1848, news arrived of the fall of Vienna, and Frederic William IV. determined to intervene in support of his kingdom. He dismissed Pfuel and placed Count William of Brandenburg, son of his grandfather Frederic William II. and of the Countess Sophia Juliana

Martial Law in Berlin Friederika of Dönhoff, at the head of a new Ministry. He then despatched 15,000 troops, under General Friedrich von Wrangel, to Berlin, the city being shortly afterwards punished by the declaration of martial law. The National Assembly was transferred from Berlin to Brandenburg. The Left, for the purpose of "undisturbed" deliberation, repeatedly met in the Berlin coffee-houses, despite the prohibition of the president of the Ministry, but eventually gave way and followed the Conservatives to Brandenburg, after being twice dispersed by the troops. Berlin and the Marks gave no support to the democracy.

The majority of the population dreaded a reign of terror by the " Reds," and were delighted with the timely opposition. They also manifested their satisfaction at the dissolution of the National Assembly, which had given few appreciable signs of legislative activity in Brandenburg, at the publication on December 5th, 1848, of a constitutional scheme drafted by the Government, and the issue of writs for the election of a Prussian Landtag which was to revise the law of suffrage. Some opposition was noticeable in the provinces, but was for the moment of a moderate nature. The interference of the Frankfort Parliament in the question of the Prussian constitution produced no effect whatever. The centres of the Right and Left had there united and taken the lead, then proceeding to pass resolutions which would not hinder the Prussian Government in asserting its right to determine its own affairs. Public opinion in Germany had thus changed;

Germany's Rejection of Radicalism there was a feeling in favour of limiting the demands that might arise during the constitutional definition of the national rights; moreover, the majority of the nation had declined adherence to the tenets of radicalism. It seemed that these facts were producing a highly desirable change of direction in the energies of the German National Assembly; the provisional central power was even able to pride itself upon a reserve of force, for the Prussian Government had placed its united forces, 326,000 men, at its disposal, as was announced by Schmerling, the imperial Minister, on October 23rd, 1848.

None the less, an extraordinary degree of statesmanship and political capacity was required to cope with the obstacles which lay before the creation of a national federation organised as a state, with adequate power to deal with domestic and foreign policy. But not only was this supreme political insight required of the national representatives; theirs, too, must be the task of securing the support of the Great Powers, without which the desired federation was unattainable.

This condition did not apply for the moment in the case of Austria, whose decision was of the highest importance. Here an instance recurred of the law constantly exemplified in the lives both of individuals and of nations, that a recovery of power stimulates to aggression instead of leading to discretion. True wisdom would have concentrated the national aims upon a clearly recognisable and attainable object—namely, the trans-

Suppressing the Hungarian Revolution formation of the old dynastic power of the Hapsburgs into a modern state. Such a change would of itself have determined the form of the federation with the new German state, which could well have been left to develop in its own way.

Russian help for the suppression of the Hungarian revolt would have been unnecessary; it would have been enthusiastically given by the allied Prussian otate under Frederic William IV. The only tasks of Austria-Hungary for the immediate future would have been the fostering of her civilisation, the improvement of domestic prosperity, and the extension of her influence in the Balkan peninsula. Even her Italian paramountcy,

The Catholic Dynasty in Germany had it been worth retaining, could hardly have been wrested from her. No thinking member of the House of Hapsburg could deny these facts at the present day. Possibly even certain representatives of that ecclesiastical power which has endeavoured for three centuries to make the Hapsburg dynasty the champion of its interests might be brought to admit that the efforts devoted to preserving the hereditary position of the Catholic dynasty in Germany led to a very injudicious expenditure of energy.

But such a degree of political foresight was sadly to seek in the winter of 1848–1849. The only man who had almost reached that standpoint, the old Wessenberg, was deprived of his influence at the critical moment of decision. His place was taken by one whose morality was even lower than his capacity or previous training, and whose task was nothing less than the direction of a newly developed state and the invention of some modus vivendi between the outraged and insulted dynasty and the agitators, devoid alike of sense and conscience, who had plied the nationalities of the Austrian Empire with evil counsel. Prince Windisch-Graetz was quite able to overpower street rioters or to crush the "legions" of Vienna; but his vocation was not that of a general or a statesman.

However, his word was all-powerful at the court in Olmütz. On November 21st, 1848, Prince Felix Schwarzenberg became head of the Austrian Government. His political views were those of Windisch-Graetz, whose intellectual superior he was, though his decisions were in consequence the more hasty and ill-considered.

FREDERIC WILLIAM IV.
King of Prussia, he declined the imperial crown offered him by the Frankfort Diet in 1849. His reign was, on the whole, a disappointing one.

His policy upon German questions was modelled on that of Metternich. The only mode of action which commended itself to the Emperor Francis Joseph I., now eighteen years of age, was one promising a position of dignity, combining all the "splendour" of the throne of Charles the Great with the inherent force of a modern Great Power. A prince of chivalrous disposition, who had witnessed the heroic deeds of his army under Radetzky, with the courage to defend his fortunes and those of his state at the point of the sword, would never have voluntarily yielded his rights, his honourable position, and the family traditions of centuries, even if the defence of these had not been represented by his advisers as a ruler's inevitable task and as absolutely incumbent upon him.

The Frankfort Parliament had already discussed the "fundamental rights." It had determined by a large majority that personal union was the only possible form of alliance between any part of Germany and foreign countries; it had decided upon the use of the two-chamber system in the Reichstag, and had secured representation in the "Chamber of the States" to the governments even of the smallest states; it had made provision for the customs union until May 18th, 1849, at latest. Among the leaders of the Centre the opinion then gained ground that union with Austria would be impossible in as close a sense as it was possible with the other German states, and that the only means of assuring the strength and unity

Secessions Among the Liberals of the pure German states was to confer the dignity of emperor upon the King of Prussia. The promulgation of this idea resulted in a new cleavage of parties. The majority of the moderate Liberal Austrians seceded from their associates and joined the Radicals, Ultramontanes, and Particularists, with the object of preventing the introduction of Prussia as an empire into the imperial constitution. Schmerling resigned the presidency of the imperial Ministry. The Imperial Administrator was forced to replace him by Heinrich von Gagern, the first president of the Parliament. His programme was announced on December 16th, and proposed the foundation of a close federal alliance of the German states under Prussian leadership, while a looser federal connection was to exist with Austria, as arranged by the settlement of the Vienna Congress.

After three days' discussion, on January 11th–14th, 1849, this programme was accepted by 261 members of the German National Assembly as against 224. Sixty Austrian deputies entered a protest against this resolution, denying the right of the Parliament to exclude the German Austrians from the German Federal State. The Austrian Government was greatly disturbed at the promulgation of the Gagern programme, and objected to the legislative powers of the Frankfort Assembly in general terms on February 7th, declaring her readiness to co-operate in a union of the German states, and protesting against the "remodelling" of existing conditions. Thus, she adopted a position corresponding to that of the federation of 1815. The decision now remained with the king, Frederic William IV.; he accepted the imperial constitution of March 28th, 1849, and was forthwith elected Emperor of the Germans by 290 of the 538 deputies present.

Frederic William Emperor of the Germans

The constitution in document form was signed by only 366 deputies, as the majority of the Austrians and the ultramontanes declined to acknowledge the supremacy of a Protestant Prussia. The 290 electors who had voted for the king constituted, however, a respectable majority. Still, it was as representatives of the nation that they offered him the imperial Crown, and they made their offer conditional upon his recognition of the imperial constitution which had been resolved upon in Frankfort. It was therein provided that in all questions of legislation the decision should rest with the popular House in the Reichstag.

The imperial veto was no longer unconditional, but could only defer discussion over three sittings. This the King of Prussia was unable to accept, if only for the reason that he was already involved in a warm discussion with Austria, Bavaria, and Würtemberg upon the form of a German federal constitution which was to be laid before the Parliament by the princes.

The despatch of a parliamentary deputation to Berlin was premature, in view of the impossibility of that unconditional acceptance of the imperial title desired and expected by Dahlmann and the professor of Königsberg, Martin Eduard Simson, at that time president of the National Assembly. The only answer that Frederic William could give on April 3rd, 1849, was a reply postponing his decision. This the delegation construed as a refusal, as it indicated hesitation on the king's part to recognise the Frankfort constitution in its entirety. The king erred in believing that an arrangement with Austria still lay within the bounds of possibility; he failed to see that Schwarzenberg only desired to restore the old Federal Assembly, while securing greater power in it to Austria than she had had under Metternich.

Where the King Blundered

The royal statesman considered Hungary as already subjugated, and conceived as in existence a united state to be formed of the Austrian and Hungarian territories, together with Galicia and Dalmatia; he desired to secure the entrance of this state within the federation, which he intended to be not German but a Central European federation under Austrian leadership.

On the return of the parliamentary deputation to Frankfort with the refusal of the King of Prussia, the work of constitution-building was brought to a standstill. The most important resolutions, those touching the head of the empire, had proved impracticable. The more farsighted members of the Parliament recognised this fact, and also saw that to remodel the constitution would be to play into the hands of the Republicans. However, their eyes were blinded to the fact that twenty-four petty states of different sizes had accepted the constitution, and they ventured to hope for an improvement in the situation. The Liberals were uncertain as to the extent of the power which could be assigned to the nation, in contradistinction to the governments, without endangering the social fabric and the existence of civic society. To this lack of definite views is chiefly to be ascribed the fact that the German National Assembly allowed the Democrats to lead it into revolutionary tendencies, until it ended

The National Assembly Led by Democrats

its existence in pitiable disruption. The Liberals, moreover, cannot be acquitted from the charge of playing the dangerous game of inciting national revolt with the object of carrying through the constitution which they had devised and drafted—a constitution, too, which meant a breach with the continuity of German historical development. They

Royal Family Expelled From Dresden fomented popular excitement and brought about armed risings of the illiterate mobs of Saxony, the Palatinate, and Baden. The royal family were expelled from Dresden by a revolt on May 3rd, and Prussian troops were obliged to reconquer the capital at the cost of severe fighting on May 7th and 8th. It was necessary to send two Prussian corps to reinforce the imperial army drawn from Hesse, Mecklenburg, Nassau, and Würtemberg, for the overthrow of the republican troops which had concentrated at Rastadt.

Heinrich von Gagern and his friends regarded the advance of the Prussians as a breach of the peace in the empire. The Gagern Ministry resigned, as the Archduke John could not be persuaded to oppose the Prussians. The Imperial Administrator had already hinted at his retirement after the imperial election; but the Austrian Government had insisted upon his retention of his office, lest the King of Prussia should step into his place. He formed a conservative Ministry under the presidency of the Prussian councillor of justice, Grävell, which was received with scorn and derision by the Radicals, who were now the dominant party in the Parliament. More than a hundred deputies of the centres then withdrew with Gagern, Dahlmann, Welcker, Simson, and Mathy from May 12th to 26th, 1849.

The Austrian Government had recalled the Austrian deputies on April 4th from the National Assembly, an example followed by Prussia on the 14th. On May 30th, 71

German "Stupidity and Ignorance" of 135 voters who took part in the discussion supported Karl Vogt's proposal to transfer the Parliament from Frankfort to Stuttgart, where a victory for Suabian republicanism was expected. In the end 105 representatives of German stupidity and political ignorance, including, unfortunately, Lewis Uhland, gave the world the ridiculous spectacle of the opening of the so-called Rump Parliament at Stuttgart on June 6th, 1849, which reached the crown-

ing folly in the election of five "imperial regents." The arrogance of this company, which even presumed to direct the movements of the Würtemberg troops, proved inconvenient to the government, which accordingly closed the meeting hall. The first German Parliament then expired after a few gatherings in the Hôtel Marquardt.

The Imperial Government, the Administrator and his Ministry, retained their offices until December, 1849, notwithstanding repeated demands for their resignation. A committee of four members, appointed as a provisional central power by Austria and Prussia, then took over all business, documentary and financial. As an epilogue to the Frankfort Parliament, mention may be made of the gathering of 160 former deputies of the first German Reichstag, which had belonged to the "imperial party," The meeting was held in Gotha on June 26th. Heinrich von Gagern designated the meeting as a private conference; however, he secured the assent of those present to a programme drawn up by himself which asserted the desirability of a narrower, "little Ger-

Proclamation of the Prussian Government man," federation under the headship of Prussia, or of another central power in association with Prussia. Upon the recall of the Prussian deputies from the Frankfort Parliament the Prussian Government issued a proclamation to the German people on May 5th, 1849, declaring itself henceforward responsible for the work of securing the unity which was justly demanded for the vigorous representation of German interests abroad, and for common legislation in constitutional form; that is, with the co-operation of a national house of representatives.

In the conferences of the ambassadors of the German states, which were opened at Berlin on May 17th, the Prussian programme was explained to be the formation of a close federation exclusive of Austria, and the creation of a wider federation which should include the Hapsburg state. Thus in theory had been discovered the form which the transformation of Germany should take. On her side Prussia did not entirely appreciate the fact that this programme could not be realised by means of ministerial promises alone, and that the whole power of the Prussian state would be required to secure its acceptance. The nation, or rather the men to whom the nation had entrusted its future, also failed to perceive that this form was the only kind of unity practically attainable, and that to it must be sacrificed those "guarantees of freedom" which liberal doctrinaires declared indispensable.

It now became a question of deciding between a radical democracy and a moderate constitutional monarchy, and German Liberalism was precluded from coming to any honourable conclusion. Regardless of consequences, it exchanged amorous glances with the opposition in non-Prussian countries; it considered agreement with the Government as treason to the cause of freedom, and saw reaction where nothing of the kind was to be found. It refused to give public support to aggressive Republicanism, fearing lest the people, when in arms, should prove a menace to private property, and lose that respect for the growing wealth of individual enterprise which ought to limit their aspirations; at the same time, it declined to abate its pride, and continued to press wholly immoderate demands upon the authorities, to whom alone it owed the maintenance of the existing social order.

The Prussians Hailed as Deliverers The Baden revolt had been suppressed by the Prussian troops under the command of Prince William, afterwards emperor, who invaded the land which the Radicals had thrown into confusion, dispersed the Republican army led by Mieroslawski and Hecker in a series of engagements, and reduced, on July 23rd, 1849, the fortress of Rastadt, which had fallen into the hands of the Republicans. The Liberals at first hailed the Prussians as deliverers; the latter, however, proceeded by court-martial against the leaders, whose crimes had brought misery upon thousands and had reduced a flourishing province to desolation. Seventeen death sentences were passed, and prosecutions were instituted against the mutinous officers and soldiers of Baden.

The "free-thinking" party, which had recovered from its fear of the "Reds," could then find no more pressing occupation than to rouse public feeling throughout South Germany against Prussia and "militarism," and to level unjustifiable reproaches against the prince in command, whose clever generalship merited the gratitude not only of Baden but of every German patriot. Even then a solution of the German problem might have been possible had the Democrats in South Germany laid aside their fear of Prussian "predominance," and considered their secret struggle against an energetic administration as less important than the establishment of a federal state, commanding the respect of other nations. But the success of the Prussian programme could have been secured only by the joint action of the whole nation. Unanimity of **Germany's Idea of Union Abandoned** this kind was a very remote possibility. Fearful of the Prussian "reaction," the nation abandoned the idea of German unity, to be driven into closer relations with the sovereign powers of the smaller and the petty states, and ultimately to fall under the heavier burden of a provincial reaction.

Austria had recalled her ambassador, Anton, Count of Prokesch-Osten, from the Berlin Conference, declining all negotiation for the reconstitution of German interests upon the basis of the Prussian proposals; but she could not have despatched an army against Prussia in the summer of 1849. Even with the aid of her ally Bavaria, she was unable to cope with the 300,000 troops which Prussia alone could place in the field at that time; in Hungary, she had been obliged to call in the help of Russia. United action by Germany would probably have met with no opposition whatever. But Germany was not united, the people as little as the princes; consequently when Prussia, after the ignominious failure of the Parliament and its high promise, intervened to secure at least some definite result from the national movement, her well-meaning proposals met with a rebuff as humiliating as it was undeserved.

The result of the Berlin Conferences was the "alliance of the three kings" of Prussia, Hanover, and Saxony on May 26th, 1849. Bavaria and Würtemberg declined to join the alliance on account of the claims to leadership advanced by Prussia; but the majority of the other German states gave in their adherence in the **Results of the Berlin Conferences** course of the summer. A federal council of administration met on June 18th, and made arrangements for the convocation of a Reichstag, to which was to be submitted the federal constitution when the agreement of the Cabinets thereon had been secured. Hanover and Saxony then raised objections and recalled their representatives on the administrative council on October 20th. However, Prussia was able to fix the meeting of the Reichstag for March 20th, 1850, at Erfurt. Austria now advanced claims in support of the old federal constitution, and suddenly demanded that it should continue in full force. This action was supported by Bavaria, which advocated the formation of a federation of the smaller states,

Proposed Federation of States which was to prepare another constitution as a rival to the "union" for which Prussia was working. The Saxon Minister, Beust, afterwards of mournful fame in Germany and Austria, who fought against the Saxon particularism, which almost surpassed that prevalent in Bavaria, and was guided by personal animosity to Prussia, became at that moment the most zealous supporter of the statesmanlike plans of his former colleague, Pfordten, who had been appointed Bavarian Minister of Foreign Affairs in April, 1849.

Hanover was speedily won over, as Austria proposed to increase her territory with Oldenburg, in order to create a second North German power as a counterpoise to Prussia, while Würtemberg declared her adherence to the "alliance of the four kings" with startling precipitancy. The chief attraction was the possibility of sharing on equal terms in a directory of seven members with Austria, Prussia, and the two Hesses, which were to have a vote in common. The directory was not to exercise the functions of a central power, but was to have merely powers of "superintendence," even in questions of taxation and commerce. The claims of the Chambers were to be met by the creation of a "Reichstag," to which they were to send deputies.

Upon the secession of the kingdoms from Prussia, disinclination to the work of unification was also manifested by the electorate of Hesse, where the elector had again found a Minister to his liking in the person of Daniel von Hassenpflug. It would, however, have been quite

The King's Desire for Peace possible to make Prussia the centre of a considerable power by the conjunction of all the remaining federal provinces had the Erfurt Parliament been entrusted with the task of rapidly concluding the work of unification. In the meantime Frederic William, under the influence of friends who favoured feudalism, Ernst Ludwig of Gerlach and Professor Stahl, had abandoned his design of forming a restricted federation, and was inspired with the

invincible conviction that it was his duty as a Christian king to preserve peace with Austria at any price; for Austria, after her victorious struggle with the revolution, had become the prop and stay of all states where unlimited monarchy protected by the divine right of kings held sway.

To guard this institution against Liberal onslaughts remained the ideal of his life, Prussian theories of politics and the paroxysms of German patriotism notwithstanding. He therefore rejected the valuable help now readily offered to him in Erfurt by the old imperial party of Frankfort, and clung to the utterly vain and unsupported hope that he could carry out the wider form of federation with Austria in some manner compatible with German interests. His hopes were forthwith shattered by Schwarzenberg's convocation of a congress of the German federal states at Frankfort, and Prussia's position became daily more unfavourable, although a meeting of the princes desirous of union was held in Berlin in May, 1850, and accepted the temporary continuance until July 15th, 1850, of the restricted federation under Prussian leadership.

Conditions of the Tsar's Neutrality The Tsar Nicholas I. was urgently demanding the conclusion of the Schleswig-Holstein complication, which he considered as due to nothing but the intrigues of malevolent revolutionaries in Copenhagen and the duchies. In a meeting with Prince William of Prussia, which took place at Warsaw towards the end of May, 1850, the Tsar clearly stated that, in the event of the German question resulting in war between Prussia and Austria, his neutrality would be conditional upon the restoration of Danish supremacy over the rebels in Schleswig-Holstein.

Henceforward Russia stands between Austria and Prussia as arbitrator. Her intervention was not as unprejudiced as Berlin would have been glad to suppose; she was beforehand determined to support Austria, to protect the old federal constitution, the Danish supremacy over Schleswig-Holstein, and the Elector of Hesse, Frederic William I., who had at that moment decided on a scandalous breach of faith with his people. This unhappy prince had already inflicted serious damage upon his country and its admirable population; he now proceeded to commit a crime against Germany by stirring up a fratricidal war, which was fed by a spirit of pettifogging selfishness and despicable jealousy. A Liberal reaction had begun, and the spirit of national self-assertion was fading ; no sooner had the elector perceived these facts than he proceeded to utilise them for the achievement of his desires. He dismissed the constitutional Ministry, restored Hassenpflug to favour on February 22nd, 1850, and permitted him to raise taxes unauthorised by the Chamber for the space of six months. The Chamber raised objections to this proceeding, and thereby gave

of turning their arms upon their fellow-citizens, who were entirely within their rights. The long-desired opportunity of calling in foreign help was thus provided ; but the appeal was not made to the board of arbitration of the union, to which the electorate of Hesse properly belonged, but to the Federal Council, which Austria had reopened in Frankfort on October 15th, 1850.

With the utmost readiness Count Schwarzenberg accepted the unexpected support of Hassenpflug, whose theories

STRIVING FOR GERMAN UNITY : THE DRESDEN CONFERENCES OF 1850

In the search after federation, which occupied the attention of the German states, the differences between Austria and Prussia created a serious difficulty. The question of federal reform was discussed in free conferences at Dresden, one of these assemblies, with the delegates from the various states concerned, being represented in the above picture.

Hassenpflug a handle which enabled him to derange the whole constitution of the electorate of Hesse. On September 7th the country was declared subject to martial law. For this step there was not the smallest excuse ; peace everywhere prevailed.

The officials who had taken the oaths of obedience to the constitution declined to act in accordance with the declaration, and their refusal was construed as rebellion. On October 9th the officers of the Hessian army resigned, almost to a man, to avoid the necessity

coincided with his own. The rump of the Federal Parliament, which was entirely under his influence, was summoned not only without the consent of Prussia but without any intimation to the Prusians Cabinet. This body at once determined to employ the federal power for the restoration of the elector to Hesse, though he had left Cassel of his own will and under no compulsion, fleeing to Wilhelmsbad with his Ministers at the beginning of September. Schwarzenberg was well aware that his action would place the King of Prussia in a most embarrassing situation. Federation and union were now in mutual opposition. On the one side was Austria, with the kingdoms and the two Hesses ; on the other was Prussia, with the united petty states, which were little better than worthless for military purposes. Austria had no need to seek occasion

Austria's Great Power in Germany to revenge herself for the result of the imperial election, which was ascribed to Prussian machinations ; her opportunity was at hand in the appeal of a most valuable member of the federation, the worthy Elector of Hesse, to his brother monarchs for protection against democratic presumption, against the insanities of constitutionalism, against a forsworn and mutinous army. Should Prussia now oppose the enforcement of the federal will in Hesse, she would be making common cause with rebels.

The Tsar would be forced to oppose the democratic tendencies of his degenerate brother-in-law, and to take the field with the Conservative German states, and with Austria, who was crowding on full sail for the haven of absolutism. To have created this situation, and to have drawn the fullest advantage from it, was the master-stroke of Prince Felix Schwarzenberg's policy. Austria thereby reached the zenith of her power in Germany.

The fate of Frederic William IV. now becomes tragical. The heavy punishment meted out to the overweening self-confidence of this ruler, the fearful disillusionment which he was forced to experience from one whom he had treated with full confidence and respect, cannot but evoke the sympathy of every spectator. He had himself declined that imperial crown which Austria so bitterly grudged him. He had rejected the overtures of the imperial party from dislike to their democratic theories. He had begun the work of overthrowing the constitutional

The Sword at the King's Throat principles of the constitution of the union. He had surrendered Schleswig-Holstein because his conscience would not allow him to support national against monarchical rights, and because he feared to expose Prussia to the anger of his brother-in-law. He had opposed the exclusion of Austria from the wider federation of the German states. He had always been prepared to act in conjunction with Austria in the solution of questions affecting Germany at large, while claiming for Prussia a right which was provided in the federal constitution—the right of forming a close federation, the right which, far from diminishing, would strengthen the power of the whole organism. And now the sword was placed at his throat, equality of rights was denied to him, and he was requested to submit to the action of Austria as paramount in Germany, to submit to a federal executive, which had removed an imperial administrator, though he was an Austrian duke, which could only be reconstituted with the assent of every German government, and not by eleven votes out of seventeen !

For two months the king strove hard, amid the fiercest excitement, to maintain his position. At the beginning of October, 1850, he sent assurances to Vienna of his readiness " to settle all points of difference with the Emperor of Austria from the standpoint of an old friend." He quietly swallowed the arrogant threats of Bavaria, and was not to be provoked by the warlike speeches delivered at Bregenz on the occasion of the meeting of the Emperor Francis Joseph with the kings of South

War on the Horizon Germany, on October 11th. He continued to rely upon the insight of the Tsar, with whose ideas he was in full agreement, and sent Count Brandenburg to Warsaw to assure him of his pacific intentions, and to gain a promise that he would not allow the action of the federation in Hesse and Holstein to pass unnoticed. Prince Schwarzenberg also appeared in Warsaw, and it seemed that there might be some possibility of an understanding between Austria and Prussia upon the German question. Schwarzenberg admitted that the Federal Council might be replaced by free conferences of the German Powers, as in 1819 ; he did not, however, explain whether these conferences were to be summoned for the purpose of appointing the new central power, or whether the Federal Council was to be convoked for that object.

He insisted unconditionally upon the execution of the federal decision in Hesse, which implied the occupation of the whole electorate by German and Bavarian troops. This Prussia could not allow, for military reasons. The ruler of Prussia was therefore forced to occupy the main roads to the Rhine province, and had already sent forward several thousand men under Count Charles from the Gröben to the neighbourhood of Fulda for this purpose. The advance of the Bavarians in this direction would inevitably result in a collision with the Prussian troops, unless these latter were first withdrawn. Count Brandenburg returned to Berlin resolved to prevent a war which offered no prospect of success in view of the Tsar's attitude. Radowitz, who had been Minister of Foreign Affairs since September 27th, 1850, called for the mobilisation of the army, and was inclined to accept the challenge to combat ; he considered the Austrian preparations comparatively innocuous, and was convinced that Russia would be unable to concentrate any considerable body of troops on the Prussian frontier before the summer.

On November 2nd, 1850, the king also declared for the mobilisation, though with the intention of continuing negotiations with Austria, if possible ; he was ready, however, to adopt Brandenburg's view of the situation, if a majority in the ministerial council could be found to support this policy. Brandenburg **Prussia's** succumbed to a sudden attack **Failure** of brain fever on November **in Germany** 6th, not, as was long supposed, to vexation at the rejection of his policy of resistance ; his work was taken up and completed by Manteuffel, after Radowitz had left the Ministry.

After the first shots had been exchanged between the Prussian and Bavarian troops at Bronzell, to the south of Fulda, on November 8th, he entirely abandoned the constitution of the union, allowed the Bavarians to advance upon the condition that Austria permitted the simultaneous occupation of the high roads by Prussian troops, and started with an autograph letter from the king and Queen Elizabeth to meet the Emperor Francis Joseph and his mother, the Archduchess Sophie, sister of the Queen of Prussia, in order to discuss conditions of peace with the Austrian Prime Minister. Prince Schwarzenberg was anxious to proceed to extremities ; but the young emperor had no intention of beginning a war with his relatives, and obliged Schwarzenberg to yield. At the emperor's command he signed the stipulation of Olmütz on November 29th, 1850, under which Prussia fully satisfied the Austrian demands, receiving one sole concession in return—that the question of federal

reform should be discussed in free conferences at Dresden. Thus Prussia's German policy had ended in total failure. She was forced to abandon all hope of realising the Gagern programme by forming a narrower federation under her own leadership, exclusive of popular representation, direct or indirect. Prussia **The Reproach** lost greatly in prestige ; the **of Frederic** enthusiasm aroused through-**William** out the provinces by the prospect of war gave place to bitter condemnation of the vacillation imputed to the king after the " capitulation of Olmütz." Even his brother, Prince William, burst into righteous indignation during the Cabinet Council of December 2nd, 1850, at the stain on the white shield of Prussian honour.

Until his death, Frederic William IV. was reproached with humiliating Prussia, and reducing her to a position among the German states which was wholly unworthy of her. Yet it is possible that the resolution which gave Austria a temporary victory was the most unselfish offering which the king could then have made to the German nation. He resisted the temptation of founding a North German federation with the help and alliance of France, which was offered by Persigny, the confidential agent of Louis Napoleon. Fifty thousand French troops had been concentrated at Strassburg for the realisation of this project. They would have invaded South Germany and devastated Swabia and Bavaria in the cause of Prussia. But it was not by such methods that German unity was to be attained, or a German Empire to be founded. Renunciation for the moment was a guarantee of success hereafter.

In his " Reflections and Recollections " Prince Bismarck asserts that Stockhausen, the Minister of War, considered the Prussian forces in November, 1850, inadequate to check the advance upon Berlin of the Austrian army concentrated in Bohemia. **Problem** He had received this informa-**of Germany's** tion from Stockhausen, and **Future** had defended the king's attitude in the Chamber. He also thinks he has established the fact that Prince William, afterwards his king and emperor, was convinced of the incapacity of Prussia to deal a decisive blow at that period. He made no mention of his conviction that such a blow must one day be delivered ; but this assurance seems to have grown upon him from that date.

THE
RE-MAKING
OF
EUROPE

EUROPE
IN
REVOLUTION
VII

REACTION IN CENTRAL EUROPE
AN ERA OF GENERAL STAGNATION

THE victory of Schwarzenberg in Olmütz gave a predominating influence in Central Europe to the spirit of the Tsar Nicholas I., the narrowness and bigotry of which is not to be paralleled in any of those periods of stagnation which have interrupted the social development of Europe. Rarely has a greater want of common sense **Hindrances to Europe's Development** been shown in the government of any Western civilised nation than was displayed during the years subsequent to 1850—a period which has attained in this respect a well-deserved notoriety. It is true that the preceding movement had found the nations immature, and therefore incapable of solving the problems with which they were confronted. The spirit was willing, but the flesh was unprepared.

The miserable delusion that construction is a process as easy and rapid as destruction ; that a few months can accomplish what centuries have failed to perfect ; that an honest attempt to improve political institutions must of necessity effect the desired improvement ; the severance of the theoretical from the practical, which was the ruin of every politician—these were the obstacles which prevented the national leaders from making timely use of that tremendous power which was placed in their hands in the month of March, 1848. Precious time was squandered in the harangues of rival orators, in the formation of parties and clubs, in over-ambitious programmes and compla- **The Mission of Liberalism** cent self-laudation thereon, in displays of arrogance and malevolent onslaughts. Liberalism was forced to resign its claims ; it was unable to effect a complete and unwavering severance from radicalism ; it was unable to appreciate the fact that its mission was not to govern, but to secure recognition from the Government.

The peoples were unable to gain legal confirmation of their rights, because they had no clear ideas upon the extent of those rights, and had not been taught that self-restraint which was the only road to success. Thus far all is sufficiently intelligible, and, upon a retrospect, one is almost inclined to think of stagnation as the result of a conflict of counterbalancing forces.

But one phenomenon there is, which becomes the more astonishing in proportion as it is elucidated by that pure light of impartial criticism which the non-contemporary historian can throw upon it—it is the fact that mental confusion was followed by a cessation of mental energy, that imperative vigour and interest were succeeded by blatant stupidity, that the excesses committed by nations in their struggle for the right of self-determination were expiated by yet more brutal exhibitions of the misuse of power, the blame of which rests upon the governments, who were the nominal guardians of right and morality in their higher forms. In truth **The Nations Suffering from Depression** a very moderate degree of wisdom in a few leading statesmen would have drawn the proper conclusions from the facts of the case, and have discovered the formulæ expressing the relation between executive power and national strength.

But the thinkers who would have been satisfied with moderate claims were not to be found ; it seemed as if the very intensity of political action had exhausted the capacity for government, as if the conquerors had forgotten that they too had been struggling to preserve the state and to secure its internal consolidation and reconstitution, that the revolution had been caused simply by the fact that the corrupt and degenerate state was unable to perform what its subjects had the right to demand.

The nations were so utterly depressed by the sad experiences which they had brought upon themselves as to show themselves immediately sensible to the smallest advances of kindness and confidence. Irritated by a surfeit of democratic theory, the political organism had lost its tone. A moderate allowance of rights and freedom would have acted as a stimulant, but the constitution had been too far lowered for hunger to act as a cure. Education and amelioration, not punishment, were now the mission of the governments which had recovered their unlimited power; but they were themselves both uninformed and unsympathetic. The punishment which they meted out was inflicted not from a sense of duty, but in revenge for the blows which they had been compelled to endure in the course of the revolution.

PROGRESSIVE AUSTRIAN MINISTERS
Count Leo Thun and A. von Bach, whose portraits are given above, were among the men of note who, after the storms of the revolutionary years, supported the enlightened policy of Joseph II. As Minister of Education, the former introduced compulsory education, put the national schools under state control, and assisted the universities.

Most fatal to Austria was the lack of creative power, of experienced statesmen with education and serious moral purpose. In this country an enlightened government could have attained its every desire. Opportunity was provided for effecting a fundamental change in the constitution; all opposition had been broken down, and the strong vitality of the state had been brilliantly demonstrated in one of the hardest struggles for existence in which the country had been engaged for three centuries. There was a new ruler, strong, bold, and well informed, full of noble ambition and tender sentiment, too young to be hidebound by preconceived opinion and yet old enough to feel enthusiasm for his lofty mission; such a man would have been the strongest conceivable guarantee of success to a Ministry of wisdom and experience capable of leading him in the path of steady progress and of respect for the national rights. The clumsy and disjointed Reichstag of Kremsier was dissolved on March 7th, and on March 4th, 1849, a constitution had been voluntarily promulgated, in which the

GEORGE V. OF HANOVER
Succeeding his father on the throne of Hanover in 1851, the blind King George V. engaged in a long struggle with his people in defence of absolutism, and died an exile in Paris in 1878.

Government had reserved to itself full scope for exercising an independent influence upon the development of the state. In this arrangement the kingdom of Hungary had been included after its subordinate provinces had severed their connection with the Crown of Stephen, obtaining special provincial rights of their own. The best administrative officials in the empire, Von Schmerling, Bach, Count Thun, and Bruck, were at the disposition of the Prime Minister for the work of revivifying the economic and intellectual life of the monarchy. No objection would have been raised to a plan for dividing the non-Hungarian districts into bodies analogous to the English county, and thus laying the impregnable foundations of a centralised government which would develop as the education of the smaller national entities advanced. The fate of Austria was delivered into the hands of the emperor's advisers; but no personality of Radetzky's stamp was to be found among them. The leading figure was a haughty nobleman, whose object and pleasure were to sow discord between Austria and the Prussian king and people, Austria's most faithful allies since 1815. It was in Frankfort, and not in Vienna or Budapest, that the Hapsburg state should have sought strength and protection against future periods of storm. Even at the present day the veil has not been wholly parted which then shrouded the change of political theory in the leading circles at the Vienna court. Certain, however, it is that this change was not the work of men anxious for progress, but was due to the machinations of political parasites who plunged one of the best-intentioned of rulers into a series of entanglements which a life of sorrow and cruel disappointments was unable to unravel. The precious months of 1850, when the nation would thankfully have welcomed any cessation of the prevalent disturbance and terrorism, or any sign of confidence in its capacities, were

The Great Tide of Reaction allowed to pass by without an effort. In the following year the national enemies gained the upper hand; it was resolved to break with constitutionalism, and to reject the claims of the citizens to a share in the legislature and the administration. In September, 1851, the Governments of Prussia and Sardinia were ordered to annul the existing constitutions.

This was a step which surpassed even Metternich's zeal for absolutism. Schmerling and Bruck resigned their posts in the Ministry on January 5th and May 23rd, 1851, feeling their inability to make head against the reactionary movement. On August 20th, 1851, the imperial council for which provision had been made in the constitution of March 4th, 1849, was deprived of its faculty of national representation. As the council had not yet been called into existence, the only interpretation to be laid upon this step was that the Ministry desired to re-examine the desirability of ratifying the constitution.

On December 31st, 1851, the constitution was annulled, and the personal security of the citizens thereby endangered, known as they were to be in favour of constitutional measures. The police and a body of gendarmes, who were accorded an unprecedented degree of licence, undertook the struggle, not against exaggerated and impracticable demands, but against Liberalism as such, while the authorities plumed themselves in the fond delusion that this senseless struggle was a successful stroke of statesmanship. Enlightened centralisation would have found

The Dresden Conferences at Olmütz thousands of devoted coadjutors and have awakened many dormant forces; but the centralisation of the reactionary foes of freedom was bound to remain fruitless and to destroy the pure impulse which urged the people to national activity.

The successes in foreign policy, by which presumption had been fostered, now ceased. During the Dresden conferences, which had been held in Olmütz, Schwarzenberg found that he had been bitterly deceived in his federal allies among the smaller states, and that he had affronted Prussia to no purpose as far as Austria was concerned. His object had been to introduce such modifications in the Act of Federation as would enable Austria and the countries dependent on her to enter the German Federation, which would then be forced to secure the inviolability of the whole Hapsburg power. Britain and France declined to accept these proposals. The German governments showed no desire to enter upon a struggle with two Great Powers to gain a federal reform which could only benefit Austria. Prussia was able calmly to await the collapse of Schwarzenberg's schemes.

After wearisome negotiations, lasting from December, 1850, to May, 1851, it became clear that all attempts at reform were futile as long as Austria declined to grant Prussia the equality which she desired in the presidency and in the formation of the proposed "directory." Schwarzenberg declined to yield, and all that could be done was to return to the old federal system, and thereby to make the dis-

Severe Punishment of Liberals creditable avowal that the collective governments were as powerless as the disjointed parliament to amend the unsatisfactory political situation. In the federal palace at Frankfort-on-Main, where the sovereignty of that German National Assembly had been organised a short time before, the opinion again prevailed, from 1851, that there could be no more dangerous enemy to the state and to society than the popular representative. The unfortunate Liberals, humiliated and depressed by their own incompetency, now paid the penalty for their democratic tendencies; they were branded as "destructive forces," and punished by imprisonment which should properly have fallen upon republican inconstancy.

The majority of the liberal constitutions which the revolution of 1848 had brought into existence were annulled; this step was quickly carried out in Saxony, Mecklenburg-Schwerin, and Würtemberg, in June, September, and November, 1850, though the Chamber continued an obstinate resistance until August, 1855, in Hanover, where the blind King George V. had ascended the throne on November 18th, 1851. The favour of the federation restored her detested ruler to the electorate of Hesse. He positively revelled in the cruelty and oppression practised upon his subjects by the troops of occupation. His satellite, Hassenpflug, known as "Hessen-Fluch," the curse of Hesse, zealously contributed to increase the severity of this despotism by his ferocity against the recalcitrant officials, who considered themselves bound by their obligations to the constitution.

In Prussia the reactionary party would very gladly have made an end of constitutionalism once and for all; but though the king entertained a deep-rooted objection to the modern theories of popular participation in the government, he declined to be a party to any breach of the oath which he had taken. Bunsen and Prince William supported his objections to a coup d'état, which seemed the more unnecessary as a constitutional change in the direction of conservatism had been successfully carried through on February 6th, 1850.

The system of three classes of direct representation was introduced at the end of April, 1849, taxation thus becoming the measure of the political rights exercised by the second Chamber. The **Prussia's House of Lords** possibility of a labour majority in this Chamber was thus obviated. The Upper Chamber was entirely remodelled. Members were no longer elected, but were nominated by the Crown; seats were made hereditary in the different noble families, and the preponderance of the nobility was thus secured. The institution of a full house of lords on October 12th, 1854, was not so severe a blow to the state as the dissolution of the parish councils and the reinstitution of the provincial Landtags in 1851.

Schleswig-Holstein was handed over to the Danes; the constitution of September 15th, 1848, and German "proprietary rights" were declared null and void by a supreme authority composed of Austrian, Prussian, and Danish commissioners. By the London protocol of May 8th, 1852, the Great Powers recognised the succession of Prince Christian of Holstein-Glücksburg, who had married Princess Louise, a daughter of the Countess of Hesse, Louise Charlotte, sister of Christian VIII. However, the German Federation did not favour this solution; the estates of the duchies, who had the best right to decide the question, were never even asked their opinion. On December 30th, 1852, Duke Christian of Holstein-Augustenburg sold his Schles-

wig estates to the reigning house of Denmark for £337,500, renouncing his hereditary rights at the same time, though the other members of the family declined to accept the renunciation as binding upon themselves. Thus the Danes gained but a temporary victory. It was even then clear that after the death of King Frederic **The "German Fleet" Exposed to Auction** VII. the struggle would be renewed for the separation of the German districts from the "Danish United States." A legacy of the national movement, the "German fleet," was put up to auction at this date. The German Federation had no maritime interests to represent.

It declined the trouble of extorting a recognition of the German flag from the maritime Powers. Of the four frigates, five corvettes, and six gunboats, which had been fitted out at a cost of £540,000, Prussia bought the larger part, after Hanoverian machinations had induced the Federal Council to determine the dissolution of the fleet on April 2nd, 1852. Prussia acquired from Oldenburg a strip of territory on the Jade Bay, and in course of time constructed a naval arsenal and harbour, Wilhelmshaven, which enabled her to appear as a maritime power in the Baltic.

These facts were the more important as Prussia, in spite of violent opposition, had maintained her position as head of that economic unity which was now known as the "Zollverein." The convention expired on December 31st, 1853. From 1849, Austria had been working to secure the position, and at the tariff conference held in Wiesbaden in June, 1851, had secured the support of every state of importance within the Zollverein with the exception of Prussia. Prussia was in consequence forced to renounce the preference for protective duties which she had evinced in the last few years, and, on September 7th, 1851, to join the free trade "Steuerverein," which Hanover had formed with Olden-**Austria's Treaty with Prussia** burg and Lippe in 1834 and 1836. The danger of a separation between the eastern and western territorial groups was thus obviated; the Zollverein of Austria and the smaller German states were cut off from the sea and deprived of all the advantages which the original Prussian Zollverein had offered. Austria now thought it advisable to conclude a commercial treaty with Prussia on favourable terms on February 19th, 1853, and to leave the smaller states to their fate. In any case their continual demands for compensation and damages had become wearisome. Nothing remained for them except to join Prussia. Thus on April 4th, 1853, the Zollverein was renewed, to last until December 31st, 1865. It was an association embracing an area containing 35,000,000 inhabitants. As after the fall of Napoleon I., so now the lion's share of the plunder acquired in the struggle against the revolution fell to the Church. Liberalism had indeed rendered an important service to Catholicism by incorporating in its creed the phrase, " the Free Church in the Free State."

The Church's Large Share of Plunder

The Jesuits were well able to turn this freedom to the best account. They demanded for the German bishops unlimited powers of communication with Rome and with the parochial clergy, together with full disciplinary powers over all priests without the necessity of an appeal to the state. Nothing was simpler than to construe ecclesiastical freedom as implying that right of supremacy for which the Church had yearned during the past eight centuries.

The Archbishop of Freiburg pushed the theory with such brazen effrontery that even the reactionary government was forced to imprison him. However, in Darmstadt and Stuttgart the governments submitted to the demands of Rome. Parties in the Prussian Chamber were increased by the addition of a new Catholic party, led by the brothers Reichensperger, to which high favour was shown by the " Catholic Contingent" in the ministry of ecclesiastical affairs—a party created by the ecclesiastical minister, Eichhorn, in 1841.

There was no actual collision in Prussia between ultramontanism and the temporal power. The Government favoured the reaction in the Protestant Church, which took the form of an unmistakable rapprochement to Catholicism. The Powers were committed to a policy of mutual counsel and support. Stahl, Hengstenberg, and Gerlach, who had gained complete ascendancy over Frederic William IV. since the revolution, were undermining the foundations of the Protestant creed, especially the respect accorded to inward conviction, on which the whole of Protestantism was based. In the " regulations " of October, 1854, the

Reaction in Protestant Church

schools were placed under Church supervision, and in the "Church Councils" hypocrisy was made supreme. When Bunsen advanced to champion the cause of spiritual freedom, he gained only the honourable title of " devastator of the Church."

In Austria the rights of the human understanding were flouted even more completely than in Russia by the conclusion of the notorious concordat of August 18th, 1855. This agreement was the expression of an alliance between ultramontanism and the new centralising absolutism. The hierarchy undertook for a short period to oppose the national parties and to commend the refusal of constitutional rights. In return the absolutist state placed the whole of its administration at the disposal of the Church, and gave the bishops unconditional supremacy over the clergy, who had hitherto used the position assigned to them by Joseph II. for the benefit of the people, and certainly not for the injury of the Church. The Church thus gained a spiritual preponderance which was used to secure her paramountcy. The example of Austria was imitated in the Italian states, which owed their existence to her. Piedmont alone gathered the opponents of the Roman hierarchy under her banner, for this government at least was determined that no patriot should be led astray by the great fiction of a national Pope. In Spain the Jesuits joined the Carlists, and helped them to carry on a hopeless campaign, marked by a series of defeats. In Belgium, on the other hand, they secured an almost impregnable position in 1855, and fought the Liberals with their own weapons. Only Portugal, whence they had first been expelled in the eighteenth century, kept herself free from their influence in the nineteenth, and showed that even a Catholic government had no need to fear the threats of the papacy.

The Strong Hand of Rome

Rome had set great hopes upon France, since Louis Napoleon's " plebiscites " had been successfully carried out with the help of the clergy. But the Curia found France a prudent friend, not to be caught off her guard. The diplomatic skill of Napoleon III. was never seen to better advantage than in his delimitation of the spheres respectively assigned to the temporal and the spiritual Powers. Even the Jesuits were unable to fathom his intentions.

HANS VON ZWIEDINECK-SÜDENHORST

SAVING THE COLOURS: THE GUARDS AT THE BATTLE OF INKERMAN IN 1854

From the painting by Robert Gibb, R.S.A., by permission of Mr. E. Bruce-Low

TO FACE PAGE 4978

The CONSOLIDATION of the POWERS

THE UNITED KINGDOM IN THE MID-VICTORIAN ERA

By Arthur D. Innes, M.A.

THE fall of Sir Robert Peel, in 1846, had been effected almost at the moment when the Duke of Wellington was persuading the House of Lords to swallow the repeal of the Corn Laws, the crowning accomplishment of Peel's career. It was achieved by a combination of angry Protectionists and angry Irishmen, who united to throw out a government measure for coercion in Ireland. The potato famine had definitely completed the conversion of both Peel and the Whigs to the doctrines of the Anti-Corn Law League, and was followed by earnest efforts for the relief of distress.

But distress itself had, as usual, intensified discontent, generating agrarian outrages, and relief and coercion were proffered simultaneously. The unconverted chiefs of what had been Peel's party saw their opportunity; and the adverse vote brought about Peel's resignation. Lord John Russell formed a Whig Ministry, with Palmerston as Foreign Secretary—which position he had occupied in Melbourne's time—and the Peelites, regarding the question of Free Trade as of primary im-

Great Britain in the Year of Revolutions portance, gave the Government a support which secured its continuity. The improvement in the condition of the working classes, coupled with the British inclination to distrust the political efficacy of syllogisms expressed in terms of physical force, made Great Britain almost the only European country where nothing revolutionary took place in the year of revolutions, 1848. The monster petition of the Chartists was its most alarming event.

The death of O'Connell, however, in the previous year had deprived the Irish of a leader who had always set his face against the methods of violence, and Ireland did not escape without an abortive insurrection headed by Smith O'Brien. The leaders were taken, condemned to death for high treason, had their sentences commuted to trans-

Lord Palmerston at the Foreign Office portation, and were subsequently pardoned—more than one of those associated with the movement achieved distinction in later years in the political service of the British Empire.

Palmerston's activities at the Foreign Office, however, were a source of considerable disquietude at this period. Forty years of parliamentary life, many of them passed in office, first as a Tory, later as a Canningite, and finally as a Whig, had not produced in that persistently youthful statesman any inclination in favour of the further democratisation of the British Constitution, or of what in his younger days would have been called Jacobinism abroad; but he was a convinced advocate of freedom as he understood it and as Canning had understood it. He saw in revolutionary movements a disease engendered by despotic systems of government; and being alive to the European ferment, he took upon himself to warn the despotic governments that they would do well to apply the remedy of constitutionalism before the disease became dangerous.

The despotic governments, recognising no difference between the disease itself and the remedy, held him guilty not only of officiousness in tendering advice which

4975

QUEEN VICTORIA AND THE PRINCE CONSORT

From the painting by Sir Edwin Landseer, R.A.

THE ROYAL VISIT TO IRELAND IN 1849: THE FLEET IN CORK HARBOUR

was unasked, but of fomenting revolution in their dominions, and were not unnaturally resentful, although, as a matter of fact, they would have profited greatly by paying heed to his well-meant warnings.

The attacks in Parliament on his "meddling" policy were successfully met in 1849, and public opinion endorsed his view that Britain ought to make her opinions felt in foreign countries — that, in fact, she would not be adequately discharging the responsibilities of her great position in the world unless she did so. Nevertheless, his methods were irritating not only to foreign potentates, but to his own sovereign, who frequently found that her Foreign Minister was committing the Government without her knowledge to declarations which she could only endorse because it would have been impossible to retract them with dignity, his colleagues being consulted as little as herself.

In 1850 the queen sent a memorandum to Russell, requiring that she should be kept adequately informed before, not after, the event, of any steps which the Foreign Minister intended to take. The immediate cause of the memorandum was connected with Palmerston's attitude on the Schleswig-Holstein question, regarding which she and her husband, Prince Albert, favoured the German view, to which Palmerston was opposed. Another incident illustrative

LORD JOHN RUSSELL
He was twice Prime Minister, first in 1846 on the formation of a Whig Ministry following the defeat of Peel, and again in 1865, on the death of Lord Palmerston. He was created Earl Russell in 1861, and he died in 1878.

THE EARL OF BEACONSFIELD
Eminent as statesman and novelist, Benjamin Disraeli, afterwards Lord Beaconsfield, made a great reputation in the political world, though his maiden speech in the House of Commons was greeted with derisive laughter. He twice held the high office of Prime Minister.

of the Foreign Minister's high-handed methods was the "Don Pacifico" affair. Don Pacifico was a Jew from Gibraltar, a British subject, residing in Greece, whose house and property were damaged in a riot. Palmerston took up his claim for compensation as an international instead of a personal affair, sent the fleet to the Piræus, the harbour of Athens, and seized Greek merchant vessels. Russia adopted a threatening attitude, to which Palmerston had no disposition to yield. The French Republic, under the presidency of Louis Napoleon, was indignant at the action of Great Britain, but still more indignant at being ignored by Russia. Palmerston accepted French mediation — not arbitration; there were further complications, in which the French thought that Albion was showing her historic perfidy; but the whole affair was too trivial to involve two great nations in a war over mere diplomatic proprieties, and the quarrel was patched up. This incident was the inciting cause of a formal attack on Palmerston's foreign policy, which resulted in a vote of censure in the Upper Chamber, in consequence of which a resolution of confidence was introduced in the Commons. Peel himself was on the side of the Opposition, but Palmerston vindicated his principles in a wonderful speech — the "civis Romanus

THE GREAT EXHIBITION OF 1851: QUEEN VICTORIA AND THE PRINCE CONSORT AT THE OPENING CEREMONY IN HYDE PARK

The Exhibition of the Industry of all Nations, which owed its inception to the enterprise and energy of the Prince Consort, did much to extend a knowledge of the world's manufactures, and gave an impetus to commercial activity. Held in Hyde Park in a building which covered nineteen acres of ground, it remained open for twenty-three weeks, and during that time was visited by upwards of six million persons. The above picture shows the inauguration of the Exhibition on May 1st, by Queen Victoria and the Prince Consort.

From the painting by H. C. Selous in the South Kensington Museum

sum " speech—which carried the House and the country triumphantly with him. The year also witnessed one of those " No Popery " waves of excitement which periodically break upon England. The Tractarian movement had produced in the mind of the Pope the recurrent delusion that the heretical island was on the verge of conversion. He issued a Bull establishing a Roman hierarchy in England, with territorial titles, an assumption of authority contravening the constitutional principle of the royal supremacy. In response to the popular excitement created, the Government introduced the " Ecclesiastical

letter till its repeal twenty years later. The queen's memorandum in the previous November, somewhat to the public surprise, had not been followed by Palmerston's resignation; apparently he had accepted the rebuke in good part, and promised to consult the queen's wishes. But his practice remained unaltered. The arrival in England of the Hungarian leader, Kossuth, was the occasion of a display of sympathy which was at best a breach of international etiquette, Kossuth being technically a rebel. At the moment when Palmerston was being taken to task for neglect of his promise to pay proper

LORD ABERDEEN'S FAMOUS COALITION MINISTRY
On the defeat of the Derby government in December, 1852, Lord Aberdeen formed a coalition Ministry of Whigs and Peelites with Gladstone as Chancellor of the Exchequer, Russell at the Foreign and Palmerston at the Home Office.
From the painting by Sir John Gilbert, R.A.   Photo by Walker

Titles " Bill, which was naturally opposed by the Roman Catholics and also by all who saw in it an interference with the principle of religious liberty. The Government, feeling its position to be somewhat precarious, took advantage of its own defeat on a snap vote—a symptom of the now growing demand for further electoral reform—to resign, and thereby to demonstrate the impossibility of any other working administration being constructed. It resumed office in February, 1851, and carried the Bill in a modified form, but the Act remained practically a dead

attention to the queen's wishes in this affair, Louis Napoleon in France carried out the coup d'état which he had been preparing, and established himself as a dictator. Palmerston persuaded himself that the British Foreign Minister could express his personal approval in a conversation with the French ambassador without committing the Cabinet, the Crown, or the country. The other parties concerned did not accept that view, and Palmerston's resignation was demanded. But he had hardly been dismissed when he got his " tit-for-tat with John Russell," as he expressed it. Napoleon's coup d'état had its alarming side for Great Britain, as a probable prelude to an aggressive French policy, of which the Napoleonic tradition would make England the primary object of hostility. A Bill was accordingly introduced for the reorganisation of the militia. The scheme proposed was not felt to be satisfactory; Palmerston headed the attack, the Ministry were defeated, and the Government was undertaken by the Conservative chief, Lord Derby, with Disraeli as his Chancellor of the Exchequer and Leader of the House of Commons, in February, 1852. The most notable of the actual achievements of the Russell administration had been the application in Australia, by an Act of 1850, of those principles of colonial government which had been inaugurated by the Canadian Act of Reunion. The new Ministry carried a new Militia Bill and then dissolved, apparently with a view to taking the sense of the country on the Free Trade policy which had brought the Liberals into office.

The Ministerialists, however, did not definitely commit themselves to a Protectionist programme, and the question was brought to a direct issue in the Commons by a resolution affirming the principle of Free Trade, which, in amended form, was accepted and carried by an overwhelming majority. Fifty years were to pass before the discovery that the revolutionary economic doctrine of 1846 to which the country declared itself definitely

converted in 1852 was an exploded antediluvian fallacy. In the interval, the scanty handful of its opponents were but feeble voices crying in the wilderness The theory of Protection being so effectively scotched as to be apparently killed, the ex Protectionists —who had maintained the old doctrine not from the manufacturing, but from the agrarian point of view—fell back on the principle that the landed interest, which the old system had protected, required relief now that the protection was withdrawn; and to this end Disraeli constructed his Budget. But his extremely ingenious redistribution of the burden of taxation failed to attract the approval of economists of other schools, or of those interests which did not desire the land to be relieved at

THE DEATH OF THE DUKE OF WELLINGTON
The long and illustrious life of the Duke of Wellington came to an end in 1852, the hero of Waterloo passing peacefully away on September 14th, in his arm-chair at Walmer. In the above picture the body of the distinguished general, who was laid to rest with great pomp in St. Paul's Cathedral, is seen lying in state at Chelsea Hospital.

their expense. The Budget debate marked conspicuously the opening of the long personal rivalry between its proposer, Disraeli, and its strongest critic, William Ewart Gladstone. The Government was defeated, and resigned in December, 1852. The Ecclesiastical Titles Bill, which had been a barrier between Whigs and Peelites, had already vanished into limbo, and the Ministry which now took office was formed by a coalition of those two parties. The Peelite, Lord Aberdeen, was its head, Gladstone its Chancellor of the Exchequer, Russell was at the Foreign Office, and Palmerston Home Secretary.

Before the fall of the Conservatives, a great figure had passed from the stage. A little more than two years after his closest political associate, Sir Robert Peel, the "Iron Duke" died in September, at the age of eighty-three. Forty years before, he had proved himself the greatest captain in Europe save one ; and his, in the eyes of Europe, had been the triumph of vanquishing that one. To him more than to anyone else France owed it that she had been generously treated when the war was ended ; his was probably the most decisively moderating influence among the statesmen whose task it was to restore order in Europe. But while he possessed high qualities of statesmanship, they were not those adapted to parliamentary government. As a Minister he was a failure ; as a counsellor his judgment always carried very great weight. His unqualified patriotism, his complete subordination of personal interests to what he conceived to be the welfare of the state, his perfect

THE DEFENDER OF SEBASTOPOL
General Todleben, a distinguished Russian soldier and military engineer, held Sebastopol against the British, displaying great resource and energy until he was severely wounded.

sincerity, his transparent honesty, and his conspicuous moral courage, made him a unique figure, and fully justified the universal popularity which came to him tardily enough, and the genuine passion of mourning with which the whole nation received the tidings of his death. Wellington had overthrown the first Napoleon. Eleven weeks after he had breathed his last, "the nephew of his uncle" was proclaimed Emperor of the French with the title of Napoleon III. The famous coalition Ministry opened its career with the first of the brilliant series of Gladstone Budgets, introduced in a speech which revealed the hitherto unsuspected fact that figures can be made fascinating. But even the charm of the Budget was soon to be overshadowed by the war clouds in the East. So far as the preliminaries of the Crimean war are concerned with French and Russian rivalries

BURIAL OF THE DUKE OF WELLINGTON: THE FUNERAL CAR ARRIVING AT ST. PAUL'S

QUEEN VICTORIA AS SHE APPEARED IN THE YEAR 1852

and with matters outside British interests, they will be dealt with in the chapter following. Here we observe that in the beginning of 1853 the Tsar was assuming a threatening attitude towards the Porte on the hypothesis that Russia was the protector of the Greek Church Christians in the Turkish dominions; and that France, in the character of protector of the Latin Christians, regarded the Russian attitude as merely a pretext for absorbing the Danube states. A similar view was entertained in England, where the Tsar had already made suggestions regarding the ultimate partition of the Turkish Empire, which he regarded as practically inevitable

England, however, and Palmerston in particular, looked upon the maintenance of the independence of Turkey as a necessity, if for no other reason because Russian expansion in the direction either of India or of the Mediterranean appeared exceedingly dangerous to the interests of Great Britain. It may be remembered that the Afghan war of 1839 had been the outcome of Persian aggressions which were universally regarded as prompted by Russia.

Russia maintained her claim to protect the Christians in the Danube provinces; Turkey declined her demand for

Napoleon would not venture on that appeal single-handed. The temper of the country, however, was clearly in favour of Palmerston's views, and in July the French and British fleets were despatched to Besika Bay. The "Vienna Note," a proposal formulated by the Powers in conference at Vienna, was amended by Turkey and rejected by Russia in August. Everywhere popular feeling was rising; an anti-Christian émeute was feared in Constantinople, and the French and British fleets were ordered to the Dardanelles in October, ostensibly to protect

THE QUEEN REVIEWING THE SCOTS GUARDS ON THEIR DEPARTURE FOR THE CRIMEA IN 1854
The aggression of Russia, involved by her claim of 1853 to be protector of the Orthodox Greek Christians in the Turkish dominions, was naturally resented by Turkey. Both Britain and France took the side of the latter, and on March 27th, 1854, declared war on Russia, whence followed all the miseries and suffering of the Crimean war.

guarantees; the rest of the Powers upheld Turkey. Negotiations failing, Russia occupied the provinces in July as a proceeding warranted by her treaty rights. The Powers might, by the exercise of joint pressure, have compelled Russia to retire, but a mere evacuation would not have satisfied either Napoleon or Palmerston. Aberdeen, on the other hand, allowed his aversion to war to be so obvious that the Tsar probably felt quite satisfied that Britain would not join France in an appeal to arms, and that

the Christians. Before the close of the month Turkey declared war on Russia, to which the Tsar replied by declaring that he would not take the offensive. The Turks crossed the Danube, and fighting began. But when a Russian squadron fell upon some Turkish ships in the harbour of Sinope and destroyed them on September 30th, the action was regarded as proving the insincerity of the Tsar's declarations. Aberdeen found himself obliged to consent to the occupation of the Black Sea by the allied fleets on December 27th. The

BEGINNING OF THE CRIMEAN WAR: THE BATTLE OF THE ALMA ON SEPTEMBER 20TH, 1854

Landing at Kalamita Bay, near the mouth of the River Alma, in September, the allied forces, consisting of 25,000 English, 25,000 French, and 8,000 Turks, began the march on Sebastopol, the great arsenal and harbour of Russia, and found a Russian army under Menschikoff between them and their goal. The struggle was not long delayed. On the 20th was fought the Battle of the Alma; victory rested with the allies, but it was dearly purchased, the British in two hours' fighting losing 2,000 men, while the French loss was returned at 1,200

From the painting by Isidore Pils in the Versailles Museum

ATTACKING THE RUSSIAN STRONGHOLD: THE SIEGE AND BOMBARDMENT OF SEBASTOPOL

After the victory of the Alma, an immediate assault on Sebastopol was contemplated, but the opposition of the dying French general, St. Arnaud, prevented this from being attempted, and the allies settled down to a siege which continued for nearly a year, and was terminated on September 8th, 1855, by the capture of Malakoff Fort, the key to the Russian position.

Reproduced from sketches by an artillery officer

NAVAL BRIGADE AT SEBASTOPOL: LORD RAGLAN VIEWING THE STORMING OF THE REDAN

From the picture by R. Caton Woodville, by permission of Messrs. Graves & Co.

precipitate action of France and Britain in presenting a joint note demanding the evacuation of the Danube provinces gave Austria an excuse for leaving them to act independently; and on March 27th, 1854, the two Western Powers declared war on Russia and proceeded to a formal alliance with the Turks, who in the meantime had more than held their own on land.

Troops were despatched to co-operate with the Turks, and it soon became evident that the Russians would have no chance of effecting a successful invasion; before the end of July it was clear that they would be obliged to evacuate the Provinces. But before that time instructions had already been sent for the invasion of the Crimea and the seizure of Sebástopol.

But the invasion could not be carried out till September; and by that time, Sebastopol had been placed in a comparatively thorough state of defence by the engineering skill of Todleben. Its capture by a coup de main was now extremely improbable. The British and French forces disembarked at Eupatoria, and found a Russian army under Menschikoff lying between them and Sebastopol. The battle of the Alma, in which the brunt of the fighting was borne by the British, left the allies masters of the field. Menschikoff withdrew his main force not to Sebastopol but to the interior. The opposition of the dying French general, St. Arnaud, prevented an immediate assault from being attempted—it was ascertained later that the attempt at that moment would probably have been successful—and the allies settled down to a siege. Their

The Charge of the Heavy Brigade numbers were not sufficient for a complete investment, and the communications between Menschikoff and the garrison remained open. The British drew their supplies from the port of Balaclava, and Menschikoff now endeavoured to effect its capture. The movement, however, was repulsed, mainly by the magnificent charge of the Heavy

LORD RAGLAN
Commander-in-chief of the British forces in the Crimea, his conduct of the war was severely condemned both by the public and the Press. He died from dysentery on June 28th, 1855.

Brigade against a column of five times their own numbers; but that splendid action was eclipsed in the popular mind by one of the most desperate, and, from a military point of view, most futile, deeds of valour on record, the charge of the Six Hundred.

In the "Valley of Death" Through the misinterpretation of an order, the Light Brigade hurled itself through a terrific storm of shot and shell upon a Russian battery, captured it, and then, because there was nothing else to be done, relinquished it, leaving more than two-thirds of their number in the "Valley of Death." Nothing whatever was gained of a calculable kind. Yet it was one of those deeds which have a moral value past all calculation, like the equally futile defence of Thermopylæ. Ten days later an attempt was made upon the British position before Sebastopol at Inkerman. The attack was made by a large Russian force in the midst of a fog so thick that none knew what was going on except close at hand. Concerted action was impossible, and men battled desperately as best they could in small groups. The fight was fought by the men virtually without commanders, and, in spite of immensely superior numbers, the Russians were triumphantly repulsed. But after Inkerman, the design, then in contemplation, of an immediate assault on Sebastopol was abandoned. And then the Crimean winter began. A winter siege had not been in the programme when the expedition was planned; the arrangements were disastrously inadequate, and their inadequacy was increased by the destruction in a gale of the stores which had reached Balaclava but had not been disembarked; while the iniquities of army contractors broke all previous records. The four winter months killed far more of the troops than the Russians were responsible for. The blame lay not at all with the officers on the spot, and only in a limited degree with the Government, but popular indignation compelled the retirement of Aberdeen; and Palmerston, the

BRITISH HEROES AT BALACLAVA: THE CHARGE OF THE HEAVY BRIGADE ON OCTOBER 25TH, 1854

The supplies for the British army were drawn from the port of Balaclava, and as its capture would have been of immense value to the Russians, Menschikoff attempted to bring this about on October 25th. The movement, however, was repulsed, mainly by the magnificent charge of the Heavy Brigade against a column of five times their own numbers,

From the picture by R. Morin

THE CHARGE OF THE LIGHT BRIGADE: THE SIX HUNDRED RIDING "INTO THE VALLEY OF DEATH"

The brilliant action at Balaclava illustrated on the preceding page was eclipsed in the popular mind by the splendid but futile charge of the "Six Hundred." Through the misinterpretation of an order, the Light Brigade hurled itself through a terrific storm of shot and shell upon a Russian battery, while "cannon to right of them, cannon to left of them, cannon in front of them volley'd and thunder'd," and then, because there was nothing else to be done, relinquished it, leaving more than two-thirds of their number in the Valley of Death.

man in whom the confidence of the country had not been shaken, became Prime Minister in February, 1855. The lesson of the early administrative blunders had been learnt, and a great improvement was soon apparent. The immense and unprecedented services of the staff of nurses organised under Florence Nightingale, who had been at work since November, mark an epoch in the history of civilised warfare. Negotiations were renewed at Vienna; but while agreement might have been reached on two of the four proposals put forward by Austria, Russia was obdurate on a third, and the belligerent allies were dissatisfied with the fourth.

A New Epoch in Warfare

The negotiations broke down, and Austria again found excuse in the attitude of the French and British for declining to join them in an offensive alliance—in their eyes a breach of faith on her part. In May, however, Sardinia joined the allies, and the British share in the operations at Sebastopol became comparatively restricted, while the British fleets found little of consequence to do. It was not till September 8th that Sebastopol fell, an event secured by the French capture of the Malakoff.

Napoleon was now satisfied with the personal security his imperial position had acquired from the war; the friendship of the new Tsar, Alexander II.—Nicholas had died in March—was of more importance to him, if not to France, than the repression of Russia. Austria cared only to have her own Balkan interests safeguarded, and it was with no little difficulty that the British were able to secure adequate checks on Russian aggression. The occasion was used for a fresh settlement of those maritime regulations which had been the cause of the " Armed Neutrality " at the close of the last century. Privateering, the one weapon which hostile Powers had been able to wield effectively against Great Britain, was abolished; and, on the other hand, it was conceded that the neutral flag should cover all goods but contraband of war, and that even on belligerent vessels neutral goods should not be liable to capture, in March, 1856.

Abolition of Privateering

The war in the Crimea had necessitated the withdrawal of British regiments from India, where, on the other hand, Dalhousie's annexations had involved an increase in the Sepoy army. A quarrel with Persia demanded an expedition to that country from India at the end of 1856, owing to the seizure of Herat by Persia—a movement attributed, as a matter of course, to Russian instigation. No difficulty was found in the military operations, which soon resulted in a treaty by which Persia resigned Herat and all claims on Afghan territory; but the war must be included among the minor circumstances which encouraged the outbreak of the great Sepoy revolt of 1857.

About the same time a war with China was brought about by what is known as the " Arrow " incident. The Arrow was a Chinese vessel which had been sailing under the British flag, and was continuing to do so though the year during which she was authorised to do so had just elapsed. The Chinese authorities, having no knowledge of this lapse, nevertheless seized the crew in Canton harbour on the hypothesis that there were persons " wanted " for piracy among its number. Reparation was demanded and refused, the British fleet was called into play, and the incident developed definitely into a war. The British Government acted on the principle that the punctilios of Western diplomacy are invariably looked upon by Orientals as signs of weakness which invite defiance; highhanded methods, however, equally invariably offend the moral ideals of a large section of the British people, and the Government was vigorously attacked by the Liberals and Peelites who had parted from the Ministry. But an appeal to the country gave Palmerston a decisive majority in April, 1857. The war was brought to a conclusion in the course of 1858.

Britain's War with China

Almost the first news, which came on the new Parliament as a bolt from the blue, was that of the great outbreak in India, the story of which has been dealt with in the earlier section of this work devoted to Indian history. The Mutiny was inaugurated by the rising of the Sepoys at Mirat on May 10th, 1857. Delhi was seized in the name of a restored Mogul Empire; a British force concentrated on the famous Ridge, which it occupied for the siege of the great city, held by forces enormously superior in point of numbers.

Above Allahabad, the whole Ganges basin was in the hands of the mutineers, and the British were soon shut up in Cawnpore or the Lucknow Residency, with the

THE VICTORY THAT SETTLED THE FATE OF SEBASTOPOL: THE CAPTURE OF THE MALAKOFF BY THE FRENCH

From the painting by Yvon

exception of the force on the ridge before Delhi and of a considerable number who took refuge at Agra. The loyalty and diplomacy of Sindhia and his minister Dinkar Rao restrained the Gwalior army from marching to Delhi. In September, Delhi was stormed and Lucknow was reinforced by the operations of Havelock and Outram.

From that time, though Sindhia was no longer able to hold back the Gwalior regiments, the tide turned. Troops were arriving from England; a contingent on its way to the Chinese war was detained for the more serious affair. In November, Sir Colin Campbell relieved the defenders of the Lucknow Residency; in the spring, the British armies were

amend the conspiracy laws; but the French had assumed an attitude of such amazing and bombastic truculence that the Conspiracy to Murder Bill was regarded as a pusillanimous submission to foreign insolence—a curious charge against the Minister who was accustomed to being himself accused of arrogance rather than submissiveness in foreign affairs, mainly to be explained by the tenacious pride with which the nation clung to its claim of offering an asylum to refugees from oppression.

The Bill was defeated, the Government resigned, and again Lord Derby took office, though his party was in a minority in the House of Commons. Under such circumstances, the Ministry had no choice

QUEEN VICTORIA RECEIVING HEROES OF THE CRIMEA AT BUCKINGHAM PALACE
From the painting by Sir John Gilbert, R.A.

everywhere triumphant, and in the summer the last efforts of the revolt were crushed.

The Mutiny brought home to the British mind the necessity for terminating the unique and anomalous dual control, by the East India Company and Parliament, of the government of India. It was time that the Crown should assume the exclusive responsibility, and in February, 1858, Palmerston brought in a Bill for that purpose. By a curious accident, he was turned out of office before the Bill could be passed. An Italian named Orsini flung bombs under the carriage of Napoleon in January; it turned out that the plot had been hatched and the bombs manufactured in England. The Government proposed to

but to seek for compromises with the Opposition. Lord Derby's India Bill, when introduced, was obviously not destined to pass, and the Act which finally ended the career of the East India Company, and transferred the Indian government to the Crown, was virtually the work of all parties combining to arrive at a settlement irrespective of party. Lord Canning, the Governor-General, who had remained at the helm throughout the Mutiny, inaugurated the new regime as the first Viceroy. In the same summer, the Lords were persuaded to pass a Bill removing the political disabilities under which the Jews still laboured, a principle repeatedly approved by the Commons

THE RULERS OF BRITAIN AND OF FRANCE AT THE OPERA IN LONDON

Arising out of their common interests in the war against Russia, a kindly feeling sprang up between Britain and France, the rulers of the two countries exchanging visits of friendship. On April 16th, 1855, the Emperor Napoleon III. and the Empress Eugénie arrived in England, visiting Queen Victoria at Windsor Castle, and in the above picture they are shown with the Queen and the Prince Consort at the Royal Italian Opera on April 19th,

QUEEN VICTORIA AND THE PRINCE CONSORT VISITING THE TUILERIES

In the August following the visit of the French Emperor and Empress to England, Queen Victoria and the Prince Consort visited France. In this picture the British queen and her husband are seen at the Tuileries, the former in the foreground on the arm of Napoleon with Prince Albert and the Empress Eugénie immediately behind.

THE ENTENTE CORDIALE IN THE MIDDLE OF LAST CENTURY

QUEEN VICTORIA DISTRIBUTING THE CRIMEAN MEDALS AT THE HORSE GUARDS
The first distribution of V.C. medals is represented in the above picture, this event taking place on May 18th, 1856; the queen is shown in the act of presenting a medal to Sir Thomas Troubridge, who had lost both his feet in action.

and rejected by the Peers during the preceding twenty-five years. Electoral Reform—that is, extension of the franchise—was a subject in which the electorate and the unenfranchised masses were more interested than Ministers. Russell and a considerable section of the Liberals were becoming more strongly disposed in that direction, but the Palmerstonians preferred to keep the question shelved as long as possible. Disraeli, however, now saw a possibility of

securing success to the conservative policy by a measure professedly democratic, but safeguarded by devices which, in the eyes of the Liberals, were intended to secure political preponderance for conservative influences. Defeated on a resolution introduced by Russell, Lord Derby appealed to the country; the party returned somewhat strengthened in numbers, but still in a minority, and the minority gave way to a new Palmerston administration, with Russell at the Foreign Office. the two

THE QUEEN AND PRINCE ALBERT VISITING BROMPTON HOSPITAL AT CHATHAM. IN 1856

liberal leaders having recognised the need of co-operation. Gladstone returned to the Exchequer.

Palmerston remained at the head of the government till his death in 1865. It was inevitable that a Franchise Bill should be introduced, but it aroused no enthusiasm in Parliament or in the country, and

in the commercial treaty with France, negotiated by Richard Cobden, which was ratified in 1860.

The Budget of that year reduced the number of articles subject to customs duties from 419 to 48, the primary object being the removal of preferential and protective duties. Financial questions, however, narrowly missed producing a serious constitutional crisis. It was proposed in 1859 to remove the tax upon paper. Being introduced in a Bill separate from the Budget, the Lords claimed the right of rejecting the proposal. The Commons claimed that the Lords could not reject separately any part of the general financial scheme. The action of the Lords in rejecting the Bill was in accordance with the law, but not with the custom of the Constitution. The crisis was averted, partly by a series of resolutions in the Commons, which pointed to the inclusion of such proposals in the Budget as security against the repetition of such action by the Lords, and partly by the inclusion of the particular pro-

"EASTWARD HO!" THE DEPARTURE OF BRITISH TROOPS FOR INDIA
When the Indian Mutiny broke out in 1857, the British army in India was not sufficiently strong adequately to cope with the rising, and reinforcements were speedily despatched from England. Farewell scenes are graphically represented in the above picture.
From the painting by Henry O'Neill, A.R.A.

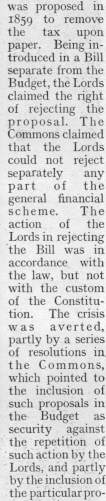

Russell, who introduced it, found an excuse for its withdrawal, after which, by common consent, reform was shelved for the lifetime of the Prime Minister. There was little legislation during Palmerston's supremacy, and domestic interest centred mainly in the systematic extension of Free Trade principles, in the Budgets, and

posal in the Budget of the following year.

These years, however, were marked by complications in the affairs of other nations which made the task of steering Great Britain successfully a difficult and delicate one. The sympathies of the country and of the Government were with the Italians in their struggle for liberty from

THE MARRIAGE OF THE PRINCESS ROYAL TO PRINCE FREDERIC WILLIAM OF PRUSSIA ON JANUARY 25TH, 1858

From the painting by John Phillip, R.A.

THE MARRIAGE OF KING EDWARD VII. AND QUEEN ALEXANDRA ON MARCH 10TH, 1863

This interesting event in the lives of the present King and Queen of Great Britain and Ireland was celebrated on March 10th, 1863, at St. George's Chapel, Windsor. The Prince of Wales, as he then was, first met Princess Alexandra of Denmark in 1861, and their union two years later, which happily remains unbroken, was welcomed by the whole nation, "the sea-king's daughter from over the sea," then winning for herself an affectionate place in the hearts of the people that has strengthened with the march of years.
From the painting by W. P. Frith, R.A.

the Austrian yoke, with Poland in her resistance to Russia, with Denmark in her hopeless contest with Prussia and Austria over Schleswig-Holstein. In the first case, the moral support of Great Britain was of considerable value to Victor Emmanuel; in the other two, the action of the Government had the unfortunate appearance of exciting an expectation of material support which they lacked the courage to carry into action.

But it was the civil war in America which most seriously threatened to involve this country. There were two grave causes of

system the more easily because it had no use for slave-labour itself, and became determined to abolish slavery. Hence the Southern States asserted the right to secede from a confederation which they had entered voluntarily; the North held that the union was federal, indissoluble, and that secession was rebellion.

In 1861, a group of the Southern States formed themselves into a confederation claiming independence, under their own president, and the great struggle began. The sympathies of the British were sharply divided. Toryism had a fellow

QUEEN VICTORIA WITH PRINCE ALBERT AND THEIR CHILDREN

disagreement between the Northern and the Southern States of the Union, which issued in a third, the gravest of all. The Northern States were manufacturing communities, and determined to protect their manufactures by the exclusion of foreign competition. The Southern States, whose products were not exposed to competition, objected to the protectionist policy which raised prices for the consumer. The Southern States lived by the production of crops cultivated by slave labour; the North was able to realise the iniquity of the

feeling for the gentry of the South. Liberalism held slavery in horror, yet the general principles of political freedom were on the side of the right of secession. The Government was firm in its resolution not to intervene, not to declare itself on either side; but it was obliged to commit itself on the question whether the Southerners were to be treated as lawful belligerents or as rebels. The position adopted was that the effective strength of the Southern States made them de facto belligerents, and that their recognition

THE LAST DRAWING ROOM ATTENDED BY PRINCE ALBERT WITH QUEEN VICTORIA AT ST. JAMES'S PALACE IN 1861

From the picture by Jerry Barrett

as such implied no judgment on the merits of the dispute ; on the other hand, the time had not yet come when their claim for recognition as a separate nation could be officially acknowledged. The justice and impartiality of this attitude proved having been negligent of set purpose. At the same time, greatly as the South benefited by the resolute impartiality of Great Britain, it felt itself hardly less bitterly aggrieved thereby than the North, since it appeared almost certain that British

acceptable neither to North nor to South. In 1862 Great Britain was all but compelled to commence hostilities by the action of the North in seizing the persons of two commissioners from the South on board a British vessel, the Trent, on which they had embarked in the neutral port of Havanna. The tardy recognition of this violation of international law and the liberation of the commissioners averted hostilities. Relations were, moreover, perpetually strained to a high pitch of intensity by the action of the Alabama and other cruisers of the same type in the Confederate service. These were vessels constructed in British dockyards, which sailed from British ports, professedly on harmless voyages, but with the actual intent of being handed over at some appointed spot to Confederate officers,

POLITICAL RIOTS IN HYDE PARK

The defeat of the Reform Bill in 1866 gave rise to a considerable amount of feeling in the country. A mass meeting in favour of reform was shut out of Hyde Park, and as a protest, the mob broke down the railings, "thereby convincing most of those who had hitherto been incredulous that the demand for the franchise was not a mere demagogic figment."

who proceeded to employ them for the destruction of the Federal mercantile marine. Since the British Government had failed to display sufficient vigilance in detaining such craft, notably the Alabama, they were regarded by the North as intervention would have decisively terminated the war in favour of the Confederates. Nothing could have been more creditable to the labouring population of the United Kingdom than the dogged determination with which they supported

LORD PALMERSTON ADDRESSING A SITTING OF THE HOUSE OF COMMONS IN THE YEAR 1860
From the painting by J. Phillip, R.A.

the Government, from the conviction that the anti-slavery cause was the cause of righteousness, in spite of the terrible sufferings entailed by the cotton famine, resulting from the Northern blockade of the Southern ports. No nobler example of self-restraint has been recorded than that of the Lancashire operatives in those cruel times; nor has the general public ever displayed its free-handed generosity more wisely and more generously than in the efforts then made for the relief of the distress prevailing. The war was brought to an end with the complete success of the North, in the spring of 1865. In the summer, Parliament was dissolved, having sat for six years, but no immediate effect was produced on the

LORD TENNYSON
Successor to Wordsworth as Poet-Laureate, Tennyson remained until his death, in 1892, the supreme English poet, challenged only by Browning, beside whom he sleeps in Westminster Abbey. In 1884 he received a peerage.

Government. That came with the death of the octogenarian Premier in October. The democratic movement, which had been held in check by general consent until his demise, at once became active. At the same time, Irish discontent assumed a somewhat more threatening shape, owing to the formation of the "Fenian Brotherhood" by the physical-force party, whose strength lay amongst the crowds of emigrants who had been driven to America, and had there been learning practical lessons of warfare in the ranks of Federal and Confederate armies alike. The Fenians set themselves to the secret organisation of armed rebellion; and the detection of the conspiracy and arrest of its leaders revealed a state of affairs

THE FENIAN OUTRAGES: ATTACK ON THE PRISON VAN AT MANCHESTER
Discontent in Ireland assumed a serious aspect towards the end of 1865, the formation of the "Fenian Brotherhood" by the physical-force party indicating the length to which the agitators were prepared to go. The Fenians set themselves to the secret organisation of armed rebellion, as well as opposing the authorities in England, the above picture showing an armed attack on the Manchester prison van for the liberation of Fenian prisoners.

THE GREAT EASTERN RECOVERING THE LOST ATLANTIC CABLE

The largest vessel in existence when built in London in 1854-7, the Great Eastern, proved of great service in laying the Atlantic cables in 1865, and recovered them, after being lost, in 1866; but the vessel was otherwise a failure.

From the picture by R. Dudley

which induced the Government to go so far as to suspend the Habeas Corpus Act in Ireland. The Reform Act of 1832 had abolished the old system of rotten boroughs, which placed the control of half the constituencies in the country in the hands of a few families; it had given representation to the great towns, which had grown up mainly in the course of the industrial revolution; it had applied uniformity to the methods of election; it had transferred the preponderance of political power from the landed to the commercial interests; incidentally it had transformed the House of Lords into a conservative organisation. But its high franchise had still completely excluded the labouring classes from the electorate. For a time, those classes had shown signs of a tendency to believe that the vote would be a panacea for all ills, but the wave of industrial prosperity which attended the repeal of the Corn Laws, and the development of Free Trade, removed the more pressing incitements to the demand for political power;

ROBERT BROWNING

One of the two great poets of the Victorian era, Browning enriched our literature with poetic thought of enduring value, his crowning achievement, the "Ring and the Book," appearing in 1869. In 1846, he married Elizabeth Barrett, also a poet of genius.

and Gladstone, now a convinced advocate of franchise extension, regarded it mainly as a measure of justice to which it would be wise to give effect while it was still not the subject of political passion. At the general election Disraeli had made it plain that the question would be forced to the front; and accordingly Lord Russell, Palmerston's successor in office, introduced a Reform Bill. Its moderation, however—it would have added less than half a million voters to the electorate — prevented it from exciting enthusiasm, and did not prevent it from exciting the determined opposition of the anti-democratic section of the Liberal party who formed the historic "Cave of Adullam." The Adullamites, in conjunction with the Conservatives, all but defeated the Bill on the second reading; when they carried an amendment against the Government in Committee, the Ministry resigned.' For the third time the Conservatives took office, with Lord Derby as their chief and Disraeli as their leader, while the party itself formed

5003

a minority in the House of Commons. The defeat of the Liberal Bill roused a fervour in the country which had not attended its introduction. A mass meeting in favour of reform was shut out of Hyde Park, whereupon the mob broke down the railings, thereby convincing most of those who had hitherto been incredulous that the demand

The Reform Bill Carried for the franchise was not a mere demagogic figment. The impression thus produced was confirmed by a series of demonstrations during the latter part of 1866, and a Reform Bill was announced as a part of Disraeli's programme for 1867.

His first intention of proceeding by resolution—that is, by obtaining the assent of the House to a series of principles on which the actual Bill was then to be constructed—was abandoned ; the Cabinet was split on the moderate Bill which Disraeli then proposed to introduce, and the secession of Lord Cranborne (afterwards Lord Salisbury) and others decided Disraeli to adopt a much more audacious scheme which would capture support from the Opposition. He had hoped to be able to introduce sundry " fancy franchises," and other securities to prevent a complete subversion of the balance of political power, but it soon became clear that if the Bill was to pass the Government would have to accede with very little reservation to the amendments demanded by the Liberals. The result was that in the boroughs the franchise was granted to all householders and to ten-pound lodgers, with a twelve-pound occupation franchise in the counties; the " fancy franchises " disappeared. The Act, indeed, went very much further than the Liberal leaders had proposed to go in their own Bill ; it definitely transformed the House of Commons into a democratic body, though the change had still to be completed by the assimilation of the county franchise to that of the

Disraeli at the Height of his Power boroughs. The same year was rendered notable in the colonial history of the Empire by the British North America Act, which eventually united the British Colonies in North America, with the exception of Newfoundland, in the federation which bears the name of the Dominion of Canada. The conduct of King Theodore of Abyssinia, who thought himself justified in seizing a number of British subjects, confining them at Magdala, and refusing to pay any attention to representations demanding their liberation, necessitated the completely successful Abyssinian expedition, under the command of Lord Napier, in the spring of the following year, 1868. By this time Lord Derby had withdrawn, leaving Disraeli, long the actual chief of the party, as its avowed head.

Renewed Fenian disturbances emphasised the unsatisfactory condition of Ireland, which was destined to occupy an exceedingly prominent position in the domestic politics of the succeeding period. In June it was clear that the Ministry was practically powerless in the face of the Opposition, and in the autumn Disraeli appealed to the new electorate. The result was that the first democratic Parliament of the United Kingdom returned the Liberals to power under Gladstone's leadership, with a decisive majority. In English history the inauguration of democracy forms an epoch, which we must respect for clearness sake as a dividing line ; but as the dividing line in Continental history is drawn by the German

Leaders of Intellectual Movements overthrow of France and the establishment of the German Empire under the Prussian hegemony, we may here note that Great Britain abstained from taking any active part in those important events.

Industrial movements are dealt with in a separate section. But in the intellectual movement of the period now under review we have to note the succession to Wordsworth as Poet Laureate of Alfred Tennyson, who held his supreme position unchallenged for the rest of his life, save in the eyes of those who recognised a still mightier genius in Robert Browning, whose crowning achievement, the " Ring and the Book," appeared in 1869. But the world at large was more deeply affected by another influence which had its birth in England. Simultaneously, Charles Darwin and Alfred Russel Wallace developed their conception, which will always be associated with the name of the former, of the evolution of species. That conception filled the minds of the orthodox with alarm, and called for an almost fundamental readjustment of ideas on the relations between " Nature, Man, and God," which a later generation has found to be in nowise subversive of the essential doctrines of Christianity.

ARTHUR D. INNES

TURKEY AFTER THE CRIMEAN WAR
ADJUSTMENT OF THE EASTERN QUESTION

THE year of revolutions, 1848, which shook Western Europe with its conceptions of freedom. had left Turkey almost untouched. Shekib Effendi held a formal conference with Pope Pius IX., in Rome in 1848, under commission from the Sultan, who would have been glad to hand over to the Pope the protectorate of the Catholics in the East ; the Holy Father had sent out the Archbishop Ferrieri with an appeal to the Oriental communities, which, however, did not end in that union which the Porte and the Pope had hoped for.

The revolt of the Boyars and of the Polish fugitives in Moldavia and Wallachia speedily resulted in the strengthening of the hospodar Michael Sturdza, and in the appointment of Kantakuzen in place of Bibeskos. The Hungarian rising, on which the Porte had staked its hopes for the infliction of a blow on Austria, came to nothing, on the capitu-

Protectors of the Catholics lation of Vilagos. On the other hand, the Sultan, encouraged by the presence of a British fleet in the Dardanelles, declined to hand over the Hungarian fugitives.

Austria and Hungary thereupon avenged themselves by taking advantage of a claim for damages which France had now set up. Two parties, the Catholics and the Greeks, were quarrelling about the Holy Places in Palestine. The powers protecting the Catholics were invariably France or the Pope, while the Greeks had been under a Russian protectorate since 1720. It was to deliver these Holy Places from the hands of the Moslems that the Crusades had been undertaken. Saladin had permitted the Latin clergy to perform service in the Church of the Holy Sepulchre in 1187, while Robert of Anjou had purchased the Holy Places from the caliph in 1342.

After the conquest of the Holy City by Sultan Selim, 1517, the Georgians secured part of Golgotha, all the other remaining places being reserved expressly to the Sultan in 1558. The title was further confirmed by the capitulations of France with the Sultans in 1535, 1621, 1629, and 1740. Violent outbreaks of jealousy took place between the Armenians, Greeks, and Catholics concerning these marks of

The Holy Sepulchre in Dispute favour and especially concerning the possession of the Holy Sepulchre. In 1808 the Greeks, after the Church of the Holy Sepulchre had been destroyed by fire, actually reduced the tombs of Godfrey of Bouillon and Baldwin to ruins. The Greeks, aided by Russian money, restored the Church of the Holy Sepulchre ; meanwhile the Latins, whose zeal was supported by France, gained possession of two chapels in 1820.

In the year 1850 the Pope and the Catholic Patriarch of Jerusalem applied first to France, and joined France in a further application to the Porte, to secure protection against the Greeks. Fear of Russia induced the Porte to decide almost entirely in favour of the Greeks, and the only concession made to the Catholics was the joint use of a church door in Bethlehem.

In the realm of the blind the one-eyed man is king ; above the reactionary governments rose the " saviour of order," who had been carried to the throne of France by the Revolution. The presidential chair, which had gained security and permanence from the coup d'état of December 2nd, 1851, was made a new imperial throne within the space of a year by the adroit and not wholly untalented

A New Throne in France heir to the great name of Bonaparte. On January 14th, 1852, he had brought out a constitution to give France a breathing space, exhausted as she was by the passionate struggle for freedom, and to soothe the extravagance of her imaginings. But this constitution needed a monarchy to complete it. The basis of a national imperial government was there in detail : a legislative body elected by national suffrage ; a senate to guarantee the constitutional legality of legislation ; an "appeal to the people" on every proposal which could be construed as an alteration of the constitution ; a strong and wise executive to conduct state business, whose "resolutions" were examined in camera, undertaking the preparation and execution of everything which could conduce to the welfare of the people.

Napoleon III. Emperor of France

The twelve million francs which the energetic senate had voted as the president's yearly income might equally well be applied to the maintenance of an emperor. When the question was brought forward, the country replied with 7,840,000 votes in the affirmative, while 254,000 dissentients appeared merely as a protest on behalf of the right of independent judgment. On December 2nd, 1852, Napoleon III. was added to the number of crowned heads in Europe as Emperor of France by the grace of God and the will of the people. No Power attempted to refuse recognition of his position. The democratic origin of the new ruler was forgotten in view of his services in the struggle against the Revolution, and in view also of the respect he had shown for considerations of religion and armed force.

Unfortunately the new monarch could not gain time to convince other Powers of his equality with themselves. The old reigning houses were not as yet sufficiently intimate with him to seek a permanent union through a marriage alliance ; yet he was bound to give France and himself an heir, for a throne without heirs speedily becomes uninteresting. Born on April 20th, 1808, he was nearly forty-five years of age, and dared not risk the failure of a courtship which might expose him to the general sympathy or ridicule. Without delay he therefore married, on January 29th, 1853, the beautiful Countess Eugénie of Teba, of the noble Spanish House of Guzman, who was then twenty-six years of age. She was eminently capable, not only of

PRINCE MENSCHIKOFF
He was in charge of the Russian forces at the battles of the Alma and Inkerman, and also took part in the defence of Sebastopol, but, in consequence of illness, he was recalled in 1855 and died in 1869.

pleasing the Parisians, but also of fixing their attention and of raising their spirits by a never-ending series of fresh devices. No woman was ever better fitted to be a queen of fashion, and fashion has always been venerated as a goddess by the French.

Nothing but a brilliant foreign policy was now lacking to secure the permanence of the Second Empire. It was not enough that Napoleon should be tolerated by his fellow sovereigns ; prestige was essential to him. There was no surer road to the hearts of his subjects than that of making himself a power whose favour the other states of Europe would be ready to solicit. For this end it would have been the most natural policy to interest himself in the affairs of Italy, considering that he had old connections with the Carbonari, with Mazzini, and with Garibaldi. But it so happened that the Tsar Nicholas was obliging enough at this juncture to furnish the heir of Bonaparte with a plausible pretext for interfering in the affairs of Eastern Europe. Napoleon III. cannot be regarded as primarily responsible for the differences which arose in 1853 between Britain and Russia. But there can be no doubt that he seized the opportunity afforded by the quarrel of these two Powers and hurried the British Government into an aggressive line of policy which, however welcome to the electorates of British constituencies was viewed with misgiving by many British statesmen, and was destined to be of little advantage to any power but the Second Empire.

The Tsar Nicholas had for a long time past regarded the partition of the Turkish Empire in favour of Russia as a step for which the European situation was now ripe. Britain and Austria were the Powers whose interests were most obviously threatened by such a scheme. But he thought that Austria could be disregarded if the assent of Britain was secured ; and as early as 1844 he had sounded the British Government, suggesting that, in the event of partition, an

The Tsar's Schemes on Turkey

understanding between that Power and Russia might be formulated with equal advantage to both. His overtures had met with no definite reply ; but he appears to have assumed that Britain would not stand in his way. It was not till 1854,

was increased by the annoyance which Napoleon felt at the arrogant demeanour of the Russian court towards himself.

But Napoleon, busied as he was at the moment with preparing for the re-establishment of the empire, could not afford to push his resistance to extremes, and it would have been the wisest course for Nicholas to make sure of the prey which he had in view by occupying the Danube principalities in force, before Austria and Prussia had finished quarrelling over the question of federal reforms. The fact was that the development of his plans was checked for a moment by the unexpected submissiveness of the Sublime Porte, when it agreed to guarantee the Greek Christians of the Holy Land in the possession of the coveted privileges. New pretexts for aggression were, however, very easily discovered ; and on May 11th, 1853, Prince Menschikoff despatched an ultimatum, demanding for Russia a protectorate over the fourteen millions of Greek Christians who inhabited the various countries under Turkish rule. Submission to such a demand was equivalent to accepting a partition of the Turkish dominions between Russia and the Sultan. Even without allies the Sultan might be expected to make a stand : and allies were

THE SHRINE OF THE HOLY SEPULCHRE AT JERUSALEM
In 1808 the Church of the Holy Sepulchre at Jerusalem, one of the shrines which the Crusaders had endeavoured to wrest from the hands of the Mohammedans, was destroyed by fire, and the Greeks, with the aid of Russian money, had the sanctuary restored.

however, that, feeling secure from further insurrections in Poland, he unmasked his batteries against the Porte. The temptation to reassert the French protectorate over the Latin Christians of the East

AFTER THE FALL OF KARS: SIR WILLIAM FENWICK WILLIAMS PARTING WITH THE GRIEF-STRICKEN CITIZENS

When the Crimean war broke out, in 1854, Sir William Fenwick Williams was sent to Asiatic Turkey to organise the Turkish army, and reaching Kars in September he immediately prepared it for defence. The siege began in June, 1855, by the Russians, under Muravieff, and after a heroic defence lasting till November 25th, Williams was compelled to surrender. The gallant soldier was idolised by the Turkish army as well as by the citizens of Kars, and their sorrow at parting with him is admirably illustrated in the above picture.

From the painting by Barker

forthcoming. Though Napoleon had been first in the field against Russia, it was from Great Britain that Abd ul-Mejid now received the strongest encouragement. Some months before the ultimatum Nicholas had confessed his cherished object to the British ambassador; and though the shock of this disclosure had been tempered by a proposal that Britain should take Egypt and Crete as her share of the spoil, the British Government was clear that, in one way or another, the integrity of the Turkish Empire must be secured. Lord Stratford de Redcliffe, the British representative at Constantinople, advised that no concession whatever should be made to Russia. The advice was taken. Although the Tsar had probably not counted upon war as a serious probability, nothing now remained but to face the consequences of his precipitation, to recall his ambassador, and to send his troops into the Danube principalities. They were invaded on July 2nd, 1853, the Tsar protesting " that it was not his intention to commence war, but to have such security as would ensure

ALEXANDER II. OF RUSSIA
The son of Tsar Nicholas I., he succeeded to the throne of Russia on March 2nd, 1855. The emancipation of 23,000,000 serfs in 1861, chiefly due to the Tsar's own efforts, was the greatest achievement of Alexander's reign.

the restoration of the rights of Russia." Unprepared as he was, he had every prospect of success if he could secure the co-operation of Austria. Had these two Powers agreed to deliver a joint attack upon Turkey, inducing Prussia, by means of suitable concessions, to protect their rear, the fleets of the Western Powers could not have saved Constantinople, and their armies would certainly not have ventured to take the field against the combined forces of the two Eastern emperors. But the Tsar overrated his own powers and underrated the capacity of the Sultan for resistance. All that Nicho'as desired from Austria was neutrality; and this he thought that he might confidently expect after the signal service which Russian armies had rendered in the suppression of the Hungarian rebellion. No advance was made on his part towards an understanding with Austria until the two Western Powers had appeared on the scene. This happened immediately after the Black Sea squadron of the Turkish fleet had been destroyed in the harbour of Sinope by

VIEW OF KARS FROM THE EAST, SHOWING THE FORTRESS, ABOUT THE YEAR 1840

Admiral Nakimoff on November 30th, 1853. The allied French and British fleets had been in the Bosphorus for a month past with the object of protecting Constantinople; now, at the suggestion of Napoleon, they entered the Black Sea in January, 1854. At this juncture Prince Orloff was despatched to Vienna, without authority to offer any concessions, but merely to appeal to Austrian gratitude. It would have needed a statesman of unusual penetration to grasp the fact that Austrian interests would really be served by a friendly response to this dilatory and unskilfully managed application; and such a statesman was not to be found at the Hofburg. Schwarzenberg had died very suddenly on April 5th, 1852, and his mantle had fallen upon the shoulders of Count Buol, who had no qualifications for his responsible position beyond rigid orthodoxy and some small experience acquired in a subordinate capacity during the brief ministry of Schwarzenberg. Buol confirmed his master, Francis Joseph, in the erroneous idea that the interests of Austria and Russia in the East were diametrically opposed. Accordingly, Prince Orloff was rebuffed, and Austria supported a demand for the evacuation of the Danubian principalities issued by the Western Powers on February 27th, 1854.

France and Britain were encouraged by this measure of Austrian support to conclude a defensive treaty with the Sultan on March 12th and to declare war on Russia on March 27th. In the first stages of hostilities they had the support of the Austrian forces. Austria accepted from Turkey a formal commission to hold the Danube principalities during the course of the war, and co-operated with a Turkish army in compelling the Russian troops to withdraw. And on August 8th, Austria joined with France and Britain in demanding that Russia should abandon her protectorate over Servia and the Danubian principalities, should allow free navigation of the Danube, should submit to a revision of the "Convention of the Straits" of July, 1841, in the interests of the balance of power, and should renounce the claim to a protectorate over the Greek Christians of the Turkish dominions. When these demands were rejected by Russia, and the war passed into its second

Austria's Rebuff to Russia

Russia Rejects the Demands of the Powers

stage, with France and Britain acting on the offensive in order to provide for the peace of the future by crippling Russian power in the East, it might have been expected that Austria would go on as she had begun. But at this point a fifth power made its influence felt in the already complicated situation. Frederic William IV. did not go to the lengths advised by Bismarck, who proposed that Prussia should restore peace by concentrating an army on the Silesian frontier, and threatening to attack whichever of the two neighbouring empires should refuse a peaceful settlement. But the King of Prussia was by no means inclined to make capital out of Russian necessities, and turned a deaf ear to the suggestions of Austria for an armed coalition against the Tsar. The result was that Austria, though she concluded, in December, 1854, an offensive alliance with France and Britain, did not take part in the Crimean War, the operations of which have already been described.

The Tsar Nicholas died, worn out with chagrin and anxiety, on March 2nd, 1855. His policy had cost Russia a loss which was officially calculated at 240,000 men; and "Generals January and February" had treated him even more severely than the allied force which he had expected them to annihilate. Negotiations were opened by his son Alexander II., who declined, however, to limit the Russian fleet in the Black Sea. The allies, therefore, proceeded with the attack upon Sebastopol; and after a third unsuccessful attack upon their position in the battle of the Tchernaya, August 16th, 1855, the Russians were compelled, by a fearful cannonade and the loss of the Malakoff, September 8th, which was stormed by the French in the face of an appalling fire, to evacuate the city. The capture of the Armenian fortress of Kars by General Muravieff in November enabled the Russians to claim more moderate terms of peace than would otherwise have been possible. On February 6th, 1856, a congress opened at Paris to settle the Eastern question, and peace was signed on March 30th of the same year.

By the terms of the Peace of Paris, the Black Sea was declared neutral and open to the merchant ships of every nation. It was to be closed against the warships of all nations, except that Russia and Turkey were permitted to equip not more than

Death of the Tsar Nicholas

ten light vessels apiece for coastguard service, and that any state interested in the navigation of the Danube might station two light vessels at the mouth of that river. The integrity of Turkey was guaranteed by the Powers, all of whom renounced the right of interfering in the internal affairs of that state, nothing beyond certain promises of reforms being demanded from the Sultan in return for these favours. For the regulation of the navigation of the Danube a standing commission of the interested Powers was appointed. Moldavia and Wallachia were left in dependence on the Sultan, but with complete autonomy so far as their internal administration was concerned. They were to pay a tribute, and their foreign relations were to be controlled by the Porte. Moldavia recovered that part of Bessarabia which had been taken from her by Russia, and in this way the latter Power was pushed back from the Danube.

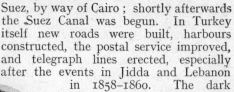

MILOS OBRENOVITCH

Prince of Servia, he was driven out by a revolution in 1839, but was subsequently recalled, and after his death, in 1860, his son Michael was acknowledged by the Porte.

In Asia Minor the action of France and England restored the frontier to the status quo ante. Turkey, henceforward received into the concert of Europe, promised further reforms in the Hatti - humayun of February 18th, 1856, and reaffirmed the civic equality of all her subjects. The " hat " was received with equal reluctance by both Ottomans and Christians. Only since 1867 have foreigners been able to secure a footing in Turkey. If any advance has been made since these paper promises, it is due not to the imperial firman but to the increase of international communication, which brought the light of civilisation to the very interior of Asia. In 1851 the first railway was built from Alexandria to

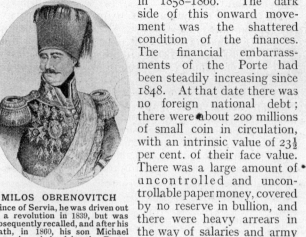

ABD UL-AZIZ

ALI PASHA

Becoming sultan on the death of his brother, Abd ul-Mejid, in 1861, Abd ul-Aziz found himself confronted by difficult tasks, and for ten years was guided by two very distinguished men, Fuad and Ali Pasha.

Suez, by way of Cairo ; shortly afterwards the Suez Canal was begun. In Turkey itself new roads were built, harbours constructed, the postal service improved, and telegraph lines erected, especially after the events in Jidda and Lebanon in 1858–1860. The dark side of this onward movement was the shattered condition of the finances. The financial embarrassments of the Porte had been steadily increasing since 1848. At that date there was no foreign national debt ; there were about 200 millions of small coin in circulation, with an intrinsic value of $23\frac{1}{2}$ per cent. of their face value. There was a large amount of uncontrolled and uncontrollable paper money, covered by no reserve in bullion, and there were heavy arrears in the way of salaries and army payments. During the Crimean War, apart from an enormous debt at home, a loan of £7,000,000 had been secured in England. Three further loans were effected in 1858, 1860, and 1861. Expenditure rose, in consequence of the high rate of interest, to £14,000,000 annually, while the revenue amounted to £9,000,000 only. In 1861 the financial strain brought about a commercial crisis; an attempt was made to meet the danger by the issue of 1,250 millions of piastres in paper money, with forced circulation. While the upper officials, bank managers, and contractors, such as Langi and Dumonceau, Eugene Bontoux, and Moritz Hirsch were growing rich, the provinces were impoverished by the weight of taxation and the unnecessary severity with which the taxes were collected. The concert of Europe had guaranteed the first state loan,

Hence in 1882 originated the international administration of the Turkish public debt; and this became the basis of the claim for a general supervision of Turkish affairs by Western Europe, which was afterwards advanced in the case of Armenia and Crete.

The Porte was thus unable to prevent the appointment of Colonel Alexander
Roumania's Rise to Prosperity Johann Cusa, at the instance of France, as Prince of Moldavia on January 29th and of Wallachia on February 17th; the personal bond of union thus established between these vassal states resulted in their actual union as Roumania in 1861. Cusa's despotic rule was overthrown on February 22nd, 1866, and under the new prince, Charles of Hohenzollern, the country enjoyed a rapid rise to prosperity, although the political incapacity of the people, the licence granted by the constitution, and the immorality of the upper classes did not conduce to general order. In Servia the Sultan's creature, Alexander Karageorgevitch, was forced to abdicate on December 21st-22nd, 1858, the family of Obrenovitch was recalled, and after the death of Milos at the age of eighty, on September 26th, 1860, Michael Obrenovitch II. was elected and acknowledged by the Porte. Under the revolutionary and literary government of the "Omladina," "youth," Servia became the scene of Panslavonic movements, hostile to Hungary, which spread to the soil of Bosnia and Herzegovina, and even endangered the absolute monarchy of Michael.

On March 6th, 1867, the last Turkish troops were withdrawn from Servian soil, in accordance with the agreements of September 4th, 1862, and March 3rd, 1867. After the murder of the prince, on June 10th, 1868, the Skupshtina appointed the last surviving Obrenovitch, Prince Milan, then fourteen years of age, and passed the new constitution on June 29th, 1869. An additional consequence was that Turkey became again involved in disputes with the Western Powers; in 1858 the occasion was the murder of the British

GEORGE I. OF GREECE
The despotic rule of King Otto led to his deposition, and in 1863 a new king was chosen in the person of George I., a son of the King of Denmark.
From an early photograph

and French consuls at Jidda, in Arabia, and in 1860 the atrocities of the Druses against the Christians in Lebanon and Damascus. To anticipate the interference of the Powers, the Grand Vizir, Fuad Pasha, one of the greatest statesmen that Turkey has produced in the nineteenth century, was sent to the spot with unlimited powers; but it was not until a French army of occupation appeared that the leaders in high places were brought to punishment, and the province of Lebanon was placed under a Christian governor. The chief service performed by Fuad was that of introducing the vilayet constitution, the division of the Ottoman Empire into sanjaks and kasas, by which means he had already produced great effects on the Danube provinces. Had it not been for the opposition of the whole company of the Old Turks, the imams, mollas, mütevelis, hojas, the dervishes, and softas, in the mosques, the schools, the monasteries, and also the coffee-houses, he would possibly have succeeded in cleansing the great Augean stable of Arabic slothfulness.

Upon the death of Abd ul-Mejid, on June 26th, 1861, his brother, the new ruler, Abd ul-Aziz, 1861–1876, was confronted by difficult tasks, and the question arose as to his capacity for dealing with them. The good-natured Abd ul-Mejid had generally allowed his Grand Vizirs to govern on his behalf, but after 1858, when the royal privy exchequer had been declared bankrupt, he relapsed into indolence and weak sensuality. Notwithstanding the shattered state of the empire, his brother and successor, Abd ul-Aziz, promised a government of
Programme of the New Sultan peace, of retrenchment, and reform. To the remote observer he appeared a character of proved strength, in the prime of life, and inspired with a high enthusiasm for his lofty calling. All these advantages, however, were paralysed by the criminal manner in which his education had been neglected. The ruler of almost forty millions of subjects was, at that time, scarcely able to write a couple of lines in his own language. The result was the failure of his first attempts

to bring some order into the administration and the finances, a failure which greatly discouraged him. Until 1871 he allowed himself to be guided by these two distinguished men, Fuad and Ali Pasha; at the same time his want of firmness and insight, his nervous excitability, which often made him unaccountable for his actions, and his senseless and continually increasing extravagance led him, not only to the arms of Ignatieff, "the father of lies," but also to his own destruction.

In the commercial treaties of 1861–1862 gunpowder, salt, and tobacco had been excepted from the general remission of duties. The salt tax, which was shortly afterwards revived, was a lamentable mistake. Sheep farmers suffered terribly under it, for the lack of salt produced fresh epidemics every year among the flocks and destroyed the woollen trade and the manufacture of carpets. The culture of the olive and tobacco also suffered under the new imposts, while internal trade was hindered by octroi duties of every kind.

A new King on the Throne of Greece To these difficulties military and political complications were added. Especially dangerous was the revolt in Crete, in the spring of 1866; in 1863 Greece had expelled the Bavarian prince and chosen a new king, George I., formerly Prince Wilhelm of Schleswig-Holstein-Sonderburg-Glücksburg, and had received the seven Ionian Islands from England in 1864; she now supported her Cretan brothers and co-religionists with money, armies, troops, and ships, notwithstanding the deplorable condition of her own finances.

Only when an ultimatum had been sent to Greece did the Porte succeed in crushing this costly revolt under pressure from a conference of the Powers in 1869. Meanwhile, Ismail Pasha of Egypt had received, in 1866 and 1867, the title of "Khedive" and the right to the direct succession. Undisturbed by English jealousy, the "viceroy" continued the projects of his predecessor, especially the construction of the Suez Canal, which had been begun by Lesseps; he increased his army, built warships, appointed his own Minister of Foreign Affairs in the person of the Armenian Nubar Pasha, travelled in Europe, and invited the courts of several states to a brilliant opening of the canal in 1869; by means of a personal visit to Constantinople, by large presents and an increase of tribute, he further secured in 1873 the sovereignty which he had assumed. In the summer of 1867 the Sultan appeared in Western Europe accompanied **The Grand Tour of the Sultan** by Fuad; it was the first occasion in Ottoman history that a sultan had passed the frontiers of his empire, not for the purpose of making conquests, but to secure the favour of his allies. He had already visited the Khedive in Egypt in 1863. Now he saw the World's Exhibition at Paris, and that of London in June, 1863. On July 24th he paid his respects to the King and Queen of Prussia at Coblentz and returned to Constantinople by way of Vienna on August 7th. The success of Fuad Pasha in inducing his master to take this step was a masterpiece of diplomacy and patriotism; unfortunately, the journey, which had cost enormous sums, did not produce the hoped-for results.

On February 11th, 1869, Fuad died, as also did his noble friend and rival, Ali, on September 6th, 1871; thereupon, simultaneously with the fall of the Second Empire, Ottoman politics entered upon that path which for Napoleon III. began before the walls of Sebastopol and ended at Sedan. In place of the influence of the Western Powers the eagles of Russia and Prussia were henceforward victorious on the Bosphorus. Upon his death-bed Fuad had written from Nizza on January 3rd, 1869, to Sultan Abd ul-Aziz: "The rapid advance of our neighbours and the incredible mistakes of our forefathers have brought us into a dangerous position; **Death-bed Warning of Fuad Pasha** if the threatening collision is to be avoided, your Majesty must break with the past and lead your people in fresh paths." The committee of officials which travelled through the provinces of the empire in 1864 expressed this thought even more bluntly: "The officials grow rich upon the taxes, while the people suffer, working like slaves under the whip. The income of the taxes is divided among the officials instead of flowing into the state exchequer."

THE WORLD'S EXHIBITION AT PARIS IN 1855: DISTRIBUTING THE AWARDS TO THE SUCCESSFUL EXHIBITORS

The Great Exhibition held at Paris in the year 1855 did much to restore the French capital to her former prestige as the Continental centre. The presentation of awards to the successful exhibitors, which ceremony took place in the Palace of Industry on November 15th, and marked the closing of the Exhibition, is illustrated in the above interesting picture.

THE SECOND EMPIRE OF FRANCE
THE ASCENDANCY OF NAPOLEON III.
AND THE WANING OF HIS STAR

FOR a short time, the diplomatic results of the Crimean war made Napoleon III. appear to be the most powerful ruler in Europe ; and he took upon himself the part of a second Metternich. He concealed his actual position and succeeded in inspiring Europe with a wholly unfounded belief in the strength of his country and himself. The World's Exhibition of 1855, and the congress which immediately followed, restored Paris to her former prestige as the centre of Europe. Pilgrims flocked to the city of pleasure and good taste, upon the adornment of which the Prefect of the Seine, Georges Eugène Haussmann, was permitted to expend £4,000,000 per annum.

The sound governmental principle laid down by the first Napoleon, of keeping the fourth estate contented by high wages, and thus securing its good behaviour and silent approval of an absolute monarchy, was followed with entire success for the moment in the "restored" empire. However, Napoleon III., like Metternich, was penetrated with the conviction that the ruler must of necessity be absolute. His greatest mistake consisted in the fact that he refrained from giving a material content to the constitutional forms under which his government was established. By this means he might have united to himself that section of the population which is not subject to the influence of caprice.

Napoleon's Greatest Mistake

The "legislative body" should have been made representative, and should have been given control of the finances and the right of initiating legislative proposals. Such a change would have been far more profitable to the heir who was born to the emperor on March 16th, 1856, than the illusory refinements which gained the Second Empire the exaggerated approbation of all the useless epicures in existence. Russia seemed to have been reduced to impotency for a long time to come, and her power to be now inferior to that of Turkey. She proceeded to accommodate herself to the changed conditions. Alexander II. assured his subjects that the war begun by his father had improved and secured the position of Christianity in the East, and proceeded with magnificent dispassionateness to make overtures to the French ruler, who had just given him so severe a lesson. The Russian politicians were correct in their opinion that Napoleon was relieved to have come so well out of his enterprises in the East, and that they need fear no immediate disturbance from that quarter.

Russia After the War

Napoleon III. showed himself worthy of this confidence. With real diplomacy he met Russia half way, respected her desires whenever he could do so, and received a tacit assurance that Russia would place no obstacle in the way of his designs against any other Power. Though Austria had not fired a shot against the Russian troops, she proved far less accommodating than France, whose troops had triumphantly entered Sebastopol. Austria had declined to repay the help given her in Hungary ; she had also appeared as a rival in the Balkans, and had only been restrained by Prussia from dealing Russia a fatal blow. Thus Austria's weakness would imply Russia's strength, and would enable her the more easily to pursue her Eastern policy. Prussia had fallen so low that no interference was to be feared from her in the event of any great European complication, though there was no immediate apprehension of any such difficulty. In a fit of mental weakness which foreshadowed his ultimate collapse, Frederic William IV. had concentrated his thoughts upon the possibility of recovering his principality of

Prussia in the Dust

GENERAL VIEW OF THE CITY OF PARIS, IN THE YEAR 1800, LOOKING NORTH-WEST ALONG THE COURSE OF THE SEINE.

Whatever Napoleon III. failed to do for France, he certainly made vast improvements in Paris. The above view shows Notre Dame in the left foreground, while beyond it, in the middle distance, the graceful shape of the Sainte Chapelle is seen, and farthest beyond we discern the tower of the Hôtel des Invalides. In the right foreground stands the Hôtel de Ville, with the broad Rue de Rivoli stretching straight ahead, and bending to the left beyond the Tuileries, we see the Champs Elysees reaching to the Arc de Triomphe in the farthest distance.

A GENERAL VIEW OF THE HEART OF PARIS AS IT WAS DURING THE BRILLIANT DAYS OF THE SECOND EMPIRE
In the above illustration the spectator is looking in the opposite direction from the view on the preceding page. The Place de la Concorde is seen in the centre of the picture, and beyond it are the Tuileries Gardens and the Louvre, while in the middle distance on the left the Grecian masonry of the Madeleine is easily distinguished, and the routes of many of the most famous thoroughfares can be readily traced, as the changes in the general aspect of this part of the city during the last half century have not been extraordinary.

Neuenberg. Success was denied him. After the ill-timed attempt at revolution, set on foot by the Prussian party in that province on September 3rd, 1856, he was forced to renounce definitely all claim to the province on May 26th, 1857. The fact that the principality was of no value to Prussia did not remove the impression that the German state had again suffered a defeat. Napoleon was one of the few statesmen who estimated the power of Prussia at a higher rate than did the majority of his contemporaries; in a conversation with Bismarck in March, 1857, he had already secured Prussia's neutrality in the event of a war in Italy, and had brought forward proposals of more importance than the programme of the union. With the incorporation of Hanover and Holstein a northern sea-power was to be founded strong enough, in

COUNT CAVOUR
A liberal statesman, he laboured strenuously for the restoration of Italian nationality, and at last, in 1861, he witnessed the summoning of an Italian Parliament.

alliance with France, to oppose England. All that he asked in return was a "small delimitation" of the Rhine frontier; this, naturally, was not to affect the left bank, the possession of which would oblige France to extend her territory and would rouse a new coalition against her. Bismarck declined to consider any further projects in this direction, and sought to extract an undertaking from the emperor that Prussia should not be involved in any great political combination. Great Britain's resources were strained to the utmost by conflicts with Persia and China, and by the outbreak of the Indian Mutiny, and she needed not only the goodwill but the friendly offices of France. For these reasons the Tory Ministry, which came into office in 1858 upon the fall of Palmerston, could not venture to disturb the

URBANO RATTAZZI
He was twice Prime Minister of Italy, in 1862 and again in 1867, but held office for only a brief period on each occasion, resigning through his opposition to Garibaldi.

good understanding with Napoleon, however strongly inclined to this course.

Napoleon was thus free to confront the apparently feasible task of increasing his influence in Europe and conciliating the goodwill of his subjects to the empire. It

was now necessary to apply the second fundamental principle of the Bonapartist rulers, to avoid any thorough investigation of internal difficulties by turning attention to foreign affairs, by assuming a commanding position among the Great Powers, and by acquiring military fame when possible. Polignac had already made a similar attempt. He had failed through want of adroitness; the capture of Algiers came too late to prevent the July Revolution. Napoleon did not propose to fail thus, and for once, at least, his attempt proved successful. Naturally the methods by which Ministers had begun war under the "old regime" were impossible for a popular emperor. Moreover, Napoleon III. was no soldier; he could not merely wave his sword, like his great uncle, and announce to Europe that this or that dynasty must be deposed. Principles must be followed out, modern ideas must be made triumphant; at the least, the subject nation must be made to believe that the individual was merely the implement of the great forces of activity latent in peoples. He had turned constitutionalism to excellent account; the struggles of the Liberal party to obtain a share in the government had ended by raising him to the throne. Another idea with which modern Europe was fully penetrated, that of nationality, might now be exploited by an adroit statesman. Napoleon neither exaggerated nor underestimated its potency; only he had not realised how deeply it was rooted in the hearts of the people. He knew that it was constantly founded upon folly and presumption, and that the participation of the people in the task of solving state problems fostered the theory that the concentration of the national strength was ever a more important matter than the maintenance of the state; hence he inferred the value of the national idea as a means of opening the struggle against

THE STATESMEN WHO ENDED THE CRIMEAN WAR: THE CONGRESS OF PARIS IN 1856

Attended by two plenipotentiaries from each of the seven Powers—Britain, France, Russia, Turkey, Austria, Prussia and Sardinia—the Congress of Paris agreed to the terms of peace that brought the Crimean war to an end. The integrity of the Ottoman Empire was guaranteed, the Danube declared free for navigation, and the Black Sea recognised as neutral.

From the painting by Dubufe in Versailles Museum

existing political institutions. But of its moral power he had no conception ; he never imagined that, in the fulness of time, it would become a constructive force capable of bending statecraft to its will. Here lay the cause of his tragic downfall—he was like the apprentice of some political magician, unable to dismiss the spirits whom he had evoked when they became dangerous.

His gaze had long been directed towards Italy ; the dreams of his youth returned upon him in new guise and lured him to make that country the scene of his exploits. It was, however, in the East, which had already proved so favourable to Napoleon's enterprises, that he was to make his first attempt to introduce the principle of nationality into the concert of Europe. Turkey was forced to recognise the rights of the Roumanian nation, of which she had hardly so much as heard when the question arose of the regulation of the government in the Danube principalities. She could offer no opposition when Moldavia and Wallachia, each of which could elect a hospodar tributary to the Sultan, united in their choice of one and the same personality, Colonel Alexander Johann Cusa, and appointed him their prince at the beginning of 1859 on January 29th and February 17th.

By this date a new rising of the kingdom of Sardinia against Austria had already been arranged for the purpose of overthrowing the foreign government in Italy. The victorious progress of the national idea in the Danube principalities, which not only

GARIBALDI
The central figure in the battle for Italian independence, Garibaldi, the son of a poor sailor, led the revolters against the Austrian rule, continuing the struggle till Italy became a nation, with Victor Emmanuel as her king, and then retiring to Caprera.

destroyed Austria's hopes of extending her territory on the Black Sea, but also became a permanent cause of disturbance in her Eastern possessions, was now to justify its application in Italy. The attempt of the Italian, Orsini, and his three associates, who threw bombs at the imperial couple in Paris on January 14th, 1858, wounding both of them and 141 others, is said to have materially contributed to determine Napoleon's decision for the Italian war. He was intimidated by the weapons which the Nationalist and Radical party now began to employ, for Orsini in the very face of death appealed to him to help his oppressed fatherland, and it became manifest that this outrage was merely the expression of national excitement.

A similar state of tension existed in the Sardinian state, its dynasty and its leader, Count Camillo Cavour, who had been the Prime Minister of King Victor Emmanuel since November 4th, 1852. At first of moderate views, he had joined the Liberals under Urbano Rattazzi and Giovanni Lanza, and had entered into relations with the revolutionary party throughout the peninsula. He had succeeded in inspiring their leaders with the conviction that the movement for Italian unity must proceed from Piedmont. Vincenzo Gioberti, Daniel Manin, and Giuseppe Garibaldi adopted Cavour's programme, and promised support if he would organise a new rising against Austria. Cavour, with the king's entire approval, now made this rising his primary object ; he was confident that Napoleon would not permit Austria to

VICTOR EMMANUEL II.
He ascended the throne of Sardinia in 1849, in succession to his father, and in 1861 he was proclaimed King of Italy at Turin, reigning until his death, which occurred in January, 1878.

THE ITALIAN CAMPAIGN OF NAPOLEON III.: DEFEAT OF THE AUSTRIANS AT THE BATTLE OF PALESTRO ON MAY 30TH, 1859

From the painting by Emilio Lapi in the Gallery of Modern Paintings, Florence

THE FRENCH ATTACK UNDER MACMAHON AT THE BATTLE OF MAGENTA ON JUNE 4TH, 1859

From the painting by Yvon in the Versailles Museum

ANOTHER SCENE IN THE BATTLE OF MAGENTA: THE ITALIAN CAMP DURING THE FIGHT

From the painting by Giovanni Fattori

THE EMPEROR NAPOLEON III. AT THE BATTLE OF SOLFERINO

From the painting by Meissonier in the Louvre

SOLFERINO: "ONE OF THE BLOODIEST CONFLICTS OF THE CENTURY"

On June 24th, 1859, was fought the battle of Solferino, "one of the bloodiest conflicts of the century." Three hundred thousand men, with nearly 800 guns, were opposed in the terrible fight, and while the French had no definite plan of action, the Austrian leaders were unable to avoid a series of blunders. Rarely, indeed, have troops been handled with so little generalship. In the battle, which ended in the defeat of the Austrians, no fewer than 12,000 Austrians and nearly 17,000 allies were killed or wounded, and 9,000 Austrian prisoners were taken, as against 1,200 Italians.

From the painting by Jules Rigo in the Versailles Museum

aggrandise herself by reducing Italy a second time. The Austrian Government played into his hands by declining to continue the arrangements for introducing an entirely autonomous and national form of administration into Lombardy and Venice, and by the severity with which the aristocratic participants in the Milan revolt of February 6th, 1853, were punished. Sardinia sheltered the fugitives, raised them to honourable positions, and used every means to provoke a breach with Austria. The schemes of the House of Savoy and its adherents were discovered by the Viennese government, but too late; they were too late in recognising that Lombardy and Venice must be reconciled to the Austrian supremacy by relaxing the severity of the military occupation. Too late, again, was the Archduke Maximilian, the enlightened and popular brother of the emperor, despatched as viceroy to Milan, to concentrate and strengthen the Austrian party. Cavour gave the Lombards no rest; by means of the national union he spread the fire throughout Italy, and continually incited the Press against Austria. The Austrian Government was soon forced to recall its ambassador from Turin, and Piedmont at once made the counter move.

In July, 1858, Napoleon came to an agreement with Cavour at Plombières; France was to receive Savoy if Sardinia acquired Lombardy and Venice, while the county of Nizza was to be the price of the annexation of Parma and Modena. The House of Savoy thus sacrificed its ancestral territories to gain the paramountcy in Italy. The term "Italy" then implied a federal state which might include the Pope, the Grand Duke of Tuscany, and the King of Naples.

THE EMPEROR NAPOLEON III.
Many improvements in internal administration were carried out under Napoleon III., but the emperor's policy was one of vacillation, and the story is told that Bismarck on one occasion described him as "an undetected incapable."

JOSEPH NAPOLEON
The son of Jerome of Westphalia, he married Clotilde, the daughter of Victor Emmanuel, thus strengthening the community of interests between France and Sardinia.

Sardinia at once began the task of mobilisation, for which preparation had been already made by the construction of 250 miles of railway lines. On January 1st, 1859, at the reception on New Year's Day, Napoleon plainly announced to the Austrian ambassador, Hübner, his intention of helping the Italian cause. On January 17th, the community of interests between France and Sardinia was reaffirmed by the engagement of Prince Joseph Napoleon —Plon-Plon—son of Jerome of Westphalia, to Clotilde, the daughter of Victor Emmanuel. Even then the war might have been avoided had Austria accepted British intervention and the condition of mutual disarmament. Napoleon dared not provoke England, and informed Cavour on April 20th that it was advisable to fall in with the British proposals. But the Cabinet of Vienna had in the meantime been so ill-advised as to send an ultimatum to Sardinia threatening an invasion within thirty days if Sardinia did not forthwith and unconditionally promise to disarm. This action was the more ill-timed, as Austria was herself by no means prepared to throw the whole of her forces into Italy. By accepting British intervention Cavour evaded the necessity of replying to the ultimatum. France declared that the crossing of the Ticino by the Austrians would be regarded as a casus belli. The crossing was none the less effected on April 30th, 1859. The war which then began brought no special honour to any of the combatants; though it materially altered the balance of power in Europe. In the first place, the Austrian army showed itself entirely unequal to the performance of its new tasks; in respect of equipment it was far behind the times, and much of its innate capacity had disappeared since the campaigns of 1848 and 1849; leadership and administrative energy were alike sadly to seek. Half-trained and often wholly uneducated officers were placed in highly responsible positions. High birth, irrespective of capacity, was a passport to promotion; a fine presence and a kind

The Austrian Army Corrupt and Incapable of dandified indifference to knowledge and experience were more esteemed than any military virtues. There was loud clashing of weapons, but general ignorance as to their proper use. The general staff was in an unusually benighted condition; there were few competent men available, and these had no chance of employment unless they belonged to one of the groups and coteries which made the distribution of offices their special business.

At the end of April, 1859, the army in Italy amounted to little more than 100,000 men, although Austria was said to have at command 520,000 infantry, 60,000 cavalry, and 1,500 guns. The commander-in-chief, Count Franz Gyulay, was an honourable and fairly competent officer, but no general. His chief of the staff, Kuhnenfeld, had been sent to the seat of war from his professorial chair in the military academy, and while he displayed the highest ingenuity in the invention of combinations, was unable to formulate or execute any definite plan of campaign.

With his 100,000 troops Gyulay might easily have overpowered the 70,000 Piedmontese and Italian volunteers who had concentrated on the Po. The retreat from that position could hardly have been prevented even by the French generals and a division of French troops, which had arrived at Turin on April 26th, 1859; however, the Austrian leaders were apprehensive of being outflanked on the Po by a disembarkation of the French troops at Genoa. Gyulay remained for a month in purposeless inaction in the Lomellina,

Napoleon and Garibaldi in Battle the district between Ticino and Sesia; it was not until May 23rd that he ventured upon a reconnaissance to Montebello, which produced no practical result. The conflict at Palestro on May 30th deceived him as to Napoleon's real object; the latter was following the suggestions of General Niel, and had resolved to march round the Austrian right wing. Garibaldi, with three or four thousand ill-armed guerrilla troops, had crossed the

Ticino at the south of Lake Maggiore. This route was followed by a division under General MacMahon, and Niel reached Novara on the day of Palestro and proceeded to threaten Gyulay's line of retreat, who accordingly retired behind the Ticino on June 1st. He had learned nothing of MacMahon's movement on his left, and thought his right wing sufficiently covered by the division of Clam-Gallas, who was advancing from the Tyrol. The battle on the Naviglio followed on June 3rd, and Gyulay maintained his position with 50,000 men against the 58,000 under the immediate command of the Emperor Napoleon in person.

MacMahon had crossed the Ticino at Turbigo, driven back Clam-Gallas, and found himself by evening on the Austrian left flank at Magenta on June 4th, 1859. Unable to rely on his subordinates for a continuance of the struggle, Gyulay abandoned his position on the following day, evacuated Milan, and led his army to the Mincio. At this point the Emperor Francis Joseph assumed the command in person; reinforcements to the number of 140,000 troops had arrived,

The terrible Battle of Solferino together with reserve and occupation troops amounting to another 100,000. With these the emperor determined to advance again to the Chiese on the advice of General Riedkirchen, who presided over the council of war in association with the old quartermaster-general Hess.

On June 24th they encountered the enemy advancing in five columns upon the Mincio, and to the surprise of the combatants the Battle of Solferino was begun, one of the bloodiest conflicts of the century, which ended in the retreat of the Austrians, notwithstanding the victory of Benedek over the Piedmontese on the right wing. Three hundred thousand men with nearly 800 guns were opposed on that day, and rarely have such large masses of troops been handled in an important battle with so little intelligence or generalship. The French had no definite plan of action, and might have been defeated without great difficulty had the Austrian leaders been able to avoid a similar series of blunders. The losses were very heavy on either side. Twelve thousand Austrians and nearly 17,000 allies were killed or wounded; on the other hand, 9,000 Austrian prisoners were taken as against 1,200 Italians.

VICTOR EMMANUEL AND HIS STAFF AT THE BATTLE OF SAN MARTINO

From the painting by Cassioli in the Palace of the Signory at Siena

THE HEIGHT OF THE CONFLICT AT SAN MARTINO ON JUNE 24TH, 1859

While the main battle was in progress at Solferino, other sections of the combatants were engaged in a prolonged and deadly conflict near San Martino, and, ignorant of the fate which had overtaken the Austrian army, Benedek, who had twice repulsed the Sardinians, continued the struggle for several hours after the issue had been decided, retiring at last when a severe storm had broken out. This engagement was noteworthy for the conspicuous part taken in it by Marshal Niel, "who distinguished himself above all the other leaders on the French side."

From the painting by Professor Ademollo in the Gallery of Modern Paintings at Florence

THE WELCOME OF PARIS TO THE FRENCH ARMY ON ITS RETURN FROM ITALY ON AUGUST 14TH, 1859

From the painting by E. Ginain in the Versailles Museum

The Emperor Napoleon had not yet brought the campaign to a successful conclusion; his weakened army was now confronted by the "Quadrilateral" formed by the fortresses of Peschiera, Mantua, Verona, and Legnago, which was covered by 200,000 Austrians. Moreover, Austria could despatch reinforcements more rapidly and in greater numbers than France. Austrian sympathies were also very powerful in South Germany, and exerted so strong a pressure upon the German Federation and on Prussia that a movement might be expected at any moment from that direction. Frederic William IV. had retired from the government since October, 1857, in consequence of an affection of the brain; since October 7th, 1858, his brother William had governed Prussia as prince-regent. He had too much sympathy with the Austrian dynasty and too much respect for the fidelity of the German Federal princes to attempt to make capital out of his

GENERAL HESS
Chief of the staff in the Austrian army under Field-Marshal Radetzky, General Hess shared with that great leader many of his victories.

neighbour's misfortunes; he had even transferred Bismarck from Frankfort to St. Petersburg, to remove the influence upon the Federation of one who was an avowed opponent of Austrian paramountcy. But he awaited some definite proposal from the Vienna government. Six army corps were in readiness to advance upon the Rhine on receipt of the order for mobilisation. The Emperor Francis Joseph sent Prince Windisch-Graetz to Berlin, to call on Prussia for help as a member of the Federation, although the terms of the federal agreement did not apply to the Lombard-Venetian kingdom; but he could not persuade himself to grant Prussia the leadership of the narrower union, or even to permit the foundation of a North German Union. A politician of the school of Felix Schwarzenberg was not likely to formulate a practicable compromise. Austria thus threw away her chance of defeating France and Bonapartism with the help of her German brethren, and of

THE MEETING OF VICTOR EMMANUEL AND GARIBALDI AT SESSIA IN 1860
From the painting by Aldi in the Palace of the Signory, Siena

remaining a permanent and honoured member of the Federation which had endured a thousand years, merely because she declined an even smaller sacrifice than was demanded in 1866.

During the progress of these Federal negotiations at Berlin the combatants had themselves been occupied in bringing the war to a conclusion. The Emperor Napoleon was well aware that the temper of the Federation was highly dangerous to himself, and that Great Britain and Prussia would approach him with offers of intervention. He therefore seized the opportunity of extricating himself by proffering an armistice and a provisional peace to the Emperor Francis Joseph.

The French Emperor's Peace Terms

After two victories his action bore the appearance of extreme moderation. Austria was to cede Lombardy to France, the province then to become Sardinian territory; the Grand Duke of Tuscany and the Duke of Modena were to be permitted to return to their states, but were to be left to arrange their governments for themselves, without the interference of either of the Powers; Austria was to permit the foundation of an Italian Federation; the desire of the Emperor Francis Joseph to retain Peschiera and Mantua was granted. On these terms the armistice was concluded on July 8th, and the provisional Peace of Villafranca on July 11th; and Napoleon withdrew.

The official account of the war of 1859 by the Austrian general staff attempts to account for the emperor's conclusion of peace on military grounds, emphasising the difficulty of continuing hostilities and the impossibility of placing an army on the Upper Rhine, in accordance with the probable demands of the Federation. This is an entirely superficial view of the question. Had Prussia declared war on France on the ground of her agreement with Austria, without consulting the Federation, and sent 150,000 men within a month from the Rhine to the French frontier, the anxieties of the Austrian army in Italy would have been entirely relieved. Napoleon would certainly have left Verona if the Prussians had been marching on Paris by routes perfectly well known to him.

Influence of the Emperor in Europe

Although the Italian policy of Napoleon III. seemed vague and contradictory, even to his contemporaries, yet he was still in their eyes entitled to the credit of being the creator of the kingdom of Italy; so that in the year 1860 he stood at the zenith of his influence in Europe. He successfully concealed from public opinion how much had really been done contrary to his wishes. It was discovered that his character was sphinx-like, and what was really weakness seemed to be Machiavellian calculation.

Cavour, indeed, saw through him and made full use of his vacillation; and years later the story was told how Bismarck, even in those days, called the French emperor "une incapacité méconnue," an undetected incapable. But as against this unauthenticated verdict we must remember that the emperor possessed a wide range of intellectual interests and a keen comprehension of the needs of his age. On the other hand, he was lacking in firmness; natures like Cavour and Bismarck easily thwarted his plans, and could lead him towards the goal which they had in view.

France as the Friend of Small Nations

Outside France, Napoleon's advocacy of the national wishes of the smaller nations of Europe made him popular. When Moldavia and Wallachia, contrary to the tenor of the treaties, chose a common sovereign, Alexander Cusa, Napoleon III., with the help of Russia, induced the Great Powers to recognise him, and protected the Roumanians when their principalities were united into a national state. Cusa, it is true, was deposed by a revolution on February 23rd, 1866. Prince Charles of Hohenzollern, who was chosen on April 20th, obtained for the youthful state, by the force of his personality, complete independence on May 21st, 1877, and the title of a kingdom on March 26th, 1881.

It was Napoleon's purpose to perform equal services for the Poles. The Tsar Alexander II., in order to conciliate them, placed, in June, 1862, their countryman, the Marquess of Wielopolski, at the side of his brother Constantine, the viceroy of Poland. Wielopolski endeavoured to reconcile his people to Russia, in order to help his countrymen to win some share, however modest, of self-government. But the passionate fury of the Poles frustrated his purpose, and he was unable to prevent the outbreak of the insurrection in January, 1863. He thereupon gave up his post, and the Russian Government adopted the sternest measures. In February, Prussia put the Russian emperor under an obligation by granting permission to Russian

THE EMPEROR AND EMPRESS OF FRANCE RECEIVING THE AMBASSADORS OF SIAM AT THE PALACE OF FONTAINEBLEAU

From the painting by Gérome

troops to follow Polish insurgents into Prussian territory. This compact, it is true, did not come into force, since it aroused the indignation of Europe; but it showed the goodwill of Prussia, and Bismarck, by this and other services in the Polish question, won the Tsar over so completely that Russia's neutrality was

How France Helped the Poles

assured in the event of a quarrel in Germany. Napoleon now induced England, and, after long hesitation, Austria also, to tender to Russia a request that the Poles should be granted a complete amnesty; but this was refused. The support of Prussia was peculiarly valuable to Russia, because France, England, and Austria resolved to intercede further for the Poles. In a note of June 27th, 1863, the three Powers recommended to Russia the grant of six demands, of which the most important were a Polish Parliament and a complete amnesty.

Palmerston supported these first steps of Napoleon, in the interests of British rule in India. In Poland he saw a wound to Russian power, which he determined to keep open. But he refused his assent to more serious measures which Napoleon pressed on his consideration, because the Polish question was not so important for the British that they would embark on a war for this sole reason; still less could Austria, since it was one of the participatory Powers, follow Napoleon on his path. The Tsar, however, was so enraged at Austria's vacillating attitude that he thereupon immediately proposed to King William an alliance against France and Austria. Bismarck advised his sovereign not to accept the Tsar's proposal, because in a war against France and Austria the brunt of the burden would have devolved on Prussia. Napoleon then proposed to the Austrian emperor, through the Duc de Gramont, that he should cede Galicia to Poland, which was to be emancipated,

The French Emperor in the Lurch

but in return take possession of the Danubian principalities. Count Rechberg answered that it was strange to suggest to Austria to wage a war with Russia for the purpose of losing a province, when it was customary to draw the sword only to win a fresh one. Napoleon thus saw himself completely left in the lurch, and Russia suppressed the rebellion with bloodshed and severity; the Governor-general of Wilna, Michael Muravjev, was

conspicuous for the remorseless rigour with which he exercised his power. It would be a mistake to consider Napoleon as a sympathetic politician who, if free to make his choice, would have devoted the resources of his country to the liberation of oppressed nations. His selfishness was revealed in the expedition against Mexico; and there, too, he tried to veil his intention by specious phrases.

He announced to the world that he wished to strengthen the Latin races in America as opposed to the Anglo-Saxons, who were striving for the dominion over the New World. He had originally started on the expedition in concert with Great Britain and Spain, in order to urge upon the Mexican Government the pecuniary claims of European creditors. The two allies withdrew when Mexico conceded their request; the French general, Count Lorencez, thereupon, in violation of the treaty, seized the healthy tableland above the fever-stricken coast of Vera Cruz, where the French had landed. General Forey then conquered the greatest part of the land, and an assembly of notables, on July

The Waning Power of Napoleon

11th, 1863, elected as emperor the Archduke Maximilian, brother of Francis Joseph. He long hesitated to accept the crown, because Francis Joseph gave his assent only on the terms that Maximilian should first unconditionally renounce all claim to the succession in Austria. After Napoleon had promised, in the treaty of March 12th, 1864, to leave at least 20,000 French soldiers in the country until 1867, the archduke finally consented to be emperor; he did not shut his eyes to the fact that monarchy would be slow to strike root in the land. Napoleon, by placing the Emperor Maximilian on the throne, pursued his object of gradually withdrawing from the Mexican affair, since the United States protested against the continuance of the French in Mexico. The reader is referred to a later volume for the history of the way in which Napoleon deserted the unhappy emperor, and incurred a partial responsibility for his execution at Queretaro. The restless ambition of Napoleon's policy aroused universal distrust in Europe. When the war of 1866 broke out, after his failures in the Polish and Mexican affair, his star was already setting; and a growing republican opposition, supported by the younger generation, was raising its head menacingly in France.

THE UNIFICATION OF ITALY
AND GARIBALDI'S BRAVE FIGHT FOR LIBERTY

THE greatest political event of the nineteenth century on the European Continent is the simultaneous establishment of the national unity of the German and Italian peoples. The aspect of Europe was more permanently changed by this than by any event since the creation of an empire by Charles the Great. The feeling of nationality is as old as the nations themselves, and the history of the two nations with their divisions and subdivisions records in almost every generation proud exhortations or plaintive appeals to assert their unity by force of arms. From Dante and Petrarch, from Machiavelli and Julius II.—"Out with the barbarians from Italy!"—down to Alfieri and Ugo Foscolo, the line is almost unbroken.

The Germans show the same sequence. But the appeals of the writers of the German Renaissance, from Hutten to Puffendorf and Klopstock, never had such **Awakening of German Nationality** a passionate ring, since the nation, even when most divided, was always strong enough to ward off the foreign yoke. At last the intellectual activity of the eighteenth century raised the spirit of nationality, and the German people became conscious that its branches were closely connected. The intellectual culture of the Germans would, as David Strauss says in a letter to Ernest Renan, have remained an empty shell if it had not finally produced the national State.

We must carefully notice that the supporters of the movement for unification both in Germany and Italy were drawn exclusively from the educated classes; but their efforts were powerfully supported by the establishment and expansion of foreign trade, and by the construction of roads and railways, since the separate elements of the nation were thus brought closer together. The scholar and the author were joined by the manufacturer, who produced goods for a market outside his own small country, and by the merchant, who was cramped by custom-house restrictions. Civil servants and military men did not respond to that appeal until much later. The majority of the prominent officials and officers in Germany long remained particularists, until Prussia **The New Regime in Italy** declared for the unity of the nation. In Italy the course of affairs was somewhat different. There the generals and officers of the Italian army created by Napoleon were from the first filled with the conviction that a strong political will was most important for the training of their people; the revolution of 1821 was greatly due to them. Similarly, the officers of the smaller Italian armies between 1859 and 1861 joined in large numbers the side of King Victor Emmanuel. The movement reached the masses last of all. But they, even at the present day in Italy, are indifferent towards the new regime; while in South Germany and Hanover, and occasionally even on the Rhine, they are still keenly alive to their own interests.

When Garibaldi marched against the army of the King of Naples, the soldiers of the latter were ready and willing to strike for his cause, and felt themselves betrayed by generals and officers. It is an undoubted fact that the Neapolitan Bourbons had no inconsiderable following among the lower classes. The Catholic clergy of Italy were divided; the leaders supported the old regime, while the inferior clergy favoured the movement. The mendicant friars of Sicily were enthusiastic for Garibaldi, and the Neapolitan general, **Garibaldi the Patriot Leader** Bosco, when he marched against the patriot leader, was forced to warn his soldiers in a general order not to allow themselves at confession to be shaken in their loyalty to their king. Pius IX. endured the mortification of seeing that in 1862 no less than 8,493 priests signed a petition praying him to place no obstacles in the way of the unification of Italy.

It was from Germany, the mother of so many ideas, that at the beginning of the nineteenth century the modern movement, of which the watchword was national and political unity, took its start. But the impulse was not given by the current of internal development ; it came from outside, through the tyranny of Napoleon. The nation recognised that it could only attain independence by union, and keep it by unity.

The conception of emperor and empire found its most powerful advocate in Stein. But he and his friends, as was natural, considered the overthrow of the foreign tyranny more important at first than formal unity. In his memorial addressed to the Tsar in 1812 he pointed out how desirable it was that Germany, since the old monarchy of the Ottos and the Hohenstauffen could not be revived, should be divided between the two Great Powers, Prussia and Austria, on a line corresponding to the course of the Main.

He would, however, have regarded this solution only as an expedient required by existing circumstances. " I have only one fatherland," he wrote to Count Münster at London, on December 1st, 1812 — " that is called Germany ; and since I, according to the old constitution, belong to it and to no particular part of it, I am devoted, heart and soul, to it alone, and not to one particular part of it. At this moment of great developments the dynasties are a matter of absolute indifference to me. They are merely instruments." Stein's efforts at the Congress of Vienna, where he vainly stood out for the emperor and the imperial Diet, remained as noble examples to the next generation. The thought of nationality radiated from Germany, where Arndt, Uhland, Körner, and Rückert had written in its spirit. But Napoleon had roused also the Italians and the Poles, the former by uniting at least Central and Upper Italy, with the exception of Piedmont, into the kingdom of Italy ; the latter by holding out to them the bait of a restored constitution. It is significant that

the first summons to unity was uttered by Murat, who, when he marched against the Austrians in 1815, wished to win the nation for himself, and employed Professor Rossi of Bologna, who was murdered in 1848, when a Liberal Minister of the Pope, to compose a proclamation embodying the principle of Italian unity. The peoples of the Austrian monarchy were subsequently roused by Germany to similar efforts.

There was this distinction between Germany and Italy—in the former the Holy Roman Empire had served to keep alive the tradition of unity, while in Italy no political unity had existed since Roman times. In Italy the movement towards unity had no historical foundation, and the " municipal spirit " was everywhere predominant until the middle of the nineteenth century. When, in 1848, a number of officers, who were not natives, were enrolled in the Piedmontese army, the soldiers long made a sharp distinction between their " Piedmontese " and their " Italian " superiors. So again in the Crimean War, when 15,000 Piedmontese were sent to fight on the side of the French and English, most of them heard for the first time that the foreign nations termed them Italians.

In Germany, again, it was a question of uniting prosperous states, but in Italy of overthrowing unstable ones—for example, the States of the Church and Naples. In Germany it was necessary to reckon with superabundant forces and the jealousy of two Great Powers ; and by the side of them stood a number of prosperous petty states where culture flourished. Italy, on the other hand, was dependent on the Austrians, who were termed Tedeschi, or Germans ; in this connection, however, the Italians were forced to admit that an organised government and a legislature, which in comparison with Piedmont itself showed considerable advance, existed only in the Austrian districts. And in addition the Italians had to struggle against the great difficulty that the papacy, as a

JOSEPH MAZZINI
The Italian patriot who suffered in the cause of liberty and unity, Mazzini devoted his whole life to the furtherance of his ideals, and, taking as his watchword "God and the People," pursued his purpose with passionate zeal.

Italy's Dependence on Austria

spiritual empire, opposed their unification. The risings of 1821 in Naples and Piedmont, as well as that of 1831 in the Romagna, aimed far more at the introduction of parliamentary forms than at the attainment of national unity. The thought of liberty was stronger then than that of nationality. Only in the background did the secret society of the Carbonari entertain the vague idea of the union of Italy. The followers of the Genoese, Joseph Mazzini, 1805–1872, claim for him the honour of being the first to follow out the idea of unity to its logical conclusion. Certain it is that Mazzini, undeterred by failures, devoted his whole life to the realisation of this idea. "I have just taught the Italians," he said, on one occasion after the war of 1859, "to lisp the word 'unity.'"

Mazzini's Great Work for Unity

It was after his arrest in 1830 by the Piedmontese Government as a member of the Carbonari, when he spent several months as a prisoner in the fortress of Savona, that he formed the plan of founding a league under the name of "Young Italy," with the object of creating an Italian republic. Animated by a faith which amounted to fanaticism, he took as his watchword "God and the People!" He described later his feelings as a prisoner: "I saw how Rome, in the name of God and of a republican Italy, offered the nations a common goal and the foundation of a new religion. And I saw how Europe, wearied of scepticism, egoism, and anarchy, received the new faith with enthusiastic acclamations. These were my thoughts in my cell at Savona." He did not shrink from employing all the weapons of conspiracy, including even assassination.

All the rebellions and conspiracies which he plotted proved failures; but even under the stress of conscientious scruples as to the right he had to drive so many highly gifted colleagues to death and long years of captivity, he was supported by the thought that only thus could the ideal of nationality

GARIBALDI

The great champion of Italian liberty, Giuseppe Garibaldi, became associated with Mazzini in the early days of the movement, and was condemned to death, but escaping, he returned later to Italy to lead his people to victory.

From a photograph

be kept before the eyes of the people. In the oath which he administered to the members of his secret league they vowed: "By the blush which reddens my face when I stand before the citizens of other countries and convince myself that I possess no civic rights, no country, no national flag . . . by the tears of Italian mothers for their sons who have perished on the scaffold, in the dungeon, or in exile . . . I swear to devote myself entirely and always to the common object of creating one free, independent, and republican Italy by every means within my power."

The league spread over Italy and every country where Italians lived. Giuseppe Garibaldi heard for the first time of Mazzini in 1833, when as captain of a small trading-vessel he was sitting in an inn at Taganrog on the Black Sea, and listened to the conversation at the next table of some Italian captains and merchants with whom he was unacquainted. "Columbus," he wrote in 1871, "certainly never felt such satisfaction at the discovery of America as I felt when I found a man who was endeavouring to liberate his country." He eagerly joined the fiery orator of that dinner-party, whose name was Cuneo, and, armed with an introduction from him, hastened to Mazzini, who was then plotting his conspiracies at Marseilles.

Garibaldi took part in one of the futile risings of February, 1834, was condemned to death, and escaped to Argentina, where he gathered his first experiences of war. He long followed the leadership of Mazzini, although the natures of the two men were too different to permit of any very intimate relations between them. Garibaldi called Mazzini the "second of the Infallibles"; but he esteemed him so highly, that at a banquet given in his honour at London in 1864 he toasted him as his master.

Mazzini was the central figure of the Italian movement only up to the middle of the fifties. After that an amelioration was traceable in the life of his nation. When the middle classes took up the cause of freedom as one man, the importance of the conspiracies disappeared and the entire system of secret societies—for the Carbonari and the Young Italy were opposed by the Sanfedists, the league of the reaction—became discredited. Public

Mazzini Condemned to Death life was now more instinct with vitality. A blind and biassed republicanism was no longer the only cry; the leaders of the movement began to take the actual conditions into account, and the Piedmontese, in particular, worked in the cause of constitutional monarchy. Mazzini, on the other hand, hated the house of Savoy equally with every other dynasty. Two of his conspiracies were aimed against Piedmont, so that sentence of death was pronounced on him by the courts of that kingdom.

The new ideas started from Piedmont. The noble priest Vincenzo Gioberti proposed the plan that all Italy should rally round the Pope, and follow him as leader in the war of independence. A number of Piedmontese nobles, Count Cesare Balbo, Marquis Massimo d'Azeglio, and the greatest of them, Count Camillo Cavour, were filled with the conviction that the government of Italy belonged by right to the constitutional monarchy of Piedmont. They had all grown up in an atmosphere of conservative ideas, respectful towards the monarchy, and filled with admiration for the army and the civil service of Piedmont. The revolutionists of 1848 were united only in their hatred of the foreign yoke; their views for the future were of the most conflicting character, and must have led to dissension if they had been clearly formulated.

The hope that Pope Pius would be permanently won for the great thought soon faded away. In the whole agitation the idea of federalism was still widely predominant. Venice and Rome under Daniel Manin and Mazzini declared for

Cavour in Public Disfavour independent republics; even Lombardy felt some reluctance to unite with Sardinia. Rossi, the papal Minister, wished merely for a league of the sovereign princes of Italy, not a united Parliament. In Piedmont the middle-class citizens opposed with suspicion the representatives of the monarchical military state, and Cavour, who defended the royal authority, was in 1849 one of the most unpopular of politicians. Even then he was opposed to

Urbano Rattazzi, who was soon destined to become the leader of the bourgeois circles. Italy thus succumbed to the sword of Radetzky. Napoleon, as President of the French Republic, put an end to the Roman Republic, since he did not wish to allow all Italy to be subjugated by the Austrians. The heroic and, for some time, successful defence of Rome by Garibaldi—on the scene of this memorable fight, at the summit of the Janiculum, a colossal monument has been erected in his honour—raised him to be the popular hero of the nation, while Mazzini's republican phrases began to seem vapid to the intelligent Italians.

The wars of 1848 and 1849 left the Italians with the definite impression that only Piedmont could have ventured to face the Austrian arms in the open field. King Charles Albert was clearly a martyr to the cause of Italian unity; he died soon after his abdication, a broken-hearted man, in a Portuguese monastery. Since his son, Victor Emmanuel, alone among the Italian princes maintained the constitution granted in 1848, the hopes of Italy

Cavour at the Goal of his Ambition were centred in him. In the year 1852, Cavour reached the immediate goal of his burning but justifiable ambition; for after he had allied himself with Rattazzi and the liberal middle class, he was entrusted with the direction of the government. He soon ventured openly to indicate Piedmont, which had been overthrown so recently, as the champion in the next war of liberation. He drew his weapons from the arsenal of the clever Ministers who, in the seventeenth and eighteenth centuries, had helped the Dukes of Savoy to hold their own between France and Austria. He was the heir of the old dynastic policy of Savoy, but in a greater age, dominated by the thought of nationality. He formed an alliance with the man whom the republicans of Italy hated intensely, and against whose life they plotted more than one conspiracy.

The question may well be asked whether the Italian blood was stirred in the veins of the Bonapartes when, in 1805, the first Napoleon created the kingdom of Italy, and when, in 1830, his nephew entered into a secret Italian alliance, and, finally, as Napoleon III., allied himself with Cavour for the liberation of Italy. It is not an unlikely supposition, although diplomatic reasons and the lust of power were the primary motives which actuated the nephew of the great conqueror in forming this alliance ; for he considered that his uncle had bequeathed to him the duty of destroying the work of the Congress of Vienna, especially in Italy, where Austria had entered on the inheritance of France.

Napoleon won friends for France on all sides when he came forward as the advocate for the idea of nationality. While he did so, there lay in the bottom of his heart the intention of increasing the territory of France on the basis of this idea, by the annexation of Belgium and Savoy, and of thus uniting all French-speaking peoples under the Empire. On the other side, he thought it dangerous to stretch out his hand to the Rhine, where the Germans, whom he called the coming race, might oppose him. He wished to free Italy from the Austrian rule, but only in order to govern it as suzerain. For this reason he declined from the outset to entertain the idea of giving political unity to the peninsula. He only agreed with Cavour at Plombières that Sardinia should be enlarged into a North Italian kingdom with from 10,000,000 to 12,000,000 inhabitants.

There was to be a Central Italian kingdom, consisting of Tuscany and the greater part of the States of the Church. Naples was to be left untouched. The Pope was to be restricted to the territory of the city of Rome and its vicinity, and in compensation was to be raised to the headship of the Italian Confederacy. Napoleon reserved to himself the nomination of his cousin, Joseph, called Jerome, to the throne of Central Italy, but concealed his intention from Cavour, while he hinted to him that he wished to place the son of King Murat on the throne at Naples. In return for his armed assistance the

French Emperor's Promises emperor stipulated for the cession of Savoy and Nice. The story of the campaign of 1859 and of its termination by the Treaty of Villafranca has been told in the last chapter. By the treaty, Napoleon's promises, therefore, were only partially fulfilled. By allowing Venetia to remain Austrian he belied the proclamation

announcing that " Italy shall be free from the Alps to the Adriatic," with which he had opened the war on May 3rd. Cavour felt himself deceived and exposed. His old opponent, Mazzini, had derided his policy before the war, and had warned the Italians not to exchange the rule of Austria for that of France. However unwise this attitude of the old conspirator might be, he now seemed to be correct in the prediction that Napoleon would deceive the Italians. The passionate nature of Cavour, which slumbered behind his half good-natured, half mockingly-diplomatic exterior, burst out in him with overwhelming force. He hurried to the headquarters of Victor Emmanuel and required him to lay down his crown, as his father, Charles Albert, had done, in order to show clearly to the world the injustice perpetrated by Napoleon. Cavour displayed such violence that the two men parted in downright anger. But Cavour, without further demur, resigned his office. That was the wisest step he could take to turn aside the reproach of treachery, which the republican party was already bringing against him. In the course of a conversation with the senator Joachim Pietri, an intimate friend of Napoleon, he gave vent to his displeasure in the most forcible terms, and threw in the teeth of the emperor the charge of deceit. " Your emperor has insulted me," he cried ; " yes, sir, insulted me. He gave me his word, and promised me to relax no efforts until the Austrians were completely driven out of Italy. As his reward for so doing he stipulated for Nice and Savoy. I induced my sovereign to consent to make this sacrifice for Italy. My king, my good and honourable king, trusted me and consented. Your emperor now pockets his reward and, lets us shift for ourselves. . . . I am dishonoured before my king. But," added Cavour, " this peace will lead to nothing ; this treaty will not be carried out."

One of the causes which led Napoleon to conclude peace so rapidly was the fear that the Italians would go far beyond his original intention and win complete

Cavour is Deceived by Napoleon III.

BARON RICASOLI

On the flight of the Grand Duke in 1859, he was made dictator of Tuscany, and was at the head of the Ministry in 1861 and again in 1866.

political independence for themselves. Cavour, in spite of his proud words about the integrity of the Piedmontese policy, had really wished on his side to outwit the emperor. For, at his instigation and in consequence of the agitations of the National Union, which he had secretly organised, not merely had Parma, Modena,

The Demand for United Italy and the Romagna risen against the Pope, but even in Central Italy, in Tuscany, in the Marches and in Umbria, the authorities had been driven out, and everywhere there was an outcry for United Italy. Victor Emmanuel had certainly, at the wish of Napoleon, refused this request, and had only accepted the supreme command of the volunteer corps which were forming everywhere.

Napoleon wished to preclude any further extension of this movement. Hence the hasty conclusion of the armistice, and the provisions of the Peace of Zürich, November 10th, 1859, that Sardinia might retain Lombardy, but not extend her territory further. In Tuscany, Parma, and Modena the old order of things was to be restored, if the people agreed to accept it ; and the States of the Church, and this condition was taken as obvious, must once more be subject to the Pope.

All Italian States were to form a Confederation, which Austria, as representing Venice, wished to join. Cavour, incensed at these fetters imposed on the Italians, said as he left the Ministry : " So be it ! they will force me to spend the rest of my life in conspiracies." And in the last letters before his retirement he secretly urged the leaders of the movement in Central Italy to collect money and arms, to wait their time loyally, and to resist the wishes of Napoleon.

Rattazzi, Cavour's successor, was an eloquent and practised advocate, of a tractable disposition, and therefore more acceptable to the king than Cavour ; he possessed a mind more capable of words

Cavour's Eloquent Successor and schemes than of action. Cavour, speaking of him, said that he was the first among the politicians of the second class. In accordance with the popular feeling Giuseppe Dabormida, the new Minister of Foreign Affairs, declared on July 23rd that Sardinia would never enter into an Italian Confederation in which Austria took any part. This policy was absolutely essential for self-preservation, since Piedmont, in a league with Austria, the Pope, and Naples,

would always have been in the minority. The new Cabinet was wavering and insecure, and so dependent on the will of Napoleon that it did not venture to take any forward step without his consent. But at this point the fact became evident that the work of unification was not dependent on the ability of individuals, but on the attitude of the whole nation.

It is astonishing with what political tact the several Italian countries struggled for union with Sardinia. The Sardinian Government was compelled to recall, immediately after the preliminary peace, the men it had sent to Bologna, Florence, Modena, and Parma to lead the agitation. These districts were consequently thrown upon their own resources ; but Tuscany found, on August 1st, 1859, in Baron Bettino Ricasoli, and the Romagna and the duchies in Luigi Carlo, a retired physician, leaders who governed the provisional commonwealths with sagacity, and guided the public voting which declared for submission to Victor Emmanuel.

Only in quite exceptional cases was any violence used against the hated tools

The Swiss Mercenaries of the Pope of the former governments; otherwise order prevailed generally, and a childlike, almost touching, enthusiasm for the unity of Italy. The Pope attempted a counter-blow, and succeeded in conquering Perugia on July 20th, 1859, by means of his Swiss mercenaries, who did not shrink from outrage and plunder.

Thereupon the Romagna, Tuscany, and Modena concluded a defensive alliance. General Manfredo Fanti organised in October, 1859, a force of 40,000 men ; so that the Pope desisted from further attacks. Since the Treaty of Villafranca left the return of the former governments open, so long as foreign interference was excluded, the Pope and the dukes calculated upon an outbreak of anarchy, which would provoke a counter-blow. They centred their hopes on the Mazzinists ; and Walewski, the Minister of Napoleon, who was unfavourable to the Italians, said that he preferred them to a party which styled itself a government. But this hope faded away before the wise attitude of the Central Italians.

The Emperor Napoleon now saw himself confronted by the unpleasant alternative of allowing the Italians full liberty, or of restoring the old regime by force. But ought the liberator of Italy to declare war on the country? And it was still more out of the question to allow the interference of the defeated Austrians. He repeatedly assured the Italians that he persisted in his intention to carry out his programme of federation.

Doubt has been felt whether the letter to this effect which he addressed on October 20th, 1859, to Victor Emmanuel really expressed his true intention. In that letter he repeated his demand for the restoration of the old regime in Central Italy and for the formation of an Italian Confederation with the Pope at its head. But it is clear that this was really his own and his final scheme; for he was too wise not to foresee that a united and powerful Italy might one day turn against France.

With this idea, therefore, he said to Marquis Napoleone di Pepoli: "If the movement of incorporation crosses the Apennines, the union of Italy is finished, and I do not wish for any union—I wish simply and solely for independence." His programme would have proved the most favourable solution for France, since it would then always have had a hand in the **The Italian** affairs of Italy, from the simple **Dislike of** reason that the North Italian **the French** kingdom, which owed its existence to him, would have had no other support against Austria and the remaining sovereigns of Italy. That was the precise contingency which Cavour most feared; and for that reason he secretly urged the leaders of Central Italy not to comply with the intentions of Napoleon. In fact, deputations from the Romagna, Tuscany, and the duchies offered the sovereignty to King Victor Emmanuel. He did not dare to accept the offer against the wish of Napoleon, and merely promised in his reply that he would represent to Europe the wishes of the Central Italians.

It is a remarkable fact that Victor Emmanuel, in these complications, entertained for a moment the idea of joining hands with Mazzini and raising the standard of revolt against Napoleon. By the agency of Angelo Brofferio, the leader of the democratic opposition in the Piedmontese Parliament, and the opponent of Cavour's diplomacy, the king negotiated with the old republican conspirator on whom first his father, and later, he himself, in 1857, had caused sentence of death to be passed on account of his organisation of a revolt in Piedmont. Mazzini showed at this crisis how greatly the welfare of his country outweighed with him all other considerations. He sent a message to that effect to the king, and only asked him to break off entirely with Napoleon, whom the Republicans regarded as Antichrist. In return Mazzini offered to raise the whole of Italy, including Rome and Naples, after which would follow the promotion of Victor Emmanuel to be **The King's** king of the peninsula. But then **Advice to** —for Mazzini expressly made **Brofferio** this proviso—he intended to fight, as previously, for the republic and for the expulsion of the House of Savoy. The king is reported to have said to Brofferio: "Try to come to an understanding; but take care that the Public Prosecutor hears nothing of it."

The negotiations, however, did not lead to the desired goal, for the game seemed to the king to be too dangerous. Mazzini certainly promised on that occasion more than he could perform; his schemes could not have been carried into execution against the express wishes of Napoleon, who would not have abandoned the Pope and Rome. Italy had only obtained the support of the emperor against Austria because the monarchical policy of Cavour offered a guarantee that in Italy at least the revolutionaries, who threatened his rule in France, were kept in restraint. The emperor, as his action in the year 1867 clearly proves, would have certainly employed force against Italy, even though Rome had been raised in rebellion; for since the French Democrats were implacably hostile to him, he was bound at least to have the clerical party on his side.

Garibaldi, who then was entrusted by the provisional government with the command of the Tuscan troops, overlooked all these considerations, and was already determined to advance on Rome. But Farini, the dictator of Romagna and of the duchies, thought his enterprise dangerous, and, going to meet him, induced him to withdraw from Central Italy. Having **Garibaldi's** returned to Turin, Garibaldi **Call** was received with consideration **to Italy** by Victor Emmanuel, who was privy to this plot; he then addressed a manifesto to Italy, in which he condemned the miserable, fox-like politicians, and called upon the Italians to place their hopes exclusively on Victor Emmanuel. That monarch, under his outward simplicity, possessed natural shrewdness enough to remain on good terms with all who wished to further the unity of Italy.

In this consists his inestimable services in the cause of the unification of Italy. Towards the end of the year 1859, Napoleon was forced to admit that he could not carry out his programme in Central Italy by peaceful methods. He thus ran the risk of losing Savoy and Nice, which had been promised him as a reward before the war. His own interests and his predilection for the Italian cause combined to induce him to leave a part, at any rate, of Central Italy to Victor Emmanuel. In order to carry out this change of policy, Walewski was dismissed and Edouard Antoine Thouvenel, a liberal who shared Napoleon's preference for Italy, was nominated Foreign Minister on January 5th, 1860. But the new policy was not possible with the Cabinet of Rattazzi, since that Minister did not possess the courage to assume the responsibility for the cession of Savoy and Nice. A bold and broad policy could only be carried out with the assistance of Cavour. The latter was already thirsting for power, while Rattazzi was vainly trying to block his road. It is true that the king was not pleased with the exchange of Ministers; he still cherished some rancour against Cavour for the "scene" which the latter had made with him after the Peace of Villafranca. Public opinion, on the other hand, more especially in Central Italy, looked to Cavour alone for the realisation of its wishes. Since his ambition was fired by the prospect of new and grand exploits, he induced his friends to work vigorously on his behalf, so that the Cabinet of Rattazzi was compelled to make way for him on January 16th, 1860. Rattazzi and his colleagues were not all so candid in their views as Dabormida, the Foreign Minister, who felt he could not compare with Cavour, and wrote at the time: " I was impatient

ADMIRAL PERSANO
Admiral of the Italian fleet, Persano, on the occasion of Garibaldi's bold expedition to Sicily, was ordered by Cavour to place his ships between Garibaldi's transports and the Neapolitan fleet.

GENERAL LAMORICIÈRE
One of the leaders of the Legitimist party in France, he was appointed commander-in-chief of the papal forces in 1860, when the Pope surrounded himself with an army of 20,000 enlisted soldiers.

to give up my place to him. But he was still more impatient than I was. I am sorry that he expended so much trouble in bursting the doors that stood open to him. But he has the right to be ambitious."

Napoleon, although not disposed to a grand and sweeping policy, had the astuteness requisite to disguise his frequent changes of front, and to veil his machinations with a semblance of magnanimity. Since he knew that the British distrusted him, and foresaw that the annexation of Savoy and Nice would appear to them the prelude to an extensive policy of aggrandisement, he lulled their suspicions by concluding a commercial treaty on free-trade principles, January 23rd, 1860. At the same time he informed the Pope that France no longer wished to insist on the restoration of the legations of the Romagna, Bologna, and Ferrara to the States of the Church.

This change in the policy of Napoleon could not have been more unwelcome to anyone than to the Pope. After all, Pius IX. had himself to blame for it, since he opposed the sensible counsels of Napoleon. The emperor had requested him in a letter of July 14th, 1859, to grant to the already rebellious legations a separate administration and a lay government nominated by the Pope. " I humbly conjure your Holiness," so the letter ran, " to listen to the voice of a devoted son of the Church, who in this matter grasps the needs of his time, and knows that force is not sufficient to solve such difficult problems. In the decision of your Holiness I see either the germs of a peaceful and tranquil future, or the continuation of a period of violence and distress." But the Curia continued obstinate, and declared that it could not break with the principles on which the States of the Church had been governed hitherto. The Pope, in fact, protested against the concession of religious liberty which had been granted by the provisional government at Bologna. Napoleon now adopted a severer tone. He published in December, 1859, a pamphlet, "The Pope and the Congress," in which it was stated that a restoration of papal rule in Central Italy had become impossible. Granted that a secular kingdom was necessary for the Pope in order to maintain his independence, a smaller territory would be sufficient for that purpose. Shortly afterwards, Napoleon addressed a second letter to Pius IX., in which he called upon the

throne. Cavour, however, met the refusal of Napoleon by a bold move, on which Rattazzi would never have ventured. Without asking the emperor, and against his will, a plebiscite was taken in March, 1860, in all the provinces of Central Italy, including Tuscany, on the question whether they wished for incorporation in the kingdom of Italy. The elections for the Parliament of Upper Italy proceeded at the same time with equal enthusiasm. All the capitals entrusted Cavour with full powers in order to express their confidence. It was no rhetorical figure when Napoleon,

THE REVOLUTION IN SICILY: RELEASED PRISONERS IN THE STREETS OF PALERMO
Rebelling against their Neapolitan rulers, the Sicilians looked eagerly for the assistance of Garibaldi, who at last decided to join the movement, sailing on May 5th, 1860, with about a thousand volunteers. In the above picture released prisoners are seen leading their gaoler through the streets of Palermo before putting him to death.

Pope on his side also to make some sacrifice for the union of Italy, which was slowly and surely progressing.

Cavour, meantime, had not reached his goal. On February 17th, 1860, Italy learnt the latest of the constantly changing programmes of Napoleon. According to this, only Parma and Modena were to be incorporated with Sardinia. Victor Emmanuel would rule the legations as Vicar of the Pope ; but Tuscany must remain independent ; at most a prince of the House of Savoy might be placed on the

in a speech delivered on March 1st, expressed his dissatisfaction at the arbitrary action of Italy. Cavour, however, had cleverly secured the goodwill of Britain, which had quite agreed to the proposal that Italy should withdraw from the influence of Napoleon. Palmerston was malicious enough to praise Cavour in the British Parliament for the boldness of his action.

Now, at length Cavour opened regular negotiations about the cession of Savoy and Nice, which had been promised by the treaty of January, 1858. What was the emperor to do ? Was he, on his side, to risk the loss of the two provinces by his obstinacy ? Perhaps even at the eleventh hour he might have prevented the incorporation of Tuscany if he had declared that under these conditions he would be contented with Savoy; but now the expectations and the covetousness of

Cavour's Magical Influence the French had been whetted, and he could not draw back. There is no question that Napoleon then abandoned the real interests of France, and was vanquished by Cavour. It had often been said, and subsequent events have proved the truth of the statement, that Cavour exercised a positively magical influence on Napoleon's vacillating mind. The Italian had probed the soul of the French emperor, and knew how far he might go. Having correctly gauged on the one hand the selfish interests of Napoleon, and on the other his sympathetic attitude towards the Italian question, Cavour could venture to play with him up to a certain point.

But there were limits to this policy. Cavour in vain tried all the arts of his diplomacy, and every expedient which his subtle mind suggested, to save Nice at least for the Italians. But here he was confronted by the definite resolution of the emperor, who would have exposed himself in the face of France, had he given in. Cavour and Benedetti signed the treaty on March 24th, 1860. When this was done, the Italian Minister, with a flash of humour, turned round suddenly and whispered in the ear of Benedetti: "We are partners in guilt now, are we not ?"

But an anxious time was in store for Cavour—the debate in the Italian Parliament. The great majority of the people, certainly, understood that King Victor Emmanuel and Cavour could not have acted otherwise. Rattazzi, however, the old rival of Cavour, placed himself at the head of the opposition; and he had a

Garibaldi Deceived by Cavour strong supporter in Garibaldi, who took his seat in Parliament with the express object of opposing the cession of Nice, his native town, to France. Henceforth he hated Cavour, who, as he said, had made him an alien in his own country. Garibaldi was not so indignant at the fact itself as he was that Cavour had deceived him; since a year previously, in answer to a direct question, the Minister had denied the cession of Nice. In no other way

could the crafty statesman have secured Garibaldi's sword for the war of liberation. On the other hand, Garibaldi esteemed the king highly, because some months later to the question, "Yes or no," he had returned the true answer. Victor Emmanuel then added that, if he as king submitted to cede Savoy, the country of his ancestors, to France, Garibaldi must be prepared to make equal sacrifices for the sake of the union of Italy.

We are told that Cavour, at this critical time, in order to soothe Garibaldi's feelings, sent him a note with the brief question, "Nice or Sicily ?" He is thus said to have incited the enthusiastic patriot to conquer the island. The story is quite improbable; for Cavour would certainly have preferred to mark time for the present, and consolidate the internal and economic conditions of the kingdom of North Italy, which consisted of 4,000,000 Piedmontese, 2,500,000 Lombards, and 4,000,000 Central Italians. This state, without the States of the Church, which were in an impoverished condition through bad administration, and without the

Sicily's Coming Revolt pauper population of Naples, would certainly have risen to considerable prosperity. It would have been well for North Italy not to have been burdened with the task of drawing the semi-civilised districts of the south into the sphere of its higher culture and its greater prosperity. "We must first organise ourselves," Cavour said at the time, "and form a powerful army; then we can turn our eyes to Venetia and further to the south, and to Rome." It was certainly, therefore, no hypocrisy when, up to March, 1860, he repeatedly sent envoys to Naples, in order to induce the Bourbons to follow a national policy and enter into an alliance with the kingdom of North Italy.

But here the genius of the Italian people took other paths. The wary statesman soon saw himself carried onward by the party of action farther than he himself had wished; for Mazzini and his partisans were incessantly scheming the revolt of Sicily. Under their instructions Francesco Crispi, who had long before been condemned to death by the Neapolitan courts, travelled through the island at great personal risk, collecting on all sides sympathisers with the cause, and preparing for the day of rebellion. The Sicilians did indeed rise in various places, but their attempts were hopeless if Garibaldi could not be induced to invade Sicily. He declared to the Mazzinists from the very first that he would only join the struggle under the standard of " Italy and Victor Emmanuel " ; in spite of his republican leanings he saw with unerring perception that Italy could only be united by means of the Piedmontese monarchy. Mazzini also declared, as in the previous year, that he wished first and foremost to conform to the expressed will of the people.

But the conscientious Garibaldi still hesitated ; he was weighed down by the enormous responsibility of leading the fiery youth of Italy to danger and to death, since all former plots against the Bourbons had miscarried and been drowned in the blood of their promoters. King Ferdinand II. of Naples, called " Bomba " since the savage bombardment of Messina in September, 1848, understood how to attach the soldiers of his army to his person ; he was hard-hearted but cunning, and by his affectation of native customs won himself some popularity with the lower classes on the mainland. The **Garibaldi's Heroic Expedition** Sicilians, indeed, hated their Neapolitan rulers from of old ; and the people gladly recalled the memory of the Sicilian Vespers, by which they had wrested their freedom from Naples in 1282. King Ferdinand died on May 22nd, 1859, and was succeeded by his weak son, Francis II., a feeble nature, with no mind of his own. Since the outbreak in Sicily was suppressed, and seemed to die away, Cavour urgently dissuaded Garibaldi from his enterprise, even though he later secretly aided it by the supply of arms and ammunition. It was Cavour's business then to decline any responsibility in the eyes of the diplomatists of Europe for the unconstitutional proposal of the general.

Garibaldi finally took the bold resolution of sailing for Sicily on May 5th,1860, with a thousand or so of volunteers. This marks the beginning of his heroic expedition, and also of the incomparable game of intrigue played by Cavour ; for the whole body of European diplomatists raised their voices in protest against the conduct of the Italian Government which had allowed a warlike expedition against a neighbouring state in time of peace. Cavour, assailed by all the ambassadors, declared, with some reason, that Garibaldi had acted against the wishes of the Government, and informed the French emperor that the Government was too weak to hinder the expedition by force, since otherwise there was the fear of a republican rising against the king. At the same time Cavour adopted measures to avert all danger from Garibaldi. Admiral Persano received commands from him to **Insurrection Among the Sicilians** place his ships between Garibaldi's transports and the Neapolitan fleet which was watching for them. To this intentionally cryptic order Persano replied that he believed he understood ; if need arose Cavour might send him to the fortress at Fenestrelles. He must have made up his mind to be repudiated, like Garibaldi, in the event of the failure of the expedition.

Garibaldi landed at Marsala, the Lilybæum of the ancients, on May 11th, 1860. He obtained but little help from the Sicilians ; when he attacked on May 15th, near Calatafimi, the royal troops, the 2,400 Sicilians who had joined him, ran away at the first shot, while he won a splendid victory with his volunteers. At Palermo, however, all was ready for the insurrection. In concert with his friends there Garibaldi, notwithstanding the great numerical superiority of the Bourbon troops, ventured on a bold attack during the night of the 27th-28th May. The people sided with him ; the troops of the king were fired upon from the houses and withdrew to the citadel, whence they bombarded Palermo. Rebellion blazed up through the whole island, and the scattered garrisons retired to the strong places on the coast, especially to Messina.

Alarmed at the revolt of the island, King Francis of Naples changed his tone ; in his dire necessity he summoned liberal Ministers to his counsels, and promised the Neapolitans a free constitution. He sent an embassy to Napoleon III. with a petition for help. The attitude of the latter was significant. He explained to the envoys that he desired the continuance **King Francis Appeals to Napoleon III.** of the Kingdom of Naples, but that it did not lie in his power to check the popular movement. The Italians, he said, were keen-witted, and knew that, after having once shed the blood of the French for their liberation, he could not proceed against them with armed force. He added : " The power stands on the national side, and is irresistible. We stand defenceless before it." He advised the King of

Naples, however, to abandon Sicily, and to offer an alliance to King Victor Emmanuel. Napoleon promised to support his proposal. This was done, and all the Great Powers assented to the wishes of France—even Great Britain, which, with all its inclination to Italy, still wished that the peninsula should be divided into two kingdoms. Cavour was in the most difficult position; it was impossible, in defiance of Europe, to refuse negotiations with Naples, yet he could not but fear to risk his whole work if he offered his hand to the hated Bourbons. He therefore consented to negotiations, for form's sake, and even induced King Victor Emmanuel to write a letter to Garibaldi, calling upon the latter to discontinue landing troops on the mainland of Naples.

Garibaldi thereupon replied to the king on June 27th: "Your Majesty knows the high respect and affection which I entertain for your person; but the state of affairs in Italy does not allow me to obey you as I should wish. Allow me, then, this time to be disobedient to you. So soon as I have accomplished my duty and the peoples are freed from the detested yoke, I will lay down my sword at your feet, and obey you for the rest of my life."

But Cavour was harassed by a still further anxiety. Garibaldi, on his march through Sicily, surrounded himself almost exclusively with partisans of Mazzini, and was resolved, so soon as Naples was liberated, to march on Rome. If then the republican party of action in this way did their best for the liberation of Italy, the fate of the monarchy was sealed. Cavour, therefore, staked everything to provoke a revolution on the mainland, by which not Garibaldi, but Persano or the king himself, should be proclaimed dictator. He entered into a compact with one of the Ministers of the King of Naples, Liborio Romano, who equally with Alessandro Nunziante, Duke of Majano, adjutant-general of Ferdinand II., was ready for treachery. Cavour hoped by aid of the latter to rouse a part of the Neapolitan army to revolt. He wrote to Persano: "Do not lose sight of the fact, Admiral, that the moment is critical. It is a question of carrying out the greatest enterprise of modern times, by protecting Italy from foreigners, pernicious principles, and fools."

But Nunziante, awakening the suspicion of the Bourbon Government, was obliged to take refuge on board the Piedmontese fleet. The king's uncle, Prince Louis,

Suspicions of the Bourbon Government

THE LIBERATORS OF SICILY: GARIBALDI WITH A GROUP OF PATRIOT HEROES

THE MISERABLE HIDING-PLACE OF THE KING AND QUEEN OF NAPLES

During the bombardment of Gaeta by the Piedmontese in 1861, the King and Queen of Naples sought refuge in the damp, unwholesome vaults illustrated in the above picture. "Their fear," says a contemporary account of the siege, "must have been very great indeed to have induced them to live in such a wretched hole. The stench, on entering, is great; and in some chambers through the doorway four generals died during the siege from the bad atmosphere and confinement."

Count Aquila was ordered by his nephew to quit the kingdom. It was thus evident that Garibaldi's services must once more be utilised in order to overthrow the Bourbons. He landed on August 19th, 1860, on the coast of the peninsula near Melito, and marched directly on Naples. The generals who were sent against him were unreliable, since their hearts were in the Italian cause. The soldiers who supported the Bourbons thought themselves betrayed, and murdered General Fileno Briganti at Mileto, August 25th, after he had concluded terms of capitulation with Garibaldi. The latter was received everywhere with enthusiasm; the common people regarded him as an invulnerable hero. When he entered Naples on September 7th, 1860, with his 18,000 volunteers, he was greeted by Liborio Romano as liberator; the king withdrew with his army of 60,000 men into a strong fortress on the Volturno. A momentous crisis had arrived. For the

Garibaldi's Entry into Naples

adherents of Mazzini in the train of Garibaldi it was of vital importance to prevent the people of Naples from being called upon to vote whether they wished Victor Emmanuel to be king. They confirmed Garibaldi in the idea of marching immediately on Rome, of driving out the French troops, and of putting an end to the hierarchy. Garibaldi's breast swelled with his previous successes; he was susceptible to flattery, and firmly persuaded himself that it was merely Cavour's jealousy if Victor Emmanuel did not follow the noble impulses of his heart and throw open to him the road to Rome and Venice.

When Cavour sent his trusted envoy, the Sicilian Giuseppe La Farina, in order to put himself in communication with Garibaldi, the latter insulted him by ordering his expulsion from Sicily. At first Garibaldi acquiesced in the dictatorship of Agostino Depretis, who was sent by the king; but on September 18th he replaced him, from suspicion of his connection with Cavour, by Antonio Mordini, an intimate friend of Mazzini. In this way Garibaldi succeeded in involving Italy simultaneously in a war with France and Austria. The Emperor Napoleon looked sullenly at Naples, where a revolutionary focus was forming that threatened his throne with destruction.

Once more Cavour faced the situation with the boldest determination. He was firmly convinced that the monarchy and the constitutional government of North Italy must contribute as much to the union of the peninsula as Garibaldi; he therefore counselled the king to advance with his army into the papal territory and

itself and its immediate vicinity, had surrounded himself with an army of 20,000 enlisted soldiers, at whose head he placed General Lamoricière, one of the leaders of the legitimist party in France. The mercenaries consisted of French, Austrians, Belgians, and Swiss; their officers were partly the flower of the legitimist nobility of France—a fact which could not be very pleasant to Napoleon. But King Victor Emmanuel sent 40,000 men, under the command of General Manfredo Fanti, against the States of the Church; and Lamoricière, who was obliged to leave half his troops

FAREWELL VISIT OF GARIBALDI TO ADMIRAL MUNDY ON THE HANNIBAL AT NAPLES

to occupy it—with the exception of Rome, which was protected by Napoleon—to march on Naples and to defeat the army of the Bourbon king, which was encamped on the Volturno. Matters had come to such a crisis that, when Victor Emmanuel sent his Minister Luigi Farini, from 1859–1860 dictator of the Emilia, and General Cialdini to Napoleon III., to expound his plan, the emperor gave a reply which showed that he was not blind to the necessity of the action taken by Victor Emmanuel.

The Pope, in order not to be entirely dependent on the help of France, which was intended merely to protect Rome

to suppress the inhabitants of the States of the Church, was attacked by a greatly superior force. He was so completely defeated at Castelfidardo on September 18th, 1860, that he was only able to escape to Ancona with 130 men, while almost the entire papal army was taken prisoners. Persano received orders to bombard Ancona; it surrendered on September 29th.

The troops of Garibaldi had in the meantime attacked the Bourbon army on the Volturno, but without any success. The Bourbon troops crossed the Volturno in order, in their turn, to attack. Garibaldi boldly held his ground with his men, and

GENERAL VIEW OF CAPRERA, GARIBALDI'S ISLAND HOME

THE RETREAT OF GARIBALDI, NEAR RAVENNA, ONE OF ITALY'S HISTORIC TREASURES

THE HOME AND REFUGE OF ITALY'S GREATEST PATRIOT

ITALY'S TRIBUTE TO GARIBALDI: THE PATRIOT'S MONUMENT ON THE JANICULUM AT ROME

the Neapolitans, although three to one, could not gain a victory ; but Garibaldi was far from being able to calculate upon a rapid success. Under these circumstances public opinion was strongly impressed when the army of Victor Emmanuel appeared on the bank of the Volturno ; the Neapolitans withdrew behind the Garigliano.

It was high time that King Victor Emmanuel appeared in Naples ; for Garibaldi was now so completely under the influence of the opponents of Cavour that he flatly refused to allow the incorporation of Naples and Sicily in the kingdom of Italy to be carried out. Mordini, his representative in Sicily, worked at his side, with the object that independent Parliaments should be summoned in Naples and Palermo, which should settle the matter. Garibaldi actually informed the king that he would not agree to the union unless Cavour and his intimate friends were first dismissed from the Ministry. By this demand, however, he ran counter to almost the entire public opinion of Italy. In Naples especially and in Sicily all prudent men wished for a rapid union with Italy, since the break-up of the old regime, in Sicily especially, had brought in its train confusion, horrors, and political murders. Garibaldi long debated with himself whether he should yield ; but when the Marquis Pallavicino—who had fretted away the years of his manhood as a prisoner in the Spielberg at Brünn and was now the leader of the party of action— and with him virtually the whole population of Naples, went over to the other side, the patriot general mastered himself and ordered the voting on the union with Italy to be arranged, October 21st.

The king would have been prepared to grant his wish and to nominate him lieutenant-general of the districts con-

GARIBALDI'S STATUE AT FLORENCE

quered by him, had not Garibaldi attached the condition to it that he should be allowed to march on Rome in the coming spring. As this could not be granted, he withdrew in dignified pride, although deeply mortified and implacably hostile to Cavour, to his rocky island of Caprera. In his farewell proclamation he called upon the Italians to rally round " Il Rè galantuomo " ; but he foretold his hope that in March, 1861, he would find a million Italians under arms, hinting in this way that he wished by their means to liberate Rome and Venice. But a fact, which many years later was disclosed in the memoirs of Thouvenel and Beust, shows how correct the judgment of Cavour was when he kept the Italians at this time away from Rome. When Garibaldi wished to march against Rome, Napoleon told the Vienna Cabinet that he had no objection if it wished to draw the sword against Italy to uphold the Treaty of Zürich—that is to say, for the papacy ; only, it could not be allowed to disturb Lombardy again. It is conceivable that Rechberg, the Foreign Minister, dissuaded the Emperor Francis Joseph from a war which could bring no gain to Austria even in case of victory. The Bourbon army could not hold its ground against the troops of Victor Emmanuel, and King Francis threw himself into the fortress of Gaeta. When he surrendered there with 8,000 men on February 13th, 1861, the Union of Italy was almost won. Cavour himself was not fated to see the further accomplishment of his wishes. He was attacked by a deadly illness not long after an exciting session of Parliament, in which Garibaldi heaped bitter reproaches on his head. In his delirium he dreamed of the future of his country. He spoke of Garibaldi with great respect ; he said that he longed, as much as the general, to go to Rome and Venice. He spoke with animation of the desirability of reconciling the Pope with Italy. When his confessor Giacopo handed him the sacrament on June 6th, 1861, he said to him : " Brother, brother, a free Church in a free state " (" Frate, frate, libera chiesa in libero stato "). These were his last words.

Cavour's Dying Words — No problem had engrossed the maker of Italy in the last months of his life so much as the Roman question. There was a section of his friends who considered it necessary to yield Rome to the Pope, in order that the secular power of the papacy might remain undisturbed. Such was the idea of D'Azeglio. Stefano Jacini thought that Rome, on the model of the Hanse towns, might be turned into a Free State, where the Pope might maintain his residence in the character of a protector and suzerain.

Cavour, on the contrary, was convinced that Italy without its natural capital was an incomplete structure. He would have granted the Pope the most favourable conditions if the latter would have met the wishes of the Italians. The Throne of Peter, which so many able statesmen had filled in the past, was now held by Pius IX., a child-like, religious nature, who allowed himself to be enmeshed by the irreconcilable ideas of Giacomo Antonelli and the Jesuits, and by his obstinacy proved the greatest obstacle to the union of Italy.

In spite of repeated pressure from the Emperor Napoleon, he refused to admit the introduction of reforms in the administration of the Papal States, or to conciliate **The Pope an Obstacle to Union** the national feelings of the Italians. Victor Emmanuel, even before his march into the States of the Church, professed his readiness to recognise the papal sovereignty within the old territorial limits, provided that the Curia transferred to him the vicariate over the provinces taken from it. It was an equally beneficial circumstance for the infant state that the Pope, by repudiating liberty of conscience and free political institutions in his Encyclical of December 8th, 1864, and in the Syllabus, *Syllabus complectens præcipuos nostræ ætatis errores*, outraged the sensibilities even of those Catholics who wished for the maintenance of the temporal power, but did not wish to plunge back into mediævalism. Liberal ideas would not have been able to continue their victorious progress between 1860 and 1870 in the Catholic countries of Austria, Italy, and France if the Papal Chair had not involuntarily proved their best ally.

Baron Bettino Ricasoli, the successor of Cavour, thought that he acted in his predecessor's spirit when he made dazzling proposals to the Pope, on condition that the latter should recognise the status quo. Ricasoli proposed a treaty, which not merely assured all the rights of the papal primacy, but offered Pius, as a reward for his conciliatoriness, the renunciation by the king of all his rights as patron, especially that of the appointment of the **Garibaldi Wounded in Battle** bishops. By this the Pope would have completely ruled the Church of Italy ; and that State would have been deprived of a sovereign right, which not merely Louis XIV., but Philip II. of Spain and Ferdinand II. of Austria, would never have allowed themselves to lose. In place of any answer the cardinal secretary, Antonelli, declared, in the official " Giornale di Roma," that the proposal of Ricasoli was an unparalleled effrontery.

This unfortunate attempt overthrew the Ministry of Ricasoli, and under his successor, Rattazzi, Garibaldi hoped to be able to carry out his design against Rome. He mustered his volunteers in Sicily, and landed with 2,000 men on the coast of Calabria ; but the Government was in earnest when it announced that it would oppose his enterprise by arms. Garibaldi, wounded by a bullet in the right foot, was forced to lay down his arms after a short battle at Aspromonte on August 29th, 1862. The road to Rome was not opened to the Italians until the power of France was overthrown by the victories of Germany.

THE
RE-MAKING
OF
EUROPE

THE
CONSOLIDA-
TION OF THE
POWERS V

PRUSSIA UNDER KING WILLIAM I.
AND COUNT BISMARCK'S RISE TO POWER

CAVOUR, on his death-bed, spoke unceasingly of the future of his country, and thus expressed himself about Germany : " This German Federation is an absurdity ; it will break up, and the union of Germany will be established. But the House of Hapsburg cannot alter itself. What will the Prussians do, who are so slow in coming to any conclusions ? They will need fifty years to effect what we have created in three years." This was the idea of the future which the dying statesman, to whom the name of Bismarck was still probably unknown, pictured to himself. It is quite possible that Germany, notwithstanding its efficiency and its culture, would have required, without Bismarck, another half-century for its union. King Frederic William I. had possessed an efficient army, without being able to turn it to account, as his great son did. Twice the tools

The Goal of King William I. were procured and ready before the master workman appeared on the scene who knew how to use them. We know precisely the goal which King William I. put before himself in the German question before Bismarck became his Minister. The plans which, as Prince Regent, he unfolded to the Emperor Francis Joseph at the conference at Töplitz, towards the end of July, 1860, were modest.

He was prepared to form an alliance with Austria which would have guaranteed to that country its existing dominions, thus including Venice. In return he required a change in the presidency of the German Federation as well as the command in the field over the troops of North Germany in future federal wars ; the supreme command in South Germany was to fall to Austria. Thus, for the future there would be no possibility of the Federation choosing a general for itself, as Austria had desired on June 6th, 1859, when Germany armed against Napoleon III. Prussia was bound to

prevent a majority in the Federation deciding the question of the supreme command of its army. Neither William I. nor his Ministers then aimed at the subjugation of Germany. But even those claims were rejected by Austria. Francis

The King's Work for the Army Joseph declared that the presidency in the Federation was an old prerogative of his house, and therefore unassailable. On the other matter no negative answer was returned, and negotiations were opened with the Federal Diet ; but Austria was certain that the Assembly would reject the proposition.

If we leave out of sight the army reforms, the inestimable work of William I., we shall observe, until the appearance of Bismarck on the scene, serious vacillation in the home policy no less than in the foreign policy of Prussia. When the Prince Regent became the representative of King Frederic William IV., he issued on October 9th, 1858, a programme which announced in cautious language the breach with the reactionary method of government. The avoidance of all canting piety produced a beneficial impression ; but there were only platitudes on the German question, among others the phrase : " Prussia must make moral conquests in Germany." When the Prince Regent soon afterwards summoned a Ministry of moderate Liberals, with Prince Anton von Hohenzollern at its head, public opinion breathed more freely, and the dawn of a " new era " was expected. The name of Count Maximilian Schwerin, Minister of the

Prussia in the Dawn of a " New Era " Interior, seemed to guarantee a broad-minded policy of reform. Count Alexander von Schleinitz, the Minister of Foreign Affairs, was, on the contrary, still firmly attached to the old system.

The Prussian people meantime understood the good intention, and the new elections to the Chamber brought a majority of moderate Liberals which was prepared to support the Government. A number of Liberal leaders intentionally refrained from standing, in order not to arouse in the Prince Regent misgivings lest a repetition of the state of things in 1848 was intended. The leading figure in the Chamber, which met in January, 1859, was Vincke, whose loyalty was beyond suspicion. Commendable political wisdom was shown in this moderation on the part of the constituencies. As a matter of fact, the new Government introduced schemes of reform touching the abolition of the land-tax privileges of the nobility and the abolition of the police powers of the owners of knight-estates. Great efforts were expended to induce the Upper House, where the Conservatives possessed a majority, to accept the reforms. In a matter of German politics, where the conscience of the people chimed in, the new era fulfilled the expectations formed of it. Prussia spoke boldly in the Federal Diet on behalf of the restoration of the constitution of Electoral Hesse, which had been meanly curtailed. The Government could not rise superior to these attacks. The Prince Regent was unable to bring himself to make a clean sweep of a set of unpopular high officials, who had been much to blame in the reactionary period for open violations of the laws. The revolt of Italy had a great and immediate effect on the German people. The founding of the National Society, with Rudolf von Bennigsen at its head, in July, 1859, was a direct consequence of the Italian war. The society aimed at the union of all German-speaking races outside the Austrian Empire under the leadership of a Liberal Prussia. The Regent, far from being encouraged, felt alarmed by the events in Italy; the revolutionary rising in Naples and Garibaldi's march repelled him. He could not convince himself that the national will was entitled to override legitimist rights. His whole policy, both at home and

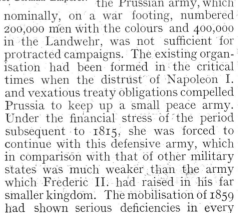

KING WILLIAM I. OF PRUSSIA
He was born in 1797, and on the death of his brother, Frederic William IV., succeeded to the throne of Prussia, being the seventh king of that country, and on January 18th, 1871, was proclaimed first German Emperor.

abroad, was thus stamped by conservatism and uncertainty. The Austrian Minister, Rechberg, at the conferences of the Emperor Francis Joseph with the Prince Regent and with the Tsar at Töplitz and Warsaw, succeeded in confirming these two monarchs in the conviction that they, too, were threatened by the national and Liberal tendencies. Austria was no longer isolated in that respect as in 1859.

All these circumstances co-operated to close the ears of the Prussian people when the king, who succeeded his brother on the throne on January 2nd, 1861, came before the Chamber with the plan of army reform. William I. was superior to the majority of his German contemporaries in recognising that a comprehensive Prussian policy could only be carried out with a strong army. Leopold von Ranke says of a conversation which he had with the king on June 13th, 1860: "The sum of his resolution was . . . to leave the German princes undisturbed in their sovereignty, but to effect a union in military matters which would conduce to a great and general efficiency. He fully grasped the idea that military power comprised in itself the sovereignty." As long before as the preparations which might have led to a war with Austria in 1850, the prince was convinced that the Prussian army, which nominally, on a war footing, numbered 200,000 men with the colours and 400,000 in the Landwehr, was not sufficient for protracted campaigns. The existing organisation had been formed in the critical times when the distrust of Napoleon I. and vexatious treaty obligations compelled Prussia to keep up a small peace army. Under the financial stress of the period subsequent to 1815, she was forced to continue with this defensive army, which in comparison with that of other military states was much weaker than the army which Frederic II. had raised in his far smaller kingdom. The mobilisation of 1859 had shown serious deficiencies in every

CORONATION CEREMONY OF KING WILLIAM I. AT KONIGSBERG, OCTOBER 18TH, 1861

direction. Besides this the Prince Regent even then, in order to remedy the most crying evils, had instituted an important reform on his own authority. Hitherto there had been few or no permanent staffs for the Landwehr regiments; so that on a fresh mobilisation the troops could not be placed in the ranks as soon as they were called out, but had first to be formed into regiments. Such a state of things seems incredible at the present day.

At the demobilisation of 1859, the Prince Regent directed that the recently formed staffs of the Landwehr regiments should be kept up. This change could not, however, go far enough; for since the members of the Landwehr were bound to be dismissed, those staffs consisted mostly of officers only, and were not sufficient to form the basis of a powerful new organisation. The attention of William I. was now directed to this point. But the War Minister of the day, Bonin, was too timid to undertake the responsibility of the necessary measures, and on December 5th, 1859, Roon had to be summoned in his place.

The new proposal came before the Prussian Diet on February 10th, 1860. One of the great drawbacks of the existing constitution of the army lay in the fact that, while annually, on the average, 155,650 men reached their twentieth year, only 20,000 men were enrolled in the army. Thus twenty-six per cent. of the young men capable of bearing arms bore the whole burden of military service, which was especially heavy, since the obligation to serve in the Landwehr lasted to the thirty-ninth year. The consequence of this was that in the first levy of the Landwehr one-half of the total numbers, and in the second levy five-sixths, were married men.

COUNT MAXIMILIAN SCHWERIN

Among the Ministry of moderate Liberals summoned by the Prince Regent in 1858 was Count Schwerin, Minister of the Interior; a "new era" was confidently anticipated, and the public looked to Schwerin for reforms.

The number of men liable to serve had remained the same for more than forty years, although the population of the country had increased from ten to eighteen millions. The obligatory period of service in the standing army, three years with the colours, two years in the reserve, was too short for the body of the army. The government therefore proposed to levy annually, instead of 40,000 men, 60,000 men—forty per cent., that is, of all those liable to serve; while in return the obligation to serve in the Landwehr was to last only to the age of thirty-five years. Besides this, the three years' service in the reserve was to be raised to five years.

This change signified a considerable strengthening of the standing army and a reduction of the Landwehr. This is shown by the figures of the full war footing which it was hoped to reach. The army was intended henceforth to consist of 371,000 men with the colours, 126,000 men in the reserve, and 163,000 in the Landwehr. The scheme demanded the attention of the Diet in two respects. On the one side a money grant was necessary, since it was impossible to enrol the numerous new corps in the old regiments, and thirty-nine new line regiments had to be raised. An annual sum, £1,350,000 sterling, was required for the purpose. Besides this, the existing law as to military service required to be considerably modified. This applied not merely to the division of the period of service between the standing army and the Landwehr, but also concerned the length of compulsory active service. At that time, in order to spare the finances, the soldiers were often dismissed after serving two or two and a half years. King William did not consider this period sufficient, and demanded the extension of the period of service to three, and in the case of the cavalry to four, years. Measures of no less importance had then been taken with regard to the tactics of the infantry. After the war of 1859, there arose the question of the conclusions to be drawn from the experiences of the Italian campaign. The defensive methods of the Austrians had proved inferior to the offensive tactics of the more dashing French. The French had often succeeded, in infantry combats, in rushing with an impetuous charge under the Austrian bullets, which had a very

Marginal heading: Reforming the Army of Prussia

curved trajectory, and in thus winning the day. For this reason it was the ordinary belief in the Austrian army that defensive tactics must once for all be given up.

The successes of the French were over-estimated, and there was a return in the years 1859–66 to "shock tactics"; these attached little importance to the preliminary musketry engagement, and con-sisted in firing a few volleys and then charging with the bayonet. Many voices even in the Prussian army advocated a similar plan. Colonel Ollech was sent by the Prussian General Staff to France in August, 1859, in order to investigate the condition of the French army. He re-turned strongly preju-diced in favour of the system of shock tactics, and advised the king to issue an order, in con-nection with a similar order issued by Frederic the Great for the cavalry, that "every infantry commander would be brought before a court-martial who lost a position without having met the attack of the enemy by a counter attack."

King William was at all times clever in discovering prominent men for leading positions. The chief of the General Staff, Lieutenant-General Helmuth von Moltke, clearly saw the risk of this advice. In his remarks on Ollech's report he laid great weight on the attacking spirit in an army; but he recognised correctly that the needle-gun, introduced in 1847, secured **Moltke's** the Prussians the advantage **Principle in** in the musketry fighting, and **Warfare** that in the reorganisation of the army stress should be laid on that point. Moltke's principle was that the infantry should make the fullest use of their superior firing power at the beginning of the battle, and should for that purpose select open country, where the effect of fire is the greatest. An advance should not be made before the enemy's infantry were shattered, and in this movement attacks on the enemy's flank were preferable. The Prussians fought in 1866 with these superior tactics, and they owed to them a great part of the successes which they

THE HISTORIAN RANKE
Professor of History at Berlin from 1825 till 1872, Leopold von Ranke was the author of many works dealing with European history.

achieved. The Prussian Landtag did not mistake the value of the proposals made by the Government, but raised weighty objections. The majority agreed to the extension of the annual recruiting, to the increase of the officers and under-officers, and to the discharge of the older members of the Landwehr. On the other hand, the great diminution in the number of the Landwehr on a war footing, and the resulting reduction of their importance, but especially the three-years' compulsory service, aroused vigorous oppo-sition. General Staven-hagen, who gave evidence for the proposal, char-acterised the two-years' service as sufficient. The Government recognised that it could not carry the Bill relating to com-pulsory service, and therefore withdrew it. It was content to demand an increase of 9,000,000 thalers — £1,350,000 sterling—in the war Budget, in order to carry out the increase of the regiments.

The Finance Minister, Baron von Patow, explained in the name of the Government that the organisation thus created was provisional, and would not assume a definite character until the Government and the popular representatives had agreed about the law itself. The Old Liberal majority of the Chamber of Representatives adopted this middle course, and sanctioned the required increase. Thus the yearly budget for the army was raised to 32,800,000 thalers—£4,920,000 sterling, or, roughly, a quarter of the entire revenue of 130,000,000 thalers—£19,500,000 sterling.

This expedient was manifestly illusory. The king at once ordered the disbanding of thirty-six regiments of Landwehr, whose place was taken by an equal number of line regiments. Altogether 117 new battalions and twelve new squadrons were formed. Obviously the king, who presented colours and badges to the new regiments on January 18th, 1861, in front of the monument of Frederic the Great, could not disband these newly formed units or dismiss their officers. The Chamber of Representatives became, in fact, suspicious, but agreed to the

5055

increased army budget once more for the next year. Since the elections to the Landtag were imminent, the final decision stood over for the new House.

It would be a mistake to treat the events which followed in the ordinary manner, relating how the king was prudent but the Chamber petty in the army question, and how in this struggle the wisdom of the Regent fortunately prevailed over the meddlesomeness of the professional politicians. The state of affairs was quite otherwise. The dispute in the matter itself was not indeed beyond settlement. In case of necessity it would have been possible to arrive at a compromise as to the amount of compulsory service, and the Prussian army would hardly have been less effective if the two-years' military service had been introduced then and not postponed until after the death of Emperor William I. This consideration does not in any way lessen the credit due to the king.

But, as the new elections showed, there was another and greater issue at stake. The influence of Liberal ideas in Europe was precisely then at its height, and public opinion tended towards the view that the royal power in Prussia must be checked, exactly as it had been in that model parliamentary state, England. The citizen class had then, it was thought, come to years of maturity, and it possessed a right to take the place of the monarchy and nobility in the power hitherto enjoyed by them. At the new elections, on December 6th, 1861, the Progressive party, in which the members of the movement of 1848 assumed the lead, was formed in opposition to the Old Liberals, who had left their stamp on the former Chamber. This political group had not yet the whole electorate on its side ; it carried a hundred seats, barely a third of the whole Assembly. The Old Liberals felt themselves meanwhile outstripped, especially since the king no longer extended his confidence to

FIELD - MARSHAL ROON
Entering the Prussian army in 1821, he revealed a thorough grasp of military matters, and his reorganisation of the army found brilliant justification in the success of the national arms in the wars of 1866 and 1870-1.
From a photograph

the Liberal Ministers, who were defeated on the army question. While this change was being effected among the citizen class, the nobility and the Conservative party on the other hand, who had been greatly chagrined at being dismissed from the helm of state after the assumption of the regency by the prince, put forward their claim not less resolutely. The great services of the Prussian nobility to the army and the civil service, to which, both before and after, it supplied first - class men, could not, of course, be disputed. But to justifiable pride at this fact was joined such intense class prejudice that even a man like Roon could not for a long time bring himself to recognise the justification of an elected representation of the people. General Manteuffel, as chief of the royal military cabinet, worked with him in the same spirit. Ernst von Gerlach and Hermann Wagener represented in the " Kreuzeitung " similar views. Karl Twesten, one of the most prominent members of the Liberal party, called General Manteuffel a mischievous man in a mischievous position—a taunt which Manteuffel answered by a challenge to a duel, in which Twesten was wounded.

The Liberal Ministers saw with concern how the king inclined more and more towards the paths of the Conservative party. They counselled him, in **Roon's Advice to the King** view of the impending struggle over the military question, to conciliate public opinion by undertaking reforms in various departments of the legislature. Roon vigorously opposed this advice, which he saw to be derogatory to the Crown. He induced the king on March 1st, 1861, to adjourn these Bills, which had already been settled upon. He unceasingly urged the king to dismiss his Liberal colleagues and to adopt strong measures. In a memorial laid before the king, dated April, 1861, he wrote of the Hohenzollern-Schwerin

Cabinet, in which, nevertheless, he himself had accepted a seat, that "it is only compatible with the pseudo-monarchy of Belgium, England, or of Louis Philippe, not with a genuinely Prussian monarchy by the grace of God, with a monarchy according to your ideas. People have tried to intimidate your Majesty by the loud outcry of the day. All the unfortunate monarchs of whom history tells have so fared; the phantom ruined them, simply because they believed in it."

Prussian Conservatives in Power The opposition was apparent as soon as the new Chamber assembled on January 14th, 1862. Opponents of the proposal were elected on the commission for discussing the Army Bill in a large majority. When the Budget was discussed, a resolution was adopted which called for more precise details of the state finances. This was a reasonable demand, and was soon afterwards conceded by Bismarck. But the Conservative advisers of the king then stigmatised the wish as an encroachment on the rights of the Crown, and the Chamber of Representatives was dissolved on March 18th, 1862, after a short term of life. At the same time the Liberal Ministry was dismissed. Its place was taken by a Cabinet in which officials preponderated, but which, on the whole, bore a Conservative character. It is certainly to the credit of Roon and Manteuffel that their influence on the king paved the way for Bismarck. But they made the beginning of his term of office more difficult for the great Minister, since he was at once drawn into the most violent antagonism to popular representation. The question must be raised whether Prussia, with her great military and intellectual superiority, would not have obtained the same results if there had been no such rupture with public opinion. The Crown Prince Frederic William held this view, and it was shared not only by Albert, the English Prince

CROWN PRINCE FREDERIC
The only son of William I., he married Victoria, Princess Royal of England, in 1858. A man of courage, he opposed the reactionary policy of Bismarck, and fought with distinction in the various wars waged by Prussia.
From a photograph

Consort, but also by the king's son-in-law, the Grand Duke Frederic of Baden, who just then was reforming his country with the help of the Liberal Ministers, Baron Franz von Roggenbach and Karl Mathy. Men of a similar type would have gladly co-operated to help King William to gain the imperial crown. King William himself felt that, in consequence of his quarrel with the Chamber, many sincere friends of Prussia were mistaken as to his country's German mission. This point was emphasised even in the National Assembly.

In order to counteract this tendency, the king had appointed Bernstorff, who advocated the union of Germany under the leadership of Prussia, to be Minister of Foreign Affairs in the place of Schleinitz, who held legitimist views. Bernstorff adopted, in fact, most vigorous measures, when several states of the German Zollverein, on the conclusion of the Free-Trade commercial treaty with France, threatened that they would in consequence withdraw from the Zollverein. They found a supporter in Austria, who would gladly have broken up the Zollverein; but they were forced to yield to Prussia, since their own economic interests dictated their continuance in the Zollverein. Bernstorff furthermore, in a note addressed to the German courts on December 20th, 1861, announced as a programme the claim of Prussia to the leadership of Lesser Germany. By this step the Berlin Cabinet reverted to the policy of union which had been given up in 1850. The party of Greater Germany collected its forces in opposition. Austria resolved to anticipate Prussia by a tangible proposition to the Diet, and proposed federal reforms: that a directory with corresponding central authority should be established, and by its side an assembly of delegates from the popular representatives of the several states. But, before this proposal should be agreed to, steps were to be taken to elaborate a common system of civil procedure and contract law for the whole of Germany. Both the Prussian note and the Austrian proposal met with opposition and a dissentient majority in the Federal Diet at Frankfort, for the secondary states did not wish to relinquish any part of their sovereignty in favour of either the Prussian or the Austrian Government. The necessary condition for the success of the Prussian policy would have been a majority in a German Parliament on the side of Prussia, as in 1849. But Bernstorff, although in his heart he favoured the plan, could not advise the king to summon a National Assembly, because, as things then stood, its majority would have approved of the opposition of the Prussian progressive party.

Ascendancy of Radical Liberalism

In the new elections to the Chamber of Representatives Radical Liberalism gained the greatest number of seats. The two sections of this party numbered together 235 members—two-thirds, that is, of the 352 representatives of the Landtag; the Old Liberals under the leadership of Vincke had dwindled to 23 votes. The new majority gladly accepted the challenge flung to them; for the idea, which Roon had erroneously termed the ultimate goal even of the moderate Liberals, was actively dominant among them. They wished for no compromise, but aimed at the subordination of the king to the Parliament. The examples of England and Belgium dominated their plans in every detail.

The army question became the outward pretext on which the two constitutional theories came into conflict with each other. Since the king did not concede the two years' compulsory service, which the Chamber demanded as a condition of the army reform, the House resolved, on September 23rd, 1862, to strike out entirely the costs of the reform, which was tantamount to disbanding the new regiments. In this way a humiliation was laid on the king, which was intended to bend or break him.

The Bold Stand of the King

King William was resolved rather to lay down the Crown than to submit to a compulsion by which, according to his view, he would have been degraded to the position of a puppet ruler. He seriously contemplated this step, when the Ministry of Hohenlohe, seeing no way out of the difficulty, asked to be dismissed.

The king doubted whether men would be found bold enough to confront the Chamber of Representatives. Whenever Roon and Manteuffel had formerly spoken of Bismarck, the king had hesitated to entrust the government to a man whom he considered to be a hot-head. Now, he told Roon, Bismarck would no longer entertain any wish to be at the head of affairs; besides that, he happened to be on leave, travelling in Southern France.

Roon, however, could assure the king that Bismarck, who had been already recalled, was prepared to enter the service of the king. Soon afterwards the latter learned that Bismarck had, immediately on his return, paid a visit, by invitation, to the Crown Prince. King William's suspicions were aroused by this, and he thought, " There is nothing to be done with him; he has already been to my son."

All doubts, however, were dissipated when Bismarck appeared before him and unfolded his scheme of government. The king showed him the deed of abdication, which he had already drafted, because, so he said, he could not find another Ministry. Bismarck encouraged him by the assurance that he intended to stand by him in the struggle between the supremacy of the Crown and of Parliament. On the day when the Chamber of Representatives passed the resolution by which the monarch felt himself most deeply wounded, on September 23rd, 1862, the nomination of Bismarck as President of the Ministry was published.

Bismarck's Rise to Power

Bismarck's work is the establishment of the unity of Germany no less than the revival of the power of the monarchy and of all conservative forces in that country. His contemporaries have passed judgment upon him according to their political attitudes. Those who regarded the advancing democratisation of Great Britain and France as equally desirable for Germany, and as the ultimate goal of its development, were bound to see an opponent in the powerful statesman. A difficult legal question was put before Bismarck at the very outset of his activity. He counselled the king to disregard the Budget rights of the Chamber of Representatives.

For the historical estimate of Bismarck it is not of primary importance whether the constitutional arguments which he employed on this occasion are tenable or not; this legal question must certainly be decided against him. He took his stand on the ground that the Budget was, according to the constitution, a law on which the Crown, the Upper Chamber, and the Chamber of Representatives must agree ; and that the authors of the Prussian constitution had on this point reversed the practice of England, where money grants are exclusively the province of the Lower House. They had not provided for the event that the three might not be able to agree and the law could thus not be passed ; there was therefore an omission. But since the state could not stand still, a constitutional deadlock had resulted, which would be fatal unless the Budget for the year were provided by the arbitrary action of the Crown.

The consequence of this theory was that the Crown could enforce all the larger Budget demands, even though the two Chambers had pronounced in favour of the smaller sum. From this point of view every theory turned on the exercise of the powers of the constitutional authorities. In the great speech in which the Prussian Minister-President **Bismarck's** explained his views, he con-**Dangerous** fronted the Chamber with his **Declaration** political principles : " The Prussian monarchy has not yet fulfilled its mission ; it is not yet ripe to form a purely ornamental decoration of the fabric of your constitution, nor to be incorporated into the mechanism of parliamentary rule as an inanimate piece of the machinery." Even the king wavered for a moment when Bismarck in the Budget commission of the Chamber of Representatives, September 30th, 1862, made his famous assertion that " the union of Germany could not be effected by speeches, societies, and the resolutions of majorities ; a grave struggle was necessary, a struggle that could only be carried through by blood and iron." Even Roon considered this phrase as dangerous.

The state was administered for four years without a constitutionally settled Budget. The Chamber of Representatives declared this procedure illegal, and great excitement prevailed throughout the country. In order to suppress the opposition, strict enactments were published on June 1st, 1863, which were directed against the freedom of the Press and of the societies. At this period the Crown Prince Frederic William joined the opponents of Bismarck, because he thought the procedure of the Ministers might provoke a new revolution in Prussia. He made a speech on June 5th, in the town hall at Danzig when receiving the municipal authorities, which was directed against the Government : " I, too, regret that I have come here at a time when a quarrel, of which I have been in the highest **The Crown** degree surprised to hear, **Prince Criticises** has broken out between **Bismarck** the Government and the people. I know nothing of the enactments which have brought about this result." The Crown Prince at the same time sent a memorandum to the king to the same effect ; but on June 30th he wrote to the Minister-President a letter full of indignation and contempt, which would have shaken the resolution of any other man than Bismarck : "Do you believe that you can calm men's minds by continual outrages on the feeling of legality ? I regard the men who lead his Majesty the king, my most gracious father, into such paths as the most dangerous counsellors for Crown and country."

The king was deeply hurt at the public appearances of his son ; he contemplated harsh measures against him, and Bismarck was compelled to dissuade him from his purpose. The Minister reminded the king that in the quarrel between Frederic William I. and his son the sympathy of the times, as well as of posterity, had been with the son ; and he showed the inadvisability of making the Crown Prince a martyr. Thus the situation in Prussia seemed to be strained to the breaking point. The Representative Chamber adopted in 1863, by a large majority, the resolution that Ministers should be liable out of their private fortune for any expenditure beyond the Budget.

It is marvellous with what independence and intellectual vigour Bismarck guided foreign policy in the midst of these commotions. We need only examine the pages **Prussia's** of history from 1850 to 1862 **Place** to find clearly how little **in History** Prussia counted as a European Power. It played, in consequence of the vacillation of Frederic William IV., a feeble rôle, especially at the time of the Crimean War. Even later, when William I. was governing the country as prince regent and as king, Cavour, who was continually forced to rack his brains with the possibilities which might effect a change in the policy of France and

Austria, Great Britain and Russia, hardly took Prussia into consideration. That state, during the Italian crisis of 1860, had little more weight than a Power of the second rank—only about as much as Spain, of which it was occasionally said that it would strengthen or relieve the French garrison in Rome with its troops.

Bismarck an Object of Ridicule Great as are the services of King William to the army and the State of Prussia, he could not have attained such great successes without a man like Bismarck. Considering the feebleness of Prussia, which had been the object of ridicule for years, every one was, at first, surprised by the vigorous language of Bismarck. When, in one of the earliest Cabinet councils, he broached the idea that Prussia must watch for an opportunity of acquiring Schleswig-Holstein, the Crown Prince raised his hands to heaven, as if the orator had uttered some perfectly foolish thing, and the clerk who recorded the proceedings thought he would be doing a favour to Bismarck if he omitted the words ; the latter was obliged to make the additional entry in his own writing.

The newspapers and political tracts of that time almost entirely ridicule the attitude of the new Minister, whom no one credited with either the serious intention or the strength to carry out his programme. His contemporaries were therefore only confirmed in their contempt for him when, on November 26th, 1862, he suddenly ended the constitutional struggle in Electoral Hesse, which had lasted several decades, by sending an orderly to the Elector Frederic William, with the peremptory command that he should give back to the country the constitution of 1831.

And now came his amazing conversation with the Austrian Ambassador, Count Aloys Karolyi. Austria, shortly before, without coming to terms with Prussia, had brought before the Assembly in Frankfort the pro-

Bombshell of the "Terrible" Bismarck posal already mentioned for federal reform. Bismarck, in that conversation, taunted Austria with having deviated from the method of Prince Metternich, who came to a previous arrangement with Prussia as to all measures concerning German affairs ; and he declared to the count that Austria would soon have to choose between the alternatives of vacating Germany and shifting its political centre to the east, or of finding Prussia in the

next war on the side of its opponents. This assertion fell like a bombshell on Vienna. Count Rechberg was not so wrong when he talked of the "terrible" Bismarck, who was capable of doing anything for the greatness of Prussia.

The two great parties in Germany were organised at the precise moment when Bismarck entered upon office. A Diet of representatives from the different German Parliaments, which was attended by some 200 members, met at Weimar on September 28th, 1862. This assembly demanded the summons of a German Parliament by free popular election, and the preliminary concentration of non-Austrian Germany ; to begin with, at any rate, Austria would have to remain outside the more restricted confederation. This assembly and the activity of the National Society led on the other side to the formation of the Greater Germany Reform Society, which came into existence at Frankfort. It demanded a stricter consolidation of the German states under the leadership of Austria. The narrow particularism of the princes and their

The Greater Germany Movement immediate followers, who were unwilling to sacrifice for the welfare of the whole body any of the sovereignty of the individual states, kept aloof from these efforts. Their underlying thought was expressed by the Hanoverian Minister, Otto, Count Borries, who, when opposing the efforts of the National Society on May 1st, 1860, went so far as to threaten that the secondary states would be forced into non-German alliances in order to safeguard their independence.

The Greater Germany movement gained adherents not merely by the constitutional struggle in Prussia but also by the movement towards liberalism in Austria. The absolute monarchy, which had ruled in Austria since 1849, ended with a defeat on the battlefield and the most complete financial disorder. The pressure of the harsh police regulations weighed all the more heavily, as the state organs, since the conclusion of the concordat with Rome, were put equally at the service of ecclesiastical purposes. The discontent of every nationality in the empire impelled the emperor, after Solferino, June 24th, 1859, to make a complete change. It would have been the natural course of proceedings if the emperor had at once resolved to consolidate the unity of the

Empire, which had been regained in 1849, by summoning a General Parliament. But the Crown, and still more the aristocracy, were afraid that in this imperial representation the German bourgeoisie would come forward with excessive claims. For this reason an aristocratic interlude followed. Count Goluchowski, a Pole, hitherto Governor of Galicia, became Minister of the Interior on August 21st, 1859, while Count Rechberg, who had already succeeded Count Buol as Minister of the Interior and of the Imperial House on May 17th, was given the post of President.

The administrative business of the entire monarchy was, by the imperial manifesto of October 20th, 1860, concentrated in a new body, the National Ministry, at whose head Goluchowski was placed, while the conduct of Hungarian affairs was entrusted to Baron Nikolaus Bay and Count Nikolaus Szécsen ; at the same time orders were issued that the provincial councils—Landtage—and a council of the empire elected from them—Reichsrat—should be summoned. These bodies were, however, only to have a **Hungary on the Verge of Rebellion** deliberative voice ; and besides that, a preponderant influence in the provincial bodies was assigned to the nobility and the clergy. It was a still more decisive step that the members of the conservative Hungarian haute noblesse, in their aversion to German officialism, induced the emperor once more to entrust the administration of Hungary and the choice of officials to the assemblies of nobles, known as " county courts," as had been the case before the year 1848. These measures produced a totally different result from that anticipated by Bay and Szécsen.

The meetings of the county courts, which had not been convened since 1849, were filled with a revolutionary spirit, and, while offering at once the most intense opposition, refused to carry out the enactments of the Ministers, because, so they alleged, the constitutionally elected Reichstag was alone entitled to sanction taxation ; and they chose officials who refused to collect taxes, or only did so in a dilatory fashion. The country in a few months bordered on a state of rebellion.

As the Hungarian Ministers of the emperor had plunged the Empire into this confusion, they were compelled to advise him to entrust a powerful personality from the ranks of the high German officials

with the conduct of affairs. Anton von Schmerling was nominated Minister of Finance on December 17th, 1860, in the place of Goluchowski. He won over the emperor to his view, which was unfavourable to the Hungarians, and carried his point as to maintaining one united constitution and the summoning **The Magyars' Expectations of Independence** of a central parliament. He proposed also that a limited scope should be conceded to the diets of the individual provinces. These were the fundamental principles of the constitution granted on February 26th, 1861. Schmerling deserves credit for having restored the prestige of the constitution in Hungary without bloodshed, even if severe measures were used.

The county assemblies were dissolved, and trustworthy native officials substituted for them. The vacillation of the emperor in 1860 strengthened, however, the conviction of the Magyars that in the end the Crown would yield to their opposition, and once more concede the independence of Hungary in the form in which it was won by the constitution of April, 1848. The leadership of this opposition in the Landtag summoned in 1861 was taken by Franz Deák ; the Landtag, in the address which was agreed upon, refused to send representatives to the central Parliament, and complete independence was demanded for Hungary.

Schmerling advanced unhesitatingly on the road which he had taken. At the same time he won great influence over the management of German affairs, and for some period was more powerful in that sphere than the Minister of the Exterior, Count Rechberg. The latter considered it prudent to remain on good terms with Prussia, and not to stir up the German question. Schmerling, on the other hand, put higher aims before himself, and wished to give Germany the desired federal reform, and to strengthen Austria's influence in Germany by the estab-**Austria's Influence in Germany** lishment of a strong central power in Frankfort. He hoped to overcome the resistance of Prussia by help of the popular feeling in non-Prussian Germany. He enlisted confidence in Germany also by the introduction of constitutional forms in Austria. Austria tried to sweep the German princes along with her in one bold rush. The emperor, in deference to a suggestion of his brother-in-law, Maximilian, the hereditary prince of Thurn and Taxis, resolved to summon all German princes to a conference at Frankfort-on-Main, and to lay before them his plan of reform. The King of Prussia in this matter was not treated differently from the pettiest and weakest of the Federal princes. The emperor communicated his intention to King William at their meeting in Gastein on August 2nd, 1863, and, without waiting for the stipulated written decision of the king, handed him by an adjutant on August 3rd the formal invitation to the Diet of Princes summoned for August 16th.

The blow aimed by Austria led to a temporary success. Public opinion in South Germany was aroused, and in some places became enthusiastic ; the sovereigns and princes gave their services to the Austrian reform. All this made a deep impression on King William ; the Bavarian queen, Marie, and her sister-in-law, the widow of King Frederic William IV., urged him on his journey from Gastein to Baden-Baden to show a conciliatory attitude towards the Austrian proposal. Nevertheless he followed Bismarck's advice, and kept away from the meeting at Frankfort. The Emperor Francis Joseph made his entry into the Free Town amid the pealing of the bells and the acclamations of the inhabitants, who favoured the Austrian cause. He skilfully presided over the debate of the princes, and King John of Saxony, 1854–1873, an experienced man of business and an eloquent speaker, confuted the protests which were preferred by a small minority. The Grand Duke Frederic Francis II. of Mecklenburg-Schwerin proposed to invite King William to make the journey to Frankfort. King John assented,

KING JOHN OF SAXONY
Under this king, who reigned from 1854 till 1873, and who was distinguished for learning and culture, many schemes for the betterment of the people of Saxony were introduced, while the army was reformed.

ANTON VON SCHMERLING
Minister of Finance, he restored the prestige of the constitution in Hungary without bloodshed.

but made two additional proposals, which were not quite friendly to Prussia. He first induced the meeting to declare that it considered the Austrian proposals suitable as a basis for reform ; and it was also soon settled that the refusal of the King of Prussia was no obstacle to further deliberation. After these resolutions, which were taken on August 18th, King John went to Baden-Baden, in order to take the invitation to the King of Prussia.

King William did not seem disinclined to accept the invitation, and said to Bismarck : " Thirty princes sending the invitation, and a king as Cabinet messenger, how can there be any refusal ? " But Bismarck saw that this surprise, planned by Austria, was a blow aimed at Prussia, and he would have felt deeply humiliated by the appearance of his monarch at Frankfort. Germany was to see that any alteration of the German constitution must prove abortive from the mere opposition of Prussia. Bismarck required all his strength of will to induce William to refuse ; he declared that if the king commanded him, he would go with him to Frankfort, but that when the business was ended he would never return with him to Berlin as Minister. The king, therefore, took his advice. What Bismarck had foreseen now occurred. It is true that the Austrian proposal was in the end discussed and accepted, against the votes of Baden, Schwerin, Weimar, Luxemburg, Waldeck, and the younger line of Reuss. But since the meeting only pledged itself in the event of an agreement with Prussia as the basis of these resolutions, Austria had failed in the achievement of her main result.

PRUSSIA & AUSTRIA ON THE EVE OF WAR
THE FATE OF SCHLESWIG-HOLSTEIN

ALL these debates and intrigues between Prussia and Austria sank into the background when the fate of Schleswig-Holstein was destined to be decided by arms. The occasion for this was given by the death of the Danish king, Frederic VII., on November 15th, 1863, with whom the main line of the royal house became extinct. The collateral line of Holstein-Glücksburg possessed the hereditary right to Denmark, while the House of Augustenburg raised claims to Schleswig-Holstein. All Germany thought that the moment had come to free Schleswig-Holstein from the Danish rule by supporting the Duke of Augustenburg. The two great German Powers were, however, pledged in another direction by the Treaty of London.

Denmark had expressly engaged by that arrangement to grant Schleswig-Holstein an independent government; on this **Denmark's Claim on the Duchies** basis the Great Powers on their side guaranteed the possession of the duchies to the King of Denmark and all his successors. The two great German Powers were to blame for having compelled the inhabitants of Schleswig-Holstein in 1850 to submit to Denmark. From hatred of Liberalism and all the mistakes it was supposed to have made in 1848, they destroyed any hopes which the inhabitants of Schleswig-Holstein might have formed for the future, after the royal house should have become extinct. Duke Christian of Augustenburg sold his hereditary rights to Denmark for 2,250,000 thalers—£500,000—although his son Frederic protested. But Denmark did not think of fulfilling her promise. The German Federation was content for years to remonstrate and propose a court of arbitration. Finally, the Federal Council resolved on armed intervention against Denmark. Hanoverian and Saxon troops occupied Holstein, but they were forced to halt on the Eider, as Schleswig did not belong to the Federation.

In Copenhagen the Eider-Danish party drew peculiar conclusions from these circumstances; since, they said, Schleswig did not belong to the Federation, the Treaty of London might be disregarded, the bond between Schleswig and Holstein **Duke Frederic and His Supporters** dissolved, and Schleswig, at any rate, amalgamated into the unified State of Denmark. Threatening crowds forced the new monarch, Christian IX., in spite of his superior insight, to consent to the united constitution. The Treaty of London was to all intents and purposes broken.

The claim of Duke Frederic of Augustenburg to Schleswig-Holstein was thus unanimously applauded by the popular voice of Germany. He declared himself ready to follow loyally the democratic constitution which the duchies had given themselves in 1848, and surrounded his person with liberal counsellors. A large proportion of the governments of the petty German states recognised the duke as the heir, and the majority of the Federal Council decided in his favour.

Prussia and Austria, indeed, as signatories of the Treaty of London, felt themselves bound by it towards Europe. They possessed, according to it, the right to compel Denmark to grant to the duchies independence and union under one sovereign; but they could exempt themselves from recognising the hereditary right of King Christian IX. Austria in particular, whose stability rested on European treaties, did not venture to admit that the right of nationality could undo those treaties. **Prussia Against the Powers** Was Prussia able to confront the other Great Powers with her unaided resources? Bismarck, with all his determination, thought such a move too dangerous. The stake in such a struggle would have been too trivial; for, as Bismarck showed the Prussian House of Representatives, Prussia would have lent its arms to establish the claims of a duke who, like the other petty states, would have mostly voted with Austria at Frankfort. "The signing of the Treaty of London," so Bismarck said on December 1st, 1863, in the Prussian House of Representatives, "may. be deplored ; but it has been done, and honour as well as prudence commands that our loyal observance of the treaty be beyond all doubt." These reasons did not, however, convince the House. It pronounced in favour of the hereditary right of the Duke of Augustenburg. Bismarck vainly put before the Opposition that, as soon as Prussia abandoned the basis of the Treaty of London, no pretext whatever could be found for interfering in Schleswig, which stood entirely outside the German Confederation.

KING FREDERIC VII.
King of Denmark from 1848, his tyrannous rule in Schleswig-Holstein was bitterly resented, and by his death, in 1863, the main line of the royal house became extinct.

The violent opposition of the House of Representatives to Bismarck's methods was due to the fact that the Conservative party, to which Bismarck had belonged, had in 1849 and 1850 condemned the rebellion of Schleswig-Holstein against Denmark ; and there was the fear that the supporters of legitimacy would once more in the end make the duchies subject to Denmark. As a matter of fact, the two great German Powers had tolerated the infringements of the Treaty of London by Denmark since 1852, and had not contributed at all to preserve the rights of the duchies. This explains the blame laid upon the two Great Powers by the committee of an assembly of representatives at Frankfort on December 21st, 1863, in an address to the German people. For twelve years, it said, the Danes had been allowed to trample under foot the Treaty of London. Now, with the extinction of the royal house, and the revival of the hereditary right of

KING CHRISTIAN IX.
He succeeded to the throne of Denmark in 1863, on the death of Frederic VII. His eldest daughter, Alexandra, married King Edward VII. of Great Britain and Ireland.
From a photograph

Augustenburg, the possibility had come of getting rid of the shameful treaty. "Now, when the execution of that treaty would be fatal to the cause of the duchies, armies were being put into the field in order to enforce its execution." This reproach against the Prussian policy

would have been justified if Bismarck had still been, as he was in 1848, a man of exclusively Conservative party politics. The German people could not know that he had become a far greater man. He had now fixed his eye on the acquisition of the duchies by Prussia, and steered steadily towards that goal which King William still considered unattainable. Just now he won a great diplomatic triumph. Austria, on the question of the duchies, was divided from the German minor states, her allies, and Bismarck widened the breach. He explained to the Vienna Cabinet that Prussia was resolved to compel Denmark to respect the Treaty of London by force of arms, and, if necessary, single-handed. Austria now could not and dared not leave the liberation of Schleswig to her rival alone, otherwise she would have voluntarily abdicated her position in Germany. Rechberg, who in any case was favourably disposed to the alliance with Prussia, induced his master, under the circumstances, to conclude the armed alliance with Prussia ; Francis Joseph was, however, disappointed that the Diet at Frankfort and the anti-Prussian policy had borne no fruits. The two Great Powers pledged themselves in the treaty of January 16th, 1864, to attack Denmark, and settled that after the liberation of the duchies no decision should be taken about them except by the agreement of the two Powers. Austria thus felt protected against surprises on the part of Prussia. The treaty met with the most violent opposition both in the Prussian and the Austrian representative assemblies. The money for the conduct of the war was actually refused in Berlin. The Austrian Chamber did not proceed to such extreme measures, but the majority held it to be a mistake that Austria adopted a hostile position against the minor states, and neglected the opportunity to make a friend of the future Duke of Schleswig-Holstein.

The army to conquer Schleswig consisted of 37,000 Prussians and 23,000 Austrians, who were opposed by 40,000 Danes. The supreme command of the invading force was held by Count Wrangel. The Danes hoped to the last for foreign help, but the threats of England to the German Powers were smoke without a fire. The Danes first attempted resistance along the Danewerk. But the Austrians in the battles of Jagel and Okerselk, on February 3rd, stormed the outposts in front of the redoubts and pursued the Danes right under the cannons of the Danewerk. Since there was the fear that the strong position would be turned by the Prussians below Missunde, the Danish general, De Meza, evacuated the Danewerk on February 5th, and withdrew northwards. The Austrians followed quickly and came up with the Danes the next day at Oeversee, and compelled them to fight for their retreat. Schleswig was thus conquered with the exception of a small peninsula on the east, where the lines of Düppel were raised, which were in touch with the island of Alsen and the powerful Danish fleet. Prussia proposed then to force the Danes to conclude peace by an investment of Jütland. The Austrian Cabinet could not at first entertain this plan. General Manteuffel, who was sent to Vienna, only carried his point when Prussia gave a promise that Schleswig-Holstein should not be wrested from the suzerainty of the Danish crown; on the contrary, the independent duchies were to be united with

FREDERIC VII. OF DENMARK AND HIS CONSORT
From a photograph

Denmark by a personal union. The allies thereupon conquered Jütland as far as the Liim Fiord, and by storming the lines of Düppel, on April 18th, the Prussian arms won a brilliant success, and the blockade of the mouths of the Elbe was relieved by the sea-fight of Heligoland on May 9th, 1864.

The future of the duchies was now the question. Popular opinion in Germany protested loudly against their restoration to the Danish king, and Bismarck now fed the flame of indignation, since he wished to release Prussia from the promise she had made. But he would not have attained this object had not the Danes, fortunately for Germany, remained obstinate. A conference of the Powers concerned met in London on April 25th, 1864. The Danish plenipotentiaries, still hoping for British support, rejected on May 17th the proposal of Prussia and Austria for the constitutional independence of the duchies, even should their possession be intended for their King Christian. The matter was thus definitely decided. Austria was now compelled to retire from the agreement last made with Prussia. The Vienna Cabinet, making a virtue of necessity, resolved to prevent Schleswig-Holstein from falling to Prussia by nominating the Duke of Augustenburg. King William had long been inclined to this course, if only Duke Frederic was willing to make some arrangement with Prussia about his army, as Coburg had already done; if he would grant Prussia a naval station and allow the North Sea Canal to be constructed; and if the duchies entered the Zollverein. The duke would certainly have agreed to these terms in order to obtain the sovereignty had not Austria on its side made more favourable promises. There was a strong wish at Vienna to prevent Schleswig-Holstein becoming a vassal state of Prussia. The duke, encouraged by this, promised the king indeed to observe those conditions, but he added the qualification that he could not know whether the Estates of Schleswig-Holstein would assent to the treaty. If not, he was ready to withdraw in favour of his son.

This additional proviso filled Bismarck with misgivings; for the farce might be repeated which had been played before, when Duke Christian of Augustenburg sold his claims to Denmark, and his son Frederic then came forward with his hereditary right to Schleswig-Holstein. The determination of the Prussian Prime Minister not to give in until the countries were incorporated into Prussia grew stronger day by day. The first step in that direction was the conclusion of peace with Denmark on October 30th, 1864; the two duchies were unconditionally resigned to Austria and Prussia, without any consideration being paid to the hereditary claims of the Houses of Augustenburg and Oldenburg. Bismarck did not want to break with Austria yet. He was sorry, therefore, to see that Count Rechberg retired on October 27th, 1864, from his office as Minister of the Exterior ; the charge was brought against him in Austria that the policy of alliance with Prussia which he followed was to the advantage of the latter state only. His successor, Count Alexander Mensdorff, had, it is true, the same aims as Rechberg ; but since he was less experienced in affairs, the opponents of Prussia gained more and more influence among his higher officials. This circumstance was the more mischievous since the two Great Powers were administering the duchies jointly—an arrangement which in any case led to

DUKE OF AUGUSTENBURG
On the death of the Danish King in 1863, the Duke of Augustenburg raised claims to the duchies of Schleswig-Holstein, but by the war of 1864 these went to Prussia and Austria.
From a photograph

friction. In February, 1865, Prussia came forward with the conditions under which she was willing to nominate the Duke of Augustenburg to Schleswig-Holstein. They contained in substance what had already been communicated to the duke. But Austria did not agree to them. Weight was laid in Vienna on the argument that the German Confederation was a union of sovereign princes, and no vassal state of Prussia could be allowed to take its place in it.

Prussia thereupon adopted stricter measures and shifted her naval base from Danzig to Kiel. Bismarck then openly declared, " If Austria wishes to remain our ally, she must make room for us." The war cloud even then loomed ominously. The Berlin Cabinet inquired at Florence whether Italy was prepared to join the alliance. The two German Powers still, however, shrank from a passage at arms immediately after a jointly conducted campaign. The result of prolonged negotiations was the Treaty of Gastein on August 14th, 1865. The administration of the duchies, hitherto carried on in common, was divided, so that Nearer Holstein was left to Austria, and Further Schleswig to Prussia. Lauenburg was ceded absolutely to Prussia for 2,250,000 thalers— £500,000. Prussia was clearly advancing on a victorious career, and the acquisition of the duchies was in near prospect. The Prussian Representative Chamber, which eighteen months previously had spoken distinctly for the hereditary right of the Duke of Augustenburg, once more in the summer of 1865 debated the affair. But now the friends of the scheme of incorporation were already so numerous that it could no longer agree to a resolution by a majority. It was seen that the foreign policy of the Progressives in Prussia had been wrecked. The king, as a recognition of his services, raised Bismarck to the rank of count, September 15th, and thus proclaimed to the outside world that he had absolute confidence in his conduct of affairs. Bismarck called the Treaty of Gastein a patching of the crack in the building. In reality the Premier had long determined on a war with Austria. Since Austria favoured the partisans of the Duke of Augustenburg as much as ever, and afforded opportunity for their agitations against Prussia, the Prussian note of January 26th, 1866, complained of the "means of rebellion" which Austria employed. It was announced in this document that Prussia claimed henceforward complete liberty for her policy. Bismarck still kept the door of peace open to himself, in case Austria was willing to withdraw from Schleswig-Holstein. But the course of proceedings at the Prussian Cabinet Council of February 28th, 1866, shows that the king was familiar with the idea of war. The Minister-President developed at this council the **The Austrian Emperor Dissatisfied** thought that no war was to be kindled for the sake of Schleswig-Holstein only ; a greater goal, the union of Germany, must be contemplated. It was resolved, first of all, to open negotiations with Italy for a defensive and offensive alliance. In this council of war, Moltke gave his unqualified vote for the war, while the Crown Prince uttered an emphatic warning against such a policy, for the reason that it rendered

probable the interference of foreigners. An important change had occurred in Austria in July, 1865. Schmerling had failed to win the emperor over permanently to his political views. Francis Joseph was dissatisfied because the Parliament raised excessive claims to a share in the government, and went too **Moltke in Favour of War** far in reducing the war Budget. The Austrian and Hungarian aristocracy joined the opponents of the united constitution, and Count Moritz Esterházy, Minister without portfolio since July 19th, 1861, used the dissatisfaction of the emperor to undermine the German Cabinet. On July 30th, 1865, the "Counts' Ministry," under the presidency of Count Richard Belcredi, was nominated in the place of Schmerling ; an imperial manifesto on September 20th, 1865, proclaimed the suspension of the constitution and adjournment of the Imperial Council. The high nobility was favoured in every branch of the government, Slavism pitted against Germanism, and the way prepared for the settlement with Hungary. Prince Esterházy in this Cabinet was the dominant figure in foreign policy, and he was influenced in an anti-Prussian direction by Biegeleben of the Foreign Office, while the weak Minister of the Exterior, Count Mensdorff, vainly spoke for the maintenance of peace.

THE CAMPAIGN AGAINST JÜTLAND: AUSTRIANS CROSSING THE LIIM FIORD

AFTER THE DEFEAT OF AUSTRIA IN 1866: BERLIN'S JOYOUS WELCOME TO THE VICTORIOUS PRUSSIAN ARMY

From a contemporary drawing.

3068

THE ADVANCE OF PRUSSIA
VICTORIOUS CAMPAIGN AGAINST AUSTRIA

ALARMED by the warlike intentions of the Prussian Government, the Austrians thought it advisable in March, 1866, to take measures for arming. Some ten battalions were transferred to Bohemia, in order to strengthen the corps stationed there, and several cavalry regiments from Hungary and Transylvania were ordered to move into the province which was first menaced. Count Károlyi, the Austrian ambassador in Berlin, was at the same time commissioned to ask if Prussia really intended to attack Austria. This precipitate procedure of Austria rendered it easier for Bismarck and the generals, who were advising war, to induce King William also to make preparations. The measures taken by the Cabinet Council of March 28th comprised the supply of horses for the artillery, the repair of the fortresses, and the strengthening of the divisions quartered in the south of the country.

Bismarck Promises Reform Bismarck answered the really objectless inquiry of Count Károlyi in the negative, but sent a circular to the German courts, in which he accused Austria of wishing to intimidate Prussia by her preparations, as she had done in 1850. He further announced that Prussia would soon come forward with a plan for the reform of the German Federal Constitution.

But more important than these measures and notes, which caused so much public uneasiness, were the secret negotiations for the conclusion of the alliance with Italy. These did not proceed smoothly at first, since Italy was afraid of being made a tool, since Prussia might use the threat of an Italian alliance to induce Austria to give way. The Italian Government, in order to avoid this, declared it could only consent to a formal and offensive alliance for the purpose of attacking Austria-Hungary. King William could not agree to this, since he did not contemplate an invasion of Austria, for which indeed there was no pretext. The Prussian Government was only prepared for a friendly alliance, which should prevent either party forming a separate convention with Austria and leaving the other in the lurch. The result was the compromise of a defensive and offensive alliance, to be

The Advice of the French Emperor valid for three months only, in case war was not declared by Prussia before that date. Italy hesitated to agree to it, and applied to Napoleon III. for advice. The French emperor desired nothing more ardently than a war in Germany, in order, during its continuance, to pursue his schemes on Belgium and the Rhine districts.

He knew that William I. would not be persuaded by Bismarck to fight unless he were previously assured of the alliance of Italy; otherwise the king thought the campaign would be dangerous, since nearly the whole remaining part of Germany stood on the side of Austria. It may be ascribed to the advice of Napoleon that the hesitating Italian Premier, La Marmora, concluded a treaty, to hold for three months, on April 8th, 1866.

Bismarck wished to employ this period in pushing on the German question. He intended to show the nation that it must look to Prussia alone for the fulfilment of its wishes for union. Prussia proposed on April 10th, in the Diet of Frankfort, to summon a German Parliament on the basis of universal suffrage. In order to separate Bavaria from Austria, a proposal was made to the former state that the supreme command of the German federal troops should be divided ; Prussia should

Liberal Mistrust of Bismarck command in the north, Bavaria in the south. But Bismarck's intention, sincere as it was, did not meet with the approval of the majority of the German people. The Liberals asserted that the conversion of Bismarck to the idea of a German Parliament with universal suffrage was not genuine, and derided the idea that a government which did not respect the right of popular representation in its own country would unite Germany under a Parliamentary constitution. So rooted was the distrust of Prussia that Bavaria refused this favourable proposal. Pfordten, the Minister, was in his heart not averse to the plan; but the court, especially Prince Charles, the uncle of the young King

Austria's Improved Prospects

Lewis II., urged an alliance with Austria. When Austria saw that her prospects of winning over to her side the minor German states had improved, the war party in Vienna gained the ascendancy, and the cautious counsels of Mensdorff were disregarded. During the course of April, however, negotiations were begun between Vienna and Berlin for a simultaneous disarmament on both sides; and, as the result of a conciliatory note of Austria, prospects of peace were temporarily disclosed. King William thought that Prussia ought not to be obstinate in resisting all attempts at an understanding.

This more peaceful tendency was nullified by the preparations of Italy, which watched with uneasiness the inauguration of better relations between Prussia and Austria. By command of King Victor Emmanuel some 100,000 men were enrolled in the army during the month of April. As a result of this, the Emperor Francis Joseph, disregarding the warnings of Count Mensdorff, ordered the mobilisation of the southern army on April 21st, and that of the northern army on the 27th.

The counsellors of King William, who were urging war, thus were given weighty reasons why Prussia could not remain behind in her preparations. The king was in any case already convinced of the necessity of crossing swords with Austria, since he contemplated even in April a sudden attack on the still unprepared imperial capital. But since he was unwilling to appear in the eyes of Europe as the breaker of the peace, he had

On the Verge of War

waited for the mobilisation of Austria. Now the same steps were taken by him between May 5th and 12th. War was thus almost inevitable. The Vienna Cabinet, which did not underrate the dangers of an attack from two sides simultaneously, resolved at the eleventh hour on a complete change of policy towards Italy. Of late years the sale of the province of Venetia had been refused, as detrimental to the honour of Austria; she was now willing to relinquish the province, in order to have a free hand for a war of conquest against Prussia. Prince Metternich, the Austrian ambassador at Paris, was commissioned to call in the mediation of Napoleon III.

The Vienna Cabinet was willing to pledge itself to cede Venetia, on condition that Italy remained neutral in the coming war and that Austria was then able to conquer Silesia. Napoleon thought it a stroke of good fortune to have received simultaneous proposals from Prussia and Austria. By a skilful employment of the situation the aggrandisement of France in the north or east was virtually assured.

When he communicated the offer of Austria to the Italian Government, the latter justly retorted that the conditional promise of a cession of Venetia did not present the slightest certainty; the conquest of Silesia by Austria was doubtful, and if it did succeed, Austria's position would be so much improved that she would certainly not feel disposed to redeem her pledge. Thereupon Austria professed readiness to

Italy Tempted by Austria

sign a treaty which should secure Venetia unconditionally to the Italians. This offer presented a great temptation to Italy, but could only be accepted at the expense of a flagrant breach of faith towards Prussia. The Italian Cabinet, after a debate of several hours, resolved on May 14th to refuse the offer, since the wish for war was already kindled in Italy, and the acceptance of the gift would certainly have been attributed by the republican portion of the population to the craven and dishonourable policy of the House of Savoy.

The negotiations, nevertheless, were so far profitable to Austria that Italy was no longer arming for a war to the knife, since she was almost certain to gain Venetia even if the result of the war was less favourable. Austrian diplomacy further succeeded in establishing closer relations with France. Napoleon once more attempted to induce Prussia to give a distinct undertaking with reference to cessions of territory on the Rhine. Bismarck, however, put him off with general promises; his " dilatory " diplomacy, as he afterwards expressed himself, aimed at rousing in Napoleon the belief that he was quite ready to be somewhat of a traitor to his country, but that the king would not hear a word of any cession of German territory to France. His policy was both bold and astute ; he secured the neutrality of the emperor, without giving him the slightest pledge which compromised Prussia.

Napoleon, like almost all Frenchmen of that time, was convinced that Austria in the struggle with Prussia had the military superiority. For that reason the emperor had induced Italy to form an alliance with Prussia, in order to restore the balance of power ; and similarly, he wished to secure his position for the probable event of an Austrian victory. Napoleon, therefore, concluded a secret treaty with the Vienna Cabinet on June 12th, in which Austria undertook to cede Venice, even in the event of a victory, to Italy, which the emperor always favoured. The scheme which he had now made the goal of his policy was as follows : Venetia was to be ceded to Italy, Silesia to Austria, Schleswig - Holstein and other North German districts to Prussia, which, in turn, would have to give up considerable territory on the Rhine to France. But instead of arming in order to carry out this desirable solution, Napoleon thought he would pose as arbitrator of Europe after the exhaustion of his rivals. That was his mistake. The Italy of 1860, unprepared and poorly armed, had been easily forced to give up Nice and Savoy ; but Napoleon never suspected that Prussia after the war would be strong enough to refuse the claims of France. His mistake lay in adopting one and the same line of policy with Cavour and Bismarck, with Italians and Germans.

The nearer the war came the more unfavourable became the diplomatic situation of Prussia. The ambassador at Paris, Count Goltz, warned his countrymen not to depend on the neutrality of Napoleon. The governments of the German secondary states felt themselves menaced by the propositions for federal reform, and public opinion in South and West

LEWIS II., KING OF BAVARIA

The history of this monarch, who succeeded to the throne of Bavaria in 1864, is a particularly sad one. He was in constant opposition to his Ministers and family, and in 1886, in a fit of insanity, drowned himself near his castle of Berg.

From a photograph

Germany was averse to Prussia. Any hope that Bavaria and Hanover would remain neutral disappeared ; Saxony was closely united with Austria. It was peculiarly painful to King William that he was besieged with petitions from Prussian towns and communities praying for the maintenance of peace. Intense aversion to the war prevailed, especially in the Catholic districts on the Rhine ; when the members of the Landwehr were called up, there was actual insubordination shown in some places. The king, therefore, considered it advisable to entertain the proposals for mediation which were being mooted.

When Anton von Gablenz, a Saxon landowner and brother of the Austrian general, came to Berlin, to recommend a partition of Germany between the two Powers, he received full authority to place this proposal before the Vienna Cabinet. But the Austrian Ministry rejected that mediation, obviously because the Government had already decided for a war, and because Austria could no longer desert the minor German states, with which she practically had come to terms, and let them be partitioned at the last moment. It was Austria now who urged on the war and rendered Bismarck's steps easier. The Vienna Cabinet thus refused the proposal, emanating from Napoleon, to send representatives to a congress, on the ground that the fate of Venetia would form the object of the negotiations ; one Great Power could not allow other states to decide on its rights of ownership.

King William still hesitated to give the signal for war. By June 5th all Prussian army divisions on the southern frontier had taken up their posts. Moltke thought that the Prussian corps should advance concentrically into Saxony and Bohemia and attack the Austrians, who could hardly be ready to fight for another three weeks. But the king preferred to await the progress of the hostile measures which the Vienna Cabinet was already taking in Schleswig-Holstein and Frank-fort. Indeed, great impetuosity was shown at Vienna. The Austrian Government summoned the Estates of Holstein to discuss the fate of the country, although by the terms of the treaty the duty was incumbent on them of exercising no control over Holstein without the assent of Prussia.

Prussian Troops in Holstein When Prussia retorted by marching troops into Holstein, the Vienna Cabinet called upon the German Confederation to order the mobilisation of the Federal Army against the violation of the Federal Treaty by Prussia. The decisive sitting of the Federal Diet was held on June 14th.

Prussia had explained to the minor states that she would regard the resolution to mobilise as a declaration of war. Nevertheless a motion of Bavaria was voted on, which, even if not expressly aimed against Prussia, still had for its object the formation of a federal army. When the motion was carried by nine to six votes, the Prussian plenipotentiary, Savigny, announced the withdrawal of Prussia from the Confederation. King William immediately afterwards gave the order for the invasion of Saxony, Hanover, and Electoral Hesse.

At the outbreak of the war some 290,000 Prussians were ready to march into Austria and Saxony; only 48,000 were intended to fight the minor states. The latter, indeed, could put about 120,000 soldiers in the field; but Moltke went on the principle that the decisive blow must be struck on the chief scene of war with superior forces. The first blow was aimed at Hanover, Electoral Hesse, and Nassau, whose sovereigns had refused to promise neutrality. The blind King George V. of Hanover declared to the Prussian ambassador that compliance with the demand of Prussia was equivalent to his being mediatised; but that he would never allow himself to be mediatised— he would rather die an honourable death. Manteuffel thereupon advanced with his division into Hanover from Holstein, while Goeben and Beyer advanced from the west. General Vogel von Falckenstein held the supreme command of these troops. The Hanoverians, 18,000 strong, retreated before this superior force towards the south, and were successful in escaping the first plan, which calculated that they would still be at Göttingen; so that

Hanoverians Retire Before the Austrians

Falckenstein actually believed they had slipped from him. He abandoned the pursuit for a time; the troops of King George might have thus reached the forest of Thuringia by way of Gotha and Eisenach, and escaped to Bavaria in safety.

It was only on Moltke's urgent warnings that Falckenstein finally sent Goeben's division to Eisenach; the road by way of Gotha was barred to them by General von Flies. King George thus saw himself surrounded. Flies, who was nearest to him, attacked him on June 27th, with 9,000 men at Langensalza. The outnumbered Hanoverians bravely held the field; but immediately afterwards the net was drawn closer round them, and King George was forced to surrender on June 29th.

The Prussian main army was faced by 248,000 Austrians, who were joined by 23,000 Saxons. The Austrian commander was Lewis von Benedek, who had reaped a rich harvest of honours in the campaigns of 1848, 1849, and 1859; in the battle of Solferino he held the field on the right wing, and did not retire until the rest of the army had left the scene of action. He had been commander-in-chief of the Austrian army in Italy, which he expected to command in the next war. He was imperturbable, experienced, and high-minded, but he recognised the limitations of his abilities. He knew that he was only adapted to be a general under less important conditions, such as on the scene of war in Upper Italy; he was lacking in the intellect and thorough military education requisite for the leader of a large army.

Limitations of the Austrian Commander

When finally against his will he accepted the supreme command against Prussia, he had to receive lectures from one of his officers on the military geography of Germany. Since popular opinion, not merely in Austria but also in South Germany, expected his nomination to the command of the northern army, the Emperor Francis Joseph begged him to overcome his scruples. He refused, and only gave way after the emperor had represented to him that he could not be allowed to desert the dynasty at a crisis. The army was stationed in Moravia, resting on Olmütz, and Bohemia was occupied only by a small number of troops. In this latter country barely one army corps was stationed, under Count Eduard von Clam-Gallas; the Saxons thereupon retreated. Moltke's original plan to open the war by an attack, and by June 6th to invade Bohemia from all sides, had not been put into practice. The divisions of the Prussian army were at this time posted in a long line of 250 miles from Halle to Neisse. According to Moltke's plan, they were to unite their forces in the enemy's country. But when the attack had to be postponed, and it was reported at the Prussian headquarters that the Austrians were in Moravia, it was thought that Benedek was aiming a blow at Silesia. The divisions of the Prussian army, therefore, which were stationed to the east, pushed towards the left and took up a very strong position on the Neisse.

This delay in taking the offensive was turned to account as soon as war was determined upon. On June 15th the advance guard of the army of the Elbe, 49,000 men, under Bitterfeld, marched into Saxony. The first army of 97,000 men assembled in Lusatia under Prince Frederic Charles; the second army, finally 121,000 strong, was stationed in Silesia under the Crown Prince Frederic William. The corps of Von der Mülbe, 25,000 men, mostly militia, followed as a reserve. All the divisions were ordered to enter Bohemia on June 21st, and the district of Jitschin was fixed as the rendezvous, where they were to meet on June 28th. In consequence of the shifting of the Silesian corps towards the south-east on the Neisse, the distance which the army of the Crown Prince had to traverse to Jitschin was longer than the lines of march of Prince Frederic Charles and of the army of the Elbe. The separate advance of the Prussian divisions into Bohemia was thus attended with considerable danger. Moltke, whose hands had been hitherto tied by diplomatic considerations, knew this; and, remaining behind at first with the king in Berlin, he directed the movements of the three armies with marvellous foresight.

Moltke's Marvellous Foresight

The Austrians received the order on June 20th to march out of their quarters in Moravia. Benedek, accurately informed by his intelligence department of the detached position of the Prussians, wished to lead his army opportunely between the advancing divisions and to defeat one after the other before they combined. The first army reached Reichenberg on June 23rd and pressed on towards the Iser; the army of the Elbe marched parallel to it. The second army was still on Silesian soil, advancing towards the passes of the Riesengebirge—the Giant Mountains. As Benedek established his headquarters at Josefstadt in Bohemia on June 26th, and Prince Frederic Charles had already traversed Northern Bohemia, the Austrian leader selected him for his first opponent.

The Plans of Austria's Commander

He ordered the two corps which he had stationed in Bohemia—the Austrian under Clam-Gallas, and the Saxon, 60,000 men in all—to face Prince Frederic Charles on the Iser in order to detain him. He himself put the main body of his army in movement towards the Iser. The troops of the Crown Prince crossed the Bohemian frontier in the passes of the Riesengebirge on June 26th; Benedek, therefore, while wishing to attack Prince Frederic Charles with six army corps in all, sent back two corps under Gablentz and Ramming to guard the mountain passes against the second army. Since the movements of the Prussians were admirably combined, and one army was eager to relieve the other, these two Austrian corps were vigorously attacked on June 27th. Thus the Prussian I. corps under General Adolf von Bonin was pitted against the Austrian corps of Gablentz at Trautenau, while General Steinmetz met Ramming's force at Nachod. These sanguinary encounters resulted in a defeat of the Austrians at the latter place, and a victory at the former.

Nevertheless, it was already clear that the Prussian tactics were far superior to those of Austria. The Prussian needle-gun fired three times as fast as the Austrian muzzle-loader; and, apart from this, the "shock tactics" of the Austrians, who tried to storm heights and belts of forest with the bayonet, were to a high degree

LEWIS VON BENEDEK

In the campaigns of 1848, 1849, and 1859 this Austrian commander greatly distinguished himself, but in the war against Prussia, when in chief command of Austria's army, he suffered humiliating defeat.

disastrous. The Prussians brought the enemy's attack to a standstill by rapid firing; they then threw themselves in smaller divisions on the flanks of their adversary, and completed his overthrow. Hence the terrible losses of the Austrians even after a successful charge. At Trautenau, although victors, they lost 183 officers and 4,231 men killed and wounded, the Prussians only 56 officers and 1,282 men; at Nachod 5,700 Austrians fell and only 1,122 Prussians. The superiority of the Prussians was manifest in the preparations for the war, in tactics, and in the better education of the officers and men.

On the evening of June 27th the gravity of these facts was not yet realised in the Austrian headquarters. Benedek therefore adhered to his plan of continuing his advance against Frederic Charles. This was, however, dangerous, because the nearer enemy, the Crown Prince, would certainly put himself more in evidence on the next day. The Austrian's alternative was to abandon the attack on the first army and to hurl himself with all available troops against the second army. If this had been done, the Crown Prince would have had to contend against an attack by superior numbers. This was known at the

Prussian headquarters, and Frederic William and his chief of the general staff, Leonhard von Blumenthal, made up their minds that they would have hard fighting on their further advance through the mountain passes. Bonin, after his reverse of June 27th, had returned to Prussian territory, whereas the Guards advanced on the road to Eipel, and Steinmetz from Nachod towards Skalitz.

The Crown Prince waited with his staff in the middle between these two columns, ready to hasten to the post of danger. The **The Crown Prince in Battle** coolness and caution of the generalship, considering the difficult position, could not be surpassed. Benedek, however, obstinately held to his original plan. He actually inspected, on the morning of June 28th, the three corps concentrated against Steinmetz, without striking a blow at him with these superior numbers. On the contrary, he ordered the greater part of these troops to march against Frederic Charles, and commissioned the Archduke Leopold in particular to take up a strong position behind the Elbe. By so doing he abandoned a favourable chance and made a miscalculation, for that very day the troops of the Crown Prince came up with the

HANOVERIAN VICTORY OVER THE PRUSSIANS AT LANGENSALZA
Attacked by the Prussians at Langensalza, on June 27th, 1866, while on their way to join the Bavarian forces, the Hanoverians held the field and gained a notable victory, the Prussians having a thousand men killed and wounded.

THE BATTLE OF SKALITZ: PRUSSIAN CAVALRY CAPTURING THE AUSTRIAN CANNON
This battle, fought on June 28th, 1866, between the Prussians and the Austrians, ended in a severe defeat of the latter, who left behind on the field no fewer than 5,000 men out of a total of 20,000 taking part in the fight.

combined Austrian forces both at Skalitz and Trautenau. Archduke Leopold, contrary to Benedek's orders, offered battle at Skalitz, and brought a complete defeat on himself; out of the 20,000 Austrians, 5,000 were left on the field of battle. At the same time Gablenz, who had been victorious on the previous day at Trautenau, was defeated by the Guards under Prince Augustus of Würtemberg near Trautenau. The Crown Prince had thus forced his way through the passes on June 28th, and as a result of this the way to the Elbe was free. Meanwhile, the advance guard of Prince Frederic Charles reached the Iser on June 26th. The army of the Austrians and Saxons tried unsuccessfully to dispute the passage in a sanguinary night encounter at Podol; but the prince followed up his victory somewhat slowly, and allowed his advance to be checked by the rearguard action, unfavourable indeed to the Austrians, at Münchengrätz on June 28th. A message from Moltke, however, made him press forward more rapidly.

Benedek Depressed by Defeat

Benedek had meantime learnt with deep inward perturbation that his three corps, which had been moved against the Crown Prince, were defeated. This news produced such an effect on him that he gave up the offensive which he had intended to assume against Prince Frederic Charles. He resolved, on the advice of Krismanic, the " strategist of positions," to take up a naturally strong defensive position on the hills above the Elbe, and to await there subsequent attacks. He also sent to the combined Austrian-Saxon army an order to retire on to the main army. But unfortunately the intelligence department at his headquarters was so dilatory that this order had not arrived when the troops of Prince Frederic Charles attacked the Saxons and the corps of Clam-Gallas on the afternoon of June 29th, at Jitschin.

The commanders of the allies must have thought that the main army was near at hand, and that they ought therefore to defend Jitschin, the junction of the roads. They accepted the battle, and at first successfully resisted. Then about seven o'clock the Austrian officer arrived and handed in the order to retreat. The Austrians now wished to discontinue the battle, but were involved in disastrous engagements by the keen advance of the Prussians and were completely beaten.

The Saxons of the Crown Prince Albert withdrew in good order; but the corps of Clam-Gallas broke up on the retreat, which lasted the whole night and the following day, and they reached the main army in a deplorable condition.

The strong position occupied in the meantime by the Austrian main army was thus rendered untenable, for the two army corps which were supposed to form the left wing were defeated, and Prince Frederic Charles could attack the Austrians in flank and rear. Benedek was therefore forced to give the order for retreat in the night of June 30th to July 1st. Since the Prussians did not follow him at once, they did not know how far he had led his army back. King William and Moltke had meanwhile reached the army of Prince Frederic Charles on July 1st.

Austria in a Sad Plight

Moltke believed that the Austrians had occupied a strong position behind the Elbe, and were waiting behind the fortresses of Josefstadt and Königgrätz for the attack. They were, however, already halting behind the Bistritz, a tributary of the Elbe, where they had arrived exhausted by a disorderly night march. Benedek, through these events, had lost all hope of victory, and decided on a further retreat behind the Elbe, and, if necessary, even to Olmütz or towards Vienna.

This gloomy state of affairs was expressed in a telegram which was sent immediately afterwards by the Austrian commander to the emperor, urgently advising him to conclude peace at any price. A disaster for the army was inevitable. Francis Joseph believed, however, that he could not own himself conquered without a pitched battle. He therefore answered : " Peace is impossible. We must retreat if necessary. Has any battle taken place ? " This expression of the emperor's will seems to have determined Benedek to accept a pitched battle, and as the Prussians were rapidly advancing he made instant preparations for it.

Late in the evening of July 2nd the news was brought to the Prussian headquarters that the Austrians were still in front of the Elbe, ready to accept the challenge. It was determined by King William and Moltke, after deliberation, to attack the enemy at once in full force, and orders were sent that night to the Crown Prince to summon him to start at once. Blumenthal had lately advised the two Prussian armies, who were no longer prevented from joining forces, to concentrate tactically to the west of the Elbe, in order thus to obviate the danger of being

Prussians Ready for Attack

separated in a pitched battle. Moltke, however, ordered that the plan of separating the armies should still be observed, but in such a way that the armies on the day of battle might join forces by a rapid march. He wanted to be able to attack the Austrians in the front with one army, and on the flank with another. The greatness of Moltke lies in this bold strategy, which aims at the complete annihilation of the enemy by enclosing him between broad advancing masses ; the application of this method enabled him in 1870 to capture entire armies.

The Austrians and Saxons on the morning of the battle of Königgrätz, July 3rd, were 215,000 men strong, drawn up in close formation. The great disadvantage of their position was that they had the Elbe in their rear ; but, of course, several bridges had been thrown across it. The centre and the left wing pointed west, and awaited the attack of Prince Frederic Charles ; the right wing, consisting of the fourth and second corps, was ordered to face north, since the advance of the second army might be expected from that quarter.

The great Battle in Progress

The Crown Prince, following the orders given him, started immediately at early morning, but he did not reach the battlefield before noon. In the meantime the first army attacked the centre ; the Elbe army, the right wing of the Austrian army. The Elbe army made good progress ; on the other hand, Prince Frederic Charles vainly exhausted his efforts against the strong centre of the Austrians. The Austrian artillery was planted in tiers on the hills of Chlum, Lipa, and Langenhof, and at once precluded any attempt at an infantry attack. Since Prince Frederic Charles was compelled to wait until the Crown Prince joined his left wing, the weak spot in his line was there, for the Austrians, temporarily superior in numbers, might outflank him.

It was fortunate for the Prussians that the seventh division was stationed there under Fransecky, who covered the weakness of his position by a determined and splendid offensive. He advanced into the Swiepwald, drove out the Austrians, and from that position harassed their right wing, which was ordered to hold its ground against the expected attack of the Crown Prince. The Austrians thereupon, in the hope of overwhelming Fransecky, made a counter attack, which was at first

KING WILLIAM OF PRUSSIA AT KÖNIGGRÄTZ LEADING THE PURSUIT OF THE DEFEATED AUSTRIANS

At the battle of Königgrätz, or Sadowa, the Austrians were completely defeated on July 3rd, 1866, and were forced to beat a retreat, King William himself leading the pursuit.

From the painting by Sell, by permission of the Berlin Photographic Co.

repelled with loss, and the wood could not be captured by the Austrians until a part of the second corps turned against Fransecky. Hitherto eleven Prussian battalions had held their ground against fifty-nine Austrian battalions.

The battle, however, at noon was extremely favourable to the Austrians. King William looked anxiously towards the north, where the Crown Prince had long been vainly expected. Benedek deliberated whether he ought not now to bring up his strong reserves and win a victory by a vigorous assault on the Prussian centre. But he felt crippled by the news, which reached him three hours earlier than King William and Moltke, that the Crown Prince was approaching. Benedek saw also, with uneasiness, how his right wing, intent upon the struggle in the Swiepwald, left great gaps towards the north.

Anxious Moments in the Fight

It thus happened that the second army, when it came on the scene at noon, was able at the first onset to overlap the Austrian right wing. The Prussian Guards and the sixth corps were in the first line ; the corps of Bonin and Steinmetz followed after. The Guards, after a short fight, captured the key of the Austrian position, the village of Chlum, and soon afterwards Lipa also. Startling as was this onslaught of the Prussians, and great as was its success, Benedek still thought it possible to retrieve the day. He brought up his reserves in order to retake Chlum. The Austrians, charging bravely, actually drove back the Guards by their superior force. They were on the point of entering Chlum when, rather late, the Prussian corps under Bonin appeared, repulsed the Austrians, and soon afterwards assured their defeat.

The army of Prince Frederic Charles, hitherto kept in check, now advanced, and the Prussian cavalry was called upon to complete the victory. Although the Austrian cavalry stopped this pursuit in the battle of Streschewitz, the masses of infantry, abandoning all order, poured down on the Elbe, looking for the bridges over the river. It was fortunate for them that they were not pursued by the Prussian infantry. The Austrians, although terrible disorder prevailed in places among them while crossing the Elbe, were able to reach the left bank of the river in the night of July 4th. Their losses were terrible ;

The Victory with the Prussians

they amounted in all to more than 44,000 men, some half of whom, wounded or unwounded, were taken prisoners. The Prussians had 1,335 killed and 9,200 wounded. Most of the Austrians had fallen during their fruitless attacks in dense masses on the Prussian needle-guns. This crushing disaster was only slightly compensated by the victory which the Austrians won over the Italians at Custoza, ten days earlier.

Francis Joseph thought it necessary after the battle of Königgrätz to call in the mediation of France. The official Paris journal announced on July 5th, 1866, that Venetia had been ceded by Austria to the Emperor Napoleon. Austria counted confidently that the French Emperor would urge Italy to neutrality, and would check the victorious career of Prussia by stationing an army on the Rhine. Advice to this effect was given to the emperor by his Minister of the Exterior, Drouyn de l'Huys. But France was not prepared for war ; the emperor was at that time incapacitated by a torturing disease, and he therefore allowed himself to be persuaded by Prince Jerome, as well as by his Ministers, the Marquis de Lavalette and Eugène Rouher, to abandon the idea of hostilities against Prussia, in order to win territorial concessions from King William by negotiations. The Prussian ambassador, Count Goltz, adroitly represented to him how much more favourable an amicable arrangement with Prussia would be for him. From this moment France had played for the last time her rôle as leading power in Europe.

France Falls from Power

Prussia was energetic in reaping the fruits of her victory. Goltz kept Napoleon in suspense by courteous hints, without pledging the Prussian Government in any matter. When the French diplomatist, Benedetti, appeared at the Prussian headquarters in Moravia, with a commission from Napoleon, the circumstance aroused fear in Bismarck that Napoleon would now come forward with his claims ; but it appeared that Benedetti had none but vague orders, and was only intended to hinder the entry of the Prussians into the Austrian capital. Meantime Benedek in his rapid retreat had reached Olmütz with his army. The second army was ordered to watch and follow him, while the first marched southward on Vienna. Since Austria thought its southern frontier was secured by the cession of Venetia, the larger part of the field army stationed in Italy, 57,000 men, was ordered to the northern theatre of war. Archduke Albert assumed the supreme command. Benedek was instructed to withdraw from Olmütz to the Danube, in order that the newly collected army might be on the defensive behind the river. But the defeated general loitered so long in Olmütz that detachments of the army of the Crown Prince were able to get in front of his army. Benedek's marching columns were attacked on July 15th, near Tobitschau, south of Olmütz, and suffered a serious reverse ; eighteen cannon fell into the hands of the Prussians. Benedek was thus forced to abandon his march southward, and withdrew towards Hungary, in order to reach the Danube by a détour along the Waag. In consequence of this, the Prussians were able to appear on the Danube earlier than he could.

Meantime the Prussians were fighting successfully against the minor states. The Bavarians were attacked and defeated by Goeben's division at Kissingen on July 10th, 1866. Although Moltke now **Conquering Army of Prussia** ordered General Falckenstein to pursue at once the main body of the enemy, the Bavarians, and crush them, Falckenstein thought it better to capture Frankfort first. He defeated the Federal Corps in the engagements of Laufach and Aschaffenburg, and entered the Free City victoriously. But since by so doing he had disobeyed the orders from the king's headquarters, he was deprived of the supreme command, and on July 19th General Manteuffel took his place. Once more the Prussians were enabled to attack individually their disunited opponents, and to defeat, first the Federal Corps at Bischofsheim and Wertheim, and then the Bavarians at Neubrunn and Rossbrunn.

Goltz, yielding to the pressure of Napoleon, had concluded with him, on July 14th, preliminary agreements as a basis for peace. The withdrawal of Austria from **Peace after the War** the German Confederation was fixed as the first condition ; but the dominions of the Austrian monarchy were not to suffer any loss except that of Venetia. Prussia, in addition, stipulated for the right to form a North-German Confederation under her own military supremacy, and to annex Schleswig-Holstein. A South-German Confederation was to be organised, with an independent position on every side. Napoleon intervened with these proposals between the two belligerent states. Bismarck would have been glad if he could have concluded peace with Austria without Napoleon, since there was always the fear that France would come forward during the negotiations with demands of territory **Austria's Serious Mistake** for herself. Bismarck explained this to the Vienna Cabinet, and added that Prussia in this case would renounce any claim for indemnification of the costs of the war. But Austria made the mistake of regarding France as a friend, and declined the offer. This was a serious error, since Napoleon was solely animated by the wish to win, through good offices to Prussia, the consent of the latter to his designs on Belgium and the Rhenish provinces.

Napoleon therefore, when King William declared that the terms agreed upon by his ambassador in Paris on July 14th were insufficient, and demanded the annexation of extensive districts of North Germany, lost no time in giving his assent to the demand ; he would have sacrificed even Saxony on these grounds without compunction. Prussia had now secured the prize of victory, and concluded an armistice with Austria. Immediately before that, Moltke wished to make another successful coup. General Fransecky was ordered to occupy Pressburg, in order that on any outbreak of war the Prussian army might secure the passage of the Danube. An engagement was fought at Blumenau on July 22nd ; but it was left undecided, since at noon both sides received the news that an armistice had been concluded.

The preliminary peace was signed in Nicholsburg. The parties were soon agreed, since Austria, after her severe defeat, was forced to consent that Prussia should have a free hand in Germany. King William would indeed gladly have acquired for Prussia some Austrian territory, **Peace after the War** especially Austrian Silesia and parts of Northern Bohemia. He only gave way at the representations of Bismarck that if he pressed his claims too much he would risk what he had already won. The last difficulty disappeared when Prussia consented to a condition laid down by Austria and recognised the inviolability of the kingdom of Saxony. The preliminary peace was concluded on this basis on July 26th. The Treaty of Prague followed on August 23rd.

The convention between Austria and Italy presented more difficulties. The Italian admiral, Persano, at the outset of the war received orders to secure a pledge for Italy by occupying the Dalmatian island of Lissa. During the bombardment of the capital of the island the Austrian admiral Tegetthoff appeared on the scene,

Bismarck's Superior Diplomacy attacked the Italian fleet on July 20th 1866, and the " Rè d'Italia " with his own flagship, and forced the Italian fleet to retire. Since Garibaldi also, on invading the Italian Tyrol, was defeated by the Austrian general Kuhn in several engagements, Italy was compelled to be satisfied with the treaty concluded on October 3rd, by which Venetia was ceded.

The superior diplomacy of Bismarck was now able, under the impression caused by the Prussian victories, to unite non-Austrian Germany, hitherto torn by factions, at any rate against the contingency of a war. Above all, he induced the king to terminate the conflict with the Prussian House of Representatives by offering the hand of friendship to it in his speech from the throne on August 5th, 1866. There were irreconcilable Conservatives who urged the king to use the foreign victory for the complete overthrow of the Liberal party; but the royal speech expressly recognised that the expenditure incurred for military purposes would have subsequently to be sanctioned by the Landtag, and therefore asked an indemnity for such expenses.

In this point the king followed, not without hesitation, the advice of Bismarck. In the conversation with the President of the House of Representatives he declared that in a similar case he would not be able to act otherwise than he had done before ; but this statement, for which Bismarck declined responsibility, was, fortunately, not made public until later. Not less

Enlarging the Prussian Territory clever was his treatment of the conquered secondary states. Bismarck set up the principle that full incorporation or a complete amnesty to the individual states was the just course; the entry of those who were chosen members of the new federation ought not to be burdened with hard conditions. Hanover, Hesse-Cassel, Nassau, and Frankfort-on-Main were fully incorporated, by which means the Prussian territory was enlarged by 27,638 square miles. On the other hand, the demands for a war indemnity imposed by Prussia on the remaining states were moderate. The greatest triumph of his negotiations was that Würtemberg, Baden, and Bavaria concluded, between the 13th and 21st August, 1866, a defensive and offensive alliance, on the basis of which their military forces were, in case of war, to be under the command of Prussia. These provisions, which were kept secret for the moment, constitute the foundation of the union of Germany.

This favourable event had been chiefly effected by the action of Napoleon, who had unwisely let the right time slip past, and only now stretched out his hands to German territory. Bismarck, with the most subtle diplomatic skill, had fed the king with false hopes until the war was decided. The emperor now demanded the price of his neutrality. His ambassador, Benedetti, in an interview with Bismarck on August 5th, demanded the Rhenish Palatinate with Mainz, as well as the district on the Saar. Bismarck

France Approaching Disaster then haughtily opposed him. He threatened that, if France insisted upon these claims, he would at once, and at any cost, make peace with the South Germans and advance in alliance with them to conquer Alsace and Lorraine. Napoleon was alarmed, since his forces were no match for the gigantic war equipment of Germany. Prussia alone had 660,000 men with the colours.

But Bismarck took care that the demands of France were published in a Paris journal, so that the national feeling of the Germans was intensely aroused. On the strength of these impressions, the above-mentioned alliances with the South German states were brought about. Germany was thus put in a sufficiently strong position to defend every inch of national soil against East and West. Napoleon III. was diplomatically defeated before he was conquered on the field of battle. Drouyn de l'Huys, since the emperor would not listen to his proposals for forcing on a war, took farewell, and said : " I have seen three dynasties come and go. I know the signs of approaching disaster, and I withdraw."

HEINRICH FRIEDJUNG

THE
RE-MAKING
OF
EUROPE

THE
CONSOLIDA-
TION OF THE
POWERS VIII

THE PRUSSIAN ASCENDANCY
AND THE AUSTRO - HUNGARIAN EMPIRE

ON October 3rd, 1866, King William formally took possession by letters-patent of Hanover, Hesse-Cassel, Nassau, and Frankfort-on-Main, which the Peace of Prague had assigned to him by the law of nations, and whose incorporation into Prussia had been sanctioned by the Landtag of the monarchy in September. The king declared in his speech to the Hanoverians on the same day that he honoured the grief which they experienced in tearing themselves from earlier and endeared connections, but that the interests of the nation dictated the firm and lasting union of Hanover with Prussia, and that Germany should be the gainer by the acquisitions of Prussia.

However correct these principles were, a large part of the Hanoverians were little inclined to recognise them and to submit to the inevitable. Devotion to the Guelfic house, above all to the king, George V., **The Blind King George V.** whose blindness made him an object of universal pity, and his spouse, the universally beloved Queen Mary; the consideration that the gentry of the country would be ousted from the exclusive possession of the high offices of state ; that the capital would be severely injured by the loss of the court ; that antiquated but familiar methods of business would be broken down on all sides by the Prussian freedom of trade and freedom of movement ; the traditional dislike of the Hanoverians for the Prussians, especially for the Berliners, who were decried as supercilious and empty-headed ; in short, personal-feeling and practical interests combined in producing the result that the Prussian rule was only endured by the nobility, the clergy, and a large part of the citizens and peasants, with a silent indignation.

The king, who had fled to the Castle of Hietzing, near Vienna, added fuel to the discontent by a manifesto to his people on October 5th, in which he declared, in opposition to the warrant of William I., that the incorporation of his land into Prussia was null and void, and expressed his confidence in the Almighty that He would restore Hanover to the Guelfic house " as He had done sixty years ago, when the same injustice from the same quarter was not allowed to continue."

Hanoverian Hatred of Prussia Societies were secretly formed throughout the country whose aim was this restoration, and it was proposed to hold a " Hanoverian Legion " in readiness, which, should a crisis arise, might be on the spot sword in hand. The hatred of the people towards Prussia was shown in the abuse showered on individuals, especially on Prussian soldiers.

It is interesting to hear that Bismarck entertained the idea, which had once been successfully realised by Cleisthenes at Athens, of breaking up the existing combinations, and creating out of them new forms of political life, which should facilitate the fusion of the old and new parts of the country. According to his speech in the House of Representatives on February 5th, 1867, he wished to re-divide all the country west of the Elbe into four large provinces, which should correspond to the mediæval tribes, and be called Old Franconia, Westphalia, Lower Saxony, and Thuringia. Old and New Prussia were to be merged in these provinces as a means of softening the contrast between them and the rest of the Prussian state. Bismarck did not succeed in carrying out this idea; the states, gradu-**Hanover Governed with a Firm Hand** ally created by political events, showed themselves stronger than the original tribes. No course was left but to govern the province of Hanover, which remained unaltered in itself, with a benevolent but firm hand, and to trust in the all-effacing power of time. Dictatorial powers in the new territorial divisions had been granted to the Government until September 30th, 1867, and the Prussian constitution was to come into force in those parts on October 1st, 1867. Advantage was taken of this circumstance to send an order to the governor-general, Von Voigt-Rhetz, that all officials on whose implicit co-operation no reliance could be placed should without further delay be removed from their posts; a number of **Punishment of Guelf Agitators** Guelf agitators also were confined in the fortress of Minden. This measure was so far effective that outward tranquillity was restored; but there were indications that among the people loyalty to the Guelfs was by no means predominant.

On October 1st, thirty-nine representatives to the Second Chamber, and seventy delegates from the communes, declared that they accepted the annexation as an unalterable fact brought on by the obstinacy of the former Government itself; and when, on October 11th, a special Hanoverian corps, the tenth, was raised, 425 out of 660 Hanoverian officers—that is to say, almost two-thirds—at once went into the Prussian service, a circumstance which, it may be well understood, caused a bitter disappointment to the banished king.

Things went far more smoothly in Electoral Hesse and Nassau than in Hanover; in the former the despotic rule of Elector Frederic William I., and in the latter the inconsiderate exercise of forest rights and the refusal to grant the Liberal constitution of 1849, whose restoration the Landtag vainly demanded, had caused the subjects to dislike their sovereigns so that the end of the system of petty states was universally felt to be a release from unendurable conditions. The feeling in Frankfort was very bitter, since the town where the ancient emperors were elected, one of the most important commercial capitals of South Germany, was reduced from a Free City to a provincial Prussian town; even the enormous development of **The Bitter Feeling in Frankfort** the city, which, as soon as it was freed from its isolation, outstripped all the other South German towns except Munich, could not banish the mortification felt at the loss of independence.

Bismarck and the king were indefatigably busy in meeting, so far as was feasible, the wishes of the annexed districts in order to win them over to the new order of things. Electoral Hesse owed to the personal intervention of the monarch

the fact that half of its state treasure was left in 1867 as a provincial fund to provide for workhouses, the maintenance of the poor, and for the national library; and the province of Hanover received in February, 1868, the yearly grant of a sum of £75,000 for purposes of local administration. Ample pecuniary compensation was also made to the deposed sovereigns. The Elector of Hesse received in September, 1867, the other moiety of the state treasure, which had accumulated from the subsidies paid by England in 1776 for the troops sent to America.

The Duke of Nassau was assigned, in September, 1867, some castles and £1,500,000 sterling, and King George in the same month a capital sum of £2,400,000, the income of which was to be paid him in half-yearly instalments, though the sum itself remained in the hands of trustees until an agreement had been made with his relations as to its administration.

It was naturally supposed, in view of these friendly concessions, which were only sanctioned by the Prussian Landtag after a hard contest, that the three princes would **Bismarck and the "Reptiles"** tacitly, if not expressly, waive all claims to their former territories. But since King George, in February, 1868, and Elector Frederic William, in September, 1868, publicly made violent attacks upon Prussia, the sums due to the two sovereigns in March and September, 1868, were sequestrated. Since George brought his Guelf legion to 750 men, and kept them in France unarmed, as "fugitives," a law of spring, 1869, provided that the interest of the sequestrated £2,400,000 should be applied to warding off the schemes devised by the king and his emissaries to disturb the peace of Prussia. From Bismarck's saying: "We will pursue these obnoxious reptiles into their holes," the sum of money in question was soon universally called the Reptile fund; it was mostly employed on newspaper articles in support of the new order of things. It was not until 1892 that the sequestration was ended in favour of Duke Ernest Augustus of Cumberland, son of George V.

In Schleswig-Holstein the feeling in favour of Duke Frederic still continued; but the certainty that the Prussian eagle would once for all protect the duchies against the detested Danish yoke, and the propaganda of a Danish nationality, which was now awakening in the Danish border districts of Schleswig, contributed slowly but surely to the end that the largely predominant German population learnt to adapt itself to the new conditions. The brave spirit of the duke, who saw his fondest hopes blighted, and scorned to foment a useless resistance to the detriment of the duchies, helped much to tranquillise men's minds and prepared them for the day when his daughter Augusta Victoria should wear the imperial Crown.

Prussia, at the moment when it withdrew from the German Confederation and began the war against Austria, had invited all the North German states to conclude a new league. In August, 1866, nineteen governments which had fought on Prussia's side in the war professed their readiness to take that step. Meiningen and the elder line of Reuss, which had stood on the side of Austria, did the same after some hesitation, and the old anti-Prussian Duke Bernhard of Meiningen abdicated in favour of his son George. Ministerial conferences were opened in Berlin on December 15th, under the presidency of Bismarck, to which representatives were sent by all the North German governments, and by Saxony and Hesse-Darmstadt for their territory right of the Main. The fundamental principles of the new federal constitution were settled in these conferences. According to it the presidency of the Confederation should belong to the King of Prussia in so far that he should represent the Confederation in foreign politics, declare peace and war in its name, superintend the execution of the Federal resolutions, nominate all officials of the Confederation, and command its army and fleet.

The Federal Council was to represent the governments, and in it, on the basis of the voting conditions in the former German Confederation, seventeen votes

GEORGE V. OF HANOVER

On the annexation of Hanover by Prussia in 1866, George V. fled to the Castle of Hietzing, near Vienna, and issued a manifesto to his people declaring the incorporation of his land into Prussia to be null and void. The king died at Paris in 1878.
From a photograph

should be given by Prussia, four by Saxony, two each by Mecklenburg-Schwerin and Brunswick, one by each of the remaining eighteen states, making forty-three votes in all. The Federal Council shared in the whole work of legislation, and represented the sovereigns of the Confederation.

The people were to share in the legislation by means of a Reichstag springing from the direct universal suffrage. This Reichstag possessed also initiative rights; it was not proposed to pay the deputies. The following were declared to be Federal matters: The army and navy, in which connection the peace strength of the army was fixed at 1 per cent. of the population of 1867, and the right of increasing it every ten years was reserved; then foreign policy, posts and telegraphs, tolls and trade. The finances were to be based on the tolls, the compulsory taxes, and the profits of the posts and telegraphs. To supply any deficit in the revenue the individual states were pledged to "register contributions" in proportion to the numbers of their population. The Federal Budget was to be sanctioned for periods of three years; the expenses of the army were estimated at the rate of £33 15s. a head in perpetuity. After different objections had been successfully raised against certain of these provisions, they were approved on February 2nd, 1867, and in that form submitted to the Constituent Reichstag elected on February 12th.

It was a matter of the greatest importance for the party conditions in this Reichstag that in the autumn of 1866, when an effort was being made to get rid of the Prussian dispute, two new parties appeared on the scene. The National Liberal party, which, breaking away from the Progressive party—now sinking more and more into a policy of barren negations —aimed at a confidential and vigorous association with the great statesman who had shown by his actions that he was not the bigoted country squire—Junker—which, according to the outcry of the Progressives, he always had been and still was. Similarly the moderate Conservatives founded the Free Conservative party—

"German Empire Party" Founded since 1871 called also the "German Empire party"— which proposed to unite the observance of sound conservative principles, respect for authority, and support of the monarchy with wise progress and the maintenance of civil liberty.

In the Constituent Reichstag the Conservatives numbered 59 deputies; the Free Conservatives, 36; the Old Liberals, who stood near them, 27; the National Liberals, 79; Progressives, only 19. In addition there were 18 Particularists, 12 Poles, 2 Danes, 1 Social Democrat, Aug. Bebel, and a number of "wild" politicians. The decision lay with the two parties whose principles brought them into touch, and who, in the phrase of the day, were termed the Right and Left Centre, the Free Conservatives, and the National Liberals.

The Reichstag chose for president Eduard Simson, who had presided at the National Assembly in Frankfort, 1848–1849, and thus was outwardly connected with the traditions of the Hereditary Imperial party. The feeling prevailed in the debates that, whatever might be the private views of the representatives, it was impossible to disregard the wishes of the state governments, and that, under all the circumstances, something must be effected by mutual concessions.

Bismarck gave vigorous expression to his feeling in his speech of March 11th, 1867, one of the most powerful which he ever made, when he appealed to those who would not sanction any

Bismarck's Powerful Appeal diminution of the Prussian Budget rights in the case of army estimates. "The mighty movements which last year induced the nations from the Belt to the Adriatic, from the Rhine to the Carpathians, to play that iron game of dice where royal and imperial crowns are the stake, the thousands and thousands of victims of the sword and of disease, who by their death sealed the national decision, cannot be reconciled with a resolution

ad acta. Gentlemen, if you believe that, you are not masters of the situation! . . . How would you answer a veteran of Königgrätz if he asked after the results of these mighty efforts? You would say to him, perhaps, ' Yes, indeed, nothing has been done about German union; that will come in time. But we have saved the Budget right of the Prussian Chamber of Deputies, the right of endangering every year the existence of the Prussian army; for this we have fought with the emperor under the walls of Pressburg. Console yourself with that, brave soldier, and let the widow, too, who has buried her husband, find consolation there.' Gentlemen, this position is an impossibility! Let us work quickly, let us put Germany in the saddle, and she will soon learn to ride."

In the course of the conferences some forty amendments to the Bill were discussed by the Reichstag. Thus the Confederation acquired the right of levying not only indirect but direct taxes; every alteration in the army and the fleet was made dependent on the express sanction of the president. Criminal jurisdiction,

The Functions of the Confederation legal procedure, and in private law contract rights at least, were transferred to the Confederation the Confederation. The Federal Chancellor was to accept by his signature the moral, not legal, responsibility for the enactments of the President.

The voting for the Reichstag was to be secret; the eligibility of officials as candidates was to be recognised. Accurate reports of the public sittings of the Reichstag were to be secure against prosecution. The deputies were to be paid. The Federal Budget was to be passed for one year only, instead of three. In military matters the proviso that one-hundredth of the population of 1867 should serve with the colours in peace time, and that the rate should be £33 15s. per head was only to be in force until December 31st, 1871. The Confederation was given the right to raise loans in urgent cases; in the case of denial of justice in any state the Confederation was bound— if a remedy could not be obtained by legal methods—to interfere and afford lawful help. As regarded the entry of one or more of the South German states into the Confederation, it was settled that this should be effected on the motion of the President, by means of a legislative act. Finally, alterations of the constitution were treated in the same way, but a two-thirds majority in the Federal Council was requisite. The federal governments accepted nearly all of these resolutions; Bismarck, in their name, lodged protests against two of them in the Reichstag on April 15th. First, against the grant of daily pay to the representatives in the Reichstag. In the eyes of the governments, the limitation of eligibility imposed by the non-granting of allowances was an indispensable counterpoise to universal suffrage. The Reichstag accordingly abandoned the daily allowances. Secondly, the governments regarded it as thoroughly inadmissible that the existence of the army after December 31st, 1871, should be dependent on the annual votes of fluctuating majorities, while the expenditure on the civil administration was legally fixed. Rudolf Gneist, a deputy, called attention to the fact that the Lower House might well refuse the expenses of a professional army, such as existed in England, but that a national army, like the German, must be regarded as a permanent institution. The governments would have preferred that, according to the original scheme, the minimum strength of the army should have been settled once for all, and a permanent provision voted for maintaining it. They finally, on April 17th, declared their agreement to the proposal of the Free Conservatives and of the National Liberals, which provided that the present peace strength of the army, fixed until December 31st, 1871, at one-hundredth of the population, and the lump sum of £33 15s. per head of the army, should be kept in force beyond that date, but only so long as they should not be altered by federal laws; but the disbursement of sums for the entire national army was to be annually fixed by state law. On April 17th, 1867, the king closed the Constituent Reichstag with a speech from the throne which expressed his satisfaction that the federal power had obtained its necessary authority, and that the members of the Confederation had retained freedom of movement in every department where it might be advantageous for them.

Closing of the Constituent Reichstag

After the Landtags of the individual states had declared their assent, the constitution became a reality on July 1st, 1867. Only about four-fifths of the German people were now united in the "North German Confederation"; but this union was closer, and hence more powerful, than any previous one in Germany; and for the first time in their history the German people possessed the assured right of co-operating in the framing of their fortunes by the mouths of freely elected representatives. The South Germans, indeed, still held aloof; but the universal feeling was expressed by a Hanoverian: "The line of the Main is no longer a spectre, but only a halting-place for us, where we can take water and coal on board, and can recover our breath in order soon to proceed further on our route."

The French Emperor's Compensations

During the deliberations of the Reichstag a heavy storm-cloud had gathered, but had happily been dispersed. The French Emperor, Napoleon III., had attempted on August 5th, 1866, to obtain "compensations" for the aggrandisement of Prussia and the union of Northern Germany by demanding Rhenish Hesse with Mainz and the Bavarian Rhenish Palatinate. Having met with a flat refusal, he had claimed, as his reward for leaving Germany to Prussia, both Belgium and Luxemburg.

Bismarck prolonged the negotiations in this matter, since he did not wish to irritate France beyond endurance, and so drive her into the arms of the enemies of Prussia. He did not return any definite answer to the offer which he simultaneously received of an offensive and defensive alliance with the French Empire; but, so far as Luxemburg was concerned, left no doubt in the mind of Count Benedetti, the French ambassador, that King William would decline to give France any active assistance in acquiring it, and at most would passively tolerate the proceeding.

But to give timely intimation to friend and foe that war would find Germany united, Bismarck published on March 19th, 1867, the offensive and defensive alliances which Prussia had concluded in August, 1866, with Bavaria, Würtemberg, and Baden, and which were joined also by Hesse-Darmstadt on April 11th, 1867. Three points were established by these treaties. (1) North and South Germany supported each other in case of war with their entire military force; (2) this force stood under the single and supreme command of the King of Prussia; (3) all the states guaranteed to each other the integrity of their respective territories.

Germany Ready for Emergencies

Napoleon, indeed, persuaded King William III. of the Netherlands to conclude a treaty, in virtue of which the latter ceded to the emperor his right to Luxemburg, in return for a compensation of £200,000 ; but the king, who very reluctantly surrendered Luxemburg, insisted on Prussia's formal assent to the treaty, and, as already mentioned, this assent was not forthcoming ; the whole nation was unanimously resolved to prevent at all hazards the smallest encroachment on German territory, even on territory which was only connected with the body of the nation by the bond of the Zollverein, as had been the case with Luxemburg after the dissolution of the German Confederation.

Napoleon III. Gives Way to Germany

Napoleon, whose military resources were not ready for a collision with Germany, finally recoiled before this determined opposition, and all the more so because Austria, where, since October 30th, 1866, the Saxon Baron von Beust presided at the Foreign Office, was not induced, even by the offer of Silesia, to form an armed alliance against Prussia. Austria had felt, too recently and too acutely, the military superiority of Prussia to venture on a new war, especially one against the entire German nation.

On the proposal of the Tsar Alexander II. a conference of all the Great Powers was summoned at London, and this decided that Luxemburg should be left to the house of Nassau-Orange, but be declared neutral. Prussia accordingly had to withdraw her garrison from the former federal fortress, Luxemburg, and to allow the destruction of its fortifications. But Luxemburg remained in the Zollverein as before. The inglorious termination of a matter far from glorious in itself was very detrimental to Napoleon's reputation ; the victories of Prussia and the formation of the North German Confederation, just as the creation of the Kingdom of Italy some few years before, were reckoned by all supporters of the doctrine of France's natural and "legitimate" hegemony in Europe as severe defeats to France. "Now," exclaimed Thiers, half in menace, half in warning, before the Chamber in March, 1867, "no further blunders may be committed." The emperor felt himself deeply injured that Prussia had refused the enlarge-

France's Severe Defeats

ment of France, which he so ardently desired. "Bismarck has attempted to deceive me," he afterwards said to Heinrich von Sybel, "but an emperor of France may not let himself be deceived." Even the Catholic party was indignant with him, because he had allowed the revolution a free hand and had left the Pope to be despoiled. The Republican opposition completely outdid itself in most venomous attacks on the emperor, of which Victor Hugo and A. Rogeard made themselves the mouthpieces.

And now, to crown all, there came the crash of the Mexican expedition. The emperor gave way before the threat of the United States that they would treat the continued presence of a French army on American soil as a casus belli. The desperate entreaties of the empress, Charlotte, who came to Europe in July, 1866, to plead her husband's cause, were useless ; when she realised her position, her reason gave way. Between the end of January and the middle of March, 1867, the French troops withdrew from Mexico, and Maximilian, who was too proud to desert his followers in the hour of danger, and still hoped to strengthen the fading influence of his party by liberal concessions, was taken prisoner at Querétaro, together with Generals Miguel Miramon and Tomas Mejia, brought before a court-martial, and shot as a rebel, on June 19th, 1867.

The French Withdraw From Mexico

In order to conciliate French public opinion, Napoleon determined upon liberal measures which ran counter to the despotic traditions of the Second Empire. He granted to the senate and the legislative body in January, 1867, the right to interpellate the Government, and gave permission that not merely the "Minister of State"— that is, the hitherto all powerful Premier— but every Minister might present the case for his policy before the Chamber, but only under "instructions from the emperor."

This concession was regarded, however, as a fundamentally important step, by which the emperor wished to introduce, in the place of his own exclusive irresponsibility, ministerial responsibility; that is to say, he wished to pass from a despotic to a constitutional, or even parliamentary, method of government. That was not, indeed, Napoleon's intention ; but one step leads to another, and the emperor's failing health made it more and more incumbent on him to relieve himself of the business of government. The politicians, who thought they must contest a change of system on political or personal grounds, now combined into a reactionary club under the name of the "Cercle de la rue de l'Arcade." The intellectual leader of these "Arcadians" was the "Vice-Emperor," the Minister of State, Rouher, while the liberalising party, le Tiers parti, which grew up in 1866 between the "Arcadians" and the Republicans, was led by the former Republican, but now "freethinking Imperialist," Emil Ollivier, a talented but ambitious and weak character.

The Paris International Exhibtion of the summer of 1867 shed a transitory brilliance over France and the emperor; but the murderous attempt of a Pole, Anton Bereszowski, on the life of the Tsar Alexander II. on June 6th, struck a discordant note in the midst of the festivities, and comments were made on the absence of the Emperor Francis Joseph, who was in mourning for his brother Maximilian, the victim of Napoleon's bad faith, and kept away from the French capital. Napoleon and his consort therefore journeyed, in August, 1867, to Salzburg to express their sympathy to Francis Joseph; they stayed there from August 18th to the 23rd, and although Napoleon had only come accompanied by General Fleury, yet through him and Beust a better understanding was brought about between the two empires—a step which was universally regarded in Germany as aimed at Prussia. But although the two parties had merely agreed that Prussia should be prevented from crossing the Main, and Russia from crossing the Pruth, yet now two camps were formed in Europe : Prussia and Russia stood in the one, Austria and France in the other. Francis Joseph paid his return visit to Paris on October 23rd. On his way he had exchanged a "flying and formal" greeting with the King of Prussia, at the latter's wish, in Oos; but he said to General Ducrot in Strassburg : "I hope that we shall some day march side by side."

The Treaty of Prague, according to the French conception of it, implied that Prussia by its terms was restricted to North Germany, and might not venture to form any union with the South German states, unless the assent of every Power participating in the treaty was obtained.

Friendly Meeting of Emperors

France reckoned herself one of these Powers, because she had intervened in July, 1866; but she had not signed the treaty—indeed, she could not have been allowed to do so, since she had taken no share in the war—and therefore possessed properly no right to superintend the execution of the treaty. Bismarck adhered strictly to the principle that Austria alone was entitled to take any action in this matter, but that even Austria might not raise any objections if all the states of the South, combined into a union, wished to form a national bond with the North. The only doubtful point was whether any single state was competent to join the North German Confederation.

The Abortive Southern Confederation

But it very soon became clear that the "Southern Confederation," planned at Prague in 1866, would not come to pass. Bavaria, as by far the largest state, would naturally have obtained the predominant position; but King Charles of Würtemberg was still less willing to acknowledge the superiority of King Lewis II. than that of the King of Prussia. The Grand Duke Frederic of Baden, son-in-law of the King of Prussia, a liberal and patriotic prince, was resolved to enter the North German Confederation at the next opportunity, and his views were shared by the majority of his subjects. His Ministers, Karl Mathy and Rudolph von Freydorf, were staunch German patriots like himself. Mathy had written to Bismarck on November 18th, 1867, asking for Baden's entrance into the Federation, but was put off with hopes for the future, and died before attaining his object, on February 4th, 1868.

In spite of all democratic and ultramontane opposition, the South and North were drawing closer to each other. Agreeably to the spirit of the treaties, all the states south of the Main introduced in 1868 universal conscription and armed their infantry with the Prussian needle-gun; in consequence of this they obtained Prussian instructors for their troops, and Hesse-Darmstadt concluded, in April, 1867, a military treaty with Prussia, by the terms of which its troops were completely incorporated into the army of the North German Confederation. The royal Saxon army, however, by virtue of the convention of February 7th, 1867, constituted from July 1st onwards the

Conscription in the Southern States

Twelfth North German Army Corps, under its own administration. In Würtemberg the new War Minister, Rudolf von Wagner, proceeded to reform the army on the Prussian model ; and the example was followed in Bavaria, despite the particularism of that kingdom by the War Minister, Sigmund von Prankh. The

Organising a United German Army preparation for a united German army proceeded without interruption. The treaty of federation with Prussia was accepted by the Chambers in the autumn of 1867, in Baden without any struggle, but in Würtemberg after violent parliamentary disputes, although the democratic party of Würtemberg foretold that the new policy of " militarism " would impose an intolerable burden on the people without securing them against France. The treaty, according to the Bavarian constitution, did not require the approval of the estates. Owing to this union of all German races in a common system of defence with such safeguards, the Zollverein, which had been renounced by Prussia, was once more established on a new basis. First of all, the so-called liberum veto of each particular state—the right to repudiate any resolution of the majority as not legally binding on the non-assenting state—was abolished ; in its place was introduced the principle that resolutions passed by the majority were binding on the minority. The work of legislating for the Zollverein was to be carried out by the Federal Council and Reichstag according to this principle.

Besides matters connected with customs, the taxation of the salt obtained within the Zollverein, and of the tobacco produced or imported into the Zollverein, fell within the competence of the Reichstag, sitting as the Customs Parliament. The duration of the customs treaty was once more fixed for twelve years, with the proviso that, if notice was not given, it would continue as a matter of course for another twelve years.

These treaties also met with opposition in Würtemberg and Bavaria from the protectionists and the particularists, who not only feared heavy economic

loss from the free-trade principles prevailing in Prussia, but also disliked the customs union with the North as a preliminary step to political amalgamation. Yet the interests of trades and industries, which obviously could not exist without the Zollverein, were so important that in the Bavarian Representative Chamber, on October 22nd, 1867, 117 votes against 17, and on the 31st, in the Würtemberg Chamber, 73 against 16, were given for the customs union.

The First Chamber in Bavaria, that of the Imperial Councillors, made a futile attempt to preserve the Bavarian "liberum veto " ; but as Bismarck declared that he would sooner renounce the customs treaty itself than allow this limitation on it, the Chamber gave way. Hungary, after the suppression of the Hungarian rebellion of the year 1849, was deprived of independence, and was, as far as possible, reduced to the constitutional status of a crown demesne, which in the last resort was governed from Vienna. The proud Magyar people had not resigned itself in silence to this lot, but continuously demanded the restoration of its independence. It absolutely refused to send representatives to the Reichsrat in Vienna, the central Parliament of the monarchy created by the constitution of February 26th, 1861. The leader of the Opposition was Francis Déak, 1803–1876, originally a lawyer and judicial assessor in his own county of Szala. He had been Minister of Justice in 1848, and became later a parliamentary politician by profession ; he was a man of shrewdness, determination, and integrity, of temperate views, resolute in advocating the rights of his people and yet unwilling to

FRANCIS DEAK
A Hungarian politician prominent in his country's struggles for liberty, he led the movement against the sending of representatives to the Reichsrat in Vienna.

Leaders in Hungarian Movements interfere with the undoubted rights of the Crown. He was opposed to the feudal abuse of serf labour no less than to the communist views rife among the Hungarian peasantry, whose supporters would have most gladly divided the property of the nobles among themselves. Some reputation was also enjoyed by Count Julius Andrássy, whose inclinations led him into the region of foreign policy. The defeat of Austria in the year 1859 broke the ice both in the western and eastern half of the Empire. Schmerling, the creator of the February constitution, consented in April, 1861, to summon once more the Hungarian Landtag, which had been dissolved in 1849. But since Deák demanded a return to the state of things which had existed before 1848, no understanding was reached, and in the year 1866 General Klapka, with Bismarck's support, organised a "Hungarian legion" to fight on the side of Prussia against the House of Hapsburg-Lorraine. The defeat of 1866 convinced the Emperor Francis Joseph that a reconciliation with Hungary was absolutely essential if Austria was not to be completely crippled by internal feuds and prevented from maintaining its already tottering position as a Great Power. "In the East," said Andrássy, "no power is less important than Austria, and yet it ought, in the interests of civilisation, to have great influence there." The Germans in Austria came to the help of the Magyars when they declared at a meeting in Aussee on September 10th, 1866: "Dualism, but not Federalism! no joint monarchy, still less a mere Federation, but two halves of the empire, compact in themselves and closely united together against the outside world."

The new Foreign Minister, Friedrich Ferdinand, Baron Beust, 1809–1866, an excessively energetic statesman, whose pride did not blind him to the needs of the time, worked towards the same end. He wished to restore Austria to its old position by settling the dissensions and by modern legislation, and to leave its forces free for a strong foreign policy, which might limit the encroachments of Prussia and Russia. The circumstance that Beust was a foreigner and a Protestant enabled him to act with greater impartiality towards the affairs of Austria than a native statesman engaged in party struggles could usually manifest, but it roused much

COUNT JULIUS ANDRÁSSY
For his share in the revolutionary movement of 1848 he was exiled from Hungary; returning to his own country in 1857, he became Prime Minister ten years later.

BARON BEUST
To this Austrian statesman belongs the credit of reconciling Hungary to Austria. Born at Dresden in 1809, he died in 1886.

prejudice and distrust against him. When he had already declared to the reassembled Hungarian Reichstag on November 19th, 1866, his willingness to conform with the wishes of the nation, having been nominated on February 7th, 1867, Prime Minister of Austria in place of Count Belcredi, he succeeded in obtaining the imperial decrees of February, 1867. According to these, Hungary recovered its independence, receiving a responsible Ministry of its own under Andrássy. Croatia, the military frontier, and Transylvania were united with it; the "Court Chancery," which existed for Hungary and Transylvania in Vienna, as well as the office of Hungarian Viceroy, were abolished from the moment the new Ministry began its official activity. The western half of the empire, for which, unofficially, the name Cis-Leithania, or the country west of the border-river Leitha, was soon adopted, naturally also received its special government.

It was proposed that foreign policy, the army—the German language to be used for words of command—the excise, and the national debt should be regarded as joint concerns of the "Austrian-Hungarian monarchy," as the official title ran. According to this agreement three imperial Ministers were created for foreign affairs, the army, and the finances. The imperial Minister for Foreign Affairs was to preside in the imperial Ministry and bear the title of Imperial Chancellor, this office being conferred on Baron Beust, as the promoter of the compromise with Hungary. The imperial Ministers were responsible to the so-called Delegations for their measures; these Delegations were bodies of thirty-six deputies each, which were elected by the Parliaments of the two halves of the kingdom, on a fixed proportion to the First and Second Chambers, and met alternately at Vienna and Pesth. They discussed the governmental proposals separately and independently ; valid resolutions could therefore only come into force by the agreement of the Delegations. The share of Hungary in the joint expenditure was fixed in 1867 at thirty per cent., that of Austria at seventy per cent. The Compromise, and

Coronation of Francis Joseph
also the Customs and Commerce Treaty of the two halves of the empire were to be valid for ten years. On June 8th, 1867, the solemn coronation of Francis Joseph and his consort Elizabeth took place. The Magyars felt themselves victors and masters in their own country. The Roumanians and the Saxons in Transylvania were destined soon to feel the heavy hand of the ruling people, which wished by conciliation or by force to make Magyars of the whole population of Hungary. The Croats, on the other hand, who formed a compact nation of two millions, and were inveterate enemies of the Hungarians, received from the Hungarians on June 21st, 1868, the concession that a special Croat Minister should sit in the Ministry at Pesth, and that forty-five per cent, of the revenues of the country should remain reserved for the country itself. Accordingly, on December 29th, 1868, the twenty-nine Croat deputies appeared in the Hungarian Reichstag, from which they had been absent for fully twenty years.

FRANCIS JOSEPH OF AUSTRIA
Born in 1830, he became Emperor of Austria in 1848, on the death of his uncle, Ferdinand I., and on June 8th, 1867, on the formation of an Austro-Hungarian State, he was crowned at Pest with the crown of St. Stephen.

The disputes between parties and nationalities in Austria were strained to the utmost. The Germans defended the centralised constitution of February 25th, 1861, and with it the predominance of their race, for which they claimed superiority to other nationalities in intellectual gifts and achievements ; politically, the majority of them were Liberals. The Slavs, on the other hand, but, above all, the Czechs, were for a form of Federalism, which would guarantee more liberty of action to the several crown lands ; and the Feudals and Clericals supported the same view. But Beust induced the Poles

by concessions at the cost of the Galician Ruthenians, who compose 43 per cent. of the 7,000,000 of Galician population, and of the other crown lands, to take their seats in the Reichsrat ; and he also succeeded in procuring a German majority in the Landtags of Bohemia and Moravia. Thus, on May 22nd, 1867, the regular " inner " Reichsrat, composed of deputies of the several Landtags, could be opened ; but the Czechs refused to sit in it.

The Ministry of Beust, in conformity with the universal change in opinion, piloted through the two Houses of the Reichsrat a series of laws during the course of the year 1867 which received the force of statutes by the imperial sanction given on December 21st, 1867. By this means, Austria, once the promised land of despotism, was changed into a modern constitutional state. Thus ministerial responsibility was introduced, and a state court of twenty-five members was created for the trial of impeached Ministers ; equality of all citizens in the eyes of the law, equal eligibility to all offices, freedom of migration, liberty of the Press and of association, liberty of conscience and religion, the inviolability of private houses, and the secrecy of letters, freedom of religion, freedom of education, the separation of the administration of justice from the government, in short, all the blessings of a modern state, were bestowed at one blow on a people which a few months before had been governed like a herd of cattle. The House of Representatives received the right of electing a president, the right

Changes in the Government of Austria
of voting taxes and recruits, the right of legislation in all important matters ; it was to be summoned annually, and its debates were to be public. The powers of the Landtags were proportionately limited.

These achievements were accompanied by a law, based on the eleventh article of the law as to the representation of the empire, dealing with the supervision of the primary schools, Volksschule, by which local, district, and national school-boards were constituted, and to all three of them not merely representatives of the Church, but also of the state and of education, were nominated. The Concordat of the year 1855 had enslaved education and given the Church full power over the schools, but, by one of the few invariable laws of history, the reaction was only the more violent.

The emperor, in a letter to the Archbishop of Vienna, blamed the bishops because, instead of being **Emperor** conciliatory, they had roused **Blames the** intense animosity, and thus **Bishops** rendered the task of the Government more arduous. A new Ministry, with the especial support of Beust, who in this connection assured the papal nuncio that according to his conviction the Austrian monarchy and the Catholic Church were sisters, carried in the Upper House in March, 1868, the laws which had been determined upon by the Lower House in 1867. By these laws (1) civil marriage was granted in the case where a priest, for reasons not recognised by the state, refused to put up the banns of an engaged couple; (2) the supreme management of a school, with exception of the religious instruction, was reserved to the state, and the post of teacher was open to every citizen of the state without distinction of denomination; (3) in mixed marriages the sons were to accept the religion of the father, the daughters that of the mother, and every citizen should have the right to change his religion on completing his fourteenth year. The emperor signed the

laws on May 25th, 1868. But when Pius IX., on June 22nd, denounced them in the most bitter terms as abominable, absolutely null, and once for all invalid, the feud between Church and State became most acute. The Pope, in view of the legislation directed against the omnipotence of the Church, felt himself only strengthened in his long-cherished intention of claiming doctrinal infallibility for the papal chair. When, however, on July 18th, 1870, this attribute was awarded him by the Vatican Council, Austria replied by a revocation of the Concordat on July 30th, and the restoration of the " placitum regium "—royal consent—as an essential condition for the validity of any papal enactment in Austria.

During these struggles the finances of Austria were reorganised by a somewhat violent measure. The proposal of Ignaz Edlen von Plener, Minister of Commerce, was accepted by a large majority in the Lower House in June, 1868; by this the entire public debt was to be transformed into one unified 5 per cent. stock, but as the interest was to pay a tax of 20 per cent., the rate of interest payable by the **Austria's** state was in fact reduced to 4 **Army** per cent. The army was re-**Re-organised** organised in December, 1868, on the basis of universal conscription, and the war strength fixed for ten years at 800,000 men. The Landwehr was to comprise not merely the older members of the line troops, but also those persons who, though available, had been rejected as superfluous, and had thus not enjoyed any thorough training in the ranks.

" GERMANIA ": THE NATIONAL MONUMENT OF THE FRANCO-GERMAN WAR

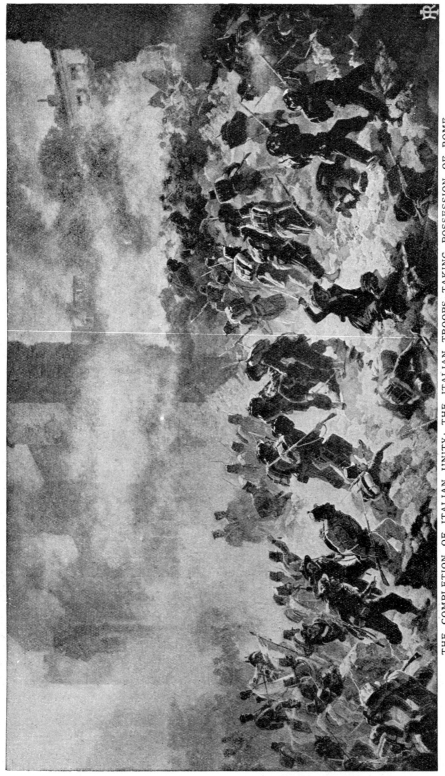

THE COMPLETION OF ITALIAN UNITY: THE ITALIAN TROOPS TAKING POSSESSION OF ROME

September 20th, 1870, stands out prominently in modern European history, marking as it does the completion of Italian unity, the troops, as shown in the above picture, taking possession of Rome in the name of the Italian nation. The defence by the Papal troops being merely the Pope's protest against violence the white flag was soon hoisted.

THE
RE-MAKING
OF
EUROPE

THE
CONSOLIDA-
TION OF THE
POWERS
IX

THE DECLINE OF NAPOLEON III.
APPROACH OF THE FRANCO-GERMAN WAR

THE Roman question was one of the most difficult with which Napoleon III. had to deal. The emperor had withdrawn his troops from Rome in September, 1864, after the Italian Government had pledged itself to remove the seat of the monarchy from Turin to Florence, which promise implied a certain abandonment of claim to the capital, Rome, and neither to attack Rome itself nor to allow it to be attacked by any other Power. The Ultramontanes in France were beside themselves at this agreement; they saw in it the withdrawal of French protection from the still existing fragment of the temporal power of the Pope, the beginning, therefore, of its end; and if they regarded this end as a heavy blow to the Church, the Chauvinist party, headed by Adolphe Thiers, which held the French leadership in Europe to be part of the order of the universe, regarded a complete victory of the Italian national state as an irrevocable hindrance to that leadership on the south side of the Alps, just as the establishment of the German national state seemed to be the end of that predominance on the east bank of the Rhine.

The French Chamber and the Pope

In February, 1866, the French Chamber under these two influences adopted the resolution that the secular sovereignty of the Pope was essential for his spiritual reputation; and after the reversion of Venice to Italy Ultramontane attacks were showered upon Liberal conceptions in general and Italy in particular. The Radical Minister of Public Instruction, Victor Duruy, who brought the Orders which concerned themselves with education under the common law, claimed for the state the education of girls, and founded national libraries of a Liberal character; but he had to guard against the pronounced hostility of the Clericals, and could not prevent, in July, 1867, the temporary closure of the " École Normale," the teachers' training institution, in which Liberal views were active.

The effect of these occurrences was, on the Italian side, that the democratic Minister Rattazzi, a friend to the French, hoped for a revolution in Rome itself, in the course of which Victor Emmanuel might come forward, as in 1859, to restore order. If his troops occupied Rome in this way, the Roman question might be solved very simply, without direct violation of the September Treaty. But Garibaldi, overflowing with fiery zeal, tore in pieces this delicate web of statecraft by entering the states of the Church in September, 1867, at the head of a band of volunteers, in order to overthrow the Pope. When Rattazzi, on being required by Napoleon III. to take counter measures in virtue of the treaty, preferred to tender his resignation, the emperor sent an army from Toulon to Rome under Failly.

Victory of the Pope's Army

This, together with the papal soldiers under General Hermann Kanzler, overtook the Garibaldians, who had immediately begun to retreat on Monte Rotondo, near Mentana, north-east of Rome, and dealt them a crushing blow, November 3rd. "The chassepots have done wonders," Failly wrote to the king. The French army was now compelled to remain in Rome, since otherwise the rule of the Pope would have immediately collapsed. A part of Napoleon's power was again firmly planted in Italy, the indignation of all opponents of the papacy against the guardian of the Pope was once again unloosed, and the dislike of the Italians for the man who prevented the completion of their unity was accentuated. The emperor vainly tried to submit the Roman question to the decision of a European congress, which he proposed to call for this purpose. No other Great Power wished to burn its fingers in this difficult affair.

Napoleon III. the Guardian of the Pope

Napoleon, meantime, conscious that France, from the military point of view, was far behind Prussia, had devised all

5093

sorts of plans to equalise this dispropor-
tion. The first scheme, which really
effected some result and went to the root
of the evil, simply aimed at the introduction of a universal conscription after the
Prussian model ; but the emperor encountered in this the opposition, both of his
generals—who for the most part were

The Radicals sufficiently prejudiced to con-
in Fear of sider a professional army as
Militarism more efficient than a national
army—and of the politicians,
who, partly out of regard for the popular
dislike of universal military service, partly
on political grounds, would hear nothing
of such a measure. All Radicals shrank
from " militarism " and every measure
which might strengthen the monarchy.

Thus the keen-sighted and energetic War
Minister, Marshal Niel, was forced in the
end, against his better judgment, to be
content with a law which proclaimed, in
principle, universal military service, and
fixed its duration at nine years, but, as a
matter of fact, at once neutralised this
reform, since each individual had the
admitted right to buy himself off from
service in the line. Only the duty of
forming part of the militia, or " garde
mobile," was incumbent on everyone.
But, from considerations of economy, this
" garde mobile " was allowed to exist on
paper only, without any attempt to call
it into existence beyond the form of
nominating the officers ; the men were
not organised or even called out for
training. It thus happened that the North
German Confederation, with 30,000,000
souls and an annual levy of 90,000, could
put an army of 540,000 into the field, but
France, with 36,000,000 inhabitants,
raised only 330,000 men.

In armament, however, the French infantry enjoyed a considerable advantage, since
it was equipped with the Chassepot rifle,
which had a range of 1,200 paces, compared
with which the needle-gun, with a range of

Deadly 400 paces only, became at long
Missiles of distances as useless as a stick ;
Warfare in addition to this, the French
weapon was superior to the
German by reason of a smaller bore, a
better breech, and its handiness. On the
other hand, the North German artillery,
whose shells only burst on striking, was
superior to the French, whose missiles
burst after a certain time, often difficult
to calculate exactly, and sometimes exploded in the air before reaching their

mark. The mitrailleuse, on which the
French founded great hopes, proved itself
in 1870 to be by no means a serviceable
weapon, and it was not considered necessary on the German side to adopt it.

The necessity of again finding stronger
support in the nation suggested to the
emperor in January, 1869, the plan of
securing the purchase and management
by the French Eastern Railway of the
Belgian private railways to Brussels and
Rotterdam. In this way Belgium would
become, first economically, and subsequently politically, dependent on France.
But the Belgian Liberal government of
Frère-Orban refused assent to the treaty
for sale ; and since in this question they
were backed by their otherwise deadly
enemies, the Ultramontane party, this
attempt also of the emperor to restore
his prestige proved a failure.

Although Prussia had entirely kept
away from any share in the whole matter,
she was accused by several French papers
of having instigated the Belgian Government to opposition. Even the treaty with
Baden, by which Badeners were allowed

Austria's to pass their terms of military
Embarrassed service in Prussia, and Prus-
Finances sians in Baden, could not successfully be represented as an
infringement of the Treaty of Prague.
Nevertheless, France, Austria, and Italy,
since the summer of 1868, had vigorously
prosecuted the negotiations for a triple
alliance directed against Prussia. But
Beust was restrained by several considerations — the embarrassed condition of
Austrian finances, the incompleteness of
the army reform, the many difficulties of
the domestic situation, the reluctance of
10,000,000 Germans in Austria to make
war on their compatriots, the aversion of
Hungary to every project for restoring the
Austrian predominance in Germany.

He saw himself quite unable to undertake
a war immediately, however much a war
might have suited his inveterate hatred of
Prussia. Such a war, according to his
view, ought to arise from a non-German
cause, some collision of Austria and
Russia in the East, when Prussia would go
over to the Russian side, and thus any
appearance of the war being waged
against German union would be avoided ;
otherwise, war was the best method of
effecting an immediate reconciliation between North and South. A war against
German unity was unacceptable to the

Italians also, since in all probability it would have been followed by a war against their own unity, and this they did not wish to see destroyed, but completed; and probably a portion of the Conservative party would only have been induced to fight against Prussia by the surrender of Rome. But the emperor, who did not venture to inflict a further wound upon the susceptibilities of his Catholic subjects, could not in any case fulfil this condition; and the majority of the Italians stood on the side of the Ministers, who declared to King Victor Emmanuel in July, 1869, that they could not be parties to obliterating the events of the year 1866.

Light is thrown on the situation by the anxiety of Beust lest Napoleon should not be playing an honourable game, but in the last instance, if Prussia, intimidated by the Triple Alliance, was inclined to concessions, should make an agreement with Prussia at the cost of Austria. Since the negotiations thus met insuperable difficulties everywhere, their continuance was, in September, 1869, indefinitely postponed, to use Napoleon's words to Francis Joseph. No terms, according to Beust's statements, had yet been signed, but a verbal agreement had been made on three points: (1) That the aim of the alliance, if ever it was concluded, should be protection and peace; (2) that the parties should support each other in all negotiations between the Great Powers; and (3) that Austria, in a war between France and Prussia should remain at least neutral.

At the moment when these negotiations had come to a standstill a great change had taken place in the internal affairs of France. At the new elections to the legis-

Election Changes in France

lative body on May 23rd, 1869, a great shrinkage of the Royalist votes was apparent; while the opposition in 1857 had received only 810,000, and in 1863 had reached 1,800,000, it now swelled to 3,300,000, and the figures of the Government party receded from 5,300,000 in the year 1863 to 4,600,000. Ollivier's "Third Party" obtained 130 seats in the Chamber of Deputies of, and, combined with the forty votes of the Republican Left, formed a

VICTOR DURUY
Historian and educationist, he became Minister of Public Instruction in France, and did much for the advancement of education by the founding of national libraries.
From a photograph

majority against the followers of Rouher. Napoleon III. need not have regarded the result of the elections as a sign of popular hostility to himself; even the Third party was imperialist. But the result was bound to endanger his position if he declared his agreement with Rouher and the "Arcadians." He therefore veered

"National Ministry" Dissolved

round, dissolved the "National Ministry" on July 17th—Rouher was compensated by the presidency in the Senate, which, on August 2nd, in a solemn session, accepted the scheme of reform settled by the Cabinet—and submitted on September 6th, 1869, comprehensive constitutional reforms to the approval of the Senate. By these, the legislative body acquired the rights of electing all its officials, of initiating legislation, of demanding inquiries, and of appropriating the supplies which it voted to specific branches of the public service. Although the constitutional responsibility of the emperor himself was not given up, yet the principle of ministerial responsibility was introduced, and provision made for the impeachment of Ministers before the Senate. The emperor himself, when speaking to the Italian ambassador, Constantin Nigra, characterised the scope of these reforms as follows: "I had the choice between war and personal rule on one side, and peace with liberal reforms on the other side. I decided for the latter." The circumstance that his experienced War Minister, Niel, died on August 14th, 1869, had at first the effect of making every warlike expedition seem doubly hazardous; it was destined to be seen that his successor, Marshal Lebœuf, possessed neither the experience nor the foresight of Niel.

The emperor summoned on January 2nd, 1870, the Ministry, which, in virtue of the decree of the Senate, was to undertake the responsible conduct of business. Its head was Emile Ollivier, who became Minister of Justice and Public Worship; Count Daru, a clever and cautious man of marked personality, received the Foreign Office; the Home Office went to Chevandier de Valdrôme, the Finances to Buffet. But since the Left demanded that the

General view of the buildings of the Louvre as seen from the Tuileries Palace.

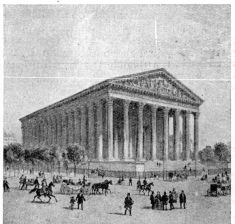

Outside the Church of the Madeleine.

Facade of the Arc de Triomphe towards the city.

General view of the Tuileries Palace as seen from the Gardens.

PARIS IN HER SPLENDOUR: IN THE DAYS OF THE SECOND EMPIRE

General view of the Place de la Concorde, showing the Rue Royale and the Madeleine in the distance.

Scene around the Gate and Boulevard of St. Denis.

Column of the Grande Armée in the Place Vendôme.

In the heart of the business quarter : The Bourse and the Place de la Bourse.

SCENES IN THE CAPITAL CITY DURING THE REIGN OF NAPOLEON III.

Chamber should receive the right of co-operating in any future alteration of the constitution, as otherwise a resolution of the Senate might recall one day what it had granted the previous day, the emperor without demur submitted the constitutional changes to a plebiscite on the ground that the nation had in his time, in 1852, approved the constitution of the empire, and had therefore a claim to say if this constitution was to be altered. The question put to the people was whether it approved of the decree of the Senate on September 6th, 1869, and whether it wished by this means to facilitate the future transmission of the crown from the emperor to his son. The answer of 7,350,142 electors was in the affirmative, that of 1,538,825 in the negative; in the army, which was also allowed to vote, 285,000 answered " Yes," 48,000 " No." Although opposition was considerable, yet it was split up into an Absolutist part, for which the decree of the Senate went much too far, and a Republican, for which the decree did not go far enough, since it not only allowed the Empire to stand, but even assisted Napoleon to consolidate his power. Against this divided opposition, which in any case was five times as large, showed to prodigious advantage, and the emperor was justified in seeing in the plebiscite of May 8th, 1870, a strong proof of the confidence of quite five-sixths of the French in his person, in his dynasty and his rule. Soon afterwards the Ministry underwent

EMILE OLLIVIER

At the head of the Ministry summoned by Napoleon III. at the beginning of 1870 was Emile Ollivier, against whom the accusation has been made that " with a light heart " he " rushed his country into war with Germany."

From a photograph

THE DUC DE GRAMONT

Soon after the formation of the Ministry in 1870, Count Daru resigned his seat at the Foreign Office, and was succeeded by the Duc de Gramont, whose policy as Foreign Minister precipitated the war with Germany.

From a photograph

an important change by the substitution of the Duc de Gramont for Daru. The latter had two motives for resignation. In the first place he had not been able to carry his point that the emperor alone was not entitled to order any future plebiscites, but that the legislative body must also be first heard in the matter. Secondly, Daru was much concerned about the Vatican Council, which Pius IX. had opened in Rome on December 8th, 1869, in order that, at the very moment when the temporal power of the papacy was diminished and even threatened with complete destruction, the spiritual power might be made unlimited through the proclamation of the Pope's infallibility in matters of faith and morals. The Bavarian Prime Minister faced, as far back as April 9th, 1869, the serious danger which threatened the independence of states if this doctrine of the papal infallibility were received, and called upon all states which had Catholic subjects to adopt a common policy towards the papal claim ; but for various reasons he only found support in Russia, which forbade its Catholic bishops to attend the Council, and he was defeated by the ultramontane and particularist majority of the Bavarian Landtag on February 15th, 1870. Daru fared no better with his warnings ; his own colleague, Ollivier, declared that the infallibility affected only the internal administration of the Church and did not concern the State—as if the Church on her side would recognise any sphere of human action as entirely belonging to the State!—and put him off with the dubious assurances of the papal Secretary of State, Count Giacomo Antonelli : "In theory we soar as high as Gregory VII., and Innocent III. ; in practice we are yielding and patient." No effect was produced by the warnings of the noble Montalembert, once so extolled by the Ultramontanes. He blamed the oppression of the State by the Church no less than that of the Church by the State. "We ought," he said, "to stem in time the stream of flattery, deceit, and servility which threatens to flood the Church." He died before his warning cry was justified by events, and Daru's successor, Gramont, was a thoroughgoing Ultramontane who, as such, hated heretical Prussia. The peace of Europe seemed, on June 30th, 1870, to be absolutely assured ; Ollivier could declare in the Chamber that no disturbance threatened it from any quarter, and Lebœuf, the War Minister, proposed to enlist in the army for 1871 only 90,000 instead of 100,000 recruits. The deputies of the Left committed themselves to the statement that the 40,000,000 Germans who had united under the leadership of Prussia were no menace to France, and Ollivier himself can almost be described as a friend of German unity. Archduke Albert of Austria, however, had visited Paris in

ARCHDUKE ALBERT
As field-marshal he commanded in Italy, and afterwards reorganised the Austrian army. Foreseeing the Franco-German war, he advised France to strike the first blow.

April, 1870, on the pretext of an educational journey to the south of France, and, in view of the possible admission of Baden to the North German Confederation, had spoken of the necessity of common measures for the observance of the Treaty of Prague. He unfolded, in this connection, the plan that if war became necessary, a French army should push on past Stuttgart to Nüremberg, in order to unite there with the Italians, who would advance by way of Munich, and with the Austrians, who would come from Bohemia ; they would then fight the Prussians in the region of Leipzig. The archduke was therefore playing with fire ; but he declared that the transformation of the Austrian army would not be

War Plans of Archduke Albert

completed for one or two years, and emphasised the necessity that, since Austria required six weeks to mobilise, France should strike the first blow alone, at any rate in the spring, in order that the Prussians might be settled with before autumn came with cold, long nights and before Russia could interfere. A council of war which Napoleon held on May 17th declared that the demand that France should first make the effort single-handed could not be entertained. General Lebrun, who was then sent to Vienna, did not find Francis Joseph inclined to waive the demand which Prince Albert had made. The Austrian emperor held it to be essential, not merely from the military but also from the political standpoint, since if he declared war simultaneously with France, the Prussians would make full use of the "new German idea" and sweep the South with it. He would have to wait for the course of the war, and then, when the French had advanced into South Germany and were welcomed as liberators from the Prussian yoke, he would take the opportunity and join in the war. The course of events in South Germany gave France room to hope for a change in popular opinion. In Bavaria, Hohenlohe had been turned out in February, and had been replaced by Count Otto Bray-Steinburg, a staunch Particularist. In Würtemberg the most inveterate Democrats gave out the watchword : "French rather than Prussian," and a mass petition, which received 150,000 signatures, demanded the introduction of a militia army on the Swiss model.

The French Emperor's War Council

King Charles replied in March, 1870, by the dismissal of Gessler, Minister of the Interior, who was accused of weakness, and by summoning Suckow to the War Ministry. The latter declared his readiness to make a reduction in the war Budget—a step to which his predecessor, Wagner, had not consented—but in other respects to maintain the army organisation on the Prussian system, which had only been introduced in 1868. A keen-sighted French observer, the military plenipotentiary, Colonel Stoffel, himself warned the Emperor Napoleon against overestimating the Particularist forces. In any case, it was very dubious whether the French could and would fulfil the conditions on which Austria made its co-operation depend— in the event, that is, of its being forced into war by the breach of the Treaty of Prague, which it postulated as the preliminary condition for any military action. The impression thus won ground even there, that, in spite of the tension in the European situation, in spite of the passions and personal influences which were making towards a war, the maintenance of peace, for the year 1870 at least, still seemed probable at the beginning of July.

The government of Queen Isabella II. of Spain had long fallen into complete disrepute owing to the unworthy character of the queen, who had openly broken her marriage vows. Since Isabella abandoned herself entirely to the reactionary party, the Liberals rose, under the leadership of Francisco Serrano and Juan Prim, on September 20th, 1868. After the defeat of the royal army at the bridge of Alcolea on the Guadalquivir, in which the commander-in-chief, General Pavia, was severely wounded on September 28th, the queen, who was just then staying at the seaside watering-place, San Sebastian, was obliged to fly, with her family and her "intendant," Carlos Marfori, to France.

The idea which the bigoted queen had still been entertaining of sending Spanish troops to Rome in place of the French was thus destroyed. The victorious Liberals did not contemplate relieving the Emperor of France from the burden of protecting the Pope. They held fast to the monarchy, nevertheless; and as all attempts to obtain as king

ISABELLA II., QUEEN OF SPAIN
Under the rule of this queen the government of Spain fell into disrepute owing to her unworthy character, and at last, in 1868, she was expelled to France, abdicating in favour of her son, Alfonso XII. She died in 1904.
From a photograph

either Duke Thomas of Genoa, the nephew of the King of Italy, who was still a minor, or the clever Ferdinand of Coburg-Gotha, the titular King of Portugal, a widower since 1853, were abortive, they offered the throne to the latter's son-in-law, the hereditary Prince Leopold of Hohenzollern-Sigmaringen, born in 1835, who was a Catholic, happily married, the father of sons, an upright and energetic man in the prime of life. During 1869, the proposal was laid privately before the hereditary prince himself and his father, the reigning prince, Charles Anthony; but it received a refusal, since the undertaking appeared far too rash. The state of affairs was not altered until a new attempt was made, in February, 1870. Salazar, the previous emissary, was now sent with letters of Prim's to the prince, the hereditary prince, King William, and Bismarck. He went first to Berlin. King William thought the offer should not be accepted; but he recognised that, according to the family laws applying to the whole House of Hohenzollern, he had, as head of the house, no right of prohibition in this case. Bismarck behaved differently. He did not, indeed, promise himself any direct military assistance from Spain if a Hohenzollern wore the Spanish Crown, but closer friendly relations between the two countries, and, as a result, a strengthening of the position of Germany by "one if not two army corps," and more especially by improved commercial intercourse. He therefore advised the hereditary prince " to abandon all scruples and to accept the candidature in the interest of Germany."

But the prince could not even yet make up his mind. It was only natural to consider the effect of such a

Vacant Throne of Spain

candidature on France. Robert von Keudell, one of Bismarck's trusted followers, expressly states that Bismarck did not foresee any danger of an outbreak of war on this ground, since Napoleon would sooner see the Hohenzollern in Madrid than either Isabella's brother-in-law, the Duke of Montpensier of the House of Orleans, or a republic. Napoleon also, who had been informed of the matter by Charles Anthony in the autumn of 1869, had said neither " yes " nor " no," and therefore seemed to raise no objection.

Bismarck's Agents In Spain

A renewed inquiry in Paris itself was impossible, since Prim had urgently begged for secrecy in the matter, in order that it might not be at once frustrated by the efforts of the Opposition. And, again, the House of Sigmaringen was so closely connected with the Bonapartes by Charles Anthony's mother, a Murat, and his wife, a Beauharnais, that the possibility was not excluded that Napoleon III. would actually consent. Bismarck now secretly sent to Spain two trusty agents, Bucher and Versen, who brought back satisfactory news ; but all this was done in a personal and private way, and the Prussian Government was not implicated. Finally, in order to escape from the candidature of the Duke of Montpensier, which was naturally unpalatable to the Spanish authorities, Salazar was once more sent to Sigmaringen at the beginning of June, 1870, and this time received the consent of Charles Anthony and of Leopold. A great moment seemed to have arrived for the House of Hohenzollern-Sigmaringen, and Leopold felt it a heavy responsibility to withdraw from a people " which, after a long period of weakness, was making manly efforts to raise its national civilisation to a higher plane " ; that is to say, to free itself from the dominion of the Ultramontanes. The candidature of Leopold was thereupon

LEADERS OF THE SPANISH LIBERALS
Francisco Serrano and Juan Prim, whose portraits are given above, led the rising of the Spanish Liberals against the reactionary party and the queen, this movement, in 1868, resulting in the dethronement and flight of Isabella and her family. Serrano twice acted as regent before the government was given into the hands of Alfonso XII.

officially proclaimed in Madrid on July 4th, and the Cortes was summoned for July 20th to elect a king.

Throughout the whole affair the point at issue was a matter which in the first instance was a completely private concern of the Spanish nation. The Spaniards could clearly elect any person they wished to be king, and if they looked for such a person among the scions of sovereign or formerly sovereign houses, all that could be demanded was that the elected king should renounce all hereditary right to another throne, in order that a union of the Spanish with another monarchy, and the consequent danger to the balance of power in Europe, might be avoided for all time to come. In the case in point no such renunciation was necessary, since the Swabian line of the Hohenzollerns possessed no hereditary rights, and the hereditary prince, Leopold, accordingly could not be called a Prussian prince.

The Prussian Government, therefore, as such took absolutely no share in the question since it could claim no right to influence the decision ; the king, the crown prince, and Bismarck had given their opinion merely as private individuals. Nevertheless the official news of the proposed candidature of Leopold fell like a thunderbolt on Paris, and Gramont was at once convinced that he had once more to do with a diabolical stratagem of Bismarck's against the interests and honour of France. Although the French representative in Madrid telegraphed that Prim declared every charge against Bismarck to be groundless, and asseverated that the candidature was the exclusive work of the Spanish nation, Gramont allowed a question to be asked him on the point, in the legislative body, on July 6th. In answer, he explained defiantly that France, with all respect for the wishes of the Spanish nation, would not allow a foreign Power to place one of its princes on the throne of Charles V., and thus disturb the equilibrium of Europe. Gramont's language inspired a general fear of approaching war, which his further procedure confirmed. He ordered Count Benedetti, who was taking the cure in Wildbad, to put the request before King William in Ems that, since he had allowed Leopold's candidature **Relations** and thus mortified France, he **of Germany** would now impress upon the **and Spain** prince the duty of withdrawing his assent. But the king obviously could not be persuaded to do that; what, according to the family laws, he could not have sanctioned, he was also unable to forbid, especially after Gramont's behaviour on July 6th. He sent, however, an intimation to Sigmaringen that he would personally have no objection to any renunciation which the prince might choose to make. Faced by the danger of plunging Germany and Spain into war if he persevered in his candidature, Leopold actually withdrew from his candidature on July 12th.

King William sent the telegram of the " Kölnishe Zeitung," which contained this news, by the hand of his adjutant Prince Anton Radziwill, to the French ambassador on the promenade at Ems on the morning of July 13th. The king considered the incident closed, and that was the view of the whole world, as it was the wish of Napoleon and Ollivier. Gramont thought differently; he insisted that the king must be brought into the affair, and therefore pledge himself never to grant his approval should the candidature be renewed. Benedetti received telegraphic orders from his superior to tell the king this on that very morning of July 13th.

He did so, and met with a refusal, but repeated it and " at last very pressingly," as the king telegraphed to Bismarck at Berlin; so that the king finally, in order to get rid of him, sent him a message by his aide-de-camp to the effect **Audacious** that he had no further com- **Behaviour of** munications to make to him. **the French** The king left it to Bismarck's discretion whether he would or would not communicate at once this new demand of Benedetti's and its rejection to the North German ambassadors among foreign Powers and to the Press. But he distinctly did not command this communication to be made. Bismarck, who had returned from Varzin in deep distress at the king's long-

suffering patience towards the French, conferred with Roon and Moltke in Berlin and was resolved to remain Minister no longer unless some satisfaction was obtained for the audacious behaviour of the French; and he deserves all credit for having never flinched for a moment. To force a war, which he regarded as a terrible calamity, if Keudell may be believed, and as likely to be the first in a long series of racial conflicts, was a policy which Bismarck would never have adopted merely for the sake of hastening that union between North and South which was certain to come sooner or later.

But now, when the war was forced upon him, when it could not be avoided without the "cankering sore" of a deep humiliation to a people just struggling into national life, he knew no scruples, and no hesitation. At eleven o'clock at night, on July 13th, the celebrated telegram from Ems was sent to the editor of the semi-official " Norddeutsche Allgemeine Zeitung " and to the embassies. The message reproduced verbatim the telegram, composed by Abeken, which the king had sent **Germany's** to Bismarck from Ems, with **Rebuff** the omission of any irrelevant **to France** matter, and ran as follows: "After the news of the resignation of Prince Hohenzollern had been officially communicated to the imperial French Government by the royal Spanish Government, the French ambassador in Ems further requested His Majesty the king to authorise him to telegraph to Paris that His Majesty pledged himself for the future never to give his assent if the Hohenzollerns should renew their candidature. His Majesty thereupon declined to grant another audience to the French ambassador, and informed the latter through his aide-de-camp that His Majesty had no further communication to make to the ambassador."

This telegram, which was known throughout Germany on July 14th, evoked on all sides the deepest satisfaction that a clear and well-merited rebuff had been given to French presumption; and this satisfaction was increased when it was learnt that Gramont had made a further demand of the ambassador, Baron Karl von Werther, in Paris, namely, that the King of Prussia should write a letter to the Emperor Napoleon, in which he should declare that he had no intention of insulting France when he agreed to the candidature of Leopold. The telegram from Ems in no way compelled the war; that was rather done by the French arrogance towards Germany; it was as Strauss wrote to Renan: " We are fighting again with Louis XIV."

The acerbity of King William's refusal to pledge himself permanently was fully felt in Paris; but the fact could not be disguised that, in view of the withdrawal of a candidature described by France as unendurable, no one in Europe would approve of the conduct of the Imperial Government if it declared itself dissatisfied. The majority, therefore, of the Ministers rejected Gramont's demand that the reserves should be called out; it was left to Gramont to put up with this reprimand for his officious procedure, or to resign.

This was in the morning of July 14th. The emperor himself also was for peace, since he knew the military strength of the Germans, and considered the pretext for the war inappropriate. Even the Empress Eugenie seems to have been unjustly accused of having urged on the war from hatred of heretical Germany, and from anxiety as to her son's prospects.

France Eager for War Yet the feeling in the Cabinet Council veered round in the course of July 14th, and late at night the resolution to mobilise was taken; the British ambassador, Lord Lyons, aptly suggested the reason in the following words: " The agitation in the army and in the nation was so strong that no government which advocated peace could remain in office."

The emperor, his heart full of evil forebodings, yielded to this tide of public opinion; Ollivier and the entire Ministry could not resist it. On the plea of a freshly arrived telegram, which in spite of the wishes of the Opposition was not produced —it cannot have been the telegram from Ems, which was already known—a motion was brought forward on July 15th in the legislative body for the calling out of the Garde Mobile and for the grant of sixty-six millions for the army and the fleet; after a stormy discussion it was carried by 245 votes against 10 votes of the Extreme Left. The French nation had forced its government into war; its representatives almost unanimously approved.

The official declaration of war against Prussia by Napoleon was announced in Berlin by the chargé d'affaires, Georges Le Sourd, on July 19th. The situation had developed with such rapidity, through Gramont's impetuosity and Benedetti's mission to Ems, that this declaration of war is the only official document which came to the Prussian Government from Paris. To judge by the official records, the war seems to have commenced like a pistol-shot, whereas, in reality, it was due to causes stretching back over past centuries. The relations of the German and the French nations, which had been steadily changing since 1552, to the disadvantage of the former, were destined to be definitely readjusted by the war, and the absolute independence of Germany from the " preponderance " of France was to be once for all established.

How Germany Received the Challenge

The whole of Germany felt at once that this was so. The declaration of war was like the stroke of a magician's wand in its effect upon the internal feuds and racial animosities by which the German nation had been hitherto divided. They vanished, and, with them, the mistaken hope of France that now, as on so many former occasions, Germany might be defeated with the help of Germans. The spokesmen of the anti-Prussian party in the South remained as perverse and obstinate as ever; but they no longer had behind them the masses, who, at the moment when the national honour and security seemed menaced, obeyed the call of patriotism with a gratifying determination, and felt that, not merely by virtue of the treaties to which they had sworn, but also by virtue of unwritten right, the cause of Germany was to be found in the camp of Prussia.

When the king travelled, on July 15th, from Ems via Coblenz to Berlin, his journey became a triumphal progress through Germany. Being informed at the Berlin railway station of the resolutions of the French Chambers, he decided to mobilise the whole Northern army, and not merely some army corps, as he had originally intended. He fixed July 16th as the first day for all preparations to be completed. That same day King Lewis II. of Bavaria, since the casus foederis had occurred and Bavaria, by the treaty, had to furnish help, ordered the Bavarian army to be put on a war footing. On July 17th, the same order was given by King Charles I. of Würtemberg, who had hastened back from St. Moritz to Stuttgart. The North German Reichstag assembled on July 19th.

Mobilising the Armies of Germany

It was greeted with a speech from the throne, which in its dignified strength and simplicity is a model of patriotic eloquence such as could only flow from the classic pen of Bismarck. "If Germany silently endured in past centuries the violation of her rights and her honour, she only endured it because in her distraction she did not know her strength. . . .

Bismarck's Historic Declaration To-day, when her armour shows no flaw to the enemy, she possesses the will and the power to resist the renewed violence of the French. . . . God will be with us as with our fathers." The Reichstag unanimously, except for the two Social Democrats, granted £18,000,000 for the conduct of the war ; the South German Landtags did the same. The enthusiastic self-devotion with which the German nation, excepting naturally the Guelf legion and the great financial houses, which even at this epoch-making moment thought only of themselves, rose up in every district to fight for honour, freedom, and unity, was, in one respect, more remarkable than that which the great days of 1813 had brought to light ; for the first time in German history Germany arose as a united whole.

While the armies were collecting, Bismarck published in "The Times" the offer which France had made him through Benedetti in August, 1866, proposing an offensive and defensive alliance between Prussia and France ; by it Luxemburg and Belgium were to be assigned to France, which in return would allow Prussia a free hand in Germany. The British ex-Minister, Lord Malmesbury, called this scheme a "detestable document," because it furnished, in spite of Benedetti's embarrassed attempts at denial, a proof that the French Government had been prepared to annihilate its neighbours, who were only protected by the law of nations, without any just claim. It was solely due to Prussia's sense of justice and astuteness that Napoleon's purpose was not successfully accomplished.

Neutrality of European Powers Such revelations contributed their share to the result that no arm was raised in Europe for France. Great Britain at once declared her neutrality, and British merchants derived large profits from the war by supplying coal and munitions of war to the French. Russia was favourably disposed to Prussia ; it feared that an insurrection of the Poles might break out on any advance of the French to Berlin, and hoped to obtain during the war an opportunity to cancel the Treaty of Paris of 1856. In Italy King Victor Emmanuel was indeed personally inclined to support the French, on whose side he had fought in 1855 and 1859 ; but his Ministers were opposed to a war which was waged against the growing unity of Germany. Any hindrance to this growth must signify a defeat of the principle of nationality, and thus become dangerous to the unity of Italy. The lowest price at which Italy could be won was in any case the surrender of Rome ; but Napoleon III. stood in awe of the clerical party, and could not make up his mind to a step which would incense them.

The policy of Austria was at least transparent. She intended to complete her preparations for war under the cloak of neutrality, without exposing herself to a premature attack from the side of Russia. The rapidity with which the French army was crushed, however, by the Germans soon stifled any wish to take part in the war which had been felt at Vienna.

On the eve of the declaration of war, on July 18th, an event involving grave issues occurred at Rome. The Vatican Council, assembled since December 8th, 1869, was oppressed from the outset by the sense of an inevitable destiny. The Opposition reckoned some 150 bishops and abbots. But it was out-voted in the ratio of three to one by the supporters of infallibility, and was itself divided, since one part alone was opposed to the dogma itself, the other part only did not wish to see it proclaimed just then. Besides this the papal plenipotentiaries conducted the proceedings in such a way as to preclude any notion of freedom in the expression of opinions or in voting. After a trial vote of July 13th had shown the result that 451 ayes and 88 noes were recorded, and a deputation of the Opposition to the Pope had produced no effect most of the Opposition left Rome.

Thus, on July 18th, 1870, amid the crashes of a terrible storm which shrouded the council hall in darkness, the dogma was accepted, by 533 votes against two, that the Pope of Rome, when he speaks ex cathedra to settle some point of faith and morals, is infallible, and that such decisions are in themselves unalterable even by the common consent of the Church.

The Papal Dogma of Infallibility

THE FRENCH SOLDIERS' UNREALISED DREAM OF VICTORY

From a photochrome of the famous painting, "The Dream," by Detaille, in the Luxemburg Gallery

TO FACE PAGE 5105

THE DOWNFALL OF THE SECOND FRENCH EMPIRE
AND THE FOUNDING OF THE THIRD REPUBLIC

IT was to be expected, from the rapidity with which France had brought on the outbreak of the war, that she would have the start of the Germans in its preparations, and would bring the war as soon as possible into Germany. Lebœuf, the Minister of War, certainly used the phrase, "We are absolutely ready to the last gaiter-button," and possibly the emperor hoped to break the spirit of Prussia by rapid blows, and then to incorporate Belgium. But it was soon shown that France was not ready. "There was a deficiency," so the French historian, Arthur Chuquet says, "in money, in food, in camp-kettles, cooking utensils, tents, harness, medicine, stretchers, everything, in short"; the existing railways were inadequate to convey to the frontiers the 300,000 men whom France had at her disposal for the war, so that half of them were obliged to march on foot. The regiments were not constructed according **France Unprepared for War** to definite and compact geographical districts: Alsatians had to travel to Bayonne in order to join the ranks of their regiments, and southerners to Brittany. The result, under the stress of circumstances, was an irremediable confusion and an unusual delay in the advance. On the other hand, the mobilisation proceeded quickly and easily among the Germans, where everything had been prepared as far as could be beforehand, and every day was assigned its proper task. Moltke made the suggestive remark that the fourteen days of the mobilisation, during which there was nothing to carry out that had not been long foreseen, were some of the most tranquil days of his life.

The French, according to the original and proper intention, formed one single army, the army of the Rhine, whose commander-in-chief was to be the emperor, with Lebœuf as chief of the General Staff; but when it came to the point, this army was divided into two forces, one of 200,000 men under Marshal Bazaine in Metz, and one of 100,000 men under Marshal MacMahon in Strassburg. The German troops were divided into three armies. The first was posted, under General Steinmetz, north-east of Trèves, round Wittlich, and was made up of the 7th and **The Three Armies of Germany** the 8th corps, from the Rhine districts and Westphalia; it numbered some 60,000 men. Next to it came the second army, under Prince Frederic Charles, which consisted of the 3rd, 4th, and 10th corps; that is to say, of Brandenburgers, Saxons from the province, and Hanoverians, and of the Guards; it took up its position round Neunkirchen and Homburg, and was 134,000 strong. Finally, the third army, 130,000 men, was placed under the command of the Crown Prince Frederic William; to it belonged the 5th and 11th corps, from Posen, Hesse, and Thuringia, as well as the Bavarians, Würtembergers, and Badeners; they were stationed at Rastatt and Landau.

The Crown Prince, before going to the front, visited the South German courts and quickly won the hearts of his soldiers by his chivalrous and kindly nature. Strong reserves stood behind the three armies—namely, the 9th and 12th corps, the Schleswig-Holsteiners and the Saxons from the kingdom, at Mainz, and the 1st, **Guarding Germany's Sea-coast** 2nd, and 6th corps, the East Prussians, Pomeranians, and Silesians, who on account of the railway conditions could not be sent to the front until the twentieth day, and were also intended to be kept in readiness for all emergencies against Austria. The sea-coast was to be guarded against the expected attacks of the French fleet by the 17th division, Magdeburg and the Hanse towns, and by the Landwehr. Moltke, as chief of the Prussian General

NAPOLEON III, EMPEROR OF THE FRENCH

From a photograph

Staff, disclaimed all idea of a minutely elaborated plan, since the execution of such a plan cannot be guaranteed, for every battle creates a new situation, which must be treated and regarded by itself.

Moltke therefore laid down three points only as of paramount importance. First, when the enemy is met, he must be attacked with full strength; secondly, the goal of all efforts is the enemy's capital, the possession of which, owing to strict centralisation of the French Government, is of paramount importance in a war against France; thirdly, the enemy's forces are, if possible, to be driven, not towards the rich south of France, but towards the north, which is poorer in resources and bounded by the sea. Since no blow was intended to be struck before

EMPRESS EUGENIE OF FRANCE
From a photograph

the advance of the entire army was completed and the full weight of a combined attack was assured, the French had for a few days apparently a free hand, and with three army corps drove back out of Saarbrücken on August 2nd the three battalions of those opposed to them. During the operations the emperor took his son, a boy of fourteen, under fire; according to the official telegram " some soldiers shed tears of joy when they saw the prince so calm." But the satisfaction was soon turned into chagrin when the third army, in order to cover the left flank of the second army, which was advancing towards the Saar, marched closer to it, and on August 4th attacked the French division of General Abel Douay, which occupied the town of Weissenburg,

NAPOLEON III.; AND THE EMPEROR AND EMPRESS WITH THEIR SON
From photographs

"À BERLIN!" THE PARISIAN CROWDS DECLARING FOR WAR WITH GERMANY

The prospect of a war with Germany roused the inhabitants of Paris to a state of the highest enthusiasm, and for weeks they deluded themselves with hopes of victory, shouting themselves hoarse with the cry, "à Berlin!" The defeats that followed brought with them terrible disillusionment, and the whole blame was laid on the Government.

and the Gaisberg lying south of it, and utterly defeated it. Among the prisoners was a number of Turcos or Arab soldiers from Algiers, whom Napoleon, though they could not be reckoned as civilised soldiers, had no scruples in employing in the war against the Germans; but they could not resist the impetuous valour of the Bavarians and Poseners. On August 6th the third army on its advance into Alsace encountered the army of Marshal MacMahon, which occupied a strong position near the small town of Wörth, on the right bank of the Sauerbach, a tributary of the Rhine. The Bavarians attacked on the right, the Prussians on the left, and in the last period of the protracted and bloody battle the Würtembergers had also the chance of intervening with success. The end was that the French, whose numerical inferiority was counterbalanced by their formidable positions on heights and vineyards, were completely defeated, and with a loss of 16,000 men and 33 cannons they poured into the passes of the Vosges in headlong flight. "After they had fought like lions," says Arthur Chuquet, "they fled like hares." The Germans paid for the brilliant victory, which gave to them Lower Alsace with the exception of Strassburg, by a loss of 10,000 men, among whom were nearly 500 officers.

On the same day the disgrace of Saarbrücken was wiped out by the German capture of the apparently impregnable heights of Spicheren, near Saarbrücken, although only twenty-seven German

MARSHAL MACMAHON
A distinguished soldier who had served France in earlier wars, he commanded the first army corps in the Franco-German War, and, defeated at Wörth, was captured at Sedan. He was elected President of the Republic in 1873.

GENERAL STEINMETZ
A Prussian general of experience and distinction, he commanded one of the three German armies in the Franco-German War, and after failing in his task at Gravelotte, was appointed Governor-General of Posen and Silesia.

battalions were on the spot against thirty-nine of the French, whose commander, since he did not wish to be cut off from Metz, saw himself compelled to make a hasty retreat, which abandoned Eastern Lorraine to the Germans. The news from the scene of war produced in Paris, where for weeks the inhabitants had deluded themselves with infatuated hopes of victory, and had shouted themselves hoarse with the cry "à Berlin!" a terrible disillusionment, and then a fierce bitterness against the Government, on whose shoulders all the blame for the defeats was laid, since that was the most convenient thing to do. The Ollivier Ministry was overthrown by a vote of want of confidence in the Chambers, which declared it incapable to organise the defence of the country; but the Republicans did not succeed in their intention of placing an executive committee of the Chambers at the head of the country, and so superseding the Empire offhand. On the contrary, the empress transferred the premiership to General Palikao, who took the Ministry of War from Leboeuf and gave him the command of a corps. The emperor wished at first to retire with his whole army to the camp of Châlons-sur-Marne, where MacMahon was collecting the fragments of his army and gathering fresh troops round him. But since the abandonment of the whole of Eastern France to its fate would have been a political mistake, Napoleon remained for the moment stationary in Metz, against which the first and second armies now were put into movement, while the third advanced through the Vosges toward Châlons. Since this latter had the longer way to march, the king issued orders that the two other armies should advance more slowly, in order that the combined German forces might compose an unbroken and continuous mass with a front of equal depth, and that the enemy might not find any opportunity to throw himself in overwhelming numbers on any one part. On August 14th the advance guard of the first army, under Goltz, had almost reached the gates of Metz, when they found the French main army preparing to retreat. In order to check them on the right bank of the Moselle and to bring on a pitched battle at Metz, Goltz, in spite of his inferior numbers, attacked the enemy. The French, eager at last to chastise the bold assailant, immediately wheeled round; but, just as at Spicheren, the nearest German regiments, so soon as they heard the thunder of the cannons, hurried to the assistance of Goltz, freed him from great danger, and drove the French back under the fort of St. Julien, which, with its heavy guns, took part at nightfall in the fierce engagement. Thus the retreat of the French was delayed by one day, and in the meantime the main body of the Germans had reached the Moselle. Napoleon, yielding to public opinion, now resigned the supreme command to Marshal Bazaine, in whom the army and navy reposed unfounded confidence, left Metz with precipitate haste on August 14th, and entered Châlons with MacMahon on the 17th. The main army itself did not leave Metz until August 15th, and then only advanced

MARSHAL BAZAINE

Resigning the supreme command of the French army and yielding to public opinion, Napoleon appointed Marshal Bazaine to that office, but the anticipated success did not follow, Bazaine capitulating to the enemy at Metz.

CROWN PRINCE OF SAXONY

In the Franco-German War the 9th and 12th Corps, as well as the Guards, were placed, as "the Meuse Army," under Crown Prince Albert of Saxony, who had the reputation of being a splendid leader.

five miles in a whole day, since the baggage train blocked all the roads. Meantime, the Third Army Corps, that of the Brandenburgers, had reached the road which leads from Metz past Vionville and Mars-la-Tour to Verdun and the valley of the Meuse, and their general, Alvensleben, determined at all hazards to block the further march of the enemy in that direction, although he was well aware that he would have four French corps opposed to him, and for a considerable time could count on no support being brought up. A desperate struggle began on August 16th. At two o'clock in the afternoon Alvensleben had not a single infantry battalion or any artillery in reserve; so that when Marshal Canrobert, with sound judgment, pressed on in order to break up the exhausted German line, the Twelfth Cavalry Brigade was compelled to attack the enemy, notwithstanding all the difficulties of a cavalry attack on infantry armed with chassepots. This "Charge of the 800" recalls that of Balaclava; only half of them came back. But here it saved the day. "Canrobert did not move again that whole day; he might have broken through, but from the furious onslaught of Bredow's six squadrons he feared to fall into a trap and kept quiet." But since gradually the Tenth Corps from the left and the Eighth Corps from the right came to Alvensleben's support, the danger passed; the Germans, who on this day faced a great army of 120,000 French at first with 29,000 and later with 65,000 men, were in possession of the field of battle. Of the roads by which Bazaine could reach Verdun from Metz, the southern was blocked against him; he could only effect

THE PRUSSIANS DEFEATING THE FRENCH AT THE DECISIVE BATTLE OF WÖRTH, ON AUGUST 6th, 1870

From the painting by Beauquesne, by permission of Messrs. Braun, Clement & Co.

"THE LAST CARTRIDGE": AN EPISODE IN THE GLORIOUS DEFENCE OF BAZEILLES BY THE FRENCH, SEPTEMBER 1ST, 1870

The incident represented in this famous picture occurred at the village of Bazeilles, situated at the crossing of the Douzy and Sedan roads. Pressed by the Bavarian attack, the French retired, but a handful of men in an isolated house to the north of Bazeilles maintained a prolonged resistance against overwhelming odds until their ammunition became exhausted.

From the painting by De Neuville

his retreat now on the northern road, by Saint-Privat. And that possibility was then taken from him, since on August 18th the two German armies, both of which meantime had crossed the Moselle above Metz, advanced to the attack on the entire front from Sainte-Marie-aux-Chênes and Saint-Privat to Gravelotte. In the course of the operations the Saxons, under the Crown Prince Albert, and the Guards, under Prince Augustus of Würtemberg, stormed the fortress-like position of Saint-Privat with terrific carnage; on the right wing at Gravelotte no success was attained.

But the main point had been achieved. The great French army had

COUNT VON MOLTKE
To his military genius Germany owed much of her success over France in the war of 1870. A great strategist and organiser, he prepared the army with wonderful skill, and thus laid the foundation of the many brilliant victories which followed.
From a photograph

been hurled back on Metz, and was immediately surrounded there by the Germans in a wide circle. The indecision of the French commander-in-chief was much to blame for this momentous issue to this prolonged struggle, in which some 180,000 men on either side ultimately took part. From fear of being finally cut off from Metz itself and surrounded in the open field, Bazaine kept a third of his forces in reserve; if he had staked these, he might, perhaps, have won the game. The casualties on either side were enormous. The Germans lost on the 14th, 16th, and 18th of August 5,000, 16,000, and 20,000 men, making a total of 41,000 killed,

NAPOLEON III. PRESIDING OVER A COUNCIL OF MINISTERS AT THE TUILERIES

A BRILLIANT ACHIEVEMENT OF GERMAN CAVALRY: THE "CHARGE OF THE EIGHT HUNDRED" ON AUGUST 16TH, 1870

This brilliant feat, accomplished by Germany's Twelfth Cavalry Brigade in an engagement with the French close to the walls of Metz, recalls the famous "Charge of the Light Brigade" at Balaclava, but in this instance the brave effort, though attended with the loss of half the brigade, was successful, as it repulsed the enemy and saved the day.

From the painting by Aimé Morot in the Museum of Luxemburg

THE BATTLE OF SEDAN: GENERAL MOLTKE DIRECTING THE OPERATIONS OF THE PRUSSIAN FORCES

From the painting by Anton von Werner, by permission of the Berlin Photographic Co.

CAPITULATION OF SÉDAN: GENERALS MOLTKE AND WIMPFFEN ARRANGING THE TERMS OF SURRENDER AT THE CASTLE OF BELLEVUE

Recognising the hopelessness of continuing the struggle at Sedan, Napoleon III. wrote to the King of Prussia that "not having succeeded in dying in the midst of my troops, nothing remains for me but to deliver my sword into your Majesty's hands." General Wimpffen was deputed to go over to the enemy's headquarters at the Castle of Bellevue, near Donchery, where he had a long interview with General Moltke, whose conditions were accepted, and thus there ensued on the following day, September 2nd, the surrender of Sedan.

From the painting by Anton von Werner, by permission of the Berlin Photographic Co.

THE FRENCH EMPEROR'S SURRENDER: NAPOLEON III. MEETING WITH BISMARCK AFTER SEDAN
Defeat after defeat fell in rapid succession upon the French in their war with Germany, and, after the humiliation and loss of Sedan, Napoleon III. gave himself up to his enemies.
From the painting by Anton von Werner, by permission of the Berlin Photographic Co.

PRUSSIA'S ROYAL CAPTIVE: THE EMPEROR NAPOLEON III. AND COUNT BISMARCK ON THE MORNING AFTER SEDAN

From the painting by Camphausen, by permission of the Berlin Photographic Co.

THE FALL OF NAPOLEON III.: THE EMPEROR OF THE FRENCH A PRISONER IN THE HANDS OF THE PRUSSIANS

The surrender of Napoleon III. was quickly followed by his deposition as Emperor of the French and the establishment of a Republic. The unfortunate emperor was for some time kept prisoner by the Prussians, but he subsequently joined the Empress Eugenie and their son at Chislehurst, Kent, where he resided until his death, on January 9th, 1873.

wounded, and prisoners; the French, 3,600, 16,000, and 13,000, some 33,000 men in all. The comparative smallness of the French losses is explained by the fact that they were mostly on the defensive, although they ought properly to have attacked, and fought behind entrenchments. The French army in Metz was lost if a hand were not stretched out to it by its comrades-in-arms outside the town; it was rumoured that Bazaine would make a renewed attempt to meet the expected relieving force at Montmédy or Sedan. All the journals in Paris declared with one voice that Bazaine must be rescued at any cost. Under the pressure of this situation Mac-Mahon, who had been reinforced at Châlons by a division recalled from the Spanish frontier and by four regiments of marines, and had been nominated commander-in-chief of all the forces outside Metz, decided not to retreat to Paris—the course which seemed to him most correct in itself —but to leave the camp of Châlons to its fate and march on Montmédy by way of Vouziers and Buzancy, and there effect a junction, if possible, with Bazaine.

King William had meantime commanded Prince Frederic Charles to invest Metz. General Steinmetz, since he was not on good terms with Prince Frederic Charles, now his superior, and especially since he had failed in his task at Gravelotte, was appointed Governor-general of Posen and Silesia. The Ninth and Twelfth Corps, as well as the Guards, were placed, as "the Meuse Army," under Crown Prince Albert of Saxony, a splendid leader, and instructions were given to him to push on towards Châlons with the third army; his task was to frustrate all attempts of the French to take up a

LEON GAMBETTA
An advanced Liberal, he took office in the Government of National Defence after the proclamation of the Republic, becoming Minister of the Interior. He later became Dictator of France, and wished to continue the war against Germany, even after the surrenders of Metz and Paris.
From a photograph

position there and advance on Metz. But when the Meuse army had passed Verdun, and the third army had reached Ste. Menehould, Headquarters, which followed these movements, learnt of MacMahon's march from Châlons and Rheims; Moltke immediately issued orders, on August 25th, that the two armies would wheel to the right, in order, if possible, to take MacMahon in the rear. This dangerous manœuvre, which extended, of course, to the baggage trains of the armies, was completely successful, without causing any confusion to the columns. MacMahon failed to see the favourable chance, which presented itself for several days, of hurling his 120,000 men against the 99,000 under the Crown Prince of Saxony and annihilating them before the third army came up. When MacMahon found no trace of Bazaine on August 27th at Montmédy, he wished to commence the retreat on Paris; but on the direct orders of Palikao, the Minister of War, and postponing military to political considerations, he continued his march in the direction of Metz, and hastened to his ruin. On August 30th the corps of General de Failly was attacked by the Bavarians and the Fourth Prussian Corps under Gustav von Alvensleben at **The French Retire to Sedan** Beaumont, and thrown back on Mouzon. The whole French army retired from that place to the fortress of Sedan, in the hope of being able to rest there and then to retire along the Belgian frontier northwards. But that was not allowed to happen. The Meuse army pressed on from the east, the third army from the west; the Eleventh Corps seized the bridge which crossed the Meuse at Donchery, and thus cut off the road to the north-west. The neighbourhood of Sedan was certainly easy to defend, since the Meuse, with other streams and gorges, presented considerable difficulties to an attack; but on September 1st the Germans, who outnumbered the French by almost two to one, advanced victoriously onwards, in spite of the most gallant resistance. The Bavarians captured Bazeilles on the south-west, where the inhabitants took part in the fight, and thus brought upon themselves the destruction of their village. The Eleventh Corps took the cavalry of Illy in the north. A great cavalry attack, under the Marquis de Gallifet, at Floing could not change the fortune of the day; the French army, thrown back from every side on to Sedan, had only the choice between surrendering or being destroyed with the fortress itself, which could be bombarded from all sides.

Victorious March of the Germans

Marshal MacMahon was spared the necessity of making his decision in this painful position; a splinter of a shell had severely wounded him in the thigh that very morning at half-past six. The general next to him in seniority, Baron Wimpffen, who had just arrived from Algiers, was forced, in consideration of the 690 pieces of artillery trained on the town, to conclude an unconditional surrender on September 2nd. In this way, besides 21,000 French who had been taken during the battle, 83,000 became prisoners of war; and with them 558 guns were captured. The French had lost 17,000 in killed and wounded, the Germans, 9,000; an army of 120,000 men was annihilated at a single blow. Two German corps were required to guard the prisoners and deport them gradually to Germany.

The Emperor Napoleon himself fell into the hands of the Germans, together with his army. It is attested, as indeed he wrote to King William, that he wished to die in the midst of his troops before consenting to such a step; but the bullets, which mowed thousands down, passed him by, in order that the man on whom, in the eyes of history, the responsibility for the war and the defeat rests, although the whole French nation was really to blame, might go before the monarch whom he had challenged to the fight, and that the latter might prove his magnanimity to

GAMBETTA PROCLAIMING THE REPUBLIC AT THE PALACE OF THE CORPS LÉGISLATIF

be not inferior to his strength. The meeting of the two monarchs took place at two o'clock in the Château of Bellevue near Frénois, during which Napoleon asserted that he had only begun the war under compulsion from the popular opinion of his country. The castle of Wilhelmshöhe near Cassel was assigned him as his abode, and the emperor was detained there in honourable confinement until the end of the war.

That evening the king, who in a telegram to his wife had given God the honour, proposed a toast to Roon, the Minister of War, who had whetted the sword, to Moltke, who had wielded it, and to Bismarck, who by his direction of Prussian policy for years had raised Prussia to her present pre-eminence. He modestly said nothing about himself, who had placed all these men in the responsible posts and rendered their efforts possible; but the voice of history will testify of him only the more loudly that he confirmed the truth of the saying of Louis XIV., " gouverner, c'est choisir "—the choice of the men and the means both require the decision of the monarch.

The victory of Sedan led to a series of momentous results. Not merely did it evoke in Germany general rejoicings, such as the capture of the monarch of a hostile state and of a great army necessarily call forth, but it powerfully stimulated the national pride and definitely shaped the will of the nation. Thousands of orators at festivities in honour of the victory and countless newspaper articles voiced the determination that such successes were partially wasted if they did not lead to the recovery of that western province which had been lost in less prosperous times, of Alsace and German Lorraine with Strassburg and Metz, and also to the establishment of that complete German unity which was first planned in 1866. Bismarck gave a competent expression

HENRI ROCHEFORT

A Radical journalist, who had found it necessary to escape from France, he was elected a member of the National Assembly in 1870; but the honour carried with it no sobering influence, and once more he escaped for his life.

to the former feeling when he declared in two notes to the ambassadors of the North German Confederation, on September 13th and 16th, that Germany must hold a better guarantee for her security than that of the goodwill of France.

So long as Strassburg and Metz remained in the possession of the French, France would be stronger to attack than Germany to defend ; but once in the possession of Germany, both towns gained a defensive character, and the interests of peace were the interests of Europe. In the second place, the victory of Sedan affected the attitude of the neutral Powers. We know from the evidence of King William's letter of September 7th, 1870, to Queen Augusta that all kinds of cross-issues had cropped up before Sedan ; that neutrals had contemplated pacific intervention with the natural object of taking from Germany the fruit of its victories. The ultimate source of these plans was Vienna, where much consternation at the German victories was bound to be felt. But they had found an echo in St. Petersburg also. The Tsar Alexander, it is true, loyally maintained friendly relations with Prussia, and his aunt, Helene, née Princess of Würtemberg, wife of the Grand Duke Michael Pavlovitch, brother of the Tsar Nicholas I., was a trustworthy support to the German party at court ; but the Imperial Chancellor, Alexander Gortchakoff, expressed disapproval of every demand for a cession of French territory, since that would prove a new apple of discord between Germany and France, and thus a standing menace to the peace of Europe.

King William made the just remark that according to this view Germany must give back the whole left bank of the Rhine, since in that case only was tranquillity to be looked for from France. The battle of Sedan put an end to all wish on the part of neutrals to interfere in a war which they had not hindered. The extraordinary efficiency of the German army and the German military organisation had been manifested after a fashion which made the idea of intervention distinctly unattractive, if Germany did not court it. And Germany was very far from courting it. The Germans had faced the war by themselves; they had fought it by themselves; in effect they had won it by themselves. German piety and German poetry attributed the victory to the fact that the God of Battles was on the side of Germany; and Germany had no sort of intention of permitting the Powers which had looked on to arrange matters for the convenience of anyone but the Germans. The third result of the day of Sedan was that the French Empire fell with a crash. The Empress Eugenie received the official news of the surrender on the evening of September 2nd. She hesitated the whole of the 3rd as to what was to be done in this position. But on the 4th the Chamber had to be allowed to speak, and Jules Favre, the leader of the Left, immediately moved that Napoleon Bonaparte and his house should be declared deposed, and that the Corps Législatif should nominate a committee, which might exercise all the powers of the government, and whose task it should be to drive the enemy from the country. The Palikao Ministry also proposed a similar committee of five members to be nominated by the legislative body, but its lieutenant-general was to be Palikoa. The latter furnished a guarantee that the committee, on

GENERAL TROCHU

After the proclamation of the Republic, General Trochu became head of the government; but he did not long hold office, resigning the governorship of Paris in 1871 and retiring into private life about two years afterwards.

which, in any case, the majority of the Chamber would elect trustworthy Bonapartists, would keep the place warm for the Empire, which might be reinstated at a fitting hour. The fear of this incited the mob to act not with the Chamber, but against it. Crowds thronged into the galleries, and finally into the chamber itself, so that Eugène Schneider, the president, declared it an impossibility to continue the debate under such conditions, and the sitting was closed. The attempt to hold an evening sitting, and exclude all disturbance, could not now be carried out; at three o'clock the Senate also had to be closed. The Republic was then proclaimed at the Hôtel de Ville; and in its name the deputies of Paris, with the exception of Thiers, who refused, met as a provisional government. The Radical journalist, Rochefort, whom it was thus hoped to win over, and General Trochu, a Governor of Paris, were nominated members of it. Trochu became head of this government, and Jules Favre was his deputy. A Ministry was formed by this government on September 5th, in which Favre assumed the Ministry of Foreign Affairs, the energetic lawyer, Léon Gambetta, that of the Interior, and General Leflô the War Office. The legislative body was at once dissolved, the Senate abolished; all officials were released from their oath to the emperor, and thirty new prefects, of strict republican views, were appointed. The German merchants who had hitherto remained in France were, so far as no special permission was granted to them, ordered to leave Paris and its vicinity within the space of twenty-four hours.

JULES FAVRE

Elected Minister of Foreign Affairs in the National Assembly of 1870, he settled the terms for the capitulation of Paris in January, 1871, and resigned office a few months later.

WILLIAM I.: KING OF PRUSSIA AND FIRST GERMAN EMPEROR
From the painting by Lenbach, photo by Bruckmann

THE BIRTH OF THE GERMAN EMPIRE
AND FRANCE IN HER HOUR OF DEFEAT

ON the burning question of the moment, whether France after these severe defeats should not seek peace, Favre declared in a circular of September 6th that if the King of Prussia wished to continue this deplorable war against France, even after the overthrow of the guilty dynasty, the Government would accept the challenge and would not cede an inch of national territory nor a stone of the fortresses. Thiers, who had volunteered for the task, was sent on September 12th to the neutral Powers, to induce them to intervene ; but in view of the above-mentioned proclamations of Bismarck of September 13th and 16th, no Power thought it prudent to meddle, since Germany desired a cession of territory as emphatically as France refused one. Any agreement between the belligerents was thus for the time totally excluded. Thiers received in London, Vienna, St. Petersburg, and Florence, courteous words, but no support. Beust, deeply concerned, then wrote : " Je ne vois plus d'Europe " ; even Gortchakoff drily advised the envoy to purchase peace without delay by some sacrifices, since later it might have to be bought more dearly.

Germans March on Paris

The Germans meanwhile were marching straight on Paris. Metz remained at the same time invested by the seven corps under Frederic Charles ; the effort of Bazaine to play into MacMahon's hand on August 31st and September 1st, by a great attempt to break through at Noisseville, proved completely futile ; 36,000 Germans had held a line of five and a half miles against 134,000 French.

Even the French fleet of ironclads, which appeared in August off Heligoland and Kolberg, could do nothing from its want of troops to land. Shattered by a terrible storm on September 9th, it returned ingloriously to its native harbours.

When the Germans, after the capture of Rheims and Laon appeared in the vicinity of Paris, Favre asked for an interview with Bismarck. Conversations between the two statesmen took place on September 19th and 20th in the châteaux of Haute Maison and Ferrières. Favre declared that cessions of territory could in any case only be granted by a National Assembly, and asked for fourteen days' armistice, in order that such an Assembly might be elected. Bismarck was ready to accede to the request, but asked, as compensation for the fact that France in these fourteen days of armistice could to some degree recover her breath, that the fortresses of Pfalzburg, Toul, and Strassburg should be surrendered. Since Favre would not hear of such conditions, the negotiations were thus broken off.

Favre and Bismarck in Conference

The Germans completed the investment of Paris on September 19th, and forced Toul to capitulate on the 23rd. Strassburg had been besieged since August 11th by the Baden troops under General Werder, and since the 23rd had been exposed to a bombardment through which the picture gallery, the library, with its wealth of priceless manuscripts, the law courts, and government buildings, and the theatre were burnt ; of the cathedral, only the roof caught fire. Four hundred and fifty private houses were ruined, and 2,000 persons killed or wounded. This misfortune was due to the fact that Strassburg was a thoroughly antiquated fortress, the bombardment of which involved the destruction not merely of the works, but also of the houses of the inhabitants. The French commander, General Uhrich, ought not, under the circumstances, to have allowed matters to go so far as a bombardment ; but in the knowledge that " Strassburg was Alsace," he offered resistance until a storm, the success of which admitted no doubt, was imminent. The capitulation was signed on September 28th at two o'clock in the morning ; it was the very day on which, 180 years before,

Bombardment and Surrender of Strassburg

Louvois had accepted the surrender of Strassburg to the army of Louis XIV. There were endless rejoicings in Germany when the good news was proclaimed that a city had been won back which had remained dear to every German heart, even in the long years when it stood under a foreign yoke. September 28th was felt

Germany's National Rejoicing to be a day of national satisfaction, a tangible guarantee that the time of German humiliation and weakness was now past for ever. Since Strassburg had fallen, the great railroad to Paris lay at the disposal of the Germans; the captures of Schlettstadt on October 24th, Verdun, November 8th, Neubreisach, November 10th, Diedenhofen, November 24th, Montmédy and Pfalzburg, December 14th, completed the reduction of the smaller fortresses of the east, with which great stores of artillery and powder fell into the hands of the victors. The communications in the rear of the Germans gained greatly in security and quiet.

This fact was the more important because, since the Battle of Sedan, the war, which hitherto had been a duel between armies, assumed another phase. Under the title of " Franc-tireurs," armed bands from among the people took part in the struggle, and caused considerable losses by unexpected attacks on isolated German outposts and rear-guards. On the German side these bands were declared to stand outside the law of nations, and villages whose inhabitants took part in the war as Franc-tireurs were, under certain conditions, burnt down as a deterrent. Even Frenchmen admit that the licentious Franc-tireurs were frequently more dangerous to the natives than to the enemy.

The chief aim of the French, now that negotiations for peace had fallen through, was necessarily the liberation of the capital, for, although among the 1,700,000 persons who were in Paris some 540,000

The Germans' Iron Girdle Round Paris were men capable of bearing arms, yet of these the 340,000 Parisian National Guards were worthless from the military point of view, and of the 120,000 Gardes Mobiles, only a part of the provincials was of any value. Thus only the 80,000 soldiers of the line were thoroughly useful, and with these alone General Trochu could not break through the 150,000, and later 200,000, picked German troops, who were drawing an iron girdle round the city,

under the supreme direction of the king, who resided at Versailles, and force them to raise the siege. Under these conditions the duty of obtaining support from outside was incumbent on the members of the Government, who had left Paris in good time, in order to conduct the arming of the country, and had taken up their seat at Tours on the Loire.

But life was not instilled into this " Delegation," consisting of three old men, until Gambetta left Paris on October 6th in a balloon, and arrived in Tours on the 9th. He immediately took on himself the Ministry of War in addition to that of the Interior, and with the passionate energy of his southern temperament and his thirty-two years, he girded himself for the task of " raising legions from the soil with the stamp of his foot," and of crushing the bold hordes who dared to harass holy Paris, " the navel of the earth." Gambetta's right hand in the organisation of new forces was Charles de Freycinet, a man of forty-two, a Protestant, originally an engineer, clever and experienced, clear and cool in all his actions, but, in con-

Gambetta's Efforts to Save France sequence of the complete wreck of the professional soldiers, full of haughty contempt for military professional knowledge, and inspired by the persuasion that now men of more independent views must assume the lead, and that a burning patriotism must replace military drill.

The thought recurred vaguely to the minds of both that 1870 must go to school with 1793, and that just as then the soldiers trained in the traditions of Frederic the Great and Laudon were repulsed by the levy en masse, so now the laurels might be torn from the soldiers of William I. by the same means. That was really a grave error. In 1793 the powers allied against France were defeated chiefly from their want of combination, not by the armed masses of the French people, which to some extent existed only on paper; and the army which was now fighting on French soil far surpassed the troops of the first coalition in number and moral quality. Gambetta's exertions did not therefore rescue France, but only prolonged her death agony, multiplied the sacrifices, and enhanced the victory of the Germans.

Besides this, it was not possible, with all his resolute determination, to turn armed men into soldiers in a moment. Since it was necessary in a country which only

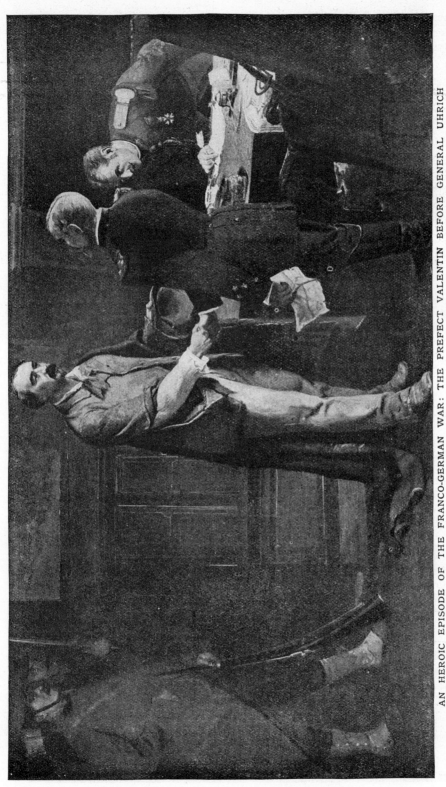

AN HEROIC EPISODE OF THE FRANCO-GERMAN WAR: THE PREFECT VALENTIN BEFORE GENERAL UHRICH

Appointed Prefect of the Department of the Lower Rhine by the Republican Government, in September, 1870, M. Valentin was desired to prove his patriotism by obtaining admission to Strassburg, then under siege. Disguised as a peasant, he made his way through the Prussian lines, and swimming across the moat under a fusillade of bullets from the French soldiers, reached the French side in safety, and as a prisoner was brought before Governor Uhrich. Turning up the sleeve of his shirt, he took therefrom the official document containing his appointment as Prefect, which was immediately recognised. Valentin, however, remained in office for about a week only, Strassburg capitulating on September 28th.

From the painting by Poilleux St. Ange, by permission of Messrs. Braun, Clement & Co.

5127

PRUSSIA'S GREAT WAR WITH FRANCE: THE DEPARTURE OF KING WILLIAM I. FOR THE FRONT IN 1870

From the painting by Adolf Menzel, photo by Schauer

GENERAL BAZAINE'S SURRENDER OF THE TOWN OF METZ TO THE PRUSSIANS, ON OCTOBER 27TH, 1870

From the painting by Conrad Freyberg, by permission of the Berlin Photographic Co.

Z 28 G

5129

possessed six batteries and 2,000,000 cartridges to procure arms and ammunition from every source, especially from England, a varied selection of weapons was the result; there were in the new army alone fifteen different kinds of guns in use. Nevertheless, Gambetta deserves admiration for having raised 600,000 men within four months; and even if all attempts were shattered against the superior strategy and the incomparable efficiency of the German troops, still Gambetta saved the honour of France, and with it the future of the republic.

Grave Danger of Paris

The Germans, shortly after Gambetta's arrival at Tours, had occupied Orleans on October 11th, and on October 18th, stormed Châteaudun, which was burnt, because the inhabitants had joined in the fight. But now troops in such superior numbers were being massed against them that at the headquarters in Versailles serious misgivings were felt as to the possibility of checking all the threatening advances upon Paris.

Under these circumstances all eyes were eagerly fixed on Bazaine, who still kept half the German army stationary under the walls of Metz. During this period all sorts of political negotiations had been conducted between Bazaine, the German headquarters, and the Empress Eugenie, now an exile in England. The gist of these negotiations was th atBazaine, supported by his army, which still remained loyal to its captive monarch, should conclude a peace and restore the empire; but the attempt failed from the numerous and great difficulties which stood in the way, and the position of the encircled army, which was unable to burst the ring of besiegers, became daily worse. From October 8th to 31st continuous rain fell in such torrents that the besiegers and the besieged, who were both encamped on the open field in miserable huts, suffered incredible hardships. Hardly any one had dry clothes; the wind whistled through the crevices; and German divisions which had only a fifth of their numbers in hospital were considered to be in an exceptionally good

PRINCE GORTCHAKOFF
The Russian Imperial Chancellor, he was one of the most powerful Ministers in Europe, and in 1871 was responsible for the secession of Russia from the Treaty of Paris, arranged in the year 1856.

condition. Among the French, the miseries of the weather were aggravated by the daily increasing want of provisions; in the end the soldiers received only one-third of their original allowance of bread, and the supply of salt was exhausted.

Bazaine therefore, after he had vainly tried to obtain the neutralisation of his army, and then its surrender, without the concurrent capitulation of Metz, was compelled to surrender himself with 173,000 men and 1,570 pieces of artillery to Prince Frederic Charles on October 27th. This was a success which surpassed the day of Sedan in grandeur, if not in glory. Germany now had in her hands the territory which she thought essential to secure her tranquillity, and the whole army of Frederic Charles was available for other theatres of war.

About this time the world was surprised by a circular from the Russian Imperial Chancellor, Prince Gortchakoff, which, bearing date October 31st, contained the declaration that the Treaty of Paris of March 30th, 1856, had been repeatedly infringed; for example, in 1859 and 1862, by the union of the two Danubian principalities of Moldavia and Wallachia into the single principality of Roumania—and that it was not Russia's bounden duty to observe merely those clauses in the treaty which were detrimental to her. She did not, therefore, consider herself bound by that provision which declared the Black Sea neutral, but would, on the contrary, make full use of her right to construct a naval harbour there. The circular showed that the authorities at St. Petersburg wished to turn to account the position of Europe, and during the weakness of France to cancel that treaty which France and England in their time had forced upon the dominions of the Tsar, since it was detrimental to the honour and power of Russia. Britain and Austria issued on November 10th and 16th a protest against this selfish policy of Russia; but the conference at London, which met at Bismarck's suggestion on January 17th, 1871, approved the action of Russia in the

Russia's Selfish Policy

DEFENDERS OF THEIR COUNTRY IN THE WAR OF 1870: TRAPPIST MONKS AT EXERCISE BEFORE JOINING THE ARMY OF FRANCE

From a photograph by the Photochrome Co. of the painting by P. G. Robinet de Poissy

MEISSONIER'S SYMBOLIC PICTURE OF THE HEROIC DEFENCE OF PARIS WHEN BESIEGED BY THE GERMANS.

5132

THE HISTORIC SIEGE OF PARIS, SHOWING THE FORTIFICATIONS ERECTED BY THE FRENCH TO PROTECT THEIR CAPITAL

From the painting by A. Binet

THE BARRIER IN THE PLACE DU TRÔNE, NOW THE PLACE DE LA NATION

A SORTIE FROM PARIS, SHOWING THE PROTECTED ARC DE TRIOMPHE

Against the heavy fire of the attacking Prussians the Parisians erected defence works in the streets of the city, and from time to time sorties were made in the hope of driving the invaders from the strong positions which they held.

THE HAVOC OF THE SIEGE: RUINED BUILDINGS AT ST. CLOUD

PLACE DE L'HOSPICE AT ST. CLOUD AFTER THE DEPARTURE OF THE PRUSSIANS

Some idea of the destruction of property resulting from the siege of Paris is given in the above pictures, showing scenes of ruin at St. Cloud after the invading army had taken its departure from the French capital.

Black Sea, and only stipulated that the Straits of the Dardanelles and the Bosphorus should be closed to the warships of all the Great Powers with the obvious exception of Turkey. The German Empire stood in this question on the side of Russia, whose emperor had indisputably facilitated the victory over France by his attitude, even if his Chancellor, Gortchakoff, tried to depreciate as far as possible the results of this victory. After the fall of Metz, Prince Frederic Charles received orders to detach a force under General Manteuffel, in order to capture the still untaken fortresses in the rear of the Germans ; he himself, with his four remaining corps, was to advance rapidly on the Loire by way of Fontainebleau and Sens. The state of things in that direction was critical. The French army of the Loire, with a strength of 60,000 men, had thrown itself on the 15,000 Bavarians of Von der Tann, defeated them at Coulmiers on November 9th, and compelled them to evacuate Orleans. The king immediately sent to the support of the Bavarians the 17th and 22nd divisions, with four cavalry divisions, which were no longer required before Paris, and entrusted the command of this "army section," including the Bavarians, to the Grand Duke Frederic Francis II. of Mecklenburg. Everything pointed to a great and decisive action. The Paris army was preparing for a sortie on a large scale, to which Gambetta wished to respond by a bold attack from Orleans ; the Germans, encamped in front of the metropolis, were to be caught, if possible, between two fires and compelled to raise the siege. But the onslaught of 58,000 French, on November 28th at Beaune-la-Rolande, under the impetuous General Jean Constant Crouzat, whom Freycinet made the mistake of restraining, proved

GENERAL WERDER
After the capture of Alsace, this German commander forced his way into Franche Comté and Burgundy, where he occupied Dijon, the capital, on October 31st.

GENERAL MANTEUFFEL
In the German war against France he commanded the army of the north and subsequently was in command of that of the south, gaining some notable victories for the Prussian arms.

ineffectual against the bravery of five German regiments and some batteries, commanded by Major Körber, a hero of Mars-la-Tour. The great sortie which General Ducrot attempted in the south-east of Paris on November 30th, against the positions of the Würtembergers and Saxons near the villages of Champigny and Brie, did not attain its object in spite of the great superiority of the French. The fire of the Würtembergers, bursting from behind the park walls of Villiers and Cœuilly, mowed down the attacking columns of the French in heaps. On December 2nd the village of Champigny, which had been lost on November 30th, was to a great extent won back by the help of the Pomeranians, and on December 3rd the army of the sortie returned back to Paris. It had lost 12,000 men, Germans 6,000, and the besiegers had to abandon all hope of breaking their way through by their unassisted strength. General Ducrot, who had vowed to conquer or to die, and exposed himself recklessly to the bullets, was compelled to re-enter Paris alive and defeated. Prince Frederic Charles defeated the army of the Loire, now commanded by the gallant General Chanzy, in the four days' battle of the 1st to the 4th of December at Loigny and Orleans, and on December 4th the Grand Duke of Mecklenburg again entered this town. German outposts bivouacked beneath the statue of the Maid of Orleans. The French army was in a most lamentable plight ; the soldiers, clothed only in linen trousers and blouses, shivered with cold and refused to fight any more. The army was finally broken into two parts, of which one, under Bourbaki, turned eastward on December 4th ; the other part, under Chanzy, retired in a north-westerly direction on the right bank of the Loire, leaving Tours to its fate ; while Gambetta

FRENCH SORTIE AT CHAMPIGNY, NOVEMBER 30, 1870: THE FIRST CANNON SHOTS
From the painting by E. Beaumetz, by permission of Messrs. Braun, Clement & Co.

THE GERMANS SUCCESSFULLY REPELLING THE FRENCH ATTACK AT CHAMPIGNY

Following up their unsuccessful attack at Beaune-la-Rolande, the French, two days later, on November 30th, made a great sortie, under General Ducrot, against the positions of the Würtembergers and Saxons near the villages of Champigny and Brie; but, though the French were greatly superior in numbers, the attack was repelled, the fire of the Würtembergers, bursting from behind the park walls of Villiers and Cœuilly, mowing down the French columns in heaps.

with the " Delegation" fled to Bordeaux on December 8th. Chanzy, pursued by the prince and the grand duke, was again defeated at Beaugency, December 7th–10th, and driven back on Le Mans. But the Germans followed him thither, along roads deep in snow and covered with ice, where the cavalry had to dismount and lead their horses, and on January 11th and 12th, 1871, won another great victory before Le Mans, in consequence of which Chanzy was compelled to retire still further west towards Brittany, to Laval. The army of the Loire was thus to all intents annihilated. Meantime there was fighting in two other districts. General Werder, after the capture of Alsace, had forced his way into Franche Comté and Burgundy, where he occupied Dijon, the capital, on October 31st. The chief command against him was held by the hero of the Italian revolution, Garibaldi, who was so much moved by the change of France into a republic that he placed his sword at the services of that very nation which in 1860 had taken his native town of Nice from the National State of Italy. But he was only a shadow of his former self, and could no longer sit a horse ; he would have done best to have remained on his rocky island of Caprera. The Garibaldian volunteers from Italy and other countries who mustered round the leader were a rabble, clothed in a picturesque uniform, who eventually proved more troublesome to the French than to the Germans. The Badeners, under General Adolf von Glümer, without allowing themselves to be stopped by these troops, took Nuits by storm on December 18th.

Garibaldi Fighting for France

The other theatre of war was the north-east of France, especially Picardy and Normandy. The resistance here, as elsewhere, was organised by emissaries from the " Delegation," and the northern army was created, so that the German headquarters sent General Manteuffel there in November. Manteuffel defeated the French, under Farre, on November 27th, at Amiens, where the " Moblots "—Gardes Mobiles—by a disgraceful flight carried the troops of the line away with them. Amiens and Rouen were occupied, and

RUDOLPH DELBRÜCK
A Prussian statesman, and for many years the right-hand man of Bismarck, he opened at Munich the official negotiations which had as their object a united Germany.

General von Goeben knew how to treat the Normans so well that they ran after him trustingly on the roads, and the peasants brought provisions to the markets —quite otherwise than in the east, where all the shutters were closed and the doors locked when the Germans approached.

The prudent and energetic General Faidherbe succeeded, it is true, in rallying and strengthening the French troops ; but on his advance from Lille he was beaten back by Manteuffel on the river La Hallue, at Port Noyelles, on December 23rd. Since his soldiers were forced to spend the night fasting, with a temperature far below freezing point, he felt himself, on December 24th, unable to fight any further ; he therefore abandoned his dangerous positions and withdrew to Arras. A second advance, on January 3rd, 1871, at Bapaume, was equally unsuccessful. General Goeben, who, after Manteuffel was sent to the south-east, received the supreme command over the two German corps, ended the war in the north by the capture of the fortress of Péronne on January 8th, and by the brilliant victory at St. Quentin on January 19th, where Faidherbe lost 13,000 men. The fortress of St. Quentin itself fell into the hands of the victors, and the French northern army was reduced to such a condition that it no longer counted for anything. The capital of France held out all this time against the Germans who were investing it. But provisions were getting scarcer and scarcer, and occasional attempts at insurrection among the populace indicated that the reputation of the Government was waning. The resistance, nevertheless, lasted far longer than was ever considered probable on the German side, and public opinion in Germany demanded with increasing emphasis that Paris should be effectively bombarded . to accelerate the capitulation. Bismarck, from the very beginning of the siege, maintained that too much energy could not be shown in attacking the enemy, since, in the first place, the investing army suffered mentally and physically from the long inaction, and, secondly, the apparently successful

Paris Under the Siege

AN EPISODE IN THE SIEGE OF PARIS: PRUSSIAN SOLDIERS IN A FRENCH HOME

From the painting by Anton von Werner, by permission of the Berlin Photographic Co.

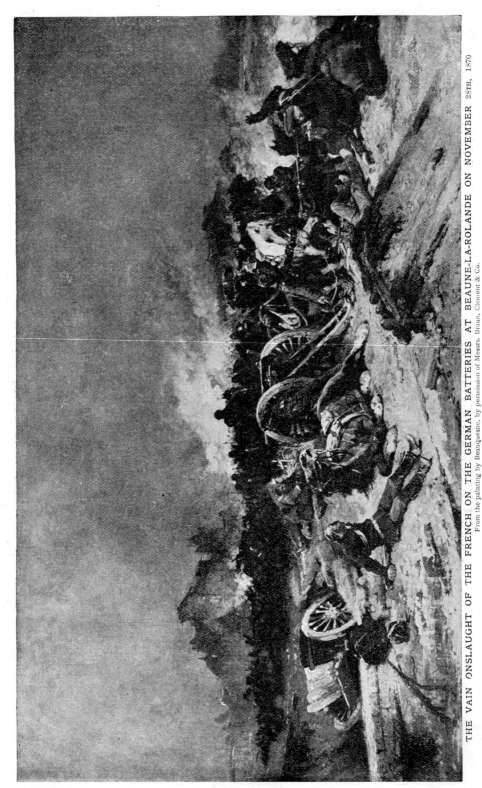

THE VAIN ONSLAUGHT OF THE FRENCH ON THE GERMAN BATTERIES AT BEAUNE-LA-ROLANDE ON NOVEMBER 28TH, 1870

From the painting by Beauquesne, by permission of Messrs. Braun, Clement & Co.

REPULSE OF THE FRENCH TROOPS AT THE BATTLE OF BAPAUME ON JANUARY 3RD, 1871

From the painting by A. Dunaresque

resistance of Paris revived the hopes of the French for an eventual victory, and once more brought up the danger of foreign intervention which was thought to have been surmounted after the day of Sedan. But the Crown Prince, Blumenthal, Moltke himself, and General von Gothberg were of opinion that a bombardment would not reach the workmen's quarter of Paris, and would thus be ineffective, and that the only means of reducing the city lay in starving it out; according to Blumenthal six weeks would be sufficient. During this time of expectancy the most important event of all, the question of the unity of Germany, was destined to

EMPEROR WILLIAM I.
From a photograph

be decided under the walls of Paris. There was a general feeling directly after the first victories that the Germans, who had marched united to the war, ought not at its close to break up again into the old disunion, but that political union ought to result from the military union as a necessary consequence and as the chief fruit of the war. From the moment when Bismarck, in the name of the Germans, demanded the cession of Strassburg and Metz as tangible guarantees for peace, the fact was established that these border fortresses of the German people could not be held without the permanent political unity of the German nation.

LOUIS ADOLPHE THIERS
In the days of French humiliation that attended the occupation of Paris by the victorious enemy, the great man of the crisis proved to be Adolphe Thiers, who succeeded in inducing the National Assembly to agree to peace on terms which Germany had practically dictated.

The current of opinion setting towards unity was strong enough to carry with it the princes, who, on account of the probable sacrifices of their sovereignty thereby

entailed, could not lightly resolve upon the decisive negotiations. These negotiations were stimulated by a large meeting held in Berlin on August 30th, which proposed as its motto that the fruits of the war must be : " A united nation and protected frontiers." The Grand Duke Frederic of Baden, whose first counsellor since the death of Mathy was the keen advocate of national unity, Julius Jolly, declared on September 2nd that he would support the constitutional union of the South German states with the North German Confederation. King Lewis II. of Bavaria and King Charles I. of Würtemberg also gave an assurance on September 5th and 7th that they were anxious to secure to Germany the fruits of victory in the fullest measure and to establish a just mean between the national coherency of the German races and their individual independence. The official negotiations were opened at Munich towards the end of September by Rudolf Delbrück, the President of the Federal Chancery of the North German Confederation, and were afterwards continued by Bismarck in Versailles. They encountered, indeed, considerable difficulties, since the Particularists were only willing to concede the most modest measure of centralisation. The Bavarians argued the superfluousness of a strict union from the very loyalty which all races had shown to the thought of nationality; in case of necessity Germany would always find all her children rallying round her. The King of Bavaria claimed as compensation for his consent to the establishment of a German federal state a sort of viceroyalty for the House of Wittelsbach, so that the Bavarian ambassadors, in the event of any impediment to the imperial ambassadors, should represent them ex officio. Prince Leopold, the uncle of the king, had suggested on January 10th, 1871, the alternation of the imperial Crown between the Houses of Hohenzollern and Wittelsbach, but had received no answer at all. In addition to Bavaria, Hesse, the Minister of which, Baron von Dalwigk, was a sworn enemy to Prussia, made as many difficulties as possible. The King of Würtemberg on November 12th, when everything seemed already settled, allowed himself to be persuaded by influence from Munich once more to delay the termination. But when Baden on November 15th signed the treaty as to the admission into the North German Confederation, and Hesse followed on the same day, the ice was broken. The Crown Prince became so impatient at the delays in the settlement of the matter that he thought that the business should be hurried on, that emperor and Empire should be proclaimed by the princes of Baden, Oldenburg, Weimar, and Coburg, and a constitution corresponding to the reasonable wishes of the people should be sanctioned by the Reichstag and the Landtags; in that case the two South German kings would have to acquiesce with the best grace they could.

The Crown Prince and Bismarck were thoroughly agreed upon the point that the King of Prussia, as President of the German Federal State, must bear the old and honourable title of emperor. The aged monarch himself had grave doubts as to relegating to the second place the comprehensive title of King

of Prussia, which his ancestor Frederic I. had created of his own set purpose, and of assuming an empty title, which his brother had declined in 1849, and which he himself had jestingly styled "brevet-major."

Bismarck maintained his own wise independence towards the father and the son. To the first he emphasised the fact that the title of emperor contained an outward recognition of the de facto predominant position of the Prussian king, on which much depended; and he asked the latter whether he could consider it wise and honourable to exercise compulsion on two allies who had shed their blood shoulder to shoulder with the North Germans. He was convinced that the new Empire would not rest on firm foundations unless all the German races joined it of their own free will, without the feeling that any compulsion was being applied to them. He therefore granted to the Bavarians and the Würtembergers by the "Reserved Rights" a privileged position in the Empire, which, although only accepted with reluctance by all determined supporters of German unity, has justified the foresight of the great statesman by affording these kingdoms the opportunity of joining the national cause without humiliation to their sense of importance.

The treaties signed on November 23rd at Versailles for Bavaria, and on November 25th, 1870, at Berlin for Würtemberg, reserved for both states the independent administration of the post office and telegraphs, and the private right of taxing native beer and brandy; this second privilege was granted to Baden also. It was further settled that the Bavarian army should be a distinct component part of the

WILLIAM I. WHEN KING OF PRUSSIA
From a photograph

THE FRENCH TROOPS ATTEMPTING TO RAISE THE SIEGE OF PARIS: THE ATTACK ON THE CHÂTEAU DE MONTBÉLIARD

From the painting by Berne-Bellecour, by permission of Messrs. Braun, Clement & Co.

German Federal army with its own military administration under the command of the King of Bavaria, and that also the Würtemberg army should form a distinct corps, whose commander, however, could only be nominated by the King of Würtemberg with the previous assent of the King of Prussia. The organisation, training, and system of mobilisation of the Bavarian and Würtemberg troops were to be remodelled according to the principles in force for the Federal army. The Federal commander possessed the right to inspect the Bavarian and Würtemberg armies, and from the first day of mobilisation onwards all the troops of North and South Germany alike had to obey his commands.

Progress of German Unity

The consideration which Bismarck showed to the kings procured him not merely their sincere confidence during the whole term of his life, a fact which was politically of much value, but also facilitated the settlement of the question of the title. Recognising that it is more palatable to the ambition of secondary states to have a German Emperor over them than a King of Prussia, King Lewis consented on December 3rd to propose to the German princes, in a letter drafted by Bismarck himself, that a joint invitation should be given His Majesty the King of Prussia to combine the exercise of the rights of President of the Federation with the style of a " German Emperor."

King William consented, waiving his scruples in deference to the universal wish of the princes and peoples of Germany. The Reichstag and the Landtags sanctioned the constitution of the " German Empire " in December and January, and on December 18th a deputation of the Reichstag appeared in Versailles, in order to transmit to the king, through the president, the good wishes of the representatives of the people for the imperial Crown. There was still friction to be smoothed away; but on January 18th, 1871—the day on which, in 1701, the Prussian monarchy had been proclaimed—in the Hall of Mirrors of the splendid Chateau of Versailles, erected by Louis XIV., the adoption of the imperial title was solemnly inaugurated in the presence of numerous German princes. The Grand Duke Frederic of Baden led the first cheer for His Majesty Emperor William. In a proclamation to the German people, composed by Bismarck, the emperor announced his resolve " to aid at all times the growth of the Empire, not by the conquests of the sword, but by the goods and gifts of peace, in the sphere of national prosperity, freedom, and culture." In the thirty years and more that have elapsed since that day the world has had opportunity to recognise that this has been no empty phrase, but the guiding star of three German emperors.

His Majesty Emperor William I.

At the moment when the Empire was revived, or, to speak more correctly, was called into existence, the French powers of resistance were everywhere becoming exhausted; even those of the capital were failing. At Christmas-time 235 heavy pieces of siege artillery were collected in Villacoublay, east of Versailles, and the bombardment of the east front of Paris was commenced on December 27th with such violence that the French evacuated Mont Avron " almost at a gallop." The bombardment of the city itself began from the south side on January 5th, and after five and a half hours Fort Issy ceased its fire. Since the shots, owing to an elevation of thirty degrees, which had been obtained by special contrivances, carried beyond the centre of the city, the inhabitants fled from the south to the north of Paris—a movement by which the difficulties of feeding them were much increased.

Bombarding the French Capital

A great, and final, sortie towards the west, which was attempted on January 19th by Trochu with 90,000 men, was defeated at Buzenval and Saint Cloud, before the French had even approached the main positions of the Germans. The bombardment of the north front began on January 21st.

Here, too, the forts were completely demolished; parts of the bastions were soon breached; the garrisons had no protection against the German shells. It was known in the city that Chanzy had been completely routed at Le Mans on January 11th and 12th, and the last prospect of relief was destroyed by the ill-tidings from the east.

General Bourbaki had marched in that direction with half of the army of the Loire; with the strength of his forces raised to 130,000 men, he hoped to compel the Germans under Werder, who only numbered 42,000, to relinquish the siege of the fortress of Belfort, and to force the Germans before Paris to retire, by

I A

WILLIAM I. PROCLAIMED GERMAN EMPEROR IN THE HALL OF MIRRORS AT VERSAILLES, ON JANUARY 18TH, 1871

From the painting by Anton von Werner by permission of the Berlin Photographic Co.

TERMINATING THE FRANCO-PRUSSIAN WAR: BISMARCK AND THIERS CONCLUDING PEACE AT VERSAILLES
From the painting by Wagner, by permission of the Berlin Photographic Co.

5147

AS INSPECTOR OF DYKES IN 1850

ENVOY AT THE GERMAN DIET IN 1858

DURING THE FRANCO-PRUSSIAN WAR

PRINCE BISMARCK AT SEVENTY

GERMANY'S "IRON CHANCELLOR" AT FOUR STAGES OF HIS CAREER

threatening their communications in the rear. But Werder attacked the enemy, three times his superior in numbers, at Montbéliard on the Lisaine, and repulsed, in the three days' fighting, from January 15th to 17th, all the attacks of Bourbaki. Not one French battalion was able to reach Belfort, where salvos had been vainly fired in honour of victory when the cannon-shots were heard.

Bourbaki commenced his retreat, dispirited and weakened; but when he learnt that Moltke had sent General Manteuffel with the Pomeranians and Rhinelanders to block his road by Gray and Dôle, and when Garibaldi, although he retook Dijon and on January 23rd captured the flag of the 61st regiment from under a heap of dead bodies, was unable to help him, he went back to Pontarlier.

But before he surrendered his army to be disarmed by the neutral Swiss, he made an ineffectual attempt to blow out his brains. His successor, Justin Clinchant finally crossed the Franco-Swiss frontier on February 1st with 80,000 men.

Famine Sufferings in Paris The last army of France was thus annihilated and the fate of Belfort sealed. Colonel Denfert-Rochereau surrendered the bravely-defended but now untenable town to General Udo von Tresckow on February 18th.

In Paris the dearth of provisions grew greater and greater during January. On the 21st a pound of ham cost 16s., a pound of butter 20s., a goose 112s. Horses, cats = 9s., dogs, and rats had long been eaten. In view of the threatened famine, Favre, the Foreign Minister, eventually appeared at the German headquarters on January 23rd, the 127th day of the siege, to negotiate the terms of a capitulation.

An agreement was at last reached on January 28th, by which an armistice of twenty-one days was granted for the election of a National Assembly, which should decide on war and peace; but, in return for the concession a high penalty was exacted, all the forts round Paris were delivered up to the Germans, and the whole garrison of the town declared prisoners of war.

The town had to hand over all its cannons and rifles within fourteen days; the only exception was made in favour of the National Guard, the disarmament of which Favre declared to be impracticable owing to

the insurrectionary spirit prevailing in that corps. Paris was thus in the hands of the Germans, although the emperor refrained from a regular occupation of it, which might easily lead to bloody encounters and hence to new difficulties, in the hope of peace being soon concluded. Permission was, of course, given for provisioning the city.

Thiers the Great Man of the Crisis Gambetta would not consent to the armistice, but was compelled by Jules Simon, who was sent by the Government to Bordeaux, to retire on February 6th. The great man of the crisis was henceforward Adolphe Thiers, who at the beginning of the war had counselled a cautious policy, and then, after Sedan, had vainly endeavoured to induce the Great Powers to intervene. He had proved himself a far-sighted patriot, to whom the country might look for its rescue.

On February 8th, twenty-six departments elected him to the National Assembly, which numbered among them 768 deputies, 400 to 500 supporters of the monarchy, Orleanists and Legitimists, but included a large majority for peace. Fully a third of France was occupied by the Germans, and Faidherbe declared that if the Government wished to continue the war in Flanders, the people would intervene and surrender to the Germans. On February 17th, Thiers was elected to the highest post in the state under the title of "Chief of the Executive," and was sent on the 21st to Versailles for the purpose of negotiating a peace.

Bismarck demanded the whole of Alsace with Belfort, and a fifth of Lorraine with Metz and Diedenhofen, in addition £240,000,000 and the entry of the German troops into Paris. After prolonged negotiations he assented to remit £40,000,000 and waive all claim to Belfort, but insisted the more emphatically on the entry into Paris, which in some degree would impress the seal on the German victories and place

The Dawn of Peace clearly before the eyes of the French their complete defeat, as a deterrent from future wars. Thiers hurried with the conditions mentioned to Bordeaux. On March 1st, the same day on which 30,000 German soldiers, selected from all the German races, marched into Paris and occupied the quarter of the town near the Champs Elysées, together with the Château of the Tuileries, the preliminary treaty for peace, which the National Assembly had adopted, after

GERMANY'S CONQUERING EMPEROR: THE TRIUMPHAL ENTRY OF WILLIAM I. INTO BERLIN ON JUNE 16TH. 1871

From the painting by Camphausen, by permission of the Berlin Photographic Co.

a stormy debate, by 546 votes to 107, was completed in Bordeaux. The official ratification of it reached Versailles on the evening of March 2nd. The Germans evacuated Paris on the 3rd, and retired behind the right bank of the Seine, which was to be the boundary of the two armies until the final peace was concluded. According to this agreement the forts to the east and north of Paris were still occupied by the Germans.

The subsequent peace negotiations were conducted in Brussels by plenipotentiaries, but proceeded so slowly that Bismarck, at the beginning of May, 1871, finally invited Favre to Frankfort-on-the-Main, in order to arrive at a clear understanding with him through a personal conference. After a short discussion the final peace was signed there on May 10th. It contained, contrary to the preliminary treaty, a small exchange of territory at Belfort and Diedenhofen, and the proviso that the evacuation of French territory by the Germans should take place by degrees, in proportion as instalments of the war indemnity were paid.

The results of the German struggle for unity were immense. In comparison with them the sacrifices of the war were not so excessive. They amounted on the German side to 28,600 killed in battle, 12,000 deaths from disease, and 4,000 missing, a grand total, therefore, of about 45,000 men; the number of wounded was calculated at 101,000. The French lost 150,000 killed and 150,000 wounded; the number of prisoners was eventually raised to more than 600,000.

Emperor William I. held a grand review of the victorious troops in the east of Paris on March 7th, and entered Berlin on March 17th. On March 21st he opened in person the first German Reichstag; on June 16th, a triumphal entry of the German army, selected out of all the German races, was made into Berlin, between two lines of 7,400 captured cannons. The age of the Holy Roman Empire of Louis XIV. and of the Napoleons was over. The new Empire of the German nation had come into being.

G. EGELHAAF

THE INTERROGATOR: AN EPISODE IN THE FRANCO-PRUSSIAN WAR

"IRRECONCILABLE"

"RECONCILED"

The horrors of war are vividly suggested by these pictures of Gustave Doré. In the first, the battle is over, leaving its carnage behind. But among the wounded are two who have fought on opposite sides, and realising each other's presence there springs up anew their hatred as they prepare to resume the struggle single-handed. But the combatants who are thus "irreconcilable" have come together in the second picture, and in their nearness to the Cross and in the presence of death have put aside their differences that they may be of service to each other.

SCANDINAVIA IN THE 19TH CENTURY
THE PROGRESS OF THE NORTHERN KINGDOMS

THE unfortunate policy of Frederic VI. had caused Denmark great reverses. She had lost her fleet, on which she had always prided herself, and had been separated from Norway, thus losing half her Scandinavian population; her prosperity had been destroyed in the wars; the national debt had assumed enormous proportions, and the financial position had been so bad that in 1813 the Government had been compelled to declare the state insolvent. Industry, too, had been paralysed, and was unable to recover for some years after the declaration of peace; commerce was almost at a standstill and to a great extent dependent on Hamburg; and agriculture, which had been very profitable during the war by reason of the high price of corn, now suffered from falling prices. But the cloud was, after all, not without its silver lining. The national extremity, and the hard struggle that **Denmark Renews its Strength** was made at the opening of the century, had a stimulating and fertilising influence on the intellectual life of the community. While political interests were unimportant and material prosperity was declining, art and literature flourished; it seemed as if the nation sought in these things consolation for its unhappy circumstances. Gradually the economic situation improved. The finances were set in order by the establishment of a national bank independent of the Government; industry prospered, and at Frederic's death, in 1839, the country had renewed its strength.

While Crown Prince, Frederic VI. had been a great friend of reform; but as king he was strongly conservative, and opposed to any changes in the constitution. But in proportion as their condition improved the people awoke to an interest in public affairs, and the desire for freedom and self-government became stronger and stronger. After the "July Revolution," the effects of which were felt in Denmark as well as in other lands, Frederic at last decided to meet the popular wish, at least in part. He therefore instituted four advisory diets—for the islands, Jütland, Schleswig, and Holstein—the first step towards a free constitution. Frederic's successor, his half-cousin Christian VIII., 1839–1848, was just as little disposed to renounce absolutism. But now **Aims of the National Liberals** the cry for a free constitution grew louder, and the National Liberals worked for the abolition of absolutism. They wished also to terminate the union of Schleswig and Holstein, and to attach more closely to Denmark that province in which the large proportion of German inhabitants endangered Danish nationality.

In the eighteenth century the two united duchies had once more come into the possession of the Danish Crown. Schleswig was, however, not incorporated with the remainder of Denmark; it remained in close connection with Holstein, and German was the official language. Frederic VI. did, indeed, give Schleswig a diet of its own, but bound the two duchies together by placing them under a Ministry and a supreme court common to both.

As the result of its long connection with Holstein, Schleswig had become more and more German, and by the nineteenth century almost half the population spoke German. When the Danes at last took measures to preserve the Danish nationality of the province, this course embittered the Germans. Thus it came about that a Schleswig-Holstein party grew up in **Denmark's German Duchies** the two duchies and demanded that Schleswig-Holstein should be made independent of Denmark, and be constituted one of the states of the German Confederation. The leaders of this party, the princes of Augustenburg, who, as descendants of a younger son, Hans the younger, of King Christian III., hoped to obtain the duchies for themselves if the royal line became extinct—which seemed likely to happen shortly—sought support in Germany, where an enthusiastic national movement in their favour was started.

The other Scandinavian countries, on the contrary, with whom the idea of Scandinavian unity at that time had great weight, were in favour of the aims of the National Liberal party in Denmark.

Schleswig's Desire for Independence The king hesitated for a long time; but at last he declared, on July 8th, 1846, that Schleswig was indissolubly bound to Denmark. In other respects, too, he met the wishes of the National Liberals; and he had just completed the framing of a constitution when death cut short his labours on January 20th, 1848.

Immediately after his death the Schleswig-Holstein party demanded the recognition of Schleswig-Holstein as a separate state. But Christian's son and successor, Frederic VII., 1848–1863, refused to separate Schleswig from Holstein, though he promised Holstein, like the other provinces, a free constitution. The Schleswig-Holstein party were, however, not willing to accept this proposal, and before long civil war broke out. Prussia supported the party of secession, and a German army entered the duchies. The Danes had to retire to Alsen, but the armistice arranged at Malmö, August 26th, through the mediation of Oscar I. of Norway and Sweden, did not lead to the conclusion of peace. In 1849 the war was renewed. Meanwhile the reactionary party had gained the upper hand in Germany; Prussia made peace on July 2nd, 1850, and by the next year the resistance of Schleswig-Holstein was overcome.

During the war Denmark had received a free constitution. The draft prepared by Christian VIII. had not met with general approval, and a Constituent Assembly summoned by Frederic VII. therefore published a constitution, dated June 5th, 1849, in which the kingdom was made a limited monarchy.

German Powers Intervene This constitution was intended for Schleswig as well as Denmark, but to this the German Powers would not consent. In 1852 it was agreed that Schleswig should not remain united to Holstein, but must not be incorporated with Denmark. On the death of Frederic VII. the whole monarchy was to fall to Prince Christian of Glücksburg and his consort Louise of Hesse-Cassel, whose mother was a sister of Christian VIII. The general constitution of July 26th, 1854, met with opposition, however, especially from the populations of Holstein and Lauenburg, whose part was taken by Prussia and Austria.

But in Denmark, where hopes were entertained, on account of the disputes existing between the chief German states, of solving the question of the constitution without German interference, the national —Eider-Danish—party, which proposed to incorporate Schleswig in the kingdom, gained the upper hand. Two days after giving his approval to a new constitution for Denmark and Schleswig, Frederic VII. died in November, 1863.

Christian IX., 1863–1906, gave way to the wishes of the Danes and signed the " November Constitution." But now Frederic—VIII.—of Augustenburg came forward with his claims to the duchies, and was supported by Prussia and Austria. These Powers refused to recognise the new king's right of succession except on condition that the November Constitution should be annulled. As the Danes did not accede to this demand, the second

Schleswig Causes a Second War Schleswig war broke out in January, 1864. Denmark had hoped to receive help from Norway and Sweden, as well as from the Western Powers, but these hopes proved to be ill founded. The Danish army, which had occupied the " Danework," retired to Düppel as early as February 5th.

Here the Danes defended themselves bravely, but were at last forced to cross to Alsen. The Prussians occupied Jütland, expelled the Danes from Alsen, and threatened to land on Zealand. The Danes could now resist no longer. At the Treaty of Vienna, October 30th, 1864, Denmark ceded the Duchies of Schleswig-Holstein and Lauenburg to Prussia and Austria; and her hope of recovering, by virtue of Article 5 of the Treaty of Prague, concluded on August 23rd, 1866, at least the northern part of Schleswig has not been fulfilled. The loss of Schleswig resulted in a change of the constitution, and on July 28th, 1866, Denmark received the fundamental law still in force.

Soon after the declaration of peace the country became involved in internal dissensions. A dispute arose in 1870 between the Government and the " Folketinget "—one of the Chambers of the Rigsdag—as to the correct interpretation of the constitution, and the struggle only ended in 1894 when the "negotiating" portion of the Left Party, which had been divided since 1878, went over to the Right. In spite of this Denmark has been on the path of progress ever since the middle of the last century. The great agricultural reforms begun in 1788 have been continued and a fixed payment substituted for forced service. The number of tenant-farmers has fallen, and the peasantry have the same political rights as the other classes of the community. Like agriculture, manufactures, commerce, and shipping are progressing satisfactorily. The obligation on artisans to join a guild has been removed, and means of communication have been improved. The merchants have become independent of Hamburg. Copenhagen, which was provided with extensive fortifications in 1886, has been a free port since 1844.

Good provision is made for national education, the general level of which is, on the whole, a high one; the people's universities, in particular, which have been imitated in Norway and Sweden, have promoted the education of the peasantry and exercised considerable influence on their intellectual life. On the accession to the Swedish throne of Charles XIII., who was old and childless, Christian Augustus, Prince of Augustenburg, was chosen as successor in 1809, but died suddenly on May 28th, 1810. It was then that a young Swedish officer, who met the Prince of Pontecorvo, Marshal Bernadotte, in Paris, offered him the Crown on his own responsibility and contrived to use his influence in Sweden **Sweden's** so that the marshal was de- **Novel Choice** signated heir to the Crown **of a King** on August 21st at a Riksdag at Orebro. Bernadotte, who called himself Crown Prince Charles John, went with his son Oscar to Sweden in October, and at once became actual ruler.

The Swedes had chosen him on the supposition that he was on friendly terms with Napoleon, and hoped that he would regain Finland for them with the help of

CHARLES XIV. OF SWEDEN

The son of a lawyer, Bernadotte, one of Napoleon's marshals, was elected heir to the throne of Sweden in 1810, and became king without opposition on the death of Charles XIII. in 1818.

the emperor. Charles John, however, had never been Napoleon's friend and did not wish to be his vassal; he therefore abandoned the idea of reconquering Finland, which, in his opinion, Sweden could never defend. He would have liked to obtain possession of Norway, which, by **Union of** reason of its situation, seemed **Sweden and** to belong rather to Sweden **Norway** than to Denmark. Accordingly he approached Alexander I. of Russia, and on April 5th, 1812, concluded a treaty with the Tsar and joined the league against Napoleon. In return for this Russia and Britain promised their assistance in the conquest of Norway. In May, 1813, he crossed over into Germany with an army, received in July chief command over the "united army of North Germany," was victorious at Grossbeeren and Dennewitz, and took part in the Battle of Leipzig. After this great battle he advanced against Denmark with part of the northern army, and by the Peace of Kiel, January 14th, 1814, compelled King Frederic VI. to relinquish the kingdom of Norway. Charles John then attached himself again to the allies, who had marched to France, and did not return to the north until the summer of 1814. In the meantime the Norwegians, who did not wish to submit to Sweden, had drawn up a free constitution and chosen the Danish prince, Christian Frederic, as their king. Charles John, who was shrewd enough to acknowledge the Norwegian constitution, succeeded in removing Christian Frederic and in bringing about the union between Sweden and Norway in a peaceful way.

By his ability as a soldier and a politician Charles John raised his new country from the lethargy into which it had been plunged by the foolish policy of Gustavus IV. to its former rank as a kingdom; he ruled with energy and discretion and furthered the welfare of the land. He was therefore admired and beloved by the people, and, foreigner though he was, he ascended the throne of Sweden as Charles XIV. at the death of Charles XIII., on February 5th, 1818, without opposition.

In time the enthusiasm for the new king declined ; he had, it is true, an attractive and lovable nature, but he was also violent in temper, intolerant of criticism, and became more and more conservative, especially after the "Revolution of July." The greatest dissatisfaction was aroused by his resistance to every proposal for altering the constitution, which on several points, particularly with respect to the organisation of the Riksdag, did not meet the requirements of the times. He, the son of the Revolution, was charged with holding narrow views.

Charles XIV Displeases His People

After 1830, a Liberal opposition was formed, which steadily increased in power, and numbered distinguished personalities among its leaders. As the Government was strongly opposed to all innovations, the indignation at last grew so great that there were serious thoughts of compelling the king to resign in 1840. However, the storm was averted, and the last years of Charles XIV. were passed in quiet. He died on March 8th, 1844, aged eighty-one years.

Under his son, Oscar I., 1844–1859, who was just as popular in Sweden as in Norway, the opposition became weaker. The king attached himself to the Liberals, surrounded himself with Ministers of broad views, and sanctioned an extension of the freedom of the Press, and triennial assemblies of the Riksdag. However, his popular proposition regarding the reconstruction of the Riksdag was rejected in 1850, and after the Revolution of February, when a reaction was sweeping over Europe, Oscar also grew more conservative and let the question of the Riksdag drop. During his reign the management of the state was successfully carried on. Oscar altered the foreign policy of Sweden by withdrawing from the Russian alliance. It was suspected that the Russians were desirous of taking possession of certain portions of the Finnish frontier lands. During the Crimean War, Sweden and Norway concluded a treaty with France and Britain, November, 1855, by which the aid of the Western Powers was assured to the united kingdoms in the event of Russia seizing any of the northern harbours. Oscar, who considered himself a thorough Scandinavian, stood on the best of terms with

Anticipating Russia's Advances

Denmark ; he acted as a mediator in the first Schleswig war, August, 1848, and later offered King Frederic VII. a defensive alliance in order to protect the Eider boundary. This offer was, however, not accepted by the Danes. Oscar's son, Charles XV., 1859–1872, was also a personal friend of Frederic VII. But the negotiations which had been opened with Denmark on account of the political situation of Europe after Frederic's death, November 15th, 1863, were discontinued, so that the king was compelled to give up the cause of Denmark in 1864.

The question of the Riksdag was finally solved in the reign of Charles XV., as at the Riksdag of 1865 all the four Estates assented to a reorganisation. The Riksdag now meets every year, and consists of two Chambers ; the king has the right of dismissing the Riksdag and issuing the writs for a new election. This reorganisation, by which the nobles were deprived of their last prerogatives, also effected a change of parties. The "Intellectuals" were supported by the cultured classes, while the "Landt-manna party" aimed chiefly at economy in the administration, particularly in the army, and a more equal division of the burden of taxation. In the reign of Oscar II., Charles' brother and successor, a violent dispute was caused by the customs policy ; several of the Landt-manna party joined the representatives of the wholesale industry and carried a law for protection. In recent years the Chambers, in which Conservatives and Liberals are now the contending parties, have introduced a new army law, by which the term of service for the "Beväring"—those who are liable to serve in the army—has been considerably lengthened. On the other hand, no agreement has yet been reached about the extension of the very limited franchise.

Sweden's Splendid Progress

Sweden, no less than Norway, has made great material progress in the nineteenth century. The legislature departed from the economic principles of an earlier age and abolished the restrictions which fettered commerce and manufacture. At the same time necessary improvements have been made in the means of communication. Trade and manufacture have opened up new paths for themselves. Agriculture, which was so neglected in the eighteenth century, has developed to such an extent that Sweden, which in the eighteenth century could not provide the corn necessary for home consumption, can now export grain. Cattle-breeding and mining, especially for iron ore, have also made great progress in recent years. As wealth has increased by the development of natural resources, provision has also been made for intellectual growth by improvement in the schools, so that in Sweden, as in the other two Scandinavian countries, popular education has now reached a high standard, and the Swedes have attained European fame in all branches of natural science. When the Treaty of Kiel, which transferred Norway from Denmark to Sweden in 1814, was proclaimed in Norway, it aroused universal indignation. The Norwegians did not wish, under any circumstances, to be subjected to the Swedes, whom they hated as enemies; the few who considered a union with Sweden advantageous were looked upon almost as traitors. Prince Christian Frederic, afterwards Christian VIII. of Denmark, who was viceroy at that time, and who was popular with the Norwegians, conceived the idea of taking advantage of the discontent against Sweden to make himself king. He accordingly summoned an assembly of the Estates of the kingdom at Eidsvold, north of Christiania, which should draw up a constitution for the country. This assembly met in April, 1814, and had completed its work by May 17th.

As a result of this constitution, which was modelled on the French constitution of 1791, Norway became a limited monarchy with one Chamber of Representatives. On this point the members of the Estates were all agreed; they all clung to the independence of Norway. But on other matters they were divided into two factions; the minority wished for

the union with Sweden and desired to postpone the election of a king, while the majority were eager to appoint Prince Christian Frederic immediately as king.

On May 17th Christian Frederic was actually elected king. When the Swedish Government heard of the proceedings in Norway they at once complained to the allies, who despatched plenipotentiaries to Christiania to put into force the decision of the Peace of Kiel, but in vain. The Norwegians armed themselves, but their army was badly equipped and without capable leaders. Christian Frederic was no general and had no inclination for war; he always hoped, like the majority of Norwegians, that the Great Powers would respect the indignation of the Norwegians against the union. Accordingly, the war only lasted a few weeks. The Crown Prince, Charles John Bernadotte, marched into Norway. The Norwegians, following the command of their king, steadily retreated, although they were consumed with the desire for battle, and in some places fought successfully. Christian Frederic did not dare to risk a decisive engagement, but agreed to an armistice On August 14th, the Convention of Moss, to the south of Christiania, was concluded. The Crown Prince, who felt that he was not strong enough to subjugate Norway completely, and who wished for peace in the north, promised in the name of King Charles XIII., before the Congress of Vienna assembled, that he would recognise the constitution of Norway; Christian Frederic, for his part, pledged himself to renounce the Crown, to convene a Storting—National Assembly—which should come to terms with the Swedish king, and to leave the country. These arrangements were carried out; the Storting made a few alterations

KING OSCAR I. OF NORWAY AND SWEDEN
The son of Charles XIV., he succeeded to the dual throne of Norway and Sweden, and, surrounding himself with Ministers of broad views, proved a good and popular ruler.

in the constitution, which necessitated the union with Sweden, and elected King Charles of Sweden as King of Norway, November 4th, 1814. The conditions of the union were more definitely stated by a National Act, the Rigsakt of 1815.

CHARLES XV.
Ascending the throne of Norway and Sweden in 1859 on the death of his father, he endeavoured to bring about closer relations between the two countries, and died in 1872.

In this way Norway came to be united with Sweden as an independent kingdom. Its constitution was one of the freest in Europe. Since that time the country has made great progress in every direction. The people successfully upheld their free constitution against the attacks of the Crown and maintained their equality with Sweden in the union. They were also able to turn the natural resources of their country to better advantage, and thus the general prosperity increased. The Norwegians have paid great attention to national education, and have taken a prominent position in art and science.

In the earlier years of the union there was often friction between the king and the people. Charles XIV., Bernadotte, who succeeded to the throne in 1818,

thought that the Norwegian constitution was too democratic, and wished to extend his power. However, his attempts to alter the constitution were frustrated by the decided attitude of the Storting, which always offered a unanimous opposition to his propositions. The Norwegians, on their part, thought that the king did too little to obtain for them the equal footing in the union which had been decreed by the constitution, and, in addition, they feared his attacks on the constitution.

Little by little, however, the relations of king and people improved; Charles John experienced in his last years many proofs of the loyalty of the Norwegians. His son, Oscar I., a liberal and kindly disposed prince, did his utmost to meet the wishes of the Norwegians. King

OSCAR II.
Charles XV. was succeeded by his brother, Oscar II., a poet and historian, who, in 1905, regretfully agreed to the demand of Norway for separation from Sweden.

and Storting worked in harmony for the welfare of the country, which was making great progress in every direction; industry, in particular, received a fresh impetus. After his death, however, there was an end of concord; the opposition in the Storting increased, and serious political struggles began which have continued almost without interruption up to the present day.

At first the official element had taken the lead in the Storting; but after the July Revolution, which had roused in Norway a more general interest in politics, and a strong national spirit, the peasants, who considered themselves the true representatives of the Norwegian people, and regarded the government officials with suspicion, founded a party in opposition to them. This party soon gained in strength by the coalition of the Liberals, who wished to extend the influence of the Storting at the expense of the executive power. It

impeached the Ministry; the Ministers were actually condemned, and the king was forced to appoint a Sverdrup Ministry, June 26th, 1884. However, no sooner did the Left come into power than they began to disagree; they split up into Moderates and Radicals, and Sverdrup was obliged to give way to a Conservative Ministry in July, 1889. But the Conservatives did not remain in power; in 1891 the Liberals came into office, which they retained till after the spring of the new century.

Almost all literary activity had ceased with the decline of the national life in the fourteenth century. The people, however, still cherished the old sagas and poems. A wealth of national poetry was

| Björn Björnson | Jonas Lie | Henrik Ibsen |

THE GREAT FIGURES IN SCANDINAVIAN LITERATURE OF THE NINETEENTH CENTURY
With the awakened enthusiasm for nationalism in the early part of the nineteenth century there dawned a new literary era in Scandinavia, the poets Björn Björnson, Jonas Lie, and others delighting in describing the characteristic traits in the life and customs of the people, while Björnson and Ibsen also achieved fame as dramatists.

now formed an opposition and established itself on the left side of the House, while what had been the official became the Conservative party, and supported the Government. The Left had a capable leader in John Sverdrup, 1876–1892; under him they became more important, and finally constituted the majority in the Storting. Consequently the relations between the Government and the Left were not over-friendly during the reign of Charles XV., 1859–1872.

Ill-feeling increased under his brother and successor, Oscar II. There were several points of dispute; the Government opposed various propositions of the Left, and could not agree with them concerning the exact meaning of a few points in the constitution. At last the Storting

springing up—songs, sagas, and fairy stories. These have been collected in recent times and furnish an interesting picture of the intellectual life of the people in earlier times. The old Norwegian language, which had remained comparatively unaltered only in Iceland, became obsolete as a literary language with the decline of literature, and survived only in dialects. The Danish language was introduced, and in the sixteenth century, when a fresh impulse was given to literary activity, the Norwegians wrote in Danish.

Thus the literature of the two countries became merged. The share which the Norwegians contributed, " Foelles litteraturen," was at first insignificant, but it increased and became more important as they gradually recovered from their inertia. But, in spite of the growing national spirit, there was as yet no effort to create a Norwegian national literature. Immediately after 1814 also, when the literary output was small, the poets showed little originality. They remained in the grooves of the eighteenth century, raved about their fatherland, and wrote

The Dawn of National Literature songs on liberty, national novels, and dramas. It was not until the year 1830 that a national literature of any importance began, with the poets Wergeland, who died in 1845, and Welhaven, who died in 1873. Both were filled with a fervent love for their country, and only differed in one point—namely, as to what would prove of most advantage to Norway. The educated classes are still strongly influenced by Danish culture, and Welhaven desired to maintain the intellectual union with Denmark; Wergeland, on the other hand, hated the Danish culture and language, and was enthusiastic about his own nationality.

Thus in 1832 there began a violent literary feud. It had some good results. On the one hand it helped to check the exaggerated enthusiasm for everything Norwegian; on the other hand it strengthened genuine self-reliance and true patriotism. With the extravagant enthusiasm for nationalism there was awakened an interest in the life of the people, in national poetry, and nature. The poets Björn Björnson, Jonas Lie, and others delighted in describing the characteristic traits in the life and customs of the people and their thoughts and feelings.

At the same time the saga period was dramatised, and Björnson and Henrik Ibsen, who died in 1906, produced a series of historical plays. Efforts were made to preserve Norwegian as the national language. From 1870 literature gradually assumed a realistic tone; the poets did not describe chiefly the life of the peasants

Finland Under the Swedes as formerly, but all classes of society. Poets such as Björnson, Ibsen, Lie, Alex Kielland, who died in 1906, and Arne Garborg, born in 1851, undertook to solve social problems. Science was studied with gratifying results at the University of Christiania. Finland, which the Swedes had conquered and converted to Christianity in the thirteenth century, was not intimately connected with the kingdom of Sweden until the sixteenth century; in the fifteenth century it was generally given to some Swedish magnate as a fief. It was not until the time of the Vasa that the royal power made itself felt in the land. Gustavus Vasa reformed the government and system of taxation, destroyed the Catholic hierarchy, and introduced the Reformation, for which M. Agricola, who died in 1557, in particular interested himself keenly; but the king's efforts to release the Finns from the oppression of their own nobles were fruitless. The situation became still worse under the sons of Gustavus, Erik XIV. and John.

At last, in 1596-1597, the Finnish peasants rose against their oppressors, and, armed with clubs, plundered the estates of the nobles; but the rising, which spread over the whole country, was suppressed, and for the second time Finland was conquered. This " Club War" cost the lives of 3,000 peasants. The conditions improved after Charles IX. became king. Assistance was given to the country, and it was united more firmly to Sweden; the power of the nobility was crushed, and Finland, which had become a

Finland's Era of Prosperity grand duchy in 1581, was governed from Stockholm, although it had its own court of justice at Abo. There in 1640 the governor-general, Per Brahe the younger, who rendered valuable services to Finland, founded a university, which soon became the intellectual centre of Finland. The Peace of Stolbowa, in 1617, fixed the frontier on the side of Russia. From that time Finland enjoyed a time of prosperity until towards the end of the seventeenth century, when the land was terribly devastated by famine and pestilence. The great Northern War came as a crowning misfortune. The country did not recover until the eighteenth century, when Swedish rule predominated. Even the war with Russia, 1741-1743, did not permanently affect the prosperity to which the country had again attained.

In the meantime desires for independence were awakening in the hearts of many Finns, who hoped, with the aid of Russia, to form an independent Finnish state under Russian protection. This wish was partly realised at the beginning of the nineteenth century owing to the indiscreet policy of Gustavus IV.; for after the unsuccessful war of 1808-1809 Sweden was obliged to cede Finland, together with the Aland Islands, to Russia by the Peace of

THE TOWN AS SEEN FROM THE HARBOUR, WHICH IS PROTECTED BY BATTERIES

THE SENATE HOUSE, WHERE LADY MEMBERS OF PARLIAMENT SIT

HELSINGFORS, THE FORTIFIED SEAPORT CAPITAL OF FINLAND

Fredrikshamn, September 17th, 1809. The Emperor Alexander I. promised at the Diet of Borga, which he opened in person, that he would maintain the constitution of the country. Finland was united to Russia as an independent grand duchy, with Helsingfors for its capital. The provinces which had been ceded by the Peace of Nystad, 1721, and the Peace of Abo, 1743, were also incorporated with the grand duchy after several years. At first Alexander I. was true to his promise and respected the constitution, but later he became a reactionary, and in this respect he was followed by Nicholas I. Better times returned with Alexander II., who decreed that from 1869 the Diet—Landtag—to which Nicholas had allowed no authority, should again be regularly convened, and should have the power of legislation with certain restrictions. In this period reforms were introduced which furthered the material and social development of the country. In the nineteenth century the Finns also distinguished themselves by their literary activity. E. Lönnrot, who died in 1884, collected the old Finnish national sagas, " Kalevala," which attracted great attention when they were published in 1835. Joh. Runeberg, who died in 1877, Finland's greatest poet, extolled in " Fänrik Stals Sägner " the exploits of the Finns in the last war against Russia. Z. Topelius, who died in 1898, has earned well-deserved renown even beyond the boundaries of Finland by his "Narratives"—Erzählungen.

In recent times a movement has been set on foot in Finland which aims at making the national language equal in importance to the Swedish. The supporters of this movement, the "Fennomanen," have been so successful in their efforts that both languages are on an equal footing in everything which immediately concerns the population of Finland. Although the people have divided into two parties on this question, they are all agreed that they must unite against the encroachments of Russia, for there are many Russians who are not pleased with the independence of Finland, and who would gladly see the country entirely incorporated with Russia. The Russian Government also made it evident that Russia would like to incorporate Finland and destroy the Finnish nationality.   HANS SCHJÖTH

A SCENE IN DENMARK'S CAPITAL: THE ROYAL THEATRE, COPENHAGEN

EUROPE SINCE 1871

THE CLOSE OF THE VICTORIAN ERA

THE TRIUMPH OF DEMOCRACY
IN THE UNITED KINGDOM

By Arthur D. Innes, M.A.

THE Reform Bill, passed in 1867, was avowedly a leap in the dark. The vote for parliamentary representatives had been bestowed on classes which had hitherto had no voice in the government of the country. Practically the whole of the urban labouring population was now entitled to vote, though the agricultural labourers, the peasantry of the three kingdoms, were still excluded. The working man had got his vote on the hypothesis that he would use it intelligently and responsibly. There was ground, on the one side, for expecting that a class numerically outweighing the rest would demand legislation in its own interests ; and, on the other, for trusting to the conservative instincts of the race to prevent such demands from being excessive.

It was evident to both the political parties that to meet the requirements of this new and preponderant element in the electorate must be a primary object with every government. It was likely that any change in the character of the representatives themselves, in the social rank to which they would belong, would be only gradual ; the actual business of government would be in the hands of the same type of legislators and administrators as before ; but they would have to satisfy the wants of new masters, and the new masters would have to be educated to a wise exercise of their newly-acquired powers.

Broadly speaking, then, at the moment when the new electorate placed Gladstone in power instead of Disraeli the attitudes of the two parties were as follows : The Liberals believed that their hands were strengthened for drastic legislation directed against what they regarded as the unjustifiable privileges of the orders of society which had hitherto held the preponderance, some of which appeared to the Conservatives in the light of necessary mainstays for the support of any orderly social fabric.

On the other hand, their foreign policy was based on the conviction that peace should be secured, and the horrors of war avoided, by carrying concession to the utmost limits compatible with national honour, and by a confidence in the equal readiness of foreign Powers to be guided by abstract conceptions of disinterested justice. The Conservatives, on the other hand, looked to the provision of methods for the amelioration of the condition of the working classes without disturbing vested interests ; and in foreign politics, having a complete distrust of our neighbours' readiness to subordinate their own interests to principles of abstract justice, they dwelt on the maxim that the best security against war is to be found in readiness for battle.

Ireland presented to Gladstone the most immediate and pressing problem. Catholic emancipation had not healed the distresses of that country, and the Fenian movement was only a more violent demonstration than usual of the intense discontent from which she was suffering. Gladstone believed the political disaffection to be the product of genuine grievances, which were attributed to the British supremacy, and

5163

KING EDWARD IN EARLY MANHOOD

corporation into which the disestablished Church was formed. Irish land presented a no less thorny problem. In Ireland, the peasant lived on, and by, his holding ; there was no demand for his labour. The alternative to living on his holding at whatever rental the landlord or his agent might demand, was emigration. Most of the peasantry were tenants at will, who could be simply evicted at six months' notice, and eviction meant the complete loss of any expenditure the tenant had incurred in improving his holding, although this state of things was locally modified by prevalent customs. The demand of the peasantry was formulated in the " Three Fs," fair rent, fixity of tenure, free sale.

The object of the Land Bill now introduced by the Government was to provide compensation for improvements in cases of arbitrary eviction, to give sundry local customs the force of law, and to assist tenants, by money loans, to

if those grievances were removed, the disaffection would die out. These sources of trouble were to be found in the agrarian and the religious systems existing. Roman Catholicism was no longer attended by serious disabilities ; but in a country where more than three-fourths of the population were Roman Catholics the religious endowments were appropriated to the established Anglican Church, while the Church to which the masses adhered was entirely dependent on voluntary support. The disestablishment of the Anglican Church in Ireland was the first important measure presented to the new Parliament in 1869. To deprive the Church of her property, to sever the connection of Church and State, to attack the supremacy of Protestantism—such, in the eyes of opponents, were the objects of the Bill, which was passed, however, part of the proposal being an arrangement under which the equivalent of some two-thirds of the Church property was returned to the new ecclesiastical

QUEEN ALEXANDRA AT THE TIME OF HER MARRIAGE
From the painting by R. Lauchert

become freeholders by purchase when the landlord was willing to sell. This Bill also was passed ; but it shared with the Act of Disestablishment the fate of being regarded as a concession, not to justice, but to violence. The activity of the secret societies was not curtailed, and even while it was under consideration it was considered necessary to pass a "Peace Preservation Act," giving considerable powers of summary jurisdiction to magistrates and otherwise restricting normal liberties in "proclaimed" districts. As an attempt at conciliation, the measures were a complete failure, and the Home Rule movement came into being — a movement distinct from Fenianism, which demanded separation, and not identical with O'Connell's old demand for the repeal of the Union, but having as its avowed object the creation of an Irish Parliament for the conduct of Irish government. In 1870 was passed the Education Act, empowering local authorities to establish schools for primary education maintained chiefly out of the rates, with the proviso that the religious instruction given in such schools should be the simple Bible teaching supposed to be common to all Christian churches and sects. Hitherto, elementary schools had been supported almost entirely by the contributions of members of different religious denominations, the bulk of them, of course, Anglican, which merely received slight assistance from government grants, In such schools it was required that parents might, under a "conscience clause," withdraw their children from religious instruction. It would be hard to name any more fruitful source of controversies, to

A ROYAL FAMILY GROUP
King Edward and Queen Alexandra in 1864, then the Prince and Princess of Wales, with their first-born child, Prince Albert Victor.

a large extent unreasonable but none the less violent, than this Education Act, associated with the name of W. E. Forster ; but these did not arise in an acute form till some years later, when the Voluntary schools began to find their own maintenance, unsupplemented by public funds, increasingly impossible.

The Nonconformist bodies protested against paying rates for the support of such schools as were allowed to maintain a "Church Atmosphere," which Anglicans and Romanists made a cardinal point of maintaining. "Undenominational" instruction being regarded as anti-Anglican, while payment for denominational instruction out of public moneys is no less objectionable from the other point of view, all efforts at a compromise between the two sides have hitherto failed; and the advocates of exclusively secular instruction as the only road to educational peace seem likely to multiply. Apart, however, from the religious question, there is a general consensus of opinion that, although elementary education by the State has not yet been turned to the best account, much good has already been done, and the machinery has been prepared for future developments. But the parents in the class for whose special benefit the system was devised have never displayed any warm appreciation of its merits; since the children are unable effectively to earn wages until their school-time is over.

Another attack on class-privilege is to be noted in the abolition of promotion by purchase in the army—a measure which was enforced by Royal prerogative in view of the probability that the House of

THE NATION'S REJOICING AT THE RECOVERY OF THE PRINCE OF WALES: THE PROCESSION TO ST. PAUL'S: PASSING LUDGATE CIRCUS

Stricken down with a severe attack of typhoid fever in November, 1871, King Edward, then "Prince of Wales, lay for several days at the point of death, and as the end seemed near, Queen Victoria and the other members of the Royal Family were twice summoned to Sandringham, where his Royal Highness was being nursed by the Princess of Wales. Happily, however, the royal patient was restored to health, and, to mark the nation's gratitude at his recovery, a thanksgiving service was held at St. Paul's Cathedral in February, 1872.

From the painting by Chevalier in the Royal Collection

Lords would prevent its enactment by process of Parliament. That a Liberal Government should appeal to prerogative to override Parliament was sufficiently paradoxical to look like a constitutional innovation. In electoral law one change of importance was made by the introduction of the ballot, which has only in part had the desired and desirable effect of sheltering those electors who do not wish it to be known how their vote has been cast.

None of the legislation recorded was of a character to excite the enthusiasm of the new electors; and the Ministers'

Conference. The result was that the Powers acquiesced in the modifications of the treaty required by Russia. Great Britain, being alone strongly interested in the maintenance of the clauses, was unable to impress her view on the other signatories; and the country felt that its prestige had been lowered in the eyes of Europe.

Somewhat similar was the effect of the Alabama claim. The Alabama, as previously related, was a vessel built in the Mersey which escaped the vigilance of the authorities, put to sea, was handed over to the Confederates, and did immense

KING EDWARD VII. AND QUEEN ALEXANDRA RIDING IN WINDSOR PARK
From the picture by Barraud, painted in the early years of their married life

conduct of foreign affairs was still less pleasing. In two separate affairs, British diplomacy had disastrous results. The Russian Government took the opportunity of the outbreak of war between France and Germany to issue a declaration repudiating certain clauses in the Treaty of Paris, which had followed the Crimean War, on the ground that altered circumstances had made them no longer binding. The claim necessitated the assembling of a conference of the Powers which had signed the treaty, held in London and known as the Black Sea

damage to the Federal shipping in the American Civil War. Very heavy claims for compensation were put in by the United States Government, while the British refused to admit that any breach of neutrality had been committed. At last, in 1871, a treaty was made by which the dispute was submitted to an international court of arbitration. In the treaty, the British Government conceded practically every one of the American demands as to the conditions of the inquiry, though denying that several of the conditions were properly applicable;

5167

and the court's decision was regarded as extravagantly favourable to the Americans.

This first great attempt to introduce the principle of arbitration in the settlement of international difficulties gave an unfortunate impression that such tribunals would be guided, not by the principles of justice, but by interest, and where Britain was concerned, by prejudice against her. The impression was intensified when a dispute as to delimitation of frontiers in the north-west of America was referred to the arbitration of the German Emperor, and was promptly decided in favour of the Americans. Thus, by

the Acts; the war raged round the doctrine of freedom of contract, which must, in the eyes of one party, be held sacred and inviolable, whereas in the eyes of the other party the "Freedom" was a fiction, the tenant or employee having practically no power to resist pressure on the part of the landlord or employer.

It was not, however, in the field of domestic legislation that the 1874 Ministry was notable. The brilliant chief of the ruling party found room for a more dazzling display of his abilities in the conduct of foreign affairs. The world was suddenly startled by the exceedingly ingenious stroke which brought the

QUEEN VICTORIA RECEIVING THE SHAH OF PERSIA AT WINDSOR, ON JUNE 20TH, 1873

the end of 1872 the Ministry had lost favour with the nation, and a dissolution at the beginning of 1874 gave Disraeli a decisive majority.

The conservative legislation proceeded on the lines of providing the working classes with opportunities for improving their condition. The fundamental difference between the attitude of Conservatism and that of advanced Liberalism became apparent in the questions of contract between landlord and tenant, or between employers and employees. The legislation systematically recognised the right of the two parties to contract themselves out of the obligations imposed by

recently constructed Suez Canal practically under British control. The canal had been constructed by Lesseps, and the natural presumption was that French influence would predominate, while the great actual preponderance lay with the Khedive of Egypt. But the Khedive was in want of cash; and on the strength of information received, Disraeli purchased his shares in the Canal Company on behalf of the British Government, which thus became very much the largest shareholder in the concern. The secrecy and the unexpectedness of the transaction gave it a peculiarly startling character, and at once aroused the excited suspicions

CABINET COUNCIL IN DOWNING STREET DISCUSSING THE EASTERN QUESTION

In 1876 a crisis of an alarming character occupied the attention of the British Government. Misrule in Turkey had brought the European provinces of the Porte into insurrection, and while one party in Britain was desirous of maintaining the rule of the Turk there was another party equally resolved to terminate the oppression at all costs.

THE CONFERENCE OF THE GREAT POWERS AT CONSTANTINOPLE IN 1876

The Eastern crisis increased in intensity when, in June, 1876, Servia and Montenegro declared war against Turkey. An armistice having been agreed upon, through the insistence of Russia, Lord Beaconsfield organised a conference of the Great Powers at Constantinople, Lord Salisbury attending it as the representative of the British Government. The conference proved abortive, the threatened Russo-Turkish war being only temporarily averted.

COUNCIL AND CONFERENCE IN LONDON AND CONSTANTINOPLE

of the political school which views with alarm any abnormal extra-parliamentary exercise of administrative power. About the same time, the Eastern question was again assuming prominence. If Russia, on the one part, succeeded, as we have seen, in securing in her own favour modifications of the post-Crimean Treaty of Paris, Turkey had succeeded in effectually evading the fulfilment of her own pledges under that instrument. The government of the Christian provinces continued to be eminently unsatisfactory, amounting practically to a military rule over a people in a state perpetually

Laurence

CHARLES STEWART PARNELL
The "uncrowned King of Ireland," Parnell exercised wonderful influence both in Parliament and throughout the country, but his appearance as co-respondent in a divorce case was the death-blow to his political career.

bordering on insurrection. Insurrection broke out in Bosnia and Herzegovina, and was repressed with circumstances of savage brutality, even when full allowance is made for inevitable exaggerations and highly coloured pictures of the cruelties practised. The European governments remonstrated, and the European populations became excited. Turkey continued to promise, and continued not to perform. The stories of the "Bulgarian atrocities" aroused a passion of indignant resentment, especially in Britain and in Russia. The governments still confined themselves to diplomatic

THE "MOONLIGHTING" OUTRAGES IN IRELAND: A VISIT FROM "CAPTAIN MOONLIGHT"
About 1880 secret societies carried out in Ireland a series of outrages, chiefly at night. The notices sent to those who were to be visited were signed "Captain Moonlight," and thus the members of these societies came to be known as "Moon ighters.'

THE EVICTION OF AN IRISH HOUSEHOLDER FOR REFUSING TO PAY HIS RENT
During the disturbed period in Ireland scenes such as that depicted above were of frequent occurrence. Rents could not be collected, and in consequence the tenants who refused to pay were forcibly evicted by officers of the police.

pressure, and Turkey still relied on their distrust of each other to secure her from anything more serious. But Russia took upon herself the obligations of Europe, and in 1877 declared war upon Turkey in the character of defender of the Christian populations.

It was precisely in this character that Russia had always intervened; British Ministers as invariably believed the philanthropic profession to be nothing but a cloak, an excuse which was to be used to advance Russian interests to the detriment of the British Empire. Suspicions of Russia prevailed over indignation against Turkey; the conviction was not unusual that Russia had deliberately fostered the disturbances, that an excuse might be provided for her own aggression. Russia flung herself against Turkey, and the magnificent defence of Plevna by Osman Pasha excited the keen admiration of a people always ready to sympathise with a

stubborn fight against heavy odds. Lord Beaconsfield—Disraeli had taken the title at the end of 1876—felt that the nation would be behind him in opposing Russia. The fleet was sent to the Dardanelles; it seemed as if a war with Russia could hardly be avoided. Blatant bellicosity got its now familiar title of Jingoism from a popular song of the day.

In the midst of the clamour the public was startled by suddenly finding the Russians and Turks embracing. The two powers had concluded the Treaty of San Stefano. But the treaty was by no means to the liking of the British, as unduly strengthening the Russian position, though not so much so as was at first feared. Lord Beaconsfield claimed that the treaty must be submitted to a conference of the Powers, who were pledged to maintain the Treaty of Paris as modified by the Black Sea Treaty. It was still far from certain that the war-clouds would disperse, and native

5171

troops were summoned from India to Malta for contingencies—a proceeding which, in the eyes of many, was a violation of constitutional principles. How far this practical demonstration of British readiness for war influenced Russia may be a matter for question ; but she assented to the British demand, and a congress of the Powers was summoned at Berlin.

Whether the objects and the methods of Beaconsfield's diplomacy were wise or unwise, the methods were successful and the objects were attained. Secret preliminary agreements were made separately with Russia and with Turkey ; and the outcome of the congress was that the Balkan States were declared independent principalities, the concessions to Russia under the Treaty of San Stefano were curtailed, and the new treaty was supplemented by an Anglo-Turkish treaty, under which Great Britain guaranteed the integrity of the Turkish dominion in Asia, in consideration of which she was to occupy the Island of Cyprus. Lord Beaconsfield returned to England, the bearer, in his own famous phrase, of "Peace with Honour," in July, 1878.

In other parts of the empire, however, Lord Beaconsfield's policy brought the Ministry more doubtful credit. The proclamation of a new title for the Queen as Empress of India at the opening of 1877 was not uncommonly regarded in Britain as a piece of cheap display ; though, on the other hand, the British mind does not find it easy to appreciate the value of even cheap display in influencing Oriental populations. But the new policy adopted towards Afghanistan by Lord Beaconsfield and his Viceroy, Lord Lytton, was fraught with danger. Ever since the restoration of Dost Mohammed in 1843, the principle of non-intervention had been maintained. But in Asia, as in Europe, Russian aggression was looked upon with increasing alarm ; Russian efforts to obtain influence at the

Court of Kabul were regarded with well founded jealousy, and there was a strong feeling in military circles that strategical requirements demanded the substitution of a " scientific frontier " for the existing one. The proposals of the British Government appeared to the Amir, Shere Ali, to be merely a cloak for annexation. A Russian mission was received at Kabul, and a British mission was stopped. Three British columns entered Afghanistan in November, 1878. Shere Ali fled, and died ; the British established his son Yakub Khan as Amir. Sir Louis Cavagnari went to Kabul as British Resident, and was very soon murdered, in September, 1879. The account of the war which followed, in which Sir Donald Stewart and Sir Frederic Roberts achieved their laurels, has been given in the history of India. A change of government in Britain in 1880 brought

The British Forces in Afghanistan

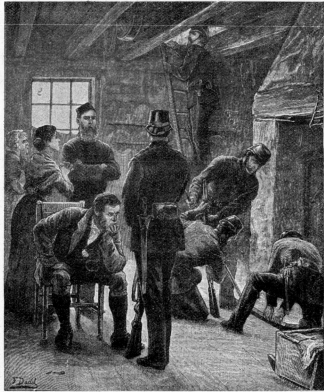

THE POLICE SEARCHING AN IRISH HOUSE FOR ARMS

a reversal of policy, and Abdurrhaman was established as an independent ruler. In South Africa the Zulu War could at best bring little prestige ; it brought disaster in the affair of Isandlhwana, though

THE ASSASSINATION OF LORD FREDERIC CAVENDISH AND MR. BURKE IN PHŒNIX PARK
The outrages which marked the disaffection of the Irish against the government in the early eighties culminated in a dastardly outrage in Phœnix Park, Dublin, on the morning of May 6th, 1882, when Lord Frederic Cavendish, Chief Secretary for Ireland, and Mr. Thomas Burke, permanent Irish Under Secretary, were assassinated by a small band of "Irish Invincibles." Twenty men were brought to trial in connection with the crime, and five of them were hanged.

the credit of British courage was indisputably confirmed by the heroic defence of Rorke's Drift. And the annexation of the Transvaal Republic was immediately afterwards to bear bitter fruit.

The social legislation had done little to satisfy the labour-class electors. The diplomatic triumph of the Berlin Congress was dimmed by the troubles in Afghanistan and South Africa. There was an uneasy sense in the country that Lord Beaconsfield was too fond of surprises and sensations, of keeping the nation in the dark, of playing with fire.

Gladstone Again in Power

The Parliament had run six years of its life when it dissolved in 1880, and the Liberals returned to power. Gladstone had retired from the leadership, but there was now no possible question that Gladstone was the leader whom the electorate demanded, and he entered upon his second administration.

The legislative efforts of the last Liberal Government had been concentrated mainly on the Irish Church Disestablishment and the Irish Land Act. Ireland was again to absorb Gladstone's attention, ultimately to the practical exclusion of other matters; while the conduct of foreign affairs was still destined to be a source of popular dissatisfaction. During the Conservative term of office the Irish Home-Rulers, though as yet the limitations of the county franchise kept their numbers low, had come to be distinctively known as the Irish members. Under the leadership of Charles Stewart Parnell, they were already consolidating into a compact and disciplined force with a large capacity for the systematic obstruction of public business. Under the new administration they rapidly became one of the most effectively organised forces on record.

The state of affairs in Ireland had not improved; agitation and organised resistance to authority had increased. The first announcement that the Government did not intend to renew the Peace Preservation Act on its lapse was regarded with grave apprehension; while the Irish members complained that there was no promise of immediately proceeding to a new Land Bill. Certain proposals brought forward by one of the Irish members were, however, embodied at an early date in the Bill for Compensation for Disturbance; but the destruction of the Bill by the Lords, coupled with the lapse of the

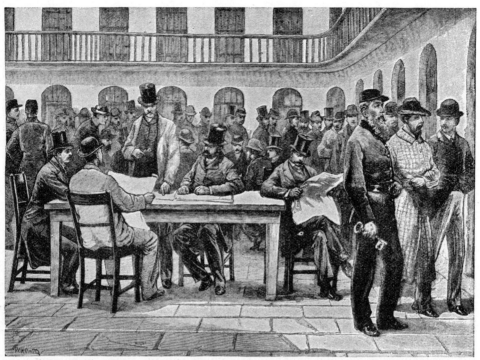

THE IRISH LAND LEAGUE: RECREATION TIME IN KILMAINHAM PRISON
A new Land Act passed by the Government in face of strenuous opposition did nothing to settle the disturbed condition of the country, and the agitation and outrages continuing, Parnell and other leaders were lodged in Kilmainham Gaol.

Peace Preservation Act, was the signal for the outbreak of a series of agrarian outrages ; and the practice of " boycotting " —a name taken from that of one of its victims—was established and carried out on an extensive scale. Rents could not be collected, and there was an immense number of evictions in consequence. The organisation known as the Land League, with which most of the Irish members were associated, was held responsible ; and, in spite of some doubt whether anything that could be brought home to them was in actual violation of the law, some of its leaders were arrested. Since there was no sort of chance that an Irish jury would convict them, the effect for the Government was somewhat ignominious.

These troubles decided the Government that coercive measures must precede the remedial. The Irish members demanded precedence for land reform, and gave warning that a measure of coercion would be met by refusal to pay rent. Nevertheless, the Coercion Bills were introduced to the accompaniment of a prolonged debate, an all-night sitting being followed by one of forty-one hours, which the Speaker brought to a close only by a summary use of his powers on his own responsibility.

This was the cause of drastic measures of procedure, intended to prevent the effective tactical use of obstruction ; but no method has yet been devised which can prevent a deliberate waste of the time of the House.

The Coercion Bills were passed after most stormy scenes, and then the new Land Act was introduced, of which the essential feature was the establishment of Land Courts to fix fair rents instead of leaving the amount as one of bargaining between landlord and tenant. The Act was passed, in spite of strenuous opposition in the House of Lords and the open withdrawal of some supporters of the Government.

The Terrible Tragedy in Phœnix Park The Parnellites refused to aid the Government; the agitation and the outrages continued ; Parnell himself and other leaders were lodged in Kilmainham ; and a manifesto was issued against any payment of rents till they should be set free. This had hardly been done when the tragedy of the Phœnix Park murders occurred, a crime emanating from extremist sources in America, and for the time extremely injurious to the Irish parliamentary party, whom a large section of the public persistently believed to be responsible. By a strange irony it fell to the Gladstone

Ministry to initiate the British occupation of Egypt. The great financial interests there of British and French had given those two countries a large control. The virtual rebellion of Arabi Pasha the bombardment of Alexandria by the British fleet, while the French fleet refused co-operation, the overthrow of Arabi by Sir Garnet Wolseley at Tel-el-kebir, and the establishment of a British control intended to be only temporary, have been narrated elsewhere. From these events the Government did not suffer ; but the same cannot be said of the later developments. The

Gordon's Death in Khartoum rise of Mahdism, the mission of General Gordon, the noble but embarrassing course of action which he adopted, and the disastrous delays, owing to which the Government expedition, despatched to his rescue, arrived at Khartoum to find that the place had been captured and the hero slain two days before, January 26th, 1885—these things dealt a disastrous blow which grievously weakened the Government's prestige.

At an earlier stage, too, it had suffered severely by the events connected with the revolt of the Transvaal Boers, the rout of British troops by a handful of farmers at Majuba Hill, and the reinstatement, in 1881, of the Boer Republic as an act of justice which, by most Boers and probably by a majority of British, was attributed to pusillanimity. That this was a misjudgment of motive, however unwise the experiment in magnanimity may have been, is sufficiently attested by the position of trusted leadership subsequently held in the Unionist party by chiefs, who at this time shared the responsibilities of the Gladstone Cabinet. The details appear in the African Division. The Penjdeh incident on the Afghan frontier, and its close by another reference to arbitration, by no means satisfactory to the British, belongs to the Indian record, but has to be noted here as the last of the series of events abroad which helped to fix on the Government the stigma of a peace-at-any-price Ministry.

Nevertheless, in spite of the dissatisfaction over foreign affairs, the Cabinet retained the support of the country by its domestic policy. Ireland having taken up its share of legislative time, the completion of the democratic reform initiated by the Conservative " leap in the dark " of 1867 was taken in hand, and a Bill was introduced in 1884 for the enfranchisement of the agricultural as well as the urban labouring classes. The Government's majority in the House of Commons was

THE NILE CAMPAIGN IN 1885: LORD CHARLES BERESFORD'S DASH TO KHARTOUM
The above picture illustrates an incident in the Nile campaign of 1885, when General Gordon was shut up in Khartoum, bravely defending it against the savage hordes of the Mahdi. Making a dash for the Nile, Sir Charles Wilson there found steamers and reinforcements from Gordon, but he was too late to save the gallant soldier. Wilson and his men being in grave danger from the enemy, an expedition under the command of Lord Charles Beresford was despatched to their assistance, and sailing up the Nile on the steamer Safia accomplished its object by rescuing the party.
From the painting by Dickenson

QUEEN VICTORIA'S JUBILEE: THE ROYAL PROCESSION ON JUBILEE DAY PASSING HYDE PARK CORNER

From a photograph by Messrs. Valentine & Sons

decisive. But franchise extension necessitated also redistribution of constituencies; and the House of Lords demanded that the Government's Redistribution Bill should take precedence of the Bill extending the franchise, the Conservatives claiming that their opposition was not directed against the principle of the Bill before them.

A serious crisis seemed imminent, and there were many angry demands for the abolition of the hereditary Chamber, or, at least, for its reconstruction on lines which would make it

Cabinet so uneasy that the opportunity was taken to resign when they were defeated on a snap vote on the Budget. Lord Salisbury, who had succeeded Lord Beaconsfield in the leadership of the Conservatives, accepted office in June. Before the dissolution of Parliament in August, a measure was passed, known as the Ashbourne Act, under which £5,000,000 were advanced by the State to facilitate the purchase of their holdings by Irish tenants; and various circumstances produced a strong impression

THE JUBILEE SERVICE IN WESTMINSTER ABBEY ON JUNE 21ST, 1887
From the painting by T. S. C. Crowther

no longer a recognised stronghold of one political party. Nevertheless, the leaders on both sides were not anxious to force a great constitutional struggle, and a practical compromise was arrived at. The Franchise Bill was again introduced and passed in the Commons, but before it was dealt with by the Lords the chiefs of the two parties agreed upon the Redistribution Bill. Honour was satisfied on both sides, and both Bills became law.

The death of General Gordon and the Penjdeh affair made the position of the

of some sort of rapprochement between the Conservatives and the Irish leader. The result of the General Election at the close of the year was embarrassing. The extended franchise had doubled Parnell's following in the House. Added to the Conservative ranks, they exactly cancelled the total Liberal majority. In effect, they could make government by either party impossible. But the effect on the Liberal leader's mind was what caused most surprise; it brought home to him that the great majority of Irishmen supported

5177

MR. GLADSTONE INTRODUCING THE HOME RULE BILL ON FEBRUARY 13TH, 1893

Mr. Gladstone's solution for the ills which afflicted Ireland was a measure of self-government for that country, and in the above picture he is seen introducing his Home Rule Bill to the House of Commons after the constituencies had sent him back to power. The Bill passed the Lower House, after long discussion, but was thrown out by the House of Lords.

From the painting by R. Ponsonby Staples, by permission of Messrs. Henry Graves & Co.

Parnell's demands—a conclusion which had not followed in the days when less than half the members from Ireland were Home Rulers. The claim of a minority had suddenly assumed the character of a national demand supported by four-fifths of the national representatives. How could England, the champion of oppressed nationalities, refuse a hearing to such a demand? From this time to the end of his life the establishment of Irish Home Rule became Gladstone's absorbing passion.

There were many members of the Liberal party who had already all but yielded to the conviction that the only solution of the Irish problem lay in Home Rule; there were some who had been actively urging at least a large delegation of powers of local self-government. But of these the most energetic had drawn the line short of the concession of a separate Irish legislature, and the Irish representatives would be content with nothing short of that. The Liberal ranks were split into these two main divisions; and those who would concede

QUEEN VICTORIA IN 1893
From a photograph by Messrs. Hughes & Mullins, Ryde

a legislature were again divided. Given an Irish Parliament, should Ireland be represented at Westminster too? If so, she would be able still to hold the balance, to control legislation in the sister kingdoms while herself free from their control. If not, she would cease to have a voice in Imperial affairs, and to realise her partnership in Imperial interests. In any case, too, a legislature elected practically by the peasantry could not be trusted to deal fairly with the question of land, any more than would a legislature elected practically by landlords.

A number of " dissentient Liberals " broke wholly with their leader, though before his intentions were realised he had been able to defeat the Salisbury Ministry, and to assume the responsibilities of office. When he introduced two Bills—one of which was to settle the land question by the State buying out the landlords and selling back the land to the peasants; while the other was to establish a Parliament in Dublin, and abolish the representation at Westminster—the combined forces of the Opposition proved too strong, and the Home Rule Bill was defeated in the House of Commons on the second reading. Parliament was dissolved. The Conservatives did not, under the circumstances, contest seats held by dissentient Liberals, and the elections returned Lord Salisbury to power with a majority virtually dependent on the consistent support of the body now known as Liberal Unionists. That combination did not cease to rule until twenty years had passed; for, although there was an interval from 1892 to 1895, during which there was again a Liberal Ministry, the Liberals, apart from Irish Home Rule members, were even then in a minority, and the House of Lords held itself warranted in refusing to recognise the composite majority which Ministers could command as representing the national will.

Whatever constitutional objections might be urged to this doctrine—virtually based on the theory that the Irish party did not count—the Lords found their practical justification when a dissolution decisively ejected the Liberals. From

THE CELEBRATION OF QUEEN VICTORIA'S DIAMOND JUBILEE: HER MAJESTY'S ARRIVAL AT ST. PAUL'S CATHEDRAL

From a photograph by Messrs. Eyre & Spottiswoode

THE ROYAL PROCESSION PASSING ALONG PALL MALL

THE COLONIAL PREMIERS AND TROOPS PASSING OVER LONDON BRIDGE

SCENES IN QUEEN VICTORIA'S DIAMOND JUBILEE PROCESSION Valentine

QUEEN VICTORIA IN THE YEAR OF HER DIAMOND JUBILEE, 1897

Photo: W. & D. Downey

EDWARD VII., KING OF GREAT BRITAIN AND IRELAND

Photo: W. S. Stuart

THE FUNERAL OF QUEEN VICTORIA: THE COFFIN BEING CARRIED INTO ST. GEORGE'S CHAPEL, WINDSOR

From the photograph by Messrs. Russell & Sons

1886 to 1892 the Conservatives held office, supported and very materially influenced by the Liberal Unionists. From 1895 to the end of 1904 Conservatives and Liberal Unionists, combined as the Unionist party, held office.

Lord Salisbury's first administration was marked by three measures in which the influence of his Liberal Unionist supporters was prominent. An Irish Coercion Act was accompanied by a Land Act authorising a revision of the rents fixed by the land court, and the provision of relief for tenants whose payments were in arrears. In 1888 a great measure was introduced giving extensive powers of local government to locally-elected bodies—county councils, district councils, and borough councils, but this was not extended to Ireland. And in 1891 it was decided that the cost of education, which was made compulsory, ought to be borne by the State. Thenceforth all parents could obtain elementary education for their children without making any direct contribution to the cost.

The period is also noteworthy in other parts of the globe for the delimitation of the spheres of influence of the various European Powers in Africa, and for the final annexation of Burma. At home, the Irish question was placed on an altered footing by the "Parnell Commission," a state inquiry which acquitted the Irish leaders of the complicity in crime with which they had been charged. The dissolution in 1892 so reduced the Unionist forces that Gladstone, with the support of the Irish, was able to eject them from office.

The new Government introduced a new Home Rule Bill, this time retaining the Irish representatives at Westminster; and on its rejection by the Lords continued to "fill up the cup," but could carry no effective legislation except in the field of finance, where constitutional practice forbade the intervention of the hereditary Chamber. Consequently the one legacy to the nation of this Ministry — led first by Gladstone, and later on, after the aged statesman's retirement, by Lord Rosebery—was the system known as the "Death Duties," which provided a substantial source of revenue from graduated charges on the value of property changing hands owing to the death of the owner. The base principles of the measure are, that all property acquired without effort on the part of the owner owes something extra to the community, and that great wealth owes not only more, but a larger percentage than moderate wealth, and moderate wealth than poverty.

KING EDWARD VII. WHEN PRINCE OF WALES
From the painting by A. Stuart Wortley, by permission of Messrs. Henry Graves & Co.

The Government majority was small at the best. A chance defeat brought about its resignation; Lord Salisbury took office, and immediately dissolved. The Unionists were returned to power with a majority of 150 over the combined Opposition; and the Liberal wing of the party now definitely amalgamated with

THE LAST CABINET OF QUEEN VICTORIA AND THE FIRST OF KING EDWARD VII.: AN HISTORIC GROUP OF MINISTERS

In the above picture are seen the members of the Cabinet in office when Queen Victoria died, in 1901. Lord Salisbury, the Prime Minister, is seated to the left of the picture with his elbow resting on the table, and his colleagues, reading from left to right, are as follow: Mr. A. J. Balfour, First Lord of the Treasury; Mr. Joseph Chamberlain, Secretary for the Colonies; Sir Michael Hicks-Beach, Chancellor of the Exchequer; Mr. C. T. Ritchie, Secretary for the Home Department; the Earl of Selborne, First Lord of the Admiralty; Lord Balfour of Burleigh, Secretary for Scotland; Lord Ashbourne, Lord Chancellor of Ireland; the Marquess of Londonderry, Postmaster-General; Mr. Walter Long, President of the Local Government Board; Mr. A. Akers-Douglas, First Commissioner of Works; Lord James of Hereford, Chancellor of the Duchy of Lancaster; Mr. R. W. Hanbury, President of the Board of Agriculture; Mr. G. W. Balfour, President of the Board of Trade; Lord George Hamilton, Secretary for India; Mr. W. St. J. F. Brodrick, Secretary for War; the Marquess of Lansdowne, Secretary for Foreign Affairs; Earl Cadogan, Lord-Lieutenant of Ireland; the Earl of Halsbury, Lord Chancellor; and the Duke of Devonshire, Lord President of the Council.

Lord Salisbury

William Ewart Gladstone

Arthur James Balfour

Lord Rosebery

Joseph Chamberlain

Sir Henry Campbell-Bannerman

Herbert Henry Asquith

EMINENT BRITISH STATESMEN OF RECENT AND PRESENT TIMES

Photos by London Stereoscopic Co., Valentine, Jerrard, Halftones, Mills and Haines

EDWARD VII. OPENING HIS FIRST PARLIAMENT: THE KING AND QUEEN IN THE HOUSE OF LORDS ON FEBRUARY 14TH, 1901

From the painting by S Begg

THE CORONATION OF KING EDWARD VII. AT WESTMINSTER ABBEY ON AUGUST 9TH, 1902

The coronation of Edward VII., who succeeded to the throne of the United Kingdom of Great Britain and Ireland at the death of Queen Victoria, on January 22nd, 1901, was arranged for June 26th, 1902, but two days before that date the startling announcement was made that the King was seriously ill, and that the ceremony must be postponed. His Majesty's condition was extremely critical, but after undergoing an operation, which, happily, proved successful, he speedily recovered, and was crowned in Westminster Abbey on August 9th.

KING EDWARD VII. AND QUEEN ALEXANDRA

Photo by W. S. Stuart

the Conservatives. The latter title almost disappeared from popular parlance, in which the official name of Unionist was gradually displaced for the old name of Tory, while the official name of Liberal yielded to that of Radical.

From the popular point of view, the succession of Irish Land Acts, whether just or unjust to the landlords, had considerably mitigated the agrarian grievances, and the consciousness that there was at any rate a large body of English and Scottish opinion favourable to Home Rule tended to discourage such violence as would be likely to alienate such sympathy. Unionist governments, however, have continued in the direction of concession to the tenant class; and an experiment was made in the Irish Local Government Act of 1898, in the hope that the delegation of large powers of local government to locally elected bodies would weaken the demand for a separate legislature. The effects of the Free Education Act were felt in the great difficulties now encountered by the voluntary schools in maintaining efficiency. Subscriptions dwindled; when the subscribers found themselves in any case required to provide money for the education of other people's children, they were not disposed to keep up their voluntary contributions as well; and the process was commenced, which has already been adverted to, of applying public funds for the relief of denominational schools.

Lord Salisbury's energies, however, were attracted to foreign affairs rather than to domestic legislation. His position and

HIS MAJESTY KING EDWARD VII.
From a photograph by W. S. Stuart

reputation enabled him to adopt a more conciliatory and less aggressive attitude than would have been easy for a party which did not represent the Beaconsfield tradition; and, on the other hand, he had the strong support of that section of Liberals who looked on Lord Rosebery as their chief when he refused to intervene forcibly—as many of the Opposition desired—in the Armenian troubles of Turkey.

The principle that the independent action of separate Powers should be checked and replaced by the concerted pressure of Europe became the guiding rule; while it suffered from the undoubted drawback that the concerted action of Europe is exceedingly difficult to set in motion. The possibilities of such a concert cannot be ignored, and serve as a check on individualist aggressiveness. These principles found expression also in connection with the Turco-Greek War, and at a later stage, when the Boxer insurrection brought about concerted European intervention in China, and considerable diplomatic skill was required to limit the general scramble for Chinese territory. Lovers of the principle of arbitration found considerable satisfaction in the adoption of that method for settling a boundary dispute with Venezuela in 1896, since the result demonstrated that anti-British decisions in such courts need no longer be regarded as a foregone conclusion.

British relations with European Powers were seriously endangered for a moment when, on the conclusion of the reconquest of the Egyptian Sudan by Lord Kitchener, a company of Frenchmen was found to have made its way to Fashoda. It was not without difficulty that the French were persuaded to recognise the decisive character of British claims in that region. In colonial affairs, the Salisbury regime was signalised by the movement towards

The Death of Queen Victoria

Federation, which took shape in the establishment of the Commonwealth of Australia; and still more memorably by the war with the Boer Republics in South Africa, which, beginning in 1899, was only terminated in 1902 with their definite incorporation in the British Empire.

Before that time, at the beginning of 1901, the great queen, whose reign was the longest in our annals—it had extended almost to sixty-four years—had passed away, and Edward VII. ascended the throne. She had become by degrees the ideal type of the constitutional monarch, save for a somewhat excessive withdrawal, not from political activity, but from publicity since the death of the Prince Consort. Her successor has displayed a singularly acute perception of the very important part such a ruler may play internationally; at least, whilst the politics of European states are largely controlled by crowned heads. The title which has been applied to him of Edward the Peacemaker is perhaps the proudest that any monarch could earn. The dissolution of Parliament had brought only a formal break in the Salisbury adminis-

Chamberlain's Tariff Reform Proposals

tration, the Ministerial majority being unimpaired. It was not very long, however, before its chief retired, his place being taken by Arthur Balfour. His primacy in the party was shared by Joseph Chamberlain, who very shortly startled England by declaring in favour of Tariff Reform—a theory of preferential or protective tariffs which was popularly supposed to be dead and buried, but now

became the object of the enthusiastic advocacy of a large number of persons who had hitherto not shown any signs of questioning the economic creed of Cobden.

While the Liberals were unanimous in upholding the doctrines of Free Trade, the Unionists were divided almost as markedly as the Liberals had been over Home Rule. Mr. Balfour achieved the feat of persuading each section of the party that his views coincided precisely with theirs. It became obvious, however, that the majority of the party were becoming converted definitely to the most extreme view that Mr. Chamberlain had advocated; and the General Election in 1905 gave an overwhelming Free Trade majority. Led by Sir Henry Campbell-Bannerman till his death, and since then by Mr. Asquith, the Liberal Government has endeavoured to deal with a series of exceedingly thorny questions, notably the education problem and the

Problem of the House of Lords

problem of licensed houses, both of which had been dealt with by the Unionist Government in a manner which had failed to satisfy the Nonconformists and the organisations which make temperance their primary object.

On the other hand, the Liberal measures have been stigmatised as confiscation and robbery, and the House of Lords has again presented itself as an insuperable obstacle to Liberal legislation, its action being supported by inferences, drawn from a series of bye-elections, that an appeal to the country would provide the same kind of justification as in 1895. But at this point the work of the historian ends, and that of the political prophet begins, and it does not appear that the Government, which retains an overwhelming majority in the House of Commons, has any intention of bringing the various vaticinations, favourable or unfavourable, to the immediate test of a dissolution.

ARTHUR D. INNES

Valentine

Baron Haymerle   Count Launay   Waddington   Prince Hohenlohe   Count   Count   Count St.   Desprez   Lothar Bucher   Von   Dr.   Count H.   Sadullah Bey   Lord Odo Russell   Lord   Karatheodori Pasha
                                             Corti   Mouy   Vallier   Holstein   Busch   Bismarck
    Count Károly   Prince Gortschakoff   Lord Beaconsfield   Von Radowitz   Baron Oubril   Count Andrássy   Prince Bismarck   Count Schuwaloff   Von Bülow   Salisbury   Mehemet Ali Pasha

"PEACE WITH HONOUR": THE REPRESENTATIVES OF ALL THE EUROPEAN POWERS ATTENDING THE BERLIN CONGRESS OF 1878

From the painting by Anton von Werner, by permission of the Berlin Photographic Co.

REACTION TRIUMPHANT IN RUSSIA
TURKEY'S EMERGENCE FROM DESPOTISM

THE expansion of Russia in Asia has already been dealt with, and before entering—as we shall do in the following pages—on the account of the Eastern Question, which is the chief concern of Russia in Europe, we must give a brief sketch of her recent domestic history.

The Tsar Alexander II., who succeeded Nicholas while the Crimean War was still in progress, was a man with liberal inclinations, but he was to a great extent the victim of a system from which a very much stronger man with the same desires would have found it next to impossible to free himself. In spite of the great measure of emancipation for the serfs, Russia remained under the iron heel of an oligarchy in spite of the theoretical semi-divine authority of the Tsar himself. The merciless repression of all freedom begot the deadliest of all foes of order—Nihilism; and Nihilism, and the terror thereof, intensified the repression of every movement, however orderly, towards liberty. In spite of the fact that Alexander was contemplating something at least in the direction of summoning a popular Assembly, he fell a victim to Nihilist plots in 1881.

Alexander II. a Victim of Nihilism

The murdered Tsar was the first ruler of Russia since 1598 who had been able to mount the throne of his fathers in peace. His father, who had felt in his own case the want of a good education, procured the best teachers for his son, and it was fortunate for Russia that the celebrated poet Shukovsky directed the training of Alexander. Alexander saw clearly the defects of his predecessor, but also understood that a thorough reform was only possible after the abolition of serfdom, and he therefore resolutely set himself to carry this out. He was spurred on by the example of the neighbouring empire of Austria, where the emancipation of the serfs had been carried out in 1781; the better class of Russians had long felt it

to be a disgrace to their country that slavery still flourished there. It was necessary to go cautiously to work, and above all to win the nobility for the cause. The Tsar therefore acted in a wise and noble manner when he expressed the wish that the nobles should take the work of emancipating the serfs into their own hands.

The Tsar's Great Work for the Serfs

There were, however, only a few who pledged themselves to the Tsar's idea. Among them were the conscientious Rostovzof Levschin, who prepared an historical account of serfdom in Russia, and the indefatigable Sergej St. Lanskoy and Tshevskin. The Grand Duke Constantine entered on the plan with great enthusiasm; the Grand Duchess Helene Pavlovna emancipated in 1859 the serfs of the estates comprised in her appanage.

All were unanimous on the question of emancipation, only there was a division of opinion, as previously under Catherine II., on the point whether the land should be given to the peasants as freehold. A secret committee was appointed by the emperor. Since this did not make any progress with its labours, a higher board, known as the Chief Commission, met, composed of more trustworthy members.

But even yet the opposition was too strong. Its leader, Prince Alexej Orlov, asserted that he would rather cut off his hand than sign the charter of emancipation. Finally, a Supreme Commission was appointed; this, being vigorously supported by the whole Press, finally completed the work. The imperial rescript of March 3rd, 1861, proclaimed the emancipation of the serfs on private estates and of the domestic slaves. By this edict more than twenty-three millions received their liberty. The peasants were required merely to pay a reasonable sum for their holdings, which now became their property. The rejoicings of the people were boundless. Wherever the Tsar appeared, he was greeted and

Millions of Serfs Emancipated

cheered as the liberator. In the year 1864 he emancipated also the peasants in Poland and Transcaucasia, and in 1866 the peasants on the imperial demesnes, and restricted the infliction of corporal punishment.

Now for the first time further reforms could be carried out. The judicial system was separated from the executive and reorganised ; trial by jury was introduced, and the taxation regulated. The economic condition and the productive power of the empire increased rapidly. The Tsar, as has recently been discovered, even thought seriously of granting a constitutional government ; his untimely assassination prevented him from carrying out his scheme. He gave the governments a sort of autonomy, and established in every district an independently elected district

ALEXANDER II., TSAR OF RUSSIA
A man of liberal inclinations, he resolutely set himself to carry out reforms, but the Nihilists were determined upon his destruction, and he was assassinated on March 13th, 1881.

diet, and a provincial diet—Zemstvo—above that in every government. Universal conscription was now introduced. It was now possible to take serious steps towards spreading culture among the people. It is true that out of a Budget of £47,139,954 in 1867, only £770,879 had been applied to educational purposes. But the figures gradually rose, and thousands of schools were founded. On the whole, even in the department of public education, a more liberal spirit prevailed. In the year 1863, a liberal statute was passed for the universities. Russia had seldom had a more philanthropic monarch. And yet the life of this Tsar, whose motto was " Justice, light, and freedom," was frequently attempted. Just as the rustic population of the

NIHILIST CONSPIRACIES IN RUSSIA: CONDEMNED MEN AND WOMEN ON THE SCAFFOLD

Russian provinces furnishes the best imaginable material for new religious sects, so the half-educated world of Russia is a fertile soil for every sort of " great ideas." The students especially, who were scrupulously prevented from receiving a sound, intellectual discipline, were often led astray by senseless oppression and still more senseless reforms. The Tsar, while in the imperial summer garden, was shot at by a student, Demetrius, on April 16th, 1866. Alexander did not allow this to divert him

POLICE SURPRISING A MEETING OF RUSSIAN NIHILISTS

was blown to pieces by a bomb thrown under his carriage on March 13th, 1881. The murder was a great blow for the free-thinking party, for the supporters of despotism and brute force were right when they asserted that the people did not yet know the proper use of liberty. The representatives of this reactionary movement, Ivan Aksakov the Slavophil and Michail Katkof, acquired more influence, especially since they had been able to impress on the educated sections of the people the idea that absolutism, orthodoxy, and many barbarous customs of the people, which it was proposed to eradicate, belonged to the essence of Russian, and, in fact, of Slavonic, life. When, therefore, Alexander's son, Alexander III., had mounted the throne, they became all-powerful, more especially their associate Constantine Pobiedonostev, who was made Procurator-General of the Holy Synod in 1880. The ship of state was once more steered into the vortex of reaction.

Alexander III. was known, like his father, to have had a leaning towards Liberal ideas ; but the manner of his father's death destroyed all prospect of his acting upon them, and severity towards everything which was suspected of association with a revolutionary propaganda was increased instead of being relaxed. The maintenance of order by an extraordinarily elaborate system of espionage and by police methods, which have had no parallel in Western Europe except during periods of religious persecution, inevitably has exceedingly ugly concomitants, and among these was cruel popular persecution of the Jews, which was encouraged instead of being checked by the Government.

Alexander III. died in 1894, and was succeeded by the present Tsar, Nicholas II. His reign has been marked by the terrible disasters of the Japanese war, which went

from the path of reform. On June 6th, 1867, a Pole, Anton Beresovsky, aimed at him, although he had bestowed benefits on the Poles. The folly of such inexperienced youths was outdone by the brutality of the police, which provoked the greatest indignation. Nihilist societies with widespread branches were founded at home and abroad. Secret newspapers were published, terrorism was preached, new assassinations were attempted, until finally the Tsar

far towards destroying the bogey of an immense and irresistible Russian power from which Western imaginations had long been suffering. On the other hand, there has been a moment when the friends of freedom were beginning to believe that by at last summoning the Duma the Tsar was intending to open the gates for a serious reform of the government. The next steps, however, pointed to a triumph of reaction; nevertheless, a hope may be admitted that in spite of the clang of bolts and bars the opening of

Syria, from the Persian frontier, from Servia, and from Bulgaria; it was obliged in consequence to agree with the other Powers to Russia's demands on March 13th, 1871, and also to lay down certain points for the regulation of the Danube traffic.

In 1873 the Russian War Minister, Miljutin, reorganised the army on the model of the German military system, introducing general conscription and considerably increasing both the number of regiments and of soldiers available in time of war. Thereupon the Eastern

THE ASSASSINATION OF ALEXANDER II., TSAR OF RUSSIA, IN 1881
In consequence of the Russian Government's severe repression of the revolutionary movements, the Nihilists determined to have revenge upon the Tsar and his officers, and on March 13th, 1881, a bomb was thrown at the emperor's carriage near his palace in St. Petersburg, Alexander II. being so severely injured that he died a few hours afterwards.

the gates is appreciably nearer at hand. Reference has already been made to the conference in London which, taking place during the Franco-Prussian War, reopened the Black Sea question, and thereby led up to a revival of the Eastern Question in general. At that conference Russia secured the abolition of the clauses of the Peace of Paris of 1856 prohibiting her from keeping warships in the Black Sea. The Porte had been forced to send a considerable body of troops to Yemen in Arabia, and was in receipt of disturbing news from

Question was again brought upon the stage by the Pan-Slavonic party. Thanks to their agitation, a revolt broke out in Herzegovina in 1875, which the Porte did not immediately suppress. When a consular commission of the Powers and Austrian intervention led to no result, the Porte took decided action, and would have restored order in Montenegro, in Herzegovina, and in Servia by superior force, had not Ignatieff opposed the use of menaces. Unfortunately for the Porte, the French and German consuls were

ALEXANDER III., TSAR OF RUSSIA

THE TSARINA OF RUSSIA

THE TSAR IN OLD RUSSIAN COSTUME

THE TSARINA IN OLD NATIVE DRESS

ALEXANDER III., TSAR OF ALL THE RUSSIAS, AND HIS CONSORT

murdered on May 6th, 1876, in the course of a riot at Salonika, and the incident cost Turkey a heavy price. Hardly had a memorandum of Gortchakoff secured a two months' armistice among the revolted parties, when the Bulgarians revolted in Drenova, Panagiurishte, Koprivshzitza, Gabrovo, and Srednagora, and were crushed by the fanatical population with dreadful cruelty—the "Bulgarian atrocities" execrated by Gladstone and the English Press.

On May 10th, 1876, the Softas, the theological students, took up arms in the capital and haughtily requested the Sultan, who was regarded as blindly devoted to Russia, to dismiss the Grand Vizir Mahmud Nedim Pasha, to send away Ignatieff, and to begin war against Montenegro. In vain did Abd ul-Aziz attempt to calm the storm by summoning Mehemet Rüshdi; the measure of his wrong-doing was full. On May 29th the new Grand Vizir and the Minister of War, Hussein Avni and Midhat Pasha, declared the Sultan deposed, and placed Murad V., the eldest son of Abd ul-Mejid, on the throne. Abd ul-Aziz was conveyed to his palace at Chiragan and there murdered, as transpired from an inquiry held in 1882; a few days after Hussein Pasha with other Ministers were assassinated in the house of Midhat. Even before the tour of the Sultan Abd ul-Aziz to Europe in the spring of 1867, a conspiracy had been discovered, directed principally against the then Grand Vizir, Ali Pasha. The chiefs of the movement called themselves Young Turks, in an opposite sense to that which is conveyed by the terms "Young Germany," or "la Giovine Italia." The objects of this conspiracy were the restoration of the old Turkish regime and of the Turkish Empire, with the complete suppression of all non-Mohammedans; the surest means to this end was proclaimed to be the arming of the Mohammedan people and the murder of the liberal-

NICHOLAS II., TSAR OF RUSSIA
Born on May 18th, 1868, he succeeded his father, Alexander III., in 1894, and has since that time witnessed the overthrow of his military forces by Japan and the constitutional revolutionary movement within his own land.

minded Ali, while the final object was war against Western Europe. After the demonstration of the Softas in 1876, the fall of Mahmud Nedim Pasha, the deposition of the Sultan, and the miserable failure of the diplomacy of the Great Powers, Chauvinism again raised its head. As early as October, 1875, the Turkish imperial newspaper, "Bassiret," had issued an inspiring and revolutionary appeal for a crusade of the Mohammedans against the infidels. Special mention was made of Algiers, East India, Java, Sumatra, and the Caucasus. In 1876 the "Sabah"—morning—threatened a general levy of 300,000,000 Mohammedans, who were to occupy England and Russia, France and Austria, and to devastate these countries, while Germany was to be spared so long as she remained neutral.

The chief persons who shared in the deposition of the Sultan Abd ul-Aziz and the enthronement of the Sultan Murad V. were Midhat, Hussein Avni Müterjim, Mehemet Rüshdi, and Zia Bey; of these the first and the last were Young Turks, while the other two were Old Turks, assuming this distinction to be possible of maintenance. Apart from these, the members of the Young Turkish party set their hopes particularly on Prince Murad, as they expected him to issue some form of constitution. As a matter of fact, when Murad had become sultan, he proclaimed his intention of granting a constitution on July 15th, 1876; but even then his mind was beginning to be overclouded, and fate willed otherwise. Midhat Pasha was the life and soul of the constitutional movement. In the winter of 1876 he drew up a memorial which he submitted to the Powers. He explained that the main cause of the decline of the Turkish Empire was to be found not in religious or racial disputes, but in a despotic government and the extravagant whims of the Sultan Abd ul-Aziz. Midhat Pasha availed himself by preference of the services of two famous

THE MARRIAGE OF THE TSAR OF RUSSIA IN THE CHAPEL OF THE WINTER PALACE, ST. PETERSBURG, ON NOVEMBER 26TH, 1894

On November 26th, 1894, Nicholas II., Tsar of Russia, was married to Princess Victoria Alice of Hesse, which event is illustrated above by an artist present on the occasion. The ceremony was performed under the direction of the Metropolitan Archbishop, with his assistant priests. Two jewelled golden crowns, adorned with medallion figures of Christ and the Virgin Mary, were held over the heads of the bride and bridegroom by several of the Russian Grand Dukes, successively relieving each other, while standing before the emperor and his bride the high-priest joined their hands beneath his stole. That part of the ceremony over, the crowns were lowered, and the holy portraits thereon kissed by the married couple.

THE TSAR NICHOLAS II. OF RUSSIA AND THE TSARINA ALEXANDRA FEODOROVNA

Photo: Russell & Sons

authors, Kemal and Zia Bey. These men were also leaders of the " Young Turkish party." Their aims, however, were not only political, but primarily literary. It is in this department that their most distinguished services were performed. They abandoned the conventionality of classical poetry and the courtly style of prose writing, and found their model either in the inexhaustible treasures of the Ottoman ballad poetry and popular language, or, as regards the " moderns," in French literature. The wealth of poetry and of moral force, and especially of the pure undefiled Ottoman language existing in the stories, satires, humorous tales, narratives, chap-books, chivalrous and political romances, ballads, puppet plays, riddles, and proverbs of the Turkish nation was only waiting the discoverer. In this respect the efforts of the Young Turks exercised a healthy influence upon Ottoman civilisation, even though their first efforts for reformation or revolution far exceeded the limits of what was permissible or possible.

Ali Suavi Effendi was a compound of Peter of Amiens and Mazzini ; but he was entirely faithful to the Koran. Zia Bey had, in the year 1859, under the title of Andalus Tarikhi, published a history of the Arab dominion in the Iberian peninsula, which was based on the somewhat superficial work of Louis Viardot, and amounted to a glorification of Moslem civilisation, characterised by a hostile attitude to Europe and Christianity. Kemal Bey, a faithful scholar of his great master and model, Shinassi Effendi, the creator of modern Ottoman literature and language, was the most important of all the Turkish poets of the modern period. He published a newspaper under the title of " Ibret " —pattern—in which he actually defended the Commune of Paris. His most important dramatic work was " Silistria " or " Vatan," the Fatherland. Though the details of the heroic defence of the Danube forts in 1854 may not be historically true, yet he secured a striking success through the exalted tone of his love for the " fatherland," a conception formerly unknown to Mohammedanism, and by the popular style of the work. Its success led to the author's banishment, after the production of this piece in Constantinople in 1873. In conjunction with Mehemet Bey, the nephew of the Grand Vizir, Mahmud Nedim Pasha, he founded the

Banishment of the Scholarly Kemal Bey

Turkish newspaper, "Mukhbir," that is, the "Reporter." The paper was suppressed when the persecution against the Young Turks was begun; the conspirators made their escape safely to Paris. There they came in contact with Fazil Mustafa, the brother of the Khedive Ismaïl, who had been banished on account of his claims to the Egyptian succession.

Persecution of the Young Turks The "Mukhbir" continued to appear in Paris and London, and thousands of copies were smuggled into Turkey; some numbers also appeared in French. To the European public at large, however, this party assumed a mask of toleration, and concealed their fanatical zeal for Mohammedanism under an appearance of free thought. Under Mahmud Pasha they were amnestied and recalled. Zia and Riza Bey, who had formerly been ambassadors in Teheran and St. Petersburg, were then the foremost in enlightening the Grand Vizir upon the complicated Bulgarian question and the problem of the Catholic Armenians. At this period there was also a Turkish

theatre at Stamboul, with a repertoire of forty to fifty pieces, partly original and partly translations of Molière by Ahmed Vesik, or of Schiller by Ahmed Midhat Effendi, the editor of the official Turkish newspaper; Vesik also published some maps in Turkish for the use of schools, and took part in the composition of a great dictionary. Münif Effendi translated part of Voltaire's "Entretiens et Dialogues Philosophiques," and followed the example of Fuad in proposing the extension and regulation of the narrow, crooked streets of Stamboul. Public libraries were founded; Abd ul-Aziz began a zoological garden, and in the medical school of the Seraglio of Galata a museum of natural objects was opened to the public.

The foundation of the "University" of Constantinople can only be described as a failure. Strangely enough, some decades later, in the movement for the emancipation of women, which found expression in 1895 in the newspaper of Tahir Effendi, "Khanimlara Makhsus Gazeta," female collaborators like Fatima Alija, Nigiar Chamin,

EXPELLING THE JEWS FROM RUSSIA: A SCENE AT THE BALTIC RAILWAY STATION

Wanderers on the face of the earth, the Jews have found their way into all parts of the world, but in few lands has their presence been welcomed, while in many countries they have been the victims of cruel treatment. Russia has been particularly unkind to the ancient people, as indicated in the above picture, persecuting them with much harshness.

THE LAST VISIT OF THE SULTAN ABD UL-AZIZ TO THE MOSQUE AT BAGDSCHA
Turkey's summary methods of high politics are well illustrated in the case of Abd ul-Aziz, who, after being deposed, was taken to his palace at Chiragan and there put to death by the new Grand Vizir and the Minister of War.

Hamijeti Zehra, Fahr-en-Nisa, Makbula Lemian, Emine Wahide, and Renesie, notwithstanding their thorough knowledge of Oriental and European languages and morals, spoke out strongly on the side of the Young Turks on behalf of the strengthening and retention of Mohammedan customs and of the avoidance of European civilisation in methods of education. At the same time Vambéry forecasts from this woman's movement an approximation to Western manners and the beginning of a beneficial reform of the state and of society.

Upon the whole, it is by no means easy to gain a clear idea of the theories and ideals of the modern Young Turkish party. Their first official leader was the Cherkess general, Hussein Pasha. He was joined by numerous

MURAD V., SULTAN OF TURKEY
When on May 29th, 1876, the Sultan Abd ul-Aziz was deposed, Murad V., the eldest son of Abd ul-Mejid, was placed on the throne. His reign, however, was brief, as he was deposed, owing to insanity, in August of the same year.
Photo: W. and D. Downey

adherents, who called themselves Fedayiji, conspirators or martyrs. Even at that time, 1860, this free federation of Ottomans was aiming at the following points : a reform of Turkey by the Turks without distinction of faith and not by Europe, the abolition of despotic government, a responsible Ministry composed of honourable statesmen, and a Chamber composed of members of all the races and religions within the Ottoman Empire. Khair ed-dîn Pasha and Khalil Sherif Pasha pursued the same objects under Abd ul-Aziz, and were supported by Zia Bey and Kemal Bey in writing and speech, and by Ali and Fuad in the government. They developed great plans, and actually succeeded in obtaining approval for some of them from the tyrannical

Safvet Pasha

General Ignatieff

Kerim Pasha

Sultan, who went so far as to summon an Armenian Christian, Agathon Effendi, to the Ministry. The programme of Midhat in 1876 was, generally speaking, based upon principles borrowed from the West; the supremacy of law, universal equality, the strengthening of the Divan against the Seraglio, freedom of the Press, independence of the judicature, reorganisation of the administrative power with respect for the Mohammedan legal code, but also in accord with Western experience, order in the palace, a change in the Eastern principle of succession, European education for the princes, marriage of the princes with European princesses, and the consequent abolition of slavery, of polygamy, of concubines, and eunuch government.

In conjunction with Fazil and Server Pasha, Midhat defended his creations, the Constitution, the Parliament, and the Senate, in his "Ittihad." He demanded a complete severance of the caliphate from the sultanate, and an abolition of theocratic government. This proposal deeply offended the strong ecclesiastical party of the Ulemas. Under the following sultan, Midhat was overthrown; and the inheritors of his ideas, the Reform Turks, or Liberals, as they preferred to be called, continued until recently the struggle to secure the liberation of the Sultan Abd ul-Hamid II. and his people from the hands of the Court Camarilla. It may be noted that in May, 1904, public attention was occupied with the rumour of the imprisonment of certain

THE FIRST STATE PASSAGE OF THE SULTAN MURAD V. TO DOLMA-BAKCHEH

Young Turks of high position. This party included Ahmed Riza, the editor of the "Meschweret," Murad Bey, a kind of political chameleon, editor of the "Misan," Theodor Kassope, the brilliant journalist of the "Haial," Ismail Kemal Bey, Vassilaki Bey, Mehemet Ubeidullah, Said Bey, Zia Bey, and Ferdi Bey, and even the Sultan's brother-in-law, Mahmud Damad, who died on January 18th, 1903, at Brussels. In sad tones does the Turkish ballad recount the deposition of the "beloved ruler Abd ul-Aziz." A gloomy fate, however, still bore heavily upon the Ottoman throne; on August 31st, 1876, Murad V., the hope of the Young Turkish party, was deposed owing to insanity, and placed in confinement until his death, on August 29th, 1904.

He was succeeded by his brother, Abd ul-Hamid II., born September 21st, 1842, the thirty-fourth sovereign of the Ottoman House and the twenty-eighth since the conquest of Constantinople. A reform of education and of the constitution, the improvement of

Midhat Pasha

Hussein Avni Pasha

Halil Sherif Pasha

Mehemet Rüshdi Pasha

MINISTERS OF THE SULTAN OF TURKEY

While holding a Cabinet Council with their colleagues at Constantinople in 1876, the four pashas whose portraits are given above were attacked by Hassan Bey, a military man who had been imprisoned for his laxity in obeying orders, and two of them, Hussein Avni Pasha and Mehemet Rüshdi, died from the wounds inflicted.

trade and economic life by a vast extension of the railway system, were the objects which this highly gifted monarch set before himself of his own free and vigorous will, for the purpose of raising "this nation of gentlemen," as Bismarck called the Ottomans, to the height of civilisation. In vain did the Sirdar Abd ul-Kerim drive back the Serbs at Alexinatz on September 1st, 1876, into the valley of the Morava. On November 1st the Bashi-bazouks had made their way beyond Junis

and Stolatz as far as the neighbourhood of Belgrade; the telegram of the Tsar Alexander II., despatched from Livadia on October 31st, commanded a cessation of hostilities. In vain did the diplomatic and peaceful Sultan resolve upon the extremity of compliance in the peace concluded on February 28th, 1877.

When the Powers demanded an independent administration for Bulgaria, Midhat Pasha, who had been Grand Vizir since December 22nd, 1876, answered this move by producing a constitution which the Sultan imposed upon his empire on December 23rd. This Representative Assembly of 200 Moslems and 60 Christians declined the proposals of the conference of the Powers. Ignatieff then went round the courts of Europe and secured their agreement to the "London Protocol," which recommended the Sublime Porte to recognise the autonomy of the two provinces of Bulgaria and Eastern Roumelia under Christian governors. However, Midhat was overthrown on February 5th, 1877, by a palace revolution, and Edhem Pasha, his successor, induced the Sultan curtly to decline the Russian proposals on April 9th.

On April 23rd the Tsar Alexander II. informed his troops at Kishineff that war had been declared. On the night of the 24th the Cossacks crossed the Pruth, and the whole army advanced into Roumania, not, as before, to secure the "liberation of the Christians," but that of their "Slavonic brothers." On April 16th Roumania had concluded with Russia a convention admitting the passage of troops, which was regarded by the Porte as a casus belli in the case of that state also. Thereupon the Chamber at Bucharest proclaimed their independence. The Turks were in position with 180,000 men along the Danube, while 80,000 troops were ready in Asia. Russia was certain of the benevolent neutrality of Germany, and in January, 1877, she had concluded the agreement of Reichstadt with Austria, which secured Bosnia and Herzegovina to Austro-Hungary in the event of her non-interference. On May 3rd the Turks declared the shores of the Black Sea to be in a state of blockade. On May 6th the Sultan assumed the title "Defender of the Faith," and proclaimed the Holy War.

At the outset the Turkish warship Seifi was attacked by Russian torpedo boats below Matchin, on the Danube, and sunk; on May 11th a Russian battery at Braila shelled the Turkish monitor Lutfi Jalil, and blew up the ship with its crew. On May 17th the Russo-Caucasian army stormed Ardakhan and invested Kars. However, the victory of Mukhtar Pasha over Loris Melikoff forced the Russians to retire to their own country in the middle of July. A Turkish fleet, supported by the revolt of the Cherkesses in the Caucasus, bombarded the Russian forts on the Abkhasian coast and captured Sukhum Kaleh; but this position was unavoidably evacuated in August, for the Russians had then recaptured Kars and made a victorious advance to Erzeroum.

Mukhtar Pasha undertook the defence of Constantinople. The Russians, indeed, had not been able to cross the Danube at Sistova and Zimnitza until June 29th, owing to the floods; but on July 7th they reached Tirnovo, and General Gurko crossed the Balkans on July 13th at the Shipka Pass.

General Schilder-Schuldner was beaten back at Plevna by Osman Nuri Pasha, and the Russian line of retreat was threatened. Had the Turkish commanders been united and able to make a decisive attack upon the Russians, the latter would scarcely have reached the left bank of the Danube. Meanwhile the Russians brought up their reinforcements and the Roumanian army, in order to capture the "Lion of Plevna," who is still celebrated in the Turkish ballad; he died April 5th, 1900. On September 11th, the birthday of the Russian Tsar, after vast preparations the great attack was begun upon the defences of Osman Pasha, and the Russians suffered their greatest defeat during the whole campaign; 16,000 dead and wounded Russians covered the battlefield, the sole result being the capture of the redoubt of Grivitza. Finally, on December 10th, the wounded Osman, whose supply of ammunition had failed, was obliged to surrender to a force three times as large as his own, with 40,000 men, 2,000 officers, and 77 guns.

The fall of Plevna encouraged the Serbs at Nisch on January 11th, 1878, and the Montenegrins made conquests on the coast

Kemal Bey   Ibrahim Effendi

Abd ul-Zia Bey   Prince Mustafa Pasha

LEADERS OF THE "YOUNG TURKISH PARTY"
The Young Turkish Party of 1867 had little in common with the movement of recent years. Aiming at restoring the ancient regime, it originated in literary idealism rather than political aspirations.

of the Adriatic on January 19th, 1878; the Greeks crossed the frontier of Thessaly on February 2nd. In Bulgaria, after endless marching, Gurko had subdued the Etropol district at the end of December, 1877, and had effected a junction with the army of Lom in Philippopolis. On January 29th, 1878, the Russians reached the Sea of Marmora at Rodosto, after the capture of the Shipka army, the destruction of the division of Suleiman, and the occupation of Adrianople. On January 31st an armistice was concluded, and then the British fleet entered the Sea of Marmora. The Russians now advanced to the neighbourhood of Constantinople, and on March 3rd dictated the Peace of San Stefano, in which they demanded complete independence for Roumania Servia, Montenegro, and Bulgaria, the cession of Armenia to Russia and of the Dobrudsha to Roumania, and would also have cut European Turkey in half by the establishment of the states of Roumelia and Macedonia. Thereupon Disraeli threatened war, concentrated Indian troops at Malta, and joined Austria in a demand for a congress. Abd ul-Hamid had dissolved the Chambers on February 14th, and had never recalled them; on May 20th he had suppressed with bloodshed the conspiracy begun by Ali Suavi in favour of Murad, and on May 25th had appointed Mehemet Rüshdi Pasha as Grand Vizir. He concluded a secret treaty with Britain on June 4th, the British undertaking the protection of

THE SULTAN ABDUL HAMID II.
Brother of Murad V., he succeeded to the throne of Turkey in 1876, and in the following year gave the country a Parliament, which was soon after withdrawn, to be restored in 1908.
Photo: W. & D. Downey

Turkey in Asia, and occupying Cyprus by way of return. The Grand Vizir, however, was replaced by Safvet Pasha on June 4th. The demands proposed in the Peace of San Stefano were considerably reduced in the Berlin Congress, June 13th to July 13th, 1878; in particular, Eastern Roumelia was left under Turkish supremacy. Austria, however, was entrusted with the occupation of Bosnia and Herzegovina, and was given the right to maintain a body of supervisory troops in the Sanjak of Novibazar, under the supremacy of the Sultan. Roumania's only reward for the valuable service which she had rendered to Russia was the acquisition of the barren Dobrudsha in return for Bessarabia, which was ceded to Russia. Greece secured the right to a better delimitation of her northern frontier, but it was not until 1880 that she secured possession of Thessaly and of the district of Arta in Epirus. The war indemnity paid by the Porte to Russia amounted to £16,080,000. In 1882, Bosnia, which had first to be conquered step by step by the Austrian troops, received a measure of civil government, under which the prosperity of this fertile district considerably increased. The Berlin Treaty was signed by representatives of all the Powers, though all were fully aware that it contained merely the germs of fresh entanglements. Prince Bismarck stigmatised the treaty as a " dishonourable fiction," while the Pan-Slavonic Party blamed the " infidelity of their German

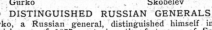

Gurko   Skobelev
TWO DISTINGUISHED RUSSIAN GENERALS
Count Gurko, a Russian general, distinguished himself in the Russo-Turkish war of 1877, capturing the fortresses of Sophia, Philippopolis and Adrianople, when the armistice of 1878 followed; while Michael Dmitrievitch Skobelev was a leader in the expeditions to Khiva and Khokand and also in the Russo-Turkish war of 1877-78.

THE SULTAN OPENING THE FIRST TURKISH PARLIAMENT

THE HOUSE IN SESSION AT CONSTANTINOPLE

Turkey's first Parliament, in 1877, as shown in the first of these two pictures, was opened by the Sultan, Abdul Hamid II., in the Grand Throne Room of the Imperial Palace of Dolma-Bakcheh. A sitting of the Parliament is illustrated in the second picture. In the side galleries were special boxes for the Sultan and other illustrious visitors.

TURKEY'S FIRST AND SHORT-LIVED PARLIAMENT OF 1877

THE SURRENDER OF OSMAN PASHA AT PLEVNA: BRINGING THE TURKISH CAPTIVE INTO THE RUSSIAN HEADQUARTERS

From the painting by Verestchagin

friend": for the unfavourable results of the Berlin Congress. Russia did not feel her military power sufficiently great to begin a war with Austria and England, after she had once lost her opportunity of occupying Constantinople. For the blunders of Russian policy, Prince Gortchakoff undoubtedly divided the responsibility with some of his younger adherents, but his freedom from blame is by no means proved.

When the German Chancellor concluded the alliance with Austria on October 7th, 1879, and shortly afterwards the Triple

of his empire by a series of innovations. In 1880 he forced the Albanian League to give in its submission and to cede Dulcigno to Montenegro. The statesmen, Midhat, Mahmud Damad, and Nuri Pasha, who had hitherto gone unpunished, were condemned to death on June 9th, 1881, and banished to Arabia. With the help of German officials, the Sultan secured in 1881 a union with the orthodox and a financial reform of high benefit to the empire. The revenue was increased by the introduction of the tobacco régie in 1883. The state was, however, chiefly

SIGNING THE TREATY OF PEACE BETWEEN RUSSIA AND TURKEY AT SAN STEFANO

Alliance in 1883, the far-sighted Sultan at once recognised that the welfare of his state was conditional solely upon the support of these most powerful influences for European peace. In 1879 the deposition of Ismaïl had indeed failed to restore the old supremacy of the Porte; the Nile Valley fell into the hands of Great Britain in 1882, and the conquest of the Sudan immediately followed; on May 12th, 1881, and June 8th, 1883, France also declared her protectorate of Tunis.

However, the Sultan loyally observed the conditions of the Berlin Congress, and attempted to increase the prosperity

strengthened by the Sultan's invitation to German officers to remodel the organisation of the army in 1880, and to elaborate a military law, which came into force in 1887. From that date, all men capable of bearing arms were forthwith assigned to a certain arm of the service, and on attaining their majority were placed under control and incorporated in troops of the line for training. In the officers' schools, which were conducted in Constantinople by the Freiherr von der Goltz from 1883 to 1895, the number of pupils rose from 4,000 to 14,000. In 1880 the old museum of antiquities was built in the

Serai gardens—Chinili Kiosk—while the new museum was constructed in 1891. In 1891 the School of Art was founded close at hand by Hamid Bey, where, notwithstanding the prohibition of the Koran against the representation of the human countenance, more than 130 young Turks were regularly instructed in painting, sculpture, and architectural design. The Sultan displayed even greater wisdom in holding aloof from the disturbances between the Balkan States, though Russian dissatisfaction with her Slavonic protectorates gave him every excuse for armed interference, and though his action on this occasion was stigmatised as "weakness" by the Young Turkish party. Roumania was proclaimed a kingdom on March 26th, 1881, as also was Servia on March 6th, 1882.

Roumania Proclaimed a Kingdam

On April 29th, 1879, the Bulgarian Sobranje had chosen Prince Alexander of Battenberg as ruler of the country. On May 9th, 1881, he overthrew the radical government and the influence of the agitators for a larger Bulgaria in Eastern Roumelia and Macedonia by means of a coup d'état. However, on September 19th, 1883, he restored the constitution of Trnovo and undertook the government of Eastern Roumelia, much against the will of Russia, on September 20th, 1885. Thereupon the jealous Servians declared war upon the Bulgarians on November 13th. After one temporary success at the Dragoman Pass, King Milan was defeated by Prince Alexander on November 18th and 19th, at Slivnitza and Pirot, driven back upon Tzaribrod, and was spared in the Peace of Bucharest, March 3rd, 1886, only at the request of Austria.

The reckless financial policy of a rapid succession of Ministers, the agitation fomented by the Radicals, the domestic quarrels in the royal family, the divorce in 1888, and the abdication of King Milan in favour of his son Alexander I. in 1889, the latter's coup d'état in 1893, and his marriage with Draga Maschin in 1900, were events which gave the unhappy country neither peace nor justice. The rise of Bulgaria and its union with Eastern Roumelia on October 5th, 1886, aroused the jealousy and the anger of the Tsar and of the Panslavists. On the night of August 21st Prince Alexander was surprised in his bed and forced to abdicate;

Abdication of King Milan

upon his return he was unable to make his peace with the Tsar, and was definitely banished from the country on December 7th, 1886; he died on November 17th, 1893.

After the short regency of Stambuloff and the disturbance caused by the appearance of the Russian general, Baron Kaulbars, the Sobranje chose Prince Ferdinand of Saxe-Coburg as their ruler. Notwithstanding the aloofness of the Sultan, the anger of the Tsar, and the outrages of the Panslavists in the country, this prince maintained his position, married Princess Louise of Parma in 1893, and from 1896 brought up his son Boris in the faith of the orthodox Church. After the murder of Stambuloff, the prince secured a reconciliation with the Tsar, his recognition by the Sultan, and was able even in Macedonia to bring about the investiture of Bulgarian bishops. Bulgaria responded by remaining neutral until 1897.

However, this fruitful country was continually disturbed by its superfluity of ambitious parliamentarians and professional politicians; only in the Macedonian question was the Bulgarian preponderance decided, and this through the dissension between the Serbs and the Greeks. But Servia and Greece displayed an attitude of greater hostility, and consequently obliged the Porte to make counter preparations and burdensome loans from the Ottoman bank. In 1889 a decision of the courts transferred the Turkish railways from the hands of Baron Hirsch to the possession of the Porte. German influence also secured the construction of the Anatolian railway, which had been pushed as far as Angora and Konia in 1896, and which, when continued to the Persian Gulf, will greatly strengthen the strategical and economic power of Turkey and increase her influence upon international trade. After the failure of the unceasing efforts of the German Commercial Company for Eastern Trade, founded 1881, the company, founded at Hamburg in 1889, of the Deutsche Levante Linie was able to issue combined tariffs for maritime and railway traffic, and thus successfully to resume commerce with the East.

German Influence in Turkey

Before, however, this decaying empire had been surrounded by the iron girdle of the railroad beyond Bagdad it was shaken to its depths by two disastrous events— the Armenian revolt and the war in Thessaly. Paragraph 61 of the Treaty of

Berlin had demanded protection from the rapacious officials, the Kurds, and Cherkesses, and reforms in the administration to help the oppressed people of the Armenians, who had shown excellent capacity for trade and manual labour. Thanks to the indolence and corruption of the authorities, these reforms were introduced with extreme slowness. In 1894 disturbances broke out in Sassun, and the cruelty with which they were suppressed immediately gave the signal for revolt in Trebizond, Gümishhane, Samsun, Agja Gune, and the Armenian vilayets;

put pressure on the Porte. On September 30th, 1895, certain Armenians gathered before the Sublime Porte, demanding reforms; on August 26th, 1896, these Armenian conspirators surprised the Ottoman Bank, and after their liberation a massacre, apparently led by the soldiers and police, was begun upon the Armenians in the capital. When the Powers protested against this bloodshed, the massacres were stopped and reforms were promised; but the Armenian question remained one of the pieces upon the political chessboard, while attention was

PRINCE ALEXANDER OF BULGARIA SIGNING HIS ABDICATION

Turkish soldiers and Kurds were massacred with the connivance of the authorities. The Armenians, entrenched in the mountains of Cilicia at Zeitun, sustained a formal siege for a long period, and from London, Athens, Paris, Geneva, and Tiflis Armenian agents carried the seeds of revolt into the distressed highlands of Upper Armenia and of the Taurus. These very towns in Western Europe served as refuges not only for the Armenian agents who were favoured by England, but also for their deadly enemies, the Young Turks, of whom France made occasional use to

soon diverted to North America, Eastern Asia, and South Africa. The Greek campaign proved more disastrous to the Christians than to the once forbearing Sultan. Two visits from the German Emperor increased and strengthened the reputation of Abd ul-Hamid II., and made German influence supreme with the Porte.

In Crete it had proved impossible to appease the animosity between the Christians and Mohammedans, notwithstanding their common descent; and the breach of the convention of Halepa of 1878, and the imposition of a constitution which limited their freedom in 1889, led to a bloody revolt; this movement was increased from 1886 by the hopes of the incorporation of the island with the mother country, notwithstanding the blockade of the Greek harbours by the Powers. On a fresh outburst of hostilities in 1896–1897, the Greek Colonel Vassos, with 2,000 men, occupied Platania in Crete on February 15th, 1897,

Turkey and Greece at War and took possession of the island in the name of King George. The Governor, George Berovitch Pasha, left Crete. The Powers protested against this violation of international law, bombarded the rebels from their ships, and blockaded the island.

When Greece declined to withdraw her troops upon an ultimatum from the Powers, the Porte declared war on April 17th, 1897. The Turkish army advanced into Thessaly under Edhem Pasha, and defeated the Greek army, which was badly disciplined and organised, under the Crown Prince of Greece, Constantine, at Turnavos, Larissa, Phersala, Domokos, and in Epirus. On May 19th an armistice was arranged by the intervention of the Powers, and a peace was concluded at Constantinople on September 17th, 1897, under the terms of which Greece lost certain frontier districts on the north of Thessaly, and undertook to pay a war indemnity of four million pounds Turkish, or £3,750,000.

The heaviest punishment inflicted upon Greece was the control of the finances imposed at the proposal of Germany, as the Germans had been the chief sufferers from the financial crisis. Greece withdrew her troops from Crete, and the island received complete independence under the suzerainty of the Sultan; Prince George of Greece was appointed as Governor. In 1893 Greece at length completed the canal through the Isthmus of Corinth. She has not yet pushed forward her railway system to a junction with the

Greece on the Road to Prosperity more developed system of the Balkan States, but is now advancing towards a more prosperous development. This short campaign had proved that the efforts of German instructors to improve the organisation, the training, mobilisation, leadership, and discipline of the Turkish troops had borne good fruit. Thus Turkey reached the close of the century. Vambéry, Adolf Wahrmund, and Von der Goltz have prophesied a new life and power for the Ottoman State under certain conditions. From the intellectual renaissance in the best men of the nation, they anticipate a revival of the powers dormant in the country and a gradual replacing of Asiatic by European ideas, a reconciliation between Mohammedanism and Christianity, and the development of a modus vivendi for these two great religions.

In view of the inexhaustible, and in many cases highly gifted, population of Asia, the protection of the empire, now limited to its own frontiers, is guaranteed by the organisation of the empire and the construction of railways and telegraphs. The weak spot in Turkey is the Bosphorus, which is unfortified on the land side, though the Dardanelles are strongly fortified. The source of all Turkish evils is to be found in the incapacity of the executive; the extensive spy system, which destroys all confidence; the lack of check upon the state expenditure; the permanent condition of insolvency, which is only concealed by forced loans and reductions of the salaries of officials; the

Turkey's Bloodless Revolution miserable condition of the population; the dishonest taxation which is the natural consequence; and especially the autocracy of the Sultan, who has, with great short-sightedness, reduced the position of Grand Vizir to a shadow. The Arab Caliphate must come to some compromise with the Ottoman Sultanate. The centre of gravity in the Turkish Empire need not necessarily be looked for in the military force at Constantinople; much rather should it be found in a body of reliable Crown advisers and capable officials. Prophecy, however, would seem to be more thoroughly impossible with regard to the Ottoman dominions than elsewhere.

The last thing which anyone expected is precisely the thing that has happened. The astonishing revolution of 1908, inaugurated apparently with the full approval of the Sultan, may be destined to give the Ottoman Empire a new lease of life by placing new ideals within the reach of the Turkish people. But Europe is still in the throes of anxiety as to the developments which may arise out of the no less sudden action of Bulgaria in proclaiming her own complete independence, and of Austria in annexing Herzegovina.

VLADIMIR MILKOWICZ

THE GERMAN & AUSTRIAN EMPIRES
THEIR SOCIAL & LEGISLATIVE DEVELOPMENT

IN the years 1871-1902 three emperors have ruled at the head of the German Empire. First, the veteran founder of the empire, William I., from 1871 to 1888; then his son, Frederic III., best known as Crown Prince Frederic William, a victim of incurable cancer, who reigned only ninety-nine days, from March 9th to June 15th, 1888; and, lastly, his eldest son, William II., born January 27th, 1859.

The differences between the characters of these three rulers are strongly marked. William I. was a man of simple character, a thorough soldier, taking no great interest in the arts and sciences, but keenly devoted to the practical business of life, full of manly amiability and loyal conscientiousness. The words he uttered on his deathbed, " I have no time to be tired," characterise his whole nature. He had the highest conception of his royal rights and duties; he read everything which he had to sign, and emphatically asserted his own views; but he was accessible to the counsel of experienced statesmen. He adhered with the greatest tenacity to the old Prussian traditions. Frederic III. was by nature and through the influence of his English consort, Victoria, the eldest daughter of Queen Victoria and Prince Albert, devoted to the liberal ideas of the time, a warm friend of all artistic and scientific effort, and a soldier so far as and no farther than his political position required.

The Brief Reign of Frederic III.

In his brief reign he allowed himself to be directed by Bismarck, from whom his father had repeatedly declared that he never wished to be separated. Differences of opinion which had earlier, especially in 1863-1866, existed between the monarch and the statesman sank so much into the background in the ninety-nine days that Bismarck asserted he had never, in his long ministerial career, known less friction between Crown and Ministry than had existed under the Emperor Frederic.

Affairs assumed quite a different shape under William II., who, coming to the throne as a young man of twenty-nine years, brought with him a thoroughly independent, indeed, despotic, nature, and in the consciousness of ample abilities and honest purpose felt competent to be his own chancellor. Thus, after only a year and a half a sharp quarrel broke out between the young monarch and the grey-haired statesman, who had so long conducted affairs with prudence and courage.

Dismissal of Prince Bismarck

From differences of opinion as to the legitimate position of the Prime Minister towards the Crown and his colleagues, and as to the social and political questions which William II. thought he was able to solve at one stroke, the feud blazed up so fiercely that the emperor on March 20th, 1890, abruptly dismissed Bismarck. Since then, Count Caprivi, Prince Hohenlohe, and, finally, Prince Bülow, have successively filled the office of Imperial Chancellor; but the importance of the office has been much diminished by the personal activity of the emperor.

Although just criticism has often been brought to bear on particular measures taken by the Government, and on its frequently slack and unsteady attitude since 1890, and although serious discontent was produced, especially under Caprivi, by its Anglophile tendencies, its indulgence towards the Poles, and its brusque treatment of Bismarck, whom the emperor took back into favour in January, 1894, yet it cannot be disguised that during this whole period the development of the German nation, in spite of disagreeable episodes of every sort, has been materially advanced. The phrase of William II., " I am leading you towards splendid prospects," was a proud but not by any means an untrue utterance. The institutions of the empire in the very first years of its existence were

The Proud Claim of William II.

completed by unceasing and generally successful legislative work. Wide local diversities could not but act as a check on the conception of real unity; and a just and very important step towards the unification was the adoption in 1872 of a universal gold standard and a universal decimal system of coinage, weights, and measures. This was followed up by the unification of civil procedure in the field of law, in 1876—a change already anticipated in criminal law by the North German Confederation—and the adoption of a uniform civil code for the empire, which came into force in the year 1900. The fixed determination of the whole nation to maintain such a military force as should secure it from attack—prompted by the knowledge, for many years after the great war, that if ever France had an opportunity of attempting to recover her lost provinces she would certainly seize it—has hitherto triumphed, though sometimes with extreme difficulty, over all attempts at reduction. Beyond this, however, William II. has declined to recognise the limitation of Germany to its European territory; alive to the immense amount of wealth and power which Great Britain has acquired by her maritime supremacy, he has resolved to give Germany a first-class navy, the growth of which is watched with some suspicion by the Power to which naval supremacy is even more vital than military supremacy to Germany. Doubts, however, may be felt as to how long the accompanying strain of taxation will be endured.

Germany's Military Strength

THE EMPEROR FREDERIC III.
His occupancy of the German Imperial throne lasted for only three months. Succeeding his father, William I., in March, 1888, his death occurred at Potsdam, from an affection of the throat, on June 15th of the same year.
Photo: Reichard & Lindner

The first decade of the new empire was largely occupied by a struggle between Church and State—the Roman Church and the Prussian State—which has been responsible for a new political term, "Kulturkampf," signifying the war between the State as representing civilisation, and the Church as representing its opposite. The struggle, however, was not confined to Prussia; the whole nation was concerned in it, and its sympathies were enlisted on one side or the other. In the first German Reichstag an almost exclusively Catholic party was formed, the Centre, which stood under the extremely clever leadership of the Hanoverian ex-Minister of State Ludwig Windthorst, 1812–1891, and immediately proved itself the refuge of Ultramontane, Guelf, and Particularist efforts.

It aimed, but unsuccessfully, at a German interference in Italy, in order to win back for the Pope his temporal power, and demanded that the articles of the Prussian constitution, which secured to the Churches complete freedom from State control, should be introduced into the Imperial constitution; but it was unable to carry its wishes either with Bismarck or in the Reichstag. It adopted, in consequence, an unfriendly attitude towards the Government. The Prussian Government further complained that the Catholic clergy in Posen and West Prussia, by an abuse of their influential position, especially in the matter of elementary schools which were under their direction, supported the national Polish movements and prejudiced the German Catholics in favour of Poland. As a result of all this agitation, Falk, the Minister of Public Worship and Instruction, carried a Bill in 1872, which strictly defined the inspection of schools as a state concern, and threw open to laymen the office of inspector, particularly in country districts. Falk then, in 1873, brought before the Landtag the four Bills, which, in spite of violent opposition on the part of the Centre and the Extreme Right, obtained a large majority and were called the "May Laws," since they received the sanction of the Crown in May, 1837. The first of these laws confined within closer limits the right of the Churches to inflict penalties on laymen in the case of contumacy; the second restricted their disciplinary power over their clergy, and

Passing the "May Laws"

AS COMMANDER-IN-CHIEF OF THE FLEET DURING HIS VISIT TO ENGLAND IN 1899

IN UNIFORM OF IMPERIAL CUIRASSIERS   A RECENT PHOTOGRAPH TAKEN IN BERLIN

HIS MAJESTY WILLIAM II., GERMAN EMPEROR

Photos by Voigt, Russell & Sons, and Neue Photo-Gesellschaft

abolished all foreign—and therefore all papal—jurisdiction over Prussian clergy. The third enacted that the clergy should no longer be educated for their profession in ecclesiastical but, in State institutions, and prohibited their attendance at foreign seminaries, especially those in Rome ; it also provided that the bishops, before making any appointment to a benefice, should give notice to the State authorities, and, if a well-founded protest was made by the State, should make another nomination. The fourth law regulated withdrawals from the Churches. Finally, in 1875 a fifth law abolished all existing religious orders in Prussia which did not devote themselves to the care of the sick, and thus in particular put an end to their activity in school matters.

Since the Pope, and the bishops following the example set them by the Pope, pronounced these laws incompatible with the principles of the Catholic Church, and in accordance with the saying : "We must obey God rather than men," refused submission to these laws, a struggle of many years' duration broke out between the State and the Church ; the vast majority of the Catholic population showed unbroken loyalty and obedience to their spiritual leaders. The struggle was waged on both sides with much bitterness, and since Catholic priests frequently used the pulpit in order to fire the believers to resist the State laws, the Prussian Government held itself bound to proceed against such agitation by penal measures. But since criminal jurisdiction

"DROPPING THE PILOT"

The great debt which Germany owes to Bismarck has been told in a preceding chapter ; the above, reproduced by permission from the famous "Punch" cartoon by Sir John Tenniel, illustrates the dismissal of the "Iron Chancellor" by the youthful and impetuous emperor, William II., on March 20th, 1890.

was one of the rights of the empire, it was inevitable that the latter should find itself entangled in the quarrel.

At the instance of Johann Lutz, the Bavarian Minister, who was engaged in a keen contest with the Bavarian Ultramontanes, the so-called "pulpit paragraph," which attached penalties to the misuse of the pulpit for inciting opposition against the Government, was inserted in the Criminal Code in November, 1871. The empire on two other occasions lent the Prussian Government its aid, first on July 4th, 1872, when it prohibited the Jesuit order and its branches from owning establishments in the dominions of the empire and from developing any activity as an order, and again on February 6th, 1875, when it introduced civil marriage in a universally binding form, not merely the so-called civil marriage of necessity. By these imperial laws it was rendered impossible for the Catholic clergy and that warlike militia of the infallible Pope, the Order of Jesuits, to agitate against the May laws ; and the influence of the Church on civil life was checked, since a marriage might be contracted and a household founded without the benediction of the Church. Bismarck during the heat of the dispute had already declared that the Government built their hopes of peace mainly on the prospect that a peace-loving Pope would once again, as had happened in past history, succeed the belligerent Pope Pius IX. This event occurred on February 20th, 1878, when, after the death of Pius, on February 7th, Cardinal Joachim

Pecci was elected Pope, and took the title of Leo XIII. He prided himself on calming by peaceful concessions the disturbances under which the reputation alike of State and Church had suffered greatly—Bismarck was, on July 13th, 1874, the object of a murderous attack by Kullmann, a fanatical Catholic.

The Nuncio at Munich, Masella, visited Bismarck at Kissingen, in July, 1878. After nine years of excessively difficult negotiations a truce was concluded in 1887, to which the most trenchant May laws were sacrificed ; for instance, the law concerning the ecclesiastical court and the preliminary training of the clergy in State institutions. But the State had by no means made an unconditional surrender to the Church; on the contrary, all the three imperial laws remained in force, and in Prussia the law as to State control of the schools, the exclusion of the orders from the schools, and the obligation of the bishops to signify beforehand to the Oberpräsident—lord-lieutenant—of the respective provinces the names of the clergy whom they proposed to appoint to vacant benefices. Bismarck had not "gone to Canossa."

The Socialist movement was rapidly swollen by the stimulus which was given to trade and industries immediately after the war of 1870, since hundreds of new factories sprang up, and thousands upon thousands of men abandoned agriculture and streamed into the factories. The reaction which set in after the second half of the year 1873 left a mass of these workmen without bread, planted bitterness and revolutionary thoughts in their hearts, and thus increased the number of those who were discontented with the existing order of things. In the year 1875 the two parties hitherto existing within the Social Democracy, the followers of Bebel and Liebknecht, and those of Lassalle, amalgamated at Gotha into the "Socialist Labour Party," and, thanks to universal suffrage, won in the elections to the

THE GERMAN EMPRESS
A princess of Schleswig-Holstein, she was married to the Emperor, William II., in 1881, and of the marriage there has been a family of six sons and one daughter.
Neue Photo-Gesellschaft

Reichstag of 1877 more than twenty seats. Two attempts on the life of the aged emperor in 1878, one by a professed Nihilist, the other by Dr. Nobeling, who escaped inquiry by committing suicide, were, as a matter of course, associated with "Social Democracy," which at once became the object of penal legislation ; with the normal result of making the organisation a secret one, but also with the effect of checking breaches of the law. The emperor and his great chancellor, however, were both aware that restrictive legislation must fail of its object unless it is accompanied by measures for curing the disease of which disorder is the symptom. Since 1883 a series of laws have protected labour and provided safeguards ; notably the insurance law of 1889 and the bank law of 1884, steps which have been opposed by the school of economists which regards them as incompatible with the pure doctrines of Individualism as supposed to have been developed at Manchester. These measures, however, have not gone far enough to satisfy the Social Democrats, who since the expiry of the restrictive law in 1890, have multiplied enormously, and in so doing have shed a good many of their early extravagances. Colonial development, in turn, has attracted some degree of German enthusiasm, never shared by Bismarck, who saw in the acquisition of colonies mainly sources of friction with other Powers, which offered in themselves little prospect of adequate economic development. Nevertheless, he somewhat reluctantly recognised the necessity for the Imperial Government to give the colonising spirit fair play under its ægis ; with the result that considerable portions of Africa are now appended to the German Empire—as related elsewhere

The Prussian State received through the mighty events of 1866 and 1870, which altered its whole framework and put new and important duties before it, a definite stimulus towards internal reforms.

The absolutism and the bureaucratic principles of the age of Frederic the Great had obtained recognition in the constitution of 1850; the landed nobility were still a privileged body. It was necessary that these anomalies should be removed and that self-government should be introduced. For example, in rural districts the lord of

New Scheme of Local Government the manor had still the right to nominate the Schultheiss—village mayor; the Landrat of the district was appointed by the king on the nomination of the chief landowner, the other inhabitants of the district being neglected; and the nobility predominated in the provincial Landtags.

The king, in his speech from the throne on the opening of the Landtag on November 27th, 1871, had pledged his word that his Government would introduce a new scheme of local government. Count Eulenburg, the Minister of the Interior, set to work to elaborate it, and although the House of Peers, under the influence of the private interests of the aristocracy, rejected the Bill at first and Bismarck had grave doubts on the point, he carried it in December, 1872, with the help of the king, who created twenty-five new peers. The king signed the Bill on December 13th. It applied at first only to the five eastern provinces—Prussia, Pomerania, Brandenburg, Saxony, and Silesia.

Anxiety as to the sentiment of the Poles forbade the grant of full self-government to the districts in Posen. According to the new law, the country communities elected their own head for the future; and only in some special cases was the landowner or his nominee still allowed to fill up this post. Country and town communities which contained under 25,000 inhabitants were for the time being constituted as a district, whose affairs were administered by a Kreistag—district council—of at least twenty-five members chosen by delegates, and therefore indirectly, from all the resi-

Electoral Privileges of the Towns dents in the district. In the Kreistags half the votes at most were to belong to the towns, the rest to the rural population. At the head stands a Landrat whom the king appoints at the nomination of the entire Kreistag; a committee of six members is assigned to the Landrat to assist him. Towns with more than 25,000 inhabitants form special "urban districts." Since the new scheme of local government worked very satisfactorily, it was extended in 1885-

1889 to the remaining six provinces; in Posen, for the reasons mentioned, narrower limits were imposed on self-government.

In the year 1875 the provincial Landtags were reformed. In future they were to consist of representatives of the Kreistags and of the municipal colleges—the magistrates and municipal officers—which met for the purpose of election in a common session; they were to assemble at least once in every two years at the royal summons and pass resolutions affecting all provincial matters, especially the construction of roads, land improvements, public institutions, public libraries, the care of monuments, and the application of the sums of money assigned to the provinces by the State in virtue of the law of dotation.

A provincial committee of seven to thirteen persons, with a provincial director as the head of all the provincial officials, was to be elected for the administration of the affairs of the province. The feature of all this legislation was that it preserved to the greatest possible degree the principle of communal self-government; there is now

The Sad Fate of Lewis II. no country in the world which, so far as laws enable it, can show so many guarantees as Prussia for the sovereignty of the law and for the effectiveness of self-government; the duty of the people now is to cultivate those characteristics which give to such laws force and vitality.

In Bavaria, under King Lewis II., born in 1845, Lutz was at the head of affairs. He was a keen antagonist of the Ultramontanes, who also met with the pronounced disfavour of the king. The latter withdrew more and more from public life, and relapsed into a dreamy existence, devoted to music and architecture, while his enormous expenditure on royal castles totally disordered the civil list. He was obliged in the end to be placed under supervision; in order to escape from it he drowned himself and his attendant physician, Bernhard von Gudden, in the lake of Starnberg on June 13th, 1886.

Since his brother Otto, born in 1848, had also long been mentally afflicted, his uncle, Prince Leopold, assumed the sovereignty as Prince Regent. He left the Liberal Ministry in office; but the Ultramontanes acquired more and more influence, and after 1899 they had even a small majority in the Second Chamber. At the urgent pressure of the Roman Catholic bishops, the State refused to recognise the Old

Catholics as belonging to the Catholic Church, and only granted them the rights of a private religious body in March, 1891. The Moderate-Liberal Minister-President, Count von Crailsheim, was compelled to resign on May 31st, 1890.

In Saxony, King John died on October 29th, 1873 ; he was succeeded by his son Albert, who had won fame in the wars of 1866 and 1870–1871, and was a capable ruler with German sympathies. In order to anticipate the imperial railway scheme, the Saxon Government bought up gradually all the private lines in Saxony by the middle of the 'seventies ; in 1894 and 1901 the class-tax and income-tax law of the year 1873 were reformed in accordance with the spirit of the times. Owing to an increase in the number of the Social Democrats, who carried in 1891–1892 eleven, and in

followed in his turn, in October, 1904, by Frederic Augustus III. In Würtemberg, under the rule of King Charles I., 1864–1891, the "German party," which combined in itself the National Liberals and the Free Conservatives, was preponderant in the Landtag, and Baron von Mittnacht, the Minister-President in agreement with this party, conducted the affairs of state in a spirit of loyalty to the empire. In the year 1891 Charles I. was succeeded by his cousin, William II., who had served in the French war and gave proof of conscientiousness, good intentions, and sound sympathy with the national cause.

In Baden Grand Duke Frederic I., born in 1826, the son-in-law of Emperor William I., a thoroughly loyal prince of national and liberal sympathies, reigned

Count Caprivi   Prince Hohenlohe   Prince von Bülow   Bieber

BISMARCK'S SUCCESSORS : THREE IMPERIAL CHANCELLORS OF GERMANY
Since the dismissal in 1890 of the great Imperial Chancellor, Prince Bismarck, the office has been successively filled by the three statesmen whose portraits are given above—Count Caprivi, Prince Hohenlohe, and Prince von Bülow.

1895 actually fourteen, out of the eighty-one electoral districts for the Landtag election, the Government and the Estates, which since 1880 were under the control of the Conservatives, resolved in 1896, notwithstanding the well-grounded protests of educated sympathisers with the social cause, to replace the universal suffrage introduced in 1868 by a suffrage graduated in three classes, which would render the third class of owners and voters quite helpless against the two upper classes. In the year 1897 the Social Democrats lost six seats at once in consequence ; and from 1901 on, no Social Democrat has sat in the Landtag. On the death of King Albert at Sibyllenort on June 19th, 1902, his brother George, born in 1832, succeeded, and was

from 1852 to 1907, when he was succeeded by Frederic II. The intense antagonism between the State and the Catholic Church led in 1876, under the Ministry of Julius Jolly, February, 1868–October, 1876, to the introduction of elementary schools of mixed denominations. Since 1881 the tension has gradually been relaxed ; but the Centre pursued unremittingly their object of reducing the ruling National Liberal party in the Landtag to a minority, by the help of the Democrats ; they lowered the majority of their rivals in 1891 to one vote, and completely attained their object in 1893.

On June 27th, 1901, there occurred a change in the Ministry in favour of Conservatism, since Arthur Brauer became

5219

Premier in place of the veteran Liberal, Wilhelm Nokk, and Alexander Dusch, Minister of Public Worship; the latter showed an inclination to fulfil the wish, of the Episcopal Curia in Freiburg and of the Centre, for the toleration of monasteries,

Disaffection in Alsace and Lorraine since he hoped in this way to get the upper hand of the more conciliatory party in the Centre. In Alsace-Lorraine, by the imperial law of June 9th, 1871, the executive power was conferred upon the emperor. The country thus became an imperial province—Reichsland—in so far that the executive power in the State, which in the other German countries is held quite apart from the executive power in the empire, coincides here with it. The Imperial Chancellor was Minister for the Reichsland; the administration of the country was conducted from 1871 to 1879, by the able and wise Eduard von Möller, who was nominated High President. In virtue of Paragraph 10 of the law of December 30th, 1871, he possessed the right of taking every measure which seemed necessary to him in case of danger to the public safety, and in the most extreme cases even to raise troops for the defence of the country. The disaffection of the inhabitants of Alsace-Lorraine, among whom in particular the "Notables"—namely, the manufacturers, large landowners, doctors, and notaries—were quite un-German, rendered this "Dictatorship paragraph" essential for a long time. On January 1st, 1874, the Imperial constitution came into force for Alsace-Lorraine; the fifteen representatives elected to the Reichstag belonged almost all to the "Protesters," who condemned the severance of the provinces from France as an act of violence.

But gradually the so-called Autonomists gained ground; these accepted the incorporation into Germany as an irrevocable fact, but wished to win the greatest amount of self-government and provincial independence for the country. Bismarck thought it wise to support the

KING ALBERT OF SAXONY
The son of King John, he succeeded to the throne of Saxony on the death of his father in the year 1873, assuming the crown with an excellent reputation won on the battlefield.
Photo: London Stereoscopic Co.

movement and by this indirect method to make the inhabitants of Alsace-Lorraine good Germans. He granted to the country in October, 1874, a popular representation—at first deliberative only, but since 1877 with powers to legislate; this was the Landesausschuss, which contains fifty-eight members—thirty-four elected by the three district councils of Upper and Lower Alsace and Lorraine, twenty by the country districts, four by the towns of Colmar, Metz, Mülhausen, and Strassburg. Universal and equal suffrage was not employed for the Landesausschuss, since that would have served to make the anti-German clerical party supreme; but the restricted suffrage gave the Notables the authority. On July 4th, 1879, the Empire granted to the imperial province the self-government which it desired. An imperial Governor-General—Statthalter—was to administer the country for the future in place of the High President; under him were placed for the conduct of affairs a Secretary of State and four Under-Secretaries of State, all to be nominated by the emperor. The Imperial Chancellor thus ceased to be Minister for the imperial province; Alsace-Lorraine was allowed to send three deliberative representatives into the Bundesrat, which thus was increased to sixty-one members. The post of governor was filled from 1879 to 1885 by the ex-Field-Marshal Manteuffel, who displayed a deplorable weakness towards the Notables. He was succeeded by Prince Hohenlohe, hitherto ambassador at Paris, whose refined and dignified manner somewhat improved the situation. When he became

A New Imperial Chancellor Imperial Chancellor in 1894, the governorship was conferred on the uncle of the empress, Prince Hermann von Hohenlohe-Langenburg. The results of the first thirty years of the incorporation of the Reichsland into the empire are not unsatisfactory, if fairly estimated. The inhabitants of Alsace-Lorraine have gradually adapted themselves more or less to the new position of affairs. The protesting party, as such, has disappeared, and if the country has not yet become German in the fullest sense, it is, at any rate, no longer French. The reasons for the slow development are clear. Threads which have been snapped for nearly two centuries can only slowly be joined together again, and the year 1870, which for Germans is a great and glorious remembrance, signifies for Alsace-Lorraine a year of defeat and oppression, and the blessings it brought with it are only slowly being realised by the people. In June, 1902, such progress, however, had been made that, from confidence in the increasing good will of the population towards the empire, the "Dictatorship paragraph" was repealed, and the inhabitants of Alsace-Lorraine now from being Germans of the "second class" became Germans of the "first class." In the Grand Duchy of Hesse-Darmstadt the Grand Duke Lewis III. died in June, 1877. Under his nephew, Lewis IV., 1877–1892, who was married to Alice, daughter of Queen Victoria of Great Britain, the long-standing dispute with the Catholic Church was settled in 1887–1888. His son, Ernest Lewis, born 1868, concluded in 1896, the railway convention with Prussia.

In Brunswick the reigning line became extinct on October 18th, 1884, by the death of Duke William, and since the next heir, Duke Ernest Augustus of Cumberland, son of the exiled King George V. of Hanover, who died in 1878, had not made any treaty with Prussia, Prince Albert of Prussia, born in 1837, a nephew of Emperor William I., was appointed regent by the Bundesrat. The interest, however, on the Guelf fund was paid over in 1892 to the Duke of Cumberland. In Mecklenburg-Schwerin the Grand Duke Frederic Francis II. died

Unfortunate Prince Alexander on April 15th, 1883. In Saxe-Coburg and Gotha, Duke Ernest II. died on August 22nd, 1893. In Lippe-Detmold, Prince Waldemar, at his death on March 20th, 1895, left a will, according to which Prince Adolf of Schaumburg, brother-in-law of the emperor, was to govern as regent for his feeble-minded brother, Prince Alexander. But Count Ernest of Lippe-Biesterfeld protested

COUNT TAAFFE
An Austrian statesman, he was summoned by the Emperor Francis Joseph to form a Ministry in 1879, and offended the Germans by wishing to grant equal rights to all.

against this, and by the decision of a court of arbitration, in which King Albert of Saxony presided over six members of the Imperial Court, Count Ernest was appointed to the regency in July, 1897. In Oldenburg, Grand Duke Peter, one of the warmest supporters of national unity, died on June 13th, 1900;

Austria's Liberal Cabinet and in Saxe-Weimar-Eisenach, Grand Duke Charles Alexander, one of the last eye-witnesses of the great age of Weimar, who had seen Goethe and breathed of his inspiration, died on January 5th, 1901. Although in Austria the German Liberal bourgeois Ministry of Herbst-Giskra resigned at the beginning of 1870, partly on account of internal dissensions, yet the Constitutional party there, resting on the German Liberals, remained at the helm until 1879. Prince Adolph Auersperg was at the head of the Liberal Cabinet from 1871 to 1879. The Czechs, who did not recognise the Constitution of 1861, absented themselves from the Reichsrat and made no concealment of their leanings towards Russia as the chief Slav power. By this means the position of the Constitutional party was gradually shaken; and when, at the beginning of October, 1878, it opposed the occupation of Bosnia and Herzegovina by Austria, it completely lost ground with the Emperor Francis Joseph, who recognised that this occupation was of vital interest to the monarchy, which had to secure a more advantageous position for itself on the Balkan Peninsula against the intrusion of Russian influence.

The emperor summoned, on August 12th, 1879, the Ministry of Count Taaffe, which aimed at the so-called reconciliation of the nationalities by the grant of equal rights to all. The Czechs, amongst whom the Conservative Old Czechs were gradually crowded out by the more radical Young Czechs, now entered the Reichsrat and usurped the power in the Landtag Chamber at Prague, in consequence of which, among other things, they carried the proposed division of the ancient German university at Prague into German and Czech sections. The Germans, on their side, did not appear for some time in the Landtag. The more radical views of the " German Popular party " and of the " Pan-German " party, which only pursued German national interests, under the clever leaders Von Schönerer, Iro, and Wolf, gained more and more the ascendancy with them, and overshadowed the Liberal Constitutional party, which placed the interests of Austria above the cause of nationality. The two former parties were at the same time strongly anti-Semitic, while the Liberal Conservative party had a large Jewish element. Taaffe fell on November 11th, 1893, since he wished to introduce universal and equal suffrage, an innovation which would have greatly weakened the parliamentary representation of the Poles, Conservatives and Liberals.

The Fall of Count Taaffe

After an attempt to govern with the Coalition Ministry of Count Alfred Windisch-Graetz until June 16th, 1895, Count Badeni, a Pole, seized the reins of government on September 29th, 1895. He conceded in 1896 the election of seventy-two representatives by universal suffrage, in addition to the 353 representatives elected under a restricted franchise, but in general conducted an administration on principles partly Slav, partly clerical, and partly feudal, and by his language ordinances of April 5th, 1897, in consequence of which all officials in Bohemia and Moravia, from 1901 onwards, were to possess a mastery of the Czech as well as of the German language, precipitated the whole Austrian monarchy into wild confusion.

In order to prevent the Czechising of the official classes, and finally of the Germans generally, which was threatened by the language ordinance, the Germans in the Reichsrat set about the most reckless obstruction of all parliamentary business, and secured on November 28th, 1897, the dismissal of Badeni and the repeal of the ordinances. But the storm was not calmed by this. The Czechs demanded the restoration of the ordinances, which would have only meant the establishment of equal rights for all ; but the Germans demanded legal recognition of the dignity of the German language as the language of the State. The Reichsrat was completely crippled for four full years by this impassable breach between the parties, since at one time the Germans, at another the Czechs, " obstructed," while by their interminable

Obstructions in the Reichsrat

speeches and motions they hindered the progress of legislation. The German Constitutional party sank more and more into the background ; Vienna was wrested from it by the Catholic " Social Christian " party under its leader Karl Lueger, whom the emperor actually confirmed in office as burgomaster, in April, 1897, and the Pan-German section was enlarged in the Reichsrat elections of 1900 from five to twenty-one representatives. While the Catholic clergy made overtures to the Slavs, a movement, advancing with the watchword, " Freedom from Rome ! " began among the Catholic German population of Bohemia and the Alpine districts ; this movement has led to the founding of numerous Protestant or Old Catholic communities in hitherto purely Catholic districts, and it is still increasing.

Since the barrenness of the Reichsrat was felt to be irksome by the electorates, whose economic interests remained unsatisfied, the Minister Ernst von Koerber, after January 19th, 1900, succeeded in 1901, by an appeal to material interests, in breaking down the spell of obstruction and making the newly elected Reichstag once more capable of work. More than £29,166,666 were granted then for railroads and canals, and in May, 1902, a Budget Bill was carried for the first time for five years. The relations of Hungary to Cisleithania depended after 1867 on the terms of a treaty concluded for ten years, which was renewed in 1877 and 1887. But the third renewal met with great difficulties, since Cisleithania demanded an increase in the share of thirty per cent. which Hungary has to pay of the common expenditure.

Hungary's Brilliant Celebrations

The celebration of the millennium of the Hungarian nation took a most brilliant form. The Germans, Roumanians, and Serbs in Hungary had indeed cause to complain of the forcible suppression of their nationality. Thus, in 1898, in virtue of a State law Magyar names were substituted for all the non-Magyar place names, and at the elections the Ministry of Desiderius Banffy, which was formed on January 14th, 1895, employed every means of intimidating and deceiving public opinion. The inevitable change of Cabinet on February 26th, 1899, which brought into power the Ministry of Koloman von Szell, led to some improvement in this respect ; the elections of 1901 were carried out for the first time without acts of violence.

FRANCE UNDER THE THIRD REPUBLIC
SPAIN'S LOST COLONIES AND
ITALY'S ECONOMIC PROGRESS

THE great majority of the French National Assembly, elected on February 8th, 1871, were in favour of monarchy, and, since Paris was republican, the Assembly fixed on Versailles as the seat of government. The threatened restoration of the monarchy, as well as the conscious pride with which Paris as the " heart of France " was opposed to the provinces, produced that terrible revolution which is called, from the municipal committee elected by the proletarian masses, the rising of the Commune. On March 28th, the " Communistic Republic" was proclaimed, which at once procured the required supplies of money by compulsory loans from the wealthy and by the confiscation of the property of the religious orders.

The Parisians had been allowed to keep their arms on the conclusion of the truce in January, 1871, at the express request of the infatuated Faure ; with these arms **Another Revolution in Paris** they resisted for nearly two months the attacks of the army led by Marshal MacMahon against the rebellious city. The troops eventually forced their way into the city after a series of murderous engagements ; but in the moment of defeat the Communards sought to revenge themselves on their conquerors by levelling the Vendôme column, burning the Tuileries, the Hôtel de Ville, and other public buildings, and shooting the clergy fallen into their hands, and foremost among them Georges Darboy, Archbishop of Paris. As a punishment for this, twenty-six ringleaders were executed by order of court-martial on the Plain of Satory, and some 10,000 who had been taken with arms in their hands were sentenced to transportation or imprisonment.

These terrible events at first only strengthened the inclination towards monarchy. Thiers, however, being convinced that in the end a Conservative republic was the form of constitution most advantageous to his country, opposed any restoration of the monarchy ; but although by a prompt payment of the £200,000,000 he contrived that France should be **Claimants to the Throne of France** evacuated by the Germans in 1873, he was compelled to retire from the post of President of the Executive in May, 1873, before the evacuation was complete. Marshal MacMahon became his successor. Since there were three parties in the ranks of the Royalists it was very difficult to set up the monarchy, which, after all, only one of these dynasties could hold.

The Orleanists, it is true, gave way to their childless cousin Henry V. of Bourbon, who, as Count of Chambord, lived at Frohsdorf, near Vienna, and MacMahon was prepared to restore the Bourbon Monarchy ; but when, in 1873, the count demanded the disuse of the national tricolour and the reintroduction of the white standard with the lilies of his house, in order that there might be a clear sign of the return of the nation to the pre-revolutionary standpoint, the courage even of the moderate Royalists failed at such a step. The republic received in 1875 its legal basis by the grant of a seven years' tenure of office to its president.

When MacMahon in 1877 made a renewed attempt to pave the way for a restoration of the monarchy, he failed, through the energy of Gambetta and the resistant power of republicanism. The elections produced a strong Republican majority, **Presidents of the French Republic** and on January 30th, 1879, MacMahon, despairing of the victory of his cause, gave way to the Republican Jules Grévy. He was followed by François Sadi Carnot, J. P. P. Casimir-Périer, Félix Faure, Emile Loubet, and finally Armand Fallières, elected in January, 1906, on the retirement of Loubet. Grévy was

A GROUP OF REVOLUTIONARIES BEING ESCORTED TO PRISON

FIGHTING IN THE RUE DE RIVOLI

The troubles of France did not end with the long series of defeats inflicted upon its armies by the Prussian troops. Following upon the national humiliation and the downfall of the Emperor, Napoleon III., there was established in Paris on March 28th, 1871, the "Communistic Republic." To suppress the revolution thus inaugurated, Marshal MacMahon attacked the rebellious city, but for two months the Parisians, armed with the weapons which they had been allowed to keep on the conclusion of the truce in the January preceding, contrived to resist the army.

THE END OF THE COMMUNE: SCENES IN THE STREETS OF PARIS

forced, through the defalcations of his stepson, Daniel Wilson, to resign on December 1st, 1887; Carnot fell on June 24th, 1894, at Lyons, under the dagger of the Italian anarchist, Santo Caserio; Casimir-Périer retired as soon as January 15th, 1895, from disgust at his office, which conferred more external glitter than real power; and Faure died on February 16th, 1899, soon after an attack of apoplexy.

The Monarchists were no longer able to obtain a commanding position, especially since Pope Leo XIII. in 1892 had ordered the Catholics to support the existing constitution. The party which

but, after the resumption of his trial, was condemned, on September 9th, 1899, to ten years' imprisonment in a fortress, only, on September 19th, to be pardoned by President Loubet. But again the Republic weathered the storm. One consequence of the Dreyfus agitation has been to increase the anti-clerical tendencies of the executive.

In June, 1899, the Social Democrat, Alexandre Millerand, actually entered the Cabinet as Minister of Commerce. In March, 1901, a law against associations was passed by the Ministry of Waldeck-Rousseau, which placed under State control the religious orders, especially those

THE BURNING OF THE TUILERIES BY THE COMMUNARDS OF PARIS

After a series of murderous engagements, the army under Marshal MacMahon forced its way into Paris and defeated the Communards. The latter, however, were determined to revenge themselves upon their conquerors, and this they did by levelling the Vendôme column, burning the Tuileries, the Hôtel de Ville, and other public buildings, and shooting the clergy who fell into their hands. In the punishments which followed twenty-six ringleaders were executed, and about 10,000 who had been taken with arms in their hands were sentenced to transportation or imprisonment.

was obedient to the Pope styled itself "les ralliés." Even the venality of Republican statesmen who allowed themselves to be paid for their support in Parliament by the company for the construction of the Panama Canal, which went bankrupt in December, 1888, was unable to overthrow the Republican government.

A crisis even more alarming was produced by the lawsuit of the Jewish captain, Alfred Dreyfus, who, on December 22nd, 1894, was found guilty of betraying military secrets, ignominiously degraded and transported to Devil's Island, near Cayenne,

inveighing against the "atheistic" Republic, punished the disobedient ones with dissolution, and deprived the orders of the instruction of the young.

A drama which is interesting from a different point of view developed round the figure of General Boulanger. He was Minister of War from January, 1886, to June, 1887, and obtained an immense popularity. He almost provoked a war with Germany in the spring of 1887, and after April, 1888, undertook to remodel the constitution with a view to the restoration of the

Empire. Wherever he appeared on his black charger the crowds greeted him with loud cheers. But at last M. Constans, the Minister, boldly laid hands on him, and arraigned him before the High Court as a conspirator against the constitution. Boulanger, from fear of condemnation, and not being bold enough to stir up a revolution, fled, on April 8th, to Brussels, where he died by his own hand on September 30th, 1891.

In the sphere of foreign policy the Third Republic was very successful in so far that on May 12th, 1881, by use of the temporarily good understanding with Germany established by the Ministry of Jules Ferry, Sidi Ali, the Bey of Tunis, who died on June 11th, 1902, was forced to accept the French protectorate, and thus the position of France on the Mediterranean was much strengthened. Tonkin, in Further India, was acquired after a checkered campaign against China, between 1883 and 1885 ; on October 2nd, 1893, Siam was driven back behind the Mekong ; and on August 6th, 1896, Madagascar was incorporated into the French colonial possessions. France also won considerable territory on the continent of Africa. In 1892 she occupied the negro kingdom of Dahomeh, while concurrently the whole Western Sudan from Timbuctoo to the Congo became French. On Lake Chad France is the predominant Power, and treaties with Germany and Britain secured its possessions. Recent troubles in Morocco have given an opportunity for French interference, which the Republic shows every intention of utilising to the utmost. Her only severe check in Africa has been that experienced from Britain in connection with the Fashoda episode.

But the originally most ardent wish of the French, to revenge themselves on

Germany and to win back Alsace-Lorraine, has not been gratified. The efficiency of the German army and the increasing numerical superiority of the German population —in 1901 there were 56,000,000 Germans to 38,000,000 French—excluded all possibility of a French victory in a duel between the two nations. Even the Dual Alliance with Russia, which was projected in 1891 under Alexander III. and concluded under Nicholas II., has freed, indeed, France from her isolation, but—according to the noteworthy confession of " Le Siècle " of September 19th, 1901—has made a reconquest of the lost provinces impossible, for the reason that Russia also must wish to stand on good terms with her neighbour Germany. A dispute with the Sultan, Abdul Hamid II., who did not satisfy the demands of some French officials, led to the despatch of a French fleet under

THE DEGRADATION OF CAPTAIN DREYFUS

Another crisis of an alarming character overtook France in 1894, when the Jewish captain, Alfred Dreyfus, was found guilty of betraying military secrets and sentenced to confinement on Devil's Island. Five years later, in September, 1899, the trial was reopened. Dreyfus was then sentenced to ten years' imprisonment in a fortress, but the punishment was not carried out, the prisoner, whose innocence had been established, receiving a pardon from President Loubet

Grévy   Carnot   Casimir-Périer

Faure   Loubet   Fallières

SIX PRESIDENTS OF THE FRENCH REPUBLIC

Since 1879 the Presidential chair of the French Republic has been occupied by the statesmen whose portraits are given above. In that year Jules Grévy was elected to the office, resigning in 1887, when he was succeeded by Francois Sadi Carnot, who was assassinated in 1894 at Lyons. Disgusted with the office, Casimir-Périer retired in January, 1895; Faure died in 1899; while Loubet retired in 1906, and was succeeded by Armand Fallières.

Photos by Pierre-Petit and Nadar

Admiral Caillard in November, 1901, to Mytilene. The Sultan gave in, granted to French schools and hospitals in Turkey the immunity from taxation which was demanded for them, and thus saved the island from the fate of the island of Cyprus, which has remained in British occupation since 1878.

The failure of the Hohenzollern candidature for the Spanish Crown had placed Ferdinand Amadeus of Savoy on the throne in December, 1870; but on February 11th, 1873, the new monarch resigned his unbearable post. The only remaining alternative was to proclaim a republic. Spanish republicanism has

GENERAL BOULANGER

Minister of War, General Boulanger was for some time a great public favourite; but, charged with conspiring against the constitution, he feared condemnation, and died by his own hand in 1891.

characteristics peculiarly its own. Its special feature, federalism, is one that is due to the Iberian soil, which brought it forth. Even to the present time the idea of a republic has drawn its strength from the hope of transforming into a republic those separate provinces of Spain which only the loosest of bonds could unite into one kingdom. A federal republic was now to be founded; though, for the moment, the founders had to content themselves, whether they would or no, with giving a republican form to the administrative and executive powers already in existence. The new republic was in a critical position. The

5227

forces of reaction had been aroused by the triumph of the Radicals, and were gathering round the man who had inherited the Carlist claims, Don Carlos the Younger, who summoned the Basque provinces to his support. Once again battalions of these mountaineers, distinguished by that classic headgear, the round cap of the Basques, flocked to the standard of the reactionary party. But once again it became manifest that their strength was in defensive tactics. An attack upon the capital was even more out of the question than during the First Carlist War. The Socialist agitators in the south, excited by the example of the Parisian Commune, thought that their time had also come, and seized several towns, in particular the arsenal of Cartagena, from which they were not easily dislodged. The army at the disposal of the republic had been utterly demoralised by the continual pronunciamentos, and had to be reorganised in part. Fortunately, neither Carlism nor communism, thanks to incompetent leadership, was able to attract many recruits; and the feeling that, at any rate, the highest positions in the state must be placed beyond the reach of ambitious intriguers grew stronger every day. Isabella had been driven out, and no one was inclined to give her another chance; but great hopes were held of the queen's son, the young Alfonso. The republic was set aside without difficulty on December 29-30th, 1874; and on January 14th, 1875, Alfonso was proclaimed king. Many might have considered this to be merely another act in the political farce; but such pessimists

FERDINAND AMADEUS AND ALFONSO XII.
The throne of Spain in the troublous days that followed the abdication of Isabella II. did not offer a very tempting prize, but Ferdinand Amadeus, the second son of King Victor Emmanuel of Italy, accepted it in 1870, abdicating in February, 1873. When the Carlist movement collapsed in the closing days of 1874, Alfonso XII. was elected king.

DON CARLOS
The brother of Ferdinand VII., he was anxious to succeed to the throne of Spain, and under pressure from the Reactionary party he raised the standard of a revolt.

were wrong. The early death of Alfonso XII., on November 25th, 1885, did not shake in any way the position of the monarchy. The Queen-widow, Maria Christina, acted as regent, at first for her daughter Mercedes, and then for her son Alfonso XIII., who was born on May 17th, 1886, and met with no opposition worthy of mention.

The period of peace, which could not be broken even by the irrepressible revolt of the remnants of the Spanish colonial empire, is a standing testimony to the fact that the economic conditions of the country are slowly but undeniably improving, and that it is beginning more and more to develop and to make use of its natural wealth. It may be that foreigners have given the impulse and are appropriating a portion of the profit; but, none the less, the advantage to the country itself is unmistakable. At this time, it is true, the social problem is a menacing danger, and its most deadly fruit, anarchism, is brought to fullest maturity in Spain; but this is partly due to the general lack of education, and is, moreover, a heritage from the sad course of Spain's earlier development. That there is an improvement is undeniable. The events of the year 1898 —the war with the United States of America and the loss of all her more important colonies—have demonstrated how small is the power of resistance that Spain can offer to a determined opponent, in spite of all her recent progress; and how inferior she is to those wealthy Powers which have acquired a great reserve of strength by establishing themselves upon a sound economic basis, and by taking a due share in the progressive movements of modern times. Calamity had long been in the air. When the American colonies were lost at the beginning of the nineteenth century, the islands of Cuba and Porto Rico were retained, partly perhaps on account of a revolt of the negro slaves in Cuba in the year 1812, which was vigorously opposed by all the white inhabitants of the island. Until the middle of the century it was only the negro population which showed any tendency to revolt. However, later on, the creole element in Cuba found that its natural course of development was impeded by the Spanish Government, and became unruly. It was supported, sometimes secretly, sometimes openly, by the United States. Every conspiracy and filibustering expedition—the first began in 1849—found ready support in North America. The American Government had even declared with praiseworthy frankness that it proposed to seize Cuba at the first favourable opportunity, but Spain was saved by the outbreak of the Civil War in the United States.

The victory of the North in this war brought about a temporary coolness between Americans and Cubans. The great revolt of 1868–78, when creoles and negroes fought together against Spain, was not supported by any attack from America. But the rich island gradually became an object of interest to American speculators, and Spain could not make up its mind to the generous concessions which would have satisfied the self-assertive creoles. The abolition of slavery in 1880 led to an economic crisis, but did not inspire the liberated slaves with any friendly feelings for Spain. So at last, in the year 1895–96, a revolt began, systematically supported by the United States; Spain gradually spent her strength in the remarkable efforts she made to meet the danger.

At the same time, 1896, a revolt broke out in the Philippines, where Spanish mismanagement, without the stimulus of any foreign influence, had driven the most enlightened and preponderant class among the natives, the Tagals, to open resistance. Notwithstanding the many tokens that foreboded ruin, the characteristic Spanish indifference to consequences was as apparent as ever. The fleet, which was the only means of salvation, continued in such utter neglect that a large number of the best ships could not be used at all

American Support for the Cubans

Spain Blind and Incompetent

LOBBY OF THE CORTES IN MADRID DURING THE BRIEF DAYS OF THE SPANISH REPUBLIC

A chance occurrence, or, according to the American theory, an act of treachery, the blowing up of the United States battleship Maine in Havana Harbour, led to the outbreak of hostilities on April 21st, 1898. With curiously clear foresight the United States had sent a considerable fleet, under Commodore Dewey, towards the Philippines. He destroyed the little Spanish squadron of Montojo at Cavite on May 1st, and, with the help of the revolted natives, obliged Manila to surrender. In Cuba the Spaniards, under Martinez Campos, Weyler, and finally, Marshal Blanco, had tried to avert calamity by the employment both of mildness and of severity. Their power in the island collapsed no less ingloriously when their little fleet, under Cervera, which had been equipped with great difficulty, had been destroyed off Santiago on July 3rd. Of Spain's immense empire, only two little colonies on the west coast of Africa now remain. The remainder of her possessions in the Pacific Ocean, the Caroline, Pellew, and Marianne islands, were sold to Germany for £850,000 on June 19th, 1899. The loss of her colonies, which was formally declared in the Peace of Paris, December 10th, 1898, is, in truth, a fortunate event for Spain. It never understood how to make proper use of its possessions. What it has lost is the happy hunting-ground of office-seekers and political parasites, passing their time discussing public affairs in the cafés of Madrid, and waiting for a revolution to further their designs. Possibly the number of these political parasites will decrease. Possibly there will be a general return to honest endeavour. The fact that the government of a woman and of a child, who has now grown to a promising manhood, was never seriously threatened, in spite of all disasters abroad, is the best testimony to the excellent spirit now prevailing in Spain. With her eyes fixed upon her own resources, Spain may now—and all signs seem to indicate

HUMBERT I. OF ITALY
The son of Victor Emmanuel II., he succeeded to the throne of Italy in 1878, and on July 29th, 1900, was assassinated at Monza by an anarchist who had been sent from America.

that she will—give an attention, too long deferred, to the training of the national mind and the development of national industry commensurate with the great natural wealth of the country and the high qualities and potency of the people.

In the Kingdom of Italy the predominant party was from 1861 to 1876 the Consorteria, or Moderate Conservative, which had been founded by Cavour. Its failures, however, and all kinds of personal jealousies enabled the Left to gain the supremacy, which was only temporarily taken from it by the renewed strength of the Right under the Marquis di Rudini. The Left abolished the duty on flour, which made the working-man's bread dear, and conferred the suffrage on all who could read and write and paid a small tax. But it could not check satisfactorily the miserable destitution of the poorer classes, especially of the labourers in the north, in the Basilicata, and in Sicily, and of the miners in the Sicilian sulphur-mines. Sicily also suffered under the reign of terror which the secret society of the Mafia established in many parts. Owing to the dearth of food, the social revolution in Milan, Ancona, the Romagna, and Southern Italy repeatedly produced open insurrection against the authority of the state. From May 6th to 12th, 1898, Milan was completely in the hands of the revolution, and order was only restored after sanguinary conflicts in which fifty-three persons were killed and hundreds wounded. The efforts of Italia irredenta, which wished to unite with the monarchy the whole " unredeemed " Italian population outside Italy, in Trieste, Dalmatia, Tirol, Ticino, and Nice, had been, especially since 1878, detrimental to a good understanding with neighbouring states ; they hindered the alliance of Italy with Austria, and so also with Germany, and gave France an opportunity to carry off, on the pretext of the depredations of the Tunisian border tribes of the Krumir, the province of Tunis, under the very eyes of the Italians, who had been trying to acquire it themselves. King Humbert I., the worthy son of Victor Emmanuel II., 1878 to 1900, being thus taught the dangers of the policy of the " free hand," concluded in March, 1887, at the advice of his Minister, Count Robilant, the Triple Alliance with Austria and Germany, which, being subsequently consolidated by the policy of Francesco Crispi, has proved hitherto a main support of the peace of Europe. It secured Italy's position in the Mediterranean, and thus effectively checked French designs on Tripoli. The attempt to place Abyssinia under Italian suzerainty gained for Italy the possession of Assab in 1881, and that of Massowah in 1885. But on March 1st, 1896, the great King Menelik with 90,000 men defeated and nearly annihilated the Italian army, 15,000 men strong, under Baratieri at Abba Garima, east of Adowah, carried 3,000 Italian soldiers as prisoners into the heart of his country, and extorted, on October 26th, 1896, a peace which secured the independence of Abyssinia and confined the Italian colony on the Red

out damage to their reputations, caused repeatedly, as in 1894, for example, considerable excitement. King Humbert was assassinated on July 29th, 1900, at Monza,

KING VICTOR EMMANUEL III. Brogi
Born in 1869, he came to the throne as successor to his father, Humbert I., in the year 1900. On October 24th, 1896, he was married to Princess Helena of Montenegro.

by Gaetano Bresci, an anarchist sent from America ; he was succeeded by his son Victor Emmanuel III., born in 1869, who by his marriage to Princess Helena of Montenegro on October 24th, 1896, has formed an alliance on the other side of the Adriatic. The economic position of Italy has made considerable progress, and a commercial treaty has been made with France. The Triple Alliance was renewed in 1902.

The papacy is bitterly hostile to the national state of Italy, which has deprived it of all secular possessions. It forbade all true sons of the Church to show any sort of recognition of the " usurping " Kingdom of Italy by taking part in the political elections to the Second Chamber. Even the Guarantee Act of May, 1871, which secures to the Pope his independence, the possession of the Vatican, and a yearly income of £118,750, has not so far been acknowledged by the Curia, since it emanates from the legislature of the monarchy, and the right of the monarchy to exist is contested by the Pope.

QUEEN HELENA OF ITALY   Brogi

Sea within narrower limits ; it now only extends from Massowah to the rivers Marab and Belesa. Bank scandals, from which even Ministers did not emerge with-

MINOR STATES OF WESTERN EUROPE
THE CLEAVAGE OF NORWAY AND SWEDEN

THE Swiss Confederation has gone through a progressive development, so far as material interests are concerned, since about 1860. It obtained a rich market for its industries by commercial treaties with its neighbours, and the great lines of mountain railways, into the Engadine, over the St. Gothard, through the heart of which a tunnel nine and one-third miles long was driven in 1882, and into the Bernese Oberland, promoted the influx of strangers, from which Switzerland derives great profits.

Switzerland and the Referendum

The constitution of the Confederation, like those of many cantons, has gradually become more democratic in the course of years. After the cantons of Zürich, Basle, Berne, and others had introduced since 1869 the Referendum, or the voting of the entire people on legislative proposals, the Federal constitution was modified on May 29th, 1874, according to the views of the Liberals and the Centre. Legislation on the subjects of contracts, bills, and trade, as well as the jurisdiction over the army and the Church, were assigned to the Confederation; it also received powers in economic matters. A supreme Federal Court and a system of registration of births, deaths, and marriages by government officials was introduced. The Referendum is allowed in all cases when either 30,000 voters or eight out of the twenty-two cantons demand that the nation itself shall say the last word on a measure approved by the Federal and National Councils. On July 5th, 1891, the popular rights were increased by the grant to the people of the initiative in the legislation on condition that 50,000 votes require it.

Increasing the Popular Privileges

This concession to democratic principles has, it must be confessed, produced the result that many useful laws which had been decided upon by the legislative bodies have been lost at the very last, especially when an increased expenditure might be expected from them. The French cantons of Western Switzerland and the Catholic cantons of Old Switzerland often came together in the attempt to hinder all progressive centralisation. The Confederation received, however, on October 25th, 1885, the monopoly of manufacturing and selling alcohol, and in 1887 the supervision of the forests and the right to legislate on the food supply; in 1898 the nationalisation of the railways and uniformity of procedure in civil and criminal cases were granted by the people.

The Confederation quarrelled with the papal throne in 1873, because Bishop E. Lachat of Basle had on his own responsibility published the Vatican decrees. The bishopric of Basle was, in consequence, abolished by the Confederation on January 29th; Kasper Mermillod, who put himself forward as Bishop of Geneva, was banished from the country on February 17th, and the papal chargé d'affaires, G. B. Agnozzi, was given his passports towards the end of November. The Old Catholic movement found great support in Switzerland, and received on June 7th, 1876, a bishop of its own, "Christian Catholic," in the person of Edward Herzog, and a special theological faculty in Berne, which was, however, only thinly attended. But in the course of time a fresh agreement was effected between Church and State; the bishopric of Basle was revived in 1884–1885, though the nunciature remained in abeyance.

Church and State Come to Terms

The social movement of the time led in 1887 to the legal restriction of the maximum working day to eleven hours, in 1881 to the adoption of a law of employers' liability, and in 1890 to the establishment of workmen's insurances against accidents and illness. On the other hand, the social democratic proposal to introduce into the constitution the " Right to Labour " was rejected by the people by 300,000 to 73,000 votes. While the Radical Democratic party was prominent, the Social Democracy generally, although it rested on the Radical Grütli-Verein, which had formally joined it in 1901, and constituted a special group in the National Council, has attained to no great influence. Since also the Conservative Liberals were able to exercise very limited power, the minority have lately directed their efforts to carry the system of proportionate voting in the Confederation as well as in the cantons, and thus to secure themselves at least a proportionate share in the popular representation and in legislation.

The kingdom of Belgium had been released by the war of 1870–1871 from the continual danger which had threatened it from the side of France. The two great parties of Liberals and Clericals were alternately in office, as had been the case for the past decades. But both parties saw themselves compelled, on political grounds, to abandon gradually the exclusive recognition of the French language in official matters and private intercourse, and to make concessions to the Flemings, who composed more than half the population of the kingdom. Accordingly, under the Clerical Cabinet of Baron J. J. d'Anethan, the use of the Flemish language was permitted in the law courts; under the Liberal Ministry of Frère-Orban, in 1878, its employment as the medium of instruction in the national schools was conceded; while under the renewed Clerical government of 1886 a royal Flemish academy for language and literature was founded. In 1892 officers were required to learn the two national languages. Frère-Orban, supported by a majority of eighteen votes, carried, on July 1st, 1879, the law which introduced **Religious Instruction in Belgium** undenominational national schools into Belgium. The religious instruction was now given outside the school hours, but classrooms were placed at the disposal of the clergy for the purpose. Owing to the ambiguous attitude of the Curia, which ostensibly exhorted the faithful to follow the law, but in secret stirred up opposition,

THE KING OF THE BELGIANS
Leopold II., King of the Belgians, founded in West Africa, with the assistance of Sir Henry Stanley, the Congo State, which was formally recognised by the Great Powers in 1885. Many terrible abuses have marked his rule there.
Numa Blanc

d'Anethan, then Ambassador at the Vatican, was recalled, and the Nuncio Serafino Vannutelli was given his passports. In 1881 the number of state gymnasia was increased, and fifty undenominational girls' schools were founded. But since the new **The Cost of Education** schools laid considerable burdens on parishes, as much as £880,000 yearly, discontent gradually was felt with the Liberal Ministry, which also opposed the introduction of universal suffrage; and the Clericals by the elections of 1884 won a majority of twenty votes.

The Clerical Cabinet of Jules Malou now passed a law, in virtue of which parishes were empowered to recognise the "free" schools—that is to say, the schools erected by the Church—as national schools in the meaning of the law of 1879; in this way the latter was practically annulled, for the parishes, from motives of economy, made such ample use of this permission, in 1,465 cases, that out of 1,933 national schools 877 were closed within a year, and were replaced by Church schools. Diplomatic intercourse with the Curia was resumed in 1885 by a Belgian ambassador to the Vatican, Baron E. de Pitteurs - Hiégaerts, and by the reappointment of a nuncio in Brussels, Domen - Ferrata. The Clerical party maintained their majority at the next elections; in fact, they grew to be more than two-thirds of the members of the Chamber.

The rise of the Social Democrats, whose influence had begun to spread far and wide through the industrial regions of Belgium, combined, with a fall of wages, to produce a disastrous revolution in Liège, Brussels, and Charleroi in March, 1886, on the occasion of a festival in honour of the Paris Commune. A new and formidable antagonist faced the Clericals in place of the Liberals, who were divided into a Moderate and a Radical section. The Government attempted to pave the way for Social Reform by the creation of courts of arbitration between workmen and manufacturers, by the introduction of state supervision over workshops, and the prohibition of the payment of wages in kind ; but the Clericals could not bring themselves to adopt really comprehensive measures of strict social justice, among which the universal liability to military service would be reckoned.

At the elections of 1892 they lost the two - thirds majority, and conceded in 1893 universal suffrage, with the proviso that electors who possessed means, were married, and academically educated, should possess a plural vote. The number of electors was increased by this law from 130,000 to 1,200,000. Since

WILLIAM III. OF HOLLAND AND QUEEN EMMA
Popular with his people, King William III. of Holland was twice married, his second bride being Princess Emma of Waldeck-Pyrmont. In 1888 it was settled by constitutional law that their daughter, Wilhelmina, born in 1880, should succeed to the throne on her father's death, which event occurred in November, 1890.

the first clause in particular helped the Clerical party in the country, it maintained its majority ; the Liberals and Social Democrats vainly endeavoured to strike the clause conceding plurality of votes out of the constitution. A general strike organised for this purpose on April 14th, 1902, had to be abandoned on the 20th ; and the new elections on May 25th resulted in a small gain for the Clericals. King Leopold II. did good service in opening up Africa, where he founded, with the help of Sir Henry Stanley, the Congo State. This state was recognised by the Great Powers at the Berlin Congo Conference in 1885, and Leopold, in virtue of a Belgian law which allowed him to bear this double title, assumed the style of Sovereign of the Congo State. The subsequent de-

QUEEN WILHELMINA
Attaining her majority on August 31st, 1898, she came to the throne, and on February 7th, 1901, married Duke Henry of Mecklenburg, who received the title of Prince Consort.

velopments have been dealt with in the African portion of this work. In the Netherlands also the institution of undenominational national schools in 1857 gave rise to excited party disputes. After that date the Catholics were completely separated from the Liberals, and among the Protestants a Christian - Conservative party, the "Anti - revolutionary," was formed, which gradually won many supporters ; its leader was the energetic and talented Abraham Kuyper, born in 1837, a pastor of the reformed religion. In March, 1888, and again in 1901, the united Catholics and Anti-revolutionaries obtained the majority. Kuyper, as Prime Minister of the Conservative Cabinet constructed on July 27th, 1901, was now able to announce their decision to procure for Christianity once more its proper influence on national life, and thus first and foremost to restore the denominational national schools. The social movement in Holland can point to comparatively little results. In 1889 a measure was passed to prohibit the excessive labour of women and children, and in 1892 a graduated scale of taxation on property and incomes was introduced. In 1896 universal suffrage was accepted, with the limitations that the electors must be twenty-five years of age and must pay some amount, however small, of direct taxation. A strike of railway employees in February, 1903, necessitated remedial legislation. In the Dutch Indies the Colonial Government in 1873-1879 and 1896 had to conduct difficult campaigns against the Sultan of Achin in Sumatra, and in 1894-1895 on the island of Lombok, where the native dynasty had been deposed.

The male line of the House of Orange since June 21st, 1884, when the Crown Prince Alexander died childless, was only represented by the king, William III. It was therefore settled in 1888 by a

throne. The anticipated event occurred on November 23rd, 1890. While in Luxemburg, where females cannot reign, the former Duke Adolf of Nassau, as head of the Walram line, and in this respect heir of the Ottonian line of the House of Nassau, became Grand Duke, the clever and popular queen-mother, Emma, took over the regency for Wilhelmina until August 31st, 1898. On that day the young queen, who then attained her majority, entered herself on her high office, and promised to rule with that same spirit of devotion to duty which endeared her ancestors to the Dutch nation. On February 7th, 1901, she gave her hand to Duke Henry of Mecklenburg, who received the title of Prince of the Netherlands, but no heir to the throne has yet been born. During the political struggle the relations of Norway and Sweden had become worse. The Norwegians had quite a different conception of the union from the Swedes, and they demanded that the two countries should be placed on an entirely equal footing. A fruitless attempt was made to come to an agreement concerning the revision of the Rigsakt of 1815. Finally, the Norwegians demanded their own consular service. This led to long and wearisome negotiations

THE ACCESSION OF KING HAAKON TO THE THRONE OF NORWAY
After the dissolution of the union between Norway and Sweden, the Storting elected to the throne of the former country Prince Charles, the second son of Frederic VII., King of Denmark, and on November 27th, 1905, he took the oath in presence of the Storting, swearing that he would govern the kingdom of Norway in accordance with its constitution and laws.

constitutional law that, on the death of William, his daughter Wilhelmina, born 1880, by the king's second marriage with Emma of Waldeck, should inherit the

between the Norwegian and the Swedish Governments. These negotiations remained ineffective because it was evident that the Swedes, instead of admitting the equality

5235

of Norway, wished to maintain their own predominance. This roused universal indignation in Norway. On May 23rd, 1905, the Storting unanimously passed a law establishing a national consular service. Upon the king's refusal to sanction the law, the Ministry of Peter Michelsen tendered their resignations. The king did not accept these, because, according to his own declaration, no Ministry could exist at that time in Norway which represented his opinions. But on June 7th, the Ministry laid its power in the hands of the Storting, which declared the personal union with Sweden dissolved, and authorised the Ministry to exercise until further notice the power appertaining to the king. Negotiations with Sweden were then entered upon. At Karlstad, on September 23rd, a treaty was concluded which settled the points of controversy raised by the dissolution of the union. King Oscar II. recognised Norway as an entirely separate state from October 27th. He renounced the Norwegian crown, and declined the request of the Storting that a younger prince of his house should occupy the Norwegian throne. On November 18th the Storting elected as king Prince Charles, the second son of Frederic VIII., King of Denmark. Prince Charles entered Christiania on November 25th, 1905, as Haakon VII., and was duly crowned on June 22nd, 1906, as King of Norway. In this way the separation of the two countries which had been united for ninety years was conclusively confirmed.

In spite of political struggles important reforms had been introduced—the establishment of the jury, new regulations in the army, in the schools, and in the elections; the material development of the country likewise did not suffer. Means of communication were greatly improved. By the erection of various agricultural, industrial, and technical schools opportunity was afforded to the people, who were actively interested in industrial pursuits, to acquire greater knowledge. By an improved utilisation of the country's

THE CORONATION OF KING HAAKON AT TRÖNDHJEM CATHEDRAL

natural resources the various branches of industry received a great impetus, especially commerce and navigation. At the present time Norway possesses the largest mercantile fleet in the world in proportion to the number of inhabitants. Next to agriculture and cattle-breeding the people depend mainly for their livelihood on fishing and forestry. The population is almost three times as large as in 1841, and successful efforts are made to encourage culture and progress.   G. EGELHAAF

THE SOCIAL QUESTION
BRITAIN'S INDUSTRIAL REVOLUTION
AND THE RISE OF THE FACTORY SYSTEM

MODERN society is characterised, technically, by the predominance of great industries and the unsuspected advantage derived from the forces of Nature; economically, by freedom of trade and right of settlement; politically, by liberty of speech and of combination, and by popular representation. On this basis, for the first time the great mass of the productive but dependent population was enabled to take a part in the important movements which make the world's history. These classes previously, leaving out of account isolated risings, had either formed only the passive foundation for all contests for political or social power, or had only been able to struggle for modest improvements in their material welfare.

Limits of Workmen's Unions It is clear that the immediate preliminary condition for an independent advance of the bulk of the people into the field of public and social life is only satisfied when they are allowed to form suitable and permanent organisations with the object of attaining their ends.

The working classes, therefore, possessed as a whole, to within the last century, no effective influence, because this condition was not fulfilled. So far as organisations generally were permitted in past ages, as was the case with the members of the guilds in the towns, their sphere of influence was restricted to social and religious requirements, relief funds, information as to work, and the improvement of some conditions of labour contracts; and guilds and authorities ensured by close superintendence and merciless severity that these narrow limits were never overstepped by the journeymen's unions.

Notwithstanding, therefore, that before this time occasionally—we may remind our readers of Rome under the Empire—a collection of masses of working men had been formed in large towns and centres of production; notwithstanding that, even earlier, wide sections of the **Power of the Ruling Classes** people had been oppressed and laid under contribution, while at the same time luxury and splendour were publicly paraded, powerful and lasting agitations by the working classes were at that time impossible.

There could be nothing more than isolated violent outbreaks, which were fated inevitably to fail, owing to the political immaturity of the rioters and the firmness of the ruling powers; for example, the Greek and Roman slave risings, or the rebellions of the peasants in Western Europe during the fourteenth to the sixteenth centuries. The ruling classes knew how to prevent any immediate repetition of these attempts by the oppressed to shatter their chains, since after every victory they applied the principle "væ victis," and exacted, with all the cruelty of the times, terrible penalties as a deterrent warning. The people thus felt their helplessness. Overawed and indifferent to all politics, the peasant went back to his plough and **The New Era of Industry** the artisan to the workshop. If state and society thus seemed in early times safely entrenched behind rampart and moat against the demands of the lower class, the modern state and its liberty offered to the people the possibility of seeing the fall of the hitherto impregnable fortress. This hope and prospect could

5237

not fail to contribute towards rousing the people from their indifference, so that, sooner or later, in all civilised nations the agitation of the lower classes was as general as the former lethargy.

Nothing, however, has been of such wide-reaching importance for the distinctive features of this movement, for its demands and its aims, as **Beginnings of Capitalistic Production** the modern industrial development, of which the marked characteristic is the method of capitalistic production. This takes place when a considerable number of workmen is employed by the same individual capital at the same time in the production of the same goods.

Historically, capitalistic production dates its beginning from the "domestic system," which began to develop itself at the beginning of the new era by the side of the handicraft of the guilds. The small exclusive economic spheres of the city states were then transformed into large uniformly administered territories, and, owing to the new colonial districts, international trade received a great stimulus. Requirements thus arose which could not be met within the old guild organisation. Thus a new form of organisation of industrial work was formed in the "domestic system." Its distinctive feature is that a contractor, called a "factor," provides a number of workmen with commissions, which they then execute in their own houses. According to this system, technically the handicraft production still predominates.

But the "domestic system," if not in the manner of production, at least in the manner of sale, denotes an advance beyond handicraft. The master handicraftsman sells his goods directly to the person who requires them; but in the "domestic system" there is always one intermediate dealer between the producer and the consumer—that is, the merchant. And **The Merchant's Place in Commerce** while the individual handicraftsman only sells a small quantity of goods, usually in an adjacent market, the merchant places large masses of goods on one or more adjacent or distant markets. With regard to selling, therefore, the domestic system represents a wholesale trade which appears excellently adapted for the supply of distant markets. And for the very reason that it combined the traditional methods of production on a small scale with a more complete method of sale in large quantities, it must have been recognised from the first as the form of industrial enterprise which, while causing the least alteration in long standing conditions, could satisfy the necessity felt in the new era for exchange of commodities between different places or nations. Persons who had some capital, and were far-sighted enough to recognise the tendency of the new want and the extent of the remunerative demand, took the lead, engaged handicraftsmen, day labourers in the towns not belonging to any guild, or hitherto unemployed members of the country population, and started the new organisation.

The "domestic system" was common in England even before the close of the fifteenth century as the method employed in the cloth industry, supplying the great markets and the export trade. Afterwards it continually spread to other trades, until it became, right up to the eighteenth century, the ordinary form of the most important industries intended to put wholesale quantities of goods on the markets. In no other **Effects of the Domestic System** country did it attain such importance, but still it prevailed to a certain degree during the seventeenth and eighteenth centuries in France and in the German-speaking countries. Since such large spheres were formed where the domestic system prevailed, the new industrial method was felt to be a considerable improvement, and its chief promoters were greeted as national benefactors. A German economist of the period wrote : "There are instances where, owing to them, splendid towns have arisen, and thousands of men have earned an honest living ; they make the country populous and productive, and are profitable members of the commonwealth, whose object is to increase and to support the 'societas civilis.'" Frederic the Great termed his Silesian weaving districts the Prussian Peru.

It has been already noticed that the method of working under the domestic system remained the same as existed before in the handicrafts, but the change in the method of the disposal of the products is connected with widely reaching social consequences. The master workman under the domestic system often, it is true, works with assistants, frequently is also owner of the tools, and even of a part of the raw material, quite like the master handicraftsman. But he no longer disposes of the goods to different customers : he delivers them, in return for payment of a previously settled wage, either to the capitalistic merchant, or to intermediate agents, "middlemen," who distribute the raw materials, superintend the work, collect the products, and pay out the wages.

Thus he is still master in his house, but he usually sells the products of his labour in accordance with the commissions received, and thus stands towards the merchant in the same relation as the workman to the employer. The result follows from this that the master workman in the domestic system can no longer hold the independent position towards the capitalistic merchant that the master handicraftsman has towards his customers. They must, therefore, in the course of time sink more and more into the position of ordinary workmen, while the merchants sweep in the substantial profits which are possible in all industries intended for a large and regular market. "On the one side, persons who know the world ; who, through their **The Social** knowledge of markets and their **Question's** solvency, relieve the small pro- **Dark Side** ducers of the anxiety of selling ; who, by their journeys, their giving credit, and their connections, transact sales, and can bear occasional losses better than the producers ; who grasp technical improvements more quickly, since they stand higher in education and are of a quicker intelligence. On the other side, small master workmen, peasants, inhabitants of small towns and of the mountains, women and children who are glad to get work, who, in addition to their industrial work are busied with agriculture and cattle breeding ; who are day labourers, with limited ideas, possessing no great technical qualifications, no large capital, no division of labour, but slow to adopt anything new, and clinging tenaciously to their old customs. The master workman in the domestic system thus is nearly always placed at a disadvantage as compared with the merchant, who knows his business and, being a capitalist, can wait his time."

The result of this is a dark side to the social question, which formerly, indeed, when merely the extent of the sales and the interests of the capitalistic producer were considered, could not have been sufficiently realised. Firstly, the lower

wages of these producers under the domestic system ; secondly, the "sweating" of these isolated, and therefore unprotected, workers by the merchant employer through reduction of wages in particular, through usurious payment for goods and deceitful calculations of the raw materials furnished ; lastly—in the **Distress** case of more unfavourable **of the Home** conditions, namely, loss of the **Workers** old markets and similar difficulties—the greatest distress existing among these very "home workers," because, wishing to turn to some account not merely their powers of work, but their tools, which usually represent their only possessions, they are compelled to accept work at any wage, even though it only affords the barest livelihood. In this way matters have gone so far that certain districts where the domestic system prevails have become the first scenes of modern pauperism on a large scale.

Attempts were made to meet the requirements of the wholesale market by yet another form of work besides the domestic system—namely, the manufactory, which, indeed, has developed more slowly than the former. It consists in the employment by one contractor of a large number of workmen for purposes of production in one building. According to this definition, it does not depend, as the domestic system, on wholesale selling, but on wholesale production. The consequences are far-reaching. In the first place, where many workmen are busied in the manufacture of one product, an extensive division of the work within the workshop itself can often be effected. The article is no longer the production of one independent craftsman who does various things, but the production of a number of craftsmen working together, each one of whom is continuously discharging one and the same part of the work. The watch which under the guild system was the individual work **Labour** of a Nüremberg craftsman **Under New** becomes in the age of manu- **Conditions** factories the production of a number of different workmen. There are now employed on it, makers of the rough material, the watch-spring, dial, main-spring, hands, case, screws, etc., a gilder, and a "repasseur," who puts the whole watch together and turns it out in a going condition. The execution is still a "handwork," and therefore dependent on the strength, dexterity, expedition, and accuracy of the individual workman in the handling of his tool. But since the same workman is always closely employed on the same separate part, the manufactory creates great skill in the particular workman. If already from this reason more goods are turned out by manufacture with a less expenditure of labour than in independent handwork, the specialisation of tools now customary must tend in the same direction ; for since the working tools are now suited to the exclusively peculiar employments of the individual workman, they thus attain a greater perfection than before, and must at the same time increase the productive power of the work.

Results of the Factory System

Since, again, the result of one man's work is the starting point for the work of another, the uninterrupted progress of the collective work presupposes that in a given working time a given result will be obtained, and that everything is systematically organised. By this inter-dependence every single man is bound to devote only the necessary time to his operation, by which means continuity, uniformity, regularity, order, and intensity in the work are created on a scale quite different from that in independent handwork.

Again, the workmen, through the division of the collective work into simple and complex, lower and higher employments, can be assigned tasks according to their natural or acquired capabilities. Thus, a hierarchy of workers is formed, to which a scale of wages corresponds. Production is, however, naturally assisted by the fact that the capitalist " can procure for himself the exact degree of strength and skill corresponding to every operation." Further, all production requires a number of simple occupations, of which every man who walks is capable; these, again, at a time when all operations are resolved into their simplest parts, develop themselves into exclusive occupations of special workmen. The manufactory thus creates a class of unskilled workmen whom the handwork system rigidly excluded. In this way the cheap labour of women and children can be employed.

A Field for Cheap Labour

Manufactories were started in considerable numbers in England after the last third of the sixteenth century, and for 200 years continually gained in importance. Since the old town corporations and the guild system hindered manufactories, they were by preference founded in ports with an export trade, or in places in rural districts where they were not under the control of the laws of the corporate towns. Government favoured them in pursuance of the mercantile doctrine, where possible, by protective tariffs and bounties on exports, and by prohibiting the production of certain industrial commodities in the colonies. The same policy towards the manufactories was adopted by the other states of Europe.

Still, we must not over-estimate the importance of manufactories at that time. Even in the eighteenth century they only partially dominated the national production among the leading civilised nations, and still rested, if we may use the expression, as an economic work of art on the broad basis of town handwork and the smaller domestic and rural industries. Even in England, where the manufactory system gained most ground, it never became so far master of the situation as to succeed in abolishing the old apprentice laws with their seven years of apprenticeship. But the manufactory system, having arrived at a certain stage of technical development, discovered methods by which it was itself surpassed. It had attained its completion in those industries which were intended to produce the tools, and especially the complicated mechanical apparatus already adopted. The stage had already been reached of setting up machines and continually perfecting them; from this moment dates the slowly and surely developing change of the greater part of manufactories into wholesale industries worked with machinery. This is the change which has impressed a distinctive stamp on the industrial production, and thus on the social life of the nineteenth century.

Coming of the Machine

The machine, with which a new era in the economic-technical development of the modern civilised world is commenced, is in the first place technically distinguished from the implement of production in earlier times, the tool. It represents a far more complete form of working implement, permits the employment of mechanical motive powers, wind, water, steam, and electricity, to a conspicuous extent, and thus enormously increases the power of production. While Adam Smith, in his day, relates with admiration that in a manufactory ten men daily turn out 48,000 needles—*i.e.*, 4,800 apiece—Karl Marx records without surprise that a machine for needle-making daily turns out 145,000 needles, and that therefore one woman, whose regular duty it is to attend to four such machines, daily produces by machinery 600,000 needles, as much as 125 of Adam Smith's men. The difference, however, between a machine and a tool, looked at from the

fact, of any human organ which moves itself during the work in the same direction as that in which the tool is moved.

The workman can, therefore, regard the tool as a supplementary organ of himself, and himself as the master of the tool. In this sense, therefore, a spinning-wheel and a hand-loom are tools, for the workman remains master of these working implements, which, besides, only serve to strengthen the movement of the human organs. But so soon as an implement effects more than such an addition of strength, as soon as the man's powers move in a direction which is entirely divergent from the movement exclusively produced by the mechanism, it becomes a machine. A locomotive, therefore, is a machine, for the handles are moved by the stoker and engine-driver in a different direction entirely from the locomotive which draws the load over the lines. Hence the differences between tool and machine, and, in connection with this, between manufactory and factory, or mill, have been summed up as follows : In a manufactory and handwork the

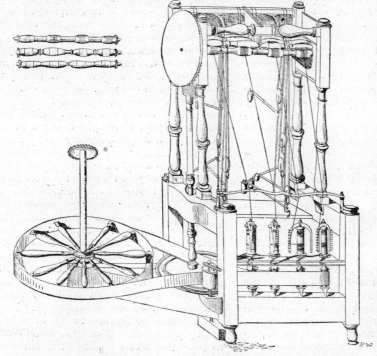

THE AGE OF MACHINERY: ARKWRIGHT'S SPINNING JENNY

The introduction of machinery marked a great advance in the industrial development of the country, though the innovation was by no means welcomed by the workers. About the year 1765, a spinning machine—the "Jenny"—was invented, which at first set six, and soon afterwards twenty-five, spindles simultaneously in movement, and could be used in the homes of the workmen. But later machines required to be housed in factory buildings, and thus there sprang up a new system of labour that spread with remarkable rapidity.

technical standpoint, is only quantitative, while from the social point of view it is qualitative. From this aspect the position of the workman who uses the implement is the criterion; and it is seen that the position of the workman occupied with the machine is distinguished, both by the nature of the employment as well as by its place in wholesale business generally, from the position of the workman using tools. A hammer, a file, and such-like are simple tools. They increase the strength of the human arm or foot, in

workman avails himself of the tool; in the factory he attends to the machine. In the former the movement of the working implement is due to him; in the latter he has to follow its movement. In a word, out of the livelong habit of guiding a special tool comes the livelong habit of "tending" a special machine. "During the manufacture period the exercise of hand labour, though distributed, remains the basis. The workmen thus form the members of a living mechanism. In the 'factory' there exists a dead mechanism independent of them, and they are incorporated into it as living appendages." In this sense a factory is defined by Andrew Ure, the first philosopher of the factory system, as a great automaton, composed of various partly mechanical, partly self-conscious organs, which work harmoniously and uninterruptedly in order to produce one and the same object. The peculiar form of combined production in this form of industry leads to the result that the factory fully develops many tendencies which are only suggested in the manufactory.

Factors in the Success of Machinery

The separation of all the mental parts of the process of production from the handwork, the resolution of all processes into their component parts—that is, into the simplest movements—and the principle of carrying out the separate operations by distinct workmen suited for the purpose, from the doctor of chemistry down to the newly engaged rustic and the child are all perfected for the first time under this system. And this again combines to make a barrack-like discipline, and, corresponding to this, a universal, uniform intensity of work, necessary if the factory system, with its various workers and all its complex operations, is to perform its functions properly. Men must now abandon their irregular habits of work, and imitate the uniform regularity of machinery.

Ure had good reason to speak of the "myriads of vassals" who are collected round the steam king in the great workshops. But it was this very peculiarity, together with the enormous increase in production, that contributed to the success of machinery and factories; for, while the work was done with a hitherto unsuspected uniformity, continuity, regularity, and speed, all the expectations of an industrial production of goods for the supply of international markets were fulfilled. The important inventions of machines, which ushered in the new age of factories, had been made in the second half of the eighteenth century in the young cotton industry. This industrial revolution had been preceded by the "ribbon mill," which served for the weaving of ribbons and trimmings. This had been worked at Danzig as early as the sixteenth century, but had been suppressed by the council on account of the damage done to competing handicraftsmen. In the seventeenth

Rise of the Cotton Industry

century it was set up at Leyden, and after various prohibitions by the council, was finally allowed by the Dutch Government. In the German Empire its use was nevertheless still forbidden, at first by municipal and then by imperial edicts, which were in force until the middle of the eighteenth century; while in England the ribbon mill had long been introduced, although it had given rise to disturbances among injured handworkers and discharged journeymen.

After the last third of the eighteenth century the inventions of the spinning and weaving machines, the forerunner of which had been the ribbon mill, followed in rapid succession. About the year 1765, a spinning-machine, the so-called "jenny," was invented, which at first set six, and soon afterwards twenty-five spindles simultaneously in movement, but could still be used in the house of a master. On the other hand, the "water frame," which was constructed by Arkwright directly afterwards, and was a machine driven by water or steam, and distinctly more effective, necessitated a special factory building. The first factory was erected by Arkwright himself at Nottingham in 1768. The new method of work was immediately adopted throughout the United Kingdom. Within twenty years England and Scotland saw not less than 142 great spinning mills founded, in which 92,000 workmen set into motion more than 2,000,000 spindles, and produced goods of more than £7,000,000 in value.

Arkwright's First Spinning Mill

The details of the machinery were now quickly perfected. After 1790, when Watt invented his steam engine, the factories were no longer dependent on water power, and thus could be erected in any place, and not merely on the banks of rivers. From this period dates the concentration of factories in the towns. In 1803, the "dressing-frame" was invented, by which means a child was enabled to attend to two looms at once, and could weave about three times as much as an industrious hand-weaver.

Other industries, the woollen industry, the cotton industry, the iron industry, the smelting and mining industries, equally shared in the development of the details of machinery, and completed the transition to the factory industry.

The introduction of the factory system had the most far-reaching results on industrial and social life. In very impor tant branches of industrial activity,

MULE SPINNING MACHINES AT WORK IN ONE OF THE EARLIEST MILLS

A VIEW OF STOCKPORT, SHOWING ITS NUMEROUS FACTORIES, IN 1834

WOMEN ATTENDING TO THE CARDING, DRAWING AND ROVING MACHINES

BRITAIN'S INDUSTRIAL DEVELOPMENT: FACTORIES IN THE YEAR 1834

especially in cotton spinning and weaving, the factory showed itself far superior to the former domestic and handwork systems. Handwork was in these departments soon put aside, or at least condemned to insignificance ; but the " domestic " industry showed distinctly more vitality, owing to its peculiar organisation. If the employ-

Ruin of the English Hand-Weavers ment of machinery in the factory reduced the cost of production for the article, the same final result was produced by the merchant-employer in the domestic industry through reduction of wages and the " sweating " of the home worker.

In this way abuses became inherent in the domestic industry, which afterwards weighed like a curse on this system of work. They became possible because the home workers submitted to the lowering of their conditions of life, for they had no way of escape. Thus Karl Marx, without any great exaggeration, could exclaim: "The history of the world shows no more terrible spectacle than the gradual ruin, which lingered on for decades, but was finally sealed in 1838, of the English handweavers, many of whom, with their families, eked out an existence on 2½d. a day. This was the effect of the factory system on the workers of competing trades."

It was equally disastrous originally to the workers in the factory. " In so far as machinery dispenses with the necessity of muscular strength, it becomes a means of employing workers without muscular strength or of immature physical development but greater suppleness of limb. Women's and children's labour was therefore the first word of the capitalistic employment of machinery." It was therefore most remunerative to exact from these cheap workers, who were the least capable of resisting, quite distinctly longer hours of labour. On this point an official report in England establishes the fact that " before the law was passed for the protection of

Apprentices from the Workhouses youthful workers, in 1833, children and young persons had to work the whole night or the whole day, or both ad libitum." John Fielden, a Liberal philanthropist from the middle class, wrote : " In Derbyshire, Nottinghamshire, and especially in Lancashire, the recently discovered machinery was set up in factories close by streams capable of turning the water-wheel. Thousands of hands were suddenly required in these places, far from the towns.

The custom crept in of obtaining apprentices from the different parish workhouses of London, Birmingham, and elsewhere. The manufacturer had to clothe his apprentices, feed them, and lodge them in an ' apprentices' house ' near the factory. Overseers were appointed to superintend their work ; but since their wages stood in proportion to the amount of results that could be extracted from the children, self-interest bade these slave-drivers make the children drudge unmercifully.

The consequence was that the children were hounded to death by overwork. The gains of the manufacturers were gigantic, but that only whetted their ghoulish voracity. They began the practice of night work—i.e., after the one batch of hands was utterly worn out by the day work, they had another batch ready for the night work ; the day batch went off to the beds which the night batch had just left, and vice versa. It was a popular tradition in Lancashire that the beds were never cold." But even the hours of labour for the men, who were unorganised, and

The Difficult Problem of Unemployment did not yet feel themselves, as later, to be a unity, were only too often enormously extended. Sober writers of this period have been able to describe the English factory hand as crushed to a lower level than that of West Indian slaves. But not even this modest existence was permanently secured to the worker. There have been, of course, at all times in the history of every civilised country cases of men, willing and able to work, being out of employment ; but only since the modern economico-technical development, and since the introduction of the corresponding legislature, has this evil, temporarily at least, assumed unsuspected dimensions. It is connected with the frequency of the occurrence of unfavourable turns of the market and of commercial crises.

These consist mainly in the impossibility of either selling the goods produced wholesale at any price approximate to the old prices, or of profitably continuing the business generally on the old extensive scale. The vendors, manufacturers, and merchants suffer heavy losses, and perhaps become bankrupt. In any case the production must be restricted, and thousands of workmen, from no fault of their own, lose their situations.

THE RISE AND FALL OF CHARTISM
AND THE FAILURE OF OWEN'S SOCIALISM

THE labour class revolted against the evils of the factory system at first in a quite barbarous fashion, by riotously attacking the manufacturers and by destroying the factories, and especially the machines, which were frequently regarded as the source of all disaster. It was only gradually that this involuntary opposition of the proletariat to the manufacturing capitalist took the form of a strike. But before the workers arrived at a full knowledge of the power of this weapon, if properly used, and acted accordingly, a movement arose which, starting from a philanthropic point of view, undertook to cure the social ills by radical proposals of reform.

Robert Owen, 1771–1858, a self-made man, who had risen while still young to be co-proprietor of a great cotton mill in New Lanark, Scotland, first made the attempt there on a limited scale after 1801

Owen's Famous Factory to remedy by a thoughtful solicitude for the workers the evils which have been described. He removed the children under ten years of age from the factory, limited the daily hours of labour for the adults to ten hours, constructed healthy dwellings as well as pleasure grounds for the workmen, arranged for the co-operative supply of provisions and other commodities, provided gratuitous attendance for the sick, and finally paid full wages to the operatives of his factory when, on account of the failure of cotton, they were obliged to remain idle.

But although Owen's factory, which, in spite of the great outlay for the welfare of the workers, had also material success, was famed throughout all Europe, and became the goal of philanthropists, statesmen, and kings on their tours, yet the example set by it was only occasionally followed by other factory owners. Owen was led by this fact to the conclusion that the deep-rooted evils could only be ended by universally binding legislation.

Thus he was the first to raise the demand for factory laws in 1813, and soon initiated a vigorous agitation with that object. After 1817 he devoted himself with peculiar energy to the problem of remedying the want of employment, which at that time, **The State's Duty to the Unemployed** just when the first commercial crisis was appearing on English soil, occupied all thoughtful minds. His proposal, which was based on earlier ones of John Bellers, required the State to provide quarters for all persons capable of work but fallen out of employment, in special rural establishments, where they might be engaged in systematic productive work, either agricultural or industrial. By following out these thoughts he came to the conception of his socialistic system, but from that time his interest in the direct amelioration of the lot of the operative by "small means" began to wane.

The fundamental principle of the system of Owen, which was supported by copious arguments in two books, "A New View of Society," 1813, and "A Book of the New Moral World," 1836–1844, assumes that the character of every man is mainly determined by appropriate education and a corresponding form of environment; indeed, Owen thinks that "children can be educated to adopt any habits and ideas that may be wished, so long as they are not absolutely contrary to human nature." Nothing, unfortunately, he finds, is done to restrain the people from the inconsiderate pursuit of their desires; the consequence is the perverted condition **Miseries of Industrial Workers** of the world at present, shown by the misery of the industrial proletariat. The reason why no steps have been taken in this matter is found in the defective insight of our rulers; they did not even know the appropriate means to perfect men's characters. But now, so Owen declares, the means are obvious to everyone since the attempt has been successfully made in New Lanark to raise the employees by moral education to a much higher level of morality.

It is merely necessary to guide men towards a correct comprehension of that personal happiness at which they all aim; that is to say, everyone should adopt that line of conduct which must promote the happiness of the community. Formerly men did not know this supreme law which governs the world ; but now it is revealed, and can easily be made clear to all, that the personal happiness of the individual can only be increased in proportion as he exerts himself to promote the happiness of his neighbours. As soon as these fundamental propositions are part and parcel of every man, the separate means are not far to seek which can procure the greatest sum of happiness for the individual as well as for all mankind.

This proposition shows quite clearly that Owen must be regarded as a genuine scion of the philosophy of the eighteenth century, who shares its rationalistic and utilitarian ideas as well as its incorrigible and ambitious optimism. He believes with all sincerity that these bald propositions might renew the religion and morality of the world. "Here," he announces, "we have a firm foundation, on which a pure, unstained religion instinct with life may be constructed, and this the only one which can grant to mankind peace and happiness without any counteracting evil." Owen was, however, far too well acquainted with practical life and its needs to content himself, like the theorists of the eighteenth century, with ethical and educational suggestions. On the contrary, he completely realised that even the moral man, if he has not the opportunity offered him of earning his living by labour, must succumb to temptation. He was therefore led to establish, by the side of his educational system, a system of state-organised labour. This culminated in the

general application of the scheme, which we have already mentioned, for the aid of the unemployed. The whole work of production was to be carried out in communities of two, three, or four thousand souls, where the adults, by eight hours' common work daily, were to obtain most of the products, industrial and agricultural, required for their own use, and were to acquire the rest by exchanging their surplus products for the surplus products of the other communities.

The leading thought in this is distinctly " that each one of these communities shall be self-supporting, and shall be held responsible for its deficiencies." No special fundamental propositions for the distribution of goods—certainly the most difficult question in any communistic organisation of society — were advanced by Owen. How could any dispute arise when all were filled with deep morality, and where, in consequence of the immense increase in production, there were goods in abundance for everyone ? It was possible, therefore, to determine the individual needs, and then to allot to each person his share in the goods of this life. In order to start his plans, Owen, himself self-sacrificing to the highest degree, turned to the upper classes, where he expected to find equally great philanthropy. It was not until this appeal to the humanity of the

Owen's Appeal to the Rich

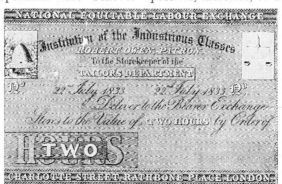

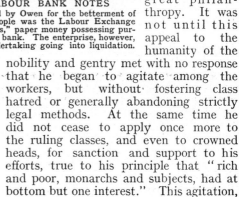

ONE OF OWEN'S LABOUR BANK NOTES

Among the many schemes started by Owen for the betterment of the conditions of the working people was the Labour Exchange Bank, which issued "labour notes," paper money possessing purchasing value in the stores of the bank. The enterprise, however, was a complete failure, the undertaking going into liquidation.

nobility and gentry met with no response that he began to agitate among the workers, but without fostering class hatred or generally abandoning strictly legal methods. At the same time he did not cease to apply once more to the ruling classes, and even to crowned heads, for sanction and support to his efforts, true to his principle that " rich and poor, monarchs and subjects, had at bottom but one interest." This agitation, which at times had been conducted with great spirit—Owen, between 1826 and 1837,

NEW LANARK AS IT WAS IN OWEN'S TIME, SHOWING HIS MODEL FACTORY

had issued 500 addresses, made 1,000 public speeches, and written 2,000 newspaper articles—met with the most vigorous opposition from the clergy, who, bitterly incensed at Owen's attacks on the Church, organised a counter movement. Even the regular popular party of the time, the Radicals, emphatically opposed Owen; for their goal was at first purely political—namely, the extension of the franchise. Owen had, however, declared the dispute for this political privilege to be unimportant, since all true popular interests could only be advanced by educational and economic reforms.

The total failure of Owen's communistic agitation was decided by the lamentable collapse of his communistic settlements, on the founding of which he was determined, since the English worker could not be convinced by doctrinaire arguments, but only by practical trial. So little was ever produced in these settle-

Failure of Communistic Settlements ments that the rations of the colonists had to be reduced to the barest limits. Thus discontent was developed, which finally led to the abandonment of the settlements, naturally not without considerable financial loss to Owen.

He did not fare better with the Labour Exchange Bank started in 1832. This was intended to apply practically the ideal principle of all exchange, the equality between the products and the profits of labour; a scheme which, if successful, would have led to the establishment of a socialistic community in the middle of capitalistic political economy. Every member of the bank could display goods in his shop, for which he at once received "labour notes," paper money issued by the bank. The amount of the labour notes paid was decided by the value of the raw material and the extent of labour required for the production of the goods in question on the average, not by the depositor himself only.

Owen's plans were therefore exposed to the ridicule whose shafts always inflict deadly wounds. The downfall of the communistic school in Britain was thus sealed. The factory population now fell under the influence of the politically revolutionary "Chartism." Owen could not support its illegal excesses and struggles for political privileges; and later, after Chartism, came the reign of trades unions and co-operative societies. While Owen's propaganda, in spite of exertions for many decades, only affected a small part of the working class—precisely its most moral and self-sacrificing members—towards the end of the "thirties" a powerful Labour party was suddenly formed in England. It happened as follows. During the violent popular movement which had carried the reform of the franchise in 1832, the working classes had been brought forward as auxiliaries by the Liberal citizens. Although the reform, in the nature of things, could only enfranchise the middle class, yet it was assumed that the interests of the working classes were to be subsequently better considered by the legislature than heretofore. Since a Bill of the Radicals to extend the circle of the franchise was rejected by a crushing majority and the reform was declared by Lord John Russell, the leader of the Liberals, to be definitely concluded, the workmen formed unions of their own. These were intended to bring about, by a fresh popular agitation, a renewed reform of the franchise, which should this time really consider the interests of the people.

Labour Unions Founded

At the head of these unions stood the "London Workmen's Association," founded in 1836, which proposed the following programme, originally drawn up by the Liberals : Universal suffrage, vote by ballot, equal electoral districts, annual elections of Parliament, abolition of property qualifications for Parliamentary candidates, and salaries for the members. This programme was proclaimed as the "People's Charter," because it was to serve the interests of the lower classes, just as, centuries before, the Magna Charta had served the interest of the aristocracy and middle classes ; and, therefore, the supporters of this programme were termed "Chartists." Their intention was to alter social legislation in favour of the masses by help of their political demands, which were intended to be realised at once. It was therefore expressly stated in the first appeal which the London Workmen's Association in 1838 addressed to workmen of the whole kingdom : "If we are fighting for an equality of political rights, this is not done in order to shake off an unjust tax or to effect a transference of wealth, power, and influence in favour of any one party. We do so in order to be able to cut off the source of our social misery, and by successful methods of prevention to avoid the infliction of penalties under unrighteous laws."

What the "People's Charter" Demanded

In all manufacturing towns, which had long been roused to violent excitement by systematic agitations against the Poor Law and the deplorable condition of the work-

men, the Chartist programme was received as a joyful message, and wherever factory chimneys smoked Chartist unions were sure to be found.

But this rapid success was only attained because the agitators had held out false hopes of immediate victory to themselves and their followers from among the working and middle classes. They calculated that, as in the reform movement of 1832, the ruling powers would once more yield to a vigorous popular movement. This was the fundamental error which was to prove disastrous to the party. When, indeed, in February, 1839, at a meeting of the "National Convention," the question of their subsequent course was raised, the inevitable result of that delusive agitation was that the party of "moral right," led by the Owenite, William Lovett, 1800–1877, with its programme of peaceful propaganda and a monster petition to Parliament, only represented the minority. The majority was composed of the party of "physical force," who took their battle-cry from Feargus O'Connor, 1796–1855, and thought themselves powerful enough to break down the strong fabric of the old system. It was resolved, in the event of the charter being refused by Parliament, to proclaim a "holy month," to strike work simultaneously in every industry. A petition for the introduction of the charter, supposed to contain more than a million signatures, was rejected, and riots immediately broke out.

Failure of Revolutionary Socialism

For some time after that the doctrine was quiescent. But in July, 1840, the party was reorganised, on the basis of the principle that the charter was to be introduced by legal means. When, however, in the year 1842, a new monster petition was absolutely rejected by the Lower House, the "party of physical force" again came to the surface

Chartism lingered on, until finally in 1848, after the February Revolution in Paris, it roused itself for a last trial of strength, but its effort was again a failure. Revolutionary Socialism in England had had its day. Nevertheless, this movement had not passed away without leaving a trace, for "it had produced one great result : it had roused the English working classes to the most outlying corners of the land from their traditional ideas of subjection, and made them realise their separate interests as a class."

THE TRIUMPH OF TRADES UNIONS
AND THE ESTABLISHMENT OF CO-OPERATION

THE movements which we have hitherto considered had met with no practical results. A better fate was reserved for one which, originating with the working classes themselves, endeavoured to attend to their interests on the basis of self-help, the movement of Labour Associations.

Trades Unions Regarded as Conspiracies Trades unions are workmen's self-defence associations for the purpose of improving the conditions of labour as well as for the protection of their professional interests generally. They were started in England, partly in connection with older journeymen's unions, in considerable numbers as early as the eighteenth century, when the first waves of the victoriously advancing capitalistic production burst on the working classes. But they were immediately resisted by legislature and heavy judicial sentences. English law extended the idea of conspiracy, which properly ought to be applied only to combinations for the commission of crimes or for the production of false evidence against third persons, to all combinations of workmen who wished to obtain higher wages.

A long list of special enactments forbidding coalitions in various trades had been issued throughout the whole eighteenth century. Finally, at the close of the century a strict general Act was passed which made all agreements between workmen, with the object of raising wages or lessening the hours or quantity of labour, punishable with imprisonment, and inflicted similar penalties on all who deterred a workman from accepting definite posts or caused him to leave them. The complete one-sidedness of these enactments is clearly seen in the fact that combinations of the employers, in order to influence wages, were only punishable by fines. The consequence of this was that at the beginning of the nineteenth century

Workmen's Coalitions Prohibited

secret trades unions had been formed everywhere, which, since all their demonstrations were treated with equal severity, employed the most reckless and reprehensible means for the attainment of their objects. Workmen who refused all complicity with their comrades, especially in strikes, the so-called "blacklegs," were actually attacked and sometimes fell victims to murderous onslaughts. The authorities naturally lost no time in proceeding to the severest counter measures. Labour coalitions could not, however, be suppressed, a sure proof that these represented in the age of capitalistic production a purely instinctive movement.

The prohibition of coalitions of workmen must have seemed to every impartial observer the more unjust, since coalitions of employers for the purpose of lowering wages were, thanks to the class justice of the English magistrates, always unpunished. A parliamentary report of 1824 states : "A number of cases have been communicated to us, in which employers of labour have been charged with combining together in order to lower the wages or to lengthen the hours of labour ; but a case could never be adduced in which any employer had been punished for this misdemeanour."

Class Justice of English Magistrates

Owing to the effect produced by a parliamentary inquiry proving the injustice and futility of the laws in question, a Bill of the Radical, Joseph Hume, was carried, which expunged from the statute book the prohibition on coalition, and threatened with imprisonment only cases of violence, menaces, or intimidation used for the purpose of forcing workmen to join a coalition, or of compelling employers to grant concessions to the workmen, in 1824. These privileges were indeed considerably restricted in the very next year, when the combinations suddenly spread over the whole country, and seemed to threaten seriously all the proprietary interests of the citizen class ; for it was now ordained that conspiracies should include " all meetings about the labour conditions of absent persons, as well as those about the persons whom a master is to employ or not to employ, and about the machines which he is to use ; and further, all agreements not to work with a definite person, or to induce other persons to suspend or refuse to accept work."

Notwithstanding that these provisions threatened with penalties many proceedings which proved to be inseparable from an effective employment of labour associations, and actually gave cause to a number of convictions, they have not been able to check the victorious career of the trades unions. It was after 1825 that the labour associations assumed the form typical of their policy and their importance in the history of the world. Up to about 1830 they were strictly local combinations of workers in similar trades. But since in this way, owing to the weakness of the union, they could not adequately meet their duties—namely, to give relief in the case of strikes, want of employ-

Trades Unions as " Unlawful " Combinations ment, sickness, or incapacity—they saw themselves compelled spontaneously to start national unions in the separate branches. Since the trades unions, safeguarding the interests of the labour class with tenacious energy, frequently caused prolonged strikes, public opinion, influenced by the daily Press, which served the middle class, was long unfavourable to them.

The courts thus treated trades unions as " unlawful " combinations, and therefore, according to the old English law, refused them legal protection. Thus, for example, thefts of the property of trades unions were not liable to prosecution. Thus, again, after excesses had been committed by members of trades unions during riots, various steps were taken to suppress the organisations. The last attempt of this kind occurred in 1866. But a Royal Commission then appointed to investigate the nature of trades unions served to destroy many popular prejudices.

The official recognition of the trades unions dates from that time. It was announced by special laws of 1871 and 1876, the latter passed under the Conservative Cabinet of Disraeli, which sought the support of the Labour party, that trades unions could not be regarded as unlawful unions. So far as no direct com-

pulsion was used, liberty to strike was permitted to the fullest extent, since, for example, the posting of " pickets " in the vicinity of factories or dwelling-houses was expressly allowed. Besides this, the privileges of a " legal entity " were granted to those trades unions which had their regulations enrolled. " They may sue and

A New Era for the Trades Unions be sued, hold personal and real property, and take summary proceedings against their officials for dishonesty."

For this reason the Congress of the Trades Unions at Glasgow expressed to the Conservative party their " fullest acknowledgments of the greatest benefit that had ever been granted to the sons of toil."

From that time the formerly persecuted unions, which comprise at the present day some 1,400,000 members, are considered in England " respectable," and have a certain share in the government ; secretaries of trades unions are promoted to be factory inspectors, justices of the peace, or even members of the Ministry. But a more important point is that the public opinion of the country sees in trades unions a necessary institution, and often in disputes with employers takes the side of the workmen's combination.

The Government, when preparing labour laws, always applies for the advice of the trades unions. In the contracts of the Government and of many communities the observance of the terms of labour required by the trades unions is a preliminary stipulation. And, in places, a sort of constitutional management has been developed since the manager of the factory usually consults with the union about any circumstances which can at all affect the interests of the workmen.

If we make it clear to ourselves what trades unionism has done, we cannot refuse to acknowledge it as a splendid proof of the practical sense and great political capacity of the British working

Labour's Debt to Owen classes. It is a special characteristic of British common-sense that the Utopian ideas prevalent only largely contributed to strengthen the power of the current of reform. The leaders of the trades unions movement were thorough-going followers of Owen, but they derived from the teaching of the great optimist merely the distant ideal of the future, while they devoted all their energies in the present to immediate practical improvements of the lot of the workman. Trades unions, in pursuing this policy, recognised for decades no alternative in the event of the refusal of their demands except a strike. When, however, the workmen had become wiser and their unions had collected large sums, the next step was that they looked for means which led to this goal without the employment of this two-edged sword. The employers also would naturally welcome, from the standpoint of their interests, any possibility of avoiding open war. " As soon as both parties merely consult their interests,

established by A. J. Mundella, at Nottingham, the centre of the manufacturing industries. This board consisted of ten representatives of the workmen and employers respectively. But every proposal as to the interpretation of the old, or the introduction of new, labour conditions had to be first brought before the so-called committee of inquiry, composed of two representatives of the workmen and the employers respectively. If this committee failed to come to an agreement, but not otherwise, the case was brought before the general meeting. The decision

SETTLING THE GREAT COAL STRIKE: THE CONFERENCE AT THE FOREIGN OFFICE

In 1893 the industries of the country were seriously interrupted by the prolonged dispute between the colliers and the mine-owners, the struggle lasting for about four months, and involving much suffering and financial loss. Lord Rosebery, at that time Secretary for Foreign Affairs in the Gladstone administration, was successful in arranging at the Foreign Office, on November 17th, a conference, over which he presided, between representatives of the Federal Coal-Owners and the Miners' Federation of Great Britain, terms being then agreed upon which ended the labour war.

they will ask themselves whether the object of the struggle—namely, to measure their strength—cannot be equally well attained by human judgment, just as the pressure of steam is ascertained by the application of some mechanism, instead of being learnt from the bursting of the boiler." From these considerations the system of "arbitration boards" grew up in Britain; these were intended to settle the disputes between labour and capital in a peaceful way. The type of many boards of this kind is the "board of arbitration" of 1860

adopted there had an absolute binding force on the disputing parties for a definite time, since the contract for work must contain the declaration of all parties thereto, that in the points at issue they will submit, without protest, to the decisions of the arbitration boards. The favourable experiences of this system, and of the system of Rupert Kettle, as county court judge, which was first tested in the building industry at Wolverhampton, led to the imitation of these systems in a number of industrial towns, and they were soon sanctioned by the

Legislature through the granting of appeals to the courts against the decisions of the chambers of arbitration by the Arbitration Act of August 6th, 1872. These systems have been finally perfected even in places where strong trades unions oppose equally close combinations of employers. Thus, in the coal industry of the counties of Durham and Northumberland, **Settling Disputes by Arbitration** a permanent committee of six representatives of each party, with a neutral president, settles all separate disputes resulting from the application of the labour contract, which holds uniformly good for the entire district. On the other hand, disputes as to the constitution of the labour contracts themselves—that is to say, as to the general principles of hours of labour and pay—are, so far as possible, settled by the full meeting of the employers in combination with the delegates of the trades unions. If no agreement results, the matter is referred to arbitration.

Each party is here represented by two arbitrators, who, for their part, choose the umpire, who delivers the final decision. A regular trial takes place before him, as before a court ; evidence is tendered, witnesses are cross-examined, and speeches are made on both sides by the aforesaid arbitrators, who in reality are counsel. " The complete technical knowledge of the parties engaged, as well as the strength of the organisations backing them up, produces the result that these proceedings are carried out with the same acuteness, and are as smoothly transacted, as dealings between the largest business houses."

The award is unconditionally carried out by the two interested groups. The existence of the trades unions presupposes this, since otherwise no one would accept the responsibility beforehand of ensuring that many thousand workmen would really submit to the award. This is, of course, valid only for a definite number of months ; after that there **Duties of the Arbitrator** must be a renewal of the old agreements, or a fresh examination of them. If the arbitrator gave his decision merely in accordance with his sympathies, this would have no lasting validity, but would only conceal in itself the germ for later conflicts. For this very reason " the arbitrator, like any third person called in to settle prices between two independent parties, has merely to ascertain that which, if he did not intervene, would be established as the natural limit of the price. Since he is called in to avoid conflict, he has to accomplish the same result as a conflict— namely, the reasonable settlement of the mutual conditions of power. Only when he has done that is he sure that his verdict will be lasting." A case in the year 1877 shows how little any awards which attempt to settle matters by moral considerations are able to arrange a dispute permanently.

Sir Farrer Herschell, as arbitrator, rejected the request of the colliery owners of Northumberland for a reduction in the wages of the miners. The owners submitted for the three months during which the award was to have validity, but immediately afterwards they renewed their demand, with the declaration that this time they must put the award out of the question, and, when the miners afterwards went on strike, they proved victorious. Parliament and Government have exerted themselves to support this development as much as possible. Thus the Act for Conciliation and Arbitration of the year 1895 was passed, which gives to the **Board of Trade's new Powers** Board of Trade the right of interfering in labour disputes. The most important proviso is that the Board of Trade may itself order the parties to nominate delegates in order to settle the dispute by mutual negotiations ; on some occasions, under the presidency of a competent person designated by the Board. The Board may also, on its own responsibility, send persons to investigate the matters in dispute, and to furnish a report on the subject ; finally, it may urge the establishment of a chamber of arbitration in districts and industries which are still without one.

The chambers of arbitration have since then become more numerous, and have frequently displayed a profitable activity ; but their actual results must not be overestimated. There is hardly any institution in the social-political field which all political and social parties so combine to recommend as these very chambers of arbitration. Nevertheless, in forty years they have not been universally adopted ; in fact, very often they have been prohibited even in the limited field where their introduction was a success. This experience has clearly demonstrated that the arbitration boards are, contrary to expectation, unable to produce social peace.

The transition from communism to social reform, seen in the trades union movement, is more conspicuously prominent in the movement towards co-operation, which was the immediate result of Owen's teaching and agitation, after the clouds of illusion had lifted. Owen had encouraged the workmen to found communities in order to provide themselves with the necessaries of life by co-operative production. After many unsuccessful attempts the fact was established that co-operative stores represented the only form of community of which the labourer was at the time capable. And when this was once known, such societies and their shops sprang up like mushrooms from the soil.

Thus a movement originated in 1826 which, in the words of its historian, Mrs. Sidney Webb, "represents the first real attempt of the British labouring classes to embody in a practical form the ideas of Owen." The spirit which animated these true pioneers of social reform is aptly described by the motto with which the regulations of the society at Warrington were introduced, running as follows: "They

Rochdale Pioneers of Co-operation helped one another, each his own brother, and each said to his brother: 'Be of good cheer!'" But the young plant which blossomed so quickly and so luxuriantly—in 1832 nearly 500 co-operative stores were already in existence—faded again rapidly, and only a few years later there was hardly a trace of the whole movement, while the labour world was intensely excited by the Chartist propaganda. Its overthrow coincides with the new impetus given to the co-operative movement, which has since lasted almost uninterruptedly to the present day.

The men who then took the lead were the "Rochdale Equitable Pioneers," as twenty-eight poor flannel weavers called themselves, who, on the day after Christmas, 1844, opened the "Old Weaver's Shop" in a back street of Rochdale, with a capital of £28 in all. The statutes announced as their object "the erection of a shop for the sale of provisions, articles of clothing, etc.; the building, purchase, and fitting up of a number of houses in which the members can live who wish to help each other in the improvement of their domestic and social position; the production of such wares as the society shall determine to make, in order to provide work for unemployed, or, especially, badly paid members; the pur-

chase or renting of plots of ground for the same purpose; lastly, the establishment by this society so soon as possible of a self-supporting colony in the country, with a co-operative system of production and distribution, or the furtherance of other attempts to found similar societies." It is clearly seen here how illusions can largely contribute to success, for they

Methods of the Co-operators gave to those poor weavers, and the many thousands who followed their example, the proud consciousness that they were the disciples of a lofty ideal and the pioneers of mankind, and inspired them with that feeling of exuberant strength which made them capable of bold action and persistent effort. This social prospect could not, however, again dim the view of practical life, as was shown from the typical constitution, so often imitated, which the Rochdale Pioneers drew up for themselves.

According to it their shop made the ordinary retail prices the basis of the sales, and then divided the profits obtained from the business among the members in proportion to the extent of the purchases effected. The purchaser received a receipt, usually a tin counter, for the amount of his purchases. At the end of every quarter the counters were given back, in order that the profits might be distributed accordingly. They usually amounted in English co-operative stores to between 5 per cent. and 15 per cent. in the three months. Anyone could be a member on payment of one shilling entrance fee. Members, therefore, practically were only customers. Of course, under this arrangement every member had an interest in the extension of the body of members, because the turnover then increased, and with it the business expenses were lessened, and so the dividend became larger. After 1872 the practice began of supplying the requirements of the wholesale societies from their own factories.

Disraeli's Service to Co-operation Co-operative societies, as opposed to trades unions, were soon favoured by the legislature. Here, too, it was Disraeli who most prominently came to their aid, and procured for them, by a series of statutes, from 1852 to 1876, the rights of corporations, after formal registration, together with all other desirable privileges, and limited the liability of members to their subscribed shares in the business.

ENGAGING DOCK LABOURERS AT THE WEST INDIA DOCKS

A FAMILIAR SCENE IN TIMES OF DEPRESSION: "WE'VE GOT NO WORK TO DO!"

From the drawing by Fred. Barnard

TWO PICTORIAL STUDIES IN THE INDUSTRIAL PROBLEM

In the first of these drawings the artist has depicted the eager competition for employment which is daily to be witnessed in times of trade depression at the Docks, where casual labour finds its most likely market, while in the second the unemployed vocalists, who complain that they have "got no work to do," have evidently abandoned the search for it.

THE MARCH OF SOCIAL REFORM
AND LABOUR'S RECOGNITION BY THE STATE

THE factory system, with its various branches, had brought with it an unprecedented increase in the labour exacted from the workers, especially from the women and children. Owen, at the beginning of his social reforms, had already abolished those evils in New Lanark, where he was master. But since he saw that such an example was only exceptionally imitated by other owners of factories, he came to the conclusion that the deep-seated distress could only be ended by legislation binding on all alike.

Thus Owen was the first who raised the cry for factory laws, and soon afterwards commenced a violent agitation for this object from 1813 to 1817. The programme which he now developed contained, first, the prohibition of the industrial labour of children under ten years, as well as of all children who could not show a certain minimum of learning ; and, secondly, the **Owen's Utopian Schemes** maximum working day of six hours for children from ten to twelve years, and of ten and a half hours for all adult factory workers. Owen in this way, although he afterwards devoted his attention almost exclusively to his Utopian schemes, introduced the idea of the protection of workers into the modern social movement.

If merely the interests of the ruling class were of weight, as the materialistic theory of history asserts, the protection of the worker would never have been introduced, so long, at least, as the labouring classes possessed no influence in Parliament. As a matter of fact, this measure was proposed and passed, thanks to moral, religious, and philanthropic reasons, aided by the far-sighted deliberations of wise statesmen. The first comprehensive factory law was enacted in 1819 at the instance of Robert Peel, the father of the famous statesman, himself a manufacturer. · This prohibited the employment of children under nine years in cotton mills, and limited the working day of young persons up to sixteen years of age to twelve hours. But the law had no effective results, since the local police authorities were far too subservient to the wholesale manufacturers. A new Factory Act was passed in 1833, which appointed special **Improving the Conditions of Labour** officials to superintend the protection of the workmen— namely, factory inspectors— an institution which has been copied by all civilised states, and fixed for all textile factories a working day of eight hours for children from nine to thirteen years, and of twelve hours for young persons from thirteen to eighteen years.

Even before this, in the " twenties " of the nineteenth century, a great popular movement in favour of a ten-hour working day had commenced, which was led by a philanthropic politician, Richard Oastler, a Tory, " the manufacturing king " ; John Fielden, Thomas Sadler, and Lord Anthony Ashley, afterwards Earl of Shaftesbury, 1801–1885, were also conspicuous. This movement, which lasted almost twenty years, roused great enthusiasm amongst the working classes, and, in view of the want of employment which prevailed towards the end of the "thirties" and the high price of bread, assumed locally forms which alarmed the governing and wealthy classes.

Thus Sir Robert Peel himself declared : "The misery and the uncertainty in the position of the labouring classes is too great. It is a disgrace and a danger to our civilisation; it is absolutely necessary to make their position less hard and less precarious. **The Chartist Agitation in England** If we cannot do everything, we can at least do something, and it is our duty to do what we are able." The Chartist agitation, which was exciting all England, served finally to make people understand the state of affairs. Chartism, indeed, which had already, in 1839, failed in its main point, had been able to effect very little direct change in the social conditions ;

but its indirect results were all the greater, for its abrupt ending made the labour classes understand that it is impossible to break the strong framework of the old constitution by the employment of force. They tried, therefore, henceforth to serve their aims by conformity to the existing institutions. On the other hand, Chartism made it clear to wide circles of the ruling classes that things could no longer go on as hitherto, that the familiar "laissez-aller" policy in social matters must be abandoned. Thus there arose in the wealthy and educated class intellectual currents which were favourable to the concession of the reasonable demands of the labouring class.

The Social Gospel of Carlyle

Thomas Carlyle signalised himself as the most mighty preacher of a healthy inner life, and to him above all the credit is due of having roused the social conscience of his time. He is distinguished from the Socialists and Radicals in the principle that he considers that human society necessarily involves some notion of rule, otherwise the society could not last. But he assumes two points—that the ruling party protects and safeguards the weaker class, and that this latter is loyal and well behaved towards its leader and protector. Both, however, only thrive on the soil of the faith and the work of all concerned. Work is necessary in order to justify our existence on earth, and faith in the ideal beyond the grave is needed in order to make the severity of labour and the miseries of our existence endurable by us.

The evils of the present day, according to Carlyle's conception, have their root in the fact that all these assumed conditions of a really human existence are not forthcoming. The old relations and ties between the feudal lords and their vassals have ceased, to give place to the unsympathetic payment of ready money as the only bond, "the cash nexus," between capitalist and workman. The poor man no longer finds any protection, but remains left to himself; the result is that he has no loyal feelings for the ruling classes, but thinks only of rebellion and revolution. Faith is tottering everywhere, even if it be not lost; and finally, work has become irksome to all, so that the proletarian does it only with reluctance, while the aristocrat tries completely to avoid it. Thus men think "this universe is a large,

Worship of Mammon

capacious cattle-stall and a workhouse with an enormous kitchen and long dining-tables, and that he alone is wise who can find his place at it."

The actual circumstance that at the present time, under the rule of selfishness, the signs of the dissolution, the transitoriness, and the unendurable burden of the existing conditions are noticeable, is for Carlyle a reassuring symptom. For now only two courses are left: either the nations, eaten up by the worship of Mammon, succumb, fall a prey to foreign conquerors, and then receive, as is right, a new faith and a new aristocracy forced on them from without; or they develop for themselves new ideals and a new social fabric, in which all sections will be knit together by the bond of mutual loyalty.

It is comprehensible that in Britain especially no contentment is found, since the prevailing doctrines and institutions are unsuitable. Carlyle heaps deadly scorn on them, one after the other. Look now at the utilitarian philosophy and the corresponding national economy; they start with a world of knaves, and wish that something honest should result! Look again at the Malthusians! They imagine that the labouring class, by sexual restraint, has it in its power to diminish the number of "hands" and to improve its position. They believe in a golden age, when twenty million workers strike simultaneously in the same domain. They needed, indeed, only to pass in an all-embracing trades union the resolution not to marry until the state of the la our market was again completely satisfactory! Or look at the constitution of Parliament! "There no British subject can become a statesman, the leader in deeds, unless he has first shown himself the leader in words! Surely this is the very worst method of election that could be devised!" Or, lastly, consider the government of the existing majority! It provides neither help nor guidance to the people, but is a thing which bobs up and down on the waves of popular favour like the body of a drowned jackass. The end is that a revolt of the people gathers, and some day bursts with fury and dashes the dead body down into the mud at the bottom.

A Golden Age for the Workers

All this must be changed. But how? Carlyle promised himself but little from Socialism. He did not wish for a Utopia, even if its realisation were possible. He wished hard work for all, since that is the destiny of mankind, and a system of subordination under the most efficient, since in no other way can the continuance and advancement of human society be ensured. The old principles of government must be revived. Formerly, the lower classes stood in countless different relations to the upper classes beyond those of buyer and seller as now—in the relation of soldier and general, tribesman and chief, loyal subject and ruling monarch. "With the complete triumph of hard cash another age has come, and thus a new aristocracy must come." This is to be the "nobility of industry," which organises and conducts a noble government, and must be responded to by the subjects with loyalty and obedience. At the time there will be a few leaders of industrial undertakings who will realise this ideal; but soon there will be more and more of them, until we, at last, shall have a noble and upright country of industry under the rule of the wisest. The motto of the nobleman of the future is, "Honourable conduct in business and warm-hearted interest in the welfare of all whom he may employ." This is the theme of Carlyle's positive social policy, which he varies from time to time with new illustrations and historical parallels, now pathetically, now sadly, now with the bold flights of idealist prophecy, now with the thundering denunciations of an Old Testament prophet. Carlyle is thus the first to announce an order of things in which the philanthropic manufacturers, filled with sympathy for the community, are to form the ruling class, the social aristocracy. From this point of view all else seems incidental, if only the leading sections of the community rise, as is anticipated, of their own impulse to the realisation of a "new code of duties." If Carlyle is therefore no political Socialist, he is yet always sufficiently a friend to the working classes to advocate the State support of the lower orders; on the other hand, he is an outspoken opponent of the democratic development, which appears to him necessary only so long as the ruling classes cannot remember their duty. If we wish to form a correct estimate of Carlyle, we must not conceive him to be a scientific philosopher or a national economist; he would have been no more able to explain the principles of modern political economy than he was capable of abstruse meditations on the last problems of willing and being. His greatness rather consisted in the fact that he was a powerful writer, who knew how to awaken enthusiasm in the social policy of the nation. All his individual ideas, on account of this defective knowledge of political economy, were of no practical use, and were far too hastily sketched to be capable of application to real life; but they were the most powerful literary means for spreading among the higher classes of the nation the feeling that the workers were unjustly suffering, and that this condition must be remedied by reforms. Carlyle himself indeed believed in a future when England would be ruled by a nobility of industry, and all England soon echoed with this new rallying cry. This was an idea which, as such, represented only an illusion of the ruling classes; but an illusion

Frederic D. Maurice   Earl of Shaftesbury

PIONEER LEADERS OF SOCIAL PROGRESS

Leader of a movement which taught that "our interests are common, and every man is full of duties towards his neighbour," the Rev. F. D. Maurice was recognised as the founder of modern "Christian Socialism," while the Earl of Shaftesbury was ever in the forefront of all causes that aimed at the uplifting and Christianising of the people.

Photos by Mansell and Elliott & Fry

E. V. NEALE

A wealthy advocate of co-operation, Edward Vansittart Neale was a true friend of the working classes, aiming at peaceful reform and making sacrifices on its behalf.

whose influence led to the rejection of the Manchester dogma in labour questions by the leading circles, and to the adoption by them of a friendly attitude towards the efforts of the workers in the direction of co-operation and coalition. Next to Carlyle must be mentioned Benjamin Disraeli, afterwards Earl of Beaconsfield, 1804–1881, the founder of the first " Social-Conservative group" in Parliament, that of the so-called "Young England." He adopts the essential points of Carlyle. But we find also much that is original in his ideas ; above all, the thought of the social kingdom comes for the first time prominently forward. In recent years, he explains, definite classes have ruled in England, and the result is that struggle between those who possess property and those who have none, which, under the dominion of free competition, has produced the unhappy condition of the people.

Disraeli as a Disciple of Carlyle

This calamity must be ended by abolishing the dominion of the classes, and therefore all class legislation. The power must be given to the king, as the only constitutional authority which represents no class interests. Under monarchical government, morality and religion will once more be established in the land. And the most powerful agent is the true nobility which embraces all that has been conspicuous in the state, whether from high birth or from talent, virtues, office, or wealth.

Disraeli, in his novels "Coningsby, or the New Generation," 1844, and "Sybil, or the Two Nations," 1845, has clearly described the results of this doctrine in practical life. In them he instances the model factories, where nothing but love and concord prevail between capitalist and worker. The manufacturer also does his best in this direction, since he takes the most comprehensive measures for the prosperity of his employees, shortens their hours of labour, prepares for them good dwelling - houses, gardens, baths, schools, reading-rooms and churches, and provides for their pleasures by musical societies, games, festivals, and dancing. Many workmen, through their master's aid, actually come to be the owners of their own houses, gardens, and small farms.

Disraeli's Model Employer

This philanthropy finds its earthly reward in the efficiency and willingness of the workers, so that Disraeli's model

manufacturer declares that from the point of view of profits this investment of capital has been one of the best he has ever made. It is the duty of the young aristocratic politicians, to whom Disraeli also directly appealed, to make such a state of affairs universal. His appeal actually fired men's enthusiasm. A number of young members of the nobility, who were fresh from the university and filled with the romantic spirit of the time, formed themselves into the "Young England" party, which honoured Disraeli as its head and teacher, and was eager for social reforms.

Another movement tried to revive the old religious feeling and to lay the only true foundation of economic reform by filling all men with a genuinely Christian spirit. The leader in it was Frederic Denison Maurice, chaplain to Lincoln's Inn, 1805–1872, who taught : " our interests are common, and every man is full of duties towards his neighbour." For this reason the opposite, and unchristian, idea of the constitution of society was to be refuted, and the coincidence of the interests of all men to be expressed in practical action. Maurice thus founded the modern "Christian Socialism." He was soon joined by other men of equal sincerity of character and of unwearying solicitude for the welfare of the workers—above all by Charles Kingsley, John Malcolm Ludlow, and Vansittart Neale—" a body of friends," as John Stuart Mill said, " chiefly clergymen and barristers, to whose noble exertions hardly enough praise can be awarded."

Founder of Christian Socialism

Since the masses of workmen in crowded meetings joined enthusiastically this crusade against the abuses of the new order of things, the reform movement of the " forties " was bound in the end to become irresistible, especially since parliamentary inquiries and official reports had proved the enormous extent to which the " sweated " labouring classes were over - worked. In vain the supporters of the prevailing doctrine of " laissez-faire," Cobden and Bright, the acknowledged leaders of the school, at their head, resisted with all their might the agitation which struck such a blow at the fundamental propositions of Manchester and was consequently decried as harmful ; in vain the great employers of labour, under the leadership of the powerful ironmaster, Lord Londonderry, took the field against " the hypocritical philanthropy which now prevails "; in vain the employers of the textile industry raised heartbreaking complaints over the threatening ruin of their trade ; in vain the learned Oxford professor, Senior, " proved " minutely by the so-called " analysis of the manufacturing process " —in reality by incorrect calculations of the costs of production and prices of manu- factured wares—that the whole net profit of the capital sunk in factories came from the twelfth hour of labour, and that there- fore that hour could not possibly be cur- tailed. Dr. Andrew Ure, the panegyrist of the factory system, tried in vain to lay stress on the interests and the morals of the protected young persons themselves, who, if too early released from the discipline of the factory, would be driven into the arms of idleness and vice.

All these forms of opposition, besides the opinion of the head of the government, Sir Robert Peel, which, being unfavourable to reform, weighed heavily in the scale, were defeated by the force of the move- ment supported by popular feeling. At the decisive voting in Parliament a part of the **Better Times for the Workers** Whigs, under the leadership of Macaulay, who in spirited words recommended the pro- tection of workmen as a means of retaining in the nation all those high qualities which had made the country great, allied themselves with the majority of the Tories and with the Radicals, in order to decree the ten-hour working day for persons from thirteen to eighteen years and for all female workers, at first only in the textile industry in 1847.

Although this law, in fact, reduced the working day to ten hours not only for the protected persons, but generally for all employees, since the protected classes composed 60 per cent. of all operatives, yet none of the consequences feared by interested or learned antagonists have ensued. The value of the British exports, reckoned before the passing of the law in 1846 at 57·7 million pounds sterling, had a few years later, in the year 1852, risen to 78 millions, an increase of 35 per cent. " If the shrewd calculation of Professor Senior had been correct," so a factory inspector remarked in his report with pointed irony, " every cotton mill in the United Kingdom would have worked for years at a loss." And with reference to the supposed degeneration of the children in consequence of too short a working day,

a report of the factory inspection of the year 1848 noted that " such uncharitable talk about idleness and vice must be stigmatised as the purest cant and the most shameless hypocrisy."

Thus, the marvellous development of industry, hand in hand with the moral and physical renascence of the factory **Marvellous Development of Industry** worker, struck the dullest eye. The laws were gradually ex- tended to the other great industries, and in 1867, under Disraeli's Ministry, partly also to the work- shops; and in 1868, at the instigation of this same Minister, the whole of this legisla- tion, which had already become somewhat confused, was consolidated and completed in the " Factory and Workshop Act."

The manufacturers, even before this, had completely reconciled themselves to the thought of the protection of workmen. Henceforth they offered no more resist- ance either on principle, by means of political agitation, or, in practical life, by infringement of the factory laws. On this head a committee appointed by Par- liament to examine the working of the existing factory laws reported in 1876 : " The numerous former inquiries into the position of the children and women engaged in the various industries of the country have disclosed conditions which produced a great outburst of public sym- pathy, and imperatively called for the intervention of the legislature."

A striking contrast to the circumstances disclosed in these reports is afforded by the present position of the persons in whose favour the various factory and workshop Acts have been passed. Some employments are still unhealthy in spite of the sanitary provisions of these Acts, and in other industries there is still occasionally a pressure of work beyond the limits defined by law, which is prejudicial to the health of the operatives. But such cases are exceptional. At the same time we have no cause for assuming that the **Fruits of Labour Legislation** legislation which has shown itself so beneficial to the workers engaged has caused any considerable damage to the industries to which it applied. On the contrary, industrial progress was clearly not checked by the factory laws ; and there are only few, even among the em- ployers, who now wish for a repeal of the chief provisions of this Act or deny the benefits produced by this legislation.

SOCIAL PROBLEMS IN FRANCE
THE STRIVINGS AFTER EQUALITY AND LIBERTY

IN France the first social movement, in the modern sense, was in connection with the great Revolution. This had tried to put into practice the ideas of Rousseau as to the Law of Nature. Man is by nature good, so Rousseau taught.

Principle of the New Constitution This good, uncorrupted man, so Robespierre added, was now personified by the lower orders only, who had remained untouched by luxury and vice. The government was, therefore, to be transferred to the lower orders by the grant of equal political privileges to all citizens, and thus the reign of everlasting equality, virtue, and happiness would dawn. The new constitution of 1793 adopted as its principle: " All men are equal by nature and by law," and " The object of society is the welfare of all." Thus, Robespierre declared: " We wish that in our country selfishness may be replaced by morality, ambition by honesty, decency by the sense of duty, contempt of misfortune by contempt of vice."

But men had not yet arrived at clear ideas of a new distribution of property. On the contrary, this result was not attained until the Directory, after the Democratic constitution of 1793 had been set aside. It was due to François Noël Babeuf, 1764–1797, a former partisan of Robespierre. Starting with the precepts of the Law of Nature, Babeuf pictured to himself the ideal society based on the following precepts : the duty of all to work; statutory settlement of the number of working hours; regulation of produc-

Babeuf's Ideal Society tion by a supreme board elected by the people; division of the necessary work among the individual citizens ; the right of all citizens to all enjoyments ; and a corresponding distribution of property among individuals, according to the standard of equality. Since even the boldest imagination hesitated to hope from one day to another

for the realisation of this ideal, Babeuf had planned a series of appropriately devised measures as a connecting link between the present and the social regeneration of the future. In the first place, a " great national community of property " was to be established, to which all State property, all property of the " enemies of the popular cause," as well as all estates which were left uncultivated, were to be attached.

Every Frenchman could join the community if he gave up his property and placed his working powers at its disposal. Besides that, the community would inherit all private estates. The members were to work in common, and would receive all the food " which composed a moderate and frugal cuisine," and other necessaries of life. Anyone who entered the community burdened with debt became exempt from all liabilities. On

An Army of Theorists and Discontents the basis of this programme, Babeuf, favoured by the circumstances described, succeeded in collecting round him many thousand followers, chiefly old supporters of the Jacobin doctrines, discontented members of the middle class, and political theorists of every rank, but only a very small proportion of artisans.

The Government interfered, alarmed at the threatening character of the movement. A secret association, the Club of the Pantheon, was therefore formed, which took steps to prepare a decisive blow. It was proposed to capture the capital by a coup-de-main, in order to plant side by side the banners of economic and political equality ; although the prepared manifesto to the people cautiously spoke only of the restoration of the overthrown constitution of 1793, in order that all who held Jacobin views might join the agitators. While the rebellion was still being secretly discussed, Babeuf and his colleagues, who had long been betrayed and watched by the police, were arrested in May, 1796. Being brought before the National Tribunal, Babeuf and his friend, Darthé, although acquitted on the charge of conspiracy, were condemned to death for inciting men to divide private property, and guillotined May 27th, 1797, and seven fellow-conspirators, among them the future historian of the movement, Filippo Buonarroti, 1761–1837, were sentenced to banishment. The young communistic movement thus become leaderless was doomed to rapid extinction.

It was not until the third decade of the nineteenth century that a large socialistic movement was again started in France, at a time when the industrial development had not yet created an enormous proletariat. This explains why it found its followers mainly among the sections of the middle and upper classes, which were steeped in idealism. Here " the young men had heard in their childhood of the portentous events of the Revolution, had lived through the Empire, and were sons of heroes or victims; their mothers had conceived them between two battles, and the thunder of cannon had ushered them into the world."

Bazard the Prophet of Socialism These youths, passionate and romantic in spirit, full of an instinctive dislike of the unscrupulous egotism and the prosaic dulness of the bourgeois society around them, were forced to offer strong opposition to the prevailing utilitarianism, and to welcome rapturously the first prophet who undertook an attack on selfishness, narrowmindedness, and the aristocracy of wealth. Such a man was Bazard in 1828, who enlisted supporters for Socialism in connection with the teaching of Saint-Simon.

Count Claude Henri de Saint-Simon, 1760–1825, who, while able to found a school, could never produce a regular movement, had stopped short of Socialism. He had never clearly understood the war between capital and proletariat. On the contrary, he included both classes under the category of "industrials"— that is, as the body of those who work at the production of material enjoyments —who, as the most numerous and productive class, ought properly to govern the State, while, as a matter of fact, the great landowners, the clergy, and the high officials possessed the power. The political background of the time favoured these ideas. At that period, 1815–1830, the decisive war in France between the

adherents to the "ancien regime" and the bourgeoisie supported by the people was being waged; while the class dispute between the property-owning orders and the proletariat, which was now first developing, had not yet made itself felt. The teaching of Saint-Simon was the theoretical expression of the aspiring **Saint-Simon's New Christianity** classes generally. The supremacy of the "industrials," which he advocated, began to assert itself in the actual economic development as the supremacy of capital. The spirit of the age, no less than the essence of Saint-Simon's nature, which was wrapped up in mysticism, required that his system should be first and foremost a religious and moral one. He therefore expressly termed it " a new Christianity." His object was to accustom mankind to a new code of ethics, in order to raise on this foundation a new political and social fabric.

" In the new Christianity," he wrote, " all morality will be directly derived from the principle that men are to regard each other as brothers. This principle, which was held by primitive Christianity, will be explained, and in its new form will lay down the fundamental proposition that religion must direct society towards the one great end, the immediate amelioration of the lot of the poorest class." Thus it was Saint-Simon's intention to perfect the material side of Christianity, and so to bring about complete earthly happiness.

Saint-Simon had not contemplated a property reform. This was first planned by Saint-Amand Bazard, 1791–1832, who also, in connection with the historico-social ideas of his master, had elaborated a special doctrine of historical development. According to this, there are two fundamental social ideas, that of selfishness, or of individualism, and that of unity, or of association. According as the latter or the former principle predominates, organic or critical **Definite Purpose of Mankind** periods in the history of nations may be distinguished. The organic epoch is characterised by the universally recognised authority of definite ideas, by the prevalence of the same thoughts in the minds of all, and by a united effort towards the same ends. Mankind here felt itself conscious of some definite purpose, and therefore proceeded to raise permanent social structures. The critical epoch was marked by criticism of the traditional principles, which were deprived of their influence over men's minds by the disappearance of public spirit and by the reign of individualism. Existing institutions were undermined, until finally the edifice which earlier times had reared crashed down. The followers of the new doctrine announced " to the

The Dreams of French Visionaries astounded world an age so full of fame and magnificence, such glorious times, such golden crops and rich harvests, such happy people, so much wealth and pleasure, so much greatness, enjoyment, and harmony, that the most indifferent opened eyes and ears and were intoxicated with these prophetic visions."

The elaboration of this doctrine in detail was chiefly due to Barthélemy Prosper Enfantin, 1796-1864, who represented all profits, rents, and dividends as a species of income which did not depend on the labour of the possessor, but on the " exploitation " of the workman. The fundamental principles which were to put an end to all this, had to be carried out by a hierarchical organisation of society, and so the contesting Saint-Simonian party had already been organised on a strict system of hierarchy, and its guidance entrusted to two high priests — pères suprèmes—Bazard and Enfantin in 1829.

But when Enfantin, becoming arrogant from the number of his followers, who were reckoned by thousands, demanded the " emancipation of the flesh," since he preached that the marriage tie should not be binding if affections grow cool, because society ought to be just to *all* natures, even to flirts and coquettes, then Bazard seceded, in 1831, disgusted at such a travesty of the true teaching. The " Globe," the organ of the school, soon preached without any further shame the bold doctrine of free love. Such a foolish and immoral deterioration could not fail to alienate the people from a doctrine stained with extravagance and

Fragments of a Great Cause indecency. Enfantin could only find forty loyal followers when he withdrew to his property at Ménilmontant, near Paris, with the fragments of what had been shortly before so flourishing a school. "Enfantin," the last number of the " Globe" declared, "is the messiah of God, the king of the nations. The world sees its Christ, and recognises him not ; therefore, he withdraws himself from you with his apostles." The last

survivors of the school, Olinde Rodrigues, Michel Chevalier, Charles Duveyrier, were finally dispersed by legal intervention, since a charge of immorality was brought against them in August, 1832. So rapidly was the movement past, and so violent was the disenchantment of the public, that " nothing was left of the whole incident except a feeling of astonishment that men could ever have paid attention to it, and a new ground for distrust of innovations. Before a year elapsed people spoke of Saint-Simonism as of a long-forgotten matter."

Charles Fourier, 1772-1837, elaborated his social theory independently of Saint-Simon. Its starting point was strictly individualistic. His aim was not the happiness of the community nor the equality of all, but the satisfaction of the impulses of the individuals, the most enjoyable life for each separate person. All individual impulses, according to Fourier, come from God, as necessarily follows from their existence, and are therefore good. It is only necessary to give them free play on a profitable field ; the result is then obtained that men can always have wishes and

Fourier's Social Theory desires, and that the earth can readily satisfy all their wishes. If at the present time men have longings which remain unsatisfied, and impulses which must be suppressed, this, in view of the harmony between wish and enjoyment which God wills, is an evil which must exclusively be attributed to the deficient organisation of human society.

The system of Fourier only attained considerable importance after the dissolution of the Saint-Simonian school. Victor Considérant, 1808–1897, had great influence on it, as he freed the master's teaching from all kinds of fantastic additions, and at the same time brought prominently forward certain vigorous ideas which could be turned to account in the popular agitation, such as the right to work and the insurance of the worker. Both these movements, Saint-Simonism as well as Fourierism, had, on the whole, found supporters only among the " intellectuals," and those members of the middle class who were theorists. The real mass of workers kept aloof from them as a rule.

The first interference of the French workmen in politics followed rather in connection with the secret societies of the Republicans. In the middle of the " twenties " a new secret society, the " Société des

Amis du Peuple," had formed itself out of the ruins of the overthrown Carbonari conspiracy, with a Jacobin programme. Its management was in the hands of a number of young men, mostly students, who succeeded in carrying their agitation into the ranks of the workmen. Out of this society, which made various attempts to effect the establishment of the Republic by concerted risings, was developed, after various intermediate steps, the " Société des Familles," the views of which advocated communism.

Filippo Buonarroti, an Italian, one of the banished members of Babeuf's party, had received an amnesty, and on his return had plunged once more headlong into the whirlpool of conspiracy. Thus he had become a Carbonaro, and he afterwards joined that republican body of conspirators. True to his old ideals, he had tried to introduce communism into these associations. But that which the speeches of the feeble old man failed to effect was accomplished by his spirited narrative of Babeuf's teaching, heroism, and martyrdom. The members of the secret clubs—the " intellectuals," the middle class,

Men who Delighted in Conspiracy and the workers—recognised that the only true result of equality for them was communism. Louis Auguste Blanqui, 1805–1881, and Armand Barbès, 1809–1870, two ex-students who had played a part in all republican plots, and had been in the forefront of every disturbance, were the leaders of these communists.

Disheartened by no failures, and crushed by no penalties, these past-masters of conspiracy used every release from prison as an opportunity to plan at once fresh murderous schemes and assassinations. These men, who wanted rather the fiendish delight of conspiracy than any object to conspire for, did not attempt to initiate any such tangible schemes of reform as even Babeuf had already started. The tactics of the secret society guided by them were to make the ruling power incapable of resistance by a skilful and bold coup-de-main at the appropriate moment, and to rouse the people to revolt. An attempt on the life of the king was advised as a preliminary skirmish before the pitched battle. The method of this political warfare is what the Socialists have since usually called " Blanquist tactics." On May 12th, 1839, the insurrection of the Blanquists, 850 in number, took place ; but since at that moment no political or economic crisis was felt, the expected response was not forthcoming, and the rising was soon quelled.

While the difficulties of association were so great, the natural disinclination of the French to form strong and permanent party combinations could not fail to produce a large variety of sects, corresponding to the many Socialistic schemes of the time. The exaggerated doctrine of Babeuf as to equality was continued by the school of Etienne Cabet, 1788–1856, which wished to attain its object by strictly legal methods, and in other points made an advantageous departure from the crudities of Babeuf's scheme. The Fourierists have been already mentioned. Next came the school of Philippe Buchez, 1796–1865, who had given a more distinct character to the shapeless propositions of the Fourierists by the effective remedy of union. Buchez insisted from 1831 onwards that the workmen ought to economise until they could form themselves into a productive association. A part of the profits of the business ought then to be applied either to the extension of the old association or to the founding of a new one, until finally all the workmen in France were owners of the capital necessary for production. This train of thought led, as Lexis pointed out, to a series of actual attempts, and certain sections of the Parisian working classes clung tenaciously to the idea.

The plan developed by Louis Blanc, 1811–1882, of founding such " productive " associations by state-given aid could not fail to meet with more support from the proletariat. For then the workman did not require to save out of his small wages ; and besides this, the labouring class was liberated at a blow. The scheme of Blanc culminated in the special point that the State should organise the workmen, so far as they wished, into workshops, which, during the first year, were to be

State aid for the Workers directed by the State, but afterwards by the workmen themselves. These " ateliers sociaux" were to be associated, to agree as to the method and extent of the production, to provide for the sick and incapable, and to help those undertakings which were depressed by crises. Since it was expected that the industries conducted by capitalists would soon be brought to a standstill by this competition, this system of associations only presented a transition stage towards pure communism, of which the principles were to be : " Production according to capabilities, consumption according to requirements."

All these schools—and this point must be strongly emphasised, for it is often overlooked—must not be considered as merely representative of the working classes; on

Aims of the Christian Socialists the contrary, they felt that they represented all classes suffering from capitalistic methods of production, the lower middle class as much as the proletariat. This is still more the case with the Radical Christian Socialists of that time, such as Pierre Leroux, 1797–1871, the Abbés Hugues Félicité Robert de Lamennais, 1782–1854, Henri Benjamin Constant de Rebecque, 1767–1830, and Constantin Pecqueur, 1801–1887. These, consciously or unconsciously, renewed the idea of Saint-Simon, that a purification of mankind by religion and morality was alone able to pave the way for future social reform ; for then only would all men regard each other as brothers, and be able to establish a new organisation, in which the possessors of wealth would consent to equalise the differences in property.

Pierre Joseph Proudhon, 1809–1865, a contemporary, appreciated more fully the interests of the middle and the lower classes, since in an ingenious but thoroughly idealist scheme he aimed at a realisation of the three main principles of the great Revolution—justice, equality, and liberty —in the economic world. He took up a position, in the interests of individual freedom, distinctly opposed to communism, against which he brought the charges that it obliterates the distinctions between individuals, fosters the indolence of all, and extinguishes personality. His intention was to preserve the improvements due to the economic system of individualism, but, on the other hand, to remove the distress and unhappiness intro-

Lamentable Error of Socialism duced by it. For this reason competition is to be maintained; but opposition and isolation are, within certain limits, to be obviated by reciprocal support and combination. For " competition and association," so he said, " support each other. Far from excluding each other, they do not even diverge. Whoever speaks of competition assumes a common goal ; competition is therefore not egotism, and it is the most lamentable error of socialism to see in it

the overthrow of society." He only attacked the unrestrained competition, where the possession of capital, as the privilege of a favoured minority, "exploits" the large, hard-working majority of the people ; where the small man, from want of credit, cannot keep his footing; and where the social disorder leads to a crisis, to the bankruptcy of employers, and to want of employment among many thousand workers.

The party of the democratic middle class led by Alexandre Auguste Ledru-Rollin, 1807–1874, saw itself compelled to make advances to Socialism. Its chief organ, the " Réforme," willingly opened its columns to Louis Blanc's social and political articles, and even its official programme clearly showed the influence of the new socialistic doctrines. " The workers," so it ran, "have been slaves and serfs; they are now labourers ; our aim must be to elevate them to the position of sharers. The State must take the initiative in industrial successes in order to introduce such organisation of labour as will raise the workers to the position of

The Golden Age of the Bourgeoisie sharers. The State must provide work for the stalwart and healthy citizen, and help and protection for the old and weak." Notwithstanding this strong socialistic current, there were at first only slight waves visible on the surface of political life ; the strict law of meetings and associations, and the franchise, which depended on a large income and was granted only to the 200,000 richest citizens in the whole of France, prevented the new ideas from being asserted with irresistible weight in ordinary times.

In the " thirties " and " forties," when Socialism and the emancipation of the lower orders were so prominent in the world of thought, the governing powers were quite unconcerned by them. At no period of the nineteenth century had the large industries and " haute finance " so ruled the governing powers as at this time, which Treitschke called " the golden age of the bourgeoisie." Indeed the labour legislation in no way served to protect the worker, but was purely directed towards the interests of the bourgeoisie. The associations of workers in the same craft for the promotion of their " presumed " common interests, as it was very significantly termed in the law, which dated from the year 1791, were still prohibited ; and this law, under the government of Louis Philippe, was still enforced merely against coalitions of the workers, and never against the employers. The prefects were instructed, in the event of strikes, to forbid meetings and to put foreigners who took part in them at once across the frontier.

The labour book was obligatory on the workmen, and in the commercial courts the employers had a secured majority. Only a feeble protective law was passed in favour of the workmen, which established a twelve hours' maximum working day for children ; and even then the official instructions for carrying it out explained that it could not be strictly observed. The ruling class in France was not at all disturbed, either by the misery of certain sections of the proletarians in the large towns, or by riots of starving workmen or risings of communistic conspirators.

This misgovernment was crowned by the insolent ignorance with which the official representatives of this rule of the great bourgeoisie flatly denied the existence of abuses and declared their world to be the best of all possible worlds. **Guizot's Arrogant Attitude** Although facing a condition of things which concealed in it most bitter class disputes, that section of society asserted that neither disabilities nor privileges existed, since everyone could become rich, and then acquire the highest political rights. " There are no more class disputes," announced François Pierre Guillaume Guizot, 1787–1874, as President of the Council, a short time before the February Revolution, " for there are no longer any conflicting interests." And when reference was made to the agitation among the people, he arrogantly thought that " we, the three powers, the Crown and the Chambers, are the only legal organs of the sovereignty of the people ; besides us there is only usurpation and revolution." And thus the demand for the extension of the franchise, which in the whole country was granted only to a bare quarter of a million of the most highly taxed, was flatly refused. No class which so obstinately asserted its privileges could rule for long ; and in fact the monarchy of July, 1830, was overturned like a house of cards by the revolutionary hurricane of the year 1848.

The upper bourgeoisie was, however, still politically the most matured class at that time. The real middle class, the poorer citizens of the towns, had, under the July monarchy, abandoned the radical opposition, which politically supported the traditions of the great Revolution. In other points it fluctuated vaguely between the maintenance of all ownership and a socialistic altruism, and had never been able to effect a union with the **Socialism the Land of Promise** peasants, by far the most numerous class in the country. The political immaturity of the middle class was exceeded by that of the working classes, who thought they could come with one mighty leap into that land of promise called Socialism.

Under such circumstances the provisional government which, put at the head of affairs by the Revolution of February, 1848, embodied primarily the middle class, and secondarily the working orders, was not able to produce any considerable results. The maximum working day, which had been fixed for all industrial undertakings, was not carried out, and the prohibition to appoint "middlemen," who overworked the men, was not observed. The gift of £120,000 to the labour associations was unable to effect any increase in co-operative systems, and the reluctant attempt to put into practice the right to work finally, when the " national workshops " established for the purpose were discontinued, led to riots.

Thus the French ship of state drifted aimlessly, without a compass, on the ocean of politics, and was at the mercy of the first man who knew how to take the helm and steer her into a safe harbour. The direction of the official social policy under Napoleon III. was determined by the fact that the sovereign himself, while still a young prince, had developed his own programme of social reform, which culminated in the creation of a nobility of manufacturers in Carlyle's sense, and in an attempt by the State to solve the labour problem by the cultivation of untilled **Napoleon III. as Social Reformer** lands. What was done, then, towards putting this project into practice, when its originator mounted the throne of France ? If we wish to answer this question correctly we must not forget that Napoleon had paved the way to his position by perjury and crime, and that consequently he had to be on his guard against revenge. This system, therefore, began with a campaign against all associations, however constituted, of workmen, who were considered the most active disseminators of revolutionary ideas. Thus, not only all their political unions but also their purely economic associations, including many flourishing co-operative stores and similar societies, fell victims to the dictatorship which "saved society." But after the first zeal to found the new empire had abated, a careful

Labour's Rights under the Empire

distinction was made between the political and the economic organisations of the proletariat, and while the former were ruthlessly nipped in the bud, no obstacles were placed in the way of the latter.

Thus, there arose under the empire a vigorous labour agitation, of which the centre of gravity lay in the combinations for obtaining higher wages and generally improved conditions of labour. Now, it is true that such coalitions were forbidden according to the already mentioned law of 1791; but they were still tacitly allowed. "Striking" workmen were pardoned and complete neutrality was enjoined on the prefects in event of suspension of work. Finally, in 1864, the prohibition on coalition itself was removed.

But beyond this the empire undertook to support the working classes by a long series of tangible measures. At one time it tried to guarantee to the metropolis cheap prices for necessary provisions. This was done especially by the establishment of the "Caisse de la boulangerie" endowed by the bakers, from which the individual masters received advances in times of high prices for corn in order to be able to maintain the low price of bread. Then an energetic attempt was made to face the labour question, not indeed in the vague form of the royal pamphlet, but by a system of public building operations. Within fifteen years more than £600,000,000 were spent in Paris alone on public edifices. The same thing happened in Lyons, Marseilles, and Bordeaux.

Great Days of the Building Industry

This measure had various important consequences from the magnificent scale on which it was carried out. Permanent and profitable employment was given to a large number of "hands," wages had an upward tendency, and the spirit of enterprise was everywhere aroused by the excitement proceeding from the building industry. All else that happened was of subordinate significance. The remaining

point most worthy of mention is the legislation on mutual help societies, which supported their members in case of sickness or, under certain circumstances, of incapacity to work. These possessed an income of £400,000 and various privileges; and their number actually increased from 2,000 in 1852 to 4,000 in 1859.

The workmen in the State workshops were compelled to insure their old age, and at the same time their wages were increased by the amount of the premiums. Besides this, state funds were available for the construction of workmen's dwellings and the erection of benevolent institutions, crèches for the children of workmen, asylums for crippled workmen. It is strange that the empire never thought about real legislation for the protection of workmen.

The most appropriate estimate of all this social policy is given by Lexis in his book on trades unions in France. "Louis Napoleon as emperor did not really need to fear that he would be reminded by the working classes of his brochure on pauperism. The social policy of the empire is by no means opposed to the

The Policy of Louis Napoleon

spirit of it. Discipline and superintendence of the workmen on the one side, amelioration of their material position on the other; that is an idea which is always upheld in the home policy of Louis Napoleon." In fact, the working class undoubtedly gained much from the new order of things; its position was incomparably improved during the years 1850–1870. Even the development of capital in the age of joint-stock companies was, on account of the number of new undertakings, not without profit to the lowest classes. For "even if one part of the shifted millions was concentrated in the coffers of the capitalistic body, another part was scattered over the mass of the wage-earning class."

Notwithstanding this, the proletariat was proof against all the allurements of the Second Empire. It was dumb to all gifts, deaf to all promises, cold to all flatteries; indeed, "the current of republican feeling, like a mighty river, swept away with it continually larger masses of the people." The lower middle class was at first furious, since, at the era of wild speculation and company promotion, when the bearers of the most renowned Bonapartist names joined in the worship of the golden calf, it had to bear the brunt of the costs. It knew nothing of the black art of gambling on the stock exchange, and would gladly make money without trouble, and therefore was caught by enticing promises and invested its hard-earned savings in rash or swindling undertakings.

The middle class, therefore, and the proletariat, to whom the illusions created by Proudhon's theories had given common ideals, and with them the possibility of common action, united, especially in Paris, for the overthrow of the Empire. When this was accomplished under the influence of the defeat to the imperial armies in 1870, those classes combined against the republic of the bourgeoisie and actually brought the Paris commune, in which the National Guard, mostly recruited from their order, held sway for some time, from March to May, 1871, under their power.

Since neither Paris nor the Government wished to yield, the result was civil war, which naturally ended with the suppression of the insurgent population of the capital. In that short time, however, the government of the besieged city, whose programme of **Liberty under the Third Republic** social policy was indistinct in other respects, had not been able to exhibit any comprehensive measures of reform. Under the Third Republic, which for the first time secured to the French working class permanent and full liberty in every direction, important political labour agitations as well as powerful economic organisations of the labouring classes were instituted. Politically, the most noteworthy event was the complete separation of the proletariat from the lower middle class. The proletariat followed out its own aims exclusively, in politics and economics, and thus acted according to the programme of class warfare.

Regard for the political influence of the masses of workmen compelled the Government to make social reforms which, in the first instance, dealt with the continuation of the protection to workmen—by the introduction of the ten-hours maximum working day for young persons under eighteen years and for all female workers in factories—and the concession of full liberty of coalition, since 1884. Besides this, the workmen have, in a number of towns, particularly in Paris, enforced various arrangements which are conducive to their interests, such as the establishment of labour exchanges at the cost of the community, as also regulations for the minimum wage and maximum working day for all men employed by the town on public works. The movement in favour of trades unions and co-operative societies has lately received a great stimulus in France; the number of workmen united **Advance of Co-operation in France** in trade associations already reaches 500,000. We may assume that the social and economic organisations of the French working classes, although they are still far from reaching the English standard, will, if given undisturbed development, attain in a few decades some such importance as the English.

It is, lastly, worthy of remark that the Socialists have succeeded in influencing the administration of the Board of Trade, so valuable for social interests, in favour of the workmen, since the Socialists have united with the democratic sections for the protection of the republic against the attacks of the military and clerical parties.

The more the working class in this way practically arrived at a comprehension of its immediate economic interests, in contradistinction to those of the richer class and without regard to any collision with those of the inferior bourgeoisie, the less satisfied could this latter class feel by the alliance with the proletariat. Thus it resulted that after the "seventies" the predominance of Proudhon's views, which earlier had effected the spiritual union between the two orders, grew less and less, and that the inferior bourgeoisie now worked for their salvation outside the socialistic organisations.

But the lower middle class did not succeed in making an organisation with a special programme of its own ; and therefore hundreds of thousands of its members cordially welcomed the demagogues, who promised them that they would oppose the great capitalists as well **Transitory Success of Boulangism** as the socialistic tendencies. This is the explanation of the transitory success of "Boulangism," in 1889, and more lately of the great prospects of the " nationalistic groups," who anticipated a revival of the French middle class from the campaign against the world of Jewish trade and finance. But this movement was so short-lived that no elucidation of its confused economic scheme was forthcoming.

SOCIAL DEMOCRACY IN GERMANY
THE RISE & SPREAD OF LABOUR MOVEMENTS

THE first labour agitation in Germany was noticeable in the "forties." It then, owing to the strict police regulations of the German Confederation, chiefly affected the German journeymen who lived by thousands in foreign countries. Its leader

Germany's First Labour Agitation was a tailor, Wilhelm Weitling, 1808–1871, who, as an emissary of the secret "Bund der Gerechten," League of the Just, at Paris, transplanted the communistic agitation to Switzerland. He organised the movement in such a way that public workmen's unions were founded under harmless designations, in which recruits were obtained for the "League of the Just." The object was to establish by revolutionary methods the communistic society, for which Weitling, in connection with the French Utopians, had drawn up a special system.

At the same time interest in communism had been roused even in the German middle classes, where the half doctrinaire, half idealist tendencies of the age had found a receptive soil in the students of philosophy and literature. In the mystic circle of the "humanistic philosophy" of Ludwig Andreas Feuerbach, 1804–1872, efforts were made to produce "humane" conditions even in social life, and the heartless capitalistic methods of business were condemned in accordance with the criticism of the French Socialists.

The positive ideal of this party, headed by the writers Moses Hess, 1812–1875, and Karl Grün, 1813–1887, was the most complete freedom of man, conceived by

The Secret "League of the Just" nature as noble, in actions and conduct, in production and consumption. This school must therefore be termed anarchist, since it preached the unqualified self-glorification of the individual and the exclusion of any compulsion. This philosophic socialism found favour first with the educated middle class, and then also with the secret "League of the Just."

But since the arguments of this kind of Socialism were necessarily unfamiliar to the workmen, Karl Marx, 1818–1883, succeeded at last in preventing this system from doing any harm in that league. Through his efforts the league, which henceforth was styled "Bund der Communisten," adopted his principles, a change which practically produced no further results then, since his success coincided with the outbreak of the revolution of February, 1848, which dispersed the members of the league in all directions.

The only independent labour movement was made quite apart from the communistic league, under the organisation of Stephan Born, a compositor, 1825–1897. By vigorous agitation he succeeded in founding a labour party, which came forward under the name of "Arbeiterverbrüderung," Labour Confraternity, and had as its immediate aim universal

Overthrow of the Democracy suffrage for all representative bodies and a ten hours' working day. The activity of the "Labour Confraternity" at that time consisted chiefly in the support of the war of the democracy against the counter revolution; and thus the league was necessarily involved in the overthrow of the democracy. It was dissolved in 1850, and all attempts to call new workmen's unions into existence were nipped in the bud.

Some attempts of Marx and others to resume the agitation in foreign countries by the revival of the old communistic league miscarried, owing to the vigilance of the police; and thus this association also soon disappeared for ever in 1853. During the whole of this decade the re-action allowed no organised labour movement to take place. This period was used by Marx for the further development of his system, which he had already sketched in the "Communistic Manifesto." His original works, which secure him a position among the first thinkers of all time, reach their highest level in his

" Materialistische Geschichtsauffassung ", and also in his " Untersuchung der kapitalistischen Produktionsweise."

From the study of Hegel, Marx had formed the fundamental conception that history depicts a ceaseless process of life, decay, and progress, in which each separate stage is absolutely necessary and relatively justified, however much it conflicts with all the accepted notions of politics or ethics. But while Hegel deduced the laws of historical movement from the " self-development of the absolute notion," Marx was converted by the philosophy of Feuerbach to the view that the man creates the ideas, and that the " idea " does not determine the history of the man.

At the same time his whole mental attitude rested on a materialistic basis, since he adopted the results of Feuerbach's investigations, that the higher beings whom our religious fancy has created are only the fanciful reflections of our own being. If man thus, unconsciously, created religion, why not all political, legal, artistic, and scientific existence ? And here Marx believes that he can discover the secret connection of all historical de-

Marx's Theory of Historic Development velopment, since he assumes that, in the first instance, politics, but more remotely all other manifestations of the spiritual, social, and intellectual life, are to be referred to the economic conditions and their development as the one ultimate cause.

The economic formation of society since the abandonment of the primitive common ownership of the soil is determined in all its previous history by the contrast between the classes, especially that between the ruled and ruling classes. But this is changed in the course of time. For each economic constitution develops from itself productive forces which are finally incompatible with the old form of production and the old form of class supremacy.

As a consequence of this the contrast between the classes culminates in a class warfare, in such a way that a crisis must follow, the result of which must be one of two alternatives : either the disruption of the existing social constitution and its change into a higher system, since the suppressed classes have overthrown the hitherto ruling classes, or the common ruin of the warring classes.

This keen inquiry into the economic system shows how conditions are at the present moment. According to it, the value of all commodities is determined by the amount of combined necessary, that is, normal, working time requisite for their production. A commodity which has cost twelve hours of combined necessary labour is worth double as much as a commodity which has cost six hours. But now in the capitalistic social system only

The Workman and the Capitalist the owners of means of production and livelihood produce commodities ; and therefore the great majority of the non-propertied class sell their only commodity, their power of work, to the propertied. "The worker," so it is said in the account of Marx's teaching by Friedrich Engels, 1820–1895, which is to be regarded as an authentic representation, " sells his power of work to the capitalist for a certain daily sum. After a few hours' labour he has produced the value of that sum. But his contract of work runs to the effect that he must drudge for a further round of hours, in order to complete his labour for the day. The value which he produces in these additional hours of excess labour is excess value, which costs the capitalist nothing, but nevertheless goes into his pockets."

The appropriation of unpaid labour is the fundamental law of the capitalistic method of production, the existence of which is inseparable from the " sweating " of the workmen. Since now, according to Karl Marx, the excess value is the only thing which interests the capitalist in the process of production, his economic transactions will always be directed towards the increase of this excessive value.

The evident results of this desire for extra profits are as follows : In the first place, the daily hours of labour will be immoderately prolonged. Then the cheap labour of women and children will be employed on an immense scale. Finally, the anarchy in co-operative production which is so significant of the modern economic

Anarchy in Co-operative Production methods will be more and more carried to extreme lengths. "The chief tool," so Engel explains Marx's views, " with which the capitalistic method of production increased this anarchy in co-operative production was the precise opposite of the anarchy ; that is, the increasing organisation of production as co-operative in every productive establishment. With this lever it destroyed the old peaceful stability. When it was introduced into a branch of industry, it allowed no other method of work besides. When it took possession of hand work, it destroyed the old hand work. The field of labour became a battle-ground. Not merely did war break out between the individual local producers, but the local wars in turn became national, the com- **The Bitter** mercial wars of the seventeenth **Wars of** and eighteenth centuries. **Industry** Wholesale industries and the establishment of the world market have made the war universal, and at the same time given it an unprecedented bitterness. Among individual capitalists, as among entire industries and whole countries, the favourableness of the natural or created conditions of production decides the question of existence. The defeated is remorselessly disregarded. The opposition between co-operative production and capitalistic appropriation now appears as the contrast between the organisation of production in the single factory and the anarchy of production in the whole society."

The consequences of this are suspensions of business and work, partly local, partly universal, which lead to the formation of an army of unemployed, the so-called " industrial reserve army." This must grow larger as time elapses. For the " bourgeoisie " surmounts the crises by two measures only : on the one side by the forced annihilation of a mass of productive forces, factories which are not working, etc., on the other side by the conquest of new markets. The crises, then, are surmounted only by preparing more widely extended and more violent crises, and the means of avoiding the crises are lessened.

The crises now afford a means of concentrating various amounts of capital in one hand. Every capitalist ruins many other capitalists. Hand in hand with this destruction of many capitalists by a few, the co-operative form of the process of labour is developed in a continually grow- **Capital's** ing scale. There is the change **Vast** of the old instruments of labour **Supremacy** suited to use by the individual into instruments adapted only for combined use, the entanglement of all nations in the net of the world market, and with this the international character of the supremacy of capital. The mass of misery grows with the continually diminishing number of great capitalists, who secure exclusively for themselves all the advantages of this change ; but at the same time sedition grows rife among the working classes, who are always swelling in numbers, and are organised by the mechanism of the capitalistic system of production. The monopoly of capital becomes a clog on the method of production, which has flourished with it and under it. It is removed, and its place is taken by the communistic social system, the principles of which are only suggested by Marx.

While Marx was developing his system in London, an attempt had been made in Germany, after the end of the " fifties " in the nineteenth century, to win over the workmen to the Liberal movement, which was assuming new importance. This was done by first founding associations for the education of workmen, and by the self-help movement initiated by a former judge of the patrimonial court, Hermann Schulze-Delitzsch, 1808–1883. The educational societies could, from their nature, only have a restricted sphere of influence. The case would have been otherwise with the self-help movement if it had been connected with the real interests of the working class, above all, with the organisa- **Lassalle the** tion of trades unions. Instead **Friend of** of this, Schulze contemplated, **the Workman** in the first instance, the establishment of money-lending banks, of societies for supply of raw materials, of co-operative shops and similar associations which considered especially the interests of the small master-workmen, while the proletarians were attracted merely to the co-operative stores which were then also founded.

The result could only be that the workmen themselves felt this representation of their class interests to be insufficient, and looked round for men to help them. The man who came forward now as their leader was a friend of Marx, Ferdinand Lassalle, 1825–1864, who had won the confidence of the proletariat by his socialistic and revolutionary antecedents. The labour agitation of the present day, and with it " Social Democracy," were the fruits of his political activity.

Lassalle began his agitation in March, 1863, with the " Open Answer " to a deputation of workmen from Leipzig, who wished to learn his views on the social question and the means of reform. This pamphlet contained also the fundamental principles of Lassalle's social programme, which are only explained, supported, strengthened, and defended in all his later writings. It was shown first of all that the average wages in a national industry depending on private capital and free competition always remain limited to the bare livelihood which is ordinarily necessary among a people for the support and continuance of life, the "iron law of wages." This was the inevitable destiny of the workmen so soon as they were in any man's pay. The workers must, therefore, Lassalle concluded, become their own masters, the house for which they work must be their own property, a "productive association"; then that distinction between the wages of labour and the profit of owners would disappear, and in its place the proceeds of the labour would form remuneration for the labour. Organisation in productive associations could only be feasible under the existing conditions, if the State advanced to the workers the money for the purchase of the firms and of everything else which belonged to the management of factories and business. The means by which this State credit was to be won was the introduction of universal, uniform, and direct franchise, which would presumably secure to the labouring class the majority in Parliament. This was the solution propounded by the "Open Answer." Lassalle, in order to propagate this doctrine, founded the "Universal German Workmen's Union," of which he became the president, with absolute powers.

The older German communists, with Marx at their head, naturally could not approve of Lassalle's teaching or his tactics. The proposition of the "iron law of wages" could not but greatly offend Marx; but still more was the proposal

Liebknecht   Bebel

GERMAN LEADERS OF SOCIAL DEMOCRACY

A loyal disciple of Marx, Wilhelm Liebknecht took a leading part in the advancement of Socialism, adopting extreme measures to secure the success of the cause and suffering two years' imprisonment, while Ferdinand August Bebel, who also has been imprisoned, has led the social democratic movement in the Reichstag and in the Press.

EDUARD BERNSTEIN

A writer remarkable for wide learning, grasp of facts, and graceful style, he led the opposition against Marxism, opposing the party view that the disruption of the bourgeois society was soon to be anticipated.

of the productive association as a remedy for all social misery bound to call forth all the indignation of the communistic thinker, who, in 1852, had declared that the proletariat ought not to meddle with doctrinaire attempts such as exchange banks and associations, but "should try to revolutionise the Old World with their own great combined means." The Communists viewed with equal suspicion the exaggerated value attached by the followers of Lassalle to universal suffrage; for Marx did not expect to lead communism to victory by parliamentary majorities, but expected all success from the continuously growing impoverishment of the masses and of the thus inevitable self-annihilation of the civil society. In accordance with this view he openly announced to the German workmen by the mouth of his most loyal disciple, Wilhelm Liebknecht, 1826–1900, that Socialism was merely a question of power, which for that reason could not be solved in any Parliament of the world. During the lifetime of Lassalle these opponents could accomplish nothing, but soon after his early death, in 1864, they began to undermine his system. The International Association of Workmen, the Red International, founded in the autumn of 1864, acted as their champion. This never indeed counted more than a thousand members in Germany, but afforded a base of operations from which the attack against the followers of Lassalle might be made. The regular troops of Marx's following were, however, first furnished by the "Federation of German Workmen's Unions." This was a labour league which, founded in 1863 by the party of Progress, had gradually been piloted to complete communism by the influence of Liebknecht on its chairman, Ferdinand August Bebel, born in 1840. In 1868, the Federation declared openly for the principles of the Internationals, and in 1869 established itself, in combination with seceded members of the Universal German **Programme of the Social Democrats** Workmen's Union and with other Socialists, as the Social Democratic Labour party. The programme of this Social Democratic party, drawn up at Eisenach towards the end of 1869, was conceived in the spirit of Marx, and only slightly corresponded with the ideas circulated by Lassalle's vigorous agitation, in order not to preclude the possibility of a future reconciliation with the powerful party of Lassalle's followers.

The programme declared expressly that the Social Democratic party regarded itself as a branch of the International Workmen's Association. Their ideal was the free Republic, which alone was able to replace the wage system of the existing industrial regime by co-operative labour, which should guarantee to each worker the full proceeds of his labour. The Eisenach programme laid down, as the immediate objects of the efforts of the party, a series of social and political requirements, which were borrowed partly from the principles of the political Radicals, partly from the doctrines of Marx and Lassalle.

The Social Democracy had begun, shortly before, to take active steps. The immediate impulse to practical action was given by an attempt, made by the Party of Progress in 1868, to found trades unions. Jean Baptista von Schweitzer, 1833–1875, and Friedrich Wilhelm Fritzsche, the leaders at the time of the " Universal German Labour Union," which was always influenced by the glorification of Lassalle, took immediate steps to establish industrial unions in order to forestall the detested **Amalgamating the Forces of Labour** bourgeois party. Finally, as the third member of the league, the "Social Democratic Labour party" of Marx appeared on the scene in order to secure its share. After this organisation of trades unions, the Social Democratic party in Germany ceased to content itself with bare criticism of the existing society, and to aim only at the final goal of their efforts, the State of the future. Henceforward it endeavoured to interfere directly with life,

since it put clearly before the workers the great advantages they could at once gain if they combined in masses according to their respective trades.

The results of the elections for the Reichstag in 1874 show how effective the trade organisation was. Although the split of the Social Democracy into the two camps of the Lassalle party and the Eisenach party still continued, socialism was already able to show a splendid army; not less than 340,000 votes were cast for it. Soon afterwards the Social Democracy entered upon the era of persecution by the courts and the police, and this, among other causes, led both parties to end the organisation of unions.

The instinct of self-preservation now impelled both sections to unite and to apply all their forces exclusively to the struggle against the common foe. The amalgamation was carried out at the congress at Gotha in 1875, where, as usually happens, the more radical party gained the ascendancy over the more moderate. The new programme showed in essential points the communistic stamp of Marx's doctrines, and only slight concessions were made to **Demands of the Working Classes** the followers of Lassalle. In fact, "Lassalleanism" ceased from that time to play any independent rôle in the history of the party. In other respects it is a feature of the Gotha programme that it pays far more attention to the protection of the workers than the earlier programmes.

Unrestricted right of coalition, ordinary length of working day, prohibition of Sunday labour, of child labour, and of all forms of female labour injurious to the health, laws for the protection of the life and health of the workers, legal liability and independent administration for all charitable funds belonging to the workers ; this was the list of requirements which the German working-classes continuously put before the Government of the day. Men began, therefore, to attach far more weight than before to an immediate and practical social reform. This change in tactics proved to be a factor of enormous significance, which was calculated to bring continuous reinforcement to the party. In the election of the Reichstag of the year 1877 the Socialistic Labour party, as the official title now was, could unite 493,000 votes in support of their candidates.

Shortly afterwards, on May 11th and June 2nd, 1878, followed the two attempts on the life of the German Emperor. Public opinion falsely made the Social Democrats responsible for this, and so the emergency law "against the common danger threatened by the Social Democracy" was passed in October, 1878. After the party seemed to be really quite broken, it recovered and effected some secret and some harmless public organisations. When, then, in 1881, the "trade associations" of the workmen were allowed by the police, the Social Democracy won back their complete freedom of action ; for the trade associations afforded excellent rallying points and recruiting grounds for the active army of the Social Democracy, although in their meetings hardly any party politics were discussed.

It is not astonishing, therefore, that the law as to the Socialists did not fulfil its primary object, the annihilation of the party. When the Social Democracy had recovered from the first shock, it advanced in an uninterrupted victorious career, until in the elections of the Reichstag of 1890 it received more than 1,400,000 votes. So it became clearer from day to day that the emergency law lacked any permanently effective result, and offered no compensation for the **Bismarck's Social Policy** tainting of political morality, which the police espionage required by the law greatly promoted. The German Emperor, William II., recognising this, determined to renounce the use of this two-edged sword on September 30th, 1890.

Prince Bismarck, simultaneously with the suppression of the social democratic labour agitation, had inaugurated a system of social policy that was intended to put into practice all the best points of the modern Labour movement.

German legislation had hitherto occupied itself but little with the working-men. In 1869 it had granted to them the right of coalition, and for the rest had been satisfied with the prohibition of the labour of children under twelve years, and with the limitation of the labour of young persons under sixteen years in factories. It was a consequence of the fundamental notions of the Imperial Chancellor that no further steps were taken in this direction, although the school of socialist professors, of whom the most important intellects were Albert Schäffle, Gustav Schmoller, Adolph Wagner, Wilhelm Lexis, and Lujo Brentano, advocated this particular reform before all others. The Chancellor wished at one time that the manufacturer should be master in his own house, and be able to conduct the business entirely at his own discretion. But then Bismarck did not abandon the view that the factory law as to the maximum working day, Sunday rest, &c., lowered the profits of the owner too greatly, and also diminished the wage-earning of the workman, even if it did not altogether render his employment precarious. **The State's Duty to the Worker** Besides this, he believed that there were only local complaints of excessive duration of labour, so that any interference was the less imperative. Bismarck considered uncertainty of existence to be the real misfortune of the modern proletariat. His programme, therefore, announced that the worker, when sick, ill, or disabled, should be cared for, and that work should be found him when out of place.

He imagined that the first requirement could be realised by the plan that millions of workers should be insured in state-organised offices against the economic results of sickness, accidents, infirmity, and old age ; the necessary costs were to be paid partly by the workmen themselves, partly by the owners of the business, partly by the empire, which was to be enabled to make ampler advances by the introduction of the tobacco monopoly and profitable taxes on spirits. The second requirement he wished to fulfil by recognition of the "right of labour," which could be put into practice by the carrying out of appropriate works, such as construction of canals and roads at the public cost in times of great scarcity of employment.

With these views of the necessity of State solicitude for working men, Bismarck combined the conviction, which had been strengthened in him by the development of the Social Democracy, that this party was in the highest degree dangerous to the State, and that, in the event of further unchecked development, it would certainly produce, sooner or later, a bloody social catastrophe. The result **Fears of a Social Catastrophe** of this view was his campaign of extermination against the Social Democracy, which, however, as has been described above, completely miscarried. His constructive social policy has, however, been unusually successful. The German working-men's insurance, which was announced in an imperial message in 1881, and was completed by 1889, must be termed "a magnificent organising structure, unique of its kind in the history of the world." We see from the numbers of the working men affected how immense a service was rendered.

In the year 1900 nine millions of workers were insured against sickness, thirteen millions against old age and infirmity, seventeen millions against accidents. The sums which on the basis of the legal claim thus established are paid to the workers merely out of the means of the employers and the empire amount at the present day to more than £10,000,000 sterling annually, and are certain soon to be increased. The only point of that programme which Bismarck did not assist in carrying out is the solution of the problem of "unemployment." But, notwithstanding this deficiency, the achievements of the first Chancellor in the field of social policy stand as a "monument more lasting than brass."

The Unsolved Problem of the Unemployed

The new regime which commenced with the retirement of Bismarck started very favourably with the working men. The socialist laws were not renewed; and William II. unfolded his programme of social policy in two public statements. According to them, "the time, duration, and nature of labour were to be so regulated by the authority of the State that the preservation of health, the laws of decency, the economic requirements of the workers, and their claim to legal privileges should be permanently upheld." Legal enactments for the adequate representation of workers were to be passed in order to preserve peace between employers and employed.

The protection of workmen was soon considerably extended, since, by the law of the year 1891, Sunday labour, as well as the labour of children under thirteen years, was prohibited, and a maximum working day of eleven hours for adult female workers in factories was introduced. In other respects also, in spite of a strong current of opposition which set in among the wealthy citizen class, social reform has been distinctly advanced by the introduction of a maximum working day of twelve hours for all journeymen bakers, the closing of shops at nine o'clock in the evening, commercial courts for labour disputes between masters and employees, and, finally, continual improvements to the system of statutory insurance of workmen. During these years the Social Democracy has slowly but surely increased in extent;

Growth of Social Democracy

at the same time, however, a distinct disintegration is perceptible in the party. The congress at Erfurt in 1891, which drew up a programme, showed the party still united round the banner of Marx; but since then the main principles of Marx have been the centre of a heated controversy.

The leader of the opposition against Marxism, which is temporarily still found in the minority, is Eduard Bernstein, born January 6th, 1850, who, on account of earlier offences under the Press laws, is forced to live out of Germany; a writer equally remarkable for his wide learning, his grasp of facts, and his graceful style. Bernstein first opposed the party view that the disruption of the bourgeois society was soon to be anticipated, and that the tactics of the party must be determined by this prospect. Social conditions, he thought, had not come to a crisis in the way assumed by Marx. "The number of property owners has not become less, but greater. The enormous increase of social wealth is not accompanied by a dwindling number of capitalistic magnates, but by a growing number of capitalists of all grades. The middle classes change their character, but do not disappear from the social scale."

Selfish Tendencies of Capital

Even in the industrial world the concentration of production, according to Bernstein, confirms in some branches only the prophecies of socialistic criticism; in others it falls far short of them; and in agriculture concentration proceeds still more slowly. Politically the privilege of the capitalistic class gives way to democratic institutions, and the purely selfish tendencies of capital are more and more limited by society itself.

And in this way there will be less necessity and opportunity for the great political crashes, which the working class moreover would not be able, at present or for a long time, to surmount. The Social Democracy, therefore, may not reckon any more on the great catastrophe, but it ought politically to organise the working class, develop it into democracy, and fight for all reforms in the State which are calculated to elevate the working class and develop the constitution in the spirit of democracy.

The most important question of tactics in this sense is, which is the best way to extend the political and industrial rights of the German working men? The fact that Bernstein, in spite of the intense hostility which he encountered, remained in the ranks of the party, and the further fact that many "men of intellect" in it had already made themselves more or less known to him, opened a reassuring prospect for the future of the German working men's movement. If, in the course of time, the great mass of the social democracy should really abandon the sterile doctrines of Marx, and aim at an honourable social reform on national soil, nothing would remain of the old Social Democracy beyond the name, and the cult of the " constitution of the future " would sink into a harmless amusement.

It had been the custom for many years in Germany to regard the economic needs and requirements of the working class simply as the " social question," which was the outcome of the development of the capitalistic conditions relating to production, exchange, and competition. When this development had brought to light unfavourable results and new needs in other professional classes also, there could no longer be any doubt that the social question covered a much wider field. The most distinct expression of this is the fact

Movements of the German Tradesmen that these professional classes begin to organise themselves in a similar way to the working class, and noisily demand—as little disinterestedly as the proletariat—that the State should intervene with its authority on their behalf in the existing economic conditions. The master tradesmen did this first, and recently the small dealers. These two classes are generally kept in view when mention is made of the movement of the middle class in Germany; a movement which, moreover, has been of incalculably less importance than that of the working men.

The movement of the tradesmen is mainly represented by two associations : the United Trading Associations and the Universal German " Handwerkerbund." The political representation of their demands is effected by the Conservative and the Clerical party, and in an especially partial way by the " German Social Reformers," the section of the regular anti-Semites. There are two prominent postulates, from which, if granted, the tradesmen class, oppressed by the modern development of factories, trade, and demand, hope to gain renewed power ; first, that a proof of qualification be demanded from every man who in the future intends to set up as a master, and, secondly,

that it be obligatory on every master to join the guild of his calling. The proof of qualification is intended primarily to guarantee the quality of the work done by the tradesman ; secondly, to limit the competition in favour of those who are already in the business. The obligation to join a guild is intended to combine

Defensive Combination of Employers all masters in the common defence of their interests, and to make every individual master share the burden of the suggested methods of promoting trade, credit departments, courses of lectures, etc., since experience has shown that when entrance is voluntary only a minority are enrolled in the guilds. At the same time the following measures are proposed : the institution of chambers of tradesmen, in order to serve as a special board of control over the guilds and to represent duly the interests of the trade in all legislative matters ; also, restriction of military workshops, prison labour, and hawking ; further, prohibition of cooperative stores, travelling booths, public auction of tradesmen's goods, and of branch establishments ; finally, regulation of the system of tender in the interest of the tradesman class, and preferential rights for the claims of tradesmen in cases of bankruptcy.

The proposal as to the proof of qualification has already found a majority in the German Reichstag. On January 20th, 1890, a motion in its favour was passed by 130 votes against 92. But the Government emphatically declined to accede to this wish.

The Prussian Government showed itself far more friendly to the second chief demand of the tradesmen, that of compulsory membership of a guild, since it proposed in the Bundesrat the introduction of this regulation for most smaller industries within a legally determined limit in 1896. The Bundesrat altered the proposal in a liberal sense. The principle of universal compulsory membership was

Aims of Compulsory Guilds allowed to drop; on the contrary, the formation of a compulsory guild was made dependent on the resolution formed by the majority of the tradesmen concerned. In this form the proposal has been law since July, 1897. Stress must be laid on the point that the compulsory guilds may not establish common branches of business in order to promote the industrial undertakings of the members of the guild, and are therefore restricted in their field of activity; also that the law realises another demand of the tradesman party, since it institutes chambers of tradesmen with a number of legal privileges.

Besides this, the German Governments have endeavoured, by the enactment of a special law, to protect those engaged in the building trade more efficiently than before.

Government Protection for the Workers The Government for the present is very cool towards the increasing demands of the tradesmen, who aim at a sort of guild privilege. They had the following propositions announced as their own programme by representatives of the Prussian Board of Trade. First, the assistants who wish to become masters are to have an opportunity of educating themselves both in the technicalities of their business and also in arithmetic and bookkeeping; next there are to be permanent exhibitions of all the power machines, apparatus, and tools employed in the smaller industries; finally, the formation of societies of the masters for common economic objects, societies for raw materials, for shops, etc., was to be supported when possible. How much of this will be passed depends to a considerable extent on the good will of the tradesmen themselves, whose corporate action is far from becoming as prominent as the political middle-class movement, which demands State coercion for the exclusion of harassing competition.

After the trades agitation came the movement of the middle-class shopkeepers, which has hitherto been less important. The agitation started here with the " Zentralverband deutscher Kaufleute," in addition to which, in the year 1898, a " Bund der Handel- und Gewerbetreibenden" was formed. So far as this movement is directed against sordid competition, it has chosen a thoroughly justifiable object, which the German Governments have supported by providing special legislation to check this evil, which manifested itself under the most various forms. On the other hand, their agitation against the large warehouses has overshot the mark, and their intemperate opposition to such useful institutions as co-operative stores is emphatically to be condemned. Since 1899 a regular campaign has been organised against the warehouses, which met with considerable success. In Saxony, a number of towns has introduced a progressive tax on the profits of the large

Progressive Taxes in Saxony

business houses. In Bavaria, the tax on trades has been modified in the same sense, and in Prussia, since 1900, a Bill with a similar object has been introduced by the Government and accepted by the Landtag.

In Austria, the prospects of the Social Democracy were more favourable than in Germany, since the heated struggle among the nationalities for years repressed any interest in other questions, and the Government, by unscrupulous exercise of their powers against the Press and the rights of association and assembly took away all air and light from the budding plant of Social Democracy. The agitation of Lassalle had found but faint echo in Austria.

On the other hand, after the concession of the right of assembly in 1867, the new Social Democratic Labour party received for the moment a great stimulus; this, however, soon died away when, after its assent to the German " Eisenach programme," that privilege was again withdrawn from it by the Minister Giskra. A revival of the party was the consequence of the milder interpretation of the laws as to associations under the Hohenwart Ministry in 1871. The stricter policy of the Ministry of Adolf Auersperg, 1871–1879, produced, however, a second decline. Under the succeeding Ministry of Taaffe, which introduced milder measures, the Social Democracy was once more in the ascendant, and for the first time gathered followers from among the Czechist workmen.

Anarchism in Austria

At this epoch Anarchism found its way into Austria through the " Freiheit " of Most, and in a few years the whole working-men contingent of the Social Democracy had wheeled into the Anarchist camp. When, however, the Anarchist party had dug their own grave in 1885, by plots of assassination which led to a stupendous reaction, the Social Democracy slowly revived. Since then, being led by Victor Adler in a strict Marxist spirit, it was able to gain an increasing body of followers, and, under the Ministry of Badeni, it won the reform of the franchise, by which a fifth group, composed of electors qualified on the basis of universal and uniform suffrage, and electing seventy-two members, was added to the existing four electoral groups in 1895. Out of these the Social Democrats, in the election of the Reichsrat of 1897, secured fourteen members. The trades movement has also received a stimulus since 1893, although up to the present little more than 100,000 workmen share in it. Much progress was made in legislation as to the protection of workmen, especially under Taaffe, when trenchant factory laws, among them the maximum twelve hours' working day for men as well as compulsory insurance against sickness and accidents were introduced.

In Austria especially the movement of the middle class has attained great importance, which—under the protection of clerical members of the high nobility and many Catholic priests—represented there at the same time the anti-Semite party. But before a strong party showed itself, as early as 1883, the two chief demands of the tradesmen class, the enforcement of which is their foremost object, namely, the proof of qualification and compulsory association, were realised in Austria. The proof of qualification was, in the words of Count Richard Belcredi, who helped this agitation to a successful issue, designed to be " a most necessary protection of honest work and of existing industries against competition and pro-

Hungary's Backward Condition duction at ruinous under- prices ; a protection against inexperience, insufficient knowledge and means, as well as indiscretion on entering into business ; a protection of consumers and purchasers against inferior commodities."

The compulsory association was to organise trade, and to promote " esprit de corps," thoroughness, and honesty in all its branches. The result of these experiments in Austria, however, has shown that the proof of qualification has nowhere helped the tradesman, but in places has rather hindered him by the separation of trades ; and the compulsory associations have certainly not become practically efficient on any considerable scale. The direction of the middle class movement towards political goals has not only failed in attaining the expected result, but has momentarily hindered the co-operative self-aid movement which was benefiting the more efficient among the small shopkeepers.

In Hungary the backward condition of industrial development, and the strength of the purely national movements, have for many years presented insuperable obstacles to an extension of the Social Democratic party. In 1868 a Labour party was founded there with the programme of Lassalle.

After the beginning of the "seventies," this party also adopted a more Marxist creed, but did not long strictly maintain it.

At the beginning of the " eighties," anarchism brought confusion into the small group, and, on the other hand, subsequently a part of the Social Democrats often made extensive compromises with the middle-class parties. On the whole, the party remained limited to the few industrial districts, especially the capital Buda-Pesth, until, at the beginning of the " nineties," the agitation was suddenly carried with great success into the ranks of the labourers on the estates of the Magyar nobility. Since then the authorities, who had already been obliged to crush some risings with armed force, have prosecuted it with the utmost severity of the law. This party can hardly take part in the parliamentary elections, since the franchise is dependent on a payment of sixteen shillings in taxes.

Government's Opposition to Labour

The organisation of trades unions is still in an early stage, and has to contend with the authorities. Altogether there are some fifty thousand working men united in the trade associations. The legislation as to the protection of workmen is still quite undeveloped. The only real progress which can be recorded in recent times is the introduction of compulsory insurance against sickness.

In Switzerland the Social Democracy, notwithstanding the most complete liberty of movement at all times, and notwithstanding the shelter afforded to so many persecuted foreign socialists, has never been able to attain real importance. The reasons for this are to be found in the difficulties of agitation, owing to the defective concentration of industry, in the steady political and social development of the country, and, finally, in the sober, practical character of the people. The Social Democracy, founded in 1865 by partisans of the International Labour Association, has very slowly increased, so that its party organisation now numbers only 6,000 members. The " Grütliverein," which is composed exclusively of Swiss citizens, and goes hand in hand with the Social Democracy, is more important ; it has at the present day 15,000 members. The Social Democracy carried four candidates in the election to the Federal National Council in 1899. Its representation in

Democratic Movements in Switzerland

the cantonal Parliaments and in the town councils is equally weak. The trade-association movement is, apart from callings such as those of printers and railway employees, not very strongly developed ; but locally, for example, in Basle, co-operative stores have become important. In Denmark the social movement stood

Labour Conditions in Denmark from the first in close sympathy with the German Social Democracy, and therefore the Social Democratic party there adopted a programme which in its main features corresponded to the German.

The trade union organisation of the Danish workmen is of still greater significance ; up to the present some 80,000 industrial workers have joined it, and have greatly improved the conditions of their labour by energetic combination.

The statutory protection of workmen has not been much developed in Denmark ; it is mainly restricted to the ten hours' working day for young persons.

In Holland the large industries have been little developed ; the economic conditions of the country are determined by the flourishing agriculture and extensive wholesale trade.

The trades union movement is of greater importance, and some 30,000 organised workmen now take part in it. The legislation on social politics has culminated in the institution of an eleven hours' maximum working day for young persons and female workers.

In Belgium, where the already existing germs of large industries had attained an enormous development in the second half of the nineteenth century, a Social Democratic Labour party of some importance was eventually founded, after various useless attempts, towards the middle of the " seventies." Its pro-

Belgium's Large Industries gramme was modelled in all essential points on the German one. After the second half of the " eighties " the party received considerable additions of strength, since it used its utmost endeavours at the same time to form and to promote trades unions and industrial associations. Several of these Belgian industrial societies are well known for their excellent management and their wide sphere of influence, as, for example, the " Vooruit " at Ghent

and the " Volkshaus " at Brussels. In the year 1893 the workmen, in combination with the Radicals, extorted, by monster demonstrations and a general strike, universal suffrage, which was not indeed granted in a direct form, but under that of the so-called franchise by "majority of votes." At the first elections which took place on that system in 1894, 350,000 votes were polled for socialist candidates, of whom 32 were able to enter the Belgian Chamber. Since that date Socialism has continually won new adherents, so that it was in a position at the later elections to unite 530,000 votes in support of its candidates, and to effect the election of 41 deputies.

Legislation for the protection of workmen is restricted in Belgium chiefly to the twelve hours' maximum working day for young persons.

In Italy, where until recently there have not yet been any noteworthy industries, the relations of the employers to their workmen in town and country were by no

Spread of Anarchism in Italy means patriarchal; on the contrary, the workmen, since they were not sufficiently organised, were " sweated " to the greatest extent. It was only since the beginning of the " eighties " of the nineteenth century, when the Anarchists, after various riots, had finally been defeated by the stringent measures of the Government, that the Social Democracy began to come into prominence.

The trades unions have become comprehensive organisations, and the Social Democracy has also numerous followers, especially in North Italy, the real centre of industry, although associations of country workers have declared their adhesion to the party. Spain, in her industrial development, stands appreciably behind Italy. In other respects the politico-social life of Spain presents in important points practically the same peculiarities as that of Italy—namely, distress among the lower orders, a lamentable want of education among the people, and the intrusion into politics of numerous disreputable scions of the " higher " classes. Anarchism has, therefore, rapidly spread here since the end of the " eighties," while the Social Democrats could not make any way. GEORG ADLER

GREAT DATES FROM THE FRENCH REVOLUTION TO OUR OWN TIME

A.D.
1789 MAY: Meeting of States-General. JUNE: Tennis Court Oath. The States-General becomes the National or Constituent Assembly. JULY 14th: Fall of Bastille. AUG.: Abolition of Feudal privileges. OCT.: Insurrection of Women.

1790 FEB.: Leopold II. Emperor. JULY: Treaty of Reichenbach. AUGUST: Mutinies, and massacre of Nanci.

1791 MARCH: Death of Mirabeau. MAY: Canada Act. JUNE: Flight of Louis to Varennes. AUG.: Conference of Pilnitz. SEPT.: Louis accepts the Constitution. OCT.: "Legislative" Assembly meets.

1792 JAN.: Treaty of Jassy. FEB.: Treaty between Austria and Prussia. MARCH: 1st, Francis II. Emperor; 29th, Gustavus III. of Sweden assassinated. APRIL: France declares war on Austria. JUNE: Mob breaks into Tuileries. JULY: 24th, Prussia declares war; 27th, Brunswick's proclamation. AUG.: Mob attack on Tuileries; Louis a prisoner. Supremacy of Paris Commune. Fall of Longwy. SEPT.: September massacres. Cannonade of Valmy. "National Convention" meets; Republic proclaimed. OCT. and NOV.: Success of Republican armies. DEC.: Trial of Louis XVI. opens.

1793 JAN.: Second partition of Poland. Louis beheaded. FEB.: Declaration of war with England and Holland. Revolt of La Vendée. MAR.: Revolutionary Tribunal. APRIL: Flight of Dumouriez. JUNE: Fall of Gironde. JULY: Revolt of Girondist departments. Death of Marat. SEPT: Law of the Suspect. Carnot. OCT.: Republican Calendar. Marie Antoinette and Girondins guillotined. NOV.: Reign of Terror. DEC.: Toulon captured.

1794 MARCH: Fall of Hébertists. APRIL: Fall of Danton: Robespierre supreme. Pichegru in Netherlands. JUNE: 1st, Howe's victory; 26th, Jourdan's victory at Fleurus; 28th, Thermidorian reaction. Fall of Robespierre; end of Reign of Terror. OCT.: Pichegru overruns Holland.

1795 JAN.: Third partition of Poland. APRIL: Peace of Basle with Prussia. JULY: Peace of Basle with Spain. Emigrés crushed at Quiberon. OCT.: Insurrection of Vendémiaire suppressed. Directory established.

1796 MAY: Bonaparte in Italy. Lodi. SEPT.: Archduke Charles repulses invasion of Jourdan and Moreau. OCT.: Spain allies with France. NOV.: Arcola; Paul I. Tsar of Russia. Gustavus IV. assumes government of Sweden.

1797 JAN.: Rivoli. FEB.: Cape St. Vincent. APRIL-JUNE: Mutinies in British Fleet. Treaty of Leoben. Repression of Venice. Cisalpine and Ligurian Republics constituted. SEPT.: Coup d'état of Fructidor. Death of Hoche. OCTOBER: Camperdown. Treaty of Campo Formio. NOV.: Frederic William III. King of Prussia.

1798 APRIL: Helvetic Republic constituted. MAY: Egyptian expedition sails from Toulon. Rebellion in Ireland. JUNE: Vinegar Hill. JULY: Battle of the Pyramids. AUG.: Battle of the Nile. Second coalition formed.

1799 JAN.: Parthenopean Republic of Naples. MARCH: Stockach. APRIL: Magnano. MAY: Bonaparte repulsed at Acre. JUNE: Trebbia. AUG.: Novi. Capture of Dutch Fleet in the Texel. SEPT.: Restoration of Naples monarchy. Withdrawal of Suwarrow. OCT.: Return of Bonaparte. NOV.: Coup d'état of Brumaire. Bonaparte First Consul.

1800 JUNE: Marengo. AUG.: Union between Great Britain and Ireland. DEC.: Hohenlinden.

1801 FEBRUARY: Resignation of Pitt. Treaty of Lunéville. MARCH: Abercrombie at Aboukir. APRIL: Nelson at Copenhagen. Alexander I. Tsar. OCTOBER: Peace preliminaries. The Batavian Republic organised.

1802 MARCH: Peace of Amiens. APRIL: French Concordat with Papacy. AUG.: Bonaparte First Consul for life. SEPT.: Piedmont annexed to France.

A.D.
1803 MARCH: Secularisation of ecclesiastical states in Germany. MAY: War declared between France and Great Britain; French occupy Hanover.

1804 FEB.: Royalist Plot of Pichegru and Cadoudal; Moreau exiled. MARCH: Murder of Duc d'Enghien. Issue of the Code Napoleon. MAY: Napoleon I. Emperor of the French. Pitt returns to office. Russia forms alliance with Prussia. NOV.: Alliance joined by Austria.

1805 MARCH: Villeneuve sails from Toulon. MAY: Italian Republic becomes a monarchy, with Napoleon king. Eugene Beauharnais viceroy. JULY: Calder defeats Villeneuve. SEPT: Third Coalition formed. OCT.: Capitulation of Ulm. Trafalgar. DEC.: Austerlitz. Treaties of Schönbrunn and Presburg. Bourbon Dynasty of Naples deposed.

1806 JAN.: Death of Pitt. End of Holy Roman Empire. APRIL: Joseph Bonaparte King of Naples. JUNE: Louis Bonaparte King of Holland. JULY: Confederation of the Rhine. OCT.: Prussia crushed at Jena and Auerstädt. NOV.: The Berlin Decree.

1807 JAN.: The Orders in Council. Act abolishing Slave Trade. FEB.: Eylau. MARCH: Portland Ministry. Canning Foreign Secretary. APRIL: Treaty of Bartenstein. JUNE: Friedland. JULY: Treaty of Tilsit. Jerome Bonaparte King of Westphalia. SEPT.: Copenhagen bombarded. OCT.: Treaty of Fontainebleau. French troops enter Spain. Stein begins his reforms in Prussia. DEC.: Junot at Lisbon.

1808 MARCH: Abdication of Charles IV. of Spain. MAY: Meeting at Bayonne. Rising of Spain. JUNE: Joseph Bonaparte King of Spain. Murat King of Naples. JULY: Capitulation of Baylen. AUG.: Vimeiro. Convention of Cintra. OCT.: Meeting of Erfurt. NOV.: Fall of Stein. Napoleon goes to Spain. DEC.: Advance and retreat of Sir John Moore. Napoleon leaves Spain.

1809 JAN.: Moore at Corunna. FEB.: Fall of Saragossa. APRIL: Wellesley at Lisbon. Austria declares war. MAY: Tyrolese revolt. Aspern. Annexation of Papal States. JUNE: Soult forced to evacuate Portugal. JULY: Wagram; Talavera. Walcheren Expedition. OCT.: Peace of Vienna. Bernadotte becomes Crown Prince of Sweden.

1810 MARCH: Napoleon marries Marie Louise. JULY: Annexation of North Sea Coast Districts. SEPT.: Busaco; Cortes meets at Cadiz. NOV.: Torres Vedras. DEC.: Tsar withdraws from Continental System.

1811 MAY: Fuentes d'Oñoro and Albuera.
1812 JAN.: Ciudad Rodrigo. APRIL: Badajoz. JUNE: Moscow Expedition starts. Liverpool Ministry. JULY: Salamanca. SEPT.: Borodino. Burning of Moscow. OCT.: Retreat from Moscow. NOV.: Bridge of Beresina. DEC.: Agreement of Tauroggen.

1813 FEB.: Treaty of Kalisch. MAY: Lützen and Bautzen. JUNE: Vittoria. Treaty of Reichenbach. AUG.: Katzbach and Dresden. SEPT.: Treaty of Töplitz. OCT.: Leipzig.

1814 JAN.: Treaty of Kiel. Norway joined to Sweden. FEB.: La Rothière. MARCH: Capitulation of Paris. APRIL: Battle of Toulouse. Napoleon goes to Elba; Bourbon restoration. MAY: Treaty of Paris. NOV.: Congress of Vienna meets.

1815 MARCH: Napoleon lands and returns to Paris. MAY: Murat overthrown at Tolentino. JUNE: Ligny, Quatre-Bras, and Waterloo. JULY: Second Bourbon restoration. Napoleon sent to St. Helena. Holy Alliance. NOV.: Peace of Paris.

1818 Congress of Aix-la-Chapelle. Evacuation of France by forces of the Allies. Pindari war in India.

1819 The Six Acts.
1820 Accession of George IV. Queen Caroline scandals. Royalist reaction in France. Revolution of Riego in Spain. Revolution in Portugal and separation from Brazil. Insurrections in the two Sicilies. Congress of Troppau, afterwards Laibach.

GREAT DATES FROM THE FRENCH REVOLUTION TO OUR OWN TIME

A.D.		A.D.	
1821	Death of Napoleon. Suppression of Italian revolts. Greek insurrection against Turkey.	1853	Turkey declares war against Russia.
1822	Canning, Foreign Secretary. Independence of South American colonies recognised. Congress of Vienna. Greek successes.	1854	Crimean war. Battles of Alma, Balaclava, and Inkerman.
1823	Ferdinand VII. of Spain re-establishes absolutism by French help. Reaction in Portugal. Huskisson's commercial policy in England.	1855	Palmerston Ministry. Fall of Sebastopol. Alexander II. Tsar.
1824	Accession of Charles X. in France.	1856	End of War. Persian and Chinese wars. Lord Canning in India.
1825	Ibrahim Pasha in Greece. Nicholas I. Tsar of Russia.	1857	Indian Mutiny ; revolt broken.
1826	Canning prevents Spanish intervention in Portugal. Fall of Missolonghi.	1858	Orsini's bomb. Derby Administration. Mutiny suppressed ; India transferred to the Crown.
1827	Canning, Prime Minister. Anglo-Russian Treaty of London. Death of Canning. Battle of Navarino.	1859	Napoleon supports Sardinia against Austria ; Magenta and Solferino. Peace of Villafranca. Palmerston's return.
1828	Wellington, Prime Minister. Test and Corporation Acts repealed. Clare election. Usurpation of Dom Miguel in Portugal. War between Russia and Turkey.	1860	Union of Savoy and Nice to France. Garibaldi in Sicily. The Commons, the Peers, and the Paper Duty.
1829	Catholic emancipation. Treaty of Adrianople. Greek independence recognised.	1861	Victor Emmanuel King of Italy. Death of Cavour. Abd ul-Aziz Sultan. William I. in Prussia. Emancipation of Russian serfs. North American Civil War.
1830	Accession of William IV. in England. Grey Prime Minister. The July Revolution. Louis Philippe King of the French. Risings in Belgium, Poland, and Sicily. Accession of Ferdinand II. in Naples.	1862	Battle of Aspromonte. King Otto expelled from Greece. Bismarck Prussian Minister. Cotton famine.
1831	Belgium recognised as an independent kingdom. Polish revolt suppressed. English Reform Bill rejected.	1863	Schleswig-Holstein war. Suppression of Poland. The Alabama.
1832	Reform Act passed.	1864	Death of Palmerston.
1833	Otto of Bavaria King of the Hellenes. Isabella succeeds in Spain. Miguel expelled from Portugal. Slavery abolished in the British Empire.	1865	Russell Ministry. Gastein Convention.
		1866	Seven Weeks' War of Prussia and Austria. Sadowa. Venetia ceded to Victor Emmanuel. French in Rome. Dual Government of Austria-Hungary.
1834	Melbourne Ministry. Poor Law Reform. On Melbourne's dismissal by the king, Peel attempts to form Ministry.	1867	Disraeli's Reform Bill. B.N.A. Consolidation Act. Abyssinian War.
1835	Melbourne Ministry returns. Palmerston in control of Foreign Affairs. Ferdinand I. Austrian Emperor.	1868	Isabella expelled from Spain. Fenian outrages. Abolition of Church rates.
1837	Accession of Victoria. Hanover separated from Great Britain. Papineau's revolt in Canada.	1869	Gladstone Administration. Irish Land Bill and Disestablishment.
1838	Lord Durham in Canada. Development of Chartism.	1870	Franco-German War ; Sedan ; Third Republic. Italy unified. English Education Act.
1839	Mehemet Ali in Syria. Abd ul-Mejid sultan. Peel and the Bedchamber question. Anti-Corn Law League.	1871	Surrender of Paris. German Empire proclaimed. Black Sea Conference.
		1872	Alabama award.
1840	Mehemet Ali checked. Marriage of Queen Victoria. Canadian Act of Reunion. Chinese " Opium " War.	1873	MacMahon President in France.
		1874	Alfonso XII. in Spain. Disraeli Administration.
1841	Kabul disaster. Peel, Prime Minister.	1875	Purchase of Suez Canal shares.
1842	Dost Mohammed restored. Peel's sliding scale. The Disruption in Scotland.	1876	Bulgarian atrocities. Abd ul-Hamid Sultan.
1843	Annexation of Sindh. Gwalior Campaign.	1877	Russo-Turkish War. Annexation of Transvaal.
1845	First Sikh War ; ended next year.	1878	Treaty of San Stefano. Berlin Congress. Afghan wars ; ended in 1880.
1846	Repeal of the Corn Laws. Pius IX. Pope. Russell administration.	1879	Zulu War : Isandhlwana.
1847	Fielden's Factory Act.	1880	Gladstone Administration.
1848	February Revolution ; Second French Republic. Risings in Sicily and Naples. March Revolution in Germany. Revolt of Schleswig-Holstein from Denmark. Revolts of Lombardy and Venice against Austria. Frankfort Parliament. Radetzky defeats Charles Albert of Sardinia at Custozza. Accession of Frederic VII. in Denmark, Francis Joseph in Austria ; Louis Napoleon President of French Republic. Dalhousie in India. Collapse of Chartist movement in England. Reaction victorious in Germany and Austria. Second Sikh War.	1881	Majuba. Retrocession of Transvaal.
		1882	Bombardment of Alexandria. Tel-el-Kebir.
		1884	Franchise and Redistribution Acts.
		1885	Death of C. G. Gordon. Penjdeh incident.
		1886	First Home Rule Bill. Salisbury Ministry.
		1888	Parnell Commission.
		1889	Annexation of Burmah.
		1893	Second Home Rule Bill.
		1894	Death Duties. Armenian atrocities.
		1895	Salisbury's Unionist Administration. Jameson raid.
1849	Hungarian revolt suppressed. Victor Emmanuel King of Sardinia. Dissolution of Frankfort Parliament. Reaction in Central Italy. Annexation of Punjab.	1896	Venezuela boundary dispute. Cretan rising.
		1898	Conquest of Sudan.
1850	North German Confederation. Convention of Olmütz. Australian Constitution Bill. The Queen's memorandum to Palmerston.	1899	Boxer rising in China. South African War begins.
		1900	Australian Commonwealth.
1851	Coup d'état in France. Palmerston dismissed. Great Exhibition.	1901	Accession of Edward VII.
		1902	End of Boer War.
1852	Schleswig-Holstein question. Cavour Minister. Death of Duke of Wellington. Napoleon III. Emperor.	1903	Russo-Japanese war.
		1904	Separation of Norway and Sweden.
		1905	Morocco and Egyptian agreements.
		1906	Grant of responsible government in S. Africa.
		1903	Constitutional Revolution in Turkey.

GLIMPSES of EUROPE'S CAPITAL CITIES

IN THE HEART OF LONDON
Valentine

VIEW FROM THE MONUMENT, SHOWING THE RIVER THAMES, THE TOWER & TOWER BRIDGE

TRAFALGAR SQUARE AND THE NELSON COLUMN AS SEEN FROM THE WEST SIDE

Valentine

ANOTHER VIEW FROM THE MONUMENT, SHOWING ST. PAUL'S IN THE DISTANCE

LONDON, THE CAPITAL OF THE BRITISH EMPIRE

PANORAMIC VIEW, SHOWING EIGHT OF THE BRIDGES ACROSS THE RIVER SEINE

Frith

THE AVENUE DE L'OPERA, WITH THE OPERA HOUSE IN THE DISTANCE

"LA VILLE LUMIÈRE": SCENES IN THE BEAUTIFUL CAPITAL OF FRANCE

A GENERAL VIEW, SHOWING THE IMPERIAL PALACE AND THE CATHEDRAL

Frith

UNTER DEN LINDEN, ONE OF THE MOST FAMOUS STREETS IN EUROPE

IN BERLIN, THE PROSPEROUS CAPITAL OF THE GERMAN EMPIRE

NEVSKII-PROSPEKT, ONE OF THE FINEST THOROUGHFARES IN THE WORLD

THE OLD ADMIRALTY BUILDING FROM ONE OF THE BRIDGES SPANNING THE NEVA

ST. PETERSBURG, THE MODERN CAPITAL OF THE RUSSIAN EMPIRE

PART OF THE FRANZENSRING, THE PRINCIPAL BOULEVARD OF VIENNA

Photochrome
BUDAPEST, SHOWING THE SUSPENSION BRIDGE ACROSS THE RIVER DANUBE

THE CAPITAL CITIES OF AUSTRIA AND HUNGARY

A BIRD'S-EYE VIEW, SHOWING THE PICTURESQUE MOSQUES AND MINARETS

ANOTHER VIEW OF THE CITY, INCLUDING THE GALATA BRIDGE

CONSTANTINOPLE, THE CAPITAL OF THE TURKISH EMPIRE

LOOKING TOWARDS THE RUINS OF THE ACROPOLIS

Photochrome

GENERAL VIEW OF THE MODERN TOWN

ATHENS, THE CAPITAL OF ANCIENT AND MODERN GREECE

ROME, SEEN FROM ST. PETER'S, SHOWING THE TIBER AND THE CASTLE OF ST. ANGELO

GENERAL VIEW OF BERNE, WITH THE BERNESE OBERLAND IN THE DISTANCE

ROME AND BERNE: THE CAPITALS OF ITALY AND SWITZERLAND

PANORAMA OF MADRID, GIVING A GLIMPSE OF THE PRADO IN THE FOREGROUND

GENERAL VIEW OF LISBON, LOOKING FROM ST. PEDRO DE ALCANTARA

MADRID AND LISBON: THE SPANISH AND PORTUGUESE CAPITALS

THE BRUSSELS PALAIS DE JUSTICE: ONE OF THE WORLD'S LARGEST BUILDINGS

THE BRONZE STATUE OF WILLIAM II. AT THE HAGUE

SCENES IN THE CAPITAL CITIES OF BELGIUM AND HOLLAND

A PICTURESQUE GLIMPSE OF BUCHAREST, THE CAPITAL OF ROUMANIA

GENERAL VIEW OF SOFIA, WITH MONUMENT TO ALEXANDER II. OF RUSSIA

PANORAMIC VIEW OF BELGRADE AS SEEN FROM THE RIVER DANUBE

THE CAPITALS OF ROUMANIA, BULGARIA, AND SERVIA

EUROPE: SEVENTH DIVISION
THE EUROPEAN POWERS TO-DAY
AND A SURVEY OF THE BRITISH EMPIRE

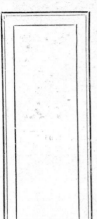

As concerns our present great geographical division—Europe—we have now reached the last historical phase. It remains for us to take the states into which that division is now split up, to give an account of their present-day characteristics, and to relate the present with the past and the immediate future. For it is not the historian's part to prophesy, though he has provided the data for prophetic inductions, within very circumscribed limits.

At this stage, therefore, we give a picture of the political and social conditions prevailing, first of all, in every Continental state, large or small, from Russia to Andorra, dwelling on those features which appear to be of the strongest interest in each individual case.

Finally, we turn to our own islands, and thence digress to an account of our world-empire, which needs to be treated as a unity, although such treatment of it has been impossible to fit into our continuous narrative of world-history built up on a geographical basis. For it is the history of an expansion into every quarter of the globe, the picture of an empire whose flag is planted on every continent, whose dominion in every continent but Europe itself extends from sea to sea, and claims to include, metaphorically at least, in that dominion the boundless ocean itself.

RUSSIA
By Dr. E. J. Dillon

TURKEY, GREECE AND THE BALKANS
By F. A. McKenzie

AUSTRIA-HUNGARY
By Henry W. Nevinson

GERMANY
By Charles Lowe, M.A.

BELGIUM, HOLLAND, LUXEMBURG, SWITZERLAND
By Robert Machray, B.A.

ITALY AND SAN MARINO
By William Durban, B.A., and Robert Machray, B.A.

FRANCE, MONACO, AND ANDORRA
By Richard Whiteing and Robert Machray, B.A.

SPAIN AND PORTUGAL
By Martin Hume, M.A.

SCANDINAVIA
By William Durban, B.A.

THE UNITED KINGDOM
By Arthur D. Innes, M.A.

THE BRITISH EMPIRE
By Sir Harry H. Johnston, K.C.B.

THE FIRST DUMA, WHICH SAT FROM MAY 10TH TILL JULY 22ND, 1906
From the drawing by L. Sabbatier

THE SECOND DUMA, WHICH LASTED FROM MARCH 5TH TILL JUNE 16TH, 1907

THE THIRD DUMA, WHICH ASSEMBLED ON NOVEMBER 1ST, 1907

RUSSIA'S PARLIAMENT: PICTURES OF THE THREE DUMAS

EUROPEAN POWERS TO-DAY
RUSSIA IN OUR OWN TIME
ITS POVERTY, CORRUPTION, AND OPPRESSION
WITH A GLOOMY AND UNCERTAIN OUTLOOK
By Dr. E. J. Dillon

THE Russia of the twentieth century is the product of manifold social forces, religious influences, and political currents, of which the most salient and obvious began to be keenly felt and generally noticed in the reign of Peter the Great. Down to that historic epoch the nation had kept studiously aloof from the progressive peoples of Europe, leading a life apart.

Unlike the Poles and Czechs, whom communion with papal Rome had brought into continuous contact with all that was stimulating in Western civilisation, Russia isolated herself by embracing Byzantine Christianity and accepting Byzantine culture. Peter the Great was the first ruler to break with this paralysing past and to endeavour to bring his people into line with their European neighbours.

Thinking Russia in Two Camps

The task was superlatively arduous, and the efforts constantly made since then to accomplish it divided thinking Russia into two camps, which towards the middle of the nineteenth century received the names of the Slavophile and the Western.

The men of the latter party yearned for the regime of France or England. Those of the former thanked God for having vouchsafed to His chosen people the best of all possible institutions : Greek orthodoxy as the most perfect Christian creed ; Russian autocracy, conceived as a paternal relation between tsar and people, and therefore the most satisfactory of all forms of government ; and the village commune as the highest type of social organism. Perfect in idea, those institutions had been abused by men, and were consequently now capable of great improvement. But to put them wholly away for Western innovations would be suicidal. Indeed, the circumstance that they constituted the exclusive heritage of the Russian race might, it was argued, be taken as a proof that Providence has destined the Slav Messiah of the nations to take the place of effete Europe in the vanguard of the cultured world.

The note of Slav thought being the universal and the absolute, it too often happens that inadequate attention is paid by Russian reformers to the concrete, the real, the relative. In this way

The Dream of the Idealists

it came to pass that the friends of Western culture in the tsardom longed not so much for the grafting of European ideas on the Russian stock as for a quick and complete break with the past and the complete regeneration of the nation on the lines of extreme Socialist theories. Orthodoxy, autocracy, and the village commune, everything Russian, was to be thrown into the melting-pot, whence a rejuvenated nation was to emerge.

When far-resonant events like the Crimean War allied themselves with these nihilistic notions, from the union of the two sprang that powerful current of anarchistic thought and feeling which openly and secretly has been undermining the bases of the Russian Empire ever since. With this tendency, which has made itself felt in all classes of society—being industriously spread by village schools and popular literature, as well as by the teachings of professional revolutionists—the names of Alexander Herzen, Nicholas Dobroliuboff, and Leo Tolstoy have been closely associated. Most of the active leaders of the reform movement, saturated

Russia's War with Japan

to the heart's core with those subversive ideas, were unwilling to make allowances for Russian ways of thought, modes of living, religious feeling, and secular customs. Midway between these two camps stood the ruling oligarchs—planless, listless, resourceless.

The war with Japan revealed and intensified the astounding weakness of the established political and social fabric, hastened the downfall of the regime, and offered the reform party a golden opportunity to put their fanciful projects to the test of realisation. When the tsar, giving way to what seemed the wishes of his people, had laid down his prerogative of absolutism and promised far-reaching political and social reforms, the ground, cleared of ancient encumbrances, presented a unique site for the erection of a stable democratic fabric.

Guided by ordinary common-sense and commanded by an unflinching will, the reform party might have successfully infused into the nation all the democratic current it was capable of absorbing. The leverage it had acquired was enormous. Some few discerned then what the many can plainly see to-day—that that party by first accepting the power, without responsibility, which was well within its reach, might have soon afterwards obtained the reins of government, and begun its grandiose and perilous experiment upon the nation.

But, confident of an easy victory, disdainful of help, impatient of advice, and chafed by delay, the Democrats violently opposed, in lieu of steadily supporting, Count Witte's administration.

Democrats in Quest of Allies

In quest of allies, they made a high bid for the support of the Jews, the peasants, the working man, the lower clergy, and the troops by promising reforms which it would have taken a century of continuous effort and untold sums of money to realise. At the best of times Russian reformers lack the saving sense of measure, but now they broke loose from all restraints and ended by alienating the sympathies of many

true Democrats who could gauge the tendency of the time and estimate the speed and the trend of the main social and political currents of semi-articulate Russia.

Since the partial revolution of 1905–6, which rendered many weighty problems acute without starting practical solutions for any of them, Russia has been passing through a transitional phase, the duration of which it is impossible to predict. That extraordinary upheaval, which may be aptly characterised as the result of a struggle not so much between two forces as between two weaknesses, between an epileptic and a paralytic organism, began in truly characteristic fashion. Whole sections of the Statute Book and State Law were abrogated by implication. Customs and traditions, hallowed by ages, were informally but effectively abolished, and nothing whatever was put in their places. In short, a sponge was passed over the slate, on which the mob was allowed to write its conflicting demands, and almost everybody was surprised to see that anarchy ensued. Some of the worst effects of the confusion which was thus

Fruits of the Recent Revolution

produced still continue to make themselves felt in the principal departments of public life. Many of the political and social questions then formulated are still pressing for answers. Between the theory and practice of the present administration many a chasm is still unbridged.

Thus it would tax the ingenuity of a Montesquieu to determine the type of monarchy which in Russia has succeeded absolutism, and the courtly Almanach de Gotha has illustrated the difficulty by offering a definition of the regime in terms which contradict each other. One may take it that the government is still an autocracy, tempered, as the rule of the first Romanoffs was, by the wishes of the people; but with this difference, that in the seventeenth century public opinion was focussed fitfully in the Zemsky Councils, whereas to-day it is permanently embodied in the Duma and the Council of the Empire.

One of the most momentous changes brought about by the revolution of 1905 affects the legislative machinery of the tsardom. Formerly the monarch was the sole fountain head of law, and although he invariably availed himself of the services of the Council of the Empire and the Senate, which drafted Bills and interpreted statutes, his influence upon law-making was paramount and unchallenged. But the charter which he bestowed upon his people in 1905 contains a promise that henceforth no measure shall be inscribed upon the Statute Book without the assent of the two representative Chambers.

That is now become one of the fundamental maxims of the Russian Constitution. But, like all such principles, it is applicable and absolute only in normal times. During periods of public trouble exceptions are provided for. For example, if in the intervals between two Dumas, the Crown believes that the needs of the empire call for special legislation, the tsar may on his own authority promulgate it, on condition that on the reassembling of the nation's spokesmen the measure be laid before them for confirmation or repeal. The one instance in which the emperor, going further, altered the fundamental laws themselves and accomplished what was technically a coup d'état, occurred in June, 1907, when he authorised M. Stolypin to change materially the electoral law. Among the arguments brought forward in defence of this bold line of action two seem **Two Dumas** especially cogent. The franchise **that** as established in 1905 had no **Failed** claims whatever to be included among the fundamental laws, which alone are "immutable." Indeed, it had been printed among them solely in consequence of a mere chancellery blunder. Moreover, by their nature the conditions which a citizen of almost any country must fulfil in order to qualify as a voter, especially when the franchise is very restricted, are not stable. They change with the times, and no serious legislator would seek to canonise them.

Another consideration that weighed with the Crown and the Premier was the danger that threatened representative institutions in Russia at that critical period of their existence. Two successive Dumas had come together, bitterly disappointed the hopes of their friends, and realised those of their enemies. And if the third experiment should fail, the grant of an elective Chamber would most probably have been suspended sine die. In order to avert this calamity it seemed necessary to get together an assembly that would consent to discharge its own functions within the narrow limits outlined by the constitution. A set of arbitrary voting qualifications was therefore drawn up by the Prime Minister, which,

however illogical, unfair, and indefensible they may be on theoretic grounds, attained the end in view. The third Duma accordingly met, passed laws, discussed Bills, increased the pay of its own members to an extent that was deemed exorbitant, and accustomed the nation to the working of a legislative **The Cabinet** assembly. The responsibility **and** attaching to that course and **its Members** the credit for these results belong principally, if not exclusively, to M. Stolypin. The Duma in its present shape, and indeed the entire machinery of government, continue to exhibit in a superlative degree signs of the haste with which they were elaborated and proofs of the faultiness of their working.

In form they are stamped with the mark of transition, in character they exhibit the defects of the qualities which render the Slavs socially popular and politically inferior. The "Cabinet," presided over by the Premier, includes only a certain number of the tsar's official advisers, and eliminates nearly all the more important ones. The Ministers of War, Marine, and Foreign Affairs, as well as the Minister of the Imperial Court are outside the Cabinet. At bottom this may be an advantage, for it makes them quite independent of the Prime Minister. If they take part in any parliamentary discussion, the act is understood to be quite spontaneous on their part, and in each case they must first obtain the express authorisation of the emperor. The Prime Minister's authority does not touch them, nor does the Crown, when appointing or dismissing them, consult him.

The autocracy as it prevailed down to 1905 has thus disappeared, but it seems impossible to define with anything approaching to precision the type of government that has taken its place. Nor would it be easier to trace the limits that divide the legislative, judicial, and executive powers from each other. The tsar, indeed, **The Tsar** still retains his old title of **Still an** Autocrat, despite the needlessly **Autocrat** bitter opposition offered to it by democratic politicians who spend most of their energy in barren tilting against windmills. But he has preserved more than the title. No measure can acquire the force of law without his assent. All authority emanates from him. He is the source of justice and mercy, and his dispensing power— of which, however, he but seldom makes use—is extensive enough to enable him indirectly to temper or annul a penal law. The tsar is the one connecting link between the Russian nation and all the foreign members of the international community. He is also the war-lord of Russia, to whom the land and sea forces owe obedience, and he is the sole judge of the acts of his Ministers, who are respon-

Disappointed Liberal Reformers sible to no other institution in the empire. What disappointed Liberal reformers most bitterly complain of is the Duma's impotence even in financial matters. And in truth its influence is chiefly negative.

The Lower Chamber may criticise, but cannot reform. If its members pass a Bill obnoxious to the Government, the Upper House is virtually certain to throw it out. A Chamber of Reconciliation is then convoked, composed of a number of members of both legislatures. If these fail to agree, everything remains as it was before, and if a money vote is in question, the Minister continues to receive the sum allotted to him by the estimates of the preceding year. That the Duma should be thus restricted to the rôle of censor is deemed to be one of the worst defects of the present system of government.

On the other hand, it cannot be gainsaid that the soft, plastic character of the Slavs, the feebleness of their social interests, and the ease with which they turn away from deeds to words, are also to some extent answerable for the barrenness of the legislative sessions. The present Speaker, M. Khomyakoff, who is himself endowed with the admirable characteristics of the Slav in an eminent degree, has frequently pointed out the evil and explained it. Speaking in November, 1908, to a publicist about the glut of Bills and the slowness with which they are dealt with, he is reported to have said : " Looking at it all round, I must say that, to my thinking, the legislative machinery should

Squabbles in the Duma be changed in some way. I cannot indicate how this is to be done . . . but it is easy to see that if on July 1st this year there remained 222 Bills untouched, and by November 1st of the same year 290 more were laid before the House, well, there is something to think about. . . But all that would be nothing if the members of the Duma hit it off together, more or less. But they are eternally squabbling, eternally fighting. With regret I am obliged

to say that of late these quarrels have increased. On the whole, however, that is in our character. Let four men come together, and the very first thing they do is to rummage each other's souls in quest of each other's defects. About the good points nobody cares, but they infallibly rake up the delinquencies."

It is almost impossible to watch the working of the administrative mechanism of to-day without seeing that the Duma has lost the fascination for Russia which it possessed in the year 1906. It was then looked up to as a sort of brazen serpent in the Desert of Bureaucracy, created in order to heal. To-day it is but one of the many state departments of which there were then too many, whose privileged members are paid high salaries by the starving people for doing little or nothing. It has ceased to be a fountain of good, and is looked upon as a source of malignant evils.

It has no hold whatever on the country, and therefore cannot act as a breakwater against the heavy rollers of the revolutionary sea which threatens to sweep away the dynasty and the monarchical regime.

The Creeping Paralysis of the Duma And as the Duma is the only rampart which the monarchy now possesses against a general democratic movement — just as the police is the only protection on which the monarch relies against terrorist plots— it follows that, parallel with the creeping paralysis of the Duma goes the perilous weakening of the monarchic regime.

Thus the Russian Autocracy might be likened to a mighty rock which after centuries of repose has just rolled from the summit of a high mountain, but has been stopped midway down. In its present precarious position it may remain for years, or it may suddenly resume its downward course to-morrow, crushing everything in its way. This latter contingency is deemed by many to be all the more likely as many forces are working deliberately, methodically, and perseveringly, to set it rolling; while most of the officials who have undertaken the task of thwarting these, are either listless, negligent, or else secretly in the service of the enemy.

Evidently, then, change is a necessity. The sole question is, who shall have the shaping of it ? At present the dynasty has the opportunity, and, to a limited extent, the ways and means, but apparently lacks the right men or else the will to appoint them. Even of the Bureaucrats, who at present wear the livery and receive the pay of the Crown, a large percentage are desirous of ulterior and far-reaching changes. A new political and social revolution is what they ardently hope for. And they would not only welcome its advent but would work actively to hasten it if they could take this step with impunity. Some of them indeed do, but stern necessity compels the majority to bide their time in relative quiescence.

This attitude is but one of many symptoms of a dangerous disorder which the ruling classes cannot, or will not, diagnose. Since the October 17th to 30th, 1905, there has been a bewildering dislocation of the political forces of the country, but it came to pass so gradually that even its occurrence—to say nothing of its significance—has not been realised or even noticed by the professional watchmen of the nation. But its effects are felt, although they are not being traced to the true cause. The Cabinet, the dynasty, the ruling classes—administrative and legislative—are now on one side, and the people are on the other. There is no organic nexus between the governing bodies and the nation. Liberty is banished to the parliamentary island of the Tavrida Palace, law to the hall of the Senate and the pages of the civil and criminal codes, justice to the world to come, and the few measures of reform with which the Duma or the Cabinet periodically toy are as indifferent to the nation as the caress of a soft and tender hand squandered on a tortoise's shell would be to the slumbering tortoise inside.

The Shadow of a Second Revolution

The nation is marching steadily along its own grooves of thought, and striving towards its own ideals, and the governing classes are moving over theirs. The link between them is purely mechanical, not organic, and that, too, seems destined shortly to snap. Even now the subterranean forces of upheaval are so active, so constant, so successful, and the resistance offered them is so feeble, that even strangers with open eyes and ears, and nimble minds, can predict with perfect confidence the coming of the second revolution.

The principal mainstay of the dynasty, and, indeed, of order in the empire, is at present the army, whose loyalty has withstood temptations that appeared irresistible. Suspected in 1905 of being honeycombed with sedition, it still constitutes not only the most efficient protection to the regime, but to all elements of peaceful progress in the nation. In 1905 vigilant observers confidently predicted the saturation of the army with anarchistic or socialistic views within three years, that being the period necessary for a complete renovation of the troops. But although the efforts of the revolutionary party are concentrated on the land and sea forces, without whose help or connivance they will find it difficult to carry out their subversive designs, the temper of the troops is still on the whole satisfactory.

Russia's Loyal Troops

But even the army is not immune from the individual efforts of such apostles of the revolution as the late Gershuni, whose almost irresistible influence might aptly be likened to that of the pied piper of Hamelin. Socialism and Anarchism are now reaching the private soldier and common man by means of the Press, which the revolutionary forces of the country can handle with surprising effects. The bulk of daily papers, as well as weekly and monthly journals, are arrayed against the government, and their present moderation of tone is solely a result of the powerful deterrents which martial law puts in the hands of governors and general-governors. A change of regime to-morrow, or even the repeal of exceptional legislation, would effect a sudden and complete transformation in their methods of warfare.

That the army still needs complete reorganisation in almost every respect is evident, and not merely to experts, but also to careful outside observers. In the course of the years 1906 and 1907, the Government removed nearly all the highest commanders from active service, the chiefs of corps and divisions, and likewise about two-thirds of the other commanding officers. But independently of this weeding-out process numbers of excellent officers have voluntarily quitted the army because of the miserly pay there, the slowness of advancement, the lack of stimulus to enterprise, and of the crushing out of individuality by rigorous centralisation. Hundreds of them found it utterly impossible to live on the pittance they received.

The Army in Need of Reform

Of these many resigned their commissions, while others plunged into debt. The life of the average officer, from the grade of major downwards, was a never-ending sequence of disillusions and hardships.

The War Ministry, when it shortened the term of service from four years to three, failed to allow for the fact that the training would have to be intensified correspondingly. Twenty-five per cent. more work was accordingly expected of the staff officers, who received neither better pay nor more help than before. Yet the staff of officers **The Army's** had nearly always been inade- **Serious** quate. As the number who are **Loss of Men** continually lacking amounts to about 4,000, the work that falls to those who are in the service is doubled and sometimes trebled. Every year the military schools send out about 2,500 young officers to the army, which is annually losing about 4,000. The deficit is therefore growing instead of diminishing, and most of those who leave the service are said to be the best educated and the most highly qualified.

From January, 1909, the pay of the Russian officers was increased, but only slightly. Lack of funds keeps them from receiving their due, for gold is one of the chief forces that move the steel of armies, and Russia is poor. Still, much larger sums might have been made available for the troops by intelligent thrift. The hundreds of millions assigned in 1908 to the building of the Amoor railway line would, in the opinion of experts and patriots, have been much better invested in raising the material and moral level of the soldiers and officers. Men of talent whom a military career was wont to attract under the first Nicholas and the second Alexander now seek at the Bar, in trade, commerce and industry, or in various departments of the civil service, a suitable field for their activity and adequate remuneration for their time and labour.

In Russia, garrison service is marked by sameness, and the efforts put forth to vary its monotony too often demoralise those who make them. Hence the **Problem** morale of the officers' corps **of Garrison** stand in quite as much need **Service** of being improved as their material condition. And unless this problem is worked out to a desirable solution, the common men, who constitute the finest fighting material in the world, will lack efficient instructors, without whom the raw stuff cannot be fashioned into a living organism. In a country like Russia, the barracks could, and should, be turned into a kind of

national school for the upbringing of the primitive beings that enter them every year. Little has been done by the tsar's military advisers in the way of profiting by the lessons of the late war. And yet most other countries have utilised Russia's painful experience. The hand grenade, for instance, proved a most useful weapon during the Japanese campaign, and the War Ministry accordingly resolved to introduce it. Two departments, therefore, undertook to supply hand grenades to the army—the artillery and the engineers' corps—but as they have been unable to agree how to set about it, the step has not yet been taken. The utility and necessity of siege artillery is another of the practical conclusions which were drawn from the experience obtained during the Manchurian campaign. But the Russian army, which was not supplied with siege guns in 1904, is not supplied with them yet.

Again, about half of the divisions are still without quick-firing guns, because there is no money to buy them, the sum needed being computed at £20,000. Yet for the new and uncouth headgear which has **Essential** recently been introduced, a **Qualities of** sum of £1,400,000 was assigned **the Politician** unhesitatingly. The police, too, which is one of the least efficient in the world, is manifestly undergoing a process of slow reorganisation. Here, however, the work of improvement is more difficult owing to the exiguity of qualified men, for in Russia no one can become a good policeman who is not a man of nerve and a citizen of more than average moral worth. And individuals endowed with such ethical and physical equipments have no motives for becoming social pariahs by donning a livery which renders them in the eyes of Russian society what the publicans were in the eyes of the Jews.

In order to be and to remain an honest and incorruptible member of the police force in Russia, a man must be heroically virtuous, wholly temptation proof. Doubtless, every department of the administration in the tsardom has its own peculiar temptations, but that of the police teems with them. The pay is absurdly small; the work is hard; the risks are great; the antipathy of the public is intense and ruthless, and if a member is dismissed by his superiors, he is virtually an outcast. During the discharge of his duties money is thrust upon him at every hand's turn, sometimes for what he does, at other times

RUSSIA'S FINEST INFANTRY: THE SEMINOVSKY BEING REVIEWED BY THE TSAR

THE TSAR, WITH AN IKON IN HIS HAND, BLESSING RUSSIAN INFANTRY

ANOTHER PICTURE SHOWING THE TSAR REVIEWING THE SEMINOVSKY REGIMENT

THE TSAR OF RUSSIA AMONG HIS SOLDIERS

for what he leaves undone, and very often on the principle on which the Chinese pay their doctors, so long as they have no need of their professional services. Under these circumstances to fall is easy, even to an immaculate citizen. And the bulk of the police are the reverse of immaculate. The secret political police organisation,

Workings of the Secret Police which at a time like the present is one of the mainstays of the regime, has been shown by recent events to be at once implicitly trusted and absolutely untrustworthy. Its workings tend to undermine the throne, which it is paid to support, and its agents—some consciously, others unwittingly—defeat the very object which the organisation exists to promote. Nor is it to be supposed that any partial reform will infuse new life into the service so long as the Government lacks men of common honesty to work as agents, money to pay them well, and an organising intellect to give direction to their efforts.

Russia's police organisation is divided into two branches, of which one deals with ordinary crime and criminals, and the other with individuals and associations whose aim is to overthrow the Government or to assassinate its members. And the influence of both divisions upon the community is now seen to be positively mischievous. In some cases the chiefs, and in most instances the agents, undisguisedly adopt measures which run counter to the principles on which society rests.

They violate the law, scoff at morality, tamper with Imperial behests, paralyse the arm of the most powerful Minister, change a judicial or administrative thunderbolt into a simple petard, open prison doors to dangerous malefactors, reveal state secrets to bloodthirsty terrorists, and finally reach a point at which public opinion, clamouring to have them punished, is uncertain whether to classify them as cunning conspirators or

Corruption Among the Police as stupid officials. The ordinary police system, which is more amenable to supervision than the political, is undoubtedly corrupt to the core. Badly-paid underlings or impecunious chiefs conspire with thieves, highwaymen, and other criminals, whom they not only screen from punishment, but aid and abet in the commission of crime. In the year 1908 some extensive conspiracies, in which members of the police took part,

were brought to light. The Government instituted strict investigations, which led to further discoveries of a nauseous kind. The accused were sent for trial, the scandal was intense and widespread, and the public mistrust of the police became more deep-rooted than before. But the system remains what it was. It may well be doubted whether the moral calibre of the Russian constable can be greatly improved before his material well-being has been adequately provided for by his employers. But if the ordinary police in Russia resembles salt that has lost its savour, the political section may be likened to a disinfectant with which a potent poison has been mixed.

True, in no country is scrupulous respect for austere morality a characteristic of the body of men whose duty it is to discover in order to frustrate political crimes. So long as they keep within certain broad limits, and refrain from committing a breach of certain rudimentary ethical principles, they are sure to be judged by an easy standard. But in the practice of the Russian secret police all restraints appear

Evil Record of the Spy Azeff to have been ignored, all breaches of human and divine law to be permitted. The Lopoukhine - Azeff scandal, which stirred the Russian nation to its inmost depths in 1909 revealed a code of maxims and a sequence of acts for which even men of lax morality find no excuse, and people of average intelligence can suggest no reasonable explanation.

The head of the police, Lopoukhine, set great store by a spy named Azeff, who was the soul and brain of the revolutionary committee which conceived and arranged some of the political outrages that preceded and accompanied the revolution. For the seven years ending in 1909, Azeff enjoyed the confidence alike of the terrorists and the police, and, so far as one can judge, achieved feats of sufficient importance to justify it in each case. He is said to have planned, among other crimes, the assassination of General Bogdanovitch, Governor of Ufa, of the Minister Plehve, from whom he was receiving large sums of money every year, and of the Grand Duke Sergius.

On the other hand, he betrayed the most successful Russian revolutionist that ever lived, Gershuni, who was proud of being his intimate friend. And while Azeff, the redoubted and redoubtable revolutionist, was thus playing false to his party on the one hand, and was procuring the murder of prominent members of the Imperial Government on the other hand, one of the most influential chiefs of the provincial police—Bakai, the assistant-director of the secret police of Warsaw—was betraying Azeff to the revolutionists. But as the revolutionary committee could not on such questionable evidence convict its trusted leader of foul play, it appealed to Lopoukhine, the police director who had been the zealous co-operator and intimate friend of the despotic Minister Plehve, and this gentleman gave evidence against the secret agent whose services he had utilised and appreciated.

Among the causes that have led to this anarchy are the lack of unity of system and moral laxity. Under Plehve, for instance, there were five different bodies of secret police, each one working by itself and directing its efforts principally against the others. These were, the force under the police department, the police of the Department of Public Safety, the police of the Minister of the Interior, the palace police, and the police of the **How Plots are Revealed** Foreign Department. It is easy to see how these bodies might unintentionally baulk each other's schemes; but that, moved by spite, hatred, or other base motives, they should deliberately play into the hands of the revolutionists is more difficult for foreigners to understand. To Russians, however, it seems not only probable, but true. And among the instances they bring forward in support of this grave accusation the following is the most striking.

While the cleverest Russian revolutionist, Gershuni, was living in a tailor's family in Kieff, planning the assassination of the Governor of Ufa, his every deed and word were revealed to the chief of the Kieff secret police. The traitors were two zealous revolutionists, the tailor and his daughter in whose house Gershuni was living. Now the chief of the Kieff police, General Novitsky, forwarded urgent telegrams to the Home Secretary, Plehve, asking for instructions and expecting to be authorised to arrest the conspirators. But Plehve, who is alleged to have had a grudge against the destined victim of the assassins, ordered the police director to stay his hand. " Observe, report, keep everything absolutely secret, but do nothing rash." Such was the gist of the Minister's mysterious behest. And during a whole month the chief of the Kieff police continued to report, and the Home Secretary went on repeating his instructions. At last the day set apart for the crime was drawing near, and the police director informed Plehve that the four conspirators whose names he had communicated **Forces that Prevent Anarchy** long before had started for Ufa to commit the deed. But still Plehve made no sign. And in May, 1903, General Bogdanovitch, Governor of Ufa, was duly shot dead by the four assassins, who went away unmolested.

As things now stand in Russia, the throne alone would seem to separate the nation from anarchy, while the police shield the throne from destruction. On the efficiency of the police, therefore, the duration of the present regime will continue to depend, unless it be laid upon some more solid groundwork.

A thorough reorganisation of the police will entail heavy expenditure. Money, therefore, is a requisite. And what is true of the army and the police is equally true of every state department in the empire : without funds, no root-reaching reform is feasible. On the other hand, without purifying reform the diseased organism cannot be healed nor the enfeebled financial forces reinvigorated. We are apparently face to face with a vicious circle.

On the finances in the first instance, and on the economic condition of the country in last analysis, the future of the nation very largely depends. For the longer needful reforms are delayed, the more intense and widespread will disaffection become, and the slighter will be the influence of the conservative elements in the country. These elements are at present almost entirely confined to the higher classes. Formerly, indeed, the peasantry, too, were included among them, but erroneously ; because the Russian **The Peasants' Idea of Politics** mooshik—this is one of the Russian terms for peasant —bore stoically what he could not alter, and dared not criticise, he was set down as a worshipper of the autocracy. And, in order to obtain a Conservative majority in the Duma, the peasant was enfranchised by the first electoral law. In the interests of the nation, that mistake had to be righted as soon as the unwelcome fact became clear that he was quite indifferent to politics, as politics, but was ready to join any party, legal or illegal, that would give or promise him gratuitously the land belonging to the squires, the Crown, or the Church.

Intellectually little better than the French or British peasant of the eleventh century, the mooshik lazily tills the land which he occupies but does not own. He is but a member of the village community in which the ownership is vested. Hence he lacks the sharp-cut notion of personal property, which to European peoples is almost an innate idea. He sees no moral wrong in sequestrating by force the land that belongs to another, especially if that other is of a different class; nor can he discern any danger to himself in that course, although underlying it is a principle which, if logically applied, would reduce him to utter poverty. On the benighted condition of the vast agricultural class which thus constitutes a formidable and proximate danger to the well-being of the nation, the third Prime Minister, M. Stolypin, concentrated his attention.

Among a set of urgent problems all pressing for instant solution, he singled out the agrarian question as the most momentous. Soon after he had accepted office he acquired the conviction that unless he could win over the peasantry to such conservatism as enlightened selfishness

engenders, the country would be ruined. But his way was blocked with many obstacles. Seemingly, the peasantry had already thrown in their lot with the enemies of the empire. Revolutionary groups had bribed them with the promise of free land, rightly feeling that to be successful the anti-monarchical movement must have the active support of the masses. And it was because having won they failed to keep that support, and the movement consequently remained a mere urban revolution, that Russia is still an autocracy. Of the 150,000,000 who now inhabit the tsardom, only 12·8 per cent. dwell in cities, the other 87·2 per cent. live in the country, and of these 74·2 per cent. are tillers of the soil. The entire peasant class of the empire amounts to 67·2 per cent., or two-thirds of the population. These figures enable one to understand the importance of the peasantry to the revolutionist leaders and the recklessness with which they made their bid for its support. Brutal anarchism was the form which the subversive movement assumed among the tillers of the soil.

Russia's Peasant Population

M. Stolypin's mode of warring against this violent outburst was to smash the last of the three idols of the Slavophiles—the village commune—to divide among

A RUSSIAN CROWD BEING HELD IN CHECK BY COSSACK SOLDIERS

A COSSACK REGIMENT RIDING THROUGH THE STREETS OF ST. PETERSBURG

individual husbandmen the land theretofore possessed in common, and thus grafting the idea of personal property on the sluggish, untutored minds of the rustics to wait until that should bring forth political and social fruit. This vast and fateful experiment is now in process of realisation. In the haste with which it had to be undertaken and the political colour that was necessarily imparted to it in consequence of the stress and strain of the moment lie the sources of its two sets of defects.

But the efforts made by the Government were praiseworthy. The domain lands of the Imperial family and extensive estates bought from wealthy noblemen were parcelled into lots by the Peasants' Bank, and are now divided among the farmers who undertake to refund the cost price to the State. The continuous migration of landless husbandmen to Siberia is also being directed and fostered by the Government, which further proposes to invite the same land-seeking class to colonise certain districts of Central Asia. The number of families that have migrated to Siberia during the year 1908 is computed by the central authorities at 74,500, or, say between 370,000 and 450,000 individuals of both sexes. The extent of land parcelled out among these is estimated at 3,000,000 dessiatines, a dessiatine being equal to 13,067 square yards, or approximately 2⅝ acres;

Emigration to Siberia Encouraged

this amounts to nearly 17,000 square miles. This salutary agrarian reform, simple though it may seem, will require the expenditure of sums of money so vast that the special agrarian fund will not suffice to furnish them. One may be pardoned for doubting whether even yet the Ministry itself fully realises the amounts that will ultimately be absorbed by this grandiose experiment, or the political changes it will bring forth. That the peasants will fail to redeem the bonds issued by the government to the noblemen who are selling their land, and that the deficit must one day be covered by the State, seems to many a foregone conclusion.

But the total cost of the transfer will probably not be limited to this loss. For the peasant, who already lives from hand to mouth, will be unable, from lack of ready money, to till the land as the noblemen tilled it. He must therefore obtain credit or sell out. Yet, in lieu of receiving the wherewithal to keep his new farm on its old level of productivity he has to saddle himself from the outset with debts which will cripple him and damage the community. The system of cultivation that still obtains in Russia may be tersely described as plunder of the soil. Much is taken, and little or nothing is given back. The three-field system, which involves enormous work, the lack of variety of crops, and the absence of artificial manures, contribute to exhaust the fertility of the land. But it is difficult to see how any Minister, situated as M. Stolypin was, could have provided funds enough for the agrarian revolution which he courageously inaugurated. It is worth noting that, contrary to expectation, the peasants do not readily

Land for the Peasants purchase the land which the Agrarian Bank acquired at its own risk from the landlords and divided into lots suited for farms. And yet the terms on which the bank offers them are very advantageous to the purchaser. Between November, 1905, and November, 1908, the bank thus bought 3,682,000 dessiatines from noblemen who had either actually suffered or were afraid of suffering from the violence of the peasantry.

Yet, of all this land, only 656,000 dessiatines have been bought by the would-be tenant farmers, or, say, 18 per cent. of the whole. The remainder, amounting to more than 3,000,000 dessiatines, remains on the hands of the bank, which has been authorised to make further purchases amounting to 2,000,000 dessiatines. In this way 5,000,000 dessiatines are in a transitional state—a result which must have a mischievous effect on the material well-being of the community.

In the Budget this dead loss figures as a minus, for the former owners of these estates have already been remunerated in government bonds, bearing interest at 5 and 6 per cent. And the interest on this debt has to be paid with regularity. The result is that the Government, in order to make good the loss of the bank, draws upon the taxpayer, and having assigned 7,000,000 roubles to the peasants' bonds in 1908, gave a subsidy of 17,500,000 in 1909.

But a more scathing criticism than could be based upon the probable financial consequence of the measure lies in the grounded fear that by its limitations it

M. Stolypin's Doubtful Experiment will demoralise the village community, which it cannot wholly abolish, will ruin the bulk of the peasant farmers, whom it cannot furnish with adequate means of tilling the newly acquired soil, will cut millions adrift from the land, deprive them of permanent work, rob them of the material and moral help which they heretofore received from the village community, and expose them unequipped for resistance to the powerful temptations

of professional revolutionists. In other words, M. Stolypin's experiment, if there were funds to ensure to it the highest degree of success, could not bring forth good fruits before a couple of generations. But realised only in part—and plainly in its subversive part—owing to the dearth of funds to carry out the whole, and relied upon as an immediate remedy for the pressing political evils of to-day, it strikes most Russian observers as a superlatively mischievous scheme, which, however, does credit to the heart of M. Stolypin.

That the peasantry is as sorely in need of culture as the land will be taken as a self-evident proposition by all who have lived among them. Crass ignorance, mediæval superstition, paralysing fatalism, and a propensity to thriftlessness and laziness, are among their negative characteristics, and also among the active causes of the poverty from which they constantly suffer. Indeed, such is the character of the Russian agricultural class that, according to a competent, but one hopes a mistaken, judge, M. Obraztsoff, the introduction of personal property

Idleness in Rural Russia among them will in three years cause about 20,000,000 of them to be landless. " The owners will exchange their farms for alcohol, just as they now exchange their carts and their garments for drink. There are families who have drunk their unsold land for twenty years in advance."

It is interesting in this connection to note the views of another authority, A. J. Savenko, who affirms that the fundamental impressions which rural Russia makes on the observer are the laziness, listlessness, and ignorance of its inhabitants. " The indolence of the majority of the peasants transcends all bounds. For dwellers in cities, who live in an atmosphere of steady toil, it is positively bewildering. The peasants are averse to doing anything. Work of any sort is distasteful to them, and they shirk it by every means in their power. Old and young are characterised by sloth, but youth takes the foremost place. In a large village you cannot find a single good worker, male or female. They will not consent to exert themselves even for most substantial remuneration, preferring to sit with folded arms at home. They live in want ; some of them beg ; but none wish to labour. . . . All in all, I think that in the course of a whole year the peasants work no more than from one to two months. The remainder of the time they spend in utter idleness, which has a stupefying effect on them.

"Cynicism is a natural consequence of this sloth and listlessness. The peasants live in incredible squalor. Their æsthetic requirements are lowered to a microscopic minimum. The need of the most elementary comforts are wholly unfelt. They lead literally the life of hogs. Brutish cynicism shows itself through the whole course of rustic existence. I do not know wherein the spiritual side of it consists. The bulk of them are not conscious of any bond between themselves and the nation or the State. Religion no longer plays the part that it once did in the life of the people. In a fairly large village there is no church, and none of the villagers are in the least put out by the lack of one. Only one necessity is everywhere felt in the gloomy existence of the peasantry—the necessity of *vodka*—and that thirst is stilled abundantly."

A correlate to the laziness of the peasant is the large number of days of rest he enjoys even during the **The Peasants** busiest months of the year when **Poor and** every hour of daylight ought **Thriftless** to be utilised to the fullest. For example, August 1st is a holiday, the sixth is a holiday; the fifteenth is a holiday, the twenty-ninth and the thirtieth are holidays. Add to these the four Sundays, and you have nine days in one month during which no work is done.

But it is not only in the country that this disregard of time is noticeable. In trade and commerce, at the Bar, in the banks, on the railways—in short, everywhere it is the same. The Board of the Siberian Railway has lately published statistics of the number of hours the trains were late on that line during two consecutive years. In 1906 they lost 2,514 hours, and in 1907, 2,335 hours, *i.e.*, in 1906, 104¾ days; and in 1907, 97 days and 7 hours. In the course of three years the Siberian trains lost exactly one year. And these statistics deal only with passenger trains.

Poverty is the correlate of sloth and thriftlessness, and it may well be doubted whether in any other country in Europe the material existence of the peasants leaves so much to be desired as in Russia. "The peasant's dwelling is a wooden or mud hut, more suited for cattle than for human beings. The peasants, with-

out distinction of sex, and oftentimes the cattle, take their rest in one narrow, mephitic room. Such a rudimentary convenience as a bed is a very great rarity in a farmer's house. The villages and hamlets in which the rural population of Russia are sheltered burn to ashes once in twenty years, completing **Russia in** its ruin. Some hygienists hold, **Contrast** however, that if Russia were **with America** not periodically thus consumed by fire she would rot away in her infected huts and cabins. . . . Nor is the food of the peasant any better. Compared with what it was, there is a certain change for the worse. . . . It consists mainly of bread and potatoes. Even such vegetables as cabbage, onions, and cucumber are disappearing from the table of the bulk of the peasants."

The wealth-creating power of the Russian husbandman is what the personal characteristics and the social conditions enumerated above would lead one to expect. Take the five principal cereals of the country—rye, wheat, oats, barley, Indian corn—and we find that in the year 1900 the total produce was but 3,269 million poods—a pood is 36 pounds; there are 62 poods in a ton—valued at 1904·7 millions of roubles. That is in Russia, where agriculture constitutes the main occupation, giving work to 74 per cent. of the entire population. Now, in the United States, where only 36 per cent. of the population till the land, the harvest of cereals in that same year amounted to 5,340 million poods, valued at 2,800 million roubles. Thus the American farmers gathered in 63 per cent. more—in weight—than the Russians. And yet the population of the tsardom is, roughly speaking, double that of the North American Republic.

If we now inquire how much of the corn is eaten by the people who raise it, we shall find the Russian husbandman **The Food** lagging far behind his rivals. **of the** In fact, one may truly say of **Peasants** him what was said of the French tiller before the revolution : " He always has too little to eat, and occasionally dies of hunger." During the year 1904 the American citizen consumed 54·3 poods of corn; the German, 28·0; Austro - Hungarian, 23·3 ; French, 23·3 ; British, 23·0 ; Russian, 18·3. The melancholy significance of these figures will become more clear when we bear in mind that together with corn foods the other peoples eat meat, fish, eggs, vegetables, butter, and fruits in much larger quantities than Russians. Nor should it be forgotten that Russia exports about 15 per cent. of the entire harvest of cereals, which amounts to about 3 to 4 poods a head of the population. The following suggestive table gives in poods the production and the consumption of the five cereals enumerated above by six nations in 1894 and 1904 :

The Scanty Fare of the Russians

Countries	Production per head		Consumption per head	
	1894	1904	1894	1904
Britain	10·8	8·2	23·9	23·0
Germany	21·1	26·1	23·7	28·0
France	27·2	28·4	27·5	23·3
Austria-Hungary ..	24·9	23·1	23·1	23·3
United States ..	51·3	72·8	42·8	54·3
Russia	26·6	26·3	22·8	18·3

The sameness and scantiness of the Russian peasant's repasts are all the more surprising that game is abundant in the interior and fish plentiful in Russian seas, rivers and lakes. The amount of fish caught in Russian waters every year is computed by the well-known expert, Borodin, at 1,120 million kilogrammes, of which about 19,000,000 kilogrammes are caught in the Caspian Sea ; 35,000,000 in the Baltic and White Seas ; 17,000,000 in the Black Sea and Sea of Azov ; over 6,000,000 in the Arctic and Pacific Oceans ; and 5,000,000 in the Ural Sea.

Carp and perch contribute about 754,000,000 kilogrammes ; herring about 152,000,000 ; salmon, about 45,000,000; sturgeon, approximately, 34,000,000 ; different other kinds, about 40,000,000 ; not counting 64,000,000 kilos of fresh-water fish. And it should be borne in mind that this wealth of fish food is obtained with a minimum of expenditure in money and labour, for fisheries and pisciculture in Russia are still in a very primitive state. The sea, like the land, is being ruthlessly plundered ; poaching is almost universal, and down to a short time ago close seasons were openly disregarded. Yet Russia supplies three times as much fish as the United States, five times as much as Great Britain, and six times as much as France. The amount of cattle possessed by the peasantry, according to the latest statistics, was

Russia's Great Fish Supply

in 1908 : in European Russia, exclusive of Poland, 25,000,000 head ; in Poland, 3,000,000 ; in Asiatic Russia, 6,000,000 ; in the Caucasus, 5,000,000 ; in Finland, 2,000,000. But although the absolute total in that year was undoubtedly greater than in any of the foregoing years, the percentage per 1,000 souls of the population had fallen perceptibly. In the sixties of the last century it was about 340 ; in the seventies, 327 ; in the eighties, 319 ; in the nineties, 311.

Fires caused by gross neglect or malice constitute one of the scourges of the tsardom. It is computed that every year fire destroys property valued at 400,000,000 roubles, about £42,000,000. Of every thousand roubles' worth insured by the various companies almost 80 per cent. of the premium is thus consumed. Assuming that the value of insured property in the tsardom amounts to sixty milliards of roubles, the yearly loss suffered by the insurance companies alone through fire is estimated by experts at 336,000,000 roubles. And this forms but a portion of the total loss, because a large amount of property is never insured. Now, a considerable percentage of these fires might be easily hindered by the application of ordinary prudence on the part of the peasants and by watchfulness on the part of the authorities, who have done little to suppress incendiarism.

Improved State of the Workers

Among the Sphinx questions of the year of the revolution, 1905, the economic condition of the Russian working man was thrust in the foreground as the most pressing of all. And, considering that the changes brought about in the social and political framework of Russia were due in large part to the strikes organised by factory hands, the mistake was pardonable. And crying evils were redressed. The Russian workman, having beaten the world's record for strikes, had most of his genuine grievances speedily remedied ; the hours of work have been shortened, the pay has been raised, the risks have been lessened, the methods of terminating his engagement have been made easy and satisfactory to him, and over and above he has dealt a stunning blow to the employers of labour, whose profits he has cut down, and whose business he has in many cases wholly ruined. But parallel with the rise in wages went the increase in prices for the necessaries of life, and some articles are further out of the workmen's reach to-day than before the revolution. In the Moscow district in January, 1897, there were 248,500 workmen receiving in wages 42,500,000 roubles, or, say, 170 roubles a year per man. In 1903 there were 293,000 men in receipt of 56,500,000, or 192 roubles a head, making a rise of 12 per cent. But during the same period the prices of food rose by 25 per cent (bread), 36 per cent. (meal), and even 50 per cent. (peas).

In consequence of the strikes of 1905–1906 a further great rise has taken place in the prices of bread, foodstuffs generally, and the necessaries of life. One of the results of the revolution was a further augmentation of the wages of workmen without any corresponding increase in their productivity. The absorbing power of the home markets was unfavourably affected by this perturbation. This was noticed at the fair of Nijni Novgorod in 1908, when the turnover fell short of the average of former years by no less than 15-20 per cent. In

Industry's Loss through Strikes 1905, women's wages were still very low, the average not exceeding 6-8 roubles a month—about 12s. 6d. to 17s. 6d. Since then the lot of the working man and woman has been very substantially bettered. In 1907 a series of far-reaching measures, calculated to improve it still further, and including insurance against accidents, was drafted by the late Minister of Trade and Industry, M. Philosofoff, and would have been laid before the Duma in the form of a Bill had it not been for his sudden death at the close of that year.

The marvellous vitality of Russian finances and the solidity of their economic basis were brought into sharp relief by the revolutionary movement of 1905, which dealt a severe blow to industry, commerce and finances. In 1905 the number of strikes totalled 13,110, while the number of workmen taking part in them amounted to no less than 2,709,695. The damage done was incalculable. This phenomenon is unprecedented in the economic history of Europe. It may well be doubted whether in any other country the financial and industrial fabrics would have successfully borne such a formidable strain. In Russia the gold standard is still intact ; trade, commerce, and in-

dustry, although passing through a protracted crisis, are seemingly regaining their buoyancy, and altogether the outlook, without being precisely inspiriting, is described by observant Russians as less depressing than might reasonably have been expected. Russia's credit in 1909 may be gauged by the terms on which she

Russia Living Beyond Her Means concluded her $4\frac{1}{2}$ per cent. loan in January of that year. The conjuncture was highly unfavourable. War clouds hung over the Balkan Peninsula. It was feared that Austria, Turkey, Bulgaria, Servia, and possibly Russia herself, might be drawn into the coming sanguinary struggle.

The Russian rente stood at $77\frac{1}{4}$, and it was known that the Finance Minister must at almost all costs raise funds abroad in order to pay off the war loan of 300,000,000 roubles contracted in France in 1904. Yet, despite these adverse conditions, a loan of 450,000,000 roubles was raised in January, 1909, of which the usual price was $89\frac{1}{4}$, the bankers' commission $3\frac{3}{4}$, and the net proceeds received by the Treasury, $85\frac{1}{2}$. And considering all the circumstances, these results are considered to be fairly satisfactory.

At the same time it cannot be gainsaid that Russia has now reached a point at which she must either live by the exertions of her own wealth-creating class, without the continuous help of foreign capitalists, or else be content, after a series of financial crushes, to find her normal level. To many who are quite unbiassed observers she appears to be now living beyond her means. The vast sums which are about to be spent on the strategic Amoor railway at a time when the army and the police have yet to be reorganised, the navy to be rebuilt, the peasants to be financed in their new character of tenant farmers, education to be cheapened and diffused, the whole system of internal administration to be remodelled, fill one with misgivings, not,

The Nation in Danger of Bankruptcy indeed, as to Russia's resources, which are enormous, but respecting the ability of her rulers to develop and utilise them sufficiently to make the revenue cover the expenditure. With reluctance I venture to utter my strong conviction that unless some genial administrator—a statesman as well as a specialist—successfully encounters the hero's task of reconstructing the financial and economic fabric of the Russian Empire, applying freely the drastic remedies by which alone the present disorders are curable, the nation, having first lost its old standard, will inevitably sink into the slough of bankruptcy and financial anarchy before the Russian constitution is twenty-four years old. That the peasant is too heavily taxed considering his present income is as

Defects in Financial System evident as it is that his present income is much too slender considering the extent to which sobriety, thrift, and industry might increase it. Another defect in the present financial system is that the tax-gathering is done in September, when the farmer is obliged to sell what he has just threshed in order to satisfy the collector. For there is no postponing the season ; it is as the laws of the Medes and Persians. Even in districts where tobacco is grown, which cannot be brought to market before November, the taxes are, for the sake of uniformity, gathered in September. The result is that in many places where ready money is not available the belongings of the farmer are distrained.

The pivot of the financial machinery is the sale to foreign countries of cereals, which contribute more than any other kind of export to pay the interest on the foreign debt. For the balance of trade in Russia must necessarily be active ; that is to say, the total value of the exports must largely exceed that of the imports. That is one of the consequences of the nation's indebtedness. Russia is forced to sell part of the harvest to her neighbours, however urgent may be her own need of it. In 1908 the exportation of corn and other foodstuffs fell off to a disquieting extent affecting the trade balance correspondingly. The following comparison of the value of the exports and imports in millions of roubles for the last four years needs no further commentary :

Year	Value of exports in million roubles	Value of imports in million roubles	Excess of exports over imports in million roubles
1905 ...	1017	583	434
1906 ...	1043·5	650·5	393
1907 .	1016·8	759·8	257
1908 ...	932	752·8	179·2

Manufactures in Russia, which were, so to say, built up by the Finance Minister, Witte, with the money of foreign capitalists, are still suffering from the strikes, the spoliation, and the incendiarism that

accompanied the revolution. The West Russian Manchester, Lodz, until 1905 one of the most prosperous manufacturing cities in Europe, was well-nigh ruined and swept out of existence by the anarchistic wave. And the recent sudden increase in the activity of the Moscow manufactures and the briskness of their trade is attributable solely to the ruin of those at Lodz.

At present, however, there are signs that Russian industry is slowly recuperating—the staple industries, metallurgy, the collieries, the Baku oil-wells, are no longer stagnant. Russian firms have competed successfully for orders from Italy and other foreign countries for railway waggons and metal rails. In short, the lowest depths of depression appear to have been reached, and the present rise, if very gradual, is at least continuous. At the same time, it should not be forgotten that a large percentage of the capital sums invested in Russian industry melted away wholly during the heat of the revolution. And yet the Russian money market still offers uncommonly favourable terms for capital.

Railway Building in Russia During a great part of the year 1908 the official rate of discount was 7½ per cent., while the private rate was still higher. Even on excellent security advances bore interest at the rate of 10 per cent.

In the tsardom there is hardly any capital available for industrial enterprises. It is mostly locked up in Government securities. About 25 per cent. of the foreign loans is held in Russia by Russians, or, say, 344,000,000 roubles ; while over a milliard and a half has been invested in internal loans during the past five years.

The building of new railways and the working of old ones generally offer a fair test of the level of a country's material prosperity. In Russia, since the war, little has been attempted in the way of constructing new lines. Some that had been begun before have been completed, such as the Moscow girdle line, the Orenburg-Tashkent, the Perm-Ekaterinburg lines, and a few others. In 1908 the grandiose Amoor railway, which is expected to cost much and bring in little, was begun. The second track of the Trans-Siberian was commenced, and a most useful line connecting Northern Russia with the Donetz coal district was undertaken by a private company. But railways, which create wealth in other countries, are not profitable in Russia. They are often ruinous, owing to the frauds in countless shapes which turn the immense profits into the pockets of dishonest schemers. Millions of passengers travel without tickets every year, and many of them lord it over those who pay their way. The railways are forced to pay enormous damages for the loss of fictitious consignments. In short, the losses needlessly incurred in exploiting the principal lines are enormous, and it is the peasant, the workman, and the manufacturer who have at last to make good this deficit. It is computed that 100,000,000 roubles are swallowed up every year by these colossal frauds. And in lieu of plucking up this abuse by the roots, the authorities, finding it less troublesome to lessen the deficit by raising the passenger tariff, have had recourse to this expedient, with undesirable results. First-class passengers are either disappearing altogether from several lines, or they are represented by the privileged people who still travel gratis.

Experts affirm that as the peasants might easily increase their slender yearly pittance by thrift, sobriety, and sheer hard work, so the Government might convert the sempiternal deficit into a handsome surplus by exploiting on businesslike principles the railways, woods and forests, the state lands, the minerals, and the fisheries of the empire, all of which are now being managed with a degree of perfunctoriness which differs little from culpable negligence. Clever railway managers like those whose names are so well known in Great Britain and the United States would soon change the annual loss of 100,000,000 roubles into a large net profit. The colossal wealth of forests which now bring in but £6,000,000

TWO CELEBRATED RUSSIAN AUTHORS
Count Leo Tolstoy and Maxim Gorky, whose portraits are given above, are both novelists who take the side of the poor and endeavour to bring about better social conditions, though the latter has not the religious enthusiasm which characterises Tolstoy's writings. Tolstoy, having resigned all privileges of rank, now lives as a poor man.

sterling might easily be made to yield twice that sum. The naphtha wells in Baku and numerous other districts could and should be made the sources of a splendid annual revenue, whereas, at present, they enrich only a few individuals.

The fisheries, which are far and away the most abundant in the world, are at present worth no more than £215,000 a year. The State mining industries are carried on at a dead loss. The financial operations of the Imperial Russian Bank do not bring in much more than £10,000,000 sterling to the state. In a word, the sources are abundant, but no one tries to tap them properly. Russia has it in her power to pay her way and prosper. But she seemingly lacks the will. The results are all the more deplorable that they could so easily be avoided.

One of these results is the enormous indebtedness of the nation. And it is increasing, not diminishing. If we compare the Russian estimates for 1909 with those of previous years, we shall find it hard to shake off the conviction that the ordinary expenditure is growing out of all proportion to the growth of the ordinary revenue. The yearly excess of ordinary revenue over ordinary outlay has been in millions of roubles in :

1903	1904	1905	1906	1907	1908	1909
148·8	111·5	99·3	145·9	146·5	74·4	4·8

Between the years 1903 and 1909 the annual income of the state went up from 2,031,080,000 roubles to 2,447,000,000, while the expenditure rose from 1,883,000,000 to 2,472,020,000. The total Budget of 1907 showed a deficit of 52,770,000 roubles ; in the following year an internal loan of 200,000,000 was required to cover the deficit ; and in 1909 a foreign loan of 450,000,000 was floated.

Russia's indebtedness is, therefore, appalling. As compared with her potentialities, it is not perhaps alarming; but contrasted with her annual revenue, and the slight wealth-creating power of the state, it is becoming disquieting. If the business management of the empire—abstraction made from politics—were in competent hands, guided by resourceful heads, there would be nothing to fear, for Russia's potential wealth is reasonably believed to be immense. But as things now are, and bid fair to continue, the symptoms are not suggestive of impending prosperity. Almost one-fourth of the yearly outlay is spent on the service of the debt, which has increased since 1903 by over 40 per cent. In the year 1902 it amounted to 6,664,000,000 roubles. In 1909 it had grown to 9,175,000,000.

Russia Blind to her Possibilities

And this enormous total would have been utterly inadequate to the needs of the empire were it not for the unpalatable fact that about 28 per cent. of the ordinary income derives from the alcohol state monopoly. This is the sale of vodka by the Government, which was conceived with the best intentions by Alexander III., but has proved, according to the testimony of the most competent authorities, a curse to the Russian nation. The number of million vedros—a vedro is 2·704 gallons—of vodka consumed yearly from 1901 to 1906 is as follows:

In 1901	49·5	In 1904	71·2
In 1902	66·0	In 1905	75·9
In 1903	71·5	In 1906	85·0

One of the most gifted and best informed Russian publicists, M. Menshikoff, writes: " It must not be supposed that the alcoholic poison has infected the lower classes only. It has tainted in a like degree the petty tradesfolk, the merchants, the clergy, the bureaucrats of cities, and it numbers many victims among the higher intelligent classes."

Widespread Curse of Drunkenness

The injury inflicted by drunkenness on the physical and moral constitution of the Russian race is incalculable, and it is clear to many that degeneration is the ultimate form it usually assumes. Disease and crime are its ordinary accompaniments. Characteristic is the fact that in many places children are among its victims. In a Zemsky Council of the province of Perm the drunkenness of school children was one of the themes discussed, and the council, having heard the report of the school inspector of the district, called for further details with a view to the adoption of repressive measures. (Cf. " Novoye Vremya," November 10th, 1908.) It is, perhaps, hardly to be wondered at that the peasantry, whose monotonous lives consist mainly of an alternation of hardship and oblivion, should seek to vary it by the artificial mirth and temporary forgetfulness bestowed by inebriety.

Against such vices as this, and the crimes to which it leads, legislation is powerless. Unless the youth of the country can be made amenable to moral influences such as will enable it to face and withstand temptation, the hope of lasting betterment is slender indeed. Religion in Orthodox Russia is doubtlessly still a beneficent force, but it seldom moulds the youthful mind or steels the tender will. And nothing has taken its place. Since the revolutionary wave passed over the land the latent symptoms of general anarchism, which long lay dormant, have been brought into the light of day. Now, therefore, there is at least hope that the hideous disease may be cured, which would otherwise induce general paralysis. But by whom? The clergy of the Orthodox Church are badly educated, badly housed, underfed, and exposed to all kinds of temptations. The ecclesiastical schools where the religious shepherds are trained have forfeited the character of educational establishments in the good sense of the term. A professor of the Ecclesiastical Academy of St. Petersburg, Professor Glubokoffsky, gives a description of their working in terms that make Russian patriots shudder. There is no teaching there, no docility, no obedience, and the morals are disgusting. Even the celebrated Ober Procuror of the Most Holy Synod, K. Pobedonostseff, deliberately stated shortly before his death that " the ecclesiastical school has become a low tavern." If the salt thus loses its savour wherewith shall it be salted?

Schools that do not Educate

The condition of ordinary secular schools is often as bad or even worse. It would, of course, be a gross exaggeration to assert that the influence of all educational establishments in Russia is the reverse of beneficial. But it is fair to say that the good schools are the exception, and one may truly add that ever since the revolution of 1905 the youth of Russia has been animated by a spirit of lawlessness and gross self-indulgence with which those teachers who strove to discharge their duties were generally powerless to cope.

Scholars of both sexes in many parts of Russia formed secret societies for the purpose of meeting together and indulging in veritable orgies. The majority, while eschewing such uncleanness, refused obedience to their teachers, came to school or absented themselves as they liked, openly criticised their masters, and sometimes turned the school into a tavern or a gambling den. In a Moscow boarding school for children of the nobility, forty scholars struck work in 1908 because they were dissatisfied with the conduct of the director. The head-master, it appears, had demurred to those boarders who failed to come home before one o'clock a.m. The indignant young gentlemen first complained of the head-master to the marshal of the nobility, and, having received no redress, quitted the school.

In one of the educational establishments at Kharkoff the boys were allowed to have their own smoking-room; but they turned it into a gambling hell, and drove away the inspector who came to **Astonishing School Revelations** see what they were doing. In Tiflis a schoolboy, having received bad marks for his lesson, protested. His comrades supported him energetically but vainly. At last they ordered the school council to expunge the bad marks and put good ones in their place, threatening unless this were done to throw bombs. And the school council complied.

In the city of Kutais the governor-general received an anonymous letter condemning him to death. Very shortly after this it came to his knowledge that the missive had emanated from the state grammar school, and that one of the fifth form boys had been deputed to kill him. His excellency, repairing to the educational establishment, entered the fifth class during a lesson, and exclaimed abruptly : "Master G., you were chosen by lot to kill me. Eh ? " The boy curled up with fear and muttered : "Pardon, your excellency, pardon, I—I—can—you know —decline—refuse—to do it." "Oh, well, it doesn't matter. I'll forgive you this time," was the astonishing reply, and, so saying, his excellency walked away majestically. And the lad was not even rebuked !

None of the very distressing phenomena that characterised the Russian revolution have challenged such widespread attention or occasioned such serious misgivings as the vicious precosity of Russian youth. Not content with aping the vices of their elders, they strove to outdo them. Even virtue and innocence, which were happily well represented during that period of unbridled licence, generally paid the toll of self-disguise to vice. The revolution, **The Vicious Precosity of Young Russia** however, merely brought out a disease that had long been latent. For many years previously the fermentation of ideas produced by the germs of revolutionary literature had been proceeding unchecked. Maxims and principles were instilled into the minds of children which were strong dissolvents of traditional morality, and, if pushed far enough, of the basis of social life.

In elementary schools the old ideals were methodically dethroned. Vice and virtue were made to derive their changeful character from the social and political views of the individual. Thus, to rob or steal was a good action if undertaken for the purpose, say, of despoiling the rich and succouring the poor man. Killing was not murder if the assassin's motives were politically or socially revolutionary. Religion and traditional ethics, which taught doctrines the reverse of these, were envisaged as a set of social shackles from which mankind could not be too soon emancipated. In a word, the baleful influence of these "educational" currents, felt for nearly forty years, cannot easily be over-estimated.

When the Press censorship was removed the sluice gates of this reservoir of turbid nihilism were suddenly burst open. For months the sphere of journalism and literature was flooded with the waters of anti-religious, anti-ethical, anti-social doctrines and sentiments. Everything that had been held sacred by former generations was anathematised as degrading or held up to derision by this. Parental affection, **Reservoir of Turbid Nihilism** conjugal fidelity, and respect for the convictions of others when those others happened to be conservatives in politics or religion, were scoffed at as irrational and antiquated. To revealed creeds, to patriotism, ethics, clean living, no quarter was given by the leading iconoclasts, who hypnotised the young generation. Free love was preached and practised by the youth of the intermediate schools, who founded "free-love leagues,"

5313

drew up by-laws which members were bound to observe, and utterly ruined many youths of both sexes. At last the Press drew attention to the evil, and the Minister of Public Instruction endeavoured to uproot it. But the mere surgery of administrative measures was unavailing. "The roots of the disease must be treated,"

The Mirror of Literature wrote one of the most widely-spread journals. "And these," it added, "are to be found in ourselves, in the whole social organism, in the decay of the family, in the depravity of fathers and mothers." Whether the cure will be successfully accomplished, it is unhappily certain that the young generation will come to the front morally and intellectually enfeebled by the ravages of one of the most malignant diseases that can befall the social organism.

The morbid feelings and subversive notions which are among the symptoms of this fell malady are necessarily mirrored in the popular literature, which therefore throws a strong light on latter-day Russia. But the Russian literature of to-day is much more than a mirror. Some sections of it might, perhaps, be aptly likened to a laboratory where noxious germs are carefully cultivated which warp the mind, disfigure the soul, and produce the monstrous shapes that excite our disgust. Characters which Wycherly and Congreve would have shuddered even to contemplate are not only described in latter-day novels and stories with artistic talent and undisguised sympathy, but they are associated with the highest of the new ideals held up to the Russian nation. To say that many of the literary productions which characterise the revolutionary epoch are public outrages on morals and religion is to put the case with studied moderation.

The British public knows something of Maxim Gorky and Leonid Andreyeff, but one may doubt whether it has ever read the works of Artsybasheff, whose

Russian Writers, Good and Bad "Sanyin" would have been confiscated by the police of Great Britain, Austria, or Germany; of Kuzmin, Sollogub, Kamenski, and a host of others. It is only fair to add that many of the works of these writers are quite free from the taint of immorality. Sollogub's "Little Devils" is a powerful story, and Kuzmin's verses are technically perfect. But such tales, for instance, as "Four," or "Leda," by A. Kamenski, or "Sanin,"

by Artsybasheff, cannot be too severely condemned, whether we view them from the ethical angle of vision or the æsthetical.

Wrought upon for decades by disintegrating forces such as those enumerated above, Russia's vital powers could not but be seriously impaired. And the present plight of the nation moves one to pity. An ardent friend of Russia, himself a Slav patriot, has put his impressions frankly upon record as follows : "What I am going to say has a paradoxical ring about it, but it is none the less true. There is no Russian nation. With an Orthodox Russian people we are indeed acquainted, a people numbering 88,000,000, whose religious convictions offer them a substitute for everything in the nature of national ideas possessed by other peoples. But we look in vain for a compact Russian nation permeated with identical interests. And the most amazing trait of this phenomenon is the circumstance that this gigantic mass of people speaks one tongue, cherishes one faith, and yet in spite of it all shows so little understanding for the common ties that bind it to the State.

Solvents of Russian Society It is no satisfactory explanation to say that lack of culture and geographical conditions are answerable for this. The fundamental causes lie deeper : it is that egotism peculiar to all Slav peoples which finds it so hard to make sacrifices for the common weal, either in the narrow or the broader sense of the term."

These are some of the solvents of Russian society with the effects of which on concrete men and women, and doubtless on the whole Russian organism, the rising generation will soon be confronted. Happily there are also several powerful factors on the other side—religious sectarianism, partial revivals in the Orthodox Church, strenuous efforts by Russian Lutherans, and even the reforming zeal of ordinary citizens who, having cultivated the moral sense, would gladly rescue their youthful compatriots from the abyss that now threatens to engulf them.

From the Orthodox Church, with its atrophied organs, its demoralised schools, and its good-natured, half-starving clergy, no miracles in the social sphere can yet be expected. The essence of Russia's religious creed—one of the facets of the trinity of which Panslavism was once composed—lies in the life to come, the world beyond the grave. Death is the starting-point of everything worth knowing, worth possessing, and therefore worth striving for. Hence, strange though it may seem, death is the central point of the orthodox faith; life is dull, grey, repellent; it is only the sunset of existence that tinges everything, not, indeed, with its own splendour, but with the ineffable glory of the world to come. It is no exaggeration to assert that of all Christian creeds and churches, there is not one that contributes less to the equipment of its adherents for the stern life struggle here below than the contemporary Orthodox Russian Church.

Panslavism, of which orthodoxy was one of the three bases, has thus been thrust from the foreground of the scene on which Russia is now playing her part. Belief in her heaven-sent mission among the effete nations of two continents may still perhaps linger on in the breasts of the veteran contemporaries of Khomyakoff and Aksakoff, but it is no longer a stimulating or an active force in the community. Had it been otherwise, it would have aroused the nation in 1908. The anti-Slav policy then **Thwarting the Balkan Confederation** struck out by the Austro-Hungarian Secretary for Foreign Affairs, Baron von Aehrenthal, when he annexed Bosnia and Herzegovina, thwarted the scheme of a Balkan Confederation, and buried the last hopes of the Southern Slavs, would have unchained an irresistible popular outburst. The Government, however firm its resolution to keep the peace, would have been driven to resist, and, if needs were, to fight, as in 1877. For the issues were

vital; the moment was critical; the choice of alternatives would be final. But nearly everything turned out as the Austrian statesman had expected. Russia's defence of her kith and kin was verbal. Bound by secret treaties to remain an inactive spectator of the incorporation of the Slav provinces, she accepted the inevitable. **Russia's Doubtful Future** She could not well begin a diplomatic campaign against a measure, however far-reaching, to which she had already deliberately given her assent. And the condition of her army, as well as the state of her finances, agriculture, and industry, forced her to eschew a disastrous military conflict, which would have been the sole alternative to any attempt at evading her treaty obligations.

From whatever angle of vision we contemplate the Russia of to-day, we are struck with the contrast between her boundless potentialities and the sordid reality, and with the vast distance between promise and achievement, which are divided by a seemingly infinite abyss. One might aptly liken the Russian nation to a very complex mechanism, forged by some latter day Vulcan, and then taken to pieces.

Properly put together, set in motion, and guided by a genial engineer, it might prove one of the main factors in the latter-day history of Europe and the human race. But of this there is no sign. The pieces still lie scattered about, half corroded with rust, and the most optimistic feeling they arouse in the minds of Russia's friends who contemplate them is a vague hope. E. J. DILLON

TYPICAL RUSSIAN PRIESTS AND MILITARY OFFICERS

ESSENTIAL INFORMATION ABOUT RUSSIA

AREA AND POPULATION. The Russian Empire contains one-seventh of the dry land of the surface of the earth, and its total area, reckoning the reduction arranged by the Treaty of Portsmouth after the Russo-Japanese War, and including the area of inland waters, is now 8,647,657 square miles. This is made up as follows :

—	Area English sq. miles.	Population.
European Russia (divided into 50 provinces)	1,862,524	109,354 600
Poland (divided into 10 provinces)	49,018	10,947,300
European Caucasus (3 provinces)	85,201	4,343,900
Trans-Caucasia (11 provinces) ..	95,402	6,114,600
Siberia (9 provinces)	4,786,730	6,740,600
Steppes (4 provinces)	710,905	2,797,400
Turkestan (4 provinces) ..	400,770	5,746,600
Trans-Caspia	213,855	397,100
Finland	125,784	2,857,200
Internal Waters (Caspian Sea, &c.)	317,468	
Total ..	8,647,657	149,299,300

The towns with a population of more than 100,000 are as follow :

EUROPEAN RUSSIA : St. Petersburg, 1,429,000 ; Moscow, 1,359,254 ; Warsaw, 756,426 ; Odessa, 449,673 ; Lodz, 351,570 ; Kiev, 319,000 ; Riga, 282,230 ; Kharkov, 173,989 ; Vilna, 162,633 ; Kazan, 143,707 ; Saratov, 137,147 ; Yekaterinoslav, 135,552 ; Kishinev, 125,787 ; Astrakhan, 121,580 ; Rostov on Don, 119,476 ; Tula, 114,733 ; Helsingfors, 106,067.

ASIATIC RUSSIA : Baku, 179,133 ; Tiflis, 159,590 ; Tashkent, 155,673.

GOVERNMENT. In 1905 the creation of the Russian Parliament, or Gosudarstvennaya Duma, laid the foundation of political liberty. The Duma is the Lower Chamber, and election to it is made by electoral bodies in the chief towns and governments. The Council of the Empire is the Upper Legislative Chamber. Half of the members are elected for nine years, and the other half are appointed by the tsar, who also appoints the President and vice-President. Members of the Upper House must be not less than forty years of age, and possess an academical degree. Members of both houses are paid. Both Houses have equal legislative powers, and both must pass any measure before it is laid before the tsar for ratification. There are also several boards or councils which are entrusted with both deliberative and executive powers—the Ruling Senate, which is also the supreme judicial authority; the Holy Synod, which is composed of bishops and supervises the religious matters of the empire ; and, the most important of all, the Council of Ministers, consisting of the 14 Ministers of State and the general directors of the most important administrations.

EMPEROR. The tsar is Nicholas II., Emperor of all the Russias, and eighth ruler of the House of Romanof-Holstein. He was born on May 18th, 1868, and succeeded his father in 1894.

DEPENDENCIES. Russia has no colonies, properly so called, but in Central Asia she has two vassal states, Bokhara and Khiva [see page 1533].

FINANCE. The revenue for the year 1906 was £354,733,680, and the expenditure was £339,610,000. The chief sources of revenue were state loans, state monopolies (sale of spirits, telegraphs and posts), state domains (railways, forests, mines), indirect taxes (customs, sugar, naphtha, matches, etc.), trade licences, and stamp and other duties. The Russian National Debt at the beginning of 1907 was about £915,000,000.

INDUSTRY AND COMMERCE. The Russian Empire has about 333,000,000 acres under crops, two-thirds of the acreage being under cereals. The chief crops of European Russia and Poland are hay, potatoes, rye, wheat, oats, and barley. In South Russia and Siberia wheat takes the place of rye as the chief cereal. Flax, hemp, tobacco, cotton, and silk are also important industries. In Russian Central Asia the growth of the cotton industry is especially remarkable, having trebled in output in four years. About half of Russia is forest land, and the state is the largest owner of forests, holding as much as 64 per cent. of the entire forest land of European Russia. The chief minerals of Russia are coal, naphtha, iron, salt, copper and zinc, but the mineral wealth of Russia and of Siberia is supposed to be as yet barely tapped. The oil-field of the Baku district is the most important known. In European Russia and Caucasia, manufactories find employment for 1,711,755 people. The chief manufactories are, in the order of their importance, in the following classes—textile, food, metal, ceramics, wood, paper, chemicals, and leather. But manufacturing industries are still in a backward state. The value of Russia's exports for the year 1907 was £110,431,572 and the value of her imports was £78,609,164. The chief articles of export were corn, timber, and wooden goods, flax, eggs, dairy produce, furs, and leather, oil-cake, naphtha, and naphtha oils, cotton, sugar, hemp, fowl and game, and horses. The chief imports were raw cotton, machinery, textiles, metal goods, wool and wool yarn, tea, coal, raw metals, leather and hides, fish, silk, and chemicals.

CURRENCY. The legal unit is the rouble, which contains 100 kopeks, and is worth 2s. 1⅙d. The usual calculation is that 9·46 roubles = £1.

	1 kopek	= ¼d.
100 kopeks	= 1 rouble	= 2s. 1⅙d.
15 roubles	= 1 imperial	= 31s. 5½d.

The rouble is a silver coin. There are new gold coins for 5 and 10 roubles. There are also issued notes for 1, 3, 5, 10, 25, 50, 100, and 500 roubles.

In Finland the coinage has the same basis as the French currency [see page 5398], except that the centime value is called a *penni*, of which 100 make a *markha*, which equals a franc. The standard is gold, though the markha is not coined in gold. The coins are (copper) 1, 5, and 10 penni ; (silver) ¼, ½, 1 and 2 markha ; (gold) 10 and 20 markha.

WEIGHTS AND MEASURES. The Finnish weights and measures follow the metric system [see page 5399], but the Russian weights and measures are as follows :

LINEAL

	1 vershok	= 1·75 inches.
8 vershoks	= 1 stopa	= 3·50 inches.
2 stopas	= 1 archine	= 28 inches.
3 archine	= 1 sagène	= 7 feet.
500 sagènes	= 1 verst	= 1,166⅔ yards or ·662878 mile.

SURFACE

	1 square archine	= 67·1 sq. ins.
9 sq. archines	= 1 square sagène	= 784 sq. ins.
2400 sq. sagènes	= 1 dessiatine	= 13,067 sq. yds.

WEIGHTS OF COMMERCE

	1 dola	= ·69 grain.
96 dola	= 1 zolotnick	= 65·83 grains.
3 zolotnicks	= 1 lotti	= 197·49 grains.
8 zolotnicks	= 1 lana	= 1 1/5th oz.(about)
12 lanas or 32 lotti	= 1 funt or pound	= ·902818 lb.
40 funts	= 1 pood	= 36 1/10th lb.
10 poods	= 1 berkovitz	= 361 1/10th lb.
3 berkovitz	= 1 packen	= 1083⅓ lb.

POSTAGE. Great Britain to Russia : Letters, papers, and samples, as for France [see page 5398]. Parcels for Russia in Europe : via Hamburg, 2s., 2s. 6d., and 3s. for 3, 7, and 11 lb. respectively ; via Ostend, Flushing, or Sweden, 2s. 3d., 2s. 9d., and 3s. 3d. To Asiatic Russia, 1s. per parcel extra.

TELEGRAMS. Great Britain to Russia in Europe, 4½d. per word ; to Russia in Asia, 1s. per word ; private telegrams in cypher not accepted.

EUROPEAN
POWERS
TO-DAY

II
TURKEY,
GREECE AND
THE BALKANS

TURKEY, GREECE AND THE BALKANS IN OUR OWN TIME
DAWN OF LIBERTY IN THE OTTOMAN EMPIRE
By F. A. McKenzie

OF all the great changes that have swept over the world during our time, two stand out as of overwhelming importance — the awakening of Asia, following on the triumphs of Japan, and the reconstruction of Eastern Europe.

The Balkan Peninsula is in the midst of a period of far-reaching transformation. Here all the races of the world seem mixed. We have the Turk, long over-lord of all, but now driven back in Europe on a territory not much more than half the size of Great Britain. In Bulgaria we find a combination of white, Mongol, and gipsy, giving us the energetic and progressive Bulgar as we now know him. Elsewhere we have Slav and Latin, the Slav ever forcing himself to greater place by his growing numbers. Greek, Roumanian, Czech, Bulgar, Serb and Albanian all dwell around these mountains. To the struggle of race is added the even more bitter struggles of conflicting creeds. The Jew has long been an element of discord. Mohammedan and Christian learned here through many ages to look at one another through a curtain of hate ; and the Christians have fought together like tiger-cats to maintain **Turkey's Wonderful Revolution** their different branches of the Eastern Church. For Christianity in the Near East has too often meant, not the religion of the individual, making for charity and good deeds, but the evolution of merciless and cruel racial prejudices.

Politically, the changes that have come, within even a year, sound more like romance than reality. In the early summer of 1908 the most optimistic prophets of the progress of humanity did not dare to whisper of hope for Turkey. Here was a land reckoned by all—so far as her European dominions were concerned—as absolutely beyond redemption. " The Sick Man of Europe " was about to die, and expectant neighbours had completed their plans for sharing his territories among themselves. Now the " Sick Man " is well on his way to recovery. Turkey, yesterday the tomb of freedom, has to-day become the cradle of liberty, and her former arch-tyrant has placed himself at the head of the party of progress. Bulgaria, once ground down by the Turk, reveals in her prosperous, sturdy, and ambitious people the emergence of the Bulgar to world place. Servia, **Servia Free from Poverty** despite the volatile life of her capital, shows us perhaps the only kingdom on earth where practically every man has enough and to spare, and where the problems of poverty are unknown. The gallantry of Montenegro, ready to risk national existence for an ideal of racial unity, commands our admiration if not our approval. Bosnia is entering on a period of definite subjection to Austria.

The most interesting figure in Eastern Europe to-day, and the one around whom much of the movement has revolved, is Abdul Hamid, Sultan of Turkey. It is but a year since he shared with King Leopold the place of the most despised European monarchs. Then they called him Abdul the Damned. To-day he is named Abdul the Blessed. Extravagant eulogy has succeeded what was possibly extravagant denunciation. But after praise and blame have been meted out, there remains an amazingly interesting character to study.

Abdul ascended the throne thirty-three years ago, at a time when it seemed as though the Turkish Empire would not endure for another decade. During his rule Turkey has lost many of its fairest provinces. Bosnia and Herzegovina have been taken by Austria. Bulgaria has become an independent kingdom; Crete has now a government of its own, and important Asiatic sections have been snipped off. Abdul long made the name of his nation reek in the nostrils of the world. His own people rose against him. Yet he is Abdul—sultan, " Shadow of God on Earth," still. Abdul was thirty-

The Sultan Hard-working and Religious four when he became sultan, and had already matured into an earnest, hard-working, deeply religious man. He did not want the crown. His uncle had been deposed and had died in mysterious fashion. His brother had been made mad and kept mad while on the throne. Abdul knew that he was stepping into a place where he would be the subject of endless intrigues and plots. He possessed, unfortunately, that vivid imagination which conjures up the vision of danger everywhere. He was essentially of a shy and retiring disposition, and he had found his happiest life communing with prophets and teachers of Mohammed in the wilderness. He feared as he took his place at the head of the nation, but he took his place though fearing.

At first the world hesitated about his character. He started by encouraging a movement in favour of giving Turkey constitutional government; but he soon tired of that. When Russia brought down her great armies on Turkey it was Abdul who led his people in the war of defence, and who, after defeat, refused to accede to humiliating Russian demands, declaring, for instance, that rather than surrender his navy, he would take his ships into the Bosphorus and blow them all up, and himself with them.

But soon worse sides of his character came more prominently to the surface. In administrative affairs he proved to be a muddler, with a passion for centralising control around himself, and often unable to make up his mind on vital issues. In

Abdul a Prisoner in His Palace private life he showed himself more and more a coward. He became obsessed with fears for his own safety, and those fears dominated his conduct. He shut himself up in his Palace of Yildiz Kiosk, refusing to go out except to the most necessary religious services. He brooded over the deaths of other sultans—how some had been hurried into sacks and thrown into the current beyond the Yildiz walls; how some had been bled to death,

some poisoned, some stabbed. A deadly fear of all men fell upon him. He would trust none. In affairs of state, his passion for centralisation did great harm. This passion was, in part, also due to his overpowering distrust of others. He tried to supervise everything himself. Business that he could not attend to must wait, and so the really important developments of the country came to a standstill.

While he was deciding whether or not bicycles should be permitted in Constantinople, his ironclads were rusting in the Bosphorus. While he was considering the regulations for a café chantant in Pera, the Powers were arranging to remove his authority from Macedonia. He could not heed the complaints from Armenia of wholesale murder because he was busy trying to make up his mind whether or not one particular telegram by a British Press correspondent should be allowed to be sent. He would hesitate, consider, reconsider, and give hours to some paltry affair that should have been settled by the sub-chief of a department in five minutes. Under this rule of the

Turkey under the Old Administration infinitely little, Turkey was apparently falling to pieces. All liberty had gone. A spy system had been introduced, the most ingenious ever known. Whenever three men met in Constantinople, one of them was probably a spy. Free speech, a free Press, and even freedom of thought were things forgotten. Taxes were largely farmed, with the abuses the farming of taxes always brings. The peasant had to cut down his date-tree to pay his tribute. Trade suffered heavily. Towns and cities, yesterday centres of prosperity, were now sinking to decay and death. Security of the person was undreamed of.

Still worse was the Turkish treatment of subject races. The many Christian peoples in the empire were exposed to the most merciless oppression. The great massacres of the Armenians horrified the world. The endless fighting and slaughtering in Macedonia at last led the Powers to intervene.

A word of caution needs to be added here. Men in other lands have been led at times to assume that in these disputes one saw the real Turkish character. This is not so. All who know the Turk as he is bear testimony to his great courtesy and kindliness in the ordinary dealings of life. His sobriety, honesty and sincerity are the admiration of all who live with him. One can no more judge the average Turk by Armenian massacres than one could measure Englishmen by the Whitechapel murders.

Macedonia affords a good example of the peculiar difficulties of Turkish rule, under the old administration. Here we have a people of mixed blood and of varied races, loving strife as other men love wealth. Three opposing forces concentrated themselves on a struggle for control: Mohammedanism, with all the strength of Turkey behind ; Greek Christianity, owning allegiance to the Greek Patriarch ; and Bulgar Christianity, acknowledging the Bulgarian Exarch. The strife between Mussulman and Christian has not been a bit more merciless than that between Greek and Bulgar. The Greeks sent their armed bands across their borders, and the Bulgars carried on their propaganda from Sofia, the Bulgarian capital.

After the great war of 1878, Macedonia hoped to become part of a great Bulgaria. The Powers, in making the Treaty of Berlin, would not permit this, but handed Macedonia back to Turkey. The people brooded, prepared, and finally **Risings and** appealed to arms. They com- **Outrages in** plained of unspeakable oppres- **Macedonia** sion. In 1902 there came one great uprising in part of Macedonia. Turkey stamped it down with an iron heel. In 1903 there came another. Whole countrysides were destroyed ; each party fought the other with the utmost bitterness. Outrages on women, the murder of children, the spitting of babes in arms, the burning to death of people shut up in their homes—all these became common. Hundreds of thousands of all ages died under the sword or from hunger.

The fights between Greek and Bulgar bands added a further ghastly horror. Revolutionary "committees" were formed throughout the province, and these committees were even more tyrannical than the Turks. Murder in its every form became commonplace. Men resorted to the most incredible methods of terror, private spites were wreaked under the name of patriotism, and a thinly veiled brigandage was carried on.

When Greek bands met Bulgars, fierce fighting followed. Take one instance of a thousand, one that happened early in 1908. The Bulgarian inhabitants of Dragarsh had a festival, and were celebrating it in the usual fashion, with dance and song.

A Greek band suddenly surrounded the place and ordered the peasants to go to their homes. The doors of the houses were then fastened up and the windows closed, the dwellings were set on fire, and men, women, and children were burnt to death. The Powers of Europe attempted to mend such matters by appointing a **Beginning** foreign-controlled gendarmerie **of Bulgaria's** in Macedonia, but racial hatreds **Freedom** were so fierce that little could be done. Let us turn to the other states at this time. Perhaps the most striking contrast to Turkey was to be found in her neighbour and former dependant, Bulgaria. Up to the time of the Russo-Turkish War, Bulgaria was governed by Turkey, and was a land of massacres, oppression, poverty, and wretchedness. The "Bulgarian atrocities," the outrages committed by Achmet Agha and the Circassian irregular troops in suppressing a minor rebellion in 1876, aroused the conscience of Europe. Mr. Gladstone, in particular, championed the cause of the miserable people, and his great campaign on their behalf was the beginning of freedom for their country.

It was on Bulgarian soil that the chief struggle of the Russo-Turkish War took place. At the end of that war the Powers made Bulgaria free in her internal affairs, a nominal suzerainty being left to Turkey. The change that has come since then has been amazing. Bulgaria, before many years, despite furious political agitation, became transformed into an exceedingly prosperous state. On the internal political struggles there is no need to dwell long. Russia sought to dominate the princedom.

The first ruler, Prince Alexander of Battenberg, was elected when, twenty-two years old, he was living as a poor German officer in Potsdam. He quickly captured the imagination and the affections of his people. He united Eastern Roumelia to Bulgaria, dared the wrath of Russia, and **Prince** fought and defeated Servia. **Alexander** He was the hero of the nation, **Abdicates** but the anger of Russia caused much trouble. Time after time his life was attempted. In the end Alexander, amid circumstances whose mystery has never yet been finally cleared up, voluntarily stepped off the throne, and retired to private life. He was succeeded by Prince Ferdinand, great-grandson on his mother's side of King Louis Philippe, and son of an Austrian nobleman. Ferdinand was the very opposite of the dashing Alexander. A man of studious temperament, a naturalist rather than a warrior, he did not succeed in kindling among the people the same devotion. Happily for him, during the first years of his reign there was one strong statesman administering affairs, the "Bismarck of the Balkans," Stambuloff. That great man died under the hand of an assassin, but not before he had firmly established Bulgaria's position.

If political life has been chequered, the social advance of the nation has been beyond expectation. Before 1878 there were not more than three score schools in the entire state ; by the beginning of the twentieth century there was an elementary school in every village and a secondary school in every town of 10,000 inhabitants. Education became free and compulsory. Public hospitals arose. The people, formerly poor, showed every sign of prosperity. Railways, commercial undertakings, universities sprang up as though by magic.

"In the days of the Turkish oppression a man was accounted rich who had £500," said M. Ghenadieff, the Bulgarian Minister of Commerce, in 1907. "Now there are plenty of rich people. Nearly £3,000,000 sterling of the public debt is in the hands of the people themselves, and the state savings-bank alone receives about £80,000 in deposits each month. That sum, of course, represents merely the savings of the poorer classes. In 1878 there was in the whole country but one printing press, and that was a hand press, which is preserved as a curiosity in the Museum of Sofia. To-day we have more than 200 printing presses of the most modern description."

The streets of Sofia, the Bulgarian capital, bright, busy, and filled with contented people, are sufficient proof of

THE SULTAN OPENING THE TURKISH PARLIAMENT
The early years of the sultan's reign were full of promise. In 1877, as shown in an earlier chapter, he granted a constitution, and, in person, opened the new Parliament. But the Assembly was short-lived, reaction setting in and overcoming the liberty from which so much was expected. In 1908, yielding to the pressure of the reformers, the sultan granted another constitution to Turkey, and in December opened the Parliament elected by the people.

the state of the land. No greater contrast could have been imagined than that between Bulgaria, free, and her neighbour, Macedonia, inhabited by her kinsmen, but under the rule of Turkey. One drop of bitterness there was in the Bulgarian cup—the suzerainty of the sultan. The Bulgarians prepared to release themselves from this. They gradually built up a strong modern army, with an available fighting force of 380,000 men out of a population of 4,500,000. This force is, in the judgment of all military critics, one of unusual efficiency, splendidly drilled, well armed, and well provided in every way.

Like Bulgaria, its neighbour Servia has had a troubled political life. Up to the beginning of the nineteenth century it was under Turkish rule, and until the Treaty of Berlin, in 1878, it was tributary to the sultan. Then it became free. It owed the beginning of its freedom to a breeder of swine, Black (Kara) George, who became the chief of its people, afterwards the prince, and who was the founder of the present royal house. In recent years Servia has been much in **Servia Under a Cloud** disfavour with the world on account of the scandals that have hung around its ruling family. The quarrels between King Milan and Queen Natalie were the talk of the seven seas. When Milan retired to Paris to seek a life of pleasure there, he handed over the throne to regents for his young son, Alexander. Alexander, at the first opportunity, seized the reins of power from the regents, and governed with all the impetuosity of the hot-blooded lad he was. His private life was such that it created misgiving even in the Balkans. He caused great offence by marrying a former lady-in-waiting to his mother, with whom he had for some time before openly maintained the closest relations. Alexander and his wife were murdered one night in their palace by a band of officers amid circumstances of almost incredible brutality, and the regicides called the present ruler, King Peter, one of the Servian royal house, to the throne.

Peter accepted the call, and the regicides went unpunished. The king in consequence was boycotted by the royal and imperial houses of Europe, and for a time foreign representatives were withdrawn from his court. Servia still lies under the shadow of the royal murder. Its capital, Belgrade, is a gay city with something of the manner of Paris. It is no injustice to say of the public life of Servia that there is a certain looseness, an absence of moral, about it, that does anything but help to make a strong nation. The very army is affected, and when one thinks of the tone of public life in the peasant state to-day, one is apt to recall the condi- **Ambition of the Servians** tion of France before the German War. The rural life of the nation is much healthier. In Belgrade one observes the acme of extravagant expenditure and blazing indiscretion. In the country there is to be found a peasantry prosperous as few other peoples are, each man with his own land, each household free from fear of famine and want.

The one overpowering ambition of the Servian people had ever been to make Servia a great kingdom, by uniting with the neighbouring tribesmen of a little mountain state, Montenegro, and by absorbing the Serb provinces of Bosnia and Herzegovina, owned by Turkey. This ambition was checked for the time by the action of the Powers of Europe when they made the Treaty of Berlin. By one of those political contradictions, over which statesmen delight and plain men puzzle, they left Bosnia and Herzegovina nominally Turkish, but handed them over to Austria to administer. One small strip of land between Servia and Montenegro, the Sanjak of Novi-Bazar, was the subject of a still more contradictory compromise. There the military occupation was to be Austrian and the civil administration Turkish. Practically, however, this did what was wanted. It prevented the junction of Servia and Montenegro.

Servia never abandoned her hope of some day obtaining Bosnia and Herzegovina for herself, and a large number of the Serb people in those two provinces sympathised with her. Meanwhile, Austria went on with her work of admin- **Results of Austrian Government** istration. About the success or otherwise of the Austrian government there is much dispute. The abuses of the old time Turkish regime have been ended. Peace has been maintained, commerce has been encouraged, schools of all kinds have been built, and much has been done to open up the provinces as tourist resorts. Great hotels have sprung up and sportsmen from all countries have been encouraged to come. Cattle-breeding and horse-breeding—particularly the latter—have been carefully fostered. But it is doubtful if the Austrians have to any extent gained the good-will of the people, or have allayed political ferment.

The little state of Montenegro shares the racial ambitions of Servia. The entire population of Montenegro is considerably less than that of Nottingham, and its size is about equal to Devon and Cornwall combined. Its capital boasts a population of 5,000, excluding the small garrison, and its public debt is £70,000. It is the land of the Black Mountains, declared independent by a prince bishop 240 years ago, and maintaining its freedom in face of all ever since. Its people held their land since 1389, when a remnant of the old Servian nobility established itself there to escape the Turkish yoke. It is so precipitous that it would be practically impossible for regular armies to invade it.

The Small State of Montenegro

It is, from end to end, one succession of mountains and valleys ; its men are all warriors ; and its principal export, as its brave ruler, Prince Nicholas, once declared, are its princesses. The daughters of Nicholas are allied to some of the greatest royal families of Europe. The picturesque and charming dress of the people and their delightful old-world ways make their land a centre of pleasure to the explorer of unbeaten tracks. The Montenegrins, bold, daring and fearless, and sturdily independent, command the good-will of the world.

While its neighbours bickered, Roumania, the great kingdom of the north, was content to foster trade and increase population. Its king, Charles, and its queen, well known in literature as " Carmen Sylva," are held in universal esteem and honour. Its population in a quarter of a century has increased between forty and fifty per cent., and is now 6,500,000. The Danube runs to the sea through its territory, its soil is exceedingly fertile, and its crops are said to be the heaviest in Europe. It has in recent years become a field of tremendous commercial enterprise, and prides itself to-day on being a strong industrial rather than a military nation. Yet it could put 650,000 men on the field if war came.

Greece Fallen from Her High Place

Greece has fallen from her high place in the world. Up to the time of her war with Turkey, in 1897, men still looked on the ancient kingdom as the possible pioneer of freedom and progress in the Eastern Mediterranean. Old traditions, old affections, and old beliefs led to the hope. The war shattered all that. It was not alone that Greece was defeated ; nations have found new birth and fresh strength in defeat before to-day. But the war revealed a cowardice, a political corruption, and a lack of preparation which disillusioned the world.

Greece, until then, had sought to pose as the protector of weaker Christian peoples against Turkey. It was the interference of Greece in the control of Crete that had brought about hostilities. She had further been fired, in common with other Eastern races, with the ambition for the political union of her race. Her ambition was greater than her capacity, her financial resources, or her self-sacrifice. She has had, as a result of the monetary cost of her war, to hand various of her revenues over to a Financial Commission, to secure the payment of interest on her external debt. Her regular army is now down to a few thousand men, and those are notoriously inefficient. Her political administration is still torn by fierce jealousies. Industrious as the Greek may be in other lands, he is all too given to taking life easily in his own. The workshops of Athens are too empty and the coffee-houses are too full. In short, Greece has been left behind, and unless some new spirit enters into the hearts of her people, she is likely to play a lesser rather than a greater part in the making of the New East.

Why Greece is Lagging Behind

Thus we arrive at the summer of 1908.

In the palace of Yildiz Kiosk sat Abdul Hamid, ever busying himself with his affairs of state, and ever becoming more the victim of his own fears. His attitude at that time was well described by one of his own court.

" He trembled at his best troops, shrunk from trusting his elder sons, his sons-in-law, brothers-in-law — who are mostly generals—and the officers who had inclination to serve him strengthened by strong personal and family interests. For some months before the revolution the troops had only blank cartridges for their rifles. This step was taken from a fear that cartridges fully charged might be used against the sultan himself. Likewise all the guns in the forts that could be turned against the Yildiz had been spiked.

Electricity is laid on in the palace. But the sultan, fearing that it might be turned against him for regicidal purposes, had the wires cut and candles exclusively used. These lights are stuck on circular pieces of cork that float on wooden buckets of water. The water will be available to cope with fire should the crime of burning down the palace or any of the sultan's numerous sleeping kiosks be malignantly attempted." It was at the moment when the darkness was apparently deepest that light

officers in the Turkish army opened up negotiations with the Young Turk leaders. Their pay was in arrears, they saw their army being ruined and their country piecemeal destroyed under the rule of Abdul, and they resolved to make common cause with the reformers. At once a secret movement began in the Turkish army without parallel in modern times. The sultan's spies were everywhere, yet the sultan got scarce an inkling of it. The reformers made their headquarters in

KING FERDINAND ANNOUNCING THE INDEPENDENCE OF BULGARIA

In 1878, at the Treaty of Berlin, the Powers of Europe created Bulgaria an autonomous principality, under the suzerainty of the Sultan of Turkey; and in 1908, when Turkey underwent such a marvellous change, Bulgaria feared that the nominal suzerainty might be made a real one. To this she was unwilling to consent, and in October, at Tirnovo, Prince Ferdinand solemnly proclaimed Bulgaria an independent kingdom, taking for himself the title of king.

came. A number of progressive Turks, driven from their country by the sultan's rule, had formed in Paris an association for bringing liberty to Turkey. "The Turk in his own land is the most oppressed of all men," they said. "He has none to help him. The Christians have the European Powers on their side, but no one stands for us."

For some time the Young Turk movement was not taken very seriously by the world. Early in 1908 certain high

the vilayet of Monastir, in Macedonia. Army corps after army corps was won over, and in the summer the reformers were ready to strike. Early in July a body of troops marched out of their barracks at Monastir, officers at their head, and formally declared a constitution for Turkey. News of this was quickly brought to Constantinople, and soldiers were despatched against them. The pasha in charge of the troops was shot, and his men made common cause with the Constitutional party. The Turkish governor—Hilmi Pasha—was given the choice between joining the reformers or being shot. He went over to reform, departed for Constantinople, and used all his influence to induce the sultan to meet the revolution in the only possible way, by yielding to it. The immediate transformation of the life of the people in Salonica and Monastir seemed more like a romance than reality. The Bulgar and Greek bands were curtly bidden to cease their strife; Christian and Turk fraternised. The racial disputes of many generations seemed swept away in a moment. Order was strictly maintained. One European present at Salonica at the time graphically described the scene in a letter home :

Changed Days for Turkey

" Until two days ago very few people here realised the seriousness and the rapidity with which the movement was developing, although about ten days earlier they began to say with satisfaction, ' Le bonheur des espions est passé.' People spoke freely in the streets and cafés and trams—a thing unknown before. During the night of the 22nd the whole town was placarded with manifestoes by officers in uniform, the text of which has probably been published in England. It is said that they were drawn up in admirable Turkish, and it was an extraordinary sight to see the crowds reading them.

" One police official who attempted to interfere was shot by an officer. In another case a policeman protested against an officer who was putting up a manifesto. ' Very well, wait till I give you a baksheesh,' said the officer, putting a cartridge into his hand. The policeman took the hint, and departed at once. This was done in the most frequented place in Salonica yesterday at noon, to the amusement of all in the cafés. Everyone looked radiant yesterday, especially the officers, who, as a rule, go about in silence and suspicion. In the afternoon and evening the people were harangued by Turks, Greeks, Bulgars, Jews and Armenians, the whole situation—bands, internal politics, etc.—being discussed with the utmost freedom and good temper. This would be of little importance elsewhere, but here in Turkey it is almost a miracle. About midnight one of Hilmi's A.D.C.'s arrived with the news that the sultan had accorded the constitution—' according to

The Sultan Yields to the Reformers

the will of the people '—and there was the greatest enthusiasm."

In a moment Abdul found that all his elaborate preparations to secure his own safety had become of no avail. His army had failed him, and without his army his power had gone. He promptly showed unexpected political wisdom. He gave in to the reformers, and in an hour changed the whole policy of his nation. He granted a constitution to Turkey. From that day Abdul came under the control of the body which had arranged the revolt, the Committee of Union and Progress.

Probably no such vital change in the affairs of a great nation has ever taken place before accompanied by so little bloodshed and violence. The leaders of the new movement—themselves, be it remembered, men of a conquering nation —declared that henceforth there was not to be in Turkey one triumphant race and others subject to it, but that men of all races were to be as brothers. Moslem and Christian forgot their old blood feud. Enemies of yesterday embraced together in the streets. Turk and Greek, Albanian and Jew fraternised, and even the Armenian was permitted to join in the rejoicing as friend and comrade, and proved himself one of the greatest forces for reform. The army of spies and petty tyrants disappeared as though by magic, and the head spy of all fled to London and told there a pitiful tale of his remorse for his past life. Men who for years had not dared to whisper their hopes now spoke out freely. A free Press began to appear as though conjured from the earth. Even the women caught the fever progress, and emerged from their hidden existences.

Rejoicings in the New Turkey

" We must each dig a grave," said one Turkish officer in addressing a crowd composed of men of many nations. " We must dig it deep and wide, and bury in it all our hatreds and all our resentments, private and public. Place over it a marble slab, bearing this inscription, ' There shall be no resurrection.' "

The political developments were equally remarkable. The constitution, made and destroyed in the early days of Abdul's reign, was restored. This was followed by a general amnesty and by a rescript declaring the equality of all Ottomans, of whatever race and religion, granting freedom from arbitrary arrest, and giving the people permission to travel freely abroad and to establish commercial associations. In December the first Parliament, duly elected by the people, met, and the sultan crowned the proofs of his resolve to be in the new movement by opening the parliament in person.

As his state coach drove through the packed crowds stretching the whole way along the four miles of narrow streets between his palace and the new Parliament House, the hated oppressor of yesterday was received everywhere with frantic enthusiasm. He spoke to the elected law-givers in the warmest manner. " I am hopeful," he declared, " that your labours will be fruitful of good for the empire and the people. With this hope, I proclaim the opening of this parliament." The renaissance of Turkey was regarded with anything but delight in various quarters. Austria, in particular, had hoped to profit much by the dismemberment of the European Ottoman Empire; now all her expectations were shattered. Bulgaria saw a possibility that the nominal suzerainty of the sultan might under reformed conditions be made a real one. This she would not allow. An official banquet was held at Constantinople for the representatives of foreign Powers, and the Bulgarian Minister was not invited. He demanded to know the reason, and was told that his status was not the same as that of others, as his country was not independent, but under Turkish suzerainty. The Bulgarian Government replied to this by promptly recalling its Minister, and by seizing part of a neutral railway between the two states. Prince Ferdinand of Bulgaria visited Vienna and was received there like a king, and shortly afterwards, in the early days of October, 1908, he proceeded to Tirnovo, the ancient capital of his people, and solemnly proclaimed Bulgaria an independent kingdom, and took for himself the title of king.

Bulgaria's Independence Declared

At the same time Austria announced that she would annex Bosnia and Herzegovina, and make them part of her empire, while retiring from Novi-Bazar. The news came like a thunder-clap to Europe. Turkey found her prestige assailed from two quarters at once. Servia and Montenegro saw all their ambition for a great Serb nation thwarted. The arrangements made by the Powers in 1878 for the permanent settlement of the Eastern Question were broken up. Had

Turkey been stronger, a declaration of war against one or both the Powers would probably have followed. The Turkish Government dared not do this, but the Turkish people showed their feelings by instituting a strict boycott of Austrian goods. The Servian and Montenegrin peoples clamoured for war. Happily for the world, it was winter-time, when campaigning was practically impossible owing to the deep snows. The weeks of waiting gave time for second thoughts.

Growing Power of the Albanians

Servia was bidden by Russia and Great Britain to keep the peace. Austria in the end agreed to pay Turkey a substantial sum for the surrender of her sovereign rights over the two provinces. Russia, under the administration of M. Isvolsky, revealed a spirit of disinterestedness and of moderation so different from her old-time Balkan campaigns that men asked in wonderment if this could be the same empire of the tsars. She threw all her influence on the side of peace.

One other factor will have to be reckoned with more and more in the Balkans—the Albanians. Direct descendants of the conquering soldiers of Alexander the Great, they retain unbroken the courage of their ancestors. The Albanians have never been really conquered; they are men of great intellectual capacity; their sons have made leaders for other nations in the past, and are likely to do so in the future. The island dependency of Crete was withdrawn from the direct rule of the sultan in 1898, and placed under Prince George of Greece, as High Commissioner. It had long dreamed of political union with Greece, and when the Turkish upheaval came, it begged the Powers to permit this. The Powers promised friendly consideration, but the plan has aroused the bitterest opposition in Turkey itself.

I write this in the early months of the New Year. In Turkey itself the growing power of the army, as shown in the summary defeat and censure of the premier, Kiamil Pasha, by Parliament, has cast some shadow over the scenes. Austria menaces Servia with war unless she definitely abandons her racial ambitions. The future is uncertain. Only one thing can be said with surety. The year 1909 will find the Balkans a centre of world attention and world interest.

What of the Future ?

F. A. McKenzie

ESSENTIAL INFORMATION ABOUT TURKEY

AREAS AND POPULATION. The area of Turkey, including all the tributary states, is estimated at 1,663,000 square miles, and the population at 41,000,000. This includes Crete, Cyprus, Egypt, Bulgaria, Bosnia, and Herzegovina ; but as Cyprus and Egypt, while tributary to Turkey, are administered by Great Britain, and as the other states mentioned have thrown off the yoke of Turkish rule, the actual area and population of Turkey is properly as follows :

	Sq. miles.	Population
Turkey in Europe	65,350 ..	6,130,200
,, ,, Asia	693,610 ..	17,683,500
,, ,, Africa	398,900 ..	1,000,000
Total	1,157,860 ..	24,813,700

The towns of over 100,000 population are—Constantinople, 1,106,000 ; Damascus, 250,000 ; Smyrna, 201,000 ; Aleppo, 200,000 ; Salonica, 150,000 ; Bagdad, 145,000 ; and Beirut, 118,800.

GOVERNMENT. On July 24th, 1908, an Imperial Iradé gave to Turkey a Constitution and an Elective Assembly. Up till that time the sole governing power was the will of the reigning sovereign, based upon the precepts of the Koran, the Multeka and the Cahon nameh, the second of these being reputed sayings of Mohammed, and the third a legal code drawn up by Soleiman the Magnificent (1520–1566). Under the new order the liberty of the individual is inviolable, and there is a free Press and a free system of education. Parliament consists of two Chambers—a Senate and a Chamber of Deputies—and sits from November 1st to March 1st, unless the session is prolonged by the sultan. The sultan has the power to nominate Senators up to one-third of the entire body. Senators must be not less than forty years of age, and must have rendered distinguished service to the state. Representation in the Lower House, or Chamber of Deputies, is on the basis of one deputy to every 50,000 male citizens. Deputies, who are elected for four years, must be not less than thirty years of age, and must be able to read and write. Members of both Houses are paid. The President and the Vice-Presidents of the Chamber of Deputies are appointed by the sultan, but their names must be on lists submitted by the Chamber. Measures must be passed by both houses, and be ratified by the sultan before they become law. In the event of dissolution, a new election must take place within six months.

MONARCH. The present sultan is Abdul Hamid II.—born 1842, succeeded to the throne 1876—the thirty-fourth of the House of Othman, the founder of the Ottoman Empire.

FINANCE. The revenue, which has not hitherto been published officially, was estimated at about £18,680,000 for the year 1906–1907. The chief sources of revenue are tithes, land and property taxes, customs and monopolies. The external debt of Turkey is about £80,000,000, and interest about £3,500,000.

INDUSTRY AND COMMERCE. The soil of Turkey is fertile, but agriculture is pursued by primitive appliances. The chief products are tobacco, cereals, cotton, figs and fruits, coffee, madder, opium and gums. The chief cereals are wheat, rye, barley, oats, and maize. Wine-growing and distilling are important industries. Silk is cultivated, rose culture—for otto of roses—and cotton growing are encouraged. Minerals are little worked, although Asiatic Turkey especially is rich in mineral resources, including chrome, silver-lead, zinc, manganese, antimony, copper and emery, coal and petroleum. Manufacturing industries are not far advanced, but there is some metal working (chiefly utensils), and Damascus textile industries—silks, cottons and woollens—employ about 10,000 hands. Fisheries include sponges, mother of pearl, and pearls. In 1906 the total imports were of the value of £28,229,419, and the exports of the value of £17,705,133. The chief exports were raw silk, grapes, grain, flour, mohair, figs, coffee, opium and hides.

CURRENCY. The money system of Turkey is as follows :

1 para	= 1/18d.
40 paras = 1 piastre	= 2·16d.
100 piastres = 1 lira turca or medgidié	= 18s.
5 lira = 1 purse	= 90s.

The coins are : (copper) 1, 5, 10, and 20 paras ; (silver) $\frac{1}{2}$, 1, 2, 5, 10, and 20 piastres ; (gold) $\frac{1}{4}$, $\frac{1}{2}$, 1, $2\frac{1}{2}$, and 5 lira.

WEIGHTS AND MEASURES. For about twenty years metric weights [see page 5399] have been compulsory for cereals ; although metric weights were also decreed compulsory for other purposes in 1892, the decree has never been enforced. The old Turkish names were applied to the metric names, thus:

LINEAL.		WEIGHTS.	
Nokta	= Milimetre	Habbe	= Centigramme
Khat	= Centimetre	Boughdais	= Decigramme
Parmak	= Decimetre	Denk	= Gramme
Archine	= Metre	Drachma	= Decagramme
Mill	= Kilometre	Ock	= Kilogramme
Farsang or Pharoagh	} = Myriametre	Batman	= Myriagramme
		Kantar	= Quintal
		Tchéki	= Millier or Tonne
SURFACE.		CAPACITY.	
Deunum = Are		Zarf	= Centilitre	Sultchek = Litre
Djerib	= Hec-tare	Kouton = Decalitre	Kile	= Decalitre
		Kileh	= Hectolitre

The old Turkish standards are complicated and confusing, there being standards for cottons and carpets different from those for silks and woollens. Many of them, such as measures of capacity and land measure, differed in different localities.

POSTAGE. Great Britain to Turkey, letters, papers, and samples as for France [see page 5398]. Parcels may be sent to British Post-office agencies in Turkey, which are at Beirut, Constantinople, Smyrna, and Salonica, the charge varying according to destination and route. The only route to Beirut is via Egypt, and the charge is 1s., 2s., and 3s. for 3, 7, and 11 pounds respectively. But there are three routes to Constantinople and to Smyrna, and the charge may be as high as 2s. 6d., 3s., and 3s. 6d. for 3, 7, and 11 pounds, the rates in force by the overland route via Belgium, Germany, Austria, and Roumania. Parcels may also be sent through Austrian agencies, which are maintained at about twenty-five different places, or by Ottoman post, which has about fifty agencies.

TELEGRAMS. Great Britain to Turkey, 6½d. per word, but private telegrams in code or cypher are not accepted.

SAMOS

Samos is a principality of the Ottoman Empire, possessing a considerable degree of independence, guaranteed by Great Britain, France, and Russia. Its status is the status of Bulgaria and of Greece before these principalities declared themselves independent from Turkey. Samos is one of the Anatolian Islands, has an area of 180 square miles, and a population of about 50,000. The capital and port is Vathy, with 25,000 inhabitants. The Prince Governor is A. Kopassy Bey. The resources are chiefly agricultural—wine, raisins, olive-oil, and tobacco. Imports and exports are each of about £200,000 value annually, and the revenue and expenditure are each about £25,000 annually.

INFORMATION ABOUT GREECE AND ROUMANIA

GREECE

AREA AND POPULATION. The area of Greece, including the islands and Thessaly, is 25,014 square miles, and the population is 2,631,952. To this may now be added the island of Crete, with an area of 3,400 square miles, and a population of 310,200, making for the entire kingdom of Greece an area of 28,414 square miles, and a population of 2,942,152. The principal towns and their populations are Athens, 170,000; Piræus, 70,000; Patras, 37,958; Canea, the capital of Crete, 24,537; and Candia, also in Crete, 22,774.

GOVERNMENT. Greece is a constitutional monarchy, the present ruler being George I.—born December 24th, 1845—who is younger brother of the present King of Denmark, and who was elected King of the Hellenes by the National Assembly at Athens in March, 1863, when he was eighteen years of age. Legislative power is vested in a single Chamber—the Bulé—of 235 paid members, who are elected by adult manhood suffrage for four years. Representatives must be not less than thirty years of age. As representation is based on one deputy for every 12,000 of the population, the Chamber expands automatically with the increase of the population. Bills become law only by the votes of an absolute majority, and the Chamber can sit only if half of the members are present.

FINANCE AND COMMERCE. The estimated revenue for 1908 was £5,465,711, and the estimated expenditure was £5,361,762. The chief sources of revenue are customs and excise, stamps, direct taxes, monopolies—salt, petroleum, matches, and playing cards—and revenue from state property. The national debt of Greece was, at the end of 1907, £28,703,300, with an annual charge of £888,708. Agriculture is the mainstay of Greece, and manufactories are of no importance. The chief cereals are wheat, barley, rye, and maize. The best crop, however, is currants. Other products are valonia—a tanning acorn—tobacco, silk, wine, olives, and fruits. The value of Greek imports for the year 1906 was £5,738,060, and the exports, £4,722,300. The chief imports are corn, yarn and tissues, coal, timber, wrought metals, and chemicals. The chief exports are agricultural products—currants, figs, tobacco; raw minerals—lead, magnesium, emery, marble; wines and spirits, olive and other oils, and hides.

WEIGHTS AND MEASURES. The weights and measures are metric [see page 5399] although the old Greek standards, which were by no means uniform, have not yet been quite done away with. The standards of weight, however, though decimal, do not quite conform to metric standards. In the others, Greek names have been given to metric quantities.

LINEAL.		CAPACITY.	
Gramma	= Millimetre	Kybos	= Millilitre
Daktylos	= Centimetre	Mystron	= Centilitre
Palame	= Decimetre	Kotylê	= Décilitre
Pecheus	= Metre	Litra	= Litre
Stadion	= Kilometre	Koilon	= Hectolitre
Skoinis	= Myriametre		

SURFACE.

Square Pechus = Square metre   Stremma = Are

WEIGHTS.

1 Drachma = 1 Gramme = 15 Grains
1,500 Drachmai = 1 Mna = 1⅓ Kilogramme = 3·306931 lb.
100 Mnâi = 1 Talanton = 1½ Quintal = 330·6931 lb.
10 Talanta = 1 Tonos = 1½ Tonneaux = 29·52615 cwts.

CURRENCY. The money currency of Greece is based upon the convention between France, Italy, Belgium, and Switzerland [see page 5398]. Thus the *drachma* is the equivalent of the French franc and the Italian lira, and the *leptâ* (100 lepta = 1 drachma) has the same value as the centime of France and the centesimo of Italy. The gold coins of Great Britain, Germany, Austria, Denmark, Russia, Spain, Turkey, Egypt, and the United States are legal tender in Greece, subject to a deduction of 5s. per cent. from their nominal value.

POSTAGE. Great Britain to Greece: Letters, papers and samples, as for France [see page 5398]. Parcel post, 2s. 3d., 2s. 9d., and 3s. 3d. for 3, 7, and 11 lb. respectively. Limit of length, breadth, or depth, 2 feet; of length and girth combined, 4 feet.

TELEGRAMS. Great Britain to Greece and the Greek Islands, 6d. per word.

ROUMANIA

AREA AND POPULATION. Roumania—the name given to the old provinces of Wallachia and Moldavia—has an area of 50,700 square miles and a population estimated at 6,585,534 for 1907. The chief towns are Bucharest (the capital), 276,178; Jassy, 77,759; Galatz, 62,545; Brạila, 56,300; Ploësti, 45,107; and Craiova, 45,579.

GOVERNMENT. The kingdom of Roumania dates from 1861, and its independence from Turkey from 1877. The present king, Carol I. (born 1839, son of Prince Karl of Hohenzollern-Sigmaringen), was elected in 1866. His queen, Princess Elizabeth von Wied, is "Carmen Sylva" of poem and prose. The government is a dual-chamber legislature. The Senate, or Upper Chamber, has 120 members, elected for eight years; and the Chamber of Deputies has 183 members elected for four years. Election for both Houses is by a system of direct vote and delegation depending upon the voter's education and property qualification. Senators must be forty years of age, and deputies twenty-five years of age. The king has the power of veto. The Executive consists of a council of eight Ministers, presided over by a Prime Minister.

FINANCE AND INDUSTRIES. The estimated revenue for 1908–1909 was £16,440,441, and the estimated expenditure was £16,349,651. On March 31st, 1907, the public debt of Roumania was £55,415,792, more than half of which is represented by public service works, chiefly railways. The climate of Roumania is extreme—excessively hot in summer, and excessively cold in winter. The chief industries are agricultural, stock raising, and mineral. The chief crops are maize, wheat, barley, oats, rye, vines, plums, and tobacco. Other crops are colza, flax, hemp, and sugar beets. Stock raising—horses, cattle, sheep, goats, and swine—is the most important single industry. The forests yield valuable timber, chiefly oak, beech, fir, and pine. Coal and petroleum industries are important, and the latter is exported in large quantities. The only manufactures of even moderate importance are those of clothing, woodwork, and metal-work. In 1906 the total imports were of the value of £16,531,900, and the exports £19,269,020. The chief exports are wheat, barley, maize, petroleum, salt, spirits, hides, wood, and cattle.

CURRENCY. The currency is on the system of the Latin Monetary Union [see page 5398], the *bano* (plural, *bani*) being equal to a centime, and the *leo* (plural, *lei*) being equal to a franc (100 bani = 1 leo).

WEIGHTS AND MEASURES. These are metric [see page 5399].

POSTAGE. Great Britain to Roumania: Letters, papers and samples, as for France [see page 5398]. Parcel post, 2s., 2s. 6d., and 3s. for 3, 7, and 11 lb. respectively if by Hamburg, and 3d. per parcel more if by Ostend or Flushing.

TELEGRAMS. Great Britain to Roumania, 3½d. per word.

INFORMATION ABOUT THE BALKAN STATES

The Balkans, in their widest sense, are the states of the Balkan Peninsula, but Greece at the southern extremity of the peninsula is not usually reckoned one of the Balkan states, and Roumania is excluded, as it is on the north side of the Danube. Thus, the Balkan states are Turkey in Europe, Bosnia and Herzegovina, Bulgaria, Servia and Montenegro. Turkey is considered separately [see page 5326]. Bosnia and Herzegovina are now attached to Austria [see page 5337], so there remain for separate treatment Bulgaria, Servia, and Montenegro.

BULGARIA

AREA AND POPULATION. The area of Bulgaria is 38,080 square miles, and the population is 4,035,620. The chief cities and towns, with their populations, are Sofia (the capital), 82,621 ; Philippopolis (the capital of Southern Bulgaria, formerly known as Eastern Roumelia), 45,707 ; Varna, 37,417 ; Rustchuk, 33,632 ; Slivno, 25,027 ; Shumla, 22,275 ; and Plevna, 21,145. Chief port is Varna, on the Black Sea.

GOVERNMENT. Bulgaria was created by the Powers of Europe at the Treaty of Berlin in 1878, an autonomous principality, under the suzerainty of the Sultan of Turkey. The prince was to be the elected choice of the people, which fell upon Ferdinand, the youngest son of Prince Augustus of Saxe-Coburg-Gotha. The mother of the prince was a daughter of King Louis Philippe of France. On October 5th, 1908, Prince Ferdinand, at Tirnovo, the ancient capital of Bulgaria, assumed the title of Tsar, and renounced all allegiance to Turkey. The Legislative House is a single Chamber, the Sobranjé, or National Assembly, the members of which are elected for five years on a universal manhood suffrage in the proportion of one member to 20,000 population. Executive power is vested in a Council of eight Ministers appointed by the prince.

FINANCE AND INDUSTRY. The estimated revenue and expenditure for 1908 were £5,090,000. The Bulgarian public debt is about £15,000,000. Over one-third of the area of Bulgaria is under cultivation, and almost one-third under timber. Agriculture provides occupation for 70 per cent. of the population. Wheat is the principal cereal, and is the chief article of export. Other prominent industries are wine-growing, tobacco and silk culture, otto of roses, cotton and rice cultivation, dairy farming, and stock-raising. All minerals are state property, but coal and salt are the only ones worked to any extent. The manufactories include the making of woollens and cottons, cords and cigarettes, flour-mills, and saw-mills. In 1906 the imports valued £4,338,975 and the exports £4,482,934. The chief exports are grain, textiles, raw silk, and live-stock.

CURRENCY. The currency is upon the same basis as that of France [see page 5398], but the Bulgarian equivalent of a franc is the lev (plural leva), and of a centime it is the stotinko (plural, stotinki).

WEIGHTS AND MEASURES. These are metric [see page 5399].

POSTAGE. Great Britain to Bulgaria, as for France [see page 5393]. Parcel post, 2s. 3d., 2s. 9d., and 3s. for 3, 7, and 11 lb. respectively if by Hamburg, or 3d. per parcel more if by Ostend or Flushing. Limit of length, breadth, or depth, 3½ feet ; of length and girth, 6 feet.

TELEGRAMS. Great Britain to Bulgaria, 4d. per word.

SERVIA

AREA AND POPULATION. Servia has an area of 18,650 square miles and a population of 2,688,025. The chief towns, with their populations, are Belgrade (the capital), 77,816, and Nisch, 21,946.

GOVERNMENT. The King of Servia is Peter I. (born 1844, and ascended the throne after the assassination of King Alexander in 1903). The constitution vests the legislative authority in the king and a National Assembly, or Narodna-Skupshtina, which has 160 paid deputies, elected by manhood suffrage for four years. The executive power vests in the king, assisted by a Council of eight Ministers.

FINANCE AND INDUSTRY. For the year 1907 the revenue was £3,618,110, and the expenditure was £3,615,500. The chief sources of revenue are monopolies, direct taxes, customs, railways, and excise. At the end of 1907 the public debt stood at £18,043,720. The country is agricultural, under a system of peasant freehold ownership. The principal crops are maize, wheat, grass, plums, barley, oats, vines, hemp and flax, and tobacco. Silk culture is also followed, and there is important stock raising for export. Mines in active operation include coal, lignite, gold, copper, lead, zinc, antimony, and silver. The industries include flour milling, brewing and distilling, sugar-works, weaving, and tanning. In 1907 the total imports were of the value of £2,823,333, and the total exports £3,259,650. The chief exports were prunes, pigs, wool, wheat, wine, hides, cattle, and horses.

CURRENCY. The currency is based on the franc and the other standards of the Latin Monetary Union [see page 5398]. The para is the equivalent of a centime, and the dinar (100 paras = 1 dinar) is the equivalent of one franc.

WEIGHTS AND MEASURES. The weights and measures are metric [see page 5399].

POSTAGE. Great Britain to Servia, as for France [see page 5398]. Parcel post, 3d. per parcel less than to Roumania [see page 5327].

TELEGRAMS. Great Britain to Servia, 3½d. per word ; code or cypher telegrams not accepted.

MONTENEGRO

AREA AND POPULATION. Montenegro has an area of 3,630 square miles and a population of 230,000. The chief towns, with their populations, are Cettinjé, 4,500 ; Podgoritza, 10,000 ; Dulcigno, 5,000 ; and Niksic, 5,000.

GOVERNMENT. Montenegro, which was recognised as independent by the Treaty of Berlin, is a hereditary constitutional monarchy, with a National Assembly, or Skupshtina, composed of seventy-four members, elected by universal suffrage for a period of four years. There are also twelve appointed members. The reigning prince is Nicholas I. (born 1841 ; succeeded his uncle 1860).

FINANCE AND INDUSTRY. The estimated revenue for 1907 was £124,166, and the expenditure was £120,370. The public debt is £70,000. Agriculture is pursued in a primitive fashion. The chief crops are maize, tobacco, oats, potatoes, barley, and buckwheat. Stock raising is important. There are practically no mining or manufacturing industries.

CURRENCY. Montenegro has a small circulation of local nickel and bronze coinage, minted in Austria, but the chief medium of exchange is Austrian silver coins and paper notes. Turkish silver and French and English gold are also legal tender.

WEIGHTS AND MEASURES. The metric system is used [see page 5399].

POSTAGE. Great Britain to Montenegro, as for France [see page 5398]. Parcel post, 2s. 3d., 2s. 9d., and 3s. for 3, 7, and 11 lb. respectively if viâ Hamburg, or 3d. per parcel more if viâ Ostend or Flushing. Size limit as for Bulgaria [see above].

TELEGRAMS. Gt. Brit. to Montenegro, 3½d. per word.

AUSTRIA-HUNGARY IN OUR TIME
AN EMPIRE OF MANY NATIONAL-
ITIES AND CONTENDING RACES
By Henry W. Nevinson

FROM its history one can see that the monarchy of Austria-Hungary is not so much a result as a residue. It embodies no conscious purpose or intention, like modern Germany. After its long and varied annals we can hardly speak of its growth, for it remains rather as a shapeless and almost accidental collection of pieces than an organic and vital whole. It is still encumbered by the tradition of former greatness in days when it stood before Europe as the Holy Roman Empire, whose monarch was equally the successor of the Cæsars and the representative of God's temporal power here on earth. It would be hard for any empire to live up to such a part as that, and the memory of an obsolete grandeur which could not be maintained has prevented the country hitherto from developing along fresh lines of progress.

We can, indeed, hardly speak of Austria-Hungary as a country at all. It lies sprawling in the middle of Europe, without natural limits or frontiers; and it has no natural character of its own, though the parts of the empire are in touch; and it possesses no colonies or foreign settlements. Almost every kind of scenery may be found within its boundaries. In the south-west are the Alpine peaks of the Tyrol; in the south-east the great ranges and forests of the Carpathians. North, in Bohemia, and south, in Bosnia, are **Austria's Varied Scenery** regions of pleasant hills and valleys, interspersed with plains. The Alförd, or central flat through which the great rivers of Hungary run, is one of the largest plains of Europe, and the outlying province of Galicia, beyond the northern Carpathians, is a vast plain of Russian character. As a complete contrast to such scenes, you may pass down one of the most beautiful and varied coastlines in the world, from the top of the Adriatic to the Mouths of Cattaro, and still you are in Austrian or Hungarian territory, for Austria stretches out an arm to reach the sea at Trieste, Hungary **Mixed Races in Austria** does the same at Fiume, and the narrow length of rocky shore and mountain, called Dalmatia, is Austria's again. This diversity of scene makes Austria-Hungary one of the most beautiful and interesting parts of Europe for the traveller, especially as it is also one of the least known. But the diversity of scene is even surpassed by the diversity of race; and though this also affords the traveller a further interest and charm, it adds considerably to the problem of government.

In fact, it *is* the problem of government, and without realising the diversity of race, it is impossible to understand what the contemporary history of the empire means. There are eight easily recognised races within the frontiers, and the list might be extended to eleven. Of the eight at least five are not merely different from each other; they are strongly nationalist, and from time to time display violent hostility towards one or all of the other races with whom they are supposed to share the glory and government of the same empire. That is the worst of an empire which has not grown by natural energy from the inside, but has been thrown together bit by bit as occasion served, often by the accident of dynasty or marriage. One remembers the well-known ironic line :

Bella gerant alii ; tu, felix Austria, nube.

Or, in English :

By others let the wars be waged ;
Thou, happy Austria, get engaged.

Such marriages were successful in adding territory, not in adding power. To form a picture of the result, you might imagine small portions of the British Empire all clustered together in the same country, so that English and Irish, French Canadians and Boers, New Zealanders and Manxmen were living side by side, without the sea to keep them comfortably tolerant and apart. Such a **Disunion in the Empire** variety of peoples, all dwelling within a small space—Austria-Hungary is only about twice the size of the British Islands—adds much to a traveller's interest. Indeed, to the student of men, no part of Europe, not even the Balkan Peninsula, is so full of varied knowledge as Austria-Hungary.

Almost every stage of European civilisation is found existing there in full vitality—the scientific and highly educated German of Vienna, the mountaineer of the Tyrol, the gipsy of the Hungarian plain, the ancestral Moslem of Bosnia, the Roumanian descendant of old Roman colonists in Transylvania, the progressive Czech of Bohemia, the unchanging Jew of Galicia, the unhappy Pole, and, finally, isolated almost in the centre of them all, unrelated to any of them, and only very dimly related to far-off Turks and Finns, stands the Magyar, surrounded by Slavs of various names, and almost continually at strife with the Emperor of Austria, who happens to be also his own king. In the whole Austrian Empire, almost the only European stock which you will not find is the Austrian. It would be hardly too much to say that such a being as an Austrian does not exist.

We may, however, use the word roughly still for the large German population which forms the centre of Austrian society and boasts itself, with some justice, the most civilised and advanced of the many nationalities. These Germans are the natural successors to the eastern province of Charlemagne's old Teutonic Empire—the East Mark, which warded off the Mag- **Advanced and Civilised Germans** yars—and they number some 9,000,000, or about a third of Austria's population, and something over 2,000,000, or about a ninth part of Hungary's. Till quite lately no one would have hesitated to call them the predominant race. German was the language, not only of the Court, society, and literature, but of all official and legal business throughout the empire. It was taught in all schools and used in every department of the army. No one would

have thought twice in describing Austria as a German Power, and it is naturally the desire of the German-speaking population to keep things as they were or to extend the German culture and influence.

But in recent years the Germans have seen themselves checked, and even driven back, not only by the Magyars of Hungary, but by the various branches of Slavs in Bohemia and the lesser states, such as Styria and Carinthia. The surprise has only intensified their Teutonism. Many have embraced the so-called Pan-German ideal, which tries to regard the cause of all the Teutonic peoples of the world as one, and would gather the Teutons, not only of the German and Austrian Empires, but of Russia, South America, South Africa, including the Boers, and of Holland and Belgium into a single fold. A favourite scheme of Pan-Germanism for some time past has been an extension of German influence throughout the old Turkish provinces to the port of Salonika, or even by way of Constantinople itself, where Germans already number some 40,000, to Asia Minor, and by a German **Enemies of the Austrian German** railway to Bagdad and the Persian Gulf. By this route they hoped to find an outlet for the German increase in lands where they would not lose their nationality, as they do in the United States. At the moment events are against the scheme, but it is a thing to be remembered in estimating the probabilities of Austrian politics. It is the ultimate goal of the " Drang nach Osten," of which we have heard so much.

For the time, however, these more ambitious designs have been checked, and the Austrian German is fighting for existence in his own country rather than for distant Pan-Germanism in the Balkans or Asia Minor. For some ten years past he has been brought into sharp and continual conflict with Czechs, Magyars, and Italians, in turn or together. It is partly a religious quarrel, and the cry of " Freedom from Rome "—" Los von Rom ! "—is one of the party's watchwords. But many good Catholics belong to the movement, too, and the conflict is, before all things, a matter of race or nationality. For some years past the section that looks to Germany rather than Austria as its national fatherland has been growing, and allegiance to the Hohenzollern of Berlin rather than to the Hapsburg is openly expressed. To unite the German part of Austria to the rest of Germany is an obvious though futile device. But for the position of Bohemia, perhaps Bismarck might have tried to realise it. But he knew that Bohemia made the thing impossible. Probably an equal obstacle lies also in the very different nature of the South German from the Prussian. For the South German of Austria, if less painfully educated and disciplined to a certain kind of capacity, has far more freedom and charm of nature, and far more imaginative power. Nor does his neighbour, the South German of Bavaria, find life under Prussian leadership exactly enjoyable.

So the Pan-German of Austria is now standing in opposition to the chief forces at work in his country. Perhaps the strongest, as well as the most recent, of these forces is Pan-Slavism. It is a similar movement, but less conscious, less wealthy, and devoid of organisation and practical aim. It is a dream of distant unity, like the Russian movement of the same name— a feeling of common brotherhood rather than a policy with a programme. Certainly it has the strength of **The Slavs Weakened by Division** numbers, for, taking the Austria-Hungary monarchy as a whole, the Slavs probably outnumber all other races by at least two millions. But, as usually happens among Slavs, they are weakened by division. The Czechs of Bohemia, the Croats, the Serbs, the Ruthenians, the Slovenes, the Slovaks, the Dalmatians, and the Poles, though all of Slav origin, now in many cases form separate nationalities, and even in language they are often unintelligible to each other, though their languages are akin.

They are also divided by religion. The great majority, such as the Czechs, the Croats, and the Poles, are Catholic ; while the Serbs and many of the Southern Slavs remain Orthodox, following the same rites and doctrines as the Greek and Russian Church. The Pan-Slavist ideal in Austria-Hungary is the formation of the empire into a kind of confederacy of states in which the Slav would predominate. At one time, like all Pan-Slavists, they looked forward to a Slav empire under the suzerainty of Russia.

But this ideal has been dimmed by the overwhelming defeat of Russia in the East and by the cruel reaction of her own government against liberty. At the present time the Slav claims are for separate nationalities. The Croats, gathered round their old capital of Agram, live in violent protest against the dominance of the Magyars in the kingdom of Hungary, to which they belong. They are nearly all Catholic ; in fact, the name Croat is used among the Southern Slavs for Catholic just as the name of Servian signifies Orthodox or Greek Church. They **Feuds of Czechs and Germans** boast a fine history, claiming to be the only Southern Slavs, except the Montenegrins, never subdued by the Turks. Indeed, they are the only Slavs in Austria-Hungary who have established some right to nationality, except the Czechs of Bohemia, and, in quite recent years, perhaps the Roumanians of Transylvania, who have become an even more painful thorn in the side of the Magyars, because there is always a danger that Roumania may adopt their cause.

But of all the Slavs in the empire, the Czechs are by far the strongest and most advanced. Their civilisation is historic, and their nations long held a high place in Europe. But the Germans have been their foes from the beginning, and the feud continues with violence to the present day. Till some thirty years ago there seemed every chance that their nationality would become absorbed under German language and manners. The national movement began with the revival of the national language, as also happened in Hungary, and is happening in Ireland now. It is strange that a literary and academic beginning should have taken so deep a hold on the populace that German is now a language under a ban and the contest between the peoples is perpetual.

As long ago as 1886 Bohemia won the privilege of special law courts and universities, together with the recognition of her language as official, though this right was again withdrawn in 1899, when the Czechs were endeavouring to introduce Czech words of command into the army. This feud against the Pan-Germans has, **Bohemia Demands a Kingship** in fact, continued ever since, breaking out with especial fury in 1902, again in 1904, when the Vienna University was closed on account of it and the Germans retaliated by smashing up Kubelik's concert-hall at Linz ; and again towards the end of 1908, when martial law was proclaimed in Prague at the very time of the emperor's Diamond Jubilee. The Czechs now demand a restoration of the old separate kingship for Bohemia on the same terms as Hungary's kingship, and it is very probable the concession will be granted by the coronation at Prague either of the present old emperor or of his successor, the Crown Prince Franz Ferdinand, who is an enthusiastic Catholic, and has also a Czech wife in **Hungary's Disputes with Austria** morganatic marriage. The estimated number of Czechs in the empire is about six million, or nearly a quarter of the population of Austria proper. But more serious for Austria even than Bohemia's nationalism has been the prolonged disagreement with Hungary.

We need not go back to the cruel repression of Hungary under Heynau after the revolutionary chaos of 1848, when the present emperor came to the throne; nor to the restoration of the constitution in 1861; nor even to the "Ausgleich," or Compromise of 1867, by which Beust hoped he had arranged a workable system of unity in separation. In 1897 the struggle was renewed, chiefly on the Hungarian demand for a separate tariff and separation in commercial affairs. It resulted in a complete block in the constitution existing between the two countries.

By that constitution there is an Austrian Parliament of two Houses— the Upper House, largely hereditary, and a Reichsrath of elected representatives; and there is a distinct Hungarian Parliament of a House of Magnates, chiefly hereditary, and a House of elected representatives, in which the Magyars have hitherto secured a majority, though they are not a majority of the population. Both Parliaments send "Delegations" of sixty members each to sit alternately at Vienna or Budapest, for the arrangement of the common financial burdens. The Delegations may vote together; but they sit separately, and do not debate together. The emperorking can personally veto all Bills passed by either Parliament; and he appoints the Ministers himself, apart from the will of the majority. Such a system may obviously lead to a deadlock on any

THE CROWN PRINCE OF AUSTRIA
The Archduke Franz Ferdinand, successor to the throne of the Austrian Empire, was recently invested with power entitling him to participate in the government of the dual monarchy.

serious question, and on the question of the tariff and the army the deadlock lasted year after year. In 1900 the emperor threatened to suspend the constitution. In 1902 Kossuth, son of the famous Hungarian liberator of 1848, and leader with Count Apponyi of the Magyar Nationalists, demanded absolute separation, except for the bond of the crown. In the next year a complete disintegration of the empire seemed probable, and the Kossuthites insisted on the use of Hungarian words of command and the employment of Hungarian officers in the Hungarian regiments of the regular army, not merely in the Honved, or local Hungarian militia, corresponding to the Austrian militia, or Landwehr. The emperor conceded the appointment of Hungarian officers and the use of national emblems, but steadily refused the use of the Hungarian word of command as destroying the unity of the army. So the deadlock on the tariff and army continued, the Hungarian Parliament going so far in 1905 as to refuse taxes and recruits. The emperor summoned the so-called Coalition to Vienna, but no terms could be arranged. In the following year, 1906, the Coalition was allowed to take office on condition that it did not oppose a measure for manhood suffrage, all males over twenty-four. This was carried largely by the emperor's personal influence, acting through the premier, Baron von Beck, an honourable statesman, who also succeeded in ending the ten years' quarrel over the tariff by a commercial treaty with Hungary, in 1907. Under this **End of a National Quarrel** treaty, each state was granted a separate tariff; but Hungary was to pay 36 per cent. of the expenses for war, defence, and foreign affairs. A court of arbitration for future disputes was also instituted. The question of the word of command in the army was held over, and is not definitely settled at the time of writing. The Magyars are, in part, very much occupied by the Slav movements directed against them in Croatia and Transylvania, and by their own endeavours to retain a majority in their Parliament by one device or another under manhood suffrage. With this object they framed a Bill in 1908 by which a fairly rich Magyar's vote will count as about thirty to one against the Slav peasant's. It is significant that in the Austrian Reichsrath the first appeal to the people under manhood suffrage produced a Parliament of twenty-six groups, the two largest being the Social Democrats—90, largely Jewish in tendency, and the Christian Socialists—65, largely anti-Semites.

The year 1908 was for many reasons one of the most remarkable in Austria's history, and much future history is likely to spring from it. For some years past Austria had

they were not intended to work. Nothing was further from the thoughts of the two most interested Powers than a reformed and resuscitated Turkey. They were only waiting for Turkey to rot till she dropped, and in the meantime they opposed any genuine reform on the ground that the integrity of the Turkish Empire must never be infringed.

THE HEART OF VIENNA

The real value of this phrase was shown in the early summer of 1908 when Count von Aehrenthal, who had lately succeeded Count Goluchowski as Foreign Minister in Austria, suddenly proposed to extend the Austrian, or rather Hungarian, railway from the frontier of Herzegovina through the Sanjak of Novi Bazar to the Turkish frontier town of Mitrovitsa. By this line Austria would at once open for herself a route to Salonika without quitting territory under her own control till she entered Turkey herself. It was a daring proposal, but Russia countered it by suggesting another railway, from the Danube, through Servia, the Sanjak and Montenegro, to Scutari and the Adriatic, thus binding together the Serb states and giving them egress to the sea independent of Austria. To such a scheme, after her own proposal, Austria could only assent with a

A SCENE IN THE AUSTRIAN CAPITAL
The Schottengasse and Währingerstrasse, two of the chief thoroughfares in Vienna, the leading city of Austria, are shown in the above illustration.

been watching the decline of Turkey into apparent ruin with peculiar attention. As one of the "two most interested Powers," she had combined with Russia to impose various schemes of reform upon the sultan, especially in regard to Macedonia, where the wretchedness and persecution of the populations had become a scandal to Europe. But the schemes of reform did not work;

sardonic smile, and so the matter rested. But suddenly all deep-laid plans and dark designs of Austria, as of other Powers regarding the Near East, were overturned by the Young Turk Revolution of July. Up to 1908—the time of writing—no revolution had ever equalled it for skill, moderation, and success. Unhappily,

Austria's Thwarted Designs success was just the last thing that the two most interested Powers desired in Turkey. They had long looked forward with apprehension to a terrible combat in sharing out the Turkish Empire, but it would be a still more terrible thing if no one was to get a share.

The details of the arrangement are, naturally, obscure. We only know that there were meetings between Baron von Aehrenthal, M. Isvolsky, the Russian Foreign Minister, and Signor Tittoni, the Foreign Minister of Italy, and that in September, Prince Ferdinand of Bulgaria, an Austrian by birth and education, visited Budapest and was received with royal honours. On October 5th, Prince Ferdinand, almost certainly at Austria's suggestion, proclaimed himself tsar of an independent kingdom, owing no fealty to Turkey and no tribute for Eastern Roumelia. On the following day, Austria formally annexed the Turkish provinces of Bosnia and Herzegovina, which she had been allowed to occupy and administer by the Treaty of Berlin since 1878.

"The rights of our sovereignty," ran the proclamation, "are extended to Bosnia and Herzegovina. Among the many cares that surround our throne, care for your material and spiritual welfare shall not be the least." At the same time, a share in the legislation was promised, together with equal rights before the law, and equal protection for religion, language, and race. The Austrian troops which had been allowed to police the Sanjak of Novi Bazar, a long, Turkish strip of land

Annexation of Turkish Territory lying between Servia and Montenegro, were also withdrawn, nominally as compensation to Turkey. The concession was valueless, for if those Serb states on either side of the Sanjak were hostile, Austria could not hold it ; and if they were friendly, she could re-occupy it without effort. But by the annexation of the two provinces, Austria tore up the Treaty of Berlin, insulted Turkey, and exposed the Young Turk government to

extreme danger from the probability of war, besides irritating Servia and Montenegro almost beyond endurance.

There are nearly 2,000,000 Servian Slavs in the annexed provinces. Less than half the population is Orthodox—the rest being Catholics or Mohammedan descendants of Serbs early converted by the Turks ; but all of them are Servian by race, descendants from subjects of the old Servian Empire that was destroyed by the Turks at the end of the fourteenth century. The annexation cut the Serb race in half, and absorbed about a third of it. Servia saw herself also cut off, hopelessly from the sea and from her heroic kinsmen in Montenegro. The Servian fighting strength is very small, probably not more than 200,000 of all arms, though Servia had lately been purchasing new batteries from France.

Austria, in the three previous years, had also spent very large sums in re-armament, and she could probably put over a million men in the field, including the Hungarian Honved. But her troops are admittedly ill-assorted and split up

Servia's Fate in the Balance by nationalist feeling, and at the time of writing it seems as though Servia may declare war any day. At the worst she could only be absorbed into Austria, and form the nucleus of a great Servian province, gradually becoming as independent as Hungary. At the best she might bring Russia into the contest as protector of the Southern Slavs.

In its ulterior aims of embarrassing the Reform Party in Turkey by war and of restoring the sultan's corrupt government, Aehrenthal's coup has hitherto failed. If there was a secret bargain between him and Isvolsky, it has so far come to nothing, because Sir Edward Grey took strong steps to demonstrate Britain's friendship to the Young Turks, and the Pan-Slavists in Russia raised an outcry against any possible bargain which would secure some advantage like the opening of the Dardanelles to the Russian fleet at the price of betraying the Southern Slavs to " the German." Isvolsky, it is true, addressing the Duma on Christmas Day, 1908, definitely refused to support Servia against the Power which had broken the Berlin Treaty, but any future designs that may have been plotted against Turkey are for the present in abeyance. At the time of writing, nothing is finally arranged, not even the conference that would give the only sanction to the arrangement, and Austria has only lost very heavily in her large Turkish trade owing to the indignant boycott of Austrian goods by the Turkish people. Probably, however, she will pay Turkey a fixed sum—about £2,250,000—as compensation for the wrong.

It is possible that the annexation was in reality a further step towards the conversion of Austria into a Slavonic rather than German Power. At all events, that will probably be its result, and it is believed to have been favoured by the Crown Prince Franz Ferdinand, who has strong Slavonic sympathies. On the other hand, we must remember that, whatever

Moslems, began to leave the country in large numbers as soon as the Turkish Revolution gave them hope of security on Turkish soil. There has always been great dissatisfaction because the recruits from the provinces are taken to serve their time in far-distant parts of Austria, while troops of other nationalities are quartered among the Bosnian villages.

Perhaps even stronger discontent has been aroused by the large numbers of Catholic churches erected by Government throughout the country, though not much more than 20 per cent. of the population are Catholic. Jesuits and Franciscans are continually spreading their propaganda, and it is an open secret that

THE HUNGARIAN HOUSES OF PARLIAMENT AT BUDAPEST

the Pan-Slavists may say, it is all of a piece with the familiar German " Drang nach Osten," and that the annexed provinces are already largely Germanised. They are filled with German officials; all newspapers, except the German, are so rigorously censored that they often appear with blank columns; the forests, which are a chief source of wealth, are sold to German contractors; many Slav schools have been suppressed; the Archbishop is an Austrian nominee, and even the Orthodox Servians refuse to accept the rites of their Church from anti-national hands.

The Bosnian Mohammedans, who number about 35 per cent. of the population and are Slav by race, though very strict

they are encouraged by the Crown Prince Franz Ferdinand, who, perhaps, aims at converting Austria-Hungary into a Catholic Slav Power as a counterbalance to the Orthodox Slavs of Russia.

Thus, Germanism and Catholicism have been thrust upon Bosnia and Herzegovina with almost equal persistence, and the inhabitants naturally look for protection to their kindred in the neighbouring states of Servia and Montenegro, or even to reorganised Turkey, which they still claim as their suzerain. It must be remembered that when Austria was permitted to occupy and administer by the Treaty of Berlin, she had to mobilise 200,000 men, so strong was the opposition

5335

of the inhabitants to a purpose which she called her mission, though the provinces had but recently freed themselves from Turkish misgovernment. English travellers have often pointed to the advantages of Austrian rule—the police, the growing commerce, the excellent roads, and other signs of advancement under Baron von Kallay, who administered the provinces for twenty years with great appearance of success. But English travellers generally take their information from the German-speaking officials, and it is also a common mistake of our race to suppose that man lives by bread alone. The hostility to Austrian rule is at the present time probably as strong as in face of the occupation thirty years ago.

The Aged Emperor Franz Joseph

With Prague in open riot, the Italian provinces deeply disturbed, the Poles violently indignant at the treatment of their countrymen by Austria's German ally, Croatia and Transylvania restless under Magyar injustice, the Magyars themselves insisting on further demands for independence, and with Bosnia-Herzegovina in a state of siege, the celebration of the aged emperor's Diamond Jubilee, in 1908, could hardly be called an auspicious occasion. Yet, in all Europe there was probably no man more widely respected than Franz Joseph. It was not merely that he had reigned for sixty years without open scandal. A man of no great intellectual power or gift of foresight, he had, within the rigid limits of Austrian Court life, devoted himself to the tasks that lay before him with an obstinate tenacity that failures and disasters made tragic, but could not shake. The mysterious death of his son and the assassination of his wife cast a deep gloom over his private life, while the loss of nearly all his Italian possessions, the annihilation of his forces by Prussia, and the collapse of Austria's old leadership among the German States, were public disasters that few dynasties could survive. Yet neither grief nor disaster turned him from the fulfilment of duties which destiny laid upon him, and long experience had endowed him with a kind of

The Emperor's Griefs and Disasters

instinct for discerning the right moment to yield or to remain firm. How far he was aware of his Foreign Minister, Baron von Aehrenthal's, sudden action that convulsed Europe with apprehension in the autumn of 1908, we cannot yet say. The stroke was so unlike the emperor's habitual restraint and moderation that it encouraged the belief in his temporary retirement from affairs and his delegation of authority to his successor. That report has been contradicted, and one can only hope that the end of a long and worthy career will not be marked by dangerous European complications which Austria's action will have chiefly contributed to bring about.

What will happen at the aged emperor's death has long been a central problem of international politics. M. Milovanovitch, the Servian Foreign Minister, while protesting against Austria's attempt to shatter the Serb nationality by annexing the provinces, said in January, 1909: "Austria-Hungary is not a Fatherland, but rather a prison of numerous nationalities all panting to escape." The description is singularly apt. As I have tried to show, the empire is hardly even a geographical expression. Never was a great Power less homogeneous or more savagely torn by contending races. It is natural to suppose that with the departure of the man who has so long held the component parts together, however loosely, a general disruption will ensue and the whole fabric of the empire collapse. But it would be unwise to prophesy any such fate. Austria-Hungary has survived so long that in all likelihood it will go on surviving, if only by habit. Besides, a disruption would imply the isolation of many enfeebled nationalities.

Problem of the Future

Patriotic as Czechs and Magyars and Serbs and Germans may be, when it came to the point they might very likely prefer to hang together rather than enjoy a short-lived separation at the cost of ultimate and perpetual absorption under the grinding imperialism of one or other of their powerful neighbours.

HENRY W. NEVINSON

ESSENTIAL INFORMATION ABOUT AUSTRIA-HUNGARY

AREA AND POPULATION. Austria, which comprises the provinces of Upper and Lower Austria, Salzburg, Styria, Carinthia, Carniola, Coastland, Tyrol and Vorarlberg, Bohemia, Moravia, Silesia, Galicia, Bukowina, and Dalmatia, has an area of 115,903 square miles, and—at the census of 1900—a population of 26,150,708. The Kingdom of Hungary, which consists of Hungary proper, with Croatia and Slavonia, has an area of 125,430 square miles, and—at the census of 1900—a population of 19,254,559. The recent annexation of Bosnia and Herzegovina by the Austro-Hungarian Government adds to the territory directly subject to the dual monarchy an area of 19,702 square miles, and a population of 1,568,092 (census of 1895). The total area of Austria-Hungary with the recently annexed provinces is 261,035 square miles, and the total population is 46,973,359.

Austria has seven towns with a population of over 100,000 : Vienna, 1,999,912 ; Prague, 228,645 ; Trieste, 205,136 ; Lemberg, 159,877 ; Gratz, 138,080 ; Brünn, 109,346 ; and Krakau, 104,836. Hungary has two : Budapest, 732,322 ; and Szeged, 102,991. The chief town and capital of Bosnia and Herzegovina is Sarajevo, with a population of 38,083.

GOVERNMENT. The Austro-Hungarian monarchy, as the dual monarchy is officially called in international affairs, consists of two distinct states—the Austrian Empire and the Kingdom of Hungary. Each state is independent of the other ; each has its own constitution, and each legislates for itself ; but in certain departments the interests are entrusted to a common executive. The interests that are considered common are : foreign affairs, the army and navy, and certain matters of finance. Two delegations—each consisting of sixty members chosen from the Upper and Lower Houses of the two respective states—deliberate on common interests, and communicate their desires and decisions one to the other. They never deliberate as a whole, but vote together as a whole only in the event of disagreement after three interchanges of views. There are three executive departments for common affairs—Foreign Affairs, War, and Finance—each under the supervision of a Minister of State.

The Austrian Parliament, or Reichsrath, has an Upper House (Herrenhaus) and a Lower House (Abgeordnetenhaus). The former is a privileged House, consisting of princes, nobles, bishops, and distinguished citizens nominated by the emperor for special services to State or Church, and has 170 members. The Lower House has 516 members, and is elected, every Austrian male citizen over twenty-four years of age and with twelve months' residence qualification having a vote. The duration of the Lower House is six years, and members are paid.

The Hungarian Parliament, or Országgyütes, has also two Chambers—an Upper House, or Förendiház, and a Lower House, or Képviselöház. The former is composed of princes, nobles, and Church dignitaries ; and the latter, with 453 members, is elected on a low franchise. Members of the Lower House are paid.

MONARCH. The reigning sovereign is Franz Josef I., or, in Hungarian, Ferencz József (born August 18th, 1830), who became Emperor of Austria on the abdication of his uncle, Ferdinand I., and the renunciation of the crown by his father on December 2nd, 1848, and who became King of Hungary on June 8th, 1867. The heir presumptive is the Archduke Franz Ferdinand (born December 18th, 1863), nephew of the Emperor Franz Josef I.

FINANCE. The estimates of revenue and expenditure for 1907, the latest year having published figures, were about £18,000,000, the three sources of revenue to the common exchequer being the customs, and the contributions of Austria and of Hungary in the respective proportions of 65·6 and 34·4 per cent. Austria and Hungary have no joint national debt, and by law no joint loan may be issued. The only common obligation resembling a public debt is the guarantee of the State notes, the value of which in circulation is about £110,000. The special debt of Austria is about £175,000,000, and of Hungary about £150,000,000.

INDUSTRIES AND COMMERCE. Agriculture stands at the head of the industries in both Austria and Hungary. In the former it provides about half of the population with employment, and in the latter almost three-quarters. In Austria the chief crops, judged by acreage under cultivation, are rye, potatoes, oats, barley, wheat, maize, pulse, vines, sugar beets, beets, and buckwheat ; in Hungary the chief crops are wheat, maize, rye, oats, barley, pulse, potatoes, vines, beets, and sugar beets. Mining is important in both countries, the chief minerals and mineral products of Austria being coal, brown coal, salt, iron, lead, silver, zinc, quicksilver, graphite, gold and copper ; and of Hungary being lignite, coal, iron, gold and silver. About 17,000 Austrians find employment in sea-fishing. The chief factory industries are the production of beer, sugar, and tobacco.

The chief exports of Austria-Hungary are timber, coal, eggs, sugar, woollens, glassware, iron and steel goods, leather goods, paper and barley ; the chief imports are raw cotton and raw wool. For the year 1908, the value of the exports was £96,874,000, and of the imports £105,518,000.

CURRENCY. The currency is on a gold standard, but the standard coin—the krone, korona, or crown—is coined only in silver. The 20-crown piece contains 60·9756 grammes of fine gold, and is worth 16s. 8d.

Bronze coins	{ 1 heller, or ½ kreuzer = 0·1d.	
	{ 2 hellers, or 1 kreuzer = 0·2d.	
Nickel coins	{ 10 hellers, or 5 kreuzer = 1d.	
	{ 20 hellers, or 10 kreuzer = 2d.	
Silver coins	{ 100 hellers, or half a gulden =	
	{ 1 krone, or korone (crown) = 10d.	
10-crown piece	.. ..	= 8s. 4d.
Single ducat (= 11 crowns 29 heller)	..	= 9s. 4¾d.
20-crown piece	.. ..	= 16s. 8d.

WEIGHTS AND MEASURES. The metric system is used [see page 5399].

POSTAGE. Letters and papers as for France [see page 5398]. Parcels, 6d. per pound higher than rates to Germany [see page 5356] ; routes and limits of size as for Germany.

TELEGRAMS. Great Britain to Austria-Hungary, 3d. per word, with 1s. minimum. Private telegrams in code or cypher are not accepted for certain provinces.

LIECHTENSTEIN

This principality is a small sovereign state sandwiched between Austria and Switzerland. It has an area of 65 square miles, and a population of 9,477. The reigning prince is John II. (born, 1840), succeeded to the throne in 1858. There is a diet of fifteen members, appointed for four years. The capital of the state is Vaduz, with a population of 1,206. Liechtenstein is closely allied to Austria by treaty, and belongs to the Austrian Customs Union. The property of the sovereign is managed by the Chancellery at Vienna, and the postal, telegraphic and telephonic systems are managed by Austria. The revenue and expenditure amount to about £26,000 a year, and there is no public debt. Agriculture, stock-raising, and textile manufacturing are the chief industries of the small state.

THE KAISER AND KAISERIN REVIEWING PRUSSIAN STAFF OFFICERS AT POTSDAM

GERMAN ARTILLERY IN THE MANŒUVRES ON THE FRENCH FRONTIER, OCTOBER, 1903

FOOTGUARD RECRUITS REVIEWED BY THE KAISER: NOTE THE "GOOSE-STEP"

CROWN PRINCE, IN THE FOREGROUND, AS AN OFFICER OF THE IMPERIAL CUIRASSIERS

GERMANY'S GREAT CONSCRIPT ARMY: SOME SCENES OF MILITARY LIFE

GERMANY IN OUR OWN TIME
THE EMPIRE'S PLACE AMONG THE WORLD POWERS & ITS MILITARY & NAVAL STRENGTH
By Charles Lowe, M.A.

BY far the most conspicuous and momentous event of the nineteenth century was the rise of the new German Reich on the ashes of the Second French Empire. The victories of the great Napoleon will shine for ever in the pages of history, though the results of those victories have all gone to dust. The Corsican was a man of tremendous, but of negative, power. He shook all Europe to its foundations, but out of its ruins evolved no new political structure to survive his own fall. He was essentially a destroying demon, while Bismarck, on the contrary—who was to succeed him as the principal wielder of one-man power in Europe—proved the genius incarnate of creation.

Napoleon had only escaped from Elba and reached the Tuileries with intent to make one more gigantic effort to crush united Europe when Bismarck was born— seven weeks exactly before Waterloo—All Fools' Day happening to be the birthday of the wisest man of his time. Little, certainly, did the Titanic Corsican then think that, far away, in an obscure hamlet of the sandy Mark of Brandenburg, a man-child had on that First of April been born, endowed with the power of building up again what he had cast down, and of shivering his upstart dynasty to atoms. All the seas of blood which flowed at the

Germany's Imperial Solidarity call of Napoleon had been shed in vain ; whereas the German Empire stands, and promises to stand, a solid result of the three wars of 1864, 1866, and 1870, which Bismarck found necessary to wage in order to unify the German people. Hence he has come to be known as the statesman of "blood and iron," as if, forsooth, omelettes could be made without eggs, or states cemented without the sacrifice of human life. If any empire more than

another, after that of Rome, has been built up by a policy of blood and iron, surely it is our own, for the long reign of Queen Victoria was one of almost continuous war in one part or another of her world-embracing dominions. It might easily be shown that without this policy of "blood and iron" it would never have been

Germany the United States of Europe possible to point to the new German Empire as the most momentous creation of the nineteenth century. It is now well-nigh forty years since this mighty empire took the place of vanquished France as the leading, because the most powerful, nation on the Continent of Europe; for, after Sedan, the centre of political gravity passed automatically from Paris to Berlin. Yet even now there are but few Englishmen who have a clear and just notion as to what sort of a thing this new German Empire really is.

It may, therefore, be said at once that it is unique of its kind ; and that it is *not* an empire in the Cæsarian or Tamerlanian, or Turkish, or Russian, or Napoleonic sense of the term. It would be much nearer the mark to describe the German Empire as the "United States" of Europe, with the King of Prussia as their perpetual president, under the title of "Deutscher Kaiser," or "German Emperor," for "Emperor of Germany" he is not. That would imply sovereignty *over* the German people, but William II.'s sovereignty is confined to Prussia. It is for this reason that neither he nor his grandfather, the first kaiser—*in*, not *of*, a united Fatherland—was ever crowned, as coronation would carry with it the idea of imperial sovereignty, which is not an attribute of the German Emperor. Nor are all Germans the "subjects" of the kaiser, as

5339

they are so often called. Every German is the subject of his own Landesvater, or native sovereign. Thus the only immediate "subjects" of William II. are his own honest Prussians, while the Saxons, the Würtembergers, and the Badeners, etc., own similar allegiance to their own respective rulers, but all enjoy the superincumbent status and privilege of imperial German citizenship. Another point to be noted is that the kaiser does not receive from the empire a single penny of his Civil List—about £800,000 —which is exclusively Prussian, and all the ceremonial expenses entailed upon him as emperor are drawn from his copious stipend as King of Prussia. The imperial dignity is an honorary title in the strict sense of the term, but the cost of maintaining it is cheerfully borne by the kaiser-king's special Prussian subjects for the honour of the family, so to speak, "et pour les beaux yeux du roi de Prusse."

The Kaiser's Loyal Prussians

It is ignorance of these and other facts essential to a clear comprehension of the subject that has caused the German Emperor to be represented as a kind of Frankenstein monster, bearing no resemblance to any man or monarch in the universe. It cannot be too emphatically declared that William II. is not an absolute or irresponsible ruler, like, for example, Nicholas II. of Russia. The best way of realising his character as a sovereign is to remember that the German Empire is but the European analogue of the United States of America, a confederation of twenty-five sovereign states—of which three, the Free Cities of Hamburg, Lübeck, and Bremen, are republics—under the title of "Deutsches Reich," with the King of Prussia, ex-officio, as its perpetual executive chief or president. Just as each State in the American Union enjoys its own legislature for the transaction of purely state affairs, so a similar system prevails in Germany, where each federal state has its own bicameral diet, or Landtag, for legislating on affairs not reserved for the Reichstag or Imperial Parliament. The Kings of Saxony, Bavaria, and Würtemberg, and the Grand Dukes and Dukes of the other federal states are just as much sovereigns in their own territories—just as much "kings in their own castles," so to speak—as the King of Prussia, with the title German Emperor, is

Germany's States and Sovereigns

in his own special Hohenzollern monarchy. The depth of popular ignorance on this head in England was revealed when the Duke of Edinburgh succeeded to the throne of Saxe-Coburg-Gotha, by the death of his uncle, and when he was written of as having now "taken an oath of allegiance" to the German Emperor, as if he had become his imperial nephew's vassal.

On the contrary, the duke became just as much of an independent sovereign in Germany as the King of Prussia himself, who is only "primus inter pares" among his fellow sovereigns in the Reich. Outside of his own particular kingdom of Prussia, William II., as German Kaiser, has no more power of interference in the civil affairs, say, of Saxony, Bavaria, or Baden, than the Khan of Tartary. Even in the Free Cities of Hamburg, Lübeck, and Bremen, the emperor cannot step in to exercise the prerogative of mercy, one of the symbols of sovereignty.

To talk about the kaiser as a despot, an autocrat, an absolute ruler, an irresponsible monarch, is to talk nonsense. The truth is that both as King of Prussia and as German Emperor William II. is a constitutional sovereign— if of a peculiar kind. When Englishmen speak of "constitutional" government they mean government by party, whereas the German conception of the same thing is government according to a written constitution, whether it includes party see-saw or not. The trouble with our own "glorious constitution" is that it is in the nature of a "lex non scripta," so that we never really know where we are; whereas, the Germans always enjoy the immense advantage of knowing, so that in cases of dubiety or dispute they simply have to turn to the "Reichsverfassung." And the same remark applies to the Prussian constitution, the outcome of the revolution of '48, when the respective powers of crown and crowd were very carefully defined; though, on the whole, the balance of power is in favour of the king in his right of absolute veto.

The Limited Powers of William II.

But as kaiser he has no such right, so that in this and some other respects, he is not so powerful as the president of the United States. The legislative body of the empire may be said to consist of two Chambers—the Reichstag, or National Assembly, representing the German people and returnable by manhood suffrage;

and the Bundesrath, or Federal Council, representing the Federal Sovereigns and Free Cities of the Fatherland. Each of these Chambers has co-ordinate and co-equal powers. The assent of both is essential to the passage of an imperial law, and any Bill would be blocked by the veto of either. Apart from these two bodies the kaiser himself, as President of the Union, has no power to veto an imperial law; and as Prussian member of the Federal Council he can only command seventeen votes out of a total of fifty-two.

It will then appear that, even in the Federal Council, the Prussian president might easily be outvoted on any question : as he was, for example, in the case of the Supreme Court of the empire, which was located at Leipzig instead of Berlin. A Bill which is passed by the Reichstag and approved by the Federal Council becomes law whether the emperor, as King of Prussia, has voted for it or not ; and then the imperial president has no separate veto power, no choice but to execute the combined decision of the German people and German princes. But now a word **Functions** as to the Reichstag, or **of the** National Asembly, of which, **Reichstag** by the way, the members are now paid, and which is often described as a mere " money voting and law-assenting machine." Nothing could be further from the truth. The power of the Reichstag to reject measures placed before it by the Imperial Government is absolute, and this Government has no means of coercing its will. True, the kaiser, with the assent of his fellow sovereigns in the Union, may dissolve Parliament, but so can our own king on the advice of his premier; and to dissolve a Parliament is not to dragoon it.

Dissolutions of the German Parliament have always taken the form of a plebiscite, a referendum, a direct appeal from the party-torn representatives of the German people to the people themselves, and in nearly all such cases the reply has been decidedly in favour of the Government. Power of purse is exercised as absolutely by the German Reichstag as by the House of Commons, and the kaiser cannot put a new warship on the sea, or add a single man to the German Army without the sanction of the German people.

The list of measures which have been rejected both by the Imperial and Prussian Parliaments is a very long one, but the Government remains in power whatever happens, seeing that the principle of government by party does not form part of the administrative machinery of any German state. Nor among sensible people is there any strong desire for it. National security is of far more importance to Germany, as a sort of " besieged fortress " **Why Germany** —to use the words of Moltke **Needs a Strong** —than government by see- **Monarchy** saw; and the problem ever before the German people and their rulers is how to combine the greatest degree of national safety with the highest degree of individual liberty. " Hemmed in," said Moltke, " between mighty neighbours, we are of opinion that we require a strong monarchy." Moreover, it cannot be doubted that Prince Bülow, on the eve of the General Election of 1907, spoke the popular mind of the nation when he said that " no one in Germany desires a personal regime, but, on the other hand, the great majority of the German people is most emphatically against a party regime."

But while it is quite true that though the German people do not, as is so often said of them, live under a personal regime, or anything like it, it is equally true that what may be called the personal power of the emperor is very great. In the purely civil and political field this power, as we have seen, is circumscribed by the written constitutions of Prussia and the empire, and not once has the kaiser-king ever sought to overstep or circumvent the limits set against his arbitrary will.

He cannot veto a measure which has received the double approval of the Reichstag and the Bundesrath ; he cannot, without the consent of his fellow sovereigns in the Union, declare an aggressive war, and most certainly those sovereigns would never allow their executive president to precipitate the nation into a wanton struggle. Well, then, but what is the nature of the power **The Kaiser** that the kaiser so palpably **Master of** exercises ? The answer is **Many Legions** that he is the representa- tive and spokesman of the German people to other countries ; above all, that he is commander-in-chief of the army and navy ; and that this " Kaiserliche Herr " also claims to be a " Kriegsherr," war-lord, or master of many mighty legions. It is the flashing of the emperor's helmet more than of his crown which sometimes tends to dazzle the eyes and bewilder the German nation, and other nations as well. It is in his administrative capacity as "Kriegsherr" that the kaiser wields most personal power within the empire; while abroad he is also comparatively untrammelled in the domain of foreign policy. In both fields the emperor is entitled by the constitution to wield great personal power, yet he has never abused it or sought to throw his sword into the scale either against the civil rights of his own people or the general rights of man as involved in the peace of the world.

And the sword of the German Emperor is a mighty one—none more so. The "German Michael," with his "mailed fist," is perhaps the most formidable fighting man the world has ever seen; and yet he is a pacific one, seeing that he has not once bared his blade for well-nigh forty years, or since his last great set-to with the Gauls beyond the Rhine. Whatever else may be said about Germany, it must at least be conceded to her credit that, with all her tremendous armed strength, she has ever been a bulwark of the European peace.

Since her war with France, Germany may be said to have become an industrial state as compared with the almost purely agricultural country which she was before; yet her greatest industry is militarism—the manufacture of soldiers, and in this respect she easily surpasses all her rivals. Of these soldiers she keeps a standing army of about 600,000, which is just about double the strength of what it was a year or two after the great war; and in time of war this force could be raised to a first fighting line of about a million and a half.

If need were, Germany could put into the field, from her reserves of various kinds, a host of over four millions of highly trained fighting men. Her standing army is divided into twenty-three army corps, all as like each other as two pins in respect of composition and efficiency, so that after a stranger has seen the march-past of one of those superb bodies of men, he may be said to have seen the whole German army. It is, of course, a conscript army, though its size is fixed by budget law, and hence it follows that, though all Germans capable of bearing arms are liable to serve, it is only the fittest who are taken to the colours, seeing that the number of available recruits always exceeds that of the time-expired men.

The Germans Under Conscription

It would be outside the scope of a sketch like this to detail the organisation of the German army; suffice to say that it is a machine which represents more brainwork than any other machine ever devised by the wit of man, and that it is just as

GERMANY'S PARLIAMENTARY BUILDINGS IN BERLIN

THE STATELY PALACE OF THE GERMAN EMPEROR AT POTSDAM

near perfection as any human institution can possibly be. But, then, as to its cost ? Do we not often hear of the frightfully oppressive burden of militarism under which the German people groan as compared with our own ? What are the facts ? One is, that our own military estimates for 1905–6 exceeded those of Germany by nearly a million sterling for the United Kingdom alone ; while our Army Budget for the whole empire was £61,500,000, as compared with the £29,000,000 of Germany and the £27,000,000 of France. "Ah, but then," exclaim the critics of militarism,

Cost of Great Armies "apart from the actual cost of the German army in positive cash, just consider the blood-tax that has to be paid by its victims in diverting two of the best years of their life from their civil occupations, and thus sterilising their productive labour !"

The answer to this is that what these victims lose in one way they gain, and more than gain, in another. For they return to civil life far better citizens than ever they were before — imbued with discipline, orderliness, respect for authority, energy, improved physique, and other qualities which soon enable them to make up, and more, for the time, not lost, but devoted to the service of their country—a citizen's first and highest duty. It is a great mistake to suppose that military service is unpopular in Germany. It may be with some, but with the vast bulk of the nation the army is its most popular institution, and its officers are readily accorded the leading position in society. In fact, the average German officer is the highest type of the German man.

But the worship of his uniform sometimes leads to strange results—witness the case of an old gaol-bird, called Voigt, a cobbler by trade, who dressed himself up as a captain in the Prussian Guards, way-laid a party of William II.'s finest soldiers, and commanded them to follow him to a little town, Köpenick, near Berlin. The soldiers obeyed like sheep or machines. At Köpenick, the cobbler-captain, saying he was the agent of the kaiser, arrested the burgomaster, and sent him and his lady under escort to Berlin, after which he coolly walked away with all the cash in the treasury, which he had previously demanded in exchange for a receipt. The feat would have been impossible in any other country save Germany, where there is a blind worship of every kind of uniform, beneath which no one ever takes the trouble to look.

This is one of the minor penalties of being a "Volk in Waffen," a people in arms, but that is a condition of things from which the Germans by no possibility can escape if they would continue to be secure of their national existence. It is just as essential for them to have the finest army in Europe as it is for us to have the strongest fleet in the world. Conscription is a sheer necessity for the Germans; and each country has its own peculiar needs and problems. As in the case of individuals, what is food for one may be positive poison for another, and it would be just as preposterous for us to seek to obtrude upon the Germans our own special form of con-

If Germany Went to War With France? stitutionalism as it would be absurd for the Germans to insist upon our adopting their system of conscription. The question is often asked : What would be the likely issue of another war between France and Germany ?

The answer to such a question must be simplified by a comparison of figures. Supposing the armies of the two countries to be pretty equal in respect of strength, organisation, and efficiency, let it nevertheless be remembered that, whereas the populations of France and Germany in 1870 were nearly the same, that of Germany is now 63,000,000, as compared with the 40,000,000 of France. Thus the answer to the question referred to will probably take this form : that the Malthusianism of decadent France has relegated her to the position of a second-rate Power vis-à-vis of virile, fruitful, and multiplying Germany.

But there is another vital consideration that bears upon the likely issue of a second struggle between France and Germany, and it is this : that in 1870 Germany had no navy worth the name, while now—leaving America out of account—her fleet is considered to be inferior in battle power, as distinguished from comparative paper strength, only to that of England. The war of 1870 was exclusively a land war, and the swift, crushing victories of the Germans had this peculiar, this unique result—that they may be said to have put the French navy entirely out of action, seeing that it had to hurry off all its best guns and men to help in the defence of Paris. But such a thing—

Why Germany Built Her Navy such a victorious walk-over on land—is never likely to occur again ; and that was why, or at least one of the reasons why, the Germans—knowing that if ever they had to fight again they would have to do so on sea as well as on land—provided themselves with a navy which M. Lockroy, French Minister of Marine, who was given special facilities for studying it, pronounced to be the " best organised in the world."

As the rise of the German Empire was the most momentous fact of modern times, so the most momentous thing in the history of this new empire was the creation of the German fleet. In 1870 Germany possessed but thirty-seven war-ships all told, and a very miscellaneous job lot they were ; while now she has no fewer than about 260 various kinds of battle-craft, built or building, including several of the Dreadnought type. In 1888 the navy was manned by only 15,000 officers and seamen, and twenty years later the number exceeded 50,000. In 1888 the ordinary naval expenditure was only £2,500,000, by 1908 it had risen to £18,000,000 ; while the total sum to be devoted to the navy between 1906 and 1917 was voted at 166 millions sterling, though supplementary Bills tend to increase these colossal figures.

To the 260 war-ships of various kinds built and building in 1907, add 100 of the finest liners of the great German shipping companies, which are retained by the Government as auxiliary cruisers in the event of war, and you will get some idea of the new and formidable phenome-

William II. Creator of the Navy non which may be said to have burst upon a startled and apprehensive Europe in the form of the Imperial German navy. And here it may be pointed out that while the army of the Fatherland is only " German," its navy is " Imperial " ; that is to say, that while the army is composed of contingents from the various states of the Union, each with its own peculiarities and privileges, the navy—recruited from the seafaring population on the same conscript principle as the army—is an imperial institution pure and simple, and is much more of a rivet to the unity of the Reich.

The difference may be further accentuated by saying that while there is no Imperial Minister of War, there is an Imperial Chief of the Admiralty. In its present form the Imperial navy may be said to be the creation of William II., and, if for nothing else, he will always be remembered for this achievement. To the eagle on the escutcheon of the Hohenzollerns he may be said to have added a swan. William I. taught Germany how to march, and it remained for his ambitious grandson to show her how to swim.

" As my grandfather," the latter said, " reorganised the army, so I shall reorganise my navy, without flinching and in

the same way, so that it will stand on the same level with my army, and that, with its help, the German Empire shall reach the place which it has not yet attained."

Other utterances of the emperor show that he was the first of his race to grasp the meaning of sea-power—the struggle for which promises to be a marked feature of the present century—utterances such as "Our future lies on the water"; "Germany, too, must have her place in the sun"; "without the consent of Germany's ruler nothing must happen in any part of the world"; "may our Fatherland be as powerful, as closely united, and as authoritative as was the Roman Empire of old, in order that the phrase 'Civis Romanus sum' may be replaced by 'I am a German citizen'"; "Neptune with the trident is a symbol for us that we have new tasks to fulfil since the empire has been welded together. Everywhere we have to protect German citizens, everywhere we have to maintain German honour; that trident must be in our fist."

These and other utterances of his clearly showed that William II. had been

The Kaiser's Passion for Sea Power

bitten by the new-born passion for sea power, though in this respect he was but acting as the spokesman of the vast majority of his people. The voice of that people found vent in the creation of a Flottenverein, or Navy League, which now numbers almost a million subscribing members, and which has an annual income of about £50,000 for the purpose of agitating in favour of an ever stronger navy. But even previous to the formation of that league the Reichstag, in response to the same popular voice, had willingly voted 8,000,000 sterling for the construction of a sixty-mile long and twenty-nine feet deep canal between Kiel Harbour and the mouth of the Elbe—a work which, begun in 1886 and inaugurated in 1895, practically doubled the value of the German fleet by enabling it to concentrate either in the North Sea or the Baltic without incurring the various risks of going round by Denmark.

And now it has been decided to deepen and broaden this Kaiser Wilhelm Canal to admit of the passage of battleships of the Dreadnought type. Moreover, the Reichstag voted £1,500,000 sterling for the fortification of Heligoland, which we surrendered to Germany in 1890 in exchange for Zanzibar.

Otherwise the Flottenverein—under the patronage of some of the highest personages in Germany, including the emperor's sailor-brother, Prince Henry—played a prominent part in preparing the public mind for successive demands of money to increase the navy. The large naval programme of 1898, providing for seventeen

Germany's Great Building Programme

new battleships, coincided with the Spanish-American War; while soon after the outbreak of our Boer War the Reichstag again voted, in 1900, something like £100,000,000 for the carrying out of a naval programme extending over sixteen years; though on two subsequent occasions, 1906 and 1907, supplementary Bills in the direction always of bigger battleships were presented to Parliament.

There was the less opposition to the immense Government demands in 1900, as the German public had been highly irritated by our seizure of several of their mail steamers, and the unloading of them at Durban in search of contraband—an incident to which the emperor thus alluded in a telegram to the King of Würtemberg: "I hope the events of the last few days will have convinced ever widening circles that not only Germany's interest, but also Germany's honour must be protected in distant seas, and that to this end Germany must be strong and powerful on the sea also." At the same time it was stated, *not* in the preamble, but in the memorandum of motives attached to the Bill of 1900, that "Germany must have a fleet so strong that even for the greatest naval Power a war with it would have such risks as to imperil its sea supremacy."

And then the fat was on the British fire. For these words were regarded as a clear warning, if not a threat, to England, and there were many who professed to believe that a war between the two countries was only a question of time. For the last quarter of a century—or from

Britain's Relations with Germany

1884–85, when Germany, in spite of much dog-in-the-manger obstruction from us, first started on her career as an oversea Power—the relations between the two peoples had been anything but cordial, and during the Boer War their estrangement reached a climax. But, truth to tell, there were faults and jealousies on both sides.

The German Empire was a political fact to which Englishmen were long in reconciling themselves, and there were but few who could lay their hands upon their hearts and call themselves its well-wishers. These feelings of coldness and suspicion were only intensified when Imperial Germany shot ahead and became our most formidable rival in the world of commerce. "That England," so Bismarck once said, "looks on in some surprise when

Germany's Progress on the Sea

we, her landlubberly cousins, suddenly take to the water too is not to be wondered at." But the Germans had not merely taken to the water. In the opinion of our Teutophobe alarmists, it was also their aim to wrest from us the trident of Neptune and destroy our tyrannical supremacy on the sea. As one writer said: "A mighty longing for larger sea power, a determination to brook no longer the overwhelming and resistless supremacy of England on the main, has seized upon the soul."

But while thus striving to make encroachments on the sea, the Germans at the same time had not been neglecting the air, and in the latter respect their most successful inventor, Count Zeppelin, was hailed by the emperor as "the foremost man of his century." For his conquest of South Africa, Lord Roberts received £100,000 from a grateful country, and that is precisely the sum which was also voted to Count Zeppelin by the German people for his conquest of the air. The degrees of these two acts of victory were very different, but still the Germans were entitled to claim that they had advanced further on the path of air-conquest than any other nation. Heine had sneered at them as a nation of dreamers, whose thoughts were always in the air, but his words had now acquired a wonderfully new significance:

The French and the Britons now lord it on land.
In the ocean the Britons are rooted;
To the Germans remaineth the region of air,
Where they domineer undisputed.

With Count Zeppelin's achievements the

The Possible Conquest of Great Britain

time, however, had now come when the most hot-headed and visionary among the Germans began to regard their partial conquest of the air as a long step in the direction of the possible conquest of Great Britain, which would thus no longer enjoy the advantages of being an island if the sky could be darkened with aerial navies.

But it is a far cry from Lake Constance to the cliffs of Kent; and, on the other hand, in a country like Germany,

there is not always perfect identity between popular aspirations and Government aims. The emperor himself disavowed all deliberate hostility to England; while his chancellor, Prince von Bülow, was still more emphatic. Replying to the charge of some Socialist speakers in the Reichstag, that the increase in the German navy was rightly regarded as directed against Great Britain, the chancellor said, December, 1905: "That we are pursuing no aggressive plans against Great Britain I have said a hundred times. I have said a hundred times that it is nonsense to father such schemes on us."

To a Press interviewer some little time after, the prince said: "I admit that we have made great strides in shipbuilding; for, like other nations, we require a fleet in proportion to the extent of our commercial interests all over the water. But, as a matter of fact, our navy is still very small in proportion to our oversea commerce—judging their relative dimensions by those of other nations. To argue, however, that Germany thinks of ever competing with England for the mastery of the sea is

Germany's Need of Sea Power

tantamount to accusing us of wishing to build a railway to the moon, including rolling-stock, sleeping-cars, etc. It is sheer nonsense, and I for one deplore that anybody should deem me capable of entertaining such a fantastic idea."

In the Reichstag also the chancellor said: "In our construction of a fleet we are not pursuing aggressive aims. We only desire to defend our own German coasts, and to uphold German interests abroad. It is, moreover, the wish of by far the greater portion of the German people that we should not be defenceless on the sea. . . . The saying, 'Our future lies on the water,' is not in any way pointed at other Powers. . . . We have not the slightest intention of driving another Power from the sea, but we have just as good a right to sail the seas of the world as other nations have. That right the Hansa had centuries ago, and that right the new German Empire also possesses."

Apart from all question of England and her sea supremacy, it must be owned that Germany had reasons enough for justifying herself in the eyes of other nations in the building of a navy commensurate with her population (63,000,000), the extent of her coast-line, the size and number of her colonies, the volume of her marine trade—

which is far superior to that of France—and her dignity as the leading Power on the Continent. Where was the logic of our grudging to Germany, with marine interests greater than those of France, a navy at least equal to the French one? Surely every country may enjoy the right of determining the means and manner of its self-defence; but human nature is a strange thing, and often prompts to the remark: "Cet animal est très méchant; quand on l'attaque, il se défend."

Since the year 1848 Germany has seen her coast blockaded on three separate occasions, including the war of 1870, when she was practically powerless at sea. Again, in 1907, the value of her sea-borne trade was £372,000,000 sterling. Of this total, £294,000,000 was carried by German merchant vessels of over 3,000,000

Atlantic, until this was recovered for us by a couple of colossal Cunarders. The value of German trade done with the British Empire alone was over £109,000,000 annually. Besides, Germany was becoming more and more dependent on foreign supplies of food and raw material for the industrial portion of her people, and in the

THE WARSHIP FRAUENLOB

event of those supplies being interrupted, she would be faced with a serious economic crisis. It would be difficult for her to withstand a Continental coalition unless she could count upon a free sea, and so for these, if for no other reasons, it was imperative for her to have a navy commensurate with her interests —a navy which nevertheless began to fill the minds of Englishmen with apprehension and alarm.

GERMAN WARSHIPS: THE KAISER KARL DER GROSSE

One of the greatest of Germany's ambitions is to possess a navy that shall be unrivalled by any other Continental Power, and under the present kaiser, William II., distinct advance has been made in this direction. The two warships illustrated above, which are shown sailing through the great waterway, the Kiel Canal, are typical examples of Germany's naval strength.

tons register, valued at over £40,000,000, and manned by 60,000 seamen. Ten per cent. of the world's commerce and 79 per cent. of German sea-borne trade was carried in German bottoms, while the liners of the Hamburg and Bremen companies were the finest that crossed the sea, and had even wrested from us the blue ribbon of the

But the popular passion for sea power was still more deeply rooted. The desire for national unity had been followed by an equally strong craving for national expansion. For several years after the establishment of the empire, Bismarck and others worked hard at its internal consolidation — witness, among other things, the codification of all the conflicting laws of Germany, a gigantic work lasting nearly thirty years, to which only German heads were equal. And no

5347

sooner had the imposing edifice of the Reich been fairly riveted within and without than the national energy began to seek an outlet in the creation of a Germany beyond the sea. For years Bismarck had been indifferent, and, indeed, positively averse, to colonial adventure; but at last he could no longer resist a popular impulse which was rapidly growing in strength. The result was that, within a year or two of this new departure, in 1884, Germany found herself included in the ranks of the colonial Powers, with territories in Africa, New Guinea, and the Pacific Archipelago aggregating an area five times the size of her empire in Europe, though nine-tenths of this area is in Africa.

Colonies of the German Empire

To this, some years later, in 1897, Germany added a ninety-nine years' " lease " of a 200-square mile foothold at Kiaochau, on the coast of China, whither the kaiser's sailor brother, Prince Henry, was despatched as the menacing apostle of the " mailed fist," with this sentence from his Majesty ringing in his ears : " Imperial power means maritime power, and maritime power and Imperial power are mutually interdependent, so that one cannot exist without the other."

Germany may thus be said to have become an oversea Power without becoming a colonial one in the British sense. It was wittily and truly said that France had colonies but no colonists ; Germany, colonists but no colonies ; while England had both colonies and colonists. It was too late in the day, as indicated by the world's clock, when Germany entered the colonial field, for by this time all the available waste spaces of the earth had already been appropriated by other Powers, especially England. What she wanted was to found a new Germany, a new Fatherland across the sea for the accommodation of those vast numbers of her surplus sons who had hitherto migrated to America and other Anglo-Saxon lands ; but it soon became apparent that none of the African territories which had now fallen to her were at all suitable for this purpose.

Vain Search for a New Fatherland

They were all sub-tropical, and fitted only to be plantation, not agricultural, colonies. Very small was the total number of Germans who went to seek their fortunes in Germany's " colonies," and even of these a large proportion were govern-ment officials employed to administer the protectorates without having first learned from us the very necessary art of ruling native races. The brusque manners of Prussian policemen and the brutal methods of some German drill-sergeants were unsuited to the black tribes of the Kamerun and Damaraland. Rebellion was frequent, and even the German army, which boasted itself to be the best in Europe, was for several years powerless to put down a native rising in South-West Africa involving the loss of thousands of German lives and millions of money.

After this experience, shame and remorse overtook those Germans who had sneered at our own protracted struggle with the Boers. Attracting few or no colonists in the ordinary sense of the term, those German protectorates on the whole have never ceased to be a financial burden to the Imperial Government, and yet their existence and the necessity of defending them continued to be one of the chief arguments in the logic-armoury of the Chauvinists and the Pan-Germanists for the strengthening of the Imperial fleet.

Germany's Bid for First Place

These Pan-Germanists deserve more than a passing notice, seeing that, in a sense, they play that part in German political thought which the advocates of a united Germany did during the period between 1815 and 1870. Their organisation, the " All-Deutscher Verband," or Pan-German League, corresponds to, and is the complement of, the " Flottenverein." According to its statutes, it " has for object the revival of German nationalistic sentiment all over the earth, preservation of German thought, ideals, and customs in Europe, and across the ocean, and the welding into a compact whole of the Germans everywhere." The official anthem of these Pan-Germans is :

" Deutschland, Deutschland über Alles,
Ueber Alles in der Welt."

In charging down on the French at Waterloo, the Scots cried : " Scotland for ever ! " In charging down on the whole world after Sedan, the Germans shouted : " Deutschland *everywhere !* " Prince Bülow once gave the toast : " The King first in Prussia ; Prussia first in Germany ; Germany first in the world ! " And, saying so, he pretty well expressed the creed of the Pan-Germanists. The emperor, too, on the twenty-fifth anniversary of the Reich, delighted their hearts by declaring : " Out of the German Empire a world-empire has arisen. Everywhere, in all parts of the earth, thousands of our countrymen reside. German riches, German knowledge, German activity, make their way across the ocean. The value of German possessions on the sea is some milliards of marks. Gentlemen, the serious duty devolves on you to help me to link this greater German Empire close to the home-country, by helping me, in complete unity, to fulfil my duty also towards the Germans in foreign parts."

But while thus voicing the splendid aims of the Pan-Germanists, the emperor and his Government have never recognised their activity to the same extent as in the case of the "Flottenverein," and for the reason that the propaganda of the "All-Deutscher Verband" is still beyond the pale of practical politics.

There are now about 92,000,000 of German-speaking men in the world, and of these only 63,000,000 live in Germany itself. The rest are divided between Austria-Hungary, 12,000,000; Switzerland, 2,320,000; Russia, Baltic Provinces, etc., 2,000,000; various other European countries, 1,130,000; United **Proposals** States and Canada, 11,500,000; **of Teutonic** South America, 600,000; Asia, **Utopians** Africa, Australia, 400,000. But how, then, do the Pan-Germanists propose to bring all these widely-scattered Teutons into a common fold? In what respect does Pan-Germanism differ from Zionism, which aims at the repatriation of the Jews, or, at least, at their collection from all the countries of Europe and agglomeration into a new Semitic nation with a Rothschild or a Hirsch for their ruler? Broadly speaking, the Teutonic Utopians propose:

First, an economic alliance with all countries in Europe inhabited by Germanic peoples, such as Austria, Switzerland, Holland, Belgium, Luxemburg. This economical alliance will lead to political union for defensive and offensive purposes.

Secondly, the formation of a Central European Customs Union, aimed primarily against England and the United States, and secondarily against Russia.

Thirdly, the union of all the Germanic peoples—Low and High Germans—in one central Germanic Confederation. As part of this policy, Deutschthum across the seas is to be reclaimed. Out of transmarine Deutschthum a greater Germany is to arise. The only way in which the

Government has hitherto shown its practical sympathy with the aims of the Pan-Germanists has been to pursue a root and branch policy of Germanisation within the empire itself—with the French of Alsace-Lorraine, the Danes of Schleswig, and, above all, with the Poles of Prussian Poland, where, by a merciless **Dangerous** process of expropriation **and Unpractical** and other forms of com-**Dreamers** pulsion, the Slavs have been placed under the Teutonic steam-roller. Otherwise, the Government has held aloof from the agitation of the Pan-Germanists as from the propaganda of unpractical and dangerous dreamers, though it has been said that what the professors think to-day will be espoused by the practical politicians of to-morrow.

At the same time, it is well to remember that both the "All-Deutscher Verband" and the "Flottenverein" are rooted in the undeniable fact that the limits of the present German Empire are too narrowly drawn for the size of its population as well as for its importance and its aspirations. In fact, both these propagandist leagues may be said to incorporate that restless spirit, that ever-growing passion for national expansion, that hungering after "fresh woods and pastures new," which can scarcely fail to bring the German people into fierce struggle-for-life competition, if not, perhaps, into actual conflict, with other nations.

Those nations have to reckon with the fact that Germany, which, up to 1884, merely was a Continental Power, has now become a Colonial one, and aims at also being a "Weltmacht," or World-Power, in the sense that Great Britain is such.

"Without the consent of Germany's ruler," said the kaiser proudly, "nothing must happen in any part of the world" —and thus he explained what is meant by saying that Germany has become a "Weltmacht"—a Power that must be **Germany as** consulted before the other **Britain's** European Powers can come **Rival at Sea** to any agreement with regard, say, to Morocco, China, or other oversea "spheres of interest." It was to lend emphasis to her voice in such consultations, and protect her dealings with the markets of the world, that Germany thought it necessary to create a navy commensurate with her interests as a "Weltmacht"—a navy which, though at first merely intended for coast defence, gradually assumed a battleship build for offensive warfare if need be, and at last grew to such formidable proportions that the British Government of Sir Henry Campbell-Bannerman, at the second Hague Conference in 1907, felt compelled to propose to Germany a mutual arrest of naval armaments and their restriction to the ratio of two to one. It is needless to say that this proposal was negatived by Germany on the ground of the inexorable " logic of facts." The truth is that Germany has become our most formidable naval rival because she had in the meantime also become our most dangerous commercial rival. Our supremacy on the sea, which we had won at Trafalgar, was still undisputed; but, on the other hand, our monopoly of the markets of the world had begun to crumble soon after Sedan.

Germany's Rise from Poverty

Having vanquished the French in the field of war, the victors of Sedan set themselves to outstrip the British at the arts of peace, and it was not long before the cry arose in this country that they were beginning to do so. Ten years after Sedan, Germany adopted a moderate protective tariff, and, whether as a consequence or not, in a few years the country became transformed. From being one of the poorest of Continental states, Germany became the richest, and, in some respects, richer even than England. Let us take a few facts and figures.

In 1882, two years after the adoption of protectionism, British shipping through the Suez Canal was over 4,000,000 tons ; in 1906 it had risen to 8,500,000, or a trifle over 100 per cent. increase. In 1882 German shipping was 127,000 tons; in 1906, 2,250,000, an increase of about 1,700 per cent. In 1882 England owned 81 per cent. of all shipping passing through the Canal ; in 1906 the percentage had sunk to 63. In 1882 Germany owned only 2½ per cent., but in 1906 this had risen to over 16 per cent. Again, the Germans proudly point to the fact that one of their shipping lines—the " Hamburg-America "—has now become the greatest in the world, far surpassing the nearest of its British rivals in the extent of its operations and the number and tonnage of its ships. The capital of the company exceeds £5,000,000, its employees exceed 18,000, and its ocean-going fleet

Shipping Enterprise in Germany

numbers 149 vessels, with a tonnage of over 725,000. In addition, there is a swarm of river vessels and tugs, with a tonnage of nearly 150,000. The entire fleet is valued at £7,000,000. There are fifty regular passenger and cargo liners, calling at over 300 harbours. In the United States alone the company employs 2,000 agents. Furthermore, ships of the Hamburg Line are trading now in waters which until quite recently were regarded as British preserves—for example, in Indian, Chinese, and Australian seas, and even in the Persian Gulf.

According to one of our own consular reports for 1906, the general economic improvement in Germany had continued steadily, and " attained a hitherto unprecedented height." In " most trades the only subject of complaint was the scarcity of workmen."

The excess of Germany's exports over her imports has been growing rapidly. Dividing the last twenty-five years into five-yearly periods, the average excess of exports over imports of manufactures, as shown in this return, is given for each period in the following table :

NET EXPORTS OF MANUFACTURES FROM UNITED KINGDOM AND GERMANY.

—	United Kingdom Million £	Germany Million £	Excess of U.K. over G. surplus Million £
1882–86	136·5	51·2	85·3
1887–91	138·4	57·3	81·1
1892–96	110·5	57·5	53·0
1897–01	110·5	77·6	33·9
1902–06	138·1	113·1	25·0

Thus, it will be seen that the lead of £85,300,000 previously enjoyed by the United Kingdom has steadily dropped till it amounted to no more than £25,000,000. But corrected estimates tend to show that, as an exporter of manufactured goods, Germany is now within £15,000,000 of the United Kingdom.

It is on the strength of these official figures that the Hohenzollern Empire has been pronounced by an expert writer— Mr. Ellis Barker, author of " Modern Germany "—to be " at present by far the wealthiest state in Europe. Germany and the individual states composing it have a very large national debt, but against that debt they possess very considerable assets. Of these the Prussian state railways alone, which earn a profit of from seven to eight per cent., would suffice to pay off the whole of the indebtedness of the empire and of all the individual states." Another indication of national wealth and prosperity is the fact that between 1885 and 1905 the German state insurance societies paid to about 19,000,000 workers, male and female, about £256,000,000 on account of illness, accident, infirmity, and old age.

In this connection be it remarked that no other country has essayed and accomplished so much for the welfare of her working classes as Germany. Under the old emperor she took the lead in the attempt to solve modern social problems by means of state legislation, thus inaugurating a sort of state Socialism in some beneficiary fields ; while William II. also hastened to make his mark as a saviour of society by summoning an international labour conference, and in Germany itself full effect was given to its recommendations by a measure for the amendment of the Industrial Code.

All this is true. Under Protection— in consequence of it, as some maintain; in spite of it, as others aver—Germany has **Stronghold of Social Democracy** grown to be the wealthiest country in Europe. In the opinion of many she is also the best governed country in Europe, in the sense that she enjoys a government best adapted to her special needs and circumstances; yet we are confronted by the puzzling facts that for every Socialist in England there are four in Germany, and that social democracy, the party of extreme discontent, is stronger in Germany than anywhere else in the world.

At the election to the first Reichstag in 1871 only three per cent. of the total votes had been given to the Socialists, and by 1881 this percentage had risen to 6·12 with a poll of 312,000. By 1890 the percentage had further bounded up to 19·74 with a poll of 1,427,300 ; while at the election of 1903 the percentage was 31·71, or well on to a third of the whole —the Socialists having secured 3,010,771 out of a total poll of 9,495,586—a percentage of 37·71. Numerically, they were thus by far the strongest of the eight or ten parties among which the 397 seats in the Reichstag are divided. Of these seats they only secured 82, but according to the law of strict proportional representation they ought to have had about 130. The development of social democracy belongs to the history of the empire

proper, but here at least it may be said that its members—formerly, in 1903, nearly a third of the whole electorate— are the men whom the emperor has repeatedly denounced as "a band of fellows not worthy to bear the name of Germans," and "enemies to the divine order of things; men without a Fatherland."

Socialists Routed at the Polls It was with the help of these "Vaterlandslose Gesellen" that the Clericals, in 1907, threw out a demand for £400,000 for the perfection and development of South-West Africa, and on this issue the Government appealed to the German people, who were told that the new General Election was to decide whether Germany was to remain merely a Great Power in Europe, or whether she was also to become a World-Power. The reply of the people was decisive, and the Government got a working majority. The Socialists suffered a sort of *débâcle*. They returned to the Reichstag shorn of about half their strength—with 43 seats instead of 82, although, out of a total of 11,262,800 votes—the highest number ever yet given in the empire—they had polled 3,259,000, or only about 29 per cent., instead of their previous 32 per cent.

Nevertheless, the election was held to furnish clear evidence that the ambition to make Germany a "Weltmacht" and an oversea Power was no longer confined to the emperor, the "Flottenverein," and the Pan-German League, but that it had also permeated the great mass of the German people. It was held to show that the working population of Germany had deliberately and emphatically endorsed the economic policy which benefits the producer.

It was further held to prove that, however bad the general state of agriculture in Germany, it was at least decidedly better than in Free-Trade England. The German people had begun to grow tired of a party which was in the **The Greed of the Socialists** main one of mere opposition and negation—a party as innocuous as it was noisy. The Socialists now appeared in the light of those who, the more they get, the more they want. "What do they want ?" inquired the Birmingham brassworkers, when they went over to inquire into the condition of the German workman. "They seem to have everything cheap, and we don't know what they are agitating for." It was seen that the poor in Germany were not becoming poorer but richer. Socialism was being overcome by social prosperity. Its decrepitude was held to be due to the fact that Germans are guaranteed high wages by their tariff, that Germany is advancing with giant strides in wealth, comfort, and prosperity, while surrendering none of the noble ideas of duty, faith, and obedience upon **A Period of** which the old emperor and Bismarck built up the empire. In **Intellectual Stagnation** fact, the material prosperity of Germany—side by side with, and partly as a result of, her militarism, which supplied her trade, industry, commerce, and agriculture with labour at once disciplined and intelligent—had begun to assume such proportions as to throw all the other phases of the national life into the shade. Militarism and money-making and materialism have absorbed all the best energies of the nation, and left it thus comparatively poor and unproductive in the various intellectual walks of life.

An American writer of German origin, Wolf von Schierbrand, is pretty near the mark when he says: "There is an astonishing uniformity of mediocre ideas in modern Germany, with little of that daring flight of thought, that love of speculative philosophy, little of that poetical sentiment, which the world was wont to consider a special province of the German mind. There has been at work a process of mental levelling down. This prevailing sameness, this dearth of genius —although it cannot be denied that it is coupled with a great increase in hard common-sense and a practical turn of mind—can be traced all through German literature, art, and science of to-day. Since the close of the Franco-German War no really great poet, author, artist or scientist has arisen in Germany. Nearly all her great names antedate that war. This, I believe, is in part owing to the influence of military training on the **Politics Before Intellect** mind of the nation at the formative period of life." But, apart from this, the mind of the nation is absorbed in its material development, its expansion, and is far more concerned with the problems of politics than with those of intellect and art. It was the same with ourselves during our Civil War and Commonwealth period, when our literature was only saved from being one exclusively of political pamphlets by a "Paradise Lost." But the German of the empire has not yet produced even a Klopstock, not to speak of a Milton, and as for Goethes and Schillers they are sadly to seek.

In an up-to-date "History of German Literature," by Edward Engel, he pronounces this to be "the first literature in the world," a judgment which can only be described as springing from the madness of national self-conceit wilfully blind to the fact that a literature with a Shakespeare at its head can never be relegated to a second rank. And then, as regards France, Germany has supplanted her as the leading, because the most powerful, nation on the Continent. The centre of political gravity has now been shifted from the Seine to the Spree. But Berlin is still far behind Paris as a "ville lumière," a centre of intellectualism, literature, art, and all the social graces; and one capital can still securely smile at the clumsy efforts of the other to add to the oak-leaves of a frowning Mars the laurels of an effulgent Apollo. Imperial Germany has now become a "Weltmacht," but it has not yet produced a "Weltliteratur," or anything like it. **Germany in the Field of Literature** During the last thirty years the number of new books published in Germany has, in round numbers, increased from 10,000 to about 30,000 per annum, but very few of these were ever heard of outside the Fatherland. It is useless for the Germans themselves to contend that this is more owing to the ignorance and indifference of outsiders than to the comparative worthlessness of their books, because literature is a ware, like any other commodity, which will readily find its level and its market wherever there is a desire—and it is a universal one among civilised nations— to enjoy the newest masterpieces of the human mind. In the field of literature, Germany's imports far exceed her exports, and, indeed, the latter are almost nil.

As between England and Germany, the balance of literary trade is immensely in favour of the former, and the same may be said of France. Shakespeare alone is far more frequently staged in Germany than any other dramatist, native or foreign. Imperial Germany has certainly produced some talented playwriters, and men like Sudermann, Hauptmann, Blumenthal, Von Schönthan, Heyse, Hirschfeld, Lubbliner, Halbe, and others; but most of them have sought their inspiration from the mysticism of Tolstoi, the pessimism of

Ibsen, the pruriency of Paris, or the rowdy-dowdy romanticism of which Herr von Wildenbruch, who may be described as the Bard of the House of Brandenburg, is the most stilted exponent. For the rest, the German drama of to-day tends to be heavy in ethical, political, and other aims, at the expense of pure art. At the same time it must be conceded that the theatre, which is a subsidised institution in all German states, has an educational value hitherto denied to the British people.

What has been said of the drama must also be applied to fiction in general, and also to poetry, of which the quality is almost in inverse ratio to the volume of its output. History has always been a congenial subject in Germany, but few of her historical writers have a style; and of them in general—though there are some exceptions—it may be remarked what Macaulay said of Niebuhr, that he was " a man who would have been the finest writer of his time if his talent for communicating truths had borne any proportion to his talent for investigating them." In the field of theology, Germany is far ahead of England with its criticism and its development of dogma in the light of science, while the religious life of the nation might be summed up by saying that in no country of Europe is there so much natural piety and belief in God, combined with so little church-going, as in Germany, especially among the educated classes. It is true that the kaiser himself sets an example of the straitest Lutheran faith; but then his Majesty has, on countless occasions, committed himself to the doctrine of divine right, of his being the German vice-regent of the Almighty, " our Ally at Rossbach," and he has had to live up to it.

Religion's Place in Germany

Asserting himself to be intimate with the counsels of the Almighty, the emperor claims to be no less acquainted with the canons of art, and hence it is interesting to learn from him, in his capacity as " Kunstherr," as distinguished from " Kriegsherr," that German sculpture is ahead of the rest of Europe. Perhaps the greatest museum of plastic art in Berlin is the open-air Siegesallée, in the Thiergarten, which is now lined on both sides with two and thirty marble statues of his Majesty's heroic Hohenzollern ancestors, as chiselled by the leading German sculptors under the general direction of their chief, Reinhold Begas. This imposing display of historical statuary is known to the caustic Berliners as the " Sea of Marmora," but is well worth seeing for all that. " This I can already tell you," the kaiser said when feasting all these creative artists after the inauguration of their work, " the impression which the Avenue of Victory makes upon foreigners is quite overpowering; on all sides a vast respect is manifested for German sculpture.... It shows that the Berlin school of sculptors can hardly have been excelled in the time of the Renaissance." But if we take the emperor as our critical guide through the present realms of German pictorial art, the judgment is much less favourable.

The Kaiser as an Art Critic

The newest tendency is towards realism, as represented by the " Secessionists "—from routine and the old regime, from the old and accepted schools of painting in Germany. Drawing their inspiration from Arnold Boecklin, a Swiss by birth, these " Secessionists"—who point to Lenbach as an exponent of their principles in the domain of portraiture—have aimed at creating a new and distinctive school of German art, freed from the mannerism of the past—serious, sincere, truthful.

This they aim at, and yet to the kaiser they are an odious, degenerate race, whose productions merit only proscription at the hands of the Government. " If civilisation," said the emperor, " is going to fulfil its entire mission, it must penetrate down to the lowest classes of the people. This it can only do when art bears a hand, when art elevates, instead of herself descending into the gutter." As gutter-artists, the kaiser, in his capacity of " Kunstherr," denounces the " Secessionists." What his Majesty wants is not realism, but idealism—as well in art as in literature, and even the present tendency of the latter is in a direction fatal to reverence for traditional ideals, divine right claims, and all the rest of it. German literature is at present in a very troubled, transitional state, and therefore it bulks not largely before the eyes of Europe. But it is otherwise in the field of science, where Germany easily holds foremost rank. From their very nature and mental composition the Germans are far more fitted to shine as scientists than as litterateurs—their very language being against them in the latter respect—and

Germany First in Science

even their soldiering draws its strength and brilliancy from the fact that it is of the scientific kind. Scientific students from all countries, who used to crowd for illumination to France, now flock to Germany, where a world-wide reputation was won for her by sons like Helmholz, Haeckel, Virchow, Buelow, Koch, Langenbeck, Tirkel, Czermat, **The Germans Not a Nation of Thinkers** Bergmann, Bunsen, and a host of others. In fact, it may be said that science and soldiering are the only two things that a Briton may study better in Germany than in his own country—those two subjects, and also music, in respect of which the Germans retain their proud pre-eminence both as creators and performers, though Imperial Germany has not yet produced another Wagner, whose genius was rooted in the period preceding the rise of the Reich.

As for the Press it may truly be described as poor and paltry by comparison with that of other nations—lacking in independence, influence, enlightenment, and political power. A daily newspaper is by no means so necessary to a German as it is to a Briton, a Frenchman, or an American. Mr. Ellis Barker is pretty near the mark when he writes: "The general intelligence and culture of a nation may be measured by the Press, which appeals to all, and which reflects the national mind as in a mirror; and I think that no educated German will contradict me when I state that the whole Press of Germany—dailies, weeklies, monthlies—is not only vastly inferior to the British Press, but is quite unworthy of the intelligence of a cultured nation. The German Press is a century behind the English Press, and the low standard of the whole German Press shows that the German nation is not a nation of thinkers."

This may sound paradoxical of a nation which has produced so many thinkers; but, to a great extent, it is true, on the **Germany's Educational Standard** principle that the exceptions prove the rule. In no country of Europe are there so few illiterates or so much book-learning as in Germany, and yet the average Englishman or American may be said to be a better educated man than the average German. On a peace footing Germany's standing army is about 600,000 men; while the standing army of German educationalists of all kinds numbers no less than 300,000. Germany has now twenty-two universities, which teach about 40,000 students, or more than three times the number of thirty years ago, so that she is now suffering from academic overproduction—what the emperor deplored as an ever-increasing and useless "proletariat of passmen." And all their professors are so omniscient.

Gott weiss viel,
Doch mehr der Herr Professor;
Gott weiss Alles,
Doch er—Alles besser!

While it may be owned that Germany is the *most* educated nation in the world, it is, nevertheless, a long way from being the same as *best* educated. To cram the head does not carry with it that development of character which is perhaps the primary, and certainly the higher, aim of English education. It all lies in the difference between *wissen* and *wollen*, between *kennen* and *können*. The general tendency of education, military training, etc., in Germany is to make machines of men, and the thinking power of machines is not high.

Germany is far ahead of this country in technical education; and yet, says an expert: "It is not without cause that the **Where Great Britain Leads Germany** best engineers in the world are the practically trained English engineers, although their theoretical knowledge is small as compared with their inferior German competitor." According to the same authority "the chief practical value of the German schools consists, not in the knowledge disseminated, but in the discipline instilled. . . . It cannot be too often and too loudly asserted that Germany has become great and powerful—not through her education as synonymous with knowledge, but through her discipline. National co-operation, the co-ordination of all the national forces, which is developed to a greater extent in Germany than in any other country, has proved stronger than individualism, which squanders the national forces in constant internecine warfare. . . . Indeed, I venture emphatically to affirm that Germany, with all her schools and universities, and with her army of 300,000 teachers, is a far less intelligent and far less cultured nation than is the British nation."

That is perfectly true; and it is equally true that, in spite of all her "Bildung" and book-learning, and splendid achievements in the field of science and literature,

Germany is still a very long way behind England in respect of that general something which we call civilisation. No Englishman can live long in Germany without feeling that he has come to a country where material and social refinement, manners, customs, and all the other graces of civilised life are at a decidedly lower level than in his own; and that in fact the Germans of to-day are only at about the same stage of development as were the English of Queen Elizabeth. That, however, is due to no inherent incapacity in the Germans to take on as good a coat of civilisation as ourselves, but simply to the fact that circumstances have been far less favourable to them than to us.

How War Has Retarded Civilisation

War is anything but a civilising agency, and the Germans hitherto may be said to have always been at war. So have we, for the matter of that; but while we have always contrived to wage our wars outside our own country, the poor Germans have generally had to submit to the devastation and depopulation of their own. It was a frequent remark of Bismarck that Germany had not yet recovered from the effects of the Thirty Years War, which is said to have reduced her population from 16,000,000 to less than 5,000,000. And then her other principal war waged within her own borders—the Seven Years War—the wars with the French kings and Napoleon, and the campaigns with Denmark and Austria, only afford us matter for astonishment that the civilisation of Germany should be so high as it really is. But her forty years' period of peace and material prosperity since her last great struggle with France has already done wonders for her. The German race is still almost original in its vigour; it is a rough diamond in the mine of European nations; and its good qualities—its bravery, piety, sincerity, intelligence, perseverance, energy, and idealism, only require the setting of a higher civilisation, resulting from circumstances of a kindlier and more emollient sort than ever blessed it before, to make it the leading nation on the Continent of Europe, and the one most devoted to the arts of peace.

So far, the highest expression of the German character, since the disappearance of Bismarck, is to be found in the man who had the tremendous courage to sign the warrant for his dismissal—William II., at once his country's greatest ornament and asset. Of him, the American Ambassador at Berlin, Mr. Andrew D. White, who had every opportunity for studying his character, spoke truly when he said: "The young monarch who is now at the head of Germany—original, yet studious of the great men and deeds of the past; brave, yet conciliatory; never allowing the mail-clad fist to become unnerved, but none the less devoted to the conquests of peace; standing firmly on realities, but with a steady vision of ideals—seems likely to add a new name to those who, as leaders of Germany, have advanced the world." CHARLES LOWE

Ideals of the German Emperor

Frith

KLEBER SQUARE, STRASSBURG, WITH THE CATHEDRAL RISING IN THE BACKGROUND

ESSENTIAL INFORMATION ABOUT GERMANY

AREA AND POPULATION. The German Empire consists of the following kingdoms, grand duchies, duchies, principalities and free towns.

	Square miles.	Population.	Members in Bundesrat.	Deputies in Reichstag.
KINGDOMS—				
Prussia	134,616	37,293,324	17	236
Bavaria	29,292	6,524,372	6	48
Saxony	5,789	4,508,601	4	23
Würtemberg	7,534	2,302,179	4	17
GRAND DUCHIES—				
Baden	5,823	2,010,728	3	14
Hesse	2,966	1,209,175	3	9
Mecklenburg-Schwerin ..	5,068	625,045	2	6
Saxe-Weimar	1,397	388,095	1	3
Mecklenburg-Strelitz ..	1,131	103,451	1	1
Oldenburg	2,482	438,856	1	3
DUCHIES—				
Brunswick	1,418	485,958	2	3
Saxe-Meiningen ..	953	268,916	1	2
Saxe-Altenburg ..	511	206,508	1	1
Saxe-Coburg-Gotha ..	764	242,432	1	2
Anhalt	888	328,029	1	2
PRINCIPALITIES—				
Schwarzburg-Sondershausen	333	85,152	1	1
Schwarzburg-Rudolstadt ..	363	96,835	1	1
Waldeck	433	59,127	1	1
Reuss Aelterer Linie ..	122	70,603	1	1
Reuss Jüngerer Linie ..	319	144,584	1	1
Schaumburg-Lippe ..	131	44,992	1	1
Lippe	469	145,577	1	1
FREE TOWNS—				
Lübeck	115	105,857	1	1
Bremen	99	263,440	1	1
Hamburg	160	874,878	1	3
Reichsland of Alsace-Lorraine	5,604	1,814,564	—	15
	208,780	60,641,278	58	397

The cities and towns with over 100,000 population are as follow :

PRUSSIA. Berlin, 2,040,148 ; Breslau, 470,904 ; Cologne, 428,722 ; Frankfort-on-Main, 334,978 ; Düsseldorf, 253,274 ; Hanóver, 250,024 ; Magdeburg, 240,633 ; Charlottenburg, 239,559 ; Essen, 231,360 ; Stettin, 224,119; Königsberg, 223,770 ; Duisburg, 192,346 ; Dortmund, 175,577 ; Halle-on-Saale, 169,916 ; Altona, 168,320 ; Kiel, 163,772 ; Elberfeld, 162,853 ; Danzig, 159,648 ; Barmen, 156,080 ; Rixdorf, 153,513 ; Gelsenkirchen, 147,005 ; Aachen, 144,095 ; Schöneberg, 141,040 ; Posen, 136,808 ; Kassel, 120,467 ; Bochum, 118,464 ; Crefeld, 110,344 ; Wiesbaden, 100,953.

BAVARIA. Munich, 538,983 ; Nürnberg, 294,426.

SAXONY. Dresden, 516,996 ; Leipzig, 503,672 ; Chemnitz, 244,927 ; Plauen, 105,381.

WÜRTEMBERG. Stuttgart, 249,286.

ALSACE-LORRAINE. Strassburg, 167,678.

BADEN. Mannheim, 163,693 ; Karlsruhe, 111,249.

BRUNSWICK. Brunswick, 136,397.

FREE CITIES. Hamburg, 802,793 : Bremen, 214,861.

GOVERNMENT. The supreme direction of political and military affairs is, by the Constitution of 1871, vested in the King of Prussia, who in nis capacity as chief of the German states is German Emperor. There are two Chambers in the German Parliament—the Bundesrat, or Federal Council, the members of which are appointed by the Governments of the separate states for each session ; and the Reichstag, the members of which are elected by universal suffrage for five-year terms. The Bundesrat has 58 members, and the Reichstag has 397 members, the representation being distributed as shown in the table appearing above. Alsace-Lorraine has in the Bundesrat four commissioners, who are appointed by the Statthalter, but who have no votes. Members of the Reichstag are paid. At the head of Imperial affairs is the Chancellor of the Empire, assisted by seven Secretaries of State and seven Presidents of Imperial bureaus. But there is no collective Cabinet or Ministry ; each Minister acts independently under the control of the Chancellor. The prerogatives of the emperor are restricted by the Constitution. He has no power of veto in respect to laws passed by the two Chambers, and can declare war only if defensive.

EMPEROR. The reigning emperor is Wilhelm II., King of Prussia, who was born on January 27th, 1859, and became emperor on June 15th, 1888. He is the third of the Hohenzollerns, and succeeded his father, Frederic III., who reigned for only three months.

COLONIES. Germany is the youngest of the Colonial Powers, her first colonies having been the African possessions acquired in 1884. None of her colonies are self-governing, all being administered by Imperial governors. They are as follow :

	Square miles.	Estimated population.
AFRICA—		
Togoland	33,700	1,000,000
Kamerun	191,130	3,500,000
South-west Africa	322,450	200,000
East Africa	384,180	7,000,000
ASIA—		
Kiauchau Bay	200	30,000
PACIFIC—		
Samoan Islands	1,000	33,000
Other Pacific Possessions, including Kaiser Wilhelm's Land, or German New Guinea, Bismarck or Low Archipelago, Caroline Islands, Pelew Islands, Marianne Islands, Solomon Islands, and Marshall Islands	95,160	356,000
Total	1,027,820	12,119,000

FINANCE. The revenue for the year 1906 was £119,756,500, and the expenditure was £119,363,550. The funded debt of the German Empire amounts to £177,175,000, in addition to about £30,000,000 Treasury bonds and other less permanent obligations.

INDUSTRY AND COMMERCE. Germany ranks high as an agricultural country, but as her own great population absorbs her agricultural produce, she does not appear as an important exporter of foods. Of the whole area of the country, 91 per cent. is productive, and only 9 per cent. unproductive. The principal crops grown, in the order of their acreage, are rye, hay, oats, potatoes, wheat, barley, vines, hops and tobacco. Yet the exports of agricultural and animal produce are less than one-fourth the value of the imports of the same class. Germany has rich mineral districts, the chief being Westphalia, Rhenish Prussia and Silesia for coal and iron, the Harz for silver and copper, and Silesia for zinc. The principal minerals raised, in the order of their importance, are coal, lignite, iron ore, potassic salt, rock salt, copper ore, zinc ore, and lead ore. The fishing industry is not important, and only 618 German boats are engaged in deep-sea fishing in the North Sea. The total number of people engaged in the fishing industry, including inland, shore, and sea fishing, is about 32,000. As a manufacturing country Germany takes a high place. Over a million people find employment in the metal and machinery trades, almost a million in textile trades, and over half a million in the manufacture of wooden ware. There are almost 400 sugar factories. In 1908 German imports aggregated £409,048,000, and her exports £332,030,000.

CURRENCY. The *mark* is worth 11¾d. of English money, and the pound sterling is equivalent to 20·43 marks. For approximate calculation, the mark is usually considered as being worth a shilling, and 20 marks as being worth an English sovereign. The *thaler* is a coin of 3 marks, the *krone* is worth 10 marks, and the *doppel-krone* is worth 20 marks. There are also silver coins of ½, 1, 2, and 5 mark pieces, and in nickel there are 5 and 10 pfennig pieces. The standard is gold, and the 20-mark piece contains 7·16846 grammes of fine gold.

WEIGHTS AND MEASURES. The metric system became the legal standard on January 1st, 1872. For British equivalents of metric values, see page 5399.

POSTAGE. From Great Britain to Germany : Letters, papers, and samples as for France, see page 5398. Parcels—by sea to Hamburg—1s., 1s. 6d., and 2s. for 3, 7, and 11 lb. respectively, or 3d. per parcel above these rates if by Ostend or Flushing.

TELEGRAMS. Gt. Britain to Germany, 2d. per word.

HOLLAND AND BELGIUM IN OUR OWN TIME

LIBERTY & PROSPERITY IN THE SMALL STATES

By Robert Machray, B.A.

A REVOLUTION in Brussels, not at first sight of a very formidable character, but symptomatic of a deep, widespread, pervasive feeling of dissatisfaction with existing conditions, brought about in 1830 a movement which, assuming a national aspect, resulted in the forcible dissolution of the union between Belgium and Holland. The Flemish people, who inhabited the North of Belgium, belonged to much the same branch of the great German family as the Dutch, and might be supposed to have greater sympathy with them than with the Walloons, who occupied the south of the country, and were of closer kin to the French than to the Teutons. But they were Roman Catholics, and the Dutch, for the most part, belonged to the Reformed Church—in itself a pronounced line of cleavage. Besides, the Dutch had not been politic; they had treated the Flemings with as little consideration as the Walloons. In fact, they had regarded all Belgium as inferior to Holland, and looked upon it as if it had been theirs by conquest.

If they had acted in a different spirit, Belgium and Holland might have been one country to-day. But the separation took place soon after the rising in Brussels, although the independence of Belgium was not acknowledged by Holland till nine years afterwards. Sometimes the union **Prosperity of Holland and Belgium** of countries has proved a great benefit, as in the case of England and Scotland; at other times their divorce has been followed by real good to both, and this is what has happened with respect to Holland and Belgium. They are small states, yet they can show, area and population considered, a prosperity, a condition of general well-being, which can hardly be matched

in the history of the world. It is extremely doubtful if this could have been said if they had remained united. The religious antagonism would alone, in all probability, have prevented it. Holland is a country with a history of which any **Holland's Brave Struggle for Independence** nation might well be proud. It is a little country, yet a great one. As is often pointed out for the example of mankind, the Dutch have fought through several centuries a finer struggle for civil liberty and national independence than has been made by any other people.

The story of their long struggle against the might of Spain is so full of a stormy grandeur, an invincible heroism, a prodigal heaping-up of the elements which are best and noblest in human character, that the mere memory of them moves the heart and fills the soul with passionate emotion. The expression, the "soul of a people," is often used, though, perhaps, not always quite accurately; but if there is a people of whom it may be said truly, it is of this people of Holland. And as the soul of Holland was in days bygone, so it is to-day—hard and proud, money-loving and money-getting, no doubt at all, but above and beyond everything instinct with the spirit of patriotism, for which no sacrifice can be too great.

The supreme desire of the Dutch is to preserve their independence, to have their Holland their very own. It is this ideal which dominates their national life, and equally inspires the two parties, Liberals and Anti-Liberals or Anti-Revolutionists, which divide its political life. They have good reason for cherishing this ideal, and never more so than at the present time. For, from the international point of view, the position of Holland is not exactly a happy one. There is the interesting question of the succession to the throne—interesting rather than difficult, for even if Queen Wilhelmina should have no heir a successor to the throne can be found in a prince, with the blood of the glorious House of Orange in his veins, who will be in sympathy with Dutch aspirations. The danger to the independence of Holland goes much deeper than this. The most marked feature of the history of these first years of the century is the growing antagonism between Britain and Germany. However much or little the fact may be realised, the fact remains, deplorable, menacing, incalculable as to result upon the world. The hope of all men of good will is that a struggle may be averted. No one can regard the question without the deepest anxiety; but the Dutch have special reason for thinking of it with foreboding ; for Holland stands between England and Germany. But it is not Britain that Holland has any need to fear. The irritation produced in Great Britain by the expression of the pro-Boer sympathies of the Dutch during the South African War has passed away, most fair-minded Britons feeling that the Dutch could hardly have acted otherwise than they did in supporting to some extent their kin. Britain has no wish that Holland should be other than independent for ever.

Danger to Holland's Independence

But the same cannot be said with equal truth of Germany. Holland holds the mouth of the Rhine, the greatest German river—" the Rhine, the Rhine, the *German* Rhine," as the song puts it. There has long been a school of German political thought which maintains that the possession of the whole river, particularly of its outlets, is necessary to Germany, and never ceases to urge that, seeing also that the Dutch are of Germanic stock, Holland should be occupied by Germany. Holland, too, holds the great ports of Amsterdam and Rotterdam, arguments that further reinforce the German claim. With this extended sea front, what might not Germany become ! Does not " manifest destiny " point this way ? The bulk of Germans, it should be said, listen to these flattering voices as if they heard them not, but the Dutch are hearing them always, and are haunted by them. If they have no serious fears, for the time being, of an

Holland in Fear of Germany

unprovoked armed annexation of their country by Germany, they dread the employment of subtler methods, commercial and diplomatic, which would bring about its gradual Germanisation. And again, at a crisis in European history, when the sacredness of treaties has been shown to be a fiction, should a war break out between Britain and Germany, what guarantee has Holland that her territory might not suddenly be seized by Germany as a base for operations against Britain ? It is questions like this, arising out of the present international situation, that disturb Holland and cause great searchings of heart.

The Dutch were never more determined than at the present time to preserve their identity as a people, and apart from the menace which hangs over them they go about their business at home and abroad in their quiet, easy, immemorial way. They remain, as they have been for many generations, great men of business ; their wealth and commerce now grow from year to year ; they have got their vast colonial empire well in hand, but their money flows into many lands—it was the capital they supplied that in large measure built the railways of the United States. Amsterdam is one of the banking centres of the world, besides being its diamond mart. The country, with its 2,000 miles of canals and 1,800 miles of railways, presents a pleasing spectacle of well-ordered life, with features of its own which differentiate it from that of every other land.

Holland the Peaceful

There is a spirit of peace, of rest, of quiet about it, especially in the interior, that is looked for in vain elsewhere. The old order changes in Holland as in other countries, but with a measured tranquillity all its own. Its windmills, its level, highly cultivated fields, its dreamy homesteads, the picturesque dress of its slow-moving, much-smoking peasants still endure—the delight of the contemplative and such as love not the fret and fuss and hurry of these times of ours, and the joy of the artist. In its great cities, such as The Hague, Amsterdam, and Rotterdam, the old-world atmosphere is scarce to be found save in some old houses and in the churches; in them the modern spirit prevails, as might be expected. Yet, speaking generally, the peace of the land is so great that nothing could have been more appropriate than the building of the world's Palace of Peace, where arbitration takes

THE TOWN OF UTRECHT SHOWING THE OLD CANAL

VIEW IN LEYDEN, WHICH STANDS ON BOTH SIDES OF THE OLD RHINE

ROTTERDAM, THE CHIEF SEAPORT OF THE NETHERLANDS

SCENES IN THE TOWNS OF THE NETHERLANDS

the place of war, in the midst of this people. Holland is a land of liberty. Though predominantly a Protestant country, any Dutchman is free to worship God according to his conscience. Commercially, Holland believes in Free Trade, and has fattened upon it. Nothing, perhaps, gives better evidence of its prosperity than the

No Poor Rate in Holland fact that it has doubled its population since the middle of last century. Its population is now not far short of six millions, in 1849 it was about three. Another notable fact which witnesses to the same thing is that there is no poor rate in Holland. Of course there are poor people, but they are cared for, as a rule, by religious societies and private charities.

Its political system is simple. At the head of the State is the sovereign; then there are two Chambers for legislation. The monarchy is constitutional and hereditary; the Parliament, known as the States-General, consists of a First Chamber of fifty members elected for nine years—one-third retire every three years—by the provinces ; and of a Second Chamber of 100 members, elected for four years by all male citizens of twenty-five and upwards who pay a direct tax to the State, or are householders, or own boats of twenty-four tons, or have a salary of about £23 yearly, or show evidence that they can support their families. This means that about one-third of the male citizens have votes.

For many years Dutch politics were largely influenced by questions arising out of their colonial empire, but this phase has passed away. Recently the most important measure passed into law is the Electoral Reform Law of 1896, which regulates the franchise as mentioned above. The Dutch attach great importance to education, which is compulsory for children from six to thirteen years of age. Their schools and universities are well organised ; their primary schools are practically free. The

Holland's Up-to-date Education Dutch are fine linguists, perhaps because their own language can take them but a little way in Europe or elsewhere. It is quite a common thing for Dutchmen of any position at all to speak fluently and correctly French, German, and English.

Belgium enjoys one great advantage over its northern neighbour, for its neutrality is guaranteed by the Treaty of London, November 15th, 1831, by Austria, Russia, Great Britain, and Prussia.

No country has made greater strides during recent years than Belgium in wealth and industrial development, thanks to its natural resources, but thanks also to the fact of its neutrality being guaranteed—a fact of which the Belgians sometimes are inclined to lose sight. During the Franco-German War, Britain prevailed upon both combatants to affirm afresh the neutrality of this little country, which otherwise might have been affected very adversely.

Under the ægis of the protecting Powers, Belgium has had full opportunity for self-development, and it must be admitted that it has taken every advantage of it. No one can visit Belgium without being struck by its prosperity, whether as regards the purely agricultural section, with its vast number of small holdings all in the highest state of cultivation, or as regards the manufacturing part, the centre of which lies about Liége, with its huge ironworks and other highly successful industries. And it must not be forgotten that infected as Belgium is with the modern spirit, it is a country with a rich historic past still living and actual in

Franchise Liberties in Belgium such cities as Ghent and Bruges, and that, in the Ardennes, it can show scenes of loveliness and rare charm that appeal to all. Its magnificent cathedrals, with their splendid pictures, will always exercise some influence on Belgian life and character, though not, perhaps, in the exact direction its " Clericals " would prefer.

Belgium came into existence, as has already been stated, on its secession from Holland. By its constitution, framed in 1831, it is a constitutional, representative, and hereditary monarchy, legislative power being vested in the sovereign and two Houses of Parliament, the upper being known as the Senate, the lower as the Chamber of Deputies or Representatives. Several changes have been made in the constitution with respect to the franchise, the last being introduced by the law of December 29th, 1899. By this law the principle of manhood suffrage has been established, qualified, however, by the *suffrage universel pluriel*, and the proportional representation of minorities founded upon a somewhat complex system.

All citizens over twenty-five who have lived for one year in any given commune have one vote. But this is not all. They have an additional vote if, first, they are thirty-five years of age, married, with legitimate offspring, and pay a tax of five francs (4s.) to the State ; or, second, are twenty-five years of age and own immovable property to the value of £80, or have a corresponding income, or for two years have received £4 a year from Belgian State funds or from the national savings bank. But the Belgian can have yet another vote if, being twenty-five years old, he possesses a diploma of higher education, or has filled some public or even private position which implies this higher education.

No Belgian can have more than three votes. Both Houses of Parliament are chosen by this electorate. Senators are elected for eight years, most of them being elected by the general body of voters, and the rest by the provincial councils. The Deputies are elected for four years, in the proportion of one member to every 40,000 of the population, and number 116, one-half of whom retire every two years. The members of Parliament are paid indemnities, and get free passes over the railways.

Though Belgium has of recent years become an intensely democratic country, it is still, as will have been seen, a long **Belgium a Stronghold of Socialism** way from the " one man, one vote " principle. Its present franchise is the result of a long and sometimes embittered struggle which, apart from the Congo, practically includes the whole political history of the country. For a lengthy period after the foundation of the kingdom under Leopold I., power was held alternately by the Clericals, or Catholics, and the Liberals, or Anti-Catholics; it was much the same during the first twenty years of the present king, Leopold II. But 1886 saw the rise of a new party, that of the Socialists, and it is this party which has made Belgium democratic ; though it did not become formidable much before 1893, it has since become a great power in the land. The state of parties may be best shown by quoting the election returns for 1908. Half the deputies had to be elected—81 seats in all. The Socialists won five seats, three from the Liberals and two from the Catholics, now in power.

The new Chamber consists of 87 Catholics, 43 Liberals, 1 Christian Democrat, and 35 Socialists. In the elections to the Upper House the Liberals lost five seats, of which the Socialists gained three, leaving the Catholics with 63 votes against the 47 of the combined opposition, or " Left." Twelve years ago the Catholics had

two-thirds of the votes in the Chamber. It is thus apparent that the " Right," or Catholics, are steadily losing ground ; they draw their strength mainly from the Flemish provinces, while the parties forming the " Left " derive theirs from the Walloon provinces. The Catholics support religious education in the schools and **Clerical Control of Education** universities, and the Church, paid by the State, is yet outside its control. The Liberals belong to the middle class and the industrial portion of the community, and are, as it were, between two stools. The Socialists preach and uphold the doctrine of collectivism, and are strongest among the working classes. All parties of the Left unite against the Clerical control of education. But the battle wages most fiercely, as for many years past, round the franchise. In 1904 M. Feron, the leader of the Left, moved the abolition of " plural " voting in favour of universal suffrage, but was defeated. In 1906 all sections of the Left combined on a common programme, the two chief " planks " in it being reform of the franchise and compulsory education free from Church control. And the end is not yet.

Perhaps it should be said that almost the entire population of Belgium belongs to the Roman Catholic faith, but full religious liberty prevails, all denominations receiving grants from the national funds. The two racial divisions, Flemish and Walloon, continue to be marked by a difference of language. Nearly 3,000,000 in the north, the country of Flanders, speak Flemish only ; while rather more than 2,500,000 in the south, the Walloon area, speak French only. About 1,000,000 Belgians speak both languages.

But it is the South chiefly that is industrial, that has the greatest wealth, that has made, and is making, Belgium what it is, and in the end it can hardly fail to establish its influence as supreme over the national **Belgium's Reactionary Priests** life. In Southern Belgium the standard of education is, on the whole, higher than in the North, as might be expected from the pressure of industrial competition. The higher branches of education are well provided for throughout the country ; it is with respect to the primary schools that the trouble comes. Primary school education is compulsory in a way, but it is too much in the hands of the priests, who, naturally, are more or less reactionary.

But the chief fact in the contemporary history of Belgium is its wonderful industrial development; this has been helped by technical education, which is in an advanced state.

Belgium has now taken upon itself the responsibilities of a great colonial empire. In 1908 the Congo Free State ceased to be independent, the sovereignty over it being transferred from the King of the Belgians to the country. The area of the Congo is estimated at 802,000 square miles, and its population at from 14,000,000 to 30,000,000. The Congo State was constituted a sovereign country under Leopold II. in 1885 by the Berlin Conference. It was declared neutral, with free trade, and the natives were protected under special rules—rules which, there is only too much reason to believe, were not observed in actual practice.

As the Congo has been thrown open to all the world, there is little ground now to suppose that there will be a continuance of the atrocities perpetrated on the natives which shocked the conscience of mankind.

THE GRAND DUCHY OF LUXEMBURG

THE great world nowadays knows very little about this small country, but rather more than forty years ago its name was on the lips of everyone; for after the war between Prussia and Austria in 1866—which resulted in the decisive defeat of the latter and a fresh grouping together of the German states— **Luxemburg's Independence Guaranteed** Napoleon III. sought "compensation" to France for the increased power of the former by attempting to buy the Grand Duchy from the King of Holland, who also was Grand Duke of Luxemburg. Prussia, however, stoutly resisted this scheme, and for a time the "Luxemburg Question," as it was called, filled the mind of diplomatic Europe with apprehensions of war. But the matter was finally settled by a conference of the Powers held in London in 1867, when it was agreed that the garrison Prussia had for many years maintained in the city of Luxemburg should be permanently withdrawn from its fortress, that the fortress itself should be dismantled and destroyed, and that the Grand Duchy should henceforth become in every sense an independent and sovereign State, with its neutrality guaranteed.

Another consequence, though not immediate, of this war was that a prince of the illustrious House of Orange-Nassau, from whom Prussia had taken the Duchy of Nassau, became Grand Duke of Luxemburg. His son, William, is the reigning sovereign at the moment when this article is written. A nice point has arisen as to the succession to the throne, for the Grand Duke's children are all daughters, and, according to the Salic Law, the Grand Duchy should pass away from his family at his death. It was by this law that Luxemburg had ceased to belong to the sovereigns of Holland, the older branch of the House of Orange, when Queen Wilhelmina succeeded William III. Like the Dutch, the "Luxemburgeois" have the fear of Germany, their most powerful neighbour, before their eyes; they have no desire to lose their national identity in the existing German Empire, as might very easily happen. Therefore, in July, 1907, their Parliament, or Chamber of Deputies, became a law unto themselves by solemnly declaring that the succession shall devolve on the present Grand Duke's daughters, and their descendants in order of birth, the Salic Law notwithstanding. And as no Power is likely to say them nay, in the Europe of to-day, the people breathe freely once more.

It is a very tiny state, this Grand Duchy, its area being just a trifle under 1,000 square miles, and its population somewhere about 250,000. It is well governed by its Chamber, which consists of forty-five members, half of whom are elected every three years; it has no army to speak of, and its debt, mostly incurred in railway building, is a mere bagatelle. It is a prosperous little country, its mining and smelting industries bringing much grist to the national mill; it is a happy little country, for its inhabitants, now that the German spectre is laid, are well content **A Country Happy and Prosperous** with their lot; it is a beautiful little country, especially the northern half of it, which forms the south-east portion of that lovely land known as the Ardennes. There is no more interesting or romantic city than the capital, also called Luxemburg, whch is remarkable alike for its natural beauty and strategic importance.

ROBERT MACHRAY

ESSENTIAL INFORMATION ABOUT HOLLAND & BELGIUM

HOLLAND

AREA AND POPULATION. The Kingdom of the Netherlands has an aggregate area of 12,648 square miles, and a population of 5,672,237. The principal towns with their populations, are: Amsterdam, 564,186; Rotterdam, 390,364; The Hague (the capital), 248,995; Utrecht, 114,692; Groningen, 73,278; Haarlem, 69,701; Arnheim, 62,279; and Leiden, 57,095.

GOVERNMENT. Holland is a constitutional hereditary monarchy. Legislative power is vested in the sovereign and Parliament, or the States-General, which is a two-chambered house. The Upper Chamber has 50 paid members, elected for nine years. One-third of the members retire every three years. The Lower Chamber has 100 paid deputies, elected for four years, the vote being held by all citizens of not less than 25 years of age who can show a small franchise qualification. The Upper House may approve or reject bills, but may not amend them.

MONARCH. The ruling sovereign is Queen Wilhelmina (Wilhelmina Helena Pauline Maria), born 1880; succeeded her father in 1890.

FINANCE. The estimated revenue for the year 1909 was £15,394,060, and the estimated expenditure was £16,714,680. The chief sources of revenue are excise, direct taxes, indirect taxes, and customs duties. The direct taxes are the land, personal, capital, and income taxes. The public debt of Holland at the beginning of 1909 was £94,014,108.

INDUSTRY AND COMMERCE. The land is low and flat, intersected by numerous canals and rivers. About 2,000,000 acres is arable land, and quite double this area is pasture land. The principal crops, reckoned from the acreage covered, are rye, potatoes, oats, wheat, beans, peas, barley, beets, and buckwheat. Holland has a fishing fleet of over 5,000 vessels, with crews aggregating over 20,000 men. There are a few state-owned coal-mines in the province of Limburg, but no other minerals. The chief manufactures are distilling, sugar refining, brewing, vinegar making, margarine, butter and cheese, cocoa, textiles (linens, damasks, cottons and woollens), tobacco; diamond-cutting is an important industry in Amsterdam. Dutch imports during 1908 were of the value of £210,289,000, and the exports were of the value of £173,662,141.

COLONIES. The Dutch colonies are as follow:

	Sq. Miles.	Population
EAST INDIES [see page 909]: Java, Madura, Sumatra, part of Borneo, Celebes, Molucca Islands, Timor Archipelago, part of New Guinea, and sundry small islands	736,400	36,000,000
WEST INDIES: Surinam, or Dutch Guiana, and the colony of Curaçao	46,463	128,931
Total	780,863	36,128,931

In the case of the East Indies, the figures of population are only conjectural.

CURRENCY. The monetary system of Holland is based upon the gulden, or florin.

1 cent = 1/5d.
100 cents = 1 gulden, guilder, or florin = 1s. 8d.
The coins in circulation are:

Bronze: ½, 1 and 2½ cents.
Silver: 5, 10, 25 cents, ½, 1 and 2½ gulden.
Gold: Ducat or 5¼ gulden and 10 gulden.
The gold ducat is worth 16s. 8d.

WEIGHTS AND MEASURES. The metric system of weights is used [see page 5399].

POSTAGE. Great Britain to Holland: Letters, papers and samples, as for France [see page 5398]; parcel post, 1s., 1s. 6d., and 2s. for 3, 7, and 11 lb. respectively. Length, breadth or depth limit, 3½ feet; length and girth limit, 6 feet.

TELEGRAMS. Great Britain to Holland, 2d. per word, with a 10d. minimum.

BELGIUM

AREA AND POPULATION. Belgium is divided into nine provinces, and has an area of 11,373 square miles, and a population of 7,238,622. The principal cities and towns, with their populations, are: Brussels (the capital), 623,041; Antwerp, 304,032; Liége, 172,039; Ghent, 163,079; Mechlin, 58,800; and Bruges, 53,486.

GOVERNMENT. Belgium is a constitutional hereditary monarchy, whose neutrality is guaranteed by Great Britain, Austria, Russia, and Prussia. Legislative powers are vested in the king, the Senate, and the Chamber of Representatives. The Senate, or Upper House, consists of 110 members, elected for eight years. Some members are elected by direct popular vote, and the remainder are elected by the provincial councils. Senators must be not less than 40 years of age, and must have a certain property qualification. The Chamber of Representatives, or Lower House, has members proportionate to the population, which may not exceed one member for each 40,000 inhabitants. They are elected for four years, one half retiring every two years, but a dissolution entails a general election. The vote is possessed by all citizens who have attained the age of 25, and certain property and educational qualifications entitle the citizen to supplementary votes. Deputies are paid. Executive power is in the hands of ten Ministers of State.

MONARCH. The king is Leopold II. (born April 9th, 1835), who succeeded his father in 1865.

FINANCE. The estimated revenue of Belgium for the year 1908 was £24,856,196, and the estimated expenditure was £24,839,906. The chief sources of revenue are the state railways, excise, customs, registration fees, property and personal taxes, succession duties, post office and trade licences. The Belgian National Debt at the beginning of 1907 was £131,418,680, mostly at 3 per cent.

INDUSTRY AND COMMERCE. More than half of the area of Belgium is under cultivation, and about 20 per cent. of the entire population is dependent upon agriculture. According to acreage, the chief crops are potatoes, rye, oats, wheat, beets, barley, tobacco, and hops. Forestry and stock raising—horses, cattle, and swine—are important industries. The chief mineral wealth of Belgium is its coal, the annual output of which is about 22,000,000 tons. Iron ore is both mined and imported, and other minerals include zinc, lead, and copper. The iron and steel works are very important. The non-metallic industries include glass manufacture, sugar refining, textiles, lace, flour, and starch mills. The imports for 1908 were of the value of £134,904,000, and the exports of the value of £103,413,000.

COLONY. The African territory known as the Congo, and formerly officially known as the Independent State of the Congo, was annexed to Belgium in September, 1908, thus becoming a Belgian colony. Its area is estimated at 802,000 square miles, and its population at from 14 to 30 millions, including under 3,000 Europeans. The towns are Boma, the capital, with a population of 3,000 (300 Europeans), and Matadi, with a population of 4,000 (250 Europeans). Three-fifths of the export trade is rubber, and the remainder is palm-kernels, palm-oil, and ivory.

CURRENCY AND WEIGHTS AND MEASURES. As for France [see page 5398].

POSTAGE AND TELEGRAPH RATES. As for Holland [see above].

TELEPHONE. Communication between London and over a dozen cities and towns in Belgium is possible at a fee of 8s. for a three minutes' conversation.

GENERAL VIEW FROM MONT BLANC BRIDGE, SHOWING ROUSSEAU'S ISLAND

THE HANDSOME PLACE NEUVE, WITH EQUESTRIAN STATUE OF GENERAL DUFOUR

ANOTHER VIEW, SHOWING THE MONT BLANC RANGE IN THE DISTANCE

SCENES IN THE FAMOUS SWISS TOWN OF GENEVA

SWITZERLAND IN OUR OWN TIME
THE FREEST COMMUNITY IN THE WORLD
By Robert Machray, B.A.

THE general impression of Switzerland is coloured far too much by the notion that it is an ideal country in which to spend a most delightful holiday, be it for a long or short period, whether the season be summer or winter. Switzerland undoubtedly stands for all this, but there is a tendency to forget or lose sight of the fact that it stands for much more. This outside point of view, largely based in England on such beguiling announcements as "A Week in Lovely Lucerne for Five Guineas, or a Fortnight for Nine," is scarcely, if at all, modified when the tourist finds himself actually on the lake and sees its beautiful mountains around him or mirrored in its blue waters. Satisfied with his excursion and his experiences, he returns home, nor stops to think of, far less ponder, the story that lies behind all this enchantment.

He has heard of Tell and the tyrant Gessler, and the apple placed on the boy's head and pierced by the shaft from the father's bow; he has heard, probably, of one or two incidents in Swiss history of a romantic sort ; but he catches scarce a glimpse of the truth that the smoothly gliding life of this land, no matter what aspect of it be considered—social, educational, political, religious, racial or commercial—is the result of some seven centuries of conflict and change. Indeed, it is a life so well ordered, so sweet in the working of all parts of the machinery that goes to complete it, so easy in its touch—the **What the Tourist does not Learn** expression "pressure" in this case is quite inapplicable—on the individual, whether citizen of the republic or stranger within its gates, that our tourist is as serenely unconscious of it as he is of the "gentle influence" of a star.

The fault is not to be charged altogether to the tourist ; it must be laid, in large measure, at the door of the Swiss themselves, though from their point of view it is no fault at all, but rather their way of playing the game. They do everything they can to encourage the belief that their land is veritably the Playground of Europe, and so great is their success in this **Switzerland the Playground of Europe** effort that vast numbers look on Switzerland as the land of the charming tour, of the delightful holiday, rather than as the country of the Swiss, one of the most interesting peoples in the world, with a civilisation more highly developed, from the political standpoint, than that of any other nation on the planet. With the Swiss, business is business, and business with them takes on the form of the admirable exploitation of that marvellous beauty with which Nature has so richly and abundantly endowed their land. So they give the casual observer the impression that they are a nation of innkeepers and waiters who understand the art of "running" hotels in the most perfect manner possible, and that their sole aim in life is to act as showmen to the wondrous natural attractions of their country.

In one of the most amusing books of pure humour ever written, "Tartarin sur les Alpes," Alphonse Daudet makes his hero, the inimitable Tartarin of Tarascon, come to the conclusion that the whole of Switzerland is the concession, so to speak, of a gigantic and enormously clever and capable catering company who, commercially, take the utmost advantage of everything at their disposal—the rosy peaks of the great mountains, the white calm of the glaciers, the green slopes of the upland pastures, the deep blue of lakes, the rolling masses of cloud, the grandeurs of sunrise and sunset, the pretty châlets and picturesque peasants—all "worked" to perfection, apparently for the benefit of the sightseer, but in reality in the interests of the concessionaires, who have skilfully brought to their aid the services of railways, steamers, guides—and the best hotels in existence, take them all in all. This conceit is certainly a pardonable one, for the exploitation of Switzerland by the Swiss is very well done indeed. Before passing from this phase of the Switzerland of our own time, a few facts respecting the hotel "industry" may be quoted. In 1880 Switzerland possessed, in round figures, 1,000 inns with some 58,000 beds; in 1890, about 1,500 inns with 70,000 beds; in 1900, nearly 2,000 inns, with 105,000 beds, representing a capital of about 600,000,000 francs, or £24,000,000 sterling.

The Great Hotel Industry

It must be remembered in this connection that the total area of the country is less than 16,000 square miles, of which almost a third is unproductive. The profits of successful hotel-keeping are notoriously large, and the stream of gold that pours into Switzerland annually, and all the year round—for somewhere in Switzerland it is always the "season"—cannot easily be measured, but it must be very great; though, of course, it varies from year to year owing to circumstances. For instance, the attractions offered by the Franco-British Exhibition held in London in 1908 sensibly reduced the volume of tourists into the country, as they did everywhere outside of England.

The Swiss are highly intelligent, particularly as to getting the most money out of anything; they have a keen eye to the main chance. This is especially true of their hotel-keeping. As an example of this, there may be noticed what has taken place with regard to their winter resorts, such as Davos, and other places of the same kind. Originally they were introduced to the world as specially suitable spots for the residence of consumptives, and great numbers of those suffering from lung affections did live in them with beneficial results. But such places are no longer the exclusive abodes of such people. On the contrary, many hotels now announce that they will not admit consumptives. So soon as the Swiss grasped the fact that Davos, and resorts like it, could be made extraordinarily attractive as a field for winter sports, such as skating, tobogganing, skiing, and so on, to the strong and the hale, they turned their attention

Business Ability of the Swiss

forthwith to the strong and the hale. So the consumptive client takes a lower place. This is not altruism; but it is business—as an American might say. However, this is not to say that there is no place remaining for the consumptive, for there are admirable sanatoria at his command. Outside of them he is not "wanted" as he used to be.

Having said so much on this aspect of the Swiss, it is time to consider another, which has already been suggested. This little nation, which is composed of some 3,500,000 souls, drawn from three races —German, French and Italian—with different languages and religions, has developed the most perfect example of a pure democracy in being to be found on the globe. This is what the ordinary tourist does not know, for it does not press itself upon him. Never was or is there a land in which government was and is so little obvious. There is hardly even a policeman to be seen, nor are there any decorations worn by the citizens —a small point, but on the Continent significant of much. In this typically democratic state there are no classes, no caste, no nobility, no exclusive privileges. Even the president of this republic is not the head of the State in the same sense as is the President of the United States or of France; he is hardly more than *primus inter pares*, and his headship, such as it is, endures for a year only.

Switzerland the Land of the Free

As has been well pointed out, the dread of the supremacy of any single man is one of the governing factors in the Swiss character. This is a country in which every man has as good a chance as another, though, to be sure, natural ability tells here as everywhere. All this has only come about gradually, and after long struggles, both external and internal. But it remains nothing less than the most extraordinary thing in the political history of mankind that this small state, with its mixture of rival races and religions, perched upon the mountains of Central Europe, hemmed in on all sides by great nations, should have become both in ideals and in fact the freest community in the world. Something of this it owes to the neutrality of the country, as indispensable to the general interest of Europe, having been guaranteed by the Treaty of Vienna, 1815, something, also, to the high state of education everywhere prevalent, even elementary education being excellent. But the explanation, in the main, lies in the history and the character of the Swiss people, history and character acting and reacting on each other, as always. Though the story of Tell and the apple be a myth, like other stories of a similar kind resolved into fictions in the crucibles of scientific research, it has a heart of truth which survives all destructive scientific processes. It stands for the Swiss character; it expresses the soul of this people better than anything else. When the Forest Cantons came together against the Hapsburgs and the might of Austria, their struggle was for freedom—the right to live out their lives in their own way. Battle after battle did they fight, and battle after battle did they win, consolidating all the while their national character, which was based on patriotism, and fusing themselves incidentally more and more into one people.

They were, and long were, great soldiers, and not in Switzerland only; as has been finely said, they were willing to sell their swords, but never their freedom. The Helvetic Republic of 1798 grew out of the old defensive **Switzerland's** league of the cantons, as **War** oak from acorn. Present- **of Religion** day Switzerland, however, begins in that year of European unrest, 1848; but this beginning included all that had gone before in Swiss history. In that year the Swiss Confederation, then consisting of nineteen entire and six half cantons, was united for federal purposes under a constitution. A revised constitution came into force in 1874, and continues, with little change, in force at the present time. In 1900, when the principle in elections known as "proportional representation" was before the country, the nation decided against it.

Since the close of the Napoleonic epoch the struggles of Switzerland have been entirely internal. There was, at the close of the first half of last century, what may be called the War of Religion, in which the Protestants triumphed over the Catholics, and caused the dissolution of the Catholic league known as the Sonderbund; and, forty years later, there was a fight between the rival Churches in the Italian canton of Ticino—Tessin. But these are merely noted in this article to bring out the point that to-day Protestant and Catholic live at peace — there being complete religious liberty—on the patriotic basis that Switzerland is greater and dearer than any Church. Apart from the religious conflict, and more important as determining the life to-day of the country, is the political struggle. The chief parties in the State are: the "Right," or Conservatives, whether Protestant or Catholic; the "Centre," or Liberals; **The Great** the "Left," or Radicals; the **Problem of** "Extreme Left," or Socialists **the Swiss** —divisions of political belief and opinion which now obtain more or less in all modern communities. In one aspect the great question before the Swiss for the last sixty years has been whether Switzerland is to be one federal state or a confederation of states—cantons—each of them a sovereign state; the same question, in fact, which the Civil War settled in the United States of North America.

From 1848 to 1872, the main political preoccupation of the Swiss was the establishment of a federal state which yet left a large amount of self-government to the cantons, a problem which was satisfactorily solved. The Federal State is supreme in matters of peace and war, in the making of treaties, in army affairs, posts and telegraphs, money issues, weights and measures, revenue, public works, patents, and other matters that affect the country as a whole; no canton can break away from the rest, but still each canton retains the power of making its own laws, apart from such subjects as appertain to the domain of the Federal government. From 1872 to the present time, the dominant note in Swiss politics is the direct rule of the people as distinguished from government by elected representatives, and as expressed by what are styled the "Referendum" and the "Initiative."

Under the Constitution of 1874, supreme legislative authority in the confederation is vested in two Chambers: a State Council of 44 members elected by the cantons— **How the** two for each canton and one for **People are** each of the half cantons, irre- **Governed** spective of their size or population; and a National Council of 167 deputies or delegates chosen by the whole Swiss people by manhood suffrage, one representative for every 20,000 of the population; these deputies are elected for three years. The two Chambers united form the Federal Assembly, which elects a Federal Council of seven members, who are not members of either Chamber, to whom is deputed the chief executive authority. The President and Vice-President are selected from the Federal Council, which sits at Berne, the head-quarters of the administration, and, by the way, the financial centre of the country. The Radicals have long controlled the government. At the elections to the National Council in October, 1908, they were returned by a large majority, but their power has been tempered by the voice of the people as given through the media of the Referendum and the Initiative.

Safeguards to National Liberty

One of the astonishing things about Switzerland is that, though the Radicals are always in the majority at the elections, yet the people have often rejected Radical measures, thus showing a certain innate and invincible conservatism. As a matter of fact, the Conservatives, though in a minority, constitute a very large proportion of the population. By the Referendum any law passed by the legislature must be referred to the direct vote of the nation if a petition to that effect is presented by 30,000 citizens, or by eight of the cantons, and the law must be altered, or even abolished, according to the result of the plebiscite. The liberty of the people is still further safeguarded, and the power of the legislature curtailed, by the Initiative, which signifies the right of any 50,000 citizens to demand a direct popular vote on any constitutional question. Taken together, the Referendum and the Initiative are the last and highest expression of the democratic spirit, and furnish an example to the rest of the world.

It must be admitted that these two political principles, or devices, if the phrase is preferred, have acted very well; but it is manifest enough that they could not be safely employed in a country where the mass of the people were not so highly educated and intelligent as are the Swiss. For instance, they could hardly be expected to act well in Russia. When they were introduced into the Swiss political system, many of the Swiss themselves thought the result would be bad, but this has not by any means been the case.

Advanced Political Privileges

A large part of the population follows agriculture; there are 300,000 peasant proprietors in Switzerland, the land being pretty equally divided amongst them, and all work very hard. The Swiss peasant is a very thrifty person, and manages to live on wonderfully little. The French and Italian Swiss are more lively than the German Swiss, who is apt to be a somewhat phlegmatic individual, but they are all as one man in patriotic feeling.

In the matter of education the Swiss, as Sir Horace Rumbold has put it, exhibit a "veritable passion." The Constitution of 1872 made education free and compulsory, though each canton makes laws for itself with respect to the way in which education is imparted. All schools make gymnastics an integral part of their curriculum, having in view the fact that the gymnasium is the nursery of the soldier; the schools teach manual labour and industries; girls are taught dressmaking.

A few words in conclusion should be said about the Swiss military system. In a sense, and a very true sense, every Swiss is a soldier. The hotel-keeper and the waiter can handle the rifle; their soldierly education begins with the gymnastic training at the school, and continues in the cadet corps. So excellent is this preparatory work that Switzerland, protected, in any case, by her guaranteed neutrality, has no regular standing army, but she has the finest militia in Europe. So good is it that the new British Territorial System is largely modelled upon it. When the Swiss lad has left the cadet corps, he joins the Auszug, or Elite, for some years, next the Landwehr for a further period, and finally is drafted into the Landsturm. He has to put in so many days each year with the colours. It is a real army, and its total strength is about half a million.

The Swiss a Nation of Soldiers

So much importance do the Swiss attach to it that one of the few changes in the country brought about by the Referendum in November, 1897, is the increase in the number of days' service each recruit must put in, in his first year. In the cavalry the recruit now serves 92 days; in the artillery, 77 days; and in the infantry, 67 days, with repetition courses of 13 days each year, instead of every second year. The recruit has been so well trained before joining the army that he makes rapid progress, and develops immediately into a fine soldier. Not the least wonderful thing about this wonderful little country is that it maintains its wonderful army for a good deal under £2,000,000 a year.

ROBERT MACHRAY

AREA AND POPULATION. Switzerland is divided into 22 cantons, of which the total area is 15,976 square miles, and the total population is 3,463,609. The principal towns, with their populations, are Zürich, 186,846; Basle, 131,687; Geneva, 116,387; Berne (the capital), 73,185; Lausanne, 54,460; St. Gallen, 52,934; Chaux-de-Fonds, 41,310; and Lucerne, 34,480.

GOVERNMENT. The government is a Federal Republic, the legislative and executive authority of which is vested in a Parliament of two Chambers—the Upper Chamber, or Ständerath, and the Lower Chamber, or Nationalrath. The Upper House consists of 44 members, representing the 22 cantons—two for each canton. These members are paid, but their remuneration, as well as their election or their appointment, varies, and is decided by the liberality or wisdom of the canton represented. The canton of Basle, or Bâle, is divided into urban and rural districts, each of which appoints one member. The two cantons of Appenzell and Unterwald are also divided into two parts, and each part of each of the two cantons returns one member. The Nationalrath, or Lower House, has 167 members apportioned among the cantons, and calculated at one deputy for every 20,000 inhabitants. Members are paid from the Federal exchequer 16s. per day of session which they attend, and expenses depending upon the mileage which they must cover to attend the sitting. Members are elected for three years, upon a franchise embracing every citizen who has reached the age of twenty-one. Clergymen are ineligible for membership. The two Chambers, collectively, are called the Bundes-Versammlung, or Federal Assembly. Although these two Houses may pass laws, the body of the people may veto these laws, and prevent them from becoming effective, the popular vote upon measures being known as the *Referendum*, which may be demanded by any petition bearing the signatures of 30,000 citizens, or any request by eight cantons. The President of the Republic and the Vice-President of the Federal Council are elected by a joint session of the two Chambers. These two men are the first magistrates of the Confederation; they are elected for one year, and may not be re-elected until the expiry of one year after they have held office. The Vice-President is usually elected to succeed the retiring President. The executive authority is vested in a Federal Council, or Bundesrath, of seven members, elected by the Federal Assembly for three years. These members, who may not engage in any other business or profession during their term of office, introduce legislative measures into the two Chambers, and fill the offices of Secretaries of State.

FINANCE. The powers of the Federal Assemblies in matters of taxation are limited. They may not impose direct taxes. In certain extreme circumstances a demand may be made to the canton authorities for contributions upon a definitely arranged scale of proportion. Certain taxes are paid over to the canton authorities. The profits of the Federal monopoly in alcohol go to the cantons, who must spend not less than 10 per cent. of the amount received upon measures to combat alcoholism. One-half of the amount collected on the score of exemption from military service is also paid to the cantons. The Federal revenue for 1906 was £5,335,820, and the Federal expenditure was £5,142,276. The chief sources of revenue are the customs and the postal and telegraph services. The National Debt at the beginning of 1907 was £4,031,038, and most of it carries an annual interest charge of 3½ per cent.

INDUSTRY AND COMMERCE.—Land tenure in Switzerland is chiefly a peasant proprietorship. About 72 per cent. of the land is productive, and of this area over one-third is grass and meadow land, almost one-third is under forest, about one-fifth grows fruit, and about one-sixth is devoted to crops and gardens. The chief crops are rye, oats and potatoes, but the output is large enough to meet the domestic market, and cereal and leguminous foods are imported largely. The principal agricultural industry is dairy farming, and the principal products are cheese and condensed milk. Stock-raising—chiefly cattle and horses—is important. The production of wine reaches the value of about £2,000,000 per annum. The Federal government exercises a paternal care over the forests. By law the area devoted to forest must be maintained, and new wood is planted where necessary, the outlay being defrayed from public funds. Pisciculture is an industry of some importance, and the establishments for its practice number over 150. The only minerals worked are salt-mines, which exist in five districts. Switzerland has developed into an important manufacturing country, and, notwithstanding the disadvantage of long railway transport for oversea merchandise, she still manages to do well in extra-European markets. The principal manufactures are silk, cotton, and linen fabrics, thread, woollens, clocks, watches, leather, gloves, pottery, tobacco, and snuff. Alcohol is a Federal monopoly. The value of Swiss imports for the year 1908 was £63,497,000, and the value of the exports was £41,537,000. The chief articles of export, according to value, were embroidery and other cotton manufactures, silk ribbons, and fabrics, watches and clocks, machinery, cheese, condensed milk, chocolate, coal tar dyes, and hides and skins.

CURRENCY. Switzerland is a member of the Latin Monetary Union, and the currency is, therefore, similar to that of France, Belgium, Italy, and Greece [see page 5398]. The centime is known also as a Rappen.

100 centimes, or rappen = 1 franc

A ten-centime piece is also known as a Batzen. Both gold and silver are legal tender to any amount. Although the coins of France, Belgium and Greece circulate in Switzerland, there is a law prohibiting the importation of 2, 1, and ½-franc Italian pieces, under a penalty of confiscation, the reason being that under the terms of the Latin Monetary Union Italy need not redeem her silver coins in gold should the Union be dissolved.

WEIGHTS AND MEASURES. The legal system is the metric [see page 5399], but there are still found in practice some of the old weights and measures, such as the centner = 100 pfunds = 110·231 lb. avoirdupois. The pfund is equal to 500 grammes, and, according to the metric system, is divisible into decimal parts, but practice follows largely the old division into halves and quarters called Halbpfund and Viertelpfund respectively.

POSTAGE. Great Britain to Switzerland: Letters, papers, and samples as for France [see page 5393]. Parcel-post, via France, 1s. 6d., 2s., and 2s. 6d. for 3, 7, and 11 lb. respectively; via Belgium and Germany, 1s. 9d., 2s. 3d., and 2s. 9d. for 3, 7, and 11 lb. respectively.

TELEGRAMS. Great Britain to Switzerland: 3d. per word, with 1s. minimum.

REFUGEES AMONG THE RUINS   THE DAMAGED POST-OFFICE

TWO VIEWS OF THE DESTRUCTION IN THE CORSO VITTORIO EMANUELE

SCENE IN THE TORRENTE CARTALEGNI   RUINED CHURCH OF SAN GIOVANNI

IMPROVISED HOSPITAL IN THE OPEN AIR   RUINS IN THE FINE VIA GARIBALDI

MESSINA AFTER THE EARTHQUAKE ON DECEMBER 28th, 1908

ITALY IN OUR OWN TIME
THE NEW KINGDOM VIRILE AND PROSPEROUS
By William Durban, B.A.

AGAIN and again the question has been asked, what is the perennial charm of Italy, that land which reckons itself the special favourite of the sun? The best answer is that the secret of Italy's enchantment lies not in its atmosphere, delightful though the climate may be; nor in its antiquity, fascinating though its countless historic relics truly are; nor in its art, even though the whole peninsula is one incomparable picture gallery; but in that perpetual renaissance which gives irresistible impression of constantly renewed youth. The Italy of to-day has amazed the world by its virility, its rejuvenation since that memorable day, March 17th, 1861, when the new kingdom sprang into being with the proclamation of Victor Emmanuel, "Il Ré Galantuomo," as king of that "Italia Unita" which had been the dream of patriots—a dream at last materialised by the policy of Cavour, the fiery crusade of Garibaldi, and the enthusiasm stirred by Mazzini and Gavazzi.

The young kingdom is one of the Great Powers. Its people are the most prolific in Europe, increasing even more rapidly than the population of Russia, and pouring forth such streams of emigrants that in Brooklyn alone is a colony of 60,000 Italians, with a great quarter to themselves, while Argentina is rapidly becoming a South American Italy. In every age Italy has renewed its youth, but never with anything like **Italy's Renewed Youth** the splendid vigour displayed during the present generation. No other land so thoroughly captivates the imagination with a multitude of monuments grey with age, but surrounded by all the evidences of youthful and irrepressible life in its most eager and strenuous demonstrations.

Though this favoured peninsula has been the subject of elaborate cultivation through all historic ages, and has from time immemorial supported teeming populations, yet it is, as we see it, even more redundantly fruitful than ever. Loveliness of aspect here blends with superabundant fertility, the land overflowing with oil and wine, from Chiasso, on the northern frontier, down to Girgenti, on Sicily's southern coast. The whole vast coastline is a delightful sea-front where oleanders, tamarisks, stone-pines, and countless **Italy a Land of Beauty and Fertility** evergreen shrubs form a verdant frame for the variegated and brilliant picture of the interior landscape. Italian topography is a study of Nature in every one of her artistic moods. This unspeakable beauty of the whole country renders Italy more than ever a favourite playground of Europe.

Each successive year, increasing numbers of tourists visit the Italian Alps, dominated by Monte Rosa, the wonderful Dolomites, the Tyrolese valleys, the resorts round Lakes Maggiore, Como, Garda, Ticino, Orta, Lugano, and Iseo; the Etruscan hill-cities, described by delighted visitors as occupying the most wonderful region in the world; the fairy villages nestling in hundreds of nooks in the Apennine chain of hundreds of miles; the Lombardian plains, sheeted with blue-blossoming flax and intersected by lines of mulberry trees on which silkworms thrive by millions; the Riviera, with its semi-tropical vegetation; the Venetian larch forest of St. Mark, and the groves of Vallombrosa; the classic scenes of Baiæ and Capri, and the insular paradise of Sicily. With her head crowned with a diadem of Alpine snow, Italy bathes her feet in the central waters of the blue Mediterranean, and her citizens draw an ever-growing revenue from crowds of seekers after health and pleasure from lands near and far.

When, in the middle of the nineteenth century, Italy was welded into one nationality, she was steeped in poverty. But, to give a quaint little illustration of the

5371

financial revolution that has been accomplished, whereas the English Christmas markets used to be stocked with immense numbers of delicious little Italian maize-fed turkeys, these are now missing, for the simple reason that "the people are rich enough to afford to consume their own poultry." That simple fact speaks volumes of the change that has come about in material conditions. There is still much poverty, but it is no longer general and deplorable. Italy has declared war on the slum, and the change effected is marvellous. The social regeneration that began in Piedmont has spread over the whole land.

An Era of Social Regeneration

At Turin a beggar is rarely seen, and in Naples, where, when Victor Emmanuel was proclaimed king, he found 90,000 professed *lazzaroni*, including criminals of every grade, with thieves, loafers, and drunkards, both beggary and squalor have been drastically dealt with. Fifty years ago the common people were almost wholly unable to read. The new regime has reduced illiteracy, until now less than one-third of the adult males, and one-half of the adult females are illiterate.

Notwithstanding that Italy lacks two indispensable elements, coal and iron, and is compelled to spend every year £8,000,000 on coal, so sturdy is her modern enterprise that her native industrial companies have £60,000,000 of paid-up capital, while foreign companies have about half that amount. The manufacturing expansion in the north has been marvellously rapid. The output of the paper-mills has more than doubled in twenty years. One of the phenomenal advances has been in applied electricity. From Volta down to Marconi, Italy has had a leading part in great discoveries in electricity. It was an Italian patriot, Antonio Meucci, who really invented the telephone ; Pacinotti constructed the first machine for the application of electro-magnetism ; and Ferraris achieved the magnificent discovery of electric dynamic rotation, generated by means of alternate currents. Professor Righi, by his wonderful experiments on electric waves, paved the way for Marconi's introduction of wireless telegraphy, the most marvellous victory over time and space ever celebrated by science. And gradually the Italians are utilising the immense hydraulic forces of their country for producing so much of the "white coal,"

Triumphs of Italian Inventors

as they call electricity, as shall help them to reduce the import of coal from England. The electricity derived from the Alpine and Apennine streams will, in time, yield enormous wealth, for the number of useful falls in Italy is 34,837. Electrical establishments have turned many dull and idle towns into busy hives of industry, with rapidly increasing populations. This is the case at Maniago, near the fall of the River Cellina, whose waters are now being used to carry torrents of life and light to Venice and to other cities on the way to the beautiful "Bride of the Sea." This colossal work cost 10,000,000 francs, £400,000, and occupied 3,000 labourers in its installation.

The first trial of the great discovery of Ferraris was made in Rome by engineer Mangarini, who conveyed the force of the famous fall of the River Aniene at Tivoli, a classic spot, over the Campagna to the city. The magic light that at evening illumines the streets and houses of Rome, and the force that impels trams and mechanism of all kinds, come from the lovely cascade so admired by travellers, near which Augustus held his tribunal, Mæcenas had the villa where he used to entertain Horace, and the Emperor Hadrian built his magnificent rural palace. Italy is a land of agriculture, but this industry has passed through a crucial crisis at the close of the nineteenth and beginning of the twentieth centuries. Methods were miserably bad, and a train of diseases struck one crop after another. The magnificent vineyards were terribly damaged by the peronospera and the phylloxera, those parasites which passed into Italy from France, which in twenty years lost thus £400,000,000.

Italy's Magnificent Vineyards

The silkworm disease, the orange-tree blight, and the fly that fatally perforates the olives have simultaneously during the present generation inflicted immense mischief. Men like Signor Solari and Signor Bizzozero have revolutionised Italian farming, as thoroughly as our own was revolutionised in the eighteenth century. And as Italian emigrants love to return home after a long absence, many of these have come back with the progressive ideas they have acquired in America, France, or Switzerland. In 1898 over 30,000 agricultural labourers returned and landed at Genoa alone, and hundreds every year cross the Atlantic for the great Argentine harvest, where they are highly paid, and then return to reap their own harvests. Small peasant farmers and labourers have all alike awakened to the new order of things. Village banks have entirely revolutionised the position of the peasants, who formerly could make no progress for want of capital with which to attempt small farming successfully. Signor Wollemborg, a Lombard village doctor who has since been Minister of Finance, founded the first Italian village bank on the model of those which Herr Raiffeisen had established broadcast in Germany.

There are now nearly 2,000, with a membership of nearly 200,000. These institutions have rescued thousands of the diligent and persevering contadini, or peasants, from the terrible grip of the usurer. And likewise of late years the artisans and small shopkeepers have built up the huge organisation of the People's Banks, with their capital of £5,000,000 and their yearly business of £50,000,000, while £70,000,000 has been accumulated in the Private Savings Banks, institutions very similar to the People's Banks. The various banks lend money on very easy terms, and by their aid immense new areas have been

Prosperity of the Rural Labourers planted as vineyards or cultivated in other ways, with profit to the worker never before possible. The rural labourers have succeeded in working out their own salvation. Out of the old sordid despair the contadini have been lifted into fair prosperity.

The favourite system of land tenure and cultivation which still prevails is the famous mezzeria. On this plan the estate is divided into a number of poderi, or fields, half the produce of which is retained by the peasant who cultivates the soil, and the other half goes to the landlord as rent. The poderi average about thirty-nine acres each. The contadino's house is on the podere, and is no mere hovel, for it provides ample accommodation for a large household. The agricultural system adopted provides occupation for the peasant-farmer for the whole year without intermission, for on the same podere he grows wheat, or maize, or rye, wine, oil, and flax, according to the qualities of the soil.

These labourers are exceedingly intelligent, and they toil indefatigably, but with the utmost cheerfulness. The women of the family rear silkworms and often make money by plaiting the beautiful straw produced in the sunny clime, and also by spinning from the fine flax. The farmer not only gives to the landlord as rent half the produce of the podere, but also a stipulated number of eggs, hams, poultry, etc., while his wife or daughter, called the massaia, or housekeeper, may, by agreement, have to wash for the landlord's household. The new prosperity

Secret of Italy's Progress of this agricultural community, the backbone of the nation, is the real secret of Italy's marvellous recent progress, as the land is mainly an agricultural one. At the beginning of the new century the attention of the whole world was drawn to a series of crucial labour troubles in Italy, which had been coming to a head for several years. A vast change came over the condition and also the spirit of the working classes during the last decade of the nineteenth century, for during that period great numbers of the peasantry became artisans, and thus a very great new industrial community arose. But very quickly discontent was propagated amongst these by the spread not only of socialism, but also of anarchist ideas. Disastrous and riotous strikes took place amongst masons, miners, and railway workers.

The peasants caught the contagion and organised a league, but this was immediately met by the formation of a landowners' league. In Rome the masons employed on the monument to Victor Emmanuel II. organised a labour league and tried to compel every workman to join it, but parliament vigorously intervened for the protection of the men who refused to be coerced, and the leaguers were defeated. The only important industry in Sicily besides agriculture is sulphur-mining in the wonderful "solfatara" district in the south of the island. The miners, many of whom are very quarrelsome, given to the use of

Armed Workmen on Strike the knife and revolver, and to gambling, revolted against what were truly hard conditions in mines fearfully hot and reeking with poisonous sulphur fumes. But when the marble quarrymen at Carrara, far away in the north of Italy, got up a sympathetic strike, they quickly resorted to violence, forming armed bands, which scoured the mountains and threatened to raid the town itself; great alarm was caused amongst the peaceful inhabitants. Martial law was proclaimed, the province was placed under the rule of General Huesch, and the wanton insurrection was speedily quelled. Great improvements have of late effectually ameliorated the lot of the toilers, and the Employers' Liability Bill has had an excellent effect. It should be noted that the Italian is a born engineer.

The Italian's Genius for Engineering He inherits the Roman faculty for construction of public works, and many of the great Continental railways, the marvellous Alpine tunnels, and our own Forth Bridge, were mainly made by operatives from Italy. It is computed that there are always about 500,000 of these frugal Italian workers scattered about Europe. There is an Italian quarter in every great city in Europe whenever important public works are being executed.

Amongst this fascinatingly interesting people political problems are perpetually challenging solution. The typical Italian delights in litigation, and in these new days of genuine constitutionalism he becomes an ardent political partisan. The Italians are a nation of orators, and their parliamentarians revel in rhetorical declamation. A payment of a rent of £6 entitles to a vote. The king and queen have achieved great popularity by their manifestations of intense sympathy with the people in every time of suffering, going freely amongst cholera-stricken patients and toiling like slaves during the terrors created by appalling earthquakes. Parliamentary institutions are peculiar, for the Senate, or Upper Chamber, is composed of members nominated by the king for life on the advice of the Premier. Thus the legislation is exceedingly democratic, yet the people feel that in emergency the Senate might be relied on to prevent reckless enactments. In the Lower House the proportion of professional men amongst the deputies is extraordinary, for these constitute two-thirds of the deputies. Only

Middle-class Members of Parliament a very few working-men have ever found their way into the Italian Parliament. Nor have very many of the aristocracy been elected. The members are mostly of the middle class. Modern United Italy has produced a succession of really great statesmen, of whom the nation is proud. The names of Cavour, Sella, Ricasoli, La Marmora, Minghetti, Depretis, Cairoli, Crispi, Di Rudini will live, and the doings of the Premiers who have succeeded each other since this century began : Saracco, Pelloux, Zanardelli, Sonnino, Fortis, and Giollotti, are fresh in European recollection.

In Italy, as the seat of the venerable Papacy, religion and politics have for ages been inevitably entangled. But the separation of Church and State under Cavour's administration, and the dissolution of the vast number of convents, wrought a most radical revolution. The quarrel with the Vatican is still in process. The present Pope, when he was Archbishop Sarto, of Venice, was esteemed for his simplicity of life and his pastoral assiduity. But as Pius X. he is constrained by the Catholic Curia to assume the same attitude of intransigent Ultramontanism which was maintained by his predecessor, Leo XIII., and before him by Pius IX. But the struggle of late years has been not so much between the Vatican and the monarchy as between the College of Cardinals and the Modernists within the Catholic Church. These ecclesiastical Liberals within Catholicism have their head-centre in France ; but in Italy the famous Abbate Murri is engaged in a chronic dispute with the Curia. He has immense in-

Famous Waldensian Church fluence over young Italy, both lay and clerical. Protestantism is comparatively feeble in Italy. It is mainly represented in modern growth by the young Chiesa Evvangelica, founded by the eloquent Padre Gavazzi in the middle of the last century, but in more ancient phase by the denomination which is the oldest Protestant communion in the world, the famous Waldensian Church, which was born in the romantic valleys of the Cottian Alps, their home being called by Michelet " that incomparable flower hidden amid the sources of the Po."

The missions of the Waldenses are dotted about all over Italy and Sicily, and of late years they have steadily multiplied. The most conspicuous ecclesiastical figure in Italy is Monsignor Merry del Val, who was born in London of Spanish parents in 1865, and educated in England. This dignitary has been indefatigable in conducting the conflict between the Vatican and the French Government over the Separation Law. He visited England as Papal Envoy on the occasions of Queen Victoria's Jubilee and King Edward's coronation. He was created a cardinal, and succeeded Cardinal Rampolla as Papal Secretary of State.

This exquisitely lovely land has in our time suffered from the convulsions of Nature more than any country has ever done in the whole history of the world. The closing week of 1908 will be marked in its annals by the record of the earthquake which visited Calabria and Sicily, destroying Reggio and Messina, wiping out Scylla, and wrecking many other towns and villages. This appalling catastrophe created unspeakable consternation throughout the world, for it was estimated that 300,000 lives were lost.

Through all the struggles, difficulties, troubles, and vicissitudes of the brief history of the young kingdom of United Italy the royal family have not failed to win deepening esteem and affection. Thus the republican ideal of Mazzini is a dead theory. The nation was plunged into impassioned grief by the tragedy enacted at Monza on July 29th, 1900, when the beloved King Humbert I. was assassinated by the anarchist Bresci. His son and successor, Victor Emmanuel III., had as Crown Prince gained abundant popularity.

He and his wife, the beautiful Princess Elena of Montenegro, are considered "the handsomest royal pair in Europe," yet the king is the smallest of Continental sovereigns, being only five feet three inches in height, while the queen is very tall, so that when seen together they present a most striking contrast. Throughout their marriage service the king stood, while the queen knelt on a cushion, and thus they were just of a height. "The only time she was able to look up at me," says King Victor, quite good-humouredly.

So immense have been his services already to his country that he has been styled, and not without reason, "The Saviour of Italy." WILLIAM DURBAN

THE REPUBLIC OF SAN MARINO

ONE of the minor events of the year 1907 was the conclusion of a fresh treaty of friendship between the Kingdom of Italy and the Republic of San Marino, and in the arrangements and discussions which preceded this settlement, as in the treaty itself, the republic, which has only an area of 33 square miles, and a population well under 12,000, appeared as a sovereign and independent state, although its separate existence is maintained solely by the benevolent protection of its big friend, Italy. Of all the numerous independent states into which the Italy of the Middle Ages was divided, San Marino alone survives to the present day; and as long as Italy, by a sort of good-humoured forbearance, permits it to remain as it is, so long, and no longer, will its name be seen on the roll-call of the nations. It is situated some ten miles or so from the historic Italian town of Rimini, and is to all intents and purposes as Italian as any part of the country. But it claims to be the oldest state of Europe, dating its pretensions as far back as 855, though its independence is of a much later date. From the point of view of age, it regards the modern kingdom as something of an upstart.

It undoubtedly can boast of being the smallest republic in the world. When the devastating presence of Napoleon passed over Italy in blood and flame, San Marino was spared. "Let it remain," said the great conqueror, "as a model of a republic." In those days it was more democratic, perhaps, than it is to-day. The eight parishes of which the republic consists return sixty members to its Parliament, called the Great Council; twenty of these representatives are drawn from its nobles, twenty from its townsmen, and twenty from its peasantry; two of them are appointed every six months as Regent-Captains with executive power. There is, besides, a smaller council, which regulates all matters pertaining to finance, law, education and war; its duties must be tolerably light, for San Marino has no debt; and, of course, it cannot go to war, though it has an army of about a thousand officers and men. Its capital, also called San Marino, has a population of 1,500, and is situated on the top of Mount Titano, a termination in that direction of the Apennines. The government Palace, rebuilt here in 1894, is a fine edifice. There is much that is interesting and picturesque about the town, and, indeed, about the whole of this small republic.

The meetings of the Council, with the "Noble Guard" in their fanciful uniforms in attendance, partake of something of the character of a pageant instinct with the suggestion of old-world romance and charm. But it need hardly be added that nobody regards this little republic very seriously; there is, in fact, a good deal about it which smacks of a Gilbertian opera. ROBERT MACHRAY

ESSENTIAL INFORMATION ABOUT ITALY

AREA AND POPULATION. Italy is divided into sixty-nine provinces, and has an area of 110,550 square miles, with a population, according to the census of 1901, of 32,475,253. It includes the islands of Sicily and Sardinia. Statistics of population do not distinguish the population of cities from the communes in which these cities are, so that the figures relating to any commune include both the urban and rural population. There are eleven communes (all capitals of provinces) of which the population is over 100,000, as follows :

Naples, 563,540 ; Milan, 493,241 ; Rome, 462,743 ; Turin, 335,656 ; Palermo, 309,694 ; Genoa, 234,710 ; Florence, 205,589 ; Bologna, 152,009 ; Venice, 151,840 ; Messina (before the earthquake of December, 1908), 149,778 ; and Catania, 149,295.

GOVERNMENT. The constitution of Italy provides for a limited monarchy. The executive power is vested in the monarch, and is exercised through responsible Ministers. The legislative power is vested in the monarch and a two-chambered Parliament, consisting of the Senato, or Upper House, and the Camera de Deputanti, or Lower House. The Senate, which is not restricted in regard to numbers, and at present consists of 346 members, including five members of the royal house, consists of princes who are of age, and members nominated by the king for life. Senators must be not less than forty years of age, must pay not less than £120 a year in taxes, or must have held high office or rendered distinguished service to the state. Electors for members of the Lower House must be at least twenty-one years of age, and must have an educational or property qualification. There are 508 deputies in the Lower House. Parliaments sit for five years, but may be dissolved by the king at any time. Business can be conducted in either Chamber only if there is an absolute majority of members present. Members receive no remuneration, but travel free on some railways. The executive power is vested in the king, assisted by eleven Ministers, each at the head of a state department.

MONARCH. The present King of Italy is Vittorio Emanuel III. (born 1869 ; succeeded his father in 1900).

FINANCE. The estimated revenue for 1908 was £80,017,780, and the estimated expenditure was £77,836,956. The chief sources of revenue are the government monopolies—tobacco, salt, lotteries and quinine—customs, excise, and octrois (or local customs), railways, and post-office service. The National Debt of Italy is £530,866,700, and the annual interest charge is £22,607,500.

INDUSTRY AND COMMERCE. Agriculture is the chief industry of Italy, and over 70 per cent. of the total area is in the productive state. The chief crops, according to the acreage covered, are wheat, vines, maize, olives, rice, and tobacco. Silk culture is important, and is expanding. Attention is paid to forestry, and government aid is given in replanting. Mining provides occupation for 66,000 people. The chief mineral industry of Italy is the sulphur mines, of which there are over 600. Other mines are zinc and lead, salt, graphite, and petroleum, mineral fuel, copper, iron, antimony, and mercury. Italian quarries employ 66,000 people, and two-thirds of the value of the total output is marble. There are about 250,000 fishing-boats and 100,000 fishermen, 6,000 of whom are engaged in deep-sea fishing. The chief industries are textile—silk, woollen, cotton, and linen—and the sugar industry is making rapid strides. Industrially, Italy is making great progress In 1908 the value of Italian exports was £74,330,000 and of Italian imports, £121,238. The chief exports are raw silk, cotton and silk fabrics, olive oil, eggs, hemp, silk waste, dried fruit, sulphur, and wine. Great Britain sells more to Italy than does any other nation ; and Switzerland is Italy's best customer.

COLONIES AND DEPENDENCIES. The only Italian colonies or dependencies are those on the east coast of Africa, and one port in China. They have little economic value.

	Area.	Population.
Eritrea (on the Red Sea) ..	88,500	450,000
Italian Somaliland	100,000	400,000
Tientsin	18	17,000
Total ..	188,518	867,000

CURRENCY. The money of Italy is upon the same basis as the French currency [see page 5398] a lira, or lire, being the exact equivalent of a franc, and a centesimi the Italian equivalent of a French centime. The coins in circulation are: bronze, 1, 2, 5, and 10 centesimi ; nickel, 20 and 25 centesimi ; silver, 1, 2, and 5 lire ; gold, 10 and 20 lire ; state-notes, 5 10, and 25 lire ; bank-notes, 50, 100, 500, and 1,000 lire.

WEIGHTS AND MEASURES. The metric system is in force [see page 5399].

POSTAGE. Great Britain to Italy, for letters, printed papers, commercial papers, and samples, the same as for France [see page 5398].

PARCEL POST (via France). 1s. 6d., 2s., and 2s. 6d. for 3, 7, and 11 lb. respectively. If by slower route, via Belgium, Germany, and Switzerland, 9d. per packet above these prices.

TELEGRAMS. Great Britain to Italy, 3d. per word, with a minimum charge of one shilling.

SAN MARINO

San Marino is an independent republic, which claims to be the oldest state in Europe, and which has placed itself under the protection of Italy. It is entirely enclosed by Italy proper, and is situated in the hills behind Rimini. Its area is thirty-three square miles, and its population 11,000. The seat of government is San Marino, a village of 1,500 population. Legislative power is vested in a council of sixty members, two of whom act as regents for six months and exercise executive power. There is a smaller council of twelve, who divide into four committees or congresses. The principal exports are wine, cattle, and stone.

FRANCE IN OUR OWN TIME
A SURVEY OF THE NATION'S SOCIAL AND POLITICAL LIFE
By Richard Whiteing

WE have followed the history of France among the nations of Europe down to our own day. Where does this great country stand at the present time?

In regard to politics the answer is simple enough. France has established the Republic after more than a century of effort, and has put it on the footing of the institutions that are taken as matters of course. This means, not that the present system is free from the liability to error and to great economic and social change, but simply that a reversion to either of the earlier forms, of monarchy or empire, is unthinkable. For good or ill the old parties have, and can have, no hope of a governing majority. The monarchy is associated with the tradition of misery; the empire with that of defeat and humiliation. The disasters of 1870–1 have had precious results on the temperament of the people; it is unlikely that the war drum will ever throb again in France in any cause but the defence of the territory. Even the lost provinces have become rather an aspiration than a purpose and a hope.

The new political ideal is the welfare of the nation as a whole, the making life better worth living for every unit of the mass of population. In his latest survey of the whole situation, M. Jaurés boasts that the country is now in full political democracy. In other words, the French people are at last in sole charge of their own destinies.

The New Political Ideal

The constitution has been fashioned into a perfect instrument for the work in hand. Its provision of the second ballot ensures the predominance of the popular will; the deputies are paid as servants of the State, not as servants of any section of the electorate. The suffrage is universal, and no man has more than one vote. The electoral machinery is of ideal simplicity. The Senate, composed of 300 members, will wholly represent the principle of popular choice in the second degree when its few surviving life members have passed away. The president is but the most eminent servant of the nation. This is not to say that none but Republican parties exist. There is a Monarchist party which, as Nationalist or Conservative in name, harps on the string of military glory, and still keeps a kind of sentimental hold on a section of the peasantry, and makes some figure in the social life of Paris. But the peasant proprietors in the mass are for the Republic, because they believe that it is for order and stability, and that they have nothing to fear from it, and a good deal to hope.

What the Republic Represents

The urban masses, again, are bound to give it their support as the progressive movement in being, though the workmen as a whole are overwhelmingly Socialist and anti-capitalistic. In the decisive election of 1906, of some 9,000,000 voters who went to the poll, nearly 6,250,000 cast their votes for Republican or Socialist candidates, without counting another million or so who represented Liberals well affected to the existing system. The poor remainder stood for all the forces of reaction. The majority were all Republicans of one shade or other, whatever else they were not, and were ready to coalesce for the defence of Republican institutions.

The Socialist section of the Republican party now includes much of the highest intellect of France, and exemplifies nearly all the varieties of that school of politics throughout the world. The racial mind has a wide range, from the utmost poise and precision of scientific thought to the most passionate enthusiasm for the idea. The Commune is the classical example.

It was a system on the one hand, and, on the other, a delirium of utter self-sacrifice. Its members died by thousands for a social millennium. The outbreak would have ruined the democratic cause for ages in any other country; in France it only gave the cause a set-back that has already become but an incident of its career.

A Great French Socialist The darkest hour found a man capable of stemming the current of disaster, and effecting the salvage of the proletarian idea. This was Jules Guesde. He had laid the causes of failure to heart, and he gradually taught his countrymen to abandon the old methods of sterile insurrectionary agitation, and to rely on organised propaganda to a definite end.

He opposed the desperate measure of the general strike, and in due course achieved the miracle of sending forty deputies to the Chamber pledged to a Collectivist programme, and to the saving idea of unity of all sections of the advanced party in the common cause. They were not, however, to co-operate with the Government; they were to convert it to Socialism, and his union of parties was still to be only a union among the elect. The thought of common action with men who were Republicans, and nothing else, was repugnant to his soul.

Then came Jaurès with the wider outlook of a scheme for union among all the supporters of the Republic. He was, and is still, a professor of philosophy, and, as such, a distinguished member of the academic body and a servant of the State. A man holding that position in France must be deeply versed in the history of nations and the history of thought, and the studies of Jaurès had taught him that practical persons with a sense of give and take always win in the long run. He urged his brother Socialists to spread their doctrines among the people in the old way, but meanwhile to work with the constituted authorities, and in Parliament for all that Parliament was worth.

The Butcher of the Commune He entered warmly into the Dreyfus agitation, on the side that ultimately triumphed, and he finally sent one of his lieutenants into the government as member of a Ministry that contained the hated De Gallifet, " the butcher of the Commune."

This proceeding scandalised the Socialists of Europe, and it led to a Titanic debate between Jaurès and the German Bebel, at the International Congress of Dresden. Bebel triumphed by carrying a resolution to the effect that Socialism should have a policy strictly independent of all other political parties, and should take no part in a " capitalist" government. Jaurès frankly accepted the vote, and, by his submission to the idea of party discipline, did much to maintain his position, and to lead his very antagonists to more practical courses. His followers are not a solid phalanx; it is his proud, though perhaps rather premature, boast that " outside of the united party" there is none deserving of the Socialist name.

Jaurès is still strictly a party man, and he constantly uses his energies as a spur to prick the sides of ministerial intent. In the summer of 1906 he held another Titanic debate with M. Clemenceau, as the head of the Government, on the great question of the rate of progress in democratic reform that still separates the labouring class of France from the middle class. There had been serious strike riots, and the Government had been compelled to intervene to preserve the peace. " Order is the Republic's first law," M. Clemenceau

Order the Republic's First Law seemed to say. " Give us the opportunity to be your friends. All that you want will come, if only you have the patience to wait for it." He carried the point by a vote that expressed the confidence of the Chamber. " You are not the Almighty," cried the defeated champion in a moment of petulance. " You are not even the Devil," was the retort.

In the elections of 1906 over 26 per cent. of those who went to the poll cast a Socialist vote, yet this was regarded as a Socialist defeat. Socialism is powerful enough to influence legislation, though not to control it. It now elects mayors by the hundred, and municipal councillors by the thousand. Its chief supporters are found among the workmen, and the " intellectuals" of the professorial group.

Trade Unionism in France, as such, is rather " on the fence" in being not frankly Socialist though in strong sympathy with the movement. It has long been political and speculative in its tendencies, and for a simple reason. Many of the benefits in higher wages and the like, which with us were the exclusive concern of such organisations, are, in France, secured by the personal thrift of the workman, and by the help of the State. The French Unionists often prefer to save for themselves, and this leaves them fancy free for the dream of a beneficial revolution which is to settle everything. Many of their comrades, however, are still for the English method of trade funds for purely trade purposes—the raising of wages, and the benefits. The first would make the unions a branch of a sort of labour party, rejecting the co-operation of all other classes but their own, and working by means of a class war. The others have the powerful support of the miners, the printers, the textile workers and the engineers.

According to Miss Scott, the latest historian of the movement, the only important unions that are distinctly revolutionary are those of the building trades. One of their spokesmen utters a warning cry against " the development of a fourth estate composed of trades economically privileged, with the unskilled and unemployed left on one side." It is no easy matter to arouse French enthusiasm for any idea of a purely utilitarian character. The tendency is always to look before and after to the complete regeneration of the race. This tendency has hindered the progress of French Co-operation. It has attained to nothing like the same rate of development as the British movement— even in the manufacturing branch, which has always been peculiarly its own.

France the Workman's Paradise

The net result is that the French workman has, on the whole, a better lot than the British. He has more of the joy of life. His government, state and municipal, does more for him, and takes care that he shall be abundantly supplied with simple pleasures—seats in the shady thoroughfares for the summer evenings, where he may smoke his pipe and see his children at play ; well-kept woods, forests and parks, where he may ramble on Sunday with his wife and family ; cheapened services of tram and train—all with ludicrously cheap holidays as the general result. If his hours of labour are longer, the pace is nothing like so hard. His home life abounds in the solid and substantial comfort of the neat and cleanly dwelling, the well-filled clothes-press and larder, the well-cooked meal, and the well-stocked market as its source of supply.

For most of these blessings, no doubt, he has to thank his admirable wife, herself a product of the most careful cultures, domestic, educational, and religious. He eats " like a prince," both in quality and in the quantity for his need. On this point the comparative statistics as to the prices of provisions in the two countries which are published in England from time to time are wholly illusory. With the French workman, two or even three courses and dessert are not the exception, but the rule. His children have the best of elementary, and often of advanced education — the former entirely free, with free meals at need—and over and above this, free access to magnificently appointed technical schools, where they may learn their trades.

Happy and Contented Workers

The spontaneous help of his comrades rarely fails him in misfortune. He is less frequently haunted by the spectre of a submerged tenth than his British brother ; indeed, that class is practically non-existent in France. "Wherever you go," says a recent observer, " you will find less evidence of poverty, of idleness, of misery than will force itself on your attention almost anywhere else in the world."

Thanks to all this, the French workman is generally content to remain in his class. It is by no means, however, the content of acquiescence. His class hatreds are strong, and, with his sense of equality, he is disposed to have " no use " for the bourgeoisie or for the aristocrats. In so far as he is a workman of the towns, he is generally socialistic and anti-capitalistic to the backbone. He belongs either to the French Working Class party, which is opposed to any sort of co-operation, political or other, with society at large, or to the Socialist Revolutionary party, which is disposed to accept such co-operation in politics, on conditions, but in each case with a view to the final triumph of equalitarian ideas. Finally, he hates war, partly on general principles, but mainly because he hates the blood tax of the conscription. Then, for the balance of power in public affairs, the workmen are effectually held in electoral check by the peasantry, whose large share of the ownership of the land gives them little liking for Socialism, and no taste for farming under the State. These are the more potent as a check, because they have all but completely rallied to the Republican idea. Successive Governments have wooed and won them by standing firmly for the security of

Peasantry Opposed to Socialism

property and for public order, and by making them objects of peculiar care in other ways. Their technical schools for farming, for instance, are on the same high level as the schools for arts and crafts.

Liberty, Equality and Fraternity are still the watchwords of the Republic, but the French are disposed to take them not exactly in this order. Equality is the passion of the people, and the goal of all their strivings and of all their hopes. Fraternity is a sentiment of only less strength, but as yet it has got no further than fraternity by classes. Among the workmen, for instance, the sense of brotherhood is a positive affection of the soul, only to be realised by those who have lived in close touch with them and witnessed its countless manifestations of courtesy, charity, and active help.

Watchwords of the Republic

It is the same among the professional and the other classes who are the brain and nerve of France, and here fraternity finds its strongest manifestation in the strength of the family tie. The family constitutes a vast insurance society for the mutual guarantee of all its members against the ills of life. Few fail to respond to the appeal, even when the claim extends to cousinships of the remoter degrees. The whole scheme of collective well-being is that in emergencies no single member of the "clan" shall have to stand quite alone. The uncle who looks after his graceless nephew as a matter of duty, and almost without expectation of gratitude, is a familiar figure of French comedy.

This, in itself, with the obligations it entails, involves a certain sacrifice of liberty, since you can hardly have it both ways—dependence, and a perfectly free course. Liberty, therefore, while it has made huge progress under the Republic, is still hampered by intolerance. The Press is free to the point of licence ; but personal freedom, especially that of public meeting, still leaves much to be desired. The Government, in its passion for public order, is fretful and meddlesome, especially as it works through the agency of the police. It regulates strikes and public meetings to the point of exasperation, and compromises the "order of the streets" by a fussy anxiety to preserve it. The ordinary prefect of police simply loses his head at the sight of two or three gathered together for public discussion. The very

Weaknesses in the Government

crowd is at fault in the same way ; and in psychological moments every man's hand seems to be against his neighbour's coat-collar in the act of arrest.

For all that, the Republic is by far the strongest French government of modern times if only for the classic reason that it divides Frenchmen the least. The vast and powerful middle class no longer stands aloof. The people, in the conventional sense of the term, are not and never have been enough to make a governing system. The power may come to them when they have all the qualifications for it ; but by that time they and the nation will be one. At present the middle class, with its backing of the moderates of all shades, is as strong as ever in affairs and in knowledge.

In all times the vast majority of the governed, as distinct often enough from their governors of the moment, have constituted a sort of natural force of conservation. They are at once eager for change and fearful of its effects ; and their very inconsistencies serve to determine the pace for progress, and to compel a due regard to the adjustments between old interests and new claims. It may be no more than the force of habit, but a force it is, for their mass makes them the predominant partner in politics. No party, however advanced, can touch the actual experience of administration without swaying to the side of this moderate norm, which represents the working mean between movement and stagnation, and which exists by no accident but by a law. When that central and all-powerful body swerves in momentary aberration to either extreme, progressive or reactionary, it begins to diminish in numbers, and to lose control. A government of abstract justice and of revolutionary upheaval, if it could be established to-morrow, would pass like the dream of a night. The chronic infirmities of human nature would still assert their rights.

Predominant Partner in Politics

The Republic is now in the safe keeping of the whole nation. Like every other government in the world, it will, of course, undergo enormous changes, but these must be gradual, and must still conform to the law of human affairs. The moderate man will ever be master in the long run. Much of the abuse of the "middle class" is due to the sense of

THE INTERIOR OF THE SENATE IN THE LUXEMBURG PALACE

EXTERIOR OF THE CHAMBER OF DEPUTIES

INTERIOR OF THE CHAMBER OF DEPUTIES

OUTSIDE AND INSIDE THE FRENCH HOUSES OF PARLIAMENT

their irresistible might. They captured the old revolution, they have already captured the new. In many respects France is fortunate in being rooted in institutions that make for stability and social peace. Her wise laws of inheritance provide for a beneficent diffusion of wealth throughout the whole of the

Thriftiest People in the World
body politic. No man may leave all his property exactly as he likes. A considerable share of it must go to his wife and children, and not to any one of them to the detriment of the rest. In this way there is an automatic check on the growth of large fortunes, and a constant diffusion of wealth, which irrigates the whole field of national well-being with a fertilising stream.

There are few French citizens, men or women, who are without " expectations " of a kind. Consequently there is no huge landless, moneyless class, filthy, feckless and forlorn, answering to our abject poor. The flower and product of this system is the national habit of thrift, which is an effect of wise legislation rather than a mere peculiarity of the national temperament. Opportunity has made the French the thriftiest people in the world. Having the means of saving, they naturally save.

This, and this alone, accounts for the enormous recuperative power of the nation as a whole. "Whereas Great Britain," says Mr. W. L. George, in his "France in the Twentieth Century," "has but just recovered from the depression following on the South African War, a comparatively cheap contest which did not entail the destruction of a single English home, France, within four years of 1870, had regained her position, after paying an indemnity nearly equal to our total Transvaal expenditure, and enduring six months' devastation of her soil." French literature is naturally best understood by a study of the French character,

The Double Nature of the Frenchman
of which it is the necessary outcome. The Frenchman has two natures in marked contrast. In one he is the child of the joy of life—all impulse, whim, and go-as-you-please; in the other, he is the most staid, orderly, respectable being in the universe. In the first he follows the wayward law of his moods and his intuitions; in the other he is almost the victim of a rigorous logic which compels him to keep his mind as tidy as his

person, and to put every idea in its place. The latter is his normal state, and it has produced his classic literature; the former has prompted him to all the revolts of reaction towards Romanticism, Naturalism, Idealism, and all the other schools that are characterised so much by the final syllable of their names. Ronsard, apart from his services to the good government of the language, came to bring life and the joy of a free course in the beauty of nature. The rather miscalled age of Louis XIV. brought discipline, law and order; our good *bourgeois* of the muse was now intent on a return to the proprieties. This mood ran its course until he made holiday again with the Romantics. "Tempted of the Devil," wrote the wrathful Nisard, of Hugo the leader of the band, "he is begetting new schools every day."

It was not to last for ever. The rebels in their turn came to repentance with the Parnassian group. The poetic mind is now once more in a state of lawlessness, or, at any rate, of unrest, which bodes another return to the righteousness of form. Banville, who succeeded Hugo as the

Banville the Successor of Hugo
master poet of his day, was still the Romantic movement, but that movement chastened by its sense of the need of flawless workmanship and of spiritual restraint. His "Petit Traité de la Poésie" was merciless in its insistence on the clearness, precision, and minute finish of detail so dear to the French mind. Leconte de Lisle was classic in spirit, call him what else you will, though a classic with a wider outlook on life than the men of the grand period.

Sully Prudhomme, the next great name, has been called, and not unhappily, a French Matthew Arnold in his sense of the good breeding of an Augustan ideal, and sometimes a Lucretius, or even a Darwin, of poetry. Coppée was the same sort of man working in a medium of scenes of humble life, a French Crabbe, touching the butcher, the baker, and the candlestick-maker, not as one of themselves, but as the Puritan of a rigorous law of art.

Sully Prudhomme died but the other day. Where is he now—at any rate, in regard to his status in this world? Before the breath went out of his body an advanced school had come to regard him as a fogey. It has yet to wreak its vengeance on Heredia, the last of the Parnassians, for the crime of popularity, but no doubt he, too, will have his hour of the wrong sort. His goldsmith's art in the fine chiselling of the phrase has carried their system to perfection; and perfection palls, to say nothing of the fact that the younger men are waiting, and that youth will have its day.

We are still with the Decadents, though in new manifestations. Beaudelaire rules our spirits from his urn; so does Verlaine, and it is estimated that at least a hundred of his pages may reach posterity. They should do so, for he at least restored the personal and the human note which had no place in the baggage of the Parnassian band. Mallarmé, sometimes coupled with him as a neo-Decadent, is far inferior.

It is now a riot of schools, if the word is not inappropriate to systems that are little more than exaggerations of the personal note. Some sing the all-importance of the *ego*, others the emptiness of life. They pass across the illuminated disc of popularity, from nothing into nothingness again, like the figures in the cinematograph. The Polychromists, who hold that the word is not merely the symbol of colour, but the thing itself, are still to **The Modern Poetic Movement** be found, though you have to look for them. The Realists yet honour Jean Richepin for his "Chanson des Gueux," and another composition in which he has written with much appreciation of the Devil and all his works. Maupassant shaped well in this school of verse at the outset of his career.

Foreigners have largely influenced the modern poetic movement. Maeterlinck is perhaps the most distinguished case in point. But there is now a promising cult, which places Whitman at the head, of Poe, Emerson and Thoreau as the four men of universal genius that America has given to the world.

The general result is that the old French prosody, the result of centuries of critical labour, has gone all to pieces, and that its chief law—one word, one vote for signification—has been repealed. Even the venerable figure of syntax has been plucked by the beard. Impression has taken the place of logic, assonance of rhyme. The reaction will follow in due course, probably in a new classical movement with larger and more generous bounds.

The same tendencies are observable in French fiction. It is a time of unrest, but the outlook is most promising. The old Naturalist school of Zola, as a school, is gone, but it has left abiding traces, most of them for good. The good ones are in the direction of respect for the facts and of a faithful rendering of detail; the bad, in sheer pornography, though this is not the founder's fault. Bourget, though no Naturalist, in regard to the observation of **French Fiction of To-Day** the things of the flesh, follows that method in regard to the things of the spirit. There is another trace of Zola in the fact that the new school is overwhelmingly purposeful. In no former time has French fiction been so much occupied with the study of social facts. This is the main line of the new departure. Even the revived study of local manners and customs, local types, is not free from the laudable suspicion of a purpose of natural regeneration. If some still write in the old way, for the pure love of story as story, and of character in and for itself, they form but a minority, though a minority with a right to their welcome.

The revival of religion has its apostles, but every one of them takes care to let you see that he is a patriot rather than a saint. The wide, wide world is not forgotten, and it has a school to itself, with Loti as its master. His work has the study of foreign race types and exotic peculiarities for its means, and a suggestion of the greater glory of France for its end and aim. That perfectly equipped writer has ever been the best of patriots; and when he writes of "India without the English," we may easily divine his regret that Providence did not vouchsafe the blessing of its being "with the French."

The social studies embrace every variety of the *genre*. Most of them have this peculiarity, that they deal with groups rather than with individuals, in the older way. Where they are historic in their setting, we have no longer the splendid personalities of the past, the heroes of the **Social Studies in Novels** world movement through the ages, but, instead, the masses of humanity, dim, but by no means dumb, who are struggling towards the light. Paul Adam and Paul and Victor Margueritte are the chiefs of the school. Their books are of races and nations, all in movement on the epic scale.

The fiction that has narrower limits of place or time has made a new departure under the leadership of M. Rod, who is not a thinker only, but a man of letters, with all the restraints that belong to the French ideal of the character. The miseries of the people, the bankruptcy of faith, the internecine struggle between capital and labour, the self-seeking of the professional politician, are among his more striking themes. M. De Vogüé has taken this last subject as the motive of his powerful work " Les Morts qui Parlent." For him the parliamentarians of to-day are but the delegates of the Convention in a new part. He is a polemist of great force, with a keen sense of actuality, which, however, does not prevent him from casting a longing, lingering look towards the past. Rod, too, is not without this tendency, but he can see good in both sides, and sympathy is his dominant note.

A Writer of National Romance

The note of sadness and of protest against a too insistent present is found again in much of the work that has provincial France for its subject, and particularly in that of M. Bazin, who stands at the head of a school. M. Bazin has written novels of great power—on the work-girls, on the exodus of the peasantry from country to town, on the religious persecution involved in the present quarrel between Church and State, on the problem of the lost provinces. The last, a mixture of history, patriotism, and philosophy, aspires to the dignity of a national romance, and as such it has been acclaimed by the most educated readers in France. But their suffrages are not enough for this writer. He has studied provincial life in all its aspects with a success that has enabled him to realise the sane and sound ambition of a wide popularity. Bordeaux is another remarkable writer of the same class.

The writers who are most read in France are Paul Bourget and Anatole France, of the earlier school, and Maurice Barrès of the new. Paul Bourget is now, whatever he was not in the past, the eloquent apologist of marriage, of the authority of the family as a social organism, of monarchy and aristocracy, and, above all, of religion. He brings to their support a delicacy and a suppleness of mind, and a perfectly equipped literary talent, which compel the attention of many who have no sympathy with his views.

France's Popular Authors

These, however, have their antidote ready to hand in Anatole France, that "august Nihilist pamphleteer," as somebody has called him, who stands supreme in literary power, and especially in eclecticism of style. He is the champion of the new ideas that seem pressing forward to victory. They could hardly do without him, for in France, as elsewhere, the cause is often of less importance than the skill of the advocate. His " sober elegance, his neat limpidity "—to translate perhaps too literally—compel the admiration of all. In a series of well-known works of fiction he stemmed the torrent of prejudice in the Dreyfus case far more effectually than even Zola, to whom his detractors have ever refused the title of a man of letters.

At any rate, what Zola did for the country at large Anatole France did for educated opinion, which still counts for much in matters of taste. He takes a side in seeming to take none, and to be wholly devoted to a detached and caustic observation of contemporary ideas. " L'île des Pingouins," one of the latest of his works, is also one of the best examples of his method, and with that, unfortunately, of a certain superfluity of coarseness that hardly deserves to be called a defect of his qualities. He is a precious asset of the cause of progress, since most of the writers who are most read stand for a sort of reaction against the ideals of the popular party. It is easier to get a hearing in that way, among the select few—still large enough to make a considerable public of themselves.

A Novelist of the New School

Maurice Barrès is perhaps the most widely read of the three. He writes, often with a strong conservative bias, in all the *genres*, and he has identified them with successive stages of his own development. He is a patriot, an ardent " regionalist," in his love of the character and colour of provincial life, an historical novelist of the new school, in his keen sense of the nations as makers of history, and his comparative indifference to their masters of court or camp. He is also a psychologist of the first order, with a deep insight into the souls of races, as distinct from the merely individual growths. The newer tendencies of cultivated thought are to be found in his pages, and especially in his strong insistence on the belief that no people can afford to forget its past. " Our individual conscience comes from the love of our country and of its dead."

Is there no place, then, for the novelists who write merely for the love of character and of incident, and especially for the love

BORDEAUX, VIEWED FROM THE TOWER OF ST. MICHAEL'S CHURCH

PANORAMIC VIEW OF LYONS FROM THE PLACE BELLECOUR

THE IMPORTANT NAVAL HARBOUR OF BREST

CHERBOURG, AS SEEN FROM THE FORT DU ROULE

SCENES IN THE GREAT CITIES AND PORTS OF FRANCE

of telling a story without any other prepossession ? Assuredly, or M. Henri Regnier would not be read. He is a subtle spirit born out of his proper time, which was the eighteenth century, and prevailing by the force of his irony and his wit, and especially of that variety of the latter which is known as the "esprit gaulois."

French Apostles of Feminism But the remorseless obligations of the subject compel us to return to another class of writers with a purpose—the apostles of "feminism." The subject looms largely in the literature of France, as distinct from the propaganda by the deed and by the platform to which it is almost wholly confined in England. Marcel Prévost led the way with " Les Demi-Vièrges " ; but, as a rule, the women have now taken the matter into their own hands.

Their studies of passion leave little to be desired, except sometimes a sense of restraint ; and the freedom for which they plead is less that of the representative assembly than of the home and the heart. Gérard d'Houville—Madame de Regnier for her familiars—writes with remarkable literary power. Madame de Noailles follows on the same side, and is much in vogue. With these are Madame de Coulevain, the author of " Éve victorieuse," and especially of " Sur la branche," and Madame Marcelle Tinayre, whose " Maison du péché " was one of the most widely read books of its year.

All of these have not only something to say, but they have learnt how to say it by the most serious reading in literature and history. They differ from earlier writers of their sex, and even from George Sand, in having a distinctly feminine point of view. They write as women, and not as women who hope to be taken for men. Such a method has its dangers ; and it must be confessed that some of their feminine followers have run into the grossest licence, as though to proclaim

Imagination's Place in Literature their independence of the precept that want of decency is want of sense. The late Madame Bentzon, though woman to the finger-tips and a champion of women, had in perfection the qualities that must always go to the making of good literature, and especially reserve.

Imaginative work is not the all in all of a literature. There are thinkers who work for thinking's sake, as there are artists who work only for the sake of art. But the peculiarity of modern France is that the apostles of ideas tend more and more to express themselves in poetry, fiction, and drama. They naturally wish to have a hearing, and they find that the average reader prefers to take even his philosophy in object-lessons. Some of them fare ill in this attempt, and succeed only in showing that they have missed their vocation. Most of the vital thought of France is enshrined in its fiction, and that fiction is so good because it is expected to be so much more than the amusement of an idle hour.

In history there has been a change from the prophetic and picturesque and the essentially literary method of Michelet to that of the minute and exhaustive study of facts with the object of leaving them to tell their own story, or, at best, of grouping them with a little malice aforethought. M. Sorel is the leading representative of this school, and he may be described as the French Stubbs. M. Lavisse, and, above all, M. Fustel de Coulanges, stand for the older and the more attractive method. But their work is still governed by a rigorously methodic purpose

A Brilliant History of France and treatment, which at least seems to obtain its effects of the picturesque by accident rather than by design. The last-named, however, though it may annoy him to hear it, is very much of a great writer. M. Gabriel Hanotaux may be said to unite the two schools. His history of contemporary France during the period of reconstruction that followed her last great war is at once one of the most brilliant and solid works of the time. Apart from these, we have any number of writers of the memoirs in which the French have always excelled. M. Bourget has entered the domain of travels in a manner characteristic at once of himself and of the new school, with his quite descriptively named " Sensations d'Italie." In criticism—philosophic and literary—M. Brunetière, though he has recently passed away, still rules, with M. Lemaître and M. Faguet.

In philosophy and science proper the French are for the moment largely dependent on the foreigner—exception made of such names of the illustrious dead as Pasteur and Claude Bernard. Darwin, Spencer, Buckner, Haeckel, Schopenhauer, Hartmann, and Nietzsche call the tune.

The French drama shows precisely the same tendencies as French literature. It is given over almost wholly to the problem and the social question. As M. Faguet has observed, there is in every age the formula in vogue; and, in a certain sense, all the theatres of France have ever, at any given period, played the same piece on the same night, the same sort of piece being understood.

In the eighteenth century the inevitable thing was a classic tragedy or a comedy of so-called character derived, not from the life, but from La Bruyère. In the nineteenth there was another variety of choice—Hugo, with the alternative of Augier, Dumas, or Sardou. To-day, in the drama as in the novel, writers are pushing out in every direction in search of the spiritual interests and preoccupations of their time. In the new comedy of manners, the lawyers, the doctors, the financiers sit to the artist, and not merely as individuals, but as members of a social group—the "world" of Bench and Bar, the world of medicine, and so on. What playgoer of us all can have forgotten the "Business is Business" of Mirbeau in its English dress? The French stage, usually in advance, has not been so closely in touch with the

Reward of the French Dramatist realities of life for many a year. It is the spirit of Molière, who dared to plunge right into the realities of his day, in bold disregard of the conventions of the old Italian comedy which then ruled the stage. There is no more intrigue for intrigue's sake. The modern French dramatist has simply opened his eyes to what is going on around him, and has reaped his reward in no longer being reduced to "faire du Scribe" or even "du Sardou" for a living. We in England are still, or were but yesterday, in the old rut; and, though we have escaped from Scribe, we are still hardly out of the toils of Sardou, with "The Scrap of Paper" and "Diplomacy" as our most successful pieces of the immediate past.

When that truly eminent hand in stagecraft died, it was but as a writer who in his own country had survived his own school. But Mr. Shaw and Mr. Galsworthy, with others of their band, have shown us the way to better things, especially now that our younger men have improved on one of their leaders by leaving themselves and their own personal idiosyncrasies of theory out of the cast, and by working purely in a medium of the actual concerns of their day. Mr. Pinero, the only one of our veterans who is always marching on, has caught up with at least the rear-guard of the

French host in "His House in Order," and has had his reward in the honour of adaptation for the Paris stage. And Mr. Barrie has made an attempt to extend his empire in the same region. He would have done better to begin with the "Admirable Crichton." The play so named, however, is rather German than British in its method;

The New Role of the Stage and something as much like it as one pea is like another has long been played in Germany. The French move faster. In the art of acting, for instance, while we are yet agitating for a school on the old lines of the Conservatoire, M. le Bargy is well on his way with a new method of rendering the passions of the scene, which is founded more directly on the study of nature.

The Théâtre Libre and the Théâtre Antoine are striking examples of the present methods of writing pieces, of mounting, and of playing them, all immediately from the life. The less ambitious Grand Guignol, and even the amateurish Théâtre Social, must be mentioned in this connection, if only as signs of the times. The French stage is, in some instances, gradually leaving the realism, to which ours is yet but gradually working its way, for a symbolism which is still true to the spirit of the universal quest in being a symbolism of the real. The names of Curel, of Portoriche, of Brieux, and of Donnay have yet to become household words on our side of the water; but we shall hear more of them, no doubt, in the course of the next quarter of a century. M. Lemaître, M. Lavedan, and M. Rostand, in the higher ranks, have already been brought to our notice, and, no doubt, all the rest will come in good time.

M. Rostand apart, no aspect of our modern life is indifferent to the newer writers. They seek their subjects on the stock exchange and the racecourse, in the religious conflict and the decay of faith, in the home, in public life, and in

Themes of Modern Writers Socialism as in all the reactions —in fact, wherever men's hearts beat with the passions of their age. Criticism follows them, as it always does a bold and successful lead; and, where it still ventures to disagree, it has to find some less hackneyed term of derision than "problem" and "tract." The big battalions of the playgoer are now with the problem; and naturally all is changed. The passion for experiment, for the eternally new, not as a mere bid for notoriety, but as research forward, as exploration, is equally characteristic of France in other arts. It is especially so in music. The new school, led by Debussy and d'Indy, with Bruneau, Charpentier, and Dukas—as composers or as critics—for captains of the host, are men for whom Wagner is already but a greybeard. They are as different **France's** from the great German master **New School** in their methods and aims as **of Music** he was from Gluck; and they have come to regard both as follies of the past. "That animal Gluck!" cries Debussy. "I know only one other composer as insupportable, and that is Wagner. Yes; this Wagner, who has inflicted on us the majestic, vacuous, insipid Wotan!"

"And what do you think of our Berlioz? He is an exception, a monster. He is not at all a musician; he gives one but the illusion of music, with his methods borrowed from literature and painting."

The new school borrows from literature, too, but only for the spirit, not for the method. Its art is sensuous, not to say sensual, and dreamy, and it aims at the rendering of states of emotion rather than of the emotions themselves. Debussy, for instance, after learning his accidence at the Conservatoire, and winning the Prize of Rome there by an orthodox academic composition—just to show he could do anything he liked—went straight into the work of his choice as soon as he had shaken himself free of academic control. He had served in the army, like every other Frenchman, and he found his first call to something new in "the blend of sonorities" produced by the barrack-yard call for "lights out" and the long-continued vibrations of a neighbouring convent bell. He sought to do in music what Verlaine and Stéphane Mallarmé were doing in poetry—the latter especially in his "Afternoon of a Faun." The verse was imitative of impressions of natural effects, and **Music's** Debussy tried to render these **Exquisite** in music in the same subjective **Fairyism** manner. "In the midst of a dream," says Bruneau, "murmuring violins rustle, and tinkling harps; pastoral flutes and oboes sing; and they are answered by forest horns," all in "an exquisite fairyism" of general effect.

Rossetti next took his turn of inspirer in chief with "The Blessed Damozel," rendered by the musician so as to give all the dreamy witchery of that masterpiece of fancy and imagination. Maeterlinck's "Pelléas and Mélisande" was inevitable after that, with its "ideas of fatality, of death, its atmosphere of sorrowful legend, its poor kings, poor people, poor inhabitants of unnamed lands whom fate leads by the hand"— fate and Maeterlinck. It is the music of people who do nothing, but feel everything, whose souls are instruments on which Nature plays in all her moods.

No wonder such a composer should ignore melody, with its beginning, middle, and end; its story, in a word. "I have been reproached," he says, "because in my score the melodic phrase is always found in the orchestra, never in the voice. Melody is almost anti-lyric, and powerless to express the constant change of emotion or life. It is suitable only for the song which confirms a fixed sentiment."

Debussy visited London in 1909, and conducted several performances of his own music. Vincent d'Indy, a Frenchman, but a pupil of the Belgian composer Franck, visited New York, and expounded similar views in a lecture at **Revolution** Harvard University. He met **in** with an interested though not **French Art** an enthusiastic reception; but critics of note predicted that the future was with the music of the school. French art has undergone a thorough revolution in the course of the last fifteen or twenty years, with Claude Monet and Rodin for its prophets, and Mauclair for its expositor. The last is the Boswell of both of these great men, and he has taken down their theories from their lips. The common note of it all, in music as in painting and sculpture, is the discovery that there are new effects of Nature to render, effects not always dreamt of in the philosophy of the modern classical schools. So the art of the day imports a revolt against the academical system in France, though not necessarily against the ancients. Its aim is the more faithful rendering of light. The new painters paint light on the presumption that there is really nothing else to paint. For them colour is but an effect of light, and they try to produce it by the very methods of Nature.

Their point of departure is the truism that in Nature no colour exists of itself. As a reality pertaining to objects, colour is a pure illusion. It is simply an effect of light in its impact on objects. The light does not illumine the colour; it

A REGIMENT OF INFANTRY ON THE MARCH

OFFICERS STUDYING THE ELEMENTS OF BIG GUN FIRING

A COMPANY OF SOLDIER CYCLISTS ON THE ROAD

SOLDIERS OF THE FRENCH REPUBLIC

brings the colour in its train. Objects are of no colour; or, rather, of all colours, as they absorb or reflect these from light. The academic system starts from the heresy that colour is something that can be laid on in compact masses, mixed for the purpose on the palette. Nothing of the sort; it is but an effect of far more art**Passion for** ful adjustments. The earlier **Reality** masters had some instinctive **in Painting** perception of this great truth, though they had not reduced it to a science. There are traces of it in Watteau, in Ruisdael, in Poussin, and especially in Turner, Constable, and Delacroix. The school is called Impressionist; but Mauclair gives good reason for thinking that the noun chromatism might suggest an adjective more to the point. And since colour is but light, so light is but form in every mode of definition. Why, then, take the trouble to paint anything else, since in this you have the all in all?

This is the principle of the revolt against mere subject in the picture. Why paint history, or symbol, or anything else that is so purely human and secondary in its source? Why not paint what is alone real? This passion for reality leads logically to the search for truth in mere human characterisation, for character is but truth in one of its forms. If you paint man, let it be man as he is, not as he should be in some fantastic theory of the ideal. Courbet must be mentioned here as a precursor, though the principle has been carried far beyond him by later men.

Claude Monet leads them all. His way of painting a landscape is to take, say, a dozen canvases, and to devote each to one particular aspect of the scene as the light marks the true hours of the painter's day. So the one landscape, after the patient labour of many days, comes out as twelve quite different scenes, according to their degrees of illumination. To **Monet's** plant yourself with but one **Artistic** canvas before a constantly **Methods** changing scene, and in protracted sittings jumble all its effects together, is but the childishness of art. Monet uses only the so-called primaries, though he is not very strict in the definition of them, and he never mixes the pigments on his palette to get a special combination. He simply lays them on in such a way as to produce by optical suggestion the effect of the combination

he seeks. Hence, when we are near them, his pictures are apt to look quite unintelligible, as an assortment of primitive colour stains without aim or purpose.

But see them at the right distance, and this confusion subsides into a perfectly ordered work flooded with light, and therefore with colour, and abounding in true form and drawing everywhere—not in the drawing of outline, of which Nature knows nothing, but in the drawing of colour, than which she knows of nothing else. The revolution, both in aims and methods, is extraordinary, and is not to be made intelligible by any description; it has to be seen. To be fair to a man almost forgotten, it dates at least from Couture, who, as any of his pupils still living might testify, often painted in this way.

Degas, another great Impressionist, shows the same solicitude for truth in regard to figure and to movement. He, too, has the horror of the crude outline, and holds firmly to the belief that form is but light and shade. He finds movement, by preference, among the ballet **Impressionist** girls, and he has painted them **School** by the hundred in all the in**of Painters** cidents of the daily practice of their art. Here, we have them at their lessons; there, waiting for their turn; and there again " on " in their fairyland of scenery, gauze, and coloured rays. He is quite pitiless in his passion for truth. Sometimes his nymphs look hungry, sometimes even quite ugly—a lower depth, no doubt, in the professional inferno—as they squat for repose, or writhe in the tortures of the gymnastics of their trade. But by-and-by we shall see them in their appropriate setting, and then all defects of detail will be lost in the illusion of the perfect scene, as their tremulous contours play hide-and-seek with the light from which they spring.

Renoir, another great painter of the Impressionist school, finds his favourite contrasts not so much in light and shade as in light against light, which is, after all, but the expression of the same truth; for shadow itself, as artists know it, is not blackness, but only another degree of light.

The school is a large one now. It has passed its apprenticeship of calumny, poverty, neglect, and it influences all the French painting of the day. It has produced great illustrators—Raffaelli, Forain, Renouard, and Cheret, who has done such wonders for the art of the poster. It is now on its way to the nirvana of absorption into the light of its origin, to make room for the incarnation of neo-Impressionism in the artists of the Pointillist group. With these, the effects of light, instead of being rendered as in Claude Monet's work by irregularly disposed blobs of colour, if one may use the phrase, are obtained by a sort of mosaic of it, composed of small touches of equal size, and of spherical form. This, in a way, is an attempt to paint the very atoms whose vibrations produce the light itself.

Rodin is Impressionism in sculpture; and he, too, like the painters, works mainly for effects of light, and for character, and so is in full revolt against the academy. Yet he still proclaims his allegiance to the Greeks, who, he declares, managed their statuary on precisely the same principles as his own. He is for new truth in one word, and his new truth is that we do wrong to treat sculpture as a mere glorified study of still life. It is emphatically, even in its most statuesque pose, a thing vibrating with movement, **Rodin's Genius as a Sculptor** a movement that comes from the play of light on its different masses. These, as they catch the ray, or lose it, form a great harmony; and the statue is to be wrought entirely to the end of the harmony so obtained.

For him there is no such thing as the one view, sole and single, of a piece of statuary. It has to be seen in all its parts, and to be judged by the entire disposition of its masses in regard to the everlasting play of light. His " Age of Bronze " was so much a conceivable thing of life, as distinct from the merely inert thing of the older school, that he was accused of having cast it bodily from his model, and he was compelled to take extraordinary pains to show that he had done nothing of the sort. After this came the " John the Baptist Preaching "—marvellous again in precisely the same way. It is a real man speaking to his fellows, and so wholly absorbed in his message that the whole body of him is in utterance with movements conformable to the working of his soul. He is not thinking of how he stands, or how he walks, for walking he is, but simply of what he has to say; and the last thing of which he is to be suspected is the consciousness of what he is doing. It is almost ridiculous in some of its sincerities, ridiculous in its suggestion of the utter absence of the sense of effect. The " Burghers of Calais " came later, as another revolt. The revolt might have counted for little with the general beholder, but the note of sincerity was manifest to all. The mythical child of Nature might have judged the work and **A Dreamer in Marble and Bronze** found it good—the burghers defiant in their dejection, dejected in their defiance, with the hanging lips of scorn and of despair. Think how such a subject might have fared in a studio of the Beaux Arts, and we shall realise the immense advance.

With the Balzac that came long after, Rodin reached his present manner, which is but the old one perfected in the sense of character and freedom of handling, in the deeper learning of the relation of masses, and withal in the profound sense of the symbol, and of the majesty and the greatness of life. He is now a sort of mystic sketching with the chisel as others sketch with the crayon, a Dante, a Blake, a Maeterlinck, dreaming in marble or in bronze. He loses himself now and then, but such misadventure is inseparable from the finding of any new thing. He has enlarged the bounds of sculpture; that is the main point.

Is this to say that he has destroyed the old idealism of the real classic schools or even of the academies ? Nothing of the sort. That was, and is, a real thing, too, in its search after one kind of perfection of proportion, and of the perfection of line. He has only shown that it has not exhausted all other possibilities of the quest. The Laocoon, with its divinely restrained anguish and its perfect beauty in distortion, is no less true to one conception of great art than Rodin's famished Ugolino, with the light almost shining through his ribs, is true to another. The point of interest in the new art of France is that it is one with the literature **Results of Experiments in Art** in being experimental, and something beyond it, in the sense of nature and in the sense of life. Expression of character now stands in the forefront, as distinct from the expression of mere ideals. All the reactions are still possible in all the arts; and the next one in painting and in sculpture may be in the direction of the old classic repose. The good of each successful experiment is that it still leaves some precious addition to the stock of ideas. There is no finality in anything, simply because there is none in the aspirations of the human spirit. The legend of Eden is still a valid one : we are ever trying to walk as gods.

If France has been less active than of old in science, as generally understood, it is perhaps only because her present quest is for science in all the arts. Everything in France turns on the religious question; it goes straight to the roots of the national life. In a sense there are only two parties in the country—believers and unbelievers. All others are merged in these. You are a clerical, an agnostic, or an atheist, in the first place ; the political badge comes after, as it may.

The Quarrel Between Church and State

The quarrel between Church and State dates from the Revolution—to go no further back. The Church estates were confiscated after the great upheaval, and parcelled out among various owners, mainly the peasantry. There was no undoing that; but when Napoleon I. came to restore the fabric of institutions, he found a way out of the difficulty. He frankly recognised all the religions—Catholic, Protestant, and Jewish—gave them the right to acquire fresh property, and paid the salaries of their priesthood from public funds as a sort of compensation for the loss of their former income. The State acquired certain privileges of control in return, needless to mention here.

This concordat, as it was called, worked fairly well until our time. Then it was found that the Church was in a way to become as rich as ever by the offerings of the faithful, and to take itself seriously once more as the censor of thought. She was at the same time suspicious of popular government, and was held to be a secret agent of reaction. Hence came a revival of the old and ominous cry of " the Republic in danger," and with it a determination to destroy the concordat, to reduce Catholicism to the status of a mere pious opinion, and to deprive that and the other faiths of all official support. This policy was found to unite all the discordant elements of the Republican majority. The popular party—as its strength was measured by votes—was opposed to all religion, as such ; the professorial and the middle class generally were scandalised by the claims of the Church to the censorship of ideas.

The War Against Religion

So the war broke out, with the result of disaster after disaster to the clerical power. The teaching orders, which had a sort of monopoly of the elementary schools, were broken up. Much of the wealth of the Catholic body began to go the old way of confiscation, though a good deal of it was saved by its confidential transfer as private property to the hands of the faithful. The Church was disestablished, the State salaries to the priesthood were withdrawn, while a pension scheme, offered as a sort of compensation for them, was rejected with contumely at the bidding of Rome.

The Protestants and the Jews readily accepted the new state of things, and undertook to make the support of their systems wholly a matter of private and voluntary concern. The Catholics, against whom these measures were really directed, resisted from first to last. But the measures were so acceptable to the governing majority, ruling through the ballot box, that all active resistance was vain. Successive Ministries lived on the policy of suppression. M. Waldeck Rousseau kept his Government together by this means ; so did M. Combes, and M. Clemenceau after him. No matter what the state of the game in party politics, each held this trump card in reserve for emergencies, and won with it. Right or wrong, it is unquestionably the policy of the masses that hold the mastery in France.

Renan the Genial Sceptic

Meantime the Church was not idle ; and the war was transferred from politics to literature. M. Rod has given us an interesting history of this new clerical reaction in his " Ideés Morales du Temps Présent." The movement found " the classes " very much under the sway of that genial sceptic, M. Renan ; it left them largely in the hands of M. Brunetière, the Catholic devotee. Renan was scepticism absolute and self-satisfied, scepticism as a dogma, and sufficient to all the needs of the intelligence, if not exactly of the soul. When his disciples began to look for something more, they found it in the pessimism of Schopenhauer. The reaction against this doctrine, with its revolutionary implications, led straight to the reverence of tradition as the convenient depository of the results of human experience and the only sure guide. M. Brunetière, a sort of pontiff of criticism and literature, boldly proclaimed Catholicism as at once a polity and a system of faith. With this, the more cultivated thought of France reached its positive current ; and at the present time of writing it has irresistible attraction for many minds. M. Bourget, as a thinker, is of that school. M. Jules Lemaître has made a new departure ; and, while insisting on the necessity of the religious idea, has found its true source and its authority in our " most distinguished sentiments." It reads like the end of a letter; it is meant for a confession of belief. But the literary reaction is nothing as compared with the solid force of custom that makes for the old cult. The mother of the family in France is, as a rule, Catholic and pious, whatever the father may be ; and this in all classes, and in town and country alike. There are two to reckon with in marriage, and when one of them insists on the blessing of the Church, the other has generally to give way.

The children thus get their Catholic teaching, no matter who gives it to them—the mother or the priest—and they make their first communion with all the modest pomp and ceremony that attend the rite. Many of the boys, no doubt, will grow up half-ashamed of it as they pass **Claims of** through the workshop; with **the Church** the girls its effects are rarely **of Rome** lost. And even among the urban masses and the politicians, the very ultras of infidelity often consent to have their daughters brought up in the Catholic faith. One other tribute to the force of custom must not be forgotten : the churches are open still and as thronged as ever, just as though nothing had happened. Probably, if Rome could be induced to abate half her claims to the absolute direction of the human spirit, her opponents would abate more than half their hostility. The conflict in its acute stage is the result of a natural intolerance and of an incapacity for give and take, of which neither side has the monopoly.

All sorts of attempts were made, both within the Church and without, to establish a basis of agreement between the disputants. The French bishops, or many of them, lent a favourable ear to schemes of compromise, but were overruled from Rome. The Liberal, or modernising Catholic party, represented if not exactly led by the Abbé Loisy, pleaded eloquently for a reconciliation with modern thought, and for an abatement of the Papal claim to supremacy in this domain. But this writer was peremptorily ordered

by the Church to lay down his pen, or to write only in defence of ecclesiastical tradition. The Abbé still protests against the deliberate opposition of Rome to the whole intellectual and scientific movement of the age. " Suppress," he says, " this policy of ideas, and cease to attempt the impossible." In saying this, however, he **The Church's** claims to be a true son of the **Methods with** Church. So does Father **its Critics** Tyrrell, whose name is mentioned in this connection only to show that the movement of modernism is by no means confined to priests of French nationality. He demands not a brand new Catholic theology, but simply one under the progressive influence of that " spirit " of Christianity which was the original principle of life and growth. Rome, however, has dealt as roundly with these individuals as it dealt in the past with the Gallican and all the other Churches claiming an organic life of their own.

The philosophers, of course, have not been able to keep out of the mêlée. M. Goutroux, a member of the Institute, has made an attempt at reconciliation in his " Science et Religion." He tries to show that the conflicting forces are not so much concretes as tendencies, and that each is a complement of the other. They do wrong to strive for victory; they should strive for harmony. He is entitled to be heard, if only for the breadth and range of his survey, which includes Comte, Spencer, Haeckel, Ritschel, and William James.

But the greatest of all the apologists of free thought is M. Guyau, who, in a series of brilliant works recently brought to a close by his death, has tried to sketch a " morality without obligation or sanction "—to translate the title of his most famous book. This, like much else that appears in France nowadays, is an implicit abandonment of all attempts to find a common understanding with revealed religion in any of its forms, and an effort **Where** to discover the basis of a new **Agnosticism** faith in the nature of man. **Fails** The known defect of agnosticism is its want of the categorical imperative for conduct and for life. It is negative at the best ; and a positive concept is the only one that can afford a foundational base.

M. Guyau accordingly offers a formula for morals which asks no support from revelation, from tradition, or from ecclesiastical authority, and which derives its ideal from the realities of existence and its ethic from the constitution of man. His point is, to put it quite briefly, that the altruism which is our higher principle of being is in no wise dependent on theology, commonly so called. It is just as much an essential part of us as the egoism which is supposed to be the lower principle. It belongs to man's nature, on

Education the Battlefield of Religion its expansive and dynamic side, as distinct from the merely self-preserving instinct of the other part of him, and is a force which carries with it the authority of a vital function. In this way he claims to have solved the problem of egoism and altruism, hitherto the philosopher's stone of speculation, for the benefit of the moralists. We could not, he argues, be completely egoist, even if we tried. To live is to spend ourselves for the good of others, and is at least quite as much a law of biology as to store and acquire for our own good. Pleasure may be a consequence of altruism, but it is not necessarily the end. The end is the sheer necessity of living according to the law—the law of our being, not of any deliverance from any messenger or any mount of God.

In France, as in England, education is the battlefield of religion ; and one section is eagerly in search of a system that may replace the teaching of the old faith. Some think that moral teaching should be given in the schools, others that it should be rigorously excluded from them. M. Compère, a member of the Institute, and a general inspector of public instruction, offers a complete treatise on education, intellectual and moral, in which all the sanctions are derived from laws which are not religious in the conventional sense of the term. Another writer, M. De Monzie, who has held high educational rank, urges the banishment from the schools of ethical teaching in every shape and form. " No more scholastic idealism," he says, " no

Conflict of Church and State more lay instruction, no more moral catechism ; let us apply the school and the school-teacher to their essential and unique function—education." So the war goes on, and Rome is still unyielding as ever. It can hardly be otherwise. It is bound by its traditional claim for uniformity, as distinct from unity, and is perhaps too deeply pledged for the possibility of change. Policy might suggest the wisdom of compromise, but consistency

forbids. In the voting masses of France, largely alienated from all faith, with whom the issue rests, the Church has encountered a power as implacable as itself. They, too, seem incapable of compromise, and their infidelity is an aggressive force. The same stern necessity is laid on both sides, and they advance to the onset under the impulsion of fate. The conflict now belongs, not so much to the history of a nation as to the history of religion itself. Here, for the first time in the course of human affairs, is a triumphant majority determined to give form and body to a new policy which is nothing less than the complete emancipation of the human spirit from the religious idea.

It is a difficult thing to take a bird's-eye view of a nation, more especially as the results must very much depend on the eye of the bird. France is described as at the height of her greatness, or in full decadence, according to the observer. Some think that with her declining population, heavy taxes, her disordered Budget, with its immense allocations for all sorts of fanciful schemes, and its annual estimates of something like £160,000,000 sterling,

Triumphant Legions of Free Thought she cannot possibly long keep her place in the van of civilisation. Others rejoice in the fact that the Republic has won the goodwill of all the nations but one, founded a huge colonial empire, and enormously increased her trade with Britain and with the world. The present system is, at least, fully entitled to give itself the benefit of the doubt, and to boast of its contribution to the national prosperity. One thing is certain—the nation is now quite self-governing for good or ill, and in the full enjoyment of the privilege of suffering for her own mistakes.

The dynastic conflict is at an end ; the religious conflict alone threatens domestic peace. It is serious—that is not to be denied. Both sides are to blame, for both have yet to learn the lesson of intellectual toleration.

But, as commonly happens in such cases, the one that wins least sympathy from the beholder is the one that has the upper hand. The triumphant legions of free thought have everything to fear from a reaction. A powerful minority of the peasantry, with the women, who are nearly a majority of the whole people, will not patiently consent to be hindered in the exercise of an old faith while a new one is still in the making. Religion is an institution, as well as a matter of private concern, and it must naturally have immense claims on the veneration of millions of struggling souls. The United States form a stronger Republican government than even France, and, with them, religion is as free as the air. No doubt they are happily exempt from some of the peculiar difficulties of the sister polity. France has had to disestablish a Church; they never made the mistake of establishing one. Confiscation would seem to be an indispensable agency of government, since it has gone on all through history; but it is still a two-edged sword whose cut is apt to be quite as deadly in the swing as in the stroke. There would be sound policy in sending the Church on her way contented, even at the cost of pecuniary sacrifice, and thenceforth in leaving her severely alone.

In education the Republic has made immense strides. The best teaching is now accessible to every citizen, high or low, according to the measure of his powers. The communal school has become a sort of starting-point of social equality; there is no great distinction of classes under its roof, and the humblest pass with little pecuniary difficulty to the higher grades. **France's Educational Strides** The "Lycée," corresponding roughly to our middle-class school and public school, is incomparably superior to these in regard to its cost and to the technical quality of the instruction. Here, too, all classes study side by side. Beyond these are the schools for the army, navy, engineering, and other specialised callings. Beyond them, again, is the university, equally accessible to all, but in practice mainly reserved for students of law and of the teaching profession, since the other establishments provide for all ordinary needs.

The whole system has but one defect— it still leaves a good deal to be desired in regard to the culture of character. It is far better than our own as a preparation for careers; not so good as a preparation for life. But it is greatly improving in the sense of the educational value of sports and games, though, in that respect, its faults have been exaggerated. The British system still aims at training a select class for the work of government and administration; the French, with its strong equalitarian bias, insists on giving a chance to all. Here, again, the religious difficulty has been the lion in the path. France has been driven by the force of circumstances to resist the clerical claim to supremacy in education. The starting-point of this movement of revolt was the law on the composition of the superior council of education. The famous Article VII. of that measure declared that no one belonging to a "non-authorised" religious congregation should take part in the management of public or free education. At that time, the public schools were in the hands of over 30,000 members of a teaching brotherhood of the Church entirely free from secular supervision. The new law brought the lay teachers into the work, and established training colleges in each department.

Social Status of the French Woman

France has not escaped a "feminist" question, though her difficulties have not reached the same acute stage as our own. One reason is that socially the French woman holds a position with which she is fairly satisfied. She keeps much more in her class, and shares the class sentiment, and the class ideals. She is fully occupied, and with the substantial aid she gives her husband in business—and is expected to give—she escapes all risk of becoming the inhabitant of a doll's house.

This state of things can hardly be said to apply to the purely industrial classes. Here we find that, while the women count something more than as one to two of the men in numbers, they are paid something less than as two to one. It was a professional humorist rather than a strict logician who pleaded that, although he came to business later, he invariably went away earlier than his brother clerks.

The most satisfactory note of progress for the foreign observer is that the country is now wedded to the idea of peace. It has not lost the old spirit of resistance to aggression, but it has unquestionably parted with the old love of fighting for fighting's sake. The embarrassments of the French Government in Morocco have **France Wedded to Peace** really been due far less to German diplomacy than to the extraordinary unwillingness of the French people to enter into a war of adventure. The yearning for peace is shown by the very excesses of the demand for it, for some fanatics would abolish the army altogether. M. Jaurès, however, who best represents the entire French democracy, has declared that a war in defence of the country would unite all Frenchmen able to bear arms. He draws the line at aggression, and he would go so far as to compel all governments to submit disputes to arbitration, at the peril of being regarded as enemies of the human race.

Enough has been said to show that France is strong, prosperous, bold in experiment in literature, science and the arts, alive in every sense.

RICHARD WHITEING

THE PRINCIPALITY OF MONACO

GEOGRAPHICALLY, this tiny principality, with its area of eight square miles, and resident population of some 16,000, is at present an " enclave " of France, as the French Department of the Alpes Maritimes surrounds it on all sides, except to the south, where it borders on the Mediterranean. It may be said to owe its present political existence and independence to the good will of France, though its language and traditions are Italian. In the days of the French Revolution it actually did belong to France, but its independence was restored by the Allies in 1814, who, in the following year, placed it under the protection of the King of Sardinia. Up till 1851 the principality included Mentone and Roquebrune, but in that year the reigning prince, Charles III., ceded his rights

over them to France for nearly £200,000. The present ruler, Prince Albert, has absolute power. There is no elective Chamber, but there is a consultative Council of five members appointed by the Prince, who governs through a functionary with the title of Governor-General. The principality consists of three towns— Monaco, Condamine, and Monte Carlo. It is through the last named that Monaco is known to all the world, for Monaco simply means Monte Carlo, and Monte Carlo simply means gambling.

Monte Carlo, which is a few miles from Nice, the beautiful town on the Riviera so much frequented by the English, sprang into general notice with the building of its famous—or infamous—Casino in 1858, though gambling had begun there two years

MONTE CARLO, THE BEAUTIFUL PLEASURE RESORT

earlier. In 1861 Charles III. granted a concession for fifty years to run the place as a gambling concern in a highly elaborate way, the concession eventually passing into the hands of a joint-stock company, taking care at the same time to do everything that was possible to add to the great natural attractiveness of the site; for there is no doubt that Monte Carlo is one of the most charming and delightful spots in Europe, with an almost perfect winter climate. The company, which is called the Société Anonyme des Bains de Mer et du Cercle des Étrangers de Monaco, was given an extension of its privileges in 1898, and this new contract does not expire until 1947.

Practically the whole cost of the government of the principality is borne by this organisation, which, in addition, pays Prince Albert an annual sum of £70,000 up to 1917, when the sum will be increased to £80,000; in 1927 it is to rise to £90,000, and in 1937 to £100,000. Besides these sums, the company paid a bonus to the prince in 1899 of £400,000, and will pay to him another bonus of the amount of £600,000 in 1913. The company has a capital of £1,200,000, and its shares are valuable. These facts are eloquent testimony that the " tables " pay their proprietors, but nobody else, save the prince and a few others; yet there is little or no diminution in the volume of gambling from year to year. The truth is that the principality is a vast gambling hell, and it is this, and not its beauty, that mainly attracts to it many thousands of visitors every year. ROBERT MACHRAY

THE REPUBLIC OF ANDORRA

PERCHED amongst the high mountains of the Eastern Pyrenees, with one foot in France and the other in Spain, this small commonwealth — for that term really describes it better than republic—has existed for something like a thousand years. Its area is no more than 175 square miles, and its population about 6,000; it has never been any larger or more populous; yet for all this length of time it has been an independent and autonomous state, undergoing practically no change— a fact which finds no parallel in history save in the somewhat similar instance of the Republic of San Marino, in Italy. It is a patriarchal and even primitive little country, with only one good road through it, and that available only in fine weather, the other means of communication being mere hill tracks more suitable for goats than human beings. The most exciting event which has occurred in Andorra since the days of Charlemagne, who is said to have given it its first charter of freedom, was its connection with France by a line of telegraph in 1893, an innovation to which not a few of its inhabitants were bitterly opposed.

Though independent, Andorra is under a sort of joint suzerainty of France, whose influence is steadily increasing in the country, and of the Bishop of Urgel, a Spanish ecclesiastic, in whose diocese it was once included; the frontier of Andorra is some sixteen miles from the town of Urgel, in Spain. The republic consists of six parishes, each of which sends four members to a council; the council elect from themselves two syndics to preside over the destinies of the land. There are two criminal judges, called *viguiers* (vicars), one of whom is appointed by France and the other by the Bishop of Urgel. A civil judge is also elected alternately by France and the Bishop of Urgel. The Andorrans, however, remain indifferent to these symbols of authority, and imperturbably preserve their immemorial independence; but of late years the children of the better classes are being sent to France for their education. The postal and telegraphic arrangements, too, are under French control. On the other hand, the money in circulation is Spanish, and the language is Catalan.

The people themselves are a cheerful and sturdy race of mountaineers, chiefly concerned with their flocks and herds— when they do not happen to be engaged in smuggling, for which Andorra affords unique opportunities. Taxation is, to all intents, nil; but a sum of £40 is paid for " protection " each year to both France and the Bishop of Urgel, and the raising of this sum constitutes the main feature of the Andorran Budget. Perhaps nothing could more clearly show just what the country is than to say that while the first floor of its Palacio is occupied by the Council Chamber, the centre of its government, the ground floor is a stable for the horses of its executive and members of Parliament. ROBERT MACHRAY

ESSENTIAL INFORMATION ABOUT FRANCE

AREA AND POPULATION. France has an area of 207,054 square miles, and had, at the census of 1906, a population of 39,252,245. The natural increase of the population is the lowest in Europe, the total increase for the five-year period ending 1906 having been only 290,300, equalling ·15 per cent. per annum. The cities and towns with a population of over 100,000, are as follow :

Paris, 2,763,393 ; Marseilles, 517,498 ; Lyons, 472,114 ; Bordeaux, 251,917 ; Lille, 205,602 ; Toulouse, 149,438 ; St. Etienne, 146,788 ; Nice, 134,232 ; Nantes, 133,247 ; Le Hâvre, 132,430 ; Roubaix, 121,017 ; Rouen, 118,459 ; Nancy, 110,570 ; Reims, 109,859 ; Toulon, 103,549.

GOVERNMENT. The government of France is republican, and the legislative power is vested in a Chamber of Deputies (a Lower House) and a Senate (an Upper House). The Chamber of Deputies—584 members—is elected for four years on an adult suffrage, every citizen who has attained his majority and is not in military service having the vote. The Senate has 300 members, consisting of 225 departmental senators and 75 senators elected for life by the two Chambers jointly ; but since 1884 vacancies in the list of life senators are filled by departmental senators, the particular department electing the senator for the vacancy being settled by lot. The departmental senators are chosen by an electoral body consisting of delegates chosen by the municipal councils and of senators, deputies, and councillors of the department. Members of both Houses are paid. The two Chambers unite in a National Assembly, or Congress, to elect a President, who holds office for a term of seven years. The duties and powers of the President as defined by law are that he elects a Ministry from the two Chambers, although he may appoint to the Ministry men who are not members of either Chamber ; that he can adjourn the Chambers for a period not exceeding one month and not oftener than twice in one Session ; that he concludes with foreign Powers treaties which do not involve changes in the territory of France or her colonies. The President cannot declare war without the consent of both Houses, and every official act must be countersigned by a Minister. The Ministry consists of the Premier, or president of the Council, and eleven Ministers of departments.

FINANCE. The Budget proposals for 1908 anticipated a revenue of £154,145,801 and an expenditure of £155,145,668. The chief sources of revenue are direct taxes (land, buildings, trade licences, mining royalties, cycle tax, &c.), registration fees (changes in ownership of property, &c.), customs, tobacco monopoly, and post office. At the beginning of 1907 the National Debt of France stood at £1,213,923,596, and the interest absorbed £49,440,000 a year.

INDUSTRY AND COMMERCE. Two-thirds of the entire area of France is under grass or crops. According to acreage, the chief crops are wheat, oats, grapes, potatoes, rye, clover, beets, barley, buckwheat, and maize. Orchards account for four million acres, and silk culture give employment to 123,761 persons. Mines employ 199,000 workers, the chief minerals being coal, iron ore, salt, zinc, antimony, lead and silver, manganese, arsenic, and copper. The total value of French imports for 1908 was £243,634,000, and of French exports £210,878,000. The chief articles of import are wool, coal and coke, raw cotton, raw silk, oil seeds, hides and furs, and timber. The chief exports are silks, cottons, raw wool, woollens, wine, raw silk, linen and clothes, furs and skins.

COLONIES. French colonies have an area of 4,397,826 square miles and a population of 56,117,740, as follow :

					Square miles.	Population.
ASIA :						
India	..	..	..	..	196	275,000
Annam	..	..	..	..	52,100	6,124,000
Cambodia	..	..	..	..	37,400	1,500,000
Cochin-China	..	..	..	..	20,000	2,968,000
Tonking	..				46,000	10,000,000
Laos	..	..	..	..	98,400	650,000
AFRICA :						
Algeria	..	..	..	..	343,500	5,158,050
Tunis	..	..	..	..	64,600	1,900,000
Sahara	..	..	..	..	1,944,000	800,000
Senegal	..	..	..	..	9,070	107,800
Senegambia and Niger		..	..	..	370,000	8,000,000
French Guinea..		..	..	..	95,000	2,200,000
Ivory Coast	..	..	..	..	120,000	2,000,000
Dahomey	..	..	..	..	65,000	1,000,000
Congo	..	..	..	..	850,000	10,000,000
Somali Coast and Dependencies		..			12,000	50,000
Réunion	..	..	..	..	970	173,200
Comoro Islands		..	..	..	620	47,000
Mayotte	..	..	..	..	140	11,640
Madagascar	..	..	..	..	228,000	2,644,700
AMERICA :						
Guiana	..	..	..	..	30,500	32,910
Guadeloupe	..	..	..	..	688	182,110
Martinique	..	..	..	..	380	203,780
St. Pierre and Miquelon		..	..	..	92	6,250
OCEANIA :						
New Caledonia ..		..	..	..	7,650	53,350
Other Pacific Islands ..		..	..	..	1,520	29,000

CURRENCY. France, Belgium, Italy, Switzerland, and Greece are members of a monetary convention, whereby it is agreed that the gold and silver coins of the respective countries shall have the same fineness, weight, diameter, and current value. The same monetary system has been adopted, partly or entirely, by Spain, Roumania, Bulgaria, Servia, Russia, Finland, and many South American States :

Bronze coins
- 1 centime = 1/10d.
- 5 centimes = ½d.
- 10 centimes = 1d.

Silver coins
- 20 centimes = 2d.
- 50 centimes = ½ franc = 5d. (almost)
- 100 centimes = 1 franc = 9 3/5d.
- 2 francs = 1s. 7 1/5d.
- 5 francs = 4s.

Gold coins
- 10 francs = 8s.
- 20 francs = 16s.

There is no coin for 1 centime. A 5-centime piece is popularly known as a sou, but it is illegal to mark merchandise in sous. The 20-centime coin and the silver 5-franc piece are seldom seen, the coinage of the latter being temporarily suspended.

WEIGHTS AND MEASURES. The weights and measures are metric [see page 5399]. This applies also to most of the French colonies.

POSTAGES. Great Britain to France. Letters 2½d. for first ounce and 1½d. for each additional ounce or part thereof. Printed papers, commercial papers, and samples, ½d. per 2 oz., with a minimum of 2½d. for commercial papers and 1d. for samples. Parcel post, 1s. 4d., 1s. 9d., and 2s. 2d. for 3, 7, and 11 lb. respectively.

TELEGRAMS. 2d. per word, with minimum charge of 10d. Telephonic communication between London and about 500 French cities and towns is possible at a fee of 8s. for a three minutes' conversation, except to Bordeaux, Lyons, Marseilles, and St Etienne, for which the charge is 10s.

MONACO

This small principality is surrounded by French territory, except on its seaward side. Its area is eight square miles, and its population is 16,000. There are three towns—Monaco, 3,292 ; Condamine, 6,218 ; and Monte Carlo, 3,794. The reigning prince is Prince Albert (born 1848 ; succeeded his father, 1889), who is an absolute monarch, and entrusts the government to a council of three. All the territory is urban, so there is no agriculture. The revenue is derived almost exclusively from the gaming-tables, which are owned by a company.

THE METRIC SYSTEM AND BRITISH EQUIVALENTS

The Metric, or decimal, System of Weights and Measures is the most scientific in use as a standard by any country. It is a legacy of the French Revolution. A committee of scientific men, appointed by the Academy of Sciences at the instance of the French Government, agreed that the quadrant of the earth's surface—from the North Pole to the Equator—measured through Paris, should be taken as the basis of the new system. The metre was supposed to be one ten-millionth part of this quadrant, although it has been ascertained that it is inaccurate to the extent of one four-thousandth part. The exact length of the metre is 39·370113 inches. The unit of surface measure is the *are*, which is the square of 10 metres (1 dekametre). The cubic unit is the *stere*, which is a cubic metre. The unit of capacity measure is the *litre*, which is the capacity of the cube of one-tenth of a metre (a decimetre). The unit of weight is the *gramme*, which is the weight of a cubic centimetre of distilled water at a temperature of 32° Fahr. From these units the metric system is built up with the help of a series of prefixes:

Milli =	÷	1,000	Deka =	×	10
Centi =	÷	100	Hecto =	×	100
Deci =	÷	10	Kilo =	×	1,000
			Myria =	×	10,000

Thus, a *centigramme* means one-hundredth part of a gramme, and a *dekametre* means ten metres.

LINEAL MEASURE

	1 millimetre =	·0394 inch.	1 inch	=	25 millimetres.
10 millimetres	= 1 centimetre =	·394 inch.	12 inches = 1 foot	=	305 millimetres.
10 centimetres	= 1 decimetre =	3·937 inches.	3 feet = 1 yard	=	914 millimetres.
10 decimetres	= 1 metre =	39·3708 in.,or about 3ft.3¼in.	5½ yards = 1 pole	=	5·029 metres.
10 metres	= 1 dekametre =	32 5/6th feet.	4 poles = 1 chain	=	20·117 metres.
10 dekametres	= 1 hectometre =	·0621, or about 1/16th mile	10 chains = 1 furlong	=	2 hectometres 1·168 metres
10 hectometres	= 1 kilometre =	·6214, or about ⅝th mile	8 furlongs = 1 mile	=	1·609343 kilometres, or
10 kilometres	= 1 myriametre =	6·214,or about 6 1/5th miles			about 1 3/5th kilometres.

SQUARE, OR SUPERFICIAL, MEASURE

	1 milliare	= 1 sq. ft. 11 sq. ins.	1 sq. inch	=	·006 milliares.
10 milliares	= 1 centiare	= 1 sq. yd. 1 sq. ft. 110 sq.ins.	144 sq. ins. = 1 sq. foot	=	·9 milliares.
10 centiares	= 1 deciare	= 11 sq.yds. 8 sq.ft. 92 sq.ins.	9 sq. ft. = 1 sq. yard	=	8 milliares.
10 deciares	= 1 are	= 119·603321 sq. yds.	30¼ sq. yds. = 1 perch	=	25·3 centiares.
10 ares	= 1 dekare	= 1196·03321 sq. yds.	16 perches = 1 sq. chain	=	4·047 ares.
10 dekares	= 1 hectare	= 2·471 acres.	2½ sq. chains = 1 rood	=	10·117 ares.
10 hectares	= 1 kiloare	= 24·71 acres.	4 roods = 1 acre	=	·40468 hectares.
10 kiloares	= 1 myriare	= 247·1 acres.	640 acres = 1 sq. mile	=	258·99848 hectares.

CUBIC MEASURE

	1 millistere	= 61 cub. ins.	1 cubic inch	=	0·164 millistere.
10 millisteres	= 1 centistere	= 610 cub. ins.	1728 cub. ins. = 1 cub. foot	=	2·8 centisteres.
10 centisteres	= 1 decistere	= 3 cub. ft. 918 cub. ins.	27 cub. feet = 1 cub. yard	=	7·65 decisteres.
10 decisteres	= 1 stere	= 35·31658 cub. ft.			
10 steres	= 1 dekastere	= 353·1658 cub. ft.			

MEASURE OF CAPACITY

	1 millilitre	=	·007 gills.	1 gill	= 1·42 decilitres.
10 millilitres	= 1 centilitre	=	·07 gills.	4 gills = 1 pint	= 5·63 decilitres.
10 centilitres	= 1 decilitre	=	·7 gills.	2 pints = 1 quart	= 1·136 litres.
10 decilitres	= 1 litre	=	1·76 pints.	4 quarts = 1 gallon	= 4·546 litres.
10 litres	= 1 dekalitre	=	1 peck 1½ pints.	2 gallons = 1 peck	= 9·092 litres.
10 dekalitres	= 1 hectolitre	=	2·750 bushels.	4 pecks = 1 bushel	= 36·388 litres.
10 hectolitres	= 1 kilolitre	=	3·4371 quarters.	8 bushels = 1 quarter	= 2·90942 hectolitres.
10 kilolitres	= 1 myrialitre	=	34·371 quarters.	4½ quarters = 1 chaldron	= 13·09237 hectolitres.

COMMERCIAL WEIGHT

	1 milligramme	=	·015 grain.	1 dram	= 1·772 grms.
10 milligrammes	= 1 centigramme	=	·154 grain.	16 drams = 1 ounce	= 28·349 grms.
10 centigrammes	= 1 decigramme	=	1·5432 grains.	16 ounces = 1 pound	= ·453592 kgrs.
10 decigrammes	= 1 gramme	=	15·432 grains.		or 9/20th kgr. (about).
10 grammes	= 1 dekagramme	=	5 drs. 18 grs.	14 pounds = 1 stone	= 6·350294 kgrs.
10 dekagrammes	= 1 hectogramme	=	3 oz. 8 dr. 12 gr.	2 stones = 1 quarter	= 12·700588 kgrs.
10 hectogrammes	= 1 kilogramme	=	2·2046 lbs.	4 quarters = 1 hundredweight	= 50·802352 kgrs.
10 kilogrammes	= 1 myriagramme	=	1·575 stones.	20 hundredweights = 1 ton	= 1016·047037 kgrs.
10 myriagrammes	= 1 quintal	=	1·96841 cwt.		
10 quintals	= 1 millier, or tonne	=	19·68411 cwt.		

APOTHECARIES' WEIGHT

In the metric system the apothecaries' weights are the same as the ordinary weights; hence the French tables below are given only that their equivalents in British apothecaries' weight may be given:

	1 milligramme	=	·015 grain.		
10 milligrammes	= 1 centigramme	=	·154 grain.	1 grain	= 65 milligrammes.
10 centigrammes	= 1 decigramme	=	1·5432 grains.	20 grains = 1 scruple	= 1·296 grammes.
10 decigrammes	= 1 gramme	=	15·432 grains.	3 scruples = 1 drachm	= 3·888 grammes.
10 grammes	= 1 dekagramme	=	2 drs.1 sc.14 grs.	8 drachms = 1 ounce	= 31·1035 grammes.
10 dekagrammes	= 1 hectogramme	=	3 ozs. 1 dr. 2 scs. 3 grs.		
10 hectogrammes	= 1 kilogramme	=	32 ozs. 1 dr. 12 grs.		

APOTHECARIES' FLUID MEASURE

	1 millilitre	= 16·3 minims.	1 minim	=	·059 millilitre.
10 millilitres	= 1 centilitre	= 2·8157 fl. drs.	20 minims = 1 fluid scruple	=	1·184 millilitres.
10 centilitres	= 1 decilitre	= 3·5 fl. ozs.	3 fluid scruples = 1 fluid drachm	=	3·552 millilitres.
10 decilitres	= 1 litre	= 35·196 fl. ozs.	8 fluid drachms = 1 fluid ounce	=	28·4122591 mills.
			20 fluid ounces = 1 pint	=	·568245 litres.

TROY WEIGHT

The metric system has no special table for troy weights, the weight of gold and other precious metals being computed by the ordinary metric weight. The tables below are given only that the metric equivalent of British troy weights may be shown:

	1 milligramme	=	·0154 grains.	1 grain	= 65 milligrammes.
10 milligrammes	= 1 centigramme	=	·1543 grains.	24 grains = 1 pennyweight	= 1·555 grammes.
10 centigrammes	= 1 decigramme	=	1·5432 grains.	20 pennyweights = 1 ounce	= 31·1035 grammes.
10 decigrammes	= 1 gramme	=	15·4323564 grs.		
10 grammes	= 1 dekagramme	=	6 dwt. 10 grs.		
10 dekagrammes	= 1 hectogramme	=	3 oz. 4 dwt. 7 gr.		
10 hectogrammes	= 1 kilogramme	=	32 ozs. 3 dwts.		

The pearl grain equals 51·83915 milligrammes; the pearl carat contains 3·16381 pearl grains, and is equal to 164·24253 milligrammes. The diamond grain is equal to 51·83916 milligrammes and the diamond carat (3·1683 diamond grains) is equal to 205 milligrammes.

ESSENTIAL INFORMATION ABOUT SPAIN & PORTUGAL

SPAIN

AREA AND POPULATION. The total area of Spain is 194,783 square miles, including the Balearic and Canary Islands, which are provinces of Spain. The total population is (census of 1900) 18,618,086. The towns with a population of over 100,000 are Madrid, 539,835; Barcelona, 533,000; Valencia, 213,530; Sevilla, 148,315; Malaga, 130,109; Murcia, 111,539. Two other towns, Carthagena and Zaragoza (Saragossa), were over 99,000 at last census, and are now probably over 100,000.

GOVERNMENT. Spain is a constitutional monarchy, legislative power being vested in the King and the Cortes, which consists of two houses—a Senate and a Congress. Half of the Senate, or Upper House, is elected by the largest taxpayers, the universities, the church, and provincial states; the other half is composed of princes who have attained their majority, grandees, high army and naval officers, and presidents of several tribunals. Half of the elected senators must retire every five years, and all the elected senators must be elected upon a dissolution of the Senate, by the king. The Lower House, or Congress, is composed of 406 members, elected for five years by male citizens 25 years of age. The executive is vested in the monarch and nine Ministers of State.

MONARCH. The King is Alfonso XIII. (born on May 17, 1886 after the death of his father), who became king at birth.

REVENUE. The estimates of revenue and expenditure for 1908 were £37,843,000 and £37,206,130 respectively. The chief sources of revenue are direct taxes on land, trade, mines, etc., customs, excise, tobacco monopoly and lotteries. At the end of 1907 the Spanish national debt was £332,057,595, involving an annual interest charge of £14,732,819.

INDUSTRY AND COMMERCE. About 80 per cent. of the soil of Spain is reckoned as productive, one-third of it being under cereal crops and gardens, 20 per cent. under fruits, 20 per cent. under natural grass, and the remainder being vineyards and olive trees. The chief cereal crops are wheat, barley, rye, maize, oats, and rice. Hemp and flax are also grown. The total production of wine—sherry, malaga and alicante—is almost 400,000,000 gallons, and the production of olive oil is about 40,000,000 gallons. Silk culture is carried on principally in the South-eastern provinces. Stock raising—horses, cattle, mules and asses, sheep, goats and pigs—is important. Spain has great mineral wealth—iron, coal, copper, zinc, cobalt, lead, quicksilver, sulphate of soda, salt, sulphur and phosphorus—the annual output being of about £8,000,000 value, but its exploitation is almost entirely in foreign hands. There are a few manufactories, including cotton, woollen and silk industries, paper and glass-making, cork turning and sugar refining. The total imports in 1908 were of the value of £38,357,000 and the exports £35,616 000 The chief exports are wine, ores, olive oil, cattle, raisins, oranges, cork, esparto, wool, salt and quicksilver.

COLONIES. Spain has still a few colonial possessions, although she was stripped of Cuba, Porto Rico, the Philippines, receiving £4,000,000 for the latter by the United States in 1898, and sold the Caroline and Pelew Islands to Germany in 1899. The Canary Islands are provinces of Spain and the sole Spanish colonies are now the few in West or Equatorial Africa, as follow:

	Sq. miles.	Population.
Rio de Oro and Adrar	70,000	130,000
Rio Muni and Cape San Juan	9,800	140,000
Fernando Po, Annabon, Corisco, Great and Little Elobey	780	21,946
Total ..	80,580	291,946

These colonies have little or no commercial or economic value to Spain and they constitute an annual charge.

CURRENCY. The currency of Spain was assimilated to that of the Latin Monetary Union, in 1871 [see page 5398]. The exquivalent of a centime is a *centesimo*, and 100 centesimos make one *peseta*, which equals a franc.

WEIGHTS AND MEASURES. The system is metric [see page 5399], but Spanish names are given to the various denominations. These names, however, differ from the French, usually only by one letter, mètre becoming *metro* (plural *metri*), centimètre becoming centimetro, and so on, aire becoming *area*, litre becoming *litro* (plural *litri*), and gramme becoming *gramo*. Some of the old Spanish measures are still found in occasional practice.

POSTAL RATES. Great Britain to Spain, letters, papers and samples as for France [see page 5398]. Parcel post, 1s. 6d., 2s. and 2s. 6d. for 3 lb., 7 lb., and 11 lb. respectively. No parcel insurance.

TELEGRAMS. Great Britain to Spain, 3d. per word with 1s. minimum.

PORTUGAL

AREA AND POPULATION. The area of Portugal, including the Azores and Madeira, which are parts of the kingdom, is 35,490 square miles, and the population is 5,423,132. The island area included in above is 1,236 square miles, and the island population is 406,865. The chief towns are Lisbon (the capital), 356,000; Oporto, 167,955; Braga, 24,202; Setubal, 22,074; Funchal (Madeira), 20,844; Coimbra, 18,144; Ponta Delgada (Azores) 17,620.

GOVERNMENT. Portugal is a constitutional hereditary monarchy, with two Legislative Chambers, the Camera dos Pares or House of Peers, and the Camera dos Deputados or House of Commons, which are known collectively as the Cortes Geraes. Hereditary peers are being abolished by a gradual process. The Upper House consists of peers who are nominated for life by the king, princes of the royal house, and twelve bishops. The Lower House consists of 148 deputies, with seven colonial deputies additional, elected for three years on a manhood, educational, and low tax-paying qualification. Deputies must have certain academic qualifications or a certain income. If a Parliament is dissolved its successor must be called within three months.

MONARCH. The reigning king is Manoel II. (Manuel is the English form). He was born on November 15th, 1889, and succeeded his father upon the assassination of his brother and father on February 1st, 1908.

REVENUE. The estimated revenue for 1908–1909 was £14,106,000, and the estimated expenditure £14,540,000. The funded debt of Portugal in June, 1908, was £154,122,800.

INDUSTRY AND COMMERCE. Portugal is a mountainous country, and almost half of the total area is waste land. Half of the remainder is in pasture or fallow, and of the rest half is devoted to cereal culture. Then comes fruit-trees, pulse, and other non-cereal crops and vineyards. The chief highland crops are wheat, barley, oats, maize, flax, hemp, and grapes. In the lowlands the chief crops are rice, olives, oranges, lemons, citrons, figs, and almonds. There is a large forest area of oak, chestnut, pine, and cork. The minerals worked are important, and consist of copper, lead, tin, antimony, coal, manganese, and slate. There are several manufactories, including gloves, fabrics of silk, wool, linen and cotton, metal and earthenware, and tobacco. In 1907 the value of the imports was £15,959,600, and the value of the exports was £9,778,600. Half the value of the exports was for wine, and the most important of the remainder were cork, cattle, copper ore, fruits, oil, sardines.

COLONIES. The colonies of Portugal are as follow:

	Square miles.	Population.
AFRICAN COLONIES:		
Cape Verde Islands	1,480	147,424
Guinea	13,940	820,000
Princes and St. Thomas' Islands	360	42,103
Angola	484,800	4,119,000
East Africa	293,400	3,120,000
ASIATIC COLONIES:		
Goa (India)	1,469	475,513
Damao and Diu (India)	169	56,285
Timor and adjacent islands	7,330	300,000
Macao (China)	4	63,991
Total ..	802,952	9,144,316

CURRENCY. The unit of money value is the *real* or *ree* (plural *reis*), but the coin has no existence in fact, its value being only one-twentieth of one penny. It is the one-thousandth part of a milreis, which is worth 4s. 5⅓d. The currency may be tabulated thus:

1 real or ree = ·05d.
1000 reis = 1 milreis = 4s. 5·3d.
1000 milreis = 1 conto = £222 4s. 5d.

The coins in use are:

Bronze: 5, 10, and 20 reis (value about ¼d., ½d., and 1d. respectively).
Nickel: 50 and 100 reis (value 2⅔d. and 5⅓d. respectively).
Silver – 200 reis = 2 testoon = 10⅔d.
– 500 reis = 5 testoon = 2s. 2⅔d.
–1,000 reis = 10 testoon = 4s. 5⅔d.
Gold: 1, 2, 5, and 10 milreis.

There is a large circulation of Bank of Portugal paper, and the British gold sovereign is legal tender for 4,500 reis. In Portuguese India the currency is the same as in British India. In other Portuguese colonies the currency is that of Portugal.

WEIGHTS AND MEASURES. The metric system is followed and the names are as in France. [See page 5399.]

POSTAL AND TELEGRAPH RATES. Great Britain to Portugal as for Spain [see above], but parcel-post rates to Portuguese Colonies are higher. Parcel-post to Portugal, if overland through France and Spain, is 6d. per parcel more than rates given above.

ANDORRA

Andorra is an interesting pocket republic in the Eastern Pyrenees, and is under the joint suzerainty of France and Spain. Its area is 175 square miles, and the estimates of its population vary from 5,000 to 15,000. The chief occupation is smuggling, with some agriculture, stock raising, and trade in wood and wool. Government is by a council of 24 members, elected by the heads of families, and they elect a President for four years.

SPAIN IN OUR OWN TIME
THE NATION'S NEW ERA OF PROGRESS
By Martin Hume, M.A.

THE revolution of 1868 in Spain, profound and disintegrating as it looked for a time, was almost purely political in its direct results. The already recognised right of private judgment in religion was, it is true, slightly extended, but in every other respect the national life was barely affected by the violent outburst which expelled Isabella II. from her throne and country. There was no radical change effected in social relations, in the organisation and compensation of labour, in the basis of taxation, or in the relations between Church and State.

The entire rearrangement of political parties, which was the principal outcome of the revolution, prepared the way for far-reaching changes which are now operative or impending. The accession to the revolutionary ranks of the "Union Liberal," or Moderate Liberals, ensured the success of the revolt, but it also involved the disappearance of the party itself as a separate entity; and on the restoration of Alfonso XII., in 1875, a new division of political parties was practically complete. The old purely Conservative party had disappeared as a governing factor, and the new Conservatives, who had brought about the restoration, were evolved as a separate political group from the moderate elements of the revolution itself. Thus Spain turned her back upon the past, and since then has been governed by parties, which, whether they call themselves Liberals, **Queen Christina as Regent** Conservatives, or Democrats, are all essentially Liberal in their dependence upon popular sentiment and their acknowledgment of the supremacy of the national will. For many years of the long regency of Queen Christina, 1885–1901, politicians of both parties chivalrously abstained from action likely to disturb or excite the public mind, the Liberal party especially postponing its convictions, both on religious and social problems, to the need for consolidating the throne of the child-king by the support of Spaniards of all opinions. The attitude of the official Liberal party led finally to the formation of a strong new group of Democrats pledged to far-reaching social reforms and **Accession of King Alfonso XIII.** to antagonism to the influence of the clergy, but on each occasion that this Democratic party—now led with conspicuous ability by Señor Canalejas—has coalesced with the traditional Liberals under Señor Moret for the purpose of forming a government, the coalition has been unable to withstand the strain imposed by divergent opinions, mainly on the question of the Church and the conventual orders.

The accession to effective kingship of Alfonso XIII., amidst the universal goodwill of his people, has not to any considerable extent altered the situation created and fixed by his wise and prudent mother during her long regency. The political parties alternate in power as before, the real differences between their respective policies in office being extremely slight, however democratic may be the professions of the Liberal party when in opposition, since both groups of politicians have agreed to rule constitutionally and accept the principle of popular government.

Both parties, it is true, are equally ready to manipulate the elections in the most unblushing manner in order to secure power and office for themselves; but to the people at large it matters little which political combination rules them, since the effect in either case is practically the same. The main aspirations of the country, indeed, are less towards political than towards social change, as the people have already lost faith, as a result of experience, in the efficiency of political convulsions to remedy the ills of which they complain. In the meanwhile the Socialist party in the country has increased enormously, especially in Catalonia and Biscay, where the manufacturing activity is most marked; and, as a consequence, projected legislation, under the guidance of either of the two great political parties, has mainly taken the form of Factory Acts, the limitation of the hours of labour, the restriction of the industrial employment of children, and other measures directed towards the social amelioration of the working classes. A remarkable instance of this is given by the Act for the compulsory Sunday closing of all business establishments, except those devoted to the sale of prepared food, and the legal enforcement of a weekly day of rest in all trades.

Establishing A Weekly Day of Rest

In this both Socialists and Clericals have co-operated, although it forms a revolution in the traditional habits of the people, and has only been rendered operative at the cost of considerable friction. Another demand persistently made by working-class politicians, but hitherto unattained, owing to party dissensions, is the regulation of the monastic establishments with the object of suppressing the unfair industrial competition with regular workmen arising out of the extensive manufactories carried on by some of the conventual houses.

The most striking change, however, in the position of Spain in the last few years is to be seen in the re-entry of the country into active participation in the concert of European nations. This had been traditionally difficult, as the mutual jealousies of France and Britain had usually stood in the way of a close co-operation between Spain and both of those countries simultaneously. The exigencies of European politics having drawn together Britain and France, the principal obstacle to the resumption by Spain of an important part in international politics was removed, and the situation, particularly as regards Mediterranean problems, was profoundly affected thereby. It had been an article of faith with Spaniards for centuries, and especially since their successful war with Morocco in 1860, that when the inevitable break up of the Moorish Empire in North-West Africa should take place Spain must inherit a considerable share of the country opposite her own shores, in addition to the places of arms she already held at Melilla

Spain and the Moorish Empire

and Ceuta. Unfortunately for her, when the Anglo-French agreement was signed on April 8th, 1904, recognising on the part of Great Britain the future preponderating influence of France in Morocco, Spain was unready and badly served diplomatically, and her traditional interests were to a great extent ignored, as indeed were those of England. But the subsequent Act of Algeciras to some slight extent recognised Spain's right to take part in the civilisation of the neighbouring Moslem country, by conferring upon her jointly with France a mandate of the Powers to police the ports in the interests of the world generally.

Spain has therefore had to sacrifice many of her hopes and dreams in this direction; but it is evident that however much French dominion may in time extend over Morocco, the proximity and long-standing intercommunication between the latter country and Spain will ensure that the predominating ethnological and civilising element will be Spanish. Nor has the sacrifice been entirely without compensation. The cordial friendship both with Britain and France, cemented in the former case by the auspicious marriage of King Alfonso XIII. with an English princess, not only ensures, as far as is humanly possible, Spain's own immunity from attack, but very greatly increases the probability of continued European peace. The reconstruction of the Spanish navy, destroyed in the Spanish-American War, has in the opinion of Spaniards become a necessity of the new international importance of their country, and several proposals with that object have been made to successive Parliaments. The financial sacrifices necessary for the purpose, however, prevented the adoption of any large naval scheme until late in 1908, when the difficulties were overcome and a large shipbuilding programme was definitely adopted. On the fulfilment of this, in the course of three or four years, Spain will once more enter into the circle of important maritime Powers.

Spain's Large Shipbuilding Programme

Although the agricultural and viticultural districts of the country are still suffering much poverty and hardship, Spain has in several unexpected ways greatly benefited by the loss of her great colonies in the West Indies and the Philippines, in addition to the relief afforded by the cessation of the drain of men and money which had continued for so many years in her effort to hold them. The sudden disappearance of the protected colonial markets for Spanish goods threw the Catalan manufacturers into a panic of fear for the very existence of their numerous industries, but matters in this respect have righted themselves in an extraordinary manner. The adoption of a protective fiscal policy, in 1892, by Spain had caused a great increase of activity in Spanish manufactures for home and colonial consumption ; but it also resulted in a restriction of foreign trade and heavy liquidations, causing a depletion of currency with the issue of quantities of small paper money, the international exchange being thereby raised to the ruinous rate of thirty-three pesetas (£1 6s. 1½d.) to the pound sterling, instead of twenty-five, which was the par value.

Although this entailed great hardship upon those, including the Government, who had to pay sums of money abroad, or who consumed foreign goods, and it made the cost of living considerably higher than it had been, it greatly stimulated Spanish manufactures, especially for export, since the low value of the Spanish currency caused the productions of Catalonia and other manufacturing centres to appear very cheap when compared with their foreign gold value. In 1899, for the first time in fifty years, the balance of trade turned slightly in favour of Spain ; and in 1906 the exports considerably exceeded the imports, the former having been 1,018,387,000 pesetas, £40,735,480, in value, and the latter 884,800,000, £35,392,000. Though this is producing an improved exchange, and a nearer approach to the long projected rehabilitation of the gold currency and equalisation of international exchange, it tends in the near future to bring its own antidote in a restriction of exports when money values in Spain and abroad are the same.

In the meanwhile, the purchasing power of wages being much reduced, and the demand for the commoner wines being diminished by the French protective duties, the condition of the working classes generally in Spain is deplorable to the last degree. This is seen in many ways, especially in the great growth of mendicancy, and in the constant increase of emigration to South America, which is fast draining whole districts of their best peasantry. The number of emigrants from Spanish ports in 1900 was 63,000, and in 1904, 87,300 ; whilst in 1905 no less than 126,000 Spaniards abandoned their homes in search of better conditions of life abroad, and in a recent voyage the present writer saw sixty Spanish stowaways on a single steamer. This poverty amongst the peasantry is contrasted sadly with the enormous increase of luxury and expenditure of the higher classes in the towns, and especially in Madrid, owing in great measure to the return to Spain of rich colonials when Spain lost her dependencies, and also to the large fortunes made by the manufacturers and capitalists since the protective tariffs were reimposed in 1892.

KING ALFONSO AND HIS HEIR
The posthumous son of Alfonso XII., he was proclaimed King on the day of his birth, May 17th, 1886; ascending the throne in 1902, he married Princess Ena of Battenberg in 1906, and in the following year the heir was born.

Throughout the history of Spain the predominating desire of the people has been for continued separate provincial existence, and most of the unrest of the country has had this desire for its origin. The demand for continued or increased local autonomy was in times past the principal support upon which the hopes of the clerical Don Carlos depended ; but in the last few years the cause of provincial home rule for Catalonia, Biscay, Galicia, etc., has turned from Carlism, which is recognised as a dying force, and has largely allied itself to the advanced Socialist party. In Catalonia, where the demand for complete autonomy has always been strongest, the cry for home rule, now almost unanimous, is bound up with the powerful provincial interest in maintaining a protective policy for the whole of Spain.

The Catalan party in the Cortes are united, active, and able, but they have naturally against them the whole of the representatives of the poorer agricultural provinces—the greater part of Spain. In the direction of literary activity

Spain has shown a remarkable change of tendency in the last few years. The more serious writers are directing their attention almost entirely to studies of sociology in its various forms, with a view, apparently, to discovering the causes and remedies of Spain's continued adversity. This constant introspection on the part of

Cause of Spanish Unrest — Spaniards at the present time to some extent provides a solution to the problem they set themselves. Whilst they are minutely discussing their national shortcomings and peculiarities, other nations are working ; whilst they are doubting and despairing, other peoples are pushing ahead in hope ; whilst they are waiting upon Providence, others are forcing Providence to wait upon them. The national character is a strange mixture of exalted idealism and utilitarian worldliness, and it has become so much afraid of its own ideality, which it calls Quixotism, as to shrink from enterprises that demand a measure of imagination and faith in the future.

A great deal of the listlessness which characterises Spanish life springs from this national lack of faith in action, unless the result to be attained is visible and immediate ; and although the sociological experts, who for the last few years have written of little else in Spain, formulate many diagnoses of the maladies of their country, there is a general consensus of opinion that the main evil that afflicts the body politic is Spain's want of that ardent belief in her own destiny which in the days of her greatness constituted the secret of her success amongst nations. The introspective note is manifested as much in the works of the modern writers of fiction in Spain as in those of the professed sociologists. The school of romantic writing which flourished in the mid-nineteenth century and drew its inspiration from France and England has now disappeared, and the modern Spanish novel deals almost

Spain's Literary Activity — invariably, in an analytical and psychological spirit, with the contrast between the fervent religious belief of old Spain and the rationalistic tendencies of to-day, between the proud Spanish traditions of grave deliberation and the bustling activity of the present age, between the patriarchal conservatism of the soil and the vociferous demands of labour for a due share of the richness and sweetness of life. The education of the people of Spain

still lags behind that of other European nations, although compulsory education was decreed as far back as 1857. The schoolmasters have always been wretchedly underpaid, and too often not paid at all, by the provincial and town councils, upon whom they depended, and the compulsory clauses have been almost entirely disregarded. Recently, however, a distinctly better spirit is being manifested in this respect, a special Ministry of Public Instruction having been formed, and the State having assumed authority over the schools. The present percentage of total illiterates is about 65 per cent. of the population, as against 75 per cent. fifty years ago. The total cost of primary education is not less than £1,000,000 sterling per annum, mostly falling upon the local authorities, the whole country being divided into ten educational districts for purposes of inspection and control of the 25,340 primary schools, the number of scholars upon the books being 1,620,000, whilst the whole population of the country is approximately 19,000,000. Spain still suffers from the lamentable

Madrid's Rapid Advance — lack of enterprise of its rural and provincial populations outside of the great industrial centres of Catalonia and Biscay. The land is still cultivated listlessly and on methods long since obsolete elsewhere. The area planted with vines is about 3,600,000 acres, the produce of which, in 1905, was 3,079,925 tons of grapes, yielding 389,482,116 gallons of wine. The area under olive trees is about 3,250,000 acres, producing on an average 39,500,000 gallons of oil ; these two products, with mineral ores and fruit, form the bulk of Spain's exports to foreign countries, England being now by far the largest consumer of Spanish produce, and the largest supplier of merchandise to Spain.

The change that within the last few years has brought Spain once more into the family of European nations of the first class has also profoundly affected the social life of the capital. Madrid has grown enormously both in size and population, the inhabitants now numbering nearly 600,000, and some of the thoroughfares and trading establishments are as handsome as any in Europe. The attachment of the present king for everything English, and the natural influence of an English-born queen, have greatly increased the adoption of English manners, fashions, sports and taste amongst the upper classes, by whom the English language is being studied very widely ; whilst the large number of English visitors and the ever-growing relations between the two countries, are already to a great extent leading Spaniards of the middle class to adopt new standards of comfort, well-being and hygiene.

The last few years, moreover, especially since the accession of Alfonso XIII., have seen a considerable diminution in the social and political power of the clergy, and Spain can at the present time in no sense be called a priest-ridden country. In the great industrial centres, and particularly in Catalonia and Valencia, free thought in religion to a great extent accompanies the advance of political Socialism, and a perfect freedom of expression on matters relating to religion is indulged in.

The bulk of the population, nevertheless, in Castile and the south, are faithful in their observance of the dictates of the Church, and an unsuccessful attempt of the Liberal Government in 1907 to pass a measure for regulating the monastic orders led to the fall of the Ministry and the accession of the Conservatives under Señor Maura to power. The number of re-

Spain's Religious Problems ligious houses now existing in the country is 3,253, of which 597 are for men, and the rest for women, there being still over 10,000 monks and 40,000 nuns in the cloisters. The relations between Rome and the Spanish Church are still those settled by the concordat of 1851, and all attempts to rearrange them in a more liberal spirit have failed before the strong Catholic feeling still prevalent in the country and Parliament. Similarly, the scanty concession granted to Protestants and other non-Catholic religious bodies after the revolution of 1868 is still the largest measure of liberty granted, non-orthodox worship being licit, but no outward sign or announcement of it being allowed.

The constitution which rules the country is still in substance that which was adopted in 1876, after the restoration of Alfonso XII., with some modifications of secondary importance. The main principle of this charter is contained in the formula : " The power to make laws resides in the Cortes and the king," the Cortes consisting of two co-legislative bodies of equal power. The popular Chamber, or Congress of Deputies, consists at present of 406 unpaid members, representing one for every 50,000 of the population of the country, the election being by secondary vote of boards elected on manhood suffrage in one-member districts, with the exception of 98 deputies, who are chosen by twenty-eight large districts where minorities are represented. The Upper Chamber, or Senate,

How the Country is Ruled consists of 180 elected members, and a lesser but indefinite number of nominated and ex-officio members. Of the elected senators, 130 are chosen by 49 provinces, the electoral body being co-opted from the provincial councillors, town councillors, and largest taxpayers, whilst the remaining thirty elected senators are chosen by Archiepiscopal Chapters, universities and chartered learned and philanthropic societies.

The Senators nominated by the Crown must fulfil certain stringent conditions of position, age, and annual income, whilst those who sit by right are grandees of Spain, possessing an income of at least 60,000 pesetas, £2,400, per annum—field-marshals, archbishops, sons of the sovereign, and the presidents of the Councils of State, Navy, and War, and of the Supreme Court.

The machinery of government is, as will be seen, democratic, as befits a nation in which social distinction is less marked than in any other in Europe ; but the invariable corruption of the elections, and the apathy of all those who are not politicians, place in the hands of the executive almost unrestrained power. That, as a rule, they do not abuse it greatly to the detriment of the governed is due mainly to the tolerant democratic spirit which pervades all classes of Spaniards, and so long as the members of each political party can in alternation enjoy the privileges and profits of power there is no danger of any attempt at oppression of the people who pay. On the

The Hard Lot of the Spaniards other hand, the mass of the population go their way with little regard for politicians of either persuasion, content if the powers that be will improve the well-being of those whose hard lot it is to live for ever on the brink of want, forming the great majority of the nation, ill-housed, ill-paid, ill-fed, ill-taught, a patient, hopeful and long-suffering people, who deserve a better fate than misgovernment in the past has brought to them.   MARTIN HUME

PORTUGAL IN OUR OWN TIME
THE FATEFUL RISING AGAINST THE MONARCHY
By Martin Hume, M.A.

PORTUGAL of to-day presents a typical example of a state wherein, the representative institutions being in advance of the general standard of enlightenment, a comparatively small class of politicians has been able, owing to the apathy and ignorance of the mass of the people, to corrupt and stultify a governing machinery ostensibly democratic. As happened in Spain, the dynastic rivalry led to the granting of a constitution on modern lines to Portugal in 1836 by Dom Pedro IV., who immediately afterwards abdicated in favour of his infant daughter, Maria da Gloria, with his Conservative and Clerical brother, Dom Miguel, as regent.

Such a combination could offer no permanency, and the dynastic struggle that ensued followed the same course as in Spain, the young queen representing the parliamentary party, and Dom Miguel the reactionaries. As a consequence of the final triumph of the former, the extremely guarded constitution of Dom Pedro was reformed on several occasions in a democratic sense; and, although the royal prerogative was maintained in legislation and administration to an extent unexampled in other modern parliamentary states, the ostensible form of government became in the end essentially democratic.

Up to the year 1884 the House of Peers, whose legislative rights were equal to those of the elected Assembly, consisted **Unlimited Power of the Peers** entirely of nobles unlimited in number, chosen for life by the sovereign, and this in conjunction with the operative right of veto by the king gave to the latter practically uncontrolled power over legislation, no matter how democratic the Lower House might be. The constitutional struggle has therefore turned for many years past upon the attempts of Democrats to reduce the royal prerogative over legislation, administration, and finance, the last

subject being that which appealed most strongly to an overburdened, poor, and laborious agricultural people. In the course of the struggle the sovereign has, of necessity, been brought into opposition with the more advanced section of his subjects; and, as a consequence, a very powerful Republican party has been developed, and the relations between the Crown and the nation at large have often become strained, notwithstanding the personal popularity and earnest good intentions of the late Dom Carlos himself. **The Late King Dom Carlos** The complete apathy of the mass of the population has allowed the rival political parties to alternate in office mainly for the benefit of their partisans, and with little regard for the public interest; the late king, Dom Carlos, being made, with lack of magnanimity, the scapegoat for each party in turn whilst it was in opposition.

His own patriotism and desire to serve the best interests of his country were unquestionable; but his position became intolerable in view of the corruption of the administrative and electoral machinery by politicians, and the ungenerous attitude of each parliamentary opposition towards him. He had abstained from exercising to the full the powerful prerogatives he possessed under the constitution, and interfered as little as possible with the acts of his administrators.

He had acquiesced in the considerable extensions of the suffrage, and in the strict limitation, and provisions for the eventual extinction, of hereditary legislative peerages; but, unlike other constitutional sovereigns, he found the political parties unwilling to present a bulwark between him and the popular discontent aroused by oppressive taxation and administrative corruption, for which he was not responsible. Upon the king, most unjustly, was cast the onus of unpopularity caused by the inevitable submission of Portugal to the British ultimatum with regard to the encroachments in East Africa in 1890. The accusation was levelled against him that he had allowed his Anglophil tendencies to override the interests of his own country; and when, as a sequel to this agitation, a dangerous Republican revolt was suppressed in Oporto early in 1891, the king was again held personally responsible for the repressive measures that followed, and for the delay in granting an amnesty to the revolutionaries.

The main source of discontent has always been financial. Portugal, being in the main agricultural, is a poor country, and past mal-administration and present-day jobbery have burdened the people with a taxation out of proportion to their means. It was found that however great were the promises made by politicians in opposition, no relief to the taxpayer was afforded by either party when in power. In this respect, too, the king was made the scapegoat. The whole administration was wasteful and corrupt; but upon the expenditure for the royal establishment most of the criticism was directed. The Civil List amounted to about £112,000 per annum, and although this was comparatively modest for a nation whose annual revenue was some £13,000,000, it formed the basis for constant attacks upon the sovereign and his family, who found it quite insufficient for their needs, and the king had consequently incurred heavy indebtedness to the State.

The Royal Family Criticised

The position had thus become intolerable. The elective Chamber of Parliament was unblushingly manipulated by both parties in succession, and was representative only in name, notwithstanding the existence of universal manhood suffrage limited only by the ability to read and write. The public offices were crowded by idle parasites of politicians, and the pension list was full of scandalous abuses. In these circumstances a coup d'état was effected by the Prime Minister, Senhor João Franco at the end of 1906, with the co-operation of the king. Representative institutions were suspended, and the king and his dictator declared that until an uncorrupted and independent parliament could be summoned they would govern Portugal by royal decree.

The bold step naturally aroused the violent opposition and protest of all classes of politicians, thus deprived of their unholy gains. Protest was met by prosecution and further measures of repression, and the country was deprived of all pretence of representative government, both in national and local affairs. The avowed policy of Senhor Franco and the king was to purify the administration and establish economy of the national resources, and the new broom swept with devastating effect into the dark corners of the government service. Unfortunately, the maintenance of such an open violation of national rights and traditions, however salutary this might be, entailed the keeping of the armed forces in a good humour, and money that was saved in one direction was squandered in another.

King in Debt to the State

The Civil List, whilst ruthlessly reduced in some of its items, was increased in the aggregate to some £137,000, and the indebtedness of the king to the State, a sum of £154,000, was extinguished by a piece of financial jugglery which reflected little credit upon either the sovereign or the Minister. The great mass of the people had long since lost faith in the efficacy of political action to redress the evils of poverty and backwardness under which they suffered; the king personally was genial, kindly, and popular, and, although politicians of all shades denounced the dictatorship in unmeasured terms, the country at large went on its laborious way without audible or visible protest against the deprivation of its liberties—liberties which they recognised had not to any extent remedied the hard conditions under which the majority of the people lived.

Attempts were made by the regular dynastic parliamentary parties to use for their ends the heir apparent, an amiable young prince, called after his great grandfather, the King of the French, Luis Philip, and in his name to form a parliamentary cabal against King Carlos. The queen, also, a gifted and popular lady of singularly noble character, was understood to be opposed to the dictatorship, which she considered endangered the stability of the throne and the life of her husband. The young Crown Prince Luis Philip was removed for a time from the intrigues of the constitutional parties by sending him upon an extensive tour of the Portuguese African colonies, and after his return to Portugal he stood aloof from all attempts to estrange him from his father.

Intrigues Against the King

Thus matters stood in January, 1908, when the royal family passed a few weeks at the ancient Braganza possession of Villa Viçosa, in the Alem-Tejo, east of Lisbon. In their absence from the capital the opposition to the dictatorship became more pronounced and active, especially amongst the Republican party, always ready to profit by the dissensions amongst the dynastic groups. The Press organs of Senhor Franco, the dictator, announced that a widespread republican conspiracy had been discovered, and a great number of arrests of political opponents of the dictatorship were effected as a precautionary measure on the eve of the king's return to Lisbon, whilst on the day previous to his expected arrival, January 31st, 1908, a decree was published suspending the personal guarantees, and declaring the right of the Government to imprison or expel citizens without form of law.

The state of affairs was known to be critical on the day fixed for the arrival of the royal family in Lisbon, February 1st, 1908, but Senhor Franco was confident of being able to preserve order, as the army and police were known to be faithful, and the great mass of the population were apathetic, knowing, as they did, that the king meant well by the nation, and that the evils that he and Senhor Franco were endeavouring to remedy by unconstitutional means were real and great.

It was in the waning light of early evening when the king and queen, with their two sons, Luis Philip and Manuel, landed at the quay on the Praça de Commercio at Lisbon from the railway station on the other side of the Tagus; and in an open carriage they traversed the great

Assassination of King and Crown Prince square at a foot pace between the lines of respectful and loyal people assembled to greet them. The way of the cortège towards the Necessidades Palace on the face of the hills overlooking the river lay by the Street of the Arsenal, a somewhat narrow thoroughfare turning sharply out of the end of the Praça de Commercio towards the left. Just as the horses of the king's carriage were about to take the turn, a signal shot was discharged in the crowd, and there leapt from behind the pillars of the arcade that forms the footway several assassins, who precipitated themselves upon the royal family. One miscreant, mounting the back of the carriage, shot

THE ASSASSINATION OF PORTUGAL'S KING, DOM CARLOS, IN THE STREETS OF LISBON
The dastardly act pictured in this illustration occurred on February 1st, 1908, when the king was driving through the streets of his capital to the royal palace of the Necessidades. Seated in the carriage with the king were the queen, the Crown Prince, and Prince Manuel, now king, and when the fatal attack was made Queen Amelie heroically threw herself in front of her sons. But her brave act was too late, as both the king and the Crown Prince had received fatal wounds.

| The late Crown Prince | Dom Carlos | The present King |

DOM CARLOS, THE LATE KING OF PORTUGAL, AND HIS TWO SONS

the king in the neck, whilst another shot, which was mortal, struck him in the spine, and Dom Carlos sank bathed in blood upon the floor of the vehicle. The queen, standing and striking at the murderers, sought to protect her husband and elder son at the risk of her own life, and, although the target of many bullets, she miraculously escaped. The heir-apparent, a youth of twenty-one, was mortally wounded by two shots, and died within a few minutes when the carriage had been driven for shelter into the gates of the arsenal near by. A

Fate of the King's Assassins cry of horror and grief went up at this unparalleled crime, and the murderers, or such of them as could be identified, were cut to pieces by the police and the onlookers. The dynastic opposition parties, which had led the protest against the dictatorship of Franco, were as much dismayed as his friends at the turn of affairs, since the agitation which they had stirred up had thus gone far beyond their calculations or desires, and they at once rallied unanimously to the throne, now to be occupied by Prince Manuel, the younger son of the murdered king.

The Republican party, the extreme members of which were generally accused of the regicide, found no public support to the crime. The populace, struck with

detestation of so dastardly an act, were deaf to all appeals to them to rise against the new king, a young sailor lad of eighteen, whose unaffected geniality had already made him popular ; and the expression common in Lisbon the day after the crime voiced a general sentiment when it said that the shots that had killed Dom Carlos had killed the republic, too.

A coalition Cabinet, chosen from moderate men of all parties, was formed. Franco for a single day only endeavoured to stand firm by the aid of the armed forces he had conciliated ; but, finding now everyone against him, he incontinently fled into hiding, and eventually to foreign lands ; whilst the Government that replaced him abrogated most of the decrees of his dictatorship, and provided for a prompt return to a constitutional government. Time alone will show whether the spirited but rash attempt of the lamented Dom Carlos and his Minister to remedy by unconstitutional means a great constitutional evil will bear fruit, notwithstanding the terrible crime that cut short the experiment.

Portugal can hardly, after what has passed, revert entirely to the bad old system of party alternation of political plunder ; but it is to be feared that, as in the case of Spain, no great and permanent improvement can be expected by legislative action alone. In each case the statute books contain most of the enactments needed for the prosperity and happiness of a progressive state.

It is not the laws that are in fault so much as the general lack of a sense of responsible citizenship and the lamentable prevalence of illiteracy **Portugal's Ample Resources** which render possible a lax administration and corrupt evasion of laws of themselves good and sufficient. Portugal, though naturally a poor country, has nevertheless ample resources to ensure the comfort and prosperity of its citizens, if the government were economical and honest. The people, especially in the north, where the land is mostly held by peasant proprietors, live hardly, it is true, but not miserably. They are laborious, frugal, honest and sober, and it is safe to say that when the present proportion of complete illiterates —78 per cent. of the population, notwithstanding so-called compulsory education —is reduced, as it might be considerably, no peasants in Europe will have more of the elements of happiness at their command than the Portuguese.

The revenue of the country has steadily increased from £7,000,000 per annum in 1889 to £14,000,000 in 1907 ; but the wasteful finance and political corruption cause the expenditure to exceed the revenue in each recurring year. The funded debt has also grown with depressing regularity from £148,000,000 sterling in 1896 to £160,000,000 in 1905 ; and after a declared suspension of the payment of interest in 1892, an arrangement was arrived at with the Council of Foreign Bondholders in London by which the service of the debt is now managed by a council sitting in Lisbon, to whom special funds are allocated to cover the three per cent. at present paid. The political constitution of the State consists **Political Constitution of the State** of the sovereign, whose veto upon legislative enactments is fully operative if notice be given on his behalf within thirty days of the submission of a Bill, of a House of Peers consisting of a strictly limited number of nominated peers alone, with a few hereditary survivals, the elective element having been eliminated, and a Congress of Deputies elected on practically universal manhood literate suffrage. The deputies are unpaid, but

5410

are disqualified unless they possess a small minimum private income. The country, which covers an area on the continent of 90,000 square kilometres —34,254 square miles—with a growing population of nearly 5,500,000, is divided for local government purposes into twenty-one districts, of which seventeen are in Portugal proper and three in the islands. These are subdivided into 306 arrondissements, and again into 3,961 parishes. A governor appointed by the Ministry presides over each district ; the arrondissements being also presided over by an administrator appointed by the central government, aided in each case by elected councils.

Both in national and local administration the principal evil is the multiplicity of underpaid and often corrupt officials appointed in turn by rival political parties ; and the lower ranks of the judiciary are similarly afflicted, there being no less than 142 *juizes de dereito*, civil magistrates, besides the judges of the high courts and court of appeal, in **The Nation's Wealth in Agriculture** addition to 809 elected justices of the peace, thus bringing up the number of judicial authorities to nearly a thousand for a population not much larger than that of London.

Possessing a climate unsurpassed in Europe for beauty and salubrity, and a soil in many districts of great richness, the future wealth of the country must depend principally upon agriculture. The methods of cultivation are still almost as primitive as in the times of the Romans, especially in the south, which is more backward than the north in all respects ; and the great need of the population is that the national resources, instead of being squandered, as at present, upon unnecessary armaments and useless functionaries, should be employed in promoting national education, improving means of communication, and lifting the burdens from industries now sorely oppressed.

Of purely intellectual movement there is little of native Portuguese origin since the death of Herculano the historian and Almeida Garrett the poet. The novels of Eça de Queiros, which promised much, have unfortunately ceased with his premature death, and beyond a few historical and sociological studies there is now little produced by the Portuguese presses but translations of foreign works.

MARTIN HUME

THE SCANDINAVIAN STATES IN OUR OWN TIME
LIFE IN NORWAY, SWEDEN AND DENMARK
By William Durban, B.A.

OF the three Scandinavian territories, it seems natural first to speak of Norway. No country is regarded with greater pride by its people than the glorious Norse Land, on which, to describe its various attractions, a great variety of epithets has been bestowed. It is fondly styled by its loving sons " Gamle Norge " (Old Norway), for its civilisations claim a mighty antiquity. It is the " Land of the Midnight Sun," the " Land of the Vikings," the " Land of Fosses," or stupendous cascades in immense number, and the " Land of Eternal Snow." It presents with its wonderful fjords the most magnificent coast scenery in the world, and its mountains in imposing splendour approach the Swiss Alps themselves ; while its glaciers know no rival, except in Alaska.

Its lakes are countless, and the sportsman finds it a veritable paradise with its salmon rivers, its elk, wild reindeer, lynxes, bears, wolves, foxes, grouse, and ptarmigan. " Beautiful everywhere ! " is the frequent exclamation of enchanted visitors. Romantic " dalen," or valleys, pine-clad mountain slopes, and immense juniper-covered plateaux, like the wild Dovre Fjeld, are elements of indescribable beauty in the whole landscape right up to the North Cape. The grandeur of aspect of the Lofoten Isles cannot be surpassed. The gigantic falls—the Voringfoss, the Rjukanfoss, the Skejgedalfoss, the Vettisfoss, etc.—are tremendous

Natural Features of Norway torrents leaping from immense heights into the grand fjords, and some of these sublime gorges run up into the interior between the mountain precipices to distances of from 200 to 300 miles, carrying Atlantic tides right into the far centre of the land. The beautiful Hardanger, the grand and gloomy Geiranger, the sublime Sör, and the romantic Nord fjords are amongst the most marvellous of these inlets on the coast. It is impossible to become acquainted with the Norwegian people without learning to admire and even to love them. They are to-day, as they have ever been,

A Country of Scattered Villages simple and unsophisticated, clinging with passionate fidelity and attachment to the primitive customs of Viking ages, are given to delightful hospitality, are indefatigably diligent, and are charmingly courteous, with a natural refinement. They are not " degenerate Vikings of to-day," as some have attempted to characterise them. There are hardly half as many people in all Norway, with its vast area of 124,000 square miles, as in London alone, and of its population of 2,240,000 only about 350,000 dwell in towns ; so that the country is mainly one of scattered villages, dotted along the feet of the fjords, or on the lonely wilderness jelds, or in the clearings of the immense forests.

Norway has only 740 square miles of ploughed land, so that the actual agriculture is comparatively insignificant. But immense quantities of valuable hay are cropped during the brief, hot summer on the great " saeters," or meadow farms on the broad slopes. The Norwegian landscape is of two varieties—slopes and precipices, and most ingeniously the people adapt their pursuits to natural conditions. The greatest of all industries is, as might be supposed, fishing ; for Norway has a coast of 3,000 miles, and the fishermen are perhaps the sturdiest on earth.

But the backbone of the population is bucolic, consisting of the splendid rustics known as the " Bonder," or peasant farmers. Domesticity and social life in this wildest north are delightful, and the people are as happy as any in the world. The nights of the very protracted winter are spent in study, in courtship by the young folk, in wood carving, in tending the sheltered cattle, in hunting game, in visiting, in sledging, and in the glorious sports of racing on snow-shoes and of ski-jumping, in which recreation the athletic young Norsemen are the finest experts existing. Many a fearless leap on skis is achieved from a height of 150 feet. The social life of the people intimately mingles with their fervent religious cult. As in all Scandinavia, the national Church is Lutheran, and the quaint and pretty wooden churches are always filled, the country sanctuaries on Sundays along the Hardanger and other fjords presenting a singular spectacle, for the costumes are truly picturesque. There are comparatively few dissenters ; and though theological controversies are of course not unknown, they are not acute.

Norway's Intellectual Standard

The intellectualism of Norway stands high. Indeed, the people proudly claim that in proportion to the population they have in our time produced more geniuses than has any other nation. The names of Grieg, Nansen, Ibsen, Björnson certainly suggest influences that have of late years potently affected the thought of the world in poetry, music, and geographical research. Elementary education is universal in Norway.

The political conditions in Norway are altogether unique, and have, since the dawn of the twentieth century, been cast by an abrupt and startling revolution into a shape which has marvellously materialised the democratic aspirations of the people. Since the union with Sweden never really satisfied the patriotic sentiments of the Norwegians, a constant agitation was sustained for separation. The dissolution took place by decree of the Storting at Christiania on June 7th, 1905. The overt cause of the rupture was a protracted dispute between the two nations as to their foreign diplomatic representation. The late King Oscar of Sweden refused to entertain the offer of the Norwegian crown to one of his own family, but the details for the repeal of the Union were amicably settled by the Karlsbad Convention. A plebiscite was held, after which the crown was offered to Prince Charles of Denmark, who accepted it under the title of Haakon VII., thus greatly

Separation of Norway and Sweden

gratifying the national sentiment of his adopted subjects by honouring the venerable Norse traditions. On July 22nd, 1896, he had married Princess Maud Alexandra, daughter of King Edward VII., so that the British and Norwegian royal houses are closely allied. The heir to the throne is Prince Alexander, born July 2nd, 1903, whose name was, on his father's accession, changed to Olaf.

It was a remarkable fact that though Nansen and Björnson are Republicans in principle, as all the nation well understood, they exerted a leading influence, through their speeches and letters during the separation and plebiscite campaigns, in favour of a King of Norway. Norway being a land of peasants, the town life is not so interesting as that of the country. Christiania is a quiet and even dull metropolis, but it is beautifully built, stands at the head of its own lovely fjord, and is the centre of intellectual culture, being the seat of a great university. By far the most important town is Bergen, which is also the prettiest, a rare thing for a busy commercial city. And Trondhjem, the ancient historic capital, is attractive with its curious quaintness. Deeply interesting is the operation of the famous Norwegian company system for controlling the liquor traffic, which is very similar to the Gothenburg system in Sweden. Licences for the sale of ardent spirits are entrusted to a company formed, not for profit, but for the benefit of the citizens. The latest legislation on the principle of local option gives all men and women over twenty-five years of age the right to vote for the exclusion of retail bar traffic in spirits from the community in which they reside.

The Drink Trade in Norway

The profits of the companies, after the shareholders have received five per cent. dividend, are distributed amongst objects of public utility, such as planting parks, sanitary improvement, industrial education, waterworks, sewers, libraries, theatres and other amusements, charities, and religious institutions. High duties are imposed on the high-grade liquors imported, and it has become very difficult for foreign distillers to sell their commodities. Formerly, in Norway and Sweden, all owners of the soil had liberty to brew and distil, and the result was that these countries had a *per capita* rate of consumption of spirits higher than that of any other nation. Sweden, with its 173,000 square miles, and a population of nearly 5,500,000, is absolutely unique in its scenery and in the manners and customs of its inhabitants. The beautiful Göta Canal, a marvel of engineering ; the romantic lakes, of which Wener and Wetter are fine inland seas with noble spruce-clad islands ; the magnificent forests ; the glorious Trollhättan Falls ; the entrancing summer landscapes ; the grand mountains of Norrland—the great Arctic section—with its noble rivers ; the sweet pasture-lands of Svealand, the middle region ; and the romantic seaboard of Götaland, the old southern territory of the Goths, form factors in the make-up of one of Europe's most interesting lands.

No nation is prouder of its metropolis than the Swedes have reason to be, for Nature has given them an incomparable site on which they have erected a superb city. Stockholm reigns easily without a rival as Queen of the Northland. Rising gently from the many islands of the little archipelago between Lake Maelar and the sea, this city has been styled the Venice of the North, but is, with its 303,000 inhabitants, palpitating with that modern **Stockholm,** life which fails to touch the **Queen of the** city of the Doges. Gothen-**Northland** burg, intersected by huge canals and doing a fine trade, reminds the visitor of a Dutch port, excepting that its quays are boulevarded with trees. With her immense forests Sweden is the greatest timber exporting country in the world. Having nearly fifty million acres of forest area, covering close on half of the land, she can and does contribute enormously to the needs of other nations in this respect. But the most valuable recent development is the manufacture of paper from wood pulp. A great factory, worked by the lovely Trollhättan Falls, makes paper from pulp. The other chief export is the famous Swedish iron. Most of the estates consist half of forest land, and saw-mills are ever at work in every section of the country. Through these grand woodlands of oak, pine, beech, and birch run fine rivers, which are one secret of the activity of the lumber trade, for they facilitate the floating in summer of the timber felled in the winter.

The Swedes are fortunate in inhabiting the healthiest country on earth, the death-rate being only 16·49 per 1,000, the lowest in the whole world, and longevity is a national characteristic. Sanitation is assiduously attended to by the municipalities under central government supervision, and the salubrious climate and absence of overcrowding contribute greatly to the felicitous condition of the national health. The habits of the people, especially during the last and present generations, are exceedingly conducive to the conservation of their physique. The old **Sweden's** and disgraceful inebriety has **Advanced** been successfully fought by the **Culture** famous " Bolag " control of the drink traffic, known as the " Gothenburg System," already alluded to in the reference to the modification adopted in Norway. The people are intensely attached to their Lutheran National Church, in which nearly all the clergy are university graduates, their minimum collegiate course being five years. The elective system regulates the appointment of the prelates, for the clergy choose the bishops. Under the late King Oscar II., who died on December 8th, 1907, Swedish royalty was identified with the most accomplished culture, for that beloved monarch was one of the most scholarly of kings.

King Gustavus V. married Princess Victoria of Baden, a first cousin of the German Kaiser. The union was very popular, because she is a descendant of the old and revered family of Vasa. In June, 1905, the king's eldest son, Prince Gustavus Adolphus, married Princess Margaret of Connaught. There are two other sons, one of whom, Prince William, married the Tsar's cousin, the Grand Duchess Marie, in May, 1908. Sweden and Denmark took a very prominent part in arranging with Russia and Germany the momentous Baltic and North Sea agreements for the preservation of the status quo in the Baltic, Britain and the Netherlands also sending delegates to the convention at St. Petersburg. The Baltic Agreement was signed at the Russian capital on April 23rd, 1908, and a parallel North Sea **The Land** Agreement afterwards at Ber-**of the** lin. The documents declared **Sea Kings** that the nations concerned were firmly resolved to preserve intact the respective rights of those countries over their continental and insular possessions in the regions in question.

Denmark, so often called by foreigners who have learned to love the country and its people " dear little Denmark," has special interest for England, because of the close affinity of the people of the two countries and the intimate alliance of their royal families. A celebrated letter written by Lord Nelson is enshrined in the archives of the Foreign Office at Copenhagen. This missive is addressed to "The Brothers of Englishmen, the Danes." Naturally, the "Land of the Sea Kings" must appeal to Anglo-Saxon hearts. Pro-

Denmark Rich and Contented verbially the little nations are the happiest, and Denmark, one of the smallest, is one of the happiest of all. Though she has been shorn of much of her outlying territory, she has never lost her integrity, never having known subjugation, and so high a place does she hold in the esteem of other nationalities, that the representatives of mighty dynasties have been proud to enter into matrimonial union with the Danish royal family.

The late king, the octogenarian Christian IX., who passed away on January 29th, 1906, was often alluded to as "father-in-law of half Europe." Denmark is a notable example of the way in which a little kingdom, surrounded by powerful rivals, can be equally prosperous in her smaller way. Her progress in our own time is a phenomenon which has astonished the world. This cold and bleak peninsula jutting into the North Sea, with its group of insular satellites, is the home of a people who have shown the world that a little nation can become rich, contented, happy, and progressive. Year by year the sturdy Dane is taking greater advantage of the opportunities afforded by a fertile soil.

Copenhagen, the "Athens of the North," is a metropolis of which any nation might be justly proud. Its population of over 500,000 is year by year increasing, and the city grows in importance. Much of the old town has passed away, and the aspect for the most part is modern. It is a city to linger in, and its very atmosphere enchants the visitor, while its people are amongst the most courteous on earth. The famous Vor Frue Kirke—Our Saviour's Church—is

The Country's Pre-eminence in Agriculture one of the sights of Europe, for it contains Thorwald-sen's majestic statue of the Risen Saviour, with the marble statues of the twelve Apostles by the same consummate artist. Copenhagen, being not on the mainland but on the island of Sjaelland, on the Sound, possesses a unique charm from its wild and romantic outlook on the northern sea. The beautiful city is filled with treasures of art.

Three modest animals have mainly founded the modern prosperity of this interesting kingdom—the cow, the pig, and the hen. Denmark produces an immense quantity of butter and cheese, bacon and hams, and sells them with countless dozens of eggs to Britain and other neighbours. Many of the Jutlanders, from starting as swineherds, have become large dealers and merchants. The nation has set the pace for the modern world in agricultural co-operation. This applies specially to dairying. There are over a thousand co-operative dairies in Denmark, with nearly 150,000 members, receiving milk from nearly a million cows. The State has done everything possible to promote the system. The aim has been to secure a high degree of perfection in the system of handling milk so as to ensure cleanliness and a properly controlled supply.

This system is one of the romances of modern industry. And now, as a result of the encouragement given to the creation of small holdings by the famous Act of 1899, there are fully 100,000 of these farms. The Danish "small holdings men" are singu-

Political Situation in Denmark larly well-trained, capable, and enlightened, and are steadily becoming more so. Another beneficent measure, passed shortly before the close of the last century, was the Old Age Pension Act, received now by $2\frac{1}{2}$ per cent. of the population. The present political position in Denmark is that of a broad, genial, practical democracy, of which the king is the popular figurehead. King Frederic VIII. has paid many visits to England, and has an Oxford degree. He fulfils his promise to reign in accordance with his father's example. Political conflicts in Denmark are restrained by the moderation and sturdy common-sense of the people, reforms being promoted in a democratic, progressive spirit, in spite of the efforts of the Social Democrats to expedite extreme radical measures. The fine system of national education is sustained under the joint influence of State, Church, and municipality, under the special supervision of the Minister for Church and Education, through local committees, in which the clergy and magistrates play the chief parts. Education is elaborately and perfectly organised. The municipal schools, the Latin schools, and the high schools cover the whole land with a complete network, and the opportunities are appreciated by all classes. WILLIAM DURBAN

ESSENTIAL INFORMATION ABOUT DENMARK

AREA AND POPULATION. The area of Denmark is 15,592 square miles, including the Faroe Islands (540 square miles), with a population of 2,605,268 (including Faroe islanders, 16,349). The chief towns, with their populations, are: Copenhagen (the capital), 514,134; Aarhus, 55,193; Odense, 40,547; Aalborg, 31,509; and Horsens, 22,327.

GOVERNMENT. Denmark is a hereditary constitutional monarchy. Legislative power vests in the Parliament or Rigsdag, which is a house of two chambers—the Landsthing, or Upper House; and the Folkething, or Lower House. The Landsthing has 66 members, 12 of whom are nominated by the king for life, and the remainder are elected for eight years by electoral bodies composed of the largest taxpayers. The Folkething has 114 members elected for three years by universal suffrage. The basis of membership is one member for every 16,000 inhabitants. Members of both houses must be not less than twenty-five years of age, and both are paid. Parliament meets every year on the first Monday in October. The executive power rests in the Statsraadet, or State Council, which consists of the king and the Ministers of nine public departments—some of whom may represent more than one department.

MONARCH. The reigning king is Frederik VIII. (born 1843), who succeeded his father in 1906. He is the second ruler of the House of Schleswig-Holstein-Sonderburg-Glücksburg.

FINANCE. The revenue for the year 1906–1907 was £5,210,989, and the expenditure was £4,739,001. The chief sources of revenue are indirect taxes—chiefly customs and excise—and interest on state assets. The public debt in 1907 was £14,329,544, carrying an annual interest charge of £443,385. The capital value of the state railways and other national investments is more than the debt.

INDUSTRY AND COMMERCE. Agriculture is the chief industry. About 80 per cent. of the entire soil is productive. The chief crops, according to acreage, are oats, barley, rye, beets, wheat and potatoes. Stock raising is important, and the stock includes cattle, swine, sheep, horses and goats. Woods cover about 7 per cent. of the entire area of the country, and the most common tree is the beech. Private owners are restricted in timber cutting. There is a good deal of peat bog land. There are no mineral industries in the country, except some quarrying of freestone and marble in the island of Bornholm. The fisheries around the coast are of some importance, and last census showed that there were 31,608 people engaged in the industry. Dairy farming has developed in Denmark very much during the last few decades. The Government has assisted by providing money for experiments and by strict inspection to maintain the quality of the products. There are thirty-eight brandy distilleries and a good number of breweries in the country. In the year 1906–1907 the total value of imports was £33,335,554, and the total value of exports was £23,121,667. The chief exports are wheat and barley, bacon and ham, flour, butter, eggs, hides, skins, corn-meal, oil-cake, horses and cattle.

FAROE ISLANDS. The Faroe Islands are, politically, an integral part of the kingdom of Denmark, and send two representatives to the Danish Rigsdag. The area of the islands is 540 square miles and the population is 16,349. The largest islands are Strömö, Osterö, Vaagö, Sandö and Suderö; the capital is Thorshavn, in Strömö, and has a population of 1,650. There is little agriculture, the islands being bleak and treeless, and storms are frequent, although the winters are not excessively severe. Sheep-farming, wild-fowling and fishing are the principal industries; the exports, chiefly to Denmark, consist of wool, feathers, salted and dried fish, train oil and skins.

COLONIES. The Danish colonies are all in the Atlantic Ocean. They do not include the Faroe Islands, which are politically part of Denmark.

	Sq. Miles.	Population.
Iceland	39,756	78,470
Greenland (coast)	46,740	11,893
West Indies: St. Croix, St. Thomas and St. John	138	30,527
	86,634	120,890

Iceland has a Legislative Assembly—the Althing —and a Minister appointed by the King of Denmark. The capital and largest town is Reykjavik, with a population of 8,000. The products are sheep, cattle, ponies and fish, and all cereal foods are imported. Minerals are not known in payable quantities. Greenland has an area the estimates of which vary from 320,000 to 850,000 square miles. The area given in the table above refers only to the Danish district round the coast. The total population is under 12,000, and most of them are Eskimos, only about 250 Europeans residing in the country. The industries of Greenland are almost exclusively connected with whales, seals and sharks. There is, however, one cryolite mine, the output of which is exported for the manufacture of soda and alum. Trade in Greenland is a Danish royal monopoly, and the exports are fish oil, seal skins, and a little eiderdown and feathers.

The three Danish West India Islands—St. Croix, St. Thomas and St. John—are of little importance. In 1902 an agreement had been reached between the Danish Ministers and the Government at Washington regarding the purchase of these islands by the United States, but the Danish Landsthing refused to ratify the agreement.

CURRENCY. The Danish standard of value is gold, but silver is legal tender up to 20 kroner.

$$1 \text{ öre} = \tfrac{2}{15}d.$$
$$100 \text{ öre} = 1 \text{ krone} = 1s. 1\tfrac{1}{3}d.$$

The bronze coins are 1, 2, and 5 öre; the silver coins are 10, 25, 40, and 50 öre, 1 and 2 kroner; and the gold coins are 10 and 20 kroner. Usual reckoning is—18 kroner equals one English sovereign.

WEIGHTS AND MEASURES. The old system of weights and measures is being discarded for the metric system [see page 5399]; but the transition is not yet complete. In the old system the standard of weight was a *pund* (1·1023lb.); of lineal measure, an *alen* (·6864 yard); of land, a *tondeland* (1.36 acre); of solid measurement, a *kubic fod* (1·0918 cub. ft.). In capacity measure the *tönde* equalled 3·827 bushels of grain, 28·9189 gallons of oil, 246·9179 lb. of butter, and 4·6775 bushels of coal.

POSTAGE. Great Britain to Denmark, or any Danish colony, letters, papers and samples as for France [see page 5398]. Parcel post: 1s., 1s. 6d., and 2s. for 3, 7, and 11 lb. respectively if via Harwich; 9d. per parcel more if by Ostend or Flushing. To Greenland, same as to Denmark; to Iceland same as Denmark rates via Harwich, and to Danish West Indies double these rates. Limit of length, 3½ feet; limit of length and girth combined, 6 feet.

TELEGRAMS. Great Britain to Denmark, 3d. per word; to Iceland, 8½d. per word; to St. Thomas, 5s. per word, and to St. Croix, 5s. 3d. per word; There is no cable service to St. John or to Greenland.

INFORMATION ABOUT NORWAY AND SWEDEN

NORWAY

AREA AND POPULATION. Norway has a total area of 124,130 square miles, and a population of 2,330,364. The chief towns, with populations, are: Christiania, 227,626; Bergen, 72,251; Trondhjem, 38,180; Stavanger, 30,613; all are seaports.

GOVERNMENT. Norway is a constitutional hereditary monarchy. The integrity of Norwegian territory is guaranteed by Great Britain, France, Germany and Russia, by a treaty of October, 1907. The parliament is known as the Storting, which consists of 123 paid members elected by popular vote; every Norwegian man or woman over 25 years of age who has paid a certain income tax, which varies for rural and urban voters, is entitled to vote. Elections are held every three years. The Storting divides itself into two bodies, one-fourth forming the Lagting, and the remaining three-fourths forming the Odelsting. Certain matters are considered only by the latter body. Failing agreement the two chambers sit together and a two-thirds majority of the joint voters decides the point. The king can veto a measure twice, but if it passes three stortings, elected by separate elections, the king has no further power of veto. The executive is vested in the king with one Minister of State and not fewer than seven Councillors of State.

MONARCH. The reigning monarch is Haakon VII. (born August, 3rd, 1872), second son of King Frederic of Denmark; he was elected King by the Storting on November 18th, 1905, after Norway had dissolved her political union with Sweden.

FINANCE. The revenue for the year 1906–1907 was £6,344,957, and the expenditure was £6,100,023. The chief sources of revenue are customs, railways, excise, post office, income tax and telegraphs. The public debt in 1907 was £18,822,160.

INDUSTRY AND COMMERCE. Three quarters of the area of Norway is unproductive and only 3 per cent. is under cultivation. The remainder—22 per cent.—is forest land. The chief crops are potatoes, oats, barley, wheat, and rye; but the produce is insufficient for domestic consumption. Three-fourths of the forest land is under pine trees and a large proportion of the area is state land, managed by the Minister of Agriculture. Industries depending upon the forests are wood pulp, matches and paper. The fisheries are important and employ over 100,000 people. Mineral industries are increasing in importance after a period of decline. The chief minerals are iron pyrites, silver, copper, apatite and nickel. There are a few factory industries, chiefly in the neighbourhood of Christiania, and the most important of them are textile factories, engineering shops, chemical works, metal works, brick works, and flour-mills. Water power is largely used in manufacturing. The value of imports for the year 1906–1907 was £21,428,211, and the value of the exports was £14,061,111. The chief exports are timber and timber manufactures, including matches, fish and fish products, chiefly cod liver oil, paper and paper pulp, skins and furs, mineral ores and stone, ice and carbide of calcium.

CURRENCY. As for Denmark [see page 5415].

WEIGHTS AND MEASURES. These are metric [see page 5399].

POSTAGE. Great Britain to Norway: Letters, papers and samples as for France [see page 5398]. Parcels post as for Denmark via Harwich [see page 5415].

TELEGRAMS. Gt. Britain to Norway, 3d. per word.

SWEDEN

AREA AND POPULATION. The area of Sweden is 172,876 square miles and the estimate of population at the end of 1906 was 5,337,055. The chief towns with their populations, are: Stockholm (the capital), 332,738; Göteborg, 156,927; Malmö, 75,691; Norrköping, 45,528; Helsingborg, 31,404.

GOVERNMENT. Sweden is a constitutional monarchy. The Parliament, or Riksdag, has two elected Chambers, possessing equal powers, but deliberating and voting separately. The Upper Chamber has 150 members, and election to it is made for nine years by the Landstings, or rural assemblies, and by the urban corporations not represented in the Landstings. The Lower Chamber has 230 members, elected by popular vote on a new franchise for three years. The members of the Lower House are paid. The king can initiate measures and can veto measures passed by the Riksdag. Executive power is vested in the king and a Council of State, which consists of a Minister and ten Councillors.

MONARCH. The King of Sweden is Gustaf V. (born 1858), who succeeded his father, Oscar II., in December, 1907.

FINANCE. The estimated revenue and expenditure for the year 1907 was £11,945,600. The chief sources of revenue are the customs, duties on spirits and beet sugar, state lands, railways and telegraphs, income tax, post office, stamps, and the profits of the National Bank. The public debt stood at £25,570,476 in January, 1908; it represents solely expenditure on railways, from which the profits more than pay the interest.

INDUSTRY AND COMMERCE. Agriculture employs quite half of the population, although less than nine per cent. of the country is under cultivation. The chief crops, according to acreage, are oats, rye, barley, potatoes, wheat and pulse. There is also considerable stock raising—cattle, sheep, horses and pigs. Dairy farming has made important progress in recent years. Over half of the whole country is forest land and Sweden exports more timber than any other European country. The fisheries are much less important than those of Norway and have experienced some bad years recently. Sweden is rich in minerals, and Swedish iron, refined by the use of charcoal, is famous throughout the world. Iron is the chief mineral worked and most of the iron ore raised is exported. Other ores worked include those of silver and lead, copper, zinc, and manganese. Coal is also found and mined. The chief industry is connected with the forests, and in the kingdom there are about 1,300 saw-mills, about 500 joinery and cabinet-making works, about 150 wood pulp factories, and some 70 paper mills. Iron, steel and machinery works claim about a thousand separate establishments. Then come textile factories—over 300 in number—devoted to cotton and wool. The exports for the year 1906 were of the value of £27,768,988, and the imports were of the value of £35,475,104. The chief exports are timber, iron and steel, butter, wood pulp, iron ore, paper, machinery (including cream separators), carpentry work, stone, metal goods and matches.

CURRENCY. As for Denmark [see page 5415].

WEIGHTS AND MEASURES. These are metric [see page 5399].

POSTAGE. Great Britain to Sweden: Letters, papers, and samples, as to France see [page 5398]. Parcel post, 1s. 6d., 2s., and 2s. 6d. for 3, 7, and 11 lb., via direct steamer to Stockholm; 1s. per parcel higher if via Ostend or Flushing.

TELEGRAMS. Gt. Britain to Sweden, 3½d. per word.

EUROPEAN
POWERS
TO-DAY

XII
THE UNITED
KINGDOM

UNITED KINGDOM IN OUR OWN TIME
A CONTEMPORARY SURVEY OF ITS POLITICAL AND SOCIAL INSTITUTIONS
By Arthur D. Innes, M.A.

THE British Empire to-day is a unique phenomenon in the history of civilised mankind, differing in essential particulars from every contemporary empire as from all that have existed in the past. In the course of 300 years the people of these islands have taken possession of vast tracts of the earth's surface. The ancient empires held their conquests by force of arms, but in her great dominions on two continents our state has no garrison at all. Wherever Rome ruled, her government was of the military type; practically it is only in India that ours falls under that category. Neither our colonial nor our Asiatic dominion presents close resemblances to the empires of other European states. except so far as Russia in Central Asia and France in North Africa hold positions more or less analogous to our own in India.

The states of which the empire is composed offer—subject to the ultimate authority of the central state, to which they stand in varying relations—examples of almost every conceivable type of polity: absolute monarchies in India, where the British raj itself is that of a racial aristocracy; while all the greater colonies are democracies. Or, if we follow the territorial method of classification, the empire will supply us at one end with federated countries in Canada **States in the British Empire** and Australia, and at the other with something not far removed from the Greek idea of the city-state in the Isle of Man and in the Channel Islands. In the course of this work we have watched England developing politically far in advance of all Continental states, while Ireland remained a subordinate, half-controlled province, and Scotland held fast to a somewhat lawless independence;

until, 300 years ago, the three kingdoms were united under one crown, and then, at intervals of a century, under one legislature—theoretically, at least, on an equality. Three hundred years ago, the only over-sea territory possessed by the people of these islands was the embryo colony of Virginia, which had existed precariously for years. The seven- **Britain's Colonial Expansion** teenth century saw a British expansion which was not itself permanent, because the colonies then established afterwards broke away from the mother country. But it also saw, on the one hand, the confirmation of British supremacy on the high seas and of parliamentary supremacy in the British polity.

In the eighteenth century Great Britain completely distanced all rivals in the competition for colonial expansion, in spite of the loss of the group of communities which formed the United States, and this supremacy was confirmed by the Napoleonic wars. In those wars Napoleon himself chose commerce as the field in which he would come to death-grips with the British, with the result that, after Waterloo, there was no competitor within measurable distance of them, and the lead thus gained was increased progressively during the nineteenth century. During that century, also, the colonial expansion continued; the whole of one continent was appropriated. In India the British passed from being merely the dominant power to being lords of the whole land between the mountains and the sea; and finally the most valuable portions of the Dark Continent fell also under their dominion. The expansion was accompanied by a change in the internal polity. The supremacy of parliament was unchallenged; but the gradual extension of the electoral body transferred the control of parliamentary majorities first from the landowners to the manufacturers and the middle class, and then from the middle to the labouring classes.

A further characteristic has to be remarked on in order to understand the position of the British Empire in the world **Britain as** at the present day. Until the **a Military** stadtholder of Holland became **Power** king of England, these islands never played a part much more than insignificant in the struggles of Continental states. In mediæval times England had fought with France on her own account; later, still on her own account, she had fought Spain, and later still Holland.

The new dynastic association with Holland, coupled with her own dynastic question, forced her into the European arena; but even then it was not the size of her armies, but the genius of her great general, Marlborough, and the wealth which supplemented the exhausted treasuries of her allies, which made her alliance valuable; and, mutatis mutandis, the same principles applied throughout the whole series of wars which were finally brought to an end in 1815. To divert the energies of her enemies she did not fight them on land, but helped her neighbours to do so. For her own hand she fought them on the sea.

It was only in the Peninsular War that she took rank as a military power, and there she was only enabled to do so because Napoleon wanted the bulk of his legions for Moscow. Moreover, in the same connection it has to be observed that, with the possible exception of 1793, Continental interests have never been the motive of her wars. In nearly every case she has fought because the interests of France collided with her own in extra-European regions. With hardly a variation, her rulers have systematically declined to intervene in foreign quarrels otherwise than through diplomatic channels. **Moulding** That rule has been broken, or is **of Britain's** in serious danger of being broken, **History** only in one corner of Europe: she would fight to prevent Constantinople from falling into the hands of Russia. We may say, then, that viewing the United Kingdom of to-day as the product of the forces which we have observed moulding its history, it forms the central state of an empire whose distinguishing characteristics are an immense transmarine colonial

system, such as no other European Power possesses; an immense lead in commerce; an established maritime supremacy, both mercantile and naval; the smallest of "regular" armies, outside of India, on the historic ground that no state has ever been able continuously to maintain both army and navy in the front rank, while to the British the navy has always proved the more effective instrument both for offence and defence. Further, this state has evolved its own polity—the system of parliamentary government—as an organic growth, without revolution and without copying the institutions of other states, except in occasional matters of detail; whereas her own institutions have been consciously adopted as models, though with appropriate modifications, in the constitution of most civilised countries.

Socially, as well as politically, her people have been, and continue to be, distinguished by the combination of a marked acknowledgment of class distinctions with exceptional facility in passing class barriers; in other words, social ranks are recognised, but are not permitted to stiffen **Intellectual** into castes, as they did stiffen **Record of the** in most European states. **British Isles** Hence "labour movements," all the movements which are apt to be labelled "Socialistic" by those who disapprove of them, are accompanied among the proletariat by a much less virulent antagonism to the well-to-do than is frequently the case in other lands.

In the intellectual field, the British Isles claim great names in science, both in its theoretic realms, such as Bacon, Newton, and Darwin, and in its practical application. In pure literature it is somewhat curious to remark that the greatest achievements of a people which prides itself on practical common sense have been in the region of imagination, of poetry, where it is not only insular prejudice that claims a supreme position for Shakespeare. Like the Shakespearian period, the hundred years which opened with the period of the French Revolution were rich in great literary names; but it cannot be said that either in literature or in science the United Kingdom in the twentieth century is showing any marked superiority to European and American rivals.

Aspects of this empire external to the United Kingdom itself remain to be treated at length hereafter; in this chapter we are concerned with our own islands.

The condition of affairs to-day is the product of the past, the outcome of organic development; and development means both continuity and change. Can we, then, analyse the elements which tend to change and to continuity respectively?

In the nineteenth century the United Kingdom became the great, almost the one, manufactory and carrier of the world. Among the various causes of this supremacy, the most decisive is probably to be found in the Napoleonic wars—partly because they devastated Europe and drained off the best human material for fighting, instead of manufacturing; while the people of these islands were, comparatively speaking, able to devote a much

trade that Free Trade was universally acknowledged to be the cause of the expansion, and the advocacy of Protection was regarded as at best a " pious opinion."

But it has not proved impossible either for European states or for America to develop manufactures on their own account which can compete with British goods in the market. It is, perhaps, difficult to realise from the figures produced that our commercial ascendancy is vanishing; but the monopoly is ours no more; and it is by no means clear that the country will not attempt to recover it by a reversion to pre-Cobdenite methods.

It is curious to observe that Germany's commercial advance in the last forty years

MEN OF THE ROYAL ENGINEERS CONSTRUCTING A SUSPENSION BRIDGE

larger share of their energies to peaceful pursuits; partly because the Berlin Decree practically involved that the British should either monopolise the carrying trade or lose it altogether.

Apart from the war, the British already had a long lead in the carrying trade, and were in front of other countries in the development of machinery and the application of steam. But the practical monopoly was the outcome of the artificial conditions created by Napoleon, and made it supremely difficult for any other nation to enter into competition. The development of the Free Trade programme by Sir Robert Peel and by Mr. Gladstone was attended by so marked an expansion of

is often attributed with equal confidence to her adoption of Protection for her manufactures. It is not probable that Tariff Reform, if it does come, will ruin either our own commerce or, alternatively, that of our competitors, who at present rely on a Protectionist policy. Perhaps from the point of view of the historian, whose business is largely with the analysis of causation, the most remarkable feature of the economic problem now dividing the country is that it was brought out of the regions of cloud-cuckoo-land into practical politics by the action of a single individual—that but for Mr. Chamberlain the merits of Protection would probably receive to-day as little public recognition as they did in that

THE SEAFORTH HIGHLANDERS ON PARADE

SQUADRON OF THE CITY OF LONDON SHARPSHOOTERS

THE ROYAL FUSILIERS ON PARADE

THE ROYAL IRISH VOLUNTEERS AT CAMP

Gale and Polden

SOME TYPES OF BRITAIN'S FIGHTING FORCES

THE 14TH—KING'S—HUSSARS PROCEEDING TO MANŒUVRES

A COMPANY OF SCOTS GUARDS

Gale and Polden

SOME BRITISH SOLDIERS ON THE MARCH

statesman's " Radical " days. Whatever school of economists prevails, it may be safely prophesied that commercial ascendancy will remain with this country so long as she holds the maritime supremacy, and will pass as soon as she loses it. That supremacy is as yet unchallenged. The practical unanimity with

Unchallenged Mistress of the Seas which the doctrine of a two-Power standard for the Royal Navy is accepted—at least, as concerns the fleets of European states—would be a mere absurdity for a country not already in possession of a decisive preponderance over any other, or lacking the means to maintain such preponderance. There is no Power which dreams of challenging the mistress of the seas single-handed on her own element, though there is one which is popularly credited with having inherited Napoleon's pre-Trafalgar programme.

Have the conditions, then, so changed that what Napoleon found to be impracticable a century ago—what had been almost unthinkable since the destruction of the Spanish Armada—is practicable to-day ? Fortresses reputed impregnable have been captured through an unsuspected entry ; before Wolfe scaled the Heights of Abraham, Quebec seemed secure against any possible attack. The chances that an attempt to invade these islands would result only in the annihilation of the invader appear to be no less overwhelming than in the past ; but the condition of security is vigilance, as the condition of successful attack is secrecy.

It can only be said that there is no present sign either that vigilance is lacking or that the secret concentration of an invading force is possible. The historic position is unaltered. Now, as always, it is the fleet which makes invasion impossible. Now, as always, a Continental army operating in this country would not find our military forces organised to offer resistance as it would on

Is England Liable to Invasion ? invading a Continental state. Parma in 1588, or Napoleon in 1805, would have found their veterans opposed by the same half-drilled and half-trained amateur soldiery which would now form the bulk of our defence at the present day. But there is no more likelihood of a Continental army getting the chance of operating in England than there was in the days of Parma or of Napoleon. Wisely or unwisely, the nation is content with

that position ; or, at any rate, shows no greater inclination than in the past to adopt the alternative policy of universal military service. It is at least probable that the recent reorganisation — with modifications which experience of its working will suggest—will produce the maximum of efficiency attainable under the purely voluntary system.

As regards the security of these islands, then, the historic position appears to be unchanged. But the United Kingdom is responsible for the defence of the empire, and here we must note that the conditions to-day are not quite what they have been in the past. Our frontiers are not, as they were, exclusively oceanic. In the eighteenth century, the possession of America and India depended entirely upon sea-power ; when our supremacy on the sea was decisively established, our rivals' successes in either continent could only be temporary.

But now the advance of Russia in Central Asia has made possible a conflict which would have to be fought out on land ; and although the idea of a war with the United States is scarcely less

Britain's Place Among the Powers unnatural than that of a civil war, the possibility, however remote, involves the question of the defence of the Canadian frontier. The conditions of our rule in India demand the presence, under all circumstances, of a large white garrison within the peninsula. At the present time, indeed, nothing is less likely than a war with Russia, except a war with the United States ; but either contingency would seem to call for military operations, as distinct from naval, on a much larger scale than we have hitherto been involved in by European complications. As concerns Europe itself, as with the defence of these islands, the historic position holds. Any conceivable combination of Powers would hesitate to challenge us by sea ; combined fleets have always proved even more difficult to handle successfully than combined armies. But no Power would be greatly perturbed by the prospect of a British invasion.

The British alliance to-day, as in the past, would be coveted where British subsidies would be desirable ; the aid of British fleets would be useful, or the hostility of British fleets would be feared ; not for the sake of the battalions that could take the field. It is to be remarked, however, that the mere fact of our naval ascendancy is, and always has been, a source of irritation ; it is probable that all Europe would regard any extensive development of our military organisation as indicating not a defensive, but an aggressive intent, precisely as we are disposed to interpret the expansion of the German Navy. We are so free from aggressive desires that we can hardly believe such charges to be made in good faith ; nevertheless, foreign nations find it exceedingly difficult to believe that we have annexed so large a proportion of the globe merely in self-defence.

At the present time, however, thanks largely to the consistency of a foreign policy, which has been maintained without regard to party for a quarter of a century, the United Kingdom has been almost cleared, in the eyes of its neighbours, of the charge of fluctuating between peace-at-any-price and blatant jingoism. The Japanese War has deprived Russian aggression of its immediate terrors, and the political reformation of Turkey which astonished the world in 1908 has minimised the danger of an Anglo-Russian quarrel over the Eastern Question. Hence our relations with the great Slav **Germany** Power have become almost **the Bogey of** cordial. With France we have **Britain** reached a happy stage in which the respective spheres of interest of the two nations have become so definitely delimited that no rational cause of quarrel arising is imaginable, and a friendliness of feeling has been developed which is the best possible safeguard against a sentimental explosion.

The rôle of bogey has been transferred to Germany. The situation emphasises the fact that the historian may go a great deal too far in insisting on a logical statesmanship as the primary factor in political action. Germany is our bogey, chiefly because she has erected us into a bogey ; and that she has done so is due largely to her historians and professors, many of whom suffer from a conviction that England designs to crown a career of cold-blooded spoliation by seeking the ruin of Germany. That is to say that, mutatis mutandis, the present German view of England is very much like what has been the normal English view of Russia. German hostility to England is based on a a wholly irrational fear of English designs, but while it exists it forces upon England an attitude which is easily interpreted as one of hostility to Germany. In neither country is the actual hostility shared either

by the controlling statesmen or by the mass of the population, and the mutual suspicion will probably wear itself out in course of time. Commonsense, the absence of any antagonistic interests, the futility of a struggle between a military and a naval Power, and the growing inclination to pay deference to the public opinion of Europe, **King Edward** should suffice to prevent **the Consummate** any momentary panic from **Diplomatist** driving two great nations into a struggle which would injure both and could benefit neither. But it would be vain to deny that such an atmosphere of mutual suspicion as now exists under the fostering care of a solid portion of the Press of both countries is eminently adapted for the cultivation of the microbe of international rabies.

Here, however, we have a very notable illustration of the invaluable services which may be rendered to the state by the crown, in the unique position which it holds to-day. A visit to the German Emperor by the consummate diplomatist who occupies the British throne has had an immediately pacificatory effect, which goes far to confirm the conviction that Anglo-German antagonisms are in no sense fundamental, but are the outcome of misunderstandings, which may be eradicated by the persistent application of commonsense.

Within its own borders, the United Kingdom presents a singular complex of nationalities. The Englishman, the Irishman, the Scot, and the Welshman, are each of them emphatic in asserting their distinct nationality, though the Englishman is somewhat apt to overlook the claim on the part of the other three when they are acting in conjunction with him, and credits their vices to themselves, and their virtues to their English connection. Except in the case of Wales, the distinction is historical rather than racial, for the Irish Kelt is not more emphatically Irish than are the descen- **Britain's** dants of Norman, English, or **Complex** Scottish settlers ; and the Scot **Nationalities** of the Lowlands is as much a Sassenach to the Highlander as the Englishman. England, wealthier, more fertile, more populous, if not larger in actual area than the other three put together, has been the " predominant partner " ever since partnership of any kind existed ; but a difference in her historic relations with the three remains apparent at the present day. Scotland, an independent state for centuries, which successfully defeated repeated attempts to subdue her, voluntarily joined England to form the single state of Great Britain, in 1707, under guarantees that her national institutions should not be altered. She has so far, at least, remained in the position of managing her own concerns that it is recognised

What Wales Claims from England

as impracticable to introduce material modifications without the assent of the majority of her representatives in the Commons. Wales, treated to some extent as a subject province from the conquest by Edward I. till the accession to the English throne of a Welshman in the person of Henry Tudor, in 1485, has formed an integral part of England since her admission to full parliamentary representation in the reign of Henry VIII., but of recent years has been claiming distinctive treatment on the ground that her people are distinct from the English in race, customs, predilections, and to some extent language, the Welsh tongue being still in popular use.

The Irish position differs from that of the Scots or Welsh. Nominally subject to the English Crown since the reign of Henry II., Ireland was treated for centuries as a subject province in which English law was more or less enforced spasmodically, and English government could hardly be described as definitely established till the beginning of the seventeenth century.

Before that time, and still more afterwards, large appropriations of the soil to Protestant English and Scottish settlers, coupled with the political disabilities attaching to Roman Catholicism—the creed of four-fifths of the population—kept the bulk of the people in constant hostility to the Government; which was intensified by the tyrannical use of their power by the Protestant oligarchy through the greater part of the eighteenth century. The Act of Union in 1800 theoretically placed Ireland on an equal footing with England and Scot-

Ireland's Place in the Union

land in the United Kingdom, but the maintenance of the Catholic disabilities for another quarter of a century intensified the hostility between the Catholic peasantry and the Protestant landlord class. Hence English and Irish agree in recognising the necessity of distinctive treatment for Ireland, but from fundamentally different points of view. For the securing of justice as between landlord and tenant the economic conditions

would make the establishment of the English land-tenure a quite futile course. What is justice from the tenant's point of view, is robbery from the landlord's; and the solution England offers is to impose upon both what she considers justice, and Irishmen do not. The solution offered by the great majority of Irishmen is that they should settle the matter for themselves without English intervention—that the " distinctive treatment" should be controlled by the Irish democracy, not by the English.

The abstract justice of this claim appeals the more readily to the foreign spectator, because under the existing conditions it appears that, unlike the position of Scotland and Wales, the wishes of the Irish democracy—that is, of the majority of their parliamentary representatives—are apt to influence the judgment of the majority at Westminster in inverse proportion to their intensity—unless the Irish happen to hold the balance between the two great parliamentary parties. The process, however, of extending large powers of self-government to local bodies has recently been applied, in the hope that

The Irish Demand for Home Rule

it may remove the urgency of demands for a separate legislature. It may be affirmed with satisfaction that the virulence of popular Irish hostility to the Government has greatly abated, though the same can probably not be said of the persistence of the demand for Home Rule; just as the personal hostility between English and Irish Members of Parliament has disappeared.

In any case, it seems certain that the increasing congestion of work in the Imperial Parliament will make it more and more necessary for parts of that work to be delegated to local bodies, and it is not improbable that a solution of this difficulty will ultimately be found in the recognition of Nationalist—not Separatist—aspirations by the establishment of Nationalist legislatures with limited powers, in subordination to the Imperial Parliament. The practical difficulties of evolving such a scheme are, however, so great that there is no present prospect of such a change being introduced.

The political party in the Imperial Parliament, which, under the leadership of Mr. Gladstone, committed itself to approval of the abstract principle of Home Rule for Ireland, is retarded from taking active steps towards its realisation by the consciousness that such plans as have hitherto been formulated might create

TYPES OF BRITISH BATTLESHIPS

In this and the following pages we give a series of drawings illustrating the leading types of vessels which constitute the strength of the British Navy, including those of the much discussed "Dreadnought" class.

H.M.S. "DRAKE"

H.M.S. "SHANNON"

H.M.S. KENT

H.M.S. "KING EDWARD VII" AT SPITHEAD.

H.M.S. "GHURKHA" T.B.D.

H.M.S. "EXMOUTH"

H.M.S. "TRIUMPH"

Lord Nelson   Dreadnought   Bellerophon   Hindustan

GREAT BRITAIN'S FIRST LINE OF DEFENCE: FOUR OF THE EMPIRE'S FIRST-CLASS BATTLESHIPS

TYPES OF BRITISH CRUISERS: H.M.S. INDOMITABLE, IN FOREGROUND, MAKING HEAVY WEATHER

IMPROVED TYPE OF SUBMARINE, SHOWING FULL HEIGHT OUT OF THE WATER

SUBMARINES ATTACKING A WARSHIP WITH DUMMY-HEADED TORPEDOES

A No. 2 SUBMARINE OF THE HOLLAND TYPE

THE SUBMARINE IN NAVAL WARFARE

Photos: Cozens and Stephen Cribb

fresh causes of friction no less serious than those they were designed to remove; while the demand for "Home Rule all round" has not hitherto been expressed by any portion of the electorate. The conception of the empire as a congeries of self-governing states, associated into federated groups according to their geographical position, having as their apex or formal bond of union the Crown and the Imperial Parliament, in which all shall be represented—this conception has not yet passed from the theorists to the practical politicians. If ever it does so, it may be assumed that the United Kingdom will be transformed into one of the federated groups, like the Dominion of Canada or the Commonwealth of Australia.

The United Kingdom of the Future

At the present day, however, the United Kingdom has one Parliament only; and the Parliament of the United Kingdom is also the Imperial Parliament—that is to say, that in conjunction with the Crown—not independently of it—it is legally recognised as the ultimate sovereign authority, not only in the United Kingdom, but throughout the empire. Whatsoever is done or ordained by the authority of the king in Parliament is lawfully done, and is legally binding in every portion of the empire to which the ordinance applies. By this authority every colony or dependency of the empire has received its present constitution, and might lawfully be deprived of it, just as by the same authority murder might be legalised and playing bridge be elevated into a capital offence.

Its own commonsense and the moral sense of the community set a practical limit to its powers; commonsense forbids it to exercise those powers in a manner opposed to the spirit of the constitution—it will be in no hurry to repeat the blunder which gave birth to the United States of America; but the law sets no limit and recognises none. Such authority has always in England been recognised as residing in the Crown and the National Council, whether that Council was the Saxon Witan, the Magnum Concilium of the Normans and early Plantagenets, or the Parliament in which the Commons appeared by their representatives. The authority of king and Council acting together has never been in dispute except by doctrinaire maintainers of the divine and inalienable right of succession to the throne, who deny that

Authority of King and Parliament

even the king in Parliament can alter the course of the succession. The constitutional struggles have been fought round the question how far the Crown can act independently of Parliament, by prerogative, and sometimes how far Parliament can act independently of the Crown.

The king in Parliament—the Crown and the two Houses of Parliament—are the ultimate authority. For the sake of brevity we shall use the term "Parliament" for this complete body, speaking of the Crown and the Houses when its component parts are referred to distinctively. The Houses would be fully described as the House of Peers and the House of the Representatives of the Commons, the latter being alternatively spoken of as "the Representative House," or "the Commons." While Parliament is the ultimate authority, it discharges directly only a part of the sovereign functions. Moreover, Parliament itself is subjected to a certain degree of external control, partly because the members of the Representative Chamber are dependent on the electorate for the continuity of their membership, partly from the influence of a public opinion which may be external even to the electorate. Thus, members will hesitate to take in the House a line which will endanger their seats at a general election, and a steady demand for the franchise by a solid body of persons excluded from the electorate is tolerably certain to be met if its existence is really indubitable. Of the three powers which, united, make up Parliament, the Commons' House is theoretically predominant.

Predominance of the House of Commons

The electorate has for half a century been constructed on a democratic basis. The House of Commons expresses the will of the electorate. The Peers and the Crown must yield to the emphatically expressed will of the Commons, as also must the Executive which is responsible to Parliament though not directly conducted by it. That is the theory which locates the effective sovereignty of the United Kingdom with the democracy; a theory which does not altogether correspond with the facts.

In theory, again, the British Constitution has these two leading characteristics: it distributes political power between the Crown, the aristocracy, and the people; and it separates the exercise of the three functions of sovereignty, the legislative, the administrative, and the judicial; while the necessary unity is

SIR JOHN FISHER

SIR PERCY SCOTT

LORD CHARLES BERESFORD

SIR WILLIAM MAY

LEADING ADMIRALS OF THE BRITISH NAVY IN OUR OWN TIME

Photos: Russell, Dinham, Gale and Polden, and Russell, Southsea

secured by enabling the people in the long run to dominate the Crown and the aristocracy, and the legislature to dominate the Executive and the Judiciary. The people, it must be observed, means in any case only that portion, large or small, of the whole community which composes the electorate.

The relative political weight of the Crown, the aristocracy, and the people, has varied very greatly; with a general tendency to reduce first the preponderance of the Crown, which the Normans established, then the preponderance of the aristocracy, and then to acquire a preponderance for the Commons. It may be said that for two hundred years the Crown has exercised not control, but only influence, greater or less according to the monarch's personality. The actual control vanished when a German king of Great Britain found that his position depended on the good will of a party over whose discussions his linguistic deficiencies made it impossible for him to preside. The preponderance remained with the aristocracy, because a large proportion of seats in the representative chamber was virtually in the gift of peers, although **Relations of** the House of Commons **the two Houses** carried more weight than **of Parliament** the House of Lords. This ascendancy of the aristocracy disappeared with the Reform Act of 1832, which created a new antagonism between the Houses which has continually been intensified with the democratising of the Commons.

The character, however, of both Houses has been so materially modified since that date that our conceptions of the character of Parliament—largely derived from Burke —require readjustment. Exponents of the constitution, so recent even as Walter Bagehot, wrote before the democratic forces called into play by the second Reform Act had had time to show how they would operate. Until then the weight of the electorate had still been controlled by the propertied classes, and though the peers had lost their pocket boroughs, a large minority among them was still in accord with the advanced party in the House of Commons. But that Reform Act, that " leap in the dark," has made that advanced party much more advanced than it was before, since the electorate is no longer dominated by the propertied classes; a fraction only of the peers is in sympathy with it, since its principles involve considerable modifications in the theory of property; and when the advanced party has a majority in the Commons, it has to reckon on the consistent antagonism of the great majority of peers to its projects.

At the same time, the House of Commons has lost its preponderance in Parliament. That preponderance was won from the Crown in virtue of the power of **The Power** the people; it was assured as **of the House** against the peers so long as it **of Lords** was practically possible to bring pressure on the Crown for the creation of a sufficient number of peers to convert a party minority into a party majority. The mere threat to do so was effective when the peers were a sufficiently patrician body to feel that their social, even more than their political, character would be lost by the creation of forty new peers. The creation of forty peers would hardly affect the character of the House to-day—neither would it affect the party majority. To swamp the majority would involve swamping the House, and would make the constitution of the Second Chamber an absurdity. Hence, that method of compulsion could only be applied by a party determined either to abolish the second chamber or to construct it *de novo* on a basis already specified and accepted. On the other hand, the still older method by which the House of Commons enforced its will—the refusal of supplies— was efficacious only when the Commons were in opposition to the administration.

The effect is that the House of Lords can refuse to pass any measures distasteful to it, however emphatically endorsed by the Commons, until it feels that its refusal will ensure the decisive support of the electorate to a specific measure for its abolition or reconstruction. Whereas it can always count on the existence of a very strong predisposition, in the electorate, in favour of a Second Chamber of some sort, a conservative preference for the maintenance therein at least of an aristrocratic or hereditary element, and a dis- **Problem** tracting division of opinion **of the House** among reconstructors as to a **of Peers** practicable basis of reconstruction. Human ingenuity would never have deliberately devised such a second chamber as the House of Peers; but it has the enormous advantage of being a natural growth, not deliberately devised at all; and to dispossess it would be an experiment in constitution-making from which the political genius of the people of the

United Kingdom has an intense aversion. Thus, the constitutional position which the United Kingdom has reached to-day would seem to be this: The House of Commons—as we shall presently see—has a control over administration, and the peers, as a House, have none. The peers cannot carry legislation against the Commons; but they can set the legislative desires of the Commons at defiance, so long as they do not thereby rouse the electorate to an overwhelming determination to be rid of them at any price. They fulfil the theoretical function of a Second Chamber as a check on hasty legislation, but only when the legislation is democratic, not when it is reactionary. Whether, and when, the democracy will discover a satisfactory solution of the problem thus presented is becoming a somewhat acute question; but it can only be said that no solution hitherto propounded has commanded anything more than the doubtful acquiescence of any large body of reformers.

The Peers a Check on Hasty Legislation

In the legislative capacity of Parliament which we have had under consideration, the third element, the Crown, has ceased to have more than a formal importance. The technical right of veto remains in the background, but no one imagines that it will ever be exercised, unless conceivably in the case of some flagrant violation of constitutional practice by the Houses—in itself a sufficiently improbable event.

We come now to the relations between Parliament, the Judiciary, and the Executive. The Judiciary need not detain us long. The judges became independent two hundred years ago. A general guarantee of fitness is provided by the fact that they are removable on an address to the Crown by both Houses, but their independence is secured by the corresponding fact that it is only on such an address that they are removable. Their appointment rests nominally with the Crown, actually with the Crown's legal advisers, and security against grossly partisan appointments is assured by the presumption that such appointments would provoke retaliation. The real seat of the Government of the country is to be found only by examining the relations between the Parliament and the Executive, in "party" and "cabinet" government, affecting legislation as well as administration. The whole administration is controlled by officers technically

How Judges are Appointed

appointed by the Crown as the head, the Crown acting through Ministers. But the will of the people is expressed through Parliament. Before the "glorious revolution" of 1688 the king might, and very often did, choose Ministers who were antagonistic to Parliament, and Parliament could get rid of them only by the process of impeachments, or by refusing supplies—a double-edged weapon at the best of times.

The problem was to secure harmony between Parliament and the administration; which, in effect, meant the majority of the House of Commons and the administration. The solution was found in the selection of Ministers exclusively from the party which had a majority in the Commons; and the actual selection was very soon transferred, on the accession of the Hanoverians, from the Crown to the chief of the dominant party. The Crown, indeed, continued to exercise, on occasion, the technical right of declining the services of distasteful Ministers and of placing the selection in the hands of someone who was not the recognised leader of the majority; but in practice that technical right was gradually eliminated. The principle had already been established that Ministers themselves were personally responsible for their acts, and could not take shelter behind orders from the Crown; and the further principle was gradually established that the whole group of Ministers are responsible for the acts of each individual Minister, a system expressed by the phrase "collective responsibility of the Cabinet."

Collective Responsibility of the Cabinet

It became the practice that Ministers should be selected from members of one or other of the Houses of Parliament, in which connection it is curious to note that there was for a long time a dislike to their appointment from among the Commons, on the ground that, as the king's servants, they would exercise a dangerous monarchical influence in the House. It required an extended experience to show that their membership of the House increased the power of the House itself instead of curtailing its independence.

The group of the principal Ministers selected by the chief formed the confidential committee, which came to be known as the Cabinet, meeting in secret conclave to decide the course of the policy which is to be adopted and the legislative measures which are to be submitted to

Parliament. There is no technical bar, it may be remarked, to the initiation of legislation which does not emanate from the Cabinet, but such legislation has very little prospect of being carried unless the Cabinet choose to adopt it as a Government measure ; so that practically and normally the initiative lies with Ministers.

In a sense, however, the control of Ministers lies with the House of Commons, because if it is dissatisfied with their conduct, it can demand their resignation—such a demand formulated by the House of Lords would either be ignored or met by an appeal to the Commons for a vote of confidence. It has not hitherto been admitted that a Ministry supported by the representative Chamber can be dismissed by the peers ; but it could not venture to defy an adverse vote in the Commons, since, inter alia, Ministers are human enough not to be anxious to retain office if they are deprived of salaries. On the other hand, the Crown, though having the technical authority to dismiss a Minister or a whole Ministry, would not venture to do so without being absolutely **When a** sure that its action would be **Ministry** endorsed by an early appeal to **Resigns** the electorate. In practice, therefore, it is to the Commons that Ministers are responsible, and the Commons have the power of dismissal. Up to a certain point it is the Commons, also, that have the power of appointment. An adverse vote in the Commons on a fundamental question will compel Ministers either to resign or to advise a dissolution. In the former case the retiring chief recommends the Crown to " send for " the official leader of the Opposition, who holds that position by the choice of his party, which now is presumably—on the hypothesis that the House is composed of two parties—in a majority, or can command at least the provisional support of a majority. In the second case, the Ministry remains in office till it meets with an adverse vote in the new Parliament, when it will resign, and a new Ministry will be formed by the leader of the Opposition. In either case the Minister who constructs the Cabinet is the man whom the party which commands a majority has chosen as its leader. If he does not command a majority, he will accept office only with a view to an early dissolution. The Minister will construct his Cabinet, and select his colleagues, in general accord with the wishes of his party ; and so far it is true that the Ministry or Cabinet, the executive body, is appointed by the House of Commons—meaning thereby the political party which commands a majority in that House. Yet the real control of the House over the administration is limited. The system **The System** is workable only on the basis of **of Party** party government, the hypo- **Government** thesis that there are two main parties, to one or other of which all minor groups will attach themselves with some consistency. It is possible under the system for a Ministry to carry a series of measures, no one of which has the actual approval of an actual majority of members. If one of those measures is defeated, the Ministry will resign, and the Opposition will assume the government. A group of members who dislike one measure but are bent on a second, will give their support to the first rather than have the second shelved by the resignation of the Cabinet. Another group will reverse the process ; and the Government will successfully carry both measures, though each would have been lost if the reluctant supporters of the Government had given their votes exclusively on the merits of the particular measure.

What is true of the House of Commons is still more true of the electorate. The electorate chooses its party, not its specific measures. The prospect of Tariff Reform or of Local Option, of Land Reform or of an Education Bill, may decide which party shall predominate in Parliament ; but the electorate does not endorse beforehand all the measures which that party may see fit to adopt before another General Election. Different projects may be the decisive factors in the choice of different constituencies which unite to bring the same party into power ; and it is possible that neither project has the direct approval of a majority of constituencies, or of a majority of members, and may yet both be part of **Decisive** the avowed programme of the **Factors at** Ministers whom the victorious **Elections** party will support in passing both. It may be noted in passing that the resignation of the Cabinet does not necessarily involve the formation of a Ministry from the Opposition. If it is the outcome of dissensions within the Cabinet, the leader of the revolt, or someone in sympathy with the revolt, may be given the opportunity of reconstructing the

INTERIOR OF THE HOUSE OF LORDS AS SEEN FROM THE THRONE

INTERIOR OF THE CHAMBER, LOOKING TOWARDS THE THRONE

GREAT BRITAIN'S UPPER HOUSE OF PARLIAMENT

INTERIOR OF THE HOUSE, LOOKING TOWARDS THE STRANGERS GALLERY

INTERIOR OF THE HOUSE, LOOKING TOWARDS THE SPEAKER'S CHAIR

SCENES IN THE BRITISH HOUSE OF COMMONS

Government. But the fundamental fact is that the House of Commons will not formally attack Government measures or administration merely because it disapproves in particulars, so long as it sees in the defeat of Ministers the prospect only of an alternative Government, of which it disapproves more strongly in general.

How the Party System Works

Hence we arrive, not at the predominance of the House of Commons as a whole, nor exactly at a predominance of the Cabinet, but at a balance between the Cabinet and the majority of the party from which it is drawn. Unless some such vital question arises as Home Rule or Tariff Reform, the minorities of the party will support the majority, and the majority will support the Cabinet. The Cabinet can go its own way so long as the threat of resignation will keep its majority solid ; but the Cabinet cannot defy a majority which is ready to demand its resignation if it does so. But beyond the House of Commons there is the House of Lords, which can render the legislation—though not the administration—nugatory so long as it does not endanger its own existence by so doing. The peers have been not infrequently threatened, but threatened men live long. It cannot well be maintained in the circumstances as expounded that a supremacy can be definitely located.

The will of the majority of the House of Commons is not necessarily, at least in particulars, that of the electorate. The vote of the majority does not necessarily express the wish even of that majority. The Cabinet is powerless unless it can command that vote, and the vote itself may be rendered nugatory by the peers. It may be seen that the system is decidedly remote from any logical ideal, and this will be further emphasised by two considerations. The first of these is the structure of the Cabinet, which conducts administration. The logician

Paradoxes in the State Departments

would set an expert at the head of each Department of state ; the system provides in each a board of expert advisers, but sets at the head someone who, as often as not, is entirely without experience in the work of that department. We may have a bookseller at the Admiralty, a metaphysician at the War Office, a warcorrespondent at the Board of Trade, a country gentleman in charge of Finance,

and an untravelled attorney in charge of India or the Colonies. Experience teaches that the practice has very high merits, but it is supremely paradoxical.

The second point is that the whole system rests on the theory that one or other of two parties can always command a majority in the Commons. Yet there is nothing in the nature of things to ensure that this shall always be the case ; on the contrary, a third party has been in existence for many years, and once at least neither of the two great parties could have conducted the Government while the third party refused its support. A fourth party has already come definitely into existence ; it can no longer be regarded as in any way certain that one party will be able to command a majority of the House.

It will be necessary for two, or possibly for three of the parties to come to terms of alliance, and the programme, or part of the programme, of a small minority may be forced 'on Ministers as the condition on which their own particular programme can be carried through. Our point is that democratisation seems

Britain's Destiny in the Future

to tend of itself to the multiplication of parties, and the multiplication of parties tends to produce legislative deadlock and extreme instability of administration. And it appears at the present moment by no means improbable that the group of questions here indicated may be rendered additionally complicated at an early date by the appearance of the women's franchise in the sphere of practical politics.

Nevertheless, we may take heart of grace. Our political constitution has always and everywhere presented an abundance of paradoxes and inconsistencies, which ought by rule to have prevented progress by locking the machinery ; yet the machinery has never been brought to a standstill, nor have the works been kept going by destroying the old machinery to replace it with a brand-new article. It has always been found possible to adapt the old machinery to the new work it had to do ; and we may confidently expect that the process of adaptation will continue, the machinery will still work without revolutionary reconstruction, and the population of these islands will not cease yet awhile to hold a foremost place among the free nations of the world, of which nations not a few will be our brothers of the British Empire. A. D. INNES

INFORMATION ABOUT THE UNITED KINGDOM

AREA AND POPULATION. The area of the constituent parts of the United Kingdom and the population at last census (1901), including the Army, Navy, and merchant seamen abroad, are as follow:

	Sq. miles	Population
England	50,903	30,811,420
Wales	7,421	1,716,423
Scotland	30,405	4,472,103
Ireland	32,360	4,458,775
Isle of Man	227	54,752
Channel Islands	75	95,618
Army, Navy, and Merchant Seamen abroad	—	367,736
Total	121,391	41,976,827

PARLIAMENT. The supreme legislative power of the British Empire vests in Parliament, which consists of the representatives of the three estates of the realm—the Clergy, the Lords, and the Commons. The Lords Spiritual, or the representatives of the clergy, and the Lords Temporal, as the lay lords are designated, make up the Upper Chamber, or House of Lords. The names on the " roll " of the House of Lords number 615 at present. The number of Lords Spiritual in the Upper House is 26, and must include the Archbishops of Canterbury and York, and the Bishops of London, Durham and Winchester. No Scottish or Irish bishops sit in the House of Lords. The Lords Temporal consist of hereditary peers, life peers and law lords. Princes of the royal house have seats in the House of Lords, and although there are three of them on the roll of the House—the Prince of Wales, the Duke of Connaught, and the Duke of Saxe-Coburg-Gotha—they never debate, and seldom take part in a division. There are 28 Irish representative peers, who are elected for life; 16 Scottish representative peers, who are elected for each Parliament; and 22 dukes, 23 marquises, 124 earls, 40 viscounts, and 333 barons—sitting by right of their peerage. The House of Commons, or Lower Chamber, is an elective assembly on a low property franchise established by the Act of 1884, which made the Commons a democratic Chamber. There are 670 members in all, distributed as follows:

	Counties	Boroughs	Universities	Total
England	234	226	5	465
Wales	19	11	—	30
Scotland	39	31	2	72
Ireland	85	16	2	103
	377	284	9	670

Of these London returns 60 members, including one member from London University. Details of electoral qualification differ in different parts of the United Kingdom. The voting qualification upon the basis of property ownership is:

England and Wales
  (a) Freehold estate worth 40s. annually.
  (b) Land held in any tenure for life and worth £5 annually.
  (c) Leasehold of £5 annual value, of which original term was for not less than 60 years.
  (d) Leasehold of £60 annual value, of which original term was not less than 20 years.

Scotland
  (a) Lands and heritages of £5 annual value.
  (b) Leasehold of £10 annual value, held for life or original term being for not less than 57 years.
  (c) Leasehold of £50 annual value, original term of not less than 19 years.

Ireland
  (a) Freehold of £5 net annual value.
  (b) Rent charges on leases for life of £10 annual value.
  (c) Leasehold of £10 annual value, originally held for not less than 60 years.
  (d) Leasehold of £20 annual value, originally held for not less than 14 years.

There is also throughout the United Kingdom an occupation and a residence qualification to vote, and lodgers renting accommodation worth £10 a year unfurnished may claim a vote after 12 months' residence prior to any July 15. Liverymen of the City of London, graduates on the electoral roll of the Universities of Oxford, Cambridge, Dublin, and London, and members of the University Court and General Council of Edinburgh, Glasgow, St. Andrews and Aberdeen, vote for the City of London, and for their respective universities.

Unless dissolved by the Crown, Parliament lasts for seven years. The sovereign summons, prorogues or dissolves Parliament, and gives the royal assent to Bills that have passed both Chambers. The Lord High Chancellor is Speaker of the House of Lords as well as principal legal adviser to the Crown; and the Speaker of the House of Commons is elected to that office by the House, and holds office until a dissolution.

GOVERNMENT. In practice, government is carried on by the Cabinet, which is really a committee of the Privy Council. The Cabinet always includes, in addition to the Prime Minister, the First Lord of the Treasury, Lord Chancellor, Lord President of the Council, Lord Privy Seal, the five Secretaries of State—Home, Foreign, Colonial, War and India—and the First Lord of the Admiralty. But it usually includes other seven or eight heads of departments, such as the Chief Secretary for Ireland, the Presidents of the Local Government Board, of the Board of Trade, and of the Board of Education and the Postmaster-General, thus making about 18 members in all. The Prime Minister is invariably the leader of the great parliamentary party that has, at the time of his assumption of power, the commanding number of votes in the House of Commons. The sovereign sends for this leader, exercising his discretion in the event of several members of the party having apparently equal claims to the ability and position of leader, and entrusts him with the formation of a Ministry, which consists of about 50 Ministers, of whom about eighteen usually form a Cabinet, as indicated above.

MONARCH. The reigning king is Edward VII., born November 9th, 1841, son of Queen Victoria and the Prince Consort—Prince Albert of Saxe-Coburg-Gotha—succeeded his mother on January 22nd, 1901. He is the seventh ruler of the House of Hanover. His official title is: Edward VII., by the grace of God, of the United Kingdom of Great Britain and Ireland, and of the British Dominions Beyond the Seas, King, Defender of the Faith, Emperor of India.

FINANCE. The total National Debt of the United Kingdom on March 31st, 1908, was £759,826,051, made up as follows:

Funded—Permanent	£625,608,890
Annuities	39,407,575
Unfunded	43,959,400
Other Capital Liabilities	50,850,186
	£759,826,051

Suez Canal shares and other assets represent value for £44,392,863, so that the net debt is £715,433,188. The funded debt is nearly all in 2½ per cent. Consols. The interest and sinking fund charge for the financial year 1907–8 was £29,500,000, which included £8,365,294 to the sinking fund.

The total national revenue and expenditure for the year 1907–8 was as follows:

REVENUE	£
Customs	32,490,000
Excise	35,720,000
Property and Income Tax	32,380,000
Estate Duties	19,070,000
Stamps	7,970,000
House Duty	1,960,000
Land Tax	730,000
Post Office	17,880,000
Telegraphs	4,420,000
Crown Lands	520,000
Interest—Suez Canal, etc.	1,190,000
Miscellaneous	2,208,000
	£156,538,000

EXPENDITURE	£
Interest on National Debt	18,591,000
Repayment—National Debt	10,999,000
Other Consolidated Fund Services	1,972,000
Payments to Local Taxation Accounts	11,155,000
Army	27,115,000
Navy	31,141,000
Civil Services	30,180,000
Customs and Inland Revenue	3,222,000
Post Office	17,527,000
	£151,812,000

CUSTOMS AND EXCISE. The Customs Duties of the United Kingdom are as follow :

Beer 8/- to 37/6 per barrel.
Chicory, raw, 13s. 3d. per cwt. ; roasted, 2d. per lb.
Cocoa and cocoa butter, 1d. per lb.
Chocolate, 2d. per lb.
Coffee, raw, 14s. per cwt. ; roasted or ground, 2d. per lb.
Currants, 2s. per cwt.
Figs, raisins, French plums and prunes, 7s. per cwt.
Playing cards, 3¾d. per pack.
Spirits, 11s. 4d. and 11s. 5d. per proof gallon, or 1s. per gallon extra if bottled.
Soap containing alcohol, 3d. per lb.
Sugar, 2s. to 4s. 2d. per cwt.
Tea, 5d. per lb.
Tobacco, raw, 3/- to 3s. 4¾d. per lb.
Tobacco and snuff, manufactured, 3s. 7d. to 6s. per lb.
Wine in cask, 1s. 3d. to 3s. per gallon.

The Excise Duties are as follow :

Beer, 7s. 9d. per barrel.
Spirits, 11s. per gallon.
Glucose, solid, 2s. 9d. per cwt. ; liquid, 2/- per cwt.
Saccharin, 1s. 3d. per oz.

There are, in addition, many exise licences such as game and gun licences, marriage licences, plate licences, pawnbrokers', auctioneers', pedlars', hawkers', and dog licences.

AGRICULTURE. The total land area of the United Kingdom is about 77,000,000 acres, and of this total quantity about 4 per cent. consists of woods and plantations, about 20 per cent. is mountain and heath land used for grazing, about 35 per cent. is permanent pasture, about 25 per cent. is arable, and the remaining 16 per cent. consists of water surface, waste land incapable of cultivation, and land containing buildings. According to the latest census (1901), the total number of persons employed in agriculture, including also those employed on stock and dairy farms, gardeners and nurserymen, seedsmen and florists, was 2,262,454. The acreage of the arable land under the principal crops was in 1907 as follows : Oats, 4,218,541 ; barley, 1,885,359 ; turnips and swedes, 1,846,128 ; wheat, 1,665,017 ; potatoes, 1,151,632 ; mangolds, 518,019 ; beans and peas, 478,292. Comparison of these figures with the averages of the five quintennial periods before 1900 show that in every crop except oats and peas and beans the acreage of 1907 was the smallest. Other crops with smaller acreage are rye, cabbage, vetches or tares, lucerne, rape, flax, and hops. In 1907 the number of livestock were : Sheep, 30,011,219 ; cattle, 11,628,483 ; pigs, 3,966,824 ; and horses, 2,088,932.

FISHERIES. The official figures relating to the sea fisheries of the United Kingdom in 1906 give the following details, which do not include fish curers, packers, sail and net makers, and others dependent on the fishing industry :

	Regular fishermen	Occasionally employed	Total
England and Wales	35,007	8,080	43,087
Scotland	28,757	10,072	38,829
Ireland	7,879	16,575	24,454
Isle of Man	603	220	823
Channel Islands	544	183	727
Total	72,790	35,130	107,920

The number of fishing boats, including trawlers, liners and drifters, in 1907, was 9,332 in England and Wales, 10,365 in Scotland, and 6,097 in Ireland. The total quantity of the fish landed in 1907 was 23,770,271 tons, not including shell-fish ; and the total value, including shell-fish, was £11,738,426.

MINERALS. The number of persons in the United Kingdom who were employed in mines and quarries in 1907 was 1,060,034 :

	Coal	Metalliferous	Quarries
Under ground	757,887	18,569	
Above ground	177,081	12,819	87,814
Females	5,650	214	—
Total	940,618	31,602	87,814

The mineral output for 1907 was as follows :

	Tons	Value		Tons	Value
		£			£
Alum shale	9,905	1,692	Gypsum	235,517	88,629
Arsenic	1,499	35,829	Igneous		
Arsenical			rocks	5,674,470	1,158,951
pyrites	1,772	2,990	Iron ore	15,731,694	4,433,418
Barium			Iron pyrites	10,194	4,489
compounds	41,974	38,440	Lead ore	32,533	419,247
Bauxite (aluminium ore)	7,537	1,884	Lime phosphate	32	46
Bog ore	6,290	1,573	Manganese		
Chalk	4,779,387	200,882	ore	16,098	16,516
Other limestone	12,509,142	1,323,624	Mica..	14,615	5,074
Chert and flint	53,664	12,705	Ochre and umber	14,692	14,408
Clay and shale	14,827,895	1,850,387	Petroleum shale	2,690,028	806,323
Coal	267,830,962	120,527,378	Salt	1,984,656	648,596
Copper ore	6,625	21,253	Sandstone	5,012,053	1,397,285
Copper precipitate	267	12,665	Slate..	443,554	1,178,609
			Sulphate of		
Diatomite	150	450	strontia	10,745	8,059
Fluorspar	49,462	23,341	Tin ore	7,080	706,700
Gold ore	12,973	5,625	Uranium ore	71	6,500
Gravel and sand	2,400,392	183,625	Wolfram ore	322	41,044
			Zinc ore	20,082	100,533

GENERAL INDUSTRIES. No official or other statistics give precise or approximate information regarding the output of the many manufacturing industries of the United Kingdom. Exports and imports are carefully tabulated, but not output. The census of Production Act of 1906 will remedy this defect in our industrial statistical system by collecting data regarding the nature and volume of our home production. Meantime, the only standards of comparison are the census returns which concern occupation. Last census (1901) showed the numbers of persons employed in various occupations to be as follow :

General or local government of the country	253,865
Defence of the country (excluding army, navy, and marines abroad)	203,993
Professional occupations and their subordinate services	733,582
Domestic offices or services (excluding domestic or outdoor service)	2,199,517
Commercial occupations	712,465
Conveyance of men, goods, and messages	1,497,629
Agriculture	2,262,454
Fishing	61,925
In and about and dealing in the product of mines and quarries..	943,880
Metal, machines, implements, and conveyances	1,475,410
Precious metals, jewels, watches, instruments and games (including electricity supply)	168,344
Building and works of construction	1,335,820
Wood, furniture, fittings, and decorations	307,632
Brick, cement, pottery, and glass	189,956
Chemicals, oil, grease, soap, etc..	149,675
Skins, leather, hair and feathers	117,866
Paper, prints, books, and stationery	334,261
Textile fabrics..	1,462,001
Workers and dealers in dress	1,395,795
Food, tobacco, drink, and lodging	1,301,076
Gas, water, and sanitary service ..	78,686
Other general and undefined workers and dealers	1,075,414
Total	18,261,146

IMPORTS AND EXPORTS. The imports of merchandise into the United Kingdom for the year 1907 were of the value of £645,807,942, and the exports were of the value of £426,035,083. Of the imports British possessions supplied 24½ per cent., and of the exports British possessions took 32 per cent. The exports are divided into three classes :

1. Food, drink, and tobacco	£22,729,648
2. Raw materials and articles, mainly manufactured	55,003,081
3. Articles wholly or mainly manufactured	342,025,273
Miscellaneous and unclassified..	6,277,081
Total	£426,035,083

The third class is further divided into groups, as follows :

Iron and steel and manufactures thereof	£46,563,386
Other metals	11,674,131
Cutlery, hardware, implements and instruments	6,434,002
Electrical goods and apparatus (not machinery and wire)	2,469,927
Machinery	31,743,233
Ships (new)	10,018,313
Manufactures of wood and timber	1,407,392
Yarn and textile fabrics—	
Cotton	110,437,092
Wool	34,158,857
Other materials	16,503,896
Apparel	7,177,764
Chemicals, drugs, dyes, and colours	17,052,755
Leather and manufactures thereof	6,599,591
Earthenware and glass	4,048,893
Paper	2,344,290
Miscellaneous	33,391,451

INFORMATION ABOUT THE BRITISH EMPIRE

AREA AND POPULATION. The area of the entire British Empire is about 11,400,000 square miles, which is about 21 per cent. of the known land surface of the globe; and the population of the entire British Empire is about 410,000,000, which is about 22 per cent. of the entire population of the globe. The area and population (estimated for 1907) of the constituent parts of the British Empire are as follow:

	Sq. miles	Population
United Kingdom	121,391	44,100,231
Gibraltar and Malta	119	225,314
Cyprus	3,580	250,590
Aden	9,080	43,970
British India	1,087,124	231,855,533
Indian Feudatory States	679,393	62,461,549
Ceylon	25,330	3,984,980
Straits Settlements, Malay States and Islands	101,110	2,152,770
Stations in China	670	568,070
Australia and British New Guinea (Papua)	3,065,120	4,479,840
New Zealand, with dependent islands	104,750	900,920
Pacific Islands—Fiji, Tonga, Solomon, and Gilbert Islands	16,670	331,840
British West Africa, with St. Helena and Ascension	486,540	16,814,360
British South Africa, with Rhodesia	1,241,750	8,288,600
Nyassaland and Uganda	399,090	6,540,000
Zanzibar, Somaliland, Mauritius, and Seychelles	70,010	903,000
Canada, Newfoundland, and Labrador	3,908,300	6,216,340
Bermuda and West India Islands	12,040	1,746,530
British Honduras	7,560	41,010
British Guiana	90,280	307,000
Falkland Islands and South Georgia	7,500	2,070

The total revenue of the British Empire is more than £400,000,000, and the National and State Debts aggregate over £1,500,000,000. The trade of the empire is more than £1,600,000,000 annually. There is more than 90,000 mileage of railway, and the total tonnage of shipping sailing under the British flag is 12,160,000 tons.

All the great self-governing colonies—Canada, South Africa, Australia, and New Zealand—have a preferential scheme of Customs duties, whereby articles of British manufacture are taxed upon a lower tariff than similar goods from foreign countries.

COLONIAL CONSTITUTIONS. Royal authority over British oversea dominions (except India) is exercised by the Secretary of State for the Colonies, who has the power of veto over all laws passed by colonial legislatures. This power of veto is, however, seldom exercised. The Secretary of State for the Colonies, or the Colonial Secretary as he is more frequently termed, presides over the Colonial Office, the state department through which he exercises his executive authority. Actual executive action is confined to the affairs of Crown Colonies and Protectorates, but the department is the channel through which the self-governing colonies arrange matters involving imperial and foreign interests. Governors of colonies are chosen by the king upon the advice of the Colonial Secretary.

The colonies and dependencies fall into seven classes, according to their constitutions:

(a) India has a constitution differing from all other colonies and dependencies, and is under the Secretary of State for India and the Indian Council, who preside over the India Office, a department independent from the Colonial Office. [See page 1363.]

(b) Self-governing colonies, where the Colonial Secretary has control over no public officer except the governor, and where the Crown has reserved only the power of disallowing legislation. These colonies are the six states comprising the Australian Commonwealth (of which Papua is a dependency), Canada, Newfoundland, New Zealand, Cape Colony, Natal, Transvaal, and Orange River Colony.

(c) Colonies with an elected House of Assembly and a nominated Legislative Council. These are Bahamas, Barbados, and Bermuda.

(d) Colonies with a partly elected Legislative Council. These colonies and dependencies are British Guiana, Fiji, Jamaica, Leeward Islands, Malta, and Mauritius. In all except British Guiana the constitution provides for an official majority in the Legislative Council. Cyprus has a constitution similar to that of British Guiana; but although administered by the British Colonial Office, it is, technically, a Turkish possession.

(e) Colonies and dependencies with Legislative Councils nominated by the British Crown. These are British Honduras, Falkland Islands, St. Lucia, St. Vincent, Trinidad, Grenada, East Africa Protectorate, Gambia, Gold Coast, Sierra Leone, Southern Nigeria, Nyassaland, Ceylon, Hong Kong, and Straits Settlements. In all these, except British Honduras, the constitution provides for an official majority.

(f) Colonies and protectorates without a Legislative Council. These are: Ashanti, Basutoland, Bechuanaland, Gibraltar, Northern Nigeria, Northern Territories of the Gold Coast, St. Helena, Somaliland, Uganda, Wei-hai-wei, and the Western Pacific Islands which are under a single high commissioner, and include the Tonga, or Friendly Islands, Union, Ellice, Gilbert, Southern Solomon, Santa Cruz, and New Hebrides Islands, Pitcairn and Ocean Island or Paanopa.

(g) Territory administered by a company, under powers conferred by Royal Charter. The only such territory is Rhodesia, which is administered by the British South Africa Company, through an administrator and four members appointed by the company, with the approval of the Colonial Secretary, assisted by a Legislative Council partly elected.

THE COLONIAL OFFICE. For convenience of administration the Colonial Office is divided into three departments (a) the Dominions Department, which is concerned with the self-governing colonies, and with those Crown Colonies and Protectorates in South Africa and the Pacific Ocean which are intimately connected with self-governing colonies; (b) the Crown Colonies Department, which is concerned with the administration of the Crown Colonies; and (c) the General Department, which is responsible for the general routine work of the office and affairs common to all Crown Colonies—i.e., banking, currency, education, posts and telegraphs.

The British Colonial Office transacts business in the United Kingdom for the following colonies and protectorates, and acts in the capacity of their commercial and financial agents: Bahamas, Barbados, Basutoland, Bechuanaland, Bermuda, British Guiana, British Honduras, Ceylon, Cyprus, East Africa Protectorate, Falkland Islands, Fiji, Gambia, Gibraltar, Gold Coast, Hong Kong, Jamaica, Labuan, Leeward Islands, Malta, Mauritius, Newfoundland, Nigeria, Nyassaland, St. Helena, Seychelles, Sierra Leone, Somaliland Protectorate, Straits Settlements, Swaziland, Tobago, Trinidad, Turks Island, Uganda, Wei-hai-wei, and the Windward Islands. The Colonial Office receives instructions direct from the colonial governments, but takes the opinion and advice of the Secretary of State for the Colonies upon important matters, and upon any question of constitutional principle.

IMPERIAL CONFERENCE. A conference, at which the British Government and the self-governing colonies are represented, is held every four years. The Prime Minister of the United Kingdom is president *ex officio*, and the Secretary of State for the Colonies is a member of the Conference, and acts as chairman in the absence of the president. The last conference was held in 1907.

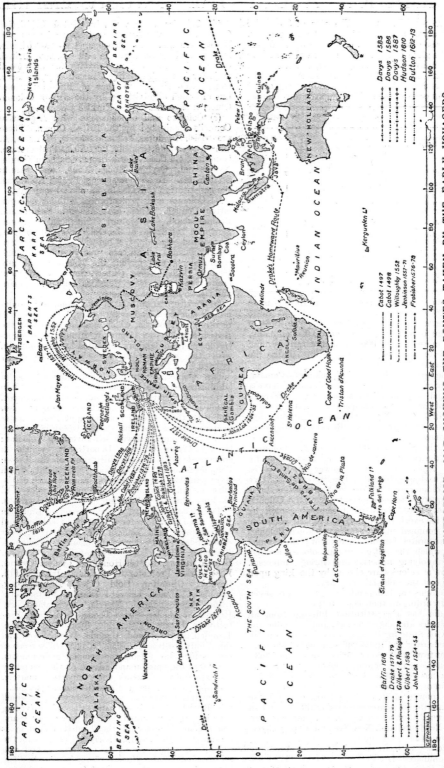

BRITAIN'S MARITIME ENTERPRISE: MAP SHOWING THE ROUTES TAKEN BY THE EARLY VOYAGERS

To the sailors who left her shores on voyages of discovery, beginning at the close of the fifteenth century, Great Britain owes a heavy debt of gratitude, for in most cases their discoveries increased the nation's territory and laid the foundations of the world-wide empire of the present day. The routes followed by these early voyagers are illustrated in the above map.

THE BRITISH EMPIRE
FROM EARLIEST TIMES TO THE PRESENT DAY
ITS EFFECT ON WORLD HISTORY
By Sir Harry Johnston, G.C.M.G.
THE EMPIRE IN THE MAKING AND THE WONDERFUL PROGRESS OF TWO CENTURIES

BEFORE considering in detail the evolution of the British Empire, and the effect of that empire on the British people and on the world at large, it may be as well to glance at the elements which have formed the present tribes of English and Keltic-speaking people of Great Britain and Ireland, who from the point of view of the extent, population, wealth, and civilisation of their empire in Europe, America, Asia and Africa have been up to the present the first among ruling races.

The people now inhabiting the British Islands are, so far as investigations go in history, archæology and palæontology, the result of many layers of humanity, belonging in the main to the white, or Caucasian, sub-species, which have inhabited England, Wales, Scotland and Ireland for the last hundred thousand years or so. Man, of a Neanderthaloid type, that is to say, a creature resembling most, of all existing races, the black Australians or the Veddahs of Ceylon, probably entered England when Great Britain, and even Ireland, were eccentric**The First Inhabitants of Britain** ally shaped peninsulas attached by isthmuses one to the other and to the north of France and Belgium. A calvarium—upper part of the skull—has been exhumed in Sligo, North-west Ireland, and is now in the British Museum of Natural History, which offers some resemblance to the Neanderthaloid crania found in Belgium, the Rhine Valley, and the Carpathians.

This early and generalised type of humanity, which some anthropologists think should be classified as a separate species of humanity, was, at any rate, near the basic stock of *Homo sapiens* before this last became differentiated into the **Men of the Early Stone Age** Negro, Mongol, or Caucasian sub-species. The Man of Neanderthal, I believe, bore a strong resemblance to the lower types of black Australians of to-day, and these last offer considerable analogies in skull form and in culture to the early palæolithic men of Britain. Whether man continuously inhabited the British peninsulas during the changes of climate which marked the Pleistocene period, with its glacial interludes of Polar conditions, is not yet clearly established. The recurring cycles of extreme cold which covered Scotland, Northern England, and the greater part of Ireland with an ice sheet may have killed out the Australoid men of the Early Stone Age; or these latter may have gradually accustomed themselves to the cold and have survived to more genial conditions.

Or the Palæolithic people, with their projecting brows, retreating foreheads, long arms and shambling legs, were perhaps exterminated not by climatic changes, but by the inrush of the first definitely "white" people of the Caucasian stock. These, it is surmised, were more or less akin to the Iberian people of Mediterranean Europe, Western (and far

North-eastern) Asia and North Africa—white men with dark hair and brown eyes. Then parts of Europe, and perhaps Great Britain, were invaded by a round-headed people, probably of Asiatic origin, who seem to have brought with them a greater number and variety of domestic animals and improved arts. Mongoloid tribes of short heads, or long - headed types like the Eskimo, may also have reached 'Great Britain from the north-east across the ice sheet, and have penetrated to Ireland. The Iberians of prehistoric days probably spoke a language allied to modern Basque or to the Berber tongues of North Africa. Some three or four thousand years ago our islands were conquered and over-run from the East by the first Aryans—long-headed Northern Europeans, with red or blond hair and blue eyes; early Kelts, in fact, who grafted their Aryan speech on to the Iberian stock, and so brought into existence the Keltic languages of the two very distinct modern branches—Scoto-Irish (Goidhelic), and Welsh (Brythonic).

Britain Three Thousand Years Ago

This amalgam of people—the earlier tribes of which resembled very much, no doubt, the modern Ainos of Japan, the Lapps of Northern Europe, the Auvergnats of Central France, the Finns, and the modern Belgians—warred, inter-married, compromised, and co-existed in innumerable tribes under petty chieftains, quite outside the history of the civilised Mediterranean world—though not out of touch with its commerce—until some five hundred years before Christ; when the coasts of Southern England may have been reached by Phœnician trading ships, who later brought back some news of Britain and even Ireland to the Greek geographers of Alexander's day and kingdom.

Then came the extension of the Roman Empire, the invasion of England by Cæsar—because the Brythonic Kelts made common cause with their Gallo-Belgian kinsmen — and the beginning of the historical period in Britain. Still, our countries continued to receive, and not to export, humanity. In the centuries that followed the Roman Conquest a few Irish missionaries, or British refugees, found their way into Northern France, where the Bretons constituted the first of British colonies. But the islands of Great Britain, Ireland and Man still attracted colonists from the outer

Cæsar's Invasion of England

world. Hordes of Germanic people occupied England and Eastern Scotland, coming from Scandinavia and the Western and North-western parts of modern Germany. Denmark and Norway between the ninth and thirteenth centuries must have contributed quite two millions of immigrants—tall, fair-haired, blue-eyed, but also occasionally tall and dark-haired (from Denmark, where an anterior Iberian people had left its traces)—to the population of Eastern England, Eastern and Northern Scotland, the Isle of Man, and all the coast regions of Ireland.

The Norman Conquest brought in its train and as its results several thousands of Frenchmen—tinged with Norse blood. The French kings of England, the Plantagenets, planted many colonies of Flemings from Belgium, or Germans from the lower Rhine ; also occasional settlers from South-west France. A few Spaniards came and remained with Philip II. of Spain, or were stranded on these shores as prisoners during the wars of the sixteenth century. Gipsies had crossed over to England at the close of the fifteenth century and had rapidly penetrated, several thousand in number, to the wilder parts of East Anglia, the Welsh Border-land, and Lowland Scotland, contributing a picturesque attenuated element of the Dravidian to a populace mostly pink and white and blond-haired.

Britain's Age of Maturity

In the wonderful Tudor period, the sixteenth century, the great race movements which had colonised these islands ceased for a time ; and Britain, having reached maturity, was ready to send its superfluous and, above all, its adventurous sons to seek new homes and found new nations. It is true that in the seventeenth and eighteenth centuries there came a few thousand French refugees from religious persecution—invaluable as individuals ; and that in the nineteenth century there has been an immigration of Germans, of Jews from Eastern and Northern Europe, and of Italians. These aliens—most of them desirable, a few undesirable—though not reaching to the sum total of a million, still have made and will make their mark on the future type of the British population, especially in the towns. But for the purposes of our survey it may be stated that the colonisation of Great Britain and Ireland ceased at the end of the fifteenth century; and that at this period began the wonderful outpouring of energy which was to create not only the largest empire that the world has ever known, but probably the biggest congeries of states under the rule of one monarch that the world will ever know until the complete federation of mankind under one earthly head is accomplished.

This résumé of the race elements in the British Islands has been necessary in order that we may arrive at some appreciation of the type of humanity which has conquered and colonised the British Empire. It is a breed retaining strains of the Iberian, even of the earliest of the prehistoric peoples of Northern Europe, but is nevertheless an amalgam in which the blond Aryan type predominates; the type which is chiefly associated at the present day with the speaking of Low German dialects. To this group English belongs. The people who founded the British Empire in the days of the Tudors and Stuarts were mainly Teutonic and Scandinavian in descent, though tinged with the Iberian in the seamen of Devon and Cornwall. The British

Founders of the British Empire colonisers and adventurers of the fifteenth, sixteenth, seventeenth, and eighteenth centuries were almost entirely drawn from Southern Scotland, England and Wales. Ireland during these centuries was itself a "champ d'exploitation" on the part of our ruthless ancestors of the larger island, though occasionally in the seventeenth century some hundreds of rebellious Irish were deported to the West Indies.

It was not until the nineteenth century that the union of Ireland with England—however unjustly it was brought about—threw open to the sons of Ireland all the advantages of the British Empire. Since then, during the nineteenth and the first few years of the twentieth centuries, the Irish, proportionately, have done more in colonising the daughter states of the empire and in administering India and the Crown colonies than the people of Great Britain.

England was the first amongst the arbitrary sub-national divisions of the now United Kingdom to think of colonising. This movement began after the European revival of learning, known as the Renaissance. As already mentioned, however, the English were not the first colonisers to leave these islands; for in

the period that immediately followed the extension of Roman civilisation in Britain, the Irish—who, though they were never actually under the sway of Rome, had become, through the Church, one of the most Romanised peoples of Western Europe—had been stirred by a strange spirit of adventure, which first took the

Ireland's Seafaring Pioneers form of missionary travels in Scotland, France and Germany, and then linked on with Norse maritime discovery; so that from Ireland came one of the first mysterious hints of a New World beyond the Atlantic. It is doubtful whether the seafaring monks or fishermen of Western Ireland ever reached the North American continent, even by following the Norse route to the Faroes, Iceland, Greenland and Newfoundland; but it does seem possible that the Irish may have sailed south-westwards past the coasts of Portugal to the Azores or Madeira, or even as far to the north-west as the once larger island of Rockall. Their more than half legendary adventures deserve mention, since they became the germ that inspired the English and Welsh raiders of the Plantagenet centuries with the idea of oversea discovery.

The Danish and Norwegian invaders of our islands were colonisers of the most successful type. They were looking for homes beyond the inclement lands of Scandinavia—inclement under ancient conditions—and they brought to the Anglo-Saxon civilisation of Alfred much knowledge of Northern geography. Through these, and through the civilised Franks of France, Alfred, the Saxon king of Southern England, was linked up (Rome helping) with the Byzantine Empire; and there is an actual tradition of Alfred having despatched, in 883, Sighelm of Sherborne as a pilgrim, via Rome, to the shrine of St. Thomas, in "India." Though Sighelm may have got no further

England's Commerce with Venice than the Nestorian churches of Mesopotamia, still even a journey to India was quite possible in the days before the Seljuk and Ottoman Turks had raised barriers of fanaticism between Christian Europe and Mohammedan Asia.

Commerce brought the England of the Plantagenets into touch with Venice—Venice which had already revealed to the world, through such travellers as Marco Polo, the existence of Asiatic kingdoms, islands and peninsulas as far as China, Sumatra and Java. Venetian maritime explorers turned their attention to the discovery of Ultima Thule, possibly as the result of some news having reached Venice of the Norwegian settlements in lands across the Northern Atlantic, also because of the important fisheries in the far North-west. In Plantagenet

Beginnings of Maritime Adventure times, however, the British lust for conquest and colonisation was slaked by the attempts to conquer and settle Scotland, Ireland, Northern and Western France. The idea of maritime adventure did not dawn on the English people till after the Wars of the Roses and the establishment of the Tudor dynasty; in fact, until the very end of the fifteenth century. Even then the mass of the people thought of no such thing. The impulse was first given by the far-sighted though stingy monarch, Henry VII., the father-in-law of an Aragonese princess, through whose relations he had heard of the conquest and settlement of the Canary Islands and Madeira, and of Spanish, Portuguese, Majorcan and Genoese adventures along the West Coast of Africa.

To the court of Henry VII. came an adventurous but disappointed Venetian mariner, John Cabot, whose famous son, Sebastian, was probably born at Bristol. In the minds of this and other Venetian navigators may have lingered the semi-legendary voyages of Nicolá and Antonio Zeno in the fourteenth century—perhaps founded on Norse traditions—which led them to habitable lands on the other side of the North Atlantic to the Vineland (Rhode Island), where grew wild grapes in profusion. Henry Tudor committed himself as grudgingly to maritime discovery as did the father-in-law of his son, Ferdinand of Aragon. John and Sebastian Cabot, however, led British crews to the discovery of Newfoundland and other points of North America, with

The Early Voyages of Discovery no very immediate results. But when the Englishmen of Devon and Cornwall, of London, Bristol, Pembroke, Cardiff, Swansea, Poole, Southampton, Tilbury, Lowestoft, and Yarmouth built better and bigger ships in imitation of, or under the teaching of, the Norman French—who, in all probability, had sailed to West Africa as early as the middle of the fourteenth century—the Dutch, Venetians, Genoese, and

Spaniards; and when, disdaining further foreign pilotage, they started forth in their own bottoms, guided by their own navigators and financed by their own capitalists, they did not for the moment turn their attention to America, but devoted themselves eagerly to the West African trade.

As I have related in other chapters, it was the longing for pepper, the desire to make money by carrying slaves, and finally the thirst for gold, that drew the British to West Africa during the reigns of Edward, Mary, and Elizabeth. At first the British adventurers hired themselves as mariners to the Portuguese, and so found out their way to the Guinea coast. Later, they would engage a Portuguese as captain or supercargo. But by the year 1554 they were sufficiently sure of themselves to undertake an all-British venture to West Africa under the command of Captain John Lok, with whom travelled Sir George Barn and Sir John York. The two ships under Captain Lok's command visited the coast of Liberia and reached the Gold Coast in 1555. In 1585 and 1588, Queen Elizabeth issued two

Royal Patron of English Trade patents, or monopolies, for trade with the Atlantic coast of Africa. The earlier dealt with Morocco; the second with the region between the Senegal and the Gambia. A third charter, or patent, issued in 1592, covered the Guinea coast between the River Nunez and, approximately, the Sherbro district.

The transportation of negro slaves from West Africa to the West Indies and Spanish America—first undertaken by Captain (afterwards Sir John) Hawkins in 1562—initiated the British into the wonders, the wealth, and the attractiveness of these lands of the Gulf of Mexico and the Caribbean Sea.

Though they never lost their grip on, or their interest in, the West African coast, the national enterprise of England during the last third of the sixteenth century and the hundred years that followed was mainly directed to the New World. Whilst Elizabeth was on the throne they snatched at many an isolated city, here and there at a promontory or an islet. But though they possessed inconceivable daring and courage, they had not the means or the national force with which to hold on to their conquests. Elizabeth, before the unsuccessful attack of the Armada, feared to take any direct government action for the founding

THE ACQUISITION OF NEWFOUNDLAND BY SIR HUMPHREY GILBERT, IN 1583

In 1578, Sir Humphrey Gilbert, a soldier and navigator, received from Queen Elizabeth a charter for discovery, to plant a colony, and be governor; but, owing to the difficulties which beset him it was not till 1583 that he achieved his purpose, taking possession, in the queen's name, of the harbour of St. John's, and two hundred leagues every way for himself his heirs and assigns for ever. The illustration shows Sir Humphrey among the rough fishermen and sailors.

From the drawing by R. Caton Woodville

of British colonies which might give umbrage to Spain, but had no wish unduly to check British maritime adventure so long as it cost her nothing but documents, messages of good will, or gilded figure-heads.

Accordingly, Sir Humphrey Gilbert —an elder stepbrother of Raleigh, who had distinguished himself by his valour in **Gilbert's** one of the wars for the sub- **Ill-Fated** jugation of Ireland—received a **Expeditions** vague charter for the discovery and colonisation of lands beyond the seas in North America " not already in the possession of any other Christian prince." This was granted in 1578, but the expeditions, financed mainly by Gilbert and Raleigh, proved to be ill-starred. Even before the first of them started, a certain Knollys, who should have served under Sir Humphrey Gilbert, treated his commander with insulting contumely, alleging that he, Knollys, being of the blood royal by descent, could not be invited to dinner by Gilbert, a simple knight.

The defection of Knollys crippled the expedition, which, though it reached the coast of Virginia, left behind a poorly equipped little colony to be starved out or killed by Indians in the course of twelve months. Sir Humphrey Gilbert made a fresh attempt in 1583, on the return from which he was drowned at sea, his vessel foundering during a gale. In the interval between the two expeditions Raleigh, with his characteristic optimism, concluded that his brother would found a great state which, in anticipation, he named Virginia, a name which was to be revived and permanently affixed to the map twenty-four years later.

As a matter of fact, Sir Humphrey Gilbert was an unsuccessful Columbus. Like Columbus, he had great ideas, but he was no coloniser or administrator. Gilbert was really bent on discovering a trans-American route to India. India, as I shall show later, was behind most men's ventures at this period as the **English** ultimate goal in all oversea **Trade** adventure. The idea of a **Expansion** chartered company to deal with the trade of India arose at the end of the sixteenth century, born of Elizabeth's notion of monopolies. Companies had been formed to trade with the Levant and Turkey; that Turkey which had opened up friendly relations with the Virgin Queen, to the great, and perhaps legitimate, disgust of the Catholics of Southern and Western Europe, who felt,

all too truly, through Pope, emperor, knightly orders and the descendants of crusading kings, that Turkey was blasting civilisation and wrecking the fairest portions of the Mediterranean world.

By 1579, Thomas Stephens, a Catholic priest of New College, Oxford, afterwards rector of the Jesuits' College at Salsette, near Bombay, had visited India, and by his letters home had excited a great interest in England in the commercial possibilities of trade with the Far East. Trading adventurers—thanks to Turkish protection—in spite of Hispano-Portuguese opposition, had reached India overland in 1583. By 1600, the English East India Company had been incorporated by Elizabeth's Royal Charter as " the governor and company of merchants of London trading to the East Indies."

Early trade relations with India had grown out of Elizabeth's alliance with the Turk, and followed an overland route through Egypt or Syria; but it was obvious that they could only be continued on a grand scale and at great profit by taking the all-sea route of the Portuguese round **Founding** the West Coast of Africa, the **the East India** Cape of Good Hope, and **Company** Madagascar. The Dutch mariners led the way in 1596, and from 1601 onwards the great sea route was followed in preference to that of the Mediterranean and Red Sea. The Dutch, after three years' undisturbed monopoly of the Indian trade, 1596-9, had raised the price of pepper against us from three shillings to six, or even eight, shillings a pound. This was the immediate cause of the foundation of the first (and chartered) East India Company.

Although the Stuarts have been much and justly censured by historians for the defects of their home policy and the deceit which characterised their foreign dealings, they cannot be accused of indifference to the creation of an empire abroad; indeed, in this respect they showed themselves much more imperial than the vaunted Elizabeth, cautious and mean as she was in her dealings and ventures. It was really under James I., the beheader of Raleigh, that the transmarine empire of the British Crown was actually founded. Our first and oldest colony, so far as continuous possession goes, is the West Indian island of Barbados, taken by an expedition in the ship Olive Blossom, in 1605, though not really occupied till 1625.

THE BRITISH IN BERMUDAS: SIR GEORGE SOMERS WRECKED ON THE ISLANDS IN 1609

One of the chief promoters of the South Virginian Company, Sir George Somers sailed in 1609, with a body of settlers, and was wrecked on the then little known islands in South America called after Juan Bermudez. In the name of King James I., he took possession of the islands, which he at once colonised, and died there in 1610.

From the drawing by R. Caton Woodville

The next oldest is the state of Virginia, definitely founded in 1607 by the building of Jamestown on May 13th of that year. The Bermuda Islands were accidentally rediscovered and occupied in 1609; the Bahamas in 1629. In 1606 an important charter was granted for the eastern coast-lands of North America, between North Carolina, Maine, and Nova Scotia. This allotted to a London company of adven-turers the regions between 34° and 38° N. Lat.; to the Plymouth Company of Devonshire, the area bounded north and south by the 45° and 41° of N. Lat.; while the intervening space was to be open to the operations of either company. It was this hesitancy about the fate of the North American coast between 38° and 41° which made it easier for the Dutch to come in a little later—1609–1621 —and create a colony on the site of New York. A portion of Newfoundland was first settled in 1623; in that year, also, was first occupied the little Leeward island of St. Christopher, which was to be the point of departure and the rallying place of so much British colonising enterprise in the West Indies during the seventeenth century.

In 1610, Henry Hudson, a navigator who, two years previously in the Dutch service, had sought vainly for a direct sea-passage to China round Siberia or across North America, was despatched by a strong joint-stock company, in which Prince Henry of Wales interested himself, to search for the China passage and inci-dentally to annex territories of value. Hudson penetrated through the Hudson Straits—really discovered twenty years earlier by John Davis—into Hudson's Bay. A mutiny on board his ship on his return caused him to be cast adrift by his crew in the Hudson Straits, and he was never more heard of. But his work of explora-tion was continued by William Baffin and other English seamen-adventurers in the three succeeding years. The marvellous energy and ubiquity of Elizabethan and Jacobean seamen are exemplified in the fate of John Davis—the great Arctic explorer and discoverer of the Falkland Islands—and William Baffin, the discoverer of Baffin's Bay and Western Greenland. Davis was one of the officers serving under the piratical Sir Edward Michelborne in the Malay Archipelago (China Chartered Company), and was himself killed by Malay

The Fate of Two Great Discoverers

Britain's Earliest Colonies

pirates off the modern British colony of Malacca; and Baffin was killed at the siege of Ormuz, when an allied Anglo-Persian force took that island from the Portuguese. Owing to the death of Prince Henry, the work of the nascent Hudson Bay Company was not vigorously prose-cuted for some years, though the growing whaling and fur-getting industries kept British interests in these regions alive.

So much for Jacobean America; the Asiatic enterprise of the British people under the same monarch was simply marvellous. In 1603 a factory had been founded at Bantam in Java, near the exit from the Sunda Straits. By the following year, the British had got possession of the Banda and Amboina Islands on the very verge of New Guinea, a foothold from which they were dislodged by the Dutch in 1623 by that "Amboina massacre" which so long rankled in the minds of the English, and was only atoned for under the reign of Cromwell. In 1606, James granted a licence to a company of merchants to trade with Cathay, China, Japan, Korea, and Cambaya—probably the first time that Japan and Korea were ever mentioned in any British official document. This China com-pany came to grief very rapidly through its leading commander, Sir Edward Michelborne, turning pirate in the Chinese seas. In 1612 the East India Company founded by Elizabeth had established a post and fort at Surat, near the coast of Western India.

Portuguese Defeated by the British

The Portuguese objected violently to this infringement of their monopoly— they had already fought with a British fleet in 1611 and been worsted—and at-tacked the British trading fleet off Swally, at the mouth of the Tapti River in 1615. The result of a terrific naval battle was an absolute victory for the British, whose right to navigate the Eastern seas was never afterwards seriously contested by the Portuguese. This victory, coupled with the diplomatic mission despatched by James I. under Sir Thomas Roe, 1615– 1618, to the court of the Mogul em-peror, Jehangir, obtained for the British company a special and an officially recognised position in the dominions of the principal ruler of the Indian peninsula.

In 1609 the right to trade at Aden had been obtained from the Arab sultan of that place, and thenceforth British ships entered the Red Sea, and in 1618 established a

ADRIFT IN THE HUDSON STRAITS: THE FATE OF A FAMOUS NAVIGATOR
Henry Hudson, a famous English navigator, who had in vain sought for a direct sea-passage to China round Siberia or across North America, was despatched, in 1610, by a joint-stock company to search for the China passage; his crew rising against him in mutiny, he was cast adrift with his son in a small boat in the Hudson Straits, named after him, and never heard of again.

British factory at Mocha. A post was founded at Jask, on the Baluchistan coast of the Gulf of Oman, in 1619. This once more roused the ire of the Portuguese, who were already on bad terms with Persia by their occupation of the islet of Ormuz and their overbearing demeanour in trying to close the Persian Gulf to all but Portuguese trade. The British—no better in commercial ethics in those days—appeared to Persian ideas as less grasping in their ambitions, and, at any rate, as a rod with which to chastise the overbearing Lusitanian. British and Persian forces combined, and Ormuz was taken from the Portuguese. The British received as a reward the right to levy customs and to trade at the port of Gombrun, near Bandar Abbas, in 1622.

Ormuz Lost to the Portuguese

In 1611, the East India Company founded a post at Masulipatam, near the mouth of the Kistna on the east coast of India, and shortly afterwards a similar post at Vizagapatam. Agencies, commercial and political, were founded at Agra and Patna in 1620. Relations with Siam—there was an English post at the Siamese-Malay state of Patani as early as 1611—Celebes, the Moluccas, and Java ripened rapidly till after the Amboina massacre. By 1623 the Dutch had expelled the British from the Malay Archipelago and the Far East, which they did not re-enter till the late eighteenth century.

In 1618, James permitted or encouraged the formation of a chartered company to trade with the Gambia River on the West African coast, the charter being based on an old patent, 1588, of Queen Elizabeth. Although neither this company nor its immediate successors were successful—indeed, by 1664 they had lost £800,000—yet these enterprises commenced under James I. laid the foundations of our future West African dominion. James I., therefore, unworthy of regard as he may be in some aspects, was the real founder of the British Empire. Under his unhappy successor, despite home troubles—partly because of them—empire building still went on. The State of Massachusetts, in North America, was founded in 1620, and Maryland in 1632. The charter of the London company had been surrendered to the Crown in 1624, that of the Plymouth company in 1635. These surrenders made it easier for the

James I. the Founder of the British Empire

Crown to deal with the organisation of the new American territories. In the West Indies, Antigua, Nevis, Anguilla, and Montserrat were colonised—mainly from St. Christopher, and farther back still in time from Bermuda—and a charter was issued to the Earl of Carlisle for certain islands in the Caribbean Sea, among them Dominica. In the East Indies a foothold was obtained at Surat, which was displaced later by Bombay, in 1614. Madras was founded in 1639; Hugli, the forerunner of Calcutta, in 1642; and an attempt, afterwards abandoned, was made in 1647 to establish a rival East India Company's depot on the coast of Madagascar.

Jamaica had been eyed for half a century by British adventurers as a prize which might be one day snatched from Spain. They had become familiar with some of its conditions by carrying thither negro slaves for sale; they realised that the Spaniards had practically exterminated the native inhabitants, that not having found minerals they had lost interest in the island, and further that many of their negro slaves had rebelled and taken to the mountains. Accordingly, two "unauthorised" raids were made on the island in 1596 and 1624. Both were repulsed by Spanish valour. Cromwell, however, took advantage of a breach of relations with Spain to send to the Gulf of Mexico a naval expedition under Admiral Penn and General Venables to seize the large island of Hispaniola. Failing in this object the expedition occupied Jamaica instead.

Charles II. as Empire Builder

Under Charles II. the empire attained a notable expansion. In North America the Dutch Colony of New Netherlands, with its two towns of Manhadoes and New Amsterdam, was acquired and turned into the English territory of New York. By the close of Charles II.'s reign, the nucleus of the original thirteen states of New England had been constituted: Carolina (North and South), Virginia, Maryland, Pennsylvania, Rhode Island, New Jersey, Delaware, New York, Connecticut, Massachusetts, Vermont, and New Hampshire. In 1670, however, Charles II. laid the foundations of a much vaster expanse of empire by granting a charter to Prince Rupert and seventeen others, incorporating them as the "governor and company of adventurers of England trading into Hudson's Bay." This was the outcome of the voyages of Davis,

THE ORIGIN OF MADRAS: THE FOUNDING OF FORT ST. GEORGE

To Francis Day, an officer of the East India Company, belongs the honour of founding Madras. In 1638 he was sent to India by that company to select a better site for their headquarters, and from the Rajah of Chandragiri he purchased a tract of land five miles long near the settlement of St. Thomé, and thereon he built a factory and a fort, which he called Fort St. George by which name Madras, which sprang from this small beginning, is still officially named.

From the drawing by R. Caton Woodville

Hudson, and Baffin, already alluded to; and the grant of this charter by Charles II. resulted in the creation of four-fifths of British North America. The company thus founded still exists; its charter—in one form or another—did not finally expire till 1859, and the bulk of its immense private territorial possessions was not finally incorporated in the lands of the Canadian people till 1870. In India, the island of Bombay and the mainland settlement of Salsette had been acquired in the dowry of Charles II.'s queen. In West Africa a new charter started afresh the British settlement at the mouth of the Gambia.

Dutch and British at War

In 1672, the broken company of British merchants trading on the Gold Coast received a charter which created a new association, known by its short title as the Royal African Company. The outbreak of the Dutch War enabled the British forces to oust the Dutch from a number of strong places where they, in their turn, had supplanted the Portuguese. Thus were obtained the fortified posts of Dixcove, Sekundi, and Accra, the beginnings of the modern colony of the Gold Coast which is now nearly as large as the joint area of England and Scotland.

All this time British trade with the Mediterranean was steadily growing. Cromwell had made Great Britain a naval power in that inland sea, so that her ships were actually able to threaten the coast possessions of the grand duke of Tuscany and the Pope, who had countenanced attacks on British shipping by Prince Rupert, and to chastise most effectually the Turkish pirates of the Barbary States. With Morocco there were occasionally war-like episodes, but, curiously enough, British intercourse with that last independent fragment of the Arabian caliph's dominions had been of a more friendly and commercial character. Nevertheless, the Moorish rovers not infrequently harried British ships engaged in the West African trade. Spain, through her vassal Portugal, which then held Tangiers and Ceuta, constantly attempted to close the Straits of Gibraltar to British ships, and thereby interfere with British trade in the Levant. Therefore, as early as the middle of the seventeenth century, there were vague longings on the part of our fellow-countrymen for some foothold in or near the Straits of Gibraltar

Spain's Opposition to Britain

which might avail to secure a free passage into and out of the Mediterranean. When Charles II. was raised to the throne, Louis XIV. of France, for mysterious reasons of his own, decided to employ the sea power of Britain to support the Portuguese monarchy against Spain. He arranged the match between Charles and Catharine of Braganza. Taking advantage of this overture, the British Ministers of the day were shrewd enough to satisfy the national longing for control over the Straits of Gibraltar by exacting as part of the princess's dowry the city and territory of Tangier.

Having gained possession of this foothold on the coast of Morocco, the government of Charles II. showed itself too frivolous, too wanting in statecraft and Imperial foresight to retain it. Had they acted more wisely as regards the Moors, it is possible that the history of North Africa might have taken a very different and a most surprising course. But, disheartened by the difficulties, and weakened by the frightful bureaucratic corruption which then prevailed in the departments of public supplies, the Ministers of Charles II. abandoned Tangier in 1684. Then it was that other British statesmen or sea-captains fixed their eyes on Gibraltar as a more tenable position. The idea remained dormant until 1704, when advantage was taken of the War of the Spanish Succession to seize and garrison Gibraltar. This step was one of the most remarkable ever taken in the history of the world, and may rank in lack of moral justification with the Napoleonic descent on Egypt and the British seizure of Aden in 1839. Beaconsfield's romantic acquisition of Cyprus might have been classed with these episodes as among the great strokes of empire-building, had it not, by the subsequent trend of British public opinion, been rendered a policy of *non sequitur*.

Britain's Seizure of Gibraltar

In the course of the eighteenth century the increasing hostility of the Turks towards even British travellers passing through their Levantine dominions, made overland communications with India so precarious and profitless that increasing attention was turned to the all-sea route round the Cape of Good Hope. Just as the Levantine and the West African trade led us to seize Gibraltar, so the development of commerce with India, China, the Malay Archipelago, and the great and small islands of the Pacific just coming within our ken, made a foothold at the southern extremity of Africa a matter of the greatest importance to the now unified kingdoms of England and Scotland.

An attempt in 1781—as unjustifiable in actual morality as the seizure and retention of Gibraltar—was made to snatch the Cape of Good Hope from the Dutch. The islands of Ascension and St. Helena—Ascension was not definitely occupied till 1815; St. Helena has been permanently in British possession since 1673—discovered by the Portuguese, and held intermittently by the Dutch, had been intermittently occupied by the British Navy or the East India Company. To the latter, in fact, St. Helena was of the highest importance as the resting place of its fleets during the eighteenth century, and longing eyes were cast on the French islands of Mauritius and Réunion, which to some extent lay midway between the Cape of Good Hope and India.

During the last half of the seventeenth century, the greed of territorial acquisition in West Africa, Eastern Asia, the South Atlantic and the West Indies, had brought **The Rich Possessions of Holland** Great Britain into violent conflict with the equally rapacious and, so far as enterprise-compared - to - means goes, more wonderful country of Holland. The British secured a hard-won victory over the Dutch in the long run, not because they were braver or more skilled as fighting seamen, but because they had a larger and richer motherland from which to draw their supplies. Holland, however, had previously plundered the Portuguese to a magnificent degree, and, even with what she had to give up to the British in the seventeenth and eighteenth centuries, was still mistress of possessions in the West Indies, South America, the southern extremity of Africa, Ceylon, Bengal, Sumatra, the Malay Peninsula, Java, and Borneo, with a kind of lien over the scarcely known continent of Australia.

During the latter part of the eighteenth century circumstances forced Holland into a position of quasi-alliance with France, some of the circumstances being the territorial ambitions of Great Britain. Putting forward the plea that the Dutch settlement of the Cape of Good Hope served as a refuge and a rallying-point for hostile French ships, the British Government attempted by two surprise attacks in 1781 to seize Cape Town. But they were beaten off. The idea, however, like that of Gibraltar, never left us, and when the French troops invaded Holland, in 1794, the British Government, in 1795, with the somewhat chary permission of the Prince of Orange, established itself in Dutch South Africa; and although for a few years our forces were withdrawn, just as the cat **The British Established in South Africa** allows the crippled mouse a moment of illusory freedom, in 1806 we made another descent on these regions, and came there to stay. The eighteenth century, however, not only saw at its close the establishment of the British at the south end of Africa—an establishment which inspired the great Portuguese traveller-administrator of Mozambique, Dr. Lacerda, in 1796, with the remarkable prophecy of the ultimate Cape-to-Cairo ambitions of the British people—but in its early years witnessed the effectual foundation of Anglo-Saxon North America, by the extension of the British colonies from the North Atlantic seaboard to the Mississippi, by maritime explorations of Vancouver Island and Oregon, which sufficed to stop Russian descent from Alaska, and Spanish ascent from California, and finally by the conclusion of the great struggle between France and Britain for predominance in North America.

Newfoundland, the first aim of British aspirations across the Atlantic, became definitely a British colony in 1728, though by previous settlement it was more justly French. The French colonies of Canada—Ontario, Quebec, and New Brunswick, which then bore the prettier name of New France—were ceded in 1763; Nova Scotia had been acquired in its entirety in 1758, together with Prince Edward's Island; Vancouver Island was not settled till 1843.

Vancouver Island having been rediscovered by Captain Cook, and ear-marked as a future British foothold on the American Pacific, the close of the eighteenth **Outlines of the Canadian Dominion** century saw the main outlines of the Canadian Dominion laid down. The Hudson's Bay Chartered Trading Company, with its four forts on the shores of Hudson's Bay and its far-reaching explorations, had established a prescriptive claim to all Arctic and sub-Arctic America except the coast of Alaska. Sir Alexander Mackenzie, the Stanley of North America and a servant of the Hudson's Bay Company, travelled overland

BRITISH SEIZURE OF JAMAICA IN 1655 AND THE SINKING OF THE SPANISH VESSELS

With sealed orders from Cromwell, in 1654, a fleet of sixty ships, commanded by Admiral Penn, and carrying about 4,000 men under General Venables, left Portsmouth on an expedition, and, sailing for the West Indies, captured Jamaica. But having failed to carry out their orders, Penn and Venables were committed to the Tower on their return.

From the drawing by R. Caton Woodville

5454

THE BRITISH ACQUISITION OF GIBRALTAR: SPANISH TROOPS MARCHING OUT

Though regarded as impregnable, during the War of the Spanish Succession, Gibraltar was taken, on July 24th, 1704, by a combined English and Dutch fleet, commanded by Sir George Rooke, who raised the British flag and claimed the town in the name of Queen Anne. The above picture shows the Marquis de Salines marching out with the Spanish troops.

From the drawing by R. Caton Woodville

to the Pacific coast in 1789-1793, first sighting the Pacific Ocean at Cape Menzies, opposite Queen Charlotte's Islands.

Vancouver Island is supposed to have been sighted by Sir Francis Drake just two hundred years before Cook, in 1578. It or the opposite coast of Oregon was christened by Drake " New

Revolt of the United States

Albion." The island was more definitely placed on the map by Juan de Fuca, a Greek sea-captain in Spanish employ, in 1592. Cook's exploration of its coasts led to no immediate settlement. It was Captain George Vancouver, R.N., in 1792-1794, who really laid the foundation of British political rights to this important island. The Hudson's Bay Company did the rest, 1821-1843.

The revolt of the United States in 1777 did not perhaps make such a great impression at the time on the British mind, because it seemed the mere alienation of a portion of the Atlantic coast lands ; it had the immediate effect of making the British still more rapacious and energetic as regards Canada. Had this revolt not occurred and been successful, it is quite possible that British energy might have languished and France have been allowed, from her tiny footholds of St. Pierre and Miquelon, and from her great possessions of Louisiana and New Orleans, to build up once again a French empire in North America. What Britain lost in the New England States she more than regained by founding the Dominion of Canada, which, in her intentions and aspirations, even before the expiry of the eighteenth century, extended from the Atlantic to the Pacific, and dwarfed the contemporaneous ambitions of the United States, baulked as they were by a Spanish Florida, Texas and California, and a French Mississippi.

With their thoughts bent on the discovery of a north-west passage which would establish an all-British route across

America's Struggling Republic

America to China, and the intention to seize the analogous southern maritime route from Atlantic to Pacific—marked by the British exploration of the Straits of Magellan, the occupation of the Malouines, or Falkland Islands, in 1765, already half-occupied and settled by France in 1763, when the celebrated Bougainville, the great French navigator of the Pacific whose name is for ever commemorated by a lovely flower, settled on West Falkland

some of the unfortunate dispossessed Acadians of Nova Scotia—and, finally, the attempt to seize Buenos Ayres during the French alliance with Spain, the existence of the struggling American Republic of the sixteen united states must have seemed to the Britain of the eighteenth century a factor of merely local importance, not more serious in a project of universal American Empire than the intermittent independence of the Transvaal was in the scheme of South African dominion.

During the eighteenth century England, in her colonial enterprise, had been powerfully reinforced by the sister kingdom of Scotland. Since the union of the two crowns, Scotland of the Lowlands had thrown herself energetically into oversea adventure. It is true that the English Government spitefully enough had baulked the attempt of the Scots—in 1698-1699 —to establish themselves on the Isthmus of Darien, there perhaps to found a Central American State ; but the bitterness resulting from this was soon forgotten, and Scots and English, without much national distinction, flung them-

Building the British Empire

selves energetically into the building up of a great British dominion in the West Indies and Northern South America. At the close of the seventeenth century Britain had only possessed in the West Indies Jamaica, the Bahamas, Barbados, and three small islands of the Leeward group.

But by the end of the eighteenth century Dominica, St. Lucia, St. Vincent, Grenada, Tobago, and Trinidad were added by conquest from France or Spain, while intermittently Cuba was held, attempts were made to take the great island of Hispaniola, the foundations of a British interest in Honduras and on the Nicaraguan coast were laid, and a swoop was at last made on Guiana, with perhaps a notion of extending that dominion later on over the adjoining Spanish province of Venezuela. So, far from the eighteenth century marking the defeat and retrogression of the British in the New World, it might more fitly be styled the American century, the second of the four great eras of the British Empire, three finished and the fourth commencing. The nineteenth century has been par excellence the age of Asian Dominion. It is quite possible that our Asiatic Empire has reached its apogee in extent, if not in population or power. The twentieth century may possibly witness the African culmination. But in the years between the death of Queen Anne and the Peace of Amiens our grandest struggles, our greatest gains, and our keenest ambitions were centred in the New World between the Straits of Magellan and the Arctic Ocean.

The desire to know more about the Pacific coast of North America, on which Russians were beginning to encroach from Eastern Siberia, while the power of Spain was obviously waning, led the British Government to send out Captain Cook to the Pacific Ocean via the Cape of Good Hope and the Malay Archipelago, and thus led to the definite discovery of Australia, New Zealand, and most of the Pacific archipelagoes, and, finally, at the end of the eighteenth century, in 1788, to the establishment of a British settlement on the coast of New South Wales—a settlement which was to be the germ of a vast Australian Commonwealth, destined to grow some day into mighty nationalities of Anglo-Saxon stock. Spanish, French, and Dutch navigators of the sixteenth and seventeenth centuries had surmised the existence to the south of New **Discovery of** Guinea and the Malay Archi- **the Australian** pelago of an island-con- **Continent** tinent, variously named in imagination Greater Java or even " Terra Australis." The actual name " Australia " was applied in the first instance to the largest island of the New Hebrides group by Quiros in 1606, in the belief that it was the promontory of a great southern continent.

Luiz Vaez de Torres, second in command of the Spanish exploring expedition led by De Quiros, the discoverer of the New Hebrides, as they were afterwards named, had passed through the "Torres Straits," discovered, and aptly named, New Guinea, and had "felt" the proximity of the real " Terra Australis." His indications were followed up ten, seventeen, and twenty-two years later by the Dutch navigators Hertoge and Carstenz, who actually located points and named features of the North and West Australian coasts.

In 1642, the Dutch navigator, Abel Janszen Tasman, skirting the western coast of Australia, penetrated so far south that he actually discovered Tasmania, which he called Van Diemen's Land, after the then governor of Java; and New Zealand—" Staaten Land." Tasman, on his return to the eastward of Australia,

derived enough information, no doubt from Malay seamen on the coasts of New Guinea, to forecast dimly the locality and area of this southern continent, " Groote Zuidland," which was soon afterwards definitely named " New Holland," Staaten Land being at the same time styled " New Zealand." In 1689 and 1699 the pirate-explorer William Dampier **What Captain** paid two visits to the North- **Cook did for** west coast of New Holland, **the Empire** and brought back some account of its peculiar peoples and products. But nothing like systematic exploration or definite discovery was accomplished in these directions until the three voyages of Captain James Cook, 1769-1777, revealed the actual coast of South-eastern Australia, and the definite outline of New Zealand. Cook also placed on the map such archipelagoes of the Pacific as had not been already made known to the civilised world by the Spanish, Portuguese, and Dutch navigators of the sixteenth and seventeenth centuries.

British exploring enterprise in these regions between the Western Pacific and the Indian Ocean had been baffled during the early eighteenth century by the rivalry of the Dutch and French. We had been obliged to fight France for predominance in India, and a fierce though unofficial warfare had been waged with Holland to keep the Dutch out of Bengal. By the middle of the eighteenth century the French had completely lost any chance of building up a great Indian empire, but the Dutch, defeated in Hindustan, still clung to Ceylon, and successfully competed with us in Java, Sumatra, Borneo, and the Moluccas.

The eighteenth century decided the fate of India, possibly for several centuries to come ; but, compared to our present Asiatic dominions, British rule in Hindustan was by no means universal, and we had but a slight foothold on **Britain's** the Malay Peninsula (Island of **Rule** Pinang, acquired 1786), and in **in India** the Malay Archipelago, Natal, Fort Marlborough, or Bencoolen, in Sumatra, and a doubtful tenancy of one or two islets off the coast of Borneo. But at the end of the eighteenth century, which, for a logical sequence, one must place at the Peace of Amiens, in 1802, the British Empire, scattered and patchy as it was, had almost the outline—the skeleton—of the empire of to-day, and was

BRITISH TROOPS MARCHING THROUGH THE SWAMPS OF BRITISH GUIANA

This colony, on the north coast of South America, once a Dutch trading outpost, was held by the British from
1781 till 1783; they again held it from 1796 till 1802, and from 1803 till 1814, when the present colony was formed.

From the drawing by R Caton Woodville

SIR GEORGE SIMPSON ESTABLISHING HIS FIRST COUNCIL OF SETTLERS IN 1835

Justly considered one of the architects of the present Canadian Dominion, Sir George Simpson had the entire management of the Hudson's Bay Company in Canada, and the rise of British Columbia was contemporary with his administration.

From the drawing by R. Caton Woodville

vastly different from the empire over which William III. was ruling in 1702. At that date this monarch, if he had called for a map of the British Empire beyond the seas, which he probably never thought of doing, would have noted a few English "plantations," or settlements, on the Atlantic seaboard of North America between Boston, **Britain's Over-** New York, and the Savan-**Seas Dominions** nah River. Other names **200 Years Ago** in clumsy writing across the Caribbean seas would have reminded him that James I. had given a charter for the Bermudas, that Charles I. had permitted the settlement of Barbados, that Cromwell had annexed Jamaica, and that under Charles II. most of the British Leeward Islands had been acquired.

In Southern Asia he would have noted the Island of Bombay—an undoubted British possession. There should also have been marked on the map factories and forts—more or less identical with political footholds—at some point on the coast of Sind, at Surat, Broach, and Ahmedabad, in Western India ; at Calcutta, Tegnapatam, Vizagapatam, Madras, and Masulipatam, on the eastern side of the Indian Peninsula ; while in the interior there were agencies at Agra and Patna. Along the shores of the Persian Gulf there were factories at Basra, Bandar Abbas, and Jask ; and, despite Dutch hostility, the East India Company still held on to trading posts at Bantam, in Java ; Macassar, in Celebes ; and Achin, in Sumatra. On the West African coast the Royal African Company possessed forts at the mouth of the Gambia, and along the Gold Coast, from Dixcovè to Accra, and at Whyda, on the coast of Dahomeh. The East India Company, moreover, had seized the island of St. Helena.

That was the extent of the British Empire in 1702, at which time Ireland still lay a depopulated, desolate, half-conquered country which was being settled on the **The Nominal** east and on the north by Pro-**Surrender of** testant English, Welsh, and **Cape Colony** Scotch settlers. Scotland herself was a separate kingdom, acknowledging only partially the direct rule of William III. The Isle of Man was a feudal kingdom under a British noble ; the Channel Islands were semi-independent piratical settlements. At the Peace of Amiens, in 1802, Great Britain, it is true, had nominally surrendered Cape Colony to the Dutch, but

had made every preparation for reoccupation, and had made that reoccupation a matter of certainty and legality by the establishment of her sea power and an understanding with the Prince of Orange.

In America she possessed the whole of the vague and vast territories of Canada, which were at any rate conceived of, under the charter of the Hudson's Bay Company, as stretching from the Atlantic to the Pacific ; besides the West India Islands already owned, she had seized and has since retained Dominica, St. Lucia, St. Vincent, Grenada, Tobago, and Trinidad, and had established a lien on the coasts of Honduras and Nicaragua.

British Honduras began in the seventeenth century as the fortified establishments of piratical British traders and timber — mahogany — cutters. Though frequently attacked by Spain, and frequently ceded to Spain by England, the British settlers held on steadfastly till, in 1786, a definitely British administration was established. She had occupied British, French, and Dutch Guiana. Far away towards the southern extremity of that **The French** continent the British Govern-**Ousted** ment had already earmarked **from Egypt** the Falkland Islands, but had been repulsed in its attempt to seize Buenos Ayres. In the Mediterranean we held, legally or illegally, Gibraltar, Malta, Sicily, and the Ionian Islands, while British naval and military action had just turned the French out of Egypt.

Here an almost unconscious intimation had been given of an intention some day to occupy that halfway station towards our growing Indian Empire. In East Africa, Britain had opened up relations with Abyssinia and Zanzibar, as also with the tribes of South Arabia and the Persian Gulf. In West Africa her forces had occupied the French colony of Senegal, and strengthened the hold over the mouth of the Gambia. As the first result of British anti-slavery enthusiasm, the colony of Sierra Leone had been founded. The forts along the Gold Coast, already mentioned, continued to be garrisoned by the Royal African (Chartered) Company. Even at the close of the eighteenth century Great Britain was beginning to think about the Niger, the upper course of which river had, in 1796, been discovered by the Scottish explorer, Mungo Park, in the direct service of the British Crown. British trade with West

Africa at that time had extended to the rivers which form the delta of the Niger, and even to the mouth of the Congo.

In 1796, as already mentioned, the great Portuguese traveller, Dr. José Lacerda, had predicted that the British would attempt to found an empire stretching from the Cape of Good Hope to Egypt. If Mungo Park discovered the main course of the River Niger, another equally distinguished Scot, an explorer of really advanced scientific attainments, James Bruce, had, in 1768-1773, rediscovered and definitely mapped the course of the Blue Nile from Abyssinia to Egypt. He was despatched on this aim by a British Secretary of State, Lord Halifax, and there is little doubt that this journey provoked a special British interest in the affairs of Egypt.

In Asia the British possessions in 1802 included a general sway over Hindustan between the Himalayas on the north and Cape Comorin on the south, between the Bay of Bengal on the east and the Indus River on the west. The actual possessions in India of the Honourable East India Company at this date over which

Expansion of one Century it ruled directly were Bengal and the Bombay and Madras provinces; a portion of the Central and North-west Provinces; parts of Rajputana. Indirectly the company controlled the affairs of Oudh, Haidarabad, and Mysore. We had even during the eighteenth century taken our first political step towards establishing British influence over Tibet; our political explorers had penetrated through Afghanistan to Bokhara, and we had acquired some influence at the court of Persia. In the Malay Archipelago we replaced the Dutch in Java and Sumatra, as also at various points on the Malay Peninsula. In North Africa, though we had no actual foothold, nevertheless, by Nelson's victories and the British occupation of Malta, we were so predominant in Tunis and Tripoli as to exercise a kind of suzerainty over those Turkish feudalities.

In 1908 the British dominions have attained an enormous area, even compared to what they were in 1802. In North America the small colonised areas of Newfoundland, Nova Scotia, New Brunswick, Upper and Lower Canada, Ontario, and the few forts of the Hudson's Bay Company, have grown into a belt of continuous colonisation and cultivation extending from the coast of Labrador to the Pacific and right up to the Arctic Circle and the eastern limits of Alaska; while the political dominion of Canada (British North America) reaches to the Polar regions, and comprises nearly half the North American Continent. In the warmer regions of the New World, vague British rights on the coast of Central

Territories Under the British Flag America at Belize have grown into the definite colony of British Honduras, while the Colony of Demerara, taken over from the Dutch, has become the large State of British Guiana, 90,260 square miles in extent. In the far south, the Falkland Islands have been definitely organised as a crown colony, and the British ægis has been thrown over the large island of South Georgia, annexed by Captain Cook in 1775. These possessions were definitely occupied and administered in 1833, because of their importance to the whaling industry in the South Atlantic.

Within the limits of Europe, though we have given up the islet of Heligoland off the German coast, we have acquired, for all practical purposes, the large island of Cyprus in the Eastern Mediterranean. The Ionian Islands, which France snatched from the dying Republic of Venice, enjoyed a British protectorate in every sense of the word for sixty odd years, and were then made over to the Kingdom of Greece. Malta, already occupied in 1802, had been definitely ceded to the British Crown in 1815.

On the continent of Asia, the large red patches of British dominion (through a chartered company), which gave to Great Britain the practical control of the peninsula of Hindustan, have grown in a hundred years to our existing Indian and colonial empire in Southern Asia. This begins almost in Africa, on the far west, with the port of Aden, the islet of Perim at the mouth of the Red Sea, and the island of Socotra off the North-east

British Rule in the Orient African coast. It extends eastwards through the British protectorate over the Aden hinterland and protectorate, or sphere of influence—established by treaty —over the whole south coast of Arabia to the vicinity of the Persian Gulf. The south-west coasts of that inlet and the Bahrein Islands are a British protectorate, and in common with the Arabian regions already referred to are attached to the vast Indian dominions, which begin on

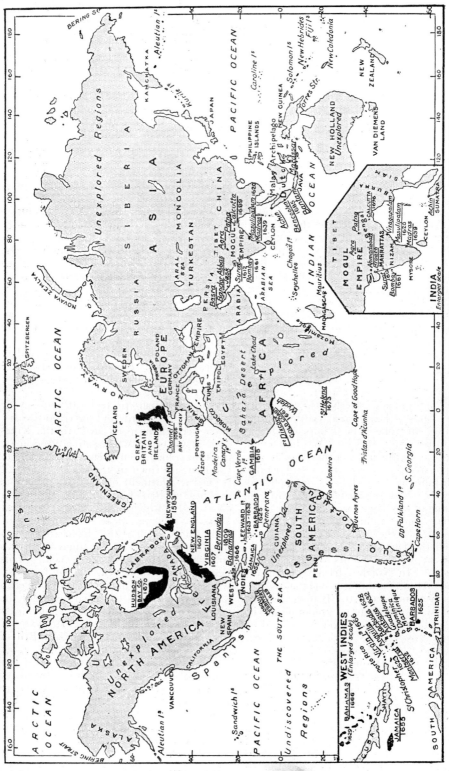

THE BRITISH EMPIRE IN 1702, ITS POSSESSIONS BEING SHOWN IN BLACK AND UNDERLINED)
Two centuries ago Great Britain had already begun her over-seas expansion, and had laid the foundations of the vast empire of the present day. In the above map, Britain's possessions in 1702 are shown in black and underlined, the figures giving the dates when the various territories were occupied and came under the British flag.

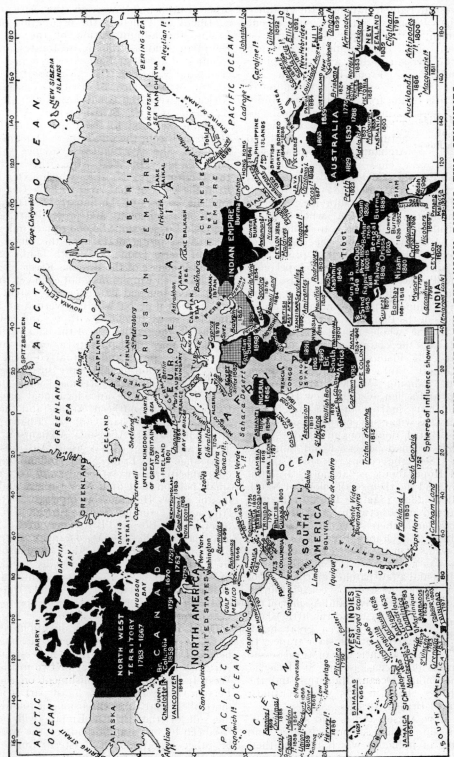

THE BRITISH EMPIRE IN 1909, ILLUSTRATING THE WONDERFUL EXPANSION DURING TWO CENTURIES

How marvellously the British Empire has extended all over the world during the past two centuries is seen by comparing the above map with that on the preceding page, both of which have been specially drawn for this History. The Empire's dominions are indicated in black and underlined, and the dates of occupation are given in every case.

the west at Baluchistan, near the entrance to the Persian Gulf. By the recent agreement with Russia, the South-east Persian coast commanding the entrance into the Persian Gulf is a British sphere of influence. From Baluchistan the Indian Empire extends continuously eastwards to the frontier of French Indo-China, and northwards to Tibet—a portion of which is actually British — and to Afghanistan, a Central Asian state in very close relations with the British Empire. Ceylon has been acquired from the Dutch, 1796-1815, and British influence now reigns supreme, directly or indirectly, over the whole Malay Peninsula from Burma to Singapore. The northern third of the island of Borneo is also under British protection.

World-Wide Range of British Power

In Australasia, and in the archipelagoes of the Pacific, the gains have also been enormous—a third part of the vast island of New Guinea with the adjacent archipelagoes of the Louisiade and the Solomon Islands, the whole inland continent of Australia, the large islands of New Zealand, the clusters of Fiji and of Tonga, the Gilbert, Santa Cruz, Ellice, Phœnix, Union, Fanning, Malden, and Hervey group, and a lien over the New Hebrides.

The last quarter of the nineteenth century has witnessed enormous accretions to the British dominions in Africa. Prior to 1875 we had possessed and built up, since 1806, the colony of the Cape of Good Hope about as far north as Kimberley, and the then small colony of Natal, founded 1824-1842. There remained unclaimed areas between Natal and Cape Colony, and there was no hold over Zululand, the Orange Free State, or the Transvaal. On the West Coast of Africa there was a patch at the mouth of the Gambia, and a few patches on the coast of Sierra Leone, a strip of coast country between the Volta River and Assinie on the Gold Coast, and the little island of Lagos, once a great head-quarters of the slave trade. In the Atlantic Ocean we possessed the islets of Ascension and St. Helena ; in the Indian Ocean, Mauritius and the Seychelles. That, in 1875, was the utmost extent of British Africa.

Growth of British Africa

By 1909 these patches and strips have grown into colonies, protectorates and spheres of influence which now in their united bulk exceed the possessions of any other European Power on the African continent, and include the occupation of Egypt, the administration of the vast Egyptian Sudan, the protectorates or colonies of Uganda, East Africa, Somaliland, and Zanzibar, the protectorate or sphere of influence of British Central Africa between the Great Lakes and the Zambesi, and all British South Africa from the Zambesi to the Cape of Good Hope, and from the outskirts of Damaraland to the Portuguese province of Mozambique. In West Africa there are the territories of Nigeria, which extend from the delta of that river to Lake Chad and the borders of the Sahara Desert—a much enlarged colony and protectorate of the Gold Coast—some 82,000 square miles in area—a protectorate over the hinterland of Sierra Leone, and both banks of the lower course of the Gambia River.

The British Empire may not even yet, in 1909, have touched its apogee of extent, and indeed if it be wisely governed and directed so as to enlist with it, and not against it, the sentiments of the backward races, it may develop into a league of peace and mutual co-operation of still more surprising vastness. It may come to include an educational protectorate over Southern Arabia and the shores of the Persian Gulf, an alliance, almost feudal, with Abyssinia, Afghanistan, Tibet, and Siam ; it may assist Australia to arrange with France and Holland on equitable terms for extended sway over a small portion of Dutch New Guinea and of the New Hebrides archipelago. In Africa, the coming South African confederation of Boer and Briton may eventually include the cognate German state of South-west Africa ; and it may also, by arrangement with Germany, link up the Uganda protectorate with the north end of Tanganyika, and thus establish the last link in the Cape-to-Cairo route.

The Coming South African Confederation

Or, if it increases in such directions as these, it may shrink in others, yielding here and there a little to France in Western Africa, to Germany an islet or two in the West Indies, or an establishment on the Persian Gulf. But for the most part it is more likely that these extensions or roundings off of the British Empire will be balanced by our standing out of the way of other ambitions in Eastern Europe and Nearer Asia, or in the Congo basin.

BRITISH TRADE AND THE FLAG
THE PIONEERS OF COMMERCE
AS MAKERS OF THE EMPIRE

THE causes and motives which have provoked the creation of this vast empire have been numerous and sometimes conflicting. The first incentive and the last have been the desire to find profitable markets for trade wherein British products or manufactures could be exchanged for foreign wares sufficiently valuable to meet the risks and expenses of sea-transport. Coupled with this has been the desire to grab at whatever good things might be going in the way of animal, vegetable, or mineral wealth not already in the possession of a nationality strong enough to defend it. Then the restless, dissatisfied or persecuted, or even criminal among us have hoped to find a happier and less trammelled existence in regions beyond the British Isles yet under the British flag. Honest commerce, eager greed for gain, naïf love of adventure, and the search for marvels—these were the provocative impulses which drove daring seamen, merchants, and soldiers of fortune beyond the seas of Britain to new worlds, new hemispheres, and strange climates during the fifteenth and sixteenth centuries.

In the seventeenth century there was superadded the desire to flee from religious or political oppression ; in the seventeenth century real colonisation took place. But in that which followed—the eighteenth —the dominant impulse once again was commerce and the rapid making of wealth in exploitable lands. This was the century of the slave trade's greatest development.

Emigration for Religious Freedom The first familiar instance of emigration for religious freedom is that of the 102 dissidents from the Church of England who emigrated in the Mayflower, in 1620, and founded Plymouth, U.S.A. The first Quakers arriving in North America, 1652–1666, were hanged, flogged, or expelled ; but from 1671 to 1681 hundreds came to America and colonised New Jersey, Delaware, and Pennsylvania. In the nineteenth century the causes of empire extension were more complex. Commerce, exploitation, the possibilities of mineral discoveries were no doubt the most powerful inducements to extend the area of British occupation ; and increasing social pressure in England and Scotland, and misery in Ireland, brought about such a rush of colonists for the vacant healthy lands in America, South Africa, and Oceania—some 16,000,000 persons in the last hundred years (of this number about 5,000,000 left between 1815 and 1850)— as our history had not yet known, the movement being enormously aided by the development of steam navigation. But there was a third factor at work in empire-building from the very beginning of the nineteenth century to its very end : sentiment—a sentimentality almost sardonic in some of its manifestations.

Factors in Empire Building

In the seventeenth and eighteenth centuries we built forts and founded colonies on the West Coast of Africa for the purpose of carrying on the slave trade in an efficient manner ; in the nineteenth century we seized important vantage points, annexed or protected enormous areas in order to suppress the trade in slaves.

The eagerness of commerce to go in front of the hampering restrictions of a regular government led to the creation of chartered companies—and chartered companies have always ended in the foundation of colonies, dominions or empires—in the seventeenth, eighteenth, and nineteenth centuries. Greed of gain was coincident with the glamour of India. India has been the mainspring of our empire, the magnet which has drawn us by such strangely devious routes that our pioneers have halted by the way, have started off at a tangent on other quests, or have become involved in the solution of other problems widely separated from those of Hindustan. The search for a quick sea route to India through North America—analogous to the Magellan Straits on the south—led Sir Humphrey Gilbert across the Atlantic, to found that Virginia which was occupied twenty-five years afterwards and which was the germ of the United States of America. The same stimulus led to the journeys of Frobisher, Davis, Baffin; and the last-named was actually killed in an attempt on the part of the East India Company's ships to found in the Persian Gulf that British sphere of influence on the approach to the Indian markets which has only become an accomplished fact in the twentieth century. Drake's attempt to find the Pacific outlet of these northern Magellan Straits, this water route across North America—which, after all, does exist, only it is too much in the frozen zone to be of any use—led to the discovery of Oregon; and, three centuries later, the same motive of research on the part of Captains Cook and Vancouver brought about the rediscovery and annexation of Vancouver Island.

The Days of Maritime Enterprise

Failing to find an easy way across the North Atlantic to the marvels of Cathay and the Middle East, the diplomacy of Queen Elizabeth was directed to an overland route through the Turkish dominions. As this proved insecure and uncertain, attention was turned towards the sea route round Africa. This led in time to the acquisition of Tangiers as a calling-place, to the settlement of St. Helena, the seizure of Gibraltar as an alternative to Tangiers, the occupation of the Cape of Good Hope, and of Mauritius.

Bonaparte, thinking to strike at Britain in India, where she was wealthiest and weakest, landed in Egypt, and may be said to have opened the overland route. From the days when the French capitulated and quitted Egypt, England could not take her eyes or thoughts off that country. The splendid private enterprise of Lieutenant Waghorn having started the overland route in 1837–47, in connection with the newly introduced steamer traffic, Great Britain found herself compelled to occupy Aden, in 1839, at the southern exit of the Red Sea, and ultimately also Perim Island. Bonaparte's action in Egypt, indeed, had far-reaching results he could never have foreseen : it brought Great Britain as a

Great Britain in Egypt

fighting power into the Red Sea. Even Abyssinia and the vaguer Ethiopian and Zanzibar regions were " looked up " at the beginning of the nineteenth century because of the bearing their alliance might have on a life-and-death war between France and Britain for the lordship of Southern Asia.

If the overland route led to an increased interest in Egypt and the turning of the Red Sea into a British lake, what was not the effect of the Suez Canal ? It made a British occupation of Egypt a matter of national necessity, a foregone conclusion to all but short-sighted British statesmen. This last came about in an odd manner, and at an unexpected juncture, and by degrees dragged us into the Sudan as far as the Congo water-parting, and compelled in time the annexation of Uganda. Indian affairs were by this time much mixed up in commerce with those of Zanzibar. Consequently, with the flanks of Egypt to be guarded, no other Power but ourselves must occupy Mombasa—already, for Indian reasons, declared a British stronghold in 1823—or the main route to the Nyanzas and the Upper Nile. Hence arose the vast British possessions in Eastern Equatorial Africa. By 1898 and 1906 the fortified harbour of Aden had grown into a protectorate or sphere of influence over the whole of the south Arabian coastlands, including the Kuriya-Muriyan Islands, from the Straits of Bab-el-Mandeb on the west and the frontiers of Oman on the east. From similar motives also has arisen the British protectorate over the Bahrein Islands in the Persian Gulf. In South Africa we could not occupy Cape Town and remain indifferent to questions of European colonisation and to the welfare of the natives within three hundred miles of the Cape Peninsula. So, in time the British flag crept along the south-east coast till it conflicted with Portuguese claims at Delagoa Bay.

British Flag in Africa

The Mediterranean route to Egypt, moreover, required other calling stations than Gibraltar. Minorca had once been ours, but it lay rather off the direct route to Egypt ; moreover, it belonged to Spain, and Spain had become our ally. Sicily would have been too large to retain and control. Napoleon had indicated just what we required then in seizing Malta. It was easy to succeed him, for the Maltese, who had little or no affection for the corrupt rule of the Knights of St. John, voluntarily offered the sovereignty of their

BRITISH OFFICIALS INSPECTING THE CISTERNS AT ADEN, BUILT IN 1700 B.C.

The story of how Aden came into possession of the British is one of some interest. In 1837, a British ship was wrecked near Aden, the crew and passengers being severely maltreated by the Arabs. On the Bombay Government demanding an explanation, the sultan agreed to make compensation and to sell the town and port to Britain, but the Turkish ruler's son, who administered the government, declined to implement the bargain, and in consequence the place was reduced by a naval and military force on January 16th, 1839. Aden, which then became an outlying portion of the Bombay Presidency, was fortified and garrisoned, and its ancient water tanks were partially restored.

From the drawing by R. Caton Woodville

little archipelago to the King of Great Britain. Beaconsfield believed he was completing the chain of naval stations and military halting places on the Mediterranean route to India by adding Cyprus, with the intention that a British dominion over Syria and a railway thence to the Euphrates valley and India should follow.

Britain's Expanding Empire Whether his successors were wiser in preferring the sea route, *via* the Suez Canal and the Red Sea, time alone can show. The affairs of India involved us, commercially first, and then politically, in those of China. This necessitated military and naval stations in Chinese waters. Hence the acquisition of Hong Kong and eventually of Wei-hai-wei. From the desire to prevent a Russian descent into Tibet and Mongolia, and thence a march towards the Himalayas—in fact, a Russian dominion over the Chinese government— arose the Japanese alliance, with all that it may yet entail. Singapore was required to safeguard the sea route between China and India; the occupation of the Straits Settlements has led to a sphere of exclusive influence over all the Malay Peninsula and a protectorate over the northern coastlands of Borneo. Burma has been annexed to obviate any other intrigues or ambitions in that quarter; while, at the risk of war with France some fifteen years ago, Siam has been maintained as a buffer state.

India has been the chief pivot of our foreign policy from the closing years of Elizabeth's reign to the rapprochement with Russia in 1907–1908: that Russia which was discovered commercially in the reign of Edward VI. by British maritime adventurers who were seeking for a north-east passage to India. The principal attraction which India and the Indian trade had for British minds in the Tudor period lay in its production of spices and pepper. It is true that many of these spices were actually derived from distant parts of the Malay

Commerce the Motive of Expansion Archipelago or from Ceylon, but these regions were considered part of India in a generalised statement, and as some of the Southern Indian ports were depots in the spice trade between Arabia, Persia, and the Farthest East, the confusion was very natural. It would be an interesting study in human history to discuss the diet of Western and Southern Europe in the later Middle Ages and down to the sixteenth century, and discover the reason of the

desire which arose for spiced food, and especially the strenuous demand for pepper. It was the desire to obtain unrestricted quantities of pepper which not only founded the East India Company—and thereby the British Indian Empire—but which first drew Britishers to West Africa : first pepper, then slaves, then gold.

Cinnamon, cloves, ginger, sandal-wood, silks, muslins, indigo, ivory, pearls, gums, carpets, and precious stones, were among the other principal Indian products which attracted the attention of European merchants from the fifteenth to the eighteenth century. The rock formations of India were believed to be excessively rich in precious stones down to quite recent times. But this natural wealth was exaggerated by Arab writers and credulous Europeans. Golconda, little more than a suburb of the modern Haidarabad, whose Mohammedan ruler was one of the first Indian princes to give the British company a trading concession, was not so much a place that produced diamonds as a centre for diamond-cutting, such as Amsterdam has since become. The sandstone region of

India's Vast Store of Wealth the Northern Deccan certainly produced diamonds ; indeed, in the sixteenth century, the Emperor Akbar received an annual royalty computed at £80,000 from the diamond mines of Panna, in Bundelkhand, on the northern edge of the ancient island of Southern India.

These mines are still worked, but are now of inconsiderable importance. Emeralds to a limited degree, rubies, sapphires, cats' eyes, and other precious stones, were to be obtained from India or the adjacent countries, besides which the accumulation of the labour and wealth of forty centuries had amassed in this wonderful peninsula— the matrix of the human race—a vast store of wealth in gold, silver, and precious stones ; and this possible plunder was one of the most potent attractions to Portuguese, Dutchman, Englishman, and Frenchman to found an empire over these patient, placable, thrifty, toiling millions of Aryanised Dravidians.

The pearl fishery was certainly one of our inducements to occupy Ceylon, one of the most notable additions to the British Empire in the early nineteenth century. Eighty years later, the ruby mines of Burma accentuated the impatience felt at the ineptitude of the native Burmese government and its intrigues with France

THE BRITISH IN CYPRUS: THE BASHI-BAZOUKS EVACUATING THE ISLAND
In terms of the Anglo-Turkish Convention, devised at the Berlin Conference, Cyprus was occupied by the forces of Great Britain on July 10th, 1878. The island is now administered as a Crown colony by a high commissioner.
From the drawing by R. Caton Woodville

and Italy. Rubies and teak forests prevailed to decide the immediate political fate of Burma. The location of gold in Australia and New Zealand came too late to be a provocative cause in the annexation of those islands, a deed already accomplished from other motives ; though it is quite possible that the early discovery

Gold the Creator of Colonies of copper in Australia may have rendered the Imperial Government more determined to secure for Great Britain the exclusive political hegemony over Australasia. Gold, however, was the creator of British Columbia, which otherwise might have slid from the feeble hold of the Hudson's Bay Company into the possession of the United States. Conversely, gold in the Yukon valley and sealskins from Alaska have been the principal reasons why the American Government has shown itself so curmudgeon in the settlement of the North-western frontier of the Canadian Dominion, so resolved not to allow Canada to achieve her natural destiny and extend to Bering Strait—an event which I predict will some day come to pass by friendly arrangement.

Diamonds in South Africa, discovered amid the sterility of the Orange Free State borderlands, suddenly changed our attitude of tolerant indifference towards the fate of the South African hinterland into one of eager unscrupulousness. Advantage was taken of the uncertain nature of the Orange State boundary and of native claims, which were assigned to Great Britain, to extend the British ægis over all the known diamondiferous territory. This opened up the route to Bechuanaland and thenceforth to the Zambesi.

We let the Transvaal go back to independence in 1881, and even waived our suzerainty in 1884. In 1886 the Johannesburg and Barberton districts were found to be rich in gold. The attitude of the British Government towards the Transvaal

South Africa's Attractive Gold-Fields immediately changed, or, more strictly speaking, was changed for it by the rise to wealth and power of Cecil Rhodes, and his British, German, French and Afrikander business associates, who, between 1889 and 1905, controlled and dominated the British Government. Lord Salisbury, in the sad autumn of 1899, may have spoken for himself in disavowing the attraction of the gold-fields as being the reason why we then found ourselves

at war with the Boers, but his colleagues must have found it difficult to preserve solemn faces as he uttered those memorable and rather pathetic words of a weary statesman of lofty ideals, aloof from the vulgar rush for wealth and a little ashamed of his yoke-fellows' greedy jingoism.

Yet to Continental critics never must British hypocrisy have seemed so needlessly patent. Of course we wanted the gold-fields, and the territory too ; but for the gold, would Jew and Gentile, Briton and German, American and Frenchman, Indian, Greek and Portuguese have flocked into the prematurely named South African Republic, or have decided rapidly—and truly—that the unadulterated government of uneducated and greedy Boers and a few peevish reactionary Hollanders was not good enough for very modern, clever, hard-working settlers, who wanted the best type and the least obstructive of existing governments—that of Great Britain ?

But for gold and diamonds—and missionaries, of whom more anon—the hinterland of South Africa might still be the

British Influence in South Africa undisputed appanage of Boer and Zulu ; there would be no railway to the Zambesi ; no British Central Africa ; but there might also be, by this time, the outline of a great German colonial empire. Possibly Afrikander children now born and getting ready for school may, in their old age, say it was lucky for the fate of the great South African nation that the passing wealth in precious metals and precious stones—perhaps by that time no longer precious—induced Great Britain as a government, but more through a few British individuals, to lay her hands on South Africa from the Vaal and the Orange rivers to the Zambesi and Tanganyika. Our intervention, though it may have been influenced by temporary greed of gain, has moulded a great nationality, the future united states of South Africa, an analogue to the fusion of Frenchman, Scot, and Englishman which will some day form the great Canadian nation.

The desire to obtain an ample supply of mahogany, logwood, and rosewood without paying toll to Spain created the British colony of Honduras. Gold and diamonds, again, enlarged the boundaries of British Guiana. Palm oil drew the British Government into a protectorate over the Niger Delta and Old Calabar.

Cloves were not without their influence on the fate of Zanzibar. Tin made it possible to develop the resources of the Malay Peninsula and impossible to brook the ingress there of any other Power. The cultivation of the sugar-cane attracted us to the West India Islands.

Codfish and lobsters have imparted an interest in the fate and prosperity of Newfoundland which might otherwise have been lacking ; cotton possibilities in Nigeria are making a chancellor of the exchequer less grim on the subject of subsidies for railway construction, especially with the happy results of the Uganda railway before his eyes ; the chance of cotton-growing in the Zambesi territories was the motive in the minds of the Ministry which despatched Livingstone and Kirk to what is now British Central Africa. The charter of the Hudson's Bay Company was the eventual outcome of Frobisher's voyages of nearly a hundred years before, when Frobisher and Queen Elizabeth, his patroness, believed he had discovered ore containing gold on the verge of the Arctic circle.

Founding of Hudson's Bay Company For more than three centuries commentators referred to this idea as a strange delusion, but the discovery of gold in the Yukon valley shows that Frobisher and Elizabeth's Italian metallurgists may not have been so very much in error. Frobisher may have picked up gold-bearing rocks on the shores of " Meta Incognita," or Baffin's Land, and the inhospitable regions of Eastern Arctic Canada may yet become as valuable as are those of the North-west.

The Hudson's Bay Company, however, was formed under Charles II. more with the object of discovering and dominating a water route to the regions of China and India across North America. But the company soon found its *raison d'être* and its claims for military and diplomatic support in the vast numbers of fur-bearing mammals which swarmed over Arctic and temperate North America. Canadians of to-day owe to the bear, fox, wolverene, lynx, marten, musquash, and mink, the political unity of their vast dominion. Nor have whales—toothed and toothless—been without their influence on the development of the empire. The Basque people of Northern Spain and South-west France seem to have been the first race in Europe or anywhere else to pursue whales on the open sea and attack them with harpoons. No doubt, at first the exploit most desired was to drive the whale on shore. The Basques seem to have had the monopoly of this pursuit from the ninth to the middle of the sixteenth century, when the whalebone **Whaling in the Arctic Seas** whale of the North Atlantic had become almost extinct. Latterly, indeed, the Basque fishermen had been wont to pursue their search for whales as far as Newfoundland, and with the growing demand for oil and whalebone the British seamen had taken up the same quest, hiring frequently the Basque pilots and harpooners to assist them. When Henry Hudson returned in 1607 from his first search for a North-west passage, he spread the news of the enormous quantities of whalebone whales and walruses which were to be found in these Arctic seas. The result was that the Arctic Ocean between Greenland, Labrador, Spitzbergen and Nova Zembla was thronged for twenty or thirty years with British whaling ships, a pursuit which not only added to our stock of hardy, resolute seamen, but increased British interest in the regions of Arctic America.

In the middle of the seventeenth century, however, whaling was almost abandoned on the part of the British, owing to the zeal with which it had been taken up by the Dutch, who became as quarrelsome and as jealous of any competition as they were in the equatorial Spice Islands.

Repeated attempts were made in the early eighteenth century to revive the whaling industry of Britain in the northern seas, and in 1725 the South Sea Company endeavoured to promote the search for whales—whalebone, introduced into English industries a hundred years before, having become an increasingly important article—by offering a subsidy. The matter **Government Bounties to Whaling Ships** was eventually taken up by the Government, whose bounties granted to whaling ships had created by 1749 the first Scottish whaling fleet, sailing from Peterhead. In the second half of the eighteenth century the spread of learning and the love of reading caused an increased demand for lamp-oil and candles. Wax was too expensive, tallow too evil-smelling ; palm oil and other vegetable fats for candle-making had not yet entered the scope of commerce. The voyages of Anson and Cook had drawn attention to the abundance of sperm whales in the south seas. In 1775 the first British whaling ships entered the Pacific round Cape Horn or through the Magellan Straits.

Discovery of Falkland Islands The pursuit of the sperm whale in the Southern seas, and the growth also of world-commerce on the east and west coasts of South America, drew the attention of navigators of several nationalities to the Falkland Islands, situated off the coast of Patagonia, so near to the extremity of South America.

These islands had been discovered by John Davis, the Arctic explorer who was killed on the coast of Malacca in 1592, and again by Sir Richard Hawkins two years later. In 1598 the indefatigable Dutchmen—led by Sebald de Wert—paid them a visit and named them the Sebald Islands. In 1690, or a little after, they received the name of Falkland Islands from Strong, a British captain.

In 1763 the French attempted to found a colony on Berkeley Sound. But by this time the Spaniards of South America considered that these islands came within their jurisdiction, and they expelled the French by force. In 1761 they had been annexed by Commodore Byron on behalf of England on the ground of their having been discovered by Davis, Hawkins and Strong; but the Spanish Government contested the British claim as vehemently as the French attempt, and prepared to go to war on the subject. Nevertheless, in 1771, the British claim to the islands was recognised by Spain in a formal convention. Either they proved to be of less importance to the whaling industry than was expected, or the distractions of the

Napoleonic Wars caused them to be forgotten, for their formal cession by Spain was not followed by any attempt at British settlement other than the chance visits of whaling ships. So much so, that in 1820 the new republic of Buenos Ayres laid claim to the Falkland Islands, and established a colony on the site of the old French settlement at Port Louis.

As no protest was made by Great Britain, the islands might have lapsed into an appanage of a South American republic had it not been that they had become a rendezvous for American whaling ships from the United States, and the masters of these ships fell out with the newly established Argentine authority. American war vessels seem to have intervened in the quarrel, and between them the Argentine settlement was destroyed. Then the British Government awoke to the importance of this forgotten outpost, with the result that the British flag was again hoisted in 1833.

The whaling industry flagged some twenty years afterwards, and was succeeded by the pursuit of the fur-bearing sea-lion. But for many years subsequently the Falkland Islands have been valued, not as a resort for whaling or sealing-ships, but as a wool, tallow, and mutton producing colony, in which a very vigorous white race is springing up which may some day play a part in the politics of South America.

Whaling's Service to the Empire The whaling industry also caused the annexation by Captain Cook in 1775 of South Georgia, a large island—the size of Cheshire—in the South Atlantic, about 950 miles to the E.S.E. of the Falkland group. Whalers have also caused the annexation, or the retention, of numerous tiny archipelagoes in the Pacific, and of Tristan d'Acunha in the South-east Atlantic

THE TOTAL POPULATION, NUMBERING EIGHTY-ONE, OF TRISTAN D'ACUNHA

THE SLAVE TRADE AS A FACTOR IN COLONIAL EXPANSION
SLAVERY UNDER THE BRITISH FLAG AND THE SUPPRESSION OF THE EVIL

THE earliest and strongest inducement to acquire territorial possessions on the West Coast of Africa was the facility for carrying on a trade in slaves with America. The search for pepper—cardamoms, grains of paradise, the seeds of the Aframomum plant—was a temporary allurement; and there was always the trade in gold-dust between Assinie and the Volta River.

But although "Guinea gold" was exported to England steadily from the time of Charles II. onwards, it was never in such large quantities as to give a serious bias to Imperial policy. The rivers and estuaries between the Senegal, Gambia, and Sierra Leone, together with a small portion of Liberia, Hwida, Dahomeh, and Benin: these were the principal resorts of British slave-traders during the sixteenth and seventeenth centuries. In the eighteenth and nineteenth the trade spread to Lagos, the Niger Delta, Calabar, Kamerun and Congo. The rapid conquests of the Spaniards and Portuguese in Central and South America had, in the course of fifty odd years, revealed one negative quality of the New World.

These lands, rich with obtrusive mineral wealth, endowed with magnificent timber, a hundred useful vegetables, and many delectable birds and beasts, were either very sparsely populated with indigenous races of man, or the Indians had not the requisite toughness of fibre to withstand the **Spanish Rulers in America** hellish slavery to which they were subjected by the conquistadores. So that, by the middle of the sixteenth century, the problem which is now exercising many minds in the development of tropical Africa worried the Spanish rulers of America: where was the labour force to come from that could toil unremittingly in a tropical climate?

The Portuguese had anticipated the question before the New World had been discovered. Indeed, the theory of slave labour had been in vigour in the Mediterranean world from a most remote period, and had received a considerable **Victims of Moorish Pirates** fillip during the Crusades and the consequent wars between the Moslems of North Africa and the Christians of Portugal, Spain, France and Italy. Moorish pirates captured Christians, fair and dark, from off the coasts of the Mediterranean and Western Europe, from Ireland to Greece, and the captives were then set to work to row the galley, build the mole, raise the fortress, decorate the palace, and make themselves generally useful in employments not always palatable to the free Moslem.

It was the great desire of the Christian to do likewise, a desire which only began to have its fulfilment when Spaniards and Portuguese first conquered the Moors within the limits of their own peninsula and then victoriously carried their crusading conflict into Morocco. Prince Henry the Navigator did not discourage his Genoese, Majorcan and Portuguese adventurers from making slaves of the Moors on whom they could lay hands in their exploring expeditions. But they soon detected the difference in servitude between Moors and Blackamoors, though generically the two were lumped together.

The captives brought back from the north of the Senegal River were found to be of noble stuff, to whom slavery meant heartbreak. The black people, trafficked in by the very Moors themselves to the south of the Senegal River, were ideal servants, accepting readily both the Christian faith and a mild form of domestic service. In fact, historically, it was the captured Moors who obtained their own freedom by offering to show the Portuguese where they might obtain slaves of the material required by them

As soon as the British seamen of Bristol, Devon, London, and East Anglia began to venture far afield in sailing ventures under the instigation of Venetian navigators, they were very curious as to the regions **Discoveries** from which the Portuguese **of Merchant** obtained spices and muscular **Adventurers** black servants; and even in the discouraging days of Edward VI. and Mary I., when much of English capital and enterprise were fettered by religious troubles and the throttling hand of Spanish diplomacy, merchant adventurers set forth to discover West Africa for themselves.

At first seamen shipped with the Portuguese and kept their own counsel till they returned ; or, later, some Portuguese commander, unfairly treated at home, would come to England to find a market for his knowledge. The excessive jealousy and hostility of the Portuguese towards any other adventurers in the West African field were somewhat tempered where the English were concerned by Portuguese rivalry with Spain, and the feeling that in the struggle that was coming, Portugal, to avoid absorption by the power of Spain, might find assistance in an alliance with the English. Moreover, in spite of religious differences, which did not really arise until the reign of Elizabeth, and of a dog-in-the-manger policy as regards oversea adventure, there had been from the twelfth century onwards the growing up of an unwritten alliance, even of written pacts, between Angevin England and Burgundian Portugal.

It may even be said that prior to the sixteenth century the rulers and the aristocracy of Portugal and England were much more nearly akin in blood, ambitions, and even speech, than they are to-day. The influence of Portugal **Trade in** on the historical development **West African** of the British Empire has been **Slaves** so important as to excuse this disquisition. By the beginning of Elizabeth's reign, though the Portuguese did not like the entry of British seamen into the West African trade, they did not treat this intervention with such hostility as might have nipped it in the bud. Consequently, Sir John Hawkins, as he subsequently became, was in a position in 1562 to tender to the Spanish rulers of

America, Imperial or Viceregal, for the supply of cargoes of West African slaves, or Moors, as they were still called.

The ventures proved profitable to the English, and so satisfactory to the Spaniards in the West Indies that the supply continued to be carried on even during periods when Spain and Britain were officially at war. Hawkins, having enriched himself over a business in which he saw no more iniquity than has been felt by many a nineteenth century purveyor of Kanaka, or negro contract labourers, was knighted by Queen Elizabeth, and assumed as his crest a " demi-Moor in bondage."

The British trade in slaves from the West African coast might have progressed much more rapidly and prosperously between 1560 and 1660 had it not been for the rivalry and ambition of the Dutch. The inhabitants of Holland and Friesland are so near akin to us in blood and language, have so many of our own virtues and faults that we need not affect surprise that a country, small indeed, but nearly as large as the England that counted **Marvellous** in the days of Elizabeth, when **Achievements** Wales and much that lay to the **of Holland** north of Lincoln were savage and sparsely populated, should have achieved the marvellous things it did in the seas of Africa, Asia, and America during the time when its people were fighting on their very thresholds against all the power of Spain and Austria. Such surprise at the achievements of bigminded men out of a tiny country savours of a complete ignorance of history. What Holland did is as wonderful, but not more so, than the staggering first successes of Portugal or the civilisation of Greece.

The Dutch, finding that they were twice as good at ship-building, shipsailing, and ship-fighting as the Portuguese, who had become the subjects of Spain—the Spaniards, except the small Basque population in the north, were indifferent navigators—grasped at transmarine empire everywhere with a greed admirable in its stupendous character. They intended to conquer the whole of Brazil, and wished to supplant Spain in Venezuela and the West Indies. At one time they took nearly all Angola from the Portuguese, and even made an attempt at the subjugation of the Congo kingdom. They usurped the place of the Portuguese in Senegambia—the island of Goree in the harbour of Dakar to this day bears the name of a small island off the Friesland coast, and on the Gold Coast. They occupied the island of St. Helena, discovered and named by the Portuguese, and probably by their maritime attacks checked any intentions on the part of poor paralysed Lusitania to occupy the Cape of Good Hope. They several times took away the island of Mozambique from the Portuguese, occupied and named Mauritius, and exterminated the Dodo. They conquered the coasts of Ceylon, established themselves in Eastern India and ousted the Portuguese flag from almost every part of the Malay Peninsula and archipelago, where it had been so proudly hoisted and so cruelly maintained by the almost superhuman valour of the great conquistadores.

Imitation has constantly been the sincerest, if most unconscious, form of flattery on the part of the British. During the Saxon period they copied the religion, arts, manners, customs, and costume of the Frankish Roman Empire. From before the Norman Conquest they had begun to watch and **Britain the** imitate the Flemings, Picards, **Pupil of** and Bretons. Every fashion **Other Nations** in dress that came from Italy ran with a rapidity, astonishing without a coach or carriageable road, through England up to Edinburgh.

From the middle of the fifteenth to the end of the sixteenth century our seamen sedulously copied in shipbuilding, in the art of navigation, and in the use of nautical terms the maritime enterprise of Italy, Portugal, and Spain, while during the seventeenth century they devoted the same spirit of assimilation to all they could learn from the Dutch. Indeed, it was not until the second half of the eighteenth century that England began to teach other nations.

Therefore, where Venice, Genoa, Portugal, and Holland led in matters of maritime discovery, and later in the slave trade, Britain followed unquestioningly. In the last-named pursuit she had anticipated the Dutch, but towards the close of the sixteenth century the Dutch took the lead, and kept it for some fifty years. It was a Dutch ship that brought the first supply of negro slaves to British North America, Virginia, in 1619. As soon as we began to get the upper hand of the Dutch in maritime warfare, or,

to put it more fairly, as soon as Dutch enterprise slackened, the British turned the temporary trading stations established at the mouth of the Gambia, in the estuary of Sierra Leone, and on the Gold Coast, into permanent fortified posts. In fact, under Charles II., James II., and William III., the British Empire in West **Traffic** Africa began mainly with the **in Slaves** intention of supplying black **and Rum** slaves to the sugar-growing West Indies, where, under Cromwell, Britain had obtained a splendid installation by the conquest of Jamaica. By 1670, we not only desired to obtain contracts for supplying Spanish America with negro labourers, but we required them in thousands for our own American possessions. Sugar was being planted everywhere in the more tropical of the West India islands, and tobacco in Virginia.

There was a growing demand for rum made from sugar. We were approaching the two centuries, the eighteenth and nineteenth, which, amongst a thousand other remarkable characteristics, good and bad, will probably be known in the perspective of history as the centuries of distilled alcohol: the two hundred odd years in which civilised and uncivilised man attempted to poison himself and his progeny, body and mind, with rum, gin, brandy, arrack, kirsch, absinthe, schnapps, and whisky. Rum, the aguardiente of the Spaniard, got a good start in the infamous race, and vastly promoted the cultivation of the sugar-cane, thus causing the British to establish at least fourteen slave-trading depôts on the West Coast of Africa during the eighteenth century, and Liverpool, London, Bristol, and Lancaster to maintain between them a fleet of nearly two hundred slave-ships.

In 1713, the Treaty of Utrecht imposed on Spain the transference from Dutch to British merchants—in the syndicate or combine, as it would now be called, Queen **Britain's** Anne had a fourth share—of the **Share** contract for the annual supply **in Slavery** of 4,800 negro slaves to the Spanish Indies. This privilege was to last for thirty years ; but for some good reasons the Spaniards repudiated it when it had only run for twenty-six. For this and other "wrongs" the British Government declared war on Spain. The long War of the Austrian Succession that followed—and later, the Wars of the Family Compact and of the American revolt—

stood in the way of the resumption of the purveying of slaves to Spanish America in British ships. The Spaniards obtained them through the French and Portuguese, and finally made arrangements with Portugal for the cession of the West African island of Fernando Po and an establishment on the African mainland at Corisco

Negroes in the British Colonies Bay, so that Spaniards could do their own slave-buying and running. But this was little loss to the British slave-traders, because, as the eighteenth century advanced towards its middle, the British-American and West Indian colonies became more and more prosperous and in need of labourers.

In the closing years of the seventeenth century rice from Madagascar had been introduced into South Carolina, and rapidly became an article of profitable culture in the sub-tropical states of British America, provided there was a sufficiency of negro labour. Between 1700 and 1776 about 2,000,000 negroes had been conveyed to the British colonies of Eastern North America by British ships, and in this same period quite 600,000 to the British West Indies —1,000,000 before the century's close.

With the American revolt the slave-market, in what were now the United States, was practically closed to Great Britain. Moreover, coincidently with this revolt arose the first determined movement against slavery in North America. The Quakers, who played such a great part in the settlement of the original States of New England, had from the first disapproved of slavery. The State of Pennsylvania practically abolished slavery within its limits in 1776, and Vermont in 1777. Slavery, in fact, would have never been recognised by the constitution of the United States but for the insistence of Georgia and South Carolina. It was possibly cotton which gave a ninety years'

America's Cotton-Growing States extension to the institution of slavery in America. The cultivation of cotton, curiously enough, though the best wild cotton-plants are indigenous to Southern North America, did not begin in Georgia and the Carolinas until 1770. After a few miscarriages of samples at Liverpool, in 1764, it became an astonishing success. Previous to this discovery of the special value of the climate of Georgia as a cotton-producing country, the small

supplies needed by the modest manufactories of cotton goods at London, Nottingham, and in Lancashire were obtained from Cyprus, Asia Minor, and the West India Islands of Barbados, Anguilla, and St. Christopher. But a simultaneous provocation to the continuous retention of slave labour in the United States arose from England itself. From 1750 onwards a series of splendid inventions—Kaye's fly-shuttle, Hargreave's carding-engine and "spinning-jenny," Arkwright's spinning-frame, mule, and throstle—revolutionised the cotton industries of England, the whole history and development of Lancashire, whither cotton manufacturers were being removed from London because of the greater cheapness of labour and the peculiar qualities of the Lancashire climate, and even the social fabric of England. Cotton spinners, American and West Indian merchants became enormously wealthy and influential, and their sons entered Parliament. Thus were founded the careers of the great Sir Robert Peel and of Gladstone. These wonderful develop-

Growth of the Cotton Industry ments of British industry caused an enormous demand for the raw material. It was before the days of steamships, though the machines with steam power invented by James Watt applied to cotton spinning were the origin of the application of steam-power to locomotion; and the sailing voyages from Turkey through a war-devastated Mediterranean, were too uncertain as a means of a large and constant supply. In the West Indies the area under British control suited to cotton cultivation was too small. As soon as the war with the American colonies could be brought to a conclusion, a trade in cotton, cultivated by slave labour, sprang up between the United States and Liverpool so enormous as to preclude for a long while any serious movement on the American side for the abrogation of the slave status.

But the prohibition of the foreign slave trade by the United States in 1794-1808, and the similar prohibition by Britain in 1808—strengthened by the provisions of the Treaty of Ghent in 1814—effected a great improvement in the position and happiness of the slave in America and in the British West Indies. Hitherto the wastage of life had been terrible. There were about 800,000 negro and mulatto slaves

BRITAIN'S PROTEST AGAINST SLAVERY: CLARKSON PRESIDING AT A CONVENTION OF THE ANTI-SLAVERY SOCIETY

The British Anti-Slavery Society, founded under the presidency of Thomas Clarkson, had as its object the universal extinction of slavery and the protection of the enfranchised population in the British possessions. Chief among those associated with him was William Wilberforce, whose labours on behalf of the cause did much to arouse public sympathy and to bring about its final triumph in 1833, when the Emancipation Act was passed, thus putting an end by gradual steps to slavery and arranging for the payment of £20,000 000 to slave-holders.

From the picture by B. R. Haydon, R.A., in the National Portrait Gallery

5477

in the British West Indies in 1791, but it required annual drafts of about 30,000 to maintain the labour force at its sufficient quota. In 1780 there were about 600,000 negroes in the Southern United States. This figure had risen in 1790, under the stimulus of cotton-planting and increased demand for slave labour—perhaps also

Great Britain's Solicitude for the Negro
to a more careful census—to 757,000. By 1800 it exceeded a million, of whom, however, more than 100,000 were already free. By 1820 there were 233,000 free negroes in the United States, to whom the ordinary franchise of free citizens was practically denied. The embarrassment thus caused was met by the foundation in 1822 of Liberia, on the West Coast of Africa, to receive back in Africa the descendants of freed slaves whom America rejected as voting citizens.

Great Britain had already felt this difficulty of conceding political rights to the freed slaves of the West India Islands, and further had to find homes for the loyalist negroes who had fought on the British side during the American War of 1777-1783. These had first been moved to Nova Scotia; then they were conveyed to London, and finally to the Sierra Leone peninsula, which had been acquired by a philanthropist chartered company for the repatriation of negroes.

The foundation of the future Colony and Protectorate of Sierra Leone, in 1787-1792, was the first episode in a new order of empire building; sentiment or sentimentality was henceforth to rank with other more practical reasons for annexing countries, large and small, to the British Crown.

The alleged philanthropic origin of some of our possessions is an explanation, which, down to a few years ago, would have called forth the snort or the sneer from home or foreign critics of the empire. But although Great Britain is rightly famed for keeping an eye on the main

Sentiment in Imperial Policy
chance in her Imperial policy, it is a fact that several of her investments in Africa and Asia in their origin have been undertaken for motives of sincere philanthropy, and not with the immediate prospect of gain. Thus, Sierra Leone was first started as a chartered company, and then grew inevitably into a crown colony. Lagos was conquered and annexed in 1861 because it remained obstinately a

stronghold of the slave trade. British intervention in the affairs of Nyassaland was largely the outcome of Livingstone's denunciation of the Arab slave trade. British missionary propaganda was in the first place the only motive in Bechuanaland and Central Zambesia.

The same may be said for the beginning of British interest in Uganda, in all probability antedating the anxiety concerning the sources of the Nile water-supply and the irrigation of the Northern Sudan and Egypt. Philanthropy—of a rather sickly kind—started the creation of British commercial and political claims over the Lower Niger, and ranged public opinion behind the vacillating British Government of the 'nineties —it would equally have stood behind them in the 'eighties—in the last century, when Lord Kitchener was allowed to undertake the reconquest and resettlement of the Egyptian Sudan. In no region of the British Empire was philanthropy more justified in urging on a conquest than in these regions of the Central Nile valley. The uprising of the bastard

British Influence in the Sudan
Arab element in this region was in all truth a revolt in favour of the reinstitution of the slave trade in its most extravagantly cruel and infamous aspects. The Mahdi's revolt had blasted and depopulated a region of the earth's surface which, under proper administration, should have been the home of populous tribes of dark-skinned people engaged in rearing large herds of camels, cattle, asses, horses, goats, and sheep, and in cultivating millions of acres of wheat or of date palms.

Its previous government by Egypt had been undertaken first of all on a purely slave-trade basis, and secondly as a speculation very much on the lines of King Leopold's rubber empire on the Congo. The British conquest, occupation, and reorganisation of the Sudan has been a very great gain to civilisation and human happiness.

Whether such a verdict shall be pronounced on all other extensions of British rule is discussed in greater detail in this survey. But it is noteworthy that many a British conquest, in order to excite the philanthropic motive in the British people, has been preceded by a blackening of the character of those about to be conquered.

THE
BRITISH
EMPIRE
IV

BY SIR
HARRY
JOHNSTON,
G.C.M.G.

COLONIES GROWN FROM CONVICT SETTLEMENTS
EFFECT OF THE OLD TRANSPORTATION SYSTEM ON THE EMPIRE'S EXPANSION

ANOTHER inducement to acquire oversea possessions should not be overlooked, as it has contributed powerfully, if at first unhappily, to the formation of British and French colonies from the early part of the seventeenth to, in the case of Britain, the last half of the nineteenth century: the transportation of criminals or political prisoners.

The fact that several of our proudest, most prosperous colonies began in this way, or were reinforced in population by these means, we need have no scruple in admitting or regret in recording, for in all the period of English history previous to the reform of the criminal laws in 1826, 1832, 1837, persons not hanged, drawn and quartered—allowed to survive their trial—could not have been so very wicked, since the death penalty in those days was frequently imposed where now three months' imprisonment would be considered ample to meet the requirements of justice, to say nothing of the enormous frequency of false witness, of miscarriages of justice, wherein a humane judge or Minister would give the prisoner the benefit of the doubt by sentencing him or her to transportation for the enforced colonisation of new lands.

Given the shocking social condition of England and France in the eighteenth and early nineteenth centuries, this plan was really a blessing in disguise. The wretched criminal, often more sinned against than sinning, was removed from a rut

Essentials in Empire Building of hopeless social disqualification, and from incessant temptation to run counter to local laws, to a region where muscle, pluck, endurance, resourcefulness—the brigand's instincts, moderately curbed—were the essentials required in empire building. At home he or she would have eventually ended a miserable career on the gallows or in the workhouse prison. In the American States, the northern West Indies, Australia or Tasmania, the transported developed in many cases into healthy, happy, virtuous, prosperous fathers, or mothers of sturdy colonists, themselves to be the ancestors, perchance, of such as shall found the mighty independent states

Two Sides of the Australian Picture of the future. Some of the finest of Australian citizens, I have been told, can trace their descent from stalwart English poachers, whom the iniquitous game laws of a pre-Victorian Britain condemned to transportation. Similar poachers nowadays, unprosecuted or mildly punished, might develop into successful and very respectable professional cricketers, football players, or golfers; or enter the army, rise to be sergeants-major or inspectors of police, and endow their not-sufficiently-grateful country with families of ten to twelve healthy children.

There was, of course, another side to the picture in Australia, and, above all, in Tasmania. A proportion of the convicts were really wicked men and women, and the partial liberty they attained on reaching the southern hemisphere enabled them to spread their wickedness like a subtle moral contamination. The special and isolated penal settlements in New South Wales, Tasmania, Norfolk Island, Moreton Bay, West Australia, became—according to writers of that and a later day, in pamphlets and in novels—" terrible cesspools of iniquity." But the ex-convicts and ticket-of-leave men became prosperous and outspoken citizens : it has been stated in reports on the transportation question that by 1835 some of the New South Wales ex-convict citizens possessed incomes of between £20,000 and £40,000, derived from houses, lands, ships, cattle, and land transport. They advocated on the platform and in the local Press views that were described as " unprincipled," but in many respects seem nowadays merely Socialism of a respectable and accepted type. The vicious members of the penal settlements mostly died out from their evil courses and left no offspring to perpetuate their moral obliquity. For the rest, the open air, the sunshine, great spaces, necessity for physical exertion, effected a bodily and mental purification. The Australia and Tasmania of the twentieth century bear no more traces in their 4,200,000 wholesome people of the sorrows, tortures, crimes, and privations of a certain section of the original colonisers than do the modern New Englanders, who are in part descended from a similar recruitment.

Britain's Policy of Transportation

Penal colonies or settlements of outlaws or mutinied soldiers were not unknown in the polity of ancient Egypt, the Greek or the Roman worlds, and here or there in legend and in history are quoted as the seed of subsequently prosperous communities. In the evolution of the British Empire the policy of transporting law-breakers to lands beyond the sea was foreshadowed by the Vagrancy Act of Elizabeth's reign, on the strength of which her successor, James I., directed that " a hundred dissolute persons " should be sent to Virginia. In 1660 and 1670, Acts of Charles II. prescribed the transportation of offenders against the laws, which then included many who were merely " lewd, disorderly, or lawless persons," or who were dissidents in religion; and from this time onwards men and women were regularly drafted to the plantations in New England.

In 1718, an Act of George I. ordained that criminals guilty of grave offences, who escaped the death penalty, were to be farmed out to labour-contractors for transport to the American colonies. The contractors were thus enabled to sell the labour of these white slaves—men at about £10 a head, and women at £8 or £9—for whatever term the judge had attached to their transportation, say, from seven to fourteen years. At the end of that period the labourer became free, theoretically, and although in many instances, no doubt, a wicked master kept his " convict " at work beyond the term of his sentence, in many others he became a free colonist long before or settled the question himself by running away to the backwoods, or joining the Indians and becoming the father of

Fate of the White Slaves

vigorous half-breeds. Convicts were also sent to Jamaica, Nova Scotia, the Bermudas, Barbados, and other islands of the British West Indies. But with the revolt of the American States, the transportation of British law-breakers across the Atlantic came to an end. The simultaneous revelation by Captain Cook of the vast Australian territories suggested a far better outlet for the energies of those unhappy convicts in whom the great philanthropist Howard was forcing his fellow citizens and government to take an interest.

The first fleet of convict settlers left England for New South Wales in 1787, and, after a voyage of seven months, landed its consignment on the site of the modern Sydney in January, 1788. In the same year another convict station was established at Norfolk Island, about 400 miles to the north-north-west of New Zealand. In 1804 the first settlement was effected in Tasmania, when 400 convicts, many of them Irish political prisoners, were established on the site of the modern Hobart. The next year the Norfolk Island convicts were removed to Tasmania, and established on the banks of the Upper Derwent.

British Criminals in Australia

As early as 1832, however, protests began to reach England from the reputable section of Australian society against the principle of transporting thither the criminals of Great Britain. There had always been alongside the deported prisoner of the State a steady influx of free colonists. Some of these came to Australia with a view to farm, by means of cheap convict labour; and no doubt by this association of white and black sheep, not a few among the latter regained their former spotlessness of fleece. It is at any rate certain, though enough emphasis has never been placed on this happy fact, that a proportion of nearly, if not quite, half the convicts sent out to Australia found their way back into the life of decent, self-respecting men and women.

It must also be remembered that between 1800 and 1820 a large number of the prisoners were political: Irish rebels or English rioters, fighters for freedom merely, and often high-minded, pureminded men. On the other hand, after the first reform of the terrible English criminal code in 1826 and 1832, the persons deemed to have merited transportation were more certainly thorough-going lawbreakers than under the former and harsher laws. So it came about that all the respectable elements of Australian society —from whatever source recruited matters not, for their lives and exploits were sufficient testimony to their character— struck at the dumping of any more convicted criminals on Australian soil. Their protests were endorsed by their judiciary, and after 1840 no more state prisoners were sent to the eastern half of Australia.

A good many of the irreclaimable convicts of New South Wales and Queensland (Moreton Bay) were removed to Norfolk Island, which continued to be a convict station till 1854. Tasmania received all the output of British convicts until 1846, when, in consequence of protests from its Government, the supply was stopped until 1848. Then it began again, especially with regard to Irish and English Chartist political prisoners. This was in 1850, when an attempt to land 250 convicts in the previous year at the Cape of Good Hope provoked almost an insurrection. After 1850 no more convicts were sent to the beautiful island of Tasmania, which, in 1825, had been thrown open to free emigrants. In Tasmania the worst features of convict colonisa-

Troublesome Convicts in Tasmania tion were certainly manifest. The indentured or assigned criminals, who were subjected to but little supervision, frequently escaped into the bush, and between 1804 and 1830 the island was terrorised by bushrangers. This precipitated trouble with the black indigenes, whose treatment, active and passive, at the hands of British officialdom will always be one of the blots on the empire's record, from the point of view of science as well as philanthropy. The worst type of convicts were herded at the penal settlement of Port Arthur, on Tasman Peninsula, under conditions graphically described by the late Marcus Clarke in his powerful novel, " His Natural Life."

Western Australia had been founded as a colony in 1829, but for many years it languished in growth owing to the superior attractions in rapid fortune-making offered elsewhere in the island-continent. It needed cheap labour above all for the development of its resources, so that when the other states of Australia were indignantly repudiating the principle of convict immigration, the legislature of the Crown Colony of West Australia actually proposed to the Home Government, in 1846,

the sending out annually of a limited number of British convicts. The proposal was eagerly accepted by the British Government in 1849, at a time when they were placed in a very awkward dilemma by the outbreak in Cape Town against the landing of convicts. Accordingly, transportation of criminals was resumed Australia-wards, and the

The System of Transportation Abolished prisoners, released on ticket-of-leave for the most part, were sent annually to Fremantle and Albany until 1865. Many of these so-called convicts were little more than boys from the reformatory prison at Parkhurst, Isle of Wight. But later the Imperial Government began to develop a plan of regular penal establishments in Western Australia for the using up of British criminals in the mass, and this contemplated procedure offended the growing national pride of Australia.

Moreover, it was complained of by the colony of South Australia, which had never been associated in its foundation with convict immigrants, but which now witnessed a permeation of its settlements by escaped criminals from West Australia. In 1865, therefore, the system of transporting convicts to Western Australia, or to any region beyond the limits of Great Britain and Ireland, came to an end for ever.

There is nothing to gird at in this record. Transportation was a plan which in the circumstances of the time, of home institutions, and colonial needs, served a purpose that in the main was beneficent. At any rate, whether or not unpleasing to British pride, it must be ranked among the principal causes which led to the colonisation of North and South Carolina, Virginia, and Massachusetts ; of Jamaica, the Bahamas, and the Leeward Islands ; of Australia and Tasmania.

But for the need to find a dumping-ground for offenders against the criminal laws or for political prisoners, Australia and

Colonies that were Lost to France Tasmania would have become French possessions ; no doubt New Zealand as well. France, with the gold and copper of Australia and the magnificent climate of New Zealand as baits for French emigrants, might have played a very different part in the world's history. It is curious to reflect on the partly forgotten causes and personalities of this movement towards Australia. After the middle of the eighteenth century there were British Ministers who took an interest in science for the mere love of knowledge. Lord Halifax, in 1768, had despatched James Bruce, British consul in Algeria and Tunis, to Egypt, to discover the source of the Nile. In the same year, partly through the influence of the same Secretary of State—who died in 1771—Captain James

The Beauty and Wonders of Australia Cook was sent with a small naval expedition to the South Seas to observe from the longitude of Tahiti the transit of Venus. On his homeward journey he discovered, or re-discovered, New Zealand and Australia. His landing at Botany Bay, near Sydney, at the beginning of the Australian autumn, when there was a renewed outburst of leaf and blossom under the influence of the rains, caused him to give, on his return to England in the summer of 1771—besides the reports of his scientific staff, among whom was Sir Joseph Banks —such a glowing account of the beauty and wonders of Australia as fascinated the attention of arm-chair geographers in England. Amongst this type of useful and enthusiastic students was a Mr. Matra, afterwards British Agent at Tangiers, who had access to the ear of Lord Sydney, the Minister then in charge of Colonial affairs.

The philanthropist John Howard, in 1777-1779, had been agitating for prison reform. The American colonies were now closed as places to which criminals could be transported. The prosperous West Indian Islands rejected this labour material, not half so useful as negro slaves; where, then, was a harassed administration, just awaking to the impulses of modern philanthropy— largely created by the Quakers—to send the wretched beings it was too humane to slaughter and too ignorant to reform? Some suggested a penal settlement at Gibraltar; others, with more sardonic intent, the Gambia River, where the climate was reported to kill one in six among the Europeans landed there. But Mr. Matra espoused the suggestions of Sir Joseph Banks that the beautiful country of New South Wales should receive a British settlement; and afterwards shaped his plans so as to incorporate Lord Sydney's suggestion that the Botany Bay colony should comprise a scheme for the transportation of large numbers of convicts. Mr. Matra seems to have been a Corsican, the relation or descendant of a Corsican patriot who sometimes fought with, sometimes against, Paoli, in the Corsican struggle for independence which preceded the French Revolution by twenty to thirty years. Matra had become domiciled in England, and, as far as can be ascertained, never was in Australia, but merely became interested theoretically in that country's possibilities and in colonisation generally. Lord Sydney, as Sir Thomas Townshend and later as a peer, was at the Foreign Office between 1782 and 1791.

Then, owing to the disgust occasioned by the issue of the American War, the Ministry of the colonies had been abolished and the oversea possessions of Great Britain were dealt with by the Foreign

The Birth of British Australasia Department. Matra, with his knowledge of French and Italian, was useful to Lord Sydney, no doubt in Mediterranean questions. His own chief preoccupation at this time, 1783, seems to have been to found a new home for the American loyalists. Lord Sydney's aim was to select a suitable portion of the globe for the reception of transported criminals. From this curious conjunction of plans and enthusiasms sprang British Australasia.

AUSTRALIAN ABORIGINES RECEIVING BLANKETS FROM THE GOVERNMENT

THE WARS OF THE EMPIRE, JUST AND UNJUST

HOW BRITAIN'S OVERSEAS DOMINIONS HAVE BEEN EXTENDED BY FORCE OF ARMS AND THE LOSS OF THE AMERICAN COLONIES

THE participation of England in the Crusades, and, indeed, all the wars carried on by Norman, Angevin, and Plantagenet kings outside the English realm, with the exception of the conquest of Ireland, Wales, and Scotland, can hardly be called wars for the foundation of the British Empire. The campaigns of Henry II., Richard I., the first three Edwards, Henry V. and VI., were undertaken as the attempts of French princes to reign in France, while their work in the Crusades was really a lingering vestige of the Western Roman Empire, a continuance of that work of Rome which was really resumed after the Saxon interregnum.

For a brief period after the Anglo-Saxons had done much to destroy Roman civilisation in Britain, Ireland may have been more civilised and prosperous than England or barbaric Caledonia. Were it not, however, for the vestiges of an undoubted and very beautiful art, the early mediæval civilisation of Ireland might be questioned, seeing how much invention and exaggeration have accumulated in the monkish legends. [Students of this part of British history would do well to read "The Elder Faiths of Ireland," by W. H. Wood-Martin; and "The Making of Ireland and Its Undoing," by Mrs. Alice Stopford Green.] With the influence of the Romanised **Roman Civilisation in Britain** Franks on the Saxon courts, Roman civilisation soon raised its head again in the realm of the Anglo-Saxon from Edinburgh to Southampton, and the new English civilisation began to infiltrate Iberian Wales and Cornwall. The necessary preliminary to a British Empire abroad was the political consolidation of Great Britain, Ireland, and Man into a single great power with a central government. Until that could be brought about in deed, if not in word, there could be no motive, no security for an empire beyond the seas of the British Archipelago. The first wars of the empire, therefore, were those which the **England at the Time of the Normans** Norman and Angevin kings, incited by the Pope, with his desire to unify the Western Christian Church, undertook for the subjugation of Ireland and Wales. For Imperial purposes, the conquest of Ireland was sufficiently achieved in the reign of Henry II. The Danes had largely prepared the way for the English. They had slain the last Keltic king of all Ireland, Brian Boru. Ireland was then, as now, composed, in a different proportion, of much the same racial elements as England, Scotland, Wales and Cornwall.

It is probable, however, that at the time of the Norman invasion Danish was a good deal spoken on the coasts of Ireland, and from that to the English of Henry II.'s period was no very difficult step. But it was really the Roman Church that kept Ireland under English control until such time as the English infiltration had grown too strong for a national resistance.

Wales had been brought into the English hegemony at the conclusion of the reign of Edward I. Anglo-Saxon, Norman, and Danish influence combined, had, between 700 A.D. and the reign of Robert Bruce, settled the question whether Scotland was to be an independent Keltic kingdom with a predominant Keltic language, or a country ruled by the English speech, by Roman and Norman ideas of law and custom, although for two centuries more she remained a power more often hostile

5483

than friendly. The Isle of Man had come within the English sphere of influence in 1344 and 1406, when it had ceased to be ruled by a Norwegian dynasty, and had been finally wrested from intermittent Scottish occupation. The Hebrides and outer islands of West Scotland were secured from Norway, and, later, from **Scotland's Union with England** independent rule — by the "Lord of the Isles"—in 1264 and 1427. The Orkneys and Shetlands were also pledged by Norway (Denmark) in 1469 as the security for the dowry of Margaret of Denmark, who married James III. The pledge was never redeemed. Thus the kings of Scotland, mainly by war prowess, between 844 and 1470 brought the entire mainland and adjacent islands of North Britain under one rule, and in 1603 united it with the Crown of England, Wales, Ireland, and the Channel Islands, and the suzerainty over Man.

Though the nominal independence of Scotland continued until the fusion of the two crowns in the person of James VI. (I.), Scotland had no Imperial policy of her own after the Battle of Flodden Field, except the unfortunate Darien expedition of 1698–1700 to the Gulf of Uraba at the southern beginning of the Isthmus of Panama, and did not actively participate in the Imperial schemes of Britain till after the Act of Union in the reign of Queen Anne. It was likewise not until the middle of the eighteenth century that Irishmen born in Ireland are found taking any prominent part in colonial expansion.

The war-worn Henry IV. had dallied with Imperial projects of trade in the Mediterranean, and had even received embassies from the Moors of North Africa ; but his death at the early age of forty-seven cut short his plans of expanding English influence. The eighty years of turmoil that followed distracted men's thoughts from any questions but those of **The Seeds of Imperial Desires** England, Scotland, France, and Burgundy. Thus the great stirrings of the Southern English—for at first all Imperial enterprise came from south of the latitude of Lincoln—towards oversea adventure and acquisitions did not make themselves felt till the reign of Henry VII. The growing relations of trading Britain with the Low Countries, with Venice, Portugal, and the Hanseatic towns, which became very marked in the reign of Edward IV., sowed

the seeds of Imperial desires. We were prompted to found an empire by giant minds of Venice and Genoa, who, eager to take their inspirations to any monarch with the power of executing them, and often thwarted or maltreated by Spain or Portugal, came to England, and attracted the inchoate desires of this people—emergent from civil wars, safe at home, and fermenting with the new learning—towards the discovery and conquest of lands across the Atlantic Ocean.

The first war undertaken for an empire beyond the shores of Britain did not occur till the early part of Elizabeth's reign, and then for a long time it was an unofficial war, waged by gallant men whose status was little superior to that of pirates. Drake and his comrades, incensed by the attempts of the Spanish monarchy to retain all America within the limits of a Spanish monopoly, boldly attacked the colossus in detail, and by surrendering to the greedy Elizabeth much of the wealth thus acquired, escaped being hanged as pirates. But after their exploits had provoked the despatch of the Spanish Armada, **The Bold Line of Queen Elizabeth** Elizabeth took a bolder line. She afforded a somewhat churlish and treacherous assistance to the struggling people of the Netherlands, and waged a war here against Spain—not by any means crowned with honour—which was probably intended, if she saw her way clear, to add the Netherlands to the dominions of the British Crown—still claiming the kingdom of France. The Dutch, after the disgraceful behaviour of Leicester, were by no means minded to pursue their original invitation to Elizabeth to become queen over the Low Countries. Outraged at the treachery displayed by Elizabeth's generals, they resolved to lean on the House of Orange and its German connections, and to pursue an independent and even a rival course to that of England.

This divergence of paths between the people speaking two Low German dialects in the deltas of the Rhine and the Ems, and the people speaking another language of the same stock in Great Britain, Scotland and Eastern Ireland, was to culminate seventy years later in some of the toughest of our colonial fights, and reverberated to its last echo, it may be hoped, in the South African War of 1899-1902. James I. probably permitted rather than encouraged the foundation of a British

Empire beyond the sea, firstly because it was difficult to check the impulses in that direction which had grown up under Elizabeth, partly because these enterprises were encouraged by his gallant eldest son, Prince Henry, who died untimely in 1612; and lastly, because the promoters of these colonial schemes had only to bribe James's favourites to get what charter they desired. James's own colonial or Mediterranean wars were unfortunate, and resulted in no advantage. He beheaded Raleigh to please Spain, and because Raleigh had discovered no gold or silver mines in Guiana.

Cromwell's first colonial war was with Holland. The effect of the massacre at Amboina in 1623 of a number of Englishmen and their followers—nine Englishmen, one Portuguese, nine Japanese, and about ninety Malays—in order that the Dutch might retain the monopoly of the spice trade, had taken some time to reach England, but had never been forgiven or forgotten. Internal troubles had prevented the exaction of any indemnity until the establishment of Cromwell's power in 1652.

Cromwell's Revenge on the Dutch
The Dutch had taken full advantage of the paralysis of England at home between 1630 and 1652, Prince Rupert aiding on behalf of Charles II. to chase British ships from the carrying trade in the Mediterranean, Atlantic and Indian Oceans.

They had, of course, added to their offences in Cromwell's eyes by receiving an envoy from Charles II. after the death of his father. Therefore, in 1651, the Commonwealth Parliament devised the extraordinary Navigation Act; which obliged all colonial or Indian produce to be carried to Great Britain in British ships only, or foreign goods to be brought in ships of the country producing those goods. Thus they dealt a severe blow at the Dutch mercantile marine, which had become the common carriers of the world.

They wished also to check the free use of British fisheries by the Dutch fishermen, and demanded as a royalty the tenth herring of every catch. They also required—which was less defensible—that the Dutch should salute the British Fleet first whenever the two squadrons met in the Channel. The results of the naval war which broke out in 1652 were very favourable to Britain, and the position of the British in the East Indies and on the east coast of North America was materially strengthened. As regards Spain, which was covertly harassing the British settlers in the Bahamas and Leeward Islands, who for their frequent raids on Hispaniola and Jamaica no doubt deserved such reprisals, Cromwell sent an expedition, 1654-1655, under Admiral Penn—the father of the founder of Pennsylvania—and General Venables to Barbados. At this island they opened their sealed orders, and found they were to attack and occupy the large island of Hispaniola. Besides the 4,000 soldiers they had on board, they were to recruit a further force from among what we should nowadays call the convict settlers of Barbados, and were further to take up more fighting men at St. Christopher.

Jamaica Seized by the English

With 10,200 men they proceeded to attack the port of San Domingo in a most blundering fashion, and at length were beaten off by the Spaniards and the results of great sickness among their men. Ashamed—or, rather, afraid—to face Cromwell with no better results than this repulse, they proceeded to Jamaica, never very strongly garrisoned by Spain. Their seizure of the island, in May, 1655, met with but a feeble resistance on the part of the Spaniards. The folk who seemed most annoyed at the arrival of the British were the negro slaves of the Spaniards who had replaced the exterminated Arawak Indians, slaves probably brought to Jamaica originally in British vessels. These fled to the mountains, and long remained recalcitrant to British rule.

A small proportion of these descendants of the Spanish slaves claim still a certain independence and peculiar privileges of their own in the bush country of Eastern and Western Jamaica. The Spaniards nicknamed runaway negroes who took refuge in the interior mountain ranges "Cimarrones," from "Cima," a mountain peak. This term was shortened and corrupted in West Indian English into "Maroons." This attack on a Spanish possession in a time of peace, and when a Spanish ambassador had been accredited to Cromwell and to the Parliament for the purpose of arriving at a settlement of all outstanding disagreements, and even of the conclusion of an alliance between the two nations, can only be described as a dishonourable and unscrupulous action which, if it had been committed against England

England's Unscrupulous Action

by Spain, British historians would never have ceased denouncing. As it is, I cannot find a word of disapproval in the work of any British historian; only expressions of regret that the drunken squabbles of the leaders of the expedition caused it to fail humiliatingly in the original purpose entertained by Cromwell—the conquest of Hispaniola. After this outrage Spain declared war. Cromwell had already (1655–6) despatched a British fleet to the Mediterranean under Blake simultaneously with the expedition under Penn and Venables to the West Indies. Blake was to punish the Barbary rovers for their attacks on British shipping, and to strike terror into the courts of Tuscany and Rome for their having given harbourage to the recusant English war vessels, the remains of Charles I.'s navy, under Prince Rupert.

England at War With Spain

Blake threatened to bombard Leghorn, but finally agreed to accept from Rome and Tuscany an indemnity of £60,000. He then proceeded to Algiers, but the Turkish dey of that country promised reparation. The dey of Tunis refused satisfaction, so the castles of Goletta and Porto Farina were battered by Blake's artillery and the shipping they protected was destroyed. Tripoli was afterwards threatened, but submitted. Blake followed up the Spanish declaration of war in 1656 by blockading Cadiz and burning a Spanish treasure fleet at Santa Cruz (Teneriffe, Canary Islands). The alliance with France which followed the outbreak of war with Spain led to the capture and retention of Dunkirk by the English. Dunkirk was then a town of the Spanish Netherlands. In 1658 Charles II. sold the place to Louis XIV. for £200,000, which he spent on his mistresses.

In 1664–1667 the war with Holland was renewed, owing in part to Charles II. reviving the Navigation Act of the Commonwealth. But hostilities were further provoked by the unfriendly attitude of the Dutch towards the newly founded Royal African Chartered Company, which was attempting to establish itself on the Gold Coast in order to take a share in the slave traffic and in the export of gold. Out in the Far East, indeed, there was constant bickering between Dutch and English, and many a spell of "unofficial" warfare between their land or naval forces occurred sometimes when the two

Unofficial Warfare in the Far East

nations were at peace with Europe. This went on until the latter part of the eighteenth century, and had for its general purpose the expulsion of the Dutch from Bengal and the driving away of the English from Ceylon and the Malay Archipelago. An example of one of these local wars was the arrival in 1759 of a Dutch flotilla in the Hugli to assist Mir Jafar to turn out the victorious English. Clive and Colonel Forde turned fiercely on the Dutch and captured or destroyed the whole flotilla. During the eighteenth century it was France rather than Holland that we had to fight for the extension of the British Empire in America, the Mediterranean, and India.

We made use of the War of the Spanish Succession at the beginning of the eighteenth century to seize Gibraltar and Minorca. The holding of Gibraltar had been once or twice suggested as the alternative to the surrender of Tangier in 1684, and the question of a secure harbour of refuge at the outlet of the Mediterranean had become more urgent to British naval policy after the defeat of Sir George Rooke by the French off Cape St. Vincent in 1693, and the capture of the British merchant fleet from Turkey, and, later, during the subsequent operations of Admiral Russell off Cadiz. But the actual capture of Gibraltar was effected rather as a side issue, and not entirely by British valour.

Gibraltar Captured by the British

In the third year, 1704, of the war, Sir George Rooke was despatched with a force of German and English soldiers under the Prince of Hesse Darmstadt to seize Barcelona. Here, however, they were repulsed by the Spaniards, who held the place for the Bourbon King Philip. They, therefore, sailed back towards England, but on their return surprised Gibraltar, which was not expecting any attack. The importance of Gibraltar was, at all events, not yet fully realised, though at the Peace of Utrecht, signed on April 11th, 1713, it was, together with Minorca, ceded to Great Britain by King Philip of Spain. Five years afterwards, the Prime Minister, Lord Stanhope, thought Gibraltar of no consequence, and proposed to retrocede it to Spain in order to pacify Cardinal Alberoni. Minorca, the second largest of the Balearic Islands, had been captured by an English force under General and Admiral

BRITAIN'S FIRST FOOTING IN CANADA: THE FRENCH SURRENDER OF QUEBEC

Making his first voyage to Canada in 1603, Samuel de Champlain founded Quebec in 1608, and subsequently became French governor of Canada. In 1629, he was compelled to surrender Quebec to British adventurers under Admiral Kirke, but the captured territory was restored to France, peace having been arrived at between the two countries.

From the drawing by R. Caton Woodville

Stanhope in 1708. It remained as a British possession till 1756, when it fell to a French attack after the defeat of Admiral Byng. At the peace of 1763 it was restored to Great Britain, again lost to the Spaniards in 1782, seized once more by British arms in 1798, and finally restored to Spanish rule in 1803, the British deciding to retain Malta as an alternative " padlock "

Founding of the South Sea Company on the Mediterranean. The results of the War of the Spanish Succession—1702–1713—also strengthened the British position in the Hudson's Bay territories, Newfoundland, and in the West Indies ; and by the Treaty of Utrecht the " Asiento " for the supply of slave labour to Spanish America seemed to the eager British to carry with it the right or the excuse to evade the jealous Spanish monopoly of trade with South America. On such a pretext as this the South Sea Company was founded to trade with the Pacific coasts of Spanish America.

But the powerful Prime Minister of Spain, Cardinal Alberoni, had no intentions of allowing this misreading of the rights obtained under the Asiento. His hostility was accentuated by the interference of George I., in 1718–1721, with the disputes between Spain and Austria as to the division and allotment of Italian territories. The ill-feeling smouldered for years, breaking out in 1727 into a four months' Spanish siege of Gibraltar, a siege which led to assistance being afforded to the British by Morocco, and to the beginning of friendly relations with that empire never since interrupted.

In 1739 war was definitely declared on Spain, the war of " Jenkins's ear," over the interpretation of the Asiento, and was not brought to a close until 1748. During this war—largely concerned as it was with the defence of the Netherlands and Rhineland against the ambitions of France, and the counter attempts of France to restore the Stuart

Anson's Famous Voyage Round the World dynasty—no additions were made to the British Empire ; but the raiding voyage of Commodore (afterwards Lord) Anson round the world again drew British attention to the possibilities of the Pacific containing unexplored lands of value.

The peace signed at Aix-la-Chapelle in 1748 was of brief duration. The territorial ambitions of France and Britain in North America were already becoming acutely hostile. The quarrel really centred on a very important principle. Were the British settlers to be allowed by France to penetrate across the Ohio River, and thus break through the ring of French forts and claims of sovereignty stretching from the St. Lawrence to the Mississippi ? If the British accepted this confinement, then Anglo-Saxon America would at most have been limited to a small portion of Eastern North America, and perhaps to Newfoundland, which had been ceded to Britain at the Peace of Utrecht in 1713 ; though it is doubtful whether the victory of the French (in a struggle which reached its climax in a British attack on Quebec in 1759) would not have ended in the eventual supremacy of France over the whole of North America.

This American war began unofficially in 1754 by skirmishes and serious fights, in which George Washington, at the age of twenty-one, was engaged, between British and French colonists and regular soldiers along the Ohio River ; and by naval combats and raids between British and French naval forces off the coasts of

Results of the Seven Years War Newfoundland and in the British Channel. In those pre-telegraph days an unacknowledged state of war could continue, in a condition strongly resembling piracy, for more than a year before it was thought necessary to issue a formal declaration of belligerency.

This war, declared in 1756, lasted until it involved Spain, besides Prussia, Russia, and Austria, and became the " Seven Years War " of the " Family Compact." Its results, ratified by the Peace of Fontainebleau, or Paris, on February 10th, 1763, led to most momentous issues : to the establishment of a vast Anglo-Saxon North America—France only retained the two little islands off the Newfoundland coast and a small portion of Western Louisiana, and Spain gave up all territory east of the Mississippi—to the empire of British India through the victories of Clive and Eyre Coote ; to the enlargement and consolidation of that Prussia which was to grow into the great modern empire of Germany ; to the British acquisition of Senegal, which first turned our thoughts towards the Niger ; and, lastly, to the beginnings of British Honduras and the acquisition of Dominica, St. Vincent, and Tobago in the West Indies. The Seven Years War, that, began in

1756, moreover, was remarkable for a fighting element on the British side which has never since been absent from our land forces in times of need—the Highland regiments, the " Berg-Schottische " that delighted and surprised the King of Prussia when they served with Hanoverian, Hessian, and Brunswick soldiers to defend the electoral dominions in Western Germany.

It was the idea of the great Pitt, derived from a suggestion made eighteen years earlier by a Scottish statesman, Duncan Forbes, to enlist in the British Army for foreign service warlike Highlanders, who only eleven years before had been invading England under Charles Edward. From this time forward dates the complete fusion of Scottish and English interests in the conquest and administration of the British Empire.

Britain's Wars on Sea and Land

Attention should also be drawn to the very important part played in all our Imperial wars of the eighteenth century, from 1704 to the struggle with Napoleon, by the German soldiers taken into British pay. It must be remembered that in the early eighteenth century there was practically no standing army in Great Britain, merely a militia. A good deal of British fighting was done at sea. Warfare was carried on in America much more by armed colonists than by means of imported British soldiers. Some thousands of British soldiers were enlisted for the wars carried on by Marlborough, the Duke of Cumberland, and George II. in Flanders and the Rhenish Provinces ; but a large proportion, also, of the troops under British generals were Dutch, Hessians, Hanoverians, Westphalians, Brunswickers. Even under Queen Anne, Hessians, commanded by their own prince, were subsidised to do the work of the British Army; and we have already noticed that it was with a force of this kind, largely composed of Germans and commanded by the Prince of Hesse, that Gibraltar was captured. When George I. and II. were on the throne, German troops were not only employed with British subsidies to defend Hanover, but were imported into England, used in Ireland, and sent over to America, just as in the latter part of George III.'s reign they were employed to garrison South Africa. Men thus employed seldom returned to Germany. They usually married English or colonial wives, and, when disbanded, remained in or migrated to British colonies, forming in time one of the best elements in the British Empire, physically and mentally.

The Mother Country at War With America

In 1763, France ceded to Great Britain all the French possessions in North America except Louisiana. Canada was thus united to Newfoundland, the thirteen colonies of New England, and to the Floridas. Three years afterwards, the Stamp Act was passed by the British Parliament. This assertion of the principle that Britain might tax her American colonies without their giving consent to such contributions either by elected representatives at Westminster, or at any provincial assembly of their own, produced serious disturbances in Massachusetts, New York, Virginia, and other of the New England " provinces " ; and, although the Stamp Act was repealed in 1766, and in 1770 all the American Imperial import duties were removed, with the exception of the duty on tea, this last was insisted on in a way which brought the conflict between Mother Country and colonies to a head. A state of war with the colonials began in 1775 with the Battle of Lexington, near Boston.

France and Spain Against England

France joined in this unhappy war in 1778, after the capitulation of Burgoyne's troops at Saratoga. French money, men, and the diversions caused by the French Navy, which took away from Great Britain several of the recently acquired Windward and Leeward Islands, ultimately decided the American struggle in favour of the colonial forces under George Washington, Gates, Sullivan, and Greene. But for the French, it is highly probable that Sir Henry Clinton, who succeeded Sir William Howe as chief in command of the British forces in North America, would eventually have got the better of the colonists, who lacked money, stores, and munitions of war. But the ultimate result would have been much the same. During the Napoleonic wars the United States, as they became from 1776, would probably have effected a completion of their independence, and might by then have won over the French Canadians, and not have left to Great Britain any foothold on the North American continent.

Spain, smarting from the losses she had sustained at the Peace of Paris in 1763, hastened to join France in attacking

England over the American question. She devoted her efforts chiefly to the great siege of Gibraltar (1780-1782) and to recapturing Minorca, in neither of which enterprises she succeeded. Nevertheless, at the end of the war in 1782, England retroceded to Spain the Island of Minorca and the two Florida provinces in North

Dutch Jealousy of Britain America, thus renouncing, in Florida, one of the most important gains of 1763. Russia showed marked unfriendliness in 1780, combining with Denmark and Sweden in the League of Armed Neutrality. Holland went farther and declared war. At this period the Dutch were much under French influence, and were bitterly jealous of the British successes in India.

The reply to the Dutch declaration of hostilities, besides the destruction of Dutch shipping in home waters, was the despatch in 1781 of a powerful squadron under Commodore Johnstone to seize the Cape of Good Hope. Owing to the treacherous communication of the British plans by a spy the French Government was enabled to forestall Johnstone. He was attacked at the Cape de Verde Islands by the great French Admiral Suffren, and his squadron was seriously crippled. Suffren then went on to South Africa, and landed men at Cape Town to assist in driving off the British, whose second attempt, in 1782, likewise failed.

After Lord Cornwallis had capitulated to the French and Americans at Yorktown in October, 1781, this war of seven years' duration drew to a close, and was concluded by the Peace of Versailles in January, 1783. It is true that during 1782 the siege of Gibraltar had been brilliantly terminated by the heroic bravery and enterprise of the besieged force under General Elliot (Lord Heathfield), and that Rodney had smashed the French fleet under De Grasse in the West Indies ; but this war of the American revolt nevertheless imposed

A Set-back to the British Empire severe losses and humiliations on the British Empire, and it is difficult to understand why the settlement at the Peace of Versailles is alluded to by British historians with complacency. As a matter of fact, it has been so far the most serious set-back that the empire has sustained. Besides the recognition of the independence of the thirteen states of New England, we retroceded the Floridas to Spain. We gave up Minorca; restored Senegal to

the French; abandoned all stipulations concerning the non-fortification of Dunkirk, and ceded to France the West India Islands of St. Lucia and Tobago, besides several posts in Eastern India.

In 1790-1794 there was nearly an outbreak of war with Spain over the question of Nootka Sound, Vancouver Island, in reality the question whether the British territories of Hudson's Bay and the Canadas should have a Pacific coast. Spain had already occupied California (called by Drake New Albion) ; Russia, under Catherine II., was establishing fur-trading stations in Alaska. Alaska was discovered in 1721 by the Danish navigator Behring, in the employ of the Russian Government.

The Emperor Paul, in 1799, issued a charter to a Russian fur-trading company to occupy Alaska. Spain was desirous of extending northwards along the Pacific coast until she met the Russian flag. She dreaded the proximity of the English. The expeditions of Cook in 1778, and of Vancouver in 1791-1792 excited her apprehensions, and perhaps for this reason as much as others she was willing, as soon as

Additions to Britain's Dominions the first horror of the French Revolution was over, to join France in 1796 in the renewed war against Great Britain. In 1793 was the beginning of those long Napoleonic wars which lasted, with the very brief interval of the Peace of Amiens, till 1815, and which enabled Great Britain to add to her dominions Heligoland, the Ionian Islands, Malta, Cape Colony, Mauritius, the Seychelles, Ceylon, Guiana, Trinidad, the remainder of the Windward Islands, and British Honduras; besides Minorca, Java and Sumatra, Senegal, the French West Indies and Cayenne, and the Island of Reunion ; all of which were restored at the Peace of Amiens or at the Congress of Vienna.

Attempts to capture the Canary Islands, Uruguay and Buenos Ayres had failed, the last-named, undertaken in 1806-1808, causing much disappointment in England. The value of temperate South America as a horse and cattle-breeding country had already been appreciated. The monopolist policy of Spain had for generations disgusted and alienated the Spanish and Portuguese colonists, and it was believed that the road lay open for the creation, through Uruguay and Buenos Ayres, of a possible British empire over the non-Portuguese part of South America.

THE SURRENDER OF MAURITIUS TO THE BRITISH IN 1810

Formerly called the Isle of France, Mauritius was discovered by the Portuguese in 1507, it being at that time without inhabitants and unknown to Europeans. Its name was changed on coming into the possession of the Dutch in 1598; they abandoned it about a hundred years later to the French. The British captured it from the French in 1810, and when hostilities ceased, in 1814, the holding of the island by Britain was one of the provisions of the Treaty of Paris.

From the drawing by R. Caton Woodville

But though the South American Spaniards had been alienated from their selfish metropolis and its new Napoleonic dynasty, they were still sufficiently Roman Catholic to loathe the supremacy of a Protestant Power, of a nation which still oppressed its own Catholic subjects in England and Ireland. Therefore they showed such a dogged resolve to resist to the death that in 1809 the British forces under General Whitelock finally abandoned the attempt to conquer the city of Buenos Ayres, and withdrew from South America, a result which covered Whitelock with altogether undeserved obloquy.

Landmark in British History

With these exceptions, by the end of the Napoleonic wars the outlines and starting points of the British Empire of to-day in America, Asia, Africa, and Oceania were pretty clearly indicated. From the fact that we have had no " colonial" war with any European or American Power since 1815, that date becomes an important landmark in the history of the British Empire; but to some extent in Imperial warfare the division between ancient and modern should rather be placed at 1763. Up to that period the share in the conquest and defence of the empire fell almost entirely on England and Wales, and more on the navy than on the army. After that date, first Scottish and then Irish soldiers took a notable part in the land warfare of Great Britain, while the Army as a whole began to play a great part in Imperial conquest and maintenance. Indeed, since 1815, the rôle of the Navy has been almost entirely a subordinate one, an unknown quantity. It has been there to serve as a means of safe transport for the army and as a warning to other Powers not to interfere and not to transgress on British claims, and as an effective security against their attempting to do so. The Napoleonic wars, so far as Great Britain was concerned, began with the murder of Louis XVI., and with the ebullition of the French Republic and its propaganda outside the limits of France. But they were waged very soon for directly Imperial purposes. Statesmen of that time saw the enormous advantages Great Britain might derive from the general upset of affairs contingent on the French Revolution. The position of the Dutch had long excited British envy. Their attitude

Britain Envious of the Dutch

towards us in Bengal, Java, and the Spice Islands had never been forgotten or forgiven. Their dogged tenacity and colonising genius in South Africa, which may some day be paralleled by the work of the Scottish planters in Nyassaland — the Scottish and Dutch are singularly alike— showed Great Britain of what vital importance Cape Colony might become to the Mistress of India as a half-way house for the provisioning and repair of squadrons and as a home for British emigrants.

The strength and the situation of Trincomali, in Ceylon, and the menace to India which it would prove in French hands decided the British to seize Ceylon in 1795–96. We also took possession then or later of the Dutch settlement in Java and Malaya. Our morality in these actions was no worse than that of the Dutch who, 200 years before, had taken advantage of poor little Portugal being in the grip of Spain to rob her of nearly all her oversea possessions, some of which the British sea-eagle has made the Dutch osprey disgorge, though they were once in the pouch of the Portuguese gannet. No colonial war has been waged with a European Power since 1815. But war for the extension or maintenance of our empire has often been so close that ultimatums have been tendered, though subsequently replaced in diplomatic tail-pockets. Wars between France and Britain over colonial questions or ambitions in the Eastern Mediterranean or Pacific Ocean were very near in the 'forties of the nineteenth century. At that period, also, began an embittered feeling between the nascent power of the United States and successive British administrations relative to the growth of Canada and of British ambitions in North America. Several times the questions of the Oregon frontier and the amount of seaboard due to British Columbia brought us to a snarling match with the government at Washington.

Britain's long Immunity from Colonial Wars

There were also questions as to the northern frontier of Maine, which projects inconveniently into eastern Canada. The great Russian possession of Alaska was bought by the United States in 1867 more to annoy Great Britain than for any other reason, and long before the existence of Klondyke gold was suspected, or seal-skin jackets had become the reward of virtue or the solace of vice. But for the threats of the United States,

Great Britain would now be in occupation of Haiti and a good deal of the disorderly republic of Venezuela. The Crimean War, as to the wisdom or unwisdom of which we cannot as yet pronounce a definite decision, was only slightly colonial, in the idea which prompted Great Britain to defend the rotten empire of the Turks.

The Turk was still the suzerain of Egypt, and Egypt, through the British-established overland route, was becoming the main road to India. What, in those days of absolute non-scruple regarding " native " rights, withheld Great Britain from accepting the proposal of the Emperor Nicholas that she should annex Crete and Egypt, and in return offer no objection to a Russian occupation of Constantinople, it is difficult to understand; unless statesmen of those days were so far-sighted, an assumption which it is not easy to deduce from their memoirs, as to feel that the abandonment of Constantinople to Russia would mean a future overwhelming impact of the Russians against the British Empire in India. It may have been an impression that France would resist à *outrance* a

Crimean War's Effect on Europe British Egypt. Yet, not long afterwards, the Emperor Napoleon himself proposed that France should occupy Morocco, Sardinia (Italy) should take Tunis, and England Egypt. Neither can this reluctance be ascribed to a period of Imperial lassitude, for whilst Russia was suggesting the division of the Turkish Empire Britain was absorbing vast territories further east.

In the opinion of the writer, the general policy of the Crimean War was right, so far as any war can be right, since it imposed a pause on European ambitions. Both Turkey and Egypt obtained a respite, during which, under wiser sovereigns, these important Mohammedan states might have developed firm and progressive governments. Probably we shall one day see Constantinople the capital of a free and civilised Balkan confederation, in which the Turk, regenerated in his civil estate, will play a leading part, in close alliance with the Bulgarian, Roumanian, and Greek states — a new quadruple alliance whose compact strength will contribute to the maintenance of the world's peace and the restoration of civilisation to the lands of the Macedonian and Byzantine Empires. There

was some menace of trouble with Spain towards the close of the 'fifties over the question of Morocco, which had just been invaded by a Spanish army (1859). Great Britain for a long time regarded Morocco as a possible protectorate, and as a means of controlling access to and egress from the Mediterranean. During

Britain's Preparations for War the 'sixties of the last century, when the Suez Canal was, in spite of the predictions of the late Lord Palmerston, approaching achievement, the British Government wobbled between a policy that should keep Spain and France out of Morocco and one which should give Great Britain a definite share in the control of Egypt.

The next menace of war on Imperial causes was again with Russia, when the internal disorders of the Turkish Empire furnished a pretext for the Russo-Turkish War. A seriously directed Russian attempt to occupy Constantinople would certainly have precipitated a fight in 1878. As it was, the Russians, the collapse of whose military power against Japan was foreshadowed by their defects of army organisation in 1877–1878, drew back from a struggle in which they would have had no ally, and Great Britain received as compensation for the £6,000,000 sterling she had spent in war preparations the lease of Cyprus, and a vague protectorate over Asia Minor, which she subsequently abandoned.

Again, in 1884–1885, the danger of war with Russia arose, this time over the safety of the Indian Empire. This was the slow-match of Russia's revenge for her enforced departure from Constantinople. The great success, administrative more than military, which had attended the extension of the Russian power over the Mohammedan sultanates in Central Asia inspired ambitious Russian soldiers with the belief that they might similarly lay hands on Afghanistan, and from this point

Extension of Russian Power of vantage win over the people of India to a preference for the supposed easy-going Russian as a ruler in place of the vexatiously interfering, moralising, educating Britisher. But Russia's belief and interest in the matter were half-hearted. Already, in 1885, her ambitions were returning towards Asia Minor and extending over Tibet and the Chinese Empire. Famines and plagues had begun to take the gilt off the Indian gingerbread.

Russia was so splendidly unattackable over the matter of the Central Asian khanates that she worried Indian officials about Afghanistan more *pour le plaisir du taquinage* than for any greater purposes. Moreover, she was already feeling her way towards a French alliance, and knew that this annoying intervention in Afghanistan would effectually stop the immediate reconquest of the Egyptian Sudan. From the close of the 'eighties of the last century British relations with France in regard to Egypt, the extension of French domination over Nigeria, and French aggression on Siam, brought us almost to the deliverance of an ultimatum in 1893.

Great Britain's Differences with France

We were probably then nearer to war with France over Imperial questions than even some five years later over the question of Fashoda. France, however, knew better than to go to war with Great Britain over affairs on which we were always ready to compromise. She knew that she had no chance against the British Fleet. On the other hand, she was equally aware that since 1884 a new factor had come into the colonial field—that Great Britain nourished a deep-seated dislike to Germany for having ousted her from the Kameruns, taken Damaraland under her very nose, and snatched at other portions of South Africa ; wrested from Great Britain a vast East African dominion, previously controlled by the potent personality of Sir John Kirk, founded a German state on the flank of the Gold Coast ; threatened the Lower Niger ; and occupied or bombarded Pacific archipelagoes which were only not British because we had not thought it worth while to hoist the flag. France knew that Great Britain did not wish to push her too far, lest a Franco-German alliance should menace the British position in Egypt.

So, between 1893 and 1899, France gave in on this point, and on that principle, and Britain surrendered some undefined claim, swallowed some disappointment, or abandoned a vague project. All danger of a conflict between the two Powers on questions of colonial policy disappeared with the withdrawal of Marchand from Fashoda, and the dropping of any intention on the part of Great Britain to maintain the independence of Morocco.

Peace Between the Powers

All things considered, Great Britain had got the better of Germany over the rush for empire in East and Central Africa.

Bismarck had indicated the 11th parallel of south latitude as the *ne plus ultra* of British extension from the Cape northwards, and he or his successors had hoped to secure Uganda and much of the Congo State for German expansion. This and that rapprochement, this and that consideration, not forgetting the serious Arab revolution in German East Africa, checked the German lust of empire over savages.

But as the German mind ruminated over the distribution of the spoil which followed the great European rush for Africa, a bitter feeling was engendered against the British. Partly to humour this, partly with an idea that it might lead to something, German Imperial policy dallied with a Boer alliance. It was felt instinctively that under their skins, Boer and Northwest German are singularly alike. If the Boers could not stand alone against England, they might throw in their lot with the future of Germany, and become the nucleus of a great German-speaking dominion in the south of Africa. Hence the intrigues with the Transvaal which provoked the foolish Jameson Raid on the part of the passionate Rhodes, and in turn the rash telegram of the German Emperor. But it is doubtful, if all the secrets of the chancelleries were known, whether there has been any serious menace of war with Germany over colonial questions since 1890, so far as the direct interests of Great Britain are concerned. There has been much more danger of an Anglo-German conflict over the position of France. Britain, in order to settle herself definitely in Egypt, "gave" Morocco to France, in the calm way in which we nations of higher culture, and consequently greater power, direct the fortunes of the backward or savage peoples. Germany at that time (1904) was giving her Imperial policy an altogether different bent.

Germany's Imperial Policy

Disappointed of dominion over Africa, choked off the conquest of China by the uprise of Japan, temporarily diverted from American enterprise by the ominous hints of the United States, she decided that the line of least resistance lay in the direction of the Balkan Peninsula, Constantinople, Asia Minor, and the Persian Gulf. For the moment, owing to the outcome of the war with Japan, Russia was helpless. France and Britain—France, for some reason, most of all—barred the way to Constantinople. Italy viewed with marked disfavour the unavowed German scheme, the *Drang nach Osten*. France was the pivot of this new alliance for the temporary preservation of the Turkish Empire. France was the easiest hit at. Thence arose the emperor's visit to Tangier, the open threat to France, and the nearest approach as yet in history to an armed conflict by land and sea between the forces of Great Britain and those of the German Empire, allied certainly with Austria-Hungary. This happily averted struggle would have been a colonial war, for it would have originated in the Egyptian question.

As regards Russia, it is doubtful whether we have ever been on the verge of war with her over Imperial interests since the Afghan settlement of 1885. We were annoyed, exasperated, bothered by the Russian designs on Northern and Western China. But had those designs been pushed to annexation of Chinese territory, and had Japan been powerless to resist, we

might have preferred to indemnify ourselves by the occupation of Tibet and a protectorate over Central China rather than by going to war with Russia. It was Germany, to a very great extent, that nipped in the bud our plans in regard to Tibet, and perhaps most of all as regards Central China.

It was by no means certain whether, in spite of our benevolent neutrality during the Spanish War, the United States would have given us any backing in regard to Chinese protectorates or spheres of influence. Consequently, finding this policy led to danger, the British Government revived the idea already suggested by Lord Rosebery of an alliance with Japan as a means of holding Russia in check and preserving the balance of power in China.

The outcome of the Japanese alliance may have momentous results, not, perhaps, in all directions palatable to Great Britain. These, however, are best discussed under another heading.

PIONEERS OF EMPIRE: THE HOME OF A BRITISH SETTLER IN THE SOUTH SEAS

5495

LORD ROBERTS CROSSING THE ZAMBURAK KOTAL IN HIS FAMOUS MARCH FROM KABUL TO KANDAHAR IN 1880
From the painting by Louis Desanges

BRITISH CONQUESTS IN THE EAST

EXPANSION OF THE INDIAN EMPIRE
AND THE OPIUM WAR WITH CHINA

WE have so far dealt with the wars undertaken against or narrowly averted with nations of white men in connection with British imperial interests. Wars of conquest waged with races that were black or yellow have been numerous since the middle of the eighteenth century. The wars with other Europeans were unmoral rather than just or unjust. Both parties quarrelled about the property of a third party, or lands that belonged to nobody worth consideration.

But the imperial wars waged in Africa and Asia have often been unjust, though there were instances of doing evil in order that presumed good might follow. On the American continent and in Australia the population has been too little in opposition to the incoming British settlers to have provoked any conflict worthy of record as a "war"; but the case has been otherwise in New Zealand and some parts of India, Burma, China, and South Africa.

Putting aside the conflicts of colonists with American Indians in Eastern-north America, our first imperial war with non-Europeans and non-Christians was the conflict against the Moors round Tangier conducted by British regiments in the reign of Charles II. This fighting, however, was not altogether unjust. The Portuguese, two and a half centuries before, had taken Tangier from the Moors, and transferred it by **Tangier Transferred to Britain** arrangement to Great Britain, probably because if Portugal had not done so the Moors would have taken it from her, as they had taken other Portuguese posts on the Atlantic coast of Morocco. Seeing, however, that our position in Morocco could only be maintained as the outcome of a practical conquest of that state, the British withdrew from the struggle and surrendered Tangier to the Moors; and although they afterwards indemnified themselves by snatching Gibraltar from Spain, still, there is no unjust war to be laid to our charge in Morocco. The next fighting with native peoples of non-European race took place in India seventy years afterwards. Here our **India the Birthplace of Man** merchants found themselves in the most splendid, thickly inhabited part of Asia. China in her best provinces might vie with India in density of population, and in her total sum of inhabitants; but the glory of China was pale before the art, the science, the history of India, and its magnificent physical endowments of fauna and flora. India should be placed first in the list of the world's countries, for she is almost certainly the birthplace of man.

But the India of the middle eighteenth century was an empire to be had for the taking. The Mohammedan power, which had begun with the irruption of Arabs, Afghans, and Tartars in the eighth and eleventh centuries, had crumbled to feebleness. The power of non-Mohammedan peoples and principalities had revived. There was no universal national spirit in India. Each big or petty prince was as ready to ally himself with the power of the European for his own advantage as, in the days before 1870, each kingdom, duchy or principality of Germany was ready to take part with France against the power of Prussia or Austria. The wars waged in India by the East India Company during the eighteenth and the first half of the nineteenth centuries were in a measure wars waged with Indians against Indians. As Sir William Hunter remarks in his great work on the Indian Empire, "the British won India, not from the Mohammedans—the Mogul dynasty—but from the Hindus." In the early part of the eighteenth century the Mogul Empire, founded by the House of Timur, the Tartar, in 1526, was falling to pieces under the attacks of the reviving Hindu power. Though Arabs, and soon afterwards Afghans, had invaded North-west India between 711 and 828, Mohammedan rule over Northern India did not begin until the year 1000. For five hundred years afterwards there were constant compromises with the many millions of Hindus, whose religion co-existed valiantly alongside militant Mohammedanism. Down to the establishment of universal British domination, there remained Hindu kingdoms and dynasties which had never been conquered or ousted by the Afghans or the Moguls.

Revival of Hindu Power

But in the middle of the seventeenth century a very definite revival of the Hindu power began in South-west India, in the hilly country to the south and west of Bombay. This was the confederation of sturdy Hindu peasant farmers, cavalry armed with spears, to be known subsequently as the "Mahrattas," apparently a corruption and shortening of Maharashtra. The Mahrattas' power was built up by a succession of warrior kings beginning with the great Rajput adventurer Sivaji. The power of this dynasty over the whole Mahratta confederation passed, early in the eighteenth century, into the hands of a Brahman prime minister—the Peshwa— and became hereditary in this form.

The French, under Dumas and Dupleix, governors of the French settlement of Pondichery on the coast of South-east India, had started the idea of interfering in the internal wars of nizams and nawabs, rajahs and wazirs. This had been carried on with such success by Dupleix himself, and by the Marquess de Bussy, that a considerable tract of Eastern India between Bengal and Madras had been made over to the French by the Nizam of Haidarabad, and the French had become the dominant power in Deccan and Southern India. But by 1761, in consequence of the brilliant military operations of Robert Clive, Colonel Forde, and Sir Eyre Coote, and the extraordinary lack of support afforded to their agents by the French Government, there was scarcely a French flag flying over any portion of India. Although at the Peace of Fontainebleau (1763) the sites of Pondichery, Chanderna-

India Free from the French

5498

gore, and two or three other trading stations were restored to France, after 1761 she had ceased to count seriously as an Indian power. The British were now face to face with the crumbling Mogul Empire —itself in the throes of a death-struggle with the new Mahratta power and its independent or semi-independent Mohammedan feudatory states, no other European nation intervening. Prominent among these independent Moslem princes, the descendants of former governors, or wazirs, under the Moguls, was the Nawab of Bengal, Suraj-ud-Daulah.

He succeeded his grandfather in 1756, and immediately afterwards quarrelled with the English of the Calcutta settlement. His capture of Calcutta, in 1756, and the episode of the " Black Hole " need not be further described here. Calcutta was recovered by Clive soon afterwards. Clive had first distinguished himself—in 1751— in surprising and afterwards defending Arcot, a native stronghold in the Madras Presidency. The series of surprising bold actions in Southern India on the part of the British had for result the complete breakdown of the French career of conquests. War having been already declared against France, Clive proceeded up country and seized the French post of Chandarnagar. This action led to Suraj-ud-Daulah and the French making common cause. At the Battle of Plassey, in 1757, Clive, with 1,000 British troops, 2,000 sepoys, and eight guns, defeated the army of the nawab, which consisted of 35,000 infantry, 15,000 cavalry, and 50 cannon. Moreover, Suraj-ud-Daulah had with him some fifty French artillerymen.

British Empire in India

This victory founded the British empire over India. After several other fights with the French and Dutch, and a series of battles with the nawab's forces, terminating with the decisive victory of Sir Hector Munro at Baxar in 1794, Clive was able to bring a good deal less than a quarter of India under British control, direct or indirect. In 1765 he became governor of Bengal, and took the Mogul emperor under the chartered company's protection.

Warren Hastings, who succeeded Clive as governor-general, lent British troops to a British ally, the wazir of Oudh, in order to check the invasions of the Rohilla Afghans, who were attempting to intrigue with the Mahrattas against the Mogul emperor and his feudatories.

British interference from Bombay in Mahratta affairs—the promotion of a British candidate for the throne of the Peshwa—precipitated the first struggle with the Mahrattas. This began in 1778 with Goddard's brilliant march across India from Bengal to Gujerat, which province, the last home of the lion, he conquered almost without fighting. One of his subordinate officers, Captain Popham, captured brilliantly the rock fortress of Gwalior, which was restored finally to the native prince, Sindhia, in 1886. In the following year, 1779, the British forces were defeated at Wargaon, and the first Mahratta War ended with the mutual restoration of all conquests, except Salsette and Elephanta Island, both near Bombay, which were retained by the British.

The two powerful Mohammedan states of the Deccan and Southern India, Haidarabad and Mysore, next assumed a hostile attitude towards the aggressive British. Warren Hastings managed to detach the Nizam of Haidarabad and minor Hindu princes from this league, and the British strength was mainly directed **Napoleon's Scheme to Seize Egypt** against Haidar Ali of Mysore, whose son, Tippu Sahib, was to prove one of our most formidable enemies in India. The Mysore army had conquered nearly all the British establishments in South-eastern India, except the actual town of Madras; but by persistent fighting all these possessions were won back by 1784. The second Mysore War began in 1790, conducted by Lord Cornwallis. By this time diplomacy had arrayed on the side of the British the important forces of the nizam and of the Mahratta confederation. Tippu Sahib, therefore, was partially conquered, and his kingdom was reduced by one-half.

He was also made to pay a war indemnity of £3,000,000. Enraged at this, he commenced a correspondence with the French Government, and his letters inspired Napoleon with the idea of seizing Egypt and attacking the British in India. The naval exploits of Nelson ruined that scheme, and in 1799 the British, under the Governor-General, Lord Mornington (Marquess Wellesley) and General (Lord) Harris, fell on the isolated Tippu and captured his last fortress, Seringapatam, in the defence of which Tippu was killed. The second Mahratta War, of 1802-1804, resulted, through the victories of Sir Arthur Wellesley (afterwards the Duke of Wellington) at Assaye and Argaum, in the Deccan, and those of Lord Lake at Aligarh and Laswari, in the removal of the Mogul emperor from the control of the Mahratta confederation to that of the East India Company, in the British control over Delhi and the North-west Provinces, and in enormous territorial gains in Eastern India. Unfortunately, it was **Britain's Wars in India** followed by a disastrous retreat of the British forces and a repulse of Lord Lake at Bhartpur, during the war with Holkar, a member of the Mahratta confederacy, in 1804-1805. The Ghurka or Nepalese Wars of 1814-1815 ended by a peace being signed, after the victories of General Ochterlony, near the capital, Khatmandu, the terms of which confined the Ghurkas to their present territory, recognised the British control over Sikkim, and secured for the Indian administration the hill stations of Simla and other Himalayan tracts, and the faithful alliance of the Nepalese people.

In Central India robber bands, rising here and there to the dignity of predatory states and known as the Pindaris, were ruining settled commerce and agriculture by their raids. They were partly formed by the débris of the Mogul Empire, and were to some extent supported by the Mahratta confederacy in their guerrilla warfare. They were finally crushed, and their leaders killed, imprisoned, or won over to allegiance by an army of 120,000 men wisely collected by the Governor-General, Lord Moira, Marquess of Hastings.

The reason for this overpowering force was the threatening aspect of the Mahratta confederacy. This attitude resolved itself into a rising—the third and last Mahratta War—in 1817. The Battle of Mehidpur (1817) and the magnificent defence of the sepoy garrison of Sitabaldi enabled the British administration to break up, once and for all, the Mahratta confederacy, and to make territorial arrangements **Mahratta Confederacy Broken up** in the Bombay Presidency and in Central India, which have lasted to this day. The peshwa, or president, of this great Hindu league surrendered and went to live near Cawnpore on a pension of £80,000 a year. His adopted son was the notorious Nana Sahib, who, in the Indian Mutiny of 1857, avenged on the bodies of English women and children the rage and disappointment he felt at not being allowed to succeed to all the emoluments and privileges of his patron and adoptive father. Coincidently with the rise of the British power in India proper, the Indian or Burmese states of Assam, Chittagong, Ava, Bhamma, Arakan, Pegu, and Tenasserim had come under the supreme control of the new Burmese dynasty of the Alaung-paya (Alompra). Elated with his **The Two** victories over quasi-Hindu states **Burmese** like Assam and Tipperah, the **Wars** Burmese monarch of Mandalay permitted or encouraged his soldiers or subsidiary chiefs to raid into territories more distinctly British. The eventual results were the first Burmese War of 1824-1826, followed by the annexation of Assam, Chittagong, Arakan, Tavoy, Mergui, and Tenasserim ; and the second Burmese War, of 1852, which further added to the Indian Empire the delta of the Irawadi, leaving only to native rule two provinces of the short-lived Burmese Empire—Upper and Lower Burma.

In 1839 took place the first invasion of Afghanistan. On the face of it this action on the part of Lord Auckland might seem foolhardy and a reckless courting of needless difficulties, except that Britain, ever since she became responsible for the maintenance of peace in India, has been forced at intervals to oppose the Afghans, from Warren Hastings' loan of British troops to attack the Rohillas in 1773 to the Mohammed border warfare of 1908. Lord Auckland endeavoured to place a prince —Shah Shuja—friendly to the British on the throne of Afghanistan, because the usurping ruler of that country, Dost Mohammed, was endeavouring to regain Peshawar, then in the power of the Sikhs, and was entertaining suspicious relations with Russia and Persia.

The installation of Shah Shuja in 1839, after several battles, in which the British were successful, meant the garrisoning of Jellalabad, Kabul, and Kandahar by **Disaster** British troops. Two years **to British** later two of the principal British **Forces** political officers were assassinated, the Kabul garrison attempted to retreat, and 4,000 British and Indian soldiers with 12,000 camp-followers perished.

Only one survived to reach the garrison of Jellalabad. The British women and children and a few sick officers had been detained as hostages by the Afghans, and, on the whole, well treated.

This disaster was avenged by the remarkable marches across Afghanistan of Generals Pollock, Nott, and England. Coming respectively from Jellalabad and Kandahar, they met at Kabul, and there blew up the bazaar and recovered the prisoners. They afterwards left Afghanistan to its own devices and the rule of Dost Mohammed. In the following year, 1843, Sind was conquered by Sir Charles Napier, the crucial battle being that of Miani, in which a British force of 2,600 men defeated 22,000 Baluchis. The battle of Miani was a glory to the British arms and the discipline of the Indian army.

The little force under Sir Charles Napier consisted of 400 British soldiers—mainly Irish—of the 22nd Regiment under Colonel Pennefather. The 2,200 Indian troops included some Bengal cavalry. The bayonet in the strong arms of the Irish, the magnificent ride of the Indian cavalry against the cannon of the Sindi army, the accuracy of the British artillery, and Sir Charles Napier won the day against an enemy of almost dauntless bravery. In 1845, the Sikhs, governed by a committee of generals since the death of Ranjit **The Great** Singh, annoyed at the British **Mutiny of the** annexation of Sind, crossed **Indian Army** the Sutlej and invaded British India. They were defeated in the bloody battles of Mudki, Firozshah, Aliwal, and finally Sobraon. A British protectorate over the Punjab followed. But, two years later, the Sikhs rose again, and the second Sikh War began with the terrible Battle of Chillianwalla, in which the British lost 2,400 officers and men, the colours of three regiments, and four guns. But less than a month later the conclusive victory of Gujerat destroyed the Sikh army and made it possible to annex the Punjab.

In 1857 broke out the great mutiny of the Indian army. In 1806 a mutiny of the native troops had occurred at Vellore in the Madras Presidency, which had commenced with a terrible slaughter of British soldiers, had been suppressed with the sternest reprisals, while discontent was afterwards appeased by concessions. The effects of this rising had been to some extent neutralised by disbanding the more tainted portions of the Madras army. In 1824 another mutiny nearly broke out in Bengal over the first Burmese War. The Hindu soldiers declared it would break their caste to cross the open sea, and eventually the difficulty had to be compounded by marching them all the way round by the northern shores of the Bay of Bengal. It is not necessary here to review all the causes of the great mutiny of 1857–1858, which for a time partially extinguished British garrisons and power in the kingdom of Oudh and in a portion of North-central India.

It was in the main an insurrection of angry soldiers, who had some real and some imaginary grievances. But it was conjoined with the fury of the dispossessed princes or princesses and nobles of Oudh and Jhansi and the treacherous enmity of the adopted son of the last peshwa of the Mahrattas, Nana Sahib. Also there was much Mohammedan fanaticism and regret for vanished glories at the court of the aged Mogul Emperor at Delhi.

The credit for the military operations which suppressed the mutiny, and the dangerous national rising which it was beginning to create, lies with Sir Henry Lawrence, who defended the Residency at Lucknow, and so detained the rebel forces of Oudh ; Sir Henry Havelock and Sir

Heroes of the Indian Mutiny James Outram, who saved the slender garrison after Lawrence's death ; Sir Colin Campbell (Lord Clyde), who rescued the Lucknow forces under Havelock and Outram and finished the reconquest of Oudh and Rohilkund ; Nicholson, the never-to-be-forgotten hero of the siege of Delhi ; and Sir Hugh Rose (Lord Strathnairn), who defeated the principal native general of the mutiny, Tantia Topi, who recaptured Jhansi and who finished the insurrection in April, 1859, in the wildest jungles of Central India. Probably the greatest of all these dauntless soldiers, and certainly the most picturesque, was John Nicholson, of Delhi.

Nothing has so much justified the abnormality of India being governed by a hundred thousand warriors and officials from islands five thousand miles away in the North Sea as the conduct of the British soldiers of all ranks, the British officials, from governor-general to Eurasian telegraph clerk, during the stress of the Indian Mutiny. One may at this distance of time see and regret the stupid blunders that provoked the mutiny, and put one's finger to a nicety on the precise measures which might have nipped the mutiny in the bud ; but once the catastrophe has occurred, one can only marvel at the qualities of officers and men in that heroic handful of British troops which twice relieved a Lucknow besieged by thousands of well-armed fanatics ; in those 8,000 men that fought their way inch by inch through the high, red walls and narrow lanes of a murderous Delhi defended by 30,000 desperate, drug-maddened sepoys,

Loyalty of the Sikh Soldiers better trained in the actual arts of war, perhaps, than the ill-educated English, Welsh, Scottish, and Irish soldiery who, by sheer force of character and strength of arm, became their conquerors. But in reviewing the history of this time of stress one must admit it was not only men born in the British Isles that crushed a revolt of savage sepoys and frantic people.

India might have been temporarily lost to us but for the co-operation of the splendid Sikh soldiers, men whose valour to the British cause was in no way inferior to the heroic behaviour of the British soldiers on their mettle. We received the loyal assistance of the great Mohammedan kingdom of Haidarabad, which had the effect of keeping Southern India out of the area of disturbance. At the same time the independent state of Nepal sent a force of Ghurkas, under Sir Jung Bahadur, to assist in restoring order in Northern India. A small war with the Himalayan state of Bhutan took place in 1864. With that exception, there was peace in India until 1878. Then once more the affairs of Afghanistan compelled attention.

Russia had despatched a mission to that country, which had been received with ostentatious honour. To have acquiesced in this situation would have been to give tacit permission to Russia to win over the country of Afghanistan to her influence, to make of it, perhaps, a vantage-point from which the invasion of India might be attempted with the Afghans as allies. Britain had nothing to offer Afghanistan

Evils of Afghan Raids but the somewhat barren privilege of isolated independence in a sterile land, with a climate of ferocious extremes. The British arm had been interposed ever since 1773 to shield India from those devastating Afghan raids which have inflicted deep and shocking wounds on her civilisation since the days of Mahmud of Ghazni. Gradually, by British diplomacy or feats of arms, Afghan rule was pushed back across the Hindu Kush and the Suleiman Hills.

And there it would have been left unmolested but for Russian ambitions turning India-wards in the thirties of the last century. In 1878 a British army entered Afghanistan and rapidly occupied Kandahar and the roads leading to Kabul. Sher Ali, the amir, fled to Turkestan and died. His son was recognised by us in his

Afghanistan Under British Protection stead, after a treaty, which practically placed Afghanistan under British protection.

But the history of 1839-41 repeated itself almost exactly, except for the disastrous retreat. The British Envoy and Resident at Kabul, Sir Louis Cavagnari, and his insufficient escort were attacked and massacred, Sir Frederick (Lord) Roberts occupied Kabul with a British army, and the new amir, Yakub Khan, abdicated.

Abd-ur-Rahman was then recognised as amir over two-thirds of Afghanistan, and the remainder, with Kandahar as a capital, was erected into a separate state. But in 1880 a severe defeat was inflicted on a British force at Maiwand, between Kandahar and the Halmand river, by Ayub Khan, a younger son of Sher Ali, and an Afghan prince who in this contest played the part of national hero better than the Russian pensioner, Abd-ur-Rahman.

The position of the British in Afghanistan in 1880 was retrieved by the splendid march of Lord Roberts from Kabul to Kandahar, which led to the total rout of Ayub Khan's army outside the precincts of Kandahar. This place was subsequently abandoned by the British and reoccupied by Ayub Khan. Then followed a conflict between Abd-ur-Rahman and Ayub, which left the former master of Afghanistan until his death, in 1901, and led to Ayub's honourable captivity in India.

In 1885 the last Burmese War took place. It was really the advance of a very strong expedition under General Prendergast up the Irawadi River to

Rising of the Dacoits Mandalay, which met with no opposition worth noting. The real Burmese War broke out afterwards in a prolonged and gallant resistance to British occupation on the part of the so-called " dacoits "— bands of irregulars commanded or inspired by Burmese nobles or princes. The distinct tribes of the Kachins and Shans took part in the four years of desultory fighting, which scarcely came to an end until 1889. The feeling of unrest produced in this

region led to an outbreak in 1891 in the adjoining state of Manipur, which was put down without much difficulty. In 1888 an expedition had to be sent against the Hazara Pathans to the north of Peshawar ; and in the same year British authority was asserted over the important little state of Sikkim, which separates Nepal from Bhutan, which has been under British influence and protection since 1815, and which the Tibetans— inspired, perhaps, both by Russia and China—were endeavouring to conquer.

The definition of the frontiers between British India and Afghanistan in 1893 and the enforcement of its results amongst the turbulent border tribes led to the protracted Tirah campaign (1895-1898) against the Waziri, Swati, Mohmand, and Afridi tribes, and the clans of the Zhob valley between Quetta and the Indus. There was also some fighting in the north-west of Kashmir (Ghilghit and Chitral). Kashmir is an important country in whose government the British had taken a more direct interest since the approximate settlement of the various frontier questions of

Russia's Intrigues in Tibet Afghanistan, Russia, Chinese Turkestan, and Tibet. In this campaign, the work of which is only half-finished, the British lost 1,050 men killed and missing, not to mention over 1,500 wounded ; while the cost amounted to over £3,000,000. The prosecution of this frontier war was accompanied or preceded by some ominous signs of disaffection amongst the peoples of North-west India.

Russia had again been intriguing with religious notabilities in Tibet at the beginning of the twentieth century, partly, no doubt, to embarrass Britain, whose alliance with Japan—projected or accomplished—was barring her way in China. It was decided, rightly or wrongly, to put an end to these anxieties which form a pendant to those of Afghanistan, and to force on Tibet the assumption of intimate diplomatic relations with British India not far removed from a protectorate —China, the recognised suzerain, being unable or unwilling to restrain the Tibetans from entering into relations with Russia.

The expedition of 1904 started in March, and was obliged to fight its way, more or less, to Lhasa, which was entered on August 3rd, 1904. Here a treaty was made, fixing a war indemnity, arranging for future commercial intercourse, and giving some recognition to British rights over the Chumbi valley, which projects into British India as a wedge between Bhutan and Sikkim. The British Government decided to submit this treaty to the sanction of the Chinese Government, and the latter, incited by the German Minister at the court of Peking, refused to agree to the conditions imposed on the Tibetans. Practically no results remain of the costly expedition to Lhasa, except a thoroughly accurate geographical survey of Southern Tibet. A treaty has been recognised by China, but it is a colourless document. To some extent, however, the Tibetan question has been settled for a long time to come by the 1907 convention with Russia. If this convention is faithfully adhered to, it will obviate any danger to India from the direction of Tibet.

In the year 1908 frontier warfare was resumed on the Afghan borders with the Zakka Khels on the south-west, and the Mohammedans on the north-east, both sections of hostile mountaineers being aided unofficially by an Afghanistan no longer efficiently controlled by the firm hand of an **Afghan Treachery and Rapacity** Abd-ur-Rahman Khan, but influenced by the fanatical dislike to the European conceived by the younger brother of the present amir, Nasir-Ullah Khan. To some extent Afghan hostility has been neutralised by the recent Anglo-Russian Convention, and a war with Afghanistan, followed by a permanent conquest of that land, which has been the source of so much woe to India, would present no serious difficulty to the Indian Government if the policy was one that commended itself to the views of the intelligent majority of Indian Mohammedans, who, if they read accurate history and profit by its lessons, must by this time be weary of Afghan treachery and rapacity.

Passing outside the political limits of the Indian Empire, the other wars in Asia undertaken by the British Government against native powers may be noted as follows. In 1838 an armed demonstration against Persia—by the despatch of a British expedition to the Persian Gulf—was rendered necessary because of an attempt on the part of the Persians to take Herat. For the same reason, in 1856, Great Britain declared war on Persia, and seized several ports on the Persian Gulf until the restitution of Herat to Afghanistan was effected. The reason of these stern measures was

that Herat was believed to be the key of India, and Persia was regarded as being merely the stalking horse of Russia. All these anxieties have been set at rest by the Anglo-Russian Convention; the British sphere in Persia suffices to maintain an orderly control over the Persian Gulf. Between 1795 and 1801 the island of Ceylon, so far as its coastal regions were **The British Occupation of Ceylon** concerned, was occupied by Great Britain as a war prize taken from Holland, a country then in the possession of France. The British had been partly assisted in these operations by the forces of the king of Kandy, the representative of the extremely ancient Singalese dynasty. This monarch, however, died in 1800 without leaving direct issue.

Interior Ceylon was, like so many Oriental countries, really governed by a powerful Minister, the adigar. The British governor of the coast districts interfered in the matter of the succession with a view to securing substantial advantages for his own Government. An expedition to Kandy was undertaken, and a small garrison left at that capital—200 British troops and 500 Malays, under the command of Major Davie. But in those days the climate of the forest regions of Ceylon was extremely unhealthy to Europeans, and the bulk of Major Davie's English soldiers were incapacitated by sickness. Then they were attacked by overwhelming numbers of Singalese, and at last obliged to capitulate and retreat. The terms of the capitulation were not observed by the cruel king of Kandy, who gave orders to massacre the entire party on the banks of the Mahaveliganga, three miles from Kandy.

Scarcely a single member of the force survived except Major Davie, who was taken back to Kandy, where he dragged out a miserable existence for another ten years. This massacre of the Mahaveliganga was not avenged by **Atrocities of the King of Kandy** the governor, whose policy in connection with Major Davie's abandonment had been most reprehensible. Consequently, the king of Kandy, encouraged by this absence of reprisals, sent armies to attack the coast possessions of the British. His forces were repulsed, and a truce was arranged which lasted for several years. But the king of Kandy gradually became ferociously cruel towards his own Ministers, nobility and people, besides causing native merchants

—British subjects—to be mutilated or killed outright. His own people rose against him in 1815, and invited and facilitated a British occupation of Kandy, which took place unopposed. The king was captured and sent as a political prisoner to Vellore, in the Madras Presidency, where he lived until 1832. The occupation of the interior of Ceylon seems to have been characterised by some tactless procedure which offended the people's religious prejudices. In addition, the chiefs and priests were rendered inimical at the diminution of their power and emoluments. Consequently, in 1817, a serious insurrection broke out in the eastern provinces of Ceylon, which it took two years of hard bush-fighting to suppress. Two other insurrections occurred in 1843 and 1845, caused by the imposition of taxes.

Ceylon's Opposition to Taxation

In 1810, a British expedition, under Sir Stamford Raffles, landed in Java and attempted to wrest that island from the Dutch. At the same time other British expeditions seized the Dutch islands of Amboina and Banda. The Dutch, however, fought fiercely near Batavia, though they were ultimately defeated, and surrendered the island, which was restored to Holland eight years afterwards.

In 1826, British commerce with the Malay Peninsula and Sumatra having suffered much at the hands of pirates coming from the Malay state of Perak, and especially from the Perak River, it was arranged that the Pangkor and Sembilan Islands should be ceded to Great Britain as a base for naval action against the pirates. These settlements, somewhat enlarged, are now known as the Dindings. In 1873-1874, the large Malay state of Perak was brought into closer political relations with Singapore Government, and agreed to accept a British resident. The official appointed to this post, Mr. J. W. Birch, was, however, murdered, with the connivance of the Malay sultan, in 1875. A punitive expedition, composed of British and Indian soldiers under General Sir Francis Colborne, divided into two columns and crossed Perak in several directions, defeating the native forces in four or five stiff engagements, warfare in this land of dense forest being peculiarly difficult. Perak was in the end thoroughly subdued, and, in 1877, the sultan, who was accessory

Malay Sultan Banished

to Birch's murder, was banished to the Seychelles Islands, another sultan being recognised in his stead. This effective piece of fighting sufficed for the assertion of the Pax Britannica on the Malay Peninsula.

The East India Company began to trade with the north of Borneo in 1609. At the end of that century they had transferred their attention to the south side of the island, whence they were driven away by the Dutch. In 1762-1775, the East India Company obtained a concession of the island of Battambang from the sultan of Sulu, together with Labuan and the territory which is now known as British North Borneo. A treaty was also entered into with the sultan of Brunei. But the people as a whole did not welcome the British, as the presence of Europeans interfered with their wide-spread piratical operations. The British were attacked and their posts demolished. The Dutch also were driven away.

The establishment of Singapore, however, in 1819, once more drew attention to the northern regions of Borneo. Trade was opened up with the sultanate of Brunei, which then included nearly all the northern regions of Borneo, except the extreme north-east. Unfortunately, all this region was, on its coast line, the seat of a vast piratical organisation, in which not only Malays, natives of Borneo (Sea Dyaks), and Chinese were engaged, but also Arabs. These pirates preyed on the extensive commerce which passed through the China Sea. They were becoming a public nuisance, and even a danger to European trade with China. This was noted by a retired official of the East India Company, James Brooke, who, wounded in the war with Burma, was travelling to China for his health. Brooke visited parts of Borneo and the Malay Archipelago, and regretted that such rich regions should be infested by these pirates, many of whom took to piracy because they had nothing else to do.

Commerce Hampered by Pirates

Having inherited his father's property, Brooke resolved to fit out an expedition of his own and visit Borneo. He reached the present state of Sarawak in 1839, and found the uncle of the sultan of Brunei at war with a rebellious officer turned pirate. Brooke's intervention gave victory to the Brunei Government, and for this service the title of Rajah of Sarawak was conferred on him (1841-42). For six years Brooke, on land and sea, co-operated with the British naval forces under Captain (afterwards Sir Harry) Keppel in attacking the Borneo pirates, who, it was found, really derived much of their strength and supplies from the town and sultan of Brunei.

Eventually the town of Brunei was bombarded by a British naval force, while the sultan's army was routed by Brooke. The sultan himself was restored to his throne after agreeing to give no more harbourage to pirates. At the same time he sold to the British Government the little island of Labuan as a base for naval operations in those waters. Sir James Brooke not only by degrees extinguished piracy along the north-west coast of Borneo, but he also, with extraordinary bravery and resolution, put down a Chinese mutiny and rebellion instigated by Chinese pirates in 1857.

He subdued two other risings, but since his death, in 1868, the peace and stability of North-western Borneo have not been seriously menaced. The British North Borneo Company, founded in 1882 as a government over North-eastern Borneo, has had to subdue several insurrectionary movements, under a leader named Mat Saleh, between 1901 and **Britain's Trade Relations with China** 1906. British trade relations with China began early in the seventeenth century by James I. chartering a company for the exclusive commerce with the regions beyond the Malay Peninsula. But this charter lapsed, and later on the trade monopoly with China was acquired by the East India Company, whose commercial relations with China, though very limited, were not much troubled by unfriendliness till the advent to power of the warlike Emperor Kin-lung. This monarch strengthened the Chinese hold over Tibet, and marched an army of 70,000 men into Nepal in 1792, the Chinese penetrating to within sixty miles of the British outposts.

At the same time the emperor allowed the agents of the East India Company to be badly treated by the viceroy and other officials at Canton. Consequently, it was deemed wise to send a special envoy to open up diplomatic relations with China, and Lord Macartney was despatched with a special mission to Peking, arriving there in 1793. But neither he nor his successor, Lord Amherst, in 1816, could obtain any alleviation of the severe disabilities imposed on European traders. In 1834, the East India Company's monopoly of the Chinese trade came to an end, and there was a considerable development of British commerce with China—on the part of British Indian subjects, among others—which necessitated the establishment of a superintendent or commissioner at Canton to watch over the affairs of the British merchants, a superintendent who became the precursor of the present highly organised and efficient Consular **China's Objection to Opium** Service. The hostility of the Chinese to British commerce was largely due to the importation of opium in large quantities from India. The Chinese officials, especially in the south of China, were becoming awakened to the serious effects of the abuse of this drug on Chinese manhood. They wished to prohibit its introduction altogether. In other directions they brought pressure to bear on British traders.

The latter, through their superintendent, agreed to surrender to the Chinese commissioner of Customs at Canton 20,283 chests of opium, which were forthwith destroyed. They also bound themselves to deal no more in this drug. Apparently, however, the semi-independent government of Canton gave no compensation for this voluntary surrender of opium, and took advantage of the superintendent's conciliatory behaviour to inflict further disabilities on British trade and even offer gratuitous violence to British shipping. The Home Government considered that the British merchants had a right to import opium ; at any rate, that the other actions of the Cantonese officials were insupportable. Accordingly they sent a British fleet to China and a small military force.

War was declared in 1840, and in that year the Chusan Archipelago, to the south-east of the mouth of the Yang-tse-kiang was occupied. In 1841 the forts guarding the entrance to the Canton River were stormed and captured, and the island of Hong Kong was seized. The Canton viceroy then agreed to **The Opium War with China** cede Hong Kong and to pay an indemnity of £1,200,000. These terms were, however, repudiated by the Imperial Government at Peking. The war therefore continued. Sir Hugh Gough occupied Canton, Amoy, Ningpo, Chapu, Shanghai, and two other coast towns. He was about to take Nanking when the Chinese emperor sent commissioners to make peace. The treaty concluded by Sir Henry Pottinger in 1842 provided not only for the cession of Hong Kong, but also for the throwing open to foreign trade of the ports of Amoy, Fuh-chau-fu, Ningpo, and Shanghai, and the payment of an indemnity of about £3,500,000. The original cause of the war—the claim to be able to trade in opium—was an indefensible one, of which Britain has since felt ashamed; but the results

The Policy that Saved China of this forcible opening of China to European commerce have, on the whole, been the salvation of that vast empire from falling into complete senile decrepitude. But the Imperial Government at Peking— for two centuries the curse of China— did not appreciate the cruel kindness of Britain. It had yielded to urgent force; now it wished to have as little as possible to do with the red-haired barbarians and their Indian subjects. Russia was a different matter; the frontiers of Russia began westwards and northwards where those of China left off. Russia, therefore, was entitled to have a diplomatic representative at Peking. As to France and England, they were small nations of sea-pirates unworthy of a place at the court of the emperor. Russia, no doubt, in revenge for the Crimean War, encouraged this attitude of disdain.

On the other hand, a great revolt had taken place in Central China, which was eventually headed by Hung-Siu-tsewen, who proclaimed himself as Tin Wang, first emperor of the Tai-ping dynasty. This was an uprising which, one would have thought, might have appealed to all the generous instincts of Britain as the champion of liberty and reform. The recent Chinese emperors had been so shockingly licentious that their moral depravity had affected the tone of public morality. The Tai-ping revolt was greatly a protest at the iniquities of the imperial court. Then, too, Hung-Siu-tsewen was a Christian, to all intents and purposes.

Revolt in Central China The behaviour of himself and his followers was admirable. His liberal-minded measures vastly encouraged foreign commerce at Nanking and Su-chau. Above all, the movement was a Chinese one, and might have led to the re-establishment of a national Chinese dynasty in the place of the Manchu Tartars, whose rule has, latterly, at any rate, done so much to arrest the growth of Chinese intellectual development and friendly, mutually-pro-

fitable intercourse with foreign nations. Yet Britain, after coquetting with the Tai-ping revolt, proceeded to lend officers —Charles George Gordon from the Royal Engineers, first and foremost—and support for its suppression, and the renewed fixing on the necks of the Chinese people of that Manchu yoke from which the more intelligent were trying to free themselves.

In 1856, the Chinese viceroy or commissioner at Canton seized, on an accusation of piracy, a sloop or "lorcha" from Macao whose captain was a British subject. It is very probable that the Arrow, as this vessel was called, was up to no good, but the Chinese commissioner, Yeh, seems to have been technically in the wrong. Sir John Bowring was then administering the government of Hong Kong and in charge of British interests in China. He decided to deal energetically with the incident of the Arrow, and requested the British admiral on the station to bombard Canton. This took place in 1857. Lord Elgin was despatched to China with a strong force to act as British plenipo-

Britain and France as Allies in China tentiary. He was diverted from his immediate object by the outbreak of the mutiny in India. The troops he brought with him proved a most welcome reinforcement to the British in Bengal. Lord Elgin, however, reached Canton towards the close of 1857, and succeeded in capturing the commissioner or viceroy, Yeh, whom he sent as a prisoner to Calcutta, where he eventually died. In 1858, France joined Great Britain in demanding redress from China for injuries suffered by French subjects and in requiring that a French representative should be accepted at Peking. At the close of 1858 the Treaty of Tientsin was negotiated. This treaty was to have been ratified by the emperor early in 1859; but when, in June of that year, the British and French representatives attempted to proceed to Peking under a strong escort, their expedition was stopped before it could land, and the British lost three gunboats and 400 men in the action which followed at the mouth of the Peiho.

Lord Elgin and Baron Gros returned in 1860, and at the head of a very strong force occupied Peking. Here the celebrated summer palace was destroyed by Lord Elgin's orders, an action which has been deplored as an offence against the canons of art. Lord Elgin, however, could think of no other means of abasing Chinese imperturbability, which was prolonging the negotiations, and, which was more serious, the sufferings of the English prisoners who had been treacherously seized by the Chinese in very bad faith.

The Treaty of Tientsin, however, was ratified in 1860, and from 1861 onwards Great Britain, France and other European Powers, besides Russia, have been represented at Peking by diplomatic Ministers. The third occasion on which we have found ourselves at war with China was in the last year of the nineteenth century. The war between China and Japan, concluded in the spring of 1895, had exposed the seeming helplessness of China.

After intervening to modify the terms of the Treaty of Shimonoseki in favour of China, Russia, France and Germany began to ask for concessions, leases, or admissions of spheres of influence ; and Great Britain, not liking to be left in the cold, required her share. Out of this Chinese scramble we came successfully, with considerable additions to the prosperous little colony of Hong Kong, and **China's Spirit Aroused** the leasehold of Wei-hai-wei. In fact, the course of events between 1895 and 1900 was thoroughly Chinese in its contrariety. We and the other land-hungry European Powers had our annexations first and our war afterwards. The national spirit of China was aroused, at any rate in the foreigner-hating Manchus of the north, and early in 1900 it broke out in the renewed murder of missionaries and native Christians, and finally in orders to the foreign representatives at Peking to leave the country.

Not wishing to trust themselves to the tender mercies of the Boxers, as the unofficial allies of the reactionary party were called, the foreign legations prepared to stand a siege in their " town-within-a-town " in Peking. The British, Japanese, Russian, American, and French authorities from their various Asiatic possessions despatched an urgency relief expedition, the British section of which was commanded by Sir Alfred Gaselee.

Peking was entered first by the British. It was found that of the 500 civilian, naval and military defenders of the different legations, 65 had been killed, and 131 were more or less severely wounded. When this trouble was over, the 20,000 German troops arrived under the command of Field-Marshal von Waldersee, but the British Government discountenanced any unnecessary coercion of China.

The acquisition of California, by the United States in 1848, led that branch of the Anglo-Saxon power to desire commercial expansion across the Pacific. In 1853–1855 a naval expedition under Commander Perry was sent to Japan **The Open Door in Japan** to force that country to enter into commercial and political relations with the United States. After some display of force Commander Perry succeeded in his famous mission—one of the turning points in world-history. In the year 1858 advantage was taken of Lord Elgin's presence in the Far East for the conclusion of a treaty between the British and the shogunate of Japan—ratified by the mikado in 1864—which obtained for Great Britain the same (limited) privileges as those granted to the United States.

But these concessions were detested by the military caste of the Samurai, by many of the Japanese nobility, and by the mikado himself when he came to hear of them. Indiscreet behaviour on the part of British traders provoked one or two outrages with loss of life. Finally, in 1863, a British naval force, under Admiral Kuper, appeared before Kagoshima and demanded redress for grievances from the shogun. Failing to receive this, Admiral Kuper reduced Kagoshima to ashes and destroyed three war steamers of the Japanese. This action brought to reason the Satsuma chieftains ; but there was another potentate acting independently—what time the titular Emperor of Japan lived sequestered in his huge harem at Kioto—and firing indiscriminately on foreign shipping passing through the straits of Shimonoseki. This was the Daimiyo, or Lord of Cho-shu or Nagato. After a preliminary chastisement at the hands of the United States, France and **Foreign Intercourse with Japan** Holland, he, as he still declined to allow foreign shipping to enter the Inland Sea of Japan, was attacked by an international squadron under the command of Admiral Sir Augustus Kuper in September –October, 1864, and utterly defeated on land as well as on the sea. The shogun's government agreed to pay an indemnity of about £700,000, and from that time onwards no serious hindrance was put in the way of foreign intercourse with Japan.

JAMESON'S LAST STAND: THE SURRENDER OF THE "RAIDERS" TO THE BOERS AT VLAKFONTEIN ON JANUARY 2ND, 1896

Prior to the South African War, the Uitlander—foreign—population, who were mostly British subjects, were refused their share of political rights, though they owned most of the property and bore the greater part of the taxation. Agitations for reform were widespread, and to enforce their claims an armed body under Dr. Jameson, at that time administrator of Rhodesia for the British South Africa Company, entered Transvaal territory on December 30th, 1895, suffering defeat by the Boers at Krugersdorp on January 1st, 1896, and again at Vlakfontein on the following day, when they surrendered conditionally. The leaders in the raid underwent trial in England, and were sentenced to terms of imprisonment.

From the painting by R. Caton Woodville by permission of Messrs. Henry Graves & Co.

BRITAIN'S CONTESTS IN AFRICA AND THE PACIFIC

THE LONG SERIES OF VICTORIES IN THE PROCESS OF EMPIRE-BUILDING

WARS of the empire undertaken against the natives of Africa, apart from conflicts in which we were really fighting European nations, may be said to have begun with Admiral Blake's chastisement of the Tunisian sea rovers of Goletta and Porto Farina in 1656. In those days, Tunisia was a kind of dependency of Turkey, having been recovered from the possession of Spain by Turkish and renegade Moslem adventurers in the employ of Turkey during the last half of the sixteenth century. Blake had also threatened Algiers and Tripoli and the Salli rovers of Morocco. The occupation of Tangier in succession to the Portuguese entailed such constant fighting with the Moors that the new possession was deemed unprofitable, and was surrendered to Mulai Ismail, sharifian sultan of Morocco, in 1684. The effective punishment of the piratical Algerine state by Lord Exmouth and the Dutch, in 1816, has already been described.

In 1808, the British Government, having thoroughly awakened to the importance of Egypt as a half-way house to India, and having regretted the easy terms which had allowed the French to withdraw, and a more or less Turkish Government to take their place, attempted, on a rather feeble pretext, to land in Egypt with the obvious intention of never withdrawing. But **Britain in Conflict with the Negro** their landing was opposed by the self-made governor, Mohammed Ali, with such spirit that the attempt was baulked and not renewed till seventy-four years later. We first came into serious conflict with the negro over South African questions. Petty skirmishes no doubt had occurred between the soldiers in the employ of the Royal African Chartered Company and the natives of the Gold Coast. Some show of force also had to accompany the definite establishment of the Sierra Leone settlements, while prior to the annexation of Sierra Leone the British Chartered Company, which was to found a West African Utopia for freed slaves, had engaged in a good deal of fighting with the turbulent natives of Bolama (Portuguese Guinea), who did not **The First of the Kaffir Wars** at all relish having an anti-slave-trade colony founded on their sea front. But the first Imperial war with the black man was undertaken in 1809 and 1811–1812 when, in order to defend the rights, or, at any rate, the claims, of the Dutch colonists, 20,000 Kaffirs were driven by British soldiers away from the " Zuurveld," and across the Great Fish River to its eastern banks. This was the first in the long series of Kaffir wars which was to culminate in the capture of Ulundi in 1880, and of Buluwayo in 1893.

In 1818–9, the second Kaffir War broke out. It originated in an internecine feud between two rival Kosa Kaffir chiefs, Gaika and Ndlambe. [Kosa is written by some South African authorities Xosa, the "X" expressing a side click. Another Kaffir name is often written Gcaleka, the "c" expressing another click. Likewise, the "C" in Cetewayo (Ketshwayo) is a click. The present writer prefers to render all these words with the gutturals, K, G, or Q]. For some reason the Cape Government sent soldiers to enforce the claims of the defeated rival, Gaika. The British force crossed the Great Fish River, and then, in revenge, the Kosa warriors under Ndlambe entered the colony and besieged Grahamstown. The Kaffirs were, of course, defeated, and their frontier was pushed farther to the east, to the Keiskamma River. The land in between the two rivers was to be regarded as neutral ground, though actually belonging to the British Crown. The Keiskamma, as a matter of fact, had been the original boundary between Kaffir and Hottentot.

In course of time certain Kaffir chiefs were permitted to settle on this neutral territory; then they were ordered to move off again. For this reason, or more probably because the Kaffirs thought they could drive the white man away altogether by attacking in force, 12,000 of them crossed the eastern frontier of the colony in December, 1834, and for a fortnight carried all before them, killing the white colonists, burning and destroying their homesteads and farms, and turning the district between Somerset East and Algoa Bay into a desert. The raid had from the white settlers' point of view been absolutely unprovoked, and there were loud cries for vengeance from Boer, German, and British colonists alike, nor did the missionaries attempt to defend the action of the invading Kaffirs. Colonel Smith, afterwards to be known as Sir Harry Smith, drove the Kaffirs back beyond the Keiskamma, and then beyond the Kei River. This was the third Kaffir War.

The Kosa Kaffirs then sued for peace. Their new frontier was drawn at the Kei River, and the land between the Kei and the Keiskamma was created a new province of the colony, and named after Queen Adelaide. But within this new province all the Kaffirs who had taken no part in the raid were allowed to remain, and, in addition, grants of land were given to the Fingo tribe, who had been enslaved and ill-treated by the Kosa.

But this settlement, approved alike by the European settlers and the missionaries, was set aside by the Colonial Secretary in England, Lord Glenelg, and Queen Adelaide province was restored to the Kosa Kaffirs, while Sir Benjamin D'Urban, the governor, was recalled. This unwise action laid the seeds of much future mischief. It was one of the causes which sent the best of the Dutch farmers out into the wilderness to carve out homes with their right hands and their guns—rifles had not come into general use—independent of the vicissitudes of a dual government wherein the man on the spot might have his policy reversed heedlessly by the man at home. The Kosa Kaffirs were not satisfied, and the Fingoes found themselves

Kaffirs on the War-path

Trouble with the Kaffirs

handed over to the tender mercies of the Kosas. In 1846-1847, war—the fourth Kaffir War—broke out again, provoked by the Kaffirs themselves. At its close the former province of Queen Adelaide was reconstituted under the name of British Kaffraria. In 1850 began the fifth Kaffir War, chiefly with the Gaika clan of the Kosa Kaffirs living in the Amatola Mountains. It extended far and wide over the eastern border districts of Cape Colony, and was marked by not a few disasters.

One of these was not directly connected with the Kaffirs, though it added to the general uneasiness and dislike with which the war was regarded at home. The troopship Birkenhead foundered in a gale off Simon's Bay, and sank with 400 soldiers and many seamen on board. By 1853, General Cathcart had captured all the Gaika strongholds in the Amatola Mountains, and had deported the Kosa Kaffirs from that district, which was afterwards settled by Hottentot half-breeds, and became known as Grikwaland East. In 1856 a terrible delusion seized on the Kosa Kaffirs through the crazy teaching of a "wizard" who had received a smattering of Christian teaching at a mission school. He predicted the coming of a millennium, in which the Kaffirs would be reinforced by their dead chiefs returning to earth with many followers, and further assisted by the Russian soldiers of the Crimean War. But to secure this millennium, the existing cattle and crops must first be destroyed. This teaching led to a terrible famine, for the deluded Kosa Kaffirs slew their cattle and cut down their crops of growing mealies. The unhappy people were obliged to emigrate to the extent of nearly 100,000, some 25,000 dying of starvation. The restless movements of these desperate men among more settled tribes brought on the sixth Kaffir War, in 1858. After the war, large numbers of Fingo Kaffirs settled in British Kaffraria, and some of the Kosas returned thither or found a home in the adjoining new Transkei province. Others migrated into Pondoland.

In 1851 and 1852 there were fights with the Basuto (Viervoet and Berea), the first of which was a defeat for the British, the second a drawn battle. In the last instance General Cathcart, after conquering the Kosa Kaffirs, had attempted to seize Thaba Bosigo in order to compel the Basuto

Kosa Kaffirs Deluded by a "Wizard"

THE FOUNDERING OF THE BRITISH TROOPSHIP BIRKENHEAD ON FEBRUARY 26TH, 1852

The disaster illustrated in the above picture occurred during a gale off Simon's Bay, South Africa, and will ever be memorable for the heroism exhibited in the face of death. On board the ill-fated steamship were nearly 500 officers and men, who stood calmly awaiting their fate while the women and children were saved. The then King of Prussia caused the splendid story of iron discipline and perfect duty to be read aloud at the head of every regiment in his kingdom.

From the painting by C. Napier Hemy, by permission of Messrs. Henry Graves & Co.

king, Moshesh, to come to terms, the Basuto having been attacking the Griqua Hottentots and Boer trekkers. The issue was not a defeat to the Basuto, but Moshesh wisely came in and agreed to a peace which has never since been broken, so far as the Imperial Government is concerned, though the Basuto had somewhat serious conflicts with the Cape Colonial Government in 1879–1880, conflicts which were eventually solved by their coming under direct Imperial control. In 1877–1878 occurred the seventh and last Kaffir War. After the terrible famine and migration of 1856–1857, a portion of the Galeka clan of the Kosa Kaffirs, under the celebrated chief Kreli, or Kareli, the son of Hintsa, who had surrendered to the British after the Kaffir raid of 1834, had been allowed, in 1865, to settle on the coast of British Kaffraria with the Fingoes and other Kaffir tribes behind them. They increased and multiplied, and in 1877 they turned round and fought the Fingoes. The British Government intervened, and the chief Kreli was deposed. Fighting spread into the colony, and was joined in by the Gaika clan under chief Sandile. This war was brought to a close in 1878 by the death of Sandile and the flight of the aged Kreli.

The Seventh and Last Kaffir War

The impartial historian of South Africa must admit that though many good qualities are inherent in the Boer people, a scrupulous consideration for the antecedent rights of the negroes is not to be attributed to them. In their eyes the natives had no rights, though, at the same time, they were not harsh if Hottentot or Basuto, Bechuana or Zulu were willing to serve for board, lodging, and occasional blankets and Cape brandy. But wherever the Boer ruled he carried on a native policy, as regards land and products, so like that of King Leopold on the Congo as to make one think that in this respect the king of the Belgians may really have borrowed his native policy from Dutch traditions. Soon after the discontented Boers left British territory, because the British Government would not evict native tribes legitimately settled on the soil in favour of incoming white men. The pioneers of the Orange River territory and the founders of the Transvaal State fell out with the warlike Basuto, the southernmost tribe of the wide-spread Bechuana stock. The British forces had repeatedly

Boers Leave British Territory

to intervene, either to save the trekking Boers from extermination by the enraged Basuto, or later to save the Basuto from being wiped out by the land-hungry Boers.

Between 1836 and 1840 the emigrant Boers, whom Lord Glenelg's foolish policy —among other causes—had driven out of the eastern parts of Cape Colony, had brushed aside the Northern Basuto, defeated the Matabele hordes of the southern Transvaal, and broken the Zulu power in Natal. As regards Matabele and Zulu, impartial history will probably say that they got no worse than they deserved. They were treacherous, cruel, devastating, and not much earlier comers in the Bechuana countries than the Boers themselves. As to the Swazi, a northern section of the Zulu-Kaffir group, they were partially protected by the Transvaal Boers from Zulu cruelty.

But in regard to Sekukuni, the government of the Transvaal behaved badly. Sekukuni ruled over a section of the North-eastern Bechuana in the country just south of the Upper Limpopo. The Transvaal Boers from the early part of the sixties were constantly seizing Sekukuni's land or people, and ignoring his rights. This chief established himself strongly in the Zoutspanberg Mountains, and after 1870 the Boer Government of Pretoria launched against this unhappy people bands of conscienceless adventurers; one of the cruellest of these was an ex-Prussian officer, Von Schlickmann, whose atrocities were a disgrace to the Boer name and will be a permanent blot on the history of South Africa. But Sekukuni held out so stoutly that he wore out the energies of the Transvaal State. As the Boer dealings with the Swazis had drawn down on them the animosity of the Zulus, it was feared by the Imperial Government that the mishandling of native affairs in the Transvaal might set going a vast negro revolt against the white man. So Sir Theophilus Shepstone was despatched with a few military officers and twenty-five mounted police to investigate. He took the bold step of annexing the Transvaal.

A Blot on South African History

The British had taken no great share in the fighting against the Zulu monarchy which had won Natal for the white man's rule. The Transvaal Boers had done that and had also installed Panda as king of the Zulus in place of the bloodthirsty Dingane. In 1873 the British Government had been represented at the installation of Cetewayo as successor to Panda. The limit of the recognised Zulu kingdom then, on the west, was the Tugela River. Of course, the colony of Natal contained hundreds of thousands of Zulu-speaking natives, but these, for the most part, had been long dissociated from Zulu rule.

In the North-west of Natal, however, there was the Hlubi clan, originally refugees from Zulu and Basuto lands. These people, under their chief, Langalibalele, began to show themselves turbulent in 1873, and had to be brought to order by the despatch of a small military force. The operations against the Gaika and Galeka clans of the Kosa Kaffirs in 1877-78 sent a thrill of racial sympathy and disturbance through Natal and Zululand, and probably decided the ill-informed king of the Zulus to make a determined fight for Kaffir independence and dominion before the white man grew too strong. It must be remembered that there is very little linguistic difference between Kaffirs and Zulus. Kaffir is an entirely artificial name. It is simply an Arab term meaning " unbeliever," which was applied to the

British Forces in Zululand

pagan Bantu along the South-east African coast by the Arabs, and by them transmitted to the Portuguese, Dutch and English. Sir Bartle Frere saw the coming danger to Natal, and resolved to forestall it by calling on Cetewayo to disarm, after giving him full satisfaction in regard to territories in dispute between the Zulus and the former Republic of the Transvaal.

No answer was received to the ultimatum. On January 22nd, 1879, the British troops under Lord Chelmsford entered Zululand. The opening of the campaign was marked by two striking incidents. The capture of the British camp at Isandlhwana, the " Hill of the Little Hand," with a loss to the British of 800 white and 500 negro soldiers ; and the defence of Rorke's Drift, on the Buffalo River, under Lieutenants Chard and Bromhead, and 120 British and Colonials against 4,000 Zulus, flushed with the victory of Isandlhwana. Another episode of this war, which has raised it in the interest of world-history far above other Kaffir wars, was the death of the Prince Imperial on a reconnoitring expedition. This sad event materially altered the course of modern French history. Zululand was conquered finally by August, 1879, in the battles of Gingihlovo,

Kambula, and Ulundi ; and the king, Cetewayo, was captured and sent into temporary retirement. Sekukuni, of the Northern Transvaal, was then tackled and finally disposed of, while the Swazis were also brought under control. Between 1879 and 1893 there was peace, except mere police operations, between the

In Contact with the Matabele

British and the natives of South Africa. All our attention was concentrated on a struggle for supremacy with the Dutch-speaking section of the white community. A British advance towards the Zambesi began in 1887-1888, a movement which brought us into contact with the Matabele power.

The Matabele were a section of the Zulus whom internecine quarrels had driven from Zululand and Natal into the Southern Transvaal. From this territory, where they had supplanted the Bechuana stock of the Bantu, the Matabele were driven by the Boers beyond the Limpopo. The Matabele in their turn, from 1840 onwards, became a predatory people, and made themselves masters of the lands between the Limpopo and the Zambesi. They enslaved more or less the pre-existing Makaranga, Mashona and kindred tribes of Nyanza stock, and were a sore affliction to the more peaceable Bechuana on their western flank.

Cecil Rhodes and his pioneers, however, had to deal with the Matabele as the effective masters of the country between the Kalahari Desert and the Eastern Portuguese dominions. Various far-reaching concessions were purchased from the greedy Matabele king, Lobengula, who was not very particular as to what he sold, because in his own mind he had determined exactly what the white men should do and what he would withhold from their scope.

But in Dr. Jameson he had a masterful person to deal with. Jameson had accurately gauged the Matabele strength, and, in a short but very brilliant campaign, con-

Dr. Jameson's Brilliant Campaign

ducted by himself and Major Forbes, and by Colonel Goold Adams—on behalf of the Imperial Government—Buluwayo was captured, and Lobengula driven towards the Zambesi, where he afterwards died. Out of a force sent in pursuit of Lobengula, a party of thirty mounted men under Captain Allan Wilson was cut off from the main body and killed by the Matabele after a heroic resistance. The Chartered Company's administration, which followed that of Lobéngula, was not in all respects quite wise, and discontent arose among the natives, Mashona as well as Matabele. After the unfortunate issue of the Chartered Company's armed entry into the Transvaal, the Matabele rose against their white rulers, and though they never succeeded in taking Buluwayo or any other fortified post, they **Unrest Among the Natives** inflicted much damage and some loss of life on the British settlers. Rhodesia was not finally restored to order until the year 1897. Since the great South African War of 1899-1902 there has been a certain amount of unrest among the natives south of the Zambesi, more especially among the Hottentots on the German borders, the Basuto, the Kaffirs of Natal, and the Zulus.

This has been caused by a multiplicity of excitants. The movement originated in certain American negroes of the Ethiopian Church, a form of Christianity which was to treat the interests of the black race as quite distinct from those of the Caucasian; the spread of education, which imparted an honest pride and capability to Christianised Hottentot and Kaffir—so that dull, stupid, violent government at the hands of German or British-Colonial officials or army officers became intolerable; the resentment felt by Zulus and Natal Kaffirs at the alleged filching of their land; lastly, the abundance and cheapness of rifles and ammunition during and after the Boer War; all these were reasons, apart from a general awakening of the negro, why movements towards turbulence and independence necessitated much vigorous police work in 1906-1908—almost amounting to warfare—on the part of British and Colonial troops in Western Bechuanaland, Natal, and Zululand.

Amongst "native" powers which the British Empire has had to fight in South Africa must be enumerated the Boers of Cape Colony, Natal, the Orange State, and **The Boers' Dislike of the British** the Transvaal. This was a vigorous, emphatically "white" race of splendid physique, compounded for the most part of men of Flemish or Dutch descent, mingled with some proportion of French Huguenots and German immigrants. The resident Boers, as distinct from the officials of the Dutch East India Company, never liked the British intrusion from the day of the first landing of British troops at Simonstown on July 14th, 1795, down to the granting of self-governing constitutions to the different states of the future South African Confederation. In 1815 the Dutch farmers had risen against the government of Lord Charles Somerset because it interfered with their summary treatment of the natives; but they were surrounded, and laid down their arms at the place since called Slachter's Nek. In spite of their surrender five of them were hanged for high treason, an act inexcusably harsh on the part of the tyrannical governor, Lord Charles Somerset, whose name for the value of his work is too much commemorated in Cape geography.

Dissatisfaction with Lord Glenelg's fatuous intermeddling and with the, often well-founded, accusations of British and Moravian missionaries as to maltreatment of natives, impelled the migration northwards and eastwards, beginning in 1836, of large numbers of Boer farmers. This led to their wresting the Orange Free State from the Basuto, the Transvaal from the Matabele hordes of Umsilikazi, and Natal from Dingane and the Zulus. Apart from the unfortunate rising of **Boer and Briton in Conflict** Slachter's Nek, Boer and Briton first came into armed conflict over Natal. The port of Durban had, it is true, been originally colonised by British and Americans; but the mighty power of the Zulus had been first broken by Boer valour. After the emigrant farmers had made themselves masters of the country now known as Natal, the intolerable shilly-shally of the home Ministers began. This was the cause in the past of many a war, large and small, and was the result of the old principles of party government and the placing of incompetent or ill-educated men for short and shifting periods at the head of great departments of state. Slowly, imperceptibly, this system has changed in favour of a trained bureaucracy—a rule of the permanent official, who shapes the policy which his temporary parliamentary chief endorses and adopts as his own.

The Natal "War" of 1842 resolved itself into a night attack by the Englishmen of Durban on the Boer position (which failed), and a siege of Durban by the Boers. This siege was raised by the arrival of a British expeditionary force. The Boers retired, and, a commissioner arriving from England in 1843, terms were arranged by which the Boers had a free hand to the north of the Drakensberg, whither

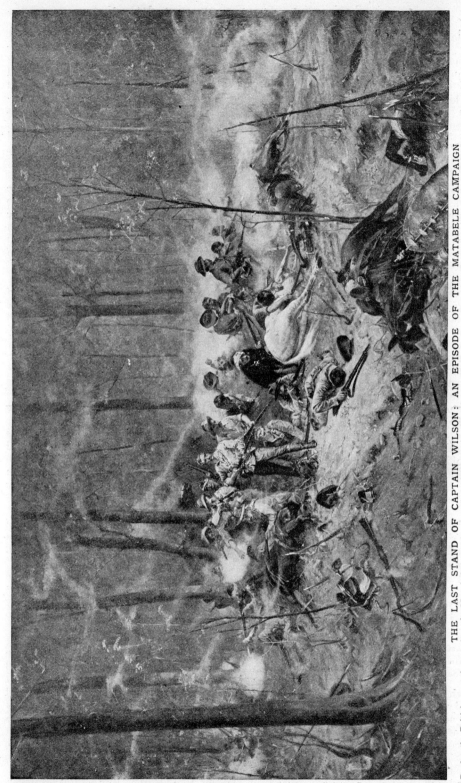

THE LAST STAND OF CAPTAIN WILSON: AN EPISODE OF THE MATABELE CAMPAIGN

During the British campaign against the Matabele in 1890, a party of thirty mounted men under Captain Allan Wilson out of a force sent in pursuit of Lobengula was cut off from the main body, and found itself surrounded by thousands of natives. All escape being cut off, the little party made its last stand on a small piece of rising ground, and died fighting like heroes.

From the painting by Allan Stewart, by permission of the Fine Art Society, 148, New Bond Street

the bolder spirits betook themselves. After well-nigh intolerable vacillation, contradictory proclamations, flag hoistings and pullings-down, treaties with native chiefs or hybrid adventurers, restraining and loosing of the justly exasperated Boers, the British Government of the Cape declared the present Orange State to be British territory in 1848.

The Boers Rise in Rebellion This action was resented by the emigrant Boers, with Pretorius at their head. They rose in rebellion, but in meeting Sir Harry Smith—one of the great names in South African history—they met one of their own kidney. After a severe fight, the Boers were defeated at the Battle of Boomplatz, and Pretorius and his men fled across the Vaal River.

The recognition of the Transvaal as an independent state in 1852, and of the Orange River Territory in 1854, are episodes in the relations of Boer and Briton which have been described elsewhere. No further armed conflict with the Boers occurred until December 20th, 1880. In 1877, the Transvaal Republic, in great difficulties over its conflict with the natives, had been somewhat summarily annexed by Sir Theophilus Shepstone on behalf of the British Government. This measure was most unpalatable to the mass of the Boer farmers under the leadership of Krüger, Pretorius, and Joubert; and they never ceased petitioning against it.

At length, encouraged by the British lassitude which had followed the Zulu War, they rose in rebellion, and after the British defeats at Bronker's Spruit, Lang's Nek, and Majuba Hill, obtained eventually the recognition of the independence of their republic, with only slight modifications, modifications which were pared away to a transparency by the Convention of London in 1884. Though this convention established more or less clearly the boundaries of the Trans-

Expansion the Aim of the Boers vaal, the Boers did not hesitate —any more than the British would have done—to trespass beyond these limits as far as British forbearance would allow, and proposed to themselves, on the one hand, to seize and monopolise the road to Central Africa, and, on the other, to conquer Zululand and thus attain access to the sea. To stop both these movements an important armed demonstration was made by the British Government in 1885,

whereby Sir Charles Warren, with a force of 4,000 men, marched up into Bechuanaland and suppressed the infant republics of Stellaland and Goshen, and substituted for them the British Protectorate of Bechuanaland, which was ultimately extended to the Zambesi. Zululand was annexed, and ultimately, in 1887–1898, Amatongaland also. The southern and western boundaries of the Orange State had, by a piece of rather sharp practice, been clipped and defined in 1869, 1871, and 1876. From 1898 a final duel between the British and the Boers for the overlordship of South Africa became inevitable. The Boers were resolved to expand, the British determined to compress them within treaty limits, and even to strangle them in their own homes.

First came about the unofficial war, the abortive raid of Jameson at the head of the Chartered Company's forces into the Transvaal in December, 1895. Then ensued four years of preparations on both sides. Those of the Boers were directed to steady armament and training, with results which certainly " staggered humanity " ; those

The Great War in South Africa of the British to sounding France, Russia, Portugal, Italy, America, and perhaps Germany as to their attitude in the event of a South African War. The outbreak of this long contemplated struggle was precipitated by the two allied Boer States delivering an ultimatum on October 9th, 1899. It is not necessary here to recount the incidents and fluctuations of this great and lengthy contest ; it is sufficient to record that the war began with a series of British defeats, retreats, and besiegements in fortified cities or camps. Then came Lords Roberts and Kitchener, and their march right into the heart of the Orange Free State, and thence by a series of successes, which went far to damp any thought of European intervention, to Pretoria, Lydenburg, Komatipoort.

By the autumn of 1900 the Orange River Republic and the Transvaal had been annexed to the British dominions, and President Krüger had fled to Europe. Most persons now thought the war at an end, but the Boers managed to keep up a guerrilla warfare for eighteen months longer, thus securing for their countrymen far better and more honourable terms of peace than would have been granted in the autumn of 1900. As military leaders, De Wet, De La Rey, Botha, Kemp, Lucas Meyer, and other Boer generals covered themselves with glory, and taught the world new lessons in warfare. But in the meantime Central South Africa was being ruined. These same men who fought so well would not carry on a hopeless struggle after the offer of reasonable terms. To the great relief of all concerned, a peace was ratified on May 31st, 1902, which has left no sting behind it to either party in the struggle. The Orange State, under a slightly different name, and the Transvaal continue to exist as self-governing communities ready to take their part as equals in any future confederation of South Africa, with Cape Colony, Natal, and Rhodesia.

The question of war between the white and the black man in trans-Zambesian Africa is, I fear, not finally laid to rest. Contemporary and later historians have frequently described this, that, or the other Kaffir war as an unjust one. There is no doubt that we sometimes fought over a wrong issue, but there is equally no doubt in the mind of the present narrator that the British power has been a great deal more anxious to do the right thing and

The Boers' Treatment of the Natives avoid injustice in its fights with the great Zulu-Kaffir congeries of peoples in the southern prolongation of Africa than it has shown itself elsewhere in the lands of Black and Yellow. In the first place, South Africa during two-thirds of the nineteenth century was not regarded as an extraordinarily valuable acquisition. The Dutch colonists, it is true, were perfectly ruthless in regard to displacing, dispossessing, killing or enslaving the black races that had preceded them.

They were no more scrupulous in this respect than the English who settled on the Atlantic coast of the United States, the Spaniards in South America, the Portuguese in India, or the Dutch in Malaya. They, the Boers, were " God's chosen people "; the yellow or black Hottentot-Bushman, or Kaffir, was a heathen, with no more claims to consideration than the beasts of the field, and both alike were shot down by the deadly accuracy of the Boer marksman. But British missionary enterprise was early afoot in South Africa, and, as I have said before, the country was not thought particularly worth taking away from its black inhabitants. No minerals of importance had been discovered prior to the diamond revelation in 1869. In many districts

horses and cattle could not live, and there European settlers could not thrive. It was a land of droughts and floods, of ice and sunstroke, of barren steppe more hopeless than the Sahara, of thorn jungle, and of man-eating lions. So far as anyone therefore is to blame for the unjustness of the Kaffir wars, it is the Dutch or Afri-

War Forced on the Zulus kander colonists, who first picked a quarrel with the natives, and then dragged the British Government into the settlement of that quarrel. Whenever the treatment was just towards the native it provoked a rising, a secession, or, at any rate, a severe disaffection amongst the white settlers.

It is true that in 1879 Sir Bartle Frere— a great and far-seeing viceroy—having annexed the Transvaal, largely because of the Boer mishandling of native rights, forced a war on the king of the Zulus. The alternative was to wait until the Zulu power, a little stronger, a little more reckless, launched itself on the colony of Natal, drowning it in blood, as Cetewayo's grandfather had done, pitiless alike to white and black, for no one has ever been so cruel to the negro as the negro.

The Chartered Company's war against the bastard Zulus of Lobengula, the descendants of the hordes led northwards by Umsilikazi or Mosilikatse, has been arraigned as unjust, except when argued on the basis of the Parable of the Talents. Lobengula and his Amandebele indunas desired to keep the white man out of the country as much as they could, except as an ivory hunter or purchaser, or possibly as one who should find minerals at his own risk and expense and hand over a handsome royalty to the king and his courtiers, who would spend it on the purchase of more oxen, more wives, and more guns and gunpowder, with which to carry out more extensive slave-raids to the north. The Chartered Company had not interfered

Chartered Company and the Zulus with the natives' rights over the land, nor had they attempted any assumption of governing rights. They were genuinely anxious—the present writer can testify—to avoid any quarrels with the Matabele, partly, to cite no higher motive, because they had greatly over-estimated the fighting strength and capabilities of the Matabele. The quarrel really arose over the position of the indigenous tribes, Mashona and Makaranga, who were treated by the

Matabele as their slaves. The Matabele theory was that if the white men wished the Mashona or other of their subject tribes to work for them as porters, labourers, or guides, their services must first be purchased from the Matabele chiefs. The Mashona and their congeners had been waiting for the white man's advent to shake off the Zulu yoke which had lain so heavily on them since about 1845.

Wars with the Matabele

Often, when pursued or plagued by the Matabele, they would fly for refuge to one or other of the white men's forts, and they were frequently followed by the Matabele and brought back. One or two episodes of this kind, though ending in bloodshed, were smoothed over by the company's officials; the Matabele warriors became more and more daring, and at last a stand had to be made. In July, 1893, a Matabele army entered the township of Victoria, and attacked the Mashonas residing there, slaughtering many before the company's police could intervene. A fight between the Matabele warriors and the mounted police ensued, resulting in considerable loss of life to the Matabele, and in an open war with Lobengula's forces, which ended in the Chartered Company becoming the government of the land in the place of these raiding Zulus who had preceded them by forty or fifty years.

In the second Matabele War, which followed in 1896, it is true that the Mashona joined hands with their former oppressors, but the discontent which provoked this war was largely caused by the company having employed an oppressive Matabele police, which, in a different uniform and with a new authority, continue to plunder the unfortunate tillers of the soil.

The foundation of the colony of Sierra Leone, in 1787-1807, for the purpose of repatriating liberated slaves led to very little trouble with the natives till Sierra Leone had been about eighty years in existence as a British colony, mainly because little attempt was made to exercise British authority beyond the Sierra Leone Peninsula and certain islands on the coast duly purchased from the native owners. The same may be said in regard to the Gambia. But as early as 1824 trouble arose on the Gold Coast with the powerful native kingdom of Ashanti. As related elsewhere, the British Crown had shirked as much as possible any direct

Trouble on the Gold Coast

responsibility for the West African settlements, though these were amongst the earliest attempts at empire beyond the British Channel. The forts and settlements were held somewhat intermittently by chartered companies. But in 1824 the governor of Sierra Leone—the Gold Coast ports were brought under the Sierra Leone government from 1821 to 1850—Sir Charles Macarthy, was forced into a conflict with the Ashanti people in order to defend the coast tribes who were under British protection. He was killed in warfare (Ensimankao, January 14th, 1824), and the British Government was obliged to avenge his death and re-establish British authority; this was the first Ashanti War between 1827 and 1831.

A short war with Lagos in 1851 was the result of an attempt to put down the slave trade. On this pretext, and also to avenge wrongs done to British merchants, the Dahomeh coast was frequently blockaded or bombarded during the third quarter of the nineteenth century, and punitive expeditions were undertaken in the Niger delta, 1886-1906, and the Congo estuary, 1875. The transfer of the Dutch possessions on the Gold Coast to Great Britain entailed another war with Ashanti

British Victories in Ashanti

in 1873-1874. This was the first occasion on which West African warfare was taken seriously. Sir Garnet Wolseley, who had distinguished himself as the commander of the Red River expedition in Central Canada, commanded a British force of about 10,000 men, 2,400 British, and the remainder negro soldiers, which, together with native auxiliaries under Sir John Glover, entered Kumasi and imposed a war indemnity which was never completely paid. Ashanti was only finally conquered after two more expeditions (1896-1900). It is now directly administered by the British Government, and has consequently increased very considerably in prosperity.

The action of France about the sources of the Niger, beginning in the early 'eighties of the last century, obliged the British Government to concern itself about the hinterland of Sierra Leone; and the various attempts to impose British influence over the warlike Temne and Mende peoples entailed a number of armed expeditions or small wars, such as the Yonni war in 1886, in what is now the rather considerable territory of the Sierra Leone Protectorate. These culminated in a regular rising of the

Temne and Mende peoples, owing to the imposition of a hut tax, in 1898. The complete subjugation of the colony which followed, coupled with the building of a railway across a portion of the hinterland, brought about the most extraordinary changes in the prosperity of the natives. Sierra Leone is now one of the best governed, most prosperous, and generally successful of the British possessions in tropical Africa. Similar attempts to open up the hinterland of the Gambia, and to protect commerce along the British banks of that river, likewise occasioned a few armed expeditions against the Mandingo or Fulbe sultans of the interior. The last of these was the expedition against Fodi Kabba in 1900.

In the hinterland of Lagos, in the Ibo territories of the Niger Delta, there were punitive expeditions, enforced conquests of natives who would not let the Britisher or his native subjects alone. These occurred mainly between 1885 and 1905, including the expedition in 1897, which rapidly conquered the blood-stained kingdom of Benin, a feat thought to be almost **Conquest of Nigeria** impossible owing to the physical difficulties of reaching Benin through leagues of forest-swamp. But amongst notable exploits of warlike enterprise on the battle-roll of Britain, nothing in this direction equalled in importance of achievements the conquest of Nigeria. As usual, the British Government had turned over to a chartered company of merchants the first responsibility of laying the foundations of the Nigerian Empire. The original attempts of 1841 and 1858 to establish something like a British protectorate or control over the banks of the Niger had failed through the frightful mortality which attacked the naval expeditions. The Lower Niger was justly regarded then as a region so impossibly unhealthy that it could not profit the British Government as a means of reaching the Nigerian Sudan.

As related elsewhere, the foundations of modern British Nigeria were laid by Captain Goldie Taubman, afterwards Sir George T. Goldie. The Royal Niger Company, which he founded, soon experienced, however, enormous difficulties in carrying their charter into effect. It was relatively easy to keep order amongst the savage cannibal negroes along the banks of the Niger and navigable Benue ; but immediately beyond these regions were the Nigerian Sudanese—the Mohammedan Nupe, Fulbe, Hausa peoples under a general Fulbe suzerainty—hordes of cavalry permeated with Mohammedan bravery. These peoples in those days were possibly egged on to try conclusions with the British company by its French and German rivals, who, in the first place, resented the British **British Rule in the Sudan** appropriation of Eastern Nigeria, and in the second, disliked most of all that the government of the country should be entrusted to a commercial company. The company had to face the situation, conquer the amir of Nupe, and impose peace by a show of force on the Fulbe sultan of Sokoto. The expedition of 1897, practically led by Sir George Goldie, was to all intents and purposes organised by the British Government, and was commanded by Imperial officers. It achieved its object after one or two pitched battles, but ran the narrowest risks of failure and disaster owing to the difficulties of transport once it quitted the navigable waterway.

When the company was succeeded by the direct rule of the British Government, Sir Frederick Lugard found it quite impossible to cry halt until, with the forces under his command, led by Colonel Morland, he had conquered the Fulbe power and established British rule over the great Hausa cities of the Central Sudan. These campaigns of 1902 and 1903 were remarkable for the extent of ground covered, the relatively small fighting force at the disposal of the British, and the effect of the victories. It would be too soon to say that the Moslem peoples of Eastern Nigeria will never again raise the standard of revolt ; but the surest way of turning their thoughts to better things, the cheapest way of maintaining our hold over this important region of Africa, is by the building of railways. As regards wars in North-east Africa within the memory of living men, the first **The Quixotic Abyssinian Expedition** to record is the somewhat quixotic Abyssinian expedition of 1864–1868. Of all the episodes in the history of the British Empire, this will seem the most difficult to explain. Its analogue in our wars of the first class with European Powers is the Crimean War. Some well-meaning but over-zealous missionaries had offended the usurping monarch of Abyssinia, Theodore. This curious personality, who, like his immediate predecessors for about seventy years back, had begun to get into touch with the civilisation of the outer world by commerce carried on through Indian traders, had invited to his court mechanics or industrial missionaries, and then, if he were capriciously displeased with them, would hold them as his captives. A British consul of Levantine or Armenian extraction,

Theodore, the Mad King of Abyssinia selected for his knowledge of Arabic and Amharic, was sent to get these captives out of Theodore's toils by negotiations. But Theodore, who was more than half a crank, and who had proposed marriage to Queen Victoria upon hearing that she was a widow, but had received no reply to his proposal, kept back the consul, too.

In a less sentimental age it might have been questioned whether, as Great Britain had at that time no desire to interfere in the affairs of North-east Africa, she was warranted in spending several millons of money, and perhaps in all about a thousand lives, in trying to rescue a few misguided Europeans who had accepted all risks in going to the court of a barbarous monarch. But there was the question of the British envoy, Mr. Rassam, and British prestige in the Eastern world.

So 16,000 (mainly Indian) soldiers, and some 15,000 non-combatants, marched through the mountains of Abyssinia till they had released the captives and captured Magdala, the last stronghold of Theodore, who committed suicide. Then, after furnishing their principal native ally, Prince Kassai, of Tigre, an Abyssinian prince of less doubtful lineage, with the means of aspiring to the throne of Ethiopia, the British forces marched back again to the Red Sea. In this achievement we were in far better circumstances than the Italians thirty years later, for the British protestations that they desired no territorial acquisitions were believed, and the mass of the Abyssinian people was on the side of the British

British Army in Egypt against the misconduct of the mad, though talented, usurper. British soldiers were not to set foot in North-eastern Africa again for fifteen years. Then, in 1882, a British force was landed at Port Said under Sir Garnet Wolseley of Ashanti, who was to become Lord Wolseley of Cairo. Here the immediate objective was the subjugation of Arabi's revolt and the reassertion of the power of the legitimate ruler of Egypt, the

khedive. The motive was absolutely not any desire to acquire more territory, but in reality to save the Suez Canal from falling under the exclusive control of France, of Turkey, or of a new Mohammedan nationality, fanatical and successful, which might be arising under the somewhat stupid colonel of artillery, Ahmad Arabi. Britain had seen between 1835 and 1840 a great military power arise in Egypt, which had conquered nearly the whole of Arabia, had wrested Syria from the Porte, and, unchecked, might have re-created from an Egyptian base a vast Mohammedan empire. It was quite possible such a thing might occur once more, with Arabi in the place of Ibrahim, the son of Mehemet Ali.

The British occupation of Lower Egypt was followed by the downfall of Egyptian rule over the Sudan, the futile despatch of Gordon, and the too-late expedition in 1884 sent to extract Gordon from a besieged Khartoum. Here, again, there was no other motive than the desire to retrieve Britain's honour, much as there had been in the case of Abyssinia. Nothing was

Gordon's Death at Khartoum desired less at that moment than the addition to the British Empire of the Egyptian Sudan. The too-late expedition, only just too late, was recalled from its natural impetus to avenge Gordon by complications with Russia in Central Asia. Little collateral wars had been carried on with the fierce Hamitic tribes of the Nubian Desert between the Red Sea coast and the Atbara, but the British and Egyptian forces were withdrawn to Wadi Halfa and the walls of Suakin, and for some years confined their efforts to repelling the attacks of the Dervishes.

The deliberate attempts at conquest of the bastard Zanzibar Arabs, descendants of the fierce Omani seamen and merchants, whose assaults on the Zanzibar coast had extinguished the power of the Portuguese in the eighteenth century, had steadily pushed inland, and had developed the slave trade to such an extent that they had scandalised the British public through the revelations of Livingstone, Speke, Grant, Stanley, Thomson and others. Ideas of empire had come to them, and they had determined to found vigorous Mohammedan slave states in Central Africa. But they knocked their heads against harder ones—the dogged Scottish pioneers of Nyassaland. It was with the

African Lakes Company at the north end of Lake Nyassa that the war broke out first between European and Arab for the possession of Central Africa. Trade had a little to do with it. The Arabs had begun to interfere between the native seller and the European purchaser ; but it is only fair to state that sheer horror at the atrocious cruelties of the Arab slave raids precipitated the fight on the part of such agents of the African Lakes Company as the late Monteith Fotheringham and the still living Moir brothers. The African Lakes Company hastily called for volunteers, and enlisted amongst others a Captain Lugard, bent on East African adventure, and a hunter of big game, Alfred Sharpe. The one became the subjugator of Nigeria and the province of Uganda, and the other is still governor of the British Central African dominions.

But the Arabs were too strong to be subdued by a rabble of undisciplined blacks officered by five or six brave English or Scotch. A drawn battle was practically the result. The slave-traders had to be attacked nearer to their base before the **Establishing a British Protectorate** Arab power could be dealt with effectually at the north end of Lake Nyassa. It fell to the lot of the writer of these chapters to head this next movement, which culminated in 1895–1896 by the defeat and death of all the Arab leaders, and the definite establishment of British dominion up to the south end of Tanganyika and the shores of Lake Mweru. A little campaign against the power of the Angoni Zulus, who had invaded Nyassaland in the early part of the nineteenth century, completed such conquests as were necessary to establish a British protectorate over the whole of British Central Africa from the upper waters of the Zambesi to the Portuguese possessions east of Lake Nyassa.

The British establishment at Aden, which was rendered necessary by the opening of the overland route to India through Egypt and the Red Sea, brought the British power into contact with the Somali coast. There had been British envoys to Ethiopia and Shoa as far back as the closing years of the eighteenth century. The coastlands and a good deal of the interior of the Somali country produced sheep, goats, camels, and even oxen, besides other commodities which were required to feed the British garrison at Aden, and also the ever-increasing number of steamers which called at Aden on their way to and from India. Therefore, as far back as the early 'fifties of the last century Great Britain, by means of official and unofficial explorations, was taking a marked interest in the fate of the Somali coast. During the period of Imperial lassitude coincident **Fall of the Egyptian Power** with the 'sixties and early 'seventies, Great Britain looked on with a shrug of the shoulders whilst Egypt, which at any rate, in our eyes, was better than France for such a purpose, attempted to make herself mistress of Somaliland.

When the Egyptian power fell, however, with the annihilation of General Hicks's army and the death of Gordon, it was necessary to do something, or else the coast opposite Aden might be jointly occupied by France and Italy. So the very oddly-shaped protectorate of British Somaliland came into existence, and, needless to say, the attempts of the British to become responsible for law and order on the Somali coast dragged them much against their will into an equal responsibility for the disorder of inner Somaliland.

A mad mullah, a robber-fanatic, beginning as so many of these Moslem leaders have done, in a very prosaic way as a disappointed store-keeper or a market gardener whose crops had been ravaged by locusts, and who in a vague way has attributed his grievances to the incoming of the British government, drew to a head the dissatisfaction of the turbulent Somalis at seeing their misgoverned country somewhat rigidly administered by the yellow soldiers and white officers of a Christian empire, or an empire synonymous in their eyes with an interfering Christianity. Had our African policy been wisely directed at the time, the mad mullah, beyond our repelling his attacks on settlements near the coast, would have been fought by a railway **Operations Against the Mad Mullah** instead of by armies of negro and Indian soldiers gallantly led by British officers into the thorny deserts over an area as large as England, in attempts, that were to a great extent vain, to grasp the mobile enemy by the throat. Troubles began in Somaliland in 1898. The operations against Sayyid Mohammed, the "Mad" mullah, now no longer regarded as mad, commenced in 1901 and did not terminate until 1904. In 1905 Sayyid

Mohammed was recognised politically by Italy and Britain as a native ruler over a defined sphere with access to the coast. So much bravery and endurance were not entirely thrown away; the Somalis received a drastic lesson. But in the light of later wisdom we now realise that the millions which this little war cost Great Britain might have been far

Civilising Influence of Railways more profitably and conclusively employed in the construction of a railway. Perhaps this lesson has been brought home to the empire. In Nigeria, in Sierra Leone, in the hinterland of Lagos, the policy of railway building has now been thoroughly understood. It is realised that a railway is the best investment of British Imperial money in these and other undeveloped countries.

It is true that the construction of a railway cannot be undertaken without a force to guard the railway workers; but it is far easier to advance from the secure base as the railway progresses, and the process requires a far smaller armed force than risky expeditions on a large scale into the unknown. The trouble in all African warfare is not the fighting when it comes to close quarters, but the question of transport in a roadless country. If you rely on native porters, they are relatively defenceless, and may bolt at the first appearance of the enemy; if on beasts of burden, mules or camels, they may be stampeded, maimed or killed by an enemy used to making such procedure the first thought in warfare. On the other hand, the railway inspires interest, curiosity, amazement, and suggests the very sweet thought of profitable commercial relations. It offers well-paid work for vigorous men, and a certain market for all native supplies.

Not long after the Arab question was settled in South-central Africa in 1896, trouble was brewing in the equatorial regions of Eastern Africa. Echoes of the revolt against the Germans in Swahili

Rising in Eastern Africa Africa amongst the so-called Arabs or Arabised negroes had spread to the British territories at the back of Mombasa. Here was wont to resort an Arab prince who was by many Moslems of East Africa regarded as the rightful occupant of the Zanzibar throne, the descendant of an Arab dynasty that had been replaced by the Sayyids of Oman. Sidi Mubarak stirred up trouble for the British. Moreover, it had been necessary to conquer by

a naval expedition a small Swahili sultanate on the Ozo River. The question of slavery and the slave trade lay at the bottom of this disaffection against British rule. When these troubles were appeased came rumours of more serious disturbances further to the west, in the Uganda Protectorate.

Sir Frederick, then Captain, Lugard had imported into the Uganda Protectorate, in the days when it was no more than a sphere of influence, a number of Emin Pasha's Sudanese soldiers. These men were brave, but they were emphatically Mohammedans, and with a few of them the old Arab dislike to the rule of the Christian still lingered. Their first easy victories in keeping order in Uganda inspired them with a contempt for the pagan or Christian negroes of that region. They also had legitimate grievances in regard to the manner in which they had been handled by one or two officers in command.

Added to this source of trouble was the extreme dislike on the part of the king of Unyoro and his counsellors and the king of Uganda to the imposition of British

Mutiny of Sudanese Soldiers control. The mass of people in Uganda, and their local chiefs or headmen, on the contrary, strongly desired a British protectorate, and were opposed to their disreputable monarch on many grounds. But the first attempts to crush the mutiny of the Sudanese soldiers provoked a formidable rising of the Banyoro and disaffected Baganda. The British force, mainly consisting of Indian soldiers and thousands of Baganda "friendlies," got the better of the mutineers in several very bloody engagements, and finally the two kings of Unyoro and Uganda were captured and deported from East Africa.

The Uganda mutiny ended, so far as serious fighting was concerned, in 1899, but a few further engagements with the remnant of the Sudanese followed, and in 1900 there was trouble with the Nandi mountaineers. In all these contests it was obvious—the writer naturally speaks as an eye-witness—that the bulk of the natives of all races and tribes of the large British Protectorate of Uganda were with the British in their attempts to introduce decent government and profitable commerce. Had it not been so, it would have required a force of 10,000 soldiers and an expenditure of ten millions of money to reduce these lands to obedience. As a matter of fact, they were pacified by a force of some 400 Indians and 3,000 native soldiers, commanded by British officers and non-commissioned officers. Moreover, an important remnant of the Sudanese remained faithful throughout to the British Government.

After the British Government advised the khedive of Egypt to withdraw his troops and officials to Wadi Halfa or the walls of Suakin, about the year 1886, no further steps of a warlike nature were taken for the reconquest of the Sudan. The task was tacitly postponed till a more convenient opportunity. Meanwhile, the present sirdar and governor-general of the Sudan, Sir Reginald Wingate, was steadily collecting information through one of the best organised intelligence departments in the world.

Emboldened by this silence, after the mahdi's death, when the Khalifa Abdallah succeeded to supreme power, a fierce attack was made on Egypt; but the Anglo-Egyptian army—that is to say, Egyptian soldiers fortified by an admixture of British non-commissioned and commissioned officers—assisted by British cavalry and commanded by General (Lord) Grenfell, inflicted on the Dervishes at Saras, about thirty miles to the south of Wadi Halfa, a defeat so overwhelming that it checked once and for all any further aspirations of the khalifa for the reconquest of the world. The battles and skirmishes with Osman Digma, between 1884 and 1897, round Suakin and in the Eastern Sudan, had no such conclusive or effective retort; but the enemy here was worn out by continual defeats, and Osman Digma abandoned the struggle and repaired to the khalifa's army on the Nile in 1897 to oppose Kitchener's main advance. He was subsequently captured in the hills behind Tokar, in January, 1900.

The Rebel Osman Digma Captured

How long this stage of waiting and preparation would have continued it is difficult to say, had not the conclusion of the drama been hastened by the action of France and the misfortunes of Italy. French rancour against the British occupation of Egypt continued to increase during the early 'nineties of the last century. It was envenomed by the opposition offered on the part of the British Government to a French annexation of Eastern Nigeria, and perhaps by the barrier we erected against the absorption of the kingdom of Siam. British inaction was mistaken for indifference or cowardice. The marvellously rapid way in which the French had opened up connections between the Atlantic coast and the Mubangi River, the great northern affluent of the Congo, and between the Mubangi and the regions of the Shari and Lake Chad, inspired them with the idea, enhanced by the similar successes of the Belgians advancing from the Congo, that the power of the Dervishes was either greatly exaggerated or was on the wane. They found that they could enter the south-western regions of the Bahr-el-Ghazal by friendly understanding with the Niam-Niam sultans, and so they conceived the idea of opening up direct trans-continental relations between the Gulf of Guinea, Abyssinia, and Somaliland, thus carrying a band of French influence right across Africa from sea to sea. It was known to the British Government, and was noted in a historic speech by Sir Edward Grey, that a French expedition was advancing to the Upper Nile.

French Expedition in Egypt

Italy, in the meantime, was aspiring to conquer and acquire the whole of Abyssinia. Her hopes were shattered at the Battle of Adawa, in 1896. The imagined consequences of this disaster at the time were probably exaggerated in the mind of the German Emperor, who strongly urged the British Government to retake the eastern portion of the Egyptian Sudan, and thus distract the Dervishes from joining forces with Abyssinia, and sweeping the Italians into the Red Sea.

Fortified by this hint on the part of a potent personage, whose moral support in Egypt counteracted the threats of French hostility, the British Government sanctioned the advance to Dongola, long prepared by Sir Herbert Kitchener, and carried into effect with a method, accuracy, punctuality, and economy which filled the British Government with admiration, and encouraged high hopes in regard to a similar advance on Khartoum. This, indeed, followed in the year 1898 as a necessary consequence of Dongola. It was the only way to prevent a French annexation of the Egyptian Sudan. Omdurman and Khartoum were retaken on September 2nd-3rd, 1898, and the episode of Fashoda followed. France bowed to the verdict of the stricken field, and

France Retires from Egypt

withdrew. But the khalifa and some of his principal lieutenants still remained at large. They had withdrawn into that ominous thorny desert of Kordofan, where Hicks's army had been lost—and the Sudan with it—in 1883. So long as they remained at large, gathering again reactionary forces for the attack, there could be no rest for the British governor at Khartoum. Consequetly, the third and last campaign that regained the Sudan for civilisation was entered upon by Sir Reginald Wingate, to the great anxiety of those who were watching afar off. A success, in its way as triumphant as that of Kitchener, settled the question once and for all. In the battle of Om Dubreikat on November 25th, 1899, the khalifa Abdallah and all his emirs were killed.

Conquerors of the Eastern Sudan

Colonel Hunter and Colonel Parsons, between them, had conquered the whole Eastern Sudan, from the Blue Nile to Kassala, in September, 1898 ; but this region required a small punitive expedition as late as 1908. The great cattle-breeding tribe of the Dinkas has elicited more than one display of Anglo-Egyptian force, and the Niam-Niams of the Western Bahr el Ghazal likewise.

The only " native " wars in Polynesia sufficiently important to be chronicled have been those which took place in New Zealand in two periods, from 1845 to 1848, and from 1860 to 1870. The indigenous New Zealand Maori population, of Polynesian origin, was certain, sooner or later, to come into conflict with the British colonists. Documents were drawn up, and received the crosses of unreflecting chiefs who thereby had disposed of large areas of communal land without realising the after effects. The unscrupulous actions of the European settlers were met by reprisals. The usual muddle took place in dealing with the great war of 1860-70 in its first stages, and before it came to a final end a good number of British soldiers and settlers had lost their lives. But, as might be anticipated, it resulted in the definite conquest of the Maori ; also in more conscientious settlement of their land questions.

No colonial war of recent years has taken place in any British American possession ; but in 1865 there was a serious danger of a wide-spreading negro revolt in the island of Jamaica. The somewhat panic-stricken and illegal actions taken by Governor Eyre and the officers under his command cost that otherwise excellent colonial official his career.

The revolt in Upper and Lower Canada between 1835 and 1838 entailed a good deal of stiff fighting. It was finally extinguished by the evident determination of the British Government, through the work of such able administrators as the Earl of Durham and Lord Sydenham, to endow the Canadas with a complete and popular form of constitutional government. In 1870 the revolt of the French half-breeds in the Red River district, under Louis Riel, entailed a military expedition commanded by the present Viscount Wolseley, then a young colonel. But Louis Riel reappeared fifteen years later, and defeated a body of Canadian mounted police and volunteers. This success rallied round him the still recalcitrant element of French half-breeds and pure blood Indians. But a body of over 5,000 Canadian militia soon overcame Riel's resistance. He was captured, tried for murder—he was practically an outlaw. having fled from justice after the murder of Thomas Scott in 1870—and hanged at Regina in November, 1885.

Fate of the Rebel Louis Riel

BRITISH HAUSA TROOPS STATIONED ON THE GOLD COAST

THE FIGHTING FORCES OF THE BRITISH EMPIRE

NAVAL ACHIEVEMENTS FROM THE TIME OF KING ALFRED TO THE PRESENT DAY

THE British, or more strictly speaking, the English Navy began in the time of Alfred as a means of counter-attack against the Danes, and continued afterwards as a collection of armed merchantmen. After the Norman conquest and under the Plantagenets it served as a method of attacking Ireland, Scotland, France, Flanders, and Spain. But as a means to the end of founding a great empire beyond the seas it only began in the time of Elizabeth. Even then there were "Queen's ships" and the vessels of private adventurers whose proceedings were either licensed or winked at by the sovereign, and who were only to be distinguished from common pirates in that their hostile actions were usually limited to the property of such nations as were at war or on bad terms with England.

The first of such sea-fights under the national flag was the battle of an English fleet under Sir John Hawkins and Sir Francis Drake against the ships of the Spanish viceroy off San Juan de Ulua, on the coast of Mexico, in 1567. This ended in a decisive victory for the British, and was the beginning of the long series of attacks on Spanish America, which continued down to 1808, and even found their echo in the United States' war against Spain **England's** on account of Cuba and Porto **Early** Rico. This particular fight at **Sea Fights** San Juan de Ulua arose over the desire of the English to carry on a trade in African slaves between Guinea and America in defiance of Spanish monopolies of commerce and privileges.

Sir John Hawkins had begun the slave trade under the indirect permit—a sub-concession from Genoese and Portuguese concessionaries—of Spain in 1562, and it had proved so profitable that Queen Elizabeth had put two of her ships and several thousand pounds into the business. This unofficial war between England and Spain, provoked by the Spanish and Portuguese monopolies of trade and communications between Europe and America, Africa, and India, was continued by Drake's piratical expeditions of 1572-1573 **Drake's** and 1577-1580, in the course **Piratical** of which he attacked and plun- **Exploits** dered the Spanish settlements of San Domingo, Florida, Cuba, and, most wonderful of all, Peru. He sailed round South America, attacked the Spaniards on the undefended Pacific coast, and then, first of all leaders of men, so far as we know, completed the circumnavigation of the globe. Magellan, the Portuguese navigator, died in the Spice Islands after discovering the Magellan Straits. His ships, not he, completed the first voyage round the world. In 1585, when Spain and England were at last at open war, followed Drake's Carthagena expedition, and in 1587 was the raid on Cadiz, in which he destroyed or captured eighty Spanish ships which were employed in preparing for the great Armada.

The exploits or outrages of Drake were among provocative causes of the dispatch of the great Armada which was effectually to subdue this nation of Protestant pirates in the Northern seas. The resistance offered to this mighty Spanish fleet may be justly regarded as one of the earliest glories of the English Navy, but we should also not forget that it was equally Dutch valour which rendered the purposes of the Armada impossible and saved England from experiencing at the hands of Spain woes such as England herself had inflicted on Ireland. Frobisher, Howard of Effingham,

Drake and Hawkins, tackled this enormous and clumsy fleet of sixty magnificent vessels as soon as it had entered the British Channel, and followed it resolutely to the Straits of Dover. Here, whilst the Spanish naval commander-in-chief was awaiting the arrival of the Duke of Parma's army for England, which was to sally out from the Flemish and Dutch seaports in shallow vessels, the brave Dutch mariners blockaded the coasts and deltas of the Netherlands, and prevented the Spanish soldiers from putting out to sea. During this hesitancy an English sea-captain, probably Winter, thought of the splendid idea—really originated some years earlier by an Italian engineer, Giambelli—of sending fireships to drift with wind and tide into the midst of the huddled and anchored Armada. This for the first time scattered the Armada. The decisive engagement and the complete rout of the fleet took place next day, though the chase was continued on the part of the English to as far north as the latitude of 56°.

Fate of the Spanish Armada

The next great naval exploit was the capture of Cadiz in 1596, by Essex, Raleigh, Effingham, and Howard, followed by a raid on Spanish shipping in the Azores Archipelago. Then for a time Spain and England were at peace. The next enemy to be encountered on the sea was Holland. An English fleet under Monk, commissioned by the Lord Protector Cromwell, defeated the Dutch off the North Foreland in 1653, and destroyed much Dutch shipping in the Texel.

All this warfare with Holland, like that with Spain, arose over the question of commercial monopolies in the Colonies and the Eastern seas. Admiral Blake proceeded to the Mediterranean in 1656 and bombarded Porto Farina and Goletta on the coast of Tunis, to punish the dey of that Turkish principality for attacks on British shipping. In 1657 Blake's fleet won a victory over the Spaniards at Cadiz. The glory of the navy has been a peculiarly English one, and perhaps accounts for the predominance of England over Ireland and Scotland. The Scandinavians, who colonised the coasts of Ireland and Scotland, did not implant there as strong a lust for a seafaring life as they did all round maritime England, from Berwick to Penzance, and from Dungeness to Lancaster. Of course, English navigation

England's Glory in the Navy

was confined pretty much to home waters —to the shores of Scandinavia, Holland, France, Spain, and Portugal—during the Middle Ages, and the first great swoops of discovery and conquest under the early Tudors were made at the instigation of Venetian, Genoese and Portuguese pilots or captains ; just as under the later Plantagenet kings the English marine learnt much from the Flemings and the Dieppois. But by the time of Elizabeth's accession the English—equally with the Dutch—were the hardiest navigators and the boldest sea-fighters in the world.

Thenceforth, though they were not too proud to learn new methods of naval construction or of maritime warfare from Holland, Spain, France, Genoa, or from the Algerine pirates, the English needed no one to show them the way into strange seas, nor, in the long run, could any other navy prevail against them. They fought and beat the Portuguese off the coasts of Africa, India, and the Persian Gulf ; they withstood the mighty ships of Spain in English and Irish waters, off the coasts of Spain and of the Mediterranean, in the Gulf of Mexico and the Caribbean Sea along the Pacific coasts of South America, amid the Spice Islands, and the archipelago of the Philippines. They won final victories over the Dutch at the close of the seventeenth and eighteenth centuries—since when, for unexplained causes, Holland has ceased to be a first-class naval power—and closed their chequered but generally successful duel with the French Navy by the battle of Trafalgar.

The Naval Triumphs of England

America fought with equal valour and address, but with infinitely smaller resources, in the war of 1812–1814, and since then, happily, has been at peace with us. Turkey received an occasional drubbing in the Eastern Mediterranean or the Red Sea between the seventeenth and the early nineteenth centuries. The Barbary rovers were finally settled by Lord Exmouth's bombardment of Algiers in 1816. Since 1806 Great Britain has held the world's championship on the open sea. And the glory till that date lay chiefly, though not entirely, with men of English birth.

In 1692, Admiral Russell defeated the French in a great naval battle off La Hogue, and thus baulked a most serious attempt on the part of Louis XIV. to restore the Stuart dynasty under conditions which would have materially crippled the British

Empire beyond the seas. The British Navy co-operated with an Anglo-German force in the capture of Gibraltar in 1704. In 1718, as a consequence of the War of the Spanish Succession and the disputes over Italy, Sir George Byng fought a successful battle which practically destroyed the Spanish fleet off the coast of Sicily.

In 1747 Admiral (Lord) Anson, Commodore Fox, and Admiral (Lord) Hawke, inflicted tremendous naval defeats and losses on the French Navy between Cape Finisterre and Belle Ile, thus cutting off France from intervention in the West Indies and North America. In the war of 1756–63, the British Navy accomplished many noteworthy feats which atoned for the feebleness displayed by Admiral Byng over the relief of Minorca. It prevented all chance of reinforcing Montcalm in Canada, or Lally in India. Lord Hawke in 1759 destroyed the main portion of the French fleet off the mouth of the Vilaine on the coast of Brittany. In 1762, Lord Albemarle and Admiral Pocock led a naval force which attacked and captured Havana, and practically the whole island of Cuba; in the **The Navy in the War with America** same year Admiral Cornish and Sir William Draper, sailing from Madras, achieved the same result with Manila and the Philippines. Both these expeditions enriched the war-chest of the British Government with several million sterling.

The luckless War of American Independence was, in its earlier stages, marked by singular ill-success on the part of the British Navy, which proved unequal to the task of preventing the transport of large bodies of French troops to America, and failed to beat or evade the French, or to seize the Cape of Good Hope as a return blow to the Dutch for joining the coalition. But, in 1781, Admiral Parker, in the battle of the Dogger Bank, administered such a severe punishment to the Dutch fleet as disabled it for the remainder of the war.

In 1782, Rodney defeated the Comte de Grasse off Dominica, in the West Indies, and thus checked the very serious depredations which the French were making on British possessions and commerce in that quarter. Nevertheless, this period of the eighteenth century (1775–1785) witnessed the greatest ascendancy of French sea power. The British naval supremacy was never so seriously threatened as between 1770 and 1892. Lord Howe's victory off Ushant on the " Glorious First of June,"

1794, upset the plans of the French Republic for the invasion of maltreated, disaffected Ireland. In the battle of Camperdown, in 1797, Admiral Duncan destroyed the efficiency of the Dutch fleet, which was then under French orders, and in the same year Admiral Jervis rendered a similar service in regard to the naval force of Spain off **The British Navy's Checks to Napoleon** Cape St. Vincent. The year 1798 saw Nelson's marvellous victory over the French battleships and transports at Aboukir Bay, a defeat which hopelessly crippled the French plans for the permanent conquest of Egypt. A detachment of the British Fleet under Sir Sydney Smith, by its watchfulness along the Syrian coast and its defence of Acre, rendered impossible what otherwise might have still taken place—a conquest by Napoleon of the empire of the Nearer East. Similarly, the naval action of the British off Valetta made it possible for the Maltese to expel the French from their island. The same force prevented Napoleon's soldiers from capturing Sicily and Sardinia.

Calder's victory over Villeneuve off Cape Finisterre in the late summer of 1805, followed by Nelson's never-to-be-forgotten achievement of Trafalgar—when the naval strength of Spain and France was ruined till the close of the Napoleonic wars—fitly closes this amazing record of victories with a crowning grace so splendid, so complete, that for one hundred and four years no sea Power or group of Powers has thought it wise to challenge our supremacy. To Nelson, more than to any other hero on the roll of fame, the British owe the extent, the stability, the wealth, and the happiness of their empire.

Since 1805, the British Fleet has fought no action of vital importance, and has, consequently, no striking victory to record over the Great Powers of the world. If the navy has had no chance to add to its laurels since 1814, except in the bombard- **Britain's Fleet the Mainstay of the Empire** ment of Russian forts in the Baltic, the interference with Turkish and Egyptian squadrons over questions of Greek and Egyptian independence, the chastisement of Arab, Malay, Chinese and negro slave-traders, and the capture of piratical South American warships; its existence and readiness for action have been the chief mainstay of the imperial forces. Without this overwhelming fleet we could never have restrained France from fresh descents on

FLAGSHIP OF THE ENGLISH FLEET AT THE TIME OF THE SPANISH ARMADA

WARSHIPS OF THE TIME OF QUEEN ELIZABETH

THE ROYAL PRINCE: A WARSHIP OF THE TIME OF JAMES I.

BRITISH SHIPS OF WAR IN THE TIMES OF ELIZABETH AND JAMES I.

THE ROYAL GEORGE: TIME OF GEORGE II.   18TH CENTURY MAN-OF-WAR

H.M.S. AGAMEMNON, THE FIRST SCREW BATTLESHIP OF THE BRITISH NAVY

FAMOUS FIGHTING SHIPS, WITH THE VICTORY IN RIGHT FOREGROUND, OFF SPITHEAD

BATTLESHIPS OF THE GEORGIAN AND EARLY VICTORIAN PERIODS

Egypt and Syria in the middle of the nineteenth century, Russia from occupying Constantinople or Peking, Germany from armed intervention in South Africa, Portugal from annexing Nyassaland, or Turkey from resuming her sway in Egypt or absorbing the Imamate of Oman. But, as before stated, it has always been behind

Checking the Algerine Pirates our land forces to ensure their victory sooner or later. Nevertheless, in this record of achievements mention might be made of the various actions of the navy in the building up of the empire since 1815. In 1816, when the anxiety of the Napoleonic struggle was at an end, it was decided to put a stop once and for all to the insolence of the Algerine pirates.

Since Blake's appearance in the Mediterranean, they had been chary of interference with British shipping, but they still interfered with the Maltese and the Ionian Islands, and continued their piracies along the coast of Naples, Sicily, and Sardinia. Thousands of wretched Maltese, Greeks, and Italians were life-long slaves of the Turkish rulers of Tripoli, Tunis, Bona, and Algiers. Lord Exmouth was proceeding to attack Algiers, after freeing the Christian slaves of Tunis and Tripoli without recourse to force, when he was joined by a small but efficient Dutch fleet under Admiral van Capellen. Together the British and Dutch smashed the fortifications of Algiers, and destroyed the dey's warships, besides exacting ample reparation for past injuries.

In 1827 the British, French and Russian Fleets destroyed the Turco-Egyptian war navy under the Egyptian Ibrahim Pasha in the Bay of Navarino or Pylus, southwest coast of Greece, with a view to establishing the independence of Greece. Then ensued a long spell of peace on the seas, scarcely broken, if at all, by the police duties of the British Navy on the West Coast of Africa—where steam vessels

Britain's Naval Wars with China were first employed in 1827— the Malay archipelago, the West Indies and the Pacific. In 1840, the British Fleet in the Mediterranean bombarded and captured that Acre which Napoleon could not take ; but this was when Britain was endeavouring to force Mehemet Ali, the viceroy of Egypt and vicarious conqueror of Syria, back into his subjection to the Porte. During the first conflict with China, British naval forces occupied the Chusan

archipelago and Hong Kong, destroyed the Bogue forts which protected the entrance to the Canton River, and eventually enabled British land forces to occupy Canton, Amoy, Shanghai and other coast towns. In the second Chinese War, the navy again occupied Canton after a bombardment. It also co-operated in the attempt to force the river access to Peking in 1859–1860, and in suppressing the Boxer revolt in 1899–1900.

The navy, in 1863 and 1864, conducted to a successful issue our only armed conflict with Japan. The dangerous Malay pirates of Borneo and the China Sea were dealt with between 1840 and 1857. A naval expedition, under Admiral Sir William Hewett, cleared out the pirates of the Congo estuary in 1875. Piracy in the Persian Gulf has also been suppressed by the patrolling of British war-vessels.

From 1826 until 1885 a detachment of our navy watched the east and west coasts of Africa to suppress the slave trade. A heavy toll of deaths from fever and climatic causes has been exacted from the west coast service, while on the

Suppression of the Slave Trade east not a few lives have been lost in the attempts to board, inspect, or capture Arab slave-daus. Occasionally, on the west coast, the measures taken to stop the sale and export of slaves have risen to the importance of small wars. Thus, the roadstead of Dahomeh was blockaded for seven years from 1876 to 1883. Lagos, a great slave-trading stronghold, was bombarded in 1851. Out of opposition to the slave raiding and trading, which were ruining interior Africa, arose the desire to combine a practical, honest commerce with philanthropic police work. It was, therefore, attempted in 1841, and later, in 1856–9, to open up the Lower Niger and Benue. In the first of these expeditions the Royal Navy and naval officers played a considerable part, while the second was also under naval supervision.

Gradually the navy, conjoined with a consular service, came to police the whole Niger Delta and the Kamerun. This state of affairs grew in the latter part of the nineteenth century into the British protectorate of Southern Nigeria. Before this protectorate possessed a properly organised police force, British war vessels inflicted salutary punishment on the eagerly commercial but very bloodthirsty negroes of the Niger Delta. There were naval expeditions to deal with the turbulent people of Opobo (1887–1892), the cannibals of Brass (1895), while an expedition mainly naval, conducted with remarkable skill, under circumstances of the acutest difficulty, put an end for ever to the blood-stained rule of Benin (1897). Gunboats and naval detachments have also maintained or restored order on the Gambia and up the Sierra Leone rivers.

In Eastern Africa the navy has played a considerable part in the operations (1891–1895) against the slave-trading Arabs and Yaos of Nyassaland. Zanzibar was bombarded in 1896 when the reactionary party among the Arabs wished to place on the throne a candidate who was not the recognised heir. Earlier than this, in 1895, a naval expedition succeeded after an exceedingly tough fight under difficulties of swamp, forest and scrub, and native ferocity—resembling the expedition to Benin—in conquering the little independent Swahili sultanate of Vitu, which had so long defied attack from Muscat or Zanzibar Arabs, Germans or British. Our navy during the whole nineteenth **The Navy's** century has policed the Red **Services** Sea, the Gulf of Aden, and the **to the State** adjoining coasts of Somaliland and Southern Arabia, administering chastisement, when they could be got at, to Arab sheikhs and Somali tribes. It has more than once intervened to maintain the Imam of Muscat on the shaky throne of Oman.

Its services during the Egyptian War of 1882 were mainly the bombardment of Alexandria and the control of the Suez Canal. It contributed a contingent to the Gordon relief expedition of 1884–1885, and intervened effectually to prevent the Dervishes from capturing Swuakin.

In the New World, since 1814, 'its services to the empire have been mainly limited to supporting the civil arm at times of ebullition and threatened revolt among the negro population of the West Indies and British Guiana ; or to exacting reparation for injuries to British commerce or British subjects on the part of the impulsive governments of Central America. Off the south Peruvian coast, H.M.S. Shah, of the British Navy, in 1877, pursued and sank the rebel gunboat of Peru, the Huascar, which had turned pirate on a large scale.

In Oceania the navy has never yet fought a great battle, but for a hundred years and more it has maintained a police of ever increasing vigilance among the many Pacific and Papuan islands under independent chiefs or British protection. It has, since 1870, protected the South Sea Islanders against unscrupulous Europeans or has chastised them for unprovoked acts of aggression against each other or against the white man. Lastly, **Science** in that nobler war, the fight **and** against ignorance, that struggle **the Navy** for the disinterested gains of pure science, the British Navy has for the last 150 years played a notable part. In 1768, Captain James Cook sailed for the Pacific in H.M.S. Endeavour (only 370 tons), in command of a scientific expedition to observe the transit of Venus across the sun's disc. The astronomical observations were completed at Tahiti, and Cook then directed his course for the scarcely known southern continent, rediscovering New Zealand on the way. The botanists and zoologists on board his ship had the privilege of first collecting and bringing back for the enlightenment of European science specimens of the extraordinary fauna and flora of Australia.

In 1773, the first directly naval expedition sailed from England for the Arctic regions, though seamen in the service of the Crown had figured much earlier in this field of research. Captain Phipps, R.N., procceeded as far north as 80° 48′ N. Lat., with the ships Racehorse and Carcass, beyond Spitzbergen. Since then the share of the British Navy in Arctic discovery has been so gigantic as to be impossible of description in a few sentences.

Among many great names on the roll of Arctic exploration may be mentioned Sir John Franklin, Sir John Ross, Sir Edward Parry, Sir George Back, Admiral F. W. Beechey, Sir Leopold McClintock, Sir R. J. McClure, Captain Austin, Sir R. Collinson, Sir Edward Belcher, Sir Albert Markham, Sir Clements Markham, and Sir George Nares—all of the Royal **Explorers** Navy, in one category or **in the** another. Between them, and **Royal Navy** with the valuable assistance of the Hudson's Bay Company, served by such men as Hearne, Mackenzie, Simpson, Dr. Rae, and Sir John Richardson, they laid down on the world's charts the greater part of the coast-line of North America and its huge annectant islands between Bering's Straits and the coast of Labrador. The Antarctic regions were first explored by Captain James Cook,

HISTORIC TYPES OF THE SCOTS GREYS, THE OLDEST CAVALRY REGIMENT

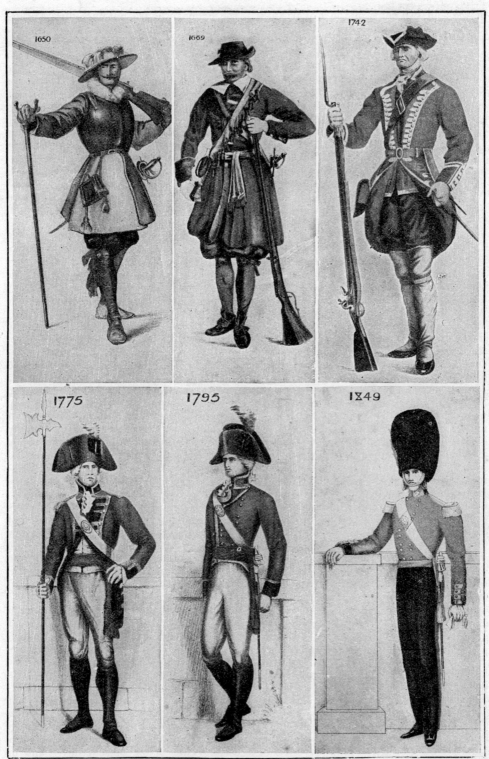

HISTORIC TYPES OF THE COLDSTREAM GUARDS, ONE OF THE OLDEST REGIMENTS

in 1773, in two ships of the Royal Navy, H.M.S. Resolution and Adventure. Captain James Ross commanded the greatest naval expedition directed towards the South Pole, that of 1839–1843. And the last explorations of these regions—English and Scottish, 1903–1904, 1908–1909—have been conducted by officers of the Royal Navy

The Historic Voyage of H.M.S. Beagle

(Captain Scott and Lieutenant Shackleton). In 1821–1822, Lieutenant Beechey, R.N., surveyed the coasts and ruins of the Cyrenaica, then, as now, one of the least known parts of Africa. A landmark in the history of human knowledge will always be the voyage of H.M.S. Beagle, in 1831–1836, with Darwin as surgeon and naturalist. Captain W. F. Owen's great surveying voyages (1822-1827) all round the continent of Africa and Madagascar were truly remarkable in their enormous additions to geographical knowledge. For the first time in history, Africa was correctly outlined in detail in almost all the intricacies of its coasts ; in the depths or shallowness, the rocks, shoals, sandbanks, deep channels, and creeks of its harbours, estuaries, river-mouths, bays, gulfs, and lagoons.

Owen's voyage was the forerunner of a general survey of the whole world of waters by the British Navy. There is not a mile of coast in the known continents and islands of both hemispheres which has not, at some time or other, been surveyed and sounded by a British ship. The charts of the Hydrographical department of the British Admiralty are in use all over the world as works of standard reference.

The four years' scientific researches carried on by the staff and crew of H.M.S. Challenger (1872–1876) were epoch-making in their results. All the great oceans were examined as to their depths, currents, temperatures, fauna (especially the living creatures of profound depths), and the conformation of their floors ; the formation

The Navy in Scientific Research

of coral islands was examined ; the action of the sun's rays on sea water was studied ; nor was the ethnology of the Pacific Islands overlooked, and the ornithology—the petrels, gulls, and pelicans—of the ocean wastes, or of oceanic rocks and atolls.

The Imperial army in its personnel and recruitment has not always been as English or as British as the navy. For example, the Foreign Legion recruited by the British Government for service during the Crimean War—not including Turkish irregulars, Bashi-Bazouks—amounted to 16,559 soldiers—German, nearly 10,000, Swiss, and Italians. Until the close of the Crimean War the British Government did not hesitate to fight its land battles by means of foreign mercenaries. Plantagenet kings accomplished much of their conquests of England, Wales, Ireland, and of Scotland with French, Gascon, Flemish, Burgundian troops ; though Henry VIII. was all English in his armed force. Mary I. employed Flemings and Spaniards abroad. Elizabeth more than once relied entirely on English valour for her incursions into the Netherlands and the American-Spanish dominions, and also for her ruthless and destructive conquest of Ireland. James I. supported his colonial seizures with English soldiers, a large proportion of whom were what we should now call convicts.

But in the times of the Stuarts—the early Stuarts especially—feudal instincts were still alive. Great nobles were still, to some extent, the rulers of shires or of smaller districts. When James I. or

Birth of a National Army

Charles I. "sold" or bestowed or chartered any West India island or North American state to an English earl, baron, or marquess, that nobleman in person or by deputy would proceed to arm and equip a number of lusty and adventurous young men from among his tenantry or hangers-on—Irish, as well as English and Welsh—and these became the first fighting force against interlopers, against Caribs, Arawaks, Mohawks, or Choctaws. Courtiers and peers who were financially interested in the East India Company furnished likewise the few fighting men, not actually sailors, who were required for the defence of the company's small forts, to defend which, later, large native armies of sepoys and Eurasians were employed.

It was really not till the struggle between king and parliament during the middle of the seventeenth century that the English national army came into being ; and this growth was to some extent checked after the Restoration. But under Charles II. two of the regiments of Lifeguards (Coldstreams—the Coldstreams were the last vestige of Cromwell's and Monk's standing army—and 1st Lifeguards) began, which have been extended and continued as a corps d'élite to the present day ; and in this reign the first regiments for foreign service, the 1st and 2nd Tangier Regiments, cavalry and infantry, "Kirke's Lambs," nowadays known as the 1st Dragoon Guards and the Queen's, or Royal West Surrey Regiment, were recruited, at first mainly from amongst the rascaldom of London and Dublin. William III. employed a large number of Dutch and Danish soldiers in his fight for the British Crown, and for some time after his coronation kept his Dutch Guards in London. In fact, he really conquered Ireland—and thereby retained England—with foreign soldiers.

George I. and George II. brought German regular soldiers to England, and, although these were eventually sent back to Hanover, the principle of recruiting German, mainly West German, mercenaries for service as, and with, the British Army abroad continued until 1857, having commenced under Queen Anne. To these German legions, their most faithful, uncomplaining service, their unswerving loyalty and unstinted bravery, the British Empire owes much. As elsewhere related, they became in many individual instances **Military Training under the Tudors** the salt of our early colonial efforts in America, South Africa, and Australia. There was no standing or professional army in England for home or foreign service until the middle of the seventeenth century. There was a militia, and in feudal days and under the Tudors nearly all the vigorous males of the community of all ranks of life were trained to arms of some kind instead of wasting their time on fruitless athletic sports, the survival in some cases of actual crude efforts to attack or defend. The serfs, peasantry, and mechanics learnt to use the bow, wield the pike, sling the stone, discharge the rude musket. They were the infantry. The gentry, successors of the knights, were the cavalry, who wielded sword or battle-axe.

This cavalry came in time to include the enfranchised yeomanry, "the upper middle class" of to-day. When a war, internecine or foreign, was toward, the king called on his barons, and they in their turn on the lesser authorities below them, to furnish from out of their serfs or tenantry the requisite number of "men-at-arms." And thus an army was gathered together. But it was less easy to do this for foreign service. Men would have come forward readily enough to fight within a few days' or even weeks' march of their own homes;

but when it came to embarking on board ship to leave for foreign parts, desertions were numerous among the militia. Moreover, the period during which feudal service could be claimed was limited, so that the English kings who carried on war in France were obliged by degrees to pay the soldiers whom they engaged to accompany them. Edward III. **First Standing Army in England** landed an army near Calais in 1346 which consisted of about 25,000 English, 4,450 Welsh, and 1,100 Irish. Their daily pay ranged from 6s. 8d. for the officers of highest rank to 3d. for the English soldiers. The Welsh, being less skilled in archery, received only 2d. a day. This was the force which won the battle of Crécy.

But, except for companies of archers, halberdiers, and showy men-at-arms, who formed part of the sovereign's household and were a guard about the palace, there was no standing army in England until the time of Cromwell's protectorship. Then there was a public force of 80,000 men.

When Charles II. came to the throne this had become in the main the army under Monk which practically suppressed the Rump Parliament and gave the throne to Charles. Nevertheless, the king made haste to disband it, only retaining out of all this force the Coldstream regiment, which became the Coldstream Guards, the oldest regiment in the British Army. He also received back to English service the Scottish soldiers who had migrated abroad after the downfall of Charles I.

After Charles II.'s marriage, however, it became necessary to raise a limited body of troops for the occupation and garrisoning of Bombay and Tangier. Men were recruited, therefore, from the wilder and more reckless remainder of Cromwell's army to form the Bombay Fusiliers—afterwards known as the 103rd Regiment—the first regular troops of the Crown maintained in India, and the two Tangier regi-**The Army of Charles II.** ments—one of cavalry (the 1st Royal Dragoons of to-day) and the other infantry (Queen Catherine's Regiment, afterwards the Queen's or the Royal West Surrey). When Tangier was restored to the Moors these regiments were brought to England, and formed part of the regular standing army, which at the end of Charles II.'s reign amounted to a total of 16,500 men. James II. raised this figure to 20,000. Much of this army went over to William III. after his landing, but for a long time he preferred to surround his person with Danish or Dutch soldiers, whose fidelity he could trust, and Ireland was conquered by him in 1689 by an army composed of Dutch, Danish, and English regiments, besides contingents from the Ulster Irish. Twenty British regiments

How the Army has Grown accompanied Marlborough to Flanders on the outset of his marvellous campaigns, campaigns which won us colonies and the outlines of empires as their ultimate results. In 1689 William succeeded in getting the Mutiny Act passed, which, renewed every year, makes the maintenance of a standing army legal, and subjects it, through its finance, to the constitutional control of the House of Commons.

Under Anne increasing bodies of regular soldiers were sent out to defend the American colonies and West Indies. By 1713 the British Colonial Army in America amounted to 11,000 men. The Home Army at this period was about 70,000 of all arms. After the Peace of Utrecht this force was disbanded, all but about 8,000, to which George I. added some regiments of German Guards.

In 1759 the 39th Regiment was raised and sent out to India to assist Clive and the forces of the East India Company. In 1793 the Home Army on a peace footing was only 17,013 men. In 1803, on a war footing, it had risen to 120,000 regulars,

78,000 militia, and 347,000 volunteers. In 1822 the standing army, home and foreign service, was only 72,000 in strength. By 1866 this total had risen to 203,500. At the present day the regular army of the United Kingdom consists of about 252,400 officers and men, of whom some 20,000 are non-combatants. Of this total about 126,000 are stationed in India (which has 80,000), and in the crown colonies, protectorates, and in South Africa.

Since the Crimean War, where European soldiery has been necessary to the situation our troops have been recruited mainly in England, Scotland, Wales and Ireland, Man and Channel Islands, Malta, Canada, Australia, and South Africa. Slowly, unwillingly, the truth is being realised that before long we must, in the United Kingdom and in all its white daughter-nations, submit to the yoke of universal, compulsory military service if we are to hold together the empire we won

The Prospect of Conscription mainly with mercenaries. As a nation we English have always disliked extremely the idea of state Socialism. Individualism has in all things been our guiding principle. So we have rebelled at all effective arrangements of militia, volunteers, and citizen armies. But by one expedient after another, cautious statesmen are bringing us nearer and nearer to the option of conscription or abdication as a ruling power beyond the limits of the United Kingdom.

A DETACHMENT OF CANADIAN NORTH-WEST MOUNTED POLICE

OUTPOSTS of EMPIRE

Being a series of photographs taken in widely distant parts of the British Empire, selected for the purpose of illustrating the diversity of the countries and climes over which the British flag is flying.

ST. JOHN'S, THE CAPITAL OF NEWFOUNDLAND

GENERAL VIEW OF VICTORIA, BRITISH COLUMBIA

5537

GENERAL VIEW OF ST. HELENA, SHOWING LADDER HILL ON THE RIGHT

VIEW OF PORT LOUIS, IN THE ISLAND OF MAURITIUS

IN THE SEYCHELLES: SCENE IN THE ISLAND OF MAHÉ

BRITISH ISLANDS IN THE ATLANTIC AND PACIFIC OCEANS

TOWN AND PORT OF ST. GEORGE'S. IN THE BERMUDAS

PUBLIC BUILDINGS AT BRIDGETOWN, IN BARBADOS

SCENES IN BRITISH ISLANDS OF THE WEST ATLANTIC

CHRISTMAS ISLAND, SHOWING THREE OF THE TEN EUROPEAN RESIDENTS

CAPE BATHURST IN THE PARRY ISLANDS OF THE ARCTIC OCEAN

WHANGAWA BAY IN THE CHATHAM ISLANDS

BRITISH TERRITORY IN THE FAR NORTH AND SOUTH

GENERAL VIEW OF HONG KONG AS SEEN FROM BOWEN ROAD

BHOTI ENCAMPMENT IN THE FARTHEST NORTH-WEST OF INDIA

SEA-COAST AND MOUNTAIN OUTPOSTS OF THE FAR EAST

ASCENSION ISLAND, WHICH IS "RATED" AS A BRITISH MAN-OF-WAR

TRISTAN D'ACUNHA: "EDINBURGH," THE ONLY SETTLEMENT ON THE ISLAND

PITCAIRN ISLAND, INHABITED BY DESCENDANTS OF MUTINEERS OF THE BOUNTY

LONELY ISLANDS OF THE OCEAN WHERE THE BRITISH FLAG FLIES

BAFFiN'S BAY, SHOWING NORTHERNMOST INHABITED HOUSE IN AMERICA

ALBERT HARBOUR, ALBERT LAND, IN THE ARCTIC REGIONS

POINTS OF BRITISH TERRITORY IN THE FROZEN NORTH

A TRADING STATION IN THE WESTERN SOLOMON ISLANDS

BUYING COPRA AT MARAN IN THE SOLOMON ISLANDS

BRITISH TRADING CENTRES IN THE SOUTH SEAS

COMPOSITION OF THE EMPIRE
THE VARIED PEOPLES UNDER THE BRITISH FLAG
THEIR CUSTOMS, LANGUAGES AND RELIGIONS

THE British Empire should be divided into two distinct sections—that which is governed from London, and that which governs itself. The first is the special appanage of Great Britain and Ireland, and the second is rapidly differentiating into a series of independent states—daughter nations—managing their own affairs, political, fiscal, commercial, with little or no concern for the requirements and interests of the metropolitan kingdom.

They are bound to us in some vaguely filial way ; bound to us mostly at present by finance, by a remarkable community of race-feeling—except possibly in those rare sections where the nationality of origin and mother tongue were different—by the use of the same language, the same irrational weights and measures, the same literature and art, the same religious beliefs and prejudices, and by the acceptance of **Britain's Vast Inner Empire** the same sovereign head. The countries of the first section, outside Great Britain, Ireland, Man, the Channel Islands, and the small Mediterranean possessions, are inhabited in the main by yellow, brown, or black men, essentially non-European in race, religion, civilisation, and languages ; those of the second section are "white men's lands," where the preponderating mass of the population is in origin of the white European stock, mainly Anglo-Keltic, and where the climate and conditions are of a nature to permit of the white man raising a vigorous progeny, which shall become the real indigenes of the land.

The first section—the Inner Empire—includes, outside Great Britain, Ireland, Man, and the Channel Islands, Gibraltar, Malta, and Cyprus; the control of Egypt, and the protectorate over the Anglo-Egyptian Sudan ; the Crown colony of the Gambia, the Crown colony and protectorate of Sierra Leone, the Gold Coast Colony, Lagos, and Southern Nigeria, the vast territories of Northern Nigeria ; the South Atlantic islands of Ascension, St. Helena, and Tristan d'Acunha ; British Central Africa, including Nyassaland ; the island of Mauritius and its dependencies, the Seychelles Archipelago ; the protectorates **Territories Under the British Flag** of Zanzibar, British East Africa, Uganda, and Somaliland ; the vast Empire of India, stretching from Aden and Perim at the southern entrance of the Red Sea and the large island of Socotra, off the Gulf of Aden, right across Southern Arabia to the Persian Gulf and Eastern Persia to Baluchistan, and thence through India proper to the frontiers of Siam and French Indo-China ; the island of Ceylon and the Maldive Archipelago ; the Malay Peninsula from Burma to Singapore (the Nicobar and Andaman Islands belong to India) and the northern third of Borneo ; the island and peninsulas of Hong Kong, the leasehold of Wei-hai-wei, in Northern China ; the Solomon Islands, the Fiji Archipelago, the Tonga group, and numerous other islands and islets in the Pacific. In the New World, Jamaica, the Bermudas, Bahamas, Turks, and Caicos islands ; British Honduras, the Leeward and Windward Islands, Barbados, Tobago, Trinidad, and the large colony of British Guiana ; and the Falkland Islands.

The second section, or Outer Empire, comprises, or will comprise before long, Newfoundland and the vast dominion of Canada ; the commonwealth of Australia, **Possessions in the Outer Empire** the dominion of New Zealand ; and British South Africa up to the Zambesi. The last, however, must, on the whole, be treated still as belonging to the first section. The Falkland Islands possess most of the conditions requisite to enable them to enter the category of the second section in course of time. There is no native race whose interests require to be safeguarded

2 D   28   D

by the Mother Country; the colony is now self-supporting. It is only a question of waiting till the population of this wind-swept but healthy dependency—as large as Wales, if its area includes the uninhabited South Georgia—reaches a sufficiently large number for it to be granted as complete powers of self-government as

The Future of South Africa Newfoundland. Considerable powers of self-government are already in the possession of British Guiana, Barbados, Bermudas, and Jamaica. The future of Guiana may, if the European population increases considerably, lie rather in the same direction as that of the dependencies of the second section—greater independence of its government from the strict control of the metropolis.

On the other hand, although it is certain and inevitable that British South Africa from the Cape up to the Zambesi will some day be a completely self-governing confederation of states, eventually including German South-west Africa and Portuguese South-east Africa—as independent of direct control from Great Britain as is Canada—that consummation cannot be completely effected till the position, claims, and rights of the aboriginal peoples have been settled to the satisfaction of Great Britain, their present protectress and guardian. Consequently, in some aspects, at the present day British South Africa does not altogether come within the second category of enfranchised daughter nations. She is not as yet entirely mistress of her own destinies.

It is very important that we should realise the distinction between these two categories. We are no longer directly responsible for what goes on in Canada and Newfoundland, in Australia and New Zealand, in Cape Colony, Natal, the Orange River State, and the Transvaal. On the other hand, we, the citizens of Great Britain and Ireland—ridiculously

Empire's Financial Burden enough, we allow no Imperial representation to Man and the Channel Islands—support alone the financial burden and the defence of the Inner Empire in the Mediterranean, Tropical Africa, Arabia, India, Malaya, Hong Kong, the Pacific archipelagoes, and Tropical and South America. We lay down the law, more or less, as to the fiscal and commercial policy in those regions, the relations between the different human races, legislation affecting

marriage and property, the maintenance or otherwise of a State Church. In fact, we are the complete masters of the destinies, down to the smallest detail, of the peoples dwelling within this first category of Imperial possessions. Their inhabitants have no independent diplomatic national representation in London similar to the agents-general of the daughter nations; the Crown colonies and protectorates are represented in the metropolis by the Crown Agents, a branch of the Colonial Office; the 300,000,000 of India and its dependencies are represented by the India Office; Egypt, the Egyptian Sudan, and Zanzibar by the Foreign Office. All treaties with foreign Powers affecting fiscal or commercial interests of these lands of the first category must be negotiated through London.

The United Kingdom acts practically as paymaster, as ultimate treasurer, to all the Inner Empire, except perhaps to India. Even the Budget of India must in a sense be submitted to the inspection and criticism of the India Office, because the United Kingdom is, in the eyes of the

India Under British Government world, responsible for the wisdom or unwisdom of Indian finance. India is governed by the Viceroy-in-Council, but that viceroy can at any moment be removed by the king on the advice of his responsible Ministers of the British Cabinet. The wishes and opinions of the British Government, to the veriest detail, are conveyed to the viceroy through the Secretary of State for India, who is aided by an advisory council. It is on this council that India might well be represented, not only by retired Anglo-Indian officials, the value of whose opinion is deservedly recognised, but by natives of India, representatives, more or less diplomatic, of Bengal, Burma, Haidarabad, Mysore, Rajputana, of the Parsees, the Sikhs, and the Punjab Mohammedans—a consultative body, at any rate, if not of the innermost council at present.

At the time of writing the Treasury of the United Kingdom, that is, the British taxpayer, finds annually about £800,000 in grants-in-aid to such Crown colonies and protectorates as cannot make both ends meet in balancing their revenue and expenditure. Besides this, occasional special grants out of British funds are made to such West Indian or African possessions as are temporarily overwhelmed by unlooked-for disasters—earthquakes, famines, fires, floods or droughts. Private British benevolence, directly instigated by royal or municipal authority, transmits from time to time to India almost as much money as, spread over the years, is paid by the Indian taxpayer to the British Indian Civil Service. Moreover, all these Imperial possessions within the first category can borrow money for their public purposes far more cheaply in the world's financial markets because of their connection with the United Kingdom, which not only controls such incurring of indebtedness, but stands as the eventual guarantor of the borrower.

Lastly, for both categories of empire the British people of the United Kingdom keep up a magnificent fleet and a standing army for foreign service, and a Diplomatic and Consular Corps. It is true that Australia, New Zealand, Cape Colony and Natal contribute small subsidies to the cost of the navy, but at present these subsidies are so small that they make no appreciable difference to our annual financial burden. No country outside Great **The Upkeep of the British Army** Britain and Ireland, except the Indian Empire, makes any contribution towards the cost of the army or of the Diplomatic and Consular Service. The Indian Empire pays for the 80,000 British soldiers serving in India, for the Indian Council sitting in London, and for a proportion of the cost of diplomatic and consular representation in Turkey, Persia, Siam, etc.

In the states of the first category no commissioned appointment of any importance is made except from London, and by the sovereign acting through the officers of the British Government. In the states of the second category all appointments to the public services are made by the sovereign through his local representative, as advised by the local responsible government. Therefore, although the Colonial Office and Crown Agents, the Foreign Office, India Office, War Office, Admiralty, Board of Trade, Trinity House, Office of Works, and other government departments may possess the power of filling all posts of any authority or emolument held by Europeans in India, Tropical Africa and America, Malaya, China, Ceylon, and the Mediterranean, they possess of right no such patronage over Australia, New Zealand, Canada, or South Africa. As a matter of actual fact, even in these great self-governing states the Mother Country is often invited to select the persons to be appointed to most of the higher posts in the civil service, armed forces and marine. An unwritten rule directs that in the postal service the higher officials shall be selected by St. **The Making of Colonial Appointments** Martin's-le-Grand; that great medical appointments shall be filled up on the advice of the Royal Society, the Crown Agents, the Royal College of Surgeons or Physicians, or the Army Medical Department; that the curators of museums, or of zoological or botanical gardens shall be recommended by the British Museum or Kew; judges and lawyers be selected from the British Bar; bishops and chaplains from the Anglican Church; customs controllers from the British Customs Service; commandants of police from the British Army, and port officers from the British Navy.

In this way, and in spite of local patriotism and that natural local clannishness which, unchecked, leads to the evolution of separate nationality, the veins of the empire—its principal arteries, at any rate—are kept flowing with British blood. Perhaps, however, it would be a happier simile to say that as yet a British brain directs the trunk and members of the British Empire.

The total land area under the ægis of the British Empire—including the Siamese portion of the Malay Peninsula, the British sphere in Persia and in South Arabia, also Egypt and the Egyptian Sudan—is approximately 13,138,900 square miles; without these last additions the area is 11,437,486 square miles. Of this sum about 3,140,900 square miles belong to the Inner Empire, and 9,998,000 to the outer or mainly self-governing division; 6,058,669 square miles lie within the temperate or Arctic regions, and 7,080,231 within the tropics. **Britain's Uninhabitable Territory** About 1,700,000 square miles of land in British North America are subject to such arctic conditions as at present these regions are either uninhabited, or merely maintain a few thousand Eskimo. About 150,000 square miles of British Arabia, 100,000 square miles of British India, 200,000 square miles of British South Africa, 600,000 square miles of Egypt and the Sudan, and one-third of the area of Australia—say 1,000,000 square miles—are at present uninhabitable by reason of the lack of rainfall and consequent sterility. These, however, are adverse conditions which the energy and works of man can abate, and even eventually cause to disappear. It is far more difficult, however, to grapple with the remains of the last Glacial Period—still holding North America and Northern Asia in its clutches—than to draw up the rain water of the Miocene and Pliocene, stored for ages under the surface formations of Australia, and therewith create a verdure which of itself attracts and precipitates the fickle rain. Roundly speaking, when all deductions for present uninhabitability are made, we are left with 9,400,000 square miles of land under the British flag, which at present supports a population of about 405,000,000.

British Areas and Populations

The proportion of population to area varies greatly. That of the United Kingdom (area, 121,390 square miles; population, 44,100,000) is 342·5 to the square mile; that of Malta and Gozo (area, 117 square miles; population, 206,690) is 1,766·8 to the square mile; of India, from Baluchistan to Siam (area, 1,766,517 square miles; population, about 297,000,000) is 179·5 to the square mile; of Australia (area, 3,065,120 square miles; population, 4,479,840) is only 1·3 to the square mile; of the Canadian Dominion and Newfoundland (area, 3,908,300 square miles; population, 6,216,340) is 1·6 to the square mile; of Trans-Zambesian South Africa (area, 1,091,770 square miles; population, 7,015,200) is 6·4 to the square mile; British Central Africa (Nyassaland and North-east Rhodesia: area, 150,000 square miles; population, 1,274,000) is 6·4 to the square mile.

In the West Indies it is 131 to the square mile; in Ceylon, 141; in British Malaya (less the Siamese Malay States and Borneo), 55; in Hong Kong, 1,121; Northern Nigeria, 62; Southern Nigeria, 101; Mauritius and Dependencies, 453; Zanzibar, 245; Gold Coast, 12; and New Zealand, nearly 9 (area, 104,750 square miles; population in 1906, 936,309).

Mixed Races Under British Rule

Of the total 405,000,000, 62,350,000 belong to the white or Caucasian race (say, 56,464,000 Germano-Kelt, and 5,886,000 Mediterranean, Iberian, Greek, Arab, Jew, Persian, Eurasian and Quadroon peoples); 282,000,000 to the dark Dravidio-Caucasic stock; about 14,500,000 to the Mongol type;

while there are approximately 1,213,000 Malays (including the Siamese Malay States); 4,000 Veddahs; 3,500 Negritoes (Malay Peninsula and Andaman Islands); 66,000 Black Australians; 550,000 Papuans and Melanesians; 100,000 Polynesians; 120,000 American Indians; and 15,000 Eskimo. In British America there are 1,901,000 Negroes and Negroids, and in Africa some 37,500,000. Of the African Negroes who are British subjects or under British control or supervision, about 29,000,000 are pure negro (Guinea, Sudanese, Nilotes, and Bantu); 8,500,000 are Negroid (Arab hybrids, Hamites, Somali, Gala, Fulbe, Mandingo, Hima, Creole half-castes); and 30,000 are Hottentot-Bushmen.

Under the British flag—somewhat imperfectly protected thereby in some cases—are the lowliest in development of all existing human races, and consequently the most interesting to students of anthropology—Veddahs in Ceylon, Australo-Papuans, Andaman and Malayan Negritoes, South African Bushmen, and Equatorial Pygmies. The same flag covers what we believe to be the handsomest people in the world to-day—English and Irish—who seem to have acquired by some mysterious process of transmission or of independent development the physical beauty of the old Greeks, possibly because they, like the extinct Greek type, are more purely Aryan in descent than the South and Central or extreme Northern Europeans of to-day. This physical beauty is equally shared by the men and women of Canada and New Zealand, if the ideal sought for is to be white of skin.

Types of Beauty in the Dominions

If, on the other hand, a dark skin is not held to diminish beauty of bodily form, then unquestionably in no part of the British dominions are there more handsome men, from the sculptor's point of view, than among certain types of Nilotic negro or Negroid, Bantu, or Fulbe. But amongst almost every group of negro peoples the women are still in an ugly stage of physical development. On the other hand, in North-western India may be seen some of the handsomest human beings in the world, women as well as men, if the monotony of the yellow-brown skin and the sleek black hair can be accepted in lieu of the blue-grey iris, the golden-brown hair, and ivory-white, pink-tinted skin of the better-looking types of England, Ireland and Scotland.

As regards the range of intellectual development, the British Empire can offer the same extremes as in bodily beauty or ugliness. There are Pygmies, Negritoes, or Bushmen, who barely know how to originate fire and who are still living in the age of stone implements, or the still earlier phase of the bamboo splinter, the natural club or twisted branch, the undressed stone or pebble, the fire-sharpened stake, the palm or fern-rind bow-string. There are negro peoples on the British verge of the Congo forest, or in the southern basin of the Benue, whose ideas of preparing food by cooking are mainly limited to partial putrefaction.

Cannibalism still prevails in parts of British Africa, Australasia, British Guiana; but the eating of human flesh, though repulsive to our modern ideas and extinct in England since, let us say, 500 B.C., and in Ireland since 100 A.D., is not necessarily a sign of low mental development. Nevertheless, Great Britain is the political guardian of at least a million professing cannibals at the present day. She is also the tutrix of another million Africans, per-

Britain the Guardian of Cannibals haps a few Negritoes, Australasians, and Guiana Amerindians, who are absolutely naked, knowing no more shame in lack of body-covering than the beasts of the field. Another 20,000,000 or so, in Africa, America, Malaya, Australia and Oceania, take little interest in clothes as a source of æsthetic delight, but adorn and vary the monotony of an exposed skin by the arts of cicatrisation, tattooing, plastering, rouging and dyeing. Some push the predilection for ear-rings to such an extent that the ear-lobes hang down in great loops of leather to the shoulders. Others ring the septum of the nose or insert large discs of wood or shell or ivory into the upper or lower lip. Quite 20,000,000 also think it more comely and convenient to knock out the upper or lower incisor teeth or to file the teeth to a sharp point. Nearly a hundred million stain their teeth orange-brown with betel nut. About ten million women and men in Scotland and England prefer to lose their front teeth or have them permanently blackened with premature decay sooner than appeal to the resources of modern dentistry.

A million women in the Eastern and Equatorial regions of British Africa think it womanly and becoming to live bald-pated, their heads continually shaved, while their husbands go burdened with chignons or natural perruques. Perhaps 2,000,000 or 3,000,000 men, Africans and Eastern Asiatics, affect the closely shaven skull, in close proximity, it may be, to other millions of males sworn never to clip their abundant locks, or obliged by custom to wear the yard-long hair in in-convenient, unsightly pigtails.

Customs of Different Peoples With these or other millions the beard is obligatory and sacred; with others it is scrupulously shaved or pulled out with tweezers. Some, like the old and dying generation of France, Italy, Spain, and Portugal, grow long finger-nails (Gibraltarese, Maltese, Malays and Chinese), to show, like the unconscious snobs they are, that they have never done manual labour.

Others wear their nails down to the quick. Two hundred millions at least of British Indians, British Africans and British Arabs keep their nails and hands and feet exquisitely manicured and pedicured, nails clipped and clean, toes cornless; others, like a proportion of the middle and lower classes of the metropolitan state, say 20,000,000 of English, Irish, Scottish, live all their lives long with dirty nails, filthy and deformed feet, and hands not fit to be grasped by a squeamish person.

Ninety-two millions of British subjects, or wards of the empire, practise circumcision as a religious or a mystic rite; about 1,000,000 of British Africans and some 50,000 black Australians pass beyond this harmless custom to elaborate mutilations described in works of technical anthropology.

About 10,000,000 out of the 44,000,000 population of men, women, and children in the British Isles are scrupulously clean as to their persons; about 250,000,000 are the same in India; personal cleanliness is the prevailing characteristic of the negro, of some Arabs, and of the Malays and Polynesians. It is fortunately a strong point with the Neo-British in

Foods of British Subjects Canada above all, in Australia, New Zealand, and some parts of South Africa. As regards food, 223,000,000 of Hindus, Burmese, Shans, Singhalese, and Tamils, are mainly vegetarian and subsist on sorghum, millet, and wheat flour, rice, butter, sugar, pulse of many kinds, pumpkins, melons and European vegetables, the egg plant, cucumbers, onions, coco-nuts, dates, mangoes, and other tropical fruits. A million and a half of British Chinese live

AN AFRICAN ZULU GIRL

AN ENGLISH BEAUTY

A FRENCH-CANADIAN GENTLEMAN

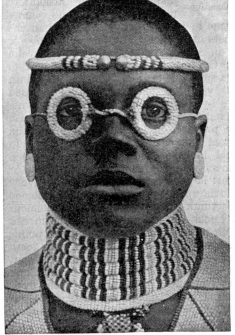

A CENTRAL AFRICAN DANDY

Photos Valentine, R. Martin, and E. N. A.

RACIAL CONTRASTS UNDER THE BRITISH FLAG

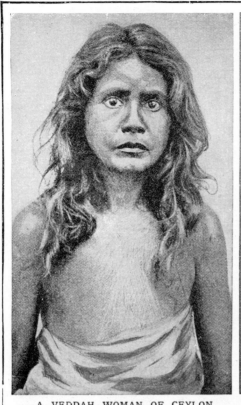

A VEDDAH WOMAN OF CEYLON   AN EGYPTIAN BEAUTY

A NUBIAN NEGRESS   SUDANESE OF UPPER NILE   WOMAN OF EASTERN SUDAN

Photo of Veddah by Drs. Fritz and Sarasin

DUSKY BEAUTY AND UGLINESS UNDER THE BRITISH FLAG

more or less omnivorously, but probably make rice the staple of their diet. The Mohammedan natives of India, the pagan and Malay natives of Eastern Asia, avoid pork if they are strict Mohammedans, but otherwise are fond of all kinds of meat and fish. The Sikhs of North-west India delight in eating pork, mutton, and goat, but share with the Hindu **Where the Ox is Sacred** the horror of touching the sacred ox. The British, Neo-British, Malays (substituting buffalo for ox), Masai, and other tribes of Equatorial East Africa, and to a certain extent the South African negroes also, are very fond of beef. Throughout the Mohammedan Mediterranean, African and Arabian regions subject to Britain, the sheep is the most common meat provider; and, of course, mutton is almost the staple of the Falkland Islands, England, Scotland, Wales, New Zealand, Australia, and parts of white South Africa. Goat's flesh is much eaten at Gibraltar, Malta, Cyprus, and throughout tropical Africa. Camel's flesh is a favourite meat in Somaliland, British Arabia, and Baluchistan.

Pork is not only eaten rapturously by the refined and lordly Sikh, but by many low-caste or pagan tribes in India. It is said even to be indulged in by the Sennaar Arabs, who have in the Eastern Sudan an indigenous type of wild boar. Wild and domesticated pigs are also eaten in the non-Mohammedan parts of North-central and West Africa. The pig, as we know, is almost the national animal of Ireland; it is a good deal favoured by the Maltese. Jambon d'York was at one time a compliment paid by the French cuisine to the pigs of the English Midlands. And, again, in the Malay Archipelago, Papua, and all the Oceanic Pacific islands, pork is the people's favourite meat. Here, also, they eat dried shark, and the hundred and one edible sea-fish of the coral-reefs and blue lagoons. Dogs **Peoples Who Feed on Dogs** are eaten in Hong Kong and Wei-hai-wei, in some of the Pacific islands, and in Equatorial Africa. The Eskimo subjects of the British Empire live on walrus and seal meat, and whale blubber; those of Tristan d'Acunha on—amongst other things—the eggs of penguins and petrels. The Indians of British Guiana will eat jaguar, if they can succeed in killing the American leopard, besides all the other wild animals of the woods. Ter-

mites (white ants), locusts, beetle-grubs, and the caterpillars of certain moths are greedily devoured by millions of negroes in British Africa from the Zambesi to Lake Tanganyika, and the Blue Nile to the Gambia.

Fish, potatoes, pork, geese, tea, milk and whisky are the principal ingredients of Irish diet; fish, mutton, milk, whisky and oatmeal the staples of the Scottish peasantry; milk, pancakes of wheaten flour, pork, potatoes, cheese, cream, whisky and cider nourish the sturdy Welsh countryfolk; bread, cheese, beer, tea, cider, beef, bacon and fish form the average sustenance of the English peasantry, a wholesome diet varied in the towns with an endless variety of tinned stuff. The Maltese live chiefly on fish, pork, goat's flesh, stirabout made of wheat or maize flour, olives and olive oil, fruit, onions, cheese and wine. The diet of the Cypriote consists of much the same as the foods of the Maltese, less pork.

The Egyptian fellahin use bread or porridge made from the flour or groats of sorghum, wheat, maize and millet as the groundwork of their daily food. They also **Varieties of Rice Foods** eat mutton, goat's flesh, pigeons, butter from buffalo and cow milk, dates, rice, vegetables of many kinds, and coarse sweet-meats made of honey or molasses, flour and olive oil. The grains and vegetables cultivated are wheat, rice, maize, sorghum and millet; pulse of several kinds, cucumbers, gourds, melons and onions. Their principal drink besides water is coffee, and for the Christians or the lax Mohammedans, arrack, a spirit made from rice, and the less heady "palm wine," the sap of the date palm.

Rice, of 250 varieties, is the staple of all coastwise India, Burma and the Malay States, also of British China. But wheat is largely grown over all North-west India; also barley (upper valley of the Ganges), sorghum or great millet everywhere below the mountains, spiked millet (pennisetum), " ragi " (eleusine), in Southern India, and paspalum and two kinds of genuine or Italian millet—panicum. There are also many oil-seeds used for food—sesamum, rape and linseed, and ten or eleven kinds of peas and beans (cicer, phaseolus, dolichos, cajanus, ervum, lathyrus and pisum). Many of these Indian grains and pulses are of ancient introduction into tropical Africa, where, with maize, they form the staple of the peoples' vegetable food. No indigenous African grain or bean is cultivated; almost the only vegetables in native dietary indigenous to that continent are the "yam" (dioscorea, also found in India), and the coco yam (colocasia), and a number of plants with edible leaves like spinach. Manioc, so much eaten in negro Africa, is the same as tapioca, and has been introduced from Brazil. Manioc is also much grown in British Malaya, and this region, with Borneo, is the home of the sago palm. The colocasia yam, really the tuber of an arum, under the name of taro, is the principal vegetable food of New Guinea and the British Pacific islands.

The citizens or the wards of the empire profess almost every known form of religious faith. There are, first of all, about 63,252,000 ostensible Christians—namely, 44,000,000 in the United Kingdom; 403,000 in Gibraltar, Malta, and Cyprus; 732,000 in Egypt and Sinai; 3,000,000 in the Indian Empire; 17,000 in China; 5,000 in Borneo; 40,000 in the Pacific islands; 920,000 in New Zealand; 4,400,000 in Australia; 1,200,000 in **Religious Faiths in the Empire** British South Africa, St. Helena, and Nyassaland; 300,000 in Uganda, East Africa, Zanzibar, Seychelles and Mauritius; 175,000 in Sierra Leone, Gold Coast, and Southern Nigeria; 6,100,000 in British North America, and about 2,000,000 in the British West Indies, Honduras, Guiana, and the Falkland Islands. Of these Christians, to quote approximate round figures only, about 11,147,616 belong to the Roman Catholic Church; 10,880,000 to the Anglican; 13,000,000 to the Free Churches—Presbyterian, 6,200,000; Baptist, 1,500,000; Methodist - Wesleyan, Congregational, Society of Friends, etc., 3,500,000—255,000 to the Orthodox Greek Church; 580,500 to the Nestorian; and 610,000 to the Coptic Church; leaving about 26,000,000 of men, women, and children undefined as to their actual sect in the Christian Church.

The British flag shelters about 290,000 Jews, of whom 196,000 dwell in the United Kingdom, 26,000 in Egypt, and 23,100 in South Africa. There are 88,000,000 Mohammedans in the British Empire and its feudatory states, mostly belonging to the Sunni division, but also including the Khojas of India, who follow the Aga Khan, a hierarchical descendant of the Old Man of the Mountain, whose adherents were the original "Assassins." The Buddhists, including the enlightened Jains of India, under the British flag number about 14,000,000. They are found chiefly in Ceylon, Bengal, Sikkim, Burma, Bhutan borders, the Northern Malay Peninsula, and Hong Kong. About **Indian Fire Worshippers** 210,200,000 natives of India, Ceylon, and Indian colonies in Africa and tropical America follow the religion of Brahma (Siva, Vishnu) in varying forms and sects. The Parsees of India, some 100,000, are still fire worshippers. A large proportion of the Polynesians and Melanesians on British Pacific islands, of Indians in the dominion of Canada, and the Caribs in British Honduras and the Windward Islands, are Christians.

Those that are not still follow vague fetishistic faiths, usually including a belief in a Supreme God of the Sky, in ancestors living again as spirits, in demigods and demons personifying natural forces and diseases, and in magic, magic being understood to be undefinable, empiric energy acting often through material means or resident in a natural object, or in one which has been shaped by man's hands. These so-called pagans really practise vague, unsuccessful religions closely akin in all their manifestations to the great stereotyped faiths of the more cultured races.

The languages of the British Empire are indeed multiform. Scarcely any great acknowledged family of human speech is unrepresented within the limits of its ægis, except the Basque, the Japanese, and the languages peculiar to the Caucasus Mountains.

Of the Aryan languages 56,810,000 in the United Kingdom, Canada, the West Indies, and British Central and South America, Australia, New Zealand, the Pacific islands, India, Mauritius, and British Africa, speak English. The living **Languages of the British Empire** Keltic tongues, Irish, Manx, Gaelic, and Welsh, are still used by about 1,811,000 people in Wales, Ireland, Scotland and Man, 1,955,000 use the French language in the Channel Islands, the Quebec, Ontario, and Manitoba provinces of Canada, in Trinidad, Mauritius, and the Seychelles, besides the large extent to which French is used in Malta and Egypt. Spanish is spoken at Gibraltar and in Trinidad. Portuguese in a rather dialectal form is much spoken by

Eurasians in parts of India and on the coast of Ceylon, also in British Guiana. Italian is a good deal employed in Malta and in Egypt ; Greek in Cyprus, Egypt, and the Egyptian Sudan. As regards the Indo-Aryan languages, Persian, with Arabic, is the language of the British sphere in South-east Persia, besides being the literary language of much of North-west India; about **India's Varied Vernaculars** 1,000,000 speak Baluchi, and 1,300,000 the Afghan or Pushtu dialect ; Sindhi is the speech of over 3,000,000 in the Sind province. The languages or dialects descended from Sanskrit, which have become the vernaculars of two-thirds of India proper are Hindi (87,240,000 people), Bengali (45,000,000), Marathi (19,000,000), Punjabi or Gurmukhi (17,000,000), Gujarati (10,500,000), Uriya (10,000,000), and Pahari or Nepalese (1,300,000), besides Kachhi (of " Cutch "), Kashmiri, Konkani (Malabar), and Singhalese, this last being spoken by nearly 2,500,000 in Ceylon.

The Uro-Altaic languages, which cover the north-eastern parts of Asia from the Baltic shores and Lapland to Bering Straits and China, and which include the outlying sub-groups of Turkish and Hungarian, are only represented in the British Empire by the much Arabised speech of the modern Turks, which is still to some extent spoken in Cyprus and—a very little—in Egypt.

The Dravidian and allied groups are wholly confined in their present range to British India, where they are spoken by about 65,000,000. The Tibeto-Burmese group of at least twenty languages furnishes the speech of something like 11,000,000 of people in Northern Nepal, Sikkim, Bhutan, Garo (part of Assam), Tipura, Naga, Manipur, and Upper and Lower Burma. Northern and Eastern Burma (the Khamti and Shan states) and the upper part of the Malay Peninsula are **Chinese Subjects of Britain** covered by the Siamo-Chinese group, which in its great Eastern branch (Chinese) is spoken by some 2,000,000 cf British subjects in the southern Malay Peninsula and Singapore, British Borneo, Hong Kong and Wei-hai-wei, to say nothing of the useful Chinese sojourners in British Columbia. The deltaic region round Rangoon and the isolated patch of Palung in Upper Burma are populated by people speaking dialects of the Mon language,

which is closely allied to the Annamese of French Indo-China. In the middle of Assam is the isolated Khasi language of uncertain affinities, spoken by about 100,000 hill people. Another isolated group is the Kolarian of Eastern and Central India, the language, in many dialects, of the Santalis, Mundaris, Savara, Kurku, etc. The Malay language is spoken by about 1,600,000 of British or British-protected peoples ; the Malayo-Polynesian languages from New Guinea to New Zealand, by 100,000 ; the Melanesian languages by another 200,000, and Papuan by 350,000.

In the heart of the Malay Peninsula there may still be lingering isolated Negrito languages ; there is certainly a Negrito speech in the Andaman Islands. A possibly Negrito dialect is still preserved by a small section, some 2,000 or 3,000, of the Veddahs of Ceylon (Rhodiyah). It would be interesting for the ethnologist to compare carefully the fragments of Negrito speech in Southernmost India, Ceylon, the Andamans, the Malay Peninsula, with the Papuan and Melanesian families, and further with what little is recorded of the **The Bantu Languages of Africa** language of the extinct Tasmanians. The diverse, but perhaps distantly interrelated, languages, in two very distinct groups, of the black Australians are spoken by about 66,000 savages and semi-savages still lingering in Australia. In British Africa we have still represented by living speakers the wonderfully interesting Bushman-Hottentot language group, so extremely unlike any other human speech of the present day by its intercalation of noisy clicks among the normal consonants and vowels. There are still, perhaps, 5,000 (British) Bushmen, and 25,000 Hottentots alive to perpetuate this primitive phonology.

The Bantu languages of Africa are spoken by about 11,000,000 negroes in British, South, Central, and Eastern Equatorial Africa ; besides a few " Semi-Bantu " of the eastern parts of British Nigeria. The languages of the Anglo-Egyptian Sudan, Uganda, and East Africa comprise the Nilotic family, about 4,300,000, ranging from the western parts of the Bahr-el-Ghazal to Masailand, near the Indian Ocean ; the unclassified Krej and Bongo groups, and heterogeneous Sudanian congeries (Niam-Niam, Mangbattu, Mundu, Madi, Lendu, Momvu, etc.). In the north-western parts of the Egyptian

Sudan is the isolated Nubian family of languages, and the Fôr and Maba of Darfur. In Northern Nigeria there are the distinct Kanuri speech of Bornu, the unclassified dialects of the lake-dwelling Buduma, the great Hausa language—spread as a trade medium from Lake Chad to the inner Gold Coast, or spoken as their native tongue by about 15,000,000 of northern Sudanian negroes, from Musgu to the south-east of Hausa, and the semi-Bantu **Dominance of the Nupe Speech** dialects, such as Ghari, of the Benue basin, north and south, down to its confluence with the Niger. The Nupe speech is the dominant language of Central Nigeria, and to the west are the Borgu dialects that are related to far-off Ashanti. In Southern Nigeria there are the languages of the Igara, Igbira, Ibo, Jekri, Ijo, and Yoruba ; and the Efik group and the semi-Bantu languages of the Cross River basin Dotted over much of British Nigeria is the Fulbe language, the range of which extends, with many gaps, for a distance of nearly 2,000 miles across Africa from the Senegal River to the borders of Wadai and Darfur.

The dialects of the Gold Coast belong in the main to four groups, the Chwi or Ashanti, the Ga (Akkra), the Mosi, and Teme. The languages of Sierra Leone are particularly interesting, and belong to the Mandingo family of Western Nigeria, and to the prefix and concord-using Temne and Bullom families. The languages of the Gambia are very little studied by a Britain which has possessed the Gambia for 200 years. They come under the Felup, Wolof, and Mandingo groups. The Libyo-Hamitic language **Speakers of Hamitic Dialects** family of North and North-east Africa is represented by such wandering Libyans of the Sahara as find their way into the dominions of the sultan of Sokoto, and by the Libyan-speaking inhabitants of the Siwah and other oases on the western outskirts of Egypt ; by the remains of Ancient Egyptian in the form of Coptic ; by the dialects of the Beja and Bishari, the Danakil and

Somali in nearly all the coast lands of the Red Sea, and all the non-Arabic-speaking tribes between Kordofan and Abyssinia ; by the closely allied Gala and the other non-Semitic Ethiopian dialects north and east of the Nilotic negro domain. Hamitic dialects are also spoken in Southern Arabia and in the island of Socotra. The Semitic languages are represented in the British domain by the Maltese language ; such Hebrew as is preserved in use by Jews in the United Kingdom, Gibraltar, and Aden ; and by the Arabic of Egypt, British Arabia, Zanzibar, and the Persian Gulf.

In British America the Eskimo language is spoken by the sparse inhabitants of the frozen shores of the Arctic Ocean between Alaska and Labrador. Of the American Indian language groups, not much more clearly interrelated than the African languages, the following are represented on British territory : The Thlinkit in the north-westernmost part of the coasts and islands of British Columbia ; the Haida of Vancouver **Languages of British America** Island and British Columbia ; the Athabascan, Tinne, or Dene of all the central and northern parts of the Canadian dominion between the Rocky Mountains and the eastern shores of Hudson's Bay ; the Algonkwin, Chippewa, or Kri, " Montagnais," of Central and Eastern Canada (using Canada in its widest sense), also in Labrador, Northern Quebec, and once in New Brunswick, Nova Scotia, and Newfoundland ; the Huron (Iroquois) of Ontario and southernmost Canada ; and the Dakota, Puan, or Siu, found still in the southern parts of Saskatchewan and Manitoba. Then there are the Maya-Kiche group on the interior borders of British Honduras ; the speech of the Caribs still lingering in a somewhat mixed type on the coast of British Honduras and in the West Indian island of Dominica and existing far more numerously in the maritime regions of British Guiana ; and the Guiana group, divided into the subgroups of Arawak, Wapiana, and Atorai.

SCENE IN BRANI, IN THE RECENTLY ACQUIRED BRITISH TERRITORY OF THE MALAY STATES

THE GUERNSEY STATES IN SESSION

HOUSE OF KEYS, ISLE OF MAN: MEETING OF THE TYNWALD COURT

MINOR PARLIAMENTS OF GREAT BRITAIN

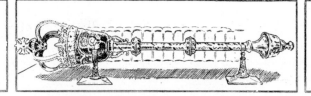

GREAT BRITAIN'S INNER EMPIRE
THE ADMINISTRATION OF THE VAST
POSSESSIONS OF THE BRITISH CROWN

IT is not necessary to delineate here the elaborate system of partially representative government in national affairs, or wholly elective administration of local provincial matters which prevails in Great Britain and Ireland. It is sufficient to point out that the Upper House in the Legislature differs from all the similar institutions in the daughter nations and colonies in that it is composed of hereditary legislators. Elsewhere the members of the Upper House, or Senate, or Legislative Council, if they are not elected by the people, are appointed for a term of years or for life by the king-emperor, or by his representative, the viceroy, or governor.

Nowhere else in the empire does this principle of hereditary legislators obtain; nowhere else would it be tolerated but in the Homeland, so tolerant of institutions which have outlived their usefulness. The Isle of Man has a Council of Public Affairs, nominated by the Crown, and a House of Keys, which is a representative assembly of twenty-four elected members. The term of sitting for this House is seven years, and the suffrage is based on a property qualification.

The island of Jersey has a lieutenant-governor and a bailiff, who is a kind of president of the legislature appointed by the Crown. The legislature consists of twelve jurats and twelve rectors of parishes elected by the people for life, and twenty-eight constables, mayors, or deputies, elected for three years. Guernsey

Independent States in the British Empire and Sark, and also Alderney, are under one lieutenant-governer, but have two separate legislatures, which consist of jurats, rectors, and sheriffs, elected indirectly, and delegates and deputies elected directly by the ratepayers. Within the far-flung net of the British Empire are a number of states practically independent as regards their home rule,

but subject to the British Government in London, directly or through the viceroy of India or the high commissioners of South Africa or of the Straits Settlements, as regards their foreign policy, and perhaps subordinated in some other

British Influence in the Sudan directions. These are: The khediviate of Egypt (area, 400,000 square miles); the petty Arab sultanates to the northeast of Aden and along the south coast of Arabia (area, about 100,000 square miles); the sultanate of Muskat and the trucial chiefs in South-east Arabia and along the Persian Gulf (area, 110,000 square miles); the British sphere in South-east Persia (area, 122,500 square miles); Baluchistan (area, 78,530 square miles); Afghanistan (area, 250,000 square miles); the sultanate of Johor (area, 9,000 square miles). Perhaps to these should be added the sultanate of Darfur, in the western part of the Egyptian Sudan, with an area of about 50,000 square miles. Afghanistan, except in regard to its foreign policy, is an absolutely independent country, and none of its statistics are included in this survey of the British Empire.

The Anglo-Egyptian Sudan is divided into thirteen provinces, the governors of which are all British officers of the Egyptian Army; the sub-governors of districts are Egyptians. The six principal judges are British; the kadis, who deal with Mohammedan law in matters of succession, marriage, and charitable endowments, are Mohammedan Egyptians or Sudanese. The governor-general over the whole of this vast area, including supervision over Darfur, is jointly appointed by the British and Egyptian Governments. He legislates by proclamation. The sultan of Darfur is practically independent in the management of the internal affairs of his country, but he is required to pay an annual tribute to the Sudan Government. The

DOUGLAS, THE BEAUTIFUL CAPITAL OF THE ISLE OF MAN   Frith

Anglo-Egyptian Sudan is entirely separate from the internationalised "capitulations" area of Egypt or other parts of the Turkish Empire; foreign consuls must be first approved by the British Government before they can receive an exequatur.

Egypt itself is still regarded as being under Turkish suzerainty. But for this theory, its native ruler, the khidewi, or khedive (Abbas Hilmi), might be regarded as an independent ruler of a country of 400,000 square. miles in area, of which only about 13,560 square miles are at present inhabited, in close and peculiar relations with Great Britain. Nominally, the khedive rules through a Ministry composed of seven members, plus a British financial adviser. But since 1883 there have been the beginnings of representative institutions. These are a legislative council—which is a consultative body, partly elected, partly nominated, qualified to pronounce opinions on the Budget and on all new laws—and the General Assembly. This last consists of the seven Ministers, the thirty legislative councillors, and forty-six popularly elected members.

The General Assembly, however, has no power to legislate, but can in a measure control all new taxation of a directly personal character or connected with land. The territories of the Persian Gulf which are within the British sphere of influence or are actual British possessions or are protectorates are : The British sphere in South-east Persia, from Bandar Abbas to Gwattar, and inland to Kerman and Birian, governed by the Shah of Persia, with British consuls at Bandar Abbas, Kerman and Malik Siah (Seistan) to watch over British interests and subjects; and, in addition, the port of Basidu on Kishm Island and the port of Jask on the Mekran coast, under the direct management of the British Indian Government; the Bahrein Islands, on the southern side of the Persian Gulf, ruled by an Arab sheikh under the control of a British political agent.

There is also the quasi-independent imamate of Oman, under a sultan, or sayyid, whose dynasty began as a sort of prince-bishopric at Muskat in the middle of the eighteenth century. Great Britain and France are mutually bound to refrain from an exclusive political control or **Britain's** annexation of the sultanate of **Kuria Muria** Muskat, but force of circum- **Islands** stances has compelled Great Britain, through the Government of India, to take the leading advisory part in the direction of the affairs of Oman. These are managed almost entirely under the advice of a British consul and political agent at Muskat. The Kuria Muria Islands, off the south coast of Oman, actually belong tc Great Britain, and their affairs are supervised from Aden. From Soham to Masirah Island, the government of Eastern Oman is carried on, more or less, by the sultan of Muskat, but the coast regions to the west as far as the Turkish frontier at Al Hasa constitute what is called Trucial Oman, a region in which the numerous **How British** petty Arab chiefs have been **Arabia** coerced by the British power **is Governed** in the Persian Gulf into an agreement not to molest each other or the sultan of Muskat. Law and order in a general way are maintained in all these regions of the Persian Gulf, and justice is administered to British subjects, by a British political resident residing at Bushire, on the south coast of Persia.

British Arabia, not connected with the geographical or political systems of the Persian Gulf, is managed by the political resident, the virtual governor and commander-in-chief, at Aden. This official depends at present on the Government of Bombay. He supervises the affairs of the Aden Protectorate and the island of Perim; those of the island of Socotra and its adjoining archipelagoes; the coast sultanates of Makalla, etc.; the Kuria Muria Islands, and the Oman coast as far east as the island of Masirah. Within

these regions of Southern Arabia there are numerous Arab sultans and sheikhs who govern their people with as little interference as possible on the part of the British, whose own direct rule does not extend over more than the island of Perim, the town and port of Aden and its hinterland, about 9,000 square miles, and the Kuria Muria Islands.

The empire of India, whose outlying spheres of influence in Persia and Arabia we have just been considering, is divided into the following types of government : There is, first of all, British India—*i.e.*, the districts actually annexed to the British Crown, with a total area of 1,097,901 square miles, and the following provinces : Bengal, Eastern Bengal and Assam, Burma, Madras, the Andamans and Nicobars, Bombay, Punjab, North-west Frontier Province, British Baluchistan, United Provinces of Agra and Oudh, Central Provinces, Berar and Coorg.

A number of small principalities within these provinces are ruled to a certain extent by their native rajahs, or by Mohammedan chiefs ; but, for the most part, this vast area is administered directly by British officials in all the principal and responsible posts, and by native officials in all the subordinate positions

THE PROCLAMATION OF LAWS ON THE TYNWALD HILL IN THE ISLE OF MAN

Then follow the feudatory states of the Indian Empire : Haidarabad (area, 82,698 square miles), ruled by the nizam ; Kashmir and Jamu (area, 80,900 square miles), ruled by a maharajah ; Baluchistan (area, 78,530 square miles), ruled by the khan of Khelat and a few small independent princes ; Jodhpur of Rajputana (area, 34,963 square miles), ruled by a maharajah; Mysore (area, 29,433 square miles), ruler, a maharajah ; Gwalior (area, 25,041 square miles), the largest Mahratta state, under a maharajah (Sindhia) ; Bikanir, a Rajputana state (area, 23,311 square miles), under a maharajah ; Jaisalmir and Jaipur, both Rajput states (respectively, 16,062 and 15,579 square miles), the first ruled by a mahalawal, the second by a maharajah; Bahawulpur, in the Punjab (area, 15,000 square miles), governed by a nawab.

In addition to the list of big feudatory states' with areas of 15,000 square miles and over, there is the old Mahratta state of Baroda, governed by the maharajah gaikwar, which has only an area of 8,226 square miles, but which ranks first on the list of feudatory states, and has a royal salute of twenty-one guns. There are eight minor states in Rajputana ; five in Central India (including the interesting little Mohammedan principality of Bhopal, under a female sovereign, the begum), and Indore, a Mahratta state under the maharajah Holkar ; three in the Bombay Presidency, the largest of which is Cutch, whose ruler is known as the rao ; five in the Madras Presidency, of which might be specially mentioned Travaniore, the southernmost portion of India, whose maharajah rules over 3,000,000 people ; one in the Central Province, Bastar (area, 13,000 square miles); Kuch Behar, in Bengal; Hill Tipura, on the borders of Burma ; Rampur and Garhwal, between Agra and Oudh ; four Sikh and three Rajput states in the Punjab ; and the interesting little Tibetan principality of Sikkim. In addition to this list, there are numerous small areas administered by minor princes, much on the lines of the smaller German duchies. The total area of feudatory India is 690,272 square miles.

British Rule in India

For the administration of British India there is the Viceroy, who rules despotically as the Governor-General-in-Council, subject to the orders of the king-emperor, as transmitted through the Secretary of State for India. The expenditure of the Indian revenues in India and elsewhere— that is to say, the annual Budget of the

N. P. Edwards
GENERAL VIEW OF ADEN, A STRONGLY FORTIFIED POSSESSION OF BRITAIN

VOLCANIC SCENERY AT ELPHINSTONE INLET IN THE GULF OF OMAN

The scenery of Elphinstone Inlet, of which the above is a typical example, has been described as the grandest but the most desolate in the world. The heat is so terrible that the native can live in the place only from November till March; a cable station was once established on Telegraph Island, but it was soon abandoned as some of the men died, while others went mad and the remainder fled. The rocks in the foreground are entirely red, while the sea is a brilliant blue.

Viceroy's government—is controlled by the Secretary of State and the Council of the India Office, who thus, in a manner, act as a kind of selected parliament to discuss and determine by a majority of votes how the revenues of India shall be spent. It is on this board of financial control—the India Office Council—that it has been suggested elected or selected native-born Indians should sit to represent the views of native-born Indians at head-quarters on matters of Indian finance and taxation. The Governor-General is assisted in his government of India by a council of seven members appointed by the Crown through the Secretary of State for India. These councillors hold their appointment ordinarily for five years, and constitute practically a Cabinet of Ministers to carry on the Viceroy's government. The seventh member of Council, for some reason called " extraordinary," is the British commander-in-chief over all the king-emperor's forces in the Indian Empire. He is practically Minister for War in the Viceroy's Council. The

Viceroy's Council of Seven

foreign affairs of the Indian Empire, which include dealing with the feudatory and allied states within and without the limits of the Indian Empire, are under the special superintendence of the Viceroy. One of the government members of Council takes charge of the finances of India, another of revenue and agriculture ; a third is the military member, charged more especially with army supply; a fourth supervises the Public Works, a fifth the Home Office and the Legislative, and a sixth commerce and industry. Each of the nine departments of state has a special secretary at the head of it. Including the Viceroy, there are only eight " Ministers " in the Executive Council.

There is further a Legislative Council nominated by the Viceroy, consisting of not more than sixteen members, or seventeen with the addition of the lieutenant-governor of Bengal. This Council has power, subject to certain restrictions, to make laws for all persons within British India, for all British subjects within the native states, and for all Indian subjects, or protected subjects, of the king in any part of the world. The members of this Council are nominated by the Viceroy under the provisions of Viscount Cross's Act of 1892, a clause of which makes it possible for the Viceroy to introduce the elective principle into the nomination of some or all of these legislative councillors. We have here a door already provided, by

Legislative Methods in India which the new measures of representative government will be prudently introduced into India. The Legislative Council, which includes the members of the Executive Council, holds its sittings in public, and the text of the Bills to be discussed must first be published for general information through the government " Gazette."

Further, no Bill, as a rule, is brought before the Viceroy's Legislative Council which has not first been subjected to the criticism of the several provincial governments. The wide development of the British Indian and vernacular Press ensures the fullest publicity for the text of all new measures, and the national voice of India to some extent thus reacts on its government, for there is no hole-and-corner legislation, and the Viceroy's Council, before placing any new law on the Statute Book, is well informed as to its popular reception.

Among the Viceroy's nominated council, natives of India probably predominate in numbers over the unofficial British members. Of these last there are generally representatives of commerce, of the Bar, and of railways. This supreme Legislative Council might undoubtedly be much larger —the maximum of sixteen, as it is, is not always attained ; it might include representatives of the larger feudatory states, of the principal religions, of native law, medicine, commerce, and industry. To a certain extent, also, the elective principle might be prudently and gradually introduced. Since these lines were written, Lord Morley's far-reaching measures for

Lord Morley and Indian Difficulties representative government in India have met most of these difficulties and have attempted to solve them. As regards the great provincial administrations, there are legislative councils in Bengal and the Central Provinces, in Burma, Eastern Bengal, the United Provinces of Agra and Oudh, the Punjab, Madras, and Bombay. The acts of these provincial legislative councils, on which there are invariably native members, can only deal with the matters of the province, and are subject to the sanction of the Governor-General. None of these legislatures may do more than discuss the financial statements of the supreme and local governments, and ask questions about them. They may not propose resolutions or call for any votes on the subject of finance.

The metropolitan state of Bengal, and all the other provinces of British India, are under governors, lieutenant-governors, or chief commissioners. With the exceptions only of the governors of Bombay and Madras, who are appointed by the king on the recommendation of the British Government, outside the ranks of the ordinary service, all these great executive posts are filled from the Indian Civil or Political Service. The Viceroy nominates and the Crown appoints the lieutenant-governors, and the Governor-General in council appoints the chief commissioners.

Each Indian province is divided into divisions under commissioners. These, again, are split up into districts, which form the unit of administration. At the head of each district is an executive

Divisions of Indian Provinces officer, styled " collector," " magistrate," or " deputy-commissioner," who has entire control of the district and is responsible to the governor or chief commissioner of the province. Associated with or subordinate to the collector are deputy-collectors, other magistrates, or assistants.

" The main functions of the collector-magistrate are twofold," says Sir William Hunter. " He is a fiscal officer, charged with the collection of the revenue from the land and other sources ; he is also a civil and criminal judge, both of first instance and in appeal ; he is the representative of a paternal, and not of a constitutional government. Police, gaols, education, municipalities, roads, sanitation, dispensaries, the local taxation, and the Imperial revenues of his district are to him matters of daily concern. He is expected to make himself acquainted with every phase of the social life of the natives, and with every natural aspect of the country. He should be a lawyer, an accountant, a surveyor, and a ready writer of state papers. He ought to possess no mean knowledge of agriculture, political economy, and engineering." There are at present some 260 districts in British India administered by these collector-magistrates. In some cases there is a collector and a magistrate, the two functions being occasionally separate. It is scarcely necessary to point out that these invaluable officials are drawn from the far-famed Indian Civil Service, the finest Civil Service in the world, entrance into which is no longer a matter of patronage, but through open competition.

The collector is the mainstay of the British Government in India. British valour won India in the first instance, and regained it after the mutiny; but the wise, incorruptibly just behaviour of the Civil Service, from its reconstruction in 1853–1858 to the present day, has done more than any feat of arms to retain the allegiance of the masses among the 200,000,000 of directly governed natives of India.

The people of the feudatory states are governed by their native princes in most cases, through a machinery of Ministers and councils, similar in degree to that of British India, except, of course, that the employés are all natives of India. In most cases justice between British Indians on the territories of the feudatory states is **Rights of the Native Princes** administered by the resident or agent of the Governor-General, who resides at the court of each feudatory prince, and advises the latter in such of his affairs as call for attention. No feudatory prince has the right to make peace or war, to send ambassadors to other feudatory princes or to external states, or to keep an armed force above a number agreed upon.

Moreover, no Europeans may reside at their courts without the sanction of the supreme government. Chiefs who oppress or misgovern their subjects, or who waste their revenues, or are unnecessarily absent from their states, are sharply taken to task; but in normal circumstances they are very little interfered with, and it is a matter of no dispute that at the present day several native states are as well and more cheaply governed than the parts of India under direct British government.

At the present date there are 760 towns in British India large and important enough to possess municipalities that have, under the Local Self-Government Acts of 1883–1884, been accorded an elective character. The majority of the members of committees are elected by the rate-payers. These municipal bodies have the charge of roads, water supply, drains, markets, and sanitation. They can impose taxes, enact by-laws, make improvements, and spend money; but the sanction of the provincial government is necessary before new taxes or new by-laws can be enforced. Very naturally, the vast majority of the members of these municipalities are Indians, and this experiment in self-government is being watched with **Experiment in Indian Government** great interest by those who hope, little by little, to induct the natives of India into the harmonious, capable, and honest administration of their home government. For rural tracts there are district and local boards which are in charge of roads, schools and hospitals. Gibraltar, a Crown colony, is little else than a garrison town—nearly two square miles in area—governed autocratically by a military governor and a civilian colonial secretary.

Malta, Gozo, and Comino are an archipelago of three islands and two islets in the Central Mediterranean (117 square miles in area; population, 206,690). The governor, always a military officer, is assisted by a lieutenant-governor (civilian), an executive council, and a council of government consisting of eleven official members, including the governor, and eight elected members. The governor has a right in case of necessity to legislate by order-in-council.

Cyprus is still theoretically a Turkish possession. By agreements concluded with the Porte between June and August, 1878, the island of Cyprus was handed over to Great Britain to be administered entirely free from Turkish control, until Russia restored to Turkey the fortress of Kars and other parts of Armenia acquired as the results of the Russo-Turkish War of 1877–78. At the present time the island is governed by a high commissioner on the lines of a Crown colony. There is an executive council consisting of the chief secretary, the king's advocate, and the receiver-general; and a legislature **British Rule in Cyprus** of eighteen members, which, besides the above-mentioned three officials, comprises the chief medical officer, the registrar-general, the principal forest officer, and twelve elected councillors—nine Christian and three Mohammedan. The voters are all male Turkish or British subjects, or foreigners who have resided at least five years on the island and are payers of land taxes. The council may be dissolved at the high commissioner's pleasure, and cannot sit for a longer term than five years. Ceylon is administered by a governor aided by an executive council of five and a legislative council of seventeen members, comprising nine officials and eight nominated unofficial members, who represent in their personalities the Singhalese, Mohammedan, Eurasian and British elements in the population. For purposes of general administration the island is divided into nine provinces, presided over by government agents who are the equivalent of the Indian collector. These in their turn are assisted by subordinate

of Singapore and Penang, though their nomination must be confirmed by the Crown. The governor of the Straits Settlements is also high commissioner for the Federated Malay States, which fact carries his commission right up to the confines of India and Siam, and for Brunei, in Central North Borneo ; and is also consul-general for the protected countries of Sarawak and North Borneo.

The Federated Malay States—except Johor—are administered by state councils composed of the native sultan, a British resident, a secretary to the resident, and

Ellis

THE COUNCIL HALL IN THE GOVERNOR'S PALACE AT VALETTA, MALTA

British, Eurasian and native officials. The Maldive Islands, 500 miles west of Ceylon, are governed by their own hereditary sultan and a cabinet of seven ministers. They are under the general supervision of the Ceylon Government, to whom the sultan is tributary.

The Straits Settlements—Singapore, Malacca, Penang, Labuan Island, Christmas Island, and the Cocos Islands—are governed much on the lines of Ceylon by a governor, with executive and legislative councils ; except that of the unofficial members of council two may be nominated by the chambers of commerce

selected native (Malay) chiefs and Chinese notabilities. A British resident-general under the control of the high commissioner supervises the general affairs of the Malay Peninsula. The state of Johor remains outside this scheme of administration. Its sultan governs the territory of Johor through native ministers and headmen, but entrusts all his foreign relations to Great Britain. The same arrangements prevail in Sarawak, a large Borneo state ruled by an English rajah. In Brunei, the country—3,000 square miles—is governed by a British resident with the co-operation of the sultan and

A SITTING OF THE CAPE PARLIAMENT: THE LATE CECIL RHODES IS INDICATED BY A X

THE LEGISLATIVE COUNCIL OF FIJI IN SESSION

PARLIAMENTS OF BRITAIN'S OVERSEAS DOMINIONS

native ministers. British North Borneo is administered by a governor, practically appointed by the Crown, and a court of directors sitting in London. The territory is divided into ten provinces, and is administered—as in Sarawak—much on the lines of a Crown colony. In Sarawak the rajah is assisted in the work of government by a nominated council of seven members. The colony of Fiji has a governor, executive and legislative councils; but six members out of eighteen are elected by the non-native settlers, and two are native representatives nominated by the governor. The native population (Fijians)—over 90,000 in number—are accorded a large share of self-government. This is arranged for by village and district councils, meetings of chiefs, and a native regulation board, which has the governor as president and four European and thirteen native members. The native legislation of the board must receive the sanction of the legislative council before becoming law.

Governing the Fiji Islands

The Fiji Islands are divided into seventeen provinces under the control of European or native commissioners. The governor of Fiji is also high commissioner for the Western Pacific, and as such controls the native governments of Tonga (which kingdom has a legislative assembly), the New Hebrides (jointly with France), the Gilbert Islands, British Solomon Islands (area, 8,357 square miles), Santa Cruz Islands, Malden Island, etc., etc. He is also assisted by resident commissioners and deputy commissioners.

The Crown Colony of Hong Kong is administered by a governor, an executive council, and a legislative council of the usual type—eight official members and six unofficial. Of these last, four are nominated by the Crown, and one is nominated by the chamber of commerce, one by the justices of the peace. Wei-hai-wei, in North China, is administered by a commissioner, who legislates by ordinance. The territory is leased by China on an uncertain term, and includes the walled city of Wei-hai-wei and an area outside of about 283 miles. Over this last the administration is mainly carried on by native headmen under the supervision of the British commissioner. The native government of the sultanate of Zanzibar, off the east coast of Africa,

China's Lease of Wei-hai-wei

is limited to the islands of Zanzibar and Pemba, though the sultan, or sayyid, is still the theoretical sovereign over the coast strip of British East Africa. The government of Zanzibar is carried on by the sultan through a British Prime Minister and native officials, judges, etc., but under the supervision of a British agent and consul-general, who also have exclusive jurisdiction over all British subjects or foreigners not the subjects of Powers having special treaty relations with the sultan's government. The Somaliland Protectorate is administered simply by a commissioner and commander-in-chief.

British East Africa (area, 177,100 square miles) has a governor and commander-in-chief, and a lieutenant-governor ; an executive and a legislative council. This last consists of eight official members and three (nominated) unofficial. The territory is divided into seven provinces under provincial commissioners, who have twenty-six collectors under them. The Uganda Protectorate is administered by a governor and commander-in-chief, but there is at present no council. The Uganda Province and portions of the Western Province (Toro and Ankole) are under native governments, except as regards jurisdiction over non-natives of the province or British or foreign subjects. These native governments are carried on under British supervision, and the British governor alone has the power of life and death. There are five provinces. In the native kingdom of Uganda there is a native parliament, or lukiko, the deliberations of which assist the king, or "kabaka," of Uganda (at present a minor) and his ministry in their government of the kingdom of Uganda, a state of great antiquity.

Uganda's Native Parliament

The territory once called British Central Africa, north of the Zambesi, is now divided into the protectorate of Nyassaland and North-east and North-west Rhodesia. The first-named is administered by a governor and commander-in-chief, an executive and a legislative council, the latter consisting of nominated and official members whose legislation is subject to the governor's veto. This virtual colony is divided into thirteen districts under the charge of residents, first, second and third class. North-east and North-west Rhodesia are governed by administrators and magistrates in the service of the British South Africa Chartered Company. Lewanika, king of the Barotse, has still a considerable amount of autonomous power over his own subjects. North-west Rhodesia comes within the purview of the South African high commissioner; North-east Rhodesia is subject to some supervision by the governor of Nyassaland, who, by arrangement, supplies the armed force for the country's defence.

The court of appeal from the courts of Nyassaland and North-east Rhodesia lies in Zanzibar; that of North-west Rhodesian justice in Cape Town. As time goes on, North-west and Southern Rhodesia will probably take their places in the great South African Confederation, while North-east Rhodesia and Nyassaland will become once more fused under their original title of British Central Africa, and will constitute a great negro state under direct British management.

The Seychelles Archipelago is administered by a governor, and executive and a legislative council, the last consisting of nominated members, three official and three unofficial, the governor **Representative Government in Mauritius** having an original and a casting vote. The island of Mauritius has an area of 705 square miles and a population of 378,000. The government is carried on by a governor, who is assisted by an executive council composed of the commander of H.M. troops, the colonial secretary, the procureur-general, the receiver-general, the auditor-general, and two elected members of the council of government. This last is almost equivalent to a lower house of legislature.

It consists, besides the governor and eight ex-officio members, of nine members nominated by the governor and ten members elected by the people on a moderate franchise. So that the Mauritians—rapidly becoming a people of Hindu, Negro and Chinese race—possess the beginnings of a representative government. The small island dependencies of Mauritius are governed by magistrates appointed by the governor.

The Transvaal is the youngest of our self-governing colonies. It has a governor, who, in this instance, is also the high commissioner for all South Africa. He governs constitutionally through a legislative council (which is to be ultimately an elective senate) and a legislative assembly of 69 members, all freely elected by the registered voters in the 69 existing electoral divisions. The franchise is limited to "white male British subjects," and the qualification is a minimum of six months' residence in the Transvaal. The registration of voters takes place biennially. The duration of **Britain's Youngest Colony** the assembly is a maximum of five years, if not dissolved earlier by the governor on the advice of his ministers. Members of the legislature are paid a maximum of £300 annually. The languages of discussion are English and Dutch, but the language of record is English. Provision is made in the Transvaal Constitution for the safeguarding of the landed and other interests of the native negroes, which in a great measure atones for the denial to them of the franchise.

The constitution and government of the Orange River Colony resemble very closely those of the Transvaal. The number of members of the legislative assembly is at present thirty-eight, elected by registered voters. Basutoland, between the Orange State and Natal, is a great negro reservation, of which the high commissioner of South Africa is governor. The territory is governed by a resident commissioner under the direction of the high commissioner, who has exclusive jurisdiction over all persons not native Basutos. To these Europeans, Asiatics, or foreign negroes, numbering in all scarcely more than 1,000, justice is administered by seven assistant commissioners who are also magistrates. The 347,000 Basutos are ruled by their own chiefs subject to appeals to the British magistrate's court.

Natal, with which the native territories of Zululand and Amatongaland and the former Transvaal district of Vrijheid are now amalgamated, is ruled by a governor, a responsible ministry, a legislative council, and an elective legislative assembly. The members of the **The Ruling Power in Natal** legislative council are summoned to act by the governor-in-council. They sit for ten years, and at present are thirteen in number. No one can be summoned to this "senate" unless he is the proprietor of at least £500 worth of immovable property within the colony. The franchise for the election of members of the legislative assembly is limited to the male sex, is apparently granted without considerations of race or literacy, and is only qualified by the possession of immovable property of the minimum value of £50, or by paying rent for such property of at least £10 per annum, or having resided at least three years in the colony, and possessing not less than £96 income per annum. The same qualifications apply to membership of the legislature. The assembly sits for not more than four years. Members of the legislature are not paid, unless they are ministers,but receive a travelling allowance. The province of Zululand is almost entirely occupied by native negroes. Only an infinitesimal part of its area—one-thirtieth—has been taken up by non-natives. One-fifth of the area of "old" Natal is set aside as a native reserve, besides large areas that have been bought by negroes from the government.

Native Negroes in Zululand

In this and other respects the negroes of Natal seem to have been very well treated by the Colonial Government ; but the means of administering justice among them, and the extent to which their interests are represented in the Natal Parliament, seem to require improvement. The negro territory of Swaziland, on the eastern side of the Transvaal (area, 6,536 square miles ; population, 85,000 negroes, 900 whites), is governed by a resident commissioner under the direction of the high commissioner of South Africa, much on the lines of Basutoland.

Cape Colony is the premier state of South Africa, and by far the oldest self-governing colony in Africa. It has possessed representative institutions since 1853, but the present form of government through responsible ministers only dates from 1872. The system, of course, starts with a governor, who receives no less than £8,000 a year, and who rules with the advice of six ministers. There is a legislative council of twenty-six elected members, who sit for seven years, the qualification being £2,000 of immovable, or £4,000 of movable property. The house of assembly consists of 107 elected members, and lasts (unless dissolved earlier) for five years. The qualification for the exercise of the franchise for the election to both houses, and for sitting in the house of assembly, is the possession of personal property (not tribal) worth at least £75 (or salary of not less than £50

The Premier State of South Africa

per annum) and a standard of literacy—ability to write one's name and address. The suffrage is still limited to males, but no race, colour, or religious distinction is made in the distribution of the franchise.

Members of both houses are paid at the rate of £1 1s. a day, with about £60 extra for travelling expenses. Local government (divisional councils, municipalities, and village-management boards) of an elaborate and efficient type is fully developed over Cape Colony and the included district of British Bechuanaland. The Bechuanaland Protectorate stretches between the northern parts of Cape Colony and the Zambesi, with an area of 275,000 square miles, and a population of 129,000 negroes and 1,000 whites. It is governed as regards the natives by six native chiefs, the most important of whom is Khama. As regards Europeans and internal or inter-tribal affairs the administration is directed by a resident commissioner, government secretary, assistant commissioners, magistrates, etc., under the general direction of the high commissioner for South Africa. The area of Southern Rhodesia is 148,575 square miles, the European population is 14,018 ; and the native population, 639,418. The country is governed by the British South Africa Chartered Company, through an administrator, an executive council of six, and a legislative council of sixteen members. Seven members out of these sixteen are elected by registered voters on a franchise which appears to be limited to European residents. The executive and legislative councils sit for three years.

Rhodesia's Limited Franchise

All laws passed must be submitted for sanction to the high commissioner of South Africa, under whose control is placed the military police. The high commissioner is represented locally by a resident commissioner. For administration Southern Rhodesia is divided into two provinces and eight districts. Native affairs are managed (under the administrator) by a department of state and thirty-one or thirty-two native commissioners. All legislation and land questions affecting natives are especially under the supervision and control of the high commissioner.

The little island of St. Helena, in the Atlantic, is 47 square miles in area, and has a population of about 4,000. Its affairs are managed by a governor and an

A NATIVE TRIAL: SCENE IN A CONSULAR COURT
N. W. Hohn

INSPECTION OF CONVICTS AT MANDALAY GAOL IN BURMA

ADMINISTERING JUSTICE TO BRITISH SUBJECT PEOPLES

executive council. The island of Ascension is administered by a naval commandant under the Admiralty. Southern Nigeria has a governor, lieutenant-governor, and colonial secretary, an executive of seven official members, and a legislative council of ten official and four nominated unofficial members, two of whom are negroes. The

Negro Kings in Northern Nigeria colony is divided into three provinces and about twenty districts, administered by three provincial commissioners and a large number of district commissioners. Northern Nigeria is governed by a high commissioner without any executive or legislative councils. The fourteen provinces are supervised by ninety-nine residents and assistant-residents. A large amount of North Nigerian territory is directly administered, so far as natives are concerned, by negro or negroid kings and rulers.

The colony of the Gold Coast has a governor, an executive council of four, and a legislative council of five official and four unofficial nominated members, of whom one is a negro. There is a department and a secretary for native affairs, and Ashanti and the northern territories are governed—under the Gold Coast governor—by chief commissioners, provincial, and travelling commissioners.

Sierra Leone, for administrative purposes, is divided into a colony of about 4,300 square miles and a protectorate of 28,110 square miles in area. Both are under the administration of the same governor, colonial secretary, and general staff ; but as regards the colony along the coast the governor is assisted by an executive council of five members and a legislative council of five official and four unofficial nominated members, of whom two are negroes. The protectorate is divided into five districts, which are administered by district commissioners, a good deal of power over the natives being still left in the hands of the native chiefs.

Bermudas an Important Naval Base In the Gambia Colony the actual " colonial " area is only about 69 square miles, and is ruled by a governor, executive council (three members), legislative council (six official, three unofficial nominated members, one of them a negro). The protectorate—3,911 square miles—is administered by the governor through a number of travelling commissioners. The lovely little archipelago of the Bermudas was really intended by Nature

for the Sea Queen's capital and the Syrens' *pied-à-terre*. It was more than that in the realms of fancy, having been chosen by Shakespeare for the scenes of " The Tempest." Instead of this, we have turned it in the course of centuries into an important naval base on the North American station, with dockyard, victualling establishment, and coaling station.

There are 360 small islands in the group, and only about twenty square miles of habitable land, with a population of 683 whites and 11,000 blacks or half-castes. The governor over this microcosm is the officer in command of the troops, and he is assisted by an executive council of six members, a legislative assembly of nine— both these are appointed by the Crown— and a house of assembly—thirty-six members—elected by the people. The franchise is dependent on the possession of freehold property of not less than £60 value. Members of the legislature are paid eight shillings a day for attendance. Representative institutions in the Bermudas date from 1620. The constitution of Jamaica, granted in 1662, was, like that of Bermuda, more suited to a

Jamaica's Enlarged Constitution large country than a small island, though Jamaica has an area of 4,207 square miles and a population, mainly negro, of 830,261. But the ancient constitution was surrendered in 1866, and, after several changes and enlargements, now stands thus :

The governor rules with the assistance of a privy council of not more than eight in number—mostly officials—appointed by the Crown ; a legislative council of the governor, six ex-officio members, ten nominated and fourteen elected. The legislative council may not sit more than five years without being dissolved. The franchise on which these fourteen representatives, as well as the members of the parochial boards, are elected is regulated by a small property qualification, residence, rate-paying, and British nationality.

Matters of local administration in Jamaica are carried out by fifteen elected parochial boards of fifteen parishes, into which the whole island is divided. The Turks and Caicos Islands are a dependency of Jamaica, with 5,287 inhabitants, the former group being administered by a commissioner and a legislative board appointed by the Crown. The Cayman Islands are likewise administered by a commissioner under the supervision of the governor of Jamaica. The Bahama Islands have a governor, an executive council of nine, a legislative council of nine, and a representative assembly of twenty-nine members elected on a small property franchise. The total area of this group is 5,450 square miles.

The Leeward Islands—area, 701 square miles ; population, 128,000—have a governor, a federal executive council nominated by the Crown, and a federal legislature of eight nominated and eight elected members. These last are elected by the unofficial members of the local legislative councils of Antigua, Dominica, and St. Kitts-Nevis. The Leeward Islands are divided for purposes of local administration into five presidencies : the island groups of Antigua, Montserrat, St. Kitts and Nevis, Virgin, and Dominica. The three first-named and Dominica possess local executive and legislative councils, the members of which, official and unofficial, are nominated. The Virgin Islands have only an executive council. There is an administrator for St.

Advanced Government in Barbados Christopher, etc., and one for Dominica, and commissioners for Montserrat and the Virgin Islands. The Windward Islands—area, 524 square miles ; population, 175,587—have a governor, who usually resides at Grenada, an administrator for St. Lucia, and an administrator for St. Vincent. In each of the three islands there are executive and legislative councils, the members of which are nominated. In all the legislative councils there are unofficial members.

The island of Barbados has an area of only 166 square miles—a little larger than the Isle of Wight—and a population of under 200,000, but it goes far beyond any other West Indian colony in representative government. It has a governor all to itself, an executive of four members besides the governor, an executive committee partly elective, a nominated legislative council of nine members, and a house of assembly of twenty four members. The last-named are elected annually by the people on a low property franchise. The executive committee has almost the functions of a responsible ministry. The non-elective element consists of the four members of the House of Assembly appointed by the governor to serve on the executive committee.

As Barbados is exceedingly prosperous, this elaborate machinery of government is apparently worth while. Trinidad and Tobago, with an area of 1,868 square miles and a population of about 273,898, have no representative institutions. Tobago Island is simply a district of Trinidad, under a district officer. The

The Prosperous Island of Trinidad two islands are under the rule of a governor, with an executive council of six members and a legislative council consisting of the governor, ten other officials, and eleven unofficial members nominated by the governor for five years. The large and prosperous island of Trinidad is divided into sixteen counties, and these are administered by nine district officers. It is therefore entirely without representative institutions.

The colony of British Honduras, on the mainland of Central America, is administered by a governor, an executive council of five members, and a nominated legislative council of three official and five unofficial members. It is divided into six districts under district commissioners.

British Guiana, on the mainland of Northern South America, is a relatively large possession, over 90,000 square miles in area, with a population of 307,000, the largest elements in which are negroes and East Indians. The administration consists of a governor, an executive council of eight members, two ex-officio, six nominated, a Court of Policy (legislative council), and a Combined Court, which deals with finance. The Court of Policy is composed of seven official and eight elected members ; the Combined Court consists of these fifteen members of the Court of Policy (which is a purely legislative body), and, in addition, of six elected financial representatives. Thus the Combined Court comprises fourteen elected unofficial members and seven officials. The functions of this Combined Court are to

How British Guiana is Governed consider the estimate of expenditure prepared by the governor in executive council and to determine the ways and means to meet it. This court alone can levy taxes. Thus, in the possession of this Combined Court, with a preponderating unofficial majority of seven elected representatives, the voting inhabitants of British Guiana come nearest of all the British possessions in Tropical America (except Barbados) to a government of popular control. But, though there are no specific principles of race exclusion, the qualifications for membership of the legislature and the franchise for electors at present render it difficult for non-Europeans to control the country's destinies.

The qualification for election to the Guianan Court of Policy consists of (1) ownership of 80 acres of land, half of which must be under cultivation ; or (2) ownership of immovable property of a value not less than £1,562 10s. ; or (3) ownership or possession under a lease for twenty-one years and upwards of a house or house and land of the annual rental value of £250. The qualification for a financial representative is the same as for a member of the Court of Policy, with the important addition that such representative must also possess a " clear annual income of £300 arising from any kind of property not mentioned in any other property qualification, or from any profession, business, or trade carried on in the colony."

The franchise which elects these fourteen members of the legislature is either " county " or " city." Its restrictions are not very severe, being either ownership or tenancy of cultivated land or houses, or a minimum income of not less than £100 (coupled with residence), or payment of twelve months' taxes of not less than £4 3s. 4d., combined with not less than six months' residence prior to date of registration. The number of registered electors at present out of a population of 307,000 is about 3,100. Only about 130 square miles of British Guiana are under cultivation. There are two municipalities, with mayor and town council—Georgetown and New Amsterdam—and local government is further provided for by fifty-four village and country district councils.

The Falkland Islands have an area (excluding the uninhabited South Georgia, 1,000 square miles) of about 6,500 square miles, and a population of about 2,100. They are administered by a governor, an executive council of four officials, and a legislative council of three officials and two unofficials appointed by the Crown.

Before passing on to consider the statistics of other parts of British America, we might note the following points about the possessions in the West Indies and Bermudas, Honduras, and Guiana. The **Mixed Races Under the British Flag** total white population of British (mainly), Portuguese, French, and Spanish descent is 62,300. Negroes and mulattoes amount to about 1,550,000 ; natives of British India, 210,000 (chiefly in Guiana, 110,000 ; Trinidad, 87,000 ; and Jamaica, 13,000) ; Chinese, 1,500 ; aboriginal Amerindians (in British Honduras, Dominica, and Guiana, about 11,000) ; mixed races, compounded of negro, East Indian, and Amerindian, 10,000.

GENERAL VIEW OF THE NEW DOCKS AT SIMON'S BAY IN SOUTH AFRICA

PARLIAMENTS OF THE OUTER EMPIRE
CANADA AND AUSTRALIA AND THEIR ADVANCED SYSTEMS OF GOVERNMENT

THE vast Dominion of Canada (nominal area, 3,745,574 square miles, though only about 2,000,000 square miles are really habitable) is perhaps the portion of the British Empire that is most independent of Great Britain. Canada makes no contribution, direct or indirect, to the Imperial fleet or army; but she shares with us the supreme rule of the king-emperor, and admits an appeal to the Judicial Committee of the Privy Council, which is almost expunged from the Australian constitution.

The rule of the king is delegated to a Governor-General, appointed usually on the advice of the British Cabinet. But this governor, once appointed, enjoys greater independence than any other delegate of regal authority, and directs the government of Canada more like a constitutional president elected for five years than a nominee of the British Colonial Office. He is assisted by a Privy Council, chosen and nominated by himself. Representing the king, he rules with the advice of responsible ministers, through a parliament of Senate and House of Commons.

The Dominion of Canada is divided at present into nine provinces and a territory (Yukon). The unorganised remainder of the far north and east is administered through the Home Office of the Dominion Ministry. With the exception of the Yukon territory, each province has a **Government in Canadian Provinces** fully-equipped local government—lieutenant-governor, responsible ministry, elected legislature. In the case of Quebec and Nova Scotia the local parliament consists of two houses—a Legislative Council equivalent to a senate, and a Legislative Assembly. All the other provinces have a Legislative Assembly only.

The Dominion Parliament has much greater and more comprehensive powers than the Senate and Congress of the United States. The provincial legislatures deal only with direct taxation within the province, provincial loans, the management of provincial lands, provincial and municipal offices, licences, public works, education, and general civil law. They also possess concurrent legislative powers with the Dominion Parliament on questions of agriculture, quarantine, and immigration. All their Bills require the assent of the lieutenant-governor, and may be disallowed within one year by the Governor-General. The **Functions of the Dominion Parliament** Dominion Parliament deals with all questions except those specifically delegated by the constitution to the provincial legislatures, and may even negotiate commercial treaties with foreign Powers or other self-governing portions of the British Empire. But all Bills passed by the Dominion Parliament require the assent of the Governor-General, and may be disallowed by the king-emperor within two years.

The Senate consists of eighty-seven members, nominated for life by the Governor-General. Their qualifications are: (1) Having attained the age of thirty; (2) birth or residence in the province for which they are appointed; (3) the possession of at least £800 worth of property.

The members of the House of Commons need no property qualification. They must be British subjects, born or naturalised, and twenty-one years of age or upwards. A member cannot sit for both a provincial legislature and the Dominion Parliament. Members are elected by ballot on a male suffrage—suffrage has not been granted to women in Canada—which is very wide, practically manhood suffrage in Ontario, Manitoba, British Columbia, and Prince Edward's Island, Saskatchewan and Alberta; a small property limit in Quebec, Nova Scotia, and New Brunswick. Since 1898, the decision as to the suffrage for election to the

Dominion Parliament has been left to the provinces to decide according to local views. Senators and members are paid : senators, £500 per annum ; members, a maximum of £500 per session. A parliament may not last longer than five years. Local government throughout settled Canada is admirably and fully developed by rural, village, town, city, and county councils. The colony of Newfoundland, with the adjoining coast strip of Labrador, is not part of the dominion of Canada, but an independent government under a governor and responsible ministry. There is an Executive Council of nine ministers, over

term for each elected assembly is four years. The majority in each assembly elects the ministry which is to serve as the governor's executive. Local government —except for the Municipal Council of St. John's—is almost entirely directed by the ministry and government departments at headquarters (St. John's).

It is interesting to note that in differences between the Dominion Parliament and the provincial legislatures an appeal to the Judicial Committee of the Privy Council resulted in a satisfactory settlement. Appeals still lie from the Supreme Court—created in 1876—of the Canadian

THE CANADIAN HOUSE OF COMMONS IN SESSION   W. J. Topley

which the governor presides ; a Legislative Council of eighteen members, nominated for life by the Governor-in-Council ; and there is a House of Assembly of thirty-six members, elected by ballot on manhood suffrage. There is a property qualification for members of a minimum value of £500, or a yearly income of £100. A payment of £24 is made in each session to each legislative councillor, and of £40 or £60— according to distance of residence—to each member of the House of Assembly. The session seldom lasts more than three months in each year, and the maximum

Dominion to the Privy Council of the United Kingdom. If this could become and remain the final court of appeal for the whole empire it would do more than any other measure to bind us together. But our law lords, our Treasury, our national indifference to pomp and show, combine to hinder the creation of an ideal Supreme Imperial Court of Appeal out of the Judicial Committee of the Privy Council. " Such a court," said Sir Edward Clarke some time ago, " should be strong in its constitution, dignified in its ceremonial, and even splendid in its surroundings,

Kerry

THE LEGISLATIVE COUNCIL OF NEW SOUTH WALES

THE LEGISLATIVE ASSEMBLY OF VICTORIA

SCENES IN TWO OF AUSTRALIA'S HOUSES OF PARLIAMENT

so as to command the respect and touch the imagination of our brethren beyond the seas." "The Judicial Committee of the Privy Council," said a morning paper recently, "which is the final court of appeal for the citizens of the Greater Britain, is one of the curiosities of our legal system. It occupies a bare, barn-like room in Whitehall; its members drop in casually and sit around a horseshoe table in their ordinary walking clothes, and there is not a solitary symbol of the dignity one would naturally expect to see associated with a tribunal of such imperial importance and world-wide jurisdiction."

Commonwealth of Australia

The Commonwealth of Australia did not attain to completion as a unified organisation until twenty years after the Canadian Dominion, by the inclusion of the great North-west, assumed its present unity and comprehensive national force. The act creating a Commonwealth of Australia came into vigour on January 1st, 1901.

The commonwealth consists of the six states of New South Wales, Victoria, South Australia, Queensland, Tasmania, and Western Australia; the little islands of Norfolk and Lord Howe—governed by New South Wales—and the territory of Papua, administered by the commonwealth government. All the six states have governors appointed directly by the Crown—i.e., on the advice of the British Cabinet; but the lieutenant-governor of Papua is appointed by the Governor-General of the commonwealth, on the advice of his Ministers. The governors of the six states may correspond direct with the Colonial Office, but must supply the Governor-General with copies of their despatches.

The Constitution of New South Wales

The constitution of New South Wales comprises a governor and lieutenant-governor, a Legislative Council of not less than twenty-one members (actually fifty-six), appointed for life by the Crown; and a Legislative Assembly of ninety elected members. The Assembly sits for three years, unless dissolved sooner. Each of the ninety constituencies only returns one member, and each member is paid £300 a year; and, like the members of Council—who are not paid any salary in their capacity of legislative councillors—can travel free on all government railways and tramways, and send their letters postage

free. The electoral franchise is conferred on men and women alike since 1902. Every man or woman, being a natural-born or naturalised subject of his Majesty, above twenty-one years of age, having resided one year in the state, and three months in a particular electoral district, is qualified as an elector, and is entitled to one vote only. Local government in New South Wales is fully provided for through the shires and municipal councils.

In the state of Victoria there are governor, lieutenant-governor, a Cabinet or Executive Council, a Legislative Council (thirty-four in number), and a Legislative Assembly. Members of the Upper House, or Legislative Council, are elected for six years. Their qualification is the possession of an estate of the net annual minimum value of £50 for one year prior to the election. Electors of the Council must be in possession of property of the rateable value of £10, if freehold, or £15 if derived from leasehold; unless, that is, they are graduates of a British or colonial university or students of the Melbourne University, ministers of religion, certificated teachers,

Victoria's Complete Local Government

lawyers, medical practitioners, or officers of army or navy; in such case they need no property qualification for the election of senators. The members of this upper house are not paid. The Legislative Assembly, which, like most of the Australian lower houses, sits for three years only, unless dissolved earlier, is composed of sixty-five members. Neither these nor their electors require any property qualification. There are the usual provisions as to being a British or naturalised British subject. Members of the lower house are paid £300 per annum. The franchise for the election of members of the lower house is practically the same as that described for New South Wales, except that it is limited to males.

Local government in Victoria is very complete, and is carried out by means of municipal and shire councils. For election to these councils—by the ratepayers—the suffrage is extended to women. In South Australia, the Legislative Council consists of eighteen members elected on much the same terms as in Victoria, except that the members elected must be at least thirty years of age, and have resided in the state for at least three years, while the property limit of the council suffrage is slightly higher, and there is no exemption therefrom for the classes of professional men as in Victoria. This suffrage, like the others, is conferred equally upon women. The House of Assembly consists of forty-two members elected for not more than three years. Qualifications and suffrage are similar to those of Victoria, except that the suffrage is also extended to women. Members of both houses are paid a salary of £200 a year whilst they serve. Local government is carried on through thirty-two elective municipal and district councils in the settled regions. In Queensland there is apparently no lieutenant-governor. The members of

A good deal of the state is divided into shires (rural districts) and municipal areas (cities, towns)—670,255 square miles in all—and over these local government, under elected councils, is fully enforced.

Tasmania has a governor, deputy-governor, and the same type of executive and legislature as the other Australian states. There is a maximum of eighteen members in the Legislative Council. This body is elected for six years. No property qualification is necessary in either house, but there is a very small property qualification attached to the Senate franchise, though, as in Victoria, this is not asked for in the case of university or professional

THE TASMANIAN HOUSE OF ASSEMBLY IN SESSION

the Legislative Council (forty-four) are all nominated by the Crown for life, and are unpaid. The Legislative Assembly comprises seventy-two members elected for a maximum period of three years, and paid at the rate of £300 a year. There is no property qualification for the members of either legislature.

The franchise is granted to all men and women, born or naturalised British subjects, from the age of twenty-one years, after twelve months' residence in the state, provided they are not insane, have not been criminally convicted or, in the case of men, have not been guilty of wife-desertion.

men. Members of the House of Assembly (35 in number) are elected for three years, the qualification being as described for South Australia, on the usual adult (male and female) suffrage. The only persons who may not sit in the legislature of Tasmania are judges of the Supreme Court, paid officials of the Crown (except responsible ministers), or contractors to Government ; neither may any member of the local legislature here or elsewhere in Australia be at the same time a parliamentary representative in the Commonweath Parliament. The local government of Tasmania is entrusted to elected municipal and rural councils. West Australia has a governor and lieutenant-governor, a Legislative Council of thirty members, and a Legislative Assembly of fifty. The councillors are elected for six years, and the members of the Assembly for three. The qualification for a councillor is. (1) to be not less than thirty years old;

Parliamentary Qualifications in West Australia (2) a resident in the state for at least two years; (3) a British subject or five-years naturalised subject. The franchise for the upper house is conferred on persons of both sexes over twenty-one, British subjects, resident in the state six months, and possessing a freehold estate of a clear value of £100, or the usual proportionate equivalent in leasehold, rent or ratepaying.

The qualification for members of the lower house is that they should be male British subjects over twenty-one who have resided in the state for twelve months ; or, if naturalised for five years, then their residence must be at least two years. The franchise for the lower house is granted to any man or woman above twenty-one—provided they are British or naturalised subjects—when they have resided at least six months in the state, and whilst they are actually resident in the district at the time of their claim. This condition about residence at the time of claiming the vote is waived for those who have a small property qualification. As throughout the rest of Australia, no elector has more than one vote for the lower house.

Members of both houses are paid £200 a year and travel free on government railways. Local government in Western Australia is entrusted to municipal councils elected by the ratepayers, and to a number of public institutions apparently depending on the Executive or the Legislature—boards of water supply and sewerage (not a very happy conjuncture !), road boards, and local boards of health. The ad-

Where Women Enjoy the Suffrage ministration of Papua consists of a lieutenant-governor and an Executive Council of six members (officials), and a Legislative Council composed of the Executive and three unofficial members appointed by the governor.

So much for the provincial administration of Australia. It will be observed that in every state with responsible government, except Victoria, the suffrage is granted on equal terms to men and women

alike, universally on the principle of one man one vote ; that the terms of duration of the elected lower houses are invariably limited to three years, and that there is no excluding property qualification attached to either membership or suffrage for the lower houses of legislature.

The federal government of Australia consists of the king (represented by a governor-general), a Senate, and a House of Representatives. The Governor-General is assisted by an Executive Council of ministers who are, or who must become within three months, members of the Federal Parliament. There are 36 senators who are elected for six years, and receive £600 a year each, unless already holding salaried posts as ministers, or salaried officers of the house.

Members of the House of Representatives are elected for three years (unless the house is dissolved sooner), and are paid at the rate of £600 a year. There are at present 75 representatives, but the numbers fluctuate in each parliament in relation to increase or diminution of the population. The number of the senators

Australia's Federal Government may be increased or diminished in the future, but always on the lines that no original state shall have less than six senators nor more than any other original state. The qualifications for senators and representatives are identical : twenty-one years of age, to be an elector, or entitled to be ; to be resident at least three years in Australia ; to be a British subject born, or a naturalised British subject of five years' standing. The federal franchise for election in both houses is universal adult suffrage (male and female), on the usual terms—twenty-one years of age and upwards, British citizenship, and a minimum of twelve months' residence.

The Canadian legislature has been commended because it left practically no loophole for dispute as to the competency of the Federal Parliament. The subjects on which the provincial parliaments could legislate were clearly stipulated, and the Federal Parliament was empowered to deal with all else which did not infringe the prerogatives of the British Crown. In the Australian Legislature, the case is reversed. The scope of the Federal Parliament is defined in thirty nine articles, and the powers of the state governments are not otherwise limited. Disputes on the interpretation of the federal constitution will have to be referred to the new High Court of Australia, which is to be an appellate, as well as an original court. An appeal to the final decision of the Judicial Committee of the Privy Council from the decisions of the High Court, or from those of the Supreme Courts of the federal states, may only be carried out on a certificate to be granted by the High Court at its own discretion. The Federal Parliament undertakes to legislate for, and to control, the naval and military defence of Australia, its trade, taxation, public debts, loans, postal service, census, and statistics, currency, banking, marriage, divorce, old age pensions, immigration, emigration, railways, regulations dealing with insolvency and corporations, departments of state, foundation of a state capital, etc. etc.

The dominion of New Zealand has an area (including all island groups attached to its administration) of about 105,249 square miles, and a population of nearly 950,000. Its government consists of a governor and commander-in-chief, an Executive Council of Ministers, a Legislative Council of 45 members, and a House of Representatives of 80 members, including four Maories. The extreme duration of membership in the upper house is seven years; the House of Representatives sits for three years, unless previously dissolved. Members of the Council are paid £200 a year, representatives £300. Councillors are appointed by the governor, representatives are elected by the people, the qualification for the last-named being that of an elector. The franchise is granted

Maories in New Zealand's Government to all men and women of European race over twenty-one years of age who have resided at least one year in the colony and three months in the electoral district. For the election of the four Maori members every adult Maori can vote who is resident in the district for which the Maori candidate is standing.

As regards local government, this also is elective on the part of the ratepayers. The dominion is divided into municipalities and counties, road districts and town districts, river drainage, water supply boards, etc. The qualifications for electors are ratepaying, residence, or the possession of property. Municipal franchise is equally extended to women. From this purview of the forms of government in every part of the British Empire and sphere

Great Britain's Advanced Daughter Nations of influence, coupled with a knowledge of the institutions of the British Islands, it will be seen that the countries with the most modern and ideally perfect type of constitution are Australia and New Zealand; next, and only inferior because it still denies the franchise to women, is Canada. The states of South Africa are not far behind, but some of them are fettered by considerations of race questions and restricted franchise. The Mother Country is still behind the more advanced daughter nations in the solution of several social problems and the simplification of administrative machinery.

India lacks an admixture of the native element in her highest councils. Trinidad is thought by some to be too purely official in its government. Gibraltar, Northern Nigeria, Uganda, and the Egyptian Sudan are administered autocratically without executive or legislative councils. Gibraltar, of course, is little else than a garrisoned fort; in Uganda there is a highly developed representative native administration, and a good deal of Northern Nigeria is still governed in parts by native princes.

The sultan of Zanzibar governs despotically through a ministry of English and Arabs, but in constant touch with the feelings and interest of the populace; the despotism of the petty Arab sultans in Aden territory, Socotra, the Hadhramaut, Oman, and Bahrein is tempered by the advice of British residents. The rest of the inner British Empire is not without some measure of elective or popular representation in its councils, and the full measure of popular government in Barbados and the Bermudas seems to have induced quiet and prosperity.

STABROEK MARKET AND THE STELLINGS AT GEORGETOWN IN BRITISH GUIANA

IN THE ROCKIES: ELBOW RIVER VALLEY AND THE THREE SISTERS

KINCHINJUNGA, THE HIGHEST POINT OF THE NEPAL HIMALAYAS IN NORTH INDIA

THE NUWARA ELIYA MOUNTAIN IN THE ISLAND OF CEYLON

MOUNTAIN RANGES IN GREAT BRITAIN'S OVER-SEAS DOMINIONS

THE
BRITISH
EMPIRE
XII

BY SIR
HARRY
JOHNSTON,
G.C.M.G.

THE SINEWS OF EMPIRE
THE RESOURCES, EDUCATION, AND DEFENCES OF GREATER BRITAIN

THE British Empire not only includes that extraordinary diversity of human races enumerated in another chapter, but it is equally diverse in its physical geography, fauna, flora, and climates. It contains deserts such as may be found in Southern Egypt, Southern Arabia, West-central India, and Australia, wherein it may not chance to rain more than once in seven years. It includes regions of mountain and forest like Assam, where the annual rainfall is the highest known— about 300 inches per annum.

It extends to the South Pole and the North Pole, and possesses territories within the equatorial belt in Africa, Eastern Asia, and South America. It takes under its ægis the highest mountains in the world, the loftiest peaks of the Himalayas, and other such notable mountains as Ruwenzori, Elgon, Kenya, Mlanje, and the Drakensberg in Africa, Mount Troödos in Cyprus, Mount Sinai in Eastern Egypt, the mountains of Penang and Perak in the Malay Peninsula, the Australian Alps, the New Zealand Alps, Roraima of British Guiana, the Blue Mountains of Jamaica, the Cockscomb Mountains of British Honduras, and the Rocky Mountains of Canada, these last unsurpassed in splendour of scenery anywhere in the world. Nor as providers of inspiring landscapes need the mountains of Scotland, Ireland and Wales, the hills of Shropshire, Derbyshire, Gloucester or Monmouth, Somerset, Devon, and Sussex be left out of the record of the empire's scenic beauty or health resorts.

Mountains of the Empire

We control half of the basins of the Niger and the Zambesi, and the sources of the Congo ; the Nile, from its twin fountains to its mouth, is wholly within the British sphere. We share Niagara with the United States, and own exclusively its only rival among the world's great waterfalls—those which David Livingstone discovered on the Zambesi. Fate has entrusted for a time to our charge—and it is to be hoped we shall be worthy of the stewardship—the largest share of the world's wonders, the choicest examples of terrestrial loveliness. At the same time the most productive regions of the world are under our sway.

Britain's Large Share of the World's Wonders

Even the seemingly unproductive, such as those as are well nigh locked in the grasp of the last Glacial Period or scorched by the sun of the Sahara Desert, are found to be rich in minerals—in gold, nitre, or precious stones.

The gold of Spanish America and California did much to increase the world's wealth in that metal, but not so much as has been obtained in the last sixty years from Australia, New Guinea, New Zealand, South Africa, British Guiana, India, and West Africa. We have silver also in Canada, Australia, New Zealand, and South Africa. Copper is obtained from Australia, from the arid South-west Africa and Northern and Southern Rhodesia, from Canada and Newfoundland ; and some day, no doubt, will be obtained from the Egyptian Sudan.

Tin, once the principal attraction to ancient explorers of the British Islands, and still much mined in Cornwall, is now found to be singularly abundant in the Malay Peninsula, and is also obtained from Australia and Northern Nigeria. Coal, the great product of the United Kingdom itself, is also now worked profitably in Australia, New Zealand, Canada, India, Borneo, Natal, the Transvaal, Rhodesia, and Cape Colony. Petroleum is found in Burma, Canada, and (in a more bituminous form) in Southern Nigeria, Barbados (West Indies), and Trinidad. Diamonds of a good second quality abound in South Africa to such an extent that the trade has

South Africa Rich in Diamonds

A BRITISH PORT IN CHINA: GENERAL VIEW OF WEI-HAI-WEI, SHOWING DOCKYARDS

to control their output. Of a better quality are those still found in India and in British Guiana, and perhaps in Australia. Australia is rich in opals. Opals, rubies, sapphires, and emeralds come from India. But I think it will be found as the civilisation of the world progresses that the so-called precious stones will deteriorate in value.

There will be a market for them where they can be used industrially, as is the case with the diamond, but as mere ornaments the educated world will be growing too sensible to spend money on them. It will prefer the pure and cheap beauty of flowers and the sensible warmth of furs. As regards this last accessory to an artificial life, the British Empire is still exceedingly rich, though it may be questioned whether it is not gobbling up its

capital at a foolish rate and making no provision for a future supply. The territories of the Canadian Dominion to the north of the fifty-second degree of north latitude are, together with Siberia, the great fur-producing regions of the world.

Hence are exported the skins of beavers, foxes, martens, stoats, otters, lynxes, wolves and bears, which provide such a large proportion of the world's fur coats, muffs, trimmings, and carriage rugs. The Canadian Government, however, might well consider whether measures should not be taken to restrict the output and preserve many valuable species of fur-bearing animals from complete extinction. This problem in regard to the skins of the sealions, exported from the Pacific coasts of Canada, has already received attention.

THE IRRIGATION WORKS AND PUBLIC RESERVOIR AT HAIDARABAD, IN INDIA

India contributes thousands of tiger, leopard, bear, deer, and antelope skins annually. Australia sends a certain proportion of the so-called opossum fur (the soft, woolly pelts of the phalanger). South Africa forwards a diminishing number of karosses made of the skins of red lynxes, foxes, jackals, and springboks. West Africa exports leopard and monkey skins; East Africa the hides of lions, leopards, cheetahs, and jackals.

But passing from the pelt that is used for its beauty and heavy fur, we may enumerate the more essential product of mere leather. Ox, antelope, and zebra hides are an export of growing importance from the territories of Uganda and East

the world, together with cattle for hides, meat, and draught purposes. Somaliland, the Egyptian Sudan, and British Arabia will also become great camel-breeding regions. This is already the case with much of West Central India—in which magnificent one-humped camels (dromedaries) are found. In far North-western India and in all the regions of Central Asia adjacent thereto, and, more or less, under British influence, there is the "Bactrian" two-humped camel, still wild in Tibet. This is an exceedingly useful beast for transport, and furnishes valuable hair for weaving fabrics and for felting. In this region also is the yak—a wild and also domesticated species of ox, which has

CLEARING AN INDIA-RUBBER FOREST IN THE STRAITS SETTLEMENTS

Africa, and enormous numbers of hides are sent to the leather markets from India, Australia, New Zealand, and South Africa.

The wool and hair products of the British Empire are a most important item. Australia and New Zealand are largely given up to the breeding of sheep—for wool as well as meat. Cape Colony and other parts of South Africa are breeding Merino sheep, and, above all, Angora goats. The great industry of the Falkland Islands is sheep and sheep products—wool, tallow, meat. It will probably be found that Somaliland and a good deal of the Egyptian Sudan will take prominent places in the future as countries furnishing goats' hair, sheep's wool, and meat to the rest of

an extravagant development of hair along the tail and sides of the body. The yak may bear some relation in origin to the bison. The bison, alas! once abounded in Southern Canada, but is now nearly exterminated.

Australia and British Arabia—later on, Somaliland, Nigeria, and parts of the Sudan—Ireland and Great Britain will produce between them sufficient horses for the needs of the empire and for all climates and purposes. If less attention were given to racing as an odious form of gambling, mixed up with so much that is disreputable and fraudulent, and greater encouragement were given by the state to honest horse-breeding for honest purposes, Great Britain ought to be able to

5583

supply herself with all the horses she needs, and not have to import any from Belgium and Hungary. As regards the domesticated birds produced by the different sections of the empire, Canada is going ahead with her fowl-breeding, not prevented, as are the people of England and Ireland, by the ridiculous cult of the fox, which checks the maintenance of so many poultry farms in the home country.

In this direction the United Kingdom lags behind its possibilities as a country for the breeding and rearing of choice poultry. India raises large quantities of peafowl, Chinese geese, and domestic fowls of various breeds. The rearing of turkeys on a considerable scale has lately made progress in Australia and New Zealand, and even on a portion of the Gold Coast in West Africa. In all the southern regions of Cape Colony and Natal poultry is usually very successful, and may before long be made an article of export. The ostrich farms of South Africa are so famous that they need no description. The wild fauna of the empire is, or should be, one of its glories, for Great Britain at present controls the fate of some of the most interesting, wonderful, and beautiful creatures still living on this planet. Our political limits include the Polar bear of Arctic Canada and the okapi of the Semliki forests; the lion, tiger, and elephants of Africa and Asia.

The white and the black rhinoceroses are still allowed to exist under the British flag in nooks and corners, and one or two game reserves, where the British sportsman (and his American, German, and Russian friends) has not as yet succeeded in exterminating them. The hippopotamus is still a nuisance to navigation in most of our African rivers. It is possible that the

Underwood

OIL-WELLS AT YANANGYET, IN BURMA

easternmost parts of Sierra Leone contain the pygmy hippopotamus of the adjoining Liberia. Somaliland, the Egyptian Sudan, British Central, and British East Africa, and the hinterland of the Gambia are marvellously rich in antelopes, giraffes, and three types of buffalo. The kangaroo is almost entirely a British subject. He may have a few arboreal cousins living under the Dutch and German flags.

Practically speaking the British ensign covers all the marsupials of the world, except the opossums of America and the cuscus of the Malay Archipelago, or the rat-like Cœnolestes of Ecuador. We possess specimens of every species of zebra and wild ass, and have but some day to extend our political influence over Tibet to throw our ægis over the only remaining wild horse. The tapir of British Guiana and the tapir of the Malay Peninsula are both citizens of the British Empire. Many a wonderful parrot or lory, a pheasant, hornbill, plantain-eater, or sunbird is entirely " British " in its range. The lyre-bird—one of the small wonders of creation — is a fellow-citizen of Australia with the kangaroo, though not yet accorded that rigid protection it deserves. As to our botanical wealth, it is stupendous.

The British flag waves over the grandest forests of the world, temperate and tropical. The pines and firs of Canada, the oaks and beeches of England, the mahogany of British Honduras and British Guiana, the Kauri pine of New Zealand, the eucalyptus and acacia of Australia, the teak of India; the ebony, the incense trees, the khayas of West Africa ; the junipers and giant yews of the East African mountains ; and the sandal-wood and bamboos of the Malay Peninsula ; the orchids of Burma and British Guiana, the roses of England and Canada,

CRUDE NATIVE METHOD OF WASHING THE RUBY-LADEN GRAVEL

Underwood

THE EUROPEAN MINING METHODS IN THE SAME PLACE

NATIVE AND BRITISH METHODS AT THE RUBY MINES OF MOGOK IN BURMA

the vines of South Africa and Australia, the wheat of British North America, the wheat of India and New Zealand, the bananas of the West Indies and of West Africa, the oranges of Jamaica and of New South Wales, the sugar of Barbados and of Queensland, the apples of New Zealand and Canada, the mangoes and mangosteens

Britain's Vegetable Wealth of India, the apples, plums, peaches of South Africa, which are some day going to be amongst her principal articles of export to a fruit-loving world ; the oil-palm of West Africa ; the rubber from the same region, from Ceylon, and from the Malay Peninsula ; the tea from Assam, Ceylon, and Natal ; coffee from Nyassaland, Uganda, and Sierra Leone ; cacao from the Gold Coast, Jamaica, and Trinidad ; rice from India and West Africa.

These are a few of the items to be recounted in our tale of vegetable wealth. It is a subject for serious consideration that the rule of the British king as directed and advised by his numerous legislatures all over the world should control such an enormous portion of the world's food supplies. In the time to come—which no living reader of this history may see—food may be more valuable than the so-called precious metals and precious stones.

The educational establishments of the British Empire, besides those of the United Kingdom and the Channel Islands, consist of the following. Gibraltar has thirteen government-aided elementary schools. In Malta there is a university, founded under the rule of the Knights of St. John in 1769, with four faculties, and a lyceum, or public school, for boys, besides two government secondary schools for boys and for girls, 167 elementary schools, four technical and art schools, and seventy-one private educational establishments.

In Cyprus there are two Boards of Education to regulate (a) the Christian and (b) the Moslem schools of the island. These consist of four Greek high schools,

State-Aided Schools in Cyprus and a Greek " gymnasium," or university ; one Moslem high school, two similar Armenian-Christian establishments (high schools for boys and girls), a third Armenian school conducted by monks, and three schools for the Maronite Christians are also state-aided. Of the 526 elementary schools, 178 are Moslem. In Egypt there were, in 1907, 2,761 Moslem elementary schools, imparting

sufficiently useful education to receive governmental assistance. There are also many government technical schools for teaching carpentry, metal work, etc.

Under the Ministry of Education there are 143 elementary schools for Moslems, thirty-four primary schools, four secondary schools, ten special and technical schools for dealing with agriculture, art, engineering, teaching, etc., and eleven professional colleges (medicine, law, military, veterinary science, engineering, teaching, etc.). In addition there are also 305 first-class schools maintained by foreigners, notably by Americans. There is the great useless Moslem university of Al Azhar, near Cairo, still wasting human time and marring the intellectual progress of modern Egypt by an antique, fanatical, unscientific, unpractical style of teaching.

Education in Egypt owes a debt to Britain mainly on account of our patience and energy in pressing on the Egyptian Government the need for rescuing knowledge from the strangling grasp of Mohammedan fanatics. But it also owes much recognition to the memory of Mehemet

The Sudan's Government Education Ali and his great-grandson, Ismail Pasha ; also equally to the personal intervention of the present khedive and his father Tewfik. And last, but not least, to private Mohammedan generosity and to the missionary efforts of America.

In the Anglo-Egyptian Sudan there are fifteen elementary Arabic schools, and six secondary. These government schools are practically secular, and Christian as well as Moslem children are educated there. There are two industrial schools, besides that which is attached to the Gordon College, and three training colleges for teachers. Gordon College itself at Khartoum includes a department for the education of the Sudanese in law and the other subjects required by them for entry into the civil service ; and also a high school for boys to be taught engineering, surveying, English, etc.

Very little seems to be done for the education of the Arabs or Somalis at Aden or in British Somaliland—practically nothing, in fact ; nor are missionaries encouraged to work there, owing to Mohammedan fanaticism. The same is the case in the Persian Gulf and in Baluchistan. In India only about 16,500,000 people out of a total population of 297,000,000 are able to read and write in any language.

NATIVE WORKMEN FILLING RAILWAY TRUCKS WITH PITCH

A STEAMER LOADING AT THE PITCH LAKE

J. White

NATIVES DIGGING THE PITCH

ONE OF THE WORLD'S WONDERS: THE PITCH LAKE AT LA TREA, TRINIDAD

Only about 25 per cent. of the boys ever attend school, and only 3½ per cent. of the girls. The best educated region is Bengal. On the whole, the Hindus are better educated than the Mohammedans. There are five universities—Calcutta, Madras, Bombay, Lahore, and Allahabad. There are 185 colleges, among which is the Mayo College for the education of the sons of princes, 115,869 government or government-aided schools, including 1,664 training and special schools for the instruction of school teachers and the teaching of many technical subjects. There are numerous government schools of art. There are also 42,604 private and charitable schools. Of the colleges, twelve only are for the education of women, for whom also there are 112 training schools, and 11,256 primary, secondary, and private schools.

In Ceylon, which has a total population of 3,578,333, there are 590 government schools, and 1,785 private schools. There is a royal college and a government training college, besides several English high schools. Less than half the population is illiterate—a great contrast to India. In the Straits Settlements, the sultanate of Johor, and the Federated Malay States there are about 245 schools of all degrees maintained by the British or the native governments (210 in the Straits Settlements). The educational establishments of Sarawak and North Borneo are almost entirely maintained by missionary societies. Hong Kong has seventy primary schools, two girls'

high schools, three high schools for both sexes, and two high schools for young people of European parentage. On the leasehold of Wei-hai-wei there are four government schools teaching English, one private school for European children, and numerous Chinese schools.

In Mauritius there is the royal college, with two preparatory schools, and there are a training college for teachers, sixty-seven government primary schools, eighty-eight state-aided schools, and one assisted Mohammedan school. Education is gratuitous but not compulsory. The Seychelles Archipelago, with a population of 22,000, maintains twenty-seven primary assisted schools, the Victoria secondary school for boys, two Catholic secondary schools, one for girls, and an efficient infants' school. There are two government scholarships of £50 a year. In Cape Colony there is a university (Cape Town), and there are five colleges and 3,750 schools, primary and secondary. In Zanzibar, and in the various Crown colonies, protectorates, and spheres of influence of Tropical Africa, except the Gambia and Sierra Leone, education is mainly in the hands of the different missionary societies, and is entirely confined to the natives of Africa. In Sierra Leone the educational establishments are excellent. There is Fula Bay College, a first-class institution; there are seventy-five primary schools, seventy-four secondary schools, four Mohammedan schools, and a college at Bô—in the interior—

A PLUMBAGO MINE AT KURUNEGALA, IN CEYLON
Photo Morgan Crucible Co.

5588

A TIN MINE NEAR KWALA LUMPUR, THE CAPITAL OF SELANGOR

G. R. Lambert & Co.

for the sons of chiefs. In the Gambia there are six elementary schools under missionary management which receive state aid. There is also one secondary school.

On the Gold Coast, in proportion to its size and wealth, education is not much fostered by the government, and were it not for the work of the Swiss Basle Mission—which for thirty years has flooded West Africa with enlightenment and education of a most practical, industrial character—the Gold Coast natives would contrast disadvantageously with the rest of British West Africans. There are seven government schools in the coast regions of this colony and 140 assisted schools. There are no government schools in Ashanti. In Southern Nigeria education has of late been taken in hand by the government with vigour and success. There is a high school at Bonny, another at Old Calabar, and a grammar school at Lagos. In addition, there are thirty-one government primary schools (four for girls) and sixty-nine assisted schools. A Mohammedan school has been opened at Lagos.

In the Bermudas, where there is a population of nearly 18,000, there are five schools for the children of the soldiers and sailors, twenty primary schools, and five secondary. There are said to be three Bermudan Rhodes scholars at Oxford. In the Bahamas the government schools number forty-six, together with twelve that receive state aid and forty-nine unaided. All this for a population of only 60,000 promises well for the advancement of the Bahamas.

In Jamaica, with a population—mainly black—of about 830,000, there are 687 government schools, three training colleges for teachers, and a high school at Kingston. There are also a large number of endowed high schools, industrial and technical institutions. Seven elementary government schools are maintained on the Turks and Caicos Islands dependent on Jamaica.

In the Leeward Islands, to a population of 134,000, there are 115 primary schools, six secondary, an agricultural college, and an industrial school. In the Windward Islands of Grenada, St. Vincent, and St. Lucia there is a population of 372,000; and there are 118 primary schools, one grammar school in Grenada, and an agricultural school in St. Vincent. Barbados has a population of 197,000, and maintains 166 primary schools, five secondary, three high schools, and Codrington College, affiliated to Durham University. Trinidad and Tobago together have a population of 328,000. There are 250 government schools, many private schools, a queen's royal college, and a Roman Catholic college. The Central American colony of British Honduras has a population of 41,000 and forty-one primary schools, together with five secondary schools. British Guiana, in

Camp Schools in the Falkland Islands
Northern South America has a population of about 307,000, 220 schools receiving state aid, and a government college in Georgetown. Besides this, the local government affords certain means to natives of the colony to pursue a university education in England.

In the Falkland Islands, near the southern extremity of the South American continent, there is a population of about 2,100, and there are five permanent schools—one Roman Catholic—besides an excellent system of camp schools, with travelling schoolmasters. Education here is compulsory.

In the little lonely South Atlantic island of St. Helena there is a native population of 3,500, for whom nine schools are maintained, partly at government expense. So much for the education of the Inner Empire; that of the self - governing daughter nations is as follows :

The dominion of Canada has an approximate population at the date of writing of 6,000,000. Her nine provinces and Yukon territory maintain 20,570 schools—public, high, and for secondary education. There are, in addition, many private schools. There are, further, thirty colleges, mostly gathered round eighteen universities. Education is compulsory throughout Canada.

The population of Newfoundland and Labrador is about 233,000 at the present time. There are 881 public and secondary schools and three colleges, supported or partly supported by state funds, but entirely managed by the local Anglican, Roman Catholic, and Methodist churches. Edu-

Cape Colony's Schools and Colleges
cation does not appear to be compulsory. In Cape Colony there is a population of more than 580,000 whites of European descent, of whom nearly 145,000 are illiterate. The total population is 2,500,000, and education—not compulsory—is state - provided in some 3,750 primary and secondary schools and in five colleges. There is an examining university in Cape Town. In Basutoland there are four government

schools, an industrial school, and 250 schools maintained—partly state aided—by missionaries. The education in Bechuanaland is entirely conducted by the London Missionary Society and the Dutch Reformed Church.

In Natal there is a European population of about 95,000; Asiatics, 112,000; negroes, 945,000. For the European children there are 295 government or state-aided primary schools, two government high schools in Durban and Pietermaritz-burg, two government art schools, 167 government or government-aided schools for negroes, and twenty-eight government-aided schools for Indian children. There are altogether forty-five schools entirely managed by the government and 469 that receive state funds. Education, though much encouraged, is not compulsory.

In the Orange River Colony education since 1905 is practically compulsory. The European population is about 145,000. There are about 170 primary schools, three residential high schools (one for girls), a training school for teachers, and the Grey University College, near Bloemfontein. Two

Compulsory Education in the Transvaal
hundred and ninety thousand inhabitants entirely of European origin in the Transvaal have their children's education attended to at 502 primary schools. There are about twelve schools specially provided for children of mixed race, and there are 209 schools for negroes. There is a normal college for the training of teachers and a Transvaal University College. Education for Europeans is compulsory. The whole character of the educational measures passed by the first Transvaal parliament, in 1906, is essentially modern and efficient.

In Southern Rhodesia there are private schools for European children at Buluwayo and at Salisbury, but of necessity the European population of the three Rhodesian provinces , (about 16,000) is at present mainly adult. The education of the great Zulu-Kaffir race in South Africa has received in general a great impulse from the Lovedale Institute of the Free Church of Scotland Mission in Eastern Cape Colony.

The commonwealth of Australia, including Tasmania and Norfolk Island, has a total population of European race of about 4,150,000. For the general and primary education of these there are 7,362 government or state-provided schools, and 2,284 recognised private schools. New South Wales has the University of Sydney

DESOLATE SOUTH AFRICA: TYPICAL KAROO SCENERY

A VAST SEA OF SAND IN THE ARABIAN DESERT

A SAND-BLOWN GRAVEYARD IN THE DESERT

DESERT SCENES IN THE BRITISH EMPIRE

and the Technical College, which last gives instruction in agriculture, among other subjects. There are schools of art in most of the principal towns. Education is compulsory. Victoria has a university at Melbourne with three colleges, a school of mines, and seventeen technical colleges. Education is compulsory, and it is said that only **Australasia's** 2 per cent. of the population is **Educational** illiterate. In Queensland education is not yet compulsory. A **Institution** university is about to be established at Brisbane. In South Australia, which has a population of nearly 385,000, education is compulsory, but it is said that nearly 17 per cent. of the people are illiterate. No doubt, under this head are included the few thousand Chinese and aborigines. This state has a university at Adelaide, and maintains a training college for teachers. In West Australia education is compulsory, and only 3 per cent. are said to be illiterate. Tasmania has a university at Hobart, two schools of mines, and two technical schools. Education is compulsory.

Little Norfolk Island, under the management of New South Wales, has one efficient government school for its population— European and Melanesian—of nearly 1,000. The dominion of New Zealand has a population of about 890,000 whites, 48,000 Maories, 2,570 Chinese, and in its dependent archipelagoes 12,340 Polynesians. Education is compulsory. There are 1,847 public primary schools, 308 private schools, 28 secondary schools, seven school of mines, four normal schools, five principal schools of art, and 11 industrial schools, besides 104 schools for Maories. There are colleges at Dunedin, Christchurch, Canterbury, and Wellington for specialist education, and these are affiliated to the university of New Zealand at Wellington.

The territory of Papua (British New Guinea) is governed by the Australian Commonwealth. It has a population of under 900 Europeans, almost all adults. **Europeans** The native population of **Increasing** Papuans is estimated at **in Fiji** 400,000. Their education is in the hands of the London Missionary Society, the Roman Catholic Society of the Sacred Heart, the Church of England Mission, and the Methodist Missionary Society of Australasia.

In the Crown colony of Fiji, the European population is steadily increasing. It numbers at present about 3,300. Education for this section of the community is provided at the cost of the community, and is directed by the school-boards of Suva and Levuka, and carried on by two government schools at these places. There are also three good Roman Catholic schools at Suva and Levuka. A government native high school has been established for some considerable time at Nasinu, near Suva, where an excellent higher education is offered to the native Fijians and the children of the Asiatic settlers (Indian coolies, mostly).

The Wesleyan and Roman Catholic missions provide entirely the primary education of the natives (Melanesians and Polynesians) throughout the Fiji and Rotuma Islands. The Wesleyans also conduct the education of the natives of the protected kingdom of Tonga. Missionaries of the Wesleyan, Presbyterian, Anglican, and Roman Catholic Churches also preside —without any grant or state assistance whatsoever—over the education of the thousands of natives of the British protected Gilbert, Solomon, and Santa Cruz Islands in the Equatorial Pacific.

The total number of armed men ready for war service—the standing armies, **Armies** 1st Reserve, colonial volun- **of the British** teers in constant training and **Empire** thoroughly efficient, also the military police—of the British Empire at the close of 1908 amounted to about 926,000, including the British Reserves, Channel Islands Militia, Honourable Artillery Company, and permanent staffs of militia, etc., but not the English Militia, Imperial Yeomanry, or Territorial Army. Of these, in the first place, should be mentioned the regular (professional) army of the United Kingdom, amounting to 216,018 combatants of all arms, and 31,348 non-combatants. This army is distributed thus : 115,148 in Great Britain, and about 15,000 in Ireland ; 3,809 at Gibraltar ; 7,099 in Malta and Crete ; 123 in Cyprus ; 76,155 in India; 1,000 in Ceylon ; 5,719 in Egypt and the Sudan ; 1,500 at Singapore ; 3,101 at Hong Kong and Wei-hai-wei ; 16,213 in South Africa; 18 at St. Helena ; 1,309 at the Bermudas; 547 in Jamaica; and about 726 in Mauritius. The total colonial contingent is 41,063 for 1908-1909, but in 1907–1908 there were 49,804 British soldiers in the colonies.

Canada has a military force on the footing of active service, including military police, of about 3,000, and an active militia of about 51,000. Australia maintains a tiny permanent army of 1,329 officers and men, and a partly paid trained militia of 15,445. Including volunteers, rifle-clubmen, cadets, and reserve of officers, the commonwealth has a potential army of 84,000 men. The six Australian states, moreover, maintain a force of about 10,000 mounted police, first-class irregular soldiers in war time. New Zealand also has a permanent militia of 341 artillery and engineers, and a regularly drilled volunteer force of not less than 18,000, notwithstanding 700 mounted police. Cape Colony—besides the Imperial troops stationed in the colony—maintains

short notice put in the field a good fighting force of at least 5,000 volunteers, mostly mounted. The Egyptian army in Egypt and the Sudan consists of a force of 19,010 rank and file, including 121 British officers. Egypt pays an approximate £150,000 a year towards the cost of the British army of occupation. Malta maintains a respectable contingent—the Royal Malta Artillery (446), the King's Own Malta Regiment (war strength, 2,258), and the Malta Militia Submarine Miners (63). The Maltese Government also pays £5,000 to the Imperial Government as a military

G. R. Lambert

OPENING OF THE FIRST STATE RAILWAY IN THE MALAY PENINSULA

a respectable armed force : 705 Cape Mounted Rifles, 1,734 Mounted Police, and a body of 5,835 volunteers in regular drill. Natal has an armed force—mounted police, mounted rifles, naval gun corps, and trained militia—of about 6,430 men. She also subsidises rifle associations (5,774 officers and men) and cadet corps (3,471). The Transvaal and Orange State together maintain the South African Constabulary, an efficient force of 2,700 officers and men. In addition, the Transvaal maintains a well-trained volunteer force, mostly ex-soldiers, of 10,000 men. Rhodesia can at

contribution. Ceylon pays about £70,000 for its Imperial garrison, and maintains in addition an efficient volunteer force of 2,333 officers and men.

India has a magnificent army of 160,000, including British officers, a military police of 56,887, a volunteer force of 34,000 Europeans and Eurasians, and contingents furnished by the feudatory states of 20,189, a total force—apart from the Imperial garrison of 76,155, for which India pays Britain about £1,395,000 annually—of 271,076 officers and men. The Straits Settlements, besides their Imperial and Indian garrison, for which they pay, have a very efficient volunteer force of about 770 Europeans, Eurasians, and Chinese. The Federated Malay States have a smart little army known as the Malay States Guides—British officers, Sikhs, Pathans, and Malays, 2,665 in all. The local military forces of British

Defenders of British Tropical Africa

South Africa, from North-west Rhodesia to Cape Colony, have already been described ; likewise those of the Egyptian Sudan. Mauritius is garrisoned by a small detachment of British troops, formerly as many as 1,394, towards the cost of which the colony paid annually £27,000, but now reduced to about 726.

The rest of British Tropical Africa is divided into two great sections, East and West. The Eastern section comprises the colonies or protectorates of Somaliland, Uganda, British East Africa, Zanzibar, and British Central Africa—Nyassaland and North-east Rhodesia. This section is defended by a regiment of negro soldiers known as the King's African Rifles. Of this at present there are five battalions, No. 1 to 6 (No. 5 is at present non-existent). The 1st and 3rd battalions are in East Africa and Zanzibar, the 2nd in Central Africa, the 4th in Uganda, and the 6th in Somaliland.

At present the total number of King's African Rifles under arms is 2,700. In East Africa there is, in addition, a military police of 1,800 under 35 British officers ; in Uganda a constabulary of 1,060 ; in Zanzibar, 500 ; in Nyassaland, 200. There is also a corps of 160 Sikh soldiers from the Indian Army stationed in Nyassaland. In the West African section the indigenous regiment, so to speak, is the West Africa Frontier Force. This is stationed in the Gambia Protectorate (126 men), the Sierra Leone Protectorate (470 men), the Gold Coast hinterland (2,175 men), Southern and Northern Nigeria (5,266 men).

The Forces in British West Africa

In addition there are the West African Regiment and the 1st battalion of the West India Regiment, besides artillery, engineers, etc., at Sierra Leone (2,612 officers and men in all). The Gambia maintains a military police of 80 men ; Sierra Leone, 240 ; Gold Coast, 621 ; Southern Nigeria, 980 ; and Northern Nigeria, 1,180. Lastly, there should also be counted with the effective forces in British West Africa

the Gold Coast volunteers (1,056 officers and men), partly paid, and maintained more or less on a war footing.

The local soldiery or military police in the West Indies and Tropical America, apart from the British garrison in Jamaica, consists of the 2nd battalion of the West Indian Regiment in Jamaica (500 officers and men), and 800 militia, besides a very efficient constabulary (1,753) modelled on that of Ireland, and, as a matter of fact, officered and sub-officered by officers and men chosen from the Royal Irish Constabulary. In Barbados there is a police force of 315, and measures are being taken to raise and maintain a small colonial force of mounted infantry.

In the Bahamas, Leeward and Windward Islands there are small forces of civil police. In Trinidad there is a constabulary of 652, and a volunteer rifle corps of 352. British Honduras maintains a constabulary of 100, and a volunteer light infantry corps (mounted and unmounted) of 260. British Guiana either fears no foe, within or without, or is very shy of disclosing its arrangements for the maintenance of

Empire's Fighting Strength

public order, for no particulars are extant as to its military and police. There are said to be militia and volunteers to the total number of 240. The Falkland Islands support a volunteer corps of 98. The total of the forces, therefore, for offence or defence throughout the empire ready for immediate action—professional army, military constabulary, volunteers or militia in constant training and available for immediate service—is about 926,300, of whom approximately 560,000 are white, and 366,000 belong to the coloured races—Indian, Egyptian, Negro, Mulatto, Malay, Chinese and Polynesian.

Behind this force there are as yet undefined potentialities which at present take the place of that actuality so necessary to the safety of the British Empire, throughout all parts of which (in the opinion of the present writer) compulsory military service on the part of all males, more or less between the ages of 19 and 40, should be an article of the constitution of every country under the British flag, most of all in the Motherland. Compulsory service in the militia is now a law of the state in New Zealand (it is projected in Australia), in Canada, in Natal, and in Cape Colony. There is something similar in the Channel Islands, where the militia in

A NATIVE OPEN-AIR SCHOOL AT OPOBO IN NIGERIA

J. A. Green

T. D. Ravenscroft

DUTCH CHILDREN AT SCHOOL IN BRITISH SOUTH AFRICA

EDUCATING THE YOUNG SUBJECTS AND CITIZENS OF GREATER BRITAIN

training amount to the respectable force of 3,163. The manhood of the United Kingdom is invited to furnish voluntarily a territorial force (314,063) for the defence of the Home Country. This, together with the militia (84,505) and militia reserve (3,413) and the Imperial yeomanry (25,195) is estimated to reach a total strength of 447,176 during 1909. Behind **Britain's** the regular army of about **Army of** 130,148 stationed in the United **Defence** Kingdom there is a reserve of about 222,850 trained officers and men, making an effective trained home army of about 352,998.

The martial spirit of the British Islands is such that in the event of real danger we could easily count on a territorial army of at least 325,000 partially trained men to stand beside our regular forces, giving us therefore a body of 677,998 fighting men for home and foreign defence; this in addition to the 118,000 British soldiers garrisoning India, South Africa, Egypt, the Mediterranean, Mauritius, West Indies, etc. To this array again might certainly be added in war time the magnificent fighting body, the Royal Irish Constabulary, numbering nearly 10,000 strong.

The navy of the empire is mainly the British Navy, to the cost of which Canada contributes nothing, while the Indian Empire pays annually £103,400, the Australian Commonwealth £200,000, New Zealand £40,000, Cape Colony £50,000, Natal £35,000, and Newfoundland £3,000. The total number of ships complete for sea in the British Navy at the close of 1908 was about 497, including 60 great battleships, 57 of which are of the most modern types. In addition to this, most of the Crown colonies or protectorates have armed vessels for police or defence purposes on their coasts, rivers, and lakes. New Zealand and Australia have a few torpedo boats. The Imperial coaling stations, more or less fortified, are (outside British waters) **Imperial** Gibraltar, Malta (possibly **Coaling** Alexandria), Aden, Karachi, **Stations** Bombay, Colombo, Rangoon, Singapore, Hong Kong, Port Darwin, Hobart, Wellington, Esquimalt, Halifax, Bermuda, Kingston, Port Louis (Mauritius), Simon's Town (Cape of Good Hope), St. Helena, Ascension, and Freetown (Sierra Leone). The additional British ports, however, at which there are supplies of coal on hand, and which are to a certain extent defended against

a naval *coup-de-main*, are far too numerous to be catalogued. The great dockyards of the empire outside British waters are at Gibraltar, Valetta (Malta), Bombay, Kidderpur (India), Hong Kong, Wei-hai-wei, Sydney, and Ascension. There is also dock accommodation at Trinkomali (Ceylon), Simon's Town (South Africa), Halifax (Nova Scotia), and Esquimalt (British Columbia).

The mercantile marine of the empire, including that of the United Kingdom, comprises about 9,511 steamers of a total tonnage of 17,001,139, many of which are easily convertible into war vessels. The nearest competitors in this respect are : Germany, 1,713, tonnage 3,705,700; United States, 1,577, tonnage, 3,160,895 ; and Norway, 1,181, tonnage, 1,264,002.

The value of the commerce of the British Empire (including Egypt and the Egyptian Sudan, Bahrein Islands, and all British Borneo), calculated in imports and exports only, amounted in the year 1906 to the amazing total of £2,189,681,147. The actual commerce of the United Kingdom reached in that year the total of £1,068,566,318. The Indian **Commerce** Empire in 1906 had a com- **of the** merce valued at £239,695,904; **Empire** British South Africa (excluding Nyassaland), £127,010,290; the Australian Commonwealth, £114,641,710 ; dominion of Canada, £113,234,930 ; Straits Settlements and Federated Malay States, £91,241,860 ; Egypt and Egyptian Sudan, £66,638,341 ; New Zealand, £33,306,540 ; British West Indies, British Honduras and Guiana, £21,027,274 ; British West Africa, £10,833,850 ; and British East Africa (Uganda, Somaliland, East Africa, Zanzibar, Seychelles, Nyassaland and Mauritius), £9,058,281. Even the little Bahrein Islands, off the Arabian east coast, did a total trade of £3,154,549 in the year 1906.

Out of all the great sections of the empire the most considerable trade with Great Britain, in 1907, was that of the Indian Empire (£106,956,000) ; the next best, the future South African confederation (£90,053,620), and the third, the Australian Commonwealth (£59,429,880). Canada came fourth with a trade between her and the United Kingdom of £41,506,980. The value of the trade between Egypt and the Egyptian Sudan and the United Kingdom is £23,717,963 approximately (1907); between us and New

Zealand for the same period, £23,050,400. The total public indebtedness of the whole empire, including that of Egypt (£96,180,000), is something like £1,611,231,869. The approximate annual revenue of the vast area (including Egypt, etc.), was, in 1907, £331,019,695 ; and the expenditure during the same period, £308,033,010 ; so that the empire as a whole is living well within its means. During this period the revenue of the United Kingdom was £144,814,073, and its expenditure £139,415,251. India, vaguely thought to be fabulously rich, with an area fourteen and a half times that of the United Kingdom (1,766,517 square miles against 121,390 square miles), and a population of nearly 297,000,000 (United Kingdom population, 44,100,231), had a revenue of only £75,626,900, which her expenditure was framed to meet exactly.

This chapter may, perhaps, fitly be closed by a few comparisons :

The World's Great Empires Area of British Empire, 13,138,900 square miles ; Russian Empire, 8,647,657 ; French Empire, 4,604,880 ; Chinese Empire, 4,227,170 ; United States, 3,567,563 ; German Empire, 1,260,603. Population of Chinese Empire,433,553,030; British Empire, 405,000,000 (approximate) ; Russian Empire, 149,299,300 ; French Empire, 96,389,985 ; United States (nearly), 84,000,000 ; German Empire, 73,200,000 (approximate); Japanese Empire and Korea, 60,000,000 (nearly).

Commerce (imports and exports), of British Empire, £2,189,681,147 ; German Empire, £712,688,015 ; United States, £669,336,930 (1907 : This was a slump year. Probably the best average annual estimate for the United States of America commerce at the present time would be £710,000,000); French Empire, £570,605,458 ; Russian Empire, £189,040,736 ; Chinese Empire, £107,440,456.

National indebtedness of British Empire, £1,611,231,869 (the actual debt of the United Kingdom is £774,164,704) ; French Empire, £1,265,630,019 ; Russian Empire and Finland, £940,556,410 ; United States, £491,437,612 ; German Empire, £179,583,330 ; Chinese Empire, £123,685,930.

Annual revenue of British Empire (1907), £331,019,695 ; Russian Empire, £214,210,000 ; French Empire, £170,727,474 ; United States, £169,345,068 ; German Empire, £120,791,550 ; Chinese Empire, £15,000,000.

Annual expenditure of British Empire (1907), £308,019,010 ; Russian Empire, £266,000,000 (approximate) ; French Empire, £168,276,097 ; United States, £152,497,750 ; German Empire, £125,863,152 ; Chinese Empire, £18,000,000 (approximate).

National Armies and Navies Nothing is known positively as to the total revenue and total expenditure of the whole empire of China. These approximate estimates deal with known results of customs, etc., and recorded Imperial expenditure.

Standing army of French Empire, soldiers, first reserve, and colonial troops, 1,300,000 officers and men (approximate) ; Russian Empire (soldiers and military police), 1,200,000 officers and men (approximate) ; German Empire (including small colonial forces), 1,180,000 officers and men (approximate) ; Austria-Hungary, 1,154,000 officers and men (approximate) ; British Empire (soldiers of regular army and reserve, Indian Army, volunteers and militia of colonies on a war footing, and military police), 926,000.

These summaries include all disciplined soldiers prepared to fight at two weeks' notice.

Navy on peace footing of British Empire, 497 ships of all classes ; French Empire, 580 (360 of these are torpedo boats or submarines) ; German Empire, 205 ; Japanese Empire, 148 ; United States, 139 ; Italy, 239 (of these 85 are old and of small account).

Mercantile marine of the British Empire (steamers over 100 tons), 9,511, tonnage, 17,001,139 ; German Empire, 1,713, 3,705,700 ; United States, 1,517, 3,160,895 ; Norway, 1,181, 1,264,002 ; Sweden, 889, 686,517 ; Japanese Empire, 829, 1,068,747 ; French Empire, 809, 1,284,368.

A FRIENDLY POWER IN EGYPT: BRITISH TROOPS MARCHING THROUGH THE STREETS OF CAIRO

From the painting by W. C. Horsley, by the artist's permission

BRITISH EXPANSION IN EUROPE
AND THE STEADY PROGRESS OF EGYPT UNDER BRITISH CONTROL

WHAT effect have the establishment and growth of the British Empire had on the world outside the limits of Great Britain and Ireland ?

In Europe, the ethnological results of the extension of British rule beyond the Irish and English Channels was inconsiderable down to about twenty years ago ; in short, down to the time that the other great nations of the White world applied themselves in all seriousness to the foundation of empires beyond the seas. They then began to adopt many British ideas, words, games, notions in art and industry, clothes, furniture, and sport. It is true that in horse-racing, railways, steamships, the training of children, farming, and agriculture we had engendered original concepts and inventions expressed in idiomatic Anglo-Saxon, and these had spread the British influence of jockeys, **British Influence Abroad** engineers, governesses, stockmen, and gardeners throughout France, Western Germany, Italy, Russia, Tunis, and Egypt; also that the success of our constitutional government had for at least 150 years turned the eyes of all reformers and political theorists towards England.

But down to twenty years ago it was rather France that set the fashions in all departments for all Europe than the Anglo-Saxon. This " British " influence abroad is at least one quarter American. It is so difficult to discriminate nowadays between what notions and ideas are started in the United States and what have their origin in British, Canadian, Australian, South African, or British-Indian brains, that for the purpose of this review the British and American Empires must be held to be one.

We started, of course, by borrowing our dominant language, our culture, industries, ideas, science, architecture, religion, rulers, laws, weapons, and cooking from France, Rome, the Netherlands, Frisia, Western Germany, and Italy. Our nearest political and racial colonies, beyond our strict geographical limits, were the Channel Islands. These were at first not so much colonies or conquests as the **Peoples of the Channel Islands** last vestiges of the Norman power which had conquered England in 1066. The Channel Islands had been peopled from quite a remote antiquity by types of the different races that overran the North of France, with which, indeed, Guernsey and Jersey were almost connected by sandbanks and fords of shallow water at the beginning of the historical period. They were taken possession of and named from the ninth century onwards by Norse rovers from Norway, and consequently came to form part of the Duchy of Normandy, of which, politically, they are the last remnant.

These Normans mingled with the preceding Iberian and Aryan Romanised Kelts. Down, therefore, to about the reign of Elizabeth, the Channel Islanders were scarcely distinguishable, anthropologically, from the Normans of Northern France. But in the sixteenth and seventeenth centuries the political troubles in England caused a number of English to settle in Jersey and Guernsey, and the complete detachment of all the Channel Islanders from the Church of Rome in the middle of the sixteenth century added to the separation from Norman France. In **The Channel Islands Secede From Rome** Alderney, Jersey, Guernsey, and Sark the people, almost without exception, belong to the Anglican Church, and here alone is the Liturgy of the Church of England rendered in French. It is somewhat surprising that this adherence to the national Church has not been rewarded by the institution of a bishop of the Channel Islands (they are under the See of

Winchester). There are, moreover, learned societies in Jersey and Guernsey which conduct their proceedings in French. From the eighteenth century onwards the islands have been garrisoned by detachments of British troops, and not a few of these soldiers or sailors from the British fleet have subsequently married and settled down in the Channel Islands, whither also during the last hundred years English families have resorted for permanent settlement because of the delightful climate, lovely scenery, low cost of living, and educational advantages. The use of the English language is spreading year by year over a larger area in these islands. As it is, Alderney is almost entirely

the use of the French language ; but all these parts of the world have retained the Roman Catholic form of Christianity. So far as language, prejudices, mode of life, and all that goes to the making of a people is concerned, the Channel Islanders of the present day—in spite of the hundred miles of sea that separate them from England—are more closely knit up with us in sympathy than are the people of half Ireland. They could never be made French citizens except by the continuous application of force, just as, in all probability, the inhabitants of Northern Lorraine will resist for centuries the attempt to coerce them into German citizenship, or the Germans of the Baltic provinces willingly

Frith

CASTLE CORNET IN THE ISLAND OF GUERNSEY

English-speaking. In Guernsey only about a quarter of the population is now unable to speak English, while another quarter can speak no French. The local language is very different from literary French, and is the old Norman speech that was introduced into the island after the Conquest. In Jersey the same thing is taking place, if anything more markedly.

In Jersey, however, if not always in Guernsey, the official language is literary French, which, by the way, is as illogical as making Italian the official language of Malta. Probably here alone in the whole world is the service of the Church of England rendered in French. Other portions of the globe have been peopled by the French and acquired by the British, and yet retain

remain subjects of the Russian Empire. Gibraltar, after two hundred years of British occupation, has had singularly little effect on the people of Spain and Portugal, beyond the neutral zone, which restricts the intercourse of the British garrison on this square mile and seven-eighths of rock with the people of the Iberian peninsula.

The British soldiers and officials for two hundred years have freely intermarried with the Genoese and Spanish women, the descendants of the original inhabitants of Gibraltar when the British took possession of it. The resulting " Rock Scorpions " vary considerably in type and social status. Several of the most beautiful and accomplished women of the world during the nineteenth century have been

MONT ORGUEIL IN JERSEY, SHOWING THE ANCIENT CASTLE

GUERNSEY'S PRINCIPAL TOWN: VIEW OF ST. PETER PORT AND HARBOUR

THE HARBOUR OF ST. HELIER, THE CHIEF PORT OF JERSEY

Frith

SCENES IN THE CHANNEL ISLANDS

GENERAL VIEW OF THE TOWN

A POPULAR PROMENADE, SHOWING PART OF MOORISH CASTLE ON THE HILL

GIBRALTAR: A VALUABLE POSSESSION OF GREAT BRITAIN

THE SIGNAL STATION ON ITS ROCKY EMINENCE

WATERPORT STREET, THE PRINCIPAL BUSINESS THOROUGHFARE

OTHER SCENES IN THE FORTRESS TOWN OF GIBRALTAR

of Gibraltar birth and descended from the unions of British officers with Spanish ladies. But these have married officials in the army, navy, or diplomatic service, and have soon passed away to spheres of influence beyond Gibraltar. There is a considerable Jewish element in the shopkeeping class, and it is these who, together with the descendants of English soldiers and Spanish women, form that type of " Rock Scorpion " that may be met with nowadays so frequently in Morocco, Algeria, Tunis above all, Malta, and the Ionian Islands. At one time there were quite a number of Gibraltarese in the regency of Tunis, attracted thither by the favourable conditions enjoyed by British

The Jewish Element in Gibraltar

the part of the Maltese people, who largely by their own personal efforts and bravery expelled the French garrison, though, of course, they had been assisted in this task by Nelson's overthrow of the French forces at sea. Fearing lest they might not be able to maintain themselves against future attacks on the part of France, and disliking very much the idea of reverting to that Neapolitan sovereignty from which the islands of Malta and Gozo were withdrawn by Charles V., the Maltese people offered their country to the King of Great Britain and Ireland. Europe confirmed this choice at the Congress of 1815. Under our rule the Maltese have prospered exceedingly. Magnificent public works have been constructed in the island

BRITISH TROOPS IN MALTA: THE MAIN GUARD AT VALETTA

commerce down to 1898. The regency of Tunis was at one time very near becoming a British protectorate, owing to the influence that radiated from Malta and the friendly relations between the beys of Tunis and the British naval officers which followed on the defeat of Napoleon Bonaparte. In the curious struggle that went on, under the surface, between France, Britain, and Italy for predominance in Tunis, Gibraltar Jews were generally the men of straw used by these conflicting influences in their attempts to acquire landed property or other stakes in the country.

The British acquisition of Malta was not—it is sometimes necessary to remind red-hot Imperialists—a conquest, but the result of a voluntary and graceful act on

of Malta—Gozo has not been so well attended to—and under the ægis of the British flag the Maltese have founded flourishing colonies—here 30,000, there 20,000, in another place 10,000—in Algeria, Tunis, Tripoli, Barca, and Egypt, and even in Crete and elsewhere in the Levant. The Maltese in Algeria tend more and more to adopt French nationality, deriving therefrom considerable commercial advantages, and finding perhaps in the French nation a more courteous foster-mother than Great Britain has been to them. " His mother was a Maltese, you know," is the sneering phrase that I have often heard from a British officer in the army or navy or in the Colonial Civil Service in

Malta's Great Prosperity Under Britain

THE BARACCA: A BEAUTIFUL VIEW IN VALETTA

A CURIOUS STREET OF STEPS AND THE HARBOUR AT VALETTA, THE CAPITAL

MARSA MUSCET, SHOWING THE STRONGLY BUILT FORTIFICATIONS

SCENES IN MALTA, BRITAIN'S CROWN COLONY IN THE MEDITERRANEAN

reference to some more or less distinguished man in the employ of the British Government. " He says she was an Italian countess, but she really was nothing but a Maltese, I can assure you." Why it should be in any sense derogatory to be born a Maltese the present writer is at a loss to understand. The population of

British Occupation of Malta these islands is considerably mixed in origin it is true, but it is derived from very noble sources—from the best of the chivalry of Aragon, France, England, Germany, and Northern Italy ; or if it be of a brunette type, then from a splendid Mediterranean stock which goes back in origin to the Phœnicians.

At one time it was thought necessary to treat Malta on very military lines ; but it has gradually been borne in on the British Government that the military and civil departments should be to some extent separated, and the time may come when Malta may have a civilian as governor, or even—why not ?—a Maltese noble or eminent citizen in that position ? But though our connection with Malta has been marked by episodes of a bad taste that seems peculiarly British—and yet not an ancient, but quite a modern trait in our race—the main results of the British occupation of Malta have been of enormous benefit to the inhabitants of the two islands. We have, in fact, definitely created a Maltese people, destined to play a very notable part in the commercial development of the Mediterranean.

If we, as the garrisoning race, should mend our manners, the Maltese might well at the same time cause an impartial history of Malta during the last hundred years to be drawn up and published, and thereby realise how much indeed they owe in gratitude to the acceptance by George III. of kingship over Malta. The British protectorate over the Ionian Islands did much the same for the Greeks

Greeks and the English Language of Corfu as for the mixed races of Arab, French, and Italian origin in Malta. It certainly spread acquaintance with and use of the English language amongst the Greeks of the Levant. Many a Greek commercial house now of world-wide importance arose from the British occupation of this archipelago, which, until the onslaught of Napoleon Bonaparte, had belonged to Venice since the time it was detached from the Byzantine Empire.

The Ionian Islands, indeed, were at last the only refuge of Greek culture from the sickening barbarism of Turkey. It is possible that but for the British occupation of these Islands, Greece would never have aspired to or have recovered her independence, would never have possessed a base from which she could organise resistance to the Turkish yoke.

Sentimentality fortunately swayed the nations of Europe in favour of Greece in the first half of the nineteenth century ; yet it is doubtful whether the spark of Hellenic nationality in Greece itself could ever have been revived and fanned into a powerful flame but for British encouragement emanating from the Ionian Islands. Nor, had this occupation not taken place, could those Greek houses of commerce have arisen to a secure affluence and have developed such a large Anglo-Hellenic trade as now exists in Western Asia Minor nor at Costantinople.

Curiously enough, Greeks are happier governed by Greeks—even if they be less well governed—than by intelligent foreigners ! We should feel it in the same way if the Germans occupied the Isle of

The Ionian Islands Under Greece Wight. They would probably do a vast deal to improve the service on the Isle of Wight Railway, and carry out much needed public works in a masterful manner, besides endowing the island with better schools than those which we give it under our existing half-hearted educational establishment. Yet—illogical and ungrateful though they might be—the inhabitants of the Isle of Wight would probably prefer to remain under or to return to the control of the British Government rather than become citizens of the German Empire.

Consequently, Great Britain acted wisely in yielding to the wishes of the Ionians that they might come under the sovereignty of Greece. Nevertheless, anyone who has visited the island of Corfu, if he be of British blood, cannot but admire the magnificent public works which we carried out on that island, and ask himself whether the material prosperity of that group might not be far higher than it is at present were the supreme administration in the hands of honest Anglo-Saxons. There is little doubt, however, that our continued retention of this protectorate would have involved us in disagreeable European complications, and certainly would have ended by offending the

VENDOR OF GOATS' MILK   A MALTESE LADY   PRIEST IN CLERICAL ATTIRE

MONK IN HIS ROBES   AN EGG-SELLER   A BOY CHORISTER

COMMON STREET PORTER   A SELLER OF SWEETS   A BRAN-SELLER

TYPICAL CHARACTERS OF THE ISLAND OF MALTA

growing power of that kingdom of Italy, with whom we desire to be connected by every tie of affection and interest. Yet, having lost the Ionian Islands, which gave us a certain hold, a useful garrison in the eastern half of the Mediterranean, we yearned for some alternative possession. The feeling burrowed underground through the tortuous channels of the official mind, and emerged at last to the surface through the romantic action of Lord Beaconsfield in 1878 in acquiring for us the leasehold—the practical possession—of the island of Cyprus. Several times before and since Great Britain has coquetted with the idea of acquiring Crete, more especially on account of the importance of Suda Bay to a great naval Power. But for unpublished—perhaps only spoken, and not written—warnings from other European Powers that the addition of Crete to Cyprus, or, as was once or twice contemplated, the substitution of this much more valuable island for the half-barren, altogether harbourless Cyprus, would mean the overflowing of the cup of bitterness and the declaration of war, Crete might now by some fiction or another be under the British flag. As it is, its destiny will be inevitably to form part of an enlarged kingdom of Greece.

Cyprus in British Hands

In Cyprus much the same effect has been produced by British rule as occurred in the Ionian Islands : magnificent public works—sometimes carried out without any regard to picturesqueness or respect for valuable historical remains—an absolutely honest, painstaking administration, the saving, just in time, of the native forests, and with them the climate, which has been rapidly deteriorating under Turkish rule from one sufficiently moist to maintain an exuberant vegetation to conditions of almost waterless sterility ; on the other, the ingratitude of the Greek, due, it is alleged, to the exclusion of Greeks from most of the posts under the British Government.

Where the Turks are Preferred

Strangely enough, we rely for local support in Cyprus not on the Greek, but on the Turkish element in the population, and we prefer much more to employ Turks than to engage Greeks in the public service, assigning as our reason that the latter are not honest and cannot be depended on for steady work ; while as a servant, a public servant, under an honest and capable employer, the Turk is

well-nigh perfection. In this case, in Cyprus, the Turk is very often simply a Mohammedan Greek. Actually, in Cyprus, in Crete, in Bosnia, and in many parts of the Balkans and Asia Minor, there is no racial difference between the good and the bad employé, the honest and dishonest merchant, but merely a question of religion.

As a master, the Mohammedan has been hitherto narrow-minded, intolerant, unprogressive, and financially corrupt ; as a servant, under an employer of the North European type, a more admirable type of faithful, quiet, industrious public officer does not exist. The British occupation of Cyprus, together with our joint occupancy of Crete at the present time, is producing this effect on the Mediterranean peoples : that it is developing the Turk in the right direction, whether or not it is producing a wholesome effect upon the Greek.

But our occupancy of Egypt, though it should properly be treated of later on in connection with African questions, has in a sense knit us up with the Greek world of commerce to such a degree that in weighing the future relations of the Greek peoples with the British Empire the peevishness of the Cypriotes will be unheard. No nationality has profited so enormously by the British conquest of Egypt and of the Egyptian Sudan, or even of East Africa generally, as have the Greeks. Since we started somewhat blindly on this Imperial movement which has led us inevitably on the path from Cairo to the Cape, Greek adventurers of commerce have marched *pari passu* with the British forces, military and naval.

Greeks as Pioneers of Commerce

There are Greek merchants as far south on the East Coast as Delagoa Bay. They penetrate to Mashonaland and to Uganda ; while on the coast of Somaliland they are more numerous than any other Europeans not of the official class. Khartoum is described as being a Greek city. Greeks and Maltese form a kind of middle-class in Egypt, between the indigenous Arabs and negroes on the one hand, and the foreign officials—British, French, and Italian—on the other. The servants of the Suez Canal Company, below the highly paid posts, if they are not Maltese are Greek.

British intervention in the affairs of Egypt and of the Egyptian Sudan, in common with that of France, really dates from Napoleon's invasion of 1799. The two countries see-sawed as to their influence over the viceroys of Egypt. France instigated the exploration and conquest of the Upper Nile, and French officers accompanied and historiographed the first expeditions despatched up the Nile by Mehemet Ali.

The British soon sent consuls to Khartoum, who drew thither other explorers and big-game hunters, who in time turned into governor-generals or other officials in Egyptian pay. French engineers constructed great canals, their masterly work

Empire. With what results ? Her extravagant debt is now, in 1908, reduced from £103,969,020 to £95,833,280, in addition to which reduction there is a general reserve fund of £11,055,413 ; her population has risen from 6,814,000 to nearly 12,000,000 ; her cultivable area from about 4,000,000 acres to 6,500,000 ; forced labour is abolished ; the rights of the peasants are absolutely secured ; justice is pure and prompt ; education enormously advanced ; canals infinitely

A LOST POSSESSION OF THE ENGLISH CROWN: GENERAL VIEW OF CORFU

culminating in the canal of Suez. The British demanded in compensation the permission to build railways and to open the overland route. The Franco-German War weakened French influence, and 1882 found Great Britain with an almost prescriptive right to interfere in the Sudan, a control of the railway system, a virtual monopoly of the steamship traffic on the Nile, and a vested right in the Suez Canal. Egyptian bankruptcy having compelled our intervention, Egypt since 1882 has been under the control of the British

extended ; railways carried to Khartoum and the Red Sea ; the Sudan reconquered and administered to the infinite blessing of its native inhabitants, the enrichment of Egypt, and the advantage of European and American trade ; and, finally, the people of the khediviate brought within sight of sound representative institutions.

The British occupation of Egypt, without the slightest doubt, has been the happiest event, in its results, which has ever befallen that country since the memorable expulsion of the shepherd kings.

BRITISH EXPANSION IN AMERICA
AND THE PASSING OF THE NATIVE RACES

IN this survey we are treating the United States historically as an outgrowth of the empire of which they formed a part down to 130 years ago. When the British first landed as colonisers on the Atlantic coast of North America, in the year **The First Britons in America** 1578, the Spaniards had already overrun Florida, and had occupied a good deal of Mexico. Otherwise, the American Continent to the north of the Gulf of Mexico was free from the presence of the Caucasian. It was at that time populated sparsely by Red Indians, who, as compared to the races conquered by the Spaniards further south, were leading the life of savages, though there were underlying indigenous civilisations in the temperate or sub-tropical portions of North America which had existed and had died away, or had been overthrown by the arrival of nomad savages from the north.

The Amerindian race probably extended in those days as far north as the Mackenzie River and the shores of Hudson's Bay. (The writer of this essay thoroughly approves the fused word of "Amerindian" to indicate the autochthonous races of North and South America. "American" is more aptly applied to the white peoples; "Indian" is too likely to lead to confusion with the Dravidian peoples. Yet physically the Amerindians are nearly connected with the Malays, Dayaks, and Mongoloid races of further India and the Malay Archipelago. "Amerindian" is a happy blend of the **Habitations of the Esquimaux** characteristics of the "American Indians.") Here they impinged on the Esquimaux, whose range in the sixteenth century was not far different from what it is at the present day—along the Greenland coasts, the great islands of the Arctic regions that lie between Greenland and the North American Continent, and along the continental shores of the Arctic Ocean as far

as Bering Straits. Southwards, the Esquimaux seem to have penetrated on the east coast of America as far as 50° N. Lat., in Newfoundland and Labrador, and to have come as a conquering race, driving before them Red Indian tribes. It was still farther to the south of these regions, where the Esquimau prevailed over the Red Indian, that the Norse colonies of the ninth and tenth centuries had been established (in Nova Scotia and Massachusetts) and had in turn been overthrown, mainly through the attacks of the Esquimaux, or at any rate of some race which in default of better knowledge we identify with the Esquimaux.

The Esquimau—the word is derived from a Red Indian nick-name meaning "eaters of raw flesh," the people's own term for themselves being Innuit—differs in the main from the Red Indian stock (which **Where the Esquimaux Originated** is identical with the existing indigenous population of America from the far north right down to Tierra del Fuego) in being moderately dolichocephalous—long-headed, instead of round or short-headed. Otherwise the Esquimaux, like the Amerindians—in a less pronounced form—seem to belong to the Mongolian sub-species of the human race. Probably the Esquimau is one of the most primitive representatives of this third main division of the human species. The straight-haired, slanting-eyed, large-cheekboned, yellow-skinned variety of humanity, which differs from the other two main divisions—the Negro and the Caucasian—in having a very sparse growth of hair on the face and body, originated in North-eastern Asia, and spread thence northwards round the Polar regions.

The type may be a very ancient one, however, that existed as far back as the time when a land connection remained between North America on the one hand, and Northern Europe on the other, by way of Iceland and Spitzbergen. The

Esquimau type indeed may even during the Glacial periods have penetrated with the glacial conditions of life into the British Islands, France, and Scandinavia.

The Amerindians (*i.e.*, all the existing indigenous races in America) belong, in the main, to a Mongoloid type, but one that has developed special features of its own, and which may have absorbed pre-existing long-headed, Aino-like tribes of a more generalised type, such Caucasoid tribes having preceded the Mongolian in the occupation of North America.

When the British colonists founded the settlement of Virginia, the Amerindians were, from our present point of view, savages, leading an existence more or less nomadic, with a preference for tents or (in the West) caves over huts. It is doubtful whether any of them dwelt in stone houses such as had once existed in the southern regions of North America, or in Mexico.

They lived largely as hunters, but probably did not number in all more than 5,000,000, if as much, throughout North America from the northern frontiers of Mexico to the Arctic Ocean. Their relations with the British settlers of

Exterminating the Amerindians the sixteenth and seventeenth centuries were in the main hostile. Tribe after tribe was gradually exterminated by diseases introduced by the Europeans, by warfare—often civil war between tribe and tribe, instigated by the European, or by alcohol.

France, late in the race for American colonisation, made up for lost time during the seventeenth century by the vigour and ability with which she colonised. By the early part of the eighteenth century she had laid the foundations of a Canadian empire and of a magnificent domain in what are now the southern states of North America. She dominated the Mississippi River from its mouth northwards so far as to bring her colonists of the south almost into touch with her colonists on the Great Lakes. Through her missionaries and her settlers she obtained a far-reaching influence over the Amerindians, with whom the French " habitants " mingled more freely—sexually—than did the Puritans or Hollanders of the Anglo-Saxon settlements.

The results are the French-speaking half-breeds of to-day in Canada — a handsome, stalwart race, often so prepossessing physically that they have been reabsorbed into the Caucasian community with little or no racial

objection. Yet the British settlers in the hinterland of New England also made friends here and there with Amerindian tribes. At last the Indians became involved in the hundred years' struggle between France and England for predominance in North America; and at this game, though the Europeans throve and increased,

England's Long Struggle for North America the Indians decreased in numbers, dying out from the extremely savage attacks of tribe against tribe, both waging that quarrel of the white man which was not theirs. By the time the United States were recognised as an independent power, and France had definitely abandoned political sway over any part of the mainland of North America—at the beginning of the nineteenth century, let us say—the Amerindians of North America had diminished in numbers both in Canada and the United States from the hypothetical 5,000,000 which were there when the white man first arrived to possibly not more than 3,000,000, distributed mainly over the countries west of the Mississippi and of the Canadian Rocky Mountains.

The middle of the nineteenth century saw the United States carrying on many an Indian war, which had arisen from the unchecked rapacity and shameless behaviour of the white colonists, who were pushing determinedly westwards towards the Pacific. Locations were set up by which it was hoped to provide a definite territory for one Indian tribe or another. A few of these locations are still maintained (87,237 square miles in 1906), but there is practically now no purely Indian territory on the soil of the United States or in Canada.

But the decrease of the Indians in the whole of North America, which may have brought their total as low as 1,300,000 somewhere about 1875—this estimate would include all Northern Mexico, with about 900,000 Amerindians—has apparently been checked of late years.

Better Times for the Indians In Canada and in the United States conscientious legislation has arrested the drink curse, and the greed of a European education is spreading amongst the Indians together with settled habits. Men and women of purely Indian blood are slightly more numerous in 1907 than they were thirty years ago. Including all Mexico, Yucatan, and Alaska, as well as the United States of America and the Canadian Dominion, there are seemingly at the present time 1,474,000 pure-blood Amerindians in North America. Yet they are less and less discernible to the traveller from abroad, inasmuch as they tend to dress and demean themselves increasingly more like the Americans of Caucasian race. They intermarry, or, at any rate, mix sexually with white men, the half-breed being of a comely type ; so that the eventual absorption of the American Indians into the Caucasian community of North America seems to be inevitable. Indeed, more than one anthropologist has considered the non-Esquimau American aborigines to have resulted from an early intermixture in far-back prehistoric days between a primitive type of Caucasian (like the Aino of Japan) and an Esquimau Mongoloid. At any rate, the cross between the Caucasian of North Europe and the Amerindian is a handsomer type of human being than the hybrid between the same race of white men and the negro.

Future of North America

The future of all English-speaking and French-speaking North America is no doubt the future of a white race, but before this result can be definitely achieved a solution will have to be found for the black problem in the United States. Within a relatively small geographical area of the United States east of the Mississippi there are at the present moment something like 9,500,000 negroes. This estimate includes some 2,500,000 persons of mixed negro and European blood. The tendency of public feeling at the present time in the United States is to lump together as negroes—" coloured people "—all men and women of recognisably negroid appearance and ancestry.

In some parts of the United States it is very awkward socially for anyone to be born with black hair and brown eyes even if they have a lively pink complexion. No doubt, many of these handsome brunettes owe their black hair and brown eyes either to Spanish intermixture or to an older strain of Amerindian. These are the explanations they strive to put forward, but woe betide them if their complexion is sallow ! During the days when slavery was an institution, the planters in the south mixed freely (sexually) with the negro or half-caste women whom they kept as their mistresses. But since the great Civil War and the emancipation of the negro, sexual intercourse between undoubted white men and

The Black Problem in America

undoubted negro women has decreased, being now forbidden by motives of racial pride—at any rate, on the side of the white man. The two races, therefore, co-exist side by side with far less tendency to intermingle than was the case when they were respectively master and slave.

But the negro has taken increasingly to the American climate and soil. Were it not for the opposition of the white man, he would have overrun the whole of the continent, and adapted himself eagerly to the most rigorous climate. His future is one of the greatest problems of the world. The white races, to begin with, are numerically as three to one with the negro. They are beginning to refuse him permission to extend as a settler beyond certain geographical limits, and even within these limits they are yearning to find some excuse to eject him from his lawful rights and expel him beyond the continental limits of North America.

If the tendencies of the extreme negrophobes rule American state policy, where will these ten millions of negroes and negroids find a permanent home ? An attempt was made to solve this problem by the institution of Liberia eighty years ago. Liberia has achieved some results, and may yet be a very valuable essay in negro self-government ; but so far she has proved a failure as a dumping ground for the American negro, for the simple reason that negroes born and bred on American soil find as great a difficulty in establishing themselves in Tropical Africa as does the European. They are almost equally subject with him to the effects of malaria, and they seem unable, as a general rule, to procreate healthy, vigorous children, unless they mingle with the indigenous races and thus allow themselves to be reabsorbed into the savage or semi-civilised negro tribes of the Dark Continent.

America's Attractions for the Negro

But the Americanised negro colonist clings instinctively, passionately, to American civilisation. He will literally die rather than give up European clothing and American notions of life, and slip back into the palæolithic or neolithic conditions of the African savage. It seems to the writer of this essay that if the cruel injustice of the white man in North America is to refuse to the negro a portion of the United States which can become his permanent home, his only resort will be the islands of the West

Indies and the states of Northern South America. Though in Africa he can scarcely withstand malaria better than the European, he can resist the sun. In America, as in Africa, the man of negro blood can perform manual labour under circumstances of heat and sun exposure which are fatal to the white man. A new Africa, therefore, may arise in Tropical America.

Great Britain is concerned with this problem, because at the present day the British West Indies are in the main peopled by negroes and negroids. In the British West Indies themselves there were very few indigenous inhabitants (Amerindian) when Britain took over the different islands, except in St. Vincent, Dominica, and perhaps Trinidad. In St. Vincent there were Caribs of more or less mixed type, sometimes hybridised with negroes. In Trinidad the few indigenous people lingering on the west coast belonged more or less to the Carib stock, but they were very few in number at the time of the British occupation of the island in 1796, and soon became absorbed in the mixed population of negroes and creoles. This island will

Mixed Races in Trinidad eventually become peopled by a homogeneous race of mixed negro, European, and East Indian origin. In British Guiana the Amerindian population forms a considerable item, perhaps 10,000 to 12,000 ; though it has probably diminished in numbers rather than increased during the hundred years of British occupation.

These people belong to the Arawak, Wapiana, Atorai, and Carib groups, related to South American stocks in the adjoining regions of the northern basin of the Amazon and to the former inhabitants of the West Indies. They do not seem to take very kindly to civilisation, and are probably destined to be absorbed into a negro or negroid peasantry, which may be further complicated by intermixture with the Indian coolie and the Portuguese colonist, the resulting race emerging as a type very like the Papuan of New Guinea or the Melanesian of the Western Pacific.

In the Falkland Islands there were no indigenes to be exterminated or saved. The islands were uninhabited by man when they became the resort of whaling ships. The present inhabitants are largely composed of British (Scottish, English, and Anglo-Saxon North American) stock, with an admixture of Spanish Americans from Uruguay. British interest in the Falkland Islands, and consequently our relations with the terminal portion of the South American continent, have, however, done a great deal to mend the lot of the miserable inhabitants of Tierra del Fuego, chiefly through the work of British missionaries. The Fuegians, a people of the

A Tribute to Missionary Enterprise Amerindian race, were first brought prominently to our notice by the writings of Darwin, who visited South America in the Beagle in 1833. At the time of his visit these people were leading a completely savage existence under miserable conditions of climate. They were almost entirely nude, and led the simple existence of the Stone Age, being unacquainted even with the use of fire, practising hardly any arts, and living the hunter's life.

The attention paid to Tierra del Fuego by the contending nations of Argentina and Chili, more especially by the Anglo-Saxon and Irish pioneers in the nominal service of those governments, led, in the second half of the nineteenth century, to the usual introduction of spirituous liquors and syphilis, and from one cause and another the Fuegians were rapidly becoming exterminated. But the advent of the South American Missionary Society has, during the last quarter of a century, not only saved the remnant from perishing but has infused into them such a degree of reasonable civilisation as may enable them to recover their numbers and better their position.

Elsewhere, in Chili or in Patagonia, the influence of British settlers, captains of industry or officials in the service of the Chilian and Argentine Governments, has stayed any tendency there might have been to provoke or extend wars between the European settlers and the local Amerindian tribes. But the inevitable tendency of these people in temperate South America, as in temperate North

Fusion of the Tribes America, will lie towards fusion with and absorption by the invading Caucasian, from whom they are not removed so far physically as the latter is from the negro ; no doubt because among the strands that go to weave the Amerindian type are Caucasian threads, traces of very ancient intermixture with the basic stock from which arose the European white man, whether that intermixture took place in far North-eastern Asia or came by way of the Pacific archipelagoes. Both routes may have been followed. The summing up, therefore, of the effect which the British Empire will have produced on humanity in the United States and British North America, in the West Indies and in South America, is this :

In the English-speaking regions of North America, north of the limits of Mexico, there will grow up a people which would be best represented at the present day by a composite photograph of all the races of Europe between Spain and Siberia, Greece and Scandinavia. The black drop in the blood of this potent race of the future will be no greater than that which has infused anciently the populations of Spain, Southern France, Sardinia, and Sicily, or which makes itself noticeable in such cities as Glasgow, Liverpool, Bristol and London, which traded with the West Indies and thereby mixed with negro slaves in the three last centuries. The Amerindian in North America will be gradually absorbed, and will improve rather than spoil the vigour and beauty of the American race. It will have much the same racial significance as the Mongolian strain which permeates parts of Scandinavia, Russia, Germany, Alsace, Brittany and Ireland.

The Canadian French and the descendants of the French colonists of Louisiana, the Spanish tinge in Texas, California, and Florida, the million or so Italians settled in America during the last fifty years, the other millions of Iberian Irish, the darker types of Hungarians, will leaven the blond masses, the descendants of the settlers from Great Britain and Northern Ireland, Russia, Poland, Scandinavia, Iceland, and Germany. The most stalwart of the peoples promise to arise in Canada ; the Canadian may be the aristocrat of the New World in the last half of the twentieth century.

"BRITANNIA'S REALM"

BRITAIN'S GREAT INDIAN EMPIRE
THE MARVELLOUS EFFECTS OF A CENTURY AND A HALF OF BENEFICENT GOVERNMENT

ON Asia, whatever may be the ultimate fate of the British Empire and the length of its duration, traces of its existence will have been left as far-reaching and ineffaceable in their nature as those of Rome on the Mediterranean world or of Macedon on the Nearer East. The peninsula of India is at once the nucleus and the starting-point of the British Empire in Southern Asia.

An inhabitant of Mars, looking at the outlines of the land surface of our planet, would certainly never have guessed that the people of the southern half of an island off the north-west coast of Europe would have made themselves the masters of Hindustan. It was virtually England that conquered India down to the close of the eighteenth century, largely as Ireland and Scotland have subsequently completed and strengthened the achievement. That a military power uprising in the

Britain's Indian Empire Balkan Peninsula should extend its sway continuously over Asia Minor, Persia and India is easily conceivable, as also that India should have fallen a prey to the Russians or the Turks of Central Asia. Yet, of course, our Indian Empire is not much more remarkable as a political achievement of the eighteenth and nineteenth centuries than is the Dutch Empire over the Malay Archipelago or what would have been a French overlordship of the Indian Peninsula. The first two conquests are the results of the development of sea power, and France, in the main, failed to take the place now occupied by Great Britain in Southern Asia because when her sea power was put to the test it yielded before that of the Anglo-Saxon.

If France has satisfied her Asiatic aspirations by the acquisition of large dominions in Indo-China—an almost sufficient compensation for what she lost to us in Hindustan—it is because at one time or another in the nineteenth century her

fleet has been sufficiently powerful to deter Great Britain from the risk of an avoidable war. In other words, in our days of imperial rapacity—the 'eighties and 'nineties of the last century—we put up with the growth of French dominion over

The Era of Imperial Rapacity Annam, Tonkin and Eastern Siam because, up to a certain point, we had too much to risk in going to war with France at sea to interpose a determined veto on her plundering of China and Siam. At such movements, of course, we expressed an unaffected disapproval with a naiveté the more extraordinary as the French activities, after all, were merely coincident with our own conquest of Burma and the Shan States and our determination to acquire undisputed political rights over the Siamese provinces of the Malay Peninsula.

In the eighteenth century we found India to be a prey to internecine war. After many invasions from the northwest, going far back into prehistoric days, the people of North Central India had been conquered by a Turkish prince at the head of an army composed of Moguls, Turks, Afghans, and Persians.

Thus in 1526 was founded the Mogul—properly spelt Mughal—Empire. Prior to this, much of Western and South Central India had been Mohammedanised and Arabised, so that the irruption of Babar slightly intensified the Mohammedan element, and enabled his descendants for the next two centuries to rule with fairly

Revival of Hindu Power undisputed sway over about 120,000,000 people, considerably more than two-thirds of whom belonged to the Hindu religion, and were thus violently opposed in their social customs and traditional beliefs to the ruling Mohammedans. The Hindu element began to revive in power and courage in the seventeenth, and above all in the middle of the eighteenth, century. Had the country been firmly united in religion under a dynasty that practised the faith of the majority of its subjects, our military and naval forces of the seventeenth and eighteenth centuries would never have been able to defeat the Portuguese, Dutch, and French, one after the other, and conquer in turn the native vassals or the foes of the Mogul dynasty till at last that dynasty became in the nineteenth century—it did not expire till 1858—the tool and pensioner of the British Chartered Company. India, speaking from the point of view of the human race and of the origin of many other important mammalian types, is perhaps the most remarkable portion of the earth's surface. It is in the main the great Mother Country —firstly, of humanity as a genus of the ape order; secondly, it may be, of human civilisation, and almost certainly of the principal religious ideas that now pulsate through the human world. In the Tertiary Epoch there seem to have arisen in India, not only the human genus and species from out of a pithec-

MAKING A PUBLIC ROAD THROUGH THE FOREST

anthropoid form, but possibly also three amongst the types of surviving anthropoid ape, and also the baboon genus. Moreover, this productive region appears to have been the birthplace of the bovine, antelopine, capricornine ruminants, several groups of carnivora, of dogs, deer, and swine.

Here, perhaps, arose the true elephant genus from out of the mastodon. Here was the great radiating centre of the gallinaceous birds. India ranks with North America and North-east Africa as one of the great evolutionary breeding grounds from which have arisen and dispersed the principal forms of animal life. Southern India, joined

it may be then with Malaysia, was almost certainly the place of origin of the human genus, and of the three species or sub-species into which modern man is divided.

When, however, the Ganges Gulf had disappeared, and the peninsula occupied very much its present form—in short, some ten to twenty thousand years ago—this portion of the world was inhabited mainly by what are styled the Dravidian races, a low type of Caucasian man, higher in development than the generalised black Australian or Veddah of Ceylon, yet not so distinctly a "white man" as the next upward step, the Iberian or brunette Mediterranean race. This last furnishes the principal racial element in the peoples of Afghanistan, Persia, North Africa, Southern and Western Europe at the present day. On these Dravidians recoiled prehistoric invasions of Mongols, of the yellow, bare-skinned, straight-haired type of humanity which may have arisen from the existing human species either in India or in Further India. These Mongolians penetrated here and there in prehistoric times amongst the Dravidian peoples, who themselves had overlaid pre-existing negroid Australoid races, for the more ancient negro type likewise originated in India ; so that here and there in Northern and Central India, and perhaps along the east coast, there are Mongolian elements older than those which penetrated India from Tibet and the Pamirs within the last 2,000 years.

At some unknown date, this side of 7,000 years ago, occurred one of the great landmarks in the unwritten history of India—the invasion of the Aryans. The name Aryan—itself of Indian origin— has been applied in past times with a

CUTTING A ROAD THROUGH THE JUNGLE IN THE FEDERATED MALAY STATES

degree of looseness which led for a while to its falling into disrepute. Its linguistic purpose was confused with a racial designation, which is probably of a far more abstruse and limited scope. One may perhaps—as a not altogether improbable theory—identify the original inventors of the Aryan tongues with the blond, grey-eyed Europeans of Russia, Central and Northern Europe. But for several thousand years Aryan languages have been spoken by all the types of Caucasian man in Europe and Western Asia, except Lapland, Finland, North-east Russia, part of Hungary, a small part of Turkey, Syria, and the borderlands of France and Spain.

The Ancient Aryan Languages

These languages seem—from such knowledge as we now possess—to have arisen somewhere in Eastern Russia or Western Asia, north of the Caucasus, and to have been the appanage of a white-skinned people of pastoral habits, physical beauty, and of a stage of culture which had reached the age of metals—copper, bronze, and perhaps iron. Some have maintained that this golden-haired or red-haired, grey-eyed people may have developed in North Africa from the brunette Mediterranean race or from some more generalised type of Caucasian man. The only clues that we possess at present as to the origin of Aryan languages would seem to lie in the direction of a Finnic or Mongolian stock.

But in prehistoric times, from 7,000 to 5,000 years ago, possibly more than that, Aryan conquerors had entered India from the north-west, and had produced much the same impression on the dark-skinned Dravidians as was made on the pristine negroes of Africa by the prehistoric invasions of Hamites from Egypt.

The Aryans introduced to the millions of Northern, Central and Western India a language of the same family as that to which Lithuanian, Slavic, Greek, Latin, and Keltic tongues belong. This language, represented pretty closely by Sanskrit, developed in the course of several thousand years into the modern dialects of India and of Southern Ceylon, leaving only outside its influence the Dravidian speech of Southern and South-eastern India and the tongues of a few aboriginal tribes. The Aryans brought with them religious ideas which modified the religion of Brahma and eventually gave rise to

Origin of the Buddha Religion

5618

that of Buddha. From them and their intrusion and infusion of superior northern blood arose the idea of caste. The original blond hair and grey eyes of the Aryans soon disappeared in their physical absorption into the millions of dark-haired, brown-eyed, swarthy Dravidians or the yellow-skinned, black-haired Mongolians. The traces of this northern physical type still linger in the highlands of Afghanistan and of the Hindu Kush. Curiously enough, these brown-haired, grey-eyed Afghans resemble strikingly the brown-haired, grey-eyed Berbers of the Atlas Mountains of Tunis and Algeria.

The Aryan influence may also have penetrated beyond India to the recesses of Siam and Cochin China ; but at the present day the mass of the population eastwards of Bengal belongs in the main to the Mongol type in varying degrees, with an underlying stratum of Negrito. The people of Bengal, the familiar "Babu" type, no doubt also have an infusion of the Mongolian in their blood. These Aryan invaders of prehistoric times were reinforced as regards language and fighting power by subsequent incursions, legendary and historical, from across the Hindu Kush. Across the lower valley of the Indus, however, at the dawn of history, races of Dravidian stock seemingly were pushing westwards through Baluchistan and Southern Persia to Mesopotamia and Eastern Arabia. Indeed, it would appear as though there had been a strong set of the Dravidian peoples towards Arabia at a remote period in the history of that peninsula, and that there may be even a Dravidian element in the blood of the Semitic and Hamitic tribes of Arabia and Ethiopia.

India at the Dawn of History

Alexander the Great definitely linked the fortunes of Europe with those of India. From his celebrated invasion onwards Europe never completely lost touch with the peninsula of Hindustan. Even Alfred the Great, King of Wessex, caused inquiries to be made about India. The invasion of the Greeks 300 years before Christ further strengthened the Aryan influence over North-western India, as is testified by the remains of a debased Greek art in the Northern Punjab and even Greek types of face amongst its people. The next great event in the history of this motherland was the invasion of the Mohammedan Arabs, which began in

BENGAL SAPPERS AND MINERS ROAD MAKING IN CHITRAL

CONSTRUCTING THE PERIYAR DAM IN SOUTH INDIA   Nicolas & Co.

SCENES IN MAN'S FIGHT AGAINST NATURE

1001 A.D., and which, carried on by the Arabised Turks and Persians, culminated in that Mogul Empire for which the British Crown was substituted in 1858 and 1876.

We found India in the seventeenth century more or less completely under the sway of the Mogul emperors. The India which they ruled, directly or indirectly, though it included Southern Afghanistan, scarcely extended to Baluchistan, and certainly stopped in the Far East at the mouth of the Ganges. It did not include Ceylon, which remained more or less governed internally by an ancient dynasty of Aryan origin and Buddhistic religion, but the coasts of which were controlled ever since the sixteenth century first by the Portuguese, then by the Dutch, and finally, in the nineteenth century, by the British. The India of the seventeenth century, ruled by the Mogul emperors, probably contained a population of 150,000,000. The Indian Empire of to-day, excluding Ceylon, extends from the Persian Gulf to the frontiers of Tonkin and contains something like 297,000,000 people. To about 150,000,000 we have brought the means at the present day of acquiring an excellent education, scarcely inferior in its scope to that which is provided for our fellow - countrymen at home. To the whole of the 300,000,000 of Baluchistan, Kashmir, Little Tibet, of the

RAILWAY SCENE IN BURMA H. C. White Co.
The above interesting picture not only shows how closely the railway system of Great Britain is copied in Burma, but also illustrates the spread of the English language in that country. Compartments reserved for women have the words "Women only" painted on the doors, while the picture of a woman above the lettering indicates the purpose of the compartment to those who have not learnt to read.

Indian peninsula proper from the Himalayas to Cape Comorin, of Burma and the Shan States we have given security of life and property to a degree never known by these Asiatic peoples in all their recorded history. Equal security has been given to the native dynasties of kings and chiefs who have accepted our suzerainty, and who

conduct the affairs of their kingdoms and principalities with decorum and justice. The wealth of India during the last hundred years, since the British became the effective masters over this region, must have increased tenfold, while the population has nearly doubled.

Magnificent public works have been carried out—thousands of miles of railways, canals for communication and irrigation, gigantic dams and reservoirs for the storage of water, bridges across rivers that are wonders of the world, the sounding, charting, and buoying of great capricious rivers up which ocean ships may travel hundreds of miles; we have developed coal-mines that have added enormously to the wealth of India; gold-mines, diamond mines. We have introduced the tea plant, and have made its cultivation one of the great industries of North-eastern India; the cinchona tree, with its fever-healing bark; the coffee-tree from Africa, and many other useful products of the tropics and the temperate zones which thrive on Indian soil. We have taken up and developed indigenous products like jute, indigo, cotton, wheat and rice. We have improved the indigenous breeds of horses; taken measures to preserve the wild elephant from extinction; checked the devastations and the numbers of harmful wild beasts and poisonous snakes. More important by far than this interference with the tiger and the viper is the tracking down of the plague, cholera, malaria and syphilis bacilli, and the war we have recently been waging on microbe-bearing rats, fleas and mosquitoes. We have fought famine in those recurring years of scarcity wherein the

NATIVE EDUCATION IN INDIA: SCENE IN A MOHAMMEDAN SCHOOL

rainfall was deficient, and we have striven to retain the rainfall necessary to the country by a careful control of the forests and the replanting of trees. When we took up the rule of India in the guise of a great amorphous trading company, India was rapidly being ruined by incessant warfare between degenerated Turkish and Afghan dynasties and their Hindu and Sikh opponents.

The country was becoming disforested by fires, by the unchecked browsing of goats and cattle, and by clearing for cultivation. And though this destruction of the woodlands could hardly affect the mighty ranges of the Himalayas or the tropical jungles of Southern India, it was, together with the neglect of irrigation, slowly extending the area of the waterless desert region in the north-west and centre. Temples and mosques and other marvels of Indian architecture at their best were crumbling into decay through the decline of art and the incessant wars between Mohammedans and Hindus. It is said, nevertheless, that the people were less taxed than they are under our existing regime, and that the population being only half what it is now, disease was not so rampant from overcrowding in towns, while famines were less frequent and severe.

It is doubtful whether these counter assertions are correct. Some of the people were no doubt lightly taxed, or paid no taxes at all, through leading the life of savages. Others again were subjected to such considerable and such irregular extortions that private enterprise was often crippled. The effects of the old regime have not quite vanished yet. Rulers and people were accustomed not only to put their savings into bullion of gold and silver, but, in the uncertainty of their lives, to trust no man, no institution, no government, with their hoards of wealth; rather to bury their gold and silver in the ground against such time as they should need it. In this way many a store of bullion has disappeared which might otherwise have been circulating through the country and stimulating commerce.

As to the records of disease, so little attention was paid to these questions in the native annals that there is scarcely any evidence on which to base a comparison between the death-rate now and the death-rate a hundred years ago. The great increase in the population, and the going to and fro, hither and thither across the Indian Empire, have no doubt spread certain diseases at one time restricted to special localities. But through the measures undertaken by British medical science some

The Fight With Disease in India diseases like small-pox have been robbed of their terrors, and others, like cholera, malaria, and the plague, are being brought gradually under control. Progress in the elimination of disease would have been quicker but for the suspicion, the prejudices, the religious fanaticism of Hindus and Mohammedans. It is scarcely an exaggeration to say that only two or three thousand natives of India out of three hundred millions have as yet grasped sufficiently the principles of natural science to realise the true causes of disease, and to be convinced that sensible people would not allow either superstition or misapplied religious principles, or foolish social customs and prejudices, to stand between an enlightened government and the elimination of such diseases as the plague.

The effect of 150 years of British rule on the peoples of India has been stupendous. We have put an end to Afghan raids which at intervals since 1001 scattered the accumulated capital, destroyed the cities and the public works of

India's Debt to Britain the industrious races, and punctuated the annals of India with holocausts of human victims. We have done away with Thuggism, widow-burning, and our influence is rapidly making child-marriage an obsolete custom. Under our rule there is complete religious liberty for all who do not want to adopt murder or torture as an article of faith. We may not last long enough to make a homogeneous undivided people out of the 300,000,000

inhabiting this sub-continent, for that is nearly as difficult as to fuse all the states of Europe into a single polity ; but, at any rate, we have set the Parsees on their feet, have raised the sect of the Sikhs to be deservedly one of the dominant forces of India, have enabled the Mohammedans of Bengal, Oudh, and Agra, and also of the Punjab and of Haidarabad, to develop their religious ideas in unfettered liberty of opinion till, if any group can save the teaching of the Arabian prophet from falling completely out of harmony with our present life, it will be the prosperous, educated, reasonable Moslems of the Indian Empire.

We may in the same way save the Hindus from themselves by sapping the intolerable nonsense of caste, of the Brahman cult, the non-hygienic principles that direct this and that restriction on wholesome food or drink, of the worship of black

Consequences of Britain's Good Rule goddesses with two dozen breasts, of all the ghastly rubbish which still reduces 200,000,000 of Hindus to a negligeable quantity in the weights of the intellectual world. We shall also have had the privilege of assisting and rendering prosperous and numerous one of the very few good and noble religions which have arisen in the world—the sect of the Jains.

The effect of the British Empire on the Malay Peninsula and in Borneo has been the abolition of piracy, the stoppage of internecine wars between one Malay sultan and another, and of the Arab slave trade ; and the great recent increase of population which has resulted from the abatement of the dense forests and their profitable exploitation, the discovery of tin and coal, and the hundredfold increase of human health, happiness, wealth and intellectual progress in these parts. If there is any portion of the British Empire without a blemish in purpose or achievement, it is the Malay Peninsula, the Straits Settlements, and all their appurtenances.

THE GOLDEN TEMPLE OF THE SIKHS AT LAHORE

BRITISH EXPANSION IN AFRICA AND THE PACIFIC
AND ITS EFFECT ON THE NATIVE RACES

THE existence of a great island or continent to the south of the Malay Archipelago had been suspected by the Portuguese early in the sixteenth century. This dim knowledge was crystallised into an allusion to "Greater Java." The Dutch were the first, in 1598, to refer to this continent to the south of New Guinea as "Australis Terra." The subsequent history of the discovery and settlement of Australia has already been given in preceding chapters.

What were the conditions of Australasia when white men in the seventeenth century were feeling their way towards fresh conquests and occupation? Why, when island after island in the Malay Archipelago was rapidly conquered and occupied by the Portuguese, Spaniards, Dutch or English, did these lands of the southern hemisphere so long evade the white man's sphere of practical politics? The westernmost promontories **Australasia's Savage Inhabitants** and islands of New Guinea were included by the Dutch within their sphere of commercial and political influence as early as the end of the sixteenth century; but the whole of the remainder of New Guinea, Australia, New Zealand, and the adjacent Pacific archipelagoes were left to themselves till the last half of the eighteenth century. The reasons for this late development were principally the savage and ferocious nature of the inhabitants, who lay utterly outside Hindu, Malay, and Mohammedan influence, and the existence of the Great Barrier Reef, which hindered approach to the coast of North-east Australia.

The extent of this reef southwards was probably over-estimated. But where it came to an end the seas were sufficiently far south to be affected by heavy gales. It was not until better and bigger ships and more scientific navigators entered these waters, with Captain Cook as a pioneer,

that any approach was made by English or French towards discovery and settlement. But the nature of the inhabitants of these Australian lands was a more powerful deterrent than the dangers of navigation. The complete absorption of the Malay Archipelago and Peninsula within the European **Mohammedan Religion Spread by the Arabs** political area in a few years after discovery had been enormously facilitated by the civilisation of the Malay race at some unknown period by Hindu influences, and, much later, by their conversion to Islam.

Just as the Islamising of the northern half of Africa shed a flood of light on a country the indigenes of which (south of N. Lat. 10°) were in a stage of early culture singularly akin to that of Australasia, so the carrying of the Mohammedan religion by Arabs through India and along the trade route to China amongst the Malay Islands did more for mediæval geography and the linking up of the worlds of Europe and the Far East than the attempts of Greece, Rome, and Constantinople or the growth of the Chinese Empire.

The conversion of the Malays to Islam definitely attached the coasts of the East Indian Islands and promontories to the civilised world. The plumes of New Guinea birds of paradise, the camphor of Formosa, the spices and even the cockatoos of the Moluccas may have reached the Persian Gulf, the Mameluke rulers of Egypt, the Greek emperors of **The Low Type of Australasian Aborigines** Byzantium, the merchants of Venice, and the Arab rulers of Grenada before the oversea exploits of the Portuguese made these regions of the Far East tributary to Western and Northern Europe. The culture which prevailed over New Guinea, excepting the small Malay sultanates of the far north-west, over all Australia and Tasmania, was of such a

low order that it might be called Palæolithic. The aborigines of New Guinea,
Australia and Tasmania were, in the main,
of a more primitive, less differentiated
character than any living races at the
present day, except their outlying relations
such as the Veddahs and Negritoes. The
lowest Australian types of men bear in
Diversity cranial formation a striking
of Race in similarity to the Neanderthal
Australia species of the genus Homo which
inhabited Europe at a very
remote period. They are, indeed, the
nearest living representatives of early
Palæolithic Man in Europe. Elsewhere
this generalised type of our species has
been developed, specialised, or exterminated. At the present day the Papuan
race of New Guinea makes a distinct
approximation towards the negro, and this
negroid type penetrates eastward and
northward, mixed in varying degrees
with the Polynesian, till it reaches
Hawai, Formosa, and Japan.

The theory sometimes advanced to
account for the physical attributes of the
extinct Tasmanians is that this negroid
type migrated southwards along the
east coast of Australia and crossed thence
to Tasmania, being afterwards succeeded
on the continent of Australia by races
with straighter hair and more prominent
noses, akin to the Dravidian.

In New Zealand there was a different
state of affairs. The first European explorers that landed on its coasts—French
and English, at the close of the eighteenth
century—observed two types amongst the
aborigines : a short, dark-skinned negroid,
and the tall, light-skinned Maori ; and
the theory was advanced some thirty years
ago that the arrival of the last named
from Polynesian archipelagoes had been
preceded by a Tasmanian immigration. But
it is inconceivable that this low race could
have constructed canoes to cross a thousand
odd miles of sea between Australia and
New Zealand's New Zealand ; it is difficult
Early enough to believe that such
Inhabitants a primitive type could even
have crossed on rafts a strait
of a few miles in width between Wilson
Promontory and Tasmania ; and it has
been surmised that their colonisation of
this island dates from a time when it was
connected by an isthmus with the Australian continent. Therefore, it is more
probable that if there was a negroid element
in New Zealand, it accompanied the Maories

5624

from the Polynesian archipelagoes. It
is the main element of the population of Fiji, and is traceable in Tonga.
The Papuans of New Guinea are fairly
abundant, of medium height, and good
proportions, though some of the tribes
of the interior tend to a shortness of
legs which recalls the forest negroes of
Africa. The skin colour is sooty brown
like that of the Australian.

The dark races of South-eastern Asia differ
from the "black" negroes in that there
is less red colour in the skin, and in the
case of the Papuans and Australians there
is a much greater projection of the brow-
ridges ; the nose, moreover, being seldom
absolutely flat in the bridge, though the
tip is wide and flat at the nostrils, and
the lips, though thick and projecting, are
not so largely everted as with the average
negro. The hair of the Papuans is black
and frizzly, and grows semi-erect, like
a mop. That of the Australians is curly
in a large way, but except for its coarse
texture grows very much like a European's.
Like the lower races of Europe and India
the Australian's body, in the male, is very
Characteristics hairy. This is one of the
of the characteristics which points
Polynesians to a basal affinity between
the Australoid and the
Caucasian. The Polynesians seem to be
a Far Eastern prolongation of Malay influence, though in physical characteristics
perhaps nearer akin to the Caucasian.
They differ from the Western Caucasian
in the relative absence of body-hair, and
a tendency to the straight, coarse head-
hair of the Mongol, Malay, and Amerindian.

It may be that before the Mongols of China,
Japan, North Asia and the Esquimaux
had become differentiated and had reached
their present habitat an early Caucasian
type threw off a smooth-skinned, straight-
haired branch which migrated to North-
eastern Asia and thence colonised much of
America, while it made its way also south
and east to the Pacific archipelagoes, to
absorb culture from the more Mongolian
Malay and mingle his blood with his.
In many of their physical characteristics
the Polynesians recall the Indians of
Western America. In modern times they
have mingled with the negroid Melanesians,
inheriting from them wider noses, undu-
lations in the head-hair, and darker skin
colour. Yet, when all has been said and
done, the best Polynesian type recalls the
European, and fundamentally the two

races may be akin, a fact which will probably have the happiest effect on the future status of the Polynesians, inter-marriage with whom will be no more prejudicial to racial beauty and mental development than the intermixture with the Amerindian or the Northern Mongol.

The effect of the British Empire on the autochthonous races of Australia and Polynesia cannot be described in terms of such glowing praise as I have applied to our altogether splendid record in India, Ceylon and Malaya. From the point of view of the anthropologist and the philanthropist it is here that our record is sorriest and most ignoble. When we invaded Australia and Tasmania the welfare, rights, and anthropological im-portance of the indigenes seem to have been completely absent from our minds.

Our Imperial conduct, in fact, in these regions ranks much lower in the scale of morality than that of the King of the Belgians, who, if he has afflicted and diminished the native tribes of the Congo, has at any rate contemporaneously illus-trated their arts, customs, and beliefs whilst **Great Britain's** such things could be re-**Black Record** corded. Our treatment of **in Australia** the Australian and Tasma-nian blacks has been stupid and brutal down to about 1896, long before which time the Tasmanians were extinct, and we deserve to be scourged for it before the world's tribunal quite as much as the Spanish nation for its treatment of the Amerindians, or Leopold of Coburg for his merciless exploitation of the Congolese. But for the missionaries and, in addition, the fighting qualities of the Maories the Polynesian inhabitants of New Zealand would have been as mercilessly dealt with.

When we laid hands on all Australia, from the point of view of keeping other European Powers out, say, in 1800, the native population of the entire island continent cannot have been less than 200,000; to-day it is computed at 65,000. Extermination seems to have been the order of the day—extermination by rum, syphilis, starvation, and later the more merciful and direct assassination by the rifle bullet. In about forty years from 1800, the natives of New South Wales, Victoria, and of South Australia, had been reduced from a possible 100,000 to about 5,000, not, of course, including those of the central and northern regions, which are still so inappropriately linked with

" South " Australia. Queensland has had as merciless a record, but here the territory was vaster, hotter, and a larger proportion of the indigenes have survived to profit by the development of Queensland public opinion on to a higher plane of thought. Their treatment now is vastly improved in this direction. Western Australia in **The Natives** the back blocks, and above all **Under Cruel** in the far north-west, has still **Treatment** much scourging to receive and atonement to make; from the half-suppressed reports of clergymen and missionaries the Westralian treatment of the natives under their control has been quite as bad as anything recorded of the Congo. But in these matters, where the great daughter nations are concerned, the British Press is inclined to complacent silence.

The black Australian, as we first found him, was certainly a savage, and an unamiable, treacherous savage. " *Ce! animal est très méchant! Quand on l'attaque il se défend!* " If our fairest coast regions were suddenly invaded by an almost irresistible race of Martians, we, in our futile defence of our homeland, might show ourselves equally treacher-ous. For a long time he was said to be an " irreclaimable " savage. But this has been shown to be as true as the dictum of King Leopold's Congo Ministers that the Bantu negroes of Congoland were " outside the pale of the family idea." The irreclaim-ability of the Australian—as announced by the white colonist—is as true as the de-pravity of the lamb in the eyes of the wolf.

Fortunately, however, there were other and nobler forces at work in Australia, and the result of their efforts, and those of the colonists and governments helping them, is that there are many police, stock-riders, trackers, farm servants, and other workers of use to the general community at the present day, who are of pure Australian blood. It is no longer probable that this wonderfully interesting race will **A Brighter** be exterminated; it is less un-**Prospect for** likely that it will be absorbed. **the Native** The half-caste between white man and Australian aborigine is not such a disappointment as are some other human hybrids, either physically or mentally. And again, from this cross to further intermixture with the whites—or, as seems now more customary, with such Afghans, Indians, Chinese, or Polynesians as the rigid immigration laws may per-mit, or fail to prevent—may in time create a small but prosperous class of dark-eyed, pale-skinned, black-haired, not uncomely people, who may find a place and a decent recognition for themselves in the future great Australian nation.

We had no recognised empire in the Pacific until we annexed New Zealand in 1840, but the unofficial influence of the **Missionaries as Builders of Empire** British on the Polynesian and Melanesian peoples began with the voyages of Cook and the first settlement of Australia. The way for the empire was prepared, unconsciously no doubt, by missionaries, whalers, and traders in small sailing ships, together with the frequent cruises of men-of-war. The missionaries, most of all, brought the Pacific islanders to the idea that their only way of political salvation—decimated as they were by their own inter-tribal quarrels, and constantly under menace of attack from European pirates—was to offer the supreme rule or wardship over their countries to the British queen.

No doubt, they were instinctively right. At any rate, if the islands had not hoisted the British flag they would have been placed under that of France, the United States, or Germany. But it is sad to think that since New Zealand became British its indigenous population has decreased from a hypothetical 100,000 to about 48,000 at the present day. The population of Fiji was estimated at about 200,000 in the middle of the nineteenth century, and is now no more than 87,125 (in 1906), and is diminishing rather than increasing. Elsewhere in the Pacific, Tonga, Santa Cruz, Solomon Islands, Gilbert Islands, Ellice Islands, the population of native strain is on the increase.

Many of these islands were depleted of their able-bodied men by the labour traffic of 1870–1890, which at first kidnapped, and later lured them for work on plantations in Eastern Tropical Australia. Many of these labourers have since returned to **The Future of the Polynesians** their homes, materially and mentally improved by their exile. There is no cause now but the inherent weakness of racial stamina why the Polynesians and Melanesians should not once more begin to increase in numbers. Yet in Hawai, under the Americans, and in Fiji under the British—both governments showing the utmost solicitude for their Polynesian wards—the native race is ceasing to have children, is dying of white men's diseases, is silently melting away before the Indian coolie, the Japanese, Chinese, and Portuguese immigrants. It is said that native women are more fertile with Japanese, Chinese or European husbands; it may chance, therefore, that the fate of this Polynesian race may be reabsorption, to form with these other racial elements another and stronger Polynesian people, an amalgam, like the predecessors, whom Cook first described, of Australoid, Caucasian, and Mongolian strains.

In other ways, the effect of the empire on New Zealand, and on these "Summer Isles of Eden set in dark purple spheres of sea," has been wholly good, so far as the general enrichment of the world is concerned. New Zealand has become in sixty-eight years a young nation of magnificent vigour, with a mighty future before her, and a population of nearly a million.

Fiji now does an annual trade in exports, such as sugar, dried coco-nut kernels, and fruit, and imports of the value of £1,213,000. This archipelago, extraordinarily endowed as to climate and healthfulness, scenery, and fertility of soil, is of the area of Wales, **Prosperous Pacific Islands** and supplies both Australia and Canada with tropical produce. The inhabitants of nearly all the other Pacific islands under British jurisdiction are converted to Christianity, and have given up cannibalism and civil war. They are, for the most part, busily engaged in the copra—dried coco-nut—trade, but a number of them still seek service in Queensland, in Pacific islands belonging to France or Germany, or even go as far afield as Mexico, confident that their British nationality will afford them ample protection.

Thus, after vicissitudes extending over more than a century—since their first discovery, or rediscovery, by British and French mariners—the Pacific islands seem to have found peace, prosperity, comparative freedom and political stability. Except in New Zealand, we have nothing to regret in our treatment of these Polynesian and Melanesian races, since a direct government control was established over the islands, large and small; but there remain some seventy or eighty years of previous unofficial British or British colonial dealings with the peoples that are a sorry record of slavery, kidnapping, alcohol-poisoning, debauchery, disease, ridiculous or even vicious wrangles between Christian sects and churches, cannibalistic outbreaks and sanguinary revenges, farcical governments got up by European or American adventurers, and floated with repudiated paper currencies.

These influences combined must have reduced the total native population of Oceania, excluding New Guinea but including New Zealand, from a possible 2½ millions to about a million at the present day. Of course, it must be remembered this 2½ millions had been living lives of useless happiness, apart from the rest of the moving world, aloof from the sorrows and struggles of the toiling thousand millions in temperate or torrid

than the nourishment of unintellectual idleness in cannibalism and sexual orgies of 2,000,000 brown Polynesians. Such fragments of the Earthly Paradise are worthier to be the home of 50,000,000 men and women endowed with the finest qualities of mind and body.

What has been the effect of the British Empire on Africa? In the west, the scene of our earliest attempts at settlement as traders and rulers, we first encouraged to an enormous extent the trade in slaves. This has led to much intertribal warfare, and even the disappearance of certain coast peoples. Between 1560 and 1860 the

G. Hughes

THE PRIMITIVE SYSTEM OF LANDING ON THE WEST AFRICAN COAST

continents. Seemingly, a policy of secluded selfishness does not enter into the scheme of the Higher Power for the development of the human race. Nature insists on a unification of the genus, and to attain this end extremes meet—the Dutchman mingles with the Hottentot, the Englishman with the Polynesian, Scotsman with West Indian negro, Portuguese with Dravidian, Arab with Bantu, Frenchman with Amerindian. The Summer Isles of Eden and the 104,000 square miles of pasture, meadow, woodland, Alp, lake, and orchard, which constitute the noble patrimony of New Zealand, were meant for better things in the destiny of man

West African slave trade certainly tended to the depopulation of parts of Guinea, Dahomeh, the Niger Delta, and the Kameruns.

The British from 1815 and the French from about 1835 set to work to suppress the slave trade they had once encouraged. This, of course, led to their increased interference in West African affairs, and by degrees to a widespread use of the English language as a medium of intercommunication. The trade in palm oil and palm kernels—said to have been invented in Liberia—was, in its early days, a British industry; and so lucrative did it become to natives as well as white men that it probably proved a more efficient corrective of the slave trade than the vigilance of the British cruisers. But the palm-oil trade gave rise to incidents and tendencies which provoked further—and often unwilling—interference on the part of the British Government with native chiefs. These last would frequently attempt to make a corner in palm oil, by preventing the interior natives from coming into contact with the white traders, who were thus compelled to deal with the oil-markets by making use of the coast negroes as intermediaries and middlemen. Thus the producing peoples of the interior received a poor price for their industry, and the European had to pay too dearly for the oil which was becoming so increasingly necessary to his home industries.

Fair Trade on the West African Coast

Now all these questions are regulated equitably. The coast men share in the general advantages of the coast government, which is partly supported by the customs duties levied on general imports and exports. The natives of the interior can dispose of their produce without let or hindrance for the prices determined by the law of supply and demand. But it is in the coast regions, above all, that the advantages of an enlightened British administration have been shown. Here a system of *petite culture* has been brought into existence, in the Gold Coast Colony especially, which has had the happiest results, especially in the cultivation of cacao. In this a trade of something like a million sterling has been developed.

A glance at the revenues and expenditures of all the British West African colonies and protectorates will at once show their prosperity. It is, above all, the prosperity of the people of the soil, whose rights have been most rigorously respected and reasonably defined. The British West African possessions are setting an example to the rest of British Tropical Africa, and to a great deal of Africa and Asia which is under other flags, of the new policy, which is going to spread like a new religion—ample recognition of the rights of the indigenous peoples to the land they live on and to the natural produce of its soil. This theory does not prevent the reservation of absolutely vacant lands or lands containing forests or mines, which must be dealt with in the general interests of the community. Such are held in trust for the community by the established government of the

New Policy of British West Africa

territory, and the proceeds or profits therefrom are publicly accounted for, and form part of the local revenue. In the administration which controls these sources of public wealth the voice of the real natives of the country will have a larger and larger part as education increases in the native community and fits the people of the soil for playing a responsible part.

Whilst foreign capital is required to fructify industries and to turn the resources of the country to profitable account, that capital must be allowed a fair representation in the local councils, and receive sufficient guarantees as to its investments; otherwise the native community will never obtain money on cheap enough terms for creating its industries. But the ambition of all these negro states under the British flag in West Africa and Nigeria should be to obtain their working capital in time through their own resources and in time to show themselves more and more worthy of home rule.

In East Africa, between the Nile Basin and the Zambesi, the chief effect on the native peoples has been produced by the abrogation of Arab authority in the coast lands and the eventual suppression of the Arab slave trade, and, finally, of slavery. The Arab treatment of East and Central Africa has followed much the same lines as European behaviour elsewhere. First of all, the land was ravaged for slaves and ivory. No thought was taken for the welfare of the indigenes at all. They were originally transported in thousands to Arabia, Persia, Madagascar, and the Comoro Islands—a few also going to Western India—and, later, they were used to develop clove, sugar, coco-nut plantations in Zanzibar and along the East African littoral from Lamu to Cape Delgado.

The Arab Oppression in East Africa

When the Arabs appreciated the possibilities of Congoland, the slaves of the populations they harried were turned on to create vast rice-fields, orange groves, lime orchards, plantations of sugar-cane, bananas, ground nuts, and maize in the valley of the Lualaba-Congo. When conquered at this epoch, the close of the nineteenth century, the domain of the Arabs on the coasts of Nyassa and Tanganyika and in Eastern Congoland presented to the British, Germans, and Belgians a certain appearance of well-being, civilisation and contentment which was in marked contrast to the savage regions outside the Arab settlements. To some extent this contrast was an unfair one to the pagan African, because the unsettled regions outside the Arab zone had been reduced to a condition of heedless savagery by the raids of the Arabs and their negro allies. The wretched remnant of the natives only secured some immunity from attack by simply offering no temptation to robbery. They accumulated no stores of food, and avoided giving any evidence of culture.

Had no European intervention taken place, matters would have taken—more slowly—the same course under the Arabs as under the white man's predominance. First, the Arabs would have cultivated millions of acres by forced labour; then, as it became more and more difficult to coerce great negro populations raised to the same level of culture as the Arabs themselves, the Arabs would have sought to work by means of hired labour. Lastly, they might have had the intelligence to perceive what we are just appreciating— thanks to the teaching of men like E. D. Morel, Albert Chevalier, Vandervelde, **Tropical Africa's Negro Problem** Charles Dilke, Fox-Bourne, and Theodore Roosevelt— that the negro is an ineradicable plant in Tropical Africa; and that, this being the case, it is better to treat him as the owner and dominant factor in the country, inspire him with the pride of ownership—individual and communal—and by means of trade allurements tempt him to exploit, as a free man and a person with a stake in his own commonwealth, the resources and riches of his dwelling-place.

This theory has its imperfections when contrasted with actual contemporary facts, but on the whole it has proved the best working hypothesis with the negro peoples of Eastern as well as Western and Central Africa. But there are other factors in the East African problem that do not exist in West Africa and the Congo Basin. Half the area of British East Africa, a quarter of Uganda, a quarter of Nyassaland are regions of considerable elevation above sea-level; and partly on this account, partly from other causes, are—or were when we entered the country —devoid of native inhabitants. To tell the truth, although the negro may have avoided settling on these elevated plateaus when he was a nearly naked savage, he has shown himself quite able to do so under

more civilised conditions. But most of these cold countries were No-man's-lands when we discovered them, and we have not felt called upon to hand them over to the black man. For thirty years there have been Scottish and English coffee planters (colonists) in Nyassaland; for seven years we have been permitting the **Unoccupied Earthly Paradises** appropriation of vacant lands by white men on the healthy uplands of East Africa. Here, as in Western Uganda and Northern Nyassaland, there are earthly paradises still awaiting the people. Consequently, the political future of Eastern Africa is likely to be far more complicated as an entity than that of West Africa, purely a black man's land, or South Africa, where the white man is quite resolved to be the predominant partner.

In British East Africa, including Somaliland and Nyassaland, there will be small, compact, powerful colonies or enclaves of Europeans and Asiatics surrounded by a very numerous, prosperous, and, I hope, friendly, population of negroes and negroids. The Arab element will remain and will permeate the leaven of the docile Bantu with a sense of self-respect and personal pride which will compel a decent treatment at the hands of the British and Indian fellow-colonists.

The effects produced by the British Empire on the native races of South Africa have been most potent. The Dutch and Huguenot settlers who preceded us had conquered the feeble Hottentot and Bushman tribes of the south-western angle of Cape Colony sufficiently to be able to dispose of the land between the little Namaqua coast, the sources of the Zak, and the Great Fish River amongst European farm settlers. These last at times were almost at war with the unsympathetic, selfish, stupid government of the Dutch East India Company. The Boer pioneers of the future white South Africa **The Racial Struggles in South Africa** shirked any contest with the powerful Bantu peoples to the east and north of the land from which they had ousted the Hottentot. Indeed, the drift of the racial struggle was rather the other way when the British first took possession of Cape Town. Should the Kaffir and Basuto be allowed to drive the Boer farmers back on to the Cape Peninsula and occupy the lands of the Hottentot in their stead? For centuries the big Bantu negroes had been pressing south from their original home in Central Africa. They had absorbed or exterminated the Hottentots and most of the Bushmen in South-eastern Africa ; on the south-west their advance was hindered by the aridity of the Kalahari Desert and Namaqualand, but they had already turned the obstacle by coming **Britain's** round the south coast of **Great Work in** the continent and advancing thus on the delect-**South Africa** able region of the Cape of Good Hope (one of the world's paradises). The Sneeuwbergen and the Great Fish River were the limits on the north and east which temporarily detained them when the Briton arrived on the scene.

But for his armed support — the resources of Britain in men, money and ships—it is doubtful whether the Boers, left to their own resources, could have stemmed this impetuous flood of Basuto and Kaffir warriors. Supposing even that Holland had remained the sovereign of Cape Colony, could the Dutch nation at that juncture have fought and vanquished two or three millions of Bantu negroes of the Zulu and Suto calibre when, even with all the resources of modern warfare and the unquestioned bravery of her troops, she has not been able to subdue the small sultanate of Achin (Sumatra) between 1815 and 1908 ?

It seems very probable that the assumption of British control over Cape Colony in 1806, and later over Natal, saved South Africa for the white man, who, in the temperate regions of the south-west, had just as much right there as the Bantu. The subsequent effect of British rule has not been to lessen the black population of Trans-Zambesian Africa. The Bushmen, already half absorbed by the Hottentots and nearly exterminated by the Bantu, are, it is true, only about 4,000 to-day, where there were perhaps 10,000 seventy years ago, and the Hottentots are a decaying people to some slight extent. They seem more likely to exist in a half-caste type, the original hybrids with the Boers —Griqua—mixing again with the pure

bred Hottentots and strengthening the race. But, thanks to the staying of civil war and mad superstitions among the Kaffirs, holocausts of slaughter and incessant murderous raids by all the Zulu clans, conquests and ravages by the different Suto or Bechuana tribes between the Upper Zambesi and the Orange River, the settled Bantu population of Southern Africa—Zambesi to Algoa Bay—has increased probably from 3,500,000, as we may compute it to have been in 1806, to nearly 6,000,000 at the present day.

The increase has been most marked in Eastern Cape Colony, Natal, Basutoland, Bechuanaland, Eastern Rhodesia, and Portuguese South-eastern Africa, where the conditions of native life have been vastly improved by the wages of the mining labour market in Kimberley, the Orange State, and the Transvaal. Unfortunately, although the Imperial rule of Britain has been—no honest person or competent judge can deny—a very great blessing to humanity in West, East, and South Africa, it has in the south and south-centre, and a little in the east, spelt ruin to the magnificent wild mammalian fauna.

The Boer hunters counted for something in this work of thoughtless destruction, but only as the disciples of British sportsmen. These were originally officers in the army, for the most part visiting the Cape on their way to or from India. India had initiated them into the joys and thrills of big-game shooting, the rifle had come into general use as a sporting weapon of precision, and thus were provoked the wonderful crusades against elephants, buffalo, **Hunters'** antelopes, rhinoceroses, giraffes, **Destructive** lions, hippopotami, zebras, **Crusades** which have ended by leaving nearly all Cape Colony with no more notable wild beasts than a few baboons, leopards, jackals, civets, springboks, and rodents ; a campaign which has placed the quagga and the blaubok on the list of extinct animals, and has brought the white rhinoceros, South African oryx, and several other interesting mammalian types very near the vanishing point.

BRITISH ENTERPRISE IN AFRICA : THE NYASSA-TANGANYIKA ROAD

MAN'S TRIUMPH OVER NATURE
THE WONDERFUL RECORD OF BRITISH ACHIEVEMENT THROUGHOUT THE WORLD

THE British nation has not merely fought with rival or recalcitrant men for the colonisation, retention, and development of its empire; it has done things more worthy of remembrance perhaps than that. It has steadily fought the reactionary forces of Nature, and has often scored a victory.

Surely something of the genius of old Rome must have left its germs in British soil and been absorbed by British men and women, whether they were Kelto-Roman, Danish, Saxon, Norman, or French in their ancestry. The Roman nature of our public works is not of to-day or the last century only. Even the roystering, dissipated, drunken, peculating soldiers and officials of Charles II. left traces of their brief occupation of Tangier in the massive masonry of the mole. Though it is 105 years since we lost Minorca, we have dowered that island with magnificent **Builders of Empire** roads, bridges, quays, and bastions. Corfu bears the impress of the practical British mind more thoroughly than any civilised influence that has preceded or followed. The public works of Aden are tremendous, awe-inspiring, even though they may be but the logical continuation of cyclopean tasks begun by prehistoric Arabs.

In Canada, before the united "dominion" days, the British and colonial governments had constructed canals across the Niagara Peninsula, alongside the rapids of the St. Lawrence. These have been subsequently extended and improved by the dominion government, until now the waters of Lake Superior—2,200 miles inland—and the other great fresh-water seas of the St. Lawrence system, including the port of Chicago, are in direct steamer communication, for reasonably small steamers, with Britain and the rest of the world.

Since Canada became a self-governing country, British capital and credit almost entirely—besides British heads and arms —have built the Canadian Pacific Railway, which has revolutionised the economics of Northern America. Energy, either of direct or indirect British origin, is combating the Glacial Period in North-western Canada, in the region of the Yukon, grappling with the permanently frozen **Possibilities of Energy and Science** soil, extorting riches and comfort from the icy north, driving back, it may be, later on, by the resources of science that hatefullest affliction of our mother earth, that possible foreshadowing of the end of all things we shall never see—the icy touch which brought about many successive glacial periods, and rendered the Polar regions, north and south, uninhabitable. It is just possible that the energy of Britons or the descendants of Britons may push back artificially the realm of ice to the shores of the Arctic Ocean, bringing in happier conditions of climate, and turning to account millions of acres of rich soil now locked in ice that has not melted for 100,000 years.

In Tropical America and the West Indies our achievements have not been so colossal. Here they should lie in the extermination of disease. We have, however, erected and endowed colleges, built railroads, roads, and bridges—Jamaica, almost from end to end, Barbados, British Honduras (uncompleted), and Trinidad— and regulated forests. In 1898 was founded the Imperial Department of Agriculture for the West Indies under **Developing the West Indies** Sir Daniel Morris. This department is at present paid for by the Imperial Government. It has rendered great services to forestry, agriculture and horticulture in the West Indies. A great deal has been done in recent years to open up the asphalt resources—the lakes of pitch —in Trinidad and Barbados, the diamond and gold mines of British Guiana, together with the water power developed by the cascades that tumble from the edges of the Venezuelan Plateau. Forestry in British Guiana, British Honduras and Trinidad, has received some attention. Horticulture has been much and wisely developed in Jamaica, and the more important of the West India Islands. From Jamaica, indeed, West and Central Africa have received most valuable contribu-

British Works in India tions in the shape of improved varieties of cotton, coffee, bananas, oranges and many useful plants for tropical cultivation. In the Falkland Islands, since our definite assumption of authority in 1833, much has been done to develop the possibilities of cattle and sheep breeding. Latterly, sheep have become more important than anything else, not necessarily for export in the form of mutton and wool, but for the rearing of good rams for breeding purposes. These are exported to South America. Here also has been made an important coaling and provisioning station for vessels going round Cape Horn.

The first great public works of Britain in India were probably trunk roads. These were begun as far back as 1790, when the East India Company settled down seriously to taking up the reins of government. The great trunk road from Calcutta and Bengal to Peshawar was first projected by an Afghan emperor, Sher Shah, and was more than half completed by the Mogul rulers. It was continued by the East India Company, and finished about 1830. A great triumph in roadmaking, achieved early in the nineteenth century, was the road up the Ghats from Bombay Island to the interior plateau. The roads of British India now run to 193,000 miles of metalled and unmetalled surface.

Canals in India followed the damming of streams—especially parallel with the sea-coast of Malabar, where they linked one lagoon to another—and then came the construction of great irrigation works. There are now 4,055 miles of

The Era of Indian Railways navigable canals in India and about 43,500 miles of irrigation canals bringing water to 13,606,000 acres. In 1850 began the era of railways. By the end of the nineteenth century the Indian Government had constructed about 25,000 miles (November, 1908, about 30,000 miles) of railways, from the hill stations of the Himalayas, such as Darjeeling and Simla, to Cape Comorin, opposite Ceylon, and from the frontier of Arakan to Quetta

and the Afghan frontier. Since then, the railways have been creeping on towards the Persian Gulf, on the one hand, and Burma on the other. Before long, no doubt, there will be direct railway communication from some port on the Persian Gulf, from which again a connection across Persia with the Russian railway system is inevitable, to Singapore.

Some of us who read these lines may yet live—still enjoying health and vigour—to travel from Calais to Singapore without changing the carriage, or, if something less " 1850 " than the present condition of the South-Eastern Railway can be brought into existence, we may enter our travelling and sleeping compartment at Charing Cross, and enjoy a marvellous panorama of the most varied landscapes, races and products of the earth's surface before we quit our compartment at the southernmost extremity of the Malay Peninsula.

The engineering works of India, such as the great bridge across the Indus at Attock, are worthy examples of the mechanical achievements of the British Empire. So is the bridging of the Zambesi

A Series of Engineering Triumphs at the Victoria Falls in South Central Africa ; so is the damming of the Nile at Assuan, Esna, Assiut and Zifta. These engineering works, conducted under the auspices of Great Britain in Egypt, have conferred enormous benefits on the peasantry and the industries of that country. Water has been brought from the foot-hills of Ethiopia to Port Sudan, and also to the town of Suakin. The Red Sea has been united with Khartoum by a railway, and Khartoum with Upper Egypt. Steamers now ply on the Nile from Khartoum to the Uganda frontier, and right into the heart of Africa up the tributaries of the Bahr-el-Ghazal or to the Abyssinian frontier on the Sobat.

On the West African coast the public works have not been altogether worthy of the British Empire until quite recently. Down to a very few years ago everyone of high and low degree who desired to land or embark on the Gold Coast had to do so more or less at the peril of his life, in heavy surf-boats, through breakers that occasionally capsized the boats and drowned the passengers. Even at the present day, Freetown, the capital of Sierra Leone, is very early nineteenth century, and compares unfavourably with the new French cities of North-west

Africa, where the ocean-going steamer can draw up alongside a magnificent quay. At Freetown the passenger has still to embark or land in a small boat. But things are moving, even in British West Africa. The public works of the Sierra Leone Protectorate are worthy of portions of India in the way of roads and bridges, and a railway of 230 miles connects Freetown with the north-western frontier of Liberia, and has already doubled the exports of the country that was once called the " white man's grave."

There is also a railway advancing from Lagos to the Niger, and from the Niger across to the commercial centres of the Hausa country, perhaps linking up some day with the railways of Egypt and of French West Africa. No enterprise would be more beneficial to the commerce and peoples of Africa than a railway from the Mediterranean to the Gulf of Guinea across the Sahara Desert ; for the railway causes the desert to blossom as the rose. If only the dread of Germany could be put aside, and Britain and France could turn their *entente* to the magnificent end of crossing the Sahara by a rail-

Linking Up the Empire way, they would have achieved a triumph over recalcitrant Nature as grand as the attacks on the Glacial Period which are going on in North-western Canada. One of the best schemes conceived by Rhodes—his own especial scheme, started and maintained by his own money—was the trans-African telegraph, a line which was to run from the Cape to Cairo.

Thus far, the communication is interrupted in several places. Through the efforts of the British South Africa Company, Cape Town is linked with Lake Nyassa and the south end of Tanganyika, and even with Ujiji in German East Africa. The next gap to fill will be from Ujiji to the telegraph system of the Uganda Protectorate. This extends no further, at present, than Lake Albert. Probably by the time these lines are in print it will have reached Gondokoro. From this point there is no further break till Alexandria is reached, near the mouth of the Nile. A land line now goes from Lagos to the heart of British Nigeria, and from Sierra Leone to the north-west frontier of Liberia.

This last will soon be linked with the French land lines of Senegambia, and these again, before many years are past, will have traversed the Sahara Desert.

A telegraph line crosses the inhospitable interior of Australia from north to south. It has seemed to the present writer that this was one of the most marvellous achievements in its way to be placed to the credit of the British Empire. The central part of Australia is a more terrible desert, perhaps, than any part of the Sahara. At the time the

Australia Spanned by the Telegraph overland telegraph line was conceived it was practically an unknown country; all that was recorded of it was the death or disappearance of explorers. It was not uninhabited, though almost uninhabitable (in its pristine conditions), but the indigenes were hostile and treacherous. Yet these difficulties were overcome, and in a few years. The spanning of Australia by this wire deserves to rank among the great Imperial achievements.

Although carried out by commercial companies and not directly by the government, mention must be made here of the deep-sea cables which are another source of gratification to our national pride. Great Britain was long the first to construct and lay a deep-sea cable. The whole conception and working out of this feat in all its parts was the work of British minds. All the great oceans, the narrow connecting seas of the world, are now spanned by British cables. Africa is girdled with them, so is South America.

Thus we have striven to conquer distance and efface time. In the course of a few hours we can send a message to the heart of Central Africa, to the watershed of the Arctic Ocean, to the hill stations of the Himalayas, and receive a reply ; and the agency principally or wholly employed will have been a British-laid cable or a British-hung land wire. We can travel from Cape Town to the Victoria Falls in five days where Livingstone fifty years ago took five months. We can traverse India from Baluchistan to the

Results of British Enterprise vicinity of Burma in another five days; or, in a period of time scarcely longer, rush from the snows of the Himalayas to the Equatorial luxuriance of Ceylon. Already Egypt, under British guidance, is feeling her way in railway construction towards Tripoli and across Arabia.

If Turkey can be brought to see the advantages of co-operation, there may be still within our lifetime a delightful alternative railway route to India, say for the winter season, when the line through France, Switzerland, Italy, Austria, Roumania, Russia, and Persia is too cold. By the alternative route we may travel via Paris, Madrid, Algeciras, Tetuan, Algiers, Tunis, Tripoli, Cairo, and Basra—unless before that time airships or æroplanes that are really safe, certain and commodious have made railways only useful for

Railways as a Civilising Influence
goods traffic. The present writer would be sorry for this. Nothing fertilises, nothing pacifies, nothing civilises like a railway. Perhaps, in fairness, something should be said about what Britain has done about steam communication at sea. The British Empire has given birth to a marvellous mercantile marine. Being of necessity the creation and dependent of sea power, this fleet of 9,000 or 10,000 steamships has always had a strong navy as its corollary. But the triumphs of peace have been those of the mercantile marine, a marine that has grown up and prospered with very little direct encouragement from the state.

The first practicable British steamers—paddle-wheelers—plied about the west coast of Scotland from 1812 onwards. In 1833 the first thorough-going steamship—*i.e.*, not a sailing vessel with auxiliary steam power—crossed the Atlantic, the Royal William, of Quebec. This steamer made the journey from Nova Scotia to Gravesend in twenty-two days. She had been entirely built by Canadians on the St. Lawrence, and was engineered by them across the Atlantic. The return voyage was first made by an Irish steamer of the Cork Packet Company. The City of Dublin Steam Packet Company had been founded in 1823, and really became the parent of the great Peninsular and Oriental Steam Navigation Company in 1826.

This line originally started by a feeble steamship service to Gibraltar, then was extended in 1839–1840 to Alexandria to meet the demand for the overland route. Others of its steamships

The Early Days of the Steamship
had painfully laboured through stormy seas round the Cape, and established themselves on the Red Sea side of the Isthmus of Suez. The General Steam Navigation Company was founded in 1824; the first steam voyage to India, round the Cape, was made in 1825; the Aberdeen Line—George Thompson—had been founded in 1824; the Harrison Line in 1830; the Royal Mail—West Indian Line—in 1839; the City Line

of Glasgow in 1839; the Cunard in 1840. In this same year the Pacific Steam Navigation Company began running steamers to South America. The Wilson Line of Hull was founded in 1845; the Natal Line—Bullard—and the Inman Line in 1850; the Bibby in 1851; the Anchor Line (Indian) and the African Steamship Company in 1852; the Union Steamship Company (of South Africa) in 1853; the Allan in 1854; the British India Steam Navigation Company in 1855. Several of these lines of steamships began as associations trading with sailing-ships, so that some of the great houses with their wonderful modern fleets of passenger and cargo steamers have a history beginning with the nineteenth century.

British statesmen have left one blot on the record of British prescience, in that they never believed in or encouraged the cutting of the Suez Canal, nor realised till the work was an accomplished fact what a marvellous gain it would be to the shipping industry of the British Empire. Ferdinand de Lesseps was one of the greatest benefactors of the British Empire.

Britain's Debt to a Frenchman
The remembrance of that fact should be an additional incitement to an everlasting friendship with France. For many years the British steamship companies held the field in regard to all long sea journeys. Then there grew up rivalry in the Mediterranean, the Red Sea, and Indian waters on the part of steamship lines from Marseilles, Trieste, Genoa, and Barcelona to Tropical America; Hamburg to the West Coast of Africa; Rotterdam to the Malay Archipelago; and, after 1880, that marvellous development of German shipping enterprise, which created first-class steamer communication between the north-eastern ports of Germany and almost all parts of the world. In speed the British vessels still hold their own, though it is a neck and neck race with Germany. In comfort, modernity of appliances, and food, it is to be feared that the German, French, and Austrian liners are superior to the British.

The Nobel Prize, however, has yet to be awarded to that steamship line which introduces the surest element of civilisation into its passenger traffic—one passenger, one cabin. It ought to be made penal to compel two, three, or four unrelated strangers to share a single sleeping compartment. In forestry and horticulture the British Empire has taken a leading

THE LANSDOWNE BRIDGE OVER THE INDUS AT SUKKUR   F. Bremner, Quetta

BRIDGE SPANNING THE ZAMBESI NEAR THE VICTORIA FALLS

THE REVERSING RAILWAY STATION AT KHANDALLA IN INDIA   Frith

OVERCOMING NATURE'S DIFFICULTIES: TRIUMPHS OF BRITISH ENTERPRISE

part, though it has frequently borrowed from Germany its adepts in forestry and economic botany, to the great advantage of British research in those directions. The names of Gustav Mann, West Africa and India; of Brandis and Kurz, the Himalayas; Sir Julius Vogel, New Zealand; Dr. Otto Stapf, Kew Gardens, will at

The King of Biological Research once occur to the mind of any reader interested in these subjects. But there have been great exponents of what might be termed Imperial botany of wholly British descent—men like Sir Joseph Banks, Sir Joseph Hooker, Professor Daniel Oliver, Sir W. Thiselton Dyer, Sir Daniel Morris, and Lieut.-Col. D. Prain.

The work of these men is of even greater fame in Germany, France, Belgium, and the United States than to the careless minds of Britishers, so indifferent in the main to scientific research. Purely scientific research, and the reading of the world's past history, the very secrets of the origin and development of living forms, have owed nearly as much to the exploring journeys of Hooker in the Himalayas and on the Atlas Mountains of Morocco as they did to the king of British biological research, Darwin—Darwin, who also qualified as an agent or servant of the empire when he accompanied the Beagle on its famous cruise in the interests of science.

Sir John Kirk, in a somewhat similar capacity in connection with Livingstone's government expeditions, opened our eyes to the wealth and the economic importance of the East African flora. British enterprise has introduced the tea-shrub into India and Ceylon, cotton into all parts of Africa and the Pacific, cacao into West Africa, coffee into Ceylon, Nyassaland, Jamaica, and Trinidad.

Sir Clements Markham won his eventual C.B. and his first renown by his splendid attempts to secure the seed of the cinchona-tree, jealously guarded as its transmission was by American In-

Blessings of Botanical Discoveries dians and South American governments. He enabled the cinchona to be planted widely over the tropical regions of the world, and brought down the price of quinine, the most potent drug yet known against malaria fever, till it eventually came within the reach of poor sufferers. If in this field of botany and agriculture there have been triumphs, what are we to say about zoology ? Well, there are two

sides to the account, though the debit balance of humanity is largely in the ascendant. We are credited, and only too truly, with having caused over Tropical Africa a devastation in the mammalian fauna which it might have taken a whole geological epoch to have brought about.

Gordon Cumming, Cotton Oswell, William Webb, William Baldwin, and F. C. Selous led the way in that crusade against the big game of the South African peninsula which has gone far to rob that future confederation of one of its most attractive possessions in the eyes of educated men and women. Oswell, Baldwin, and Selous were, at any rate, naturalists who greatly—Selous very greatly—enriched scientific zoology with specimens and information as to life and habits.

The rampant desire to kill, kill, kill, to have the joy of hearing the bullet go plunk into a mighty carcass, or some form of marvellous beauty and swiftness, still animates the minds of most South African pioneers who are carrying on the work of empire ever nearer to the Equator. Much of the big game of Somaliland near the coast

Leaders in the Realm of Natural History has been killed out. Everyone who has been divorced or who wishes to divorce, who is threatened with a breach of promise action, or has made an ass of himself—in the phrase of his relations— hies to EastAfrica to wipe out an unpleasant little piece of past by big-game shooting.

There are, and have been, of course, important exceptions to this category— men who have shot wisely and well, and who have observed and annotated, and have thus enriched not only our museums with important specimens—skins, bones, and pickled corpses—but who have given us the life history of the animals they pursued. Natural history, a better term in this last respect than biology, owes much to the writings of Livingstone, Sir Samuel Baker, W. C. Oswell, Baldwin, Selous, J. G. Millais, R. Crawshay, Alfred Sharpe, Alfred Neumann, E. N. Buxton in Africa, Sir Emerson Tennant in Ceylon, Sir Samuel Baker, Dr. W. T. Blanford, B. H. Hodgson, and R. Lydekker in India and Central Asia. One of the leaders in this modern movement of the camera versus rifle, himself distinguished as a shot and pursuer of shy beasts over difficult ground, is Edward North Buxton, who has illustrated the rare wild beasts of Corsica, Sardinia, Central Africa, and the

Sinai Peninsula, besides those of Eastern Africa. J. G. Millais has perhaps done the most striking work of all, in founding a school in the artistic and faithful portrayal of the wild life of beasts and birds in Britain, South Africa, and Newfoundland.

As regards great naturalists—biologists if you will—men to whom the study of all living things was one, indifferent as to whether they exercised their wits on geology, botany, zoology, anthropology— what a crown of glory will rest over the British Empire as long as British records remain! Darwin at the apex, Huxley, Sir Charles Lyell, Sir Joseph Hooker, Alfred Russel Wallace, Sir John Murray of the Challenger—a Canadian, Sir Richard Owen, Sir William Flower, Henry Walter Bates, Sir E. Ray Lankester, Alfred Garrod, W. A. Forbes, P. L. Sclater, E. B. Tylor, Alfred Newton, F. M. Balfour, and Wyville Thomson. Our men first revealed the curious water fauna of Lake Tanganyika—J. E. Moore and Dr. W. Cunnington—and then that of the Victoria Nyanza, not less remarkable because of its coincidence. They—Falconer, Lydekker, Bain, Dr. Anderson, Dr. Lyons, Capt. Gregory, and others—discovered, elucidated, and illustrated the wonderful extinct mammalian fauna of North-west India, the strange beast-reptiles of South Africa, the early elephants, Sirenia, hyraces of Eocene Egypt, the extraordinary giant marsupials and birds of Pleiocene Australia. These achievements not only led to the purest of all joys, the increase of abstract knowledge, but have aided us in our fight against the real reactionary Nature.

Deadly Foes of Man

For, in the most part the deadliest foes of man are the minutest organisms at the bottom of the tree of life, simple developments of living matter scarcely to be classified as animal or vegetable. In the fight against the bacillus, spirillum, amœba, coccidium, treponema and trypanosome, the British Empire has taken a leading place—a dominant place almost, not forgetting the splendid cooperation of France, Germany, Italy, and America. Sir Patrick Manson, Ronald Ross, and others, discovered the whole process by which amœboid spores are introduced into the human system by such agencies as the mosquito, tick, and flea, thereby producing malarial fever and other dread diseases. Sir David Bruce elucidated the mystery of the tsetse disease and, in concert with Drs. Nabarro and Castellani, solved the problem of sleeping sickness. An Indian army medical officer, Colonel Lambkin, has discovered a means of inoculating for syphilis—syphilis, like sleeping sickness, is produced by a flagellate protozoon, in this case a treponema—which may eventually stamp out that horrible malady. Our eagerness to open up Equatorial Africa brought the sleeping sickness into Uganda, and has cost that protectorate in all nearly 100,000 lives. This is a terrible item at first sight, but one we can balance at once by discounting the (at least) 100,000 lives probably lost in Uganda and Unyoro during the reigns of the kings Mtesa, Kabarega, and Mwanga, by the internecine wars, poison ordeals, slave-raids, famines, and other causes of depopulation which have been abolished by the introduction of law and order under the British ægis.

The Toll of Sleeping Sickness

It is a mistake to suppose also that the indigenous population of Africa was exempt from these awful visitations of disease before we mixed them all up; before we opened routes this way and that way across the continent, which conveyed disease through insect agencies from one lot of people to another, hitherto separated by mutual distrust or by pathless forests. On the contrary, before the white man arrived on the scene, the population of Africa was, I surmise from native legends and traditions, constantly being wiped out by epidemics, first of one disease, then of another; by famines due to unexpected droughts, locusts or other insect plagues, or by attacks on food crops by herds of elephants, and the destruction of livestock by lions and leopards.

These are all evils which have been or are being abated by British energies. I confidently expect that we shall soon have mastered the mysteries of sleeping sickness, blackwater fever, cholera, and many other diseases, and be able to prevent them or to cure them with certainty. In India it has been realised for the last ten years that sanitation, a cleanliness which would suppress the flea, other precautions which would exterminate the mosquito, might reduce the mortality from plague, cholera, and other dreadful maladies of the tropics to small dimensions, ever dwindling to cessation; and this has been

Sanitation the Enemy of Disease

one of the hardest, most disinterested, most thankless tasks which the British Empire has taken on its shoulders. Unhappily, though the education of India has advanced by leaps and bounds, the masses of ignorant Moslems and fanatical Hindus do not appreciate the value of

Indian Opposition to Science science and of a scientific conduct in our lives, any more than do the peasants of Ireland, of some parts of England still, of Spain, Italy, or Russia. India has once or twice been brought nearer to general revolt by honest and sincere attempts to get rid of plague and cholera than she has by the imposition of salt taxes or the insufferable snobbishness of " mem-sahibs " or eyeglassed officers.

Our efforts to improve the breeds of horses, cattle, sheep, pigs, goats, dogs, and many domestic birds are world-famous. We have domesticated the ostrich, introduced the Angora goat into South Africa, the Merino sheep into Australia, New Zealand, and South Africa ; the camel into Australia ; the horse into South and South Central Africa, Australia, and New Zealand ; deer into New Zealand and Mauritius. The mountain streams of New Zealand, British Central and East Africa have been abundantly stocked with trout. We have systematised the preservation of the Indian elephant, his capture and training for industrial purposes.

When we first took Cyprus in hand, the forests and the native agriculture were disappearing under the combined attacks of domestic goats and swarms of locusts. The goats were soon kept outside the protected area, but the fight against the locusts was a struggle that lasted for many years. This hateful insect pest is now practically extinct in Cyprus, to the very great gain of the island's prosperity. We are now bracing ourselves for an attack on

Wealth in Natural Products the mosquitoes, rats, sparrows, flies, fleas, and other small but significant pests of the empire. The mineral discoveries of the British have already been alluded to in the chapters dealing with their economic aspects. Our exploitation of the gold of India, British Columbia, Australia, New Zealand, West Africa, South Africa, Egypt, British Guiana, and the Far Northwest of Canada has added appreciably not only to the wealth of the world in general, but to that of the indigenous peoples of the gold areas. The same may be said about the tin of the Malay Peninsula, the coal of India, Natal, Borneo, Australia, and British Central Africa. We have discovered and worked petroleum and bitumen in Burma, Nigeria, and Barbados.

Copper has enabled us by its intrinsic value to gain for the general use of man the ghastly deserts of South-west Africa and Australia. Diamonds have brought water, trees, flowers, livestock, human settlers, and the amenities of a highly civilised life to bare, stony, lifeless plateaus of inner South Africa. Their attraction is enabling us to combat the choking vegetation of British Guiana.

It is impossible in the space at my command to enumerate the names and the individual services of those British subjects whom the special conditions of the empire have impelled to wonderful discoveries in all the unenumerated branches of pure science—philology ; comparative study of religious beliefs, mythology, and folk lore ; comparative anthropology, and

Britain's Predominance in the World all branches of human anatomy and medical jurisprudence ; in medicine and surgery, in law and the framing of legal codes ; in military and naval strategy ; industrial appliances ; electricity ; ship construction ; the invention and improvement of locomotives, steam-engines, bicycles, automobiles, and turbines ; in chemistry and metallurgy ; in sanitary engineering ; in architecture, photography, painting, etching, engraving, book illustrating, printing, cabinet-making, tailoring, dressmaking, and upholstery (the carpets of the British Empire deserve a special mention) ; in the drama and literature, prose and poetry.

Innumerable works of reference would show either the active participation or the predominance of British citizens in all the spheres of great intellectual and practical achievements. It is to this record we appeal in maintaining that—with all its imperfections, shortcomings, blunders, or episodes of wrongdoing, violence, or injustice fully discounted—the British Empire has been a greater blessing to the world at large and to all the countries within its scope than any congeries of states under one head that has preceded it in history.

CIVILISATION AND CHRISTIANITY
EMPIRE'S DEBT TO MISSIONARY ENTERPRISE

IT has been the custom until quite recently to sneer at missionaries, propagandists of the Christian religion, in all circles except those of the professedly devout. The late Lord Salisbury, in veiled terms, once or twice described them as a nuisance. They have often been regarded as such by statesmen who conducted our foreign or colonial affairs. I am not going to deny that there has been misdirected zeal in the past, and that in some cases the wrong kind of missionary did a great deal of harm and put Great Britain to much anxiety and expense.

Elsewhere I have animadverted on the somewhat crack-brained, uneducated missionaries who wandered into Abyssinia to convert the Abyssinians to a different kind of Christianity to that which they already professed, and who involved Great Britain and the British taxpayer in a war which cost quite a thousand lives and several millions sterling. This is the **The Good Work of Missions** only case I can call to mind where missionary enterprise was excessively ill-directed, and where it gave just ground for the animadversions of the 1860 type of statesman, who would not dream of omitting attendance at church on a Sunday morning, yet was perfectly indifferent to the spiritual or moral welfare of the myriads of black or brown people with whose affairs Great Britain was beginning to interfere politically.

When our descendants are able to look back on things from the large end of the telescope, and the history of the nineteenth and twentieth centuries is concentrated into a single readable volume, I think a very large part of that volume will be taken up with the results of mission work, possibly a larger space than is accorded to the successful campaigns of great conquerors by sea or land. The point of view from which I write is a peculiar one, which will probably please no one set of thinkers. I know it is no longer fashionable to denounce Mohammedanism or idol-worship, just as any lively interest in a new metrical arrangement of the Psalms is almost impossible to find, even in the unexplored parts of New England. My own lawless views, if I may obtrude them without impertinence, would be rendered **The Supreme Power of Christianity** thus: That nearly all religions have been a great burden, an incessant clog on the upward progress of humanity, and the only teaching which seems to the present writer to be in consonance with progress is the teaching of Christ and the words of such of His apostles as caught His spirit. Christ's teaching, like two or three other great utterances of humanity, seems the goal of which we are never quite abreast; it is always a little ahead of the ideals of true Socialism; it is a religion which is an expression of the truest Liberalism.

Many versions of Christianity have developed into fetish worship and fatuous formalities, mystic rites bordering on sorcery, Judaism run mad; the letter has killed the spirit; the Incarnate Love has been lost in fanatical hate. Still, this religion, even in its most violent or foolish phases, has never quite left the skirts of commonsense, the middle path of sanity along which man advances, with occasional checks and deviations, towards the goal of the Millennium.

What has Mohammedanism done for the world? What has been accomplished of permanent good by Buddhism, and by the wild, raving, nightmare nonsense of **Religions of the East** Hinduism? It is true that the Arabs less than a century after the death of Mohammed absorbed Persian and Byzantine culture, and spread this through Syria, Egypt, North Africa, and Spain. It is also true that, to a limited extent, they kept the lamp of civilisation burning, some of the old Greek culture living with them, while Roman civilisation in Northern and Western Europe was overwhelmed by the

Goth, Hun, Frank, and Lombard. To a great extent the civilisation of the Arabs in pre-Turkish days was the distorted civilisation of Rome. Rome and Byzantium, the direct inheritors of Hellas, had implanted their civilisation too strongly along the shores of the Mediterranean for it to be annihilated by that mixed herd of Saracens, which after all only included a proportion of Arabs of the desert in its ranks, and was recruited largely from the Mediterranean world.

But there was something in the Mohammedan religion which prevented intellectual advance. Like the other great religions of Asia, it was a case of arrested development. The results are plain to the minds of all but fantastic perverts. Why is the Christian—real or nominal—top dog to-day ? Because he is healthier, stronger, far wiser, much superior in mental capacity to the millions of Asia and Africa. What have the Turks invented ? They have conquered mainly by Christian weapons, by the arts invented and perfected under the comparative freedom of Christianity.

The Japanese have emerged from the vassaldom of Asia because they have copied the arts and sciences of Christendom, because they are unhampered by any binding religion which makes it impossible for them to live after the manner of Christians. It was the more primordial and pure type of Christianity that, consciously or unconsciously, the great Protestant and Catholic missions of the British Empire

have sought to implant in the backward and foolish places of the world during the religious revival of the nineteenth century. The Christian propaganda of the Crusades was, of course, no better in any one whit than the holy wars of the Moslems.

If anything, the Christians of the eleventh to the thirteenth centuries conducted themselves worse in Syria and the Holy Land than did the Mohammedans, when it was their turn to be uppermost. They practised a form of religion which in many aspects was a degrading fetish worship and an instigation to deeds of violence and oppression essentially unChristian. The Crusaders' type of Christianity lasted down to the sixteenth century and the Spanish discovery and conquest of Tropical America.

The Quakers as Pioneers of Missions

It was the Quakers that really started on the missionary path the churches outside the pale of Rome. They seem, first of all, to have conceived—apart from the Jesuits, Capuchins, and Franciscans of the seventeenth and eighteenth centuries—the idea of peoples of a different race and a dark-coloured skin enjoying equal rights of humanity with the conquering Caucasian.

The Society of Friends—"Quakers" is a silly nickname which might surely be allowed to die—in fact, had not long been in existence as a definite sect of thinkers before they had begun a crusade against the slave trade, which was never to die out or even perceptibly to slacken

THE ROMAN CATHOLIC CATHEDRAL AT LAGOS IN WEST AFRICA   N. W. Helm

THE HANDSOME MISSION CHURCH AT BLANTYRE IN BRITISH CENTRAL AFRICA

until the trade in slaves was exterminated. The Anti-Slavery Society of Great Britain and Ireland, which exists to this day, was founded and has been mainly supported by Quakers. In the eighteenth century—the unsectarian missionary Society for Promoting Christian Knowledge was founded in 1698 ; the Society for the Propagation of the Gospel in Foreign Parts, in 1701 —other Nonconformist bodies in the West Indies and the United States championed the cause of the negro. It was not until the time of Wesley that any section of the Church of England interested itself actively in humanitarian propaganda. The interest that the Quakers, Baptists, and Wesleyans took, more especially in the fate of the West Indian and North American negro, drew them inevitably to the coasts of Africa, firstly to repatriate negroes who had attained freedom, and who found themselves outcasts in the body politic of white men's colonies or states ; and secondly—with a much greater enthusiasm and success—to evangelise the indigenous savage negroes of West Africa.

Missionary Interest in the Negroes

India offered an immense field for missionary enterprise. The kings of Denmark, from 1705 to the early part of the nineteenth century, promoted actively Danish, German, and Nonconformist British missions to the east coast of Hindustan. For some fifty years after the British dominion had been founded by Clive, anything like a Christian propaganda was sternly discouraged by the honourable East India Company from the fear that it would arouse Mohammedan and Hindu fanaticism ; also because in England itself interest in religion had very much slackened, and official Christianity was not considered an *article d'exportation*.

The Church of England had no zeal for propaganda amongst the heathen as a body, though there were a few notable exceptions amongst its clergy who went abroad. Bishop Heber (1783-1826) was probably the first to arouse the sympathy of the members of the National Church in regard to the deplorable condition of the natives of India. The Church Missionary Society was founded in 1799. Its first field of operations was India. It was supported by the Low Church rather than the High, and in its early days it drew down a certain amount of ridicule on mission work by, possibly, an excess of sentimentalism.

In its desire to make up to the negro for the wrongs that he had suffered at the hands of the white man for the two centuries, during which the exponents of Anglican teaching were too much inclined to stand behind the slave-owner, the negro was placed on a pedestal by the Church Missionary Society, and credited with qualities of head and heart that he did not, unfortunately, always possess. The Baptist Missionary Society, founded in 1792, began a great educational work in India at the close of the eighteenth century, and soon afterwards began to work among the West Indian negroes. It laid the foundations of a negro civilisation in Fernando Po during the middle of the nineteenth century, which even under the once unfriendly rule of Spain and many other difficulties grew slowly to its modern developments. The same thing

Livingstone the Great Missionary was done for the coast country of the Kameruns, and is being done now for the central basin of the Congo. The educational work of the same society in India and China is also being conducted on a gigantic scale.

The London Missionary Society came into existence in 1795, and represented the aspirations of the Congregationalists and Wesleyans. One of its first great pioneers was David Livingstone. It is difficult to exaggerate the benefits that the Bechuana tribes in South Central Africa and the peoples of the Nyassa-Tanganyika Plateau and of Madagascar have owed to the agents of the London Missionary Society.

The Universities' Mission was founded in 1860, after the appeal of Livingstone in 1856, and has since taken a large share in the evangelisation of East Africa and Nyassaland. The great missions of the Presbyterian churches have done much for education in India, China, British Central Africa, Nigeria, and South Africa. The evangelisation of the Pacific has been largely the work of the Church of England and of the Wesleyans. Most people nowadays have read of the success of the Church of England in Uganda.

There is an English Catholic Mission, directed from Mill Hill, at work in the eastern section of the Uganda Protectorate. Some mention should be made of the struggling North African Mission, which, I believe, has also sent exponents of Protestant Christianity to Persia and the Turkish dominions. It has been an up-hill task for the brave men and women of this

The Value of Medical Missions band to fight against Mohammedan prejudice, superstition, and ignorance, especially in matters of hygiene. This mission, so far as it has succeeded, has done so by following the only means of access to the citadel of the Mohammedan heart— a thorough-going knowledge of Arabic, of the history of Islam and the features of its faith, and of medical science. Medical missions indeed, during the last quarter of a century, have developed to a

remarkable degree in India, China, and Africa. Along these lines of approach it is not easy to overestimate the sheer good that has been effected by Christian missions. This leads me to my plainest speaking and the core of my argument.

The whole of the Christian world itself is far from being in agreement on even fundamental dogmas of its religion, and so long as each sect, branch, or church adhered rigidly to the exposition of its own version of Christian dogma and of that alone, so long much of its work with intelligent non-Christian races was fruitless and even baneful, since it revived the dislike and distrust of the Christian as an official or ruler. But when, as has been the case almost universally for the last thirty years, each mission in its turn thought more of the teaching of Christ as a means of beginning, and endeavoured to deal fraternally rather than paternally with the people it had come to teach, Christian propaganda began to achieve success by leaps and bounds. When some historian of the world sums up its results a hundred years or so hence, he will—I say with confidence—

A Testimony to Missionary Achievement be able to show that the great Christian missions emanating from Europe and America have conferred on the 'backward countries of the world, to say nothing of the savage regions, a veritable renaissance, an education, an elevation which has been conveyed in a better and more salutary manner than it could have been by soldiers or officials, whose teaching was imposed by force and not persuasion.

I am well aware that that is not the verdict of to-day in all respects. Missionary efforts, in China especially, have not only been extremely obnoxious to the indigenous governing class and to uninformed public opinion in that region of 400,000,000 conservative, industrious people, but the troubles which have ensued have entailed armed intervention on the part of European nations. For these wars the missionaries have been held to blame. Several European and American statesmen have told them that they were not wanted in China, and had much better go away.

Yet, a hundred years hence, even if the missionaries were to depart from China to-morrow, it will be realised that they have done much to lay the foundations of a new China, to harmonise the ideas of China with those of Europe and America.

They have broken down more completely than any other force the isolation of China from the world's movements; and surely it is not well for the progress of the human race that 433,000,000 out of a total of 1,200,000,000 should be entirely out of touch with the rest?

What has been the result to China of her isolation and her degenerate pursuit of false knowledge? That at the present day, though she numbers 433,000,000 of people under the nominal sway of the Chinese Emperor, she is more or less under the thraldom of Japan (50,000,000), with an alternative of being under the thumb of Russia (150,000,000). Take one instance alone of the false culture that missionary teaching has attempted to remove—the cramped foot of the Chinese woman. There may be some variation in a code of morals or accepted canons of beauty.

The ultimate test of the value of both probably is the prosperity and happiness of the people that adopt them. Put to this test, it must surely be admitted that the taste, morality, and good sense of the white races of Europe and America are superior to those of the backward **What Chinese** peoples. The alternative is to **Women Owe** admit oneself ignorant or of **to Missions** unbalanced mind. We must cling to some standard in these things, and all the evidence which can be submitted to reasonable, sane men points to the fact that the European standard has generally been the best. Well, according to the European standard the cramped foot of the Chinese woman is as silly as the precautions against defilement on the part of the Brahmans, the law which forbids the eating of beef to the Hindus, the Levitical prohibitions of the pig, the hare, and the oyster, the Moslem disapproval of pictures and statues, or the fetishistic practices of negro Africa. When Chinese women all over China are able to walk about with the ease and comfort intended by Nature, they should put up some commemorative tablet to the memory of the Christian missionaries whose advice and influence abolished this and other preposterous mistakes in the perverted culture of the Chinese.

I have ventured in other places to call the missionaries the tribunes of the people. Mission influence created Exeter Hall, and all which that now vanished place of meeting portended in the attitude of the British Empire towards indigenous and inferior races. This policy, one may hope, will still be maintained by the Aborigines Protection Society. Again and again the responsible rulers of the British Empire have been prevented by its influence from committing acts of injustice, or allowing colonists or colonial officials to do so, against the previous occupants of **Rights** the soil. Many of these had **of Native** never been conquered, but had **Races** accepted the advent of the British Empire peacefully, and even with acclamation, as a force which would maintain law and justice.

Unfortunately, the first instinct of the impetuous colonist or pioneer has been to deprive these prior inhabitants of their just rights. There has been, no doubt, exaggeration on both sides. It would have been manifestly unfair to attribute to inactive, ignorant savages the whole of the vested rights over vast areas which have only been turned to profitable use by the expenditure of British capital and British lives. In some few instances the European missionaries may have been unjust towards the European pioneer or trader, and have denied him the reward to which he was entitled for his supreme efforts in the cause of civilisation. On the other hand, these lay colonists would have reduced the indigenes to miserable, landless serfs, have denied them a common humanity with us—though that this tie existed was soon shown by the hybrids which sprang up—but for the outcries of the missionary and the philanthropist.

The final test of the right to survive can only be physical and mental fitness; but it is advisable that there should be a brake on the reckless advance of the Caucasian, and this drag is provided by both the teaching and the true practice of the principles of Christianity. There should be a real Christian science, not the blasphemous, nauseous fraud which passes under that name in America, **A Plea for** which should apply the prin- **More** ciples of Christianity to the wild **Missionaries** flora and fauna of the world. Every human race and every type of animal or plant should be given a chance to show if it cannot find some niche in the mosaic of the wide world. There should be missionaries of biology as well as missionaries of Christianity, and both alike should plead the cause of the overwhelmed, the backward, the imperfect that may yet be made perfect.

THE FUTURE OF THE EMPIRE
PROBLEMS OF GREATER BRITAIN THAT DEMAND ATTENTION AND SOLUTION

A GROWING difficulty, the principal unsolved problem of the immediate future, is the regulation of the interrelations between the different states, colonies, protectorates, and other divisions of the empire in regard to mutual defence, or a common action of offence, the conduct of Imperial diplomacy, and, **The Question of Imperial Federation** above all, inter- and extra- Imperial commerce. When through such workers on the imagination as Lord Beaconsfield and Sir Charles Dilke (in his " Greater Britain ") an idea of the majesty, the marvellous scope of the British Empire began to permeate the minds of educated people, the question of Imperial Federation became, and has remained, an important political idea.

The desire was born in England, and has remained until recently an English aspiration, not as yet warmly espoused in Scotland, and only shared by that small portion of Ireland that is English in sympathies. South Africa in the 'seventies of the last century was so strongly Dutch in feeling, and so inherently hostile to England, that the late Lord Carnarvon was unable to bring into existence even a confederation of the South African states, though he had solved that difficulty between French and English in Canada.

A certain Irish element that prospered in South-eastern Australia, and by its talent and influence directed a good deal of the local Press opinion, threw cold water on the Imperial Federation idea so **Proposed Grounds of Union** far as it concerned Australia. India at that time possessed no vehicle for the expression of Indian opinion. It merely spoke through the mouths of Anglo-Indian officials. Nevertheless, the idea made progress up to a certain point. It was discussed on two lines: A commercial union and the universal participation of all parts of the empire in the common support of the armed forces by land and sea. The desire to promote Imperial unity of purpose induced several statesmen, such as Lord Randolph Churchill, Jan Hofmeyr, and Joseph Chamberlain, in 1885, 1892, and 1903, and also important organs of the Press to modify their views on Free Trade, and to advocate the restoration of differential duties, in favour of the colonies and India, at the ports of Great Britain and Ireland—in short, Protection.

So long as there was any chance of the great raw-material-producing portions of the empire like India, Australia, and New Zealand and Canada caring nothing about the fostering of local industries, but agreeing to devote all their energies to the production of raw materials which might be manufactured by the looms, forges, and factories of Great Britain and the North of Ireland, there was much to be said in favour **The Colonies and Self-Protection** of a commercial union of the whole empire which would discriminate in all its customs Houses against the goods arriving from countries not belonging to the Imperial pact. Great Britain would then have become a privileged market for the sale of colonial produce (raw material), and the colonies would have absorbed the bulk of the British manufactured goods. There would have been small local sacrifices, but such a bond as this would have knit the empire together, and the wealth and power derived from this close commercial association would have made it irresistible by land and sea—the mistress of the world.

Unhappily, as some think, India, Australia, New Zealand, and Canada did not share these views. They wished not only to produce enormous quantities of raw material, but to be equally endowed with highly organised industries to manufacture that raw material. They wished to protect these nascent industries by a relatively high tariff wall which would make it very nearly impossible for the Mother Country to compete against local manufactures. It is true that a somewhat illusory preference was to be granted to British goods in comparison to those coming from other countries, but this preference was not enough to make Australia, New Zealand, or Canada a better market for the manufactures of Britain than any other civilised country of the world. In India, as the government of King Edward has the supreme controlling power, while there has been fair play to local Indian industries and administrative independence, Free Trade has been maintained throughout all Southern Asia under British influence, and British manufactures are still able to find a profitable market under the British flag. There has also been less attempt on the part of the self-governing colonies in South Africa to shut out British manufactured goods than has been the case with Australia, Canada, and New Zealand.

Friend of Colonial Commerce This being the general position, therefore, the policy of Protection has fallen to the ground—inevitably—since our trade with the non-British world is at present as three to one in comparison with our trade with the rest of the British Empire. If we broke our commercial treaties in order to discriminate in our home ports in favour of our daughter nations, colonies, or protectorates, we should probably be ruined as an industrial nation, for the self-governing portions of the empire offer us practically nothing in exchange.

Unfortunately, to those who still take an interest in Imperial federation, the great daughter nations are setting their faces towards the ideal of fiscal independence and isolation. It may be, from the point of view of all humanity, that this is the best plan to cherish. If persisted in, it will mean that every separate section of the empire which is independent of monetary subsidies or help from the British Parliament will frame its own tariff and initiate its own commercial relations, with the point of view solely of local advantages, and without any regard to the commercial welfare of the empire as a whole.

If Jamaica can make better terms for her sugar, fruit, or other products by joining the Customs Union of the United States, to the disadvantage of British imports, she will do so. Perhaps, from the Jamaican standpoint, she will be right. New Zealand or Australia may also enter into special arrangements with the United States, to the disadvantage of Britain, but to the gain of local manufactures or products. India may enter into closer arrangements with the empire of China or with Japan—in matters of commerce—than with the two islands in the North Sea. South Africa may conclude a commercial alliance with Canada or with Australia, to the great advantage of all these regions, but very much to the detriment of purely British commerce. The very unfair part of the entirely self-seeking views now in vogue with colonial statesmen is that to the British taxpayer—almost alone—is left the onerous charge of supporting a navy which mainly exists to defend the overseas possessions of Great Britain, and an army which must be ready to strike at foes of the empire in any or all of the continents when called upon to do so.

Burdens of the British Taxpayer

If the self-governing sections of the empire contributed proportionately to their population and their commerce to the Imperial cost of the Imperial army and navy, then there would be less hardship to us, their creditors and creators, in their utter disregard of our commercial requirements. But to continue to leave us almost the entire expense and responsibility of defending the empire, and maintaining law and order within its limits, is a policy which must in the long run split up the British Empire. There is a limit to our resources in money, as well as in men.

Case for an Imperial Council Colonial statesmen argue that there shall be no taxation without representation; that they have no unbounded faith in the wisdom, economy, or talent of the Board of Admiralty, the War Office, or the Ministries for Foreign Affairs or for the Colonies; they are not disposed to furnish funds from out of their own internal revenues to be spent at the discretion of the government sitting in London. If they are to contribute, they must be proportionately represented at some Imperial council stationed in London, and be able to influence the general policy of the empire in all matters that might lead to interstate trouble or external wars. The opposition to any such Imperial policy and to the intervention of delegates from the daughter nations or dependent kingdoms or empires in bureaucratic affairs comes entirely from Britain itself, chiefly from that great and important body of permanent civil servants, trained by generations to exceeding discretion, reserve, and prudence. Statesmen from the great colonies are often widely different in nature from the men that serve King Edward in the Home Country. They are negligent of official secrets, daring in public speeches, and **Indiscretions of Colonial Statesmen** reckless of consequences, for the very good and sufficient reason that, situated where they are, they are so absolutely safe. They can say and do the most imprudent things to foreign Powers, and leave Great Britain to bear the brunt of their reckless actions.

The statesmen of Canada know that a punitory expedition or a great invasion of Canada by another Power from across the seas is an almost impossible feat, though it may be much easier for Germany or France to bombard London. Australia and New Zealand also know that they are immune from serious attack on the part of the United States, Japan, Russia, Germany or France. On the other hand, the two home islands are exceedingly vulnerable, more so, perhaps, than the mass of their population or some short-sighted Ministers believe.

Whatever course may be taken by events, there is no real danger to the independence of Australia, New Zealand, South Africa, and Canada. If Great Britain were driven out of India as a governing power she would not be replaced by any other European nation. It is possible that in course of time strong commercial relations may grow up between South Africa and Australia. Both countries may maintain fleets, with New Zealand, perhaps, as a third, which would be sufficient to prevent the hostile action of Asiatic or European Powers in the southern seas. The only danger to Canadian independence is from the United States, which, however, is hardly likely to **Danger to Canadian Independence** waste blood and money in an unprofitable war for the annexation of Canada. If the Imperial Federation idea is not revived and carried through to ultimate success with an Imperial council that will be a real working element, and with some sacrifices on the part of the component daughter nations, the next stage or phase of the British Empire to be reviewed by historians may be its restriction to the control of India and Southern Asia,

Egypt, and all existing British Africa down to the River Zambesi, the Mediterranean Islands, Gibraltar, the Falkland Archipelago, the West Indies, Guiana and British Honduras, together with the commercial outposts in China and the Pacific.

And here, again, we must not look for finality. In all these regions we are simply playing the part of educators. Our descendants will have to face the idea of a universally educated, self-governing India, wherein the British Empire may be only a subject of grateful remembrance, local nomenclature, and innumerable votive statues. Perhaps the English language, if all European tongues have not been set aside for a universal Esperanto, may remain as the commercial medium in India. We shall have left on that vast region of Southern Asia, the original matrix of Man, an impress more lasting and more creditable than the effect of the Roman Empire on our own land and kindred European countries.

The only way to counteract such a fate —and, as it may not come about for a hundred years, it need not unduly agitate **The Better Government of India** the readers of this History— would be the suspension of race or religious prejudices, the inculcation of courtesy, sympathy, and unswerving justice in all the civil and military officials sent from Great Britain to serve in India, and the patient education of the peoples of India to see the world a little more through our eyes, to take advantage of our own painfully acquired knowledge.

On our part, we must associate the educated classes of India more and more with the administration of our Indian Empire ; we must give them a share in the councils which regulate the finance and taxation of their native land. India at the present day is not ripe for complete self-rule ; the withdrawal of the British Civil Service and soldiery would merely lead to devastating warfare between the Mohammedans on the one side and the Sikhs and Hindus on the other, either or both of these sections enslaving and oppressing the unwarlike races of Southern India or Burma.

Much the same may be said about the future of Egypt and of British Tropical Africa ; we are only in Egypt as educators. But this is a land which by climate, even as far as some parts of the Sudan, is as favourable to the settlement of the races of Southern Europe as it is to the indigenous people, who are compounded of an ancient mingling of European, Asiatic and negro elements. There may be a steady set of Greek, Maltese and Italian settlers towards the lands irrigated by the Nile and its tributaries. A new European nation may be compacted; it will contain very little that is North European and British in its physical elements, and it will some day ask to stand alone.

In Uganda, Nigeria, Sierra Leone, with the kindred Liberia alongside, working on similar lines, we are building up educated negro nationalities. Little by little they will get a larger and larger share in their own self-government, until at last, like India and Egypt, they may thank us warmly for all we have done for them, and request to be allowed to manage their own internal and external affairs in future.

Such, likewise, may be the fate of a new Cyprus, and of a Malta, which was never conquered, but placed herself unreservedly and trustingly in British hands, and therefore deserves all sympathy within the limits of reason in the protection of **A Possible Alliance of the Future** her well-marked nationality and many claims to self administration. A day may dawn when British men and women may no longer be sent from these shores to govern, control and educate races that are no longer backward in the march towards a universal civilisation. It is to be hoped, however, that if we have played our part fairly, these races and peoples that we have raised up from a condition either of savagery or of hopeless confusion may unite with us on some basis of strict and honourable alliance, together with our white daughter nations ; an alliance which shall only be framed and directed for the maintenance of the world's peace and the study of the world's happiness.

Until the question of the internal administration of Ireland, Scotland, England and Wales has achieved a proper and fairly complete settlement it can hardly be said that we are fully prepared for the responsibilities of empire outside these islands. To some extent, almost enough for practical purposes, Scotland has attained Home Rule, and Wales is well on the way towards it. The arrangements for quick legislation in and for England as regards purely English requirements are still very imperfect. But the question of Ireland is an urgent one. In this case we

have an island blest with a temperate and a healthy climate, set in seas remarkable for their wealth of fish, a country of 32,605 square miles, which, if handled scientifically in the way of agriculture, forestry and horticulture, ought to support a prosperous, robust, and intellectual population of 20,000,000. As it is, its **Desperate State of the Irish** people (4,458,000) are less in number than the inhabitants of London. Such as they are, they are a notable race. Though they differ much in physical type, all their types can be paralleled in the adjacent island of Great Britain. Religion is mainly to blame for the desperate case of the Irish, and the intolerance on the part of all the principal religious bodies in Ireland still stands to some extent in the way of a fusion of interests.

Home Rule would have been restored long ago but for the extremists of the Nationalist party—that is to say, the party of Irishmen mostly, but not entirely, Roman Catholics, who have openly clamoured not only for the right to administer their own internal affairs—which, with some reservations, is clearly due to them— but for the power to sever their political connection with Great Britain. This demand is so wholly unreasonable from the racial, the religious, commercial and political points of view that it is little wonder it has been resisted so far by the majority of the electorate in Great Britain.

The Ulster minority in Ireland represents an enormous amount of profitable industry ; it stands for the prosperous and well populated portion of the island. Racially speaking, it is less Iberian and autochthonous than the rest of Ireland. Historically, its colonisation from the adjacent coasts of Wales, England and Scotland was much more recent than other settlements from these directions. This minority declines to place itself under the rule of the National party, since it **Ireland's Need of Home Government** fears injustice in fiscal and religious matters. Extended measures of local government would probably clear away this danger. The administration of their own internal affairs must be eventually accorded to the Irish people, coupled with the same participation in the affairs, responsibilities and charges of the United Kingdom as a whole, and of such of the British Empire as is equally administered by Scotland, Wales and England.

Beyond the seas, the idea of Home Rule is no new one. The states of British origin that now compose the United States of America all had their local assemblies and considerable powers of self-administration; but a foolish king and an ignorant Minister fought the battle of taxation without representation in the eighteenth century, and lost it. This implanted an idea in the minds of British subjects beyond the seas that has never been allowed to die. The representative institutions of the component parts of the empire outside the British Islands have been described elsewhere. It only remains to glance at their past history and at the problems they may raise in the immediate future.

Home Rule Beyond the Seas

Assemblies of an elective and fully representative character were early brought into existence in the West Indies at various dates from 250 years ago. It is possible that in these instances the idea of Home Rule was premature and carried to extremes. Area, population, and the future race-elements of the population were not taken into consideration in granting these rights: and at various times during the nineteenth century the representative institutions—except in the Bahamas and Barbados—were abrogated or seriously limited.

A constitution and elective lower houses of parliament were conceded to the two organised provinces of Canada in 1792; and responsible government for Upper and Lower Canada, New Brunswick, Nova Scotia, and Prince Edward Island was introduced in 1841, after what might almost be called a series of rebellions between 1837 and 1839. But for this wise concession, the vast provinces of Canada would long ago have been part of the United States, to the detriment of British commerce and British influence on the fate of the North American Continent. A constitution was given to Newfoundland in 1832, and full Home Rule in 1855. Home Rule was accorded also in a reasonable degree to the colony of British Guiana in Northern South America in continuation of the Dutch Constitution already in force in 1803. This was modified or extended in 1812, 1826, 1831, and 1891.

Constitutions in the Colonies

The provinces or colonies that now compose Australia received constitutions, and finally Home Rule, as soon as they were able to show indications of the power to maintain orderly government. These rights were granted to New South Wales in 1824, 1842, and 1855; to Victoria in 1851 and 1855; South Australia (Northern Territories added in 1861-1863) in 1856; and Tasmania in the same year; Queensland in 1859; and West Australia in 1850 and 1890. The enfranchisement of the six colonies culminated in the recognition by Great Britain of the Australian Commonwealth as a whole in the year 1900. New Zealand received Home Rule in 1882, and the status of a dominion in 1907.

South Africa has presented greater difficulties in the framing of responsible government because of the two rival types of European colonists—British and Britannicised Germans speaking English; and Boers, with the descendants of Huguenot Frenchmen, speaking Dutch. Further, there were the millions of indigenous negroes to be taken into consideration. Cape Colony, which was by far the "whitest" of the South African states, was erected into the position of a self-governing colony in 1853 and a responsible government in 1872. Natal did not receive full responsible powers of self-government till 1893. The Orange Free State and the Transvaal were respectively accorded the position of independent nations in 1854, and 1852-1858.

Self-Governing States of South Africa

When the Transvaal was annexed in 1877, it was the intention of the British Government to bestow on it a few years afterwards much the same powers of self-government as were already under consideration for Natal. This solution of the difficulty, which would have probably saved us the South African War, was prevented by the Boer uprising in 1881. Before the Orange River Colony and the Transvaal could be brought into line with the rest of our colonies in South Africa they had to be conquered and annexed. They were then as speedily as possible (Transvaal in 1906, Orange River Colony in 1907) re-erected into responsible self-governing states, in the same quasi-independent position as Cape Colony and Natal.

There still remain subject to a great extent to the direct administration of Downing Street, Basutoland, Bechuanaland, and the vast Rhodesian territories to the north and south of the Zambesi. Bechuanaland and Basutoland will no doubt remain for a very long time to come, black states, wards of the British Empire, with the guardianship either remaining in London or eventually entrusted to the White Confederation of South Africa—not, however, until such time as we can trust the colonists to give fair play to their black neighbours and fellow-citizens, and until they are entirely able to relieve the Mother Country of the cost and responsibility of intervention. The Rhodesian provinces south of the Zambesi will eventually become self-governing white man's lands of the same status as those other great states that will with them form the Confederation of South Africa. The provinces north of the Zambesi will, no doubt, be grouped under the general government of British Central Africa, and eventually be dealt with on much the same lines as the country of the Basuto and Bechuana.

They, at any rate, emphatically are black man's lands, and should certainly be regarded as a future home and privileged reserve for such negro peoples of South Africa as may choose to migrate thither, seeking a refuge from the incompatible white man. The statesmen and **The Hindu** thinkers of the British Empire **Demand for** are now beginning to face the **Home Rule** question of self-government in such territories under the administration of the empire as are not inhabited in the main by white men and Christians. The lands of the Mohammedan have certainly the best of the premature claims to self-government, because the Mohammedan religion is less unreasonable than that of the Hindu or the Buddhist. But at present the cry for Home Rule is louder and more menacing from the educated Hindus of East Central India than it is from lands where the Mohammedan influence predominates.

As regards the Straits Settlements (Malay Peninsula and Borneo) and much of the surface of India, the question is partially solved by the preservation and education of native rulers. Such, probably, will be the course followed in Egypt, in Southern Arabia, in the Persian Gulf, and in Zanzibar. We shall not grab at the land of these countries, nor seek to substitute a white man for a yellow or black as settler or colonist.

We shall work for free play and full protection for the white man's commerce and commercial agents, and also maintain as far as is reasonable the principle of Free Trade. But we shall strive by our advice, our threats (if necessary), our cash influence to educate the native dynasties in the ever better government and administration of the lands subjected to them. If these native rulers consider it advisable by degrees to enlarge their native councils into elective **Britain's** legislative assemblies, such a **Wise Policy** course will not be opposed by **in Uganda** Great Britain, provided the native legislatures show themselves prudent and observant of treaty obligations. In Uganda the present writer was permitted to restore the indigenous legislature, and more clearly to define and strengthen the prerogatives of the native king. Other supreme chiefs were set up by himself or by his successors as administrators, and the peace and quiet which have followed have shown the wisdom—in this part of Africa, at any rate—of trusting to native dynasties to rule their own people. A similar course has been followed in the protectorate of Sierra Leone, and is, no doubt, being adopted in Nigeria.

Besides the questions of interstate commercial relations and Home Rule there are other problems and dangers to be faced and solved—not perhaps with a rush, but as occasion serves. One of these is the colonisation of vacant lands, and consequently the distribution of the world's racial types. Within the vast limits of the Canadian Dominion there are perhaps a million square miles of fertile land with a healthy climate still uninhabited by men.

Most notable perhaps are the coast-lands and islands of British Columbia, an earthly paradise for scenery, climate, and wealth of natural products. British Columbia, calculated on its endowment by Nature, should be a country with the population of France, and should be one of the envied nations of the world. At present it is inhabited by about 200,000 men and women, mainly of British origin—there are also 13,000 Chinese, and 4,600 Japanese—some of whom have **Mixed Races** come direct from the Mother **in British** Country, others by way of the **Columbia** Eastern Canadian provinces, or from the United States. There is, in addition, an Indian population of about 29,000, living very much the life of gypsies. This Indian type will—I venture to predict—become fused into the general community without harm to it. Physically, it does not differ very much more from the modern type of British colonist than do some of the cotter fishing folk of North-western Scotland and Western Ireland from the more modern race types of the British Islands.

Still, 200,000 British colonists and 29,000 Amerindians are not a sufficient population for the area and extraordinary natural advantages of British **Japan's** Columbia and its dependen- **Overflowing** cies. The Japanese divined this **Population** long ago. The limits of Japan are all too small for its overflowing population. Korea may receive some of the overflow; China, on the other hand, may resist Japanese immigration, and is quite vigorous and numerous enough in her peoples to do so. Even if Japan should wrest the Philippine Islands from the United States—as she may yet try to do—this region does not offer great possibilities for the building up of a powerful people. It is small wonder, therefore, that Japan has hoped, little by little, by degrees, unobtrusively, to infiltrate the lands of British Columbia, Alaska, and the North-western part of the United States, and thus in time create a new Japan beyond the seas which might resist aggression by the eventually effete races of Europe.

Canada and British Columbia, and also the United States, are alive to this difficulty, and seemingly resolved to resist it. This movement has done something to weaken the Anglo-Japanese Alliance, and it may considerably embarrass the Asiatic policy of the British Government. Yet the problem of Canadian-British Columbian colonisation will not be solved by our keeping out the Japanese and Chinese.

The alternative seems simple: "Encourage white immigration." But the emigration of poor whites, labourers, competitors with the working men already in possession, is not encouraged; rather the reverse. One can understand the **Problem of** objection of Canadian citizens **Canadian** to having their Motherland **Colonisation** made the dumping ground for white refuse. This they have every right to reject. But if they are not to admit for menial work, or for the less attractive walks of life, the Oriental races—also an exclusion with which we can sympathise—then something must be done to attract large numbers of white settlers who will come ready to work, though with no more capital than their head and limbs.

The objection to this policy—of throwing open the Canadian Dominion to all white immigrants on the easiest terms subject to the indispensable conditions of healthiness and morality—arises from the labour leaders and trade unions of Canada. "We will not have labour cheapened" is the substance of their outcry. Their argument would probably be that they do not want to repeat in Canada the miseries of the Old World. "All labour shall be highly paid in future," almost equally paid, whether it be hair-cutting, wood-sawing, teaching mathematics, painting pictures, composing operas, writing books, reaping corn, preaching sermons, pleading or defending at the Bar.

Perhaps they are right. But meantime agricultural, mining, domestic work is almost at a standstill in the Far West while these laudable attempts are being made to solve the social problem, to create a white Canada in which there shall be no distinctions between skilled and unskilled labour—for that is what the argument resolves itself into in the long run. Already young native Canadians are **Canada's** migrating to Mexico, and the **Social** young married womanhood of **Conditions** the western parts of the dominion is wearing itself into old age and ugliness in the endeavour to be cook, washerwoman, housemaid, governess, nurse and wife in one. These are the complaints voiced by many private letters, by signed and unsigned contributions in the colonial Press. The population of Canada has not increased proportionately by anything like the same ratio as that of the United States, though there is an almost equal area of territory suited to the habitation of the white man.

Japan may also turn her attention to the colonisation of Australia, but the lands left open to her here do not offer one tithe of the advantages and attractions of British Columbia or of North-west America generally. They are arid and extremely hot, and in some parts very unhealthy. Possibly Japan may hope for a tropical future. It is a people of extremely mixed elements, as likely to develop into a tropical race as into a people of the temperate zones. In that case, Japan may accept in return for a promise to leave America severely alone the overlordship of the Philippine Islands, and little by little become the mistress of the Dutch, German, and perhaps a part of the British

Empire in that region of Malaya between Australia and New Guinea on the south-east and Cochin China on the north-west. Meantime, if any movement should be directed by the Imperial statesmen of Great Britain, it should be the direction of British emigration towards British Columbia—one of the world's paradises.

There is a future before Trans-Zambesian Africa, from a white man's point of view, that is scarcely realised. Before many years have passed, science will have found a means of extirpating such local germ-diseases as affect man and beast. The climate over nearly the whole of this region from the Zambesi to the southern ocean is magnificent. Where the soil is arid it is packed with precious metals, but much of the aridity is caused by the ill-regulated water supply. Afforestation is already producing a change in this respect, and increasing the rainfall. In fact, the rainfall may be equalised by a moderate de-foresting of the too tropical eastern coast-belt coincident with the planting up of the interior deserts. The streams produced by the heavy tropical or temperate rains will be made to supply **The White Man's Prospects in Africa** water for the irrigation of the less favoured regions. The coexistence of a negro population of some five or six million within these limits is, together with the general question of unskilled labour, one of the problems that the empire has to face and solve before long. About 1,500 years ago, in all probability, there were very few big black negroes dwelling in the lands to the south of the Zambesi. This sub-continent then was sparsely peopled by a Hottentot-Bushman race of low or arrested physique, and of poor intellectual development.

These men were leading the almost animal life of the Stone Age. Then came successive rushes of the powerful Bantu negroes from the north and east, and a good deal of the centre and east of South Africa was populated by black men, the ancestors of the modern Bechuana, Zulu, and Nyanja tribes. The Hottentots in the south-west had made a more determined resistance, and when the European first arrived on the scene, in the sixteenth century, much of the south-western part of this sub-continent was still outside the Bantu sphere. The persecution or the control of the Hottentots by Dutch and British indirectly assisted the attempts of the Kaffirs to extend further and further to the south-west. Speaking, however, racially, some sections of the Zulu-Kaffir-Bechuana peoples are no earlier colonists of South Africa than the Dutch and even the British. Some sections of them have inherently no better right to the soil of a No-man's-land than we have ; both alike have entered into the inheritance of a vanished Bushman type, if one can **The Early Colonists of South Africa** seriously ascribe full territorial rights to a race of wandering human nomads, as much, and no more, entitled to the fee-simple of the soil they roved over than the wild beasts they were attempting to dispossess.

In deciding such grave questions it has always seemed to the present writer that a very great distinction must be made between nomads and agriculturists. An agricultural race that has distinctly benefited the land it has occupied, by subduing Nature and making the country fit for intelligent human occupation, has acquired a fee-simple in the soil ; not so the nomad, who is a mere hunter. Pastoral peoples should be given reservations in return for the care they have bestowed on domestic animals, and for their having subdued more or less the wild beasts that would make the keeping of these flocks and herds impossible ; or they may have uprooted poisonous herbs, and have mitigated marsh or thorny scrub.

To reduce a long argument into as few words as possible, the future settlement of race distribution in Trans-Zambesian Africa should follow these lines : The existing agricultural races should be granted definite areas of land, which would become as much theirs as land similarly taken up by white men ; but every inducement of teaching, all fair persuasion, should be used towards these negro tribes to leave the high, cold regions or the temperate coast lands and migrate little by little to the tropical eastern belt, and, most of all, to the basin of the Zambesi, especi- **A Black Central Africa** ally the magnificent territories of British Central Africa. This is a climate well suited to negro physical development, not so well suited to the white man. As compensation for the gradual creation of a white South Africa, the building up of a black Central Africa should be carried on simultaneously. No injustice should be done to Basuto or Zulu, to Bechuana or Baronga. But actual inducements may be offered to the more vigorous and

5651

enterprising amongst the black men to migrate a little farther to the east and north in return for a good substantial grant of land. In exchange, the vacant soil of the high cold plateaux might be disposed of to European settlers. Gradually in this way the two races might draw apart, the black men living more to the east and north, and the white to the south and south-west. As in India, so in South Africa, the alternative to this policy is the setting aside of racial prejudice and the free interbreeding of black and white; the same education, the same laws, the same social organisation being made to apply to both.

Bonds of Union for Black and White

This consummation is less and less in favour. The blacks dislike interbreeding with the whites quite as much as the reverse is the case, and so far the result of such intermixture between the absolute negro and the absolute white man has not been happy either in its physical attributes or its political status.

On the other hand, the retention of five, six, ten millions of negroes as a permanently servile force has likewise ceased to be possible. Sufficient education has been brought amongst them by the white man, he has departed sufficiently from the ideas of the seventeenth and eighteenth centuries, to have made the reinstitution of negro slavery a physical impossibility. The negroes would resist it to the death, and the white man has not the numbers, the strength, or the money to reimpose such a condition on his still slightly inferior brother, whom at one time he would, if he could, have reduced once more to the level of a beast.

Of course, if the white peoples decide for a white South Africa they must face and settle the problem of unskilled labour. Either they must consent to work with the pick and shovel, the mason's trowel, the bricklayer's hod, the gardener's spade, to perform all the menial functions of domesticity, to police, to be signalman, pointsman and guard, telegraph clerk and messenger, postman, groom, carter, shepherd, vine-dresser, ostrich attendant, and dock labourer; or they must decide for a partnership on equal terms with the black and possibly the yellow man so far as South Africa is concerned. The Chinaman need have no say in the development of South Africa. He has quite a large enough sphere in Eastern

The Ideal of a White South Africa

and Central Asia, but if the "White South Africa" ideal is to be lowered because the white man dislikes to work as an unskilled labourer, the Indian must be readmitted to take his share in the development of this neglected region.

There are few problems now to be solved in British West Africa since we have most wisely decided it is the black man's country, to be owned and developed by the negro and negroid. In Uganda the same principle is in force, but in East Africa the future is much more complicated; a parti-coloured policy may be the wisest to adopt. The rights to land, communally and individually, on the part of the indigenous blacks and browns are already recognised and have been secured.

There still remain territories, collectively as large as Ireland—situated at altitudes between 6,000 and 13,000 feet above sea-level, above sunstroke and most tropical diseases, except malaria, which is a matter of infection—which are in every way suited to European settlement. Owing to former wars between tribe and tribe, and to the cold climate, there are no existing native inhabitants. Shall we actively promote the colonisation of these still vacant lands by homeless Britishers or shall we let them drift into the possession of Boers, Italians, Greeks, or Russian Jews? Then in East Africa is also the Asiatic problem.

East Africa's Asiatic Problem

Are we then to encourage, discourage or remain indifferent to the immigration on a large scale of natives of India, who shall come not merely as employés, merchants or soldiers, but as settlers, bringing their women-folk and determined to find in East Africa that America we are denying them in Natal and the Transvaal. Can we refuse them this satisfaction? Are we as Imperialists to shape new homes for white men only? Or should we expect the overplus of India to be content with new fields of energy nearer home—Southern Arabia, Southern Persia, Malaya, Borneo, Fiji, Northern Australia, Mauritius; or in Tropical America—Honduras, Jamaica, Trinidad, Guiana, leaving Africa to the Negro, Negroid and Caucasian?

Egypt is one of the knottiest problems that offer themselves for our solution. We have raised a Mohammedan people from the dust, have forced on it education, law and order, security and affluence, have even assiduously taught it what it had forgotten since it was submerged and denationalised by Islam (that lava flow of human history), that the lands of the Lower Nile and the people generated from Nile mud and sand were once the cradle and the exponents of a mighty civilisation. By our intervention this modern Egyptian race has been saved from dwindling into virtual extinction, bled to death by heartless Turkish pashas and their Circassian and Armenian servants.

Now, under an enlightened prince, who, like his father, has Egyptian blood in his veins, and administered by a new school of Egyptian, Armenian, and Turkish ministers, Egypt desires to be allowed to run alone. The Sudan, it is virtually acknowledged, is a totally different question; it has its own outlet to the sea at Port Sudan and via Uganda and Mombasa. The Sudan administered by Britain will relieve Egypt from one great menace on the south. If, argue some Egyptians, the British troops were removed from Cairo and Alexandria to the other side of the Suez Canal, in short, if the Sinai peninsula were definitely ceded **British** to Great Britain and Egypt **Officials** became an absolutely inde- **in Egypt** pendent kingdom, the British would obtain means of defending the Red Sea route to India and the Suez Canal and yet might relieve the administration of Egypt of that admixture of British officials, which, by its crushing superiority of attainments and ideals, galls the rising generation of the upper and middle classes of the native-born Egyptians.

There are other Egyptians who say or write that they are in no hurry to lose the British civilian employés of the khedive's administration; the admirable qualities of these as judges, financiers, engineers, or police officers, are fully recognised. It is the military officers who, for some reason, have made themselves disliked through want of tact, consideration, or sympathy. It is the army of occupation rather than the British officered Egyptian army which is the thorn in the wound. "If the British soldiers were removed to the Sinai Peninsula," say the Young Egyptians, "we should be content to remain for some further period under British tutelage: but let the khedive be master in his own house."

This much is clear to us in the United Kingdom, that Egypt, by its mere geographical position, is the central connecting link of our empire in Europe, Africa, and Asia. Under present circumstances, and until the navigation of the air is a commonplace fact—when there may be universal peace and a world-federation—it is vital to the continued existence of the British Empire abroad that we should neutralise the geographical advantages of Egypt by controlling the destinies and the foreign policy **Egypt** of that country. So much so, **Under British** that, if need be, violence must **Rule** be done to the finer feelings of the Egyptians by the declaration of an actual protectorate or suzerainty —a clear intimation to the khedive and his people that they are, and must remain, for an indefinite period within the diversified confederation which we call the British Empire. We justify this high-handed action by an appeal to the civilised powers that count in the world's councils.

We ask educated India, Australia, East Africa, Uganda, British Central and South Africa, Zanzibar, Mauritius, New Zealand, and even Canada, to consider what would happen to them and to their commerce if the Suez Canal were under the control of an absolutely independent power which could close it at any moment to British ships; or else in the keeping of a state so feeble and so disorganised that it was at the mercy of a *coup-de-main* on the part of any strong Mediterranean nation.

With the proviso, however, of the full recognition of Great Britain's supremacy, there is no reason whatever why Egypt should not receive in time full representative government under the khedive, who might well be raised to the rank of sultan, and even exercise almost completely independent powers in regard to internal administration and the foreign affairs of Egypt proper. Perhaps the best arrangement in the long run would be the cession to England of the Sinai Peninsula and the Sudan, the British troops being withdrawn from the sultanate of Egypt, but the sultan of that country acknowledging the over- **Italy's Place** lordship of the British Em- **in the** peror, just as Bavaria does **Mediterranean** that of the German Emperor. Provided our vital rights of control over Egypt and Southern and Eastern Arabia are recognised, the British people would welcome most heartily the regeneration of Turkey. It may be necessary to the peculiar position of Italy in the Mediterranean that Turkey shall cede some rights in Tripoli to the Italian kingdom, in return for assurances that Italy will not interfere in Albania. It may also come about that Crete is definitely assigned to Greece, as Bosnia has been to Austria, and Novi Bazar to the Serbs, the right to build the Bagdad railway to Germany, and the free passage of the Dardanelles and Bosphorus to the warships of the whole world. This really means curtailing by very little the actual extent of the present administrative area of the Turkish Empire. In return for these concessions — including the recognition on the part of the Powers of a French protectorate over Morocco—the capitulations, and later the special post offices, and all other extra-territorial privileges of the foreign Powers in Turkey might be abrogated, and Turkey left free to attend whole-heartedly to internal reform and the peaceful exploitation of her wealth in natural products.

The Factor of the German Empire

Behind all these projects stands the German Empire, without whose acquiescence much of this planned settlement of world affairs is idle chatter. The necessary entente with Germany, following on the still more necessary understandings with France and Russia, should now be the object of every British statesman's desire. Every reasonable effort must be made to frame an understanding with Germany; if possible, one which shall embrace and settle for at least a hundred years to come the aspirations of France, Belgium, Holland, Russia, America, and Japan. Then we may be able to think about relative disarmament, and the concentrating of our forces on the development of all the backward places of the world.

When such a guarantee of the world's peace is attained as the understanding between Britain and Germany, then, indeed, we ought to turn our attention more vigorously than ever to the reforms which are needed in our own Imperial domains. Besides those already touched on—local administration, commercial interrelations, and secular technical education—we must aim at making the English language a universal medium of intercommunication. It must become eventually the one official language of the whole empire. This need not lead to the neglect of other forms of speech; on the contrary, for purposes of literature, science, history, and the right understanding of diverse minds and intellects, language study—not merely

Plea for a Uniform Language

Hebrew, Ancient Greek, or Latin—must be enforced on all persons in the Imperial service. But English should be taught everywhere in all government or state-aided schools, and all higher instruction be accessible in that language.

And we must put our own pride in our pocket and make on our part concessions to commonsense. English must have its standard pronunciation fixed for a hundred years, and must then be spelt phonetically in the Roman alphabet, just as we spell African and Indian languages phonetically. Moreover, there must be but one alphabet, one printing type all over the empire. At present we tolerate the Irish alphabet in Ireland; the Greek letters in Cyprus; Coptic in Egypt; Arabic in Arabia, Egypt, India, Central Africa, and Malaya; about fifty different alphabets in India and Ceylon; and the Chinese syllabary in Hong Kong. This leads to a sickening waste of time, and to an obscurantism beloved of schoolmasters, clerics, cranky professors, pedantic prigs, sulky bonzes, rebellious Hindus, intriguing Arabs, and all those who are really opposed to the enlarged study of languages and their rapid acquisition by people in a hurry. No one can accuse me of a narrow nationalism in advocating the universal use of the so-called Roman alphabet, because this elegant, clear, easily recognised type was invented in Italy, and as regards its adaptation to the phonetic rendering of all known languages is a German invention by the great Lepsius.

Reforms that Would Benefit the Empire

Besides a uniform alphabet we want a uniform coin of standard value, uniform weights and measures, and postal rates. This last reform is nearly accomplished. In weights and measures we might very well adopt the metric system, and thus put ourselves in harmony with France and the whole Latin world, Germany, Latin America, Turkey, the Balkan States, Roumania, Austria-Hungary, and Japan. In regard to coinage, see how ridiculously the empire differs one portion from another. In Great Britain, Gibraltar, Malta, Cyprus, British Central Africa, South Africa, West Africa, St. Helena, the West Indies, Falkland Islands and British Guinea, Australia, New Zealand, Fiji and the Western Pacific, we have a gold standard and the pound sterling as unit of calculation, and a very sensible unit, too. In Egypt and the Egyptian Sudan there is a monetary system nearly in accord with that of Britain, but the Egyptian pound is worth about threepence more than the English sovereign. It is divided into 100 piastres. In British Arabia, the Central Sudan and Zanzibar the Maria Theresa dollar of an approximate 3s. 8d. still lingers. But throughout the Aden territory, British East Africa, Zanzibar, Seychelles, Mauritius, Persian Gulf, Ceylon, and the whole Indian Empire, the silver rupee of a more or less fixed exchange —value of fifteen rupees = £1—is the established currency.

In the Straits Settlements and the federated Malay States the official currency is a dollar, worth 2s. 4d. At one time there were three kinds of dollar in circulation as legal tender : the Mexican dollar, say 4s. ; the British dollar, value about 2s. 6d. ; and the Hong Kong dollar, value about 2s. These are still, with varying values, the currency of Hong Kong.

In 1902 a committee sat at the Colonial Office to consider and make recommendations regarding the currency question in **Currency in the Straits Settlements** the Straits Settlements. They recommended a return to the gold standard, but, for some inscrutable reason, instead of taking this occasion to introduce the Imperial coinage, they started this great Malayan colony off on a fresh currency of its own, equivalent to the British dollar of an approximate value of 2s. 4d.—another unit of independent value added to the Canadian dollar, the pound sterling, the rupee, the Hong Kong dollar, the five-franc piece, (which is much used in British Gambia and in Jersey). It is actions like these that stand in the way of Imperial federation. The currency of Hong Kong and Wei-hai-wei is enough to make the brain whirl, and must cause many a suicide among cashiers and accountants. The Hong Kong dollar is at present worth about 1s. 11¾d. Two other dollars of totally different and constantly varying value equally pass current. The copper coinage is shamefully bewildering. British Borneo shares the dollar standard of the Straits Settlements.

Canada has from its entry into the empire adopted the dollar of the United States as its unit. Newfoundland also keeps its accounts in dollars and cents (American), but British sterling is legal tender. British Honduras likewise employs the American dollar of an approximate 4s. 2d. as its unit of value. Thus throughout the British Empire we have the following units and values—often fluctuating—for monetary media and the keeping of accounts : The pound sterling, value 20s. ; the five-franc piece, value 4s. ; **Money Values Throughout the Empire** the Egyptian pound, value £1 0s. 3d. ; the Maria Theresa dollar, 3s. 8d. (?) ; the Mexican dollar, 4s. (?) ; the British dollar, 2s. 4d. ; the Hong Kong dollar, 1s. 11d. to 2s. ; and the dollar of British America, about 4s. 2d. For lesser coins in copper, bronze, and nickel there are many values and names—pence, cents, piastres, annas.

In some parts of West, East, and Central Africa the kauri shell is not demonetised. In Nigeria, 1,000 kauris are worth threepence ! This will give some idea of what a worry they can be as cash or in accounts. In British China there are copper coins representing one-hundredth part of the 2s. dollar—less than a farthing, and one-thousandth part of the same coin, or one forty-first part of a penny ! On the other hand, in South Africa there is a distressing dearth of small cash, no coin below a silver threepence being in circulation.

Will no great Imperial statesmen arise, will no council of broad views and dominant authority come into existence which will cause the empire to agree on :

1. A phonetic spelling and writing of the English language.

2. Uniform weights and measures (metric).

3. Uniform coinage and unit values in calculation (decimal).

4. A single alphabet—the Roman—for writing and printing all languages on an identical phonetic system, the same that is applied to English ?

I doubt if there are great men to devise great measures, and if this magnificent but **The Drift of Empire** unwieldy empire, too loosely compacted, too perversely individualistic in all its parts, be not drifting on to eventual dissolution for the want of men in its supreme councils " with head, heart, hand ; like some of the simple great ones gone ; for ever and ever by," who will impose unity in essentials and allow liberty of judgment in what is unessential.

HARRY JOHNSTON

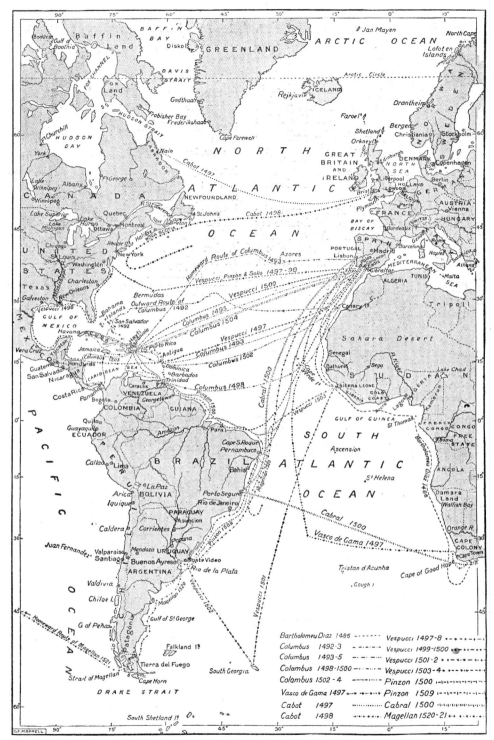

THE ATLANTIC OCEAN, SHOWING THE ROUTES FOLLOWED BY EARLY VOYAGERS

Separating the Old World from the New, and extending from one Polar circle to the other, the Atlantic Ocean has, since the sixteenth century, been the chief commercial highway of the world ; but even earlier than that period, hardy voyagers were bold enough to venture on its waters in their quest for lands unknown. In the above map the routes taken by the various discoverers are distinctly shown, while the dates of their famous voyages are also given.

THE ATLANTIC OCEAN
AND ITS PLACE IN HISTORY
By Dr. Karl Weule
THE ATLANTIC BEFORE COLUMBUS

THE Atlantic may be regarded as a long canal which winds, in the form of a letter S, and preserving an almost uniform breadth, between the Old World and the New. It extends from one Polar circle to the other. Such a configuration, when once it became known to mankind, was bound to favour international communications. The narrowness of the Atlantic has had momentous results for the history both of states and of civilisation. But it was long before the shape of the Atlantic was realised, and this for two reasons. First, the Atlantic has few islands, and this is particularly true of the zone which was the first to be attempted by navigators, the zone lying opposite the mouth of the Mediterranean. Secondly, the Mediterranean was a poor school for explorers. The broken coasts and the numerous islands of that sea make navigation too easy. The Mediterranean peoples did not, therefore, obtain that experience which would have fitted them for the crossing of the outer ocean.

Their explorations were never extended more than a moderate distance from the Pillars of Hercules, either in the Greco-Roman period or in more recent times. Almost the same obstacles existed to the navigation of the northern zone **Difficulties in the Way of Navigation** of the Atlantic. The North Sea and Baltic are not easily navigated; they presented difficulties so great that for a long time they discouraged the inhabitants of their littorals from taking to the sea. The dolmen builders, indeed, showed some aptitude for maritime enterprise; and much later we find that the men of the

Hanse towns and their rivals in Western Europe made some use of the sea for trade. But maritime enterprise on a great scale was not attempted by these peoples. In the days before Columbus, only the inhabitants of Western Norway made **Features of the Atlantic** serious attempts to explore the ocean. They were specially favoured by Nature. A chain of islands, the Faroes, Iceland, and Greenland, served them as stepping-stones. But the voyage from Norway to the Faroes is one of more than 400 miles over a dangerous ocean; and this was a much more difficult feat than the voyage of the ancients from Gades to the Isles of the Blest, if indeed that voyage was ever made. The evidence for it is by no means of the best.

The Atlantic is not merely remarkable for its narrowness and dearth of islands, but also for the great indentations which are to be found in its coasts on either side. These have exercised a great and a beneficial influence on the climate of the Atlantic seaboard. Those of the American coast-line balance those of the Old World to a remarkable degree. It is true that the eastern coast of South America bends inward with a sweep less pronounced than that of the west coast of Africa.

But there is a striking parallelism; and the same phenomenon strikes us when we study the shores of the Nor h and Central Atlantic, in spite of the fact that broken and indented coast-lines make it difficult to perceive the broad similarities at the first glance. Thus the Mediterranean corresponds to the immense gulf which separates North and South America.

The part which the Mediterranean of the Old World has played in history is so important that it has demanded special treatment in a previous chapter. The Mediterranean of America has no such claim upon the attention of the historian. It facilitated the conquest and settlement of the Spanish colonies. It has favoured the development of those motley

Linking the Atlantic with the Pacific communities which fringe its shores from Cuba and Florida on the north to the Cape of San Roque on the south. But when we have said this we have exhausted the subject of its historical importance. More important it doubtless will be in the future. Even at the present time it affords the sole outlet for the Central and Southern States of the American Union ; and when the Panama Canal is completed, this sea will become the natural high-road between the Atlantic and the Pacific—a great factor in political and economic history. It will be what the Eastern Mediterranean was in the early days of the Old World. But we are concerned with history and not with prophecy.

North of the latitude of Gibraltar the two shores of the Atlantic present a remarkable symmetry. In shape the Gulf of St. Lawrence and Hudson's Bay resemble the North Sea and the Baltic. Labrador, Newfoundland, Nova Scotia, and Cape Breton Island may be compared with North-western Europe. The chief difference between the two coast-lines is one of scale. Hudson's Bay, for example, is considerably larger than the North Sea and the Baltic put together. This does not detract from the importance of the symmetry which we have pointed out. It is all the more important because it is most striking on those lines of latitude which have been most important in the history of mankind.

The Northern Atlantic Ocean has influenced the development of our general civilisation in two directions—namely,

The Ocean's Influence on Civilisation by those physical characteristics which originate from its configuration, and by its situation with reference to the other countries on the globe. The extensive fishing grounds which it affords have been a source of wealth to European populations. Even when we take into account the colossal proportions of modern international trade, deep-sea fishing is none the less an industry of note, and makes a very important difference in the profit and loss

accounts of many a northern country. Three hundred, and even two hundred, years ago the fishing fleets of the Northern Sea, which were then numerous though clumsy, gathered, no doubt, a harvest in no degree greater than do the steam fishing-boats of the present day ; but at that time the profits made a much more appreciable difference to the national wealth, and the safety of the national food supply was more largely dependent upon their efforts.

Much more important, from a historical point of view, is the influence on character of this trading in the difficult northern seas ; for the Teutonic nations of North-west Europe and for the French, it was the best of all possible schools of seamanship, and largely contributed to the fact that these nations were able to play a leading part in the general annexation of the habitable globe which has taken place during the last three centuries.

The fisheries are here in closest communication with that other attempt, which, historically at least, exercised influence no less enduring, to find a passage round North America or round Northern Europe and

England's Supremacy of the Seas Asia to the east shore of Asia. Nothing did so much to promote the maritime efficiency of the British nation as the repeated attempts that were made to find the North-west and North-east passages, which began with the voyage of the elder Cabot, and continued to the middle of the nineteenth century. To the Atlantic as a whole belongs the high service of having led the civilised peoples of the Old World out to the open sea from the confines of the Mediterranean and other land-locked waters ; from the time of Columbus it has been a school of technical skill and self-reliance. However, its most northern part, storm-lashed and ice-bound as it is, is in no way inferior to the whole, in this respect at least, that it gave to one sole nation not otherwise particularly strong, to the English, the supremacy over the seas of the world within a short three centuries.

The Atlantic Ocean may be regarded as a broad gulf dividing the western and eastern shores of the habitable world, conceived as a huge band of territory extending from Cape Horn to Smith Sound ; this implies a limitation of our ideas regarding the age of the human race. Its share in universal history does not begin before the moment when the keel of the first Norse boat touched the shore of Greenland or Helluland. Thus, this sea, so important in the development of the general civilisation of modern times, is, historically speaking, young, and its significance in the history of racial intercourse is not to be compared with that of the Pacific or the Indian Ocean.

When compared with those ages during which these two giants, together with our Mediterranean, our Baltic and North Seas, made their influence felt upon the course of history, traditional or written, the thousand years during which the Atlantic has influenced history become of minor importance. The investigator, indeed, who is inclined to regard as " historical " only those cases in which the literary or architectural remains of former races have left us information upon their deeds and exploits will naturally be inclined to leave the Atlantic Ocean in possession of its historical youth. He, however, who is prepared to follow out the ideas upon which this work has been based, and to give due weight to all demonstrable movements and meetings of peoples, which form the first visible sign of historical activity upon the lower **Beginnings of Mankind** planes of human existence, will consider the importance of the Atlantic Ocean as extending backwards to a very remote antiquity. Our views of historical development, in so far as they regard mankind as the last product of a special branch of evolution within the organic world, have recently undergone a considerable change; the most modern school of anthropologists conceives it possible to demonstrate, with the help of comparative anatomy, that the differentiation of mankind from other organisms was a process which began, not with the anthropoid apes—that is to say, at a period comparatively late both in the history of evolution and geologically— but at a much earlier point within the development of the mammals.

From a geological and palæontological point of view, however, this conclusion carries us far beyond the lowest limits previously stated as the beginnings of mankind. We reach the Tertiary Age, a lengthy period, interesting both for the changes which took place within organic life and for the extensive alterations that appeared upon the surface of the earth. The nature and extent of these changes must, in so far as the new theory is correct, have been of decisive importance for the earliest distribution of existing humanity. If the theory be true that during the Tertiary Age two broad isthmuses extended from the western shore of the modern Old World to modern America, then from the point of view of historical development there can be no difficulty in conceiving these isthmuses as inhabited **The Atlantic as a Gulf of Division** by primeval settlers. That point of the globe over which at the present day the deep waters of the Atlantic Ocean heave would then, in fact, have been not only the earliest but also the most important scene of activity for the fate of mankind.

As regards the later importance of the Atlantic Ocean, the collapse of these two isthmuses marks the beginning of a period which is of itself of such great geological length that those first conditions which influenced the fate of our race appear to its most recent representatives as lost in the mists of remote antiquity. After the Atlantic Ocean appeared in its present form, the inhabitants of the Old World had not the slightest communication with the dwellers upon the other shore. The Atlantic Ocean then became in fact a gulf dividing the habitable world.

In all times and places mystery and obscurity have exercised an attraction upon mankind, and thus, too, the Atlantic Ocean, bounding as it did the civilisation gathered round the Mediterranean, attracted the inhabitants of those countries from an early period. As early as the second millennium before the birth of Christ we find the Phœnicians on its shores, and soon afterwards their western branch, the Carthaginians.

The inducement to venture out upon its waves was the need of tin, the demand for which increased with the growing use of bronze; and the rarity of this metal induced them to brave the dangers of the unknown outer sea. However, these two branches of the great commercial nations of Western **Italy's Dread of the Sea** Asia did not attain to any great knowledge of the Atlantic Ocean. We are reminded of the reluctance of the towns and republics of Italy to pass through the Straits of Gibraltar, though the high seas had long been sailed by the Portuguese and Spaniards, or the cowardice of the Hanseatics, who hardly dared to approach the actual gates of the ocean, when we find these two peoples who ruled for so many centuries over the Mediterranean, which is itself of no small extent, unable to advance any material distance beyond the Pillars of Hercules. Even as regards the tin trade, the chief labour was probably undertaken by the seafaring coast-dwellers of separate parts of Western Europe. How small in reality were the achievements of both nations upon the Atlantic

The Days of Greek Civilisation is shown by the amount of praise lavished upon the coasting voyage of Hanno, which, however important for geographical science, was no great achievement of seamanship. It is a characteristic feature of all landlocked seas to limit not only the view, but also the enterprise of the maritime peoples upon their shores.

In Greek civilisation the Atlantic Ocean, as such, is only of theoretical importance. A few explorers did, indeed, advance from the Mediterranean northwards and southwards into the Atlantic. Such were Pytheas of Massilia (about 300 B.C.), who journeyed beyond Britain to the fabulous land of Thule; his compatriot and contemporary, Euthymenes, followed by Eudoxos of Cyzicus (about 150 B.C.) and the historian Polybius (about 205–123 B.C.) succeeded in reaching different points upon the west coast of Africa ; but none of these undertakings led to any practical result. The reason for this fact is to be found in the length of a voyage from the coast of Greece, which was a far more difficult undertaking for the sailors of those days than it now appears. Especially important, moreover, is the fact that the Greeks, although they were the general heirs of the Phœnician colonial policy, never attempted to overthrow the supremacy of the Carthaginians in the western half of the Mediterranean Sea.

For them, therefore, the great western ocean remained permanently wrapped in the obscurity of distance, a fact which enabled them to people its illimitable breadth with creations of fancy, such as

Rome's Struggles With Carthage the "Atlantis" of Plato ; but distance was too important an obstacle to be successfully overcome by their instinct for colonisation and discovery. The Atlantic Ocean came into the purview of the Romans at the moment when their struggles with Carthage for the Iberian Peninsula ended definitely in their favour (210 B.C.); it was not until then that this rapidly developing Power in the west of the Mediterranean was able to advance

from the east coast of Spain to the interior of the country and thence to its western coast. Notwithstanding the activity of Rome in colonisation, her supremacy in Iberia led to no enterprises by sea ; nor were any such undertaken by the Romans until they had established themselves in Gaul, and had thus gained possession of a considerable seaboard upon the Atlantic Ocean.

It was in 54 and 55 B.C. that Julius Cæsar made his voyages to Britain ; a few decades later came the advance of Drusus and of Germanicus into the North Sea. The nature of these conquests precluded adventure upon the open sea. The Romans were attempting only to secure their natural frontier against the threatened encroachments of the Germanic tribes, and confined their explorations to the southern portion of the North Sea.

During the first thousand years after the birth of Christ the North Sea is the only part of the Atlantic Oecan which can be demonstrated to have had any enduring influence upon the history of Western Europe. The Veneti, and other tribes inhabiting the western coast of Spain,

Atlantic Ocean in Legend Gaul, and Germany, certainly adventured their vessels upon the open sea southward in continuation of the primeval trade in tin and amber ; even the Romans, before indefinitely retiring from Britain, made one further advance during the expedition which Cn. Julius Agricola (84 A.D.) undertook in the seas and bays surrounding Great Britain. Of other nations, however, we hear nothing during this age which would lead us to conclude that they carried on communication by means of the ocean to any important extent.

The age preceding the tenth century A.D. is entirely wanting in maritime exploits, with the exception of the expedition of the Norsemen, but is, on the other hand, rich in legends, the locality of which is the Atlantic Ocean. These are important to the history of civilisation by reason of their number ; they are the most striking proof of that general interest which was excited, even during the "darkest" century of the Middle Ages, by the great and mysterious ocean upon the west. Historically, too, they are of importance for the influence which their supposed substratum of geographical fact has exercised upon the course of discovery. This interest appears, comparatively weak at first, in the "Atlantis" legend. The legend, together with many other elements forming the geographical lore of classical Greece, was adopted by the Middle Ages, but cannot be retraced earlier than the sixth century. For nearly one thousand years it disappears, with Cosmas Indicopleustes, that extraordinary traveller and student in whose works the attempt to bring all human discovery into harmony with the Bible, an attempt characteristic of patristic literature, reaches its highest point. In the " Atlantis " of Plato, Cosmas apparently sees a confirmation of the teachings of Moses, which had there placed the habitation of the first men ; it was not until the time of the Deluge that these men were marvellously translated to our own continent. The ten kings of Atlantis were the ten generations, from Adam to Noah.

The power of legend as a purely theoretical force continued after the first millennium A.D. only in the north-eastern borders of the Atlantic Ocean. The Baltic, owing to its Mediterranean situation, was at that period the theatre of so much human activity and progress that it has already received special treatment. The **The Vikings in the North Sea** North Sea, regarded as a land-locked ocean, was not so greatly benefited by its position as it has been in the later ages of inter-oceanic communication ; at the same time, the coincidence of advantages, small in themselves, but considerable in the aggregate, have made it more important than any other part of the Atlantic Ocean as an area of traffic. These advantages included one of immeasurable importance to early navigation—namely, a supply of islands which, as formerly in the Mediterranean, conducted the navigator from point to point ; a further advantage was the character of its inhabitants, who were far too energetic to be contented with a country which was by no means one of those most blessed by nature.

Hence we need feel no surprise at the fact that the North Sea was navigated in all directions as early as the eighth century by the Vikings ; their excursions to Iceland, Greenland, and to that part of North America which here projects farthest into the ocean, are fully intelligible when we consider the training which the stormy North-eastern Atlantic Ocean offered to a nation naturally adventurous.

The example of the Norsemen was not generally imitated in Europe at that time. Charles the Great launched, it is true, a fleet upon the North Sea to repulse their attacks, and this was the first step made by the German people in the maritime profession ; though we also see the merchants of Cologne from the year 1000 sending their vessels down the Rhine and over the straits to London, the commercial rivalry of Flanders and Northern **Opening up the Atlantic** France following them in the thirteenth century, and about the same time the fleets of the Easterlings visiting the great harbour on the Thames. For the immediate estimation of existing transmarine relations on the Atlantic side of Europe, these expeditions are useful starting-points ; they have, however, nothing to do with the Atlantic Ocean as a highway between the Eastern and Western Hemispheres. The navigators who opened up the Atlantic for this purpose started from the point which past history and the commercial policy of civilised peoples indicated as the most suitable ; that is, from the Mediterranean.

The sudden expansion of the Mohammedan religion and the Arabian power over a great portion of the Mediterranean gave a monopoly of the whole of the trade passing from east to west to the masters of Egypt and of the Syrian ports ; a considerable alteration took place in those conditions under which for more than a century commercial exchange had quietly proceeded between the Far East and the West—an alteration, too, greatly for the worse. Commercial intercourse became so difficult that the chief carrying peoples of the Mediterranean, the commercial city-states, began to consider the possibility of circumventing the obstacles presented by the Moslem Power, which not even the Crusaders had been able to shatter.

From the year 1317 the traders of Venice and Genoa regularly passed the Straits of Gibraltar to secure their share of that extensive trade in England and Flanders which **Traders of the Fourteenth Century** had everywhere sprung into prosperity north of the Alps, owing to the great economic advance made by North-west Europe. Almost a generation earlier they had advanced from Gibraltar southwards in the direction which should have brought them into direct communication with India, according to the geographical knowledge of that day. This idea is the leading motive in the history of discovery during the fourteenth and fifteenth centuries, so far as the history was worked out upon the sea. We see it realised in the voyage of the brothers Vadino and Guido de Vivaldi of Genoa in 1281, and that of Ugolino Vivaldi, who in 1291 sailed down the west coast of Africa in a ship of Teodosio Doria with the object of discovering the sea route to India ; it is an idea

Arabs as the Teachers of the West apparent in the voyages made by the Italians to Madeira, to the Canaries, and to the Azores, enterprises both of nautical daring and of geographical importance. Mention must also be made at this point of the several advances upon the west coast of Africa made by Henry the Navigator ; this series of attempts occupied the whole life of that remarkable prince.

It is true that the Portuguese of the fifteenth century, like the Italians before them, proposed to use the Atlantic Ocean as a means of communication only up to that point where an imaginary western mouth of the Nile came forth from the Dark Continent. Not in vain were the Arabs the teachers of the West, both in what they did and in what they did not understand ; their additions to the knowledge of river systems are even more superficial than those made by European geographers of the Dark Ages. The mistake of the Arabs most fruitful in consequences was their division of the Upper Nile into three arms—one flowing into the Mediterranean from Egypt, one flowing into the Red Sea on the coast of Abyssinia, and one flowing into the Atlantic Ocean on the coast of North-west Africa. This hydrographical myth, of which a hint had been given long before by Ptolemy, was transmitted to the West immediately by the Arabs.

It is to the influence of this strange theory we must ascribe the attempts made by the Italians and also by Prince Henry ; they hoped to find a short cut to the realm of Prester John

The Atlantic Regarded as Illimitable and the Elysium of Southern Asia. A common feature in all the theories of the time about the Atlantic Ocean is the tendency to consider it as the illimitable western boundary of the habitable world. In the history of discovery, this mental attitude continues until the time of Columbus, whose westward voyage cannot for that very reason be compared with any similar undertaking, because it was based upon the conception of the world

as a closely united band of earth. However, in the scientific treatment of the great sea upon the west, views and conceptions of the world as a united whole had made their influence felt almost two centuries earlier. The fact that elephants are to be found both in Eastern India and Western Africa had led Aristotle to suppose that the two countries were separated by no great expanse of ocean.

After the Patristic Age, the theory was revived by scholasticism upon the basis of Asiatic and Greek geography. As transmitted by the Arabs, this theory respecting the configuration of the ocean assumed that form which was bequeathed by Marinus of Tyre about 100 A.D. and by Ptolemy to the Caliphs. The Western Ocean, upon this theory, was not reduced to the narrow canal which Seneca had conceived ; but, compared with the length of the continent which formed its shores, it yet remained so narrow that a man with the enterprise of Columbus might very well have entertained the plan of finding the eastern world by crossing its waters westwards.

The Coming of Columbus Ptolemy had given the extent of the continent between the west coast of Iberia and the east coast of Asia as 180° of longitude ; thus one-half of the circumference of the globe was left for the ocean lying between. He had thus considerably reduced the estimate of his informant Marinus, who had assigned 225° longitude for the whole extent of land, thus leaving only 135° for the ocean.

Columbus was more inclined to rely upon Marinus, as Paolo Toscanelli had estimated the extent of land at very nearly the same number of degrees as the Tyrian. Relying upon the stupendous journeys of Marco Polo and the travelling monks of the thirteenth and fourteenth centuries, he observed that Marinus had estimated his 225° of longitude only for that part of Eastern Asia which was known to him ; whereas the fact was that this continent extended far beyond the eastern boundary assumed by Marinus, and should therefore be much nearer the Cape Verde Islands than was supposed. This view strengthened Columbus in that tenacity and endurance which enabled him to continue working for his voyage during ten years full of disappointments, and it gave him that prudent confidence which is the most distinguishing feature of his character.

THE AGE AFTER COLUMBUS
THE INFLUENCE OF THE ATLANTIC ON THE WORLD'S COMMERCE DURING FOUR CENTURIES

ONE of the most remarkable facts in the history of geographical discovery is the failure of the discoverer of the New World to recognise it in its true character as an independent portion of the earth's surface ; Columbus died in the belief that he had sailed on four occasions to the eastern and southern shores of Asia, and to his last breath remained faithful to that picture of the globe which has already been described.

His contemporaries were under the same delusion. This adherence to old beliefs regarding the hydrography of the globe has produced the characteristic circumstance that, in political history and in the history of exploration, the Pacific and Atlantic are closely linked, until the year 1513, when Nuñez de Balboa descended from the heights of Darien to the shore of the southern sea. The Pacific and Atlantic Oceans were considered as forming one sea, which lay between the western and eastern shores of an enormous continental island, the Indian Ocean being nothing more than an indentation facilitating communication to the western shore. It was not until the return of the Victoria from the voyage of circumnavigation undertaken by Magalhaès that Europe learnt that between the western and eastern shores of their own world there lay, not the narrow sea they had expected to find, but two independent oceans, divided by a double continent, narrower and running more nearly north than south, and possessing all the characteristics of an independent quarter of the globe.

Epoch-Making Voyage of the Victoria

An entirely new picture of the world then arose before the civilisation of the age—new in the influence it was to exert upon the further development of the history of mankind, which had hitherto run an almost purely continental course. In every age, from that of the early Accadians to that of Hanseatic ascendancy in the Baltic, the sea has ever been used as a means of communication. Before the year 1500 A.D. we see the Mediterranean and the Indian Ocean with all their branches, as well as the North Sea and the Baltic, in constant use by mankind, and during that long period we know of a whole series of powers founded upon purely maritime supremacy. But the political and economic history even of those peoples whose power was apparently founded upon pure maritime supremacy has been everywhere and invariably conditioned by changes and displacements in their respective hinterlands ; even sea powers so entirely maritime as the Phœnician and Punic mediæval Mediterranean powers and the Hanseatics have been invariably obliged to accommodate themselves to the overwhelming influence of the Old World.

The Power of Maritime Nations

To those peoples their seas appeared, no doubt, as mighty centres of conflict ; but to us, who are accustomed to remember the unity underlying individual geographical phenomena, these centres of historical action give an impression of narrow bays, even of ponds. On and around them a vigorous period of organic action may certainly have developed at times, but their importance to the geographical distribution of human life surpasses very little their spatial dimensions.

After the age of the great discoveries history loses its continental character, and the main theatre of historical events is gradually transferred to the sea. At the same time, the co-existence of separate historical centres of civilisation comes gradually to a close, and history becomes world-wide. The leap, however, which the population of Europe was then forced to make from its own convenient landlocked seas to the unconfined ocean was too great to be taken without some previous training. This training the Atlantic Ocean provided in full ; in fact,

The Atlantic as an Agency of Education

during the sixteenth century its historical importance begins and ends with the task of educating European nations to capacity for world supremacy. No other sea upon the surface of the globe has exercised such an influence, nor was any sea so entirely suited as a training ground by configuration or position. The Pacific Ocean lies entirely apart from this question: From 1513 the task naturally placed before the white races was that of learning to sail this sea, the greatest of all oceans, and apparently the richest in prospects. Its importance is chiefly as a battlefield; it has nothing to do with military training.

The Pacific Greatest of all Oceans

In this respect the Indian Ocean can also be omitted particularly for geographical reasons, though at the same time the chief obstacle to its extensive use by European nations is its lack of some natural communication with the Mediterranean. Compared with these hindrances, the political obstacles, varying in strength but never wholly absent, raised by the Moslem powers of Syria and Egypt are of very secondary importance. How important the first obstacle has ever been is shown by the results of the piercing of it in modern times by an artificial waterway, which is kept open by treaty to the ships of every nation.

Speaking from the standpoint of universal history, we may say that the Mediterranean has exercised a retrograde influence upon humanity, even more so than the Baltic. Both seas conferred great benefits upon the inhabitants of their shores, and indeed the Mediterranean gave so much that we may speak of a Mediterranean civilisation which had lasted for thousands of years, and did not end until the growing economic, political, and intellectual strength of Northern and Southern Europe transferred the historical centre of gravity from this inlet of the Atlantic Ocean to the Atlantic Ocean itself.

Influence of the Mediterranean on Humanity

But neither of these two seas enabled the inhabitants on its shores to take the lead upon the ocean, when the fulness of time appeared with the westward voyage of Columbus, the eastward voyage of Vasco da Gama, and the circumnavigation of the globe by Magalhaēs. These seas renounced the claims which they preferred before that great decade, if not to be regarded as the transmitters of civilisation and history, yet to be considered as a history and as a civilisation. We do not see either Venice or Genoa crossing the Straits of Gibraltar, or the Hanseatics crossing the Skagerrack or the Straits of Dover, with the object of taking their share in the struggle that was beginning for maritime supremacy. Those powers were sufficiently skilled in seamanship to maintain their supremacy within their own narrow circles, but their experience was insufficient to enable them to venture upon the open seas surrounding the globe.

A strict and thorough maritime education has been from the age of discovery the fundamental condition for the attainment of the position of a modern civilised power in the hard struggle between races and peoples. Of the nations whose voices are heard with respect in the councils of peoples, there is none which does not consider itself permanently equipped and armed for the wide and mighty political and economic struggle upon the stage of the world; for of the original combatants on the scene those who have obviously remained victorious were forced to gain their early experience in the hard school of maritime struggle. These original combatants were Spain and Portugal upon one hand, Holland, England, and France upon the other, and the scene of struggle was the Atlantic Ocean. As regards Spain and Portugal, it is a remarkable fact that this sea concerned them only temporarily and within definite limits, thanks to the Papal edict of May 6th, 1493, which divided the world between the two Romance powers at the outset of their career of colonisation on conditions which placed their boundaries within the Atlantic Ocean itself.

The Atlantic as a Battlefield

This line of demarcation was to run from north to south at a distance of 100 leagues from the Cape Verde Islands, extended to 370 by the Treaty of Tordesillas of June 7th, 1494. Thus, as soon appeared, the main portion of the New World fell within the Spanish half, and only the east of South America was given to the Portuguese. The importance of their American possessions was naturally overshadowed by the far more important tasks which fell to the share of the little Portuguese nation in the Indian Ocean during the next 150 years. Brazil served primarily as a base for the further voyage to India and the Cape of Good Hope. It was impossible to make it a point of departure for further

Portuguese acquisitions, as the Spaniards opposed every step in this direction on the basis of the treaties of partition.

During the first half of the sixteenth century other European powers besides England and Holland crowded into the north of the Atlantic Ocean in pursuit of the same objects ; we find not only French explorers and fishermen, but also Spaniards and Portuguese, in the Polar waters of the American Atlantic. However, none of the other nations pursued their main object with such tenacity as the two first-named peoples, above all, the English ; the period between 1576 and 1632 belongs entirely to them, and was occupied without interruption by their constant endeavours to discover the north-west passage.

The reward, however, which the English people gained from their stern school of experience in the northern seas was one of high importance. England then was unimportant from a geographical point of view, and a nonentity in the commercial relations of the world at large ; but it was not until the middle of the nineteenth century that clear evidence **England's** was forthcoming that the com- **Great Power** munication by water between **on the Sea** Baffin Bay and the Bering Straits, though existing, was of no use for navigation. But the high nautical skill, the consciousness of strength, and the resolve to confront any task by sea with adequate science and skill—in short, the unseen advantages which the English nation gained from these great Arctic expeditions, and from their slighter efforts in the first half of the sixteenth century, proved of far higher importance than the tangible results achieved. It was these long decades of struggle against the unparalleled hostilities of natural obstacles that made the English mariners masters on every other sea, and taught the English nation what a vast reserve of strength they had within themselves.

In considering the historical career of this extraordinary island-people from the sixteenth century onwards, we are forced to regard modern history as a whole from the standpoint of national Arctic exploration, although this is far too confined for our purposes as compared with the sum total of forces operative throughout the world. During the age when maritime skill was represented by the city republics in the Mediterranean and the Northmen in the

North Sea and the Northern Atlantic Ocean, the Spaniards and Portuguese were already fully occupied with their own domestic affairs, the Moorish domination. Their first advance in the direction of nautical skill was not made until a considerable time after the liberation of Lisbon from the Moorish yoke (1147), when **Decadence** the magnificent harbour at the **of Spain and** mouth of the Tagus had be- **Portugal** come more and more a centre for Flemish and Mediterranean trade ; even then it was found necessary to call in all kinds of Italian teachers of the nautical art. It was only slowly and at the cost of great effort that Spain and Portugal became maritime peoples ; and their subjects were never seafarers in the sense in which the term is applied to the English and Dutch of the present day, to the Norwegians, or even to the Malays.

Indeed, the period of their greatness gives us rather the impression of an age of ecstasy, a kind of obsession which can seize upon a whole nation and inspire them to brilliant exploits for a century, but which results in an even greater reaction so soon as serious obstacles to their activity make themselves felt. Only thus can we explain the fact that these two peoples, once of world-wide power, disappeared with such extraordinary rapidity and so entirely from the world-wide ocean. The last Spanish fleet worthy of consideration was destroyed off the Downs by the Dutch lieutenant-admiral, Marten Harpertzoon Tromp, in 1639 ; about the same period the Portuguese were also considered the worst sailors in Europe.

The Dutch and the French held their ground more tenaciously. In both cases Arctic training ran a somewhat different course than in the case of the English. During the sixteenth and seventeenth centuries they certainly took part in the attempt to discover the north-west and north-east passages ; with a tenacity **The Age of** highly praiseworthy they ap- **Maritime** plied themselves to the more **Enterprise** practical end of Arctic deep-sea fisheries and sealing. That such occupations could provide a good school of maritime training is proved by the energy with which the Dutch, and afterwards the English and the French, made the great step from the Atlantic to the Indian Ocean ; further evidence is also to be seen in the unusually strong resistance which the two colonial powers in the seventeenth and eighteenth centuries were able to offer to their most dangerous rival, the rapidly growing power of Great Britain.

Towards the end of the sixteenth century the historical character of the Atlantic Ocean undergoes a fundamental change. From the beginning of the period of great discoveries its special destiny had been to **A Period** provide a maritime training **of Licensed** for the nations of North-west **Piracy** Europe, and to make these nations sufficiently strong for successful resistance to the two powers of Spain and Portugal, for whom the supremacy of the world seemed reserved by their geographical position, the world-wide activity of their discoverers, and the pronouncements of the Pope. Maritime capacity they had attained by their bold ventures in the Arctic and Antarctic waters of the Atlantic Ocean ; the struggle was fought out by these nations independently or in common in the seas to the south either of their own continent or of the West Indies.

We refer to the great epoch of the English and Dutch wars against the " invincible " fleets of Philip II. ; it was a period, too, of that licensed piracy, almost equally fruitful in political consequences, which was carried on in the waters of East America by representatives of all the three northern powers. The North Sea, the Baltic, and the Mediterranean have all been scourged by pirates at one time and another ; and in all three cases the robbers plied their trade so vigorously and for so long a time that the historian must take account of them.

This older form of piracy was undertaken by ruffians beyond the pale of law, who were every man's enemy and no man's friend, and plundered all alike as opportunity occurred, it being everybody's duty to crush and extirpate them when possible. But towards the end of the sixteenth century a different state of affairs prevailed on **Powers** the Atlantic Ocean. After the **Seeking a** discovery of America as an inde-**New Route** pendent continent, it became a question of life and death for the North-west European powers, which had grown to strength in the last century, to find an exit from the Atlantic Ocean to the riches of the eastern countries of the Old World. It was possible that this exit was to be found only in the south, in view of the constant ill-success of expeditions towards the Pole ; and to secure the pos-

session of it in that quarter was only possible by the destruction of the two powers that held it. This attempt was undertaken and carried through in part by open war, in part by piracy, which was not only secretly tolerated but openly supported by governments and rulers.

No stronger evidence is forthcoming for the value attached to these weapons and the free use of them during the last ten years of Elizabeth's reign than the honourable positions of Sir Thomas Cavendish, Sir Francis Drake, Sir John Hawkins, and Sir Walter Raleigh. On April 4th, 1581, the maiden queen went on board Drake's ship, concerning which the Spanish ambassador had lodged a complaint of piracy on its return from the circumnavigation of the globe, and dubbed him knight.

This irrepressible advance on the part of the North-west powers towards the east of the Old World is closely connected with the fact that the struggle for maritime supremacy was confined to the Atlantic Ocean only for a short period ; no sooner had England and Holland become conscious of their strength than we find both **Scenes of** powers in the East Indies, and **the Nations'** on the west coast of America ; **Conflicts** in short, wherever it was possible to deprive the two older powers of the choicest products of their first and most valuable colonies. So early as 1595 Cornelis de Houtman sailed with four Dutch ships to Java and the neighbouring islands ; he was followed shortly afterwards by the English and Danes.

When the North-west European powers began to extend their encroachments beyond the limits of the Atlantic Ocean, this latter naturally ceased to be what it had been for a century past—the main theatre of the naval war ; not that it became any more peaceful during the next two centuries. On the contrary, the struggles which broke out amongst the victorious adversaries after the expulsion of the Portuguese and Spaniards from their dominant position were even more violent and enduring than those of earlier days. This conflict, too, was largely fought out in the Indian Ocean, but it was waged with no less ferocity on the Atlantic.

The great length of the two coast lines which confine the Atlantic Ocean, and the general strength and growing capacity of the states of North-west Europe, led to the result that, during the course of the last three centuries, repeated changes have taken place both in the locality and vigour of the struggle for the supremacy of this ocean, and also in the personality of the combatants. Among these latter we find Portugal and Spain long represented after their rapid decadence. In the first decades of the seventeenth century the Portuguese colonies on the coast of Upper Guinea fell quickly one after the other into the hands of the Dutch ; Elima was conquered in 1537 ; in 1642 Brazil fell into the hands of Holland, after eighteen years' struggle, though nineteen years later it was restored to Portugal for an indemnity of £800,000 ; in 1651 the Dutch seized and held for 115 years the important position of the Cape of Good Hope.

In the West Indies the division of the Spanish possessions began from 1621 with the foundation of the Dutch West Indian Company, "that band of pirates on the look-out for shares." In the course of the next ten years the majority of the Lesser Antilles were taken from their old Spanish owners. In 1655 Cromwell took possession of Jamaica. The rest of the Greater Antilles remained Spanish for a considerably longer period ; Hayti **Fight for the** held out its eastern part until **Supremacy** 1821, and Cuba and Porto Rico **of the Seas** remained Spanish until 1898. The combatants in North-west Europe are divided into groups, according to their respective importance ; on the one hand, the three powers of England, Holland, and France, each of which has made enormous efforts to secure the supremacy of the Atlantic and Indian Oceans, and, on the other hand, Denmark, Sweden, and Prussia, which pursued objects primarily commercial and on a smaller scale. Their efforts on the African coast are marks of the rising importance then generally attached to trans-oceanic enterprise, and form points of departure of more or less importance in the histories of the states concerned ; but in the history of the Atlantic Ocean all of these are events of but temporary importance compared with the huge struggle between the other three powers.

The beginnings of this struggle, as far as England and Holland are concerned, go back to the foundation of the English East India Company ; the first serious outbreak took place upon the promulgation of the Navigation Act by the commonwealth on October 9th, 1651. Henceforward English history is largely the tale of repeated efforts to destroy the Dutch supremacy, at first in home waters, afterwards upon the Atlantic, lastly on the Indian Ocean. This policy produced the three great naval wars of 1652-1654, 1664-1667, and 1672-1674, which, without resulting in decisive victory for the English, left them free to proceed with the second portion of their task, the overthrow of French sea power and **England's** the acquisition of predomin-**Wars on** ance in the commerce of the **Land and Sea** world. Judged by the prize at stake, this struggle must rank amongst the greatest of modern times. It began in 1688, when Louis XIV. opened his third war of aggression ; it continued, with some cessations of hostilities, until the Congress of Vienna (1814-1815).

The struggle was carried on at many points. A land war in India (1740-1760) decided the future of the Indian Ocean. The contest to secure communications with that ocean was fought out in Egypt (1798-1801) and at the Cape (1806) ; but the main conflicts were waged on the seaboard of the Atlantic or on its waters. Supremacy in the Atlantic meant supremacy in the world until the age of steam began and the Suez Canal opened a new route to the Farther East.

Some events which are otherwise of secondary importance deserve notice because they prove how much the current estimate of the Atlantic's importance changed in the course of the struggle. Tangier came into the hands of England in 1662 as the dowry of Catharine of Braganza, the queen of Charles II. ; it was given up in 1684 on the ground that it cost more than it brought in. Twenty years later English opinion as to the value of Tangier had been materially modified ; and Gibraltar, on the opposite shore, was seized in 1704. Since then England has never relaxed her hold upon this fortress ; it has been repeatedly strengthened and defended under the greatest difficulties. Were Tangier an English possession to-day, **Gibraltar's** English it would certainly re-**Value** main, even though it were to cost **to Britain** infinitely more than the yearly vote of £40,000 which England has expended on Gibraltar for the last two centuries. Equally significant is the attitude of England towards the solitary isle of St. Helena. The Portuguese, by whom it was discovered in 1502, were content to found a little church on the island ; the Dutch noticed St. Helena so far as to destroy the church in 1600. But

5667

the East India Company, upon acquiring it in 1650, recognised its importance by establishing upon it the fort of St. James. The island, however, was not appreciated at its full value until the English supremacy in the Indian Ocean and until Australia had been founded ; that is, not before the beginning of the eighteenth century.

St. Helena a British Possession The taking over of St. Helena by the English Government in 1815 was the logical sequel to the occupation of the Cape. Both of these new possessions were intended to serve as calling stations on the main line of ocean traffic. It was not until the opening of the Suez Canal that this line declined in importance. The main route now runs from Gibraltar, by Malta and Cyprus, to Egypt, Perim, and Aden.

The eastern part of the Atlantic has served, like the Indian Ocean, as an ante-room to the Pacific. The first explorers of the Atlantic, and those powers which first seized strategic points in it, had the Pacific for their ultimate object. The opening of the Suez Canal has taken away this characteristic of the Atlantic, which is now important for its own sake alone.

The political history of the Atlantic begins upon its western seaboard, though not so early as the history of exploration might lead us to expect. In the Spanish and Portuguese colonies of South and Central America a vicious system of government acted as a bar to political and economic development. In the French and English colonies of North America progress was slow, owing to the existence of physical obstacles. Independent development began in the American continent with the Declaration of Independence.

The American War of Independence marks from yet another point of view a turning-point in the history of the Atlantic Ocean. After the Convention of Tordesillas, in 1494, Spain had ruled supreme in the Atlantic, and had almost put her **France's Shattered Navy** authority in a position above the possibility of challenge when she attempted to use Holland as a base for attacking England, the second of her rivals as an instrument for the destruction of the first. The Treaty of Paris (1763) gave England a similar position of predominance in the North Atlantic, since it definitely excluded the French from North America and left their navy in a shattered condition. The treaty created a *mare clausum* on a great

scale, and for the last time ; under it England for the first time realised the object towards which her policy had been directed for the last two hundred years. This situation, the most remarkable which the Atlantic had witnessed since the days of Columbus, lasted for over thirteen years. It was not at once destroyed by the Declaration of Independence (1776), but the growth of the United States introduced a change into the existing conditions.

England's position was altered for the worse ; and the North Atlantic began to play a new part in the history of the world. Hitherto there had been a movement from east to west ; this was now reversed by slow degrees. Europe had acted upon America ; America began at the opening of the nineteenth century to react upon Europe ; and now, at the beginning of the twentieth century, America has become a factor, sometimes a disturbing and unwelcome factor, in European complications.

The American War of Independence was a chapter in the conflict for colonial and commercial power between England and **Brilliant Era in British History** France. The United States were largely indebted to French support for their victory. The desire to obliterate the humiliation of the Treaty of Paris and to avenge the loss of vast tracts of territory in America and India had proved too much for the French. Their interference was repaid with interest by the British ; for a long period the French marine was swept from the seas ; for a considerable portion of the nineteenth century Britain monopolised the seas of the whole world. Next to the period of Atlantic supremacy, from 1763 to 1776, that which followed the Peace of 1815 is the most brilliant in the " rough island story " of the British. Geographical conditions were favourable to them. But they also showed a quality which few nations have possessed—the power of not only recognising, but also of securing, their true interests.

With the two conventions of peace concluded at Paris on May 30th, 1814, and November 20th, or with the closing act of the Vienna Congress on June 9th, 1815, the Atlantic Ocean begins a new period of its historical importance. In those conventions Britain had certainly condescended to return to her former masters some portion of the colonial prizes that she had gained during the last twenty years. These concessions were, however, of very little importance compared with the extent and the economic and strategical value of that increase to which the island kingdom could point upon the Atlantic Ocean alone. Even at that time these concessions were more than counterbalanced by Britain's retention of the Cape, and the claims which such a position implied to the whole of South Africa.

Tobago and Santa Lucia in the West Indies, and Guiana in South America were to be considered, under these circumstances, as accessions all the more welcome to Britain. These possessions could not compensate for the irrevocable loss of the North American colonies, but they implied an increase in the area of operations from which she could contentedly behold the development of the strong and independent life in the New World. The rocky island of Heligoland, which had been united to Britain in 1814 for seventy-six years, narrow as it was, was only too well placed to dominate commercially and strategically both the Skagerrack and particularly the mouths of the Weser and Elbe; it gave England the position, so to speak, of guardian over the slow growth of Germany and the no less slow recovery of Denmark. Britain's maritime predominance after the conclusion of the great European wars was so strong, and the transmarine relations into which she had entered in the course of the seventeenth and eighteenth centuries were also so numerous, that this energetic nation could not fail to draw the fullest possible advantage in every quarter of the world from the position which she occupied at the moment.

Britain Predominant on the Ocean

The period of England's unlimited predominance in the Atlantic Ocean, which she had gained at some cost to her own strength by the wars against France (1755–1763), had been too short for the completion of those transmarine objects which she had in view; but after 1815 she alone of all the powers not only found herself at the height of her strength, but had also the additional advantage of being able to avail herself of a longer period of time to strengthen her position in other respects precisely as she pleased. Then it was that Britain extended her Indian colonial empire in every direction, founded an equally valuable sphere of rule in Australia, and established herself in South Africa and on the most important points

along the Indian Ocean. In view of these undertakings, which claimed the whole of her attention, Britain had but little energy to spare during this period for the Atlantic Ocean. The occupation of the Falkland Islands to secure the passage of the Straits of Magellan, in 1833, the occupation of Lagos as the obvious exit from the Sudan district of Central Africa in the year 1861, and finally the beginning of the further development of a limited trade on several other points on the West Coast of Africa—these were at that time the only manifestations of British activity on the Atlantic shores.

The Rapid Growth of Steam Power

The increase in the value of the Atlantic Ocean to the nations of the world at large only began with the coincidence of a large number of new events. Of these the earliest is the surprisingly rapid growth of steam power for the purpose of transAtlantic navigation. Not only were the two shores of the ocean brought considerably nearer for the purpose of commercial exchange than was ever possible with the old sailing-vessels, but passenger traffic was increased; emigration from Europe to the New World on the scale on which it has been carried out since 1840 was only possible with the help of steam traffic.

The European Powers of the last two-thirds of the nineteenth century have not yet fully realised the importance, either from an economic or political point of view, of the emigration to the United States, a phenomenon remarkable not only for its extent, but for the unanimity of its object; yet the states thereby chiefly affected had already drawn general attention to the fact. This process of emigration and its results only forced themselves upon the general notice upon either side of the ocean after the youthful constitution of the United States of North America had coalesced into a permanent body politic and had developed a new race, by a fusion, unique in the history of humanity, of that growing population which streamed to it from every country of the world; and, finally, when this new nation had applied its energies to the exploitation of the enormous wealth of natural riches in its broad territory.

A New Race Developed in America

This highly important point was reached considerably earlier than any human foresight could have supposed, owing to the unexampled rapidity of the development of the United States ; and its importance holds good not only for the Atlantic Ocean but for the habitable globe. So early as 1812 the United States, when scarcely out of its childhood, had declared war upon the mighty maritime power of Britain, for reasons of commercial politics. In consequence, the United

The United States Secede from Britain States seceded, somewhat ingloriously, and paid for its first attempt at trans-oceanic aggression by confining itself to its own internal affairs for a long period ; in particular, the proclamation of the Monroe doctrine on September 2nd, 1823, is to be considered as a political act materially affecting the Atlantic Ocean.

As a matter of fact, the doctrine still remains in force, notwithstanding the selfish demands of France upon Mexico in 1861, and certain views apparently entertained by Britain and Germany with regard to South America, as the American Press affirmed, during the disturbances concerning Venezuela. To this sense of their own military and naval insufficiency is chiefly to be ascribed the fact that the transmarine efforts of the United States were applied first of all to the Pacific Ocean, which is turned away from Europe, although the European side still forms their historical coast. Between 1870 and 1880 America secured her influence in Hawaii, while at the same time she succeeded in establishing herself in Samoa. It was not until she advanced to the position of a leading state in respect of population and resources that she ventured any similar steps upon the Atlantic side, and even then her attacks were directed only against the Spaniards, who had grown old and weak.

The war of 1898 was the first great transmarine effort on the part of the United States. By their action at that time they openly broke with their former tradition of self-confinement to their own territory ; for that reason, above all

America a Factor in World Politics others, the United States have become a factor in the politics of the rest of the world, not on account of the military capacity which they then displayed : any European power could have done as much either by land or sea. Far more important to European civilisation than their military development is the economic development of North America, which has advanced almost in geometrical progression. The immediate consequence of that development has been that home production not only suffices for the personal needs of the United States, but has introduced a formidable and increasing competition with European wares in Asia, Africa, and the South Seas, or has even beaten them on their own ground ; moreover, the abundance of economic advantages has transformed the previous character of trans-Atlantic navigation materially to the advantage of the United States.

It is hardly likely that the bewildering number of trans-Atlantic lines of steam and sailing ships will in any way diminish in the face of the North American trust, which was carried out in 1902. But American control over British trans-Atlantic lines and certain Continental lines most certainly implies a weakening of European predominance. Henceforward the Atlantic Ocean loses its old character and becomes a great Mediterranean sea. The teaching of history shows us that its further development is likely to proceed in this direction ; so much is plain from the development of circumstances on either side of the

The Atlantic's Future Development Atlantic. Our European Mediterranean and Baltic are not, perhaps, entirely parallel cases, owing to their comparatively smaller area ; yet the history which has been worked out upon their respective shores is in its main features nearly identical. Whether we consider the Phœnicians and Carthaginians, the Ionic Greeks, or the modern French on the shores of the Mediterranean, or turn our attention to the Hanse towns or the Swedes upon the Baltic, the result is the same. First of all, we find tentative efforts at occupation of the opposite shores. Phœnicia occupies Carthage ; Greece colonises Asia Minor ; France, Algiers and Tunis ; and Sweden, Finland and Esthonia. In this way permanent lines of communication are slowly developed, though the mother country for a long period remains the only base.

Independent commercial and individual life on the part of the colony only appears as a third step. Both the Carthaginians and the Greeks of Asia Minor surpassed their mother countries not only in the extent and organisation of their economic development but also by the boldness with which they carried it out. Applying these conclusions to the Atlantic Ocean, the prospects before the Old

World seem somewhat doubtful; even to-day, many an individual might find good reason for characterising the once boundless ocean as a future *mare clausum,* access to which is to depend upon American favour. In any case, the times when the European Powers could rightly regard the Atlantic Ocean as their special domain by right of inheritance are past for ever. Probably, after the opening of the Central American Canal, the Pacific Ocean and the countries upon its shores will become more prominent than hitherto; however, the general direction of American life will remain as before, directed towards Europe and the Atlantic Ocean.

The reasons for this are both historical and geographical. Historically speaking, the closest national and political relations conjoin both shores of the Atlantic Ocean. It is true that, when viewed in the light of the rapid growth of modern life, the dates of the foundation of the South and North American colonies appear considerably remote. None the less, Brazil at the present day considers herself a daughter of Portugal, and the united provinces of Canada recognise **Prosperous** their origin upon the other **States of North** side of the Atlantic. These **America** old ties of relationship tend to reappear with renewed force. In the financial year 1890–1891 2·4 per cent. of the United States imports went through New Orleans, 6 per cent. through San Francisco, but no less than 81·5 per cent. through the great harbours of the Atlantic coast. Moreover, notwithstanding the rapid development of the West, the most populous and the most commercially powerful colonies and states of North America are to be found on the Atlantic coast; the great towns, the most important centres of political and intellectual life, are also situated upon the shores that look towards Europe.

The indissoluble character of these historical relations is reflected almost identically in the geographical conditions. To a modern steamship even the great breadth of the Pacific is but a comparative trifle, and this means of rapid communication is proportionately a more powerful influence in the narrower seas. It was not until steam navigation had been developed that the full extent of the Indian and Pacific Oceans was explored. In the case of the Atlantic the date of exploration is much more remote, but this ocean has profited to an infinitely greater

extent than the two former by the new means of communication. The advantage of friendly shores lying beyond its harbours favoured extensive sailing voyages ever since 1492, and this advantage naturally exists in increased extent for steam navigation. The general shortness of the lines of passage is more than a mere **Relations of** geographical phenomenon. **the Old and** Politically and economically, **New Worlds** it brings the countries and continents into closer relation. Britain and North America are not only more closely related anthropologically and ethnographically, but at the present day they carry on a larger interchange of commercial products than any other two countries. Improved communication between the harbours of these two countries is certainly not the ultimate cause of the two phenomena above mentioned.

Upon the west of the Atlantic Ocean the achievements of technical skill in steam navigation, together with the political and economic advance of the United States, has increased the importance of this sea to an unforeseen extent; so, too, upon the east the achievement of connecting the Mediterranean and Red Sea, and the political progress implied in the rise of the German Empire, have led to the same result. To the southern part of the ocean as a whole the opening of the Suez Canal implied at first some loss; since 1870 the old lines of steamship traffic from Europe to India and the Pacific, by way of the Cape, have been deserted; sailing lines carrying heavy cargo to the south and eastern shores of Asia and the steamship lines bringing Europe into direct communication with the west coast of Africa have remained.

Notwithstanding the rise of a commercial movement from west to east and a consequent lessening of the importance of the eastern ocean, the Suez Canal may in a certain sense be regarded as the primary **Suez Canal's** cause of the greater value **Commercial** which has been recently at- **Importance** tached to the eastern Atlantic Ocean and its shores. The opening of this canal—of no use to sailing-ships—through the old isthmus at the end of the Red Sea was certainly not the first and only cause of the remarkable sudden rise in oceanic communication, which is a feature as distinctive of the years 1870 to 1880 as is the decay in communication by sail that then began; this advance in trans-oceanic communication is much rather to be ascribed to progress in the art of naval construction. The fact, however, remains that since that period the Indian and Pacific Oceans, which had formerly been unknown to the maritime nations of Europe, with the exception of peoples like the English and Dutch who **The Modern** had sailed on them for nearly **Empire** three centuries, have now been **of Germany** thrown open to the maritime world at large; these powers required but a very mild stimulus to become aspirants for colonial possessions instead of desiring merely commercial activity.

This impulse is now visible as an influence affecting every district of the world that still awaits division, and it was Germany that performed the historical service of giving it ; we refer, not to the old " geographical idea," but to the modern united empire of Germany, which has realised the necessity of making strenuous efforts if it is not to go unprovided for in the general division of the world. All the old and new colonial powers at once gathered to share in the process of division, so far as it affected the islands and surrounding countries of the two eastern oceans—a fact that proves the importance of the new line of communication which had immediately given an increased value to the districts in question.

These attractions were nowhere existent in the case of the west coast of the Dark Continent, which has only recently been opened, and perhaps not yet entirely, to commerce ; they would, no doubt, have remained unperceived even yet had it not been for the surprising rapidity with which Germany established herself on different points of the long shore, and thereby attracted the attention of others to that locality. So quickly did the value of the continent rise that in the short space of a **Partition** year not a foot of the sandy shore **of Africa's** remained unclaimed. Since that **Interior** date, almost the whole of the interior of Africa, which had remained untouched for four centuries, has been divided among the representatives of modern world policy. Owing to the massive configuration and primeval character of the district, the greater portion of its history has so far been worked out within the continent itself behind its sandhills and mangrove forests ; at the same

time, this discovery of modern politics, which in our own day implies an immediate commercial development, has again made the adjoining area of the Atlantic Ocean a prominent factor in the great struggle for the commerce of the world, more prominent, indeed, than could have been imagined two decades previously.

The conquest of the ocean was successfully carried out for the first time at a point where geographical configuration favoured the passage, while also demanding that maritime capacity which can only be acquired in a hard school of training. Such a school was provided for nearly a century by the Northern Atlantic Ocean for those nations who were forced to stand aside—even after the discovery of the New World, and the clear delineation of its hydrographical conditions, by two enthusiastic and highly favoured nations of the south had greatly increased the sphere of influence of the white races.

In the event, neither enthusiasm nor good fortune proved for success in this **Destiny** labour; the honour due to the **of the** final conquerors of the Atlantic **Atlantic** Ocean and the sea in general belongs chiefly to the English nation after its training in the Arctic school. The Atlantic Ocean has lost its Old World character as a boundary sea or oceanus ; at the present day it is a Mediterranean dividing the two worlds. In the Old World, the narrow area of the European-African Mediterranean once gathered the material and intellectual wealth of antiquity upon its shores, and became the nurse of widely differentiated civilisations; so at the present day the Atlantic Ocean, especially on its northern shores, has become the intermediary of our civilisation, which embraces the world.

This ocean is now the permanent means of communication between the two great centres of civilisation, and the promoter of every advance in culture. We ask whether this is to be permanent ? The value of the Indian and Pacific Oceans, of the Baltic and Mediterranean, to humanity in the past can be traced without difficulty, while their value at the present is clearly apparent, but what their influence will be upon humanity hereafter, how their relations may be adjusted with the Atlantic Ocean, their latest and most successful rival, only time can show.   KARL WEULE

END OF SEVENTH VOLUME